AF247518

Sommario

Nomenclatura delle località citate e carta della regione
Alphabetisches Ortsverzeichnis und Übersichtskarte

Inhaltsverzeichnis

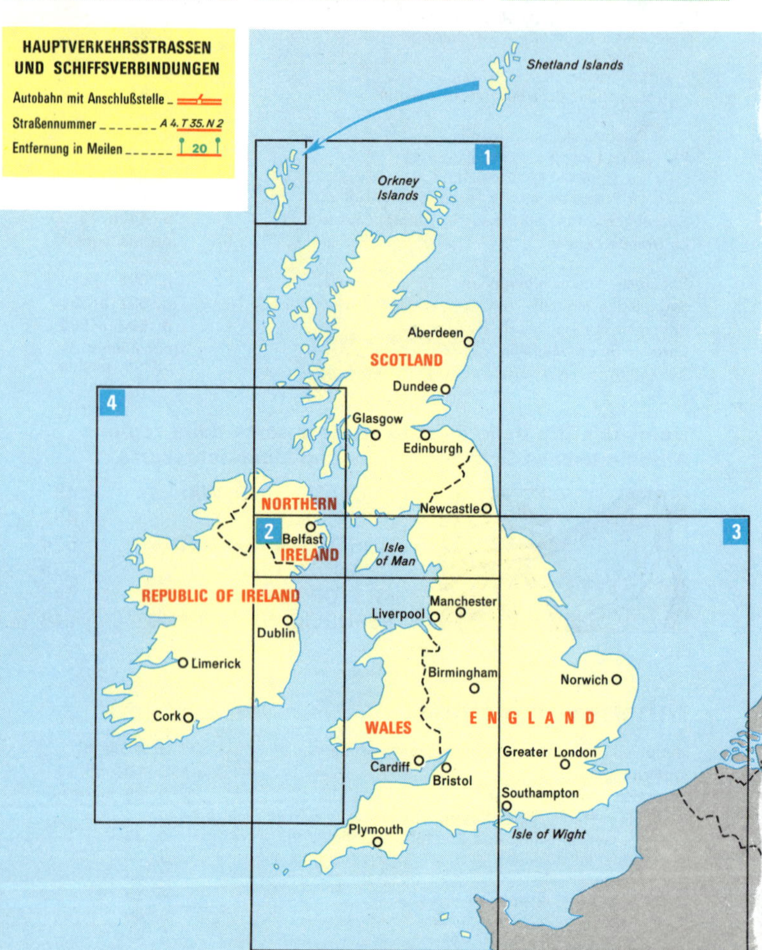

GREAT BRITAIN : the maps and town plans in the Great Britain Section of this Guide are based upon the Ordnance Survey of Great Britain with the permission of the Controller of Her Majesty's Stationery Office. Crown Copyright reserved.

NORTHERN IRELAND : the maps and town plans in the Northern Ireland Section of this Guide are based upon the Ordnance Survey of Northern Ireland with the sanction of the Controller of H.M. Stationery Office.

REPUBLIC OF IRELAND : the maps and town plans in the Republic of Ireland Section of this Guide are based upon the Ordnance Survey of Ireland by permission of the Government of the Republic, Permit number 3301.

1
SHETLAND ISLANDS
Unst
Yell
Whalsay
Mainland
Lerwick
Aberdeen
Westray
Rousay
Sanday
Stronsay
Mainland
Stromness
Kirkwall
ORKNEY ISLANDS
Hoy
Thurso
A 836
18
A 882
Wick
40
58
A 9
139
Loch Shin
Brora
Stornoway
Lewis
NORTH MINCH
Tarbert
Ullapool
32
A 835
99
A 9
Elgin
35
Banff
Fraserburgh
North Uist
Uig
Garve
28
39
18
Nairn
Keith
21
A 98
Lochmaddy
Skye
Portree
Inverness
62
A 95
A 96
49
78
57
A 82
41
Loch Ness
A 9
44
South Uist
Lochboisdale
Kyle of Lochalsh
54
Spey
A 87
Armadale
Invergarry
Kingussie
Dee
ABERDEEN
Lerwick
Rhum
Mallaig
25
A 86
52
Dee
Stonehaven
Castlebay
Sea of the Hebrides
A 830
49
Fort William
A 9
73
65
A 94
A 92
67
Coll
SCOTLAND
48
A 82
50
Loch Tay
Tiree
Mull
A 85
17
Lochearnhead
Perth
22
DUNDEE
Craignure
Oban
41
48
52
A 85
75
St.Andrews
A 849
36
A 83
48
33
A 9
29
A 91
50
Colonsay
Tarbet
A 84
45
Stirling
Lochgilphead
37
Kirkcaldy
Greenock
Falkirk
Dunfermline
Port Askaig
Jura
Tarbert
Skelmorlie
69
28
13
EDINBURGH
Rothesay
GLASGOW
36
Berwick upon Tweed
55
Islay
Largs
M 8
37
Port Ellen
A 83
Millport
Brodick
Ardrossan
33
32
A 70
Motherwell
40
A 7
33
A 699
Arran
51
A 77
A 74
62
Peebles
A 72
41
45
Campbeltown
Ayr
A 713
Abington
17
Hawick
A 698
63
A 77
53
36
42
A 702
37
A 701
58
43
A 7
62
A 68
Bergen
Stavanger
Kristiansand
Coleraine
A 2
New Galloway
Dumfries
A 74
75
A 69
58
Tynemouth
30
A 26
29
Waterfoot
Cairnryan
45
14
18
35
NORTH CHANNEL
Ballymena
A 6
Larne
88
Stranraer
58
A 75
CARLISLE
NEWCASTLE
12
71
30
A 8
Liverpool
33
A 596
SUNDERLAND
Lough Neagh
Bangor
19
Penrith
40
M 1
Ballygawley
BELFAST
42
Workington
A 66
39
52
A 66
Darlington
54
M 1
A 3
Strangford Lough
Whitehaven
Keswick
M 6
Armagh
56
Banbridge
A 595
ENGLAND
18
A 25
Newcastle
61
Kendal
33
Monaghan
39
52
Isle of Man
28
A 1
A 2
Douglas
Barrow
in Furness
13
A 65
Lancaster
Dundalk
13
Liverpool
Heysham
18

2
BELFAST
Bangor
Armagh
Banbridge
Newcastle
Monaghan
Dundalk
Kells
Drogheda
Naas
DUBLIN
Bray
Wicklow
Carlow
Arklow
Enniscorthy
Wexford
Rosslare
Isle of Man
Douglas
Barrow in Furness
Heysham
IRISH SEA
Holyhead/
Caergybi
Caernarfon
Colwyn Bay
Dolgellau
Aberystwyth
Llandrindod Wells
Llandrindod
WALES
Fishguard/
Abergwaun
Carmarthen/
Caerfyrddin
Milford Haven/
Milffwrd
Brecon
Aberhonddu
Merthyr Tydfil
SWANSEA
ABERTAWE
Newport/
Casnewydd
CARDIFF
CAERDYDD
ST GEORGE'S CHANNEL
le Havre
Cherbourg
Cork
Bristol Channel
Ilfracombe
Minehead
Bude
Newquay
Penzance
Falmouth
Isles of Scilly
Roscoff
PLYMOUTH
EXETER
Exmouth
Torquay
Taunton
Yeovil
Honiton
Dorchester
Weymouth
BOURNEMOUTH
Salisbury
Wells
Bath
BRISTOL
Swindon
Gloucester
Cheltenham
Stratford
upon Avon
Warwick
COVENTRY
Worcester
Ross
Hereford
Ludlow
BIRMINGHAM
Dudley
WOLVERHAMPTON
Shrewsbury
Welshpool
Trallwng
DERBY
STOKE
ON TRENT
Matlock
SHEFFIELD
Stockport
MANCHESTER
Wakefield
Halifax
BOLTON
Burnley
BRADFORD
LEEDS
Southport
LIVERPOOL
Birkenhead
Warrington
Chester
Mold/
Yr Wyddgrug
Wrexham/
Wrecsam
BLACKPOOL
PRESTON
HARROGATE
Lancaster
Kendal
ENGLAND
Workington
Whitehaven
Keswick
Penrith
Darlington
Isle of Man
THAMES
ENGLISH CHANNEL
Rosslare
Alderney
Guernsey
St.Peter-Port
Sark
Jersey
St.Hélier
Cherbourg
St.Malo
River Boyne
River Wharfe
Severn
Wye
Avon

3
Hartlepool
Middlesbrough
52
Scarborough
N   D
York
41   A 64   A 165
47
24
KINGSTON UPON HULL
M 62   31   A 63
13
Ouse
16
Immingham
Rotterdam
Zeebrugge
18
37   M 180   18   Grimsby
Doncaster
29   A 15   31   A 16
11
39
A 158   30
A 614   37   A 46   Lincoln   11   Skegness
33   A 1
99   54   Boston
69
NOTTINGHAM   A 17
49   A 16   A 17
LEICESTER   Wisbech   King's Lynn   44   NORWICH
41   Stamford   34   20   Great Yarmouth
52   A 47   13   Peterborough   A 10   48   A 11   A 140   42   A 12   Lowestoft
51   A 43   36   A 1   45   Ely   53
8   Ouse
5   Bury St.Edmund's
22   A 6   13   A 45   40
Northampton   92   29   CAMBRIDGE   Ipswich
42   Bedford   16   18   12   Felixstowe
A 43   55   55   M 11   Colchester   19   Harwich
52   A 10   47   55
Aylesbury   73   A 1   A 12   Chelmsford
A 418   M 1   55
OXFORD   GREATER LONDON   A 127   41   Southend on Sea
55   Tilbury
READING   THAMES   Margate
M 4   Windsor   Sheerness   Ramsgate
M 3   27   M 2   Canterbury   Deal
61   38   33   75   98   Dover
A 31   Guildford   44   A 21   Maidstone   A 20   7
Winchester   A 3   54   Royal-   45   Folkestone   Calais
40   A 23   Tunbridge Wells   65   37
SOUTHAMPTON   BRIGHTON   Hastings
Chichester   37   A 27   Eastbourne
18   45   Worthing   40   Newhaven
PORTSMOUTH
Newport
Isle of Wight   St-Malo
NORTH   SEA
Scheveningen
Göteborg
Zeebrugge
Bremerhaven
Esbjerg
Hoek van Holland
Hamburg
NEDERLAND
Vlissingen
Zeebrugge
OOSTENDE   BRUGGE
51   64   GENT
N 63   E 5
Dunkerque   N   75   BELGIË
Gravelines   A 25   BELGIQUE
40   E 3
St-Omer   66   E 41
N 42   79   LILLE
51   A 43   108
Boulogne   85   101   A 26   Valenciennes
D 928   66   A 2
80   N   N 39   116   Arras   36   Cambrai
Abbeville   76   N 39
63   N 25   45   D 929   69
Dieppe   62   AMIENS   49   Somme   St-Quentin
106   D 915   N 29   D 934   41
36   79
D 925   37   38   86   59   N 44
N 15   N 28   N 31   30   Beauvais   57   Compiègne   N 31
86   50   N 31   53   Soissons
Rosslare
CHANNEL
LE HAVRE   ROUEN   Senlis
139   N 1   N 2   7
119   N 13   73   A 13   73   92   D 915   76
CAEN   Lisieux   N 13   SEINE   174   49
N 174   49   FRANCE

ATLANTIC OCEAN

NORTH CHANNEL

Oban
Mull
Colonsay
Lochgilphea
Jura
Port Askaig
Tarbert
A 83
Islay
51
Campbeltow

97
Letterkenny
Coleraine
Waterfoot
A 2
30
A 26
29
Londonderry
N 56
17
A 5
88
32
A 6
Ballymena
Cairnryan
Stranraer
N 15
34
14
71
Larne
Donegal
A 8
30
Liverpo
NORTHERN
T 35
37
IRELAND
Omagh
Lough
Neagh
Bangor
N 15
40
27
15
BELFAST
42
Ballygawley
54
M 1
Strangford
Lough
N 16
Enniskillen
33
A 4
18
A 3
56
Sligo
41
A 4
Armagh
Banbridge
L. Allen
36
30
Monaghan
A 1
39
A 25
Ballina
N 59
37
T 53
60
N 54
N 2
31
A 2
52
Newcastle
98
N 4
24
Cavan
68
13
L 133
Boyle
41
25
T 24
Dundalk
IRISH
N 5
25
98
26
Edgeworthstown
71
Kells
N 52
22
Westport
N 17
N 3
T 24
Drogheda
L. Mask
N 60
59
27
58
N 51
SEA
Clifden
90
Roscommon
N 55
26
42
Boyne
29
N 59
48
48
18
River
N 63
Lee
20
N 4
Mullingar
11
N 1
DUBLIN
Galway
N 6
Athlone
N 6
20
14
18
Liverpool
Holyhead
57
Ballinasloe
24
7
37
N 4
T 21
70
Tullamore
20
Bray
Lisdoonvarna
N 67
41
28
27
54
Naas
N 11
113
N 18
39
Roscrea
24
N 80
77
Ennis
N 62
45
N 7
31
Wicklow
Kilkee
23
N 7
43
Carlow
N 9
Arklow
N 68
68
Thurles
N 8
T 19
56
N 80
L 105
N 69
LIMERICK
Suir
Kilkenny
N 11
69
N 21
20
38
N 24
Cashel
58
41
30
99
L 30
36
Enniscorthy
Tralee
62
Cahir
N 76
36
Dingle
77
N 8
39
N 24
14
Wexford
104
89
Carrick
on Suir
38
Killarney
N 72
27
Fermoy
N 25
12
13
Lismore
63
N 72
Waterford
Rosslare
72
N 70
20
R. Blackwater
59
N 8
Fishguard
55
N 22
22
77
Glengarriff
84
CORK
N 25
Youghal
Bantry
N 71
Cobh
Milford Haven

REPUBLIC OF IRELAND

Swansea

le Havre
Cherbourg

ST GEORGE'S CHANNEL

CELTIC SEA

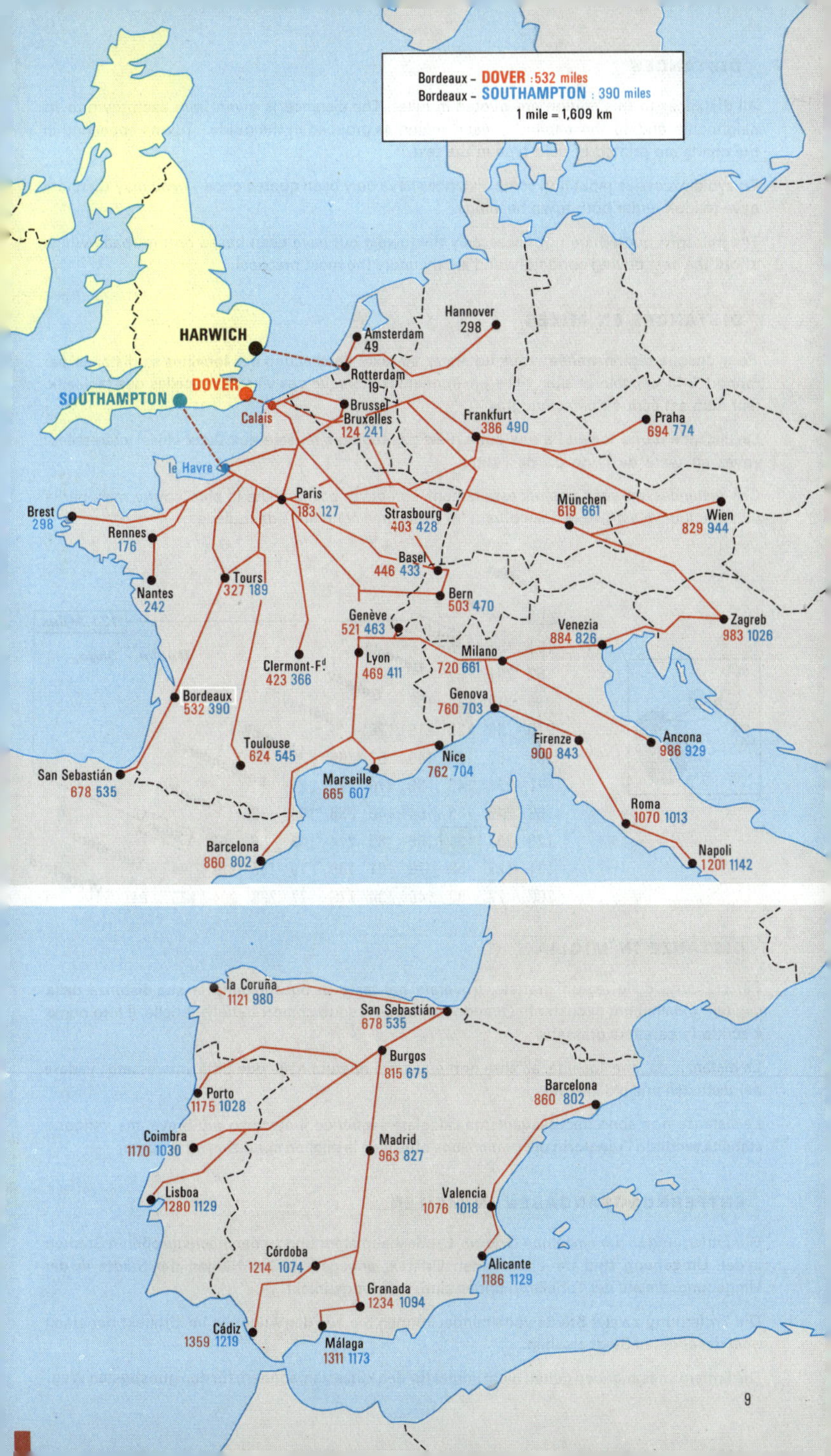

Bordeaux – DOVER : 532 miles
Bordeaux – SOUTHAMPTON : 390 miles
1 mile = 1,609 km

HARWICH
SOUTHAMPTON
DOVER
Calais
Amsterdam 49
Rotterdam 19
Brussel Bruxelles 124 241
le Havre
Hannover 298
Frankfurt 386 490
Praha 694 774
Paris 183 127
Strasbourg 403 428
München 619 661
Wien 829 944
Brest 298
Rennes 176
Nantes 242
Tours 327 189
Basel 446 433
Bern 503 470
Genève 521 463
Zagreb 983 1026
Clermont-F^d 423 366
Lyon 469 411
Milano 720 661
Venezia 884 826
Bordeaux 532 390
Genova 760 703
Firenze 900 843
Ancona 986 929
Toulouse 624 545
Nice 762 704
San Sebastián 678 535
Marseille 665 607
Roma 1070 1013
Barcelona 860 802
Napoli 1201 1142

la Coruña 1121 980
San Sebastián 678 535
Burgos 815 675
Porto 1175 1028
Barcelona 860 802
Coimbra 1170 1030
Madrid 963 827
Lisboa 1280 1129
Valencia 1076 1018
Córdoba 1214 1074
Alicante 1186 1129
Granada 1234 1094
Cádiz 1359 1219
Málaga 1311 1173

DISTANCES

All distances in this edition are quoted in miles. The distance is given from each town to its neighbours and to the capital of each region as grouped in the guide. Towns appearing in the charts are printed in bold type in the text.

To avoid excessive repetition some distances have only been quoted once — you may therefore have to look under both town headings.

The mileages quoted are not necessarily the lowest but have been based on the roads which afford the best driving conditions and are therefore the most practical.

DISTANCES EN MILES

Pour chaque région traitée, vous trouverez au texte de chacune des localités sa distance par rapport à la capitale et aux villes environnantes. Lorsque ces villes sont celles des tableaux, leur nom est écrit en caractère gras.

La distance d'une localité à une autre n'est pas toujours répétée aux deux villes intéressées : voyez au texte de l'une ou de l'autre.

Ces distances ne sont pas nécessairement comptées par la route la plus courte mais par la plus pratique, c'est-à-dire celle offrant les meilleures conditions de roulage.

	Belfast	Cork	Dublin	Dundalk	Galway	Killarney	Limerick	Londonderry	Omagh	Sligo	Tullamore
Cork	253										
Dublin	103	161									
Dundalk	52	201	51								
Galway	196	119	132	155							
Killarney	270	55	190	218	126						
Limerick	201	62	121	149	57	69					
Londonderry	71	277	145	96	176	290	221				
Omagh	69	245	113	64	146	258	189	32			
Sligo	128	203	131	106	88	214	145	88	68		
Tullamore	131	122	59	79	81	139	70	155	123	94	
Waterford	200	77	99	148	134	116	77	236	204	175	81

131 Miles

Dublin - Sligo

DISTANZE IN MIGLIA

Per ciascuna delle regioni trattate, troverete nel testo di ogni località la sua distanza dalla capitale e dalle città circostanti. Quando queste città sono comprese nelle tabelle, il loro nome è scritto in carattere grassetto.

La distanza da una località all'altra non è sempre ripetuta nelle due città interessate : vedere nel testo dell'una o dell'altra.

Le distanze non sono necessariamente calcolate seguendo il percorso più breve, ma vengono stabilite secondo l'itinerario più pratico, che offre cioè le migliori condizioni di viaggio.

ENTFERNUNGSANGABEN IN MEILEN

Die Entfernungen der einzelnen Orte zur Landeshauptstadt und zu den nächstgrößeren Städten in der Umgebung sind im allgemeinen Ortstext angegeben. Die Namen der Städte in der Umgebung, die auf der Tabelle zu finden sind, sind fettgedruckt.

Die Entfernung zweier Städte voneinander können Sie aus den Angaben im Ortstext der einen oder der anderen Stadt ersehen.

Die Entfernungsangaben gelten nicht immer für den kürzesten, sondern für den günstigsten Weg.

DISTANCES BETWEEN MAJOR TOWNS
DISTANCES ENTRE PRINCIPALES VILLES
DISTANZE TRA LE PRINCIPALI CITTÀ
ENTFERNUNGEN ZWISCHEN DEN GRÖSSEREN STÄDTEN

Example — Esempio
Exemple — Beispiel

Edinburgh - Southampton

428 Miles

	Aberdeen	Ayr	Birmingham	Blackpool	Brighton	Bristol	Cambridge	Cardiff	Carlisle	Coventry	Dover	Dumfries	Dundee	Edinburgh	Glasgow	Inverness	Ipswich	Kingston upon Hull	Leeds	Leicester	Liverpool	London	Manchester	Middlesbrough	Newcastle	Norwich	Nottingham	Oban	Oxford	Plymouth	Portsmouth	Sheffield	Southampton	Stoke on Trent	Swansea
Aberdeen																																			
Ayr	175																																		
Birmingham	419	287																																	
Blackpool	317	185	126																																
Brighton	577	458	176	297																															
Bristol	499	367	84	206	150																														
Cambridge	465	350	110	216	125	164																													
Cardiff	520	388	105	227	182	43	196																												
Carlisle	226	94	193	91	364	273	256	294																											
Coventry	437	305	18	144	154	91	88	118	211																										
Dover	591	480	198	319	81	201	124	233	386	176																									
Dumfries	205	59	228	126	399	308	291	329	35	246	421																								
Dundee	65	115	359	257	514	439	403	460	166	377	529	145																							
Edinburgh	124	77	291	189	452	371	341	392	98	319	467	77	62																						
Glasgow	141	34	289	187	460	370	352	391	96	307	482	75	81	43																					
Inverness	106	199	454	352	611	534	500	555	261	472	626	240	130	159	168																				
Ipswich	517	402	163	268	132	198	53	230	308	141	129	343	455	393	404	552																			
Kingston upon Hull	362	247	133	140	243	217	139	238	153	139	265	188	300	238	249	397	170																		
Leeds	331	216	112	84	250	194	146	215	122	116	271	157	269	207	218	366	198	60																	
Leicester	420	305	43	143	159	117	68	143	211	26	181	246	358	296	307	455	123	94	93																
Liverpool	350	218	99	57	270	179	202	200	124	117	292	159	290	222	220	385	254	126	70	116															
London	514	403	121	242	54	125	58	157	309	99	75	344	452	390	405	549	73	188	194	104	215														
Manchester	343	211	86	50	257	166	174	187	117	104	279	152	283	215	213	378	226	98	42	103	36	202													
Middlesbrough	269	184	167	121	306	251	195	272	90	173	328	125	207	145	187	304	247	85	61	150	148	251	120												
Newcastle	232	147	199	136	338	283	227	304	58	205	360	88	170	108	149	267	279	124	93	182	180	283	152	39											
Norwich	493	378	160	243	177	222	61	254	284	143	171	319	431	369	380	528	42	149	173	117	229	111	201	223	255										
Nottingham	394	279	50	137	188	143	88	164	185	55	210	220	332	270	281	429	140	90	67	24	110	133	69	124	156	124									
Oban	175	124	382	280	553	463	445	484	189	400	575	168	115	122	93	114	497	342	311	400	313	498	306	280	242	473	374								
Oxford	484	352	63	191	99	69	78	101	258	50	152	293	424	361	354	519	129	181	158	68	164	58	151	215	247	136	97	447							
Plymouth	612	480	197	319	211	120	282	156	386	204	319	421	552	484	482	647	316	330	307	230	292	243	279	364	396	340	256	575	187						
Portsmouth	566	434	145	273	49	97	147	138	340	132	130	375	506	443	436	601	161	263	240	150	246	77	233	297	329	188	179	529	81	170					
Sheffield	370	263	85	102	224	169	121	190	169	91	246	204	308	246	265	405	173	66	34	68	79	169	40	100	132	148	42	358	133	282	215				
Southampton	551	419	130	258	63	76	130	117	325	117	146	360	491	428	421	586	158	248	225	135	231	84	218	282	314	188	164	514	66	148	20	200			
Stoke on Trent	378	246	45	85	216	125	150	146	152	63	238	187	318	250	248	413	203	143	87	57	58	161	38	165	197	174	50	341	110	238	192	60	177		
Swansea	548	416	133	255	221	82	235	41	322	146	272	357	488	420	418	583	269	266	243	171	228	196	215	300	332	293	192	511	140	195	177	218	156	174	
Wick	229	308	566	464	737	647	623	668	373	584	749	363	253	282	277	123	675	520	489	578	497	672	490	427	390	651	552	223	631	759	713	528	698	525	695

The Michelin Guide, created for the motorist, offers a wide range of information including a selection of hotels and restaurants.

In order to get the most benefit from our guide please read the explanatory chapters that follow and pay particular attention to the symbols and characters, which in bold or light type, in red or black, have different meanings.

This book is not a list of all hotels and restaurants. We have made a choice amongst establishments of all classes in order to provide a service for all motorists.

We wish you a pleasant journey, and on your return please write to us at:

Michelin Tyre Co Ltd.

Tourism Department

81 Fulham Road, LONDON SW3 6RD

Your opinions, whether praising or criticising, are welcomed and will be examined on the spot by our inspectors in order to make our Guide even better.

Thank you in advance.

Choosing
your hotel
or restaurant

We have classified the hotels and restaurants with the travelling
motorist in mind. In each category they have been listed in order
of preference.

CLASS, STANDARD OF COMFORT

	Luxury	
	Top class	
	Very comfortable	
	Comfortable	
	Good average	
	Plain but adequate	
	Other recommended accommodation, at moderate prices	

without rest.   The hotel has no restaurant
with rm   The restaurant has bedrooms

HOTEL FACILITIES

Hotels in categories , , , usually have every comfort and exchange facilities; details are not repeated under each
hotel.

In other categories, the listed facilities are usually to be found
only in some of the rooms; these hotels generally have a bathroom
or a shower for general use.

Postal code	LL35 0SB
Telephone number	64622
Number of rooms	**30 rm**
Lift (elevator)	
Television in room	
Private bathroom with toilet, private bathroom without toilet	wc
Private shower with toilet, private shower without toilet	wc
External phone in room	
Bedrooms accessible to the physically handicapped	
Tennis	
Outdoor or indoor swimming pool	
Golf course and number of holes	18
Fishing available to hotel guests. A charge may be made	
Garden	
Private park	park
Garage available (usually charged for)	
Car park	
Equipped conference hall (minimum seating 25)	
Period during which a seasonal hotel is open	*May-October*
Probably open for the season — precise dates not available	*season*

Where no dates or season are shown, the establishments in bold
type are open all the year round

AMENITY

A stay in certain hotels in this guide will, without doubt, be particularly pleasant or restful.

Such a quality may derive from the hotel's fortunate setting, its decor, welcoming atmosphere and service.

Such establishments are distinguished in the guide by the symbols shown below.

Pleasant hotels

Pleasant restaurants

Particularly attractive feature

Very quiet or quiet, secluded hotel

Quiet hotel

Exceptional view

Interesting or extensive view

The establishments shown in red e.g. 🏠🏠, 💥💥 with rm, or in a very quiet situation 🦢 are indicated on the maps preceding each geographical area.

We do not claim to have indicated all the pleasant, very quiet or quiet, secluded hotels which exist.

Our enquiries continue. You can help us by letting us know your opinions and discoveries.

*Choosing
your hotel
or restaurant*

CUISINE

The stars for good cooking

We indicate by ✳ or ✳✳, establishments where the standard of cooking, whether particular to the country or foreign, deserves to be brought especially to the attention of our readers.

In the text of these establishments we show some of the culinary specialities, to a maximum of three, that we recommend you to try.

An especially good restaurant in its class

✳

This symbol indicates restaurants particularly worthy of a break in your journey. Beware of comparing the star of a luxury establishment with that of a more simple one. In either case an effort is made to serve you a meal of quality in relation to the price charged.

Excellent cooking, worth a detour

✳✳

First class products and preparations... Do not expect meals of this quality to be cheap.

Your opinions and suggestions concerning restaurants that we recommend will be extremely welcome, so do not hesitate to let us know of them. Thank you in advance.

For our part, our enquiries continue.

The red « M »

Whilst appreciating the quality of the cooking in restaurants with a star, you may, however, wish to find some serving a perhaps less elaborate but nonetheless always carefully prepared meal.

Certain restaurants seem to us to answer this requirement. We bring them to your attention by marking them with a red « M » in the text of the guide.

Alcoholic beverages-conditions of sale

Licensed premises, where alcoholic drinks may be bought and consumed (public houses or pubs, hotels and restaurants), may remain open at the discretion of the landlord but may only sell drink within legally prescribed hours.

Children under 14 are not allowed in the bar of licensed premises during the prescribed hours but this prohibition does not extend to a separate restaurant or to any other part of the premises.

The sale or consumption of intoxicating liquor by persons under 18 is prohibited in the bar of licensed premises but persons over 16 may buy and consume alcoholic drink with a meal in a separate restaurant.

N.B.: Unlicensed hotels and restaurants are not permitted to serve alcoholic beverages, including beer, even accompanying meals.

Licensing hours during which alcoholic beverages may be sold: see opening pages of each region.

Choosing your hotel or restaurant

PRICES

Hotels and restaurants whose names appear in bold type have supplied us with their charges in detail and undertaken to abide by them, wherever possible, if the traveller is in possession of this year's guide.

Valid for late 1979 the rates shown may be revised if the cost of living changes to any great extent. In any event they should be regarded as basic charges.

Where no mention **s.**, **t.** or **st.** is shown, prices are subject to the addition of service charge, V.A.T., or both (V.A.T. does not apply in the Channel Islands).
If you think you have been overcharged, let us know. Where no rates are shown it is best to enquire about terms in advance.

Principal **credit cards** accepted by establishments:
Access – American Express – Diners Club – Visa (Barclaycard).

Prices are given in £ sterling, except for the Republic of Ireland (see p. 548).

Meals

M 4.50/6.00

Set meals – Lowest price 4.50, and highest price 6.00 for set meals – including cover charge, where applicable - served at normal hours (12.30 to 2.30 pm and 7 to 9 pm).

s. Service only included.

t. V.A.T. only included.

st. Service and V.A.T. included (net prices).

M 6.00/8.00 See page 15.

M a la carte 6.00/8.50 **A la carte meals** – The first figure is for a plain meal and includes light entrée, main dish of the day with vegetables and dessert.

The second figure is for a fuller meal and includes hors-d'œuvre, a main dish, cheese or dessert. These prices include a cover charge where applicable.

1.80 Price of 1/2 bottle or carafe of ordinary wine.

1.50 Charge for breakfast (i.e. not included in the room rate).

rm 15.00/21.00 **Rooms** – Lowest price 15.00 for a comfortable single and highest price 21.00 for the best double room (including bathroom when applicable).

rm 17.00/25.00 Breakfast is included in the price of the room.

P 20.00/27.50 **Full-Board** – Lowest and highest price per person, per day in the high season.

Meals

Ask for menus including set meals and a la carte menus with the prices clearly marked if they are not produced automatically.

Hotels

Breakfast is generally included in the price of the room, even if it is not required.

Full-board

Full-board comprises: bedroom, breakfast and two meals. Terms usually only apply to a stay of three days or longer.

High season rates usually operate between June and September. It is always advisable to agree terms in advance with a hotelier.

Reservations

Hotels: Reserving in advance, when possible, is advised. Ask the hotelier to provide you, in his letter of confirmation, with all terms and conditions applicable to your reservation.

In seaside resorts especially, reservations usually begin and end on Saturdays.

Certain hoteliers require the payment of a deposit. This constitutes a mutual guarantee of good faith. Deposits, except in special cases, may amount to 10 % of the estimated hotel account.

Restaurants : it is strongly recommended always to book your table well ahead in order to avoid the disappointment of a refusal.

Animals

It is forbidden to bring domestic animals (dogs, cats...) into Great Britain and Ireland.

Seeing
a town
and its surroundings

TOWNS

986 ③④	Section number on Michelin map 986
403 404 M 27	Co-ordinates on Michelin maps 403 404
pop. 1.057	Population (last published census figures)
ECD : Wednesday	Early closing day (shops close at midday)
✉ York	Post office serving the town
✆ 0225 Bath	STD dialling code (name of exchange indicated only when different from name of the town)
BX A	Reference letters locating a position on a town plan
❊, ≼	Panoramic view, viewpoint
⛳₁₈	Golf course and number of holes (visitors unrestricted)
✈	Airport
⛴	Shipping line (passengers and cars)
⛵	Shipping line (passengers only) *see list of companies at the end of the Guide*
🚗 ☎ 218	Place with a motorail connection; further information from telephone number listed
ℹ	Tourist Information Centre

SIGHTS

Star-rating

***	Worth a journey
**	Worth a detour
*	Interesting
AC	Admission charge

Tourist sights and where to find them

See	Sights in town
Envir.	On the outskirts
Exc.	In the surrounding area
N, S, E, W	The sight lies north, south, east, west
A 22	Go by road A 22, indicated by the same symbol on the Guide map
2 m.	Mileage
h, mn	Walking time there and back (h : hours ; mn : minutes)

Standard Time

In winter standard time throughout the British Isles is Greenwich Mean Time (G.M.T.). In summer British clocks are advanced by one hour to give British Summer Time (B.S.T.). The actual dates are announced annually but always occur over weekends in March and October.

Town Plans

CONVENTIONAL SIGNS

Roads

Some streets are only shown by their beginning
Through route or by-pass – Dual carriageway . . . .
Motorway and interchange number . . . .
Street under construction – pedestrian street – one-way street . . . .
No entry, unsuitable for traffic or subject to restrictions . . . .
Railway crossing : Level crossing, road crossing rail, rail crossing road . . . . . .
Gateway – Street passing under arch – Tunnel . . . .
Shopping street – Public car park . . . .

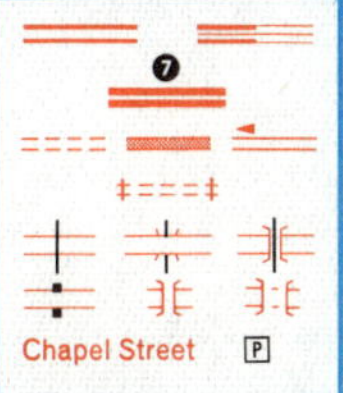

Sights - Hotels

Place of interest and its main entrance
Cathedral or church . . . . } Reference letter on the town plan . . .
Reference letter locating hotels and restaurants on the town plan . . . .

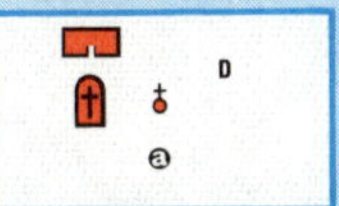

Various signs

Cathedral - Church - Hospital – Poste restante, telegraph, telephone . . . . . .
Public buildings located by letters :
  County Council Offices – Town Hall . . . .
  Police (in large towns police headquarters) – Museum . . . .
  Theatre – University, Colleges . . . .
Tourist Information Centre . . . .
Cemetery – Open woodland, park . . . .
Lighthouse – Sports ground, stadium . . . .
Golf course (visitors unrestricted) – (with restrictions for visitors) . . . .
Racecourse – Panorama – View . . . .
Landing stage : Passenger and car transport – Airport. . . . .
Underground station. . . . .

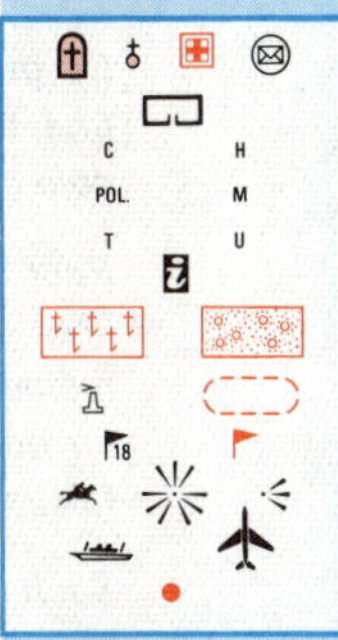

London - Special signs

Borough – Area . . . .
Borough boundary – Area boundary . . . .
Underground station. . . . .

For your car

In the text of many towns are to be found the names of **garages**
or motor agents with a breakdown service.
For your tyres refer to the pages bordered in blue.

Travelling by car

The major motoring organisations in Great Britain are the
Automobile Association and the Royal Automobile Club. Each
provides services in varying degrees for non-resident members
of affiliated clubs.

AUTOMOBILE ASSOCIATION   ROYAL AUTOMOBILE CLUB
Fanum House   83-85 Pall Mall
BASINGSTOKE, Hants., RG21 2EA   LONDON SW1Y 5HW
☎ (0256) 20123   ☎ (01) 930 4343

Ami Lecteur

Ce guide, conçu pour le voyage, vous propose une multitude de renseignements et en particulier un choix d'hôtels et de restaurants.

Pour tirer le meilleur parti de nos informations lisez attentivement les pages explicatives. Un même symbole, un même caractère en rouge ou en noir, en gras ou en maigre n'ont pas tout à fait la même signification.

Sachez aussi que cet ouvrage n'est pas un répertoire de tous les hôtels et restaurants. Nos listes sont le résultat de sélections effectuées parmi toutes les classes d'établissements afin de mieux rendre service à tous les automobilistes.

Bonne route et dès votre retour, écrivez-nous.

Services de Tourisme Michelin

46, avenue de Breteuil

75341 PARIS CEDEX 07

Vos louanges comme vos critiques seront examinées sur place par les Attachés de nos Services de Tourisme afin que ce guide soit encore meilleur dans l'avenir.

Merci d'avance!

Le choix
d'un hôtel,
d'un restaurant

Notre classement est établi à l'usage des automobilistes de passage. Dans chaque catégorie les établissements sont classés par ordre de préférence.

CLASSE ET CONFORT

🏰	Grand luxe	XXXXX
🏛	Luxe	XXXX
🏠	Très confortable	XXX
🏠	De bon confort	XX
🏠	Assez confortable	X
🏠	Simple mais convenable	
🏠	Autre ressource hôtelière conseillée, à prix modérés	

without rest.   L'hôtel n'a pas de restaurant
with rm   Le restaurant possède des chambres

L'INSTALLATION

Les hôtels des catégories 🏰, 🏛, 🏠, possèdent tout le confort et assurent en général le change, les symboles de détail n'apparaissent donc pas au texte de ces hôtels.

Dans les autres catégories, les éléments de confort indiqués n'existent le plus souvent que dans certaines chambres.
Ces établissements disposent de douches et de salles de bains communes.

Code postal de l'établissement	LL35 0SB
Numéro de téléphone	☎ 64622
Nombre de chambres	**30 rm**
Ascenseur	🛗
Télévision dans la chambre	TV
Bain et wc privés, bain privé sans wc	🛁wc 🛁
Douche et wc privés, douche privée sans wc	🚿wc 🚿
Téléphone dans la chambre communiquant avec l'extérieur	☎
Chambres accessibles aux handicapés physiques	♿
Tennis	🎾
Piscine : de plein air ou couverte	🏊 🏊
Golf et nombre de trous	⛳18
Pêche ouverte aux clients de l'hôtel (éventuellement payant)	🎣
Jardin	🌳
Parc	park
Garage (généralement payant)	🚗
Parc à voitures	Ⓟ
L'hôtel dispose d'une ou plusieurs salles de conférences (25 places minimum)	🏛
Période d'ouverture d'un hôtel saisonnier	*May-October*
Ouverture probable en saison mais dates non précisées	*season*

Les établissements indiqués en caractères gras, dont le nom n'est suivi d'aucune mention, sont ouverts toute l'année.

Le choix
d'un hôtel,
d'un restaurant

Certains établissements sélectionnés dans ce guide sont tels que le séjour y est particulièrement agréable ou reposant.

Cela peut tenir à leur environnement extérieur, à leur décoration, à leur situation, à l'accueil et au service qui y sont proposés.

Ils se distinguent dans le guide par les symboles indiqués ci-dessous.

Hôtels agréables

Restaurants agréables

Élément particulièrement agréable

Hôtel très tranquille ou isolé et tranquille

Hôtel tranquille

Vue exceptionnelle

Vue intéressante ou étendue

Les établissements signalés en rouge, ex: , with rm ou très tranquilles ont été repérés sur les cartes placées au début de chacune des régions traitées dans ce guide.

Nous ne prétendons pas avoir signalé tous les hôtels agréables, ni tous ceux qui sont tranquilles, ou isolés et tranquilles.

Nos enquêtes continuent. Vous pouvez les faciliter en nous faisant connaître vos observations et vos découvertes.

Le choix
d'un hôtel,
d'un restaurant

LA TABLE

Les étoiles de bonne table

Nous marquons par ❀ ou ❀❀ les établissements dont la qualité de la table nous a paru mériter d'être signalée spécialement à l'attention de nos lecteurs, qu'il s'agisse de cuisines propres au pays ou étrangères.

Au texte de ces établissements nous indiquons quelques spécialités culinaires, trois au maximum, que nous vous conseillons d'essayer.

Une très bonne table dans sa catégorie

❀

Ce symbole marque une bonne étape sur votre itinéraire. Ne comparez pas l'étoile d'un établissement de luxe avec celle d'une petite maison, mais dans un cas comme dans l'autre un effort est fait pour vous servir une cuisine de qualité en rapport avec les prix demandés.

Une table excellente, mérite un détour

❀❀

Produits et préparations de choix... Attendez-vous à une dépense en conséquence.

Vos avis et suggestions au sujet des tables que nous recommandons seront les bienvenus, ne manquez pas de nous en faire part. Merci d'avance.

De notre côté nos enquêtes continuent.

Le « M » rouge

Tout en appréciant les tables à « étoiles » on peut souhaiter trouver sur sa route un repas plus simple mais toujours de préparation soignée. Certaines maisons nous ont paru répondre à cette préoccupation.

Un « M » rouge les signale à votre attention dans le texte de ce guide.

La vente de boissons alcoolisées

Les lieux autorisés à la vente des boissons alcoolisées pour la consommation sur place (Public houses – pubs – hôtels, restaurants) peuvent être ouverts et fermés à la convenance de leurs gérants mais la vente de ces boissons n'y est permise que durant certaines périodes de temps fixées par la loi. Les enfants de moins de 14 ans n'ont pas accès au bar d'établissements possédant licence, durant les heures permises, mais cette interdiction ne s'applique pas au restaurant si celui-ci est séparé ou à toute autre partie de l'établissement.

Toute personne âgée de moins de 18 ans ne peut acheter ou consommer des boissons alcoolisées au bar d'un établissement possédant licence durant les heures permises, mais toute personne âgée de plus de 16 ans peut acheter ou consommer ces mêmes boissons à l'occasion d'un repas au restaurant, si séparé du bar.

NOTA : Les hôtels ou restaurants sans licence (unlicensed) ne peuvent servir aucune boisson alcoolisée, y compris bière, même à l'occasion d'un repas.

Heures de vente permises. Se reporter au début de la nomenclature de chacune des régions traitées dans ce guide.

LES PRIX

Les hôtels et restaurants figurent en caractères gras lorsque les hôteliers nous ont donné tous leurs prix et se sont engagés à les appliquer aux touristes de passage porteurs de notre guide.

Les prix que nous indiquons dans ce guide ont été établis en fin d'année 1979. Ils sont susceptibles d'être augmentés ou modifiés si le coût de la vie subit des variations importantes. Ils doivent, en tout cas, être considérés comme des prix de base.

Lorsque les mentions **s.**, **t.**, ou **st.** ne figurent pas, les prix indiqués peuvent être majorés d'un pourcentage pour le service, la T.V.A. ou les deux. (La T.V.A. n'est pas appliquée dans les Channel Islands).

Prévenez-nous de toute majoration paraissant injustifiée.
Si aucun prix n'est indiqué, nous vous conseillons de demander les conditions.

Principales **cartes de crédit** acceptées par l'établissement :
Access – American Express – Diners Club – Visa (Carte Bleue Internationale).

Les prix sont indiqués en livres sterling (1 £ = 100 pence), sauf en République d'Irlande (voir p. 548).

Repas

M 4.50/6.00   **Prix fixe** – Minimum 4.50 et maximum 6.00 des repas servis aux heures normales (12 h 30 à 14 h 30 et 19 h à 21 h) y compris le couvert éventuellement.

s.   Service compris.

t.   T.V.A. comprise.

st.   Service et T.V.A. compris (prix nets).

M 6.00/8.00   Voir page 23.

M a la carte 6.00/8.50   **Repas à la carte** – Le 1er prix correspond à un repas simple mais soigné, comprenant : petite entrée, plat du jour garni, dessert. Le 2e prix concerne un repas plus complet, comprenant : hors-d'œuvre, plat principal, fromage ou dessert. Ces prix s'entendent couvert compris s'il y a lieu.

1.80   Prix de la 1/2 bouteille ou carafe de vin ordinaire.

1.50   Prix du petit déjeuner, s'il n'est pas compris dans celui de la chambre.

rm 15.00/21.00   **Chambre** – Prix minimum 15.00 d'une chambre pour une personne et prix maximum 21.00 de la plus belle chambre (y compris salle de bains s'il y a lieu) occupée par deux personnes.

rm 17.00/25.00   Le prix du petit déjeuner est inclus dans le prix de la chambre.

P 20.00/27.50   **Pension** – Prix minimum et maximum de la pension complète par personne et par jour en haute saison.

Au restaurant

Réclamez les menus à prix fixes et la carte chiffrée s'ils ne vous sont pas présentés spontanément.

A l'hôtel

Le prix du petit déjeuner est généralement inclus dans le prix de la chambre, même s'il n'est pas consommé.

Pension

La pension complète comprend: la chambre, le petit déjeuner et deux repas. Les prix de pension sont donnés à titre indicatif et sont généralement applicables à partir de trois jours mais il est indispensable de s'entendre à l'avance avec l'hôtelier pour conclure un arrangement définitif.

Les prix haute saison sont habituellement pratiqués de juin à septembre.

Réservations

Hôtels : Chaque fois que possible, la réservation préalable est souhaitable. Demandez à l'hôtelier de vous fournir dans sa lettre d'accord toutes précisions utiles sur la réservation et les conditions de séjour. Dans les stations balnéaires en particulier, les réservations s'appliquent généralement à des séjours partant d'un samedi à l'autre.

A toute demande écrite il est conseillé de joindre un coupon-réponse international.

Certains hôteliers demandent parfois le versement d'arrhes. Il s'agit d'un dépôt-garantie qui engage l'hôtelier comme le client. Sauf accord spécial le montant des arrhes peut être fixé à 10 % du montant total estimé.

Restaurants : il est vivement recommandé de réserver sa table aussi longtemps que possible à l'avance, de façon à éviter le désagrément d'un refus.

Animaux

L'introduction d'animaux domestiques (chiens, chats...) est interdite en Grande Bretagne et en Irlande.

LES VILLES

986 ㉞	Numéro de la carte Michelin et numéro du pli
403 404 M 27	Numéro des cartes Michelin et carroyage
pop. 1,057	Population totale (dernier recensement officiel publié)
ECD : Wednesday	Jour de fermeture des magasins (après-midi seulement)
✉ York	Bureau de poste desservant la localité
☎ 0225 Bath	Indicatif téléphonique interurbain suivi, si nécessaire, de la localité de rattachement
BX A	Lettres repérant un emplacement sur le plan
☀, ≼	Panorama, point de vue
⛳18	Golf et nombre de trous (accès permis à tous visiteurs)
✈	Aéroport
⛴	Transports maritimes (passagers et voitures)
⛴	Transports maritimes (passagers seulement) *Voir liste des compagnies en fin de guide*
🚗 ☏ 218	Localités desservies par train-auto – Renseignements au numéro de téléphone indiqué
ℹ	Information touristique

LES CURIOSITÉS

Intérêt

★★★	Vaut le voyage
★★	Mérite un détour
★	Intéressante
AC	Entrée payante

Situation des curiosités

See	Dans la ville
Envir.	Aux environs proches de la ville
Exc.	Excursions dans la région
N, S, E, W	La curiosité est située : au Nord, au Sud, à l'Est, à l'Ouest
A 22	On y va par la route A 22, repérée par le même signe sur le plan du Guide
2 m.	Distance en miles
h, mn	Temps de parcours à pied, aller et retour (h : heures, mn : minutes)

Heure légale

En hiver durant une période de temps fixée chaque année et s'étendant d'octobre à mars, les visiteurs devront tenir compte de l'heure officielle, égale à l'heure G.M.T. (une heure de retard sur l'heure française).

Les plans

Voirie

Certaines rues ne sont qu'amorcées
Rue de traversée ou de contournement – à chaussées séparées . . . .
Autoroute et numéro d'échangeur . . . .
Rue en construction – piétonne – à sens unique . . . .
Rue interdite, impraticable ou à circulation réglementée . . . .
Passage de la rue : à niveau, au-dessus, au-dessous de la voie ferrée . . . . . .
Porte – Passage sous voûte – Tunnel . . . .
Rue commerçante – Parc de stationnement public . . . .

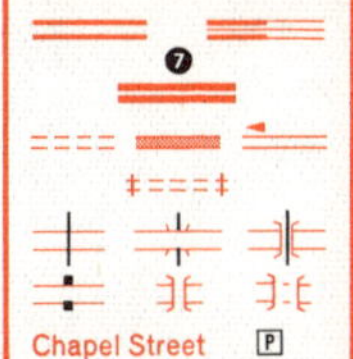

Curiosités - Hôtels

Monument intéressant et entrée principale .
Cathédrale ou église . . . . } Lettre les repérant sur le plan . . .
Lettre repérant les hôtels et les restaurants sur le plan . . . .

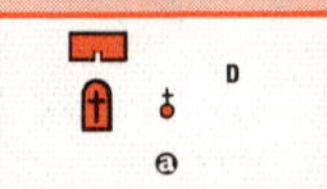

Signes divers

Cathédrale – Eglise – Hôpital – Poste restante, télégraphe, téléphone . . . . .
Edifices publics repérés par des lettres :
    Bureau de l'Administration du comté – Hôtel de ville . . . .
    Police (dans les grandes villes, commissariat central) – Musée . . . .
    Théâtre – Université, grande école . . . .
Information touristique. . . . .
Cimetière – Espace boisé, parc . . . .
Phare – Stade . . . .
Golf (accès permis à tous visiteurs) – (réservé) . . . .
Hippodrome – Panorama – Vue . . . .
Embarcadère : Transport de passagers et voitures – Aéroport . . . .
Station de métro. . . . .

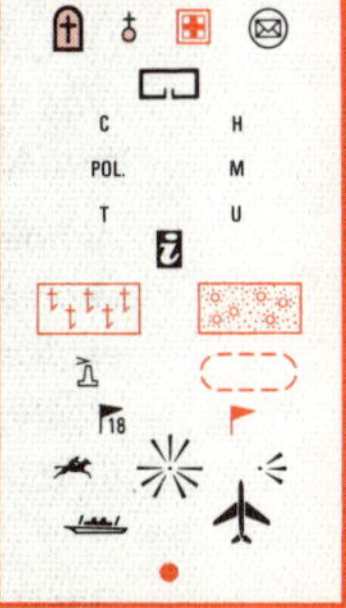

Londres - Signes particuliers

Nom d'arrondissement (borough) – de quartier (area) . . . .
Limite de « borough » – d' « area » . . . .
Station de métro. . . . .

Pour votre voiture

Au texte de la plupart des localités figure une liste des garagistes ou concessionnaires automobiles pouvant, éventuellement, vous aider en cas de panne.
Pour vos pneus, consultez les pages bordées de bleu.

Voyages en voiture

Les principales organisations de secours automobile dans le pays sont l'Automobile Association et le Royal Automobile Club, toutes deux offrant certains de leurs services aux membres de clubs affiliés.

AUTOMOBILE ASSOCIATION	ROYAL AUTOMOBILE CLUB
Fanum House	83-85 Pall Mall
BASINGSTOKE, Hants., RG21 2EA	LONDON SW1Y 5HW
☏ (0256) 20123	☏ (01) 930 4343

La nostra classificazione è stabilita ad uso dell'automobilista di passaggio. In ogni categoria, gli esercizi vengono citati in ordine di preferenza.

CLASSE E CONFORT

⛨	Gran lusso	XXXXX
⛨	Lusso	XXXX
⛨	Molto confortevole	XXX
⛨	Di buon confort	XX
⛨	Abbastanza confortevole	X
⛨	Semplice ma conveniente	
⛨	Altra risorsa, consigliata per prezzi contenuti	

without rest.   **L'albergo non ha ristorante**

with rm   **Il ristorante dispone di camere**

INSTALLAZIONI

I ⛨, ⛨, ⛨ offrono ogni confort ed effettuano generalmente il cambio di valute; per questi alberghi non specifichiamo quindi il dettaglio delle installazioni.

Nelle altre categorie, gli elementi di confort indicati esistono, il più delle volte, soltanto in alcune camere; questi alberghi dispongono tuttavia di docce e bagni comuni.

Codice postale dell'esercizio	LL35 0SB
Numero di telefono	☏ 64622
Numero di camere	**30 rm**
Ascensore	🛗
Televisione in camera	TV
Bagno e wc privati, bagno privato senza wc	🛁wc 🛁
Doccia e wc privati, doccia privata senza wc	🚿wc 🚿
Telefono in camera comunicante con l'esterno	☎
Camere d'agevole accesso per i minorati fisici	♿
Tennis	🎾
Piscina: all'aperto, coperta	🏊 🏊
Golf e numero di buche	⛳18
Pesca aperta ai clienti dell'albergo (eventualmente a pagamento)	🎣
Giardino	
Parco	
	park
Garage (generalmente a pagamento)	🚗
Parcheggio per auto	Ⓟ
L'albergo dispone di una o più sale per conferenze (minimo 25 posti)	🛝
Periodo di apertura di un albergo stagionale	
Apertura in stagione, ma periodo non precisato	*May-October*
	season

Gli esercizi in carattere grassetto senza tali indicazioni sono aperti tutto l'anno.

La scelta di un albergo, di un ristorante

Il soggiorno in alcuni alberghi si rivela talvolta particolarmente ameno o riposante.

Ciò può dipendere dalle caratteristiche dell'edificio, dalle decorazioni non comuni, dalla sua posizione, dall'accoglienza e dal servizio offerti.

Questi esercizi sono così contraddistinti:

Alberghi ameni

Ristoranti ameni

Un particolare ameno

Albergo molto tranquillo o isolato e tranquillo

Albergo tranquillo

Vista eccezionale

Vista interessante o estesa

Gli esercizi indicati in rosso es.: 🏨, ✕✕ with rm, o molto tranquilli 🐾 sono riportati sulle carte che precedono ciascuna delle regioni trattate nella guida.

Non abbiamo la pretesa di aver segnalato tutti gli alberghi ameni, nè tutti quelli molto tranquilli o isolati e tranquilli.

Le nostre ricerche continuano. Le potrete agevolare facendoci conoscere le vostre osservazioni e le vostre scoperte.

*La scelta
di un albergo,
di un ristorante*

LA TAVOLA

Le stelle di ottima tavola

Abbiamo contraddistinto con ❀ o ❀❀ quegli esercizi che, a nostro parere, meritano di essere segnalati alla vostra attenzione per la qualità della cucina, che può essere tipicamente nazionale o d'importazione.

Nel testo di questi esercizi indichiamo alcune specialità culinarie, non più di tre, che vi consigliamo di provare.

Un' ottima tavola nella sua categoria.

La stella indica una tappa gastronomica sul vostro itinerario. Non mettete a confronto la stella di un esercizio di lusso con quella di un piccolo esercizio, ma in entrambi i casi vi verranno serviti piatti di qualità, proporzionati al prezzo.

Tavola eccellente : merita una deviazione.

Prodotti e menu scelti... Aspettatevi una spesa in proporzione.

Ci saranno molto graditi i pareri ed i suggerimenti che vorrete segnalarci, in relazione alle vostre esperienze negli esercizi da noi raccomandati.

Da parte nostra le ricerche continuano.

La « M » rossa

Pur apprezzando le tavole a « stella », si desidera alle volte consumare un pasto più semplice ma sempre accuratamente preparato.

Alcuni esercizi ci son parsi rispondenti a tale esigenza e sono contraddistinti nella guida da una « M » in rosso.

La vendita delle bevande alcooliche

I locali autorizzati alla vendita di bevande alcooliche da consumarsi sul posto (Public houses – pubs – alberghi, ristoranti) aprono e chiudono secondo l'orario che i loro gestori preferiscono ma la vendita di queste bevande non vi è consentita che durante certi periodi di tempo fissati dalla legge. I ragazzi inferiori ai 14 anni non possono accedere al bar di esercizi con licenza durante le ore permesse, ma tale divieto non viene applicato al ristorante a condizione che sia separato o completamente a parte dal bar.

I giovani inferiori ai 18 anni non possono acquistare o consumare bevande alcooliche al bar di un esercizio con licenza durante le ore permesse, ma se superano i 16 anni possono acquistare o consumare le suddette bevande durante i pasti in un ristorante con bar separato.

N. B. : Gli alberghi o ristoranti senza licenza (unlicensed) non possono servire nessuna bevanda alcoolica, compresa la birra, nemmeno durante i pasti.

Orari di vendita autorizzati. Vedere all'inizio della nomenclatura di ciascuna delle regioni trattate in questa Guida.

La scelta di un albergo, di un ristorante

I PREZZI

Gli alberghi e ristoranti figurano in carattere grassetto quando gli albergatori ci hanno comunicato tutti i loro prezzi e si sono impegnati ad applicarli ai turisti di passaggio in possesso della nostra pubblicazione.

Questi prezzi, redatti alla fine dell'anno 1979, possono venire modificati qualora il costo della vita subisca notevoli variazioni. Essi debbono comunque essere considerati come prezzi base.

Quando non figurano le lettere **s.**, **t.**, o **st.** i prezzi indicati possono essere maggiorati per il servizio o per l'I.V.A. o per entrambi. (L'I.V.A. non viene applicata nelle Channel Islands).

Segnalateci le maggiorazioni che vi sembrino ingiustificate Quando i prezzi non sono indicati vi consigliamo di chiedere preventivamente le condizioni.

Principali **carte di credito** accettate da un albergo o ristorante: Access – American Express – Diners Club – Visa (BankAmericard).

I prezzi sono indicati in lire sterline (1 £ = 100 pence) ad eccezione per la Repubblica d'Irlanda (vedere p. 548).

Pasti

M 4.50/6.50 — **Prezzo fisso** – Minimo 4.50 e massimo 6.50, per pasti serviti ad ore normali (dalle 12.30 alle 14.30 e dalle 19 alle 21) compreso il coperto se del caso.

s. — Servizio compreso.

t. — I.V.A. compresa.

st. — Servizio ed I.V.A. compresi (prezzi netti).

M 6.00/8.00 — Vedere p. 31.

M a la carte 6.00/8.50 — **Alla carta** – Il 1° prezzo corrisponde ad un pasto semplice comprendente: primo piatto, piatto del giorno con contorno, dessert.

Il 2° prezzo corrisponde ad un pasto più completo comprendente: antipasto, piatto principale, formaggio e dessert.
Questi prezzi comprendono, se del caso, il coperto.

1.80 — Prezzo della mezza bottiglia o di una caraffa di vino.

1.50 — Prezzo della prima colazione se non è compreso nel prezzo della camera.

rm 15.00/21.00 — **Camere** – Prezzo minimo 15.00 per una camera singola e prezzo massimo 21.00 per la camera più bella (compreso il bagno se c'è) per due persone.

rm 17.00/25.00 — Il prezzo della prima colazione è compreso nel prezzo della camera.

P 20.00/27.50 — **Pensione** – Prezzo minimo e massimo della pensione completa per persona e per giorno in alta stagione.

Al ristorante

Chiedete i menu a prezzo fisso e la carta coi relativi prezzi se non vi vengono spontaneamente presentati.

All'albergo

Il prezzo della prima colazione, anche se non viene consumata, è generalmente compreso nel prezzo della camera.

La Pensione

Comprende la camera, la prima colazione e due pasti. I prezzi di pensione sono dati a titolo indicativo e sono generalmente applicabili a partire da 3 giorni di permanenza: è comunque indispensabile prendere accordi preventivi con l'albergatore per stabilire le condizioni definitive.

I prezzi di alta stagione vengono generalmente praticati da giugno a settembre.

Le prenotazioni

Alberghi : appena possibile, la prenotazione è consigliabile; chiedete all'albergatore di fornirvi, nella sua lettera di conferma, ogni dettaglio sulla prenotazione e sulle condizioni di soggiorno. Nelle stazioni balneari in particolar modo, le prenotazioni si applicano generalmente a soggiorni che vanno da un sabato all'altro.

Si consiglia di allegare sempre alle richieste scritte di prenotazione un tagliando risposta internazionale.

Alle volte alcuni albergatori chiedono il versamento di una caparra. E' un deposito-garanzia che impegna tanto l'albergatore che il cliente. Salvo accordi speciali, l'ammontare della caparra può venire fissato nella misura del 10 % dell'ammontare totale previsto.

Ristoranti : è sempre consigliabile prenotare con un certo anticipo per evitare uno spiacevole rifiuto all'ultimo momento.

Animali

Non possono accedere in Gran Bretagna e Irlanda animali domestici (cani, gatti...)

Per visitare
una città
ed i suoi dintorni

LE CITTÀ

986 ③④	Numero della carta Michelin e numero della piega
403 **404** M 27	Numeri delle carte Michelin e del riquadro
pop. 1,057	Popolazione totale (ultimo censimento ufficiale pubblicato)
ECD : Wednesday	Giorno di chiusura settimanale dei negozi (solo pomeriggio).
⊠ York	Sede dell'ufficio postale
✆ 0225 Bath	Prefisso telefonico interurbano (nome del centralino indicato solo quando differisce dal nome della località)
BX A	Lettere indicanti l'ubicazione sulla pianta
☀. ⋞	Panorama, punto di vista
⌗18	Golf e numero di buche (accesso consentito a tutti)
✈	Aeroporto
⛴	Trasporti marittimi (passeggeri ed autovetture)
⛵	Trasporti marittimi (solo passeggeri) *Vedere la lista delle compagnie alla fine della Guida*
🚗 ☏ 218	Località con servizio auto su treno. Informarsi al numero di telefono indicato
i	Ufficio informazioni turistiche

LE CURIOSITÀ

Grado d'interesse

★★★	Vale il viaggio
★★	Merita una deviazione
★	Interessante
AC	Entrata a pagamento

Situazione delle curiosità

See	Nella città
Envir.	Nei dintorni della città
Exc.	Nella regione
N, S, E, W	La curiosità è situata : a Nord, a Sud, a Est, a Ovest.
A 22	Ci si va per la strada A 22 indicata con lo stesso segno sulla pianta
2 m.	Distanza in miglia
h, mn	Tempo per percorsi a piedi, andata e ritorno (h : ore, mn : minuti)

Ora legale

In inverno, per un periodo che va da ottobre a marzo ed è determinato di anno in anno, viene applicata l'ora ufficiale, uguale all'ora solare del meridiano di Greenwich (G.M.T.). I visitatori dovranno considerare 1 ora di ritardo sull'ora normale italiana.

Le Piante

SEGNI CONVENZIONALI

Viabilità

Per certe strade noi indichiamo solamente l'inizio
Via di attraversamento o di circonvallazione – a doppia carreggiata . . . .
Autostrada e numero di svincolo . . . . . .
Via in costruzione – pedonale – a senso unico . . . .
Via vietata, impraticabile o a circolazione regolamentata . . . .
La via passa : a livello, al disopra, al disotto della ferrovia . . . .
Porta – Sottopassaggio – Galleria . . . .
Via commerciale – Parcheggio pubblico . . . .

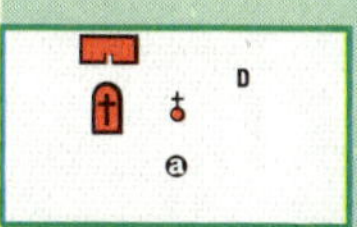

Curiosità - Alberghi

Monumento interessante ed entrata principale } Lettera di riferimento sulla pianta .
Cattedrale o chiesa . . . .
Lettera di riferimento degli alberghi e ristoranti sulla pianta . . . .

Simboli vari

Cattedrale – Chiesa – Ospedale – Fermo posta, telegrafo, telefono . . . .
Edifici pubblici indicati con lettere :
   Sede dell' Amministrazione di Contea – Municipio . . . .
   Polizia (Questura, nelle grandi città) – Museo . . . .
   Teatro – Università, grande scuola . . . .
Ufficio informazioni turistiche
Cimitero – Zona alberata, parco . . . .
Faro – Stadio . . . .
Golf (accesso consentito a tutti) – riservato . . . .
Ippodromo – Panorama – Vista . . . .
Imbarcadero : Trasporto passeggeri ed autovetture – Aeroporto . . . .
Stazione della Metropolitana . . . .

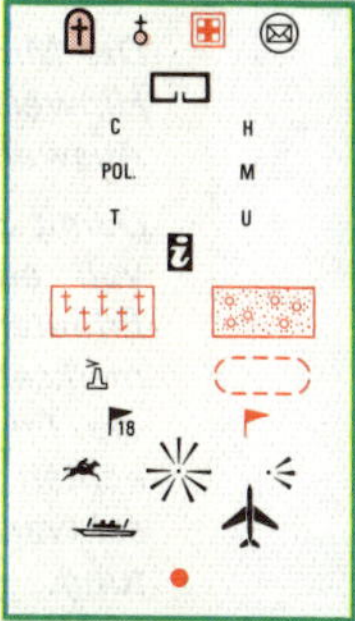

Londra - Segni particolari

Nome del distretto amministrativo (borough) – del quartiere (area) . . . .
Limite del « borough » – di « area » . . . .
Stazione della Metropolitana . . . .

Per la vostra automobile

Nel testo di molte località abbiamo elencato gli indirizzi di garage o concessionari in grado di effettuare il traino o le riparazioni.
Per i vostri pneumatici, consultate le pagine bordate di blu.

Viaggi in automobile

Le principali organizzazioni di soccorso automobilistico sono l'Automobile Association ed il Royal Automobile Club: entrambe offrono alcuni loro servizi ai membri dei club affiliati

AUTOMOBILE ASSOCIATION
Fanum House
BASINGSTOKE, Hants., RG21 2EA
☎ (0256) 20123

ROYAL AUTOMOBILE CLUB
83-85 Pall Mall
LONDON SW1Y 5HW
☎ (01) 930 4343

Der Michelin-Führer bietet Ihnen viele nützliche Hinweise für die Reise und eine umfangreiche Auswahl an Hotels und Restaurants.

Damit Sie die Vielfalt der gegebenen Auskünfte voll ausnützen können, bitten wir Sie, die Erläuterungen auf den folgenden Seiten aufmerksam durchzulesen und dabei besonders auf die Erklärungen der verwendeten Zeichen zu achten : diese haben, fett oder dünn gedruckt, in schwarz oder in rot, immer eine andere Bedeutung.

Wie auch die anderen Roten Michelin-Führer ist er kein vollständiges Verzeichnis aller Hotels und Restaurants. Um den Ansprüchen aller Reisenden gerecht zu werden, empfehlen wir Häuser jeder Kategorie, wobei wir uns jedoch jeweils auf eine Auswahl beschränken mußten.

Wir wünschen Ihnen eine gute Fahrt. Bitte teilen Sie uns nach Ihrer Rückkehr Ihre Eindrücke mit.

Michelin Tyre Co Ltd.
Tourism Department
81 Fulham Road, GB - LONDON SW3 6RD

Ihre Hinweise, Ihr Lob und Ihre Kritik werden von unseren Inspektoren an Ort und Stelle überprüft ; sie helfen uns, die Angaben im Michelin-Führer noch besser, noch exakter zu machen.

Besten Dank im voraus.

Unsere Auswahl ist für Durchreisende gedacht. In jeder Kategorie drückt die Reihenfolge der Betriebe eine weitere Rangordnung aus.

KLASSENEINTEILUNG UND KOMFORT

Großer Luxus	
Luxus	
Sehr komfortabel	
Mit gutem Komfort	
Bürgerlich	
Einfach, ordentlich	
Preiswerte, empfehlenswerte Gasthäuser und Pensionen	

without rest.	Hotel ohne Restaurant
with rm	Restaurant vermietet auch Zimmer

EINRICHTUNG

Für die geben wir keine Einzelheiten über die Einrichtung (wc wc) an, da diese Hotels im allgemeinen jeden Komfort besitzen. Außerdem besteht die Möglichkeit, Geld zu wechseln.

In den Häusern der übrigen Kategorien sind die genannten Einrichtungen oft nur in einem Teil der Zimmer vorhanden. Diese Häuser verfügen meist über ein Etagenbad oder eine Etagendusche.

Angabe des Postbezirks (hinter der Hoteladresse)
Telefonnummer
Anzahl der Zimmer
Fahrstuhl
Fernsehen im Zimmer
Privatbad mit wc, Privatbad ohne wc
Privatdusche mit wc, Privatdusche ohne wc
Zimmertelefon mit Außenverbindung
Für Körperbehinderte leicht zugängliche Zimmer
Tennis
Freibad, Hallenbad
Golfplatz mit Lochzahl
Angelmöglichkeit für Hotelgäste, evtl. gegen Gebühr
Garten
Park

Garage (wird meist berechnet)
Parkplatz

Konferenzraum (für mind. 25 Personen)

Öffnungszeit eines Saisonhotels
Unbestimmte Öffnungszeit eines Saisonhotels

Die fettgedruckten Häuser, hinter deren Namen keine Zeitangabe steht, sind ganzjährig geöffnet.

LL35 OSB
64622
30 rm

wc
wc

park

May-October season

ANNEHMLICHKEITEN

In manchen Hotels ist der Aufenthalt wegen der schönen, ruhigen Lage, der nicht alltäglichen Einrichtung und Atmosphäre und dem gebotenen Service besonders angenehm und erholsam.

Solche Häuser und ihre besonderen Annehmlichkeiten sind im Führer durch folgende Symbole gekennzeichnet:

Angenehme Hotels
Angenehme Restaurants

Besondere Annehmlichkeit

Sehr ruhiges, oder abgelegenes und ruhiges Hotel
Ruhiges Hotel

Reizvolle Aussicht
Interessante oder weite Sicht

Auf den Übersichtskarten in der Einleitung zu den einzelnen Landesteilen sind die Orte, in denen sich mindestens ein angenehmes Haus mit rotem Symbol (z. B. 🏨, ✗ with rm) oder ein sehr ruhiges Haus (🐦) befindet, eingezeichnet.

Wir wissen, daß diese Auswahl noch nicht vollständig ist, sind aber laufend bemüht, weitere solche Häuser für Sie zu entdecken; dabei sind uns Ihre Erfahrungen und Hinweise eine wertvolle Hilfe.

KÜCHE

Die Sterne für gute Küche

Mit ✿ oder ✿✿ kennzeichnen wir die Häuser mit landesüblicher oder ausländischer Küche, deren Qualität wir der Aufmerksamkeit der Leser besonders empfehlen möchten.

Im Text der einzelnen Häuser geben wir einige – höchstens drei – kulinarische Spezialitäten an, die Sie versuchen sollten.

Eine sehr gute Küche : verdient Ihre besondere Beachtung

✿✿

Der Stern bedeutet eine angenehme Unterbrechung Ihrer Reise. Vergleichen Sie aber bitte nicht den Stern eines teuren Luxusrestaurants mit dem Stern eines kleinen oder mittleren Hauses, wo man Ihnen zu einem annehmbaren Preis eine ebenfalls vorzügliche Mahlzeit reicht.

Eine hervorragende Küche : verdient einen Umweg

✿

Ausgesuchte Spezialitäten, erstklassige Zubereitung... Angemessene Preise.

Teilen Sie uns bitte Ihre Ansicht und Ihre Vorschläge bezüglich der von uns ausgezeichneten Küchen mit.

Wir danken Ihnen dafür im voraus.

Das rote « M »

Wir glauben, daß Sie neben den Häusern mit Stern auch solche Adressen interessieren werden, die einfache, aber sorgfältig zubereitete Mahlzeiten anbieten.

Auf solche Häuser weisen wir im Text durch das rote « M » hin.

Ausschank alkoholischer Getränke

Betriebe mit Ausschanklizenz für alkoholische Getränke (Public houses – pubs – Hotels und Restaurants) können zwar ihre Öffnungs- und Schließungszeiten selbst bestimmen, der Ausschank alkoholischer Getränke jedoch ist nur während gesetzlich festgelegten Zeiten erlaubt. Kindern unter 14 Jahren ist der Zutritt zu den lizensierten Hotelbars während der Ausschankzeiten untersagt. Dies gilt jedoch weder für das Hotel-Restaurant, wenn dieses von der Bar abgetrennt ist, noch für den übrigen Hotelteil.

Jugendliche unter 18 Jahren dürfen in der Bar eines lizensierten Betriebes während der Ausschankzeiten alkoholische Getränke weder kaufen noch konsumieren. Dagegen ist es Jugendlichen ab 16 Jahren erlaubt, zu einer Mahlzeit in einem Restaurant alkoholische Getränke zu trinken, vorausgesetzt, das Restaurant ist von der Bar abgetrennt.

Zur Beachtung : Hotels und Restaurants ohne Ausschanklizenz (unlicensed) dürfen alkoholische Getränke und Bier auch zu den Mahlzeiten nicht ausschenken.

Ausschankzeiten : Übersichtstabellen in der Einleitung zu den einzelnen Landesteilen.

Wahl eines Hotels, eines Restaurants

Die Namen der Hotels und Restaurants, die ihre Preise genannt haben, sind fett gedruckt. Gleichzeitig haben sich diese Häuser verpflichtet, die angegebenen Preise den Benutzern des Michelin-Führers zu berechnen.

Die in diesem Führer genannten Preise wurden uns Ende 1979 angegeben. Sie können sich 1980 erhöhen, wenn die allgemeinen Lebenshaltungskosten steigen. Sie können aber in diesem Fall als Richtpreise angesehen werden.

Wenn die Buchstaben **s., t.,** oder **st.** nicht hinter den angegebenen Preisen aufgeführt sind, können sich diese um den Zuschlag für Bedienung und/oder MWSt erhöhen (keine MWSt auf den Channel Islands).

Verständigen Sie uns von jeder Preiserhöhung, die unbegründet erscheint. Wenn kein Preis angegeben ist, raten wir Ihnen, sich beim Hotelier nach den Bedingungen zu erkundigen.

Von Hotels und Restaurants angenommene **Kreditkarten:** Access – American Express – Diners Club – Visa (BankAmericard).

Die Preise sind in Pfund Sterling angegeben (1 £ = 100 pence) mit Ausnahme der Republik Irland (s.S. 548).

Mahlzeiten

M 4.50/6.50 **Feste Menupreise** – Mindest- 4.50 und Höchstpreis 6.50 (inklusive Couvert) für die Mahlzeiten, die zu den normalen Tischzeiten serviert werden (12.30 - 14.30 und 19 - 21 Uhr).

s. Bedienung inbegriffen.

t. MWSt inbegriffen.

st. Bedienung und MWSt inbegriffen (Inklusivpreise).

M 6.00/8.00 Siehe Seite 39.

M a la carte 6.00/8.50 **Mahlzeiten «à la carte»** – Der erste Preis entspricht einer einfachen aber sorgfältig zubereiteten Mahlzeit, bestehend aus kleiner Vorspeise, Tagesgericht mit Beilage und Nachtisch.

Der zweite Preis entspricht einer reichlicheren Mahlzeit mit Vorspeise, Hauptgericht, Käse oder Nachtisch («couvert» ist in den Preisen enthalten).

⌕ 1.80 Preis für 1/2 Flasche oder eine Karaffe Tafelwein.

⌕ 1.50 Frühstückspreis, wenn dieser nicht im Übernachtungspreis enthalten ist.

rm 15.00/21.00 **Zimmer** – Mindestpreis 15.00 für ein Einzelzimmer und Höchstpreis 21.00 für das schönste Doppelzimmer (mit Bad).

rm ⌕ 17.00/25.00 Übernachtung mit Frühstück.

P 20.00/27.50 **Pension** – Mindest- und Höchstpreis für Vollpension pro Person und Tag in der Hochsaison.

Im Restaurant

Verlangen Sie die Karte der Tagesmenus zu Festpreisen und die Speisekarte, wenn sie Ihnen nicht von selbst vorgelegt werden.

Im Hotel

Im allgemeinen ist das Frühstück (auch wenn es nicht eingenommen wird) im Zimmerpreis enthalten.

Pension

Die Vollpension umfaßt Zimmer, Frühstück und zwei Mahlzeiten. Die angegebenen Vollpensionspreise sind Richtpreise und gelten im allgemeinen bei einem Aufenthalt ab 3 Tagen. Es empfiehlt sich jedoch, sich zuvor mit dem Hotelier über den endgültigen Pensionspreis zu einigen.

Hochsaisonpreise werden im allgemeinen von Juni bis September berechnet.

Zimmerreservierung

Hotels : Es ist ratsam, wenn irgend möglich, die Zimmer reservieren zu lassen. Bitten Sie den Hotelier, daß er Ihnen in seinem Bestätigungsschreiben alle seine Bedingungen mitteilt.

Besonders in Seebädern wird Vollpension im allgemeinen nur wochenweise, von Samstag zu Samstag gewährt.

Bei schriftlichen Zimmerbestellungen empfiehlt es sich, einen Freiumschlag oder einen internationalen Antwortschein beizufügen.

Einige Hoteliers verlangen eine Anzahlung (etwa 10 % wenn nichts anderes vereinbart wird) auf den voraussichtlichen Endpreis. Sie ist als Garantie für beide Seiten anzusehen.

Restaurant : Es empfiehlt sich, Tische immer und so früh wie möglich vorzubestellen.

Tiere

Das Mitführen von Haustieren (Hunde, Katzen u. dgl.) bei der Einreise in Großbritannien und Irland ist untersagt.

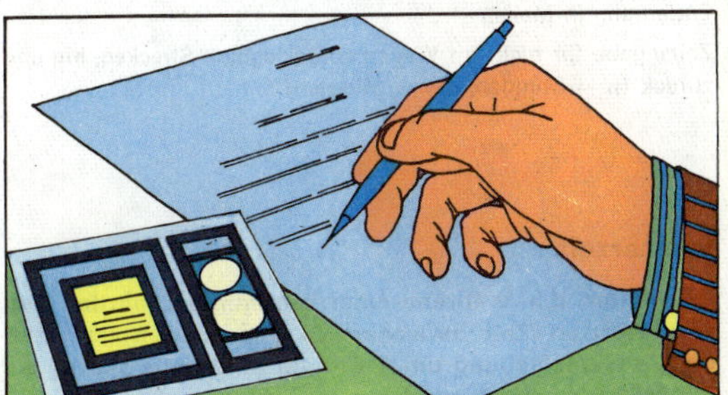

STÄDTE

986 ㉞	Nummer der Faltseite auf der Michelin-Karte **986**
403 404 M 27	Nummern der Michelin-Karten und Koordinaten des Gratfeldes
pop. 1,057	Einwohnerzahl (nach der letzten offiziellen Volkszählung)
ECD : Wednesday	Tag, an dem die Läden nachmittags geschlossen sind
✉ York	Zuständiges Postamt
✆ 0225 Bath	Zuständiges Fernsprechamt
BX **A**	Markierung auf dem Stadtplan
☀, ≼	Rundblick, Aussichtspunkt
18	Öffentlicher Golfplatz und Lochzahl
✈	Flughafen
⛴	Personen- und Autofähre
⛵	Personenfähre *Liste der Schiffahrtsgesellschaften am Ende des Führers*
🚗 218	Ladestelle für Autoreisezüge - Nähere Auskünfte unter der angegebenen Telefonnummer
🛈	Informationsstelle

HAUPTSEHENSWÜRDIGKEITEN

***	Eine Reise wert
**	Verdient einen Umweg
*	Sehenswert
AC	Eintritt (gegen Gebühr)

Lage

See	In der Stadt
Envir.	In der Umgebung der Stadt
Exc.	Ausflugsziele
N, S, E, W	Im N = Norden, S = Süden, E = Osten, W = Westen der Stadt
A 22	Zu erreichen über die Straße A 22
2 m.	Entfernung in Meilen
h. mn.	Zeitangabe für nicht im Wagen zurücklegbare Strecken, hin und zurück (h = Stunden, mn = Minuten)

Winterzeit

Im Winter, d.h. während einer bestimmten, jährlich neu festgesetzten Zeit zwischen Oktober und März, muß die Zeitverschiebung um 1 Stunde (1 Stunde später als die MEZ) beachtet werden.

Stadtpläne

ZEICHENERKLÄRUNG

Straßen

Nebenstraßen sind nur angedeutet
Durchfahrts- oder Umgehungsstraße – Straße mit getrennten Fahrbahnen. . . . . .
Autobahn und Nummer der Anschlußstelle . . . .
Straße im Bau – Fußgängerzone – Einbahnstraße . . . .
Straße für Kfz gesperrt, nicht befahrbar oder mit Verkehrsbeschränkungen
Bahnübergang : schienengleich, Überführung, Unterführung . . . .
Tor – Passage – Tunnel . . . .
Einkaufsstraße – Öffentlicher Parkplatz, Parkhaus

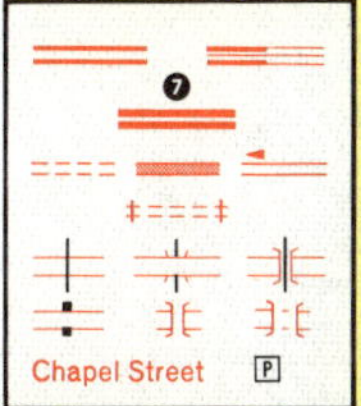

Sehenswürdigkeiten - Hotels

Sehenswertes Gebäude mit Haupteingang .   } Referenzbuchstabe auf dem Plan . .
Kathedrale – Kirche . . . . }
Markierung der Hotels und Restaurants auf dem Plan . . . .

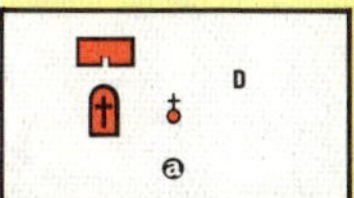

Sonstige Zeichen

Kathedrale – Kirche – Krankenhaus – Postlagernde Sendungen, Telegraph, Telefon . .
Öffentliche Gebäude, durch Buchstaben gekennzeichnet :
  Sitz der Grafschaftsverwaltung – Rathaus.
  Polizei (in größeren Städten Polizeipräsidium) – Museum . . . .
  Theater – Universität, Hochschule . . . .
Informationsstelle . . . .
Friedhof – Grünfläche mit Baumbestand, Park . . . .
Leuchtturm – Sportplatz . . . .
Öffentlicher Golf – Golf (Zutritt bedingt erlaubt) . . . .
Pferderennbahn – Rundblick – Aussicht . . . . . .
Anlegestelle : Personen- und Autofähre – Flughafen . . .
U–Bahnhof . . . .

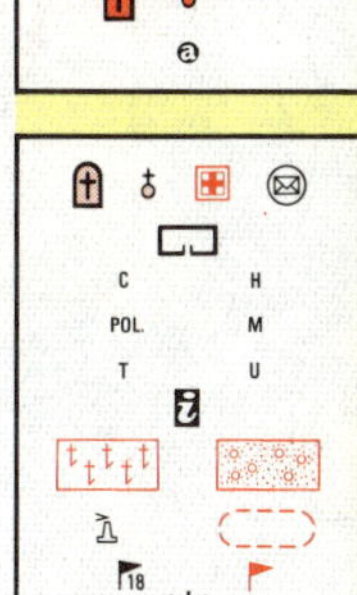

London - Besondere Symbole

Name des Verwaltungsbezirks (borough) – des Stadtteils (area) . . . .
Grenze des „ borough " – des „ area ", ...
U–Bahnstation . . . .

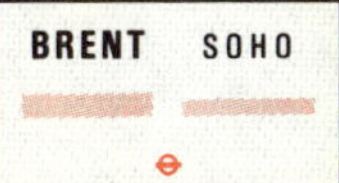

Für Ihren Wagen

Bei den meisten Orten geben wir die Adressen der Kfz-Vertrags-
werkstätten mit Abschlepp- bzw. Reparaturdienst an.
Hinweise für Ihre Reifen finden Sie auf den blau umrandeten
Seiten.

Reisen mit Ihrem Wagen

Die wichtigsten Automobilclubs des Landes sind die Automobile
Association und der Royal Automobile Club, die den Mitgliedern
der der FIA angeschlossenen Automobilclubs Pannenhilfe leisten
und einige ihrer Dienstleistungen anbieten.

AUTOMOBILE ASSOCIATION   ROYAL AUTOMOBILE CLUB
Fanum House   83-85 Pall Mall
BASINGSTOKE, Hants.,RG21 2EA   LONDON SW1Y 5HW
☎ (0256) 20123   ☎ (01) 930 4343

MOTORWAY SERVICE AREAS
RIFORNIMENTO SULLE AUTOSTRADE
RAVITAILLEMENT SUR AUTOROUTES
TANKEN UND RASTEN AN DER AUTOBAHN

NORTH
SEA
ATLANTIC
OCEAN
ENGLISH CHANNEL

GLASGOW
Harthill
M 8
EDINBURGH
Hamilton
Bothwell
M 74
CARLISLE
NEWCASTLE
Washington-Birtley
Southwaite
A1
Tebay West
Killington
Burton West
M 6
Forton
Hartshead Moor
LEEDS
Anderton
M 62
Charnock Richard
M 62
Woolley Edge
M 61
Birch
Burtonwood
Woodall
Knutsford
Sandbach
Keele
Trowell
M 6
Hilton Park
M 1
Leicester Forest East
Frankley
Corley
M 6
Watford Gap
Rothersthorpe
M 5
Newport Pagnell
M 1
Strensham
Toddington
Scratchwood
Michael Wood
Leigh Delamere
Heston
Aust
M 4
GREATER LONDON
BRISTOL
Membury
M 2
Gordano
Farthing Corner
M 3
Fleet
DOVER
Rownhams
Taunton Dene
M 27
SOUTHAMPTON
M 5
Exeter

Location		Hotel	Town	Details see page
M 1				
Scratchwood Service Area		TraveLodge	Hendon (L.B. of Barnet)	276
Junction 6 – NE : 1 m. on A 405		Noke	St. Albans	371
Junction 8 – W : ½ m. on A 4147		Post House	Hemel Hempstead	196
Junction 11 – E : ¼ m. on A 505		Luton Crest Motel	Luton	303
Junction 11 – E : ¾ m. on A 505		Luton Eurocrest	Luton	303
Newport Pagnell Service Area 3		TraveLodge	Newport Pagnell	330
Junction 18 – E : ¼ m. on A 428		Post House	Rugby (at Crick)	369
Junction 21/21A – NE : 2 ½ m. on A 46		Post House	Leicester (at Braunstone)	222
Junction 25 – W : ¼ m. on A 52		Post House	Nottingham (at Sandiacre)	339
Junction 25 – S : ½ m. on B 6002		Novotel	Nottingham (at Long Eaton)	339
Junction 40 – E : 1 m. on A 638		Post House	Wakefield	422
A 1 (M)				
Junction A 1, A 638 – N : 2 ½ m. on A 1		TraveLodge	Wentbridge (at Barnsdale Bar)	427
A 1 (M) via A 66 (M) – E : 2 m. on A 66		Europa Lodge	Darlington	154
A 1 (M) via A 167 – S : ¾ m. off A 167		Hall Garth Country House	Darlington (at Coatham Mundeville)	154
M 2				
Junction 1 – W : ¼ m. on A 2		Inn on the Lake	Shorne	386
M 3				
Junction 3 – N : 1 m. on A 30		Cricketers'	Bagshot	71
Junction 6 – SW : 1 ½ m. at junction A 30 and A 339		Hampshire Moathouse	Basingstoke	75
M 4				
Junction 3 – N : 1 ½ m. off A 312		Arlington	Heathrow Airport (L.B. of Hillingdon)	283
Junction 4 – S : ½ m. on B 379		Post House	Heathrow Airport	283
Junction 4 – N : ½ m. on B 379		Holiday Inn	Heathrow Airport	282
Junction 5 – NW : ¼ m. on A 4		Holiday Inn	Slough	389
Junction 9A – NE : ½ m. on Shoppenhangers Rd		Maidenhead Eurocrest	Maidenhead	306
Junction 11 – N : ½ m. on A 33		Post House	Reading	361
Junction 15 – N : 2 m. on A 345		Post House	Swindon	408
Junction 19 – SW : 2 ½ m. by M 32 on A 4174		Bristol Eurocrest	Bristol (at Hambrook)	111
Junction 24 – E : 1 ½ m. on A 48		New Inn Motel	Newport (Gwent) (at Langstone)	330
Junction 24 – S : ½ m. on A 48		Gateway Motor Motel	Newport (Gwent)	330

Location	Hotel	Town	Details see page
M 5			
Junction 1 – W: 1 m. on A 41	Europa Lodge	Birmingham (at West Bromwich)	92
Junction 5 – SW: 1 m. on A 38	Château Impney	Droitwich	162
Junction 11 – Γ: 1 m. on A 40	Golden Valley	Cheltenham	133
Junction 14 – N: 3 ½ m. on A 38 by B 4509	Newport Towers Motel	Berkeley (at Newport)	81
Junction 14 – SW: 1 ½ m. on A 38 by B 4509	Park	Falfield	172
M 6			
Junction 2 – S: 1 ½ m. on A 46	Coventry Eurocrest	Coventry (at Walsgrave-on-Sowe)	147
Junction 3 – S: 1 m. on A 444	Novotel	Coventry (at Longford)	147
Junction 7 – N: ¼ m. on A 34	Post House	Birmingham (at Great Barr)	92
Junction 14 – SE: ½ m. on A 5013	Tillington Hall	Stafford	396
Junction 15 – N: ¼ m. on A 519	Post House	Newcastle-under-Lyme	324
Junction 15 – S: ¾ m. on A 519	Clayton Lodge	Newcastle-under-Lyme	324
Charnock Richard Service Area	TraveLodge	Charnock Richard	132
Junction 27 – E: ¼ m. on B 5239	Casinelli's Almond Brook Motor Inn	Standish	397
Junction 38 and 39 – N: 1 m. of junction 38	Tebay Mountain Lodge Motel	Tebay	410
Junction 31 – W: ¼ m. on A 59	Tickled Trout	Preston (at Samlesbury)	359
Junction 44 – N: ¼ m. on A 7	Carlisle Crest Motel	Carlisle (at Kingstown)	128
M 20			
Junction with A 20 – NW: ½ m. on A 20	with rm Moat	Wrotham	448
M 23			
Junction with A 23 – S: ½ m. on A 23	Crawley Forest	Crawley (at Pease Pottage)	152
M 32 (this hotel also under M 4)			
Junction 1 – W: ½ m. on A 4174	Bristol Eurocrest	Bristol (at Hambrook)	111
M 40			
Junction 2 – E: 1 ¾ m. on A 40	Bellhouse	Beaconsfield	78
Junction 7 – NW: ½ m. on A 40	Belfry	Milton Common	319
M 56			
Junction 5 – on Airport Approach Road	Excelsior	Manchester (at Airport)	313
Junction 11 – N: ¼ m. on A 56	Lord Daresbury	Daresbury	154
Junction 12 – SE: ¼ m. off A 557	Runcorn Eurocrest	Runcorn	370
M 61			
Junction 5 – NE: 1 m. on A 58	Bolton Crest	Bolton	96
M 62			
Junction 24 – S: ¼ m. on A 629	Pennine President	Huddersfield	203
Junction 26 – N: 1 m. on M 606	Novotel	Bradford	102
Junction 30 – N: 1 m. on A 639	Leeds Crest Motel	Leeds (at Oulton)	217
Junction 34 – N: ¾ m. on A 645	Maine Motor Inn	Whitley Bridge	431
M 63			
Junction 9 – by approach Rd	Post House	Manchester (at Northenden)	313

TOWNS INCLUDED IN THE GUIDE

To keep the full, distinctive flavour of the separate kingdoms, principality, province, republic and islands which go to make up the British Isles, the Guide has been divided into sections each preceded by a separate map.

The maps show the towns and places with establishments included in the Guide, and those particularly selected for their general attractiveness, quiet atmosphere and good food.

A map of Great Britain and the Republic of Ireland at the beginning of the Guide shows major roads and main passenger and car ferry routes.

LES VILLES CITÉES

Chaque royaume ou Etat composant les Iles Britanniques garde sa personnalité propre; aussi sont-ils présentés en faisant précéder la nomenclature de chacun d'eux par une carte.

Cette carte signale les localités retenues et, pour chacune d'elles l'existence éventuelle d'établissements recommandés pour leur agrément, leur calme ou leur bonne cuisine.

Une carte générale de la Grande-Bretagne et de la République d'Irlande figure en outre au début de ce Guide et donne les principales voies de communications terrestres et maritimes.

LE CITTÀ COMPRESE NELLA GUIDA

Ogni Reame o Stato che compone le Isole Britanniche mantiene la sua propria personalità; perciò abbiamo ritenuto opportuno presentarli facendo precedere una carta geografica alla nomenclatura di ciascuno di essi.

Questa carta segnala le località selezionate e, per ognuna di esse, l'eventuale esistenza di esercizi particolarmente raccomandabili per la loro amenità, la loro tranquillità o la loro buona cucina.

Inoltre, una carta generale della Gran Bretagna e della Repubblica d'Irlanda figura all'inizio della Guida ed indica le principali vie di comunicazione terrestri e marittime.

DIE IM MICHELIN-FÜHRER ERWÄHNTEN ORTE

Jedes einzelne der Länder, die unter dem Begriff « Britische Inseln » zusammengefaßt sind, hat seinen eigenen Charakter; wir haben dem Rechnung getragen, indem wir dem Ortsverzeichnis jedes « Landes » eine Übersichtskarte vorangestellt haben.

Auf dieser Karte finden Sie alle im Führer erwähnten Orte, Orte mit besonders angenehmen oder ruhig gelegenen Häusern, sowie solche mit besonders guter Küche.

Eine Gesamtkarte Großbritanniens und der Republik Irland mit den wichtigsten Verkehrsverbindungen (Land- und Seewege) finden Sie in der Einleitung.

England and Wales

COUNTY ABBREVIATIONS

ABBREVIAZIONI DELLE CONTEE

ABRÉVIATIONS DES COMTÉS

ABKÜRZUNGEN DER GRAFSCHAFTEN

ENGLAND

Avon	Avon
Bedfordshire	Beds.
Berkshire	Berks.
Buckinghamshire	Bucks.
Cambridgeshire	Cambs.
Cheshire	Cheshire
Cleveland	Cleveland
Cornwall	Cornwall
Cumbria	Cumbria
Derbyshire	Derbs.
Devon	Devon
Dorset	Dorset
Durham	Durham
East Sussex	East Sussex
Essex	Essex
Gloucestershire	Glos.
Greater Manchester	Greater Manchester
Hampshire	Hants.
Hereford and Worcester	Heref. and Worc.
Hertfordshire	Herts.
Humberside	Humberside
Isle of Wight	I. O. W.
Kent	Kent
Lancashire	Lancs.
Leicestershire	Leics.
Lincolnshire	Lincs.
Merseyside	Merseyside
Norfolk	Norfolk
Northamptonshire	Northants.
Northumberland	Northumb.
North Yorkshire	North Yorks.
Nottinghamshire	Notts.
Oxfordshire	Oxon.
Salop	Salop
Somerset	Somerset
South Yorkshire	South Yorks.
Staffordshire	Staffs.
Suffolk	Suffolk
Surrey	Surrey
Tyne and Wear	Tyne and Wear
Warwickshire	Warw.
West Midlands	West Midlands
West Sussex	West Sussex
West Yorkshire	West Yorks.
Wiltshire	Wilts.

WALES

Clwyd	Clwyd
Dyfed	Dyfed
Gwent	Gwent
Gwynedd	Gwynedd
Mid Glamorgan	Mid Glam.
Powys	Powys
South Glamorgan	South Glam.
West Glamorgan	West Glam.

LICENSING HOURS - WHEN DRINKING ALCOHOLIC BEVERAGES IS PERMITTED IN PUBS AND BARS AND OTHER ON-LICENSED PREMISES (The General Rule).

HEURES PERMISES POUR LA CONSOMMATION DES BOISSONS ALCOOLISÉES (Règle Générale).

ORARI CONSENTITI PER LA CONSUMAZIONE DI BEVANDE ALCOOLICHE (Regola Generale).

AUSSCHANKZEITEN FÜR ALKOHOLISCHE GETRÄNKE (Allgemeine Regelung).

	from de	to à	from de	to à	Possible extension to Extension possible jusqu'à	
Weekdays (other than Good Friday and Christmas Day) Jours de semaine (autres que Vendredi-Saint et Jour de Noël)	11.00	15.00	17.30	22.30	23.00	Giorni della settimana (esclusi Venerdì Santo e Natale) Wochentags (außer Karfreitag und Weihnachten)
Sundays, Good Friday, Christmas Day Dimanches, Vendredi-Saint, Jour de Noël	12.00	14.00	19.00	22.30		Domeniche, Venerdì Santo, Natale Sonntags, Karfreitag und Weihnachten
	dalle von	alle bis	dalle von	alle bis	Estensione possibile fino alle Verlängerung möglich bis	

Wines and beverages may be taken with meals until 15.00 hours in on-licensed premises.

RESIDENTS : There are no time restrictions in licensed hotels for residents and their private friends.

SUNDAYS IN WALES: as in England in Clwyd, Gwent, Powys, Mid/South Glamorgan and parts of Dyfed, Gwynedd and West Glamorgan. Full day closure in parts of Dyfed, Gwynedd and West Glamorgan.

Boissons au cours des repas: jusqu'à 15 h dans les lieux autorisés.

RÉSIDENTS : aucune restriction dans l'hôtel de résidence si celui-ci possède une licence, y compris pour leurs amis privés.

DIMANCHE au PAYS DE GALLES : mêmes horaires qu'en Angleterre pour les comtés de Clwyd, Gwent, Powys, Mid/South Glamorgan et une partie des comtés de Dyfed, Gwynedd et West Glamorgan. Fermeture totale dans les autres parties du Dyfed, Gwynedd et West Glamorgan.

Bevande durante i pasti : fino alle 15 nei locali autorizzati.

RESIDENTI: nessuna restrizione nell'albergo di residenza se ha la licenza, anche per gli amici.

DOMENICA nel GALLES : stessi orari dell' Inghilterra per le contee di Clwyd, Gwent, Powys, Mid/South Glamorgan e una parte delle contee di Dyfed, Gwynedd e West Glamorgan. Chiusura totale nelle altre parti del Dyfed, Gwynedd e West Glamorgan.

Getränke zu den Mahlzeiten : bis 15 Uhr in den lizensierten Betrieben.

HOTELGÄSTE : Keine Beschränkung für den Gast und dessen persönliche Freunde im Hotel selbst, sofern dieses lizensiert ist.

SONNTAGSREGELUNG in WALES : gleiche Regelung wie in England für die Grafschaften Clwyd, Gwent, Powys, Mittel/Süd Glamorgan sowie für einen Teil der Grafschaften Dyfed, Gwynedd und West Glamorgan. In den übrigen Teilen dieser Grafschaften sind die Ausschankbetriebe geschlossen.

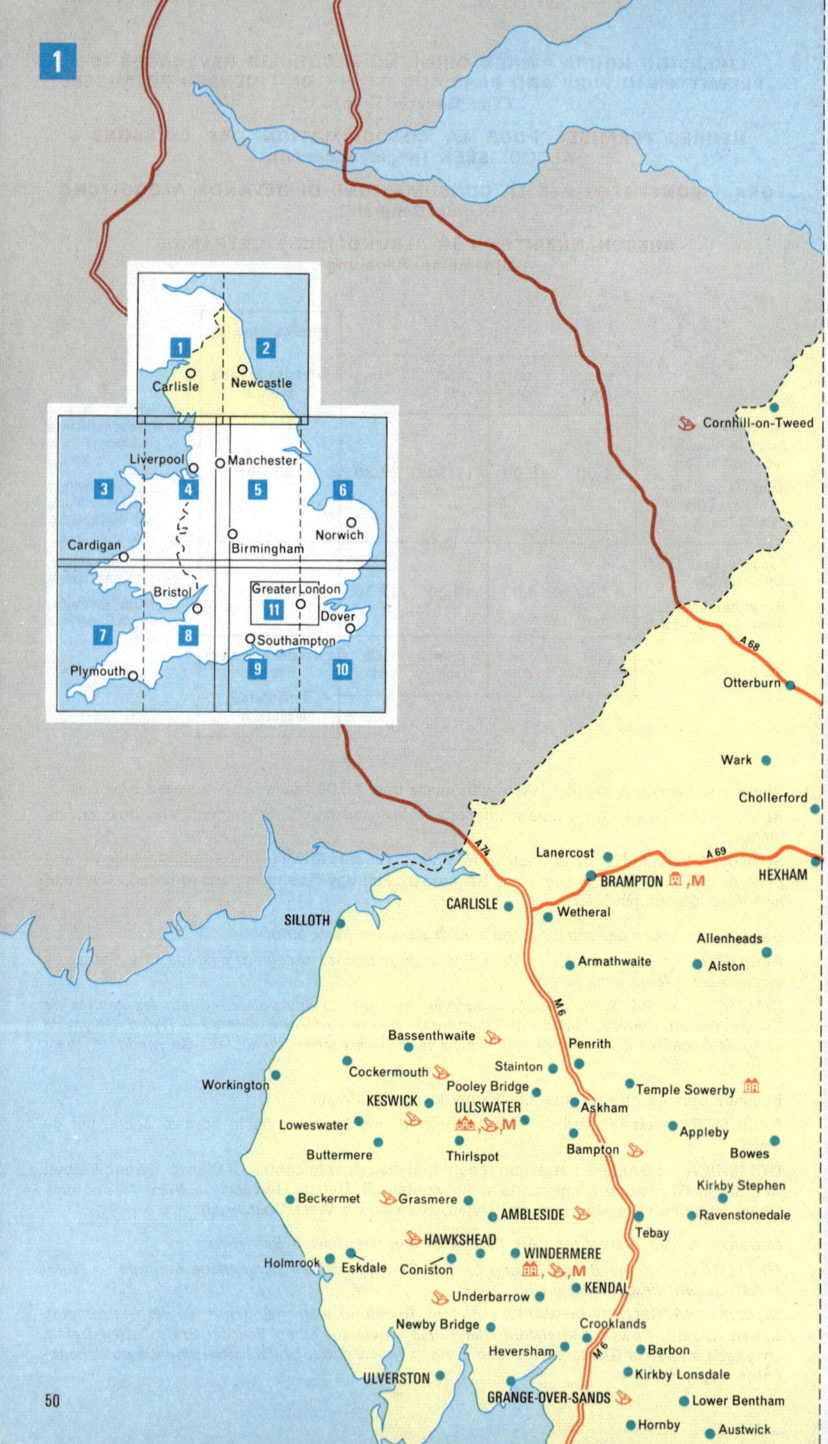

1
1 Carlisle
2 Newcastle
3
4 Liverpool
Manchester
5
6
Cardigan
Birmingham
Norwich
Bristol
Greater London
11
Dover
7
8
Southampton
9
10
Plymouth
Cornhill-on-Tweed
A 68
Otterburn
Wark
Chollerford
A 74
Lanercost
A 69
HEXHAM
BRAMPTON ,M
CARLISLE
Wetheral
SILLOTH
Allenheads
Armathwaite
Alston
M 6
Bassenthwaite
Penrith
Cockermouth
Stainton
Workington
Pooley Bridge
Temple Sowerby
KESWICK
ULLSWATER
Askham
Loweswater
,M
Appleby
Buttermere
Thirlspot
Bampton
Bowes
Kirkby Stephen
Beckermet
Grasmere
AMBLESIDE
Ravenstonedale
HAWKSHEAD
Tebay
Holmrook
WINDERMERE
Eskdale
Coniston
,M
KENDAL
Underbarrow
Newby Bridge
Crooklands
Heversham
M 6
Barbon
ULVERSTON
Kirkby Lonsdale
GRANGE-OVER-SANDS
Lower Bentham
Hornby
Austwick

Place with at least :

one hotel or restaurant .... ● Durham
one pleasant hotel .... 🏠 , ✗ with rm.
one quiet, secluded hotel ....
one restaurant with .... ❀, ❀❀, M
See this town for establishments
located in its vicinity .... RICHMOND

Localité offrant au moins :

une ressource hôtelière .... ● Durham
un hôtel agréable .... 🏠 , ✗ with rm.
un hôtel très tranquille, isolé ....
une bonne table à .... ❀, ❀❀, M
Localité groupant dans le texte
les ressources de ses environs .... RICHMOND

La località possiede come minimo :

una risorsa alberghiera .... ● Durham
un albergo ameno .... 🏠 , ✗ with rm.
un albergo molto tranquillo, isolato ....
un'ottima tavola con .... ❀, ❀❀, M
La località raggruppa nel suo testo
le risorse dei dintorni .... RICHMOND

Ort mit mindestens :

einem Hotel oder Restaurant .... ● Durham
einem angenehmen Hotel .... 🏠 , ✗ with rm.
einem sehr ruhigen und abgelegenen Hotel ......
einem Restaurant mit .... ❀, ❀❀, M
Ort mit Angaben über Hotels und Restaurants
in seiner Umgebung .... RICHMOND

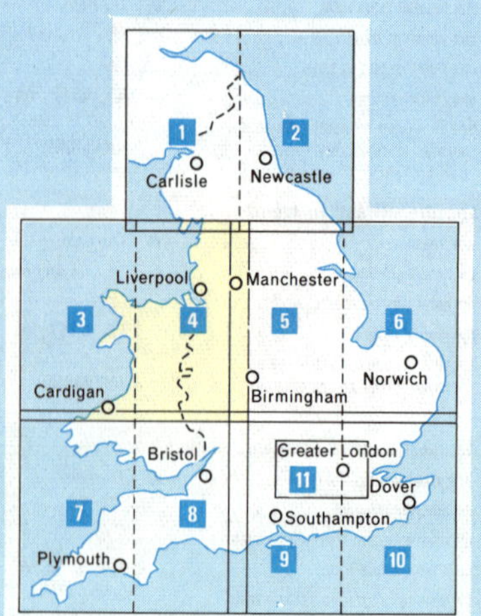

1
Carlisle
2
Newcastle
Liverpool
Manchester
3
4
5
6
Norwich
Cardigan
Birmingham
Bristol
Greater London
11
Dover
7
8
Southampton
Plymouth
9
10

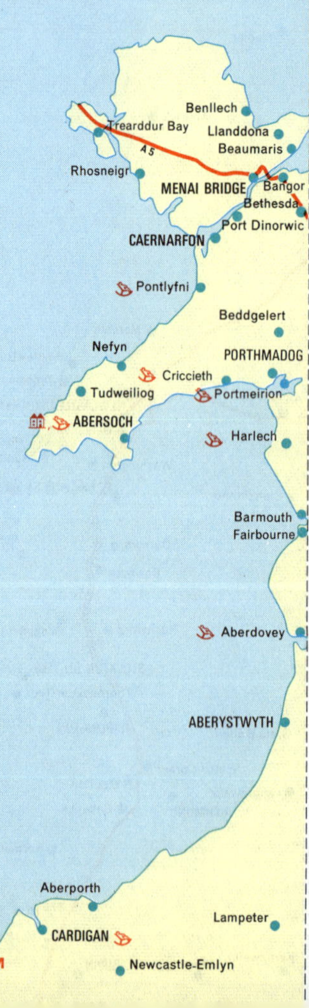

Benllech
Trearddur Bay
Llanddona
Beaumaris
A5
Rhosneigr
MENAI BRIDGE
Bangor
Bethesda
Port Dinorwic
CAERNARFON
Pontlyfni
Beddgelert
PORTHMADOG
Nefyn
Criccieth
Tudweiliog
Portmeirion
ABERSOCH
Harlech
Barmouth
Fairbourne
Aberdovey
ABERYSTWYTH
Aberporth
Lampeter
CARDIGAN
FISHGUARD
Newport M
Newcastle-Emlyn

4
Hornby
Austwick
Claughton
Settle
Morecambe
Burnsall
Lancaster
Dunsop Bridge
Gargrave
Gisburn
Whitewell
Fleetwood
Waddington
Little Thornton
St. Michael's-on-Wyre
M ,
CLITHEROE
Goosnargh
Hurst Green
Barton
Blackpool
PRESTON
Burnley
LYTHAM ST. ANNE'S
Blackburn
Mere Brow
Charnock Richard
Southport M
Birtle
Parbold
BOLTON
MILNROW
Standish
Skelmersdale
Oldham
Wigan
Worsley
MANCHESTER
Kirkby
Leigh
St. Helens
Denton
Stockport
Birkenhead
LIVERPOOL
Marple
Hoylake
WARRINGTON
ALTRINCHAM
Bramhall
Thurstaston
Greasby
Lymm
Disley
Heswall
Thornton-Hough
Daresbury
WILMSLOW
LLANDUDNO
Parkgate
Runcorn
KNUTSFORD
Alderley Edge
Rhyl
Babell
Prestbury
Penmaenmawr
Puddington
Hartford
COLWYN-BAY
St.Asaph
Macclesfield
CONWY
Afon-Wen
Tal-y-Cafn
Nannerch
CHESTER
Tarporley
Llanrwst
Congleton
Llanrhaeadr
Beeston
Crewe
Ruthin
BETWS-Y-COED
A 5
Wrexham
XXX with rm
Nantwich
STOKE-ON-TRENT
Dolwyddelan
Ruabon
Newcastle-under-Lyme
Corwen
Llangollen
Erbistock
Stone
Whitchurch
Bala
Llwynmawr
Chirk
Market Drayton
Llanarmon Dyffryn Ceiriog
Ternhill
Oswestry
Weston-under-Redcastle
Lake Vyrnwy
Newport
Llanfyllin
STAFFORD
DOLGELLAU
SHREWSBURY M
Tal-y-Llyn
Mallwyd
Telford
Welshpool
Buttington
Shifnal
R. Severn
MACHYNLLETH
WALSALL
WOLVERHAMPTON
CHURCH STRETTON
BIRMINGHAM
Caersws
Bridgnorth
Himley
Dudley
NEWTOWN
Kingswinford
Rowley Regis
Ponterwyd
Ditton Priors
STOURBRIDGE
Devil's Bridge
Pant Mawr
Hagley
Ludlow
Bewdley
KIDDERMINSTER
Stourport-on-Severn
Knighton
Abberley
Bromsgrove
Tenbury Wells
M Great Witley
Presteigne
Ombersley
DROITWICH
Leominster
Grimley
Knightwick
Worcester
M , M LLANWRTYD WELLS
Weobley
M , MALVERN
Pershore
Llangammarch Wells
Bredwardine
Hereford
Upton upon Severn
Crug-y-bar
Ledbury
53

5
Ramsgill
RIPON
Boroughbridge
Malton
Whitwell on the Hill
Bridlington
Threshfield
Burnsall
Knaresborough
Driffield
Skipton
Bolton Abbey
Ilkley
HARROGATE M
WETHERBY M
YORK
Pocklington
Steeton
Pool in W. M
Harewood
Market Weighton
Beverley
Bramhope
Holme upon
Spalding Moor
Aldbrough
Bingley
LEEDS
Selby
North Newbald
BRADFORD
Monk Fryston
Howden
A 63
KINGSTON-UPON-HULL
HALIFAX
Whitley Bridge
M Ripponden
Wakefield
Darrington
SCUNTHORPE
Immingham
M 62
HUDDERSFIELD
WENTBRIDGE
Brigg
MILNROW
BARNSLEY
DONCASTER
Redbourne
Oldham
Holmbridge
Denton
Bawtry
Stockport
SHEFFIELD
Blyth
Barnby Moor
Disley
Hope
Market Rasen
Castleton
Hathersage
Dronfield
East Retford
Prestbury
Grindleford
Barlborough
LINCOLN
Buxton
Baslow
Horncastle
Macclesfield
CHESTERFIELD
Tuxford
Bakewell
Ollerton
Woodhall Spa
Longnor
Rowsley
Higham
Congleton
MATLOCK
Farnsfield
Newark-on-Trent
STOKE-ON-TRENT
Thorpe
Southwell
Cauldon Lowe M
Belper
Sleaford
A 17
Alton
Stone
NOTTINGHAM
Grantham
Billingborough
DERBY
Uttoxeter
Sudbury
Shardlow
Castle Donington
Grimsthorpe
STAFFORD
Tutbury
Newton Solney
Loughborough
Melton Mowbray
Bourne
Spalding
BURTON-UPON-TRENT
RUGELEY
Ashby de la Zouch
Market Deeping
Measham
STAMFORD
Lichfield
Newtown Linford
Rothley
Oakham
WOLVERHAMPTON
LEICESTER
PETERBOROUGH
WALSALL
Uppingham
BIRMINGHAM
Dudley
Coleshill
NUNEATON
Oundle
Rowley Regis
M 6
M 69
MARKET HARBOROUGH
Corby
Hagley
Lutterworth
Husbands Bosworth
Thrapston
SOLIHULL
COVENTRY
Kettering
KNOWLE
RUGBY
Keyston
Hockley Heath
Kenilworth
M 1
Huntingdon
Bromsgrove
Wellingborough
Brampton
Henley-in-Arden M
Royal Leamington Spa   with rm.
Buckden
REDDITCH
Warwick M
NORTHAMPTON
Castle Ashby
DROITWICH
Barford
Daventry
ST. NEOTS
Alcester
Kislingbury
Horton M
A 428
Wilmcote
Wellesbourne Hastings
Olney
Pershore
Stratford-upon-Avon
Towcester
BEDFORD
Pebworth
Evesham
Cow Honeybourne
Newport Pagnell
Shipston-on-Stour
Stony Stratford
Wicken
CHIPPING CAMPDEN
BANBURY

6
1
Carlisle
2
Newcastle
Liverpool
Manchester
3
4
5
6
Cardigan
Birmingham
Norwich
Bristol
Greater London
11
Dover
7
8
Southampton
Plymouth
9
10
Grimsby
Cleethorpes
Louth
Sutton-on-Sea
Hogsthorpe
Skegness
Coningsby
Boston
BLAKENEY
Weybourne
West Runton
Hunstanton
Titchwell
Kelling
CROMER
Holt
Aldborough
Fakenham
Hillington
Neatishead
Lenwade Great Witchingham
Wroxham
King's Lynn
East Dereham
A47
Horning
South Walsham
Wisbech
Shipdham
Swaffham
NORWICH
GREAT YARMOUTH
Bunwell
A11
Beccles
LOWESTOFT
Thetford
Ely
Mildenhall
Diss
Fressingfield
Southwold M
ST·IVES
EYE
Halesworth
Walberswick
Bury St·Edmunds
Framlingham
A45
NEWMARKET
A45
Wickham Market
Aldeburgh
CAMBRIDGE
A11
Lavenham
Woodbridge
Cavendish
Bildeston
Orford
Melbourn
Long Melford
Tuddenham
M11
Clare
IPSWICH
Saffron Walden
SUDBURY
Kersey
Shottisham
Great Yeldham
Hintlesham
Hadleigh
55

Newcastle Emlyn

FISHGUARD
Newport **M**

Brechfa

ST.DAVID'S
Wolf's Castle

Carmarthen
Pont-ar-Gothi
A 40

Haverfordwest

Narberth with rm.

A 48

LITTLE-HAVEN

MILFORD-HAVEN

Pembroke
Saundersfoot
Pembrey
Tenby
Llanelli

MANORBIER

Horton
Mumbles

Locator map

1 Carlisle
2 Newcastle

Liverpool
Manchester

3
4
5
6

Cardigan
Norwich
Birmingham

Bristol
Greater London
11
Dover

7
8
Southampton

9
10

Plymouth

Heddon's Mouth
ILFRACOMBE
WOOLACOMBE
Combe Martin
Putsborough
Saunton
Wrafton
BARNSTAPLE
Appledore
Westward Ho
BIDEFORD

HORNS CROSS

Bradworthy
Torrington
Milton Damerel
Iddesleigh
BUDE
HATHERLEIGH

Boscastle
Clawton
Crackington Haven
Belstone
Lewdown
Sourton
Tintagel
Lydford
Camelford
Lifton

PORT ISSAC

Pendoggett

PADSTOW
ROCK
TAVISTOCK
Treyarnon Bay
Gunnislake
Mawgan Porth
Calstock
St. Wenn
Wadebridge
BODMIN
Pillaton
Watergate Bay

Lostwithiel
Lanreath
NEWQUAY
ST. AUSTELL
PLYMOUTH
A 30
Polkerris
ST. AGNES
LOOE
FOWEY
Cawsand
Polperro
Illogan
Newton Ferrers
Truro
Tregony
Gwithian
VERYAN
Portloe
ST. IVES
Camborne
Portscatho
PENZANCE
Marazion
FALMOUTH
St. Mawes
Mousehole
Praa Sands
Rosudgeon
Helford **M**
Sennen
Lamorna Cove
Mullion

Lizard

ISLES OF SCILLY

Tresco
St. Mary's

8

Crug-y-bar
A 40
Llandovery
Llangadog
BRECON
LLANDEILO
Crickhowell
Abergavenny
MONMOUTH
Merthyr Tydfil
Llandogo
Usk
Neath
Cwmbram
Blackwood
Caerleon
Swansea
M
PORT TALBOT
NEWPORT
Bridgend
M 4
CARDIFF
PORTHCAWL
Cowbridge
PENARTH
Llantwit Major
Barry
Weston-super-Mare
Hereford
Ledbury
Upton upon Severn
Tewkesbury
ROSS-ON-WYE
with rm. CHELTENHAM
GLOUCESTER
Symonds Yat
Newnham
Painswick
Coleford
Frampton on Severn
STROUD
Lydney
BERKELEY
Avening
Tintern
Stone
Stinchcombe
Wotton under Edge
Chepstow
Falfield
TETBURY
Thornbury
MALMESBURY
Alveston
Dunkirk
Chipping Sodbury
M 4
Castle Combe
Chippenham
BRISTOL
Keynsham
Calne
Clevedon
Lacock
BATH
Shaw
Stanton Wick
Devizes
Blagdon
Axbridge
Farrington Gurney
Wedmore
Emborough
Frome
Wells
Warminster
LYNTON
Minehead
Woody Bay
Watchet
Porlock Weir
Dunster
Holford
Shepton Mallet
Simonsbath
Exford
Bilbrook
Williton
BRIDGWATER
Glastonbury
Winsford
Street
Evercreech
Hawkridge
Castle Cary
South Molton
Brushford
Somerton
Mere
Hindon
Chittlehamholt
with rm. TAUNTON
Long Sutton
Milton on Stour
Martock
Ilchester
Wincanton
Witheridge
Wellington
South Petherton
Horsington
Shaftesbury
Winkleigh
TIVERTON
M, YEOVIL
SHERBORNE
Donyatt
Seavington St.Mary
North Tawton
Bickleigh
Crewkerne
Sturminster Newton
Coleford
Thorverton
Weston
Honiton
Hawkchurch
Broadwindsor
with rm. M
Tedburn St. Mary
Wilmington
Milton Abbas
WIMBORNE MINSTER
South Zeal
Gittisham
Beaminster
Piddletrenthide
Drewsteignton
Ottery St. Mary
COLYTON
Charmouth
BRIDPORT
EXETER
Venn Ottery
A 35
CHAGFORD
M
Newton Poppleford
Seaton
LYME REGIS
Wareham
POOLE
SIDMOUTH
Dorchester
MORETONHAMPSTEAD
Branscombe
West Lulworth
Postbridge
Budleigh Salterton
WEYMOUTH
Bovey Tracey
Exmouth
Dawlish
A 38
Portland
M 5
M
A 30
Two Bridges
Teignmouth
Buckland in the Moor
Combeinteignhead
Ashburton
Newton Abbot
Buckfastleigh
TORQUAY
Staverton
TOTNES
South Brent
Paignton
A 38
Harberton
Harbertonford
BRIXHAM
MODBURY
DARTMOUTH
KINGSBRIDGE
Torcross
SALCOMBE
57

9
Broadway
CHIPPING CAMPDEN
BANBURY
BRACKLEY
Wicken
Steppingley
Blockley
Flitton M
Letchworth
Moreton-in-Marsh, M
Buckingham
Woburn
HITCHIN
Winchcombe
Chipping Norton
STOW-ON-THE-WOLD
Middleton Stoney
Bicester
Whitchurch
Linslade
STEVENAGE
Kingham
Chadlington
Dunstable
Luton
CHELTENHAM with rm.
Bourton-on-the Water
Chesterton
Mentmore
Shipton-under-Wychwood
Charlbury
Woodstock
Ivinghoe
Harpenden
Welwyn
Burford
Minster Lovell
Painswick
Fossebridge
South Leigh
Bibury
Clanfield
CIRENCESTER
Avening
Fairford
Lechlade
M 1
TETBURY
Faringdon
GREATER
Cricklade
Wantage
MALMESBURY
SWINDON
11
M 4
Chippenham
Ramsbury
M 4
Calne
Kintbury M
MARLBOROUGH
Hungerford
Lacock
Hamstead Marshall
Devizes
M 3
Warminster
Andover
Elstead
Godalming
Amesbury
Newdigate
Middle Wallop
Alton
Hindon
Stockbridge
Churt
Chiddingfold
Alresford
Alfold Crossways
Winchester
Haslemere
SALISBURY
Rake
Petworth
Horsham
Brook
Billingshurst
Shaftesbury
Ampfield
Romsey
M Midhurst
Pulborough
West Chiltington
Chandler's Ford
Fittleworth
Thakeham
M 27
Bramshaw
Bishop's Waltham
ASHINGTON
Fordingbridge
Cadnam
Stoney Cross
SOUTHAMPTON
RINGWOOD
A 31
Ashurst
M 27
A 27
Burley
Lyndhurst
WIMBORNE MINSTER
BEAULIEU
Ferndown
Brockenhurst
New Milton
Barton
LYMINGTON
M CHRISTCHURCH
Milford on Sea
Yarmouth
POOLE
Bournemouth
Colwell Bay
Freshwater Bay
Wareham
Totland Bay
Studland
Swanage
Botley
Schedfield
Amberley
Small Dole
Wickham
Storrington M
Steyning
Waterlooville
A 27
ARUNDEL
M 27
Fareham
CHICHESTER M
WORTHING
Climping
Portsmouth
Middleton-on-Sea
Rustington
Lee-on-the-Solent
Hayling Island
Bognor Regis
Cowes
Whippingham
Ryde
Selsey
Newport
Bembridge
Carisbrooke
Sandown
ISLE OF
Shanklin
WIGHT
58 Chale
VENTNOR ,M
Niton

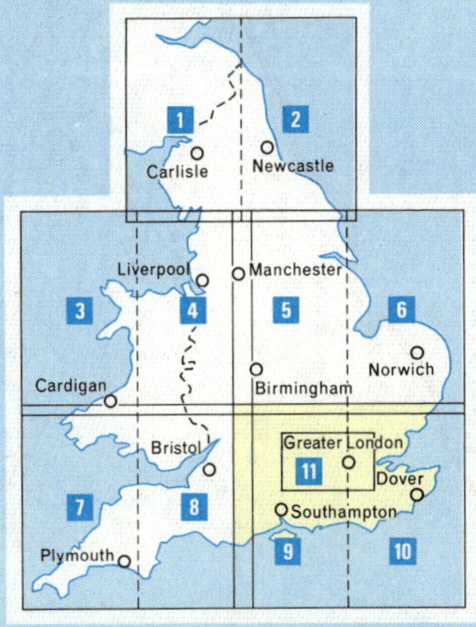

10
Saffron Walden
Great Yeldham
Dedham
Felixstowe
Harwich and Dovercourt
Baldock
Halstead
Great Bardfield
Coggeshall
COLCHESTER
Bishop's Stortford
Braintree
Messing
FRINTON-ON-SEA
Great Dunmow
CLACTON-ON-SEA
Ware
WITHAM
CHELMSFORD
Maldon
INGATESTONE
Stock
Burnham-on-Crouch
Rochford
Basildon
LONDON
Stanford le Hope
SOUTHEND-ON-SEA
North Stifford
Gravesend
MARGATE
A 2
Herne Bay
BROADSTAIRS
Shorne
Birchington-on-Sea
Sittingbourne
WHITSTABLE
Ramsgate M
Burham M
M 2
Sandwich
CANTERBURY
MAIDSTONE
Chilham
Deal
Wye M
A 2
St. Margaret's Bay
M 23
Horley
PENSHURST
DOVER
EAST GRINSTEAD
Goudhurst
ASHFORD
Biddenden
CRAWLEY
ROYAL TUNBRIDGE WELLS
Cranbrook
Folkestone
Lamberhurst
Hythe
FOREST ROW
Crowborough
Hawkhurst
Haywards Heath
Mayfield
Bodiam
NEW ROMNEY
Burwash
Sedlescombe
UCKFIELD
Rushlake Green
RYE
Halland
Battle
A 259
HERSTMONCEUX
Ninfield
A 23
LEWES
A 27
Hastings and St.Leonards
BRIGHTON AND HOVE
Alfriston
Wilmington
BEXHILL
Rottingdean
Peacehaven
Newhaven
EASTBOURNE M
Seaford
1 Carlisle
2 Newcastle
Liverpool
Manchester
3
4
5
6
Cardigan
Birmingham
Norwich
Greater London
Bristol
11
Dover
7
8
9 Southampton
Plymouth
10

11
GREATER LONDON M
Thames
Thames
60
Horton-cum-Studley
AYLESBURY
Aston Clinton
Tring
Redbourn
Welwyn Garden City
Hertingfordbury
HARLOW
Oxford
Milton Common
Thame
Owlswick
St. Albans
Hatfield
Hemel Hempstead
Saunderton
South Mimms
Radlett
Epping
ABINGDON
Aston Rowant
M 40
Amersham
Chenies
Watford
Borehamwood
Totteridge
Abridge
Watlington
Chigwell
Brentwood
Benson
Fingest
Rickmansworth
Buckhurst Hill
Wallingford
High Wycombe
Chalfont St. Giles
GREATER
BEACONSFIELD
Chalfont St. Peter
Bourne End
Gerrards Cross
Bulphan
Fawley
MARLOW
New Denham
A 5
A 11
Cookham
Henley-on-Thames
Hurley-on-Thames
Iver Heath
Thames
Knowl Hill
Maidenhead
Burnham
Purfleet
Bray-on-Thames
Slough
M 4
A 4
Pangbourne
Sonning-on-Thames
WINDSOR
Datchet
A 2
Yattendon
Winkfield
A 316
Reading
Staines
LONDON M
M 4
Sunbury-on-Thames
Egham
Newbury
Ascot
SHEPPERTON
Swanley
Swallowfield
Walton-on-Thames
Yateley
Bagshot
Weybridge
ESHER
Halstead
Silchester
Epsom
A 23
Wrotham
Camberley
Cobham
BANSTEAD
Heckfield
Woking
Chipstead
Hartley Wintney
Ripley
Ockham
M 3
Fleet
FARNBOROUGH
Redhill
GODSTONE
Westerham
SEVENOAKS
BASINGSTOKE
ODIHAM
GUILDFORD
DORKING
M 23
OXTED
FARNHAM
Gomshall
Salfords
Tonbridge

ABBERLEY Heref. and Worc. 403 404 M 27 – pop. 558 – ECD : Wednesday – ⊠ Worcester – ☎ 029 921 Great Witley.

London 137 – Birmingham 27 – Worcester 13.

- **The Elms** ⹁, WR6 6AT, W: 2 m. on A 443 ☎ 666, ≤, « Tasteful decor », ✗, ☞, park – TV P. ⚱. ◨ AE ① VISA
  M 4.95/9.80 t. ♨ 1.50 – ☞ 2.40 – **20 rm** 20.20/34.00 **st.** – P 31.40/34.60 **st.**

ABERDOVEY (ABERDYFI) Gwynedd 403 H 26 – pop. 927 – ECD : Wednesday – ☎ 065 472.
See : Afon Dovey's mouth (site**). **Envir. :** Llanegryn (church*) N : 8 m – Dolgoch Falls* NE : 10 m.

🛈 Snowdonia National Park and Wales Tourist Centre, The Wharf ☎ 321 (Easter-September).

London 230 – Dolgellau 25 – Shrewsbury 66.

- **Trefeddian** ⹁, LL35 0SB, W: 1 m. on A 493 ☎ 213, ≤ golf course and sea, ✗, ◨, ☞ – ▤ ◨wc ⴵ, ⬡ P. ◨
  April-mid October – **M** 4.50/6.60 **st.** ♨ 1.60 – **48 rm** ☞ 8.90/27.40 **st.** – P 16.70/22.40 **st.**
- **Plas Penhelig** ⹁, LL35 0NA, E: 1 ½ m. on A 493 ☎ 676, ≤, ✗, ☞, park – ◨wc ⊛ P. ◨ VISA
  M *(closed Sunday dinner to non-residents)* 5.75/8.60 t. – **12 rm** ☞ 18.60 t. – P 29.00/32.00 t.

ABERGAVENNY (Y-FENNI) Gwent 403 K 28 – pop. 9,401 – ECD : Thursday – ☎ 0873.
Envir. : Llanthony Priory* N : 10 m.
🛈 Llanfoist, ☎ 3171, S : 2 m.
🛈 Brecon Beacons National Park and Wales Tourist Board Centre, 2 Lower Monk St. ☎ 3254 (Easter-September).

London 163 – Gloucester 43 – Newport 19 – Swansea 49.

- **Angel** (T.H.F.), 15 Cross St., NP7 5EN, ☎ 2613 – TV ◨wc ⊛ P. ◨ AE ① VISA
  M 3.75/4.55 **st.** ♨ 1.65 – **31 rm** ☞ 13.50/22.00 **st.**
- **Park,** 36 Hereford Rd, NP7 5RA, ☎ 3715, ☞ – P
  7 rm ☞ 5.00/7.00 **s.**
- **Lamb and Flag** with rm, Brecon Rd, NP7 5DB, NW: 1 ½ m. on A 40 ☎ 4255 – ◨wc P. AE
  M *(closed Sunday dinner)* a la carte 4.40/6.50 ♨ 1.40 – **3 rm** ☞ 10.00/14.00 **s.**

MORRIS Brecon Rd ☎ 2126   RENAULT Monmouth Rd ☎ 2323
PEUGEOT Penpergwm, Gobion ☎ 087 385 (Gobion) 287

ABERGWAUN Dyfed – see Fishguard.

ABERGWESYN Powys 403 I 27 – see Llanwrtyd Wells.

ABERHONDDU Powys – see Brecon.

ABERMO Gwynedd – see Barmouth.

ABERMULE (ABER-MIWL) Powys 403 K 26 – see Newtown.

ABERPORTH Dyfed 403 G 27 – pop. 1,618 – ECD : Wednesday – ☎ 0239.
See : Site*. **Envir. :** Llangranog (cliffs*) NE : 4 m.
London 249 – Carmarthen 29 – Fishguard 26.

- **Morlan Motel,** SA43 2EN, ☎ 810611 – TV ◨wc �𝄞wc P. ◨ AE VISA
  M a la carte 3.25/6.05 t. ♨ 1.10 – ☞ 1.75 – **40 rm** 10.00/15.00 **t.**
- **Highcliffe,** SA43 2DA, ☎ 810534 – TV ◨wc ⊛ P
  M *(bar lunch)* approx. 5.00 **st.** – **16 rm** ☞ 10.00/17.60 **t.**
- **Ffynonwen** ⹁, SA43 2HT, SE: 1 m. by A 4333 ☎ 810312, ≤ – ◨wc P
  12 rm ☞ *(dinner included)* 10.00/20.00 **t.**

ABERSOCH Gwynedd **403** G 25 – pop. 800 – ECD : Wednesday – ☎ 075 881.
Envir. : Llanengan (church* : twin aisles rood screen) W : 2 m. – Hell's Mouth* W : 3 m. –
Aberdaron (site*) W : 10 m. – Braich y Pwll (≤** from 2nd car park) W : 12 m.
� Pwllheli, ☎ 0758 (Pwllheli) 2520, NE : 7 m. – � Pwllheli, ☎ 2622.
London 265 – Caernarfon 28 – Shrewsbury 101.

 🏠 **Harbour,** LL53 7HR, ☎ 2406 – ➪wc ⋔wc **P**. **AE** **⊙** ⌀ 1.50 – **21 rm** ⌕ 10.25/22.00 **t.**
 Easter-late September – **M** (bar lunch) approx. 5.20 **st.** ⌀ 1.50 – **21 rm** ⌕ 10.25/22.00 **t.**

 ☙ **Craig-y-Môr,** Lôn Pont Morgan, LL53 7AD, ☎ 2666, ≤, ☞ – ➪wc **P**
 season – **7 rm.**

 ⋔ **Llysfor,** Lôn Garmon, LL53 7AL, ✉ Pwllheli ☎ 2248, ☞ – **P**. **VISA**
 Easter-October – **8 rm** ⌕ 6.00/13.00 **st.**

 ✕✕ **Bronheulog** ⤳ with rm, Lôn Garmon, LL53 7UL, W : 1 ½ m. ✉ Pwllheli ☎ 2177,
 ☞ – **P**
 March-October – **M** *(closed Sunday)* (dinner only) a la carte 6.60/8.00 **st.** ⌀ 2.00 –
 5 rm ⌕ 8.50/17.00 **st.**

 at Bwlchtocyn S : 2 m. – ✉ Pwllheli – ☎ 075 881 Abersoch :

 🏨 **Porth Tocyn** ⤳, LL53 7BU, ☎ 2966, ≤ Cardigan Bay and mountains, ✕, ⤓ heated,
 ☞ – ➪wc ⋔wc **P**. **◪** **AE** **⊙**
 closed November, December and mid week from January to Easter – **M** (buffet lunch)
 approx. 9.20 ⌀ 1.90 – **17 rm** ⌕ 16.80/32.40 – P 23.70/25.20.

ABERTAWE West Glam. – see Swansea.

ABERTEIFI Dyfed – see Cardiff.

ABERYSTWYTH Dyfed **403** H 26 – pop. 10,688 – ECD : Wednesday – ☎ 0970.
See : ≤* from the National Library. **Envir. :** Vale of Rheidol* SE : 6 m.
� Brynmore, ☎ 615104 N : ½ m.
☑ Avondale, Marine Terrace ☎ 612125 (Easter-September).
London 238 – Chester 98 – Fishguard 58 – Shrewsbury 74.

 🏨 **Belle Vue Royal** (Best Western), Marine Ter., SY23 2BA, ☎ 617558, ≤ – ➪wc **P**. ⌂
 48 rm.

 ☙ **Four Seasons,** 52 Portland St., SY23 2DX, ☎ 612120 – ➪wc **P**
 closed 24 December-2 January – **M** (dinner only) 6.00 **s.** – **17 rm** ⌕ 6.50/16.00 **s.**

 ⋔ **The Groves,** 44-46 North Par., SY23 2NF, ☎ 617623 – **P**
 closed 23 December-4 January – **16 rm** ⌕ 7.65/17.60 **t.**

 at Chancery (Rhydgaled) S : 4 m. on A 487 – ✉ ☎ 0970 Aberystwyth :

 🏨 **Conrah Country** ⤳, SY23 4DF, ☎ 617941, ≤, « 18C country house », ☞, park – ▯
 ➪wc ⋔wc ☏ **P**. ⌂. **◪** **⊙** **VISA**
 March-October – **M** *(closed Monday lunch)* (bar lunch) 4.50/6.50 **t.** ⌀ 1.70 – **25 rm**
 ⌕ 9.25/26.00 **st.** – P 18.50/26.00 **st.**

AUSTIN-MORRIS-MG-JAGUAR-ROVER-TRIUMPH   FORD North Parade ☎ 4171
Park Av. ☎ 4841   VAUXHALL Pier St. ☎ 612747
FIAT Llanfarian ☎ 612311

ABINGDON Oxon. **403** Q 28 – pop. 18,610 – ECD : Thursday – ☎ 0235.
☑ 8 Market Pl. ☎ 22711.
London 64 – Oxford 6 – Reading 25.

 🏨 **Upper Reaches** (T.H.F.), Thames St. OX14 3TA, ☎ 22311, ⤳ – ▯ ➪wc ☏ **P**. ⌂. **◪**
 AE **⊙** **VISA**
 M 4.50/5.30 **st.** ⌀ 1.85 – **21 rm** ⌕ 16.00/23.00 **st.**

 at Frilford W : 4 m. on A 415 – ✉ Abingdon – ☎ 0865 Frilford Heath :

 ✕✕✕ **Noah's Ark,** OX13 5NZ, S : ½ m. on A 338 ☎ 391470, Italian rest., ☞ – **P**. **AE** **⊙**
 closed Sunday dinner and Monday – **M** a la carte 6.90/10.40 **t.** ⌀ 2.00.

RENAULT Southmoor ☎ 820386   VAUXHALL The Vineyard ☎ 20176

ABRIDGE Essex **404** U 29 – pop. 2,900 (inc. Lambourne) – ECD : Wednesday – ☎ 037 881
Theydon Bois.
London 15 – Chelmsford 19.

 ✕✕✕ Roding, Market Pl., RM4 1UA, ☎ 3030.

VW, AUDI Market Pl. ☎ 037 881 (Theydon Bois) 2722

ACKLAM Cleveland – see Middlesbrough.

ACOCKS GREEN West Midlands **403** **404** O 26 – see Birmingham.

AFON-WEN Clwyd **403** K 24 – ⊠ Mold – ☎ 035 282 Caerwys.
London 207 – Chester 11 – Denbigh 5 – Wrexham 22.

  XX **Fisheries** 🖾 with rm, E: ¾ m. off A 541 ℡ 461. ≼, ◁, 🚗 – 🚪wc ℗
    M *(closed Sunday and Monday)* (dinner only) 3.50/10.00 **s.** ⬩ 2.00 – **5 rm** ⊊ 9.00/16.00.

AIGBURTH Merseyside **403** L 23 – see Liverpool.

ALBRIGHTON Salop – see Shrewsbury.

ALCESTER Warw. **403** **404** O 27 – pop. 19,122 – ECD: Monday, Thursday and Saturday – ☎ 078 971.
Envir.: Ragley Hall★★ (17C) *AC,* SW: 2 m.
London 104 – Birmingham 20 – Stratford-upon-Avon 8 – Worcester 18.

  🏛 Cherrytrees Garden, Stratford Rd, B49 6LN, E: 1 m. on A 422 ℡ 2505 – 📺 🚪wc 🛁wc
    ☏ ℗
    22 rm.

AUSTIN-MORRIS-MG Evesham Rd ℡ 2209

ALDBOROUGH Norfolk **404** X 25 – pop. 404 – ⊠ Norwich – ☎ 026 376 Hanworth.
London 129 – Cromer 11 – Norwich 17.

  X **Old Red Lion,** The Green, NR11 7AA, ℡ 451 – ℗
    closed Monday except Bank Holidays – **M** a la carte 7.00/9.00 **t.** ⬩ 1.85.

ALDBROUGH Humberside – pop. 930 – ECD: Tuesday – ⊠ Hull – ☎ 040 17.
London 192 – Kingston-upon-Hull 12.

  🍸 **George and Dragon** (S & N), 1 High St., HU11 4RP, ℡ 230 – 🚪wc ℗. 🅂 VISA
    M (bar lunch) a la carte approx. 6.15 **st.** – **6 rm** ⊊ 10.10/18.10 **st.**

ALDEBURGH Suffolk **404** Y 27 – pop. 2,791 – ECD: Wednesday – ☎ 072 885.
🏌 at Thorpeness ℡ 2176, N: 2 ½ m.
London 97 – Ipswich 24 – Norwich 41.

  🏨 **Brudenell** (T.H.F.), The Parade, IP15 5BU, ℡ 2071. ≼ – 📶 📺 🚪wc ☏ ℗. 🅂 ᴀᴇ ⓪
    VISA
    M 5.00/5.50 **st.** ⬩ 1.65 – **47 rm** ⊊ 17.50/28.00 **st.**

  🏨 **Wentworth,** Wentworth Rd, IP15 5BB, ℡ 2312. ≼ – 🚪wc 🛁wc ☏ ℗. ⓪
    closed January – **M** (buffet lunch) 4.00/6.50 **t.** – **33 rm** ⊊ 12.75/26.80 **st.** – P 21.00/
    24.50 **st.**

  X **Granville** with rm, 243-247 High St., IP15 5DN, ℡ 2708
    closed 1 week at Christmas – **M** a la carte 4.75/8.30 **t.** ⬩ 1.50 – **9 rm** ⊊ 8.00/20.00 **t.**

TALBOT High St. ℡ 2721

ALDERLEY EDGE Cheshire **403** **404** N 24 – pop. 4,470 – ECD: Wednesday – ☎ 0625.
Envir.: Capesthorne Hall★ (18C) *AC,* S: 4 ½ m.
London 187 – Chester 34 – Manchester 14 – Stoke-on-Trent 25.

  🏨 De Trafford Arms, Congleton Rd, SK9 7AA, on A 34 ℡ 583881 – 📶 📺 🚪wc ☏ ℗
    33 rm.

  🏨 Edge, Macclesfield Rd, SK9 7BJ, ℡ 583033. 🚗 – 📺 🚪wc 🛁wc ☏ ℗
    27 rm.

  ↑ Milverton House, Wilmslow Rd, SK9 7QL, on A 34 ℡ 583615 – 🚪wc 🛁wc 🚙 ℗
    14 rm.

  XX **Le Rabelais,** 75 London Rd, SK9 7DY ℡ 584848. French rest. – 🅂 ⓪
    closed Saturday lunch, Sunday, mid August-mid September and Bank Holidays for lunch
    – **M** a la carte 7.20/9.90 ⬩ 1.85.

AUSTIN-JAGUAR-LAND ROVER-MORRIS-TRIUMPH   OPEL-VAUXHALL Knutsford Rd ℡ 582691
London Rd ℡ 582218   VOLVO 77 London Rd ℡ 583912

ALFOLD CROSSWAYS Surrey **404** S 30 – pop. 1,122 – ⊠ Cranleigh – ☎ 0403 Loxwood.
London 43 – Guildford 10 – Horsham 10.

  XX **Chez Jean,** Horsham Rd, GU6 8JE, on A 281 ℡ 752357. French rest. – ℗. 🅂 ᴀᴇ ⓪ VISA
    closed Sunday dinner, Monday and 26 December – **M** a la carte 6.65/10.75 **t.** ⬩ 2.00.

ALFRISTON East Sussex **404** U 31 – pop. 763 – ECD: Wednesday – ⊠ Polegate – ☎ 0323.
London 66 – Eastbourne 9 – Lewes 10 – Newhaven 8.

  🏨 **Star Inn** (T.H.F.), High St., BN26 5TA, ℡ 870495 – 📺 🚪wc ☏ ċ. ℗. 🅂 ᴀᴇ ⓪ VISA
    M 4.50/5.30 **st.** ⬩ 1.85 – **34 rm** ⊊ 16.50/25.00 **st.**

  X **Moonrakers,** High St., BN26 5TD, ℡ 870472
    closed Sunday, Monday, 2 weeks May, 2 weeks November and Tuesday, Wednesday
    from December to February – **M** (dinner only) 7.50 **t.** ⬩ 2.00.

ALLENHEADS Northumb. – pop. 1,470 – ECD : Tuesday – ⊠ Hexham – ☎ 043 485.
London 289 – Carlisle 41 – Newcastle-upon-Tyne 39.

  ☂ **Allenheads Inn,** NE2 5AE, ☏ 200 – **℗.** ⚡ *VISA*
    closed 19 December-6 January – **M** (bar lunch) 3.50/4.50 t. ◊ 2.25 – **9 rm** ⌧ 8.50/15.00 t.

ALLESLEY West Midlands **403 404** P 26 – see Coventry.

ALLESTREE Derbs. **403 404** P 25 – see Derby.

ALL STRETTON Salop **403** L 26 – see Church Stretton.

ALNWICK Northumb. **986** ⑮ – pop. 7,190 – ECD : Wednesday – ☎ 0665.
See : Castle** (Norman) *AC.* **Envir. :** Dunstanburgh Castle 14C-15C (ruins ; coastal setting*) *AC*
1 ¼ m. walk from Craster, no cars, NE : 7 ½ m. – Warkworth (castle* 12C) *AC,* SE : 7 m. – Roth-
bury (Cragside gardens* : rhododendrons) *AC,* SW : 12 m.
☖ Foxton Hall ☏ 066 573 (Alnmouth) 231, SE : 5 m. – ☖ Swansfield Park , Alnwick.
🛈 The Shambles, Northumberland Hall ☏ 3120 (summer only).
London 320 – Edinburgh 86 – Newcastle-upon-Tyne 34.

  🏨 Hotspur, Bondgate Without, NE66 1PR, ☏ 2924, ⇛ – ⌂wc ☏ ℗
    28 rm.

AUSTIN-MORRIS-ROVER-TRIUMPH South Rd ☏ 2683   PEUGEOT Powburn ☏ 066 578 (Powburn) 214
FORD ☏ 2294

ALRESFORD Hants. **403 404** Q 30 – pop. 3,684 – ECD : Wednesday – ☎ 096 273.
☖ Cheriton Rd ☏ 3153, S : 1 m.
London 61 – Southampton 19 – Winchester 8.

  ☂ Bell, West St., SO24 9AT, ☏ 2429
    6 rm.

  XX O'Rorkes, 34 Pound Hill, SO24 9BW, ☏ 2293 – **℗.**

AUSTIN-MORRIS-ROVER-TRIUMPH 47 West St. ☏   SAAB The Dene Ropley ☏ 096 277 (Ropley) 2307
2601   VOLVO Broad St. ☏ 3444

ALSTON Cumbria **986** ⑲ – pop. 1,916 (inc. Garrigill) – ECD : Tuesday – ☎ 049 83.
Envir. : High Force** (waterfalls) *AC,* SE : 16 m.
☖ Alston Moor ☏ 228, N : 2 m.
🛈 Railway Station ☏ 696.
London 309 – Carlisle 28 – Newcastle-upon-Tyne 45.

  🏨 **Lowbyer Manor,** Hexham Rd, CA9 3JX, ☏ 230, ⇛ – ⌂wc ℗
    May-November – **M** (dinner only) a la carte 4.05/7.55 **s.** ◊ 1.75 – **11 rm** ⌧ 12.00/
    20.00 **s.**

  ☂ Hillcrest, Townfoot, CA9 3RN, ☏ 251, ⇛ – ℗
    12 rm.

ALTHORPE Humberside **404** R 23 – see Scunthorpe.

ALTON Hants. **404** R 30 – pop. 9,920 – ECD : Wednesday – ☎ 0420.
☖ Old Odiham Rd ☏ 82042, N : 2 m.
London 53 – Reading 24 – Southampton 29 – Winchester 18.

  🏨 **Swan** (Anchor), High St., GU34 1AT, ☏ 83777, Group Telex 858875 – 📺 ⌂wc ℗. ⚡
    AE ⓞ *VISA*
    M a la carte approx. 6.00 **st.** – **26 rm** ⌧ 13.00/25.50.

ASTON-MARTIN, PEUGEOT Station Approach   FORD Ackender Rd ☏ 83993
☏ 82222   TALBOT, MORRIS Four Marks ☏ 62354
AUSTIN-LAND ROVER-MORRIS-MG-ROVER-
TRIUMPH-WOLSELEY Butts Rd ☏ 84141

ALTON Staffs. **403 404** O 25 – pop. 1,195 – ⊠ Stoke-on-Trent – ☎ 0538 Oakamoor.
See : Alton Towers (gardens**) *AC.*
London 157 – Derby 21 – Stafford 20 – Stoke-on-Trent 13.

  XX **Wild Duck Inn** with rm, New Road, ST10 4AF, ☏ 702218 – **℗.** AE ⓞ *VISA*
    closed Sunday dinner and Monday to non-residents – **M** a la carte 5.75/10.05 **st.**
    ◊ 1.20 – ⌧ 2.00 – **5 rm** ⌧ 7.40/12.40 **st.**

ALTRINCHAM Greater Manchester **403 404** M 23 – pop. 40,787 – ECD : Wednesday – ☎ 061
Manchester.
☖ Stockport Rd, Timperley ☏ 928 0761 – ☖ Dunham Forest ☏ 928 2605, W : 1 m.
☖ Hale Mount, Hale Barns ☏ 980 4468, SE : 2 m.
London 191 – Chester 30 – Liverpool 30 – Manchester 8.

George and Dragon, 22 Manchester Rd, WA14 4PH, on A 56 ℘ 928 9933 – ⌷ TV ⌷wc
☏ ℗ – **45 rm.**

Cresta Court (Best Western), Church St., WA14 4DP, on A 56 ℘ 928 8017, Telex
667242 – ⌷ TV ⌷wc ☏ ℗. ⚠. ⬛. AE ⓪ *VISA*
M a la carte 2.70/5.25 st. – **134 rm** ⊊ 16.00/24.00 st.

Pelican, West Timperley, WA14 5NH, N : 2 m. on A 56 ℘ 962 7414 – TV ⌷ ☏ ℗.
⬛ AE ⓪ *VISA*
M 2.50/4.00 st. ⌽ 2.00 – **52 rm** ⊊ 16.00/21.25 st.

Bollin, 58 Manchester Rd, WA14 4PJ, ℘ 928 2390 – ℗
10 rm ⊊ 8.00/16.00 t.

Portofino, The Downs, WA14 2QG, ℘ 928 1511, Italian rest. – ℗. AE ⓪ *VISA*
closed Sunday, 5 to 26 August and Bank Holidays – **M** a la carte 6.65/8.85 t. ⌽ 2.20.

at Hale SE : 1 m on B 5163 – ⌷ Altrincham – ☎ 061 Manchester :

Ashley, Ashley Rd, WA15 9SF, ℘ 928 3794 – ⌷ TV ⌷wc ☏ ℗. ⚠. ⬛ AE ⓪ *VISA*
closed 27 to 29 December – **M** *(closed Saturday lunch)* 3.50/5.00 t. ⌽ 2.10 – **49 rm**
⊊ 19.00/25.00 t.

Evergreen, 169-171 Ashley Rd, ℘ 928 1222, Chinese rest.

at Hale Barns SE: 2 m. on A 538 – ⌷ Altrincham – ☎ 061 Manchester :

Borsalino, 14 The Square, WA15 8ST, ℘ 980 5331, French Bistro.

at Bowdon SW: 1 m. – ⌷ Altrincham – ☎ 061 Manchester:

Bowdon, Langham Rd, WA14 2HT, ℘ 928 7121 – TV ⌷wc ☏ ℗. ⚠. ⬛ AE ⓪
M 4.25 s. ⌽ 2.00 – **41 rm** ⊊ 11.25/23.00 s.

Bowdon Croft ⤸, Green Walk, WA14 2SN, ℘ 928 1718, « 19C house and grounds »,
⇶ – TV ⌷wc ☏ ℗
8 rm.

Alpine, Park Rd, WA14 4JE, ℘ 928 6191 – TV ⌷wc ☏ ℗. ⚠. ⬛ AE ⓪ *VISA*
closed Sunday – **M** *(closed Bank Holidays for lunch)* a la carte 4.10/6.75 t. ⌽ 1.10 –
14 rm ⊊ 14.00/19.50 t.

AUSTIN-MORRIS 18 Old Market Pl. ℘ 928 2662
AUSTIN-DAIMLER-JAGUAR-MORRIS-ROVER-
TRIUMPH Victoria Rd ℘ 928 7124
DATSUN Manchester Rd ℘ 973 3021

FORD 44 Hale Rd Bridge ℘ 928 2275
HONDA, SAAB Bancroft Rd, Hale ℘ 980 8004
PEUGEOT Atlantic St. ℘ 928 3265

ALVESTON Avon ⁴⁰³ ⁴⁰⁴ M 29 – pop. 2,776 – ECD : Wednesday – ⌷ Bristol – ☎ 0454
Thornbury.

London 127 – Bristol 11 – Gloucester 23 – Swindon 42.

Post House (T.H.F.), Thornbury Rd, BS12 2LL, on A 38 ℘ 412521, ⤢ heated – TV
⌷wc ⌷wc ☏ ℗. ⚠. ⬛ AE ⓪ *VISA*
M 4.25/5.30 st. ⌽ 1.65 – ⊊ 2.25 – **75 rm** 18.00/25.20 st.

Alveston House, BS12 2LJ, on A 38 ℘ 415050, ⇶ – TV ⌷wc ⌷wc ☏ ℗. ⬛ AE ⓪
VISA
M *(closed Sunday dinner to non-residents)* 4.35/4.75 ⌽ 1.95 – **16 rm** ⊊ 14.50/22.50.

AMBERLEY West Sussex ⁴⁰⁴ S 31 – pop. 510 – ⌷ Arundel – ☎ 079 881 Bury.
London 58 – Brighton 23 – Chichester 12 – Worthing 14.

La Capanna, Houghton Bridge, BN18 9LR, SW: ¾ m. on B 2139 ℘ 790, ≤, Italian
rest. – ℗. ⓪
*closed Sunday, Monday from November to March, 24 December for 3 weeks and Bank
Holidays)* – **M** *(dinner only)* a la carte 4.40/6.45 ⌽ 1.65.

AMBLESIDE Cumbria ⁹⁸⁶ ⑲ – pop. 2,657 – ECD : Thursday – ☎ 096 63.
Envir. : Tarn Hows** (lake) SW: 6 m. by A5 93 AY – Langdale Valley** W: 7 m. by B 5343 AY.
⚹ The Old Courthouse, Church St. ℘ 2582 (summer only).
London 278 – Carlisle 47 – Kendal 14.

Plan on next page

Kirkstone Foot ⤸, Kirkstone Pass Rd, LA22 9EH, NE: ¼ m. ℘ 2232, ⇶ – ⌷wc ℗.
⬛ AE ⓪ *VISA*   **AZ c**
April-October – **M** *(buffet lunch)* approx. 6.75 st. ⌽ 1.80 – **20 rm** ⊊ *(dinner included)*
16.00/35.00 st.

Vale View, Lake Rd, LA22 0BH, ℘ 3192 – ⌷wc ⌷wc ℗. ⬛   **AZ e**
Mid March-October – **M** *(bar lunch)* approx. 4.80 st. ⌽ 2.00 – **20 rm** ⊊ 8.75/16.00 st.

Elder Grove, Lake Rd, LA22 0DB, ℘ 2504 – ⌷wc ℗. AE ⓪   **AZ a**
April-October – **9 rm** ⊊ 9.00/18.00 t.

Compston House, Compston Rd, LA22 9DJ, ℘ 2305   **AZ i**
closed February – **10 rm** ⊊ 5.30/10.60 t.

AMBLESIDE
GRASMERE

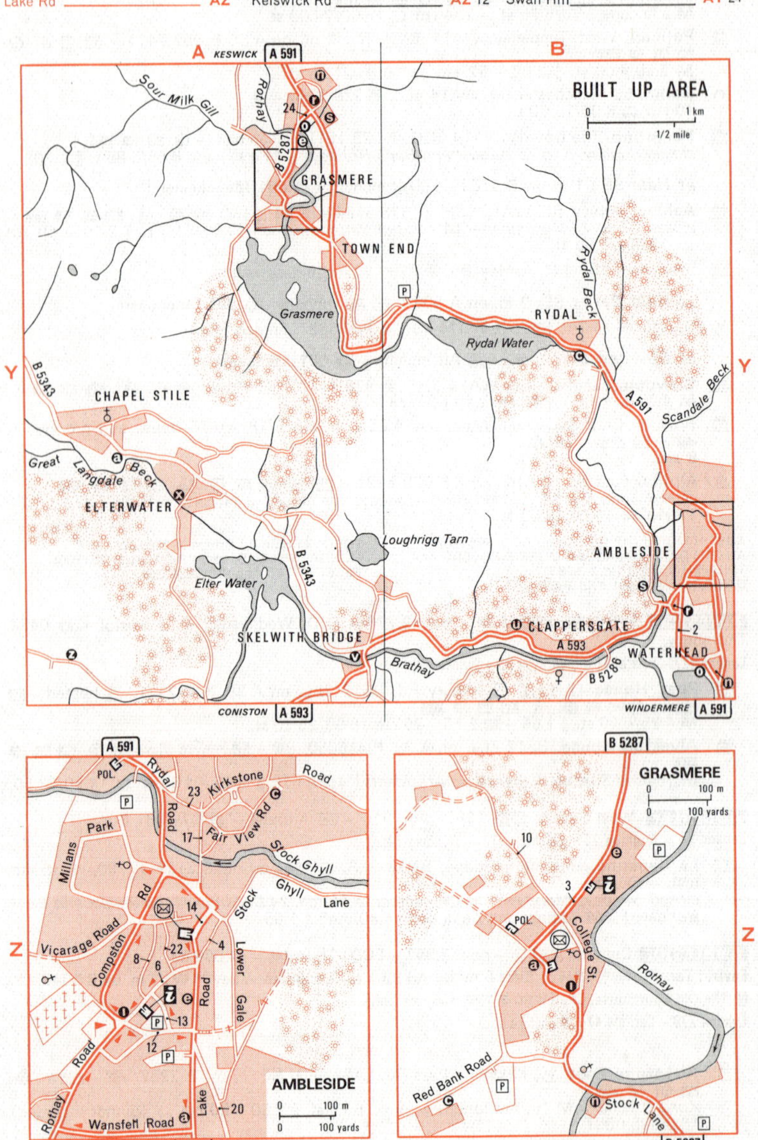

Town plans : *roads most used by traffic and those on which guide listed hotels and restaurants stand are fully drawn ; the beginning only of lesser roads is indicated.*

at Waterhead S : 1 m. on A 591 – ✉ ☎ 096 63 Ambleside :

🏨 **Waterhead** (Best Western), LA22 0ER, ☎ 2566, ≼, 🛥 – 🛏wc 🛁wc ☎ 🅿. 🔌 AE ⓪ VISA — BY **n**
M 4.60/6.85 st. 🍷 1.50 – **28 rm** ⇌ 14.80/29.60 st. – P 23.00/25.00 st.

🏨 Wateredge, Borrans Rd, LA22 0EP, ☎ 2332, ≼, « Part 17C Fishermans cottages, lake-side setting », 🛥 – 🛏wc 🅿. 🔌 — BY **o**
March-November – **M** (buffet lunch) 7.50 t. – **20 rm.**

at Rothay Bridge S : ½ m. on A 593 – ✉ ☎ 096 63 Ambleside :

↑ **Riverside** ❀, Gilbert Sear, Under Loughrigg, LA22 9LJ, N: ¼ m. off. A593 ☎ 2395, 🛥 – 🛏wc 🅿 — BY **s**
March-October – **10 rm** ⇌ 10.50/20.00 t.

XXX **Rothay Manor** with rm, LA22 0EH, ☎ 3605, ≼, 🛥 – 📺 🛏wc ☎ 🅿. AE ⓪ — BY **r**
closed January and February – **M** (buffet lunch) 3.00/10.00 t. 🍷 2.00 – **12 rm** ⇌ 24.00/36.00 t.

at Clappersgate W : 1 m. on A 593 – ✉ ☎ 096 63 Ambleside :

🏨 Nanny Brow Country House ❀, LA22 9NF, ☎ 2036, ≼ Beathay Valley and Langdale, ✖, 🎾, 🛥 – 🅿 — BY **u**
closed first 2 weeks November and first 2 weeks February – **15 rm** ⇌ 9.50/19.00 s.

at Skelwith Bridge W : 2 ½ m. on A 593 – ✉ ☎ 096 63 Ambleside :

🏨 Skelwith Bridge, LA22 9NJ, ☎ 2115, ≼, 🛥 – 🛏wc 🅿 — AY **v**
26 rm.

at Elterwater W : 4 ½ m. off B 5343 – ✉ Ambleside – ☎ 096 67 Langdale :

⚐ **Britannia Inn** ❀, LA22 9HP, ☎ 210, ≼ – 🅿 — AY **x**
March-October, Christmas and 1 January – **M** (bar lunch) 2.50/6.25 t. 🍷 2.25 – **10 rm** ⇌ 9.50/19.00 t.

at Little Langdale W: 4 ½ m. off A 593 – ✉ ☎ 096 67 Langdale :

⚐ **Three Shires Inn** ❀, LA22 9TS, ☎ 215, ≼, 🛥 – 🅿 — AY **z**
Early March-mid November – **M** (bar lunch) approx. 7.50 s. – **7 rm** ⇌ 9.00/18.00 st.

at Chapel Stile W : 5 m. on B 5343 – ✉ Chapel Stile – ☎ 096 67 Langdale :

🏨 **Langdales** ❀, Great Langdale, LA22 9JF, ☎ 253, ≼, 🛥 – 🛏wc 🅿 — AY **a**
M 4.00/7.50 t. 🍷 2.50 – **22 rm** ⇌ 12.50/17.50 t.

at Rydal NW: 1 ½ m. on A 591 – ✉ ☎ 096 63 Ambleside :

↑ **Rydal Lodge,** LA22 9LR, ☎ 3208, 🛥 – 🅿. 🔌 — BY **c**
April-October – **8 rm** ⇌ 9.00/16.00 st.

☛ *To go a long way quickly, use* **Michelin maps** *at a scale of 1/1 000 000.*

AMERSHAM (Old Town) Bucks. 🔢404 S 28 – pop. 17,254 – ECD : Thursday – ☎ 024 03.
London 29 – Aylesbury 16 – Oxford 33.

🏨 **Crown** (T.H.F.), High St., HP7 0DH, ☎ 21541 – 📺 🛏wc ☎ 🅿. 🔌 AE ⓪ VISA
M 4.25/5.25 st. 🍷 1.65 – **17 rm** ⇌ 13.50/24.00 st.

XX **King's Arms,** High St., HP7 0DJ, ☎ 6333 – 🅿. 🔌 AE ⓪ VISA
closed Sunday dinner, Monday and Tuesday after Bank Holidays – **M** a la carte 4.95/7.30 t. 🍷 1.55.

AUSTIN-DAIMLER-JAGUAR-MORRIS-ROVER-TRIUMPH London Rd ☎ 5911
RENAULT The Broadway ☎ 4656

TALBOT 4/8 White Lion Rd ☎ 024 04 (Little Chalfont) 4666

AMESBURY Wilts. 🔢403 🔢404 0 30 – pop. 5,540 – ECD : Monday – ☎ 098 02.
Envir. : Stonehenge (Megalithic Monument)*** *AC,* W: 2 m.
⛳ Tidworth ☎ 098 04 (Tidworth) 2321, NE: 7 m.
🛈 Redworth House, Flower Lane ☎ 3255.
London 88 – Bristol 52 – Southampton 31 – Taunton 61.

🏨 **Antrobus Arms,** Church St., SP4 7EY, ☎ 3163, 🛥 – 🛏wc 🚗 🅿. 🔌 AE ⓪ VISA
closed 25 and 26 December – **M** 4.00/5.00 st. – **19 rm** ⇌ 13.50/28.75 st.

RENAULT Salisbury St. ☎ 2525

AMPFIELD Hants. 🔢403 🔢404 P 30 – pop. 1,460 – ECD : Wednesday – ✉ Romsey – ☎ 042 15 Chandler's Ford.
London 79 – Bournemouth 31 – Salisbury 19 – Southampton 11 – Winchester 7.

🏨 **Potters Heron Motor,** SO5 9ZF, on A 31 ☎ 66611 – 📺 🛏wc ☎ 🅿. 🔌 AE ⓪ VISA
M 5.80 t. 🍷 1.80 – **42 rm** ⇌ 19.90/31.50 st.

ANDOVER Hants. 403 404 P 30 – pop. 25,881 – ECD : Wednesday – ☎ 0264.
London 74 – Bath 53 – Salisbury 17 – Winchester 11.

   White Hart (Anchor), Bridge St., SP10 1BH, ☏ 2266, Group Telex 858875 – 📺 🛏wc
   ☎ 🅿. 🔌 ᴁ ⓪ *VISA*
   M 4.00 st. – **22 rm** ☲ 13.00/25.00.

ALFA-ROMEO, FIAT Salisbury Rd ☏ 61166   FORD West St. ☏ 3525
AUSTIN-MG-ROVER-TRIUMPH-WOLSELEY 278 Weyhill   MORRIS-MG-WOLSELEY 94 Charlton Rd ☏ 3603
Rd ☏ 2326   VAUXHALL New St. ☏ 4233

ANGMERING-ON-SEA West Sussex 404 S 31 – see Worthing.

APPLEBY Cumbria 986 ⑲ – pop. 1,949 – ECD : Thursday – ☎ 0930.
🏌 ☏ 51432, S : 2 m. – 🛈 Moot Hall, Boroughgate ☏ 51177.
London 285 – Carlisle 33 – Kendal 24 – Middlesbrough 58.

   Appleby Manor ⌂, Roman Rd, CA16 6JD, NE : ½ m. off A 66 ☏ 51571, ≤, 🚗 –
   🛏wc 🅿
   M *(closed Christmas and 3 weeks January)* a la carte 5.35/6.65 **t.** ⌁ 2.40 – **24 rm** ☲
   12.25/20.80 **st.**

   Tufton Arms, Market Sq., CA16 6XA, ☏ 51593, ⌂ – 🛏wc 🅿. 🔌 ᴁ ⓪ *VISA*
   M 4.00/5.00 **st.** ⌁ 1.60 – **28 rm** ☲ 11.00/22.00 **st.**

   Royal Oak Inn, Bongate, CA16 6UN, ☏ 51463 – 🅿
   M (grill rest. only) a la carte approx. 6.10 **st.** – **8 rm** ☲ 7.00/14.00 **st.**

   Courtfield, Bongate, CA16 6UP, ☏ 51394, 🚗 – 🅿. 🔌 *VISA*
   M *(closed Sunday lunch)* (bar lunch) 6.00 **st.** ⌁ 1.40 – **13 rm** ☲ 8.00/16.00 **st.**

AUSTIN-MORRIS-MG, FORD The Sands ☏ 51133   TALBOT The Sands ☏ 51460

APPLEDORE Devon 403 H 30 – pop. 2,172 – ECD : Wednesday – ✉ ☎ 023 72 Bideford.
London 235 – Bideford 4 – Exeter 47 – Plymouth 62.

   Seagate, The Quay, EX39 1QS, ☏ 2589 – 🅿
   27 April-5 October – **M** (bar lunch) 4.50/6.00 **st.** ⌁ 1.50 – **10 rm** ☲ 9.25/16.50 **st.**

ARBERTH Dyfed – see Narberth.

ARDSLEY South Yorks. 404 P 23 – see Barnsley.

ARMATHWAITE Cumbria – pop. 150 – ✉ Carlisle – ☎ 069 92.
London 305 – Carlisle 10 – Penrith 12.

   Duke's Head Inn, CA4 9PB, ☏ 226 – 🅿
   M (bar lunch) approx. 5.40 – **8 rm** ☲ 8.00/15.00.

   Red Lion, CA4 9PY, ☏ 204, ≤, ⌂ – 🅿
   closed 24 to 26 December – **M** (bar lunch) 3.50/5.50 – **11 rm** ☲ 8.00/13.50.

ARMITAGE Staffs. 403 404 O 25 – see Rugeley.

ARUNDEL West Sussex 404 S 31 – pop. 2,434 – ECD : Wednesday – ☎ 0903.
See : Castle* (keep 12C, ≤* 119 steps, State apartments*) *AC* – St. Nicholas' Church (chancel
or Fitzalan chapel* 14C). **Envir. :** Bignor (Roman Villa : mosaics** *AC*) NW : 7 m.
🛈 61 High St. ☏ 882268. – **London 58** Brighton 21 – Southampton 41 – Worthing 9.

   Norfolk Arms, 22 High St., BN18 9AD, ☏ 882101 – 📺 🛏wc ☎ 🅿. 🏋. 🔌 ᴁ ⓪ *VISA*
   M 3.25/5.00 **t.** ⌁ 1.95 – **23 rm** ☲ 13.50/24.00 **t.**

   Golden Goose, Station Approach, BN18 9JL, E : ½ m. on A 27 ☏ 882588 – 📺 🛏wc
   🛏wc 🅿 – **10 rm.**

   at Walberton W : 3 m. on B 2132 by A 27 – ✉ Arundel – ☎ 0243 Yapton :

   Avisford Park ⌂, BN18 0LS, ☏ 551215, ≤, ⌂, ⌐ heated, 🚗, park – 📺 🅿. 🏋. 🔌 ᴁ *VISA*
   M 5.00/6.00 **st.** – ☲ 1.95 – **60 rm** 18.50/27.00 **st.**

MAZDA-SUZUKI Fontwell ☏ 024 365 (Slindon) 289

ASCOT Berks. 404 R 29 – pop. 15,630 – ECD : Wednesday – ☎ 0990.
🏌 Downshire ☏ 0344 (Bracknell) 24066, W : 4 m.
London 36 – Reading 15.

   Berystede (T.H.F.), Bagshot Rd, Sunninghill, SL5 9JA, S : 1 ½ m. on A 330 ☏ 23311
   Telex 847707, ⌐, 🚗, park – 🛎 📺 🅿. 🏋. 🔌 ᴁ ⓪ *VISA*
   M 4.75/5.75 **st.** ⌁ 1.50 – ☲ 2.50 – **96 rm** 22.50/28.00 **st.**

   Royal Foresters, London Rd, SL5 8DR, W : 1 ½ m. on A 329 ☏ 03447 (Winkfield Row)
   4747 – 📺 🛏wc ☎ 🅿. 🔌 ᴁ ⓪ *VISA*
   M 5.00 **st.** ⌁ 2.00 – **34 rm** ☲ 21.55/31.50 **st.**

AUSTIN-MG-WOLSELEY Ascot Motor Works ☏ 20324   PEUGEOT 71/75 High St. ☏ 21481
DATSUN Station Approach ☏ 24791   VAUXHALL Lyndhurst Rd, Station Approach ☏ 22257

ASHBURTON Devon **403** I 32 – pop. 3,518 – ECD: Wednesday – ☎ 0364.
Envir.: Dartmeet Bridge (site *) NW: 6 m.

London 220 – Exeter 20 – Plymouth 23.

 🏨 **Holne Chase** ⌂, TQ13 7NS, NW: 2 ½ m. on B 3357 ☎ 036 43 (Poundsgate) 280, ≼,
  🚗, park, ⌲ – ⌸wc 🛁wc **P**. ⊠ AE ⑩ VISA
  M 4.20/5.50 **s.** ⫶ 1.75 – **15 rm** �> 14.30/34.00 **t.**

 🏨 **Dartmoor Motel**, TQ13 7JW, on B 3357 ☎ 52232 – ⌸wc 🛁wc **P**. AE ⑩ VISA
  M a la carte 5.50/6.75 **t.** ⫶ 1.50 – **19 rm** �>= 10.50/18.00 **st.**

 ⌂ **Tugela House**, 68-70 East St., TQ13 7AX, ☎ 52206
  10 rm �>= 6.00/16.00 **st.**

ASHBY DE LA ZOUCH Leics. **403 404** P 25 – pop. 7,490 – ECD: Wednesday – ☎ 053 04.
London 119 – Birmingham 29 – Leicester 18 – Nottingham 22.

 🏨 Royal (Crest), Station Rd, LE6 5GP, ☎ 2833, 🚗 – ⌸wc ☏ **P**. ⊠ AE ⑩ VISA
  30 rm �>= 12.80/21.20 **st.**

 ✗ **Fallen Knight**, 16 Kilwardby St., LE6 5FR, ☎ 2230 – **P**. ⊠ AE
  closed Saturday lunch and Sunday dinner – **M** a la carte 5.75/9.45 ⫶ 2.95.

AUSTIN-JAGUAR-MORRIS-ROVER Bath St. ☎ 2770   DAF, MAZDA Tamworth Rd ☎ 2108

ASHFORD Kent **404** W 30 – pop. 31,240 – ECD: Wednesday – ☎ 0233.
Envir.: Hothfield (St. Margaret's Church: memorial tomb* 17C) NW: 3 m. – Lenham
(St. Mary's Church: woodwork*) NW: 9 ½ m.

London 56 – Canterbury 14 – Dover 23 – Hastings 29 – Maidstone 19.

 🏨 County, High St., ☎ 20047 – 📺
  17 rm.

 🏨 George, 68 High St., TN24 8TB, ☎ 25512 – **P**
  14 rm.

 ✗✗ **Old Cottage**, 20 North St., TN24 8JR, ☎ 20347 – ⊠ AE ⑩ VISA
  closed Sunday dinner, Monday and last 2 weeks August – **M** a la carte 3.70/6.95 **t.**
  ⫶ 1.25.

 at Kennington NE: 2 m. on A 28 – ✉ ☎ 0233 Ashford :

 🏨 **Spearpoint**, Canterbury Rd, TN24 9QR, ☎ 21833, 🚗, park – 📺 ⌸wc 🛁wc **P**.
  ⊠ AE ⑩ VISA
  M a la carte 5.35/8.65 **st.** ⫶ 1.85 – **25 rm** �>= 12.50/26.50 **st.**

 ⌂ **Downsview**, Willesborough Rd, TN25 4PD, ☎ 21953, 🚗 – 🛁wc **P**. VISA
  17 rm �>= 7.50/12.50.

 ⌂ **Croft**, Canterbury Rd, TN25 4DU, ☎ 22140, 🚗 – ⌸wc 🛁wc **P**
  closed 1 week at Christmas – **21 rm** �>= 8.00/14.00.

 at Charing NW: 6 m. on A 252 by A 20 – ✉ Ashford – ☎ 023 371 Charing :

 ✗✗ **Luigi**, Charing Hill, TN27 0NG, ☎ 2286, ≼, Italian rest. – **P**. ⊠
  closed Sunday, Christmas Day and Bank Holidays – **M** a la carte 5.10/7.15 ⫶ 1.30.

AUSTIN-JAGUAR-MORRIS-ROVER-TRIUMPH Chart DAF, SKODA Hamstreet ☎ 023 373 (Hamstreet) 2207
Rd ☎ 20624/23121   FORD Station Rd ☎ 25111
AUSTIN-MORRIS-PRINCESS-ROVER-TRIUMPH 20-46 RENAULT Maidstone Rd ☎ 34177
New St. ☎ 20334   VAUXHALL Faversham Rd ☎ 23173
CITROEN Beaver Rd ☎ 34000

ASHINGTON West Sussex **404** S 31 – pop. 1,470 – ECD: Wednesday – ✉ Pulborough –
☎ 0903.

London 50 – Brighton 20 – Worthing 9.

 🏨 **Mill House** ⌂, Mill Lane, RH20 3BZ, ☎ 892426, 🚗 – 📺 ⌸wc **P**. AE VISA
  M *(closed Sunday dinner)* a la carte 5.80/7.30 **t.** ⫶ 1.80 – �>= 1.90 – **7 rm** 13.00/19.00 **t.**

 at Washington S : 1 ¾ m. on A 24 – ✉ Storrington – ☎ 0903 Ashington :

 ✗✗ **Old Smithy**, Old London Rd, RH20 3BN, ☎ 892271 – ⊠ VISA
  closed Sunday, Good Friday and 25-26 December – **M** (dinner only) a la carte 6.60/
  9.00 **t.** ⫶ 1.95.

ASHURST Hants. **403 404** P 31 – pop. 2,659 – ECD: Monday – ✉ Southampton – ☎ 042 129.
London 92 – Bournemouth 23 – Southampton 6.

 ✗✗ **Happy Cheese**, 189 Lyndhurst Rd, SO4 2AR, on A 35 ☎ 3232 – **P**. ⊠
  closed Saturday lunch, Sunday and Bank Holidays – **M** a la carte 5.55/9.90 **t.** ⫶ 2.25.

ASKHAM Cumbria – pop. 392 – ✉ Penrith – ☎ 093 12 Hackthorpe.
London 288 – Carlisle 23 – Kendal 28.

 🏨 **Queen's Head Inn**, CA10 2PF, ☎ 225 – **P**
  M *(closed Sunday dinner)* (bar lunch) 2.50/6.00 ⫶ 3.00 – **8 rm** �>= 9.25/17.50.

ASTON CLINTON Bucks. **404** R 28 – pop. 2,473 – ECD : Wednesday – ⊠ ✆ 0296 Aylesbury.
London 42 – Aylesbury 4 – Oxford 26.

   Bell Inn, HP22 5HP, ☎ 630252, « Courtyard and gardens » – 📺 **P**. 🏛. 🔊 _VISA_
   M a la carte 13.00/18.50 **s**. ▮ 2.00 – ⌑ 4.00 – **21 rm** 25.00/42.00 **s**.

ASTON ROWANT Oxon. **404** R 28 – pop. 704 – ⊠ Lewknor – ✆ 0844 Kingston Blount.
London 43 – Aylesbury 15 – Oxford 16 – Reading 18.

   Lambert Arms, OX9 5SB, junction A 40 and B 4009 ☎ 51496, 🚗 – 📺 ⌑wc ☎
   P
   9 rm.

ASTWOOD BANK Heref. and Worc. **403 404** O 27 – see Redditch.

AUSTWICK North Yorks. – pop. 509 – ⊠ Lancaster (Lancs.) – ✆ 046 85 Clapham.
London 237 – Kendal 26 – Lancaster 23 – Leeds 47.

   Traddock ⌘, LA2 8BY, ☎ 224, 🚗 – ⌑wc **P**
   11 rm ⌑ 6.50/15.00.

AVENING Glos. **403 404** N 28 – pop. 775 – ⊠ Tetbury – ✆ 045 383 Nailsworth.
London 116 – Bristol 30 – Gloucester 16 – Oxford 49.

   XX **Four Seasons** , High St., GL8 8TR, ☎ 3070 – 🔊 _AE_ ① _VISA_
   closed Saturday lunch, Sunday and Monday – **M** 4.15/6.95 **t**.

AXBRIDGE Somerset **403** L 30 – pop. 1,097 – ✆ 0934.
Envir. : Cheddar (Gorge*** – Gough's Caves** _AC_) E : 3 m.
London 142 – Bristol 17 – Taunton 31 – Weston-super-Mare 10.

   X **Oak House** with rm, The Square, BS26 2AP, ☎ 732444, Telex 449748 – ⌑wc ⌂. _AE_ ①
   closed 26 December-5 January – **M** _(closed Sunday dinner to non-residents)_ a la carte
   5.00/7.00 **t**. – **12 rm** ⌑ 8.25/18.75 **t**.

AYLESBURY Bucks. **404** R 28 – pop. 40,569 – ECD : Thursday – ✆ 0296.
Envir. : Waddesdon Manor (Rothschild Collection***) _AC_, NW : 5 ½ m. – Ascott House**
(Rothschild Collection**) and gardens* _AC_, NE : 8 ½ m. – Stewkley (St Michael's Church*
12C) NE : 12 m.

🏌 New Rd, Weston Turville ☎ 24084, SE : 2 ½ m.

🛈 County Hall, Walton St. ☎ 5000.

London 46 – Birmingham 72 – Northampton 37 – Oxford 22.

   Bell (T.H.F.), Market Pl., HP20 1TX, ☎ 82141 – 📺 ⌑wc ☎. 🔊 _AE_ ① _VISA_
   M 3.75/4.55 **st**. ▮ 1.65 – **22 rm** ⌑ 13.50/22.00 **st**.

   King's Head (Crest), Market Sq., HP20 1TA, ☎ 5158 – **P**. 🔊 _AE_ ① _VISA_
   M _(closed Sunday dinner, Monday lunch and Bank Holidays)_ – **15 rm** ⌑ 12.80/20.20.

   at Stoke Mandeville S : 3 ¼ m. by A 413 on A 4010 – ⊠ Aylesbury – ✆ 029 661 Stoke
   Mandeville :

   Belmore, Princes Risborough Rd, HP22 5UT, ☎ 2258, ⌑ heated, 🚗 – 📺 ⌑wc ☎ & **P**.
   🔊 _AE_ ① _VISA_
   closed Christmas – **M** (dinner only) 3.85 – ⌑ 1.40 – **14 rm** 12.60/22.50.

   at Hartwell SW : 2 m. on A 418 – ⊠ Aylesbury – ✆ 029 674 Stone :

   X Bugle Horn (Embassy), HP17 8QP, ☎ 209, 🚗 – **P**.

AUSTIN-DAIMLER-JAGUAR-MG-ROVER-TRIUMPH-
WOLSELEY Buckingham Tring Rd ☎ 84071
DAF, PEUGEOT 159 Tring Rd ☎ 84050
DATSUN 13/19 Buckingham St. ☎ 24226
FORD 54/56 Walton St. ☎ 4604
MORRIS-MG-WOLSELEY Bicester Rd ☎ 81641

RENAULT Little Kimble ☎ 029 66 (Stoke Mandeville)
2239
TOYOTA, VAUXHALL 143 Cambridge St. ☎ 82321
VOLVO Stocklake ☎ 5344
VW, AUDI-NSU Bicester Rd ☎ 23434

BABBACOMBE Devon **403** J 32 – see Torquay.

BABELL Clwyd **403** K 24 – pop. 225 – ✆ 035 282 Caerwys.
London 217 – Birkenhead 29 – Chester 21.

   XX **Black Lion**, CH8 8PZ, ☎ 239 – **P**. _AE_
   closed Sunday, Monday, 2 weeks mid August, first week November and Bank Holidays –
   M a la carte 5.00/9.50 **t**.

BACKFORD CROSS Cheshire **403** L 24 – see Chester.

BAE COLWYN Clwyd – see Colwyn Bay.

BAGINTON Warw. **403 404** P 26 – see Coventry.

BAGSHOT Surrey **404** R 29 – pop. 21,074 – ECD : Wednesday – ☎ 0276.
London 37 – Reading 17 – Southampton 49.

- **Pennyhill Park,** College Ride, GU19 5ET, off A 30 ☎ 71774, Telex 928872, ≼, ✗, ⊠ heated, ⊠, ⊠, ⊠, park – TV P. ⊠. ⊠ AE ① VISA
M 6.50 ≬ 2.95 – � 3.45 – **34 rm** 25.00/34.00.

- **Cricketers'** (T.H.F.), London Rd, GU19 5HR, N : ½ m. on A 30 ☎ 73196, ⊠ – TV ⊟wc
⊠ P. ⊠ AE ① VISA
M 5.50/6.00 **st.** ≬ 1.65 – **26 rm** ⊟ 13.50/24.00 **st.**

BAKEWELL Derbs. **403 404** O 24 – pop. 4,249 – ECD : Thursday – ☎ 062 981.
Envir. : Chatsworth★★★ : site★★, house★★★ (Renaissance) garden★★★ *AC*, NE : 2 ½ m. – Haddon Hall★★ (14C-16C) *AC*, SE : 3 m. – Eyam (Celtic Cross★ 8C) N : 5 m.
⊠ Station Rd ☎ 2307.
London 160 – Derby 26 – Manchester 37 – Nottingham 33 – Sheffield 17.

- **Rutland Arms,** The Square, DE4 1BT, ☎ 2812 – TV ⊟wc ⊠ P. ⊠. ⊠ AE ① VISA
M approx. 6.00 **st.** ≬ 2.50 – ⊟ 3.20 – **33 rm** 16.00/22.00 **st.**

BALA Gwynedd **403** J 25 – pop. 1,578 – ECD : Wednesday – ☎ 067 82 (3 fig.) or 0678 (6 fig.).
See : Site★. – ⊠ Penlan ☎359.
🛈 Snowdonia National Park and Tourist Centre, High St. ☎ 367 (Easter-September).
London 216 – Chester 46 – Dolgellau 18 – Shrewsbury 52.

- **White Lion Royal,** High St., LL23 7AE, ☎ 520314 – ⊟wc ⊠wc ⊠ P. ⊠ AE ① VISA
closed Christmas and 1 January – M 3.50/4.60 **t.** ≬ 1.25 – **22 rm** ⊟ 14.50/19.50 **t.**

- **Bala Lakeside Motel** ⚕, SW : 1 ¼ m. on B 4403 by B 4391 ☎ 520344, ≼, ⊠, ⊠ –
⊠wc P
closed 1 week at Christmas and February – **M** *(closed lunch from November to March)*
a la carte 4.70/6.75 **s.** – **12 rm** ⊟ 12.25/18.25 **s.**

- **Plas Teg,** Tegid St., LL23 7EN, ☎ 520268, ⊠ – P. ⊠ AE VISA
closed Christmas – **8 rm** ⊟ 6.00/12.00 **s.**

FORD High St. ☎ 06784 (Llanuwchllyn) 777

BALDOCK Herts. **404** T 28 – pop. 6,428 – ECD : Thursday – ☎ 0462.
Envir.: Ashwell (St. Mary's Church★ 14C: Medieval graffiti) NE : 4 ½ m.
London 42 – Bedford 20 – Cambridge 21 – Luton 15.

- **Butterfield House** without rest., 4 Hitchin St., SG7 6AE, ☎ 892701, ⊠ – TV ⊟wc ⊠ � P
⊟ 0.90 – **11 rm** 10.00/17.00 **s.**

PEUGEOT 74 Icknield Way ☎ 893511

BAMBURGH Northumb. **986** ⑮ – pop. 458 – ECD : Wednesday – ☎ 066 84.
See : Castle★★ (12C-18C) *AC*. – ⊠ ☎ 378.
London 337 – Edinburgh 77 – Newcastle-upon-Tyne 51.

- **Lord Crewe Arms,** Front St., NE69 7BL, ☎ 243 – ⊟wc P
Easter-October – M 3.90/6.25 **st.** ≬ 2.25 – **26 rm** ⊟ 11.50/24.50 **st.**

- **Sunningdale,** 21-23 Lucker Rd, NE69 7BS, ☎ 334 – ⊟wc
18 rm ⊟ 8.00/18.00.

BAMPTON Cumbria – pop. 337 – ⊠ Penrith – ☎ 093 13.
London 285 – Carlisle 26 – Kendal 25.

- **Haweswater** ⚕, CA10 2RP, SW : 4 m. ☎ 235, ≼ Haweswater reservoir, ⊠, ⊠ – ⊠ P.
⊠ ① VISA
M (bar lunch) approx. 5.50 **t.** ≬ 1.75 – **16 rm** ⊟ 9.30/18.60 **t.**

BANBURY Oxon. **403 404** P 27 – pop. 29,387 – ECD : Tuesday – ☎ 0295.
Envir. : Upton House (pictures★★★, porcelain★★) *AC*, NW : 7 m. – East Adderbury (St. Mary's Church : corbels★) SE : 3 ½ m. – Broughton Castle (great hall★, white room : 1599 plaster ceiling★★) and St. Mary's Church (memorial tombs★) *AC*, SW : 3 ½ m. – Wroxton (thatched cottages★) NW : 3 m. – Farnborough Hall (interior plasterwork★) *AC*, NW : 6 m.
🛈 8 Horsefair ☎ 52535 ext 250.
London 76 – Birmingham 40 – Coventry 25 – Oxford 23.

- **Whately Hall** (T.H.F.), Horsefair, by Banbury Cross, OX16 0AN, ☎ 3451, Telex 837149,
« Part 17C Hall », ⊠ – ⊠ TV P. ⊠. ⊠ AE ① VISA
M 5.75/7.00 **st.** ≬ 2.00 – **78 rm** ⊟ 13.00/27.50 **st.**

- **Manor,** 27 Oxford Rd, OX16 9AH, ☎ 59361, Telex 837450 – TV. P. ⊠. ⊠ AE ① VISA
M *(closed Sunday)* a la carte 5.85/8.75 **t.** ≬ 1.90 – ⊟ 2.25 – **28 rm** 17.00/26.50 **st.**

- **White Lion,** High St., OX16 8JW, ☎ 4358 – TV ⊠ P
M a la carte 3.40/6.80 ≬ 2.00 – **16 rm** ⊟ 12.00/20.00 – P 15.00/23.00.

- **Lismore,** 61 Oxford Rd, OX16 9AJ, ☎ 2105
closed 1 week at Christmas – **8 rm** ⊟ 7.50/14.00 **s.**

at Wroxton NW: 3 m. on A 422 by A 41 – ⊠ Wroxton – ☺ 029 573 Wroxton St. Mary :

🏨 **Wroxton House,** Silver St., OX15 6PZ, ☏ 482, 🍴 – 📺 🛏wc 🕿 🅿. 🔼 AE ⓪ VISA
M 4.25/4.75 ⌀ 1.75 – **12 rm** ⌷ 12.00/23.00.

AUSTIN-DAIMLER-JAGUAR-MORRIS-MG-ROVER-
TRIUMPH-WOLSELEY Southam Rd ☏ 51551
BMW, TALBOT Southam Rd ☏ 53511
CITROEN, VAUXHALL 8 Middleton Rd ☏ 3551
FORD Warwick Rd ☏ 4311

LANCIA, LOTUS, SAAB 21/27 Broad St. ☏ 50733
RENAULT 15/16 Southam Rd ☏ 50141
VOLVO Main Rd, Middleton Cheney ☏ 710452
VW, AUDI-NSU Broad St. ☏ 51251

BANGOR Gwynedd **403** H 24 – pop. 14,558 – ECD: Wednesday – ☺ 0248.
🛝 ☏ 0248 (Llanfairfechan) 680 144, 7 m. off A 55.
🛈 Bron Castell ☏ 52786 (summer only).

London 247 – Birkenhead 68 – Holyhead 23 – Shrewsbury 83.

🏩 **Ty-Uchaf,** Tal-y-Bont, LL57 3UR, SE: 2 m. on A 55 ☏ 52219 🛏wc – 🅿
closed 24 December-16 January and 3 weeks before Easter – **M** a la carte 4.00/6.50 **t.**
⌀ 1.85 – **10 rm** ⌷ 7.00/14.00 **t.**

BANSTEAD Surrey **404** T 30 – pop. 45,052 – ECD: Wednesday – ☺ 073 73 Burgh Heath.
🛝 Kingswood ☏ Mogador 2188, S: 3 m.

London 17 – Brighton 39.

✖✖ **Red Coach,** 51 Nork Way, SM7 1PE, off A 2022 ☏ 57188 – 🅿. 🔼 AE ⓪ VISA
closed Sunday, Monday and Bank Holidays – **M** a la carte 6.85/10.35 **t.** ⌀ 2.45.

at Burgh Heath S: 1½ m. on A 217 – ⊠ Tadworth – ☺ 073 73 Burgh Heath :

🏨 **Pickard Motor** (Best Western), Brighton Rd, KT20 6BW, on A 217 ☏ 57222, Telex
929908 – 📺 🛏wc 🕿 🅿. 🔥 🔼 AE ⓪ VISA
M a la carte approx. 3.70 **t.** ⌀ 2.20 – ⌷ 2.25 – **33 rm** 12.00/24.00 **t.**

TALBOT 24 High St. ☏ 51414

BARBON Cumbria – pop. 221 – ECD: Thursday – ☺ 046 836.
London 262 – Kendal 13 – Lancaster 20 – **Leeds** 61.

✖✖ Barbon Inn ⌂ with rm, LA6 2LJ, ☏ 233, « 17C country inn », 🍴 – 🅿
9 rm.

BARFORD Warw. **403** **404** P 27 – pop. 1,108. – ECD: Thursday – ⊠ Warwick – ☺ 0926.
London 99 – Birmingham 22 – Coventry 13 – Stratford-upon-Avon 7.

🏠 Glebe, Church St., CV35 8BS, ☏ 624218, 🍴 – 🛏wc 🚿wc 🅿 – **11 rm.**

BARFORD ST. MARTIN Wilts. – **403** **404** O 30 – see Salisbury.

BAR HILL Cambs. **404** U 27 – see Cambridge.

BARLBOROUGH Derbs. **403** **404** Q 24 – pop. 1,778 – ECD: Wednesday – ⊠ ☺ 0246 Chesterfield.

Envir. : Worksop (Priory Church: Norman nave*) NE: 7 m.
🛝 at Worksop ☏ 0909 (Worksop) 5531, E: 7 m.

London 154 – Derby 31 – Nottingham 27 – Sheffield 11.

✖ **Royal Oak Inn,** High St., S43 4ET, ☏ 810425 – 🅿. 🔼 ⓪
closed Sunday dinner – **M** 4.00/5.00 **t.** ⌀ 2.00.

BARMOUTH (ABERMO) Gwynedd **403** H 25 – pop. 2,150 – ECD: Wednesday – ☺ 0341.
See : Site** – Panorama walk**.
🛈 Wales Tourist Office, The Promenade ☏ 280787 (Easter-September).

London 231 – Chester 74 – Dolgellau 10 – Shrewsbury 67.

🏨 Cors y Gedol, High St., LL42 1DP, ☏ 280402 – 🛗 📺 🛏wc 🅿
25 rm.

AUSTIN-DAIMLER-JAGUAR-MORRIS-MG-ROVER-TRIUMPH Park Rd ☏ 280449

BARNARD CASTLE Durham **986** ⑲ – pop. 5,270 – ECD: Thursday – ☺ 083 33.
See : Bowes Museum** *AC* – Castle* (ruins 12C-14C). **Envir. :** Raby Castle* (14C) *AC,*
NE: 6 m.
🛝 Harmire Rd ☏ 2237.
🛈 43 Galgate ☏ 38481.

London 258 – Carlisle 63 – Leeds 68 – Middlesbrough 31 – Newcastle-upon-Tyne 39.

Hotels see: Darlington E: 16 ½ m.

AUSTIN-MORRIS-MG 19 Galgate ☏ 2129

VAUXHALL Newgate ☏ 3504

BARNBY MOOR Notts. 403 404 Q 23 – pop. 280 – ✉ ☎ 0777 Retford.
London 151 – Leeds 44 – Lincoln 27 – Nottingham 31.

- 🏨 **Ye Olde Bell** (T.H.F.), DN22 8QS, ☏ 705121, Telex 56446, 🚗 – 📺 🛏 wc 🕿 🅿. ⚄.
  🄽 AE ⓪ VISA
  M 4.25/6.35 st. ♦ 1.65 – **57 rm** ⌷ 14.00/22.00 st.

BARNSDALE BAR West Yorks. 404 Q 23 – see Wentbridge.

BARNSLEY South Yorks. 404 P 23 – pop. 75,395 – ECD : Thursday – ☎ 0226.
📓 Staincross ☏ 022 678 (Darton) 2856, N : 4 m.
🛈 Civic Hall, Eldon St. ☏ 6757. — London 177 – Leeds 21 – Manchester 36 – Sheffield 15.

- 🏨 Queen's (Anchor), Regents St., S70 2HQ, ☏ 84192, Group Telex 858875 – 📺 🛏 wc 🕿.
  ⚄. 🄽 AE ⓪ VISA
  31 rm ⌷ 16.50/23.50 st.

- 🏨 Royal (Anchor), Church St., S70 2AD, ☏ 203658, Group Telex 858875 – ⚄. 🄽 AE ⓪ VISA
  M approx. 3.50 st. – **17 rm** ⌷ 12.00/20.00.

  at Ardsley E: 2 ½ m. on A 635 – ✉ ☎ 0226 Barnsley :

- 🏨 **Ardsley House,** Doncaster Rd. S71 5EH, ☏ 89401, Telex 547762, 🚗 – 📺 🚙 🅿. ⚄. 🄽
  AE ⓪ VISA
  M 3.50/5.00 st. – ⌷ 2.20 – **42 rm** 16.50/24.00 st.

AUSTIN-MORRIS-MG-ROVER-TRIUMPH 12A Regent St. ☏ 5561
DAIMLER-JAGUAR-MORRIS-MG-WOLSELEY 101 Old Mill Lane ☏ 6746
FIAT, MERCEDES-BENZ Peel St. ☏ 43317

FORD Dodworth Rd ☏ 5741
RENAULT Doncaster Rd ☏ 5915
TALBOT, FIAT Stairfoot ☏ 6675
VW, AUDI-NSU Huddersfield Rd ☏ 203855

BARNSTAPLE Devon 403 H 30 – pop. 17,317 – ECD : Wednesday – ☎ 0271.
Envir. : Swymbridge (church : carved woodwork* 15C) SE : 4 ½ m.
London 222 – Exeter 40 – Taunton 51.

- 🏨 **Imperial** (T.H.F.), Taw Vale Par., EX32 8NB, ☏ 5861 – 🛗 📺 🅿. ⚄. 🄽 AE ⓪ VISA
  M 3.95/5.75 st. ♦ 1.65 – **56 rm** ⌷ 16.00/26.00 st.
- 🏨 **Barnstaple Motel,** Braunton Rd, EX31 1LE, NW : 1 m. on A 361 ☏ 76221, 🄽 – 🛏 wc
  🅿. ⚄. 🄽 AE ⓪ VISA
  M a la carte 5.10/7.10 st. ♦ 1.35 – **60 rm** ⌷ 12.10/24.15 st.
- 🏛 Royal and Fortescue, Boutport St., EX31 1HG, ☏ 2289 – 🛗 🛏 wc 🅿 – **54 rm**.
- ✕✕ **Lynwood House,** Exeter Rd, EX32 9DZ, on A 377 ☏ 3695 – 🅿. 🄽 AE ⓪ VISA
  closed Saturday lunch, Sunday dinner, 2 weeks mid November and first week January –
  M a la carte 5.20/8.25 t. ♦ 2.25.

  at Bishop's Tawton S : 2 m. on A 377 – ✉ ☎ 0271 Barnstaple :

- 🏨 **Downrew House** 🐾, EX32 0DY, SE : 1 ½ m. on Chittlehampton Rd ☏ 2497, « Country
  house atmosphere », ✎, ⊃ heated, 🚗, park – 🛏 wc 🅿
  · *Mid March-October* – M approx. 6.85 ♦ 2.00 – **14 rm** ⌷ 12.00/14.00.

AUSTIN-DAIMLER-JAGUAR-MORRIS-MG-ROVER-TRIUMPH Boutport St. ☏ 73232
AUSTIN-MG-MORRIS Bear St. ☏ 3038
BMW Abbey Rd ☏ 4070
FIAT, TOYOTA, VOLVO Pottington Industrial Estate, Billand Way ☏ 71551

FORD Taw Vale ☏ 4173
OPEL 42 Boutport St. ☏ 4366
RENAULT Bear St. ☏ 2375/3739
SKODA 8 Boutport St. ☏ 3329
TALBOT Newport Rd ☏ 5363
VAUXHALL Pilton Bridge ☏ 2433

BARRY (BARRI) South Glam. 403 K 29 – pop. 41,681 – ECD : Wednesday – ☎ 0446.
📓 Port Rd, The Colcot ☏ 735061.
🛈 Vale of Glamorgan Borough Council, Woodlands Rd ☏ 730311 (Easter-September).
London 167 – Cardiff 10 – Swansea 39.

- 🏨 **International,** Port Rd, Rhoose, CF6 9BT, W : 2 m. off A 4226 ☏ 710787 – 📺 🛏 wc
  🕿 🅿. 🄽 AE VISA
  M a la carte 6.15/7.85 s. ♦ 1.90 – **30 rm** ⌷ 13.50/18.50 s.
- 🏨 **Water's Edge,** The Knap, CF6 8YY, ☏ 733392, ≼ – 🛗 📺 🛏 wc 🕿 🅿. 🄽 AE VISA
  M approx. 3.50 ♦ 1.50 – **38 rm** ⌷ 14.50/19.50.
- 🏨 **Mount Sorrel,** Porthkerry Rd, CF6 8XY, ☏ 740069 – 📺 🛏 wc 🚻 wc 🕿 🅿. 🄽 AE ⓪ VISA
  M 4.00/6.00 st. ♦ 1.60 – **39 rm** ⌷ 17.95/23.45 t.
- 🏨 **Cwm Ciddy Tavern Motel,** Port Rd, CF6 9BA, ☏ 732892 – 📺 🛏 wc 🅿
  M 5.00 s. ♦ 1.50 – **14 rm** ⌷ 11.50/19.00 s.

AUSTIN-DAIMLER-JAGUAR-MORRIS-MG-ROVER-TRIUMPH-WOLSELEY Brook St. ☏ 734365

BARTON Lancs. – pop. 2,010 – ☎ 0772 Broughton.
London 228 – Blackpool 18 – Lancaster 16 – Preston 4.5.

- 🏨 **Barton Grange,** Garstang Rd, PR3 5AA, ☏ 862551, ✎ – 🛗 📺 🛏 wc 🕿 🅿
  M *(closed Sunday dinner)* a la carte 4.05/8.75 st. – **60 rm** ⌷ 11.00/24.00 st.

BARTON-ON-SEA Hants. 403 404 P 31 – pop. 4,294 – ECD : Thursday – ☎ 0425 New Milton.
18 Marine Drive ℡ 615308.
London 108 – Bournemouth 11 – Lymington 8 – **Southampton 23.**

- **Red House** (Best Western), Barton Court Av., BH25 5SD, ℡ 610119, ← – ⊟wc ☎ Ⓟ. ⛹. AE ⓓ VISA
  M 3.75/4.85 **st.** 🌢 2.00 – **45 rm** ⊐ 13.00/21.00 **st.**

BARWICK Somerset 403 404 M 31 – see Yeovil.

BASILDON Essex 404 V 29 – pop. 88,000 – ECD : Wednesday – ☎ 0268 – 18 Kingswood ℡ 3297. – **London 30** – Chelmsford 17 – Southend-on-Sea 13.

- Essex Centre (Centre), Cranes Farm Rd, SS14 3DG, NW : 2 ¼ m. off A 176 and A 1235 ℡ 3955, Telex 995141 – 🛗 TV ⊟wc ☎ Ⓟ. ⛹. AE ⓓ VISA
  ⊐ 1.65 – **120 rm** 18.40/24.15 **st.**

AUSTIN-MG-ROVER-TRIUMPH-WOLSELEY Southern Hay ℡ 22661
DATSUN, OPEL Nethermayne ℡ 22261
FORD Cherrydown ℡ 23451
TALBOT Great Oakes ℡ 21241
VAUXHALL High Rd, Laindon ℡ 42481

BASINGSTOKE

London Street	Y	19
Upper Church Street	Y	24
Winchester Street	Y	27
Aldermaston Road	Z	2
Beaconsfield Road	Y	3
Buckland Avenue	Z	5
Chequers Road	Y	6
Church Street	Y	7
Churchill Way East	Z	9
Churchill Way West	Z	10
Council Road	Y	12
Cross Street	Y	13
Fairfield Road	Y	14
Houndwills Road	Z	17
New Street	Y	20
Reading Road	Z	22
Victoria Street	Y	25
Wote Street	Y	28

By spring 1981 this guide will be out of date. Get the new edition.

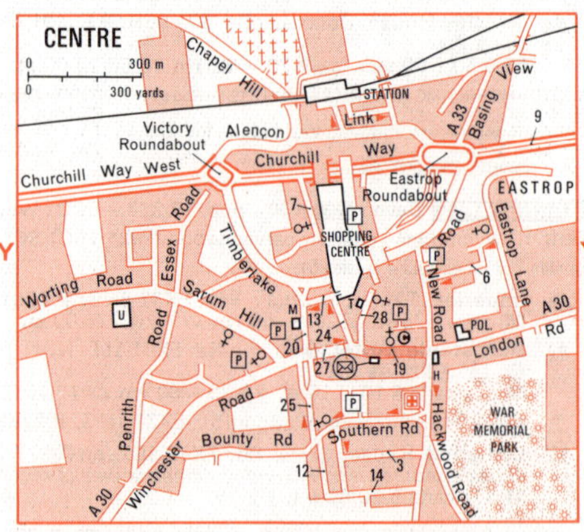

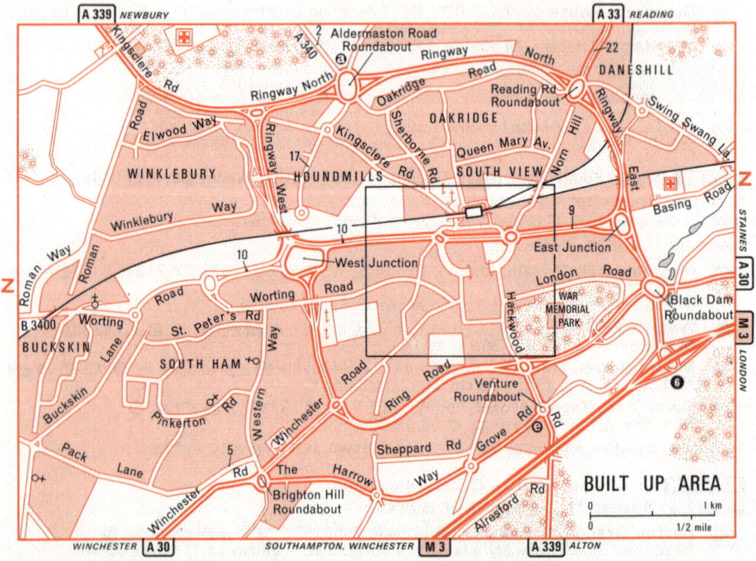

BASINGSTOKE Hants. 403 404 Q 30 – pop. 52,587 – ☺ 0256.

ｒ₉ Bishopswood Lane ℡ 073 56 (Tadley) 5213, N : 6 m. off A 340 z.

London 55 – Reading 17 – Southampton 31 – Winchester 18.

Plan opposite

- **Hampshire Moat House,** Grove Rd, RG21 3EE, SW : 1 m. junction A 339 and A 30 ℡ 68181 – 🖭 ⅋ 🅿. 🛁 ⬛ AE ⓪ VISA   **z e**
  M *(closed Saturday lunch and Christmas)* a la carte 5.60/11.00 **t.** ⅃ 1.95 – **85 rm** ⌘ 18.65/ 25.00 **t.**

- Ladbroke Mercury Motor Inn, Aldermaston Roundabout, RG24 9NV, N : 2 m. junction A 339 and A 340 ℡ 20212 – ❘⬛ 🖭 ⊟wc ☏ 🅿. 🛁 – **82 rm.**   **z a**

- **Red Lion** (Anchor), 24 London St., RG21 1NY, ℡ 28525, Group Telex 858875 – 🖭 ⊟wc ⋔wc ☏ 🅿   **Y c**
  M a la carte 6.00/9.00 **st.** – **43 rm** ⌘ 14.50/26.50.

  at Sherfield-on-Loddon NE : 6 m. off A 33 – z – ✉ Basingstoke – ☺ 025 684 Turgis Green :

- **Wessex House** without rest., Old Reading Rd, RG23 2AF, ℡ 243, 🚗 – 🖭 ⊟wc 🅿
  8 rm ⌘ 13.50/19.15.

  at Oakley W : 5 m. on B 3400 – z – ✉ ☺ 0256 Basingstoke :

- **Beach Arms Motor Inn,** RG23 7EP, on B 3400 ℡ 780210, 🚗 – 🖭 ⊟wc ⋔wc ☏ ⅋ 🅿. ⬛ AE ⓪ VISA
  M 5.25 **st.** ⅃ 2.00 – **17 rm** ⌘ 16.00/23.00 **st.**

AUSTIN-DAIMLER-MG-WOLSELEY Houndmills ℡ 65991
BMW South Warnborough ℡ 045 824 (Long Sutton) 249
DAF Turgis Green ℡ 267
FIAT, LANCIA London Rd ℡ 3896
FORD Lower Wote St. ℡ 3561
JAGUAR-MORRIS-MG-WOLSELEY New Loop Rd ℡ 24561

OPEL, VAUXHALL West Ham ℡ 62551
RENAULT 1/3 Winchester Rd ℡ 23211
ROVER-TRIUMPH London Rd ℡ 24444
SAAB Church St. ℡ 64822
TALBOT Reading Rd ℡ 65454
VOLVO London Rd ℡ 3661

BASLOW Derbs. 403 404 P 24 – pop. 1,166 (inc. Bubnell) – ECD : Wednesday – ✉ Bakewell – ☺ 024 688.

Envir. : Froggat-Edge (❄*) N : 3 m.

London 161 – Derby 27 – Manchester 35 – Sheffield 13.

- **Cavendish,** DE4 1SP, on A 619 ℡ 2311, ⬉, « Tasteful decor », ⅃, 🚗 – 🖭 ⊟wc ⋔wc ☏ 🅿. AE VISA
  M a la carte 4.90/8.80 ⅃ 1.25 – ⌘ 2.50 – **13 rm** 20.00/25.00.

BASSENTHWAITE Cumbria – pop. 518 – ☺ 059 681 Bassenthwaite Lake.

London 300 – Carlisle 24 – Keswick 7.

- **Armathwaite Hall** 🦢, CA12 4RE, W : 1 ½ m. on B 5291 ✉ Keswick ℡ 551, ⬉ Bassenthwaite Lake, « Stately home in extensive grounds », ✕, ⅃, 🚗, park – ❘⬛ 🖭 �car 🅿. ⬛ AE ⓪ VISA
  M 4.25/7.00 **t.** – **37 rm** ⌘ 15.00/29.00 **t.** – P 25.00/31.00 **t.**

- **Castle Inn,** CA12 4RG, W : 1 m. at junction A 591 and B 5291 ✉ Keswick ℡ 401, Telex 64103, ⬉, ✕, ⅃ heated, 🚗 – 🖭 ⊟wc ☏ 🅿. ⬛ AE VISA
  closed November and 4 days at Christmas – **M** 4.50/6.50 **st.** ⅃ 2.00 – **21 rm** ⌘ 17.00/ 25.00 **st.**

- **Pheasant Inn,** CA13 9YE, SW : 3 ¾ m. by B 5291 and A 66 ✉ Cockermouth ℡ 234, « 16C inn », 🚗 – ⊟wc 🅿
  closed Christmas Day – **M** 3.90/6.10 **st.** ⅃ 1.35 – **20 rm** ⌘ 11.00/24.60 **st.**

- **Overwater Hall** 🦢, CA5 1HH, NE : 2¼ m. on Uldale Rd ✉ Ireby, ℡ 566, ⬉, 🚗, park – ⊟wc ☏ 🅿. ⬛ VISA
  closed January and February – **M** *(closed to non-residents)* 3.50/6.00 **s.** ⅃ 2.00 – **13 rm** ⌘ 12.50/18.00 **s.**

- **Bassenfell Manor** 🦢, CA12 4RL, W : 1 m. at junction A 591 and B 5291 ℡ 366, ⬉, 🚗, park – ⋔wc 🅿. ⬛ ⓪ VISA
  Mid March-December – **M** (dinner only) 4.50 **t.** ⅃ 1.80 – **19 rm** ⌘ 7.70/18.50 **t.**

BATH Avon 403 404 M 29 – pop. 84,670 – ECD : Monday and Thursday – ☺ 0225.

See : The Georgian city*** : Royal Crescent*** (N° 1 Georgian House* *AC*) v – Circus** v – Prior Park* (Palladian Mansion ⬉*) *AC* z – Lansdown Crescent (⬉*) Y – Camden Crescent (⬉*) v – Pulteney Bridge (⬉*) x – Assembly Rooms v M² (chandeliers* 18C : Ballroom and Great Octagon), Museum of Costume** – Abbey Church* 16C x B – Roman baths* (Pump Room) *AC* x D – Holburne Museum* *AC* v M¹. **Envir. :** Claverton Manor (American Museum**) *AC*, E : 2 ½ m. z – Dyrham Park* (17C) *AC*, N : 8 m. by A 46 Y – Bradford-on-Avon (St. Lawrence's Church* : Saxon, Tithe Barn* 14C) SE : 9 m. by A 4 Y and A 363 – Tropical Bird Gardens* *AC*, SE : 10 m. by A 4 Y and A 363 in Rode Manor gardens.

ｒ₁₈ Sham Castle ℡ 25182, SE : 1 ½ m. Y – ｒ₁₈ Lansdown ℡ 25007, NW : 3 m. by Lansdown Rd Y.

🛈 8 Abbey Churchyard ℡ 62831 and 60521.

London 119 – Bristol 13 – Southampton 63 – Taunton 49.

BATH

A 4
CAMDEN CRESCENT
19
Julian Road
7
ROYAL CRESCENT
Oxford Rw
41
Walcot Street
Avon
Bathwick Street
A 36
6
A 36
(A 36)
51
M¹
CIRCUS
Royal Avenue
Henrietta St.
HENRIETTA PARK
CRESCENT GARDENS
23 24
25
22
M²
10
Up. Bristol Rd
A 4
33
27
Laura Pl.
A 4
38
44
PULTENEY BRIDGE
26
14
34
54 36
28
H
Road
37
12
53
15 39
B
32
56
Stall St.
D
A 3118
A 367
Green Park Rd
3
North Parade Rd
Avon
42
46
30
A 36
Lower Bristol Road
2
48
49
Pulteney
A 367
9
35
31
17
STATION
45
A 36
18
A 3062
400 m
400 yards
A 367

(M4, M5) A 46 STROUD
Swainswick Lane
UPPER WESTON
Lansdown Lane
CHARLCOMBE
Road
Bailbrook Lane
A 4
CHIPPENHAM
WESTON
High St.
Lansdown Road
St. Saviours Rd
Gloucester
TOLL BRIDGE
Weston Road
LANSDOWN CRESCENT
Road
BATHAMPTON
Y
Y
BRISTOL
Kelston Road
Avon
A 36
WARMINSTER
A 431
Newbridge Hill
London
Warminster Road
A 4
Newbridge Rd
Combe Park
ROYAL VICTORIA PARK
Road
18
Open 12-1980
Up. Bristol Rd A 36
North
U
Newton Road
Bristol
Bathwick
TWERTON
Hill
The Avenue
The Hollow
Widcombe Hill
Whiteway
Greenway La.
Road
PRIOR PARK
N
N
Englishcombe
Lane
Wellsway
Claverton
Down
Rd
Rush Hill
Frome
A 3062
COMBE DOWN
A 3067
Bradford Road
B 3110
Rd
1 km
1 mile
A 367 EXETER

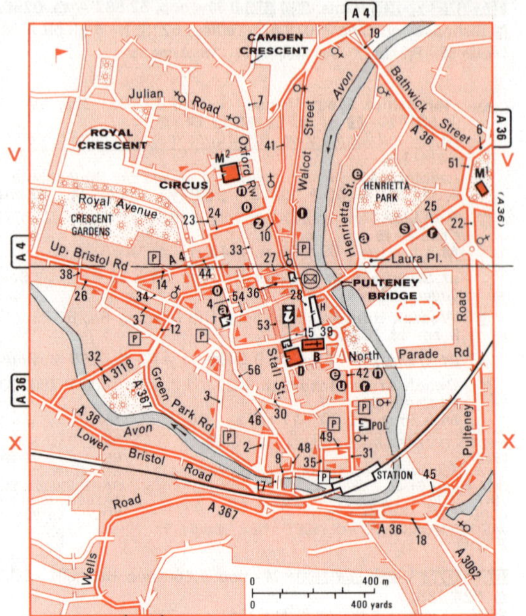

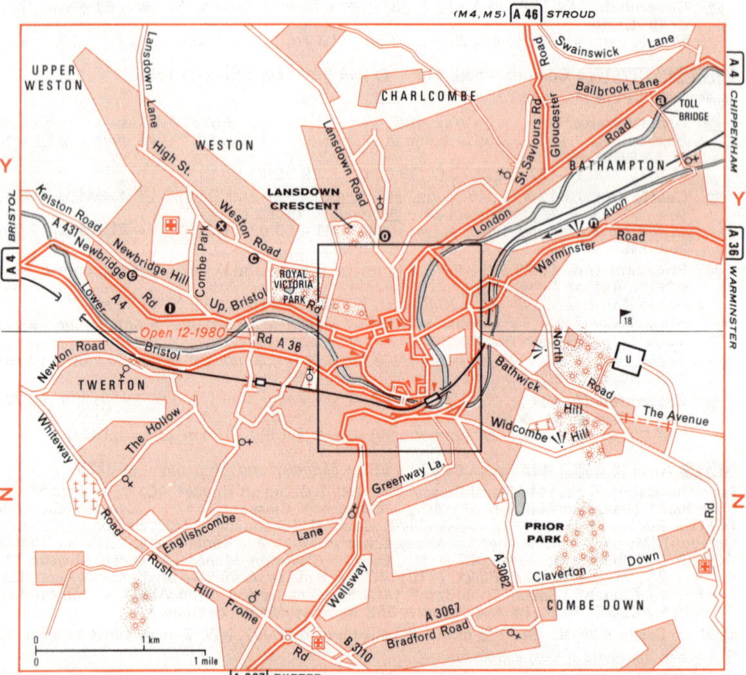

Francis (T.H.F.), Queen Sq., BA1 2HH, ℡ 24257, Telex 449162 – 🛗 TV 🅿. 🛁. 🔝 AE ① VISA **X o**
M 4.20/5.50 **st** 🍾 2.25 – 🍽 2.50 – **66 rm** 21.00/30.50 **st.**

Beaufort (Myddleton), Walcot St., BA1 5BJ, ℡ 63411, Telex 449519 – 🛗 TV. 🛁. 🔝 AE ① VISA **V i**
M 4.50/6.00 **st.** 🍾 1.40 – 🍽 2.75 – **123 rm** 20.35/31.90 **s.**

The Priory, Weston Rd. BA1 2XT, ℡ 21887. ≤, 🏊 heated, 🚗 – TV 🅿 **Y c**
closed 23 December-3 January – **M** (dinner only) a la carte 8.50/10.00 **s.** 🍾 1.80 –
🍽 2.50 – **15 rm** 21.00/35.00 **s.**

Lansdown Grove (Best Western), Lansdown Rd BA1 5EH, ℡ 315891, 🚗 – 🛗 TV **Y o**
🛏wc 🕾 🚗 🅿. 🛁. 🔝 AE ① VISA
M 3.90/5.90 **st.** 🍾 1.50 – 🍽 2.65 – **47 rm** 19.30/32.35 **st.**

Redcar, 27 Henrietta St., BA2 6LR, ℡ 65432 – TV 🛏wc 🕼 🕾 🅿. 🛁 **V a**
35 rm.

Pratt's, South Par., BA2 4AB, ℡ 60441 – 🛗 🛏wc 🕾. 🛁. 🔝 AE VISA **X r**
M 3.10/5.25 **st.** 🍾 1.50 – **51 rm** 🍽 13.25/26.50 **st.**

Royal York (Norfolk Cap.), George St., BA1 2DY, ℡ 61541, Group Telex 23241 – 🛗 **V z**
🛏wc 🕾. 🛁. 🔝 AE ① VISA
M 3.75/4.50 **st.** 🍾 1.75 – **56 rm** 🍽 13.75/29.70 **st.**

Fernley, 1 North Par., BA1 1LG, ℡ 61603 – 🛗 🛏wc 🕼wc 🕾. 🛁 **X e**
M (bar lunch) approx. 4.00 **st.** – **47 rm** 🍽 13.70/28.75 **st.**

Gainsborough, Weston Lane BA1, 4AB, ℡ 311380, 🚗 – TV 🛏wc 🕼wc 🕾 🅿. 🔝 AE VISA
closed 25 and 26 December – **M** (Sunday lunch by reservation only) 5.00/10.50 **t.** 🍾 2.00
– **13 rm** 🍽 15.00/30.00 **t.** **Y x**

North Parade without rest., 10 North Par., BA2 4AL, ℡ 60007 – 🕼. 🔝 AE VISA **X n**
closed December and January – **17 rm** 🍽 7.50/15.50 **st.**

St. Monica's 53-54 Gt. Pulteney St. BA2 4DN, ℡ 62092 – 🛏wc **V r**
M (bar lunch) 3.25 **t.** – **23 rm** 🍽 8.75/19.50 **t.**

Villa Magdala without rest., Henrietta Rd, BA2 6LX, ℡ 25836, 🚗 – TV 🛏wc 🕼wc
🚗 🅿. 🔝 **V e**
closed Christmas – **8 rm** 🍽 17.00/22.00 **st.**

Ashley Villa, 26 Newbridge Rd, BA1 3JZ, ℡ 21683, 🏊 heated – TV 🛏wc 🕼wc 🕾 🅿. 🔝 **Y i**
VISA
18 rm 🍽 14.00/23.00 **st.**

Apsley House, Newbridge Hill, BA1 3PT, ℡ 21368, 🚗 – 🅿 **Y e**
11 rm 🍽 9.50/19.00 **st.**

Richmond, 11 Great Pulteney St., BA2 4BR, ℡ 25560 – 🛏wc. 🔝 **V s**
30 rm 🍽 8.00/17.75.

Tasburgh, Warminster Rd, Bathampton, BA2 6SH, NE: 1 ½ m. on A 36 ℡ 25096, 🚗 – **Y n**
🅿
12 rm.

Popjoy's, Beau Nash House, Sawclose, BA1 1EY, ℡ 60494 – 🔝 AE **X a**
closed Sunday, Monday lunch and 24 December-21 January – **M** (dinner only from
September to March) a la carte 8.50/11.75 **st.** 🍾 2.20.

Old Mill with rm, Toll Bridge Rd, BA1 9DE, NE: 2 m. off A 4 ℡ 858476, ≤, 🌊, 🚗 – **Y a**
🛏wc 🕼wc 🅿. 🔝 AE VISA
M 4.25/7.00 **t.** 🍾 2.20 – **16 rm** 🍽 10.10/23.00 **st.**

Woods, 9-13 Alfred St., ℡ 314812 – 🔝 AE VISA **V n**
closed Sunday, Monday and 24 to 30 December – **M** a la carte 3.20/6.20 **t.**

Laden Table, 7 Edgar Buildings, George St., BA1 2EE, ℡ 64356 – 🔝 VISA **V o**
closed Sunday, Monday and 2 weeks at Christmas – **M** (dinner only) 8.50 **t.** 🍾 2.00.

Ainslie's, 12 Pierrepont St., BA1 1LA, ℡ 61745, Bistro – 🔝 AE ① VISA **X u**
closed Monday, 25-26 December and 1 January – **M** (dinner only) a la carte 5.80/8.40 **t.**
🍾 1.70.

at Lower Limpley Stoke S: 6 ¾ m. by A 36 – **z** – off B 3108 – ✉ Bath – ☎ 022 122
Limpley Stoke :

Cliffe (Best Western) 🦢, BA3 6HY, ℡ 3226, Telex 8814912, ≤, 🏊 heated, 🚗 – TV
🛏wc 🕼wc 🕾 🅿. 🔝 AE ① VISA
closed 5 days at Christmas – **M** (bar lunch) 6.50/7.25 **st.** 🍾 2.50 – 🍽 2.25 – **10 rm**
12.50/31.00 **st.**

Danielle, The Bridge, BA3 6EU, ℡ 3150 – 🅿. 🔝 AE ① VISA
closed Sunday from 1 July-15 September, Monday and first 2 weeks January –
M (dinner only and Sunday lunch) a la carte 7.45/10.15 **t.** 🍾 2.00.

at Woolverton S: 10 m. on A 36 – **y** – ✉ Bath – ☎ 037 383 Beckington :

Woolverton House with rm, BA3 6QS, ℡ 415, 🚗 – TV 🛏wc 🅿. 🔝 AE ①
M *(closed Sunday)* (dinner only) a la carte approx. 8.50 **st.** 🍾 1.90 – 🍽 1.75 – **8 rm**
18.00/27.00 **st.**

at Hunstrete W: 8 ½ m. by A 4 – Y – and A 39 off A 368 – ✉ Pensford – ☎ 076 18 Compton Dando :

🏰 **Hunstrete House** ⌂, BS18 4NS, ☏ 578, ⋖, « Country house atmosphere, gardens ». ✗, ⌇ heated, ✎, park – TV & ⇦ P. ⌂. AE
closed 23 December-4 January – **M** *(closed Sunday dinner to non-residents)* (buffet lunch Monday to Saturday) a la carte 8.00/11.00 **s.** ⌀ 1.60 – ⌑ 1.85 – **19 rm** 28.75 **st.**

ALFA-ROMEO Wellsway ☏ 29187	FORD 5/10 James St. West ☏ 61636
AUSTIN-DAIMLER-JAGUAR-MG-ROVER - TRIUMPH-	RENAULT Margarets Buildings, Circus Pl. ☏ 27328
WOLSELEY Newbridge Rd ☏ 26143	VAUXHALL Upper Bristol Rd ☏ 22131
CITROEN Prior Park Rd ☏ 29552	VOLVO Bathwick Hill ☏ 65814
DATSUN Lower Bristol Rd ☏ 25864	VOLVO, MAZDA Dorchester St. ☏ 66229

BATTLE East Sussex 🗺 V 31 – pop. 4,987 – ☎ 042 46.
See: Abbey★ (11C-14C) *AC* (site of the Battle of Hastings 1066).
🛈 Langton House, High St. ☏ 3721.
London 57 – Brighton 31 – Folkestone 43 – Maidstone 29.

🏠 **George** (T.H.F.), 23 High St., TN33 0EA, ☏ 2844 – TV ⌑wc. AE ⓞ VISA
M 3.75/4.45 **st.** ⌀ 1.65 – **15 rm** ⌑ 13.50/22.00 **st.**

AUSTIN-MORRIS 32 High St. ☏ 2425

BAWTRY South Yorks. 🗺 🗺 Q 23 – pop. 1,497 – ✉ ☎ 0302 Doncaster.
🛈 Austerfield, ☏ 710 841, NE: 2 m. off A 614.
London 158 – Leeds 39 – Lincoln 32 – Nottingham 36 – Sheffield 22.

🏨 **Crown** (Anchor), High St., DN10 6JW, ☏ 710341, Group Telex 858875, ⇦ – TV ⌑wc
☎ P. AE ⓞ VISA
M approx. a la carte 6.00 **st.** – **58 rm** ⌑ 17.50/25.50 **st.**

✗✗ **Dower House,** Market Pl., DN10 6JL, ☏ 710497 – P. AE ⓞ
closed Sunday, 4 days at Christmas and 2 weeks February – **M** a la carte 5.85/8.30 **t.** ⌀ 2.45.

BEACONSFIELD Bucks. 🗺 S 29 – pop. 12,640 – ECD : Wednesday and Saturday – ☎ 049 46.
London 26 – Aylesbury 19 – Oxford 32.

🏰 **Bellhouse** (De Vere), Oxford Rd, HP9 2XE, E: 1 ¾ m. on A 40 ☏ (Gerrard's Cross) 87211, Telex 848719, ⇦ – ⌾ TV & P. ⌂. AE ⓞ VISA
M 5.75/6.25 **st.** ⌀ 1.75 – **120 rm** ⌑ 24.00/32.00 **st.**

🏨 Beaconsfield Crest Motel (Crest), Aylesbury End, HP9 1LW, ☏ 71211 – TV ⌑wc ☎ P.
⌂. AE ⓞ VISA
⌑ 2.40 – **41 rm** 18.50/25.20 **st.**

at Beaconsfield New Town N : ¾ m. on B 474 – ✉ ☎ 049 46 Beaconsfield :

✗✗ **Jasmine,** 15a Penn Rd, HP9 2PN, ☏ 5335, Chinese rest. – AE ⓞ VISA
M a la carte 4.35/9.00 **t.** ⌀ 2.00.

AUSTIN-MORRIS-MG-WOLSELEY Penn Rd ☏ 5272	FIAT 15 Gregories Rd ☏ 5538
DAIMLER-JAGUAR-ROVER-TRIUMPH, JENSEN 55	VAUXHALL Knotty Green ☏ 3730
Station Rd ☏ 2141	

BEAMINSTER Dorset 🗺 L 31 – pop. 2,346 – ECD : Wednesday – ✉ Bridport – ☎ 0308.
London 149 – Dorchester 19 – Exeter 40 – Taunton 31.

✗✗ **Pickwicks,** The Square, DT8 3AX, ☏ 862094 – AE VISA
closed Sunday and Monday except Bank Holidays – **M** (dinner only) 5.50 ⌀ 1.50.

BEAULIEU Hants. 🗺 🗺 P 31 – pop. 1,083 – ECD : Tuesday – ✉ Brockenhurst – ☎ 0590.
See : Beaulieu Abbey★ (ruins 13C) : Palace House★ 14C, National Motor Museum★★, Buckler's Hard Maritime Museum *AC*.
🛈 John Montagu Building ☏ 612345.
London 102 – Bournemouth 24 – Southampton 13 – Winchester 23.

🏰 **Montagu Arms,** Palace Lane, SO4 7ZL, ☏ 612324, ⇦ – TV P. AE ⓞ VISA
M 4.50/6.00 **s.** ⌀ 2.25 – **26 rm** ⌑ 14.00/25.00 **s.**

at Bucklers Hard S: 2 ¼ m. – ✉ Brockenhurst – ☎ 059 063 Bucklers Hard :

🏨 **Master Builder's House** ⌂, SO4 7XB, ☏ 253, ⋖, ⇦ – ⌑wc ☎ & P. ⌂. AE ⓞ VISA
M (bar lunch) a la carte 5.60/8.60 **t.** – **23 rm** ⌑ 13.50/27.00 **st.**

During the season, particularly in resorts, it is wise to book in advance.
However, if you find you cannot take up a hotel booking you have made,
please let the hotel know immediately.
If you are writing to a hotel abroad enclose an International Reply Coupon
(available from Post Offices).

BEAUMARIS Gwynedd **403** H 24 – pop. 2,102 – ECD : Wednesday – ✪ 0248.

See : Castle★ (13 C) *AC*.

⬙₉ ☏ 810231, NW : 1 m.

London 253 – Birkenhead 74 – Holyhead 25.

🏰 Bulkeley Arms, 19 Castle St., LL58 8AW, ☏ 810415, ⬙ Menai Strait, ⏏ – 🖃 🛏wc **P**. ⛱
42 rm.

🏨 **Bishopsgate House,** 54 Castle St., LL58 8AB, ☏ 810302 – 🛏wc **P**. AE *VISA*
March-November – **M** (bar lunch) 2.95/7.00 **t.** ⚱ 1.00 – **11 rm** ⌣ 6.75/15.00 **s.** –
P 11.00/13.50 **s.**

✗ Hobson's Choice, 13 Castle St., LL58 8AP, ☏ 810323.

BECCLES Suffolk **404** S 26 – pop. 8,015 – ECD : Wednesday – ✪ 0502.

London 113 – Great Yarmouth 15 – Ipswich 40 – Norwich 18.

🏨 **Waveney House,** Puddingmoor, NR34 9PL, ☏ 712270 – 📺 🛏wc 🛏wc ☏ **P**. 🔲 AE
① *VISA*
M *(closed Sunday dinner to non-residents)* 3.95/4.50 **t.** ⚱ 2.00 – **14 rm** ⌣ 14.50/27.50 **t.**

FORD VAUXHALL Station Rd ☏ 712268   MORRIS-MG-WOLSELEY Beccles Rd, Barnby ☏ 050 276 (Barnby) 204

BECKERMET Cumbria – ECD : Tuesday and Thursday – ✉ ✪ 094 684.

London 326 – Carlisle 45 – Kendal 62 – Workington 17.

🏨 **Royal Oak,** CA21 2XB, ☏ 84551 – 🛏wc ☏ **P**
8 rm ⌣ 11.20/18.00 **t.**

BEDDGELERT Gwynedd **403** H 24 – pop. 671 – ECD : Wednesday – ✪ 076 686.

Envir. : NE : Llyn Dinas valley★★ – Llyn Gwynant valley★. **Exc. :** Blaenau Ffestiniog (site :
slate quarries★) E : 14 m. by Penrhyndeudraeth. – London 249 – Caernarfon 13 – Chester 73.

🏰 **Royal Goat,** LL55 4YE, ☏ 224 – 🛏wc ☏ **P**. 🔲 AE ① *VISA*
M 3.50/5.50 – **27 rm** ⌣ 10.00/19.00 – P 17.50/19.20.

⚘ **Tanronen,** LL55 4YB, ☏ 347 – **P**
M 3.00/5.00 **t.** ⚱ 2.45 – **10 rm** ⌣ 8.00/16.00 **t.**

BEDFORD Beds. **404** S 27 – pop. 73,229 – ECD : Thursday – ✪ 0234.

See : Embankment★ – Cecil Higgins Art Gallery (porcelain★ 18C). **Envir. :** Elstow (Abbey
Church★ 11C, Moot Hall : John Bunyan Museum *AC*) S : 1 ¼ m. – Ampthill (Houghton House :
site★, ⬙★) S : 5 m. – Old Warden (St. Leonard's Church : woodwork★; Aeroplane Museum,
near Biggleswade Aerodrome : the Shuttleworth collection★ *AC*) SE : 7 ½ m.

⛳ Green Lane ☏ 54010, N : 2 m. on A 6 – ⛳ Mowsbury, Cleat Hill ☏ 771042, N : 3 m.

🛈 Town Hall, St. Paul's Sq. ☏ 67422 ext 250 – The Museum, The Embankment ☏ 53323 (weekends).

London 59 – Cambridge 29 – Colchester 73 – Leicester 51 – Lincoln 95 – Luton 20 – Oxford 52 – Southend-on-Sea 78.

🏰 Bedford Moat House, St. Mary's St., MK42 0AR, ☏ 55131, Telex 825243, ⬙ – 🛗 📺 **P**.
⛱ – **80 rm.**

🏰 **Swan,** High St., MK40 1RW, ☏ 46565 – 🛏wc ☏ **P**. ⛱. 🔲 AE ① *VISA*
M 3.80/4.20 **s.** ⚱ 1.85 – **103 rm** ⌣ 11.45/18.50 **s.**

🏨 **De Parys,** 41 de Parys Av., MK40 2UA, ☏ 52121, ⏏ – 🛏wc ♿ **P**. ⛱. 🔲
closed 1 week at Christmas – **M** 4.00/4.50 ⚱ 2.00 – **44 rm** ⌣ 10.00/21.00.

🏨 Embankment (Crest), The Embankment, MK40 3PD, ☏ 61334 – 🛏wc **P**. ⛱. 🔲 AE
① *VISA*
M *(closed Bank Holidays)* – **21 rm** ⌣ 11.60/18.00 **st.**

at Wilshamstead (Wilstead) S : 5 m. by A 6 – ✉ ✪ 0234 Bedford :

⌂ **Old Manor House,** Cotton End Rd, MK45 3BT, ☏ 740262 – **P**
9 rm ⌣ 7.00/14.00.

at Houghton Conquest S : 6 ½ m. by A 6 – ✉ ✪ 0234 Bedford :

✗✗ **Knife and Cleaver,** MK45 3LA, ☏ 740387, ⏏ – **P**
closed Saturday lunch, Monday dinner, Sunday and Bank Holidays – **M** a la carte 5.65/
8.35 **st.** ⚱ 2.05.

at Turvey W : 7 m. on A 428 – ✉ Bedford – ✪ 023 064 Turvey :

🏨 **Laws,** MK43 8DB, ☏ 213, ⏏ – **P**. 🔲 ①
closed Sunday, 2 weeks mid August, 1 week at Christmas and Bank Holidays – **M** a la carte
5.25/7.75 **t.** – **11 rm** ⌣ 12.00/18.00 **t.**

at Clapham NW : 2 m. on A 6 – ✉ ✪ 0234 Bedford :

🏰 **Woodlands Manor,** Green Lane, MK41 6ET, ☏ 63281, ⅃ heated, ⏏ – 📺 🛏wc 🛏wc
☏ **P**. ⛱. 🔲 AE ① *VISA*
M *(closed Saturday lunch)* 4.75/5.75 **t.** ⚱ 1.65 – **18 rm** ⌣ 17.50/27.00 **t.**

P.T.O. ⟶

at *Milton Ernest* NW : 5 m. on A 6 – ✉ Bedford – ☎ 023 02 Oakley :

XX **Milton Ernest Hall** ⌂ with rm, MK44 1RF, ☏ 4111, ≤, « Victorian gothic country house », ⌂, ☞, park – ⌂wc ℗ . ◹ *VISA*
closed Easter, first week September, Christmas, first 2 weeks January and Bank Holidays – **M** *(closed Sunday dinner and Monday)* a la carte 4.75/7.70 ₰ 1.40 – **6 rm** ⌷ 20.00/30.00.

at *Bletsoe* NW : 6 ½ m. on A 6 – ✉ ☎ 0234 Bedford :

XX **Falcon Inn,** Rushden Rd, MK44 1QN, ☏ 781222 – ℗ . ◹ ◉
closed Saturday lunch and Sunday dinner – **M** a la carte 5.00/6.85 **st.** ₰ 1.80.

MICHELIN Branch, Kingfisher Wharf, London Rd, MK42 0PE, ☏ 51541.

ALFA-ROMEO, BMW, ROLLS ROYCE, BENTLEY
Shuttleworth Rd, Goldington ☏ 60412
AUDI-NSU, MERCEDES-BENZ, ROLLS ROYCE,
VAUXHALL Barker's Lane ☏ 50011
AUSTIN-MG-WOLSELEY Station Rd, Oakley ☏ 023 02
(Oakley) 3118
AUSTIN-MORRIS-ROVER-TRIUMPH Bromham Rd
☏ 63299
AUSTIN-DAIMLER-JAGUAR-MG-ROVER-TRIUMPH-

WOLSELEY 120 Goldington Rd ☏ 55221
DAF, HONDA, VOLVO Windsor Rd ☏ 45454
DATSUN 180 Goldington Rd ☏ 60121
FORD 8/10 The Broadway ☏ 58391
PEUGEOT Kingsway ☏ 212636
RENAULT 87 High St., Clapham ☏ 54257
TALBOT 1 The Kingsway ☏ 58581
VW, AUDI-NSU 20 Grove Pl. ☏ 51431

BEESTON Cheshire **403** **404** L 24 – pop. 221 – ✉ Tarporley – ☎ 0829 Bunbury.
London 186 – **Chester** 15 – **Liverpool** 40 – Shrewsbury 32.

XXX Wild Boar Motor Lodge, with rm, CV6 9NW, on A 49 ☏ 260309, Telex 61455, ☞ –
TV ⌂wc ☏ ♿ ℗
30 rm.

BELFORD Northumb. **986** ⑮ – pop. 960 – ECD : Thursday – ☎ 066 83.
London 335 – **Edinburgh** 71 – **Newcastle-upon-Tyne** 49.

🏠 Blue Bell (Swallow), Market Sq., NE70 7NE, ☏ 543, Group Telex 53168, ☞ – ⌂wc
☏ 🚗 ℗
13 rm.

BELPER Derbs. **403** **404** P 24 – pop. 24,723 – ✉ ☎ 077 382.
London 141 – **Derby** 8 – **Manchester** 55 – **Nottingham** 17.

XX **Remy's,** 84 Bridge St., ☏ 2246, French rest. – ◬
closed Saturday lunch, Sunday, last 2 weeks July, first week August, last 2 weeks February and Bank Holidays – **M** a la carte 5.45/10.30 **t.** ₰ 1.50.

BELSTEAD Suffolk **404** X 27 – see Ipswich.

BELSTONE Devon **403** I 31 – pop. 282 – ✉ Okehampton – ☎ 083 784 Sticklepath.
London 221 – **Exeter** 20 – **Plymouth** 34 – Torquay 30.

🏠 **Skaigh House** ⌂, EX20 1RD, ☏ 243, ≤, ⌓, ☞, park – ℗
16 March-14 October – **M** *(closed lunch to non-residents)* approx. 5.50 **t.** ₰ 1.20 –
10 rm ⌷ 12.00/29.00 **t.**

BELTON Norfolk **404** Z 26 – see Great Yarmouth.

BEMBRIDGE I.O.W. **403** **404** Q 31 – see Wight (Isle of).

BENLLECH Gwynedd **403** H 24 – pop. 2,554 – ECD : Thursday – ☎ 024 874 Tynygongl.
London 258 – **Caernarfon** 17 – **Chester** 70 – Holyhead 22.

🏠 **Bay Court,** Beach Rd, LL74 8SW, ☏ 2573 – ⌂wc ℗
M (bar lunch) a la carte 4.60/7.40 **s.** ₰ 1.85 – **22 rm** ⌷ 10.00/22.00 **s.**
🏠 Glanrafon, LL74 8TF, on A 5025 ☏ 2364 – ⌂wc ℗
22 rm.
🏠 **Rhostrefor,** LL74 8SR, on A 5025 ☏ 2347, ≤, ☞ – ℗
Easter-October – **M** (buffet lunch) 2.50 **s.** – **10 rm** ⌷ 7.50/15.00 **s.**
🏠 Hafod Wyn, LL74 8SD, W : ¾ m. on B 5110 ☏ 2357 – ⌂wc ℗
10 rm ⌷ 6.75/15.00 **s.**

BENSON Oxon. **403** **404** Q 29 – pop. 4,603 – ECD : Wednesday – ☎ 0491 Wallingford.
Envir. : Dorchester-on-Thames (Abbey Church* 14C) NW : 3 ½ m.
London 52 – **Oxford** 13 – **Reading** 14 – Swindon 35.

🏠 **White Hart,** 1 Castle Sq., OX9 6SD, ☏ 35244, ☞ – ℗ . ◹ ◬ ◉ *VISA*
M *(closed dinner Sunday and Monday to non-residents)* (buffet lunch) a la carte 3.10/
5.75 **t.** – **10 rm** ⌷ 9.00/16.25 **t.**

at *Roke* E : 2 m. off B 4009 – ✉ Dorchester – ☎ 0491 Wallingford :

XX Home Sweet Home Inn, OX9 6JD, ☏ 38249, ☞ – ℗.

BERKELEY Glos. **403** **404** M 28 – pop. 1,449 – ECD : Wednesday – ✆ 045 381.
See : Castle** (12C) *AC*.
London 134 – Bristol 20 – Gloucester 16 – Swindon 49.

   ⌂ **Berkeley Arms,** 4 Canonbury St., GL13 9BG, ☏ 291 – ⌷wc **P**. 🖭 *VISA*
   M 3.50/4.50 st. ⌀ 1.50 – **13 rm** ⌷ 8.00/13.50.

   at Newport SE : 2 m. on A 38 – ✉ ✆ 045 381 Berkeley :

   ⌂ Newport Towers Motel, GL13 9PX, on A 38 ☏ 575, 🍴 – 📺 ⌷wc ☏ **P**. 🛗 – **60 rm.**

BERKSWELL West Midlands **403** **404** P 26 – see Coventry.

BERRYNARBOR Devon **403** H 30 – see Ilfracombe.

BERRY POMEROY Devon **403** J 32 – see Totnes.

BERWICK-UPON-TWEED Northumb. **986** ⑮ – pop. 11,647 – ECD : Thursday – ✆ 0289.
See : City Walls* 16C. **Envir. :** Norham Castle* (12C) SW : 7 m.
⛳ ☏ 028 287 (Ancroft) 256, S : 5 m. – ⛳ Magdalene Fields ☏ 5109.
🛈 Castlegate Car Park ☏ 7187 (summer only).
London 349 – Edinburgh 57 – Newcastle-upon-Tyne 63.

   ⌂ **Turret House,** Etal Rd, TD15 2EG, S : ¾ m. off A 1 on B 6354 ☏ 7344, 🍴 – 📺 ⌷wc ☏
   P. 🅰🅴 ⓪ *VISA*
   closed February – **M** *(closed Saturday lunch, Sunday lunch and Tuesday dinner)* (dinner
   only in winter) 8.10 st. ⌀ 1.60 – **11 rm** ⌷ 17.00/30.00 st.

   ⌂ **King's Arms** (Best Western) 43 Hide Hill, TD15 1EJ, ☏ 7454, 🍴 – 📺 ⌷wc ☏ **P**. 🛗
   🅰🅴 ⓪ *VISA*
   M 4.80/7.00 st. ⌀ 2.10 – **37 rm** ⌷ 15.00/30.00 st. – P 26.80/30.00 st.

   ⌂ Castle, Castlegate, TD15 1LF, ☏ 6471 – **15 rm.**

AUSTIN-MORRIS-MG Tweedside Trading Estate   VAUXHALL 12 Silver St. ☏ 7436
☏ 7561   VOLVO Tweed St. ☏ 7537
FORD Castle Garage ☏ 7459   VW, AUDI-NSU Spittal ☏ 7214
RENAULT Golden Sq. ☏ 7371

BETHESDA Gwynedd **403** H 24 – pop. 4,190 – ECD : Wednesday – ✆ 0248.
See : Slate quarries*. **Envir. :** Nant Ffrancon Pass** SE : 4 m.
London 241 – Chester 60 – Holyhead 29 – Shrewsbury 77.

   ⌂ **Snowdonia Park Motel,** Ty'n Maes, Nant Ffrancon, LL57 3LX, S : 2 m. on A 5
   ☏ 600548, ≼ – 📺 ⌷wc 🚿wc **P**. 🅰 ⓪ *VISA*
   M (dinner only) a la carte approx. 6.95 t. ⌀ 2.70 – ⌷ 1.85 – **30 rm** 10.00/15.00 t.

RENAULT Bangor Rd ☏ 600451

BETWS-Y-COED Gwynedd **403** I 24 – pop 729 – ECD : Thursday – ✆ 069 02.
Envir. : Fairy Glen and Conway Falls* *AC*, SE : 2 m. - Swallow Falls* *AC*, NW : 2 m. - Nant y
Gwryd valley* W : by Capel Curig.
⛳ ☏ 556, ½ m. off A 5.
🛈 Wales Tourist Office ☏ 426.
London 226 – Holyhead 44 – Shrewsbury 62.

   ⌂ **Waterloo,** LL24 0AR, on A 5 ☏ 411 – ⌷wc ☏ **P**. 🛗. 🅰 🅴 ⓪ *VISA*
   closed 3 days at Christmas – **M** (buffet lunch) a la carte 6.45/7.45 t. ⌀ 2.00 – ⌷ 1.00 –
   28 rm 13.50/21.00.

   ⌂ **Craig-y-Dderwen** 🐟, LL24 0AS, SE : ¼ m. on A 5 ☏ 293, ≼, 🍴 – 📺 ⌷wc 🚿wc **P**.
   🅰 🅴 ⓪ *VISA*
   M (bar lunch) 3.85/4.85 t. ⌀ 1.00 – **21 rm** ⌷ 8.00/18.40 t. – P 20.00/24.00 t.

   ⌂ **Parkhill,** Llanrwst Rd, LL24 0ND, NE : 1 m. by A 5 on A 470, ☏ 540, ≼ Vale of Conwy,
   🍴 – ⌷wc **P**. 🅰 🅴
   10 rm ⌷ 8.50/20.00 t.

   ⌂ **Henllys,** LL24 0AL, ☏ 534, « Converted courthouse and jail », 🍴 – 🚿wc **P**. 🅰 *VISA*
   closed December and January – **10 rm** ⌷ 6.50/9.00 t.

   at Capel Curig NW : 6 m. on A 5 – ✉ ✆ 069 04 Capel Curig :

   ⌂ **Bryn Tyrch,** LL24 0CL, ☏ 223, ≼, 🎣, 🍴 – ⌷wc **P**. 🅰 🅴 ⓪ *VISA*
   M (bar lunch) approx. 5.75 st. – **14 rm** ⌷ 10.00/21.00 st.

BEVERLEY Humberside **986** ㉔ – pop. 17,132 – ECD : Thursday – ✉ ✆ 0482 Kingston-
upon-Hull.
See : Minster** 13C-15C – St. Mary's Church* 14C-15C.
⛳ ☏ 881390.
🛈 The Hall, Lairgate ☏ 882255.
London 188 – Kingston-upon-Hull 8 – Leeds 52 – York 29.

BEVERLEY

🏨 **Beverley Arms** (T.H.F.), North Bar Within, HU17 8DD, ☏ 885241 – ▯ 📺 ⇔wc ☎ 🅿.
▵. 🔳 AE ⓪ VISA
M 3.75/5.15 **st.** 🍷 1.65 – **61 rm** ⌣ 17.00/23.50 **st.**

🏠 **Lairgate,** Lairgate, HU17 8EP, ☏ 882141 – ⇔wc ☎ 🅿. ▵. 🔳 VISA
M *(closed Sunday dinner to non-residents)* (buffet lunch) 4.70 **t.** 🍷 2.00 – **20 rm** ⌣
12.25/18.40 **t.**

⚲ King's Head, Market Pl. ☏ 883103 – 🅿 – **9 rm.**

AUSTIN-DAIMLER-JAGUAR-MORRIS-MG-ROVER-
TRIUMPH 20 Norwood ☏ 886222
FORD Wednesday Market ☏ 883211

VAUXHALL Swinemoor Lane ☏ 882207
VOLVO North Bar Within ☏ 881208

BEWDLEY Heref. and Worc. **403 404** N 26 – pop. 7,237 – ECD : Wednesday – ☸ 0299.
🛈 The Library, Load St. ☏ 403303.

London 140 – Birmingham 20 – Worcester 16.

⚲ **Black Boy,** Kidderminster Rd, DY12 1AG, ☏ 402119 – ⇔wc 📶 🅿. 🔳 VISA
M 3.45/4.55 **st.** 🍷 1.60 – **25 rm** ⌣ 8.75/21.00 **t.** – P 16.75/21.80 **t.**

RENAULT Severn Bridge ☏ 403016

BEXHILL East Sussex **404** V 31 – pop. 32,898 – ECD : Wednesday – ☸ 0424.
🏌 Cooden Beach ☏ 042 43 (Cooden) 2040.
🛈 De La Warr Pavilion, Marina ☏ 212023.

London 66 – Brighton 32 – Folkestone 42.

at Cooden W : 2 m. on B 2182 – ✉ Bexhill – ☸ 042 43 Cooden :

🏨 **Cooden Beach,** Sea Rd, TN39 4TT, ☏ 2281, ≼, ⌇ heated, 🚗 – 📺 ⇔wc ☎ 🚗 🅿. ▵.
🔳 AE ⓪ VISA
M 6.00 /8.00 **st.** 🍷 1.35 – **37 rm** ⌣ 15.00/30.00 **st.**

AUSTIN-DAIMLER-JAGUAR-MORRIS-ROVER-
TRIUMPH Cooden Beach ☏ 2224
AUSTIN-MORRIS-MG-PRINCESS 68 Sackville Rd
☏ 212255
AUSTIN-MORRIS-MG 21 Station Rd ☏ 210098
CITROEN, PEUGEOT Ninfield Rd ☏ 0424 (Ninfield)
892177

DAIMLER-JAGUAR-ROVER-TRIUMPH 57-69 London
Rd ☏ 212000
FIAT London Rd ☏ 213577
RENAULT London Rd ☏ 210485
TALBOT, TOYOTA 25 Bell Hill ☏ 215252

BIBURY Glos. **403 404** O 28 – pop. 599 – ECD : Wednesday – ✉ Cirencester – ☸ 028 574.
See : Arlington Row* 17C.

London 86 – Gloucester 26 – Oxford 30.

🏨 **Swan,** GL7 5NN, ☏ 204, « Garden and Trout Stream », ⌇ – ⇔wc ☎ 🅿. 🔳 VISA
M 5.00/6.50 **t.** 🍷 1.85 – **24 rm** ⌣ 14.25/26.50 **t.**

BICESTER Oxon. **403 404** Q 28 – pop. 7,530 – ECD : Thursday – ☸ 086 92.
London 61 – Birmingham 55 – Northampton 31 – Oxford 14.

🏠 **Kings Arms** (Embassy), Market Sq., OX6 7A, ☏ 2015 – 🅿. 🔳 AE ⓪ VISA
closed Christmas – M 5.05/6.35 **st.** – **14 rm** ⌣ 10.50/14.50 **st.** – P 19.70 **st.**

BICKLEIGH Devon **403** J 31 – pop. 230 – ECD : Tuesday – ✉ Tiverton – ☸ 088 45.
London 195 – Exeter 9 – Taunton 28.

🏠 **Fisherman's Cot,** EX16 8RF, on A 296 ☏ 237, ≼, ⌇, 🚗 – 📺 ⇔wc ☎ 🅿. 🔳 AE ⓪
VISA
M a la carte 4.30/7.30 **t.** 🍷 2.00 – **8 rm** ⌣ 8.50/22.00 **t.**

BIDDENDEN Kent **404** V 30 – pop. 2,154 – ✉ Ashford – ☸ 0580.
London 51 – Folkestone 29 – Hastings 25 – Maidstone 13.

✗✗ **Ye Maydes,** 13 High St., TN27 8AL, ☏ 291306 – 🔳
closed Sunday dinner, Monday and Bank Holidays – M a la carte 7.40/9.35 **t.** 🍷 1.75.

BIDEFORD Devon **403** H 30 – pop. 11,802 – ECD : Wednesday – ☸ 023 72.
Envir. : Clovelly (site**) W : 11 m.
🛈 The Quay ☏ 77676 (summer only).

London 231 – Exeter 43 – Plymouth 58 – Taunton 60.

🏨 **Durrant House,** Heywood Rd, EX39 3QB, Northam N : 1 m. on A 386 ☏ 2361, ⌇
heated – 📺 🅿. ▵. 🔳 AE ⓪ VISA
M a la carte 5.30/8.15 **t.** 🍷 1.00 – **58 rm** ⌣ 17.85/27.60 **t.**

🏨 **Yeoldon House** (Best Western) ⌇, Durrant Lane, EX39 2RL, Northam N : 1 m. on A 386
☏ 4400, ≼ Taw estuary, 🚗 – ⇔wc 📶 🅿. 🔳 AE ⓪ VISA
closed 4 days at Christmas – M (bar lunch) 6.00 **st.** 🍷 2.00 – **10 rm** ⌣ 15.50/25.75 **st.**

at Instow N : 3 m. – ⊠ Bideford – ☉ 0271 Instow :

🏨 **Commodore,** Marine Parade, EX39 4JN, ☏ 860347, ⋖ Taw and Torridge estuaries, 🚗 –
TV ℗. ⚐. AE
M 3.90/5.00 s. ₰ 2.40 – **20 rm** ⊑ 11.50/24.00 – P 23.40/26.40.

AUSTIN-MG-ROVER-TRIUMPH-WOLSELEY Kingsley   TALBOT Bridgeland St. ☏ 2016
Rd ☏ 2546/37304   VAUXHALL Handy Cross ☏ 2282
SAAB Meddon St. ☏ 2467

BILBROOK Somerset 403 J 30 – pop. 100 – ⊠ Minehead – ☉ 098 44 Washford.
London 181 – Minehead 5 – Taunton 19.

XX **Dragon House** with rm, TA24 6HQ, ☏ 215, « Part 18C house with gardens » – ⊟wc
🛏wc ℗. ⚐ AE ⓪ VISA
closed 3 to 24 January – **M** a la carte 6.35/8.35 ₰ 1.60 – **12 rm** ⊑ 11.50/25.50 **st.** –
P 21.50/34.75 **st.**

BILDESTON Suffolk 404 W 57 – pop. 865 – ⊠ Ipswich – ☉ 0449.
London 77 – Cambridge 42 – Colchester 22 – Ipswich 15 – Norwich 45.

✗ **Bow Window,** 116 High St., IP7 7EB, ☏ 740748 – ℗. ⚐ VISA
closed Sunday and Monday – **M** (dinner only) a la carte 5.25/6.25 ₰ 1.35.

BILLINGBOROUGH Lincs. 404 S 25 – pop. 1,008 – ECD : Thursday – ☉ 052 94.
London 109 – Boston 18 – Leicester 48 – Nottingham 41.

✗ **Fortescue Arms,** High St., NG34 0QB, ☏ 228 – ℗
closed Sunday and Monday – **M** a la carte 5.00/7.10 ₰ 1.50.

BILLINGHAM Cleveland – pop. 38,107 – ⊠ ☉ 0642 Stockton-on-Tees.
London 255 – Middlesbrough 3 – Sunderland 26.

🏨 **Billingham Arms** (Thistle), Town Sq., TS23 2HD, ☏ 553661, Group Telex 53567 – |$| TV
⊟wc 🛏wc ☎ ℗. ⚐. ⚐ AE ⓪ VISA
M *(closed Saturday lunch)* 4.25/5.50 **st.** – ⊑ 3.00 – **63 rm** 17.50/24.50 **st.**

MORRIS-MG-WOLSELEY ☏ 553959   RENAULT ☏ 553071

BILLINGSHURST West Sussex 404 S 30 – pop. 4,421 – ECD : Wednesday – ☉ 040 381.
London 44 – Brighton 30 – Guildford 20 – Portsmouth 40.

XX **The Jennie Wren,** Pulborough Rd, RH14 9EU, S : ½ m. on A 29 ☏ 2571 – ℗. ⚐ AE
⓪ VISA
closed Saturday lunch, Sunday, Monday and 25-26 December – **M** a la carte 5.50/8.50 **t.**
₰ 2.10.

AUSTIN-JAGUAR-LAND ROVER-MORRIS-MG-   MERCEDES-BENZ, PORSCHE, SCIMITAR High St.
ROVER-TRIUMPH 62 High St. ☏ 2022   ☏ 3341
                                             TALBOT Five Oaks ☏ 2075

BINGLEY West Yorks. – pop. 20,420 – ECD : Tuesday – ⊠ Bradford – ☉ 097 66.
🏌 St. Ives, ☏ 2506 – 🏌 Beckfoot ☏ 3212, near Cottingley Bridge.
London 204 – Bradford 6 – Skipton 13.

🏨 **Bankfield** (Embassy), Bradford Rd, BD16 1TU, ☏ 7123, 🚗 – TV ⊟wc 🛏wc ☎ ℗. ⚐.
⚐ AE ⓪ VISA
closed 25 to 27 December – **M** 4.30 **st.** ₰ 2.00 – **73 rm** ⊑ 17.00/22.50 **st.**

LANCIA Park Rd ☏ 3556

BINHAM Norfolk 404 X 25 – see Blakeney.

BIRCHINGTON-ON-SEA Kent 404 X 29 – pop. 7,923 – ECD : Wednesday – ☉ 0843 Thanet.
See : In Quex Park : Powell-Cotton Museum* of African and Asian natural history and ethno-
logy, *AC.*
London 70 – Maidstone 38 – Margate 4.

🏨 Bungalow, Lyell Rd, CT7 9HX, ☏ 41276, ⧆ heated, 🚗 – TV ⊟wc ☎ ⅄ 🚗 ℗. ⚐
25 rm.

AUSTIN-MORRIS-MG 214 Canterbury Rd ☏ 41241

BIRKENHEAD Merseyside 403 K 23 – pop. 137,852 – ECD : Thursday – ☉ 051 Liverpool.
🏌 Arrowe Park ☏ 677 1527 – 🏌 93 Bidston Rd ☏ 652 5797.
🛈 Birkenhead Library, Borough Rd ☏ 652 6106. – **London** 211 – Liverpool 2.

🏨 **Bowler Hat,** 1 Talbot Rd, Oxton, L43 2HH, ☏ 652 4931, 🚗 – TV ℗. ⚐. ⚐ AE ⓪ VISA
M *(closed Saturday lunch and Sunday dinner)* 4.25/5.25 ₰ 1.80 – ⊑ 2.25 – **29 rm** 16.25/
23.50.

AUSTIN-MG-ROVER-TRIUMPH Park Rd North   FORD Hind St. ☏ 647 9851
☏ 647 9445   RENAULT Renshaw St. ☏ 709 9944
PEUGEOT 222 New Chester Rd ☏ 645 5991 and 644 9333   VAUXHALL 6 Woodchurch Rd ☏ 652 2366

BIRMINGHAM West Midlands 403 404 O 26 – pop. 1,014,670 – ECD : Wednesday – © 021.
See : Museum and Art Gallery** JZ M¹ – Museum of Science and Industry* JY M² – Cathedral
(stained glass windows* 19C) KYZ E.

Alcester Rd South, King's Heath ☏ 444 3584, S : 6 ½ m. by A 435 FX – Church Rd
☏ 454 1736, S : 1 m. FX – Eachelhurst Rd, Walmley ☏ 351 1014, NE : 7 ½ m. DT – Elmdon
Lane, Marston Green ☏ 779 2449, E : 7 m. by East Meadway HV – Vicarage Rd, Harborne
☏ 427 1204, SW : 5 m. EX – Warley Park, Bearwood ☏ 429 2440, W : 5 m. BU.

Birmingham Airport : ☏ 743 4272, E : 6 ½ m. by A 45 DU. – ☏ 643 4444 ext 2593.

110 Colmore Row, B3 3 SH, ☏ 235 3411/3412 – National Exhibition Centre ☏ 780 4141.

London 121 – Bristol 84 – Liverpool 99 – Manchester 86 – Nottingham 50.

Town plans: Birmingham pp. 2-7
Except where otherwise stated see pp. 6 and 7

Albany (T.H.F.), P.O. Box 149, Smallbrook Queensway, B5 4EW, ☏ 643 8171,
Telex 337031, ≼, ◪ – ⧄ TV. ≋. ◪ AE ⓪ VISA
M 5.75/6.25 t. ◊ 1.70 – ☲ 2.50 – **253 rm** 26.50/33.00 st.   JKZ **a**

Plough and Harrow (Crest), 135 Hagley Rd, Edgbaston, B16 8LS, W : 1 ½ m. on A 456
☏ 454 4111, Telex 338074, ⇌ – ⧄ TV ♿ ⓟ. ≋. ◪ AE ⓪ VISA   p. 4 EX **a**
☲ 3.50 – **44 rm** 33.80/42.30 st.

Midland, 128 New St., B2 4JT, ☏ 643 2601, Telex 338419 – ⧄ TV ♿. ≋. ◪ AE ⓪ VISA
M 6.50/7.50 ◊ 1.10 – **116 rm** ☲ 26.95/35.00 st.   KZ **r**

Holiday Inn, A.T.V. Centre, Holliday St., B1 1HH, ☏ 643 2766, Telex 337272, ≼, ◪ –
⧄ TV ♿ ⓟ. ≋.
304 rm.   JZ **z**

Strathallan (Thistle), 225 Hagley Rd, Edgbaston, B16 9RY, W: 2 m. on A 456 ☏ 455 9777,
Telex 336680 – ⧄ TV ⓟ. ≋
171 rm.   p. 4 EX **i**

Grand (Gd. Met.), Colmore Row, B3 2DA, ☏ 236 7951, Telex 338174 – ⧄ TV ⓟ.≋. ◪
AE ⓪ VISA
M 4.50/5.00 st. ◊ 1.55 – **154 rm** ☲ 18.50/23.50 s.   JKY **c**

Royal Angus, St. Chad's Queensway, B4 6HY, ☏ 236 4211, Telex 336889 – ⧄ TV. ≋
140 rm.   KY **s**

Apollo Motor, 243-247 Hagley Rd, B16 9RS, W: 2 ¼ m. on A 456 ☏ 455 0271 – TV
⇱wc ☎ ♿ ⓟ. ◪ AE ⓪ VISA   p. 4 EX **o**
closed Christmas – **M** (closed Saturday and Sunday lunch) 4.75/5.25 st. ◊ 1.95 –
90 rm ☲ 19.50/25.50 s.

Birmingham Centre (Centre), New St., B2 4RX, ☏ 643 2747, Telex 338331 – ⧄ TV ⇱wc
☎. ≋. ◪ AE ⓪ VISA
☲ 1.65 – **200 rm** 18.10/23.25 st.   KZ **u**

Norfolk, 257-267 Hagley Rd, Edgbaston, B16 9N, W: 2 ¼ m. on A 456 ☏ 454 8071,
Telex 339715, ⇌ – ⧄ ⇱wc ⇱wc ☎ ♿ ⓟ. ≋. ◪ VISA   p. 4 EX **u**
M approx. 4.50 s. – **212 rm** ☲ 15.55/23.00 st.

Cobden, 166-170 Hagley Rd, Edgbaston, B16 9NZ, W: 2 m. on A 456 ☏ 454 6621,
Telex 339715, ⇌ – ⧄ ⇱wc ⇱wc ☎ ⓟ. ≋. ◪ VISA   p. 4 EX **n**
M 2.50/4.50 s. – **146 rm** ☲ 15.55/23.00 st.

Plaza, 313 Hagley Rd, Edgbaston, B16 9LQ, W: 2 ½ m. on A 456 ☏ 455 0535, ⇌ –
⇱wc ☎ ⓟ   p. 4 EX **c**
20 rm.

Berrow Court ⌂, Berrow Drive, off Westfield Rd, B15 3UD, W: 2 ¾ m. off A 456
☏ 454 1488, ⇌ – ⓟ   p. 4 EX **e**
15 rm.

Hagley Court without rest., 229 Hagley Rd, Edgbaston, B16 9RP, W: 2 m. on A 456
☏ 454 6514 – ⇱wc ⓟ. VISA   p. 4 EX **s**
closed 25 and 26 December – **24 rm** ☲ 9.80/20.70 st.

Wentworth, 103 Wentworth Rd, Harbourne, B17 9SU, ☏ 427 2839, ⇌ –⇱ ⓟ p. 4   EX **x**
closed 1 week at Christmas – **22 rm** ☲ 6.60/14.00 s.

Dormy, 304-306 Hagley Rd, Edgbaston, B17 8DJ, W: 2 ¾ m. on A 456 ☏ 429 4455, ⇌ –
ⓟ. ◪   p. 4 EX **r**
30 rm ☲ 8.00/15.00 s.

XXX **Rajdoot,** 12-22 Albert St., B4 7UD, ☏ 643 8805, Indian rest. – ◪ AE ⓪ VISA   KZ **c**
closed Sunday lunch and 25-26 December – **M** a la carte 6.00/7.00 t. ◊ 2.00.

XX **Lorenzo's,** 3 Park St., B5 5JD, ☏ 643 0541, Italian rest. – ◪ AE ⓪ VISA   KZ **o**
closed Saturday lunch, Sunday and mid July for 3 weeks – **M** a la carte 4.55/8.70 ◊ 1.80.

XX La Capanna, 43 Hurst St., B5 4BJ, ☏ 622 2287, « Plaster-work murals », Italian rest. KZ **n**

X **Pinocchio,** 8 Chad Sq., off Harborne Rd, B15 3TQ, W: 2 ¾ m. off A 456 ☏ 454 8672,
Italian rest. – ⓟ   p. 4 EX **v**
closed Sunday and Bank Holidays – **M** a la carte 5.80/9.75 t. ◊ 1.90.

Except where otherwise stated see pp. 2 and 3

at Streetly N: 7 m. on A 452 – ⊠ Sutton Coldfield – ✆ 021 Birmingham:

Parson and Clerk (Ansells) without rest., Chester Rd North, B73 6SP, S: 1 ½ m. on
A 452 ☏ 353 1747 – 🛗wc 🅿. 🔺 ᴀᴇ   **CT s**
31 rm � 15.55/19.70 **t.**

at Walmley NE: 6 m. off B 4148 – ⊠ Sutton Coldfield – ✆ 021 Birmingham:

Penns Hall (Embassy) ⊗, Penns Lane, B76 8LH, ☏ 351 3111, ⌂ – 🛗 📺 🅿. 🏊. 🔺 ᴀᴇ
① ⱽⁱˢᵃ   **DT v**
M *(Sunday dinner closed to non-residents)* 4.90/5.50 **st.** ⏐ 2.50 – ⊇ 2.15 – **70 rm** 18.00/
24.00 **st.**

at Sutton Coldfield NE: 8 m. by A 38 – ⊠ Sutton Coldfield – ✆ 021 Birmingham:

Belfry (Best Western) ⊗, Lichfield Rd, Wishaw, B76 8BR, E: 3 m. on A 446 ☏ 0675
(Curdworth) 70301, Telex 338848, ←, 🛏, ⌂, park – 📺 🅿. 🏊. 🔺 ᴀᴇ ① ⱽⁱˢᵃ   E: 3 m.
M 4.60/7.50 **st.** ⏐ 2.10 – **59 rm** ⊇ 22.00/28.00 **st.** – P 32.25/43.50.   on A 446   **DT**

Moor Hall (Best Western) ⊗, Moor Hall Drive, B75 6LN, NE: 1 m. off A 453 ☏ 308 3751
⌂ – 📺 🛏wc ☎ 🅿. 🏊. 🔺 ᴀᴇ ① ⱽⁱˢᵃ   **DT r**
M 4.25/5.75 **t.** ⏐ 1.45 – **55 rm** ⊇ 19.95/27.90 **t.**

Standbridge, 138 Birmingham Rd, B72 1LY, ☏ 354 3007, ⌂ – 🅿   **DT a**
closed 1 week at Witsun and 1 week at Christmas – **9 rm** ⊇ 8.25/12.50 **st.**

La Gondola, Mere Green Precinct, 304 Lichfield Rd, B74 2UW, N: 2 m. on A 5127
☏ 308 6782, Italian rest. – 🔺 ᴀᴇ ① ⱽⁱˢᵃ   **DT o**
closed Sunday dinner – **M** a la carte 6.15/8.25 ⏐ 2.20.

at National Exhibition Centre E: 9 ½ m. on A 45 – **DU** – ⊠ ✆ 021 Birmingham:

Metropole, Blackfirs Lane, Bickenhill, B40 1PP, ☏ 780 4242, Telex 336129, ← – 🛗
📺 ♿ 🅿. 🏊. 🔺 ᴀᴇ ① ⱽⁱˢᵃ
M a la carte 6.15/12.05 **s.** ⏐ 1.65 – ⊇ 2.00 – **500 rm** 36.75/48.50 **s.**

Warwick, Blackfirs Lane, Bickenhill, B40 1PP, ☏ 780 4242, Telex 336129 – 🛗 📺 🛏wc
☎ 🅿. 🔺 ᴀᴇ ① ⱽⁱˢᵃ
M a la carte 6.15/7.70 **s.** ⏐ 1.65 – ⊇ 2.00 – **200 rm** 28.75 **s.**

Arden Motel, Coventry Rd, Bickenhill, B92 0EH, S: ½ m. on A 45 ⊠ Solihull ☏ 067 55
(Hampton-in-Arden) 2912 – 📺 🛏wc ☎ 🅿. 🔺 ᴀᴇ ① ⱽⁱˢᵃ
closed Christmas – **M** 7.00 **st.** ⏐ 2.20 – ⊇ 2.20 – **24 rm** 13.00/18.50 **st.**

Heath Lodge, 117 Coleshill Rd, Marston Green, B37 7HT, W: 1 m. by A 452 ☏ 779 2218,
⌂ – 🛗 🅿
15 rm ⊇ 9.75/12.75.

at Acocks Green SE: 4 ½ m. on A 41 – **DU** – ⊠ ✆ 021 Birmingham:

Kerry House, 946 Warwick Rd, B27 6QG, ☏ 707 0316 – 🛗 🅿
20 rm ⊇ 8.50/15.00 **s.**

at Sheldon SE: 6 m. on A 45 – **HX** – ⊠ ✆ 021 Birmingham:

Wheatsheaf (Ansells), 2225 Coventry Rd, B26 3EH, ☏ 743 2021 – 🛗wc 🅿. 🔺 ᴀᴇ
M 3.70/4.40 **t.** ⏐ 1.80 – **100 rm** ⊇ 18.75/23.00 **t.**   p. 5 **HX a**

La Caverna, 2327 Coventry Rd, B26 3PG, ☏ 743 7917, Italian rest. – 🅿. 🔺 ᴀᴇ ① ⱽⁱˢᵃ
closed Saturday lunch and Sunday – **M** a la carte 5.40/7.30 ⏐ 1.60.

at Birmingham Airport SE: 7 m. on A 45 – **DU** – ⊠ ✆ 021 Birmingham :

Excelsior (T.H.F.), Coventry Rd, Elmdon, B26 3QW, ☏ 743 8141, Telex 338005 – 📺 🅿. 🏊.
🔺 ᴀᴇ ① ⱽⁱˢᵃ
M 4.10/5.35 **st.** ⏐ 1.65 – ⊇ 2.75 – **141 rm** 21.00/28.50 **st.**

at Kings Heath S: 3 ½ m. on A 435 – ⊠ ✆ 021 Birmingham:

Giovanni's, 27 Poplar Rd off High St., B14 7AA, ☏ 443 2391 – 🔺 ① ⱽⁱˢᵃ   p. 4 **FX a**
*closed Sunday dinner, Monday, 17 February-4 March, 2 weeks August and 2 days Bank
Holidays* – **M** a la carte 5.20/9.85 **t.** ⏐ 1.70.

at Northfield SW: 6 m. off A 38 – **CU** – ⊠ ✆ 021 Birmingham:

Norwood, 87 Bunbury Rd, B31 2ET, off Church Rd ☏ 475 3262, ⌂ – 🅿
15 rm.

at Smethwick W: 3 ½ m. off A 456 – ⊠ Warley – ✆ 021 Birmingham:

La Copper Kettle, 151 Milcote Rd, Bearwood, B56 5BN, ☏ 429 7920, French rest. p. 4 **EV a**

P.T.O. ⟶

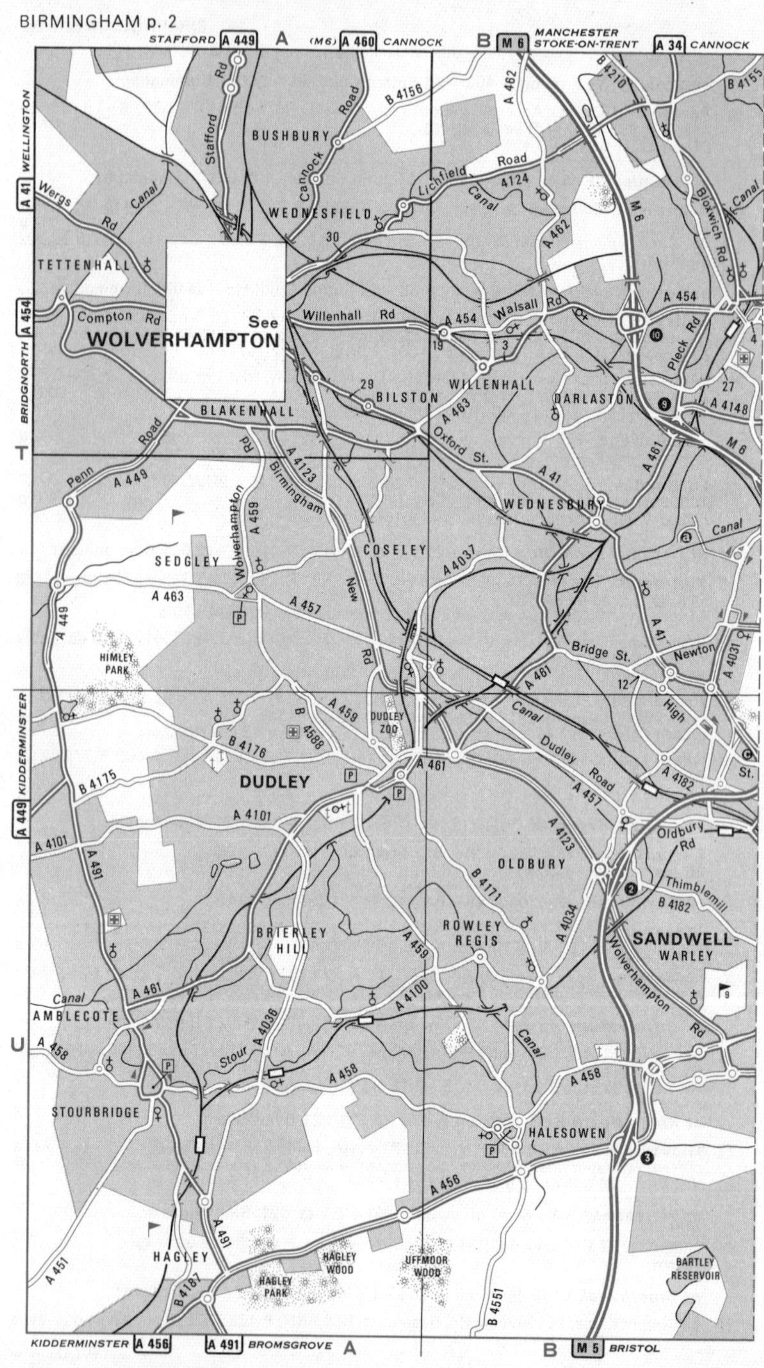
STAFFORD A 449 A (M6) A 460 CANNOK B M 6 MANCHESTER STOKE-ON-TRENT A 34 CANNOCK
A 41 WELLINGTON
Wergs
Stafford Rd
Cannock Road
B 4156
A 462
B 4210
B 4155
BUSHBURY
Canal
WEDNESFIELD
Lichfield
Road
4124
A 462
M 6
Bloxwich Rd
Canal
30
TETTENHALL
See WOLVERHAMPTON
A 454 BRIDGNORTH
Compton Rd
Willenhall Rd
A 454 Walsall Rd
10
Pleck Rd
4
Wolverhampton
A 459
19
3
WILLENHALL
29
BILSTON
A 463
DARLASTON
9
A 4148
BLAKENHALL
Oxford St.
M 6
T
Penn
A 449
Rd
A 4123
Birmingham
A 41
WEDNESBURY
A 461
Newton
A 4031
SEDGLEY
New
A 457
COSELEY
A 4037
Canal
Bridge St.
A 41
A 463
Rd
12
KIDDERMINSTER
HIMLEY PARK
A 449
A 459
B 4588
DUDLEY ZOO
A 461
High
St.
A 449
B 4176
A 461
Dudley Road
A 4182
B 4175
DUDLEY
P
A 461
Canal
A 457
A 4101
P
A 4101
A 491
Oldbury Rd
A 4123
OLDBURY
B 4171
2
Thimblemill
B 4182
BRIERLEY HILL
A 459
ROWLEY REGIS
A 4034
Wolverhampton
SANDWELL WARLEY
9
Canal
A 461
A 4100
AMBLECOTE
Stour
A 4036
Canal
A 458
U A 458
A 458
A 458
STOURBRIDGE
P
HALESOWEN
P
3
A 456
A 451
A 491
HAGLEY
HAGLEY WOOD
UFFMOOR WOOD
HAGLEY PARK
B 4551
BARTLEY RESERVOIR
B 4187
KIDDERMINSTER A 456 A 491 BROMSGROVE A B M 5 BRISTOL

BIRMINGHAM AND WOLVERHAMPTON
ENLARGED AREA

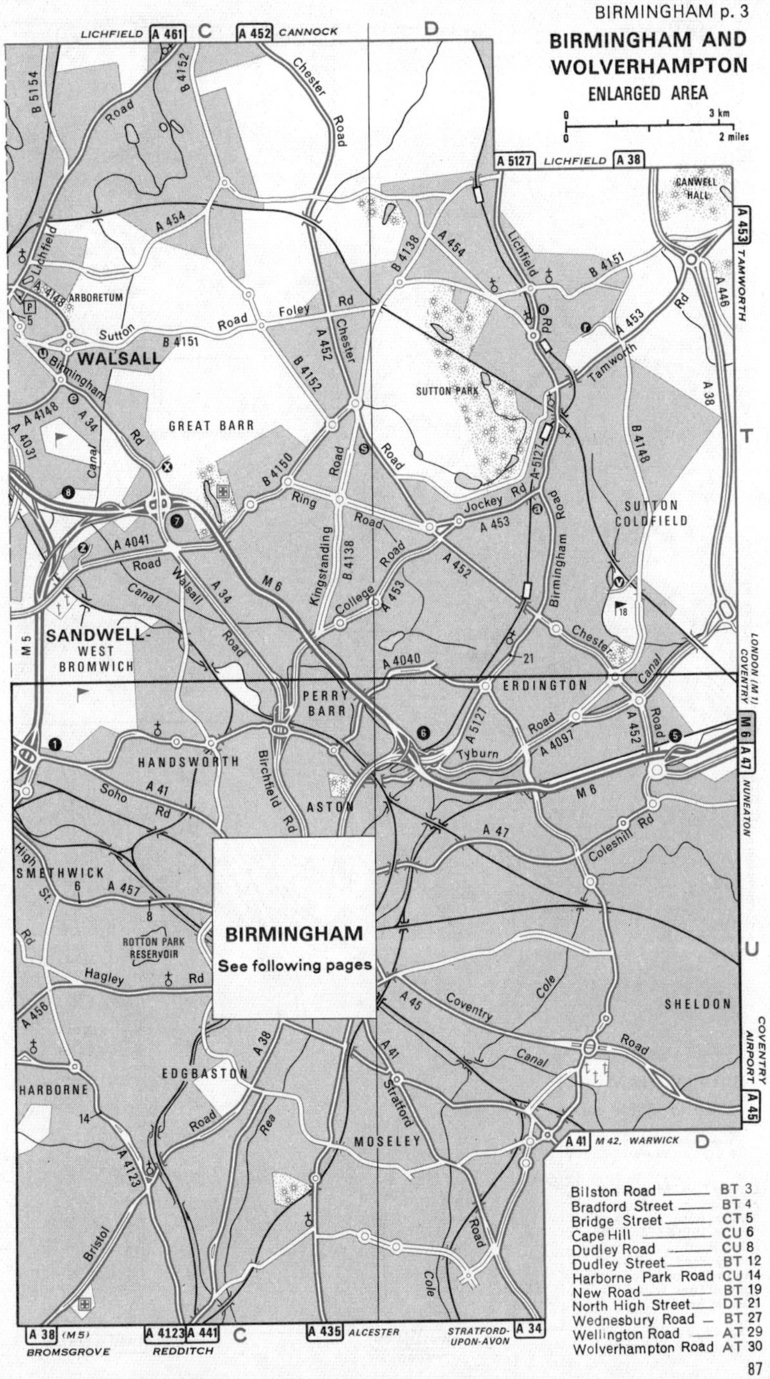

Bilston Road	————	BT 3
Bradford Street	———	BT 4
Bridge Street	———	CT 5
Cape Hill	——	CU 6
Dudley Road	———	CU 8
Dudley Street	——	BT 12
Harborne Park Road		CU 14
New Road	————	BT 19
North High Street	——	DT 21
Wednesbury Road	—	BT 27
Wellington Road	——	AT 29
Wolverhampton Road		AT 30

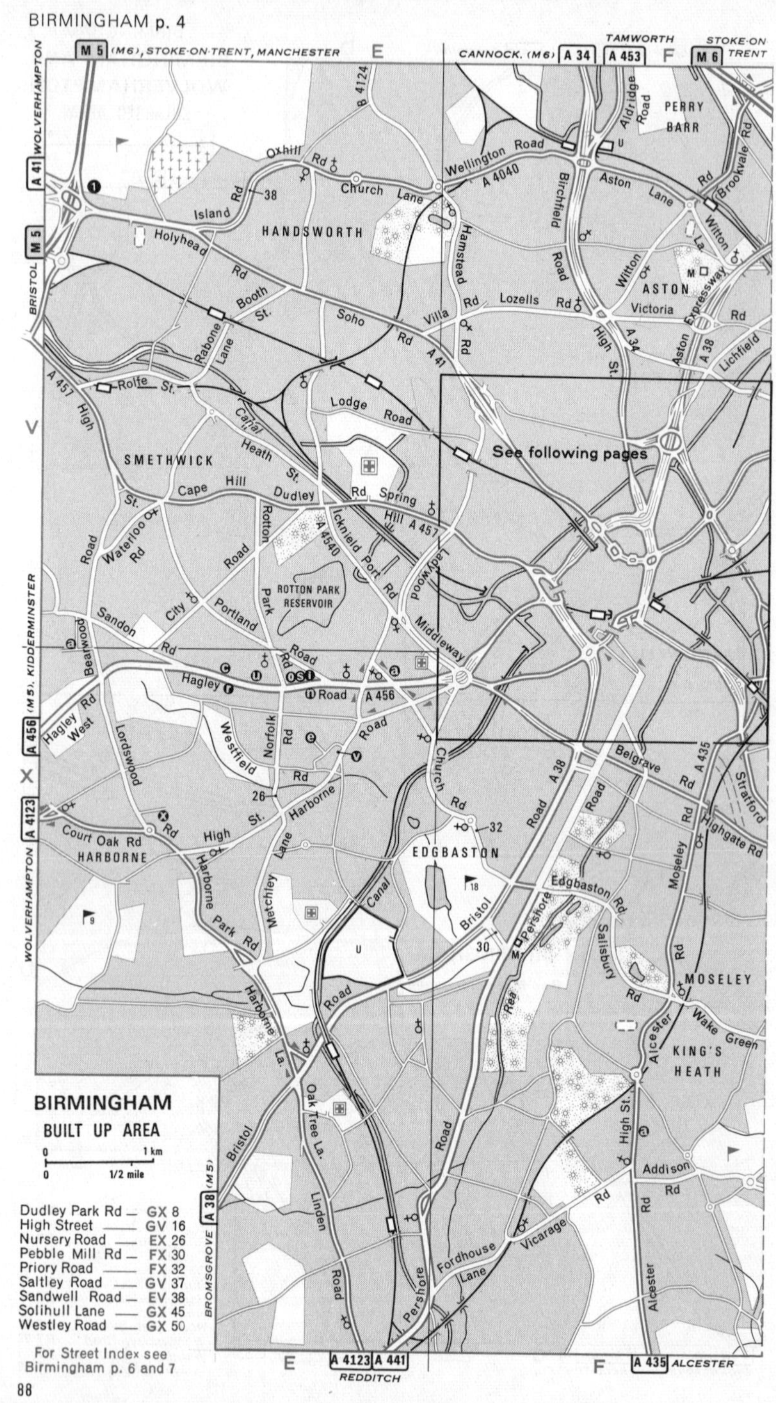

BIRMINGHAM
BUILT UP AREA

0 ———————— 1 km
0 ———————— 1/2 mile

Dudley Park Rd — GX 8
High Street ——— GV 16
Nursery Road ——— EX 26
Pebble Mill Rd — FX 30
Priory Road ——— FX 32
Saltley Road ——— GV 37
Sandwell Road ——— EV 38
Solihull Lane ——— GX 45
Westley Road ——— GX 50

For Street Index see
Birmingham p. 6 and 7

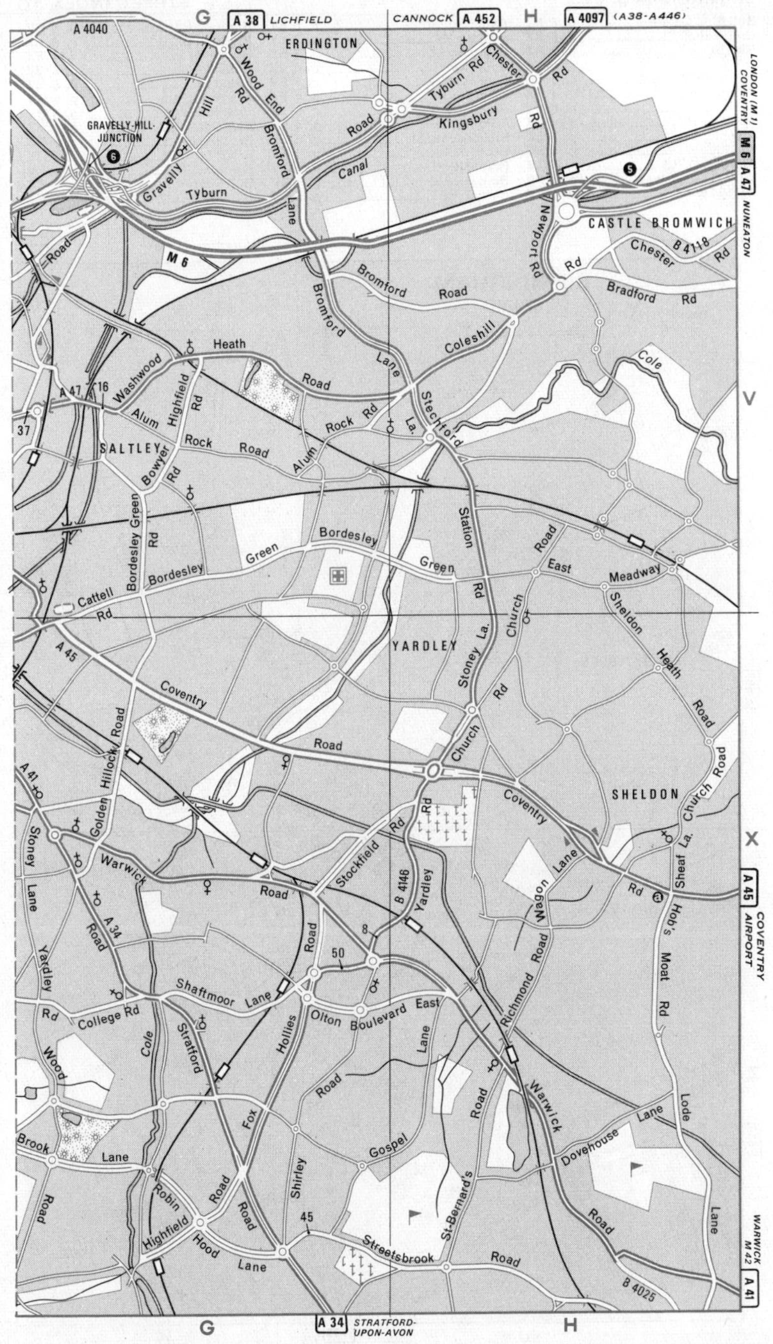
A 4040
G
A 38 LICHFIELD
CANNOCK A 452 H
A 4097 (A38-A446)
ERDINGTON
Tyburn Rd
Chester Rd
Road
Kingsbury
Wood End Rd
Bromford
Canal
LONDON (M I)
COVENTRY
M 6 A 47
NUNEATON
GRAVELLY HILL JUNCTION
6
Gravelly Hill
Gravelly
Tyburn Lane
M 6
5
Newport Rd
CASTLE BROMWICH
B 4118
Road
Bromford Road
Chester Rd
Bradford Rd
Bromford Lane
Coleshill
Cole
Heath Road
Washwood
Alum
Highfield Rd
Rock Rd
Stechford
V
A 47 16
SALTLEY
Bowyer Rd
Rock Road
Alum Rock Rd
La.
37
Bordesley Green Rd
Bordesley
Green Bordesley
Green Rd
Station
Road
East
Meadway
Cattell Rd
YARDLEY
Stoney La.
Church Rd
Sheldon
Heath Road
A 45
Coventry
A 41
Golden Hillock Road
Road
Church Rd
Church
Coventry
SHELDON
X
A 45
COVENTRY
AIRPORT
Stoney Lane
Warwick Road
A 34
Stockfield Rd
Rd
B 4146 Yardley Rd
Wagon Lane
Sheaf La. Church Road
Hob's Moat Rd
Yardley Rd
Road
8
50
Shaftmoor Lane
Olton Boulevard East
Hollies Road
Richmond Road
Warwick Road
Dovehouse Lane
College Rd
Cole Stratford Rd
Fox Road
Shirley Road
Gospel Lane
Lode Lane
Wood Lane
Brook Lane
Robin Hood Lane
Highfield Road
45
Streetsbrook Road
St Bernard's Road
Warwick Road
WARWICK
M 42
B 4025
A 41
G
A 34 STRATFORD-UPON-AVON
H

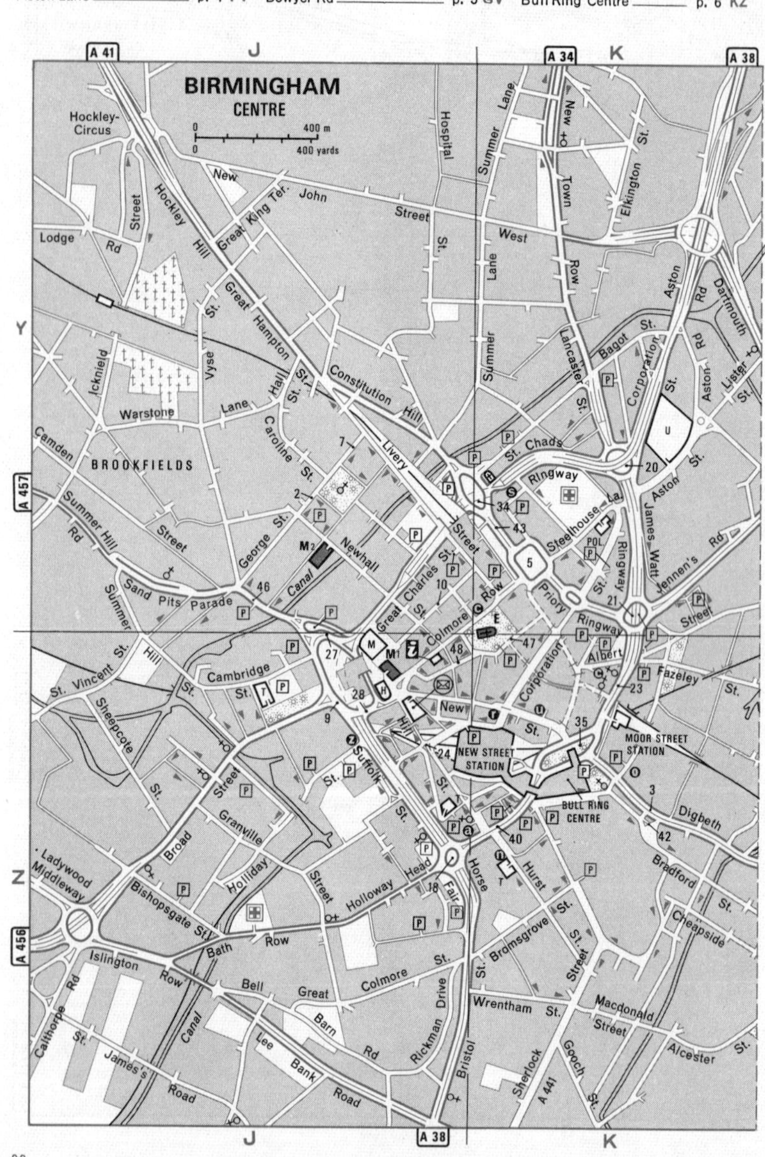

BIRMINGHAM
CENTRE
400 m
400 yards
A 41
J
A 34
K
A 38
Hockley-Circus
Hockley Hill
Street
Lodge Rd
New
Great King Ter.
John
Street
Hospital
Summer Lane
New Town Row
Elkington St.
Y
Icknield
Vyse St.
Great Hampton St.
Hall St.
Constitution Hill
West
Summer Lane
Aston
Rd
Dartmouth
A 457
Camden
Warstone Lane
BROOKFIELDS
Caroline St.
Livery Street
St. Chad's
Ringway
Lancaster St.
Bagot St.
Corporation St.
U
Aston St.
James Watt
20
Summer Hill Rd
George St.
Newhall
M2
Canal
S
34
43
Steelhouse La.
POL.
Ringway
21
Jennen's Rd
Sand Pits Parade
Summer Row
Great Charles St.
Colmore Row
C
E
5
Priory
Ringway
Street
46
27
M
M1
48
47
Albert
Fazeley St.
28
H
New St.
Corporation St.
23
St. Vincent St.
Cambridge St.
9
35
MOOR STREET STATION
Sheepcote St.
Suffolk St.
Hill St.
24
NEW STREET STATION
BULL RING CENTRE
3
Z
Ladywood Middleway
Bishopsgate St.
Broad St.
Granville St.
Holliday St.
Street
Head
Horse Fair
40
Digbeth
42
Bradford St.
A 456
Islington Row
Bath Row
Bell
Great
Barn
Colmore St.
Rickman Drive
Bristol St.
Bromsgrove St.
Cheapside
Calthorpe Rd
James's
Canal
Lee Bank
Road
Road
Wrentham St.
Sherlock St.
Gooch St.
Macdonald Street
Alcester St.
A 441
J
A 38
K

BIRMINGHAM TOWN PLANS

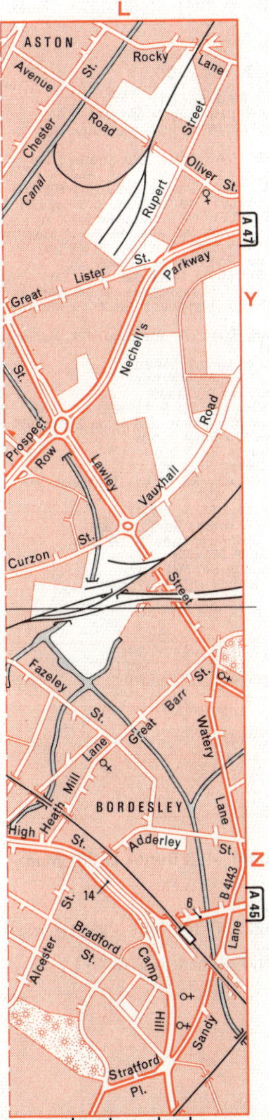

at West Bromwich NW: 6 m. on A 41 – ⊠ West Bromwich – ☎ 021 Birmingham :

🏨 **Europa Lodge** (County), B70 6RS, SE : 1 m. off A 41, ☏ 553 6111, Telex 336232 – 📶 TV 🛏WC ☎ 🅿. 🅰. 🆂 🅰🅴 ⓘ 𝐕𝐈𝐒𝐀
M 4.20/5.50 **st.** 🍷 1.55 – **133 rm** ⊃ 17.50/22.00 **s.**
BU **c**

✗✗ **Manor House** (Ansells), Hall Green Rd, B71 2EA, N: 2 m. off A 41 ☏ 588 2035, « 13C timbered manor house » – 🅿.
BT **a**

at Great Barr NW: 6 m. on A 34 – ⊠ Great Barr – ☎ 021 Birmingham :

🏨 **Post House** (T.H.F.), Chapel Lane, B43 7BG, ☏ 357 7444, Telex 338497, ⤢ heated, 🚗 – TV 🛏WC ☎ & 🅿. 🅰. 🆂 🅰🅴 ⓘ 𝐕𝐈𝐒𝐀
M 5.50/7.00 **st.** 🍷 1.65 – ⊃ 2.25 – **204 rm** 18.00/25.50 **st.**
CT **x**

🏨 **Barr**, Pear Tree Drive, Newton Rd, B43 6HS, W: 1 m. off A 4041 ☏ 357 1141, Telex 336406, 🚗 – TV 🛏WC 📶WC ☎ 🅿. 🅰.
90 rm.
CT **z**

MICHELIN Branch, Valepits Rd, Garretts Green, B33 0YD, ☏ 784 7900.

ASTON-MARTIN, OPEL 1-3 Woodthorpe Rd ☏ 444 2715
AUSTIN-DAIMLER-MG-WOLSELEY 71 Aston Rd North ☏ 359 2011
AUSTIN-DAIMLER-JAGUAR-MORRIS-MG-PRINCESS-ROVER-TRIUMPH, ROLLS ROYCE Manor Lane, Halesowen ☏ 550 7611
AUSTIN-MG-ROVER-TRIUMPH-WOLSELEY 1014/1018 Kingsbury Rd ☏ 747 2065
AUSTIN-TRIUMPH-JAGUAR-MORRIS-ROVER Aston Hall Rd ☏ 328 0833
AUSTIN-MORRIS-ROVER-TRIUMPH 479 Bristol Rd ☏ 472 1331
AUSTIN-MORRIS-MG-WOLSELEY 367 Moseley Rd ☏ 440 1131
AUSTIN-MORRIS 8/50 Cherrywood Rd ☏ 772 3394
AUSTIN-MG-WOLSELEY Hagley Rd West, Quinton ☏ 422 7171
AUSTIN-PRINCESS-MORRIS-MG Warwick Rd, Tyseley ☏ 706 4331
AUSTIN-MORRIS-MG 283 Broad St. ☏ 643 5111
AUSTIN-MORRIS-MG Alcester Rd, Moseley ☏ 449 6115
COLT 264 Oxhill Rd ☏ 554 3539
DATSUN 4 Birmingham Rd ☏ 357 4049
DATSUN 504/508 College Rd ☏ 373 2542
DATSUN Newall St. ☏ 236 7548
DATSUN 120/126 Alcester Rd ☏ 449 4751
DATSUN 110/124 Victoria Rd ☏ 327 3591
DATSUN Summer Lane ☏ 359 4848
FIAT Roebuck Lane, West Bromwich ☏ 525 5757
FIAT 979 Stratford Rd, Hall Green ☏ 777 6181
FIAT 35 Sutton New Rd, Erdington ☏ 350 1301
FIAT Station Rd ☏ Berkshaw 33145
FORD 156/182 Bristol St. ☏ 622 2777
FORD Long Acre ☏ 327 4791
FORD Wolverhampton Rd, Warley ☏ 429 7111

FORD Kingsbury Rd ☏ 382 1111
HONDA Hagley Rd, Hasbury ☏ 550 6416
JAGUAR-ROVER-TRIUMPH 1507 Coventry Rd ☏ 706 5441
MERCEDES, OPEL, VAUXHALL 870 Stratford Rd ☏ 777 3361
MERCEDES, VAUXHALL Charles Henry St. ☏ 622 3031
MORRIS-MG-WOLSELEY 193/194 Broad St. ☏ 643 4971
MORRIS-MG-WOLSELEY 884 Warwick Rd ☏ 706 8271
PEUGEOT 2119 Coventry Rd, Sheldon ☏ 742 5533
PEUGEOT Fordhouse Lane, Stirchley ☏ 459 1611
RENAULT Chester Rd North ☏ 354 4427
RENAULT Old Walsall Rd, Great Barr ☏ 357 5411
RENAULT Station Rd, Marston Green ☏ 779 2261
RENAULT, BEDFORD Kenilworth Rd ☏ (Berkshaw) 32118
SAAB, SCIMITAR, TOYOTA 138 Soho Hill, Handsworth ☏ 554 6311
TALBOT 10 Church Lane ☏ 554 2182
TALBOT Newport Rd ☏ 747 4712
TALBOT Coventry Rd ☏ 772 4388
TALBOT 90/94 Charlotte St. ☏ 236 4382
TALBOT 103 Goosemoor Lane, Erdington ☏ 382 1919
TALBOT Old Walsaw Rd ☏ 357234
TOYOTA 490 College Rd ☏ 350 4214
VAUXHALL 18 Stewart St. ☏ 454 4351
VAUXHALL 364 Chester Rd, Castle Bromwich ☏ 747 4601
VAUXHALL 16 Ryland St. ☏ 455 7171
VAUXHALL 203/217 Lozells Rd ☏ 523 9231
VAUXHALL 291 Shaftmoor Lane ☏ 777 1074
VOLVO Bristol St. ☏ 622 4491
VW, AUDI Digbeth ☏ 643 7341
VW, AUDI-NSU Barnes Hill ☏ 427 6201

This Guide is not a comprehensive list of all hotels and restaurants,
nor even of all good hotels and restaurants in Great Britain and Ireland.

Since our aim is to be of service to all motorists,
we must show establishments in all categories and so we have made a
selection of some in each.

BIRTLE Greater Manchester 🗺404 N 23 – pop. 1,989 (inc. Ashworth) – ⊠ Bury – ☎ 061 Manchester.

London 217 – Bolton 10 – Manchester 11.

🏨 **La Normandie** ⚓, Elbut Lane, BL9 6UT, N: 1 m. off B 6222, ☏ 764 3869 – 📶 TV 🛏WC 📶WC ☎ & 🅿. 🆂 🅰🅴 ⓘ 𝐕𝐈𝐒𝐀
closed 3 weeks July – **M** *(closed Saturday lunch and Sunday)* a la carte 5.55/9.40 🍷 1.60 – **17 rm** ⊃ 14.00/28.00.

BISHAM Bucks. 🗺404 R 29 – see Marlow.

BISHOP'S CLEEVE Glos. 🗺403 🗺404 N 28 – see Cheltenham.

BISHOP'S HULL Somerset 🗺403 K 30 – see Taunton.

BISHOP'S LYDEARD Somerset 🗺403 K 30 – see Taunton.

BISHOP'S STORTFORD Herts. **404** U 28 – pop. 20,750 – ECD : Wednesday – ☎ 0279.

✈ Stansted Airport : ☏ 502380, Telex 81102, NE : 3 ½ m.

London 34 – Cambridge 27 – Chelmsford 19 – Colchester 33.

🏠 Foxley, Foxley Drive, Stansted Rd, CM23 2DS, N : ¾ m. on B 1184 ☏ 53977, 🚗 – ⊟wc
Ⓟ
12 rm.

🏠 **Dane House**, Hadham Rd, CM23 2QD, W : ¾ m. on A 1250 ☏ 52289, 🚗 – ⊟wc Ⓟ.
AE ⓪
closed 1 to 10 January – **M** 3.50/4.00 ⫯ 1.50 – **14 rm** ⋤ 12.50/21.50 **st.**

🍴 **Brook House**, 29 Northgate End, CM23 2LD, ☏ 57892, 🚗 – ⊟wc Ⓟ
M *(closed Saturday and Sunday)* (dinner only) a la carte 2.45/4.50 **t.** ⫯ 1.10 – **15 rm** ⋤
9.20/17.25 **st.**

AUSTIN-DAIMLER-JAGUAR-MG-ROVER-TRIUMPH   PEUGEOT 26 Northgate End ☏ 53494
123 South St. ☏ 58441   RENAULT Northgate End ☏ 53127
DATSUN London Rd ☏ 54181   TALBOT Dunmow Rd ☏ 54335
FIAT Spelbrook ☏ 54424   VAUXHALL The Causeway ☏ 52304
FORD London Rd ☏ 52214   VW, AUDI Dane St. ☏ 54680

BISHOP'S TAWTON Devon **403** H 30 – see Barnstaple.

BISHOP'S WALTHAM Hants. **403** **404** Q 31 – pop. 3,910 – ☎ 048 93.

London 71 – Portsmouth 17 – Southampton 11.

🍴🍴 Crown Inn, The Square ☏ 2548 – Ⓟ.

BISHOPTHORPE North Yorks. – see York.

BLACKBURN Lancs. **986** ㉓ – pop. 101,816 – ECD : Thursday – ☎ 0254.

🔟 Beardwood Brow, ☏ 51122 – 🔟 Pleasington ☏ 21028, W : 3 m.

🛈 Town Hall, Library St. ☏ 53272/55201 ext 382/248.

London 228 – Leeds 47 – Liverpool 39 – Manchester 24 – Preston 11.

🏨 **Saxon Inn Motor**, Preston New Rd, Yew Tree Drive, BB2 7BE, NW : 2 m. at junction
A 677 and A 6119 ☏ 64441, Telex 63271 – 🛗 TV Ⓟ. ⟐. 🔊 AE ⓪ VISA
M approx. 3.40 **s.** ⫯ 2.00 – ⋤ 1.75 – **100 rm** 15.00/19.00 **s.**

AUSTIN-DAIMLER-JAGUAR-MG-ROVER-TRIUMPH   RENAULT Gt. Harwood ☏ 886590
Park Rd ☏ 662721   SUBARU Lower Darwen ☏ 57021
FORD Montague St. ☏ 57021   TALBOT King St. ☏ 52981
MERCEDES-BENZ Harwood Rd, Rishton ☏ 88420   TALBOT, FIAT 52/56 King St. ☏ 667782
MORRIS-MG-WOLSELEY Simmons St. ☏ 52121   VAUXHALL Quarry St., Eanam ☏ 51191
MORRIS-MG-WOLSELEY Accrington Rd ☏ 57333   VW, AUDI-LADA 854 Whalley New Rd ☏ 48091

BLACKPOOL Lancs. **986** ㉓ – pop. 151,860 – ECD : Wednesday – ☎ 0253.

See : Illuminations★★ (late September and early October) – Tower★ (❄★) *AC* **AY A.**

🔟 Devonshire Rd ☏ 51017, N : 1 ½ m. from main station **BY** – 🔟 Stanley Park ☏ 33960,
E : 1 ½ m. **BY**.

🔟 Poulton-le-Fylde ☏ 0253 (Poulton) 891629, E : 3 m. by A 586 **BY**.

✈ Blackpool Airport : ☏ 43061, S : 4 m. **BZ**.

🛈 Central Promenade ☏ 21623.

London 242 – Leeds 84 – Liverpool 57 – Manchester 50 – Middlesbrough 121.

Plan on next page

🏨 Imperial, North Promenade, FY1 2HB, ☏ 23971, ⩤, 🔊 – 🛗 TV Ⓟ. ⟐   **AY c**
146 rm.

🏨 **Savoy**, Queens Promenade, FY2 9SJ, ☏ 52561 – 🛗 ⊟wc ⊟wc Ⓟ. ⟐. 🔊 VISA   **AY a**
M 2.75/4.50 **st.** ⫯ 1.50 – **140 rm** ⋤ 11.50/24.20 **st.**

🏨 Clifton, Talbot Sq., FY1 1ND, ☏ 21481 – 🛗 ⊟wc ☎. ⟐   **AY i**
80 rm.

🏠 Gables, Balmoral Rd, FY4 1HP, ☏ 45432 – TV ⊟wc ☎   **AZ r**
72 rm.

🏠 **Warwick**, 603-609 New South Promenade, FY4 1NG, ☏ 42192, 🔊 – ⊟wc Ⓟ. ⟐.
AE   **BZ u**
closed 2 to 23 November and 2 to 18 January – **M** (bar lunch Monday to Saturday) 3.50/
4.25 **st.** ⫯ 1.80 – **77 rm** ⋤ 10.50/22.00 **st.**

🍴 Stuart, Clifton Drive, South Shore, FY4 1NT, ☏ 45485 – Ⓟ   **AZ a**
25 rm.

🏠 Mimosa, 24a Lonsdale Rd, FY1 6EE, ☏ 41906 – TV ⊟wc Ⓟ. VISA   **BZ c**
closed 23 to 28 December – **15 rm** ⋤ 14.00/18.75 **st.**

🏠 **Sunray**, 42 Knowle Av., off Queen's Prom., FY2 9TQ, ☏ 51937 – Ⓟ   **BY c**
April-October – **6 rm** ⋤ 5.80/12.70.

P.T.O. →

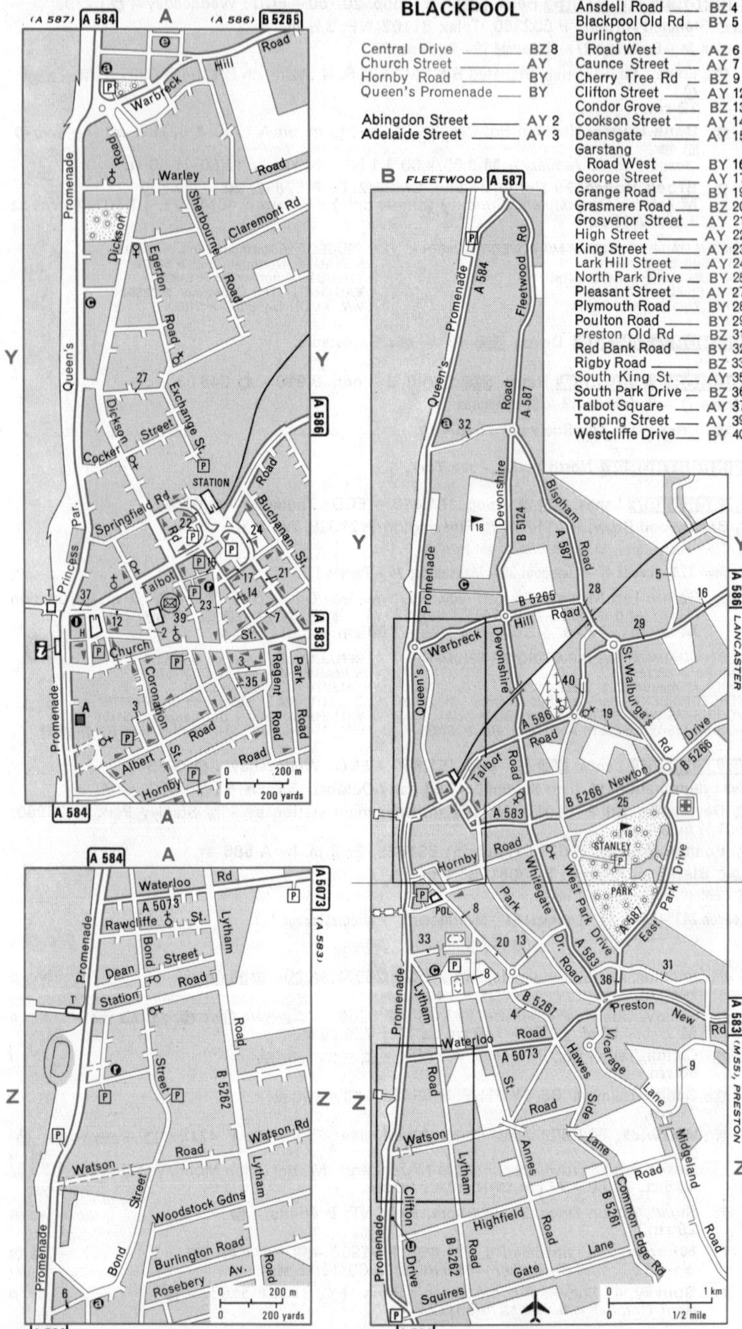

BLACKPOOL

Central Drive — BZ 8
Church Street — AY
Hornby Road — BY
Queen's Promenade — BY

Abingdon Street — AY 2
Adelaide Street — AY 3

Ansdell Road — BZ 4
Blackpool Old Rd — BY 5
Burlington Road West — AZ 6
Caunce Street — AY 7
Cherry Tree Rd — BZ 9
Clifton Street — AY 12
Condor Grove — BZ 13
Cookson Street — AY 14
Deansgate — AY 15
Garstang Road West — BY 16
George Street — AY 17
Grange Road — BY 19
Grasmere Road — BZ 20
Grosvenor Street — AY 21
High Street — AY 22
King Street — AY 23
Lark Hill Street — AY 24
North Park Drive — BY 25
Pleasant Street — AY 27
Plymouth Road — BY 28
Poulton Road — BY 29
Preston Old Rd — BZ 31
Red Bank Road — BY 32
Rigby Road — BZ 33
South King St. — AY 35
South Park Drive — BZ 36
Talbot Square — AY 37
Topping Street — AY 39
Westcliffe Drive — BY 40

⋔ **Denely,** 15 King Edward Av., FY2 9TA, ☏ 52757 – 🏵 🅿   AY e
   8 rm ⌂ 7.75/13.00 **st.**

⋔ **Manxonia,** 248 Queens Prom., Bispham, FY2 9HA, ☏ 51118 – 🅿   BY a
   Easter, mid May-October and Christmas – **20 rm** ⌂ 5.95/11.00 **st.**

✕ **Trattoria da Vinci,** 27-29 King St., FY1 3EJ, ☏ 21602, Italian rest.   AY r
   closed Sunday and first 2 weeks June – **M** (dinner only) a la carte 7.40/9.20 🍾 2.00.

ALFA-ROMEO, RELIANT-RENAULT Cherry Tree Rd ☏ 28401
AUSTIN-MG-WOLSELEY Cherry Tree Rd ☏ 67811
CITROEN 145/147 Dickson Rd ☏ 21469
DAF, SAAB, SKODA 181 Waterloo Rd ☏ 41081
DAIMLER-JAGUAR-ROVER-TRIUMPH 159 Devonshire Rd ☏ 34301
DATSUN 234 Talbot Rd ☏ 26688
FORD Whitegate Drive ☏ 63333
MERCEDES-BENZ Church St. ☏ 22257
PEUGEOT 79/83 Breck Rd, Poulton-le-Fylde ☏ 882571
TALBOT Squires Gate Lane ☏ 45544
TOYOTA Devonshire Rd, Bispham ☏ 51870
VW, AUDI-NSU Rigby Rd ☏ 21417

BLACKWOOD (COED-DUON) Gwent **403** K 28 – pop. 12,700 – ECD : Thursday – ☏ 0495.
🏌 Maesycwmmer, Hengoed ☏ 225590.

London 158 – Cardiff 15 – Newport 13.

🏩 **Maes Manor** ⌖, Maes Rudded, NP2 0AG, N : 1 ¼ m. off A 4048 by Rocks Inn,
   ☏ 224551, 🚗, park – 📺 🛏wc 🏵 ☎ 🅿. ⛱. ◪ ᴀᴇ ⓪ 𝗩𝗜𝗦𝗔
   M a la carte 5.30/6.65 **t.** 🍾 2.00 – **26 rm** ⌂ 15.50/24.50 **t.**

AUSTIN-DAIMLER-JAGUAR-MORRIS-MG 5/6 Pentwyn Rd ☏ 223388

BLAGDON Avon **403** L 30 – pop. 1,238 – ECD : Saturday – ✉ Bristol – ☏ 0761.
London 138 – Bath 19 – Bristol 17 – Taunton 39.

🏩 Mendip ⌖, Street End, BS18 6TS, ☏ 62688, ⪡ – 📺 🅿. ⛱
   40 rm.

BLAKENEY Norfolk **404** X 25 – pop. 677 – ECD : Wednesday – ✉ Holt – ☏ 0263 Cley.
London 127 – King's Lynn 37 – Norwich 28.

🏩 **Manor,** The Quay, NR25 7ND, ☏ 740376, 🚗 – 🛏wc ♿ 🅿
   closed 2 weeks mid November and Christmas week – **M** (bar lunch Monday to Saturday)
   3.00/4.00 🍾 1.70 – **22 rm** ⌂ 10.50/22.00.

🏩 **Blakeney,** The Quay, NR25 7NE, ☏ 740797, ⪡, ⬛, 🚗 – 🛏wc 🏵 🅿. ◪ ᴀᴇ ⓪ 𝗩𝗜𝗦𝗔
   M 4.60/6.00 **s.** 🍾 1.70 – **53 rm** ⌂ 11.40/29.10 **s.**

   at Binham SW : 4 m on B 1388 – ✉ ☏ 032 875 :

🏠 **Abbey House** ⌖, NR21 0DG, ☏ 467, 🚗 – 📺 🛏wc 🅿. ᴀᴇ
   closed January – **M** *(closed dinner Thursday and Sunday to non-residents)* (buffet lunch
   Monday to Saturday residents only) 5.00 **t.** – **5 rm** ⌂ 10.50/25.00 **t.**

BLANCHLAND Northumb. – pop. 167 – ECD : Monday – ✉ Consett (Durham) – ☏ 043 475.
London 293 – Middlesbrough 49 – Newcastle-upon-Tyne 25.

🏠 Lord Crewe Arms (Swallow), DH8 9SP, ☏ 251, « 12C inn », 🚗 – 🛏wc ☎
   14 rm.

BLETSOE Beds. **404** S 27 – see Bedford.

BLOCKLEY Glos. **403** **404** O 27 – pop. 1,853 – ECD : Thursday – ✉ Moreton-in-Marsh –
☏ 038 676.
London 89 – Birmingham 40 – Gloucester 29 – Oxford 33.

✕✕ **Lower Brook House** ⌖ with rm, Lower St., GL56 9DS, ☏ 286, 🚗 – 🛏wc 🅿. ◪
   closed 24 December-24 January – **M** *(closed Sunday dinner and Monday lunch to non-
   residents)* a la carte 7.50/10.00 **t.** 🍾 1.75 – **6 rm** ⌂ 11.25/25.00 **t.**

BLOFIELD Norfolk **404** Y 26 – see Norwich.

BLUNDELLSANDS Merseyside **403** K 23 – see Liverpool.

BLUNSDON Wilts. **403** **404** O 29 – see Swindon.

BLYTH Notts. **403** **404** Q 23 – pop. 1,131 – ECD : Wednesday – ✉ Worksop – ☏ 090 976.
🏌 ☏ 2356, turn left from Plessy Rd.
London 154 – Leeds 41 – Lincoln 29 – Nottingham 31 – Sheffield 21.

🏠 **Fourways,** High St., S81 8EW, ☏ 235 – 🅿. ᴀᴇ 𝗩𝗜𝗦𝗔
   M 5.00/7.00 **t.** 🍾 2.50 – **9 rm** ⌂ 13.00/17.00 **t.**

BODIAM East Sussex 404 V 30 – pop. 303 – ✆ 058 086 Hurst Green.
See : Castle★ 14 C (ruins) *AC.*
London 54 – Folkestone 36 – Hastings 12 – Maidstone 23.

  XX **Curlew,** Robertsbridge, TN32 5UY, E: ½ m. on A 229 ☏ 272 – **P**
      M a la carte 5.75/10.50 ⌑ 1.50.

BODINNICK-BY-FOWEY Cornwall 403 G 32 – see Fowey.

BODMIN Cornwall 403 F 32 – pop. 9,207 – ECD : Wednesday – ✆ 0208.
London 273 – Exeter 63 – Penzance 47 – Plymouth 30.

  🏠 **Westberry,** Rhind St., PL31 2EL, ☏ 2772 – ⊟wc 🛁wc 🕿 **P**
     closed 1 week at Christmas – **M** (bar lunch) a la carte 4.20/6.00 **s.** ⌑ 1.40 – **26 rm** ⌸
     7.50/16.00 **s.**

     at Tredethy N : 5 m. by A 389 off B 3266 – ✉ Bodmin – ✆ 020 884 St. Mabyn :

  🏠 **Tredethy Country** ⤴, PL30 4QS, ☏ 262, ≼, « Country house atmosphere », ☒ heated,
     🚗, park – ⊟wc 🛁wc **P.** ⑩
     M 5.00/6.00 ⌑ 1.50 – **12 rm** ⌸ 8.00/14.00.

BOGNOR REGIS West Sussex 404 R 31 – pop. 39,150 – ECD : Wednesday – ✆ 024 33.
🛈 Belmont St. ☏ 23140. – **London 65 – Brighton 31 – Portsmouth 25 – Southampton 37.**

  🏠🏠 **Royal Norfolk,** The Esplanade, PO21 2LH, ☏ 26222, ≼, ☒ heated, 🚗 – 🛗 📺 **P.** ⚹
     🔄 AE ⑩ VISA
     M 4.50/5.25 ⌑ 1.75 – **49 rm** ⌸ 15.00/30.00 – P 20.00.

  🏠 **Royal,** The Esplanade, PO21 1SZ, ☏ 4665, ≼ – 🛁. 🔄 AE ⑩ VISA
     M (*closed Saturday lunch*) 4.00/4.50 ⌑ 1.60 – **34 rm** ⌸ 9.50/22.00.

  🏠 **Clarehaven,** Wessex Av., PO21 2QW, ☏ 23265 – ⊟wc
     M 3.80/5.00 **st.** ⌑ 1.85 – **34 rm** ⌸ 13.70/29.80 **st.** – P 15.00/19.20 **st.**

AUSTIN-MG-ROVER-TRIUMPH 65 Aldwick Rd ☏ 4041
MORRIS-MG-WOLSELEY Lennox St. ☏ 4641
PEUGEOT 131 Elmer Rd, Middleton-on-Sea ☏ 024 369
(Middleton-on-Sea) 2432
VAUXHALL High St. ☏ 5515
VW, AUDI-NSU 126 Felpham Way ☏ 024 369 (Middleton-on-Sea) 3185

BOLHAM Devon 403 J 31 – see Tiverton.

BOLTON Greater Manchester 404 M 23 – pop. 154,199 – ECD : Wednesday – ✆ 0204.
Envir. : Hall I'Th'Wood★ (16C) AC, N : 1 ½ m.

🛈₁₈ Links Rd ☏ 42336 – 🛈₁₈ Off Junction Rd, Deane ☏ 61944, W : 4 m. – 🛈₁₈ Longworth Lane,
Bromley Cross ☏ 53321, N : 3 m. – 🛈₁₈ Lostock Park, ☏ 43278, W : 3 ½ m.
🛈 Town Hall, ☏ 22311 ext 211/485. – **London 214 – Burnley 19 – Liverpool 32 – Manchester 11 – Preston 23.**

  🏠🏠 Bolton Crest (Crest), Beaumont RD, BL3 4TA, W : 2 ½ m. on A 58 ☏ 651511, Telex 635527
     – 📺 ⊟wc 🕿 **P.** ⚹. 🔄 AE ⑩ VISA
     ⌸ 2.40 – **100 rm** 19.20/25.20 **st.**

  🏠🏠 **Pack Horse,** 1 Nelson Sq., BL1 1DP, ☏ 27261 – 🛗 📺 ⊟wc 🕿. ⚹. 🔄 AE ⑩ VISA
     M 4.00/5.00 **st.** ⌑ 2.00 – **90 rm** ⌸ 17.00/27.00 **st.**

     at Bromley Cross N : 4 m. by A 676 – ✉ ✆ 0204 Bolton :

  🏠🏠 **Last Drop Village,** Hospital Rd, BL7 9PZ, ☏ 591131, Telex 635322, « Converted
     farm », 🚗 – 📺 ⊟wc 🕿 **P.** ⚹. 🔄 AE ⑩ VISA
     M a la carte 2.75/8.50 **st.** ⌑ 2.50 – **69 rm** ⌸ 22.00/31.00 **st.**

AUSTIN-DAIMLER-JAGUAR-MORRIS-MG-ROVER-TRIUMPH Blackburn Rd ☏ 387011
AUSTIN-MORRIS-MG-ROVER-TRIUMPH-WOLSELEY Manchester Rd ☏ 32241
AUSTIN-MORRIS-MG-ROVER-TRIUMPH-WOLSELEY Manchester Rd ☏ 384512
BMW, DATSUN Moor Lane ☏ 33941
CITROEN Thynne St. ☏ 25090
COLT 154/160 Crook St. ☏ 24686
FORD 54/56 Higher Bridge St. ☏ 24474
OPEL Halliwell Rd ☏ 26566
TALBOT-LANCIA Bradshawgate ☏ 31323
TOYOTA Radcliffe Rd ☏ 382234
VW, AUDI Blackburn Rd ☏ 31464
VW, AUDI St. Helens Rd ☏ 62131

BOLTON ABBEY North Yorks. 986 ㉓ – pop. 136 – ✉ Skipton – ✆ 075 671.
See : Bolton Priory★ (ruins) and woods (the Strid★ and nature trails in upper Wharfedale).
London 215 – Harrogate 17 – **Leeds 22** – Skipton 6.

  🏠 **Devonshire Arms,** Bolton Bridge, BD23 6AJ, ☏ 265, ≼, ⤧, 🚗 – 🕿 **P.** AE ⑩ VISA
     closed 14 January-February – **M** a la carte 7.40/10.95 **st.** ⌑ 2.50 – ⌸ 2.95 – **11 rm** 12.50/
     27.50 **st.**

BONCHURCH I.O.W. 403 404 Q 32 – see Wight (Isle of) : Ventnor.

BONTDDU Gwynedd 403 I 25 – see Dolgellau.

BONT-FAEN South Glam. – see Cowbridge.

BOREHAM STREET East Sussex 404 V 31 – see Herstmonceux.

BOREHAMWOOD Herts. 404 T 29 – pop. 1,858 – ECD : Thursday – ○ 01 London.

ℹ Civic Offices, Elstree Way ☎ 207 2277.

London 15 – Luton 21.

🏨 Thatched Barn, Barnet by-Pass, WD6 5PE, E: 1 ½ m. at junction A 1 and A 5135 ☎ 953 1622, ⌇ heated – 📺 ⌷wc ☎ 🅿. ⌂ – **60 rm.**

XX Grosvenor, with rm, 148 Shenley Rd, WD6 1EQ, ☎ 953 3175 – 🅿 – **25 rm.**

XX **Signor Baffi,** 195 Shenley Rd, WD6 1AW, ☎ 953 8404, Italian rest. – ◥ AE ⓪ VISA
closed Sunday – **M** a la carte 4.85/7.25 ⌷ 1.35.

BOROUGHBRIDGE North Yorks. 986 ㉓ – pop. 1,864 – ECD : Thursday – ○ 090 12.

London 216 – Leeds 26 – Middlesbrough 35 – York 17.

🏨 **Three Arrows** (Embassy) ⌇, Horsefair, YO5 9LL, ☎ 2245, ⛨, park – 📺 ⌷wc ☎ ⟿
🅿. ◥ AE ⓪ VISA
M 3.70/4.70 st. – **19 rm** ⌂ 11.00/20.00 st.

MAZDA ☎ 2327

BORROWASH Derbs. 403 404 P 25 – see Derby.

BORROWDALE Cumbria – see Keswick.

BOSCASTLE Cornwall 403 F 31 – ○ 084 05.

London 260 – Bude 14 – Exeter 59 – Plymouth 43.

🏛 **Bottreaux House,** PL35 0BG, ☎ 231 – 🅿. ⓪
M (lunch by arrangement for residents only) approx. 2.00/5.00 **s.** ⌷ 2.00 – **11 rm** ⌂ 7.45/17.00 **t.**

⌂ **St. Christopher's Country House,** PL35 0DB, ☎ 412 – 🅿
March-October and Christmas – **6 rm** ⌂ 11.00/24.00 **st.**

⌂ **Tolcarne,** PL35 0AS, ☎ 252, ⛨ – ⌂ 🅿
14 rm ⌂ 7.50/17.00 **t.**

BOSTON Lincs. 404 T 25 – pop. 26,025 – ECD : Thursday – ○ 0205.

See : St. Botolph's Church** 14C. – ⌷ ☎ 62306, N : 2 m. on A 16.

ℹ Assembly Rooms, Market Pl. ☎ 62354 (summer only).

London 122 – Lincoln 35 – Nottingham 55.

🏛 **New England** (Anchor), Wide Bars, PE21 6SH, ☎ 65255, Group Telex 858875 – 📺
⌷wc ☎ 🅿. ◥ AE ⓪ VISA
M a la carte approx. 6.00 – **11 rm** ⌂ 12.50/24.00 **st.**

ALFA-ROMEO, JENSEN, PEUGEOT, MERCEDES-BENZ
6 Horncastle Rd ☎ 64708
AUSTIN-DAIMLER-MORRIS-MG-ROVER-TRIUMPH-
WOLSELEY Wide Bargate ☎ 66677
CITROEN London Rd ☎ 722233
FORD 57 High St. ☎ 63991
JAGUAR-MORRIS-MG-ROVER-TRIUMPH-WOLSELEY
Leverton ☎ 226

MORRIS-MG-WOLSELEY Sutterton ☎ 249
RENAULT Sleaford Rd ☎ 61901
TALBOT Main Ridge ☎ 638 67
TOYOTA Tawney St. ☎ 68626
VAUXHALL Bargate End ☎ 63851
VW, AUDI-NSU 200/2 London Rd ☎ 63293

BOTLEY Hants. 403 404 Q 31 – pop. 2,163 – ECD : Thursday – ✉ Hedge End, Southampton –
○ 048 92.

London 83 – Portsmouth 17 – Southampton 6 – Winchester 11.

🏨 Botleigh Grange, Hedge End, SO3 2GA, W: 1 m. on A 334 ☎ 5611, ≼, ⌇, ⛨, park –
📺 ⌷wc ⌂wc ☎ 🅿 – **52 rm.**

X **Cobbett's,** 13-15 The Square, SO3 2EA, ☎ 2068 – 🅿. ◥ VISA
closed 2 weeks August, 2 weeks February and Bank Holidays – **M** (dinner only Saturday,
Sunday and Monday) a la carte 6.90/9.60 ⌷ 1.45.

AUSTIN-DAIMLER-JAGUAR-MG-ROVER-TRIUMPH   RENAULT Shamblehurst Lane ☎ 3434
Southampton Rd ☎ 5111, 5115

BOURNE Lincs. 404 S 25 – pop. 5,420 – ECD : Wednesday – ○ 077 82.

London 101 – Leicester 42 – Lincoln 35 – Nottingham 42.

🏠 **Angel,** North St., PE10 9AE, ☎ 2346 – 🅿. ◥
M *(closed Sunday dinner)* a la carte 3.75/6.95 **t.** ⌷ 1.50 – **10 rm** ⌂ 9.00/14.00 **st.**

X **Golden Dragon,** 11 South St., PE10 9LY, ☎ 3466, Chinese rest. – ◥ AE ⓪ VISA
M a la carte 1.65/2.65 **s.** ⌷ 1.20.

AUSTIN-MORRIS ☎ 2852
FORD Spalsing Rd ☎ 3921

MORRIS-MG-WOLSELEY North St. ☎ 2129
TALBOT Abbey Rd ☎ 2675

BOURNE END Bucks. 404 R 29 – ○ 062 85.

London 31 – Maidenhead 4 – Oxford 31 – Reading 16.

X **Piccolo Mondo,** The Parade, SL8 5SS, ☎ 22100, Italian rest. – ◥ AE ⓪ VISA
M a la carte 6.60/7.45 **t.** ⌷ 1.45.

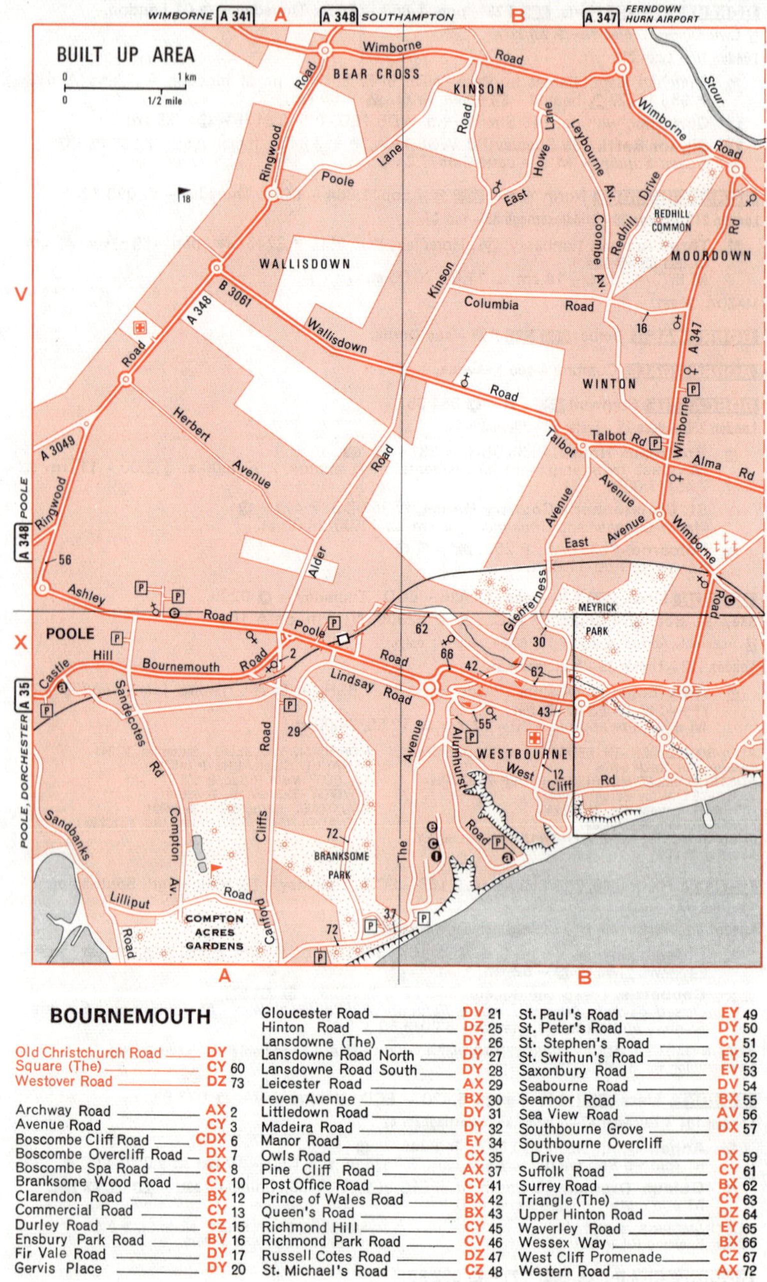

BOURNEMOUTH

Old Christchurch Road — **DY**
Square (The) — **CY** 60
Westover Road — **DZ** 73

Archway Road — **AX** 2
Avenue Road — **CY** 3
Boscombe Cliff Road — **CDX** 6
Boscombe Overcliff Road — **DX** 7
Boscombe Spa Road — **CX** 8
Branksome Wood Road — **CY** 10
Clarendon Road — **BX** 12
Commercial Road — **CY** 13
Durley Road — **CZ** 15
Ensbury Park Road — **BV** 16
Fir Vale Road — **DY** 17
Gervis Place — **DY** 20

Gloucester Road — **DV** 21
Hinton Road — **DZ** 25
Lansdowne (The) — **DY** 26
Lansdowne Road North — **DY** 27
Lansdowne Road South — **DY** 28
Leicester Road — **AX** 29
Leven Avenue — **BX** 30
Littledown Road — **DY** 31
Madeira Road — **DY** 32
Manor Road — **EY** 34
Owls Road — **CX** 35
Pine Cliff Road — **AX** 37
Post Office Road — **CY** 41
Prince of Wales Road — **BX** 42
Queen's Road — **BX** 43
Richmond Hill — **CY** 45
Richmond Park Road — **CV** 46
Russell Cotes Road — **DZ** 47
St. Michael's Road — **CZ** 48

St. Paul's Road — **EY** 49
St. Peter's Road — **DY** 50
St. Stephen's Road — **CY** 51
St. Swithun's Road — **EY** 52
Saxonbury Road — **EV** 53
Seabourne Road — **DV** 54
Seamoor Road — **BX** 55
Sea View Road — **AV** 56
Southbourne Grove — **DX** 57
Southbourne Overcliff
  Drive — **DX** 59
Suffolk Road — **CY** 61
Surrey Road — **BX** 62
Triangle (The) — **CY** 63
Upper Hinton Road — **DZ** 64
Waverley Road — **EY** 65
Wessex Way — **BX** 66
West Cliff Promenade — **CZ** 67
Western Road — **AX** 72

Town plans : the name of main shopping streets are printed in red at the beginning of the list of streets.

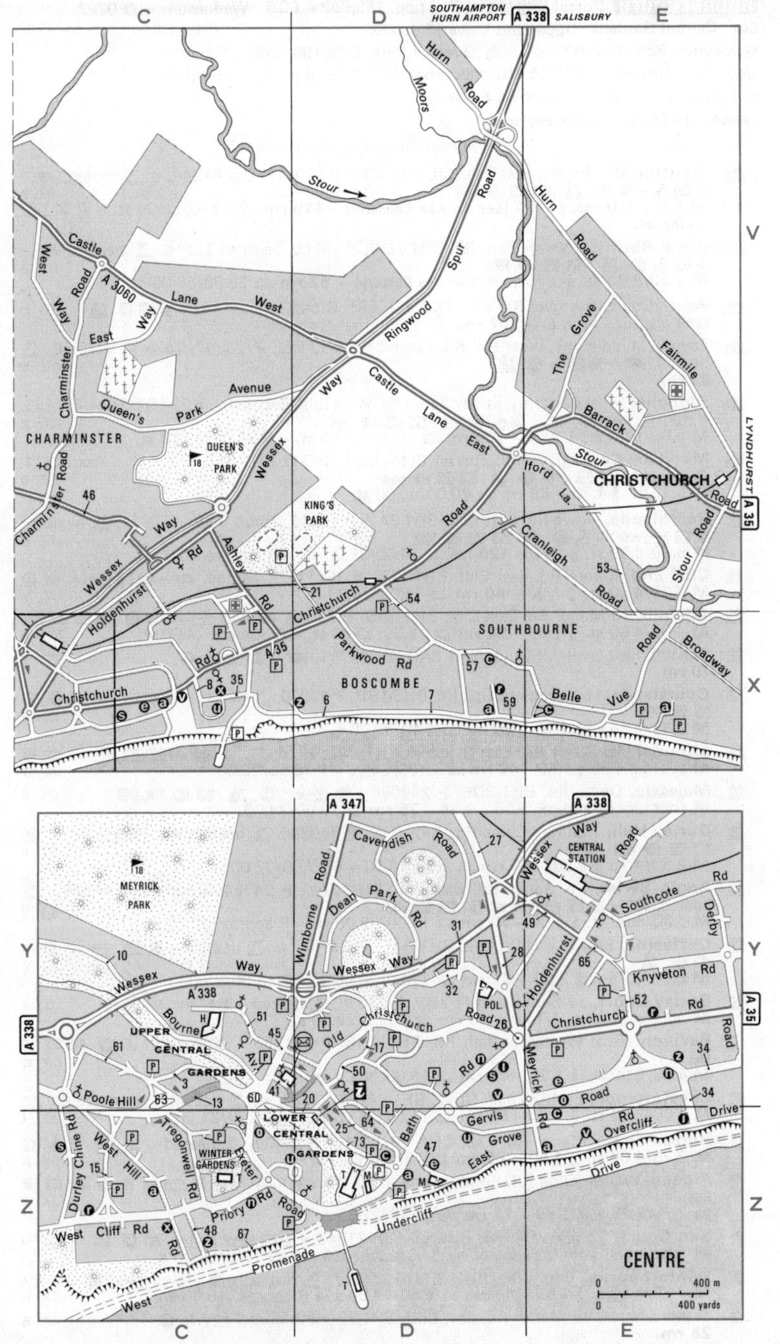

SOUTHAMPTON
HURN AIRPORT
A 338
SALISBURY
C
D
E
Hurn Road
Moors
Spur Road
Hurn Road
The Grove
Fairmile
Stour
V
West
Castle Road
A 3060
Way
Way
East
Lane
West
Ringwood
Charminster
Queen's
Park
Avenue
Wessex
Way
Castle
Lane
East
Barrack
Stour
CHARMINSTER
QUEEN'S PARK
18
Iford La.
CHRISTCHURCH
Charminster Road
KING'S PARK
Road
Cranleigh
LYNDHURST
A 35
46
Way
Ashley Rd
Christchurch
21
54
53
Stour Road
Wessex
Holdenhurst
Rd
Christchurch
A 35
Parkwood Rd
SOUTHBOURNE
Road
Broadway
V
35
8
57
Belle Vue
X
Christchurch
6
7
59
BOSCOMBE
A 347
A 338
Cavendish Road
27
Wessex Way
CENTRAL STATION
Road
Rd
Wimborne Road
Dean
Park Rd
Southcote
Derby
18
MEYRICK PARK
31
49
Y
10
Wessex Way
28
Holdenhurst
65
Knyveton Rd
Y
Wessex
A 338
Way
Wessex Way
32
POL
52
A 35
Bourne
H
51
45
Christchurch Road
26
Christchurch Road
UPPER
61
CENTRAL
Av.
Old
17
Rd
Meyrick Road
34
GARDENS
3
50
Poole Hill
63
13
60
41
20
Bath
Gervis
East
Grove
Overcliff Drive
34
Durley Chine Rd
LOWER
25
64
Road
West Hill
CENTRAL
73
Tregonwell Rd
GARDENS
47
WINTER GARDENS
Exeter Rd
15
Priory Rd
Road
48
West Cliff Rd
67
Undercliff Drive
Promenade
West
CENTRE
0   400 m
0   400 yards
C
D
E

See : Central Gardens (Upper and Lower)* CDYZ.

🏌 Meyrick Park ☏ 20871 CY – 🏌 Queen's Park ☏ 36198, NE : 2 m. CV.

✈ Hurn Airport : ☏ 020 16 (Northbourne) 71177, N : 5 m. by Hurn Rd DV.

🛈 Tourism Department, Westover Rd ☏ 291715.

London 113 – Bristol 78 – Southampton 31.

Plans on preceding pages

🏰 **Carlton,** Meyrick Rd, East Overcliff, BH1 3DN, ☏ 22011, Telex 41244, ≤, 🛆 heated, 🚗 – 🛗 📺 �&ᴄ 🚘 🅿. 🛆. 🔲 AE ⓪ VISA — EZ a
    M 8.50/10.00 st. ⌾ 2.50 (see also **La Causerie**) – **110 rm** ☕ 33.50/60.00 st. – P 41.00/50.00 st.

🏰 **Royal Bath** (De Vere), Bath Rd, BH1 2EW, ☏ 25555, Telex 41375, ≤, 🛆 heated, 🚗 – 🛗 📺 ᴅ 🅿. 🛆. 🔲 AE ⓪ VISA — DZ a
    M 7.50/8.00 st. ⌾ 1.75 (see also **The Buttery**) – **82 rm** ☕ 25.00/50.00 st.

🏰 **Palace Court,** Westover Rd, BH1 3BZ, ☏ 27681, Group Telex 41141 – 🛗 📺 🅿. 🛆 — DZ c
    (see also La Taverna) – **107 rm.**

🏰 **Savoy** (Myddleton), West Hill Rd, West Cliff, BH2 5EJ, ☏ 20347, Telex 418220, ≤, 🛆 heated, 🚗 – 🛗 📺 ᴅ 🅿. 🛆 — CZ x
    93 rm.

🏰 **Highcliff** (Best Western), St. Michael's Rd, West Cliff, BH2 5DU, ☏ 277 02, Telex 417153, ≤, ✗, 🛆 heated, 🚗 – 🛗 ᴅ 🅿. 🛆. 🔲 AE ⓪ VISA — CZ z
    M 5.00/6.00 st. ⌾ 3.00 – **100 rm** ☕ 19.50/36.50 st. – P 29.00/30.50 st.

🏰 **Marsham Court** (De Vere), Russell Cotes Rd, East Cliff, BH1 3AB, ☏ 22111, Telex 22121, 🛆 heated – 🛗 📺 🚘 🅿. 🛆. 🔲 AE ⓪ VISA — DZ e
    M 5.75 st. ⌾ 1.75 – **89 rm** ☕ 20.00/40.00 st.

🏨 **Heathlands,** Grove Rd, East Cliff, BH1 3AY, ☏ 23336, Group Telex 418261, 🛆 heated – 🛗 📺 ⇋wc 🕾 ᴅ 🅿. 🛆. 🔲 AE ⓪ VISA — EZ c
    M 5.00/6.00 st. ⌾ 2.50 – **120 rm** ☕ 14.00/28.00 st. – P approx. 20.00 st.

🏨 **Cliff End,** Manor Rd, East Cliff, BH1 3EX, ☏ 39711, 🛆 heated, 🚗 – 🛗 📺 ⇋wc 🕾 🅿 — CX v
    M 3.25/4.50 st. ⌾ 1.90 – **40 rm** ☕ 12.00/24.00 s.

🏨 **Adelphi,** 30 Manor Rd, East Cliff, BH1 3JD, ☏ 26546, 🚗 – 🛗 ⇋wc 🕾 🅿. 🔲 AE ⓪ VISA — CX e
    M 4.00/4.50 st. ⌾ 2.50 – **54 rm** ☕ 16.50/33.00 st. – P approx. 24.00 st.

🏨 **Suncliff,** East Overcliff Drive, BH1 3AG, ☏ 291711, 🚗 – 🛗 ⇋wc 🅿 — EZ v
    70 rm.

🏨 **Courtlands,** 16 Boscombe Spa Rd, BH5 1BB, ☏ 33070, 🛆 heated – 🛗 ⇋wc 🕾 ᴅ 🅿. 🔲
AE VISA ⓪ — CX u
    M 3.65/4.85 s. ⌾ 1.70 – **50 rm** ☕ 9.10/20.70 s.

🏨 **Miramar,** 19 Grove Rd, East Overcliff, BH1 3AL, ☏ 26581, ≤, 🚗 – 🛗 📺 ⇋wc 🕾 🅿 — DZ u
    M approx. 4.50 ⌾ 1.50 – **42 rm** ☕ 15.50/34.00 – P 18.50/20.00.

🏨 **Majestic,** Derby Rd, BH1 3QE, ☏ 292090 – 🛗 ⇋wc 🅿. 🛆. 🔲 AE ⓪ VISA — CX s
    M (bar lunch) approx. 5.00 ⌾ 1.25 – **75 rm** ☕ 22.60/34.00.

🏨 **Durley Hall,** 7 Durley Chine Rd, B42 5JS, ☏ 766886, 🛆 heated, 🚗 – 🛗 ⇋wc 🕾 🅿. 🔲 AE ⓪ VISA — CZ s
    M 3.50/4.75 ⌾ 2.20 – **81 rm** ☕ 8.00/18.00 – P 17.00/22.00.

🏨 **Anglo-Swiss,** 16 Gervis Rd, East Cliff, BH1 3AY, ☏ 24794, Group Telex 418261, 🛆 heated, 🚗 – 🛗 📺 ⇋wc 🕾 🅿. 🔲 AE VISA — EY e
    M 5.00/6.00 st. ⌾ 2.50 – **70 rm** ☕ 14.00/28.00 st. – P approx. 20.00 st.

🏨 **Cliffeside,** East Overcliff Drive, BH1 3AQ, ☏ 25724, ≤, 🛆 heated – 🛗 📺 ⇋wc 🛁wc
🕾 🅿. 🛆 — EZ v
    M 6.00/6.75 t. ⌾ 2.00 – **61 rm** ☕ 12.50/28.00 t. – P 18.00/23.00 t.

🏨 **Burley Court,** 29 Bath Rd, BH1 2NP, ☏ 22824, 🛆 heated – 🛗 ⇋wc 🕾 ᴅ 🅿 — DY i
    M approx. 4.50 s. ⌾ 1.40 – **45 rm** ☕ 14.25/29.00 s.

🏨 **Pavilion** (Best Western), Bath Rd, BH1 2NS, ☏ 291266 – 🛗 📺 ⇋wc 🕾 🅿. 🔲 AE ⓪
VISA — DY n
    M 4.00/5.50 st. ⌾ 1.95 – **49 rm** ☕ 16.00/35.00 st.

🏨 **Chesterwood,** East Overcliff Drive, BH1 3AR, ☏ 28057, ≤, 🛆 heated – 🛗 ⇋wc 🅿. 🔲 — EZ i
    M 4.00/5.00 st. ⌾ 1.70 – **59 rm** ☕ 11.65/24.40 st. – P 16.00/21.00 st.

🏠 **Hinton Firs,** 9 Manor Rd, East Cliff, BH1 3HB, ☏ 25409, 🛆 heated – 🛗 ⇋wc ᴅ 🅿 — EY n
    M 3.25/4.00 st. ⌾ 1.60 – **56 rm** ☕ 13.00/28.00 st.

🏠 **Albany,** Warren Edge Rd, Southbourne, BH6 4CU, ☏ 428151 – 🛗 ⇋wc 🕾 🅿. 🔲 AE ⓪
VISA — EX a
    M 2.75/3.75 s. ⌾ 1.70 – **17 rm** ☕ 10.75/21.50 s.

🏠 **Sun Court,** 32 West Hill Rd, BH2 5PH, ☏ 21343 – 🛗 📺 ⇋wc 🛁wc 🕾 🅿. AE — CZ a
    M (bar lunch only May-October) 3.00/4.25 – **36 rm** ☕ 7.50/19.00 s.

🏠 **Winterbourne,** Priory Rd, BH2 5DJ, ☏ 24927, 🛆 heated – 🛗 ⇋wc 🛁wc 🅿. 🔲 VISA — CZ n
    M 3.25/4.50 s. ⌾ 1.60 – **48 rm** ☕ 6.50/14.00 s. – P approx. 15.00 s.

🏠 **Manor House,** 34 Manor Rd, East Cliff, BH1 3EZ, ☏ 36669 – ⇋wc 🅿 — CX a
    28 rm.

🏨 Whitehall, Exeter Park Rd, BH2 5AX, ☏ 24682 – 🛗 🛏wc Ⓟ – **46 rm.**   **CZ u**

🏨 **Fircroft,** Owls Rd, BH5 1AE, ☏ 39771 – 🛏wc Ⓟ   **CX x**
M (bar lunch) 2.50/3.50 t. ▯ 1.50 – **47 rm** ☲ 9.50/17.00 t. – P 16.00/17.00 t.

🏨 Cliff Court, 15 West Cliff Rd, BH2 5EX, ☏ 25994 – 🛗 🛏wc Ⓟ – **43 rm.**   **CZ r**

🏨 **Southwood Lodge,** 36-38 Southwood Av. Southbourne, BH6 3QB, ☏ 422213 – Ⓟ.
🔄 VISA   **DX r**
February-September – **M** 2.50/3.50 ▯ 1.65 – **32 rm** ☲ 6.00/12.00.

🏨 New Somerset, Bath Rd, BH1 2NW, ☏ 21983 – 🛗 🛏wc Ⓟ   **DY s**
38 rm.

🏠 **Wood Lodge,** 10 Manor Rd, East Cliff, BH1 3EY, ☏ 20891, 🚗 – 🛏wc 🚿wc Ⓟ   **EY z**
Easter-mid October – **15 rm** ☲ (dinner included) 10.25/25.50 t.

🏠 **Tudor Grange,** 31 Gervis Rd, BH1 3EE, ☏ 291472, 🚗 – Ⓟ   **EY o**
March-October – **12 rm** ☲ 9.50/20.50 **st.**

🏠 **Alumcliff,** 121 Alumhurst Rd, Alumchine, BH4 8HS, ☏ 76477, ≼ – 🛏wc 🚿wc Ⓟ. 🔄
AE VISA   **BX a**
closed 12 to 27 April and first 2 weeks November – **17 rm** ☲ 8.25/19.00 s.

🏠 **Naseby Nye,** Byron Rd, Boscombe Overcliff, BH5 1JD, ☏ 34079, 🚗 – 🛏wc   **DX z**
13 rm ☲ 7.50/18.00 s.

🏠 **Arundale,** 38 Christchurch Rd, BH1 3PD, ☏ 28088 – Ⓟ   **EY r**
39 rm ☲ (dinner included) 10.50/21.00.

🏠 **Bursledon,** Gervis Rd, East Cliff, BH1 3DF, ☏ 24622 – 🚿wc Ⓟ   **DY v**
23 rm ☲ 9.00/18.00 s.

🏠 Sandy Beach, Overcliff Drive, Southbourne, BH6 3QB, ☏ 424385, ≼ – 🚿wc Ⓟ   **DX a**
season – **16 rm.**

🏠 **Mariners,** 22 Clifton Rd, Southbourne, BH6 3PA, ☏ 420851 – Ⓟ   **EX c**
February-October – **15 rm** ☲ 6.50/13.00 s.

🏠 **Moorings,** 66 Lansdowne Rd North, BH1 1RS, ☏ 22705 – Ⓟ. 🔄 AE ⓪ VISA   **BV c**
18 rm ☲ 6.90/13.80 t.

🏠 **Blinkbonnie Heights,** 26 Clifton Rd, Southborne, BH6 3PA, ☏ 426512, 🚗 – Ⓟ   **EX c**
12 rm ☲ 7.50/17.00 s.

✗✗✗ **La Causerie** (at Carlton Hotel), Meyrick Rd, East Cliff, BH1 3DN, ☏ 22011 – Ⓟ. 🔄 AE
⓪ VISA   **EZ a**
M a la carte 9.80/16.10 st. ▯ 2.50.

✗✗✗ **The Buttery** (at Royal Bath Hotel), Bath Rd, BH1 2EW, ☏ 25555 – Ⓟ. 🔄 AE ⓪ VISA
M a la carte 6.85/11.00 st. ▯ 2.50.   **DZ a**

✗✗ La Taverna (at Palace Court), Westover Rd, BH1 3BZ, ☏ 27681, Italian rest.   **DZ c**

✗✗ **Opus One,** 31 Southbourne Grove, BH6 3QT, ☏ 421240 – 🔄 AE ⓪ VISA   **DX c**
closed Sunday, Monday, 1 week spring Bank Holiday, first week September and 25-26 December – **M** (dinner only) a la carte 5.55/9.20 t. ▯ 2.00.

✗ **Crust,** 1 Bus Station Arcade, Exeter Rd, BH2 5AE, ☏ 21430 – 🔄 AE ⓪ VISA   **CZ o**
closed Sunday from Christmas to Easter and 6 to 20 January – **M** a la carte 5.35/6.75 **t.**
▯ 1.90.

BENTLEY, ROLLS ROYCE 26 Oxford Rd ☏ 25748
BMW Exeter Rd ☏ 24433
COLT Columbia Rd ☏ 56561
DAIMLER-JAGUAR-MG-MORRIS-ROVER-TRIUMPH
16/18 Poole Rd ☏ 766031
DAIMLER-JAGUAR 38 Poole Hill ☏ 25405
FORD 9 Palmerston Rd ☏ 34262
FORD Poole Rd ☏ 762442
JENSEN, VOLVO 33 R. L. Stephenson Av. ☏ 763344
LANCIA 318/320 Holdenhurst Rd ☏ 33304
MAZDA 216/218 Tuckton Rd ☏ 429234

MORRIS-MG-WOLSELEY 235 Castle Lane West, Redhill
☏ 510201
PEUGEOT 25/27 Palmerston Rd, Boscombe ☏ 37206
PORSCHE 382/386 Charminster Rd ☏ 510252
RENAULT 1114 Christchurch Rd, Pokesdown ☏ 49241
TALBOT 14 Carbery Row ☏ 423243
TALBOT 35 Holdenhurst Rd ☏ 26566
VAUXHALL 521 Christchurch Rd ☏ 35362
VAUXHALL Castle Lane West ☏ 526434
VAUXHALL 984 Christchurch Rd ☏ 423201
VAUXHALL Poole Rd ☏ 763361
VW, AUDI-NSU 723 Wimborne Rd ☏ 516222

BOURTON-ON-THE-WATER Glos. 🔢 403 🔢 404 0 28 – pop. 2,251 – ECD : Saturday – ☏ 0451.
London 91 – Birmingham 47 – Gloucester 24 – Oxford 36.

🏨 **Old Manse,** Victoria St., GL54 2BX, ☏ 20642, 🚗 – 🛏wc ☎ Ⓟ. 🔄
M a la carte 7.30/12.80 t. ▯ 1.80 – ☲ 1.30 – **9 rm** 21.55 t.

🏨 **Old New Inn,** High St., GL54 2AF, ☏ 20467, « Bourton model village », 🚗 – 🚙 Ⓟ
M 4.50/5.50 t. ▯ 1.60 – **24 rm** ☲ 9.90/21.00 **st.**

🏨 **Chester House,** Victoria St., GL54 2DQ, ☏ 20286 – 📺 🛏wc Ⓟ. 🔄 AE VISA
April-November – **M** 4.35 t. ▯ 2.10 – **16 rm** ☲ 10.70/18.10 t.

🏠 **Brookside,** Riverside, GL54 2BS, ☏ 20371, 🚗 – 🛏wc 🚿 Ⓟ – AE VISA
M 4.70/7.60 t. ▯ 2.00 – **10 rm** ☲ 8.00/17.20 t. – P 15.25/16.35 t.

✗ **Rose Tree,** Riverside, GL54 2BX, ☏ 20635
closed mid January-February and dinner Sunday and Monday – **M** (bar lunch Monday to Friday) a la carte 5.15/6.85 t. ▯ 1.95.

TALBOT ☏ 20366

BOVEY TRACEY Devon **403** 32 – pop. 3,834 – EDC : Wednesday – ✉ Newton Abbot – ☎ 0626.

🛈 Lower Car Park ☎ 832047 (summer only).

London 214 – Exeter 14 – Plymouth 32.

- 🏠 **Prestbury Country House** 🦢, Brimley Lane, TQ13 9JS, ☎ 833246, « Country house atmosphere », 🍽 – 🚻wc 🚗 🅿
March-October – **M** (bar lunch) approx. 5.25 **s.** 🍷 1.50 – **10 rm** ☲ 8.00/24.00 **s.** – P 15.50/18.50 **s.**

- 🏠 **Coombe Cross**, TQ13 9EY, ☎ 832476, 🍽 – 🚻wc 🅿. ⭤ AE
closed 23 December-12 February – **M** *(closed Monday lunch)* (buffet lunch) approx. 5.00 **st.** 🍷 2.00 – **20 rm** ☲ 11.00/22.00 **st.** – P 16.00 **st.**

BOWBURN Durham – pop. 5,060 – ✉ ☎ 0385 Coxhoe.

London 265 – Durham 3 – Middlesbrough 20.

- 🏨 Bowburn Hall, DH6 5NT, E : 1 m. off A 177 ☎ 770311, 🍽 – TV 🚻wc ⭤ 🅿
19 rm.

BOWDON Cheshire **403** **404** M 23 – see Altrincham (Greater Manchester).

BOWES Durham **986** ⑲ – pop. 409 – ECD : Wednesday – ✉ Barnard Castle – ☎ 0833 Teesdale.

London 258 – Carlisle 54 – Newcastle-upon-Tyne 44.

- 🏠 **Bowes Moor**, DL12 9RH, W : 3 m. on A 66 ☎ 28331, ✎ – 🅿. *VISA*
closed February – **M** a la carte 2.80/4.70 **t.** 🍷 1.20 – **10 rm** ☲ 10.00/18.00 **t.** – P 16.50/17.50 **t.**

BOWNESS-ON-WINDERMERE Cumbria **986** ⑲ – see Windermere.

BRACKLEY Northants. **403** **404** Q 27 – pop. 4,615 – ECD : Wednesday – ☎ 0280.

London 72 – Northampton 20 – Oxford 25.

- 🏨 Old Crown (County), Market Pl., NN13 5AB, ☎ 702210 – ⭤ 🚗 🅿. 🛡
15 rm.

  at Brackley Hatch NE : 5 ¼ m. on A 43 – ✉ Brackley – ☎ 028 05 Syresham :

- ✗✗ **Green Man Inn** with rm, NN13 5TX, ☎ 209 – 🚻wc 🅿. 🛡. ⓘ *VISA*
closed Christmas Day – **M** a la carte 6.00/8.70 **t.** 🍷 1.50 – **7 rm** ☲ 10.00/16.50 **t.**

FIAT 71 High St. ☎ 702 27

BRADFORD West Yorks. **986** ⑫ and ㉓ – pop. 294,177 – ECD : Wednesday – ☎ 0274.

Envir. : Haworth (Brontë Parsonage Museum★) *AC*, W : 10 m. by B 6144 AX.

🏌 Chellow Grange, Haworth Rd ☎ 427671, NW : 3 m. by B 6144 AX – 🏌 Hawksworth, Guiseley ☎ 0943 (Guiseley) 73817, N : 8 m. by A 6037 BX – 🏌 Scarr Hall, Pollard Lane ☎ 68313 BX – 🏌 South View Rd ☎ 681023, SE : 4 m. on plan of Leeds BX.

✈ Leeds and Bradford Airport : ☎ 0532 (Leeds) 503431, NE : 6 m. by A 658 BX – **Terminal :** Chester St., Bus Station, Bradford.

🛈 Central Library, Princes Way ☎ 33081 ext 45 – Information City Hall ☎ 29577 ext 425.

London 200 – Leeds 9 – Manchester 37 – Middlesbrough 70 – Sheffield 44.

Plan of Bradford opposite

Plan of Enlarged Area : see Leeds

- 🏨 **Norfolk Gardens** (Stakis), Hall Ings, BD1 5SH, ☎ 34733, Telex 517573 – 🛗 TV 🚿. 🛡. ⭤ AE ⓘ *VISA*   BZ **e**
M 3.50/5.25 🍷 2.00 – **124 rm** ☲ 20.50/28.00 **t.**

- 🏨 **Baron**, Highfield Rd, Idle, BD10 8OT, N : 2 ½ m. ☎ 613456, Telex 517229, ⭤ – TV 🚻wc ⭤ 🅿. AE ⓘ   on plan of Leeds AV **i**
M *(closed Sunday and Bank Holidays)* (bar lunch) a la carte 3.90/6.25 **st.** 🍷 1.50 – **60 rm** ☲ 21.50/28.50 **s.**

- 🏨 **Novotel**, Merrydale Rd, BD4 6SA, SE : 3 m. off M 606 ☎ 683683, Telex 517312, ☲ heated – 🛗 TV 🚻wc ⭤ 🚻 🅿. 🛡. ⭤ AE ⓘ *VISA*   on plan of Leeds AX **a**
M 5.00/6.00 **st.** 🍷 2.80 – ☲ 2.10 – **131 rm** 17.75/24.00 **st.** – P 26.00/29.00 **st.**

- 🏨 **Victoria** (T.H.F.), Bridge St., BD1 1JX, ☎ 28706 – 🛗 TV 🚻wc ⭤ 🅿. 🛡. ⭤ AE ⓘ *VISA*
M 4.50/5.05 **st.** 🍷 1.70 – **67 rm** ☲ 15.00/23.50 **st.**   BZ **c**

- 🏠 **Maple Hill** 🦢, Park Drive, BD9 4DP, ☎ 44061, ☲ heated, 🍽 – 🅿   AX **o**
10 rm ☲ 6.20/10.50 **t.**

  at Thornton W : 2 ¾ m. on B 6145 – ✉ ☎ 0274 Bradford :

- ✗✗✗ **The Cottage**, 869 Thornton Rd, BD13 3NW, ☎ 832752 – 🅿. 🛡 AE *VISA*
closed Saturday lunch and Tuesday – **M** approx. 8.25 🍷 2.90.   on plan of Leeds AV **a**

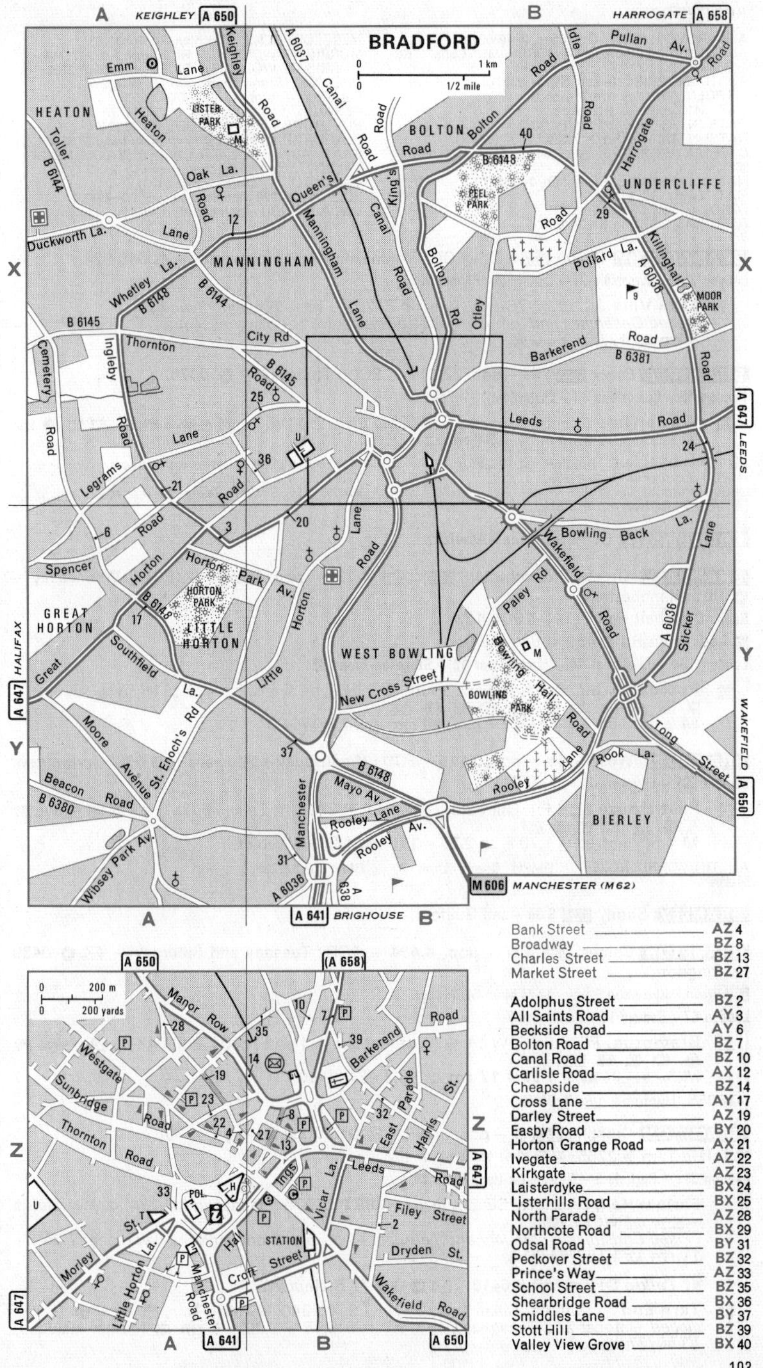

KEIGHLEY A 650
HARROGATE A 658
BRADFORD
0 1 km
0 1/2 mile
HEATON
Emm
Lane
LISTER PARK
M
Heaton
Toller
B 6144
Oak La.
Queen's
Road
Duckworth La.
Lane
12
MANNINGHAM
Manningham
Lane
Whetley La.
B 6148
B 6144
B 6145
Ingleby
Thornton
City Rd
Road
B 6145
25
Lane
U
36
Legrams
21
Road
6
Spencer
Road
3
20
Horton
Horton Park
Av.
HORTON PARK
B 6148
GREAT HORTON
17
LITTLE HORTON
Southfield
Little
La.
St. Enoch's Rd
Moore
Avenue
Beacon
Road
B 6380
Wibsey Park Av.
37
Manchester
Mayo Av.
B 6148
Rooley Lane
Rooley
Av.
31
A 6036
A 638
Keighley Road
A 6037
Canal
Road
Road
King's
Road
Canal
Road
BOLTON
Road
Bolton
Bolton
B 6448
PEEL PARK
40
29
UNDERCLIFFE
Pollard La.
A 6038
Killinghall
9
MOOR PARK
Barkerend
Road
B 6381
Leeds
Road
A 647
LEEDS
24
Bolton Rd
Otley
Lane
Horton
Road
Road
WEST BOWLING
New Cross Street
Paley Rd
Wakefield
Bowling Back
La.
Lane
Bowling
Road
BOWLING PARK
M
Bowling Hall Road
A 6036
Sticker
Rook La.
Tong
Street
Rooley
Lane
BIERLEY
WAKEFIELD A 650
A 647 HALIFAX
Great
A 641 BRIGHOUSE
M 606 MANCHESTER (M 62)
A 650
(A 658)
0 200 m
0 200 yards
Manor Row
28
10
7
P
35
39
Barkerend
Road
14
Westgate
19
Sunbridge
P 23
Thornton
Road
22 4
8
32
East Parade
Harris
St.
Z
27
13
Leeds
Vicar La.
Road
A 647
33
POL
H
i
C
Filey
Street
2
STATION
Dryden
St.
Morley
St.
Little Horton La.
Hall
Croft
Manchester
Road
Wakefield
Road
A 647
A 641
A 650

BRADFORD

ALFA-ROMEO, BMW Oak Lane ☎ 495521
AUSTIN-DAIMLER-JAGUAR-MORRIS-MG Canal Rd ☎ 33488
AUSTIN-MORRIS Nelson St. ☎ 22271
CITROEN Whetley Hill ☎ 495543
DAF 341 Leeds Rd ☎ 26812
DATSUN 88 Thornton Rd ☎ 27302
DATSUN Queens Rd ☎ 20376
DATSUN, PORSCHE, VAUXHALL Parry Lane ☎ 392321
FIAT Keighley Rd, Frizinghall ☎ 41337
FIAT Leeds Rd ☎ 663391
FORD 44 Bowland St ☎ 25131
FORD 146/148 Tong St. ☎ 681601

MERCEDES-BENZ Thornton Rd ☎ 498103
MORRIS-MG-WOLSELEY Gt. Horton Rd ☎ 71749
MORRIS-MG-WOLSELEY St. Enoch's Rd ☎ 22234
OPEL 230 Manningham Lane ☎ 491432
PEUGEOT Thornton Rd ☎ 493933
RENAULT Frizinghall Rd ☎ 495711
ROVER-TRIUMPH Frizinghall Rd ☎ 42404
ROVER-TRIUMPH 38 Manningham Lane ☎ 32444
SAAB Apperley Lane, Yeadon ☎ 0532 (Leeds) 502231
TALBOT 150 Manningham Lane ☎ 27181
VAUXHALL Thornton Rd ☎ 34201
VOLVO 226/228 Manningham Lane ☎ 491301
VW, AUDI-NSU Ingleby Rd ☎ 491414

BRADWORTHY Devon **403** G 31 – ECD : Wednesday – ✉ Holsworthy – ☎ 040 924.
London 251 – Barnstaple 27 – Exeter 50 – Plymouth 47.

  Lake Villa, EX22 7SQ, E: ½ m. ☎ 342, – TV wc wc P
  closed December and January – **M** (dinner only) (booking essential) 6.00 st. 1.75 –
  8 rm 12.00/28.00 st.

BRAINTREE Essex **404** V 28 – pop. 22,310 – ECD : Thursday – ☎ 0376.
London 45 – Cambridge 38 – Chelmsford 12 – Colchester 15.

  White Hart (T.H.F.), Bocking End, CM7 6AB, ☎ 21401 – TV wc P. AE ① VISA
  M 4.25/5.00 st. 1.70 – **34 rm** 13.50/21.00 st.

AUSTIN-MORRIS-MG Bradford St. ☎ 25701
FORD Coggeshall Rd ☎ 21202
OPEL South St. ☎ 21313
RENAULT Railway St. ☎ 21819

ROVER-TRIUMPH Rayne Rd ☎ 24444
TALBOT 253 Coggeshall Rd ☎ 25480
VAUXHALL 277/281 Rayne Rd ☎ 21456

BRAITHWAITE Cumbria – see Keswick.

BRAMHALL Greater Manchester **403** **404** N 23 – pop. 39,619 – ECD : Wednesday – ☎ 061 Manchester.
See : Bramhall Hall* (14C-16C) *AC.*
Ladythorn Rd ☎ 439 4057.
London 194 – Liverpool 44 – Manchester 10 – Stoke-on-Trent 33.

  Pownall Arms, Bramhall Lane South, SK7 2EB, on A 5102 ☎ 439 8116, Telex 666691 –
  TV wc P. AE ① VISA
  M 2.85/3.95 2.10 – 2.25 – **40 rm** 14.25/20.00.

BRAMHOPE West Yorks. – pop. 3,115 – ECD : Wednesday – ✉ Leeds – ☎ 0532 Arthington.
London 201 – Harrogate 11 – Leeds 7.5.

  Post House (T.H.F.), Otley Rd, LS16 9JJ, ☎ 842911, Telex 556367, – TV wc
  P. AE ① VISA
  M 4.50/5.50 st. 1.70 – 2.25 – **120 rm** 18.50/27.00 st.

AUSTIN-MORRIS-ROVER-TRIUMPH Breary Lane ☎ 842696

BMW ☎ 842238

BRAMLEY Surrey **404** S 30 – see Guilford.

BRAMPTON Cambs. **404** T 27 – pop. 4,494 – ECD : Tuesday and Saturday – ✉ ☎ 0480 Huntingdon.
Allison Pottery and Studio, 32/34 Main St. ☎ 2685.
London 67 – Bedford 19 – Huntingdon 2.

  Brampton, PE18 8NH, W : 1 ½ m. at junction A 1 and A 604 ☎ 810434 – TV wc
  P. AE ① VISA
  M 3.75/4.95 st. 1.95 – **17 rm** 18.25/24.50 st.

CITROEN Huntingdon Rd ☎ 53132

BRAMPTON Cumbria **986** ⑲ – pop. 3,895 – ECD : Thursday – ☎ 069 77.
Talkin Tarn ☎ 2255. – 32-34 Main St. ☎ 2685.
London 317 – Carlisle 9 – Newcastle-Upon-Tyne 49.

  Farlam Hall, CA8 2NG, SE: 2 ¾ m. on A 689 ☎ 06976 (Hallbankgate) 234, « Gardens »
  – wc wc P.
  closed Christmas, 1 January and February – **M** (dinner only and Sunday lunch) 7.25 t. –
  11 rm 10.50/24.00 t.

  at Talkin S : 2 m. off B 6413 – ✉ ☎ 069 77 Brampton :

  Tarn End with rm, Talkin Tarn, CA18 1LS, ☎ 2340, Talkin Tarn, – P
  closed October and Christmas Day – **M** 3.75/5.75 1.20 – **6 rm** (dinner included)
  13.50/27.00.

BRAMSHAW Hants. 403 404 P 31 – pop. 602 – ECD: Tuesday – ✉ Lyndhurst – ☎ 042 127 Cadnam.
London 93 – Salisbury 13 – Southampton 11 – Winchester 21.

    Bramble Hill ⑤, Bramble Hill, SO4 7JG, W: ½ m. ☏ 3165, ≤, « Former hunting lodge »,
    🐎, park – 🅿
    Easter-5 November – **M** (bar lunch Monday to Saturday) approx. 5.00 **t.** 🍷 1.80 – **16 rm**
    ☕ 11.25/23.00 **t.**

BRANDON Warw. 403 404 P 26 – see Coventry.

BRANSCOMBE Devon 403 K 32 – pop. 477 – ECD: Thursday – ✉ Seaton – ☎ 029 780.
London 167 – Exeter 20 – Lyme Regis 11.

    Masons Arms, EX12 3DJ, ☏ 300, 🐎 – 🛏wc 🅿
    M (bar lunch Monday to Saturday) 3.50/7.00 **t.** 🍷 1.90 – **22 rm** ☕ 9.50/24.00 **s.**

BRANSTON Lincs. 404 S 24 – see Lincoln.

BRANSTON Staffs. 403 404 P 25 – see Burton-upon-Trent.

BRAUNSTONE Leics. 403 404 Q 26 – see Leicester.

BRAY-ON-THAMES Berks. 404 R 29 – pop. 5,818 – ✉ ☎ 0628 Maidenhead.
London 34 – Reading 13.

    Monkey Island, SL6 2EE, SE: 1 m. off Monkey Island Lane ☏ 23400, « Island on River
    Thames », 🔌, 🐎 – TV 🛏wc 🕾 🅿. 🏊. ⟋ AE
    M 8.50 **st.** – **24 rm** ☕ 24.00/36.00 **st.**

XXXX   ❀❀ **Waterside Inn,** Ferry Rd, SL6 2AT, ☏ 20691, ≤, « Thames-side setting », 🐎,
    French rest. – 🅿. ⟋ AE ① VISA
    closed Monday and 26 December-23 January – **M** a la carte 15.20/25.65 **st.**
    Spec. Goujonnette de sole au Sauternes, Filets de lapereau grillé aux marrons glacés, Soufflé chaud aux framboises.

XX   Hind's Head, High St., SL6 2AB, ☏ 26151 – 🅿.

BRECHFA Dyfed 403 H 28 – pop. 175 – ✉ Carmarthen – ☎ 026 789.
London 223 – Carmarthen 11 – Swansea 30.

XX   **Ty Mawr** ⑤ with rm, ☏ 332, 🔌, 🐎 – 🛏wc 🅿
    closed 2 weeks October and 2 weeks February – **M** (bar lunch residents only) a la carte
    7.50/9.55 **st.** 🍷 1.80 – **5 rm** ☕ 13.25/16.50 **st.**

BRECON (ABERHONDDU) Powys 403 J 28 – pop. 6,304 – ECD: Wednesday – ☎ 0874.
See : Cathedral* 13C. Envir. : Bwlch (≤* of the Usk Valley) SE: 8 ½ m. – Road* from Brecon
to Hirwaun – Road* from Brecon to Merthyr Tydfil – Craig-y-Nos (Dan-yr-Ogof Caves* AC)
SW: 18 m. – ⌗₁₈ Penoyre Park ☏ 3658, NW: 2 m. – ⌗₉ Llanfaes ☏ 2004, ½ m. on A 40.
🄸 Brecon Beacons Mountain Centre, near Libanus ☏ 3366 – Brecon Beacons National Park, 7 Glamorgan St.
☏ 2763 (Easter-September).

London 183 – Cardiff 41 – Gloucester 62 – Swansea 44.

    at Libanus SW: 4 m. on A 470 – ✉ ☎ 0874 Brecon :

    Mountains, LD3 8EN, ☏ 4242, ≤ – TV 🛏wc 🛁wc 🕾 ♿ 🅿. ⟋ AE ① VISA
    M 3.00/4.00 🍷 1.70 – ☕ 1.00 – **26 rm** 13.00/19.50 – P 21.00.

AUSTIN-MORRIS-MG   Ship St. ☏ 2166   TALBOT   The Watton ☏ 2266
FORD   Struet St. ☏ 2401

BREDWARDINE Heref. and Worc. 403 L 27 – pop. 172 – ✉ Hereford – ☎ 098 17 Moccas.
London 150 – Hereford 12 – Newport 51.

    Red Lion ⑤, HR3 6BU, ☏ 303, 🔌, 🐎 – 🛏wc 🛁wc 🅿
    M (bar lunch) approx. 6.00 – **15 rm** ☕ 9.00/20.00.

BRENTWOOD Essex 404 U 29 – pop. 51,330 – ECD: Thursday – ☎ 0277.
⌗₁₈ King George's Park ☏ 218714. – London 22 – Chelmsford 11 – Southend-on-Sea 21.

    Brentwood Moat House, London Rd, CM14 4NR, SW: 1 ¼ m. on A 1023 ☏ 225252,
    Telex 995182, 🐎 – TV 🅿. 🏊. ⟋ AE ① VISA
    M a la carte 5.55/10.15 **t.** 🍷 2.00 – ☕ 3.00 – **25 rm** 20.50/28.50 **st.**

    Post House (T.H.F.), Brook St., CM14 5NF, SW: 1 ¾ m. on A 1023 ☏ 210888,
    Telex 995379, 🏊 heated – 🛗 TV 🛏wc 🕾 ♿ 🅿. 🏊. ⟋ AE ① VISA
    M 5.00/5.50 **st.** 🍷 2.00 – ☕ 2.25 – **120 rm** 18.00/25.50 **st.**

XX   Headley Arms (Gd. Met.), Warley Rd, Great Warley, CM14 0AR, S: 1 ½ m. on B 186
    ☏ 216104, Dancing (Friday and Saturday) – 🅿.

ALFA ROMEO, FIAT, JENSEN 2 Brook St. ☏ 216161   ROVER-TRIUMPH-WOLSELEY Kings Rd ☏ 221401
AUSTIN-MORRIS-MG-WOLSELEY 110 Shenfield Rd,   RENAULT 121/5 Kings Rd ☏ 225546
Shenfield ☏ 222424   VAUXHALL Brook St. ☏ 227290
FORD Brook St. ☏ 215544   VW, AUDI-NSU Shenfield ☏ 218686

■ BRIDGEND (PEN-Y-BONT) Mid Glam. **403** J 29 – pop. 14,544 – ECD : Wednesday – ✆ 0656 Pencoed.

London 177 – Cardiff 20 – Swansea 23.

XXX **Coed-y-Mwstwr** ⚬ with rm, Coychurch, CF35 6AF, E: 2 ¼ m. ☎ 860621, ◁, ✗, ⌷ heated, 🚗, park – TV ⌷wc ☎ P. ⚐. ⊠ AE ⓪ VISA
closed Christmas and Bank Holidays – **M** *(closed Saturday lunch and Sunday dinner)*
a la carte 9.00/14.00 **st.** ⌷ 1.75 – **9 rm** ⌷ 22.00/38.00 **st.**

■ BRIDGNORTH Salop **403 404** M 26 – pop. 9,400 – ECD : Thursday – ✆ 074 62.
Envir. : Claverley (Parish church : wall paintings* 13C-15C) E : 5 m. – Much Wenlock : Wenlock priory* (ruins 11C) *AC*, NW : 8 ½ m.

☜ Stanley Lane ☎ 3315, N : 1 m. – 🛈 Bridgnorth Library, Listley St. ☎ 3358.

London 146 – Birmingham 26 – Shrewsbury 20 – Worcester 29.

🏛 **Falcon,** St. John St., Low Town, WV15 6AG, ☎ 3134 – ⌷wc P. ⊠ AE ⓪ VISA
M 3.50/5.00 **st.** ⌷ 2.25 – **14 rm** ⌷ 12.00/22.00 **st.**

XX **Bambers,** 65 St. Mary's St., WV16 1JB, ☎ 3139
closed Sunday, Monday, September and first week January – **M** *(dinner only)* a la carte
3.60/6.05 **t.** ⌷ 1.65.

AUSTIN-DAIMLER-JAGUAR-LAND ROVER-MORRIS   BMW, FIAT Hollybush Rd ☎ 4343
MG-ROVER-TRIUMPH 52 West Castle St. ☎ 2207

■ BRIDGWATER Somerset **403** L 30 – pop 26,642 – ECD : Thursday – ✆ 0278.
Envir. : Burnham-on-Sea (St. Andrew's Church : Gibbon's sculptures*) N : 9 m.

☜ Enmore Park ☎ 027 867 (Spaxton) 244, W : 3 m. – London 160 – Bristol 39 – Taunton 11.

🏛 **Royal Clarence,** High St., Cornhill, TA6 3AT, ☎ 55196, « Tastefully decorated interior » –
TV ⌷wc 🕭wc ☎ ⇌ P. ⚐. ⊠ AE ⓪ VISA
M a la carte 5.20/7.65 **st.** ⌷ 1.80 – **28 rm** ⌷ 12.90/26.15 **st.**

at West Huntspill N : 6 m. on A 38 – ✉ High Bridge – ✆ 0278 Bunham-on-Sea :

⚘ **Sundowner,** 74 Main Rd, TA9 3QU, on A 38 ☎ 784766 – P. ⊠
closed 2 weeks May and 2 weeks November – **M** 3.00/3.75 **t.** ⌷ 1.95 – **6 rm** ⌷ 6.50/
13.00 **t.** – P 12.00/14.00 **t.**

AUSTIN-MG-ROVER-TRIUMPH 52 Eastover ☎ 2218   FORD 37 Frian St. ☎ 51332
AUSTIN-MORRIS-MG-WOLSELEY Market St. ☎ 2125   RENAULT Cannington ☎ 652228
BMW Cannington ☎ 0278 (Combwich) 652233   VAUXHALL Monmouth St. ☎ 56301
FIAT 38 St. John St. ☎ 3312   VOLVO Bristol Rd ☎ 55333

■ BRIDLINGTON Humberside **986** ㉔ – pop. 26,776 – ECD : Thursday – ✆ 0262.
See : Priory Church* 12C-15C. Envir. : Burton Agnes Hall* (Elizabethan) *AC*, SW : 6 m.
☜ Belvedere ☎ 72092, 1 m. Bridlington Station. – ☜ Flamborough Head ☎ 850333, NE : 5 m.
🛈 Garrison St. ☎ 73474 and 79626 (summer only). – London 236 – Kingston-upon-Hull 29 – York 41.

🏛 **Expanse,** North Marine Drive, YO15 2LS, ☎ 75347, ◁ – 🛗 ⌷wc ☎ P. ⊠ AE VISA
M 3.50/4.50 **st.** – **45 rm** ⌷ 9.60/18.65 **st.** – P 16.80/17.50 **st.**
🏛 **Monarch,** South Marine Drive, YO15 3PJ, ☎ 74447, ◁ – 🛗 ⌷wc ☎ P. ⊠ VISA
M 3.20/4.20 **st.** – **42 rm** ⌷ 9.50/18.80 **st.**

AUSTIN-JAGUAR-MORRIS-MG-ROVER-TRIUMPH-   TALBOT, CITROEN, HONDA, VAUXHALL Hilder-
WOLSELEY 7 Prospect St. ☎ 72267   thorpe Rd ☎ 78141
DATSUN Quay Rd ☎ 70331   TOYOTA 52 Quay Rd ☎ 72022
FORD Hamilton Rd ☎ 75336   VOLVO Pinfold Lane ☎ 70351

■ BRIDPORT Dorset **403** L 31 – pop. 6,369 – ECD : Thursday – ✆ 0308.
☜ West Bay ☎ 22597, S : 1 ½ m. – London 150 – Exeter 38 – Taunton 33 – Weymouth 19.

⌂ **Roundham House,** Roundham Gdns, West Bay Rd, DT6 4BD, ☎ 22753, 🚗 – P
closed 1 December-7 January – **8 rm** ⌷ 6.00/12.00 **st.**

at West Bay S : 1 ½ m. on B 3157 – ✉ ✆ 0308 Bridport :

🏛 **Haddon House,** DT6 4EN, ☎ 23626 – TV ⌷wc P. VISA
M 3.45/5.25 **st.** – **10 rm** ⌷ 9.50/19.00 **st.**

at Eype SW : 1 ½ m. – ✉ ✆ 0308 Bridport :

⚘ **Eype's Mouth,** DT6 6AL, ☎ 23300, ◁ – ⌷wc P. ⊠ AE ⓪ VISA
M 2.40/3.25 **st.** ⌷ 1.40 – **27 rm** ⌷ 9.50/11.10 **st.** – P 14.00 **st.**

■ BRIGG Humberside **404** S 23 – pop. 4,795 – ECD : Wednesday – ✆ 0652.
🛈 Council Offices, Bigby St. ☎ 52441.

London 167 – Kingston-upon-Hull 21 – Leeds 62 – Lincoln 24 – Sheffield 53.

⚘ **Angel,** Market Pl. DN20 8LD, ☎ 53118 – 🕭 P – **13 rm.**

AUSTIN-MG-ROVER-TRIUMPH-WOLSELEY Bigby Rd   FORD Market Pl. ☎ 52396
☎ 52066   MORRIS-MG Bridge St. ☎ 52295
DAF, VOLVO Greetwell ☎ 54665

See : Royal Pavilion* (interior**) *AC* **CZ** B – Aquarium* *AC* **CZ** A – Booth Museum (bird collection)* **BV** M – Preston Manor (Chinese collection*) **BV** D – The Lanes **CZ**. **Envir. :** Stanmer Park (site*) N : 3 ½ m. by A 27 **CV** – Clayton (church of St. John the Baptist : frescoes* 14 C) N : 6 m. by A 23 **BV**.

🏌 Roedean ☎ 63989 **CV** – 🏌 Hollingbury Park ☎ 552010 **BV** – 🏌 N : by Dyke Rd **BV** ☎ 079 156 (Poynings) 296 – 🏌 Dyke Rd ☎ 556482 **BV**.

⚓ Shipping connections with the continent : to Dieppe (Seajet).

🛈 Marlborough House, 54 Old Steine ☎ 23755 – Sea Front, Kings Rd ☎ 26450 (summer only).

🛈 at Hove : Town Hall, Church Rd ☎ 775400.

London 54 – Portsmouth 49 – Southampton 63.

Plans on following pages

🏨 **Grand** (De Vere), 97-103 King's Rd, BN1 2FW, ☎ 26301, Telex 877410, ≼ – 🛗 📺 🈂. 🔥 AE ⓞ *VISA*   **BZ** s
M 6.00/7.25 **st.** 🍾 1.75 – **165 rm** 🍽 24.00/40.00 **st.**

🏨 **Royal Crescent,** 100 Marine Par., BN2 1AX, ☎ 606311 ≼ – 🛗 📺. 🔥 AE ⓞ *VISA*   **CV** c
M 4.75/5.75 **st.** 🍾 1.90 – 🍽 3.00 – **66 rm** 19.00/29.65 **st.** – P 29.00 **st.**

🏨 **Wheeler's Sheridan,** 64 King's Rd, BN1 1NA, ☎ 23221, ≼ – 🛗 📺. 🔥 AE ⓞ *VISA* **BZ** e
closed 25 and 26 December – M (see **Wheeler's Sheridan Tavern**) – **34 rm** 🍽 24.00/44.00 **st.**

🏨 **Old Ship** (Best Western), King's Rd, BN1 1NR, ☎ 29001, Telex 877101, ≼ – 🛗 📺 🚗 ⓟ. 🔥. 🔥 AE ⓞ *VISA*   **CZ** n
M 5.50/6.60 **st.** 🍾 2.00 – **156 rm** 🍽 24.00/36.00 **st.**

🏨 **Norfolk Continental,** Kings Rd, BN1 2PP, ☎ 738201, Telex 877247, ≼ – 🛗 📺 🛏wc ☎ ⓟ. 🔥   **BZ** c
M (coffee shop lunch) 6.50 **s.** 🍾 1.75 – **65 rm** 🍽 20.00/35.00 **s.**

🏨 **Curzon** (T.H.F.), Cavendish Pl., BN1 2HS, ☎ 25788 – 🛗 📺 🛏wc ⓟ. 🔥 AE ⓞ *VISA* **BZ** v
M 3.90/4.20 **st.** 🍾 1.65 – **44 rm** 🍽 13.00/22.50 **st.**

🏨 **Madeira,** 19-23 Marine Parade, BN2 1TL, ☎ 607853, Telex 87491, ≼ – 🛗 🛏wc 🛏wc ☎ ⓟ. 🔥   **CZ** u
47 rm.

🏨 **Regency** without rest., 28 Regency Sq., BN1 2FH, ☎ 202690 – 🛏wc   **BZ** n
🍽 1.50 – **14 rm** 10.00/20.00 **st.**

🏠 **Marina,** 8 Charlotte St., BN2 1AG, ☎ 605349   **CV** n
10 rm 🍽 5.50/11.00 **st.**

🏠 **Downlands,** 19 Charlotte St., BN2 1AG, ☎ 601203   **CV** i
10 rm 🍽 5.00/10.00 **st.**

🏠 **Ellesmere,** 8 New Steine, BN2 1PB, ☎ 607812   **CZ** r
closed December and January – **14 rm** 🍽 5.25/12.50 **t.**

🏠 **Aston,** 3 Lower Rock Gdns, Marine Par., BN2 1PG, ☎ 681957   **CZ** c
14 rm 🍽 6.35/12.65 **t.**

XXX **Wheeler's Sheridan Tavern,** 64 King's Rd, BN1 1NA, ☎ 28372, Seafood – 🔥 AE ⓞ *VISA*   **BZ** e
closed Christmas – M a la carte 8.15/15.90 🍾 0.90.

XX **French Connection,** 11 Little East St., BN1 1HT, ☎ 24454 – 🔥 AE   **CZ** o
closed Sunday – M (dinner only) a la carte 6.95/9.50.

XX **Wheeler's,** 17 Market St., BN1 1HH, ☎ 25135, Seafood – 🔥 AE ⓞ *VISA*   **CZ** s
closed Christmas – M a la carte 8.15/15.90 🍾 0.90.

XX **Bannister's,** 77 St. George's Rd, BN2 1EU, Kemptown ☎ 687382 – AE   **CV** e
closed last week January - first week February – M (dinner only Tuesday to Saturday) a la carte 5.50/6.80 🍾 1.45.

XX **Dolce Vito,** Corner of Bedford Pl., 106c Western Rd, BN1 2AA, ☎ 737200, Italian rest. – 🔥 AE ⓞ *VISA*   **BY** u
M a la carte 8.15/12.95 **t.** 🍾 2.30.

X **Le Grandgousier,** 15 Western St., BN1 2PG, ☎ 772005, French rest. – 🔥 AE *VISA* **BY** x
closed Saturday lunch, Sunday and 11 to 28 August – M 5.75 **t.** 🍾 1.75.

X **Foggs,** 5 Little Western St., BN1 2PU, ☎ 735907 – 🔥 AE   **BY** a
M (dinner only) a la carte 4.50/5.65 🍾 1.40.

X **Christopher's,** 24 Western St., BN1 2PG, ☎ 775048 – 🔥 AE   **BY** z
closed Monday from November to Easter, Wednesday, 2 weeks March, last 2 weeks October and 24 to 26 December – M (dinner only) a la carte 4.75/8.30 **t.** 🍾 1.75.

X **Tureen,** 31 Upper North St., BN1 3FG, ☎ 28939, Bistro – 🔥 AE *VISA*   **BY** r
closed Sunday dinner, Monday and Bank Holidays – M a la carte 5.35/7.85 **t.** 🍾 1.75.

P.T.O. →

BRIGHTON AND HOVE

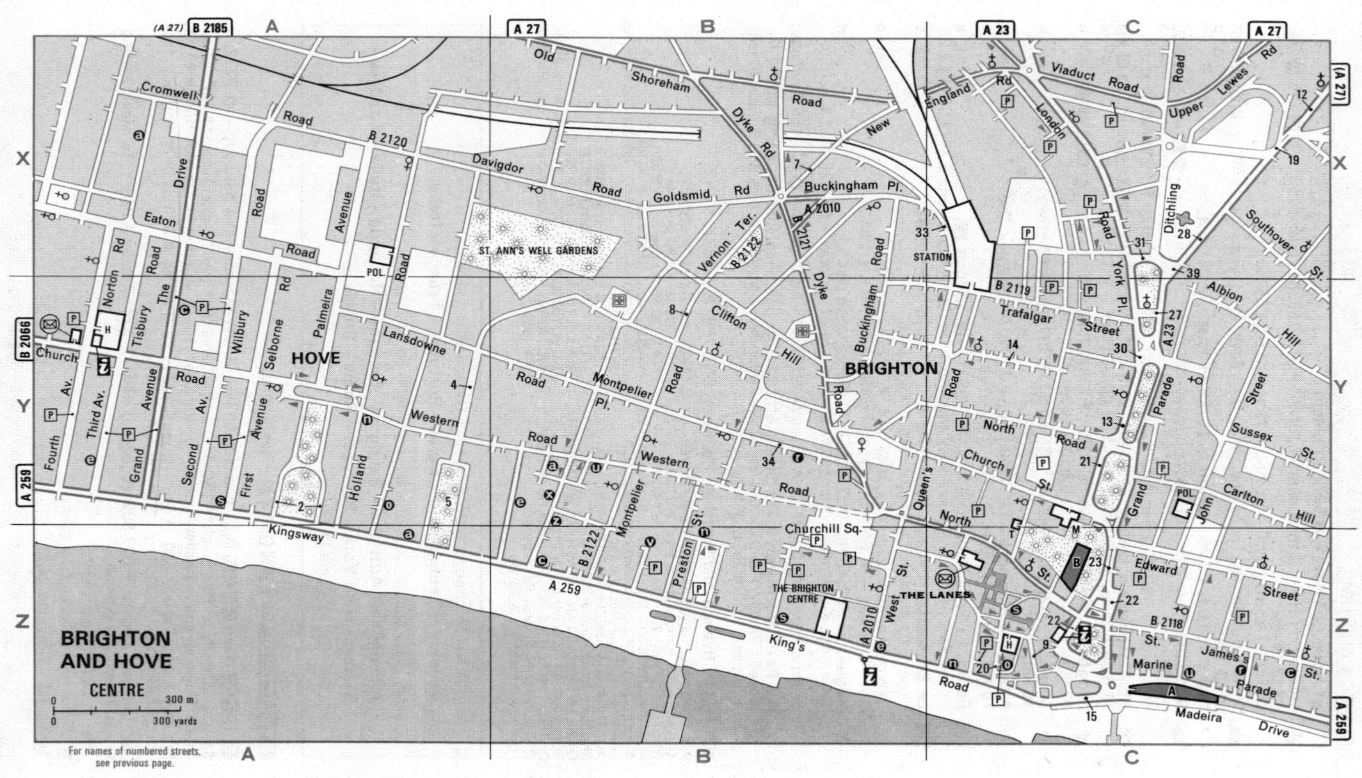

BRIGHTON AND HOVE
CENTRE
300 m
300 yards
For names of numbered streets,
see previous page.
HOVE
BRIGHTON
THE LANES
THE BRIGHTON CENTRE
ST. ANN'S WELL GARDENS
STATION
Churchill Sq.
Cromwell Road
Eaton Road
Drive
Norton Rd
Tisbury Road
The
Church Av.
Third Av.
Fourth
Grand Avenue
Second Av.
First Avenue
Wilbury Road
Selborne Rd
Palmeira
Lansdowne
Holland Road
Western Road
Western Road
Montpelier Pl.
Montpelier Road
Davigdor Road
Goldsmid Rd
Vernon Ter.
Clifton Hill
Dyke Rd
Old Shoreham Road
New England
Buckingham Pl.
Buckingham Road
Dyke Road
Queen's Road
North Road
Church St.
West St.
Preston St.
Kingsway
King's Road
Madeira Drive
Marine Parade
York Pl.
Trafalgar Street
Grand Parade
London Road
Viaduct Road
Upper Lewes Rd
Ditchling
Southover St.
Albion Hill
Sussex St.
Carlton Hill
Edward Street
James's St.
North Road
Church St.
A 27
A 23
A 259
A 2010
B 2185
B 2066
B 2120
B 2118
B 2119
B 2121
B 2122
POL.
STATION
2
4
5
7
8
9
12
13
14
15
19
20
21
22
23
27
28
30
31
33
34
39
X
Y
Z
A
B
C

BRIGHTON AND HOVE

at Hove – ⊠ Hove – ☎ 0273 Brighton :

🏨 **Dudley** (T.H.F.), Lansdowne Pl., BN3 1HQ, ☎ 736266, Telex 87537 – 🛗 TV 🚙 Ⓟ. 🏊.
🔽 AE ⓪ VISA   AY o
M 5.25/7.25 **st.** 🍾 2.00 – ☷ 2.50 – **78 rm** 20.50/27.50 **st.**

🏨 **New Courtlands,** 19-27 The Drive, BN3 3JW, ☎ 731055, Telex 87323 – 🛗 TV. 🚙 🔽
AE ⓪ VISA   AY c
M 4.80/5.50 **t.** 🍾 2.25 – **62 rm** ☷ 20.00/35.00 **st.** – P 29.00 **st.**

🏨 **Sackville** (Best Western), 189 Kingsway, BN3 4GU, ☎ 736292, ⪡ – 🛗 TV 🚙.🏊. 🔽 AE
⓪ VISA   AV n
M a la carte 7.90/10.15 **st.** 🍾 1.95 – **48 rm** ☷ 19.20/31.90 **st.** – P 25.55/30.35 **st.**

🏨 **St. Catherine's Lodge,** Kingsway, BN3 2RZ, ☎ 778181 – 🛗 TV ⌷wc ⬠. 🔽 AE VISA
M 3.65/5.25 **st.** 🍾 2.20 – **55 rm** ☷ 12.00/28.00 **st.** – P 18.50/21.00 **st.**   AV a

🏨 **Langfords,** 8-16 Third Av., BN3 2PX, ☎ 738222, 🚗 – 🛗 ⌷wc ⬠. 🏊. 🔽 AE ⓪ VISA   AY e
M 4.50 🍾 1.50 – **70 rm** ☷ 12.50/23.00 – P 19.50/22.00.

🏠 **Sherlock,** 28-29 Brunswick Ter., BN3 1HJ, ☎ 70784, ⪡ – TV ⌷wc   AZ a
46 rm.

🏠 **Albany,** St. Catherine's Ter., BA3 2RR, ☎ 773807 – TV ⌷wc 🛁wc   AV c
10 rm ☷ 9.75/17.00 **st.**

XXX **Eaton,** 13 Eaton Gdns, BN3 3TN, ☎ 738921 – Ⓟ. 🔽 AE ⓪ VISA   AX a
closed Sunday dinner, Good Friday and Christmas Day – **M** a la carte 6.80/9.05 **t.** 🍾 2.25.

XXX **La Brasserie,** Kingsway Court, First Av., ☎ 775764 – 🔽 AE VISA   AY s
closed Sunday dinner – **M** a la carte 7.00/11.50 **t.**

X **Lawrence,** 40 Waterloo St., BN3 1AY, ☎ 772922 – AE VISA   BY e
closed Sunday – **M** (dinner only) a la carte 5.15/7.10 **t.** 🍾 1.85.

X **Vogue,** 57 Holland Rd, BN2 1JE, ☎ 775066, French rest.   AY n
closed Sunday, Monday, 1 to 15 March and 1 to 21 October – **M** 3.25/4.65 **t.** 🍾 1.85.

at Poynings NW : 8 ½ m. by A 23 – BV – off A 281 – ⊠ Brighton – ☎ 079 156 Poynings :

X **Au Petit Normand,** 2 The Street, BN4 7AQ, ☎ 346, French rest. – 🔽 AE VISA
closed Monday, February and first week September – **M** (dinner only and Sunday lunch)
a la carte 5.20/8.25 **t.** 🍾 1.90.

MICHELIN Branch, Old Shoreham Rd, Hove, BN3 7EE, ☎ 778871.

AUSTIN-DAIMLER-JAGUAR-MORRIS-MG-ROVER-
TRIUMPH 117 Holland Rd at Hove ☎ 778421
AUSTIN-MORRIS 233 Preston Rd ☎ 553021
AUSTIN-MORRIS-MG Longridge Av.,Saltdean ☎ 31061
AUSTIN-DAIMLER-JAGUAR-MORRIS-MG-ROVER-
TRIUMPH 1a Lewes Rd ☎ 64131
AUSTIN-JAGUAR-MORRIS-MG-TRIUMPH 154 Old
Shoreham Rd at Hove ☎ 26264
DAIMLER-JAGUAR-LAND ROVER-ROVER-TRIUMPH,
ROLLS ROYCE Russell Sq. ☎ 21222
DATSUN, MERCEDES-BENZ Victoria Rd ☎ 414911
DATSUN 21/29 Preston Rd ☎ 685985
FIAT 24 Bedford Pl. ☎ 731118

FIAT Edward St. ☎ 63322
FIAT 100 Lewes Rd ☎ 63244
FORD 90/96 Preston Rd ☎ 506331
MAZDA 42/43 George St. ☎ 681766
OPEL, RENAULT, VAUXHALL 100 Old Shoreham Rd
☎ 416242
RELIANT 7 Church Pl. ☎ 684022
RELIANT Woodingdean ☎ 37777
RENAULT Stephenson Rd ☎ 692111
TALBOT-VOLVO 270-272 Old Shoreham Rd ☎ 737555
VW, AUDI, PEUGEOT 62/66 Station Rd, Portslade
☎ 413833

BRIMSCOMBE Glos 🔢403 🔢404 N 28 – see Stroud.

BRISTOL Avon 🔢403 🔢404 M 29 pop. 426,657– ECD : Wednesday and Saturday – ☎ 0272.
See: St. Mary Redcliffe Church** 13C-15C DZ B – Cathedral* (the Chapter House** 12C) DZ A –
Bristol Museum and Art Gallery* CZ M – Bristol Zoo* AC AY – Clifton Suspension Bridge ⪡* AY.
🏌18 Long Ashton ☎ 027 580 (Long Ashton) 2229, S : 3 m. by A 370 AY – 🏌18, 🏌9 Tracy Park
☎ 027 582 (Abson) 2251, E : 8 m. by A 420 BY.
✈ Lulsgate Airport : ☎ 027 587 (Lulsgate) 4441/7, SW : 7 m. by A 38 AY. **Terminal:** Marlborough Street Bus Station.
🚗 ☎ 291001 ext 2479.
🛈 Colston House, Colston St. ☎ 293891.

London 125 – Birmingham 84.

Plans on following pages

Holiday Inn, Lower Castle St., Old Market, BS1 3AD, ☎ 294281, Telex 449720, ☒ – 🛗 TV ⴕ 🅿 ☑
299 rm.
EZ s

Ladbroke Dragonara, Redcliffe Way, BS1 6NJ, ☎ 20044, Telex 449240 – 🛗 TV 🅿 ☑. ☒ AE ⑩ VISA
M a la carte 4.15/8.80 **st.** 🍷 2.10 – ☕ 3.50 – **210 rm** 28.00/33.00 **s.**
DEZ n

Unicorn (Rank), Prince St., BS1 4QF, ☎ 294811, Telex 44315 – 🛗 TV 🅿 ☑. ☒ AE ⑩ VISA
M 5.75 **st.** 🍷 2.00 – ☕ 3.00 – **193 rm** 18.50/27.75 **st.**
DZ i

Grand (Best Western), Broad St., BS1 2EL, ☎ 291645, Telex 449889 – 🛗 TV 🚗 🅿 ☑
180 rm.
DZ a

St. Vincent's Rocks (Anchor), Sion Hill, Clifton, BS8 4BB, ☎ 39251, Group Telex 858875 – TV 🚻wc ☎ 🅿 ☒ AE ⑩ VISA
M a la carte approx. 6.00 – **48 rm** ☕ 14.00/25.00 **st.**
AY c

Avon Gorge (Mt. Charlotte), Sion Hill, Clifton, BS8 4LD, ☎ 38955, Telex 444237, ≼ – 🛗 TV 🚻wc ☎. ☑. ☒ AE VISA
M a la carte 4.30/6.00 🍷 2.40 – **74 rm** ☕ 16.50/24.20.
AY x

Royal (Norfolk Cap.), College Green, BS1 5TH, ☎ 23591, Group Telex 23241 – 🛗 🚻wc ☎. ☑. ☒ AE ⑩ VISA
M 3.75/4.50 **st.** 🍷 1.75 – **128 rm** ☕ 13.50/24.75 **st.**
DZ e

Seeley's, 19-27 St. Pauls Rd, Clifton, BS8 1LX, ☎ 38544, ⇌ – TV 🚻wc 🚻wc 🚗
closed Sunday and 1 week at Christmas – **M** 2.75/3.95 **s.** 🍷 1.85 – **60 rm** ☕ 6.30/12.65 **t.** – P 12.20/17.70 **s.**
CZ z

Rodney, Clifton Down Rd, Clifton, BS8 4HY, ☎ 35422, ⇌
closed Christmas and 1 January – **30 rm** ☕ 7.00/12.00.
AY r

Oakfield, 52-54 Oakfield Rd, Clifton, BS8 2BG, ☎ 33643 – 🅿
closed 27 to 30 December – **27 rm** ☕ 6.00/11.00 **s.**
AY n

Pembroke, 13 Arlington Villas, Clifton, BS8 1EG, ☎ 35550
14 rm.
CZ a

XXX **Harvey's**, 12 Denmark St., BS1 5DQ, ☎ 277665 – ☒ AE ⑩ VISA
closed Saturday lunch, Sunday and Bank Holidays – **M** a la carte 8.15/11.55 **t.**
DZ c

XX **Rajdoot**, 83 Park St., BS1 5PJ, ☎ 28033, Indian rest. – ☒ AE ⑩ VISA
closed Sunday lunch, 25-26 December and Bank Holidays for lunch – **M** a la carte approx. 4.85 **t.**
CZ u

XX **Du Gourmet**, 43 Whiteladies Rd, BS8 2LS, ☎ 36230 – ☒ AE ⑩ VISA
closed Sunday, Monday, Good Friday and 1 week at Christmas – **M** (dinner only) a la carte 5.10/7.60 🍷 1.75.
AY v

XX **Rossi's**, 35 Princess Victoria St., Clifton, BS8 4BX, ☎ 30049, Italian rest. – ☒ AE ⑩ VISA
closed Sunday, Easter and 3 weeks August – **M** a la carte 4.45/7.25 **t.** 🍷 1.70.
AY a

X **Trattoria da Renato**, 19 King St., BS1 4EF, ☎ 298291, Italian rest.
closed Saturday lunch, Sunday, 2 weeks August and Bank Holidays – **M** a la carte 3.20/7.25 **t.**
DZ r

X **Rossi's N° 10**, 10 The Mall, Clifton, BS8 4DR, ☎ 36273, Italian rest. – ☒ AE ⑩ VISA
closed Sunday and Monday – **M** a la carte 3.40/4.90 **t.** 🍷 1.70.
AY e

at Hambrook NE: 5 ½ m. on A 4174 by M 32 – ✉ ☎ 0272 Bristol :

Bristol Eurocrest (Crest), Filton Rd, BS16 1QG, ☎ 564242, Telex 449376, ⇌, park – 🛗 TV 🚻wc 🚻wc ☎ ⴕ 🅿 ☑. ☒ AE ⑩ VISA
☕ 2.90 – **156 rm** 21.20/27.90 **st.**
BX o

MICHELIN Branch, Central Trading Estate, Pennywell Rd, BS5 0UB, ☎ 559802.

ALFA-ROMEO, SAAB 54/56 Redcliffe St. ☎ 27166
AUDI-NSU, MERCEDES-BENZ 20 Whitehouse St. ☎ 669331
AUSTIN-MG 36-56 West St. ☎ 662261
AUSTIN-MG 74-80 Staple Hill Rd 654776
AUSTIN-MG Station Rd, Kingswood ☎ 569911
AUSTIN-MG Feeder Rd ☎ 48051
AUSTIN-DAIMLER-JAGUAR-MORRIS-MG-ROVER-TRIUMPH, ROLLS ROYCE 11/15 Merchants Rd, Clifton ☎ 30361
AUSTIN-DAIMLER-JAGUAR-MORRIS-MG-ROVER-TRIUMPH 156 Cheltenham Rd ☎ 48051
BMW 33 Zetland Rd ☎ 45561
BMW, PEUGEOT Gloucester Rd North ☎ 692234
CITROEN 20 Whitehouse St. ☎ 669331
CITROEN, FIAT 724 Fishponds Rd ☎ 657247
DAIMLER-JAGUAR-MORRIS-MG-ROVER-TRIUMPH Avon St. ☎ 26531

DATSUN 168/176 Coronation Rd ☎ 631101
FORD 175/185 Muller Rd, Horfield ☎ 41175
FORD College Green ☎ 293881
LANCIA 47 Whiteladies Rd ☎ 37199
MORRIS-MG Church Rd ☎ 556381
MORRIS-MG 135 High St. ☎ 670011
MORRIS-MG Vale Lane ☎ 665070
OPEL Westbury Rd, Westbury-on-Trym ☎ 626172
RENAULT Marlborough St. ☎ 421816
ROVER-TRIUMPH 676 Fishponds Rd ☎ 655439
TALBOT 176-178 Kellaway Av. ☎ 49068
TALBOT 84 Downend Rd ☎ 567088
TOYOTA Gloucester Rd Patchway ☎ 693704
VAUXHALL Avon St. ☎ 70411
VAUXHALL Gloucester Rd ☎ 694331
VOLVO Berkeley Pl. ☎ 294191
VW, AUDI-NSU 55 Victoria St. ☎ 292956

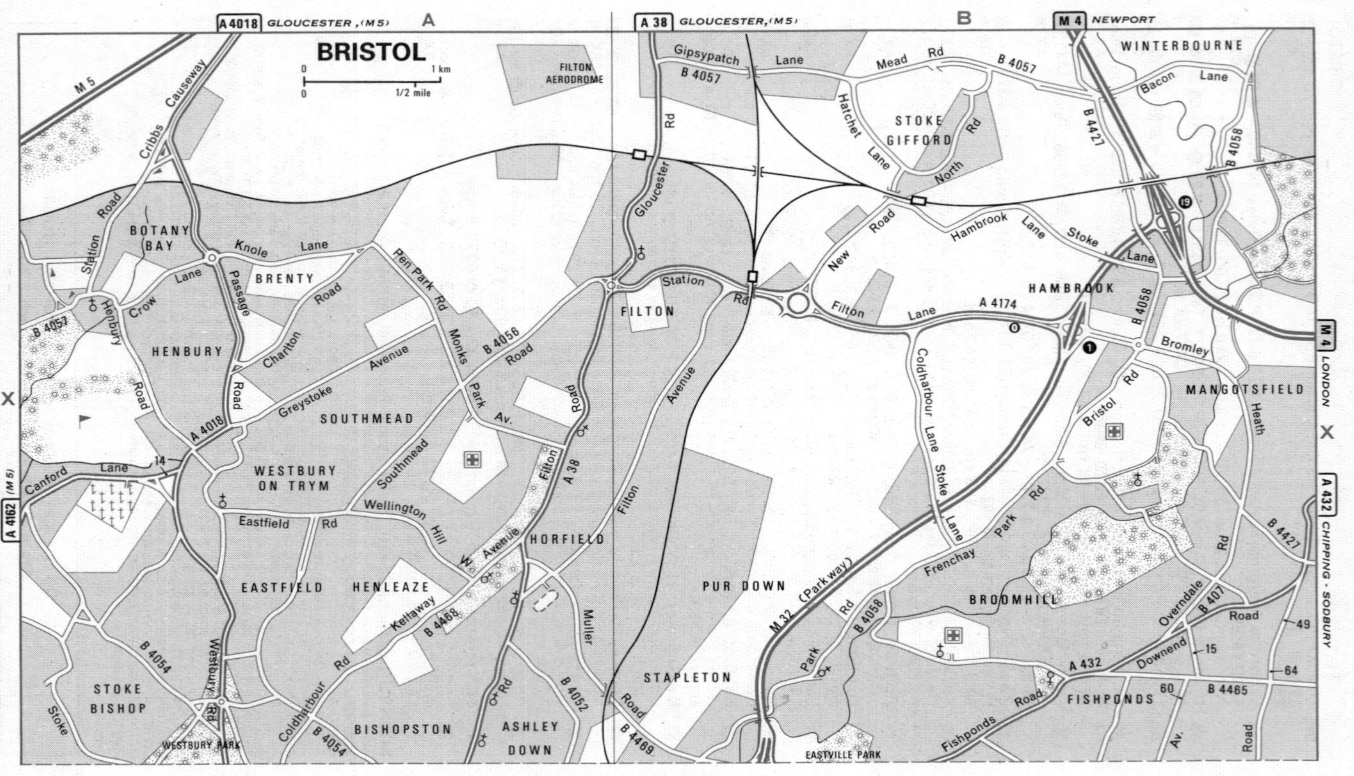
112
A 4018 GLOUCESTER ,(M5)
A
A 38 GLOUCESTER ,(M5)
B
M 4 NEWPORT
BRISTOL
1 km
1/2 mile
0
FILTON AERODROME
Gipsypatch Lane
B 4057
Mead Rd
B 4057
WINTERBOURNE
Bacon Lane
B 4427
B 4058
Hatchet Lane
STOKE GIFFORD
North Rd
Gloucester Rd
Road
Hambrook Lane
Stoke Lane
19
M 5
Cribbs Causeway
Station Road
BOTANY BAY
Knole Lane
BRENTY
Passage
Crow Lane
New
Filton Lane
HAMBROOK
A 4174
B 4058
M 4 LONDON
Henbury
B 4057
HENBURY
Charlton Road
Pen Park Rd
Monks Road
B 4056
Station Rd
FILTON
Bristol Rd
Bromley
MANGOTSFIELD
Heath
X
Greystoke Avenue
SOUTHMEAD
Park Av.
Road
A 38
Filton
Avenue
Coldharbour Lane Stoke Lane
Park Rd
B 4427
A 4162 (M 5)
Canford Lane
14
WESTBURY ON TRYM
Wellington Hill
HORFIELD
Filton
PUR DOWN
Frenchay
X
A 432 CHIPPING - SODBURY
Eastfield Rd
W. Avenue
Muller
M 32 (Parkway)
B 4058
BROOMHILL
Overndale Rd
B 407
Road
49
EASTFIELD
HENLEAZE
Kellaway
B 4468
Rd
B 4052
Park Rd
A 432
Downend
15
64
B 4054
Westbury Rd
Coldharbour Rd
B 4054
Road
STAPLETON
Fishponds Road
60
B 4465
STOKE BISHOP
Stoke
WESTBURY PARK
BISHOPSTON
ASHLEY DOWN
B 4469
EASTVILLE PARK
FISHPONDS
Av.
Road

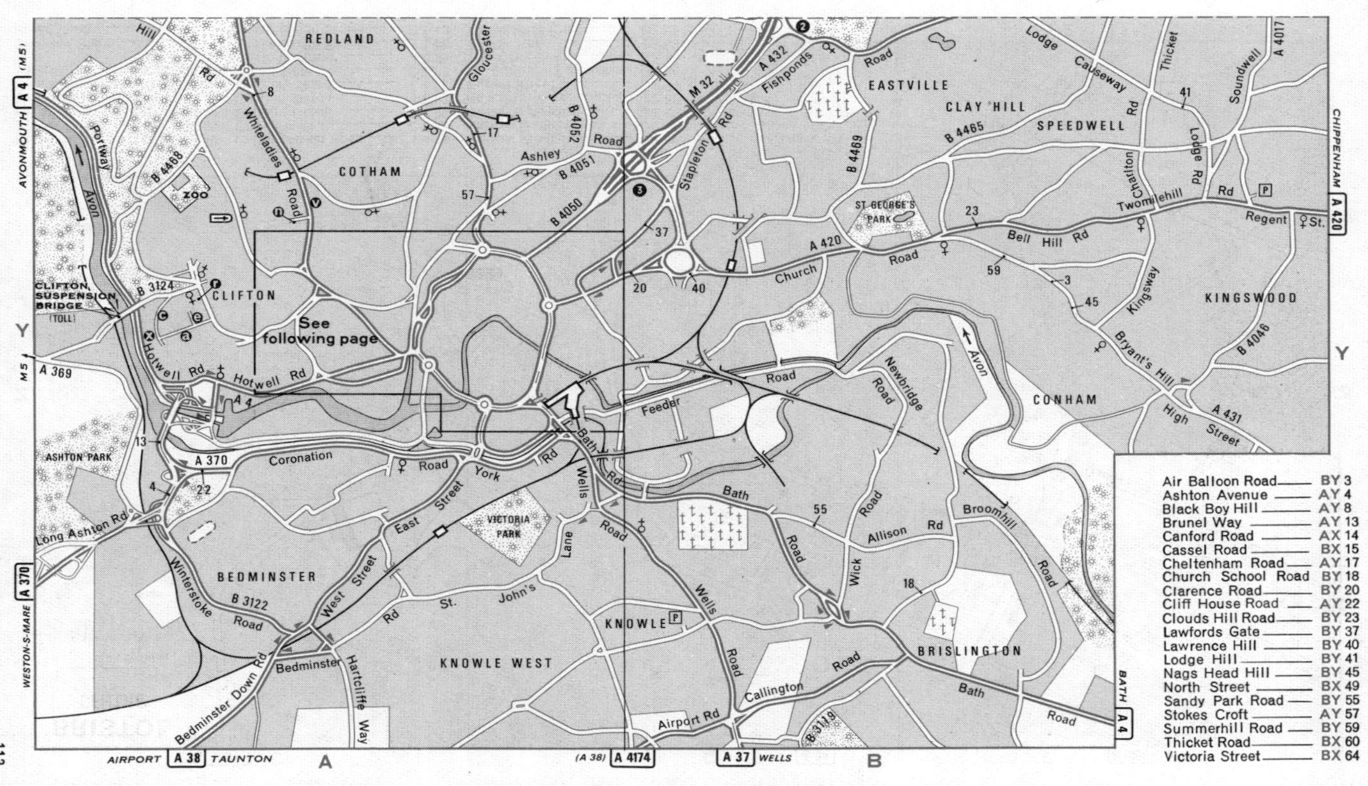

REDLAND
Gloucester Road
Hill
Portway
Avon
B 4468
ZOO
COTHAM
Ashley
Whiteladies Road
B 4052
B 4051
B 4050
Road
Stapleton Rd
M 32
A 432
Fishponds
EASTVILLE
CLAY HILL
B 4469
B 4465
SPEEDWELL
Lodge Causeway
Thicket
Soundwell
A 4017
CHIPPENHAM A 420
Lodge Rd
Chariton Rd
Twomilehill
Regent St.
ST GEORGE'S PARK
A 420
Church Road
Bell Hill Rd
Kingsway
Bryant's Hill
KINGSWOOD
B 4046
CLIFTON SUSPENSION BRIDGE (TOLL)
B 3124
CLIFTON
Hotwell Rd
Hotwell Rd
A 4
A 369
M 5
AVONMOUTH A 4 (M5)
A 4
See following page
Newbridge Road
Avon
CONHAM
High Street
A 431
Feeder
Bath Rd
ASHTON PARK
A 370
Coronation Road
York Street
East Street
Long Ashton Rd
WESTON-S-MARE A 370
BEDMINSTER
B 3122
Winterstoke Road
West Street
Rd
St. John's Lane
Wells Road
Bedminster Down Rd
Hartcliffe Way
Bedminster
KNOWLE WEST
VICTORIA PARK
Bath
Wells Road
Allison Rd
Wick Road
Broomhill Road
Road
Bath Road
B 3119
KNOWLE
Airport Rd
Callington Road
BRISLINGTON
AIRPORT A 38 TAUNTON
(A 38) A 4174
A 37 WELLS
BATH A 4
Air Balloon Road — BY 3
Ashton Avenue — AY 4
Black Boy Hill — AY 8
Brunel Way — AY 13
Canford Road — AX 14
Cassel Road — BX 15
Cheltenham Road — AY 17
Church School Road — BY 18
Clarence Road — BY 20
Cliff House Road — AY 22
Clouds Hill Road — BY 23
Lawfords Gate — BY 37
Lawrence Hill — BY 40
Lodge Hill — BY 41
Nags Head Hill — BY 45
North Street — BX 49
Sandy Park Road — BY 55
Stokes Croft — AY 57
Summerhill Road — BY 59
Thicket Road — BX 60
Victoria Street — BX 64
Y
Y
A
B

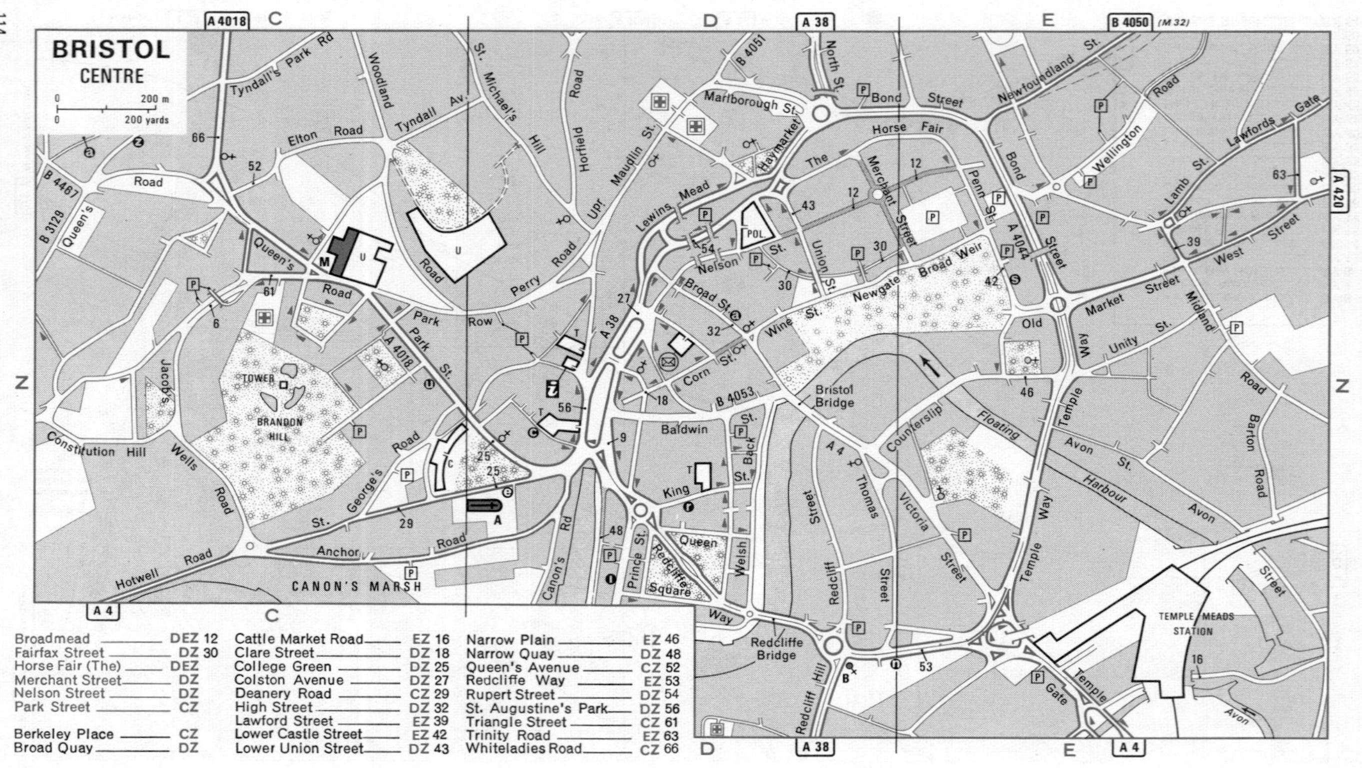

BRISTOL
CENTRE
200 m
200 yards
Broadmead —— DEZ 12
Fairfax Street —— DZ 30
Horse Fair (The) —— DEZ
Merchant Street —— DZ
Nelson Street —— DZ
Park Street —— CZ
Berkeley Place —— CZ
Broad Quay —— DZ
Cattle Market Road —— EZ 16
Clare Street —— DZ 18
College Green —— DZ 25
Colston Avenue —— DZ 27
Deanery Road —— CZ 29
High Street —— DZ 32
Lawford Street —— EZ 39
Lower Castle Street —— EZ 42
Lower Union Street —— DZ 43
Narrow Plain —— EZ 46
Narrow Quay —— DZ 48
Queen's Avenue —— CZ 52
Redcliffe Way —— EZ 53
Rupert Street —— DZ 54
St. Augustine's Park —— DZ 56
Triangle Street —— CZ 61
Trinity Road —— EZ 63
Whiteladies Road —— CZ 66

BRIXHAM Devon **403** J 32 – pop. 12,000 – ECD : Wednesday – ☎ 080 45.

⑦ Brixham Theatre, Market St. ☏ 2861 (summer only).

London 230 – Exeter 30 – Plymouth 32 – Torquay 8.

Quayside, 41-49 King St., TQ5 9TJ, ☏ 3051, ≼ harbour – ⓉⓋ ⌂wc ☎ Ⓟ. ◪ AE ⓪ VISA
M 4.25/4.50 s. ▯ 1.50 – **41 rm** ☷ 10.50/21.50 s.

Smuggler's Haunt, Church Hill East, TQ5 8HH, ☏ 3050 – ⌂wc
M a la carte 2.05/6.45 t. ▯ 1.40 – **14 rm** ☷ 9.05/18.10 t.

XX Randalls, 3 The Strand, ☏ 3357, French rest. – ◪ AE ⓪ VISA
closed Monday dinner, 2 weeks September and 2 weeks February – **M** (dinner only) a la carte 6.15/7.00 ▯ 2.30.

at Churston Ferrers W : 2 m. off A 3022 – ✉ Brixham – ☎ 0803 Churston :

Broadsands Links ⑤, Bascombe Rd, TQ5 0JT, ☏ 842360, ≼, 🗶, 🛋 – ⌂wc ☎ Ⓟ
25 rm.

Churston Court, TQ5 8DB, ☏ 842186, 🛋 – ⌂wc 📶 Ⓟ
8 rm.

AUSTIN-DAIMLER-JAGUAR-MORRIS-MG-ROVER-   FORD Churston Ferrers ☏ 0803 (Churston) 842245
TRIUMPH Milton St. ☏ 2474/3971   RENAULT New Rd ☏ 2266

BROADSTAIRS Kent **404** Y 29 – pop. 20,048 (inc. St. Peter's) – ECD : Wednesday – ☎ 0843 Thanet.

See : Bleak House (stayed in by Charles Dickens) *AC.*

🔟₈ North Foreland ☏ 62140, 1 ½ m. Broadstairs Station.

⑦ Pierremont Hall ☏ 68399.

London 77 – Dover 22 – Maidstone 46 – Margate 3.

Castlemere ⑤, Western Esplanade, CT10 1TD, ☏ 61566, ≼, 🛋 – ⓉⓋ ⌂wc Ⓟ
M (bar lunch Monday to Saturday) 4.30/5.55 st. ▯ 1.50 – **40 rm** ☷ 14.10/28.20 st.

Velindré, 10 Western Esplanade, CT10 1TG, ☏ 61485, ≼, 🛋 – 📶 Ⓟ. ◪ VISA
M (buffet lunch) 3.00/4.50 ▯ 1.65 – **15 rm** ☷ 8.50/9.50 t. – P 10.50/12.50 t.

Royal Albion, Albion St., CT10 1LU, ☏ 62116, ≼, 🛋 – ⓉⓋ ⌂wc 📶wc ☎ Ⓟ. ◪ AE ⓪ VISA
M 3.95/4.35 st. – **22 rm** ☷ 10.00/20.00 st. – P 17.00/20.00 st.

↑ Corner Ways, 49-51 Westcliff Rd, CT10 1PY, ☏ 61612
closed November and December – **12 rm** ☷ 6.25/12.50 s.

↑ Bay Tree, 12 Eastern Esplanade, CT10 1PS, ☏ 62502, ≼, 🛋 – Ⓟ
9 rm ☷ 6.00/20.00 t.

↑ Keston Court, 14 Ramsgate Rd, CT10 1PS, ☏ 62401 – Ⓟ
10 rm ☷ 6.50/13.00 st.

XX Marchesi, 18 Albion St., CT10 1LU, ☏ 62481 – Ⓟ. ◪ AE ⓪ VISA
M a la carte 5.55/9.25 t. ▯ 1.45.

at Kingsgate N : 2 m. on B 2052 – ✉ Broadstairs – ☎ 0843 Thanet :

Castle Keep, Joss Bay Rd, CT10 3PQ, ☏ 65222, Telex 896570, ≼, ⌁ heated, 🛋 – ⌂wc ☎ Ⓟ. ◪ AE ⓪ VISA
M 4.50/5.50 st. ▯ 2.50 – **30 rm** ☷ 21.50/26.00 st.

XX Fayreness with rm, Marine Drive, off Kingsgate Av., CT10 3LG, ☏ 61103, ≼, 🛋 – ⓉⓋ ⌂wc 📶wc Ⓟ. ◪ AE ⓪ VISA
closed Sunday dinner and Monday – **M** 4.50/7.50 t. ▯ 2.00 – **8 rm** ☷ 10.50/20.00 t.

FIAT ☏ 623 33   TALBOT Ramsgate Rd ☏ 63531

BROADSTONE Dorset **403 404** O 31 – see Poole.

BROADWATER Herts. **404** T 28 – see Stevenage.

BROADWAY Heref. and Worc. **403 404** O 27 – pop. 2,503 – ECD : Thursday – ☎ 0386.

London 93 – Birmingham 36 – Cheltenham 15 – Worcester 22.

Lygon Arms, High St., WR12 7DU, ☏ 852255, Telex 338260, « Part 15C inn », 🗶,
🛋 – ⓉⓋ ♿ Ⓟ. ⚓. ◪ AE ⓪ VISA
M 5.50/8.25 st. – ☷ 4.00 – **67 rm** 26.50/45.00 st.

Broadway, The Green, WR12 7AB, ☏ 852401, 🛋 – ⌂wc ☎ Ⓟ. ◪ AE ⓪ VISA
M 4.60/6.15 t. ▯ 1.85 – **24 rm** ☷ 13.00/24.00 t.

Collin House ⑤, Collin Lane, WR12 7DB, W : 1 ¼ m. on A 44, ☏ 858354, 🛋 – ⌂wc
Ⓟ. ◪ AE
closed 24 December-January – **M** (bar lunch) 4.00/7.40 t. ▯ 3.00 – **6 rm** ☷ 16.50/27.00 t.

Milestone House, 122 High St., WR12 7AL, ☏ 853432, 🛋 – Ⓟ
closed Christmas-January – **M** 4.00/6.00 st. ▯ 1.50 – **6 rm** ☷ 14.00/21.00 st. – P 18.00 st.

↑ Halfway House, 89 High St., WR12 7AL, ☏ 852237 – Ⓟ
6 rm ☷ 10.00/14.00 st.

XX Hunters Lodge, High St., WR12 7DT, ☏ 853247, 🛋 – Ⓟ. ◪ AE ⓪ VISA
closed Sunday dinner, Monday and 2 to 23 January – **M** a la carte 3.40/4.45 ▯ 1.60.

AUSTIN-MORRIS Cheltenham Rd ☏ 2424

BROADWINDSOR Dorset 🄰🄳🄳 L 31 – pop. 1,021 – ✉ Beaminster – ☏ 030 86.
London 148 – Exeter 37 – Taunton 26 – Weymouth 26.

⚓ **Broadwindsor House** ⌖, Beaminster Rd, DT8 3TX, ☏ 353, ≼, ⌗ – ⌂wc Ⓟ
closed February – **M** (bar lunch Monday to Saturday) 5.00 – **12 rm** ⇌ 9.20/25.40.

BROCKENHURST Hants. 🄰🄳🄳 🄰🄳🄳 P 31 – pop. 2,599 – ECD : Wednesday – ☏ 059 02.
🚗 ☏ 0703 (Southampton) 27948.
London 99 – Bournemouth 17 – Southampton 14 – Winchester 27.

🏨 **Balmer Lawn** (Myddleton), Lyndhurst Rd, SO4 7ZB, ☏ 3116, ≼, ⌗, ⌇ heated, ⌗ –
🅑 📺 🚗 Ⓟ. 🅰. 🅰 AE ⓞ VISA
closed 29 December-5 January – **M** 5.20/6.50 st. ⌕ 2.00 – **60 rm** ⇌ 23.00/42.00 st.

🏨 **Brockenhurst** ⌖, Rhinefield Rd, SO4 7ZF, ☏ 2557, ⌗ – ⌂wc Ⓟ. 🅰 AE ⓞ VISA
March-October – **M** (dinner only and Sunday lunch) 6.95 t. ⌕ 2.50 – **14 rm** ⇌ 11.50/
25.00 t.

🏨 **Carey's Manor**, Lyndhurst Rd, SO4 7RH, ☏ 3551, Telex 47442, ⌗ – 📺 ⌂wc ☎ ♿
Ⓟ. 🅰 AE ⓞ VISA
M 3.95/6.95 st. ⌕ 2.45 – **57 rm** ⇌ 16.95/29.90 st.

🏨 Forest Park, Rhinefield Rd, SO4 7ZG, ☏ 2108, ≼, ⌗, ⌇ heated, ⌗ – 📺 ⌂wc ☎ ♿ Ⓟ
40 rm.

🏠 Watersplash, The Rise, SO4 7ZP, ☏ 2344, ⌇ heated, ⌗ – ⌂wc ♿ Ⓟ. 🅰 VISA
M 3.50/4.50 st. ⌕ 1.80 – **27 rm** ⇌ 12.50/28.00 st. – P 14.50/17.50 st.

AUSTIN-MORRIS-MG-WOLSELEY Sway Rd ☏ 3344   SAAB 24 Brookley Rd ☏ 3464

BROME Suffolk 🄰🄳🄳 X 26 – see Eye.

BROMLEY CROSS Greater Manchester 🄰🄳🄳 M 23 – see Bolton.

BROMPTON-BY-SAWDON North Yorks. – pop. 572 – ✉ ☏ 0723 Scarborough.
London 242 – Kingston-upon-Hull 44 – Scarborough 8 – York 31.

✗ Brompton Forge, YO13 9DP, ☏ 85409 – Ⓟ.

BROMSGROVE Heref. and Worc. 🄰🄳🄳 🄰🄳🄳 N 26 – pop. 30,210 – ECD : Thursday – ☏ 0527.
🄸 47/49 Worcester Rd ☏ 31809.
London 117 – Birmingham 14 – Bristol 71 – Worcester 13.

🏨 Perry Hall (Embassy), 8 Kidderminster Rd, B61 7JN, ☏ 31976 – 📺 ⌂wc 🕳wc ☎ Ⓟ. 🅰
50 rm.

AUSTIN-MORRIS 126 Worcester Rd ☏ 31313   SAAB Windsor St. ☏ 75210
AUSTIN-MG-ROVER-TRIUMPH-WOLSELEY 52 Bir-   VAUXHALL 137 Birmingham Rd ☏ 71244
mingham Rd ☏ 72212   VW, AUDI 212 Station St. ☏ 72071
FORD 184/188 Worcester Rd ☏ 31178

BROOK Hants. 🄰🄳🄳 🄰🄳🄳 P 30 – pop. 572 – ECD : Tuesday – ✉ Lyndhurst – ☏ 042 127
Cadnam.
🅁, 🅁 Bramshaw ☏ 3252.
London 81 – Bournemouth 33 – Southampton 13.

🏨 Bell, SO4 7HE, ☏ 2214, 🅁 – ⌂wc Ⓟ
M 4.00/6.50 t. ⌕ 1.85 – **11 rm** ⇌ 13.00/28.00 t.

BROXTON Cheshire 🄰🄳🄳 L 24 – see Chester.

BRUSHFORD Somerset 🄰🄳🄳 J 30 – pop. 457 – ✉ ☏ 0398 Dulverton.
London 195 – Exeter 24 – Minehead 18 – Taunton 24.

🏨 Carnarvon Arms, TA22 9AE, ☏ 23302, ⌗, ⌇ heated, ⌐, ⌗, park – ⌂wc Ⓟ. 🅰E
closed 3 days at Christmas – **M** 5.30/7.00 t. – **27 rm** ⇌ 12.00/27.00 t. – P 21.00 t.

🏠 Three Acres Country House ⌖, TA22 9AR, ☏ 23426, ≼, « Country house atmosphere »
⌗' – Ⓟ
May-October – **M** (bar lunch) approx. 6.00 t. ⌕ 1.40 – **7 rm** ⇌ 7.50/15.60 t. – P 16.00 t.

BRYNBUGA Gwent 🄰🄳🄳 L 28 – see Usk.

BUCKDEN Cambs. **404** T 27 – pop. 2,010 – ECD : Wednesday – ✉ ☺ 0480 Huntingdon.
London 65 – Bedford 16 – Huntingdon 4.5.

   🏠 **Lion** (T.H.F.), Great North Rd, PE18 9XA, ☏ 810313 – 📺 ☎ **P**. 🔌 AE ⓪ *VISA*
   M 4.25/8.50 ◊ 1.65 – **11 rm** ☲ 13.50/18.00 st.

   🏠 **George,** High St., PE18 9XA, ☏ 810304, 🚗 – **P**. 🔌 *VISA*
   M *(closed Sunday dinner and Monday to non-residents)* (bar lunch) 5.00 **t.** ◊ 2.30 –
   12 rm ☲ 10.75/18.70 st.

BUCKFASTLEIGH Devon **403** I 32 – pop. 2,656 – ECD : Wednesday – ☺ 036 44.
See : Buckfast Abbey (the Sacrament Chapel*).
London 223 – Exeter 23 – Plymouth 20.

   ⌂ Furzeleigh Mill, Dart Bridge, TQ11 0JP, NE: ¾ m. on old A 38 ☏ 2245, 🚗 – **P**
   18 rm.

   ✗ **Country Fare,** 54 Fore St., TQ11 0BS, ☏ 2383 – 🔌 AE ⓪ *VISA*
   closed Monday – **M** a la carte 4.45/6.00 **t.** ◊ 2.10.

BUCKHURST HILL Essex **404** H 29 – pop. 11,683 – ECD : Wednesday – ☺ 01 London.
London 13 – Chelmsford 25.

   🏨 **Roebuck** (T.H.F.), High Rd, IG9 1QX, ☏ 505 4636 – 📺 ⛁wc ☎ **P**. 🛁. 🔌 AE ⓪ *VISA*
   M 3.75/4.45 st. ◊ 1.65 – **26 rm** ☲ 14.50/22.00 st.

BUCKINGHAM Bucks. **403** **404** R 27 – pop. 5,076 – ECD : Thursday – ☺ 028 02.
Envir. : Claydon House* (Rococo interior** : Chinese Room** staircase***, Florence Nightingale Museum) *AC,* SE : 8 m. – Stowe School 18C (south front*, Marble Saloon*, park :
monuments* 18C, ≼* from the Lake Pavilions) *AC,* NW : 4 ½ m.
London 64 – Birmingham 61 – Northampton 20 – Oxford 25.

   🏠 **White Hart** (T.H.F.), Market Sq., MK18 1NL, ☏ 2131 – 📺 ⛁wc ☎ **P**. 🛁. 🔌 AE ⓪ *VISA*
   M 5.50/8.50 st. ◊ 1.65 – **21 rm** ☲ 13.50/21.00 st.

   ⚓ **Swan and Castle,** Castle St., MK18 1BS, ☏ 3082 – **P**. 🔌 AE ⓪ *VISA*
   closed Sunday and Bank Holidays – **M** a la carte 3.35/6.10 **t.** – **7 rm** ☲ 8.70/16.00 st.

AUSTIN-MORRIS-MG 14/18 High St. ☏ 3153   VAUXHALL School Lane ☏ 2209
AUSTIN-MORRIS-MG-ROVER-TRIUMPH Chandos Rd
☏ 2121

BUCKLAND IN THE MOOR Devon **403** I 32 – pop. 79 – ☺ 0364 Ashburton.
London 225 – Exeter 25 – Plymouth 28.

   🏠 **Buckland Hall** 🐾, TQ13 7HL, ☏ 52679, ≼ countryside and Holne Moor, 🚗, park –
   ⛁wc **P**
   Easter-mid October – **M** (buffet lunch) approx. 6.00 ◊ 1.50 – **6 rm** ☲ 14.00/24.00 –
   P 19.00/22.00.

BUCKLERS HARD Hants. **403** **404** P 31 – see Beaulieu.

BUCKLOW HILL Cheshire **403** **404** M 24 – see Knutsford.

BUDE Cornwall **403** G 31 – pop. 4,069 – ECD : Thursday – ☺ 0288.
▯₁₈ ☏ 2006 – ▯₉ Holsworthy ☏ 0409 (Holsworthy) 253177, E: 8 ½ m.
🛈 Bencoolen Rd ☏ 4240 (summer only).
London 252 – Exeter 51 – Plymouth 44 – Truro 53.

   🏨 **Strand,** The Strand, EX23 8RU, ☏ 3222 – 📶 📺 ⛁wc ☎ **P**. 🔌 AE ⓪ *VISA*
   M 4.50/8.00 ◊ 1.70 – **40 rm** ☲ 17.00/27.50 st.

   🏨 **Falcon,** EX23 8SD, ☏ 2005, 🚗 – ⛁wc ▥wc **P**. AE ⓪ *VISA*
   May-September – **M** (buffet lunch) approx. 5.50 **s.** ◊ 1.65 – ☲ 2.30 – **47 rm** 9.45/22.20 **s.**

   🏨 **Hartland,** Hartland Terrace, EX23 8JY, ☏ 2509, 🏊 heated – 📺 ⛁wc ▥wc **P**
   Easter-September – **M** 3.60/4.80 ◊ 1.40 – **30 rm** ☲ 14.80/27.60 – P 20.80/23.00.

   🏠 **Burn Court,** Burn View, EX23 8DB, ☏ 2872 – ⛁wc ▥wc **P**
   closed 4 November-8 December and Christmas – **M** *(closed Sunday lunch)* 3.25/4.75
   ◊ 1.50 – **34 rm** ☲ 11.50/30.00.

   🏠 **Maer Lodge,** Maer Down, EX23 8NG, ☏ 3306, 🚗 – ▥ **P**
   Easter-September – **M** (bar lunch) approx. 3.50 **s.** ◊ 1.50 – **23 rm** ☲ 7.50/16.00 **s.** –
   P 10.50/12.00 **s.**

   ⌂ **Grosvenor,** Summerleaze Crescent, EX23 8HH, ☏ 2062 – ▥wc **P**
   April-October – **12 rm** ☲ 7.00/16.50 **st.**

   ⌂ **Florida,** 17-18 Summerleaze Crescent, EX23 8HJ, ☏ 2451 – ▥wc **P**
   Easter-October – **20 rm** ☲ 6.50/14.50 **s.**

   ⌂ **Chough,** Marine Drive, EX23 0LZ, S: 1 ½ m. on coast Rd ☏ 2386, 🚗 – ⛁wc **P**
   30 May-September – **12 rm** ☲ 7.50/17.00.

at Widemouth Bay S : 2 ½ m. – ✉ Bude – ☎ 028 885 Widemouth Bay :

⋔ **Trelawny,** Marine Drive, EX23 0AH, ☏ 328, ⋖ – **P**. ◪ AE VISA
Easter-September – **10 rm** � 8.50/17.00 **st.**

AUSTIN-DAIMLER-JAGUAR-MORRIS-MG-ROVER-
TRIUMPH Bencoolen Rd ☏ 2146

DAF Widemouth Bay ☏ 028 885 (Widemouth Bay) 279
FORD Bencoolen Rd ☏ 2914

BUDLEIGH SALTERTON Devon **403** K 32 – pop. **4,157** – ECD : Thursday – ☎ 039 54.
Envir. : Bicton Gardens* *AC*, N : 3 ½ m.
🛈 Rolle Car Park, High St. ☏ 5275 (summer only).
London 215 – Exeter 16 – Plymouth 55.

🏨 **Rosemullion** ⌁, Cliff Rd, EX9 6JX, ☏ 2288, ⋖ – ▯ ⌂wc ☎ **P**
30 rm.

🏛 **Southlands,** 9 Marine Par., EX9 6NS, ☏ 3497, ⋖ – ⌂wc **P**
M 4.50/5.30 **st.** ⌕ 1.50 – **20 rm** ⊸ 10.60/23.50 **st.**

⋔ **Nattore Lodge,** 11 West Hill, EX9 6BT, ☏ 2736, 🚗 – ⌂wc **P**
April-mid October – **9 rm** ⊸ 8.15/18.50.

AUSTIN-MG ☏ 2277

BUDOCK VEAN Cornwall **403** E 33 – see Falmouth.

BULKINGTON Warw. **403 404** P 26 – see Nuneaton.

BULPHAN Essex **404** V 29 – ✉ Upminster – ☎ 0375 Grays Thurrock.
London 26 – Chelmsford 17.

🏨 Ye Olde Plough House Motel, Brentwood Rd, RM14 3SR, ☏ 891592, ✗, ⊿ heated,
🚗 – TV ⌂wc ▥wc ☎ **P**. ◪ AE ⓞ VISA
60 rm.

BUNWELL Norfolk **404** X 26 – pop. **738** – ECD : Monday and Wednesday – ☎ 095 389.
London 102 – Cambridge 51 – Norwich 16.

🏛 **Bunwell Manor** ⌁, Bunwell St., NR16 1QU, NW: 1 m. off B 1113 ☏ 317, 🚗 –
⌂wc ▥ **P**. ◪ VISA
closed January – **M** (bar lunch) approx. 4.50 **st.** – **10 rm** ⊸ 9.50/21.00 **st.**

BURBAGE Wilts. **403 404** O 29 – see Marlborough.

BURFORD Oxon. **403 404** P 28 – pop. **1,255** (inc. Upton and Signet) – ECD : Wednesday –
☎ 099 382.
See : St. John's Church* 12C-14C.
Envir. : Swinbrook (church : Fettiplace Monuments*) E : 3 ½ m. – Cotswold Wildlife Park* *AC*,
S : 2 m.
⛳ ☏ 2149.
🛈 The Burford Welsh Shop, High St. ☏ 2168.
London 76 – Birmingham 55 – Gloucester 32 – Oxford 20.

🏨 **Bay Tree,** Sheep St., OX8 4LW, ☏ 3137, 🚗 – ⌂wc ⌁ **P**
M 2.60/4.45 **t.** – **24 rm** ⊸ 14.00/28.00 **st.**

🏛 **Inn For All Seasons,** The Barringtons, OX8 4TN, W: 3 ¼ m. on A 40 ☏ 045 14
(Windrush) 324, 🚗 – ⌂wc **P**. AE
closed 24 to 31 December – **M** a la carte 3.20/5.00 **st.** ⌕ 2.00 – **8 rm** ⊸ 14.00/22.00 **st.**

🏛 Winter's Tale, OX8 4PH, SE: ½ m. on A 40 ☏ 3176 – ⌂wc **P**
8 rm.

🏛 Bull, High St., OX8 4RH, ☏ 2220 – ⌂wc
12 rm.

🏛 **Lamb Inn,** Sheep St., OX8 4LR, ☏ 3155, 🚗 – ⌂wc ⌁
M 4.50 **t.** ⌕ 1.30 – **14 rm** ⊸ 10.00/22.00 **st.** – P 17.00/18.00 **st.**

🍴 **Corner House,** High St., OX8 4RJ, ☏ 3151
closed January and first 2 weeks February – **M** a la carte 4.10/4.50 **t.** ⌕ 1.80 – **10 rm** ⊸
7.50/17.00 **t.**

BURGH HEATH Surrey **404** T 30 – see Banstead.

BURHAM Kent **404** V 30 – pop. **1,843** – ✉ Rochester – ☎ 0634 Medway.
London 35 – Maidstone 5.

🍴🍴 **Toastmaster's Inn,** Church St., ME1 3SD, ☏ 61299 – **P**. VISA
closed Sunday, Monday, 2 weeks September and 1 week at Christmas – **M** (booking essential) a la carte 7.15/8.55 ⌕ 2.25.

BURLEY Hants. 403 404 0 31 – pop. 1,552 – ECD : Wednesday – ✉ Ringwood – ☎ 042 53.
☞₉ ☏ 2431.
London 102 – Bournemouth 17 – Southampton 17 – Winchester 30.

- 🏠 **Moorhill House** ⤵, BH24 4AH, ☏ 3285, 🚭 – 🛏wc 🛁wc 🅿. 🔄 AE ⓪ VISA
  M (bar lunch) 3.00/7.00 **st.** 🍷 1.45 – **25 rm** ⌧ 13.50/27.00 **t.** – P 22.00/24.00 **st.**
- ⚲ **Highcroft** ⤵, Highcroft Woods, BH24 4AG, ☏ 2525, ⟨, 🍽, 🚭 – 🅿
  closed Christmas – **11 rm** ⌧ 9.00/18.50 **st.**
- ⚲ **Tree House,** The Cross, BH24 4AB, ☏ 3448, 🚭 – 🅿. 🔄 AE
  8 rm ⌧ 8.50/16.00 **st.**
- ✗✗ **White Buck Inn** with rm, Bisterne Close, BH24 4AX, SE: 1 m., ☏ 2264, 🚭, Dancing
  (Saturday) – 📺 🛁wc 🅿. 🔄 AE ⓪ VISA
  M (buffet lunch) 5.95/9.00 **st.** 🍷 2.00 – **7 rm** ⌧ 15.00/27.00 **st.**

BURN BRIDGE North Yorks. – see Harrogate.

BURNHAM Bucks. 404 S 29 – pop. 17,751 – ECD : Thursday – ☎ 062 86.
London 33 – Oxford 37 – Reading 17.

- 🏠 **Burnham Beeches** ⤵, Grove Rd, SL1 8DP, ☏ 3333, 🍽, 🚭, park – 🛏wc 🕿 🅿. 🅰. ⓪
  VISA
  M 6.00/7.00 🍷 2.00 – ⌧ 3.00 – **54 rm** 18.00/24.00.
- ✗✗ **Grovefield** with rm, Taplow Common Rd, SL1 8LR, ☏ 3131, 🚭 – 🛏wc 🕿 🚗 🅿.
  🔄 AE ⓪ VISA
  closed 3 to 26 August and Bank Holidays – **M** *(closed Saturday lunch and Sunday)* a la
  carte 6.40/10.65 **t.** 🍷 2.65 – **8 rm** ⌧ 17.00/27.50 **st.**
- ✗ **La Baguette,** 21 High St., SL1 8TD, ☏ 3507, French rest.
  closed Monday dinner, Sunday, 1 week at Christmas and Bank Holidays – **M** a la carte
  4.15/5.90 🍷 2.00.

AUSTIN-MORRIS-MG-WOLSELEY 46/48 High St. ☏ 5255   VAUXHALL 71 Stomp Rd ☏ 4994

Si vous cherchez un hôtel tranquille,

ne consultez pas uniquement les cartes p. 50 à 60,

mais regardez également dans le texte les établissements indiqués avec le signe ⤵.

BURNHAM-ON-CROUCH Essex 404 W 29 – pop. 4,619 – ECD : Wednesday – ☎ 0621 Maldon.
London 52 – Chelmsford 19 – Colchester 32 – Southend-on-Sea 25.

- ✗✗ **Contented Sole,** 80 High St., CM0 8AA, ☏ 782139
  closed Sunday dinner, Monday, 2 weeks July and 23 December-February – **M** 4.50 **s.**
  🍷 1.45.
- ✗ **Boozles,** 4 Station Rd, CM0 8BG, ☏ 783167
  closed Sunday dinner, Monday except Bank Holidays and first 3 weeks January – **M** a la
  carte 4.75/5.95 🍷 1.20.

MORRIS-MG-WOLSELEY Station Rd ☏ 782130

BURNLEY Lancs. 986 ㉓ – pop. 76,513 – ☎ 0282.
Envir. : Towneley Hall* (16C-18C) SE: 1 m.
🏌 Towneley Park ☏ 38473 E: 1 ½ m. – 🏌 Glen View ☏ 21045.
London 228 – Bradford 32 – Leeds 37 – Liverpool 55 – Manchester 25 – Middlesbrough 85 – Preston 22 – Sheffield 67.

- 🏠 Burnley Crest (Crest), Keirby Walk, BB11 2DH, ☏ 27611 – 🛗 📺 🛏wc 🕿 🅿. 🅰. 🔄 AE
  ⓪ VISA
  ⌧ 2.40 – **48 rm** 18.00/24.50 **st.**
- ⚲ Rosehill House ⤵, Rosehill Av., Manchester Rd, BB11 2PW, ☏ 27116, 🚭 – 🅿
  11 rm.

AUSTIN-MG-WOLSELEY Church St. ☏ 21312   FORD Caldervale Rd ☏ 28311
CITROEN, TOYOTA Trafalgar St. ☏ 33311   MORRIS Todmorden Rd ☏ 36131
FIAT Accrington Rd ☏ 27328   VAUXHALL Accrington Rd ☏ 27321
FIAT, POLSKI Manchester Rd ☏ 26020   VW, AUDI-NSU Accrington Rd ☏ 31141

BURNSALL North Yorks. – pop. 109 – ECD : Tuesday – ✉ Skipton – ☎ 075 672.
🅸 Burnsall Car Park ☏ 295 (summer only).
London 223 – Bradford 26 – Leeds 29.

- ⚲ Red Lion, BD23 6BU, ☏ 204, 🚭 – 🅿
  8 rm.

BURTON-UPON-TRENT Staffs. 403 404 P 25 – pop. 50,201 – ECD : Wednesday – ☎ 0283.
🅸 Town Hall ☏ 45369.
London 128 – Birmingham 29 – Leicester 27 – Nottingham 27 – Stafford 27.

- ⚲ **Edgecote,** 179 Ashby Rd, DE15 0LB,E: 1 m. on A 50 ☏ 68966, 🚭 – 🅿
  closed Sunday dinner – **12 rm** ⌧ 7.50/14.00 **st.**

BURTON-UPON-TRENT

at Branston S : 2 ¼ m. off A 5121 (A 38) – ⊠ 🕾 0283 Burton-upon-Trent :

XXX **Riverside Inn** with rm, Riverside Drive, DE14 3EP, ☎ 63117 – 📺 ⇔wc 🅿. 🔄 *VISA*
M *(closed Sunday dinner)* a la carte 7.50/11.00 **st.** ⌕ 2.20 – **22 rm** 🖙 13.00/19.00 **st.**

XXX Stanhope Arms, with rm, Ashby Rd East, DE15 0PU, E : 2 ¼ m. on A 50 ☎ 217954,
🚗 – 📺 ⇔wc ⋔wc 🐾 🅿. ⚒
19 rm 🖙 15.00/21.00 **st.**

at Rolleston-on-Dove N : 2 ½ m. off A 50 – ⊠ 🕾 0283 Burton-upon-Trent :

XXX **Brookhouse Inn** ⌂ with rm, Brookside, DE13 9BD, ☎ 814188 – 📺 ⇔wc 🐾 🅿. 🔄
🔺 *VISA*
M *(closed Saturday lunch and Sunday)* a la carte 6.00/9.85 ⌕ 1.70 – **8 rm** 🖙 16.00/
24.00.

AUSTIN-JAGUAR-MORRIS-ROVER-TRIUMPH Moor St.
☎ 45353
AUSTIN-MORRIS-MG-WOLSELEY Derby Rd ☎ 45353
DATSUN   Scalpcliffe Rd ☎ 66677
FIAT   All Saints Rd ☎ 31336
FORD   Horninglow St. ☎ 61081

PEUGEOT   Tutbury Rd ☎ 61565
RENAULT   118 Horninglow Rd ☎ 67811
TALBOT, MERCENDES-BENZ, OPEL Derby Rd ☎
65432
VAUXHALL 12 Lichfield St. ☎ 61655
VOLVO   New St. ☎ 62282

BURWASH East Sussex 🗺 V 31 – pop. 1,140 – ⊠ Etchington – 🕾 0435.
London 55 – **Brighton** 27 – **Hastings** 19 –**Maidstone** 27 – **Royal Tunbridge Wells** 20.

🏨 **Burwash Motel,** High St., TN19 7HT, ☎ 882540 – 📺 ⇔wc 🐾 🅿
M a la carte 3.30/6.25 **t.** ⌕ 1.50 – 🖙 2.00 – **8 rm** 10.00/16.00 **st.**

Orte mit ruhigen und abseits gelegenen Hotels
finden Sie auf der Karte S. 50-60 ;
die ruhigen Hotels sind im Text durch das Zeichen ⌂ *gekennzeichnet.*

BURY ST. EDMUNDS Suffolk 🗺 W 27 – pop. 25,661 – ECD : Thursday – 🕾 0284.
See : St. Mary's Church★ 15C (the Angel roof★★).
Envir. : Ickworth House★ (18C) *AC*, SW : 3 m.
🏌 Westley Rd ☎ 5979, W : 2 m.
🛈 Abbey Gardens, Angel Hill ☎ 64667 (summer only).
London 79 – **Cambridge** 27 – **Ipswich** 26 – **Norwich** 41.

🏨 **Angel,** 3 Angel Hill, IP33 1LT, ☎ 3926, Telex 81630 – 📺 🅿. ⚒. 🔄 🔺 ⓞ *VISA*
M a la carte 5.95/10.45 – **44 rm** 🖙 20.00/30.00.

🏨 **Suffolk** (T.H.F.), 38 The Butter Market, IP33 1DC, ☎ 3995 – 📺 ⇔wc 🐾 🅿. 🔄 🔺
ⓞ *VISA*
M 4.00/5.20 **st.** ⌕ 1.65 – **41 rm** 🖙 14.00/22.50 **st.**

AUSTIN-DAIMLER-JAGUAR-MG-ROVER-TRIUMPH
76 Risbygate St. ☎ 31015
FIAT   Mildenhall Rd ☎ 3280
FORD   5 Fornham Rd ☎ 2332
MORRIS-MG-WOLSELEY Eastgate St. ☎ 3913

RENAULT   The Sheet Horringer ☎ 028488 (Horringer)
VAUXHALL Cotton Lane ☎ 5621
VOLVO   Out Risbygate ☎ 62444
VW, AUDI-NSU Northern Way, Bury St. ☎ 63441

BUTTERMERE Cumbria 🗺 ⑲ – pop. 257 – ⊠ Cockermouth – 🕾 059 685.
See : Lake★.
London 306 – **Carlisle** 35 – **Kendal** 43.

🏨 **Bridge.** CA13 9UZ, ☎ 252, ≼ – ⋔wc 🅿
April-October – **M** (bar lunch) approx. 6.50 **t.** ⌕ 2.00 – **24 rm** 🖙 11.50/24.00 **t.** – P 17.50 **t.**

🏠 **Dalegarth** ⌂, CA13 9XA, SE : 1 ¼ m. on B 5289 ☎ 233, ≼, 🚗, park – 🅿
April-October – **9 rm** 🖙 7.50/11.75 **st.**

BUTTINGTON Powys 🗺 K 25 – pop. 1,256 – ⊠ Welshpool – 🕾 093 874 Trewern.
London 180 – **Birmingham** 62 – **Shrewsbury** 17.

🏠 **Garth Derwen,** SY21 8SU, on A 458 ☎ 238, 🚗 – 🅿
closed mid December-mid January – **8 rm** 🖙 8.00/15.00 **st.**

BUXTON Derbs. 🗺 🗺 O 24 – pop. 20,324 – ECD : Wednesday – ⊠ Stockport – 🕾 0298.
Envir. : Tideswell (Parish church★ 14C) NE : 9 m.
🏌 Townend ☎ 3453, NE : on A 6 – 🏌 Gadley Lane ☎ 3494, ¾ m. Buxton Station.
🛈 St. Ann's Well, The Crescent ☎ 5106.
London 172 – **Derby** 38 – **Manchester** 25 – **Stoke-on-Trent** 24.

🏨 **Lee Wood,** 13 Manchester Rd, SK17 6TQ, on A 5002 ☎ 3002, 🚗 – 🛎 ⇔wc ⋔wc 🅿. ⚒.
🔄 🔺 ⓞ
M 4.50/5.60 **st.** ⌕ 1.50 – **40 rm** 🖙 13.50/25.00 **st.**

🏨 **Hartington,** 18 Broad Walk, SK17 6JR, ☎ 2638 – ⇔wc 🅿
closed 24 December-3 January – **M** (dinner only) 4.60 **st.** ⌕ 1.50 – **14 rm** 🖙 7.50/17.00 **st.**

AUSTIN-MORRIS Brierlow Bar ℡ 3801
AUSTIN-JAGUAR-MORRIS-ROVER-TRIUMPH Spring
Gardens ℡ 2321
FIAT 26 Lightwood Rd ℡ 2460

HONDA, SAAB Leek Rd ℡ 2494
OPEL Leek Rd ℡ 3466
RENAULT The Old Court House ℡ 3947
TALBOT 9 Scarsdale Pl. ℡ 2796

BWLCHTOCYN Gwynedd **403** G 25 – see Abersoch.

CADNAM Hants. **403** **404** P 31 – pop. 2,500 – ECD : Wednesday – ☼ 042 127.
London 91 – Salisbury 16 – Southampton 8 – Winchester 19.

　XX **Le Chanteclerc,** Romsey Rd, SO4 2NX, on A 31 ℡ 3271, French rest. – **P.** AE VISA
　　closed Saturday lunch, Sunday, Monday, 2 weeks August and 2 weeks January – **M** a la
　　carte 7.25/9.45 **t.** 1.90.

CAERDYDD South Glam. – see Cardiff.

CAERFFILI Mid Glam. – see Caerphilly.

CAERFYRDDIN Dyfed – see Carmarthen.

CAERGYBI Gwynedd – see Holyhead.

CAERLEON Gwent **403** L 29 – pop. 4,700 – ECD : Thursday and Saturday – ☼ 0633.
See : Roman Amphitheatre* *AC.* – ℡ 420 342, W : 3 m. off M 4, junction 25.
London 144 – Cardiff 17 – Newport 3.

　　The Priory, High St., NP6 1XD, ℡ 421241, – TV wc **P.** AE ① VISA
　　M 3.70/4.15 **st.** 1.85 – 2.20 – **21 rm** 12.00/16.00 **st.**

ALFA-ROMEO Ponthir Rd ℡ 420563

CAERNARFON Gwynedd **403** H 24 – pop. 9,260 – ☼ 0286.
See : Castle*** 13C-14C (Royal Welsh Fusiliers Regimental museum*) *AC* – City walls*.
Envir. : SE: Snowdon (ascent and ☀***) 1 h 15 mn by Snowdon Mountain Railway (*AC*)
from Llanberis (Pass**) SE : 13 m. – Dinas Dindle * SW: 5 m.
🛈 Wales Tourist Office, Slate Quay ℡ 2232 (Easter-September).
London 249 – Birkenhead 76 – Chester 68 – Holyhead 30 – Shrewsbury 85.

　　at Llanwnda SW : 3 ½ m. off A 487 on A 499 – ✉ Caernarfon – ☼ 0286 Llanwnda:

　X **The Stables** with rm, LL54 5SD, ℡ 830711, – TV wc **P.** AE
　　M *(closed Sunday dinner to non-residents)* 5.00/6.00 **t.** 2.00 – **12 rm** 13.50/22.00 **t.** –
　　P 23.50/30.00 **t.**

CAERPHILLY (CAERFFILI) Mid Glam. **403** K 29 – pop. 29,400 – ☼ 0222.
See : Castle** 13C.
🛈 Twyn Car Park ℡ 863378 (Easter-September).
London 157 – Cardiff 8 – Newport 11.

　　Hotels and restaurants see : Cardiff S : 8 m.
　　　　　　　　　　　Newport (Gwent) E : 11 m.

CAERSWS Powys **403** J 26 – pop. 1,205 – ECD : Thursday – ☼ 068 684.
London 202 – Aberystwyth 38 – Newtown 6.

　　Maesmawr Hall , SY17 5SF, E : 1 m. on a 489 ℡ 255, , « 16C manor house in
　　large garden », park – wc wc **P.** AE ① VISA
　　M 3.75/7.60 1.50 – **22 rm** 11.50/23.00 – P 20.00/25.00.

AUSTIN-MORRIS-MG-WOLSELEY ℡ 345

CALNE Wilts. **403** **404** O 29 – pop. 9,688 – ECD : Wednesday – ✉ Chippenham – ☼ 0249.
Envir. : Bowood Mansion* (18C) *AC.* W : 3 ½ m.
🛈 Bishop's Cannings ℡ 038 086 (Cannings) 627, SE : 1 m. from A 4.
London 98 – Bristol 33 – Southampton 56 – Swindon 19.

　　Lansdowne Arms, The Strand, SN11 0EH, ℡ 812488 – **P**
　　16 rm.

AUSTIN-MORRIS Curzon St. ℡ 812791
DATSUN London Rd ℡ 814455

ROVER-TRIUMPH Main Rd, Cherhill ℡ 812254

CALSTOCK Cornwall **403** H 32 – pop. 4,079 (inc. Gunnislake) – ☼ 0822 Gunnislake.
London 246 – Plymouth 22 – Tavistock 7.

　　Danescombe Valley without rest., PL18 9RY, W : ½ m. by Riverside Rd, ℡ 832414,
　　 river Tamar, « Country house atmosphere » – wc **P**
　　April-November – **7 rm** 7.50/18.00 – P 13.00/16.50.

CAMBERLEY Surrey **404** R 29 30 – pop. 44,967 (inc. Frimley) – ECD : Wednesday – ☎ 0276.
Envir. : Sandhurst (Royal Military Academy : Royal Memorial Chapel*) NW : 1 ½ m.
London 40 – Reading 13 – Southampton 48.

   Frimley Hall (T.H.F.), Portsmouth Rd, GU15 2BG, E : ¾ m. off A 325 ☏ 28321,
Telex 858446, ⇔ – TV ⌷wc ☎ P. ☺. 🗑 AE ⓪ VISA
   M 4.75/5.75 **st.** ¶ 1.80 – **77 rm** ⌷ 18.50/24.50 **st.**

   ✗ **Villa Romana,** 20 Park St., GU15 3PL. ☏ 24370, Italian rest. – 🗑 AE ⓪ VISA
   closed Sunday and 25 December-1 January – **M** a la carte 3.25/6.45 **t.** ¶ 1.25.

AUSTIN-MORRIS-MG-ROVER-TRIUMPH London Rd ☏ 63443

CAMBORNE Cornwall **403** E 33 – pop. 16,631 – ECD : Thursday – ☎ 0209.
London 306 – Falmouth 12 – Newquay 19 – Penzance 13 – Plymouth 63 – Truro 12.

   Tyack's, Church St., TR14 7DQ, ☏ 712628, ⇔ – ⌷wc ☞ P. 🗑 VISA
   M 3.25/5.00 **t.** ¶ 1.50 – **11 rm** ⌷ 7.50/8.50.

AUSTIN-MORRIS-MG-WOLSELEY Church St. ☏ 712066   RENAULT Rosewarn Rd ☏ 713769

CAMBRIDGE Cambs. **404** U 27 – pop. 98,840 – ECD : Thursday – ☎ 0223.
See : Colleges Quarter*** : King's College** (King's Chapel***) z L – Queens' College**
(Cloister Court) z P – St. John's College** (Gateway*) Y S – Fitzwilliam Museum** *AC* z M¹ –
Trinity College** (Wren Library**, Chapel*, Great Court and Gate*) Y U – Holy Sepulchre*
(12C round church) Y E – Senate House* Y S – The Backs* YZ – Jesus College (Chapel*) Y K –
Christ's College (Gatehouse) YZ A.
Envir. : Anglesey Abbey 12C (interior** and park* *AC*) NE : 6 m. by A 1303 x and B 1102.
🚩 Bar Hill ☏ 0954 (Crafts Hill) 80555, NW : 5 ½ m. by A 1307 x – 🚩 Dodford Lane ☏ Girton
76169, N : 3 m. by A 1307 x.
🅸 Wheeler St. ☏ 358977 and 353363.
London 58 – Coventry 88 – Kingston-upon-Hull 139 – Ipswich 53 – Leicester 68 – Norwich 61 – Nottingham 88 –
Oxford 78.

Plan opposite

   Garden House, Granta Pl. off Mill Lane, CB2 1RT, ☏ 63421, Telex 81463, ≼, ⇔ –
🛗 TV ⅙ P. ☺. 🗑 AE ⓪ VISA   **z n**
   closed 25 December-1 January – **M** 5.75/6.00 **t.** ¶ 2.75 – ⌷ 2.00 – **55 rm** 26.00/
36.50 **t.**

   University Arms, Regent St., CB2 1AD, ☏ 51241, Telex 817311 – 🛗 TV P. ☺. 🗑 AE
⓪ VISA   **z e**
   M 4.50/5.20 **t.** ¶ 1.50 – **120 rm** ⌷ 14.25/28.50 **st.** – P 20.50/27.50 **st.**

   Gonville, Gonville Pl., CB1 1LY, ☏ 66611 – 🛗 ⌷wc ☎ P. ☺. 🗑 AE ⓪ VISA   **z r**
   closed Christmas – **M** 4.65/4.90 **t.** ¶ 2.55 – **62 rm** ⌷ 19.00/28.50 **st.**

   Blue Boar (T.H.F.), 17 Trinity St., CB2 1TC, ☏ 63121 – TV ⌷wc ☎. 🗑 AE ⓪ VISA **Y s**
   M 4.20/5.00 **st.** ¶ 1.65 – **48 rm** ⌷ 15.00/24.50 **st.**

   Arundel House, 53 Chesterton Rd, CB4 3AN, ☏ 67701 – TV ⌷wc 🛁wc ☎ P. 🗑 VISA
   closed Christmas – **M** 4.45 ¶ 1.40 – ⌷ 0.95 – **59 rm** 8.60/20.65.   **Y u**

   May View, 12 Park Parade, CB5 8AL, ☏ 66018 – ⌷wc 🛁wc   **Y v**
   6 rm ⌷ 7.00/16.00 **s.**

   Helen, 167-169 Hills Rd, CB2 2RJ, ☏ 46465 – P   **X c**
   closed 10 December-10 January – **M** (bar lunch) 4.50 **st.** – **24 rm** ⌷ 8.50/17.00 **st.**

   Lensfield, 53 Lensfield Rd, CB2 1EN, ☏ 355017 – 🛁wc ☞ P. 🗑 VISA   **z a**
   closed 2 weeks at Christmas – **29 rm** ⌷ 8.00/16.00 **st.**

   Guest House, 139 Huntingdon Rd, CB3 0DQ, ☏ 352833 – P   **X a**
   closed 1 week at Christmas – **13 rm** ⌷ 8.50/17.00 **st.**

   ✗✗ **Don Pasquale,** 12 Market Hill, CB2 3NJ, ☏ 67063, Italian rest. – 🗑 AE ⓪ VISA **Y a**
   closed Sunday and 25-26 December – **M** a la carte 6.70/9.50 **t.** ¶ 1.90.

   ✗ Oyster Tavern, 21-24 Northampton St., ☏ 53110, Seafood.   **Y c**

   ✗ **Peking,** 21 Burleigh St., ☏ 354755, Chinese rest.   **Y o**
   closed Monday, 2 weeks September-October, 1 week at Christmas and Bank Holidays –
   M a la carte 4.30/6.90.

   at Trumpington S : 1 ¾ m. on A 1309 – x – ✉ – ☎ 0223 Cambridge :

   ✗ **Coach and Horses,** High St., CB2 2LP, ☏ 840388 – 🗑 AE VISA
   closed Sunday, Christmas dinner and Bank Holidays – **M** a la carte 6.80/8.90 **t.** ¶ 1.75.

P.T.O. ⟶

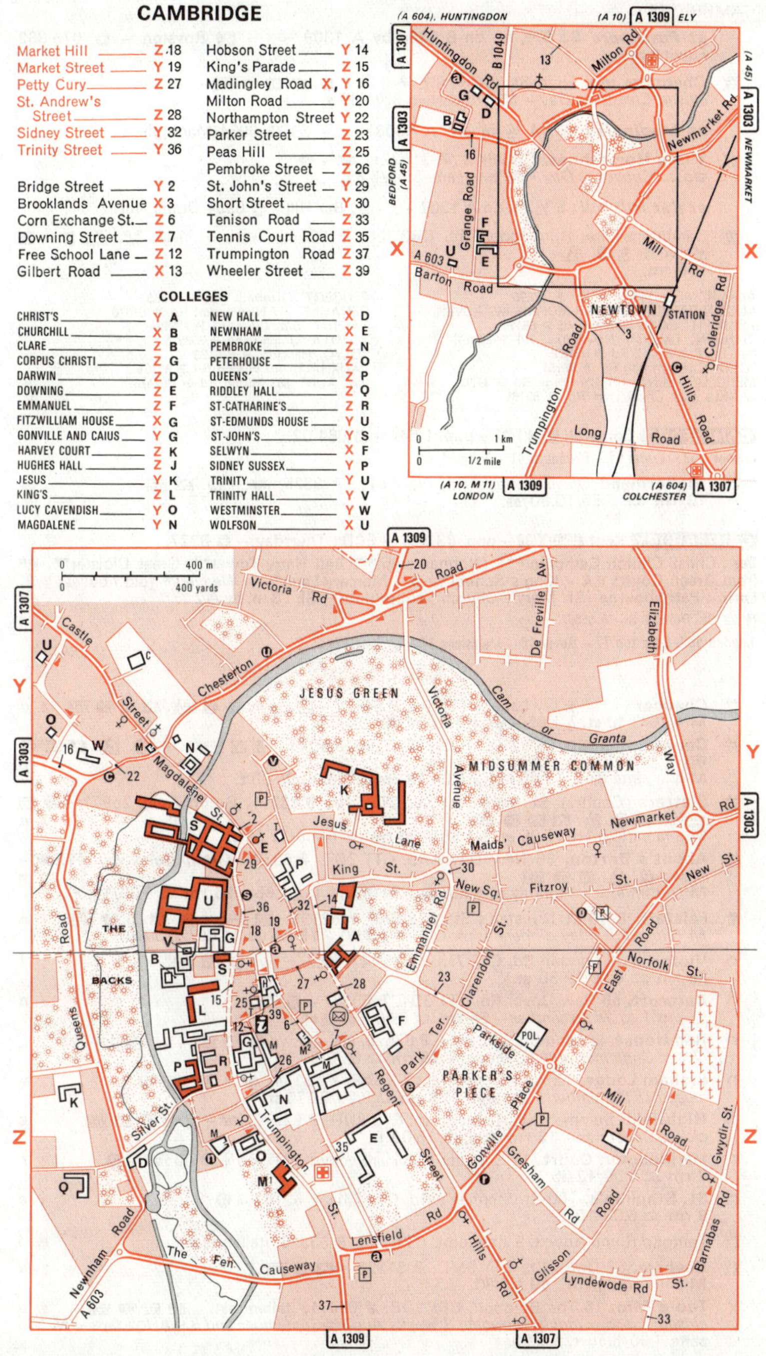

CAMBRIDGE

Market Hill — Z 18
Market Street — Y 19
Petty Cury — Z 27
St. Andrew's Street — Z 28
Sidney Street — Y 32
Trinity Street — Y 36

Bridge Street — Y 2
Brooklands Avenue X 3
Corn Exchange St. — Z 6
Downing Street — Z 7
Free School Lane — Z 12
Gilbert Road — X 13

Hobson Street — Y 14
King's Parade — Z 15
Madingley Road X, Y 16
Milton Road — Y 20
Northampton Street Y 22
Parker Street — Z 23
Peas Hill — Z 25
Pembroke Street — Z 26
St. John's Street — Y 29
Short Street — Y 30
Tenison Road — Z 33
Tennis Court Road Z 35
Trumpington Road Z 37
Wheeler Street — Z 39

COLLEGES

CHRIST'S — Y A
CHURCHILL — X B
CLARE — Z B
CORPUS CHRISTI — Z G
DARWIN — Z D
DOWNING — Z E
EMMANUEL — Z F
FITZWILLIAM HOUSE — X G
GONVILLE AND CAIUS — Y G
HARVEY COURT — Z K
HUGHES HALL — Z J
JESUS — Y K
KING'S — Z L
LUCY CAVENDISH — Y O
MAGDALENE — Y N

NEW HALL — X D
NEWNHAM — X E
PEMBROKE — Z N
PETERHOUSE — Z O
QUEENS' — Z P
RIDDLEY HALL — Z Q
ST-CATHARINE'S — Z R
ST-EDMUNDS HOUSE — Y U
ST-JOHN'S — Y S
SELWYN — X F
SIDNEY SUSSEX — Y P
TRINITY — Y U
TRINITY HALL — Y V
WESTMINSTER — Y W
WOLFSON — X U

(A 604), HUNTINGDON
(A 10) A 1309 ELY
A 1307
Huntingdon Rd
B 1049
Milton Rd
13
(A 45) A 1303 NEWMARKET
A 1303
Newmarket Rd
Grange Road
16
Mill Rd
Barton Road
A 603
NEWTOWN
STATION
3
Coleridge Rd
Trumpington Road
Hills Road
Long Road
0 1 km
0 1/2 mile
(A 10, M 11) LONDON
A 1309
A 1307
(A 604) COLCHESTER
Bedford (A 45)

A 1309
400 m
400 yards
A 1307
Castle
Victoria Rd
Road
20
De Freville Av.
Elizabeth
JESUS GREEN
Chesterton Street
Cam or Granta
MIDSUMMER COMMON
Victoria Avenue
Way
Magdalene St.
Jesus Lane
Maids' Causeway
Newmarket
A 1303
Jesus
King St.
New Sq.
Fitzroy St.
New St.
30
Emmanuel Rd
Clarendon St.
Regent St.
Norfolk St.
THE BACKS
East Road
POL.
Queens' Road
Silver St.
PARKER'S PIECE
Parkside
Trumpington
Gonville Place
Gresham Rd
Mill Road
Gwydir St.
Newnham Road
A 603
The Fen Causeway
Lensfield
Hills Rd
Glisson Rd
Barnabas Rd
Lyndewode Rd
37
33
A 1309
A 1307

at Fowlmere S: 8 ¾ m. on B 1368 by A 1309 – x – ✉ Royston – ✆ 076 382 Fowlmere:

✕✕ **Chequers Inn,** High St., SG8 7SR, ℡ 369 – **P**. ⬛ AE ⓪ *VISA*
closed Christmas Day – **M** a la carte 5.85/6.80 **s.**

at Madingley W: 4 ½ m. off A 1303 – x – ✉ ✆ 0954 Madingley:

✕✕ **Three Horseshoes,** CB3 8AB, ℡ 210221, 🚗 – **P**
closed Christmas Day – **M** a la carte 5.95/6.85.

at Bar Hill NW: 5 ½ m. on A 1307 – x – ✉ Bar Hill – ✆ 0954 Crafts Hill:

🏨 Cambridgeshire, Huntingdon Rd, CB3 8EU, ℡ 80555, Telex 817141, ✕, ⬛, 🔞 – 📺
🛏wc 🕿 ♿ **P**. ♨
100 rm.

ALFA-ROMEO 146 Hills Rd ℡ 47296
AUSTIN-DAIMLER-JAGUAR-MORRIS-MG-ROVER-
TRIUMPH 400 Newmarket Rd ℡ 65111
CITROEN, TALBOT Newmarket Rd ℡ 59151
DATSUN 315 Mill Rd ℡ 42222
FORD Cherryhinton Rd ℡ 48151
MERCEDES-BENZ 121/129 Perne Rd ℡ 47268
LANCIA 121 Chesterton Rd ℡ 69761

PEUGEOT Elizabeth Way ℡ 68686
RENAULT 217 Newmarket Rd ℡ 51616
TALBOT Babraham Rd ℡ 47072
TOYOTA Union Lane ℡ 356225
VOLVO Harston ℡ 870123
VAUXHALL 137 Histon Rd ℡ 66751
VW, AUDI 383 Milton Rd ℡ 354473

CAMELFORD Cornwall **403** F 32 – pop. 1,544 – ✆ 084 02.

London 258 – **Exeter** 57 – **Plymouth** 41 – **Truro** 34.

🏠 **Highermead** 🦢, 5 College Rd, PL32 9TL, ℡ 3325, 🚗 – **P**. ⬛ *VISA*
10 rm ⭍ 6.50/10.80 **st.**

CANTERBURY Kent **404** X 30 – pop. 33,176 – ECD: Thursday – ✆ 0227.

See : Christ Church Cathedral★★★ (Norman crypt★★, Bell Harry Tower★★, Great Cloister★★, ≤★ from Green Court) Y **A** – King's School★ Y **B** – Mercery Lane★ Y – Weavers★ (old houses) Y **D**.
Envir. : Patrixbourne (St. Mary's Church : south door★) SE : 3 m. by A 2 z.

🛈 22 St. Peter's St. ℡ 66567.

London 59 – **Brighton** 72 – **Dover** 16 – **Maidstone** 27 – **Margate** 17.

Plan opposite

🏨 **Chaucer** (T.H.F.), Ivy Lane, CT1 1TU, ℡ 64427 – 📺 🛏wc 🕿 **P**. ♨. ⬛ AE ⓪ *VISA* z c
M 4.20/5.40 **st.** 🍷 1.65 – **51 rm** ⭍ 14.00/23.50 **st.**

🏨 **County,** High St., CT1 2RX, ℡ 66266, Telex 965076 – 📶 📺 🛏wc 🕿 **P**. ♨. ⬛ AE ⓪
VISA Y n
M a la carte 8.15/13.65 **t.** 🍷 2.10 – **73 rm** ⭍ 20.00/30.00 **t.**

🏨 **Slatters** (County), St. Margaret's St., CT1 1AA, ℡ 63271, Group Telex 25971 – 📶 📺
🛏wc 🕿 **P**. ♨. ⬛ AE ⓪ *VISA* z e
M a la carte 5.10/11.05 **st.** 🍷 1.55 – **30 rm** ⭍ 14.00/22.00 **s.**

🏨 **Abbot's Barton,** 36 New Dover Rd, CT1 3DT, ℡ 60341, Group Telex 957141, 🚗 –
🛏wc **P**. ♨. AE ⓪ *VISA* z a
M (buffet lunch Monday to Saturday) 3.60/4.75 **t.** 🍷 1.65 – **35 rm** ⭍ 9.00/19.00 **t.**

🏠 **Falstaff,** 8-10 St. Dunstan's St., CT2 8AF, ℡ 62138 – 📺 🛏wc **P**. ⬛ AE ⓪ *VISA* Y a
M *(closed Sunday dinner)* approx. 3.75 🍷 2.00 – **16 rm** ⭍ 11.00/25.00 **t.**

🏠 **Victoria,** 59 London Rd, CT2 7HG, ℡ 65447, 🚗 – 🛏wc **P**. ⬛ *VISA* Y i
25 rm ⭍ 9.00/19.50 **st.**

🏠 **Barcroft,** 56 New Dover Rd, CT1 3DT, ℡ 69177 – **P**. AE z n
closed 1 to 25 December – **14 rm** ⭍ 8.50/15.00 **st.**

🏠 **Red House,** London Rd, CT2 8NB, ℡ 63578, 🚗 – 🛏wc **P**. ⬛ *VISA* by London Rd Y
closed Christmas and 1 January – **18 rm** ⭍ 8.00/20.00.

🏠 **Ersham Lodge,** 12 New Dover Rd, CT1 3AP, ℡ 63174, 🚗 – 🚿wc 🕿 **P** z v
closed 15 December-5 January – **26 rm** ⭍ 9.20/20.70 **st.**

🏠 **Highfield,** Summer Hill, Harbledown, CT2 8NH, ℡ 62772, 🚗 – 🚿wc **P**. ⬛ *VISA* Y c
closed Christmas – **12 rm** ⭍ 8.25/15.00 **t.**

🏠 **Harbledown Court,** 17 Summer Hill, Harbledown, CT2 8NN, ℡ 60659 – **P** Y r
7 rm ⭍ 5.00/12.00.

🏠 **St. Stephen's,** 100 St. Stephen's Rd, CT2 7JL, ℡ 62167 – **P** Y e
9 rm ⭍ 6.00/10.00.

✕✕ **Trattoria Roma Antica,** 9 Longport, CT1 1PE, ℡ 63326, Italian rest. z i

✕✕ **Beehive,** 52 Dover St., CT1 3MD, ℡ 61126 – ⬛ AE *VISA* z s
M a la carte 4.10/7.60 🍷 2.80.

✕ **Tuo e Mio,** 16 The Borough, CT1 2DB, ℡ 61471, Italian rest. – ⬛ AE ⓪ *VISA* Y o
closed Tuesday lunch, Monday, 3 weeks August-September and Bank Holidays – **M** a la carte 4.90/8.55 **t.** 🍷 2.90.

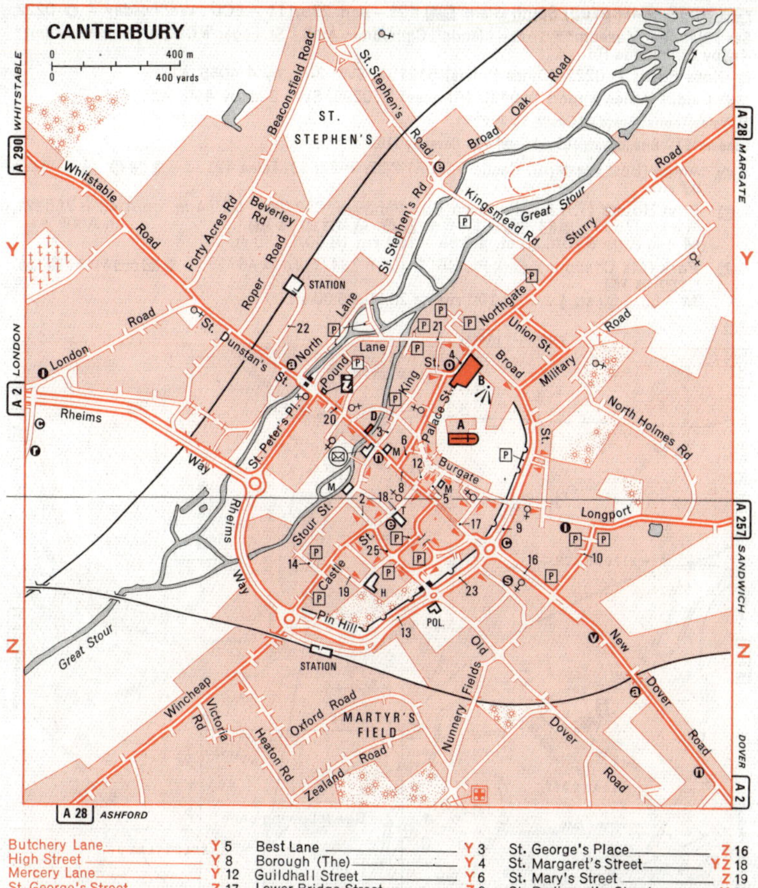

Butchery Lane — **Y** 5
High Street — **Y** 8
Mercery Lane — **Y** 12
St. George's Street — **Z** 17
St. Peter's Street — **Y** 20

Beercart Lane — **YZ** 2

Best Lane — **Y** 3
Borough (The) — **Y** 4
Guildhall Street — **Y** 6
Lower Bridge Street — **Z** 9
Lower Chantry Lane — **Z** 10
Rhodaus Town — **Z** 13
Rosemary Lane — **Z** 14

St. George's Place — **Z** 16
St. Margaret's Street — **YZ** 18
St. Mary's Street — **Z** 19
St. Radigund's Street — **Y** 21
Station Road West — **Y** 22
Upper Bridge Street — **Z** 23
Watling Street — **Z** 25

at Fordwich NE: 3 m. off A 28 – **Y** – ✉ ☎ 0227 Canterbury :

George and Dragon, CT2 0BX, ☎ 710661, « 16C village inn », — ⊟ wc **P**. 🔲 ⓞ **VISA**
closed 25 and 26 December – **M** *(closed Sunday dinner)* (buffet lunch) 4.00/9.00 **t.** ⌀ 2.70
– **13 rm** ⊡ 9.55/21.10 **t.**

at Pett Bottom S: 4 ½ m. off A 2 via Bridge Village – **z** – ✉ ☎ 0227 Canterbury :

✕ ❊ **Duck Inn**, CT4 5PB, ☎ 830354 – **P**. ⓞ
closed Monday, Tuesday, 2 weeks March, 2 weeks October and Christmas – **M** 8.50/
11.80 ⌀ 1.95
Spec. Civet de fruits de mer, Caneton rôti à l'ananas flambé au Cognac, Petit pot au chocolat.

AUDI-NSU, HONDA Rose Lane ☎ 65544
AUSTIN-DAIMLER-JAGUAR-MG-ROVER-TRIUMPH-
5 Rose Lane and 28/30 St. Peters St. ☎ 66161
DATSUN Island Rd ☎ 710431
FIAT, CITROEN, FERRARI, ROLLS ROYCE-BENTLEY
41 St. Georges Pl. ☎ 66131
FORD 23 Lower Bridge St. ☎ 51777
LANCIA The Friars ☎ 62977
MAZDA Sturry Rd ☎ 64977

MORRIS-MG New Dover Rd ☎ 66711
OPEL-VAUXHALL Ashford Rd, Chartham ☎ 022 789
(Great Stour) 331
RELIANT Sturry Rd ☎ 62845
RENAULT Northgate ☎ 65561
TALBOT The Pavillon ☎ 51791
TOYOTA Union St. ☎ 61993
VOLVO Vauxhall Rd ☎ 54341
VW Fordwich Rd ☎ 710240

CAPEL CURIG Gwynedd **403** I 24 – see Betws-y-Coed.

CARBIS BAY Cornwall **403** D 33 – see St. Ives.

CARDIFF (CAERDYDD) South Glam. **403** K 29 – pop. 279,111 – ECD: Wednesday – ☎ 0222.

See : National Museum★★ **BY** M – Llandaff Cathedral★ **AY** B – St. Fagan's Castle (Folk Museum)★ AC by St. Fagans Rd **AY**.

🏌 Dinas Powis ☎ 0222 (Dinas Powis) 512157, SW : 3 m. by A 4055 **AZ**.

✈ Cardiff-Wales Airport ☎ 0446 (Rhoose) 710296, SW : 8 m. by A 48 **AZ**

🛈 Wales Tourist Board, 3 Castle St. ☎ 27281.

London 157 – Birmingham 105 – Bristol 43 – Coventry 118.

🏨 Angel (Best Western), Castle St., CF1 2QZ, ☎ 32633, Telex 49132 – 📺 📶 🅿. ♨   **BZ a**
97 rm.

🏨 Post House (T.H.F.), Pentwyn Rd., Pentwyn, CF2 7XA, NE : 4 m. on A 48 ☎ 750121, Telex 497633 – 📺 📶 📧 wc ♨ wc ☎ 🅿. ♨   on A 48 **AY**
M a la carte 6.70/8.30 st. ♨ 1.65 – **150 rm** 18.00/25.50 st.

🏨 Park (Mt. Charlotte), Park Pl., CF1 3UD, ☎ 23471, Telex 497195 – 📺 📶 📧 wc ☎ 🅿. ♨   **BZ c**
♨ AE ① VISA
M 4.50/5.50 st. ♨ 2.00 – **100 rm** ⬜ 20.00/35.00 st.

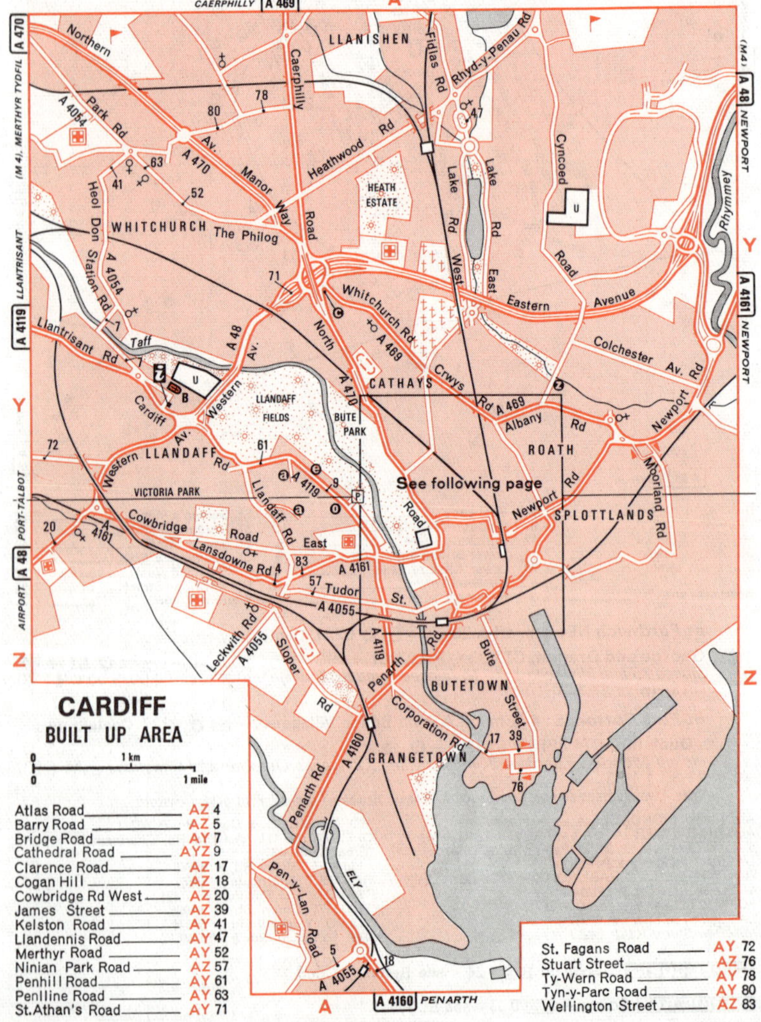

🏨 **Royal** (Embassy), St. Mary St., CF1 1LL, ☎ 23321 – 劇 TV ⬛wc 🛁wc ☎. &. ⬛. AE ⓘ VISA
M a la carte 6.55/10.00 st. ▯ 2.20 – **68 rm** ⬚ 17.00/24.00 st. – P 21.05/27.80 t.   **BZ n**

🏨 Cardiff Centre (Centre), Westgate St., CF1 1JB, ☎ 388681, Telex 497258 – 劇 TV ⬛wc
🛁wc ☎. &. 🅿. ⬛. AE ⓘ VISA   **BZ i**
⬚ 1.65 – **160 rm** 17.80/23.00 st.

🏠 Beverley (Crest), 75 Cathedral Rd, CF1 9PG, ☎ 43443 – TV ⬛wc ☎ 🅿. ⬛. AE ⓘ VISA
19 rm ⬚ 14.00/29.10 st.   **AZ o**

🏠 **Alva**, 130-132 Cathedral Rd, CF1 9LQ, ☎ 23413 – 🅿   **AY e**
closed 2 weeks at Christmas and New Year – **27 rm** ⬚ 8.50/16.00 st.

🏠 **Pen-y-Lan**, 82 Pen-y-Lan Rd, CF2 5HX, ☎ 496444   **AY z**
14 rm ⬚ 7.75/9.75 st.

CARDIFF
CENTRE

0 ——— 300 m
0 ——— 300 yards

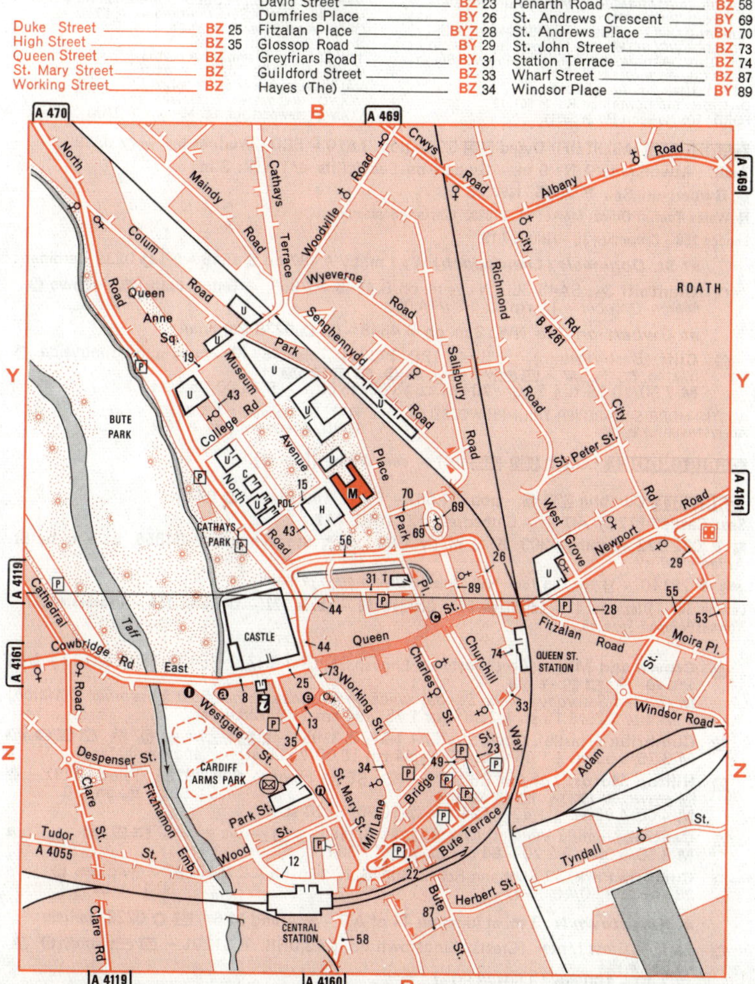

✗ **Harvesters,** 5 Pontcanna St., off Cathedral Rd, CF1 9HQ, ☎ 32616 — AY **a**
closed Sunday, Monday, 3 weeks August and Christmas – **M** (dinner only) a la carte 5.30/
7.30 ▯ 1.60.

✗ **Gibson's,** 8 Romilly Crescent, Canton, CF1 9NR, ☎ 41264, Bistro – AE VISA ⦿ — AZ **a**
closed Sunday, Monday, Tuesday after Bank Holidays and 24 December-1 January – **M** a la
carte 6.45/8.55 **t.** ▯ 1.80.

✗ Positano, 9 Church St., CF1 2BG, ☎ 35810, Italian rest. — BZ **e**

✗ **Savastano's,** 302 North Rd, Gabalfa, ☎ 30270, Italian rest. — AY **c**
closed Sunday – **M** a la carte 4.40/6.90 **t.** ▯ 1.30.

at Castleton (Cas-Bach) (Gwent) NE: 7 m. on A 48 – AY – ✉ Cardiff – ☎ 0633
Castleton:

🏨 **Ladbroke Mercury Motor Inn,** CF3 8OQ, ☎ 680591 – TV ⌷wc �📶wc ☏ Ⓟ. ♿. ◲ AE
⦿ VISA
M a la carte 5.20/8.05 **st.** – ☲ 2.45 – **55 rm** 17.55/23.00 **st.**

MICHELIN Branch, Garth St., Adamsdown, CF1 2UN, ☎ 33948.

ALFA-ROMEO, BMW 325 Penarth Rd ☎ 23122
AUSTIN-JAGUAR-MORRIS-MG-ROVER-TRIUMPH
52 Penarth Rd ☎ 43571
AUSTIN-DAIMLER-JAGUAR-MORRIS-MG-ROVER-
TRIUMPH-WOLSELEY 501 Newport Rd ☎ 495591
AUSTIN-MORRIS-MG-ROVER-TRIUMPH-WOLSELEY
89/103 City Rd ☎ 492676
DAF 134/148 City Rd ☎ 30022
DATSUN 516 Cowbridge Rd ☎ 561212
FORD 505 Newport Rd ☎ 59511

FORD 281 Penarth Rd ☎ 21071
MERCEDES-BENZ, PEUGEOT 14 Station Rd ☎ 566260
MORRIS-MG-WOLSELEY Rhiwbina ☎ 63232
OPEL West Bute St. ☎ 33221
SAAB Crwys Rd ☎ 35725
TOYOTA Llantrisant Rd ☎ 562345
VAUXHALL 2/12 City Rd ☎ 20531
VAUXHALL Sloper Rd ☎ 387221
VOLVO Grangetown ☎ 388932
VOLVO Newport Rd, St. Mellons ☎ 77183

CARDIGAN (ABERTEIFI) Dyfed **403** G 27 – pop. 3,810 – ECD : Wednesday – ☎ 0239.

Envir. : Mwnt (site★) N: 6 m. – Gwbert-on-Sea (cliffs ⟨★) NW: 3 m.

🏌 Gwbert-on-Sea ☎ 2035, NW: 3 m.

🛈 Wales Tourist Office, Market Pl. ☎ 3230 (Easter - September).

London 250 – Carmarthen 30 – Fishguard 19.

at St. Dogmaels (Llandudoch) W: 1 m. by A 487 on B 4546 – ✉ ☎ 0239 Cardigan:

⌂ **Glanteifi** ⚒, SA43 3LL, N: ½ m. on B 4546 ☎ 2353, ⟨ Teifi estuary, ⚒ – ⌷wc Ⓟ
March-October – **11 rm** ☲ 5.50/14.00.

at Gwbert-on-Sea NW: 3 m. on B 4548 – ✉ ☎ 0239 Cardigan:

🏨 **Cliff** (Best Western) ⚒, SA43 1PP, ☎ 3241, Telex 48440, ⟨ bay and countryside, ⌇
heated, ▯₉, ⚒, 🎣 – TV ⌷wc �📶wc ☏ Ⓟ. ◲ AE ⦿ VISA
M 7.50/10.75 **t.** ▯ 2.00 – **70 rm** ☲ 13.60/35.00 **t.** – P 16.00/35.00 **t.**

AUSTIN-MORRIS-MG-ROVER-TRIUMPH-WOLSELEY
Aberystwyth Rd ☎ 2365

FIAT St. Dogmaels ☎ 2025
FORD Aberystwyth Rd ☎ 2206

CARISBROOKE I.O.W. **403 404** Q 31 – see Wight (Isle of).

CARLISLE Cumbria **986** ⑲ – pop. 71,582 – ECD : Thursday – ☎ 0228.

See: Castle★ (12C) AC AY – Cathedral★ 12C-14C AY E.

🏌 ☎ 022 872 (Scotby) 303, E: 2 m. by A 69 BY – 🏌 Stoneyholme ☎ 34856, E: 1 m. by St.
Aidan's Rd BY.

🚗 ☎ 25146. – 🛈 The Old Town Hall, Green Market ☎ 25517 or 25396.

London 309 – Blackpool 91 – Edinburgh 98 – Glasgow 96 – Leeds 122 – Liverpool 124 – Manchester 117 –
Newcastle-upon-Tyne 58.

Plan opposite

🏨 **Crown and Mitre** (Best Western), English St., CA3 8HZ, ☎ 25491, Telex 64183 – ▯ TV
☏ Ⓟ. ♿. ◲ AE ⦿ VISA — BY **a**
M *(closed Saturday lunch, Sunday lunch and Sunday dinner from November to March)*
a la carte 3.25/8.15 **st.** ▯ 2.55 – ☲ 1.75 – **94 rm** 19.00/28.45 **st.**

🏨 **Cumbrian** (Thistle), Court Sq., CA1 1QY, ☎ 31951 – ▯ TV ⌷wc ☏ Ⓟ. ♿. ◲ AE ⦿ VISA
M 3.75/5.50 **st.** ▯ 1.65 – ☲ 3.00 – **64 rm** 18.00/25.00 **st.** – P approx. 30.00 **st.** BZ **u**

🏨 **Hilltop Motor,** London Rd, CA1 2PQ, SE : 1 m. on A 6 ☎ 29255, Telex 64292 – ▯
TV ⌷wc ☏ Ⓟ. ♿. ◲ AE ⦿ VISA — SE: 1 m. on A 6 BZ
M 4.00/4.95 **st.** ▯ 1.50 – **124 rm** ☲ 10.90/19.20 **st.**

🏨 **Central,** Victoria Viaduct, CA3 8AL, ☎ 20256 – ▯ TV ⌷wc ☏ 🚗. ◲ AE VISA — BZ **a**
M 3.50/5.00 **t.** ▯ 2.20 – **84 rm** ☲ 9.25/17.30 **t.**

⌂ **Cumbria Park,** 32 Scotland Rd, CA3 9DG, N: 1 m. on A 7 ☎ 22887 – �📶wc 🚗 Ⓟ
28 rm ☲ 9.50/18.00 **t.** — N: 1 m. by A 7 BY

at Kingstown N: 3 m. at junction 44 of A 7 – BY – and M 6 – ✉ ☎ 0228 Carlisle:

🏨 Carlisle Crest Motel (Crest), Kingstown Rd, CA3 0HR, ☎ 31201 – TV ⌷wc ☏ Ⓟ. ♿.
◲ AE ⦿ VISA
☲ 2.40 – **100 rm** 18.50/23.80 **st.**

CARLISLE

Botchergate	BZ
Castle Street	BY 6
English Street	BY 13
Scotch Street	BY 19
Annetwell Street	AY 2
Bridge Street	AY 3
Brunswick Street	BZ 4
Caldcotes	AY 5
Charlotte Street	AZ 7
Chiswick Street	BY 8
Church Street	AY 10
Eden Bridge	BY 12
Lonsdale Street	BY 14
Lowther Street	BY 15
Port Road	AY 16
St. Aidan's Road	BY 17
St. Nicholas Street	BZ 18
Spencer Street	BY 20
Tait Street	BZ 21
Victoria Viaduct	ABZ 24
West Tower Street	BY 26
West Walls	ABY 27

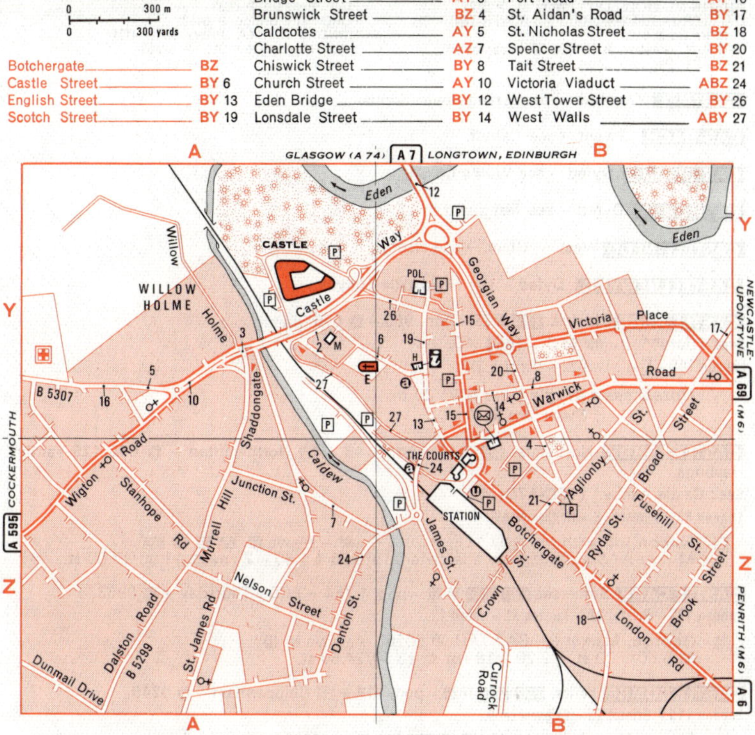

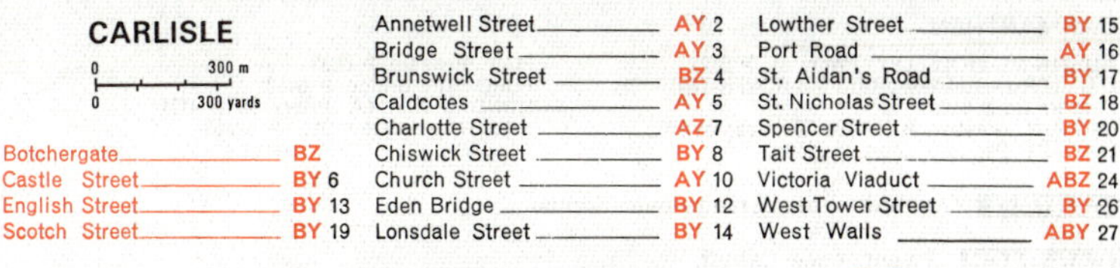

at Crosby-on-Eden NE: 4 ½ m. by A 7 – BY – on B 6264 – ✉ Carlisle – ☎ 022 873 Crosby-on-Eden:

XX **Crosby Lodge** with rm, CA6 4QZ, ☎ 618, ≤, « 18C country mansion », – wc wc Ⓟ. AE ⓓ
closed Easter Monday and 24 December-last week January – **M** *(closed Sunday dinner)* 4.75/7.50 **s.** 2.50 – **11 rm** 16.00/26.00 **s.**

at Faugh E: 8 ¼ m. off A 69 – BY – ✉ Carlisle – ☎ 022 870 Hayton:

String of Horses Inn, Heads Nook, CA8 9EG, ☎ 297, « Elaborately furnished 17C inn » – TV wc wc ☎ Ⓟ. AE ⓓ VISA
M a la carte 3.30/6.30 1.85 – **13 rm** 14.60/23.00.

MICHELIN Branch, Willow Holme Industrial Estate, CA2 5RT, ☎ 20477.

BMW, VAUXHALL Viaduct Estate ☎ 29401
DAIMLER-JAGUAR-ROVER-TRIUMPH Rosehill Estate ☎ 24387
DATSUN Lowther St. ☎ 31469
FIAT Church St., Caldewgate ☎ 25092
FORD Warwick Circus ☎ 24234
MERCEDES-BENZ, VOLVO Victoria Viaduct ☎ 28234
MORRIS-MG, ROLLS ROYCE Botchergate ☎ 26131
OPEL Wigton Rd ☎ 26269
PEUGEOT Warwick Bridge ☎ 60434
RENAULT Church St. ☎ 22423
TALBOT 37 Warwick Rd ☎ 25177
VW, AUDI-NSU Lowther St. ☎ 26104

CARLYON BAY Cornwall 403 F 33 – see St. Austell.

CARMARTHEN (CAERFYRDDIN) Dyfed 403 H 28 – pop. 13,081 – ECD: Thursday – ☎ 0267.

18 Blaenycoed Rd ☎ 87214, NW: 4 m.

Wales Tourist Board, Old Bishop's Palace, Abergwili ☎ 31557 (Easter-September).

London 220 – Fishguard 45 – Swansea 27.

Ivy Bush Royal (T.H.F.), 11-13 Spilman St., SA31 1LG, ☎ 5111, Telex 48520 – TV wc wc ☎ Ⓟ. AE ⓓ VISA
M 5.00/6.00 **st.** 1.65 – **103 rm** 14.00/24.50 **st.**

AUSTIN-MG-WOLSELEY Priory St. ℡ 6622
DAIMLER-JAGUAR-MORRIS-MG-ROVER-TRIUMPH
Pensarn Rd ℡ 6456
DATSUN Glasfryn ℡ 026 786 (Llanddarog) 370
DATSUN Penguin Court ℡ 7356

FIAT Pensarn ℡ 6633
FORD The Bridge ℡ 6482
HONDA, TOYOTA Priory St. ℡ 4171
VAUXHALL Water St. ℡ 32668

CARTMEL Cumbria – see Grange-over-Sands.

CAS-BACH Gwent – see Cardiff.

CAS-BLAIDD Dyfed – see Wolf's Castle.

CASMORYS Dyfed – see Fishguard.

CASTELL-NEDD West – Glam. – see Neath.

CASTELLNEWYDD Dyfed – see Newcastle Emlym.

CASTLE ACRE Norfolk **404** W 25 – pop. 955 – ☉ 076 05.
See: Priory★★ (ruins 11C - 14C) *AC.*
London 101 – King's Lynn 20 – Norwich 31.

  Hotels see : King's Lynn NW : 20 m.
   Swaffam S : 4 m.

CASTLE ASHBY Northants. **404** R 27 – pop. 148 – ✉ Northampton – ☉ 060 129 Yardley
Hastings.
See : Castle Ashby★ (16C-17C) *AC.*
London 68 – Bedford 16 – Northampton 8.

 XX **Falcon Inn** with rm, NN7 1LF, ℡ 200, ≤, 🍽 – 🛁wc **P**. 🔄 AE ① *VISA*
   M *(closed Sunday dinner)* a la carte 5.15/8.25 ⅃ 1.80 – **7 rm** � 11.00/17.00 **st.**

CASTLE CARY Somerset **403** **404** M 30 – pop. 1,754 – ECD : Thursday – ☉ 0963.
London 125 – Bristol 28 – Taunton 31 – Yeovil 13.

 🏛 **George,** Market Pl., BA7 7AH, ℡ 50761 – 🛁wc 🕿 **P**
   M 5.50/9.00 **st.** ⅃ 2.20 – **18 rm** ⊑ 13.50/24.50 **st.**

CASTLE COMBE Wilts. **403** **404** N 29 – pop. 414 – ✉ Chippenham – ☉ 0249.
London 110 – Bristol 23 – Chippenham 6.

 🏰 **Manor House** ⑤, SN14 7HR, ℡ 782206, Telex 44220, « Part 14 C manor house in park »,
  %, ⌇ heated, ⌇, 🍽 – 📺 **P**. 🔄 AE ① *VISA*
  closed first 2 weeks January – M a la carte 8.65/12.70 **t.** ⅃ 2.30 – **34 rm** ⊑ 21.35/47.25 **st.**

CASTLE DONINGTON Leics. **403** **404** P 25 – pop. 5,113 – ✉ ☉ 0332 Derby.
✈ East Midlands, ℡ 810621.
ℹ East Midlands Airport ℡ 810621 ext 220/230.
London 123 – Birmingham 38 – Leicester 23 – Nottingham 13.

 🏠 **Donington Manor,** High St., DE7 2PP, ℡ 810253 – 📺 🛁wc **P**. ⚠. 🔄 AE ① *VISA*
  closed 23 to 31 December – M 2.50/3.25 **s.** ⅃ 2.00 – **37 rm** ⊑ 12.85/18.00 **s.** – P 14.75/
  19.00 **s.**

CASTLE MORRIS (CASMORYS) Dyfed **403** E 28 – see Fishguard.

CASTLETON Derbs. **403** **404** O 23 – pop. 729 – ECD : Wednesday – ✉ Sheffield (South
Yorks.) – ☉ 0433 Hope Valley.
Envir. : Blue John Caverns★ *AC,* W : 1 m.
London 173 – Manchester 27 – Sheffield 16.

 🏠 **Ye Olde Nag's Head,** Cross St., S30 2WH, ℡ 20248 – **P**. 🔄 AE ①
  M 3.50/4.10 **st.** ⅃ 1.75 – **10 rm** ⊑ 10.65/20.25 **st.**

CASTLETON (CAS-BACH) South Glam. **403** K 29 – see Cardiff.

CATTERICK North Yorks. – pop. 2,391 – ECD : Wednesday – ✉ ☉ 0748 Richmond.
🏌 Leyburn Rd ℡ 833268, W : 5 m.
London 239 – Darlington 11 – Leeds 49 – Northallerton 14.

 🏠 **Bridge House** (Embassy), Catterick Bridge, DL10 7PE, N : 2 ½ m. on A 6136 ℡ 818331 –
  📺 🛁wc 🕿 **P**. ⚠. 🔄 AE ① *VISA*
  closed 4 days at Christmas – M a la carte 4.45/8.30 **st.** – **18 rm** ⊑ 10.50/19.00 **st.**

AUSTIN-MORRIS-MG-PRINCESS 14 Richmond Rd ℡ 074 883 (Catterick Camp) 3219

CAULDON LOWE Staffs. 408 404 O 24 – ✉ ✆ 053 86 Waterhouses.
London 153 – Derby 21 – Manchester 44 – Stoke-on-Trent 16.

✗ **Jean-Pierre**, ST10 3EX, ☎ 338, French rest. – **P**
closed Saturday lunch, Sunday, last week September and Christmas Day – **M** (booking essential) a la carte 6.60/10.45 **s.** 🍷 2.10.

CAVENDISH Suffolk 404 V 27 – pop. 701 – ✉ Sudbury – ✆ 0787 Glemsford.
London 66 – Cambridge 29 – Ipswich 28.

✗✗ **Alfonso's**, High St., CO10 8BB, ☎ 280372, Italian rest. – 🆎 ⓪
closed Sunday dinner and Monday lunch – **M** a la carte 5.40/10.00 **t.** 2.50.

CAWSAND Cornwall 408 H 33 – pop. 600 – ✉ ✆ 0752 Plymouth.
London 253 – Plymouth 10 – Truro 53.

🏠 Criterion ⌖, Garrett St., PL10 1PD, ☎ 822244, ≼ Plymouth Sound, « Converted fishermen's cottages » – 🛁wc
8 rm.

CHADLINGTON Oxon. 408 404 P 28 – pop. 717 – ✆ 060 876.
London 74 – Cheltenham 32 – Oxford 18 – Stratford-upon-Avon 25.

🏵 **Chadlington House**, OX7 3LZ, ☎ 437, 🏊 – **P**. 🆅🆂🅰
M (bar lunch) 4.50/7.00 **t.** 🍷 2.00 – **12 rm** ⌑ 10.00/20.00 **t.**

CHADWICK END West Midlands 408 404 O 26 – see Knowle.

CHAGFORD Devon 408 I 31 – pop. 1,250 – ECD : Wednesday – ✆ 064 73.
London 218 – Exeter 17 – Plymouth 28.

🏰 **Gidleigh Park** ⌖, TQ13 8HH, NW: 2 m. on Gidleigh Rd, ☎ 2367, ≼, « Country house atmosphere », ✗, ⌖, 🏊, park – 📺 🛏wc **P**
M (buffet lunch only) approx. 10.00 **s.** 🍷 2.00 – **11 rm** ⌑ 15.00/42.00 **s.**
🏠 **Teignworthy** ⌖, Frenchbeer, TQ13 8EX, SW: 2 ½ m. ☎ 3355, ≼, « Country house atmosphere », ✗, ⌖, 🏊, park – 📺 🛏wc **P**
M (buffet lunch) 5.50/10.50 **t.** 🍷 2.50 – **7 rm** ⌑ (dinner included) 20.00/25.50 **t.**
🏡 **Greenacres** ⌖, TQ13 8AS, ☎ 3471, 🏊 – 🛁wc **P**. 🆂 ⓪ 🆅🆂🅰
12 rm ⌑ 9.10/20.00 **t.**

at Easton Cross NE : 1 ½ m. on A 382 – ✉ ✆ 064 73 Chagford :

🏠 **Easton Court**, TQ13 8JL, ☎ 3469, « 15C thatched house », 🏊 – 🛏wc **P**. 🆂 🆎 ⓪ 🆅🆂🅰
M (buffet lunch) approx. 6.00 **t.** 🍷 1.75 – **8 rm** ⌑ 9.00/13.00 **t.**

at Sandypark NE : 1 ½ m. on A 382 – ✉ ✆ 064 73 Chagford :

🏰 **Mill End** ⌖, TQ13 8JN, ☎ 2282, « Country house with water mill », ⌖, 🏊 – 🛏wc
🚗 **P**. 🆂 🆅🆂🅰
closed 1 week at Christmas – **M** 4.00/6.75 **s.** 🍷 2.15 – ⌑ 2.65 – **18 rm** 8.75/21.00 **s.**
🏰 **Great Tree** ⌖, TQ13 8JS, ☎ 2491, ≼, « Country house atmosphere », 🏊, park –
📺 🛏wc **P**. 🆂 🆎 ⓪ 🆅🆂🅰
M 4.50/6.00 🍷 1.75 – **15 rm** ⌑ 13.00/27.00.

CHALE I.O.W. 408 404 Q 32 – see Wight (Isle of).

CHALFONT ST. GILES Bucks. 404 S 29 – pop. 8,500 – ✆ 024 07.
See : Milton's Cottage *AC*.
London 26 – Aylesbury 18.

✗✗ **Le Relais**, London Rd, HP8 ANJ, ☎ 2590, French rest. – **P**. 🆂 🆎 ⓪ 🆅🆂🅰
closed Saturday lunch and Sunday – **M** a la carte 8.25/11.35 **t.** 🍷 1.90.

MORRIS-MG-WOLSELEY London Rd ☎ 3045

CHALFONT ST. PETER Bucks. 404 S 29 – pop. 18,760 – ✆ 024 07 Chalfont St. Giles.
London 22 – Oxford 37.

🏠 **Greyhound Inn**, High St., SL9 9RA, ☎ 028 13 (Gerrards Cross) 83404 – 📺 **P**. 🆂 ⓪ 🆅🆂🅰
M *(closed Sunday dinner and Monday dinner)* (bar lunch Monday to Saturday) a la carte 5.75/8.85 **t.** – **10 rm** ⌑ 10.45/20.85 **st.**
✗✗ **Water Hall**, Amersham Rd, SL9 0NY, N: 1 m. on A 413 ☎ 2820 – **P**. 🆂 🆎 ⓪ 🆅🆂🅰
closed Saturday lunch, Sunday, Monday, 1 week summer and 1 week at Christmas – **M** a la carte 5.50/7.35 🍷 1.50.

CITROEN High St. ☎ 028 13 (Gerrards Cross) 85581   OPEL Gravell Hill, Amersham Rd ☎ 028 13 (Gerrards Cross) 85372

CHANCERY (RHYDGALED) Dyfed 408 H 26 – see Aberystwyth.

CHANDLER'S FORD Hants. **403** **404** P 31 – pop. 7,200 – ECD : Wednesday – ⊠ Eastleigh –
✪ 042 15.
London 79 – Southampton 6.5 – Winchester 7.

XX King's Court, 83 Winchester Rd, SO5 2GG, on A 33 �🕿 2232 – **P**.

FORD Bournemouth Rd �🕿 2901   RENAULT Hursley Rd �🕿 3853

CHAPEL STILE Cumbria – see Ambleside.

CHARING Kent **404** W 30 – see Ashford.

CHARLBURY Oxon. **403** **404** P 28 – pop. 2,249 – ✪ 060 881.
London 72 – Birmingham 50 – Oxford 15.

🏨 **Bell,** Church St., OX7 3PP, �🕿 278, « Tasteful decor » – ⇔wc 🛏wc ☎ **P**. 🅰. **VISA**
M (buffet lunch) 3.80/8.50 **st.** ⌕ 1.75 – **14 rm** ⊐ 15.00/31.00 **st.**

CHARLTON West Sussex **404** R 31 – see Chichester.

CHARLTON KINGS Glos. **403** **404** N 28 – see Cheltenham.

CHARMOUTH Dorset **403** L 31 – pop. 1,017 – ECD : Thursday – ⊠ Bridport – ✪ 0297.
London 157 – Dorchester 22 – Exeter 31 – Taunton 27.

🏠 **Fernhill,** DT6 6BX, W : ¾ m. on A 3052 ⚏ 60492, ≋ heated – ⇔wc 🛏 **P**
March-October – **M** (bar lunch Monday to Saturday) a la carte 6.00/7.65 **t.** ⌕ 1.85 –
15 rm ⊐ 9.50/30.00 **t.**

🏠 Queen's Arms, The Street, DT6 6QF, ⚏ 60339, ㎡ – ⇔wc **P**
March-October – **M** 2.50/5.00 **s.** ⌕ 1.75 – **15 rm.**

🏠 **Sea Horse,** Higher Sea Lane, DT6 6BB, ⚏ 60414, ≼, ㎡ – **P**
April-October – **M** (bar lunch) approx. 4.50 **st.** ⌕ 2.00 – **16 rm** ⊐ 7.00/16.00 **t.**

🏠 **Newlands House,** Stonebarrow Lane, DT6 6RA, ⚏ 60212 – 📺 ⇔wc 🛏wc **P**
April-October – **8 rm** ⊐ 6.00/12.00 **st.**

CHARNOCK RICHARD Lancs. – pop. 1,684 – ✪ 0257 Coppull.
London 215 – Liverpool 26 – Manchester 24 – Preston 10.

🏨 **TraveLodge** (T.H.F.) without rest., Mill Lane, PR7 5LQ, on M 6 ⚏ 791746 – 📺 ⇔wc
☎ ♿ **P**. 🅰 AE ⓪ **VISA**
108 rm ⊐ 14.50/20.00 **st.**

CHELMSFORD Essex **404** V 28 – pop. 58,194 – ECD : Wednesday – ✪ 0245.
London 33 – Cambridge 46 – Ipswich 40 – Southend-on-Sea 19.

🏨 **South Lodge,** 196 New London Rd, CM2 0AR, ⚏ 64564, Telex 99452 – 📺 ⇔wc ☎ **P**.
🅰 AE ⓪ **VISA**
M 3.50/4.00 ⌕ 1.50 – ⊐ 1.90 – **33 rm** 16.50/22.00.

🏠 **County,** 29 Rainsford Rd, CM1 2QA, ⚏ 66911, Telex 995430 – ⇔wc 🛏wc ☎ **P**. 🅰.
🅰 AE **VISA**
M 4.25/4.90 **s.** ⌕ 1.50 – ⊐ 1.50 – **49 rm** 9.50/20.00 **s.**

🏠 **Oaklands,** 240 Springfield Rd, CM2 6BP, ⚏ 352004 – **P**
closed Easter and Christmas – **8 rm** ⊐ 8.90/14.95 **st.**

🏠 **Beechcroft,** 211 London New Rd, CM2 0AJ, ⚏ 352462 – **P**
closed Christmas – **26 rm** ⊐ 8.95/15.20 **s.**

🏠 **Tanunda,** 217-219 New London Rd, CM2 0AJ, ⚏ 354295 – ⇔wc 🛏wc **P**
closed Christmas – **20 rm** ⊐ 8.50/17.50 **t.**

at Great Waltham N : 3 ¾ m. on A 130 – ⊠ ✪ 0245 Chelmsford :

XX **Windmill,** CM3 1AB, ⚏ 360292 – **P**
closed Saturday lunch, Sunday and Bank Holidays – **M** a la carte 3.70/9.55 ⌕ 1.50.

at High Easter NW : 10 m. off A 414 – ⊠ Chelmsford – ✪ 024 531 Good Easter :

XX **Punch Bowl,** CM1 4QW, ⚏ 222 – **P**
closed Sunday dinner, Monday dinner and first 2 weeks January – **M** a la carte 6.45/
8.95 ⌕ 1.70.

AUSTIN-MORRIS-MG-WOLSELEY 74 Main Rd,   OPEL Baddow Rd ⚏ 52959
Broomfield ⚏ 440571   PEUGEOT Bridge St. ⚏ 421233
DAF, VOLVO Braintree Rd, Little Waltham ⚏ 024534   RENAULT Southend Rd, Sandon ⚏ 71113
(Great Leighs) 534260   TALBOT 145 Moulsham St. ⚏ 61822
CITROEN Galley Wood ⚏ 68366   VAUXHALL Duke St. ⚏ 353674
FIAT, MERCEDES-BENZ 47 Springfield Rd ⚏ 55622   VW, AUDI-NSU Colchester Rd, Springfield ⚏ 468151
FORD 39 Robjohns Rd ⚏ 64111

Red Lion   **If the name of the hotel
is not in bold type,
on arrival ask the hotelier his prices.**

See : Pittville Park* A – Municipal Art Gallery and Museum* B **M. Envir. :** Elkstone (Parish church : doorway* and arches* 12C) SE : 7 m. by A 435 A.

⊠ Cleeve Hill ☏ 024 267 (Bishop's Cleeve) 2025, N : 3 m. by A 46 A.

✈ Staverton Airport : ☏ 0452 (Churchdown) 713351, W : 3 ½ m. by A 40 A and near M 5 Motorway, intersection № 11 – **Terminal :** Royal Wells.

🛈 Municipal Offices, The Promenade ☏ 22878.

London 99 – Birmingham 48 – Bristol 40 – Gloucester 9 – Oxford 43.

Plan on next page

Queen's (T.H.F.), Promenade, GL50 1NN, ☏ 54724, Telex 43381, 🚗 – 📶 📺 🅿. 🏊. 🔽 AE ⓪ VISA   B n
M 4.25/5.00 **st.** ⋮ 1.65 – ⌲ 2.50 – **76 rm** 21.00/31.00 **st.**

Golden Valley (Thistle), Gloucester Rd, GL51 0TS, W : 2 m. on A 40 ☏ 32691, Telex 43410 – 📶 📺 🅿. 🏊. 🔽 AE ⓪ VISA   by A 40 A
M 4.75/5.95 **t.** ⋮ 1.75 – ⌲ 3.00 – **103 rm** 24.50/31.50 **st.**

Carlton, Parabola Rd, GL50 3AQ, ☏ 54453, 🚗 – 📶 📺 ⌷wc ☎ 🅿. 🏊. 🔽 VISA   B r
M 4.40/5.50 **s.** ⋮ 1.75 – **49 rm** ⌲ 16.50/26.40 **s.**

George (T.H.F.), St. George's Rd, GL50 3DZ, ☏ 35751 – 📺 ⌷wc ☎ 🅿. 🔽 AE ⓪ VISA
M 4.50 **st.** ⋮ 1.85 – **42 rm** ⌲ 14.00/24.00 **st.**   B u

Overton, 88 St. George's Rd, GL50 3EA, ☏ 23371, 🚗 – 📶 🅿. AE   B e
closed 25 December-1 January – **M** *(closed Sunday lunch)* 3.00/4.50 **t.** – **12 rm** ⌲ 11.25/ 21.25 **t.** – P 16.50/18.75 **t.**

Wellesley Court, Clarence Sq., GL50 4JR, ☏ 31632, 🚗 – 📶 🅿   C a
20 rm.

The Priory with rm, 37 London Rd, GL50 3JT, ☏ 43451 – ⌷wc. 🔽 AE VISA   C s
closed Tuesday – **M** *(dinner only)* 8.00 ⋮ 2.50 – **5 rm** ⌲ 12.50/25.00.

Smiths, 4 Montpellier St., GL50 1SX, ☏ 28856 – 🔽 AE ⓪ VISA   B v
closed Sunday, Monday and Bank Holidays – **M** a la carte 4.95/7.30 **t.**

Aubergine, Belgrave House, Imperial Sq., GL50 1QB, ☏ 31402, Bistro – AE ⓪   B a
closed Sunday and Monday lunch – **M** a la carte 5.90/8.00 **t.** ⋮ 2.85.

Food for Thought, 10 Grosvenor St., GL52 2SG, ☏ 29836   C o
closed Sunday, Monday, 2 weeks late summer, Christmas and 1 January – **M** *(dinner only)* 9.00 **st.** ⋮ 2.00.

at Bishop's Cleeve N : 3 ½ m. on A 435 – A – ⊠ Cheltenham – ☎ 024 267 Bishop's Cleeve :

Cleeveway House with rm, 22 Evesham Rd, GL52 4SA, ☏ 2585, « Tasteful decor », 🚗 – ⌷wc 🅿. AE ⓪
closed Sunday, Monday and 3 weeks September – **M** a la carte 3.90/6.80 ⋮ 1.40 – **3 rm** ⌲ 10.00/20.00.

at Prestbury NE : 2 m. on A 46 – ⊠ ☎ 0242 Cheltenham :

Prestbury House ⟫ with rm, The Burgage, GL52 3DN, ☏ 29533, 🚗 – ⌷wc 📶wc ☎ 🅿   A i
closed Bank Holidays – **M** *(closed Saturday lunch and Sunday dinner)* 5.40/5.65 ⋮ 1.60 – **10 rm** ⌲ 10.00/20.00.

at Southam NE : 3 m. on A 46 – A – ⊠ ☎ 0242 Cheltenham :

De la Bere, GL52 3NH, ☏ 37771, « Tudor manor house », ✗, ⛱ heated, 🚗, park – 📺 🅿. 🏊. 🔽 AE ⓪ VISA
M a la carte 6.20/8.60 **st.** ⋮ 2.90 – **25 rm** ⌲ 18.00/37.00 **st.**

at Cleeve Hill NE : 4 m. on A 46 – A – ⊠ Cheltenham – ☎ 024 267 Bishop's Cleeve :

Malvern View with rm, GL52 3PR, ☏ 2017, ≤ Severn Valley to Malvern hills, 🚗 – ⌷wc 📶wc 🅿. AE
closed 3 weeks at Christmas – **M** *(closed Sunday dinner to non-residents)* *(dinner only)* 7.50 **st.** ⋮ 2.45 – **7 rm** ⌲ 15.00/25.00 **st.**

at Charlton Kings SE : 2 ¼ m. on A 435 – ⊠ ☎ 0242 Cheltenham :

Lilley Brook, Cirencester Rd, GL53 8EH, ☏ 25861, ≤, 🚗, park – 📺 ⌷wc 📶wc ☎ 🅿. 🏊   A a
33 rm.

at Shipton SE : 7 m. off A 40 – A – ⊠ Cheltenham – ☎ 024 282 Andoversford :

Frogmill, GL54 4HT, W : ¾ m. junction A 436 and A 40 ☏ 547 – ⌷wc ☎ 🚙 🅿. 🏊. AE
M *(buffet lunch)* 5.00/7.50 **t.** ⋮ 1.70 – **15 rm** ⌲ 12.00/27.50.

at Withington SE : 10 m. by A 435 – A – ⊠ Cheltenham – ☎ 024 289 Withington :

Mill House, GL54 4BE, ☏ 204, « 15C Stone mill house », 🚗 – 🅿. 🔽 AE ⓪ VISA
closed Sunday dinner and Monday – **M** a la carte 5.15/6.95 **s.** ⋮ 2.00.

P.T.O. →

CHELTENHAM

High Street —— BC
Pittville Street —— C 27
Portland Street —— C
Henrietta Street —— BC 28
Promenade (The) —— C 38
Winchcombe Street ——

Ambrose Street —— B 2
Berkeley Street —— C 4
Clarence Road —— C 5

Clarence Street —— C 6
Crescent Terrace —— B 7
Deep Street —— A 9
Dunalley Street —— C 10
Henrietta Street —— C 13
High Street (PRESTBURY) —— A 14
Keynsham Road —— C 15
Montpellier Avenue —— B 16
Montpellier Walk —— B 18
North Street —— C 20
Norwood Road —— B 21

Oriel Road —— C 22
Parabola Road —— B 23
Park (The) —— B 25
Park Place —— B 26
Regent Street —— C 29
Royal Well Road —— BC 30
St. George's Parade —— B 31
St. George's Place —— B 32
St. Margaret's Road —— C 33
Sandford Mill Road —— C 34
Sandford Terrace —— C 35
Thatcham Lane —— A 36

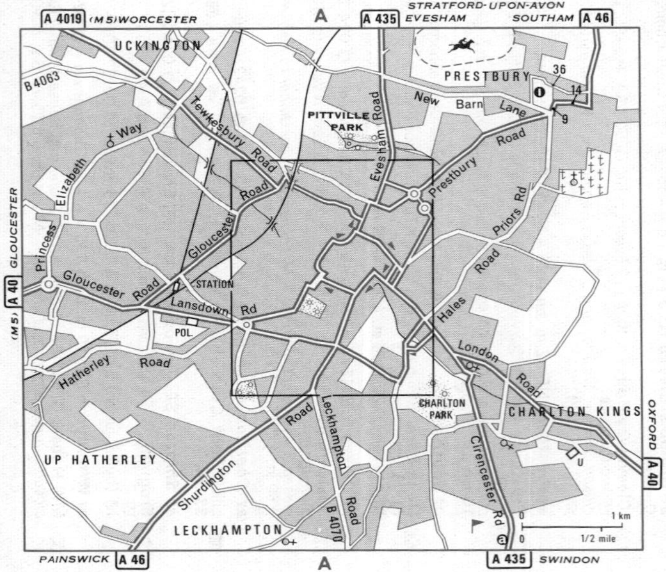

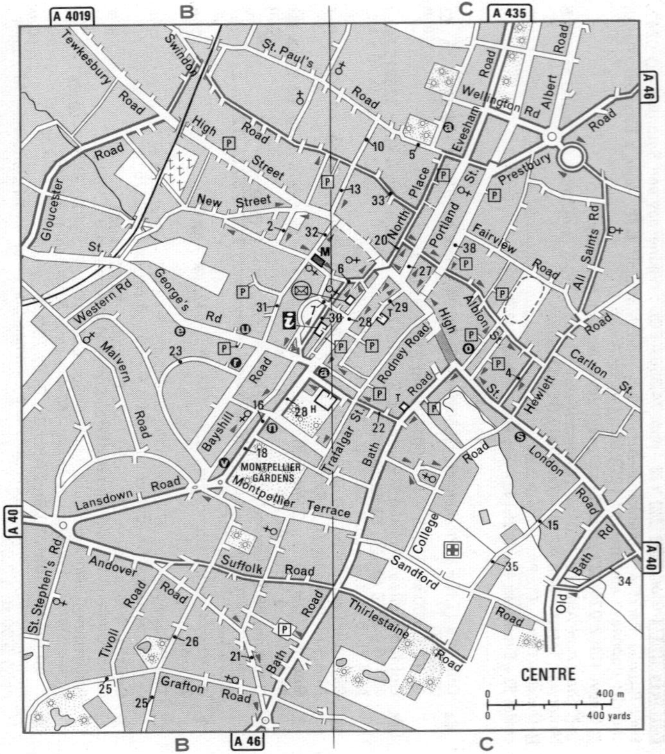

at Shurdington SW: 3 ¾ m. on A 46 – A – ✉ ✆ 0242 Cheltenham :

🏨 **Greenway** ⑤, GL51 5UG, ☏ 862352, ≼, « Country house atmosphere, gardens », park –
TV 🛏wc ☎ P. VISA
M 4.00/5.00 **s.** 🍶 1.75 – **13 rm** ⌷ 15.00/26.00 **s.** – P 32.00/34.00 **s.**

AUSTIN-MORRIS-MG-ROVER-TRIUMPH Princess
Elizabeth Way ☏ 20441
CITROEN 16/28 Bath Rd ☏ 55391
DAIMLER-JAGUAR Montpellier Spa Rd ☏ 21651
DATSUN 60/66 Fairview Rd ☏ 53880
FIAT 172 Leckhampton Rd ☏ 23365
FORD 71 Winchcombe St. ☏ 27061
LANCIA Swindon Rd ☏ 32167

OPEL 379 High St. ☏ 22666
PEUGEOT Kingsditch Lane ☏ 28945
ROLLS ROYCE-BENTLEY 62/68 Swindon Rd ☏ 55374
SAAB-HONDA Townsend St. ☏ 24348
SUBARU Andoversford ☏ 04515 (Guiting Power) 274
TALBOT Imperial Sq. ☏ 21121
VOLVO-TOYOTA 38 Suffolk Rd ☏ 27778
VW, AUDI North St. ☏ 55301

CHELWOOD GATE East Sussex 404 U 30 – see Forest Row.

CHENIES Bucks. 404 S 28 – pop. 1,099 – ECD : Thursday – ✉ Rickmansworth – ✆ 092 78
Chorleywood. – London 30 – Aylesbury 18 – Watford 7.

🏨 **Bedford Arms** (Thistle), WD3 6EQ, ☏ 3301, 🚗 – TV P. 🔲 AE ⓪ VISA
closed Christmas dinner – **M** a la carte 7.45/12.65 **t.** 🍶 1.75 – ☕ 3.00 – **10 rm** 24.00/
32.50 **t.**

CHEPSTOW Gwent 403 L 28 – pop. 8,480 – ECD : Wednesday – ✆ 029 12.
See : Castle* (stronghold) *AC.*
🛈 Tourist Information Centre, Old Arch Building, High St. ☏ 3772 (summer only).
London 131 – Bristol 17 – Cardiff 28 – Gloucester 34.

🏨 **Two Rivers,** Newport Rd, NP6 5PR, ☏ 5151 – 🛗 TV 🛏wc ☎ P. 🔥 🔲 AE ⓪ VISA
M a la carte 4.35/7.95 **s.** 🍶 1.20 – **31 rm** ⌷ 15.50/25.00 **s.**

🏨 **George** (T.H.F.), Moor St., NP6 5DB, ☏ 2365 – TV 🛏wc P. 🔥 🔲 AE ⓪ VISA
M 3.75/4.55 **st.** 🍶 1.65 – **20 rm** ⌷ 13.50/22.00 **st.**

AUSTIN-MORRIS-MG-WOLSELEY Station Rd ☏ 3159
FORD Newport Rd ☏ 2861
OPEL Bulwork Rd ☏ 5251

TALBOT Tutshill ☏ 3131
VAUXHALL St. Lawrence Rd ☏ 3889

CHESTER Cheshire 403 L 24 – pop. 62,911 – ECD : Wednesday – ✆ 0244.
See : Cathedral** 14C-16C (choir stalls and misericords**) B – St. John's Church* 12C D –
The Rows* – City Walls* – Grosvenor Museum (Roman gallery*) M[1]. Envir. : Upton (Chester
Zoo**) *AC,* N: 3 m. by A 5116.

🛈 Upton Lane ☏ 23638, by A 5116 – 🛈 Vicars Cross ☏ 35174, E: 2 m. by A 51 – 🛈 Tower's
Lane ☏ 092 82 (Helsby) 2021, NE: 8 m. by A 56 – 🛈 Ellesmere Port. Chester Rd ☏ 339 7502,
N: 9 m. by A 5116. – 🛈 Town Hall, ☏ 40144 ext 2111 and 49026 (evenings and at weekends).
London 196 – Birkenhead 19 – Birmingham 80 – Liverpool 21 – Manchester 39 – Preston 55 – Sheffield 75 –
Stoke-on-Trent 37.

Plan on next page

🏨 **Grosvenor,** Eastgate St., CH1 1LT, ☏ 24024, Telex 61240 – 🛗 TV ♿ 🔥 🔲 AE ⓪ VISA a
M *(closed Christmas)* a la carte 8.90/10.25 **t.** 🍶 2.25 – ☕ 3.25 – **100 rm** 25.00/40.50 **t.**

🏨 **Queen** (T.H.F.), City Rd, CH1 3AH, ☏ 28341, Telex 617101, 🚗 – 🛗 TV 🛏wc ☎ P. 🔥
🔲 AE ⓪ VISA
r
M 4.25/4.85 **st.** 🍶 1.65 – **91 rm** ⌷ 19.00/28.50 **st.**

🏨 **Post House** (T.H.F.), Wrexham Rd, CH4 9DL, S : 2 m. on A 483 ☏ 674111, Telex 61450 –
TV 🛏wc ☎ ♿ P. 🔥 🔲 AE ⓪ VISA
M 4.10/5.30 **st.** 🍶 1.65 – ☕ 2.50 – **56 rm** 17.00/24.50 **st.**

🏨 **Mollington Banastre** (Best Western), Parkgate Rd, CH1 6NN, NW : 2 m. on A 540
☏ 851418, 🚗 – 🛗 TV 🛏wc ☎ P. 🔥 🔲 AE VISA
closed 12 to 30 December – **M** a la carte 4.80/8.45 **st.** – **53 rm** ⌷ 17.50/28.00 **st.**

🏨 **Blossoms,** St. John St., CH1 1HL, ☏ 23186 – 🛗 TV 🛏wc ☎. 🔲 AE ⓪ VISA
e
M 4.50/5.50 **st.** 🍶 2.30 – **75 rm** ⌷ 20.00/32.50 **st.**

🏨 **City Walls** without rest., 14 Stanley Pl., ☏ 313416 – 🛗 TV 🛏wc ☎
o
20 rm ⌷ 15.00/17.50 **st.**

🏨 **Oaklands** (Thistle), 93 Hoole Rd, CH2 3BN, ☏ 22156, 🚗 – 🛏wc P. 🔲 AE ⓪ VISA c
M 2.95 **t.** – **19 rm** ⌷ 9.50/16.50 **st.**

🏨 Ye Olde King's Head, 48-50 Lower Bridge St., CH1 1RS, ☏ 24855, « 16C inn » – P s
11 rm.

🏨 **Weston,** 82 Hoole Rd, CH2 3NT, ☏ 26735 – TV 🛏wc P n
closed Christmas and 1 January – **16 rm** ⌷ 10.00/17.50 **st.**

🏨 **Green Bough,** 60 Hoole Rd, CH2 3NL, ☏ 26241 – 🛏wc P. 🔲 i
closed 24 December-1 January – **11 rm** ⌷ 7.00/14.00 **st.**

at Backford Cross N: 4 ½ m. by A 5116 junction A 41 and A 5117 – ✉ Chester –
✆ 0244 Great Mollington :

🏨 **Wirral Ladbroke Mercury Motor Inn,** CH1 6PE, ☏ 851551 – TV 🛏wc ☎ ♿ P. 🔥
🔲 AE ⓪ VISA
M a la carte 4.95/7.85 **t.** 🍶 1.95 – ☕ 2.45 – **122 rm** 16.25/21.00 **s.**

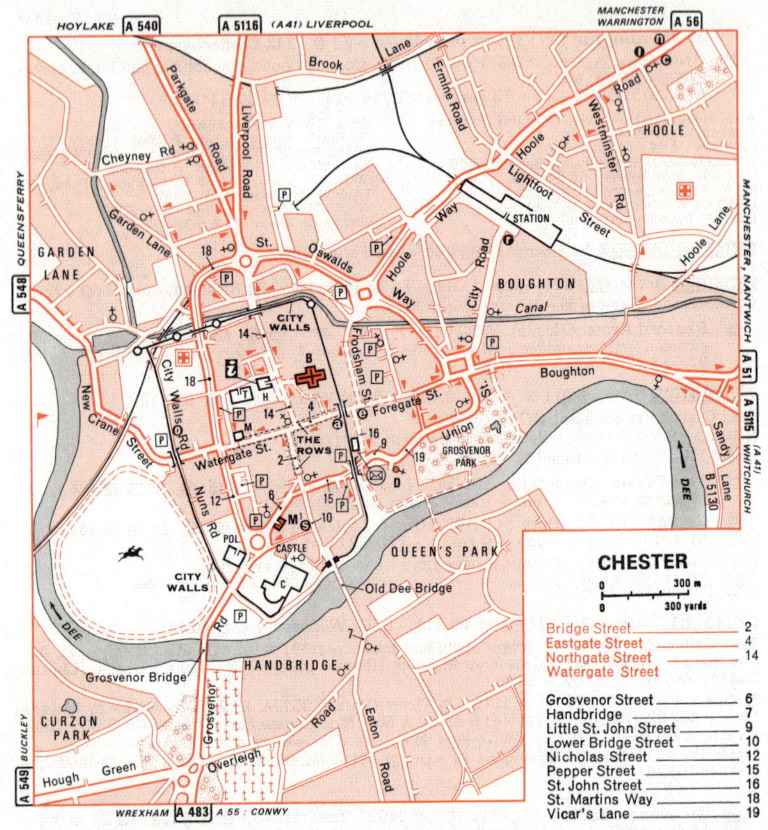

at Christleton E: 2 m. on A 41 – ✉ ☎ 0244 Chester:

🏨 **Abbots Well Motor Inn,** Whitchurch Rd, CH3 5QL, ☏ 32121, Telex 61561, 🚗 – 📺
& 🅿. ⚒. 🎱 AE ① VISA
M a la carte 7.20/11.30 **s.** 🍾 3.20 – 🍽 3.20 – **133 rm** 18.60/28.50 **t.**

at Broxton SE: 10 m. junction A 41 and A 534 – ✉ ☎ 082 925 Broxton:

XX Egerton Arms, ☏ 241, 🚗 – 🅿.

AUSTIN-MORRIS-MG-ROVER-TRIUMPH-WOLSELEY
17/23 Nicholas St. ☏ 315477
AUSTIN-MORRIS-MG-ROVER-TRIUMPH The Northgate ☏ 45051
CITROEN, DATSUN Border House ☏ 672977
DAIMLER-JAGUAR, ROLLS ROYCE 8 Russell St. ☏ 25262
FORD The Newgate ☏ 20444

OPEL 21 Garden Lane ☏ 46955
RENAULT Hamilton Pl. ☏ 317661
SAAB Western Av. ☏ 375744
TALBOT Victoria Rd ☏ 22622
VAUXHALL Hoole Lane, Broughton ☏ 24611
VOLVO 36 Tarvin Rd ☏ 25201
VW, AUDI-NSU Saughall Rd ☏ 377363

CHESTERFIELD Derbs. 🗺403 🗺404 I 24 – pop. 70,169 – ECD: Wednesday – ☎ 0246.
Envir. : Chatsworth★★★ : site★★, house★★★ (Renaissance), garden★★★ *AC*, W : 7 m. – Hardwick Hall★★ 16C (tapestries and embroideries★★) *AC*, SE : 8 m – Bolsover Castle★ (17C) *AC*, E : 6 m.
🏛 Murray House, Tapton Park ☏ 73887. – ℹ Central Library, Corporation St. ☏ 32047 and 32661.
London 152 – Derby 24 – Nottingham 25 – Sheffield 12.

🏨 Station, Corporation St., S41 7UA, ☏ 71141 – ⚒ 🛏wc ☎ 🚗 🅿. ⚒ – **64 rm.**
🏠 **Portland** (Anchor), West Bars, S40 1AY, ☏ 34502, Group Telex 858875 – 📺 🛏wc 🅿.
🔲 AE ① VISA
M a la carte approx. 6.00 **st.** – **24 rm** 🍽 13.00/22.50 **st.**

at Stonedge SW: 4 ½ m. by A 632 on B 5057 – ✉ ☎ 0246 Chesterfield:

XX Red Lion Inn, S45 0LW, ☏ 6142 , Dancing (Saturday) – 🅿.

AUSTIN-MORRIS-MG-WOLSELEY 221 Sheffield Rd ☎ 77241
CHRYSLER-SIMCA 361 Sheffield Rd ☎ 450383
CITROEN, SAAB Pottery Lane, Whittington Moor ☎ 51611
DATSUN Ringwood Rd ☎ 77386
FIAT Soresby St. ☎ 34351
FORD Barker Lane ☎ 76341
JAGUAR-ROVER-TRIUMPH Holywell St. ☎ 77241

MORRIS-MG-WOLSELEY Park Rd ☎ 73428
OPEL-VAUXHALL Chesterfield Rd, Staveley ☎ 024687 (Staveley) 3286
PEUGEOT Pottery Lane ☎ 74181
PORSCHE Broombank Rd ☎ 451611
RENAULT North Wingfield Rd ☎ 850208
TALBOT 361 Sheffield Rd ☎ 450383
VAUXHALL 464 Chatsworth Rd ☎ 79201

CHESTER-LE-STREET Durham ⑨⑧⑥ ⑲ – pop. 21,320 – ECD : Wednesday – ☎ 0385.

Envir. : Lambton Lion Park** *AC*, NE : 2 m. – Lumley Castle* (14C) *AC*, E : 1 ½ m. – Beamish (North of England open Air Museum*) *AC*, NW : 3 m.

🏌 Lumley Park ☎ 883218, E : ½ m. – 🏌 Beamish Park ☎ 020 73 (Stanley) 2552, NW : 3 m.

London 275 – Durham 7 – Newcastle-upon-Tyne 8.

🏰 Lumley Castle, DH3 4NX, E : 1 m. on B 1284 ☎ 885326, « 14C castle », ☁ heated, 🐎, park – 📺 🛏 wc 🏛 wc ☎ 🅿 🎿.
50 rm.

FIAT, VAUXHALL 187 Front St. ☎ 884221

CHESTERTON Oxon. ④⓪③ ④⓪④ Q 28 – pop. 497 – ✉ ☎ 086 92 Bicester.

🏌 ☎ 41204.

London 65 – Northampton 33 – Oxford 13.

XX **Kinchs,** OX6 8UE, on A 4095 ☎ 41444, « Tastefully converted barn » – 🅿
closed Sunday dinner, Monday and first week January – **M** (dinner only and Sunday lunch) 6.75/8.00 **t.** 🍷 2.00.

carte	Hotels and restaurants offering set meals generally also serve « a la carte ».

CHICHESTER West Sussex ④⓪④ R 31 – pop. 20,649 – ECD : Thursday – ☎ 0243.

See : Cathedral* 11C-15C BZ **A** – Market Cross* BZ **B. Envir. :** Fishbourne Roman Palace (mosaics*) *AC*, W : 2 m. AZ **R** – Goodwood House* (18C) *AC*, NE : 4 m. by A 27 AY and A 285.

🛈 The Council House, North St. ☎ 782226.

London 69 – Brighton 31 – Portsmouth 18 – Southampton 30.

CHICHESTER

East Street	BZ	Fishbourne Road	AZ 8	St. John's Street	BZ 23
North Street	BYZ	Florence Road	AZ 10	St. Martin's Square	BY 24
South Street	BZ	Hornet (The)	BZ 12	St. Pancras	BY 25
		Kingsham Road	BZ 13	St. Paul's Road	BY 27
Birdham Road	AZ 2	Lavant Road	AY 14	Sherborne Road	AZ 28
Bognor Road	AZ 3	Little London	BY 15	Southgate	BZ 29
Chapel Street	BY 6	Market Road	BZ 16	South Pallant	BZ 31
Chichester Arundel Road	AY 7	Northgate	BY 17	Spitalfield Lane	BY 32
		North Pallant	BZ 19	Stockbridge Road	AZ 33
		Priory Lane	BY 20	Tower Street	BY 35
		St. James's	AZ 21	Westhampnett Road	AYZ 36

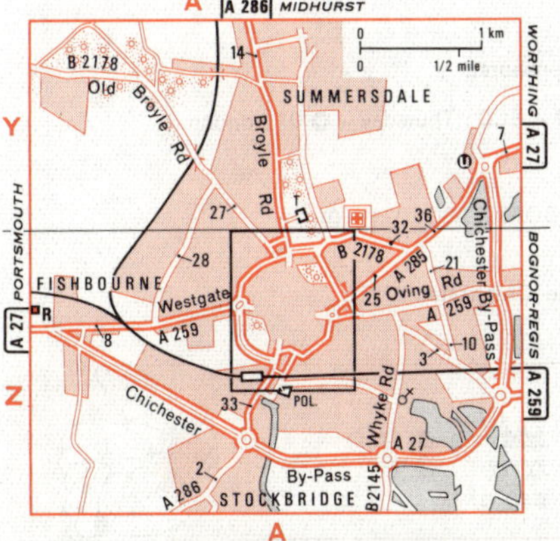

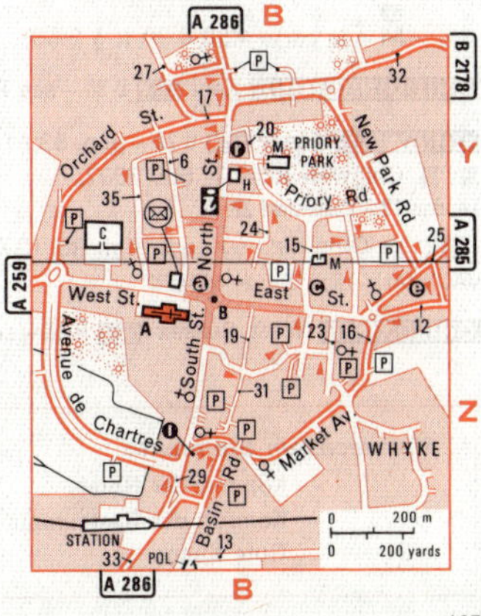

🏨 **Dolphin and Anchor** (T.H.F.), West St., PO19 1QE, ☎ 785121 – 📺 ⌷wc ☎ Ⓟ. 🏃.
🔥 AE ⓪ VISA
M (Carvery Rest) 4.00/5.00 **st.** ▯ 1.50 – **54 rm** ⌷ 14.00/23.50 **st.**
BZ a

🏨 **Chichester Lodge,** Westhampnett Roundabout, PO19 4UL, ☎ 786351 – 📺 ⌷wc ☎ &
Ⓟ. 🏃. 🔥 AE VISA
M 4.00/4.80 **t.** ▯ 1.10 – **34 rm** ⌷ 16.80/22.90 **st.**
AY u

🏠 **Ship,** North St., PO19 1NH, ☎ 782028, Telex 957141 – ▯ ⌷wc ☎ 🚗 Ⓟ. AE ⓪ VISA
M 3.60/4.75 **t.** ▯ 1.65 – **28 rm** ⌷ 9.00/19.00 **t.**
BY r

☺ **Bedford,** Southgate, PO19 1DP, ☎ 785766 – 🍴
M 3.25/3.90 **t.** ▯ 1.45 – **27 rm** ⌷ 8.00/16.00 **t.**
BZ i

XX **Little London,** 38 Little London, PO19 1PL, ☎ 784899
BZ c
closed Sunday, Monday, 2 weeks October, 23 to 26 December and Bank Holidays – M a
la carte 8.60/10.55 **t.** ▯ 1.80.

XX **Christopher's,** 149 St. Pancras, PO19 1SH, ☎ 788724 – 🔥 AE ⓪ VISA
BZ e
closed Monday dinner from October to April and Sunday all year – M 5.00/10.00 **st.** ▯ 1.35.

*at **Chilgrove*** N : 6 m. on B 2141 by A 286 – AY – ✉ Chichester – ☎ 024 359 East Marden :

XX **White Horse,** PO18 9HX, ☎ 219 – Ⓟ. 🔥 AE ⓪ VISA
closed Sunday, Monday, February and Bank Holidays – M a la carte 5.60/9.40 **t.**
▯ 2.20.

*at **Charlton*** N : 6 ¼ m. off A 286 – AY – ✉ Chichester – ☎ 024 363 Singleton :

☺ **Woodstock House** 🦢, PO18 0HU, ☎ 666, 🚗 – ⌷wc Ⓟ
closed January – M (dinner only) 5.00 ▯ 1.75 – **12 rm** ⌷ 7.50/16.00 – P 12.00/15.00.

*at **Goodwood*** NE : 4 m. off A 285 by A 27 – AY – ✉ Chichester – ☎ 024 353 Halnaker :

🏨 **Richmond Arms,** PO18 0QB, ☎ 361 – 📺 ⌷wc ☎ Ⓟ. 🏃. 🔥 AE ⓪ VISA
M a la carte 5.80/9.25 **t.** ▯ 2.25 – **20 rm** ⌷ 16.00/28.60 **t.** – P 28.85 **t.**

*at **Old Bosham*** W : 4 m. off A 27 – AZ – ✉ Chichester – ☎ 0243 Bosham :

🏨 **Millstream** (Best Western), Bosham Lane, PO18 8HL, ☎ 573234, « Tasteful decor »,
🚗 – 📺 ⌷wc ☎ Ⓟ. 🔥 AE ⓪ VISA
M a la carte 6.55/8.60 **st.** ▯ 1.60 – **16 rm** ⌷ 11.50/28.00 **st.**

*at **Funtington*** NW : 4 ½ m. on B 2178 – AY – ✉ Chichester – ☎ 024 358 West
Ashling :

XX Hallidays of Funtington, PO18 9LF, ☎ 331 – Ⓟ.

AUSTIN-DAIMLER-JAGUAR-MORRIS-MG-ROVER-
TRIUMPH Westhampnett Rd ☎ 781331
FIAT Northgate ☎ 784844
FORD The Hornet ☎ 788100
LANCIA Delling Lane, Bosham ☎ 573271

MERCEDES-BENZ, VOLVO Lavant Rd ☎ 527370
RENAULT 113 The Hornet ☎ 782293
TALBOT Market Rd ☎ 786622
VAUXHALL 55 Fishbourne Rd ☎ 782241
VW, AUDI-NSU 51/54 Bognor Rd ☎ 787684

CHIDDINGFOLD Surrey 🗺 S 30 – pop. 2,449 – ☎ 042 879 Wormley.

London 45 – Brighton 40 – Guildford 12.

XXX **Crown Inn** with rm, The Green, Petworth Rd, GU8 4TX, ☎ 2255, « 13C inn » – ⌷wc ☎ Ⓟ.
AE ⓪
M *(closed Monday and Tuesday except Bank Holidays)* a la carte 7.30/11.90 **st.** ▯ 2.50 –
⌷ 2.00 – **4 rm** 22.00/29.50 **st.**

X **Crown Bistro** (at Crown Inn), The Green, Petworth Rd, GU8 4TX, ☎ 2255 – Ⓟ. AE
⓪
M a la carte 4.50/6.30 **t.** ▯ 2.50.

CHIDDINGSTONE Kent 🗺 U 30 – see Penshurst.

CHIGWELL Essex 🗺 U 29 – pop. 53,818 – ECD : Thursday – ☎ 01 London.
🏌, 🏌 Chigwell Row ☎ 500 2097.

London 13 – Chelmsford 22.

XXX Ye Olde King's Head, High Rd, IG7 6OA, ☎ 500 2021 – Ⓟ.
VAUXHALL High Rd ☎ 500 4122

CHILGROVE West Sussex 🗺 R 31 – see Chichester.

Verwechseln Sie nicht:

Komfort der Hotels   : 🏨🏨🏨 . . . 🏠, ☺, ⭓

Komfort der Restaurants : XXXXX . . . X

Gute Küche   : ❀❀, ❀, M

CHILHAM Kent 404 W 30 – pop. 1,410 – ⊠ Canterbury – ✆ 022 776.
See : Village Square*, Castle* (17C) *AC*.
London 59 – Canterbury 6,5 – Folkestone 24 – Maidstone 21.

↑ **Cona** ⑤ Goldups Lane, Shottenden, CT4 8JG, NW: 1 ½ m. off A 252 ☏ 405, ☵ –
⋔wc **P**
10 rm ☲ 6.50/14.50 **s.**

CHILLINGTON Devon 403 I 33 – see Kingsbridge.

CHIPPENHAM Wilts. 403 404 N 29 – pop. 18,696 – ECD : Wednesday – ✆ 0249.
🏠 Malmesbury Rd ☏ 2040, N : 1 m.
London 106 – Bristol 27 – Southampton 64 – Swindon 21.

🏛 **Angel Motel** (Norfolk Cap.), 8 Market Pl., SN15 3HD, ☏ 2615, Group Telex 23241 – 📺
⌂wc **P**. ⚑ Æ ⓪ *VISA*
M a la carte 4.95/7.40 **st.** ⑧ 1.75 – **41 rm** ☲ 19.50/22.30 **st.**

FIAT Pewsham ☏ 2115   ROVER-TRIUMPH Station Hill ☏ 2215
FORD Cocklebury Rd ☏ 3255   VAUXHALL 16/17 The Causeway ☏ 3241
RENAULT London Rd ☏ 51131   VOLVO Malmesbury Rd ☏ 2016

CHIPPING CAMPDEN Glos. 403 404 O 27 – pop. 1,956 – ECD : Thursday – ✆ 0386 Evesham.
See : High Street*. **Envir.** : Hidcote Manor Garden* *AC*, NE : 2½ m.
London 93 – Cheltenham 21 – Oxford 37 – Stratford-upon-Avon 12.

🏛 **King's Arms,** The Square, GL55 6AW, ☏ 840256, ☵ – ⌂wc **P**. ⚑ Æ ⓪ *VISA*
closed January and February – **M** (bar lunch) approx. 6.75 **t.** ⑧ 1.40 – ☲ 1.20 – **14 rm**
12.50/30.35 **st.**

🏛 **Cotswold House,** The Square, GL55 6AN, ☏ 840330, ☵ – ⌂wc **P**. ⚑
M (bar lunch Monday to Saturday) 5.20 ⑧ 1.90 – ☲ 1.50 – **25 rm** 12.20/30.00 **s.**

🏛 **Noel Arms,** High St., GL55 6AT, ☏ 840317 – ⌂wc **P**
M 3.00/4.25 ⑧ 2.00 – **21 rm** ☲ 10.50/23.00.

🏛 Seymour House, High St., GL55 6AH, ☏ 840429, ☵ – ⌂wc **P**
20 rm.

at Mickleton N : 3 m. by B 4035 and B 4081 – ⊠ Chipping Campden – ✆ 038 677
Mickleton :

🏛 **Three Ways,** Chapel Lane, GL55 6SB, on A 46 ☏ 231, ☵ – ⌂wc **P**. ⚑ Æ *VISA*
M 5.00/6.00 ⑧ 2.00 – **49 rm** ☲ 12.00/27.00 – P 23.00/25.00.

AUSTIN-MORRIS-ROVER-TRIUMPH High St. ☏ 840213

CHIPPING NORTON Oxon. 403 404 P 28 – pop. 4,767 – ECD : Thursday – ✆ 0608.
London 77 – Birmingham 44 – Gloucester 36 – Oxford 21.

🏛 **White Hart** (T.H.F.), High St., OX7 5AD, ☏ 2572 – ⌂wc **P**. ⚑ Æ ⓪ *VISA*
M 4.25/4.75 **st.** ⑧ 1.80 – **22 rm** ☲ 13.50/22.00 **st.**

TALBOT ☏ 2014   VAUXHALL Burford Rd ☏ 2461

CHIPPING SODBURY Avon 403 404 M 29 – pop. 3,836 – ECD : Thursday – ✆ 0454.
Envir. : Dodington House* (18C) *AC*, SE : 1 m.
London 117 – Bristol 11 – Cardiff 50 – Gloucester 27.

↑ **Moda,** 1 High St., BS17 6BA, ☏ 312135 – Æ *VISA*
closed Christmas – **10 rm** ☲ 7.50/15.00 **s.**

PEUGEOT Badmindon Rd ☏ 312552

CHIPSTEAD Surrey 404 T 30 – pop. 4,129 (inc. Hooley) – ✆ 073 75 Downland.
London 15 – Reigate 6.

XX **Dene Farm,** Outwood Lane, CR3 3NP, ☏ 52661, ☵ – **P**. ⚑ Æ ⓪ *VISA*
M a la carte 6.10/9.10 **t.**

CHIRK (WAUN) Clwyd 403 K 25 – pop. 3,440 – ECD : Saturday – ⊠ Wrexham – ✆ 069 186.
See : Castle* (gates*) *AC*. **Envir.** : W: Vale of Ceiriog*.
London 188 – Chester 22 – Shrewsbury 24 – Welshpool 21.

XX **Hand** with rm, Church St., LL14 5EY, on A 5 ☏ 3472, ☵ – ⋔wc **P**
closed 25 and 26 December – **M** *(closed Sunday dinner to non-residents)* a la carte 4.85/
8.45 ⑧ 2.75 – **14 rm** ☲ 11.00/25.00 **t.**

CHITTLEHAMHOLT Devon 403 I 31 – pop. 146 – ⊠ Umberleigh – ✆ 076 94.
London 216 – Barnstaple 14 – Exeter 28 – Taunton 45.

🏛 **Highbullen** ⑤, EX37 9HD, ☏ 248, ≤, « Country house atmosphere » ✂, ⚑, ☒ heated,
🏌, ☵, park – 📺 ⌂wc **P**
M (bar lunch) approx. 7.00 **st.** ⑧ 2.00 – **25 rm** 18.00/24.00 **st.**

CHOLLERFORD Northumb. – ⊠ Hexham – ✆ 043 481 Humshaugh.
London 303 – Carlisle 36 – Newcastle-upon-Tyne 21.

   George (Swallow), NE46 4EW, ✆ 205, Group Telex 53168, ≤, « Riverside gardens », ⥼ –
   TV ⊟WC ☎ & ⟺ Ⓟ
   54 rm.

CHRISTCHURCH Dorset **403 404** O 31 – pop. 31,463 – ECD : Thursday – ✆ 020 15 (4 and
5 fig.) or 0202 (6 fig.)
See : Priory Church* (Norman nave**).
ⁿ₉ Iford Bridge, ✆ 3199.
🛈 Caravan, The Saxon Sq. ✆ 75555 (summer only).
London 111 – Bournemouth 6 – Salisbury 26 – Southampton 24 – Winchester 39.

   King's Arms (Crest), Castle St., BH23 1DT, ✆ 484117 – 💲 TV ⊟WC ☎ Ⓟ. ⚐. ⚞ AE ◍
   VISA
   32 rm ⌷ 13.25/24.50 **st.**

   Park House, 48 Barrack Rd, BH23 1PF, ✆ 482124, ⥼ – Ⓟ
   10 rm ⌷ 8.50/17.00 **st.**

   White Gates, 1 Westfield Gardens, Lyndhurst Rd, BH23 4SF, NE : 2 ½ m. on A 35 ✆ 5205 –
   Ⓟ – **7 rm.**

   ✕ Splinters, 12 Church St., BH23 1BW, ✆ 483454
   closed Sunday and 25-26 December – **M** (dinner only) a la carte 4.70/6.50 **t.** ♭ 1.70.

   at Mudeford SE : 2 m. – ⊠ ✆ 020 15 Christchurch :

   Avonmouth (T.H.F.), BH23 3NT, ✆ 483434, ≤ Christchurch harbour, ⌁ heated, ⥼ –
   TV ⊟WC ☎ Ⓟ. ⚐. ⚞ AE ◍ VISA
   M 4.10/4.85 **st.** ♭ 1.75 – **48 rm** ⌷ 15.00/29.50 **st.**
BRITISH LEYLAND Lyndhurst Rd ✆ 04252 (High-   CITROEN Barrack Rd ✆ 4515
cliffe) 71371   FIAT Highcliffe ✆ 04252 (Highcliffe) 72333

CHRISTLETON Cheshire **403** L 24 – see Chester.

CHURCH STRETTON Salop **403** L 26 – pop. 3,346 – ECD : Wednesday – ✆ 069 42.
ⁿ₁₈ Links Rd ✆ 2281.
🛈 Shropshire Hills, Information Centre, Church St. ✆ 2535 (summer only).
London 166 – Birmingham 46 – Hereford 39 – Shrewsbury 14.

   at All Stretton NE : 1 m. on B 4370 – ⊠ ✆ 069 42 Church Stretton :

   Stretton Hall ⤸, Old Shrewsbury Rd, SY6 6HG, ✆ 3224, ⌁ heated, ⥼, park – ⊟WC Ⓟ.
   ◍ VISA
   M 7.25/10.50 **st.** ♭ 1.20 – ⌷ 2.80 – **11 rm** 15.80/32.90 **st.** – P 31.40/38.50 **st.**

   at Little Stretton SW : 1 m. on B 4370 – ⊠ ✆ 069 42 Church Stretton :

   Mynd House, Ludlow Rd, SY6 6RB, ✆ 2212, ⥼ – 🛎 Ⓟ
   closed January – **12 rm** ⌷ 6.90/15.40 **st.**
AUSTIN-MORRIS-MG-ROVER-SHERPA-TRIUMPH-WOLSELEY 11 Burway Rd ✆ 2255

CHURSTON FERRERS Devon **403** J 32 – see Brixham.

CHURT Surrey **404** R 30 – pop. 3,443 (inc. Hindhead) – ECD : Wednesday – ⊠ Farnham.
Envir. : Devil's Punch Bowl (≤*) SE : 4 ½ m.
London 50 – Farnham 6 – Portsmouth 34 – Southampton 43.

   Frensham Pond (Best Western) ⤸, GU10 2QD, N : 1 ½ m. off A 287 ✆ 025125
   (Frensham) 3175, Telex 858610, ≤, « Tasteful decor », ⥼ – TV Ⓟ. ⚐. ⚞ AE ◍ VISA
   M a la carte 6.15/9.30 **st.** ♭ 2.20 – **19 rm** ⌷ 19.20/31.60 **st.**

   Pride of the Valley Inn (T.H.F.) ⤸, GU10 2LE, E : 1 ½ m. off A 287 via Hale House
   Lane, ✆ 042873 (Hindhead) 5799, ⥼ – TV ⊟WC ☎ Ⓟ. ⚞ AE ◍ VISA
   M 4.00/4.20 **st.** ♭ 1.65 – **10 rm** ⌷ 13.50/22.00 **st.**

CIRENCESTER Glos. **403 404** O 28 – pop. 11,990 – ECD : Thursday – ✆ 0285.
See : Parish Church* (Perpendicular) – Corinium Museum*.
Envir. : Northleach (SS. Peter and Paul's Church : south porch and the brasses* : Perpendicular)
NE : 10 m. – Chedworth (Roman Villa*) *AC*, N : 7 m.
ⁿ₁₈ Cheltenham Rd ✆ 3939, N : 1 ½ m.
🛈 Corn Hall, Market Pl. ✆ 4180.
London 101 – Bristol 37 – Gloucester 19 – Oxford 37.

🏨 **King's Head** (Best Western), 24 Market Pl., GL7 2NR, ☎ 3322, Telex 43470 – 🛗 📺 🅿️. 🛁.
🔄 AE ① VISA
M 5.20/6.75 **st.** 🍷 2.80 – **73 rm** ⊇ 15.75/34.00 **st.** – P 24.75/25.75 **st.**

🏨 **Fleece** (T.H.F.), Market Pl., GL7 4NZ, ☎ 2680 – 📺 ⌂wc ☎ 🅿️. 🔄 AE ① VISA
M 4.25/4.75 **st.** 🍷 1.65 – **23 rm** ⊇ 13.50/22.50 **st.**

🏨 **Corinium Court**, 12 Gloucester St., GL7 2DG, ☎ 4499, 🍴 – ⌂wc 🅿️. 🔄 AE ① VISA
closed Christmas and 1 January – **M** *(closed Sunday dinner)* a la carte approx. 6.50 **t.**
🍷 2.00 – **9 rm** ⊇ 10.00/24.00 **t.**

🏠 **La Ronde**, 52-54 Ashcroft Rd, GL7 1QX, ☎ 4611
10 rm ⊇ 8.50/12.50 **t.**

at Ewen SW: 3 ¼ m. off A 429 – ✉ Cirencester – ☎ 028 577 Kemble :

🍴🍴 **Wild Duck Inn** with rm, GL7 6BY, ☎ 364, 🍴 – 📺 ⌂wc 🅿️. 🔄 ①
M 4.50/5.50 **t.** – ⊇ 2.25 – **7 rm** 22.75/24.75.

at Stratton NW: 1 ¼ m. on A 417 – ✉ ☎ 0285 Cirencester :

🏨 **Stratton House**, Gloucester Rd, GL7 2LE, ☎ 61761, 🍴 – ⌂wc ☎ 🅿️. 🛁. 🔄 AE ① VISA
M 5.00/7.00 **st.** 🍷 1.60 – **31 rm** ⊇ 11.50/26.50 **st.**

AUSTIN-MORRIS-MG-ROVER-TRIUMPH Tetbury Rd ☎ 2614
CITROEN Perrotts Brook ☎ 028583 (North Cerney) 219
ROVER-TRIUMPH, VAUXHALL 7 Dyer St. ☎ 3314
TALBOT Market Pl. ☎ 3271

CLACTON-ON-SEA Essex **404** X 28 – pop. 38,070 – ECD : Wednesday – ☎ 0255.
See : Sea front (gardens)★.
🅱 Town Hall, Station Rd ☎ 25501 – Central Seafront ☎ 23400 (summer only).
London 71 – Chelmsford 38 – Colchester 16.

🏨 Royal (Gd. Met.), Marine Par., CO15 1PU, ☎ 21215 – 🛗 ⌂wc ☎ 🅿️
47 rm.

at Holland-on-Sea NE: 1 ½ m. – ✉ ☎ 0255 Clacton-on-Sea :

🏨 **Kings Cliff**, 55 Kings Par., Esplanade, CO15 5JB, ☎ 812343, ≤ – 🅿️
M 2.70/3.00 **t.** 🍷 1.80 – **13 rm** ⊇ 8.00/16.00 **t.**

🏠 **York House**, 19 York Rd, CO15 5NS, ☎ 814333, 🍴 – 🅿️. 🔄 AE VISA
closed November, January and February – **6 rm** ⊇ 6.00/12.00 **st.**

AUSTIN-MORRIS-MG-WOLSELEY 107 Old Rd ☎ 24128
DAIMLER-JAGUAR-ROVER-TRIUMPH 65-69 High St. ☎ 22422
VAUXHALL Pallister Rd ☎ 20444

CLANFIELD Oxon. **403** **404** P 28 – pop. 607 – ECD : Wednesday and Saturday – ☎ 036 781.
London 76 – Oxford 20 – Swindon 17.

🍴🍴🍴 **Plough**, with rm, OX8 2RB, on A 4095 ☎ 222, 🍴 – 🅿️
6 rm.

CLAPHAM Beds. **404** S 27 – see Bedford.

CLAPPERSGATE Cumbria – see Ambleside.

CLARE Suffolk **404** V 27– pop. 9,796 – ✉ Sudbury – E CD : Wednesday – ☎ 078 727 (3 and 4 fig.) or 0787 (6 fig.).
London 63 – Cambridge 26 – Ipswich 31.

🏨 **Bell**, Market Hill, CO10 8NN, ☎ 7741 – 📺 ⌂wc ☎ 🅿️. 🔄 AE ① VISA
M 4.00/5.00 🍷 1.90 – **20 rm** ⊇ 14.00/25.00.

CLAUGHTON Lancs. – pop. 115 – ✉ Lancaster – ☎ 0468 Hornby.
London 248 – Lancaster 6.

🍴🍴 **Old Rectory** with rm, LA2 9LA, ☎ 21455, 🍴 – 📺 ⌂wc ☎ 🅿️
closed 1 week spring, 1 week summer and 1 week autumn – **M** *(closed Sunday dinner and Monday to non-residents)* a la carte 5.65/7.95 **t.** – **4 rm** ⊇ 9.00/19.00 **t.**

CLAWTON Devon **403** GH 31 – pop. 303 – ✉ Holsworthy – ☎ 040 927 North Tamerton.
London 240 – Exeter 39 – Plymouth 36.

🏨 **Court Barn** 🦢, EX22 6PS, W: ¼ m. off A 388 ☎ 219, « ≤ country house and gardens » – ⌂wc 🅿️
April-October – **M** a la carte 4.60/7.00 **s.** 🍷 1.40 – **8 rm** ⊇ 12.00/32.00 **s.**

CLEADON Tyne and Wear – pop. 4,494 – ✉ Sunderland – ☎ 0783 Boldon.
🏌 Dipe Lane, East Boldon ☎ 4182.

London 285 – Newcastle-upon-Tyne 10 – Sunderland 4.

　　✗　**French Blackboard,** 63 Front St., SR6 7PG, ☎ 367397, French rest.
　　　　closed Sunday, 25-26 December and 1 January – **M** (dinner only) a la carte 4.55/6.05 **t.**
　　　　🍷 1.60.

CLEETHORPES Humberside 404 T 23 – pop. 35,837 – ECD: Thursday – ☎ 0472.
🖂 Alexandra Rd ☎ 66111 and 67472.

London 171 – Boston 49 – Lincoln 38 – Sheffield 77.

Plan : see Grimsby

　　🏨　**Kingsway,** Kingsway, DN35 0AE, ☎ 62836, 🛏 – ▮ TV 🖛WC ☎ 🚗 🅿. 🛁. 🔊 AE ① VISA
　　　　M 5.50/7.50 **st.** 🍷 2.00 – **57 rm** � 15.75/28.00 **st.**　　　　　　　BZ　a
　　🏠　**Wellow,** Chichester Rd, DN35 0HL, ☎ 65589 – TV 🖛WC ☎ 🅿. 🔊 VISA
　　　　M 4.80 **st.** 🍷 1.50 – **10 rm** ☘ 12.10/19.20 **st.**　　　　by Chichester Rd　Y

CITROEN 80 Brereton Av. ☎ 55558　　　　　　　　VAUXHALL 50 Taylors Av. ☎ 62961
LANCIA Grimsby Rd ☎ 63592

CLEEVE HILL Glos. 403 404 N 28 – see Cheltenham.

CLEVEDON Avon 403 L 29 – pop. 13,070 – ECD: Wednesday – ☎ 0272.
London 138 – Bristol 15 – Taunton 34.

　　🏨　**Walton Park,** 1 Wellington Terrace, BS21 7BL, ☎ 874253, ≼, 🛏 – ▮ 🖛WC 🚗 🅿.
　　　　🔊 VISA
　　　　M 4.00/5.50 **t.** 🍷 1.50 – **36 rm** ☘ 12.50/21.25 **t.** – P 18.40/20.40 **t.**
　　🏠　**Highcliffe,** 31 Wellington Terrace, BS21 7PU, ☎ 873250, ≼ – 🖛WC 🅿. 🔊 VISA
　　　　M a la carte 4.80/6.15 **t.** 🍷 1.95 – **19 rm** ☘ 11.50/20.50 **t.** – P 15.00/23.00 **t.**

AUSTIN-MORRIS-MG-ROVER-TRIUMPH Old Church　　TALBOT, FORD Bristol Rd ☎ 873701
Rd ☎ 872201

CLIFTON-UPON-DUNSMORE Warw. 403 404 Q 26 – see Rugby.

CLIFTONVILLE Kent 404 Y 29 – see Margate.

CLIMPING West Sussex 404 S 31 – pop. 963 – ✉ ☎ 090 64 Littlehampton.
London 64 – Bognor Regis 5 – Brighton 23.

　　🏨　Bailiffscourt 🦢, BN17 5RW, ☎ 3952, « Reconstructed medieval manor », ✗, 🏊 heated,
　　　　🛏, park – TV 🖛WC ☎ 🅿. 🛁. 🔊 AE ① VISA
　　　　M 7.00/14.00 **st.** – **23 rm.**

CLITHEROE Lancs. 986 ㉓ – pop. 13,194 – ECD: Wednesday – ☎ 0200.
🏌 Whalley Rd, ☎ 22618, SW: 2 m.
🖂 Information Office, Church St. ☎ 25566.

London 236 – Blackpool 35 – Leeds 44 – Liverpool 49.

　　🏠　**Roefield,** Edisford Rd, BB7 3LA, SW: 1 m. on B 6243 ☎ 22010, 🏊, 🛏 – TV 🖛WC ☎ 🅿. 🔊
　　　　AE ① VISA
　　　　M (bar lunch) 3.50/7.25 🍷 1.85 – **22 rm** ☘ 12.50/20.00.

　　　　at Sawley NE: 4 m. off A 59 – ✉ ☎ 0200 Clitheroe:

　　✗✗　**Spread Eagle,** BB7 4NH, ☎ 41202 – 🅿
　　　　M a la carte 6.65/8.00 **st.** 🍷 1.65.

AUSTIN-MORRIS-MG-WOLSELEY Whalley Rd ☎ 23883　　VAUXHALL Duck St. ☎ 22222

COATHAM MUNDEVILLE Durham – see Darlington.

COBHAM Surrey 404 S 30 – pop. 14,580 – ECD: Wednesday – ☎ 093 26.
London 24 – Guildford 10.

　　🏨　**Seven Hills Motel,** Seven Hills Rd South, KT11 1EW, SW : 1 m. off A 3 ☎ 4471,
　　　　Telex 929196, ≼, ✗, 🏊 heated, park – ▮ TV 🖛WC 🖛WC ☎ 🅿. 🛁. 🔊 AE ① VISA
　　　　M 5.75/6.75 **t.** 🍷 2.15 – **97 rm** ☘ 22.50/30.50 **st.**
　　✗✗✗　Fairmile (T.H.F.), Portsmouth Rd, KT11 1BW, NE: 1 m. on A 307 ☎ 2487, 🛏 – 🅿.
　　✗✗✗　San Domenico, Portsmouth Rd, KT11 1EL, SW: 1 m. on A 3 ☎ 3285, Italian rest. – 🅿.
　　✗✗　**La Capanna,** 48 High St., KT11 3EF, ☎ 2121, Italian rest. – 🅿
　　　　closed Sunday and 25-26 December – **M** a la carte 8.40/11.90 **t.**

ALFA-ROMEO, PEUGEOT 42 Portsmouth Rd ☎ 4493　　BMW, VW, AUDI 22 Portsmouth Rd ☎ 7141
AUSTIN-MORRIS-MG-PRINCESS-ROVER-TRIUMPH,　　DODGE, TALBOT The Tilt ☎ 4244
VANDEN PLAS Between St. ☎ 4444

 Cumbria 986 ⑲ – pop. 5,750 – ECD: Thursday – ☎ 0900.

☒₁₈ Embleton ⌖ 059 681 (Bassenthwaite Lake) 223, E: 4 m.

🛈 Riverside Car Park, Market St. ⌖ 822634 (summer only).

London 306 – Carlisle 25 – Keswick 13.

　🏨　**Trout,** Crown St., CA13 0EJ, ⌖ 823591, ⌖ – 📺 ⌂wc 🅿
　　　　M 4.00/7.00 **st.** ⌽ 2.00 – **17 rm** ⊏⊐ 10.50/22.00 **st.** – P 21.50/24.00 **st.**

　🏨　**Globe,** Main St., CA13 9LE, ⌖ 822126 – ⌂wc 🅿. ⛊ *VISA*
　　　　M 3.00/5.80 **t.** ⌽ 2.25 – **32 rm** ⊏⊐ 9.50/17.50 **t.** – P 15.30/16.50 **t.**

　🏨　**Wordsworth,** Main St., CA13 9JS, ⌖ 822757 – 📺 🕸 🅿. *VISA*
　　　　M (bar lunch) 4.00/6.00 **st.** ⌽ 1.60 – **14 rm** ⊏⊐ 6.50/15.00.

　⌂　**Hundith Hill** ⌖, Lorton Lane, CA13 9TH, SE: 2 m. by B 5292 ⌖ 822092, ⤙ Vale of
　　　　Lorton and Buttermere Fells, ✗, ⌖, park – ⌂wc 🅿. AE
　　　　March-November – **20 rm** ⊏⊐ 7.50/18.00 **t.**

AUSTIN-MG Crown St. ⌖ 822282　　　　　　　　MORRIS-MG-WOLSELEY Station Rd ⌖ 823042
BMW Derwent St. ⌖ 82366　　　　　　　　　　　PEUGEOT Gote Rd ⌖ 823017
FORD Lorton St. ⌖ 822033

 Gwent – see Blackwood.

 Essex 404 W 28 – pop. 3,643 – ECD: Wednesday – ☎ 0376.

London 49 – Braintree 6 – Chelmsford 16 – Colchester 9.

　🏨　**White Hart,** Market End, CO6 1NH, ⌖ 61654, « Part 14C Guild Hall » – 📺 ⌂wc 🕸wc
　　　　📞 🚗 🅿. ⛊ AE ⓞ *VISA*
　　　　closed 1 week at Christmas – **M** *(closed Sunday)* 7.00/12.00 ⌽ 1.95 – **24 rm** ⊏⊐ 15.00/
　　　　30.00 **st.**

 Essex 404 W 28 – pop. 76,531 – ECD: Thursday – ☎ 0206.

See: Roman Walls*. **Envir.**: Layer Marney (Marney Tower* 16C) SW: 7 m.

☒₉ Birch Grove, Layer Rd ⌖ 020 634 (Layer-de-la-Haye) 276, S: 2 m.

🛈 4 Trinity St. ⌖ 46379.

London 55 – Cambridge 48 – Ipswich 18 – Luton 67 – Southend-on-Sea 41.

　🏨　George (County), 116 High St., CO1 1WJ, ⌖ 78494, Group Telex 25971 – 📺 ⌂wc
　　　　📞 🅿. ⛴ ⛊ AE ⓞ *VISA*
　　　　M (Carvery rest.) – **35 rm** ⊏⊐ 17.00/20.75 **s.**

　🏨　**Rose and Crown,** East St., CO1 2TZ, ⌖ 76677 – ⌂wc 🕸wc 🅿. ⛊ AE ⓞ *VISA*
　　　　M *(closed Christmas dinner to non-residents)* (buffet Sunday dinner) approx. 4.00 ⌽ 1.70
　　　　– **29 rm** ⊏⊐ 8.00/17.50.

　✗✗　**Wm. Scraggs,** 2 North Hill, CO1 1NH, ⌖ 41111, Seafood – ⛊ AE *VISA*
　　　　closed Sunday and Bank Holidays – **M** a la carte 7.25/8.75 **t.**

　　　　at Wivenhoe SE: 4 m. by A 133 and B 1027 – ✉ Colchester – ☎ 020 622 Wivenhoe:

　✗　Smugglers, 47 High St., CO1 1DH, ⌖ 3582.

　✗　**Casserole,** 30 The Avenue, CO3 3PA, ⌖ 2221 – 🅿. ⛊ ⓞ
　　　　closed Sunday, Monday, last 2 weeks August, 24 December-1 January and Bank Holi-
　　　　days – **M** *(dinner only)* 7.25 **t.** ⌽ 1.75.

　　　　at Marks Tey W: 5 m. by A 12 on B 1408 – ✉ ☎ 0206 Colchester:

　🏨　**Marks Tey,** London Rd, CO6 1DU, ⌖ 210001, Telex 987176 – 📺 ⌂wc 📞 ⅙ 🅿. ⛴.
　　　　⛊ AE ⓞ *VISA*
　　　　M 4.00 **s.** ⌽ 1.50 – **106 rm** ⊏⊐ 14.25/20.35 **s.**

　　　　at Nayland (Suffolk) NW: 6 m. by A 134 – ✉ Colchester – ☎ 0206 Nayland:

　✗✗　**Bear,** Bear St., CO6 4HX, ⌖ 262204, ⌖ – 🅿
　　　　closed Sunday, Monday and Tuesday – **M** (dinner only and Sunday lunch) a la carte
　　　　4.25/5.60 ⌽ 1.55.

MICHELIN Branch, Gosbecks Rd, CO2 9JT, ⌖ 78451/4.

BRITISH LEYLAND East Gates ⌖ 77484　　　　　　FORD Magdalen St. ⌖ 71171
BRITISH LEYLAND Cowdray Av. ⌖ 76291　　　　　HONDA ⌖ 70745
CITROEN Butt Rd ⌖ 76803　　　　　　　　　　　　LANCIA, PEUGEOT Gosbecks Rd ⌖ 46455
DAIMLER-JAGUAR-ROVER-TRIUMPH Elmstead Rd　OPEL-VAUXHALL Ipswich Rd ⌖ 61333
⌖ 76281　　　　　　　　　　　　　　　　　　　　RENAULT Ipswich Rd ⌖ 68555
DATSUN 78 Military Rd ⌖ 77295　　　　　　　　TALBOT Wimpole Rd ⌖ 7082
FERRARI, PORSCHE, TOYOTA Auto Way, Ipswich　TALBOT Middleborough ⌖ 77391
Rd ⌖ 48141　　　　　　　　　　　　　　　　　VOLVO 10 Osborne St. ⌖ 77287
FIAT ⌖ 72208　　　　　　　　　　　　　　　　　VW, AUDI-NSU 83/85 East Hill ⌖ 77665

 Devon 403 I 31 – pop. 417 (inc. Colebrooke) – ✉ Crediton – ☎ 036 34 Cop-
plestone.

London 207 – Barnstaple 28 – Exeter 12.

　🏨　**Coombe House Country** ⌖, EX17 5BY, ⌖ 487, ⌇ heated, ⌖ – ⌂wc 📞 🅿. ⛊ ⓞ *VISA*
　　　　M (lunch by arrangement) a la carte 4.50/5.50 **t.** – **11 rm** ⊏⊐ 9.25/19.00 **t.**

COLEFORD Glos. **403** **404** M 28 – pop. 3,627 – ECD: Thursday – ⊠ Gloucester – ☉ 059 43 (4 fig.) or 0594 (5 fig).

ᵣₛ Coalway ☏ 3689, ½ m. on Parken Rd.

London 143 – Bristol 28 – Gloucester 19 – Newport 29.

　　🏛　**Speech House** (T.H.F.), Forest of Dean, GL16 7EL, NE: 3 m. on B 4226 ☏ 0594 (Cinderford) 22607, 🚗 – TV ⇔wc **P**. 🔊 AE ⓪ *VISA*
　　　　M 3.45/4.50 st. ⌕ 1.65 – **14 rm** � 14.00/23.00 st.

　　🏛　Bells, Lord's Hill, GL16 8BD, ☏ 2353, ✗, ⅃, ᵣₛ – ⇔wc **P**
　　　　25 rm.

　　🏚　**Lambsquay,** Forest of Dean, GL16 8QB, S: 1 ¼ m. on B 4228 ☏ 059 43 (Dean) 3127,
　　　　🚗 – ⇔wc **P**
　　　　M a la carte 5.00/6.50 t. ⌕ 2.20 – **11 rm** � 10.00/15.00 t. – P 20.00/21.50 t.

　AUSTIN-MORRIS-MG ☏ 42468　　　　　　　　　　　DATSUN ☏ 33517

COLESHILL West Midlands **403** **404** O 26 – pop. 6,297 – ECD: Monday and Thursday – ⊠ Birmingham – ☉ 0675.

London 113 – Birmingham 8 – Coventry 11.

　　🏨　**Swan** (Ansells), High St., B46 3BL, ☏ 62212 – TV 🏛wc **P**. 🔊 AE
　　　　M 3.45/4.00 t. ⌕ 1.80 – **34 rm** � 13.40/18.05 t.

COLLYWESTON Lincs. **404** S 26 – see Stamford.

COLWELL BAY I.O.W. **403** **404** P 32 – see Wight (Isle of).

COLWYN BAY (BAE COLWYN) Clwyd **403** I 24 – pop. 25,564 – ECD: Wednesday – ☉ 0492.

See : Zoo*. Envir. : Bodnant gardens** *AC*, SW: 6 m.

ᵣₛ Tan-y-Goppa Rd, Abergele ☏ 0745 (Abergele) 824034, E: 6 m. – ᵣ₉ Old Colwyn ☏ 55581.

🎭 Prince of Wales Theatre ☏ 30478 (Easter-September) – Wales Tourist Office ☏ 55719 (Easter-September).

London 237 – Birkenhead 50 – Chester 42 – Holyhead 41.

　　🏨　**Norfolk House,** 39 Princes Drive, LL29 8PF, ☏ 31757, Telex 61254, 🚗 – 🛗 TV ⇔wc
　　　　🏛wc ☎ **P**. 🔊 AE *VISA*
　　　　closed 22 December-4 January – **M** (bar lunch) approx. 7.00 t. ⌕ 1.80 – **35 rm** � 15.00/
　　　　27.00 t.

　　🏛　**Hopeside,** 63-65 Prince's Drive, LL29 8PW, ☏ 33244, Telex 61254 – TV ⇔wc 🏛wc ☎ **P**.
　　　　🔊 *VISA*
　　　　closed 22 December-8 January – **M** 5.00/8.00 st. ⌕ 2.25 – **20 rm** � 14.00/26.00 st. –
　　　　P 20.00/22.00 st.

　　↑　**Clevedon,** 18-20 Hawarden Rd, LL29 8NA, ☏ 2368
　　　　13 rm � 6.60/13.20 t.

　　　at Penmaenhead E: 2 m. on A 55 – ⊠ ☉ Colwyn Bay :

　　🏨　**Hotel 70°,** LL29 9LD, ☏ 56555, ≼ – TV **P**. 🔊 AE ⓪ *VISA*
　　　　M a la carte 5.70/10.45 st. ⌕ 2.50 – **44 rm** � 17.50/31.50 st.

　　　at Rhos-on-Sea (Llandrillo-yn-Rhos) NW: 1 m. – ⊠ ☉ 0492 Colwyn Bay :

　　↑　**Cabin Hill,** 12 College Av., LL28 4NT, ☏ 44568 – 🏛wc
　　　　April-October – **10 rm** � 5.60/13.00 s.

AUDI-NSU, MERCEDES-BENZ Abergele Rd ☏ 30456　　　PEUGEOT 268 Conwy Rd ☏ 44278
AUSTIN-MG-ROVER-TRIUMPH-WOLSELEY 394 Aber-　　FORD Conwy Rd ☏ 2201
gele Rd ☏ 55292　　　　　　　　　　　　　　　　　JAGUAR-MORRIS-MG-WOLSELEY, Conwy Rd ☏ 2281
DAIMLER-LAND ROVER, ROLLS-ROYCE, ROVER-　　VAUXHALL Princes Drive ☏ 30164
TRIUMPH 60 Princes Drive ☏ 30322

COLYFORD Devon **403** K 31 – see Colyton.

COLYTON Devon **403** K 31 – pop. 2,112 – ☉ 0297.

London 160 – Exeter 23 – Lyme Regis 7.

　　XX　**Old Bakehouse** with rm, Dolphin St., EX13 6NA, ☏ 52518 – **P**
　　　　March-October – **M** *(closed Sunday)* (dinner only) a la carte 7.35 ⌕ 1.70 – **7 rm** � 10.50/
　　　　23.00 **st.**

　　　at Colyford S: 1 m. by B 3161 on A 3052 – ⊠ ☉ 0297 Colyton :

　　🏛　Elmwood, Swan Hill Rd, EX13 6QV, ☏ 52750, 🚗 – ⇔wc **P**
　　　　12 rm.

　　🏚　**Old Manor** ⌂, Swan Hill Rd, EX13 6QQ, ☏ 52862, ≼, « Converted 15C manor house »,
　　　　✗, 🚗 – ⇔wc **P**
　　　　March-October – **M** (bar lunch) (residents only) approx. 4.00 t. ⌕ 1.20 – **10 rm** � 8.70/
　　　　17.00 t.

　　↑　**St. Edmunds,** Swan Hill Rd, EX13 6QQ, ☏ 52431, 🚗 – **P**
　　　　Easter-September – **10 rm** � 5.00/10.00 s.

COMBEINTEIGNHEAD Devon **403** J 32 – pop. 400 – ✉ Newton Abbot – ☎ 062 687
Shaldon.

London 219 – Exeter 19 – Plymouth 34 – Torquay 10.

🏠 **Netherton House** ⌂, TQ12 4RN, W: ¾ m. off B 3195 ☏ 3251, ✗, ⌇ heated, ☞, park –
⌷wc ⌷wc **P**. *VISA*
March-October – **M** *(closed Sunday dinner to non-residents)* approx. 6.50 **t.** ⌂ 1.65 –
11 rm ⌷ 15.00/17.50 **st.**

COMBE MARTIN Devon **403** H 30 – pop. 2,207 – ECD: Wednesday – ✉ Ilfracombe –
☎ 027 188.

London 218 – Exeter 56 – Taunton 58.

🏠 **Higher Leigh**, EX34 0NG, SE: 1 ¼ m. on A 399 ☏ 2486, ≤, ☞, park – **P**
M 3.75/6.50 **s.** ⌂ 2.00 – **11 rm** ⌷ *(dinner included)* 12.00/24.00 **s.**

↑ **Coulsworthy Country House** ⌂, EX34 0PD, E: 2 ½ m. on A 399 ☏ 2463, ⌇ heated,
☞ – ⌷wc **P**
12 rm ⌷ 9.00/22.00 **t.**

✗✗ **La Gallerie** with rm, Victoria St., EX34 0JT, ☏ 2566, « Tasteful decor » – **P**. ⌦ **AE**
① *VISA*
closed Sunday and Monday in winter – **M** a la carte 5.55/7.05 ⌂ 1.80 – **4 rm** ⌷ 6.00/
12.00 **st.**

BRITISH LEYLAND Borough Rd ☏ 2391   VAUXHALL Borough Rd ☏ 3257

COMPTON Surrey **404** S 30 – see Guildford.

CONGLETON Cheshire **403** **404** N 24 – pop. 20,010 – ECD: Wednesday – ☎ 026 02.
Envir. : Little Moreton Hall** (16C) *AC*, SO: 4 m.

☞ Biddulph Rd ☏ 3540, S: 1 ½ m. on A 527.
🛈 Market Square ☏ 71095.

London 178 – Liverpool 46 – Manchester 25 – Stoke-on-Trent 12.

✗✗ **Lorenzo's**, CW12 6AN, Moody Hall, Moody St., ☏ 77364, Italian rest. – **P**. ⌂. ⌦ **AE**
① *VISA*
closed Sunday dinner and Monday – **M** a la carte 6.35/8.80 **t.** ⌂ 1.80.

CONINGSBY Lincs. **404** T 24 – pop. 3,029 – ☎ 0526.
London 134 – Leicester 61 – Lincoln 29 – Nottingham 54.

✗✗ **Rattys**, 43 High St., LN4 4RB, ☏ 42285 – **P**. ⌦ ①
closed Sunday, Monday and Bank Holidays – **M** *(dinner only)* a la carte 4.20/6.50 **t.** ⌂ 1.70.

CONISTON Cumbria **986** ⑲ – pop. 1,063 – ☎ 096 64.
Envir. : Tarn Hows** (lake) NE: 3 m.
🛈 Main Car Park ☏ 533 (summer only).

London 285 – Carlisle 55 – Kendal 22 – Lancaster 42.

🏠 Sun ⌂, LA21 8HQ, ☏ 248, ≤, ☞ – **P**
10 rm.

AUSTIN-MORRIS-MG Coniston Lake ☏ 253

CONSTANTINE BAY Cornwall **403** E 32 – see Padstow.

CONWY Gwynedd **403** I 24 – pop. 12,206 – ECD: Wednesday – ☎ 049 263.
See : Site** – Castle** (13C) *AC* – St. Mary's Church* 14C. Envir. : Sychnant Pass* W: 2½ m.
☞18 ☏ 3400 – ☞9 Penmaenmawr ☏ 049 265 (Penmaenmawr) 3330, W: 4 m.
🛈 Snowdonia National Park Office, Castle St. ☏ 2248 (Easter-September).

London 241 – Caernarfon 22 – Chester 46 – Holyhead 37.

🏠 **Castle** (T.H.F.), High St., LL32 8DB, ☏ 2324 – 📺 ⌷wc ☎ **P**. ⌦ **AE** ① *VISA*
M 3.75/4.50 **st.** ⌂ 1.65 – **28 rm** ⌷ 13.50/22.00 **st.**

↑ **Llys Gwilym**, 3 Mountain Rd (off Cadnant Park), LL32 8PU, ☏ 2351 – **P**
6 rm ⌷ 4.85/9.70 **s.**

✗ **Alfredo's**, Lancaster Sq., LL32 8DE, ☏ 2381
closed Sunday dinner – **M** a la carte 6.25/8.10 **s.** ⌂ 2.70.

at Tal-y-Bont S: 5 ¼ m. on B 5106 – ✉ Conwy – ☎ 049 267 Tyn-y-Groes:

✗✗ **Lodge** with rm, LL32 8YX, ☏ 476, ☞ – 📺 ⌷wc **P**. ⌦ **AE** ① *VISA*
closed January and February – **M** a la carte 4.50/7.50 **t.** ⌂ 2.25 – ⌷ 1.25 – **10 rm** 14.50/
21.50 **t.**

COODEN East Sussex **404** V 31 – see Bexhill.

COOKHAM Berks. 404 R 29 – pop. 5,500 – ECD : Wednesday and Thursday – ⊠ Maidenhead
– © 062 85 Bourne End.
Envir. : Cliveden House* 19C (park**) *AC,* SE : 2 m.
⊺₁₈ Winter Hill, Grange Lane ℐ 27613.
London 36 – High Wycombe 7 – Reading 16.

XXX **Bel and The Dragon,** High St., SL6 9SQ, ℐ 21263
M a la carte 7.50/12.55 **t.**

X **Le Radier,** 19-21 Station Hill Parade, SL6 9BR, ℐ 25775
closed Sunday, 3 weeks September and Bank Holidays – **M** (dinner only) a la carte 6.15/
7.70 ₤ 2.20.

CITROEN High St. ℐ 22984   VW-AUDI High St. ℐ 22029

COPDOCK Suffolk 404 X 27 – see Ipswich.

COPTHORNE West Sussex 404 T 30 – see Crawley.

CORBRIDGE Northumb. 986 ⑲ – pop. 3,177 – ECD : Thursday – © 043 471.
Envir. : Hadrian's Wall** with its forts and milecastles (Chesters Fort*, museum *AC*) NW : 8 m. –
Corstopitum Roman Fort* *AC,* NW : 1 ½ m.
⊺₁₈ at New Ridley ℐ 066 15 (Stocksfield) 3101, SE : 6 m.
🛈 The Vicars Pele Tower ℐ 2815 (summer only).
London 300 – Hexham 3 – Newcastle-upon-Tyne 18.

 Angel Inn (S & N), Main St., NE45 5LA, ℐ 2119 – **P.** ◪ AE ⓞ VISA
M a la carte 3.40/7.10 **t.** ₤ 1.45 – **7 rm** ⊊ 10.50/15.00 **t.**

XX **Ramblers,** 18 Front St., NE45 5AP, ℐ 2424 – ◪ VISA
closed Sunday, Monday and 2 weeks October – **M** (dinner only) a la carte 6.55/8.75
₤ 1.05.

ALFA-ROMEO, BMW, SAAB Stagshaw ℐ 043472 AUSTIN-MORRIS-MG-ROVER-TRIUMPH-WOLSELEY
(Great Whittington) 216   Main St. ℐ 2068

<table>
<tr><td>Carte</td><td>Negli alberghi e ristoranti per i quali
indichiamo dei pasti a prezzo fisso,
è generalmente possibile ordinare anche alla carta.</td></tr>
</table>

CORBY Northants. 404 R 26 – pop. 53,500 – ECD : Wednesday – © 053 66.
Envir. : Kirby Hall* (ruins 16 C) NE : 4 ½ m.
⊺₁₈ Stamford Rd ℐ 5222.
London 93 – Leicester 27 – Northampton 22.

 Strathclyde, George St., NN17 1QQ, ℐ 3441 – ▯ ⊺ⅴ ⇌wc 🛆wc ☎ **P.** 🛆
40 rm.

AUSTIN-MORRIS-MG-ROVER-TRIUMPH-WOLSELEY   FORD Southern By-Pass ℐ 2332
Occupation Rd ℐ 2050   VAUXHALL Rockingham Rd ℐ 2531

CORNHILL-ON-TWEED Northumb. – pop. 320 – ECD : Thursday – © 0890 Coldstream.
London 345 – Edinburgh 49 – Newcastle-upon-Tyne 59.

 Tillmouth Park 🔥, TD12 4UU, NE : 2 ½ m. on A 698 ℐ 2255, ⪡, « Country house in
extensive grounds », 🔧, 🐎, park – ⇌wc ☎ **P.** ◪ AE ⓞ VISA
closed December and January – **M** 5.00/6.50 **st.** ₤ 1.75 – **16 rm** ⊊ 15.20/18.35 **st.** –
P 25.30/30.50 **st.**

 Collingwood Arms (Swallow), Main St., TD12 4UH, ℐ 2424, Group Telex 53168, 🐎 –
⇌wc ☎ **P**
16 rm.

BMW, SAAB ℐ 2146

CORSE LAWN Glos. 403 404 N 28 – see Gloucester.

CORSHAM Wilts. 403 404 N 29 – pop. 6,360 – ECD : Wednesday – © 0249.
See : Corsham Court** (Elizabethan) *AC.*
London 110 – Bristol 22 – Swindon 25.

 Hotels and restaurants see Bath : SW : 9 m.

CORWEN Clwyd 403 J 25 – pop. 2,164 – ECD : Wednesday – © 0490.
London 203 – Chester 33 – Holyhead 67 – Shrewsbury 39.

 Crown, LL21 0AH, ℐ 2403 – **P**
closed Sunday October-March – **M** a la carte 3.70/7.35 **t.** ₤ 1.30 – **6 rm** ⊊ 8.50/16.00 **t.**
– P 15.00 **t.**

See : St. Michael's Cathedral*** (1962) : tapestry*** AV A – Old Cathedral* (ruins) AV A – St. John's Church* 14C-15C AV B – Old houses* 16C-17C AV DEF.

Copeswood ☎ 451465, E : BY. – Forest of Arden ☎ 0676 (Meriden) 22118, N : 7 m. on A 45 AX.

Coventry Airport : ☎ 301717, S : 3 ½ m. by Coventry Rd BZ.

36 Broadgate ☎ 25555 ext 2398/9 or 20084/51517.

London 99 – Birmingham 18 – Bristol 91 – Nottingham 55.

Plans on following pages

De Vere (De Vere), Cathedral Sq., CV1 5RP, ☎ 51851, Telex 31380 – 🛗 📺. 🍴. AE ⓪ VISA AV n
M a la carte 5.00/10.00 st. 1.75 – **213 rm** � 26.00/36.50 st.

Leofric (Embassy), Broadgate, CV1 1LZ, ☎ 21371, Telex 311193 – 🛗 📺 🅿. 🍴. AE ⓪ VISA AV c
M 4.90/5.60 st. 2.90 – 2.15 – **90 rm** 18.00/26.50 st.

Hylands, 153 Warwick Rd, CV3 6AU, ☎ 501600 – 📺 🛏wc 🅿 AZ e
M (Carvery rest.) – **56 rm.**

Falcon, 13-19 Manor Rd, CV1 2LH, ☎ 58615 – 📺 🛏wc 🛏wc 🅿 AV s
M (Carvery rest.) – **35 rm.**

Fairlight, 14 Regent St., CV1 3EP, ☎ 24215 – 🅿 AV i
12 rm 5.50/10.00 st.

Grandstand, Coventry F.C., King Richard St., CV2 4FW, ☎ 27053 – 🅿. AE ⓪ VISA BY a
closed Saturday, Sunday and Bank Holidays – **M** (lunch only) a la carte 5.70/11.25 s.
2.00.

at Longford N : 4 m. on A 444 – ✉ ☎ 0203 Coventry :

Novotel, Wilsons Lane, CV6 6HL, junction 3 of M 6, ☎ 88833, Telex 31545, 🏊 heated –
🛗 📺 🛏wc 🅿. 🍴. AE ⓪ VISA BV v
M 5.50/5.75 st. 1.90 – 2.05 – **100 rm.**

at Walsgrave-on-Sowe NE : 3 m. on A 46 – ✉ ☎ 0203 Coventry :

Coventry Eurocrest (Crest), Hinckley Rd, CV2 2HP, NE : ½ m. ☎ 613261, Telex
311292 – 🛗 📺 🛏wc 🅿. 🍴. AE ⓪ VISA BX e
2.80 – **163 rm** 19.90/26.45 st.

at Brandon E : 6 m. off A 428 – BZ – ✉ ☎ 0203 Coventry :

Brandon Hall (T.H.F.) , Main St., CV8 3FW, ☎ 542571, Telex 31472, park – 📺
🛏wc 🅿. 🍴. AE ⓪ VISA BV
M 4.50/5.00 st. 1.65 – **67 rm** 18.00/25.50.

at Willenhall SE : 3 m. on A 423 – ✉ ☎ 0203 Coventry :

Coventry Crest (Crest), London Rd, CV3 4EQ, ☎ 303398 – 📺 🛏wc 🅿. 🍴. AE ⓪ VISA
2.40 – **69 rm** 18.00/24.50. BZ u

at Baginton S : 4 ½ m. off A 423 – ✉ ☎ 0203 Coventry :

Old Mill Inn, Mill Hill, CV8 3AH, ☎ 303588, « Converted water mill », – 🅿. AE
⓪ VISA BZ n
closed Saturday lunch and Sunday dinner – **M** a la carte 7.20/14.50 t.

at Berkswell W : 6 ¾ m. off A 4023 – AZ – ✉ Coventry – ☎ 0676 Berkswell :

Bear Inn, Spencers Lane, CV7 7BB, ☎ 33202 – 🅿. AE ⓪
closed Sunday – **M** a la carte 6.05/10.45 t. 1.75.

at Allesley NW : 3 m. on A 4114 – ✉ Coventry – ☎ 0203 Allesley :

Post House (T.H.F.), Rye Hill, CV5 9PH, ☎ 402151, Telex 31427, – 🛗 📺 🛏wc 🅿.
🍴. AE ⓪ VISA AXY s
M *(closed Sunday dinner)* 5.00/6.50 st. 1.55 – 2.25 – **196 rm** 17.00/24.50 st.

Allesley, Birmingham Old Rd, CV5 9GP, ☎ 403272 – 📺 🛏wc 🅿. 🍴. AE ⓪
closed Christmas Day – **M** 4.90/6.35 t. 2.10 – **45 rm** 10.75/24.05 st. – P 24.20/
34.50 st. AY r

at Keresley NW : 3 m. on B 4098 – AX – ✉ Coventry – ☎ 020 333 Keresley :

Royal Court , Tamworth Rd, CV7 8JG, ☎ 4171, – 🛏wc 🅿. 🍴. AE ⓪
closed Christmas Day – **M** 4.45/5.45 1.90 – **19 rm** 12.00/19.00 – P 21.00/27.00.

Beechwood, Sandpits Lane, CV6 2FR, ☎ 4243, – 📺 🛏wc 🅿. AE VISA
M 3.50 1.90 – **28 rm** 9.00/18.00.

at Meriden NW : 6 m. on B 4102 by A 45 – AX – ✉ – ☎ 0676 Meriden :

Manor (De Vere), Old Birmingham Rd, CV7 7NH, ☎ 22735, Telex 311011, 🏊 heated,
– 📺 🅿. 🍴. AE ⓪ VISA
M 4.00/4.95 st. 1.75 – **32 rm** 22.00/32.00 st.

COVENTRY

Broadgate — AV 6
Corporation Street — AV
Shopping Precincts — AV

Bayley Lane — AV 3
Bishop Street — AV 5
Burges — AV 7
Canterbury Street — AV 9
Earl Street — AV 10
Fairfax Street — AV 12

Far Gosford Street — AV 13
Gosford Street — AV 15
Greyfriars Lane — AV 16
Hales Street — AV 17
Harnall Lane — AV 19
High Street — AV 22
Ironmonger Row — AV 23
Jordan Well — AV 26
Leicester Row — AV 29
Light Lane — AV 30
Little Park Street — AV 31
Oxford Road — BZ 32
Primrose Hill Street — AV 33

Queen Victoria Road — AV 35
St. Johns (Ringway) — AV 38
St. Nicholas (Ringway) — AV 39
Swanswell (Ringway) — AV 40
Trinity Street — AV 41
Upper Well Street — AV 43
Vecqueray Street — AV 45
Victoria Street — AV 46
Warwick Road — AV 48
Warwick Row — AV 49
White Street — AV 51
Windsor Street — AV 52
White Friars (Ringway) — AV 54

CENTRE
300 m
300 yards
A 4170   A 444
A 4114
St. Nicholas
Foleshill Rd
Stoney Stanton Rd
B 4109
NAUL'S MILL PARK
Radford Rd
Rgwy Hill Cross
Holyhead
Barras Lane
Rgwy Rudge
Butts   Rd
A 4023
Croft Rd
SHOPPING PRECINCTS
MARKET
Corporation St.
SPORTS CENTRE
New Union St.
Rgwy Queen's
Rgwy St. Patricks
SPENCER PARK
STATION
(A 444)   A 429
Raglan   St.
Lower Ford   St.
Cox St.
Much Park   St.
Park   Side
Quinton Rd   Mile   Lane
London   Rd
Gulson   Rd
A 46   A 427   A 423

BIRMINGHAM   A 444   NUNEATON
BUILT UP AREA
1 km
1 mile
B 4113
Coventry Cal
Coventry   Rd
B 4109
LONGFORD
Aldermans Green   Rd
Oxford Cal
Shilton   Lane
LEICESTER   M 69   A 46
M 6   LONDON (M1)
Longford   Bedworth   Rd
FOLESHILL
Holbrooks   Lane
Lockhurst La.
EDGWICK
A 444
Church   Rd
Old   Rd
Bell   Green
Sewall
Henley
Deedmore   Rd
Hinckley Rd
Road

BIRMINGHAM   A 45
(A 51)   B 4098   TAMWORTH
KERESLEY
Brow's   Lane
Keresley
Burnaby   Rd
Beake   Av.
Road
COUNDON

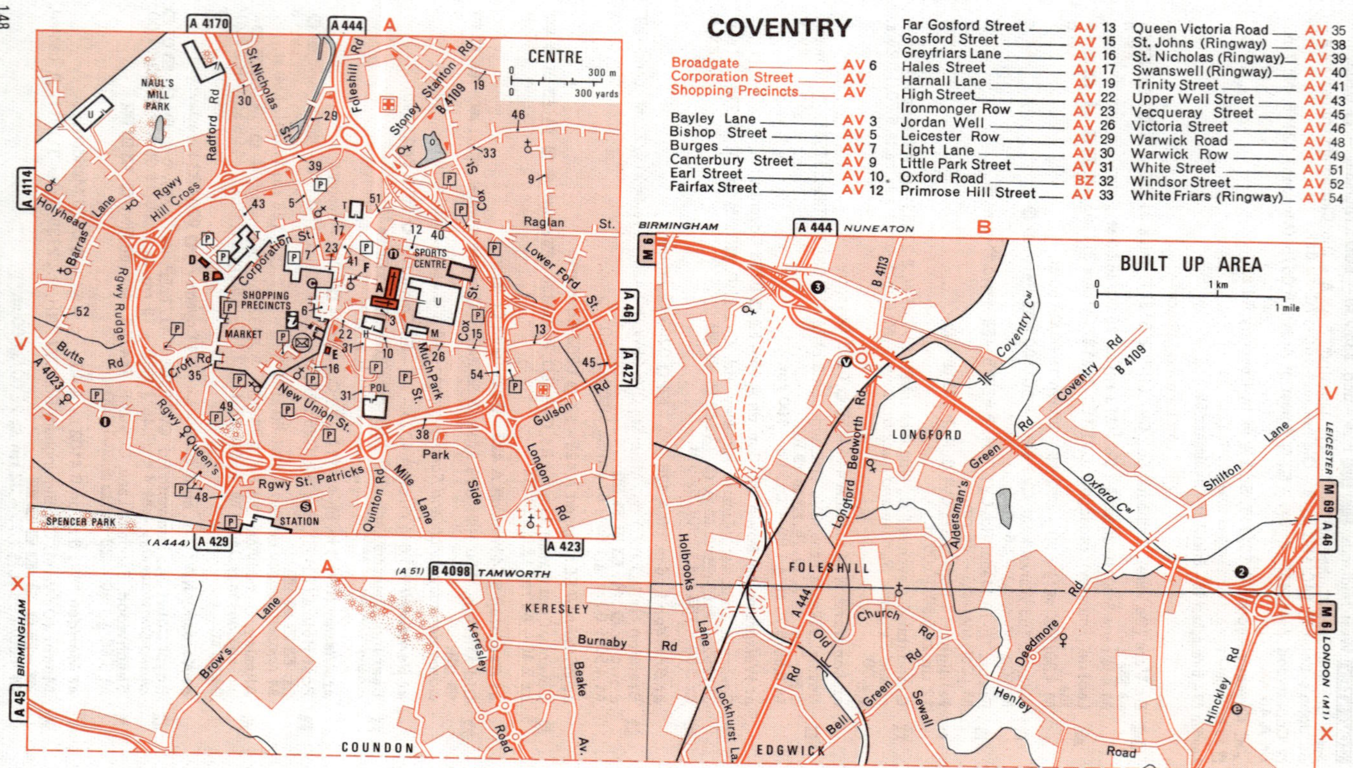

148

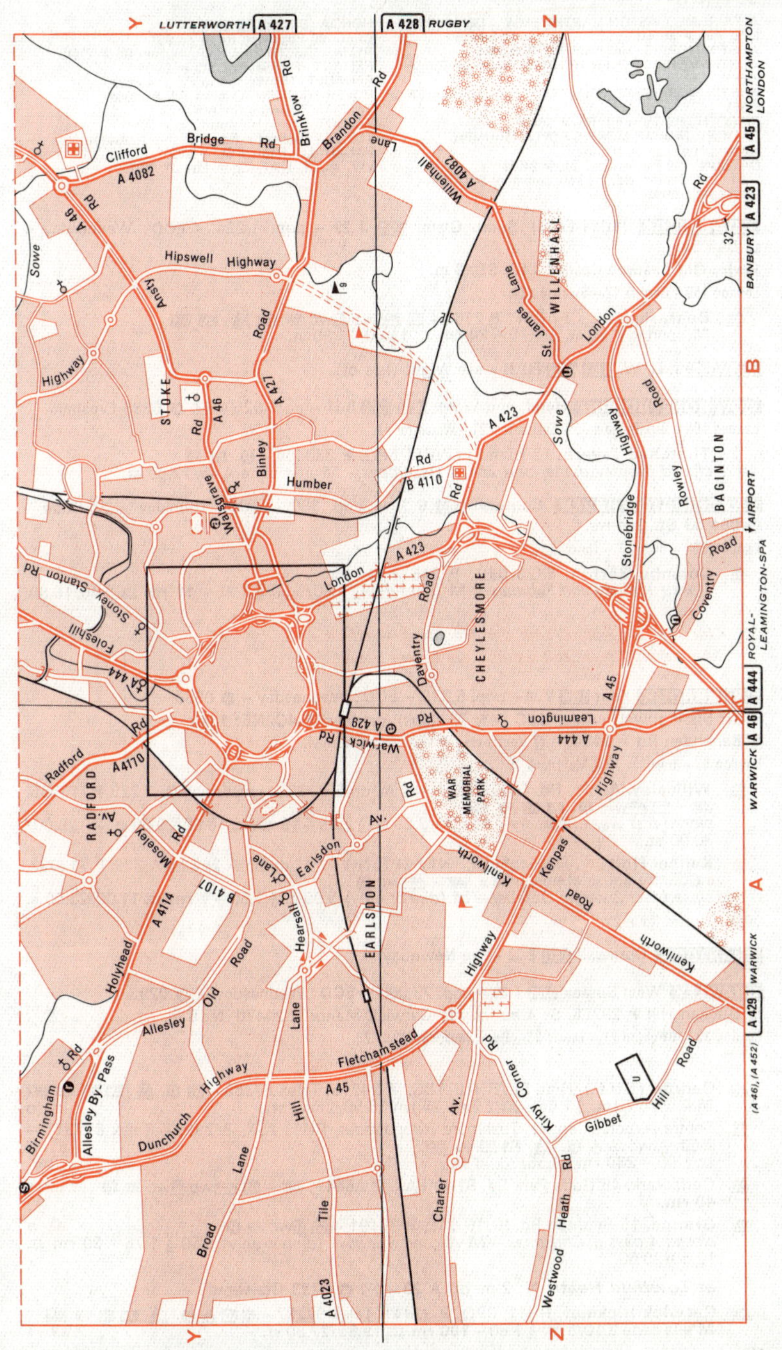

LUTTERWORTH A 427
A 428 RUGBY
Y
N
NORTHAMPTON
LONDON
A 45
BANBURY A 423
32
Clifford
Bridge Rd
Brinklow Rd
Brandon Lane
Willenhall A 4082
A 4082
WILLENHALL
St. James Lane
London Rd
A 46 Rd
Sowe
Hipswell Highway
Road
Ansty
STOKE
A 46 Rd
A 427
Highway
Binley
Humber
Rd
B 4110
A 423
Sowe
Stonebridge Highway
Rowley Road
BAGINTON
Coventry Road
Walsgrave
London Road
A 423
CHEYLESMORE
Daventry Road
B
AIRPORT
ROYAL-
LEAMINGTON-SPA
A 444
Stoney Stanton Rd
Foleshill
A 444
Warwick Rd
A 429
Leamington
Rd
A 444
A 45
Highway
WARWICK A 46
A 444
Radford
A 4170
RADFORD
Moseley Rd
B 4107
Earlsdon Lane
Av.
WAR MEMORIAL PARK
Kenilworth
Kenpas
Rd
A
WARWICK
Holyhead
A 4114
Hearsall Lane
Old Road
EARLSDON
Kenilworth Road
Highway
Allesley
Allesley By-Pass
Birmingham Rd
Dunchurch
Highway
Hill Lane
Tile
Fletchamstead Highway
A 45
Charter Av.
Kirby Corner Rd
Gibbet Hill Road
U
Westwood Heath Rd
A 4023
Y
N
A 429
WARWICK
(A 46), (A 452)

COVENTRY

ALFA-ROMEO, ASTON-MARTIN, BMW   138 Sutherland Av. ☎ 461441
AUSTIN-MORRIS Holyhead Rd ☎ 592501
AUSTIN-MORRIS-ROVER-TRIUMPH Warwick Rd ☎ 28661
AUSTIN-MORRIS-MG-WOLSELEY Lockhurst Lane ☎ 88851
CITROEN 105 Foleshill Rd ☎ 26417
DAIMLER-JAGUAR-MORRIS-ROVER-TRIUMPH Kenpas Highway ☎ 411515
DATSUN 149 Far Gosford St. ☎ 24552
FIAT 324 Station Rd, Balsall Common ☎ 0676 (Berkswell) 33145

HONDA Bishop St. ☎ 364004
OPEL 20 Edgewick Rd ☎ 663969
RELIANT, SCIMITAR, TVR Gulson Rd ☎ 27518
RELIANT Far Gosford St. ☎ 25308
RENAULT 158 Walsgrave Rd ☎ 458600
ROVER-TRIUMPH Queens Rd ☎ 23366
TALBOT Daventry Rd ☎ 503522
TALBOT Lower Holyhead Rd ☎ 28581
TOYOTA Bennetts Rd, Keresley ☎ 334204
VAUXHALL Raglan St. ☎ 25361
VW, AUDI, FIAT, Spon End ☎ 56325

COWBRIDGE (BONT-FAEN) South Glam. 🗺403 J 29 – pop. 1,224 – ECD: Wednesday – ✆ 044 63.

Envir : Old Beaupré Castle* 14C, SE : 3 m.

London 169 – Cardiff 12 – Swansea 27.

Bear, High St., CF7 7AF, ☎ 2169 – TV ⊨wc ⋔wc ☎ P. 🗠. ☒ VISA
M approx. 4.50 st. ▯ 1.75 – **24 rm** ⊆ 11.50/21.50 st.

COWES I. O. W. 🗺403 🗺404 PQ 31 – see Wight (Isle of).

COW HONEYBOURNE Heref. and Worc. 🗺403 🗺404 O 27 – pop. 925 – ✉ ✆ 0386 Evesham.
London 100 – Birmingham 35 – Cheltenham 21 – Worcester 21.

✗ **Thatched Tavern,** 12 High St., WR11 5PQ, ☎ 830454 – P. ☒ ◉
closed Sunday dinner and 25-26 December – M a la carte 4.45/12.60 st.

CRACKINGTON HAVEN Cornwall 🗺403 G 31 – pop. 380 – ECD: Thursday – ✉ Bude – ✆ 084 03 St. Gennys.
London 262 – Bude 11 – Truro 42.

Coombe Barton, EX23 0JG, ☎ 345 – P
closed January and February – M (bar lunch) 3.60/5.50 ▯ 1.75 – **11 rm** ⊆ 9.40/18.80.

Im Juli und August sind die Hotels oft überfüllt.
Außerhalb dieser Zeit werden Sie besser bedient.

CRANBROOK Kent 🗺404 V 30 – pop. 5,326 – ECD : Wednesday – ✆ 0580.
Envir: Sissinghurst : castle* 16C (◁*, 78 steps), gardens** AC, NE : 1 ½ m.
🛇 Benenden Rd ☎ 3434. – 🄸 Vestry Hall ☎ 2538 (summer only).
London 53 – Hastings 19 – Maidstone 15.

Willesley, Angley Rd, TN17 2LE, N : ¾ m. on B 2189 at junction with A 229 ☎ 713555,
🚐 – TV ⊨wc P. ☒ AE ◉ VISA
closed first week February – M 4.30/7.25 st. ▯ 2.55 – **16 rm** ⊆ 16.50/29.00 st. – P 25.00/30.00 st.

Kennel Holt 🗠, Flishinghurst, TN17 2PT, NW : 2 ¼ m. on A 262 off A 229 ☎ 712032,
« Country house atmosphere », 🚐 – ⊨wc P
closed first 2 weeks October – M (dinner only) 5.00 s. ▯ 1.50 – **7 rm** ⊆ 11.00/25.00 s.

OPEL Carriers Rd ☎ 2322

CRANTOCK Cornwall 🗺403 E 32 – see Newquay.

CRAWLEY West Sussex 🗺404 T 30 – pop. 73,000 – ECD: Wednesday – ✆ 0293.
🛇 Buchan Hill ☎ 28256, S : 4 m. AZ – 🛇 Gatwick Manor ☎ 24470, N : 5 m. AY.
London 33 – Brighton 21 – Lewes 23 – Royal Tunbridge Wells 23.

Plans on following pages

George (T.H.F.), High St., RH10 1BS, ☎ 24215, Telex 87385 – TV P. 🗠. ☒ AE ◉ VISA   BZ o
M 4.55/5.20 st. ▯ 1.65 – ⊆ 2.25 – **75 rm** 18.50/25.50 st.

Centre Airport (Centre), Tushmore Roundabout, RH11 7SX, ☎ 29991, Telex 877311 –   BY n
⌷ TV ⊨wc ☎ & P. 🗠. ☒ AE ◉ VISA
⊆ 1.65 – **230 rm** 19.55/26.45 st.

Goffs Park, 45 Goffs Park Rd, RH11 8AX, ☎ 35447, 🚐 – TV ⊨wc ⋔wc ☎ P   BZ s
40 rm.

Grange, 15 Brighton Rd, RH10 6AL, ☎ 35191 – TV ⋔wc ☎ P   BZ a
closed 4 days at Christmas – M (closed Sunday) (dinner only) 5.50 ▯ 1.75 – **30 rm** ⊆ 12.50/20.00.

at Lowfield Heath N : 2 m. off A 23 – ✉ ✆ 0293 Crawley:

Gatwick Hickmet, RH11, 0PQ, ☎ 33441, Telex 87287 – ⌷ TV & P. 🗠. ☒ AE ◉ VISA   AY i
M a la carte 3.10/5.50 ▯ 1.80 – **100 rm** ⊆ 19.85/27.80 st.

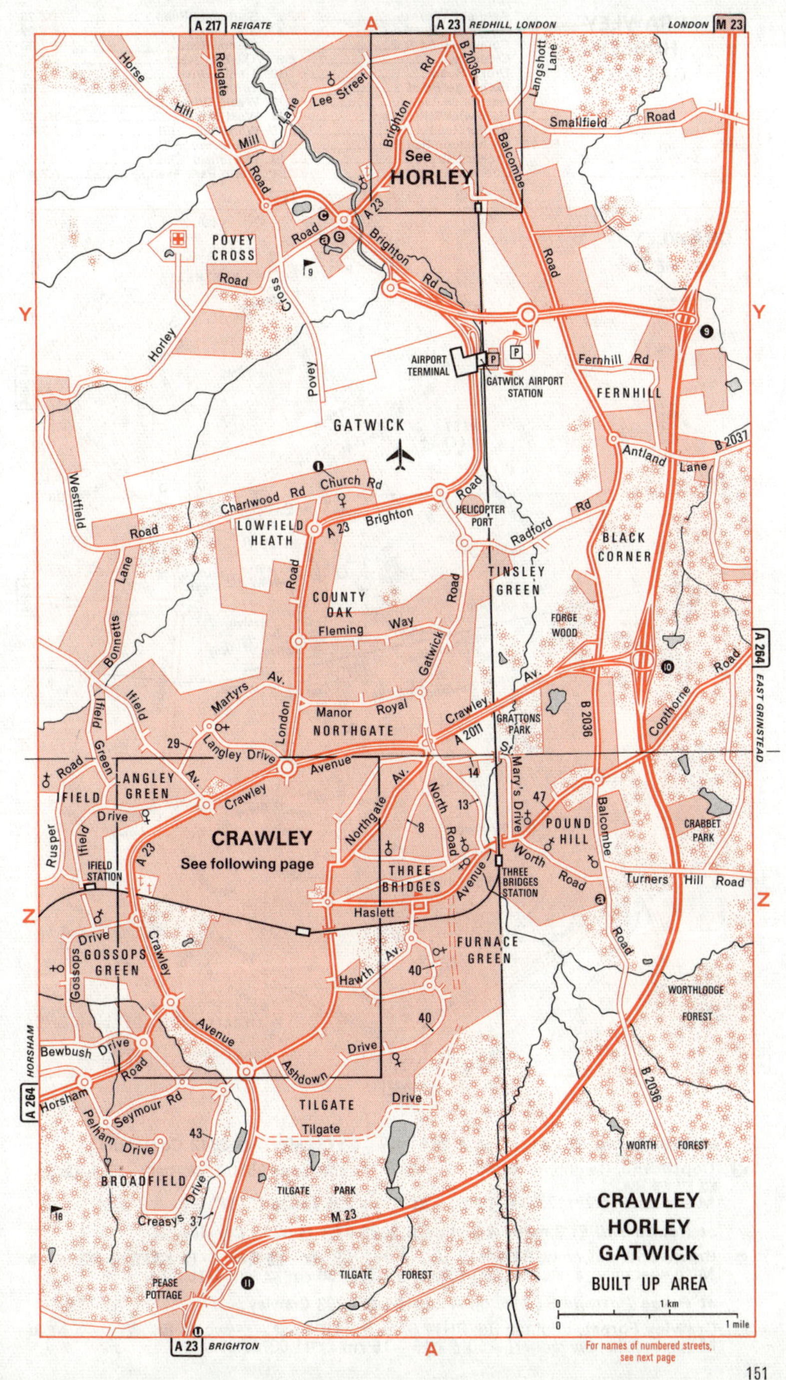
A 217 REIGATE
A
A 23 REDHILL, LONDON
LONDON M 23
Horse
Hill
Mill
Road
Reigate Lane
Lee Street
Brighton Rd
B 2036
Langshott Lane
Smallfield Road
Balcombe
See HORLEY
A 23
POVEY CROSS
Cross Road
Road
Brighton Rd
Road
9
Horley Road
Povey
Fernhill Rd
FERNHILL
Westfield
Road
Charlwood Rd
Church Rd
GATWICK
AIRPORT TERMINAL
P
P
Gatwick Airport Station
HELICOPTER PORT
Antland Lane
B 2037
LOWFIELD HEATH
A 23
Brighton
Road
Radford Rd
BLACK CORNER
Lane
Bonnetts Lane
COUNTY OAK
Fleming Way
Gatwick Road
TINSLEY GREEN
FORGE WOOD
Road
B 2036
Copthorne Road
A 264 EAST GRINSTEAD
Ifield Green
Martyrs Av.
London Road
Manor Royal
NORTHGATE
Crawley Av.
A 2011
GRATTONS PARK
10
Ifield Road
29
Langley Drive
Avenue
14
St. Mary's Drive
47
POUND HILL
CRABBET PARK
FIELD
LANGLEY GREEN
Drive
Crawley Av.
Northgate Av.
North Road
13
8
Balcombe Road
Rusper Road
Ifield
A 23
IFIELD STATION
CRAWLEY
See following page
THREE BRIDGES
Avenue
Worth Road
Turners Hill Road
Z
Haslett
THREE BRIDGES STATION
Gossops Drive
GOSSOPS GREEN
Crawley
Hawth Av.
40
FURNACE GREEN
WORTHLODGE FOREST
Bewbush Drive
Avenue
40
Drive
A 264 HORSHAM
Horsham Road
Seymour Rd
Pelham Drive
43
Ashdown Drive
TILGATE
Tilgate
Drive
B 2036
BROADFIELD
Drive
Creasys
37
18
TILGATE PARK
M 23
WORTH FOREST
PEASE POTTAGE
11
TILGATE FOREST
CRAWLEY
HORLEY
GATWICK
BUILT UP AREA
0   1 km
0   1 mile
A 23 BRIGHTON
A
For names of numbered streets,
see next page

CRAWLEY
HORLEY
GATWICK

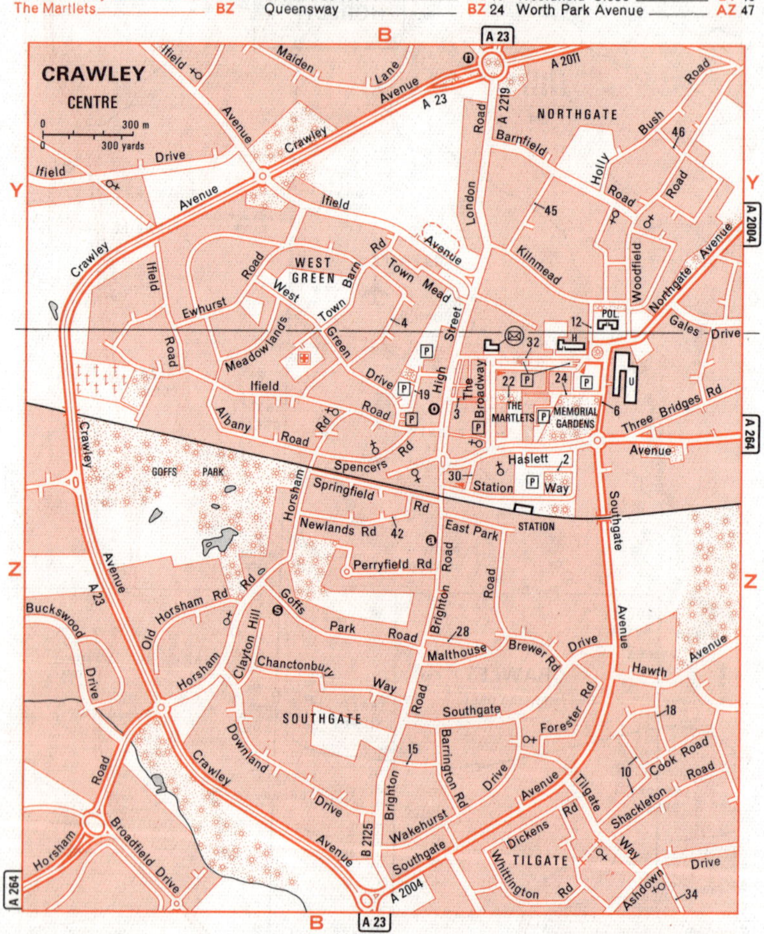

at Copthorne NE: 4 ½ m. on A 264 – AY – ✉ Crawley – ☎ 0342 Copthorne :

Copthorne, Copthorne Rd, RH10 3PG, ☎ 714971, Telex 95500, ☞, park – TV ⅖ Ⓟ. ♨.
⚉ AE ⓪ VISA
M a la carte 10.25/12.70 t. 🍷 2.20 – 🍽 2.75 – **230 rm** 26.25/37.10 t.

at Pound Hill E: 3 m. by A 264 on B 2036 – ✉ ☎ 0293 Crawley :

Barnwood, Balcombe Rd, RH10 4RU, ☎ 882709, ☞ – TV 🍴wc ☎ Ⓟ. ♨ AE ⓪ VISA AZ a
M (dinner only) a la carte 2.80/5.60 s. 🍷 2.50 – **30 rm** 🍽 12.50/16.50 s.

at Pease Pottage S: 2 m. on A 23 – ✉ ☎ 0293 Crawley :

Crawley Forest, Brighton Rd, RH11 9AD, ☎ 24101, ☞ – 🛁wc ☎ Ⓟ. ♨ AZ u
M (closed Sunday dinner) 7.50 🍷 2,15 – **15 rm** 🍽 11.00/20.00.

AUSTIN-MORRIS-MG-WOLSELEY 263/269 Haslett Av. Three Bridges ☎ 27101
CITROEN ☎ 25533
CITROEN 163/165 Three Bridges Rd ☎ 36437
DAIMLER-JAGUAR-LAND ROVER-MORRIS-MG-ROVER-TRIUMPH 41 Ifield Rd ☎ 20191

DATSUN 5 Brighton Rd ☎ 35264
FORD ☎ 28381
RENAULT Orchard St. ☎ 23323
TOYOTA Overdene Drive, Ifield ☎ 37521
VAUXHALL, OPEL Fleming Way ☎ 29771
VW ☎ 515555

CRESSAGE Salop 🔢 🔢 M 25 – see Shrewsbury.

CREWE Cheshire 🔢 🔢 M 24 – pop. 51,421 – ECD: Wednesday – ☎ 0270.
Envir. : Sandbach (Two Crosses* 7C, in Market Place) NE : 4 ½ m.
🚗 ☎ 4343.
🛈 Delamere House, Delamere St. ☎ 583191.
London 174 – Chester 24 – Liverpool 49 – Manchester 36 – Stoke-on-Trent 15.

🏨 **Crewe Arms** (Embassy), Nantwich Rd, CW1 1DW, ☎ 213204 – 📺 🛏wc 🚿wc ☎ 🅿. 🛴.
🅂 AE ⓪ VISA
M *(closed Saturday and Sunday lunch)* 4.80 **st.** 🍷 2.80 – **35 rm** ☐ 15.00/20.00 **st.**

AUSTIN-MORRIS-MG Nantwich Rd ☎ 56521
AUSTIN-MORRIS-MG-ROVER-TRIUMPH-WOLSELEY Newcastle Rd ☎ 841320
AUSTIN-MORRIS-MG High St. ☎ 214064
BMW, POLSKI, VW, AUDI West St. ☎ 214317
FIAT, POLSKI, SUBARU Earle St. ☎ 584414

CITROEN Woolstanwood ☎ 213495
DATSUN Cross Green ☎ 583437
FIAT Stewart St. ☎ 60688
FORD Macon Way ☎ 583511
PEUGEOT 613 Crewe Rd, Wist aston ☎ 68651
TALBOT, COLT High St. ☎ 213241

CREWKERNE Somerset 🔢 L 31 – pop. 4,821 – ECD : Thursday – ☎ 0460.
London 145 – Exeter 38 – Southampton 81 – Taunton 20.

🏨 Old Parsonage, Barn St., TA18 8BP, ☎ 73516 – 🛏wc 🅿 – **8 rm.**

☛ *Pour aller loin rapidement, utilisez les* cartes Michelin à 1/1 000 000.

CRICCIETH Gwynedd 🔢 H 25 – pop. 1,505 – ECD : Wednesday – ☎ 076 671.
See : Castle ≼** *AC.*
🏌 Ednyfed Hill ☎ 2154.
London 249 – Caernarfon 17 – Shrewsbury 85.

🏨 **Bron Eifion** 🦢, LL52 0SA, W : ½ m. on A 497 ☎ 2293, ≼, « 19C country house in large garden », park – 🛏wc 🚿wc ☎ 🅿
M 4.25/6.50 **st.** 🍷 2.50 – **19 rm** ☐ 18.00/40.00 **st.**

🏨 Lion, Y Maes, LL52 0AA, ☎ 2460, 🚗 – 🛗 🛏wc 🅿
38 rm.

🏚 **Parciau Mawr** 🦢, High St., LL52 0RP, W : ½ m. on A 497 ☎ 2368, 🚗 – 📺 🛏wc 🚿wc 🅿
2 March-15 October – **M** *(dinner only)* 5.70 **st.** 🍷 1.30 – **13 rm** ☐ 13.15/23.70 **st.**

🏚 **Mynydd Ednyfed** 🦢, LL52 0PH, N : ¾ m. on B 4411 ☎ 2200, ≼, 🚗 – 🚿 🅿
M *(buffet lunch)* 3.50/5.80 – **10 rm** ☐ 13.00/26.00.

🏠 **Bron-Aber,** Pwllheli Rd, LL52 0RR, W : ¼ m. on A 497 ☎ 2539 – 🚿 🅿
Easter-October – **16 rm** ☐ 7.00/14.00.

🏠 **Glyn-y-Coed,** Porthmadoc Rd, LL52 0HP, ☎ 2870 – 🅿
Easter-September – **10 rm** ☐ 4.50/9.00.

AUDI, MERCEDES-BENZ Caernarfon Rd ☎ 2516   VW-VOLVO Llanystumdwy ☎ 2733

CRICK Northants. 🔢 🔢 Q 26 – see Rugby.

CRICKHOWELL Powys 🔢 K 28 – pop. 1,286 – ECD : Wednesday – ☎ 0873.
Envir.: Tretower Court and castle ✳, NW : 2 ½ m.
London 169 – Abergavenny 6 – Brecon 14 – Newport 25.

🏨 **Gliffaes** 🦢, NP8 1RH, W : 3 ¾ m. off A 40 ☎ 0874 (Brecon) 730371, ≼, « Large garden », ✖, 🦢, park – 🛏wc 🅿
14 March-December – **M** 4.80/6.70 **st.** – **21 rm** ☐ 10.30/20.60 **st.** – P 16.00/24.50 **st.**

🏨 Gwernvale Manor, Brecon Rd, NP8 1SE, W : 1 m. on A 40 ☎ 810212, ≼, 🚗 – 🛏wc ☎ 🅿. 🛴.
14 rm.

🏚 **Bear,** High St., NP8 1BW, ☎ 810408, 🚗 – 🛏wc 🚿wc ☎ 🅿
M *(bar lunch)* a la carte 5.45/6.80 **t.** 🍷 1.50 – **12 rm** ☐ 8.50/18.00 – P 17.50/22.00.

CRICKLADE Wilts. 🔢 🔢 O 29 – pop. 2,431 – ECD : Saturday – ☎ 079 375.
London 94 – Bristol 41 – Gloucester 26 – Swindon 8.

🏚 White Hart, High St., SN6 6AA, ☎ 206 – 🅿
15 rm.

CROMER Norfolk 404 X 25 – pop. 5,376 – ECD: Wednesday – ☎ 0263.
See : SS. Peter and Paul's Church (tower ≼*). **Envir.** : Blickling Hall* (Jacobean) SW: 10 ½ m.
🏌 at Mundesley ☏ 720279, S: 7 m.
🛈 North Lodge Park ☏ 512497.
London 134 – King's Lynn 44 – Norwich 22.

 🏨 **De Paris,** Seafront, NR27 9HG, ☏ 513141, ≼ – 📶 ⌷wc 🎬 ☎ **P.** ◪ AE ① VISA
  M 4.50/6.75 t. ⅃ 2.50 – **55 rm** ☲ 10.75/24.20 t. – P 17.30/19.90 t.

  at Northrepps SE : 3 m. off A 149 – ✉ Cromer – ☎ 026 378 Overstrand :
 XX Church Barn, ☏ 588 – **P.**

AUSTIN-MORRIS-MG 16 Church St. T 512203   RENAULT Cabbell Rd ☏ 2557

CROOKLANDS Cumbria – ✉ Milnthorpe – ☎ 044 87.
London 258 – Kendal 6 – Lancaster 15.

 🏨 **Crooklands,** LA7 7NW, on A 65 ☏ 432 – TV ⌷wc 🎬 **P.** ◪ AE ① VISA
  M a la carte 5.60/9.00 t. ⅃ 2.00 – ☲ 2.20 – **21 rm** 9.50/22.00 t.

CROSBY-ON-EDEN Cumbria – see Carlisle.

CROWBOROUGH East Sussex 404 U 30 – pop. 11,540 – ECD: Wednesday – ☎ 089 26.
London 45 – Brighton 25 – Maidstone 26.

 🏨 **Crest,** Beacon Rd, TN6 1AD, on A 26 ☏ 2772, 🚗 – 📶 ⌷wc 🎬 **P.** ◪ AE ① VISA
  closed 24 and 25 December – M 4.15/5.15 st. ⅃ 2.30 – **30 rm** ☲ 12.65/24.20 st.
AUSTIN-MORRIS Beacon Rd ☏ 2777   TALBOT Church Rd ☏ 3424
RENAULT Crowborough Hill ☏ 2175

CRUG-Y-BAR Dyfed 403 I 27 – pop. 200 – ECD: Saturday – ✉ Llanwrda – ☎ 055 83 Talley.
London 213 – Carmarthen 26 – Swansea 36.

 ♨ **Glanrannell Park** ⚘, SA19 8SA, SW: ½ m. off B 4302 ☏ 230, ≼, ⚲, 🚗, park – **P**
  April-October – M *(closed Sunday lunch)* (bar lunch) 3.50/5.50 st. ⅃ 2.00 – **11 rm** ☲
  9.50/19.00 st. – P 15.00/18.00 st.

CWMBRAN Gwent 403 K 29 – pop. 45,000 – ECD: Wednesday – ☎ 063 33.
🏌 Pontnewydd ☏ 2170.
🛈 Torfaen District Council, 42 Gwent Sq. ☏ 67411.
London 149 – Bristol 35 – Cardiff 17 – Newport 5.

 🏨 **Commodore,** Mill Lane, Llan-yr-Afon, NP4 2SH, ☏ 4091 – 📶 TV ⌷wc 🏠wc 🎬 **P.** ⚒
  ◪ ① VISA
  M 3.50/4.00 s. ⅃ 1.40 – **42 rm** ☲ 16.85/23.35 s.

DALTON North Yorks. – see Richmond.

DARESBURY Cheshire 403 404 M 23 – pop. 330 – ✉ ☎ 0925 Warrington.
London 197 – Chester 16 – Liverpool 22 – Manchester 25.

 🏨 Lord Daresbury, WA4 4BB, on A 56 ☏ 67331 – 📶 TV 🚹 **P.** ⚒ – **108 rm.**

DARLINGTON Durham 986 ⑲ – pop. 85,938 – ECD: Wednesday – ☎ 0325.
🏌 Briar Close ☏ 64464, S: 1 m. on A 66 – 🏌 Stressholme, Snipe Lane ☏ 53073, S: 2 m.
✈ Tees-side Airport: ☏ 032 573 (Dinsdale) 2811, E: 6 m by A 67.
🛈 District Library, Crown St. ☏ 62034 and 69858.
London 251 – Leeds 61 – Middlesbrough 14 – Newcastle-upon-Tyne 35.

 🏨 **Europa Lodge** (County) ⚘, Blackwell Grange, DL3 8QH, SW: 2 m. on A 66 ☏ 60111,
  Telex 587272, 🚗 – 📶 TV 🚹 **P.** ⚒ ◪ AE ① VISA
  M 5.00/6.25 st. ⅃ 1.55 – **96 rm** ☲ 18.00/27.00 s.
 🏨 King's Head, Priestgate, DL1 1NW, ☏ 67612 – 📶 TV ⌷wc 🎬 **P.** ⚒ – **72 rm.**

  at Coatham Mundeville N : 4 m. off A 167 – ✉ Darlington – ☎ 0325 Aycliffe :
 🏨 **Hall Garth Country House** ⚘, DL1 3LU, ☏ 313333, « Country house atmosphere »,
  🚗 – TV ⌷wc 🎬 **P**
  closed 23 December-3 January – M 5.25/6.75 ⅃ 1.65 – ☲ 1.75 – **11 rm** 12.55/28.75 t.

  at Middleton One Row E : 5 m. off A 67 – ✉ Darlington – ☎ 032 573 Dinsdale :
 🏨 Devonport, The Front, DL2 1AS, ☏ 2255 – ⌷wc **P**
  19 rm.

  at Teesside Airport E : 5 ½ m. off A 67 – ✉ Darlington – ☎ 032 573 Dinsdale :
 🏨 **St. George,** DL2 1RH, ☏ 2631, ✂ – TV ⌷wc 🎬 🚹 🚗 **P.** ⚒ ◪ AE ① VISA
  M 9.40 ⅃ 2.35 – **55 rm** ☲ 16.00/24.75.

AUSTIN-MORRIS-MG 24/26 Bondgate ℡ 60921
AUSTIN-MORRIS-MG Grange Rd ℡ 69231
DAIMLER-JAGUAR-ROVER-TRIUMPH Croft Rd ℡ 62728
DATSUN Haughton Rd ℡ 63384
FIAT Woodland Rd ℡ 62928
FORD St. Cuthberts Way ℡ 67581
OPEL Whessoe Rd ℡ 66044

PEUGEOT 201/209 Northgate ℡ 67757
RENAULT Valley St. North ℡ 67477
SAAB 182 Woodland Rd ℡ 62440
TALBOT, BMW 28/56 West Auckland Rd, Faverdale ℡ 53737
VAUXHALL 163 Grange Rd ℡ 66155
VW, AUDI-NSU Chesnut St. ℡ 53536

DARRINGTON West Yorks. – pop. 1,095 – ✆ 0977 Pontefract.

London 184 – Doncaster 12 – **Leeds 18.**

- **Darrington** (S & N), WF8 3BL, on A 1 ℡ 71458 – TV ⌂wc ☎ P. ◪ VISA
  M a la carte approx. 6.05 **st.** – **17 rm** ☷ 11.70/17.60 **st.**

DARTINGTON Devon 403 I 32 – see Totnes.

DARTMOUTH Devon 403 J 32 – pop. 5,707 – ECD : Wednesday and Saturday – ✆ 080 43.

🛈 The Quay ℡ 2281 (summer only).

London 236 – Exeter 36 – **Plymouth 35.**

- **Dart Marina** (T.H.F.), Sandquay, TQ6 9PH, ℡ 2580, ≼ – TV ⌂wc ☎ P. ◪ AE ① VISA
  M 4.35/7.00 **st.** 🍷 1.65 – **33 rm** 14.00/28.00 **st.**
- **Royal Castle** (Anchor), 11 The Quay, TQ6 9QD, ℡ 2397, Group Telex 858875, « 1639
  coaching inn » – TV ⌂wc ☎ P. AE ① VISA
  M approx. 6.00 **st.** – **20 rm** ☷ 13.00/25.50.
- **Victoria**, Victoria Rd, TQ6 9EJ, ℡ 2572 – ◪ VISA
  closed 24 to 26 December – **M** 2.00/5.50 **t.** 🍷 1.25 – **8 rm** ☷ 7.00/14.00.
- **XX** ❀ **Carved Angel**, 2 South Embankment, TQ6 9BH, ℡ 2465, ≼
  closed Sunday dinner, Monday and January – **M** a la carte 7.50/12.50 **st.** 🍷 2.75
  Spec. Provençal fish soup, Poulet basquaise, Salmon in pastry with ginger and currants (March-September).
- **X** **Taylor's**, 8 The Quay, TQ6 9PS, ℡ 2748 – ◪ AE ① VISA
  closed Tuesday, 25-26 December, 1 January and mid January-mid February – **M** a la carte
  6.40/8.10 **t.** 🍷 2.20.

    at Kingswear E : over ferry – ✉ Dartmouth – ✆ 080 425 Kingswear :

- **Redoubt** ⟅, TQ6 0DA, ℡ 295, ≼ Dartmouth and estuary, « Country house atmosphere »,
  ☞, park – ⌂wc P
  May-September – **M** (bar lunch) 5.00/6.50 **s.** 🍷 1.80 – **11 rm** ☷ (dinner included) 13.80/
  32.50 **s.**

AUSTIN South Embankment ℡ 2181   VAUXHALL Mayor's Av. ℡ 2134

DATCHET Berks. 404 S 29 – pop. 3,737 – ECD : Wednesday – ✉ Windsor – ✆ 0753 Slough.
London 26 – Windsor 2.

- **Manor**, The Green, SL3 9EA, ℡ 43442 – TV ⌂wc P. ◪ AE ① VISA
  M a la carte 5.75/9.55 🍷 1.75 – **20 rm** ☷ 13.00/24.00 **st.**

DAIMLER-JAGUAR-MORRIS-MG-ROVER-TRIUMPH-   TOYOTA The Green ℡ 44568
WOLSELEY 18 Horton Rd ℡ 43254

DAVENTRY Northants. 403 404 Q 27 – pop. 18,625 – ✆ 032 72.
🛆 ℡ 3161, S : 1 m, of A 425.

London 82 – **Coventry 17** – **Leicester 29** – Northampton 14 – Oxford 40.

- **John O'Gaunt**, London Rd, NN11 4EN, SE : 1 ¼ m. on A 45 ℡ 77333, Telex 312228 –
  ▤ TV ⌂wc ☎ P. ⌂. ◪ AE VISA
  M 5.00/6.50 **st.** 🍷 2.00 – **100 rm** ☷ 20.50/30.00 **st.**

DAWLISH Devon 403 J 32 – pop. 9,519 – ECD : Thursday and Saturday – ✆ 0626.
🛆 ℡ 862255, E : 1 ½ m.
🛈 The Lawn ℡ 863589 (summer only).

London 215 – Exeter 13 – **Plymouth 40** – Torquay 11.

- **Lynbridge**, 8 Barton Villas, The Bartons, EX7 9QJ, ℡ 862352, ☞ – ◪
  Easter-September – **10 rm** ☷ 5.20/10.00 **st.**

DEAL Kent **404** Y 30 — pop. 25,432 — ECD : Thursday — ✆ 030 45.

🛈 Time Ball Tower, Sea Front ✆ 61161 ext 263.

London 77 — Dover 9 — Maidstone 45 — Margate 15.

🏨 **Royal,** Beach St., CT14 6JD, ✆ 5555, Telex 957141, ≼ – ⇌wc 🚗 🅿. AE ⓞ VISA
M 3.60/4.75 **t.** 🍷 1.65 – **27 rm** ⌓ 9.00/19.00 **t.**

AUSTIN-MORRIS-MG Queen St. ✆ 2214   RENAULT Sandown Rd ✆ 4239/62840
AUSTIN-MORRIS-MG The Marina ✆ 63166   VAUXHALL 48 Dover Rd ✆ 3366

DEDHAM Essex **404** WX 28 — pop. 1,641 — ECD : Wednesday — ✉ ✆ 0206 Colchester.

🛈 Countryside Centre, Duchy Barn ✆ 323447 (summer only).

London 63 — Chelmsford 30 — Colchester 8 — Ipswich 12.

🏨 **Maison Talbooth** ⤳ without rest., Stratford St. Mary Rd, CO7 6HN, W: ½ m.
✆ 322367, ≼, 🎄 – 📺 ⇌wc 🕾 🅿. 🔊 AE ⓞ VISA
closed 24 to 29 December – ⌓ 2.00 – **10 rm** 25.00/55.00 **t.**

🏨 **Dedham Vale** ⤳, Stratford St. Mary Rd, CO7 6HW, W: ¾ m. ✆ 322273, ≼, 🎄 –
⇌wc 🕾 🅿. 🔊
M *(closed first week January)* 3.75/6.00 🍷 1.75 – **12 rm** ⌓ 8.00/20.00.

XXX ❀ **Le Talbooth,** Gun Hill, CO7 6HP, W: 1 m. ✆ 323150, ≼, « Tudor house on riverside »,
🎄 – 🅿. 🔊 VISA
closed 22 to 29 December – **M** a la carte 7.70/18.10 **t.** 🍷 2.10
Spec. Fresh game broth with horseradish (October-February), Truite braisée Mon Ecluse, Bitter chocolate granita.

DEGANWY Clwyd **403** I 24 — see Llandudno.

DENTON Greater Manchester **403** **404** N 23 — pop. 38,154 — ECD : Tuesday — ✉ ✆ 061
Manchester.

London 204 — Manchester 6 — Sheffield 34.

🏨 **Old Rectory** ⤳, Meadow Lane, Haughton Green, M34 1GD, S: 2 m. off A 6017
✆ 336 7516, Telex 668615, 🎄 – 📺 ⇌wc 🕾 🅿
closed 24 to 31 December – **M** *(closed Saturday lunch, Sunday and Bank Holidays)* a la
carte 5.00/7.00 **st.** 🍷 1.75 – **24 rm** ⌓ 16.50/23.50 **st.**

> **Red Lion**
>
> Si le nom d'un hôtel figure en petits caractères,
> demandez à l'arrivée
> les conditions à l'hôtelier.

DERBY Derbs. **403** **404** P 25 — pop. 219,582 — ECD : Wednesday — ✆ 0332.

Envir.: Kedleston Hall** (18C) *AC*, NW: 5 m. by Kedleston Rd X – Melbourne (St. Michael's
Church : Norman nave*) S : 8 m. by A 514 X.

🏌 Allestree Park, ✆ 50616, N: 2 m. on A 6 X – 🏌 by Sinfin Lane X ✆ 21226 – 🏌 Mickleover
✆ 53339, W: 3 m. by A 38 X. – 🏌 Moor Rd, Morley ✆ 832235, NE: 3 m. off A 38 X.

✈ East Midlands, Castle Donington ✆ 810621, SE: 12 m. by A6 X.

🛈 Central Library, The Strand ✆ 31111 ext 2185/6 and 46572.

**London 133 — Birmingham 39 — Coventry 55 — Leicester 32 — Manchester 59 — Nottingham 16 — Sheffield 46 —
Stoke-on-Trent 34.**

Plan opposite

🏨 **Midland** (B.T.H.), Midland Rd, DE1 2SQ, ✆ 45894, 🎄 – 🛗 📺 ⇌wc 🕾 🅿. 🛁. 🔊 AE
ⓞ VISA   **Z i**
closed 25 and 26 December – **M** a la carte 6.30/8.00 **st.** 🍷 2.25 – **63 rm** ⌓ 22.55/29.00 **s.**

🏨 Pennine, Macklin St., DE1 1LF, ✆ 41741 – 🛗 📺 ⇌wc 🚿wc 🕾 🅿. 🛁   **Z e**
100 rm.

🏨 Gables, 119 London Rd, DE1 2QR, ✆ 40633 – 🚿wc 🅿   **Z o**
closed 23 December-1 January – **M** a la carte 2.40/5.30 🍷 1.20 – **60 rm** ⌓ 6.50/10.00.

🏨 Clarendon, Midland Rd, DE1 2SL, ✆ 44466 – 🅿. 🔊 AE ⓞ VISA   **Z a**
M (buffet lunch) 2.20/3.75 **st.** 🍷 1.60 – **45 rm** ⌓ 9.75/19.50 **st.**

🏨 York (Embassy), Midland Rd, DE1 2SL, ✆ 42716 – 📺 ⇌wc 🅿. 🛁. 🔊 AE ⓞ VISA
M *(closed Sunday)* 3.50/4.25 **st.** 🍷 1.40 – **39 rm** ⌓ 12.50/19.00 **st.**   **Z u**

XX **La Gondola,** 220 Osmaston Rd, DE3 8JX, ✆ 32895, Italian rest. – 🅿. 🔊 AE ⓞ   **X c**
closed Sunday and Bank Holidays – **M** a la carte 6.25/10.45 **st.** 🍷 1.55.

X San Remo, 5 Sadler Gate, DE1 3NF, ✆ 41752, Italian rest.   **Y n**

at Allestree N : 2 m. on A 6 – X – ✉ ✆ 0332 Derby :

XXX Palm Court, Duffield Rd, DE3 1ET, ✆ 58107 – 🅿.

at Borrowash SE : 4 m. on A 6005 by A 52 – X – ✉ ✆ 0332 Derby :

XX **Stable** (at Wilmot Arms), DE7 3HA, ✆ 672222 – 🅿. 🔊 AE ⓞ VISA
closed Saturday lunch, Sunday and Monday dinner – **M** a la carte 6.75/8.25 **t.** 🍷 1.70.

P.T.O. →

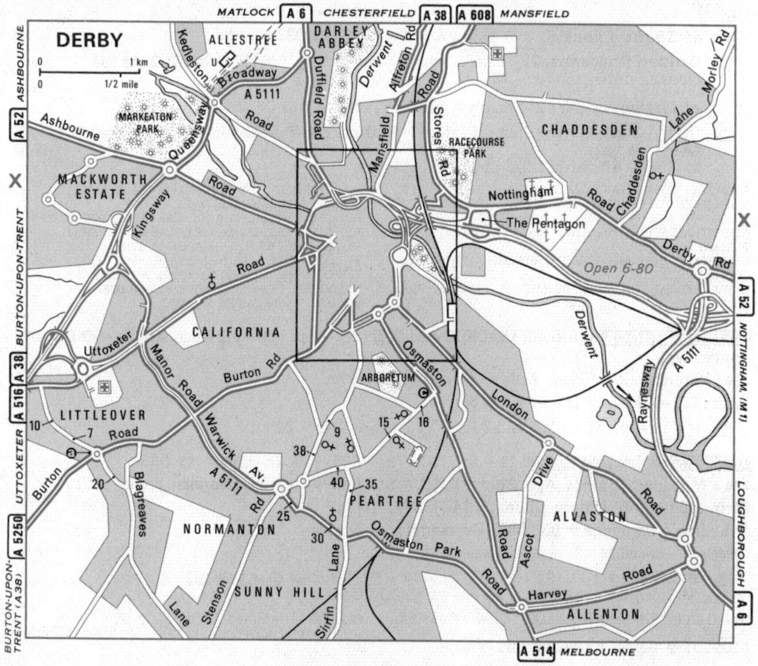

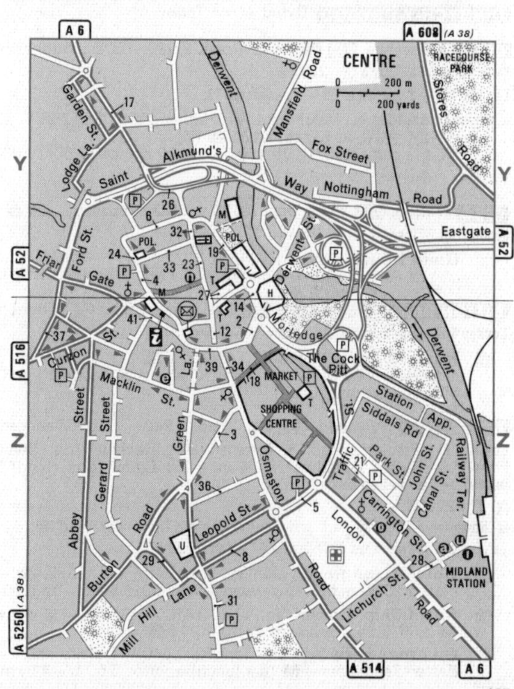

DERBY
MATLOCK A 6   CHESTERFIELD A 38   A 608   MANSFIELD
ASHBOURNE
A 52
1 km
1/2 mile
ALLESTREE
DARLEY ABBEY
Kedleston
Broadway
A 5111
Duffield Road
Derwent
Alfreton Rd
Road
Stores Rd
MARKEATON PARK
Ashbourne
Queensway
Road
RACECOURSE PARK
CHADDESDEN
MACKWORTH ESTATE
Kingsway
Mansfield
Nottingham
Road Chaddesden
X
X
Road
The Pentagon
BURTON-UPON-TRENT
A 516   A 38
Road
Open 6-80
Derby Rd
A 52
NOTTINGHAM, (M 1)
Uttoxeter
CALIFORNIA
Manor Road
Burton Rd
Osmaston
London
Derwent
Rayneswav
A 5111
LITTLEOVER
Warwick Av.
ARBORETUM
Road
Drive
ALVASTON
LOUGHBOROUGH
10   7
A 5111 Rd
38   9   15   16
Road
A 5250
Burton
Blagreaves
25   40   35
PEARTREE
Ascot
Road
A 6
NORMANTON
30
Osmaston Park
Road
Harvey
Road
Lane   Stenson   Lane   Sinfin   SUNNY HILL
ALLENTON
BURTON-UPON-TRENT (A 38)
A 514   MELBOURNE

A 6
CENTRE
A 608 (A 38)
RACECOURSE PARK
Derwent
Mansfield Road
Stores Road
200 m
200 yards
Garden St.
17
Lodge La.
Alkmund's
Fox Street
Way
Nottingham
Road
Y
Y
Saint
26
Eastgate
A 52
A 52
Friar
Ford St.
6
P
32
M
POL
19
Derwent St.
P
24   POL
33   23
Morledge
H
Gate
4   M   27   14   2
The Cock Pitt
A 516
Curzon   41   37   39   34   18
MARKET
Station
Macklin   St.   Green   Lane   SHOPPING CENTRE
Siddals Rd
App.
Street   Gerard Street   3
Railway Ter.
Z
Z
Abbey   Road   Osmaston   Leopold St.   5   London   Road
36   Traffic   Park St.   John St.   Canal St.
29   8   28   MIDLAND STATION
Burton   Mill Hill Lane   31   Litchurch St.   Road
A 5250 (A 38)
A 514
A 6

at Shelton Lock S : 3 ½ m. on A 514 – x – ✉ ☎ 0332 Derby :

XX   **Golden Pheasant**, 221 Chellaston Rd, DE2 9EE, ☏ 700112 – **P**. ⚑ AE ⓪ *VISA*
closed Sunday dinner – **M** a la carte 4.25/9.90 **t**. ⌕ 1.90.

at Littleover SW : 2½ m. on A 5250 by A 38 – ✉ ☎ 0332 Derby :

🏛   Derby Crest Motel (Crest), Pasture Hill, DE3 7BA, ☏ 513834, 🚗 – 📺 ⌂wc ☏ **P**. ⚐.
⚑ AE ⓪ *VISA*   x a
⊊ 2.40 – **40 rm** 18.00/24.50.

AUDI, CITROEN, FIAT, VW 35 Ashbourne Rd ☏31282
AUSTIN-DAIMLER-JAGUAR-MORRIS-ROVER-
TRIUMPH, ROLLS ROYCE London Rd ☏ 4747
AUSTIN-MORRIS, HONDA, TOYOTA Derwent St.
☏ 31166
AUSTIN-MORRIS-MG-ROVER-TRIUMPH 158/160 Bur-
ton Rd ☏ 43224
BMW, ROVER-TRIUMPH, SCIMITAR Uttoxeter New
Rd ☏ 32421

DAF, HONDA 275 Nottingham Rd ☏ 44248
FORD Normanton Rd ☏ 40271
PEUGEOT Nottingham Rd, Chaddesden ☏ 671221
RENAULT 1263 London Rd, Alvaston ☏ 71847
ROVER-TRIUMPH Queen St. ☏ 31166
TALBOT, OPEL Old Chester Rd ☏ 47007
TOYOTA Raynesway, Spondon ☏ 671225
VAUXHALL Castle Donington ☏ 810221
VOLVO Kedleston Rd ☏ 32625

DEVIL'S BRIDGE (PONTARFYNACH) Dyfed **403** I 26 – pop. 150 – ✉ Aberystwyth – ☎ 097 085
Ponterwyd.

See: Nature Trail (Mynach Falls and Devil's Bridge)★★.

London 230 – Aberystwyth 12 – Shrewsbury 66.

🏚   Hafod Arms (Crest), SY23 3JL, ☏ 232, ≼, 🚗 – **P** – **22 rm**.

DEVIZES Wilts. **403** **404** NO 29 – pop. 10,179 – ECD : Wednesday – ☎ 0380.

See : Museum (Bronze Age Room★) *AC* – St. John's Church (Norman choir★ *AC*).

Envir. : Edington (Priory Church★ 14C) SW : 10 m.

🏌 Bishop's Cannings ☏ 038 086 (Cannings) 627, N : 5 m.

London 98 – Bristol 38 – Salisbury 25 – Swindon 19.

🏚   **Bear,** Market Pl., SN10 1HS, ☏ 2444 – 📺 ⌂wc ☏ **P**. ⚑ ⓪ *VISA*
M 3.50/4.50 **s**. ⌕ 2.25 – **26 rm** ⊊ 12.00/20.00.

DAIMLER-MORRIS-MG-WOLSELEY New Park St.
☏ 3517
PEUGEOT ☏ 038 081 (Lavington) 2336

TALBOT The Green, Escort St. ☏ 3667
VAUXHALL, BEDFORD Lydeway ☏ 038084 (Chirton)
203

DINBYCH-Y-PYSGOD Dyfed – see Tenby.

DISLEY Cheshire **403** **404** M 23 – pop. 3,986 – ECD : Wednesday – ✉ Stockport – ☎ 066 32.
🏌 Jackson's Edge ☏ 2071.

London 187 – Chesterfield 35 – Manchester 12.

🏛   **Moorside** ⌬, Mudhurst Lane, Higher Disley, SK12 2BY, SE: 2 m. ☏ 3000, Telex 668822,
≼ – 📺 ⌂wc ☏ **P**. ⚐. ⚑ AE ⓪ *VISA*
M a la carte 6.60/10.95 **t**. ⌕ 2.00 – **20 rm** ⊊ 16.50/23.00 **st**.

MAZDA Fountain Sq. ☏ 2327

DISS Norfolk **404** x 26 – pop. 4,470 – ECD : Tuesday – ✉ ☎ 0379.
London 98 – Ipswich 25 – Norwich 21 – Thetford 17.

X   **Guild House,** Market Hill, IP22 3JZ, ☏ 2411 – ⚑ *VISA*
closed Tuesday lunch, Sunday dinner and Monday – **M** a la carte 5.55/8.45 **t**. ⌕ 1.90.

DITTON PRIORS Salop **403** **404** M 26 – pop. 693 – ✉ Bridgnorth – ☎ 074 634.
London 154 – Birmingham 34 – Ludlow 13 – Shrewsbury 21.

XX   **Howard Arms,** WV16 6SQ, ☏ 200 – **P**
closed Sunday dinner, Monday, 2 weeks September and Christmas dinner – **M** (dinner
only and Sunday lunch) 7.30 ⌕ 2.00.

DOLGELLAU Gwynedd **403** I 25 – pop. 2,340 – ECD : Wednesday – ☎ 0341.
Envir. : N : Precipice walk★★, Torrent walk★, Rhaiadr. Ddu (Blach Waterfalls★), Coed-y-Brenin
Forest★ – Bwlch Oerddws★ E : 4 m. – S : Cader Idris (road★★ to Cader Idris : Cregenneu
lakes) – Tal-y-llyn Lake★★.
🏌 ☏ 422603.
ℹ Snowdonia National Park and Tourist Centre, The Bridge ☏ 422888·

London 221 – Birkenhead 72 – Chester 64 – Shrewsbury 57.

🏛   **Golden Lion Royal,** Lion St., LL40 1DN, ☏ 422579, 🚗 – 📺 ⌂wc **P**. AE *VISA*
closed 20 December-2 January – **M** 5.00/6.50 **s**. – ⊊ 2.00 – **29 rm** 9.60/25.50 **s**.

🏛   **Royal Ship,** Queens Sq., LL40 1AR, ☏ 422209 – 🛗 ⌂wc **P**
M 3.00/5.25 **t**. – **25 rm** ⊊ 10.00/14.00 **t**.

🏚   **Gwernan Lake** ⌬, Cader Idris Rd, LL40 1TL, SW : 2 m. ☏ 422488, ≼, ⌇, 🚗 – **P**
Easter-September – **M** (bar lunch) approx. 6.50 **t**. – **11 rm** ⊊ 9.00/18.00.

at Ganllwyd N: 6 m. on A 470 – ⊠ Dolgellau – ☎ 034 140 Ganllwyd:

⚘ **Dolmelynllyn Hall** 🦆, LL40 2HP, ⌕ 273, ⪕, 🚗 – **P**
Easter-October – **M** (dinner only) 4.50 🍶 1.35 – **15 rm** ⊆ (dinner included) 11.00/16.00.

at Rhydymain NE: 6 m. on A 494 – Dolgellau – ☎ 034 141 Rhydymain:

XX **Rossi's** with rm, LL40 2AR, NE: 2 m. on A 494 ⌕ 667, ⪕, Italian rest. – **P**. 🅿 AE ⓪ VISA
M a la carte 7.15/8.60 🍶 1.50 – ⊆ 1.50 – **8 rm** 12.50/20.00.

at Penmaenpool W: 2 m. on A 493 – ⊠ ☎ 0341 Dolgellau:

X **George III** with rm, LL40 1YD, ⌕ 422525, ⪕ Mawddach Estuary, 🍴 – ⛵wc ☎ **P**. 🅿 AE
⓪ VISA
M *(closed Sunday dinner to non-residents)* a la carte 5.50/7.70 – **12 rm** ⊆ 10.75/21.00.

at Bontddu W: 5 m. on A 496 – ⊠ Dolgellau – ☎ 034 149 Bontddu:

🏠 **Bontddu Hall**, LL40 2UF, ⌕ 661, ⪕ estuary and garden, « Victorian mansion in large gardens » – 📺 ⛵wc ⛵wc ☎ **P**. AE ⓪
May-October – **M** (buffet lunch) approx. 5.95 🍶 1.95 – **26 rm** ⊆ 14.05/25.30.

⚘ **Halfway House**, LL40 2UE, ⌕ 635 – ⛵wc **P**
Easter-December – **M** *(closed Sunday lunch)* a la carte 3.15/6.30 🍶 1.50 – **6 rm** ⊆ 6.50/17.00.

AUSTIN-LAND ROVER-MORRIS-MG-ROVER-TRIUMPH Arran Rd ⌕ 422631

DATSUN Bala Rd ⌕ 422681
PEUGEOT Bontddu ⌕ 49278

DOLWYDDELAN Gwynedd 🔟🔟🔟 I 24 – ECD: Thursday – ☎ 069 06.
London 232 – Holyhead 51 – Dolgellau 24 – Llandudno 27.

🏠 **Elen's Castle**, LL25 0EJ, on A 470 ⌕ 207, ⪕, 🍴, 🚗 – ⛵wc ⛵wc **P**
Easter-October and Christmas – **M** (buffet lunch) 4.00 **t.** 🍶 1.00 – **10 rm** ⊆ 6.00/14.50 **t.**

DONCASTER South Yorks. 🔟🔟🔟 O 23 – pop. 82,668 – ECD: Thursday – ☎ 0302.
🏌 Armthorpe Rd ⌕ 831 203, E : 3 m. – 🏌 Crookhill Park ⌕ 070 286 (Conisbrough) 2974, W: 3 m. on A 630.
🛈 Central Library, Waterdale ⌕ 69123.

London 173 – Kingston-upon-Hull 46 – Leeds 30 – Nottingham 46 – Sheffield 19.

🏠 **Earl of Doncaster** (Anchor), Bennetthorpe, DN2 6AD, ⌕ 61371, Group Telex 858875 – 📺 ⛵wc ☎ **P**. 🅿. 🅿 AE ⓪ VISA
M 3.50 **st.** – **45 rm** ⊆ 17.50/25.00 **st.**

🏠 **Punch's** (Embassy), Bawtry Rd, DN4 7BS, SE: 3 m. on A 638 ⌕ 55235, 🚗 – 📺 ⛵wc ☎ **P**. 🅿. 🅿 AE ⓪ VISA
M 4.25/5.00 **st.** 🍶 2.00 – **25 rm** ⊆ 12.00/19.50 **st.**

🏠 **Danum** (Embassy), High St., DN1 1DN, ⌕ 62261 – 🛗 📺 ⛵wc ☎ **P**. 🅿. 🅿 AE ⓪ VISA
M (buffet Sunday dinner) approx. 4.60 **st.** 🍶 1.75 – **70 rm** ⊆ 12.50/20.00 **st.**

at Sprotbrough W: 3 m. off A 630 – ⊠ ☎ 0302 Doncaster:

X **Edelweiss**, 4 Main St., DN5 7RF, ⌕ 853923 – 🅿 AE ⓪ VISA
closed Monday – **M** (dinner only) a la carte 6.80/10.55 **t.**

at Hampole NW: 7 m. on A 638 – ⊠ ☎ 0302 Doncaster:

XX **Hampole Priory**, DN6 7EP, ⌕ 723740 – **P**. 🅿
closed Sunday and Monday – **M** (dinner only) a la carte 6.50/7.55 **st.** 🍶 1.50.

AUSTIN-MORRIS-MG-PPRINCESS Church Way ⌕ 21541
DAIMLER-JAGUAR-ROVER-TRIUMPH York Rd ⌕ 66861
DATSUN Bawtry ⌕ 710181
FIAT York Rd ⌕ 23418
FORD Bennethorpe ⌕ 4411

LADA, MAZDA Amershall Rd ⌕ 66405
PEUGEOT Bawtry Rd ⌕ 55241
RENAULT Thorne ⌕ 0405 (Thorne) 812110
TOYOTA Thorne Rd, Hatfield ⌕ 840348
VAUXHALL York Rd ⌕ 67483
VW, AUDI York Rd Roundabout ⌕ 64141

DONYATT Somerset 🔟🔟🔟 L 37 – pop. 342 – ⊠ ☎ 046 05 Ilminster.
London 147 – Exeter 33 – Taunton 11 – Yeovil 17.

XX **Thatchers Pond**, TA19 0RG, ⌕ 3210, 🚗 – **P**
closed 10 to 20 May and 23 December-1 February – **M** *(closed Sunday dinner and Monday)* (buffet lunch) 5.00/5.50 **t.** 🍶 1.60.

En dehors des établissements désignés par
XXXXX...X,
il existe dans de nombreux hôtels,
un restaurant de bonne classe.

DORCHESTER Dorset **403** **404** M 31 – pop. 13,736 – ECD : Thursday – ○ 0305.

See : Dorset County Museum* *AC*.

Envir. : Hardy Monument ❅ ** SW : 5 m. – Maiden Castle (prehistoric fortress*) *AC*, SW : 2 m.

🛈 Antelope Yard, South St. ℡ 66969.

London 135 – Bournemouth 27 – Exeter 53 – **Southampton 53.**

🏛 **King's Arms,** 30 High East St., DT1 1HF, ℡ 5353 – ⛁wc ☎ **P.** ♨
M 3.45/6.00 **st.** ♦ 1.80 – **27 rm** ⌕ 12.45/25.30 **st.** – P 19.90/21.90 **st.**

ALFA-ROMEO, FIAT, MERCEDES-BENZ Trinity St.
℡ 4494
AUSTIN-MG-PRINCESS 21/26 Trinity St. ℡ 3031
CITROEN, PEUGEOT Puddletown ℡ 456
DAF, VOLVO Bridport Rd ℡ 5555

DATSUN London Rd ℡ 66066
FORD Prince of Wales Rd ℡ 2211
MORRIS-MG-PRINCESS-WOLSELEY 6 High East St.
℡ 3913
VAUXHALL, BEDFORD 45 High West St. ℡ 3556

DORE South Yorks. **403** **404** P 24 – see Sheffield.

DORKING Surrey **404** T 30 – pop. 22,530 – ECD : Wednesday – ○ 0306.

Envir. : Box Hill ⦤** NE : 2 ½ m. – Polesden Lacey** (19C) *AC*, NW : 4 ½ m.

London 26 – Brighton 39 – Guildford 12 – Worthing 33.

🏛🏛 **Burford Bridge** (T.H.F.), Box Hill, RH5 6BX, N : 1 ½ m. on A 24 ℡ 4561, Telex 859507,
⌇ heated, 🍴 – TV **P.** ♨. ⬛ AE ⓪ **VISA**
M 4.75/5.75 **st.** ♦ 1.80 – ⌕ 2.50 – **30 rm** 20.50/26.00 **st.**

🏛 **White Horse** (T.H.F.), High St., RH4 4BE, ℡ 81138, ⌇ heated – TV ⛁wc ☎ **P.** ♨.
⬛ AE ⓪ **VISA**
M 4.45/5.20 **st.** ♦ 1.65 – **68 rm** ⌕ 18.50/23.50 **st.**

at Peaslake SW : 8 m. off A 25 – ✉ Guildford – ○ 0306 Dorking :

🏛 **Hurtwood Inn** (T.H.F.) ॐ, Walking Bottom, GU5 9RR, ℡ 730851, 🍴 – TV ⛁wc **P.** ⬛
AE ⓪ **VISA**
M 4.00/4.20 **st.** ♦ 1.65 – **16 rm** ⌕ 13.50/22.00 **st.**

at Wotton W : 3 m. on A 25 – ✉ ○ 0306 Dorking :

XXX Wotton Hatch, RH5 6QQ, ℡ 5665, 🍴 – **P.**

BRITISH LEYLAND 105 South St. ℡ 2244

CITROEN, MERCEDES-BENZ, VAUXHALL Reigate
Rd ℡ 5022

DORRINGTON Salop **403** L 25 – see Shrewsbury.

DOVER Kent **404** X 30 – pop. 34,395 – ECD : Wednesday – ○ 0304.

See : Castle** 12C (⦤*) *AC* Y. **Envir.** : Barfreston (Norman Church* 11C : carvings**) NW :
6 ½ m. by A2 z – Bleriot Memorial E : 1 m. z A.

🚗 ℡ 01 (London) 603 4555 – ℡ 0904 (York) 53022 ext 2631.

🛥 Shipping connections with the Continent : to Boulogne (P & O Ferries : Normandy Ferries)
(Sealink) (Seaspeed Hovercraft) – to Calais (Sealink) (Seaspeed Hovercraft) (Townsend
Thoresen) – to Dunkerque (Sealink) – to Oostende (Sealink) – to Zeebrugge (Townsend
Thoresen).

🛈 Townwall St. ℡ 205108 Portakabin, A2 Diversion, Whitfield ℡ 820650 (summer only) – Town Hall ℡ 206941.

London 75 – Brighton 81.

Plan opposite

🏛🏛 **Holiday Inn,** Townwall St., CT16 1SZ, ℡ 203270, Telex 96458, ⬛ – ▮ TV ♿ **P.** ♨. ⬛ AE
⓪ **VISA**   Y z
M a la carte 5.15/9.35 **st.** ♦ 2.85 – ⌕ 3.25 – **83 rm** 21.00/28.25 **s.**

🏛 **White Cliffs,** Sea Front, CT17 9BW, ℡ 203633, Telex 965422, ⦤ – ▮ TV ⛁wc ☎
P. ⬛ AE ⓪ **VISA**   Y a
M approx. 4.30 **st.** – **63 rm** ⌕ 11.75/22.00 **st.**

🏛 **Granham Webb,** 161-165 Folkestone Rd, CT17 9SJ, ℡ 201897, 🍴 – TV ⛁wc 🚿wc **P.**
⬛ AE ⓪ **VISA**   Y e
M *(closed Sunday lunch)* a la carte 6.75/9.70 **t.** ♦ 1.50 – **29 rm** ⌕ 10.50/24.00 **st.** –
P 18.00/28.00 **st.**

🏛 **St. James,** 2 Harold St., CT16 1LF, ℡ 204579 – TV ⛁wc 🚿wc ☎. ⬛ AE ⓪
M (bar lunch) a la carte approx. 8.00 ♦ 2.00 – **20 rm** ⌕ 10.50/22.00 **t.**   Y i

🏛 **Mildmay,** 78 Folkestone Rd, CT17 9SF, ℡ 204278 – TV ⛁wc **P.** AE **VISA**   Y n
M (bar lunch) 3.50/5.50 **st.** ♦ 2.50 – **23 rm** ⌕ 10.00/22.00 **st.**

🏛 **Dover Stage** (County), Camden Crescent, CT16 1LS, ℡ 201001, Group Telex 25971 –
▮ ☎ **P.** ♨. ⬛ AE ⓪ **VISA**   Y u
M 5.00 **st.** ♦ 1.55 – **42 rm** ⌕ 10.00/17.00 **s.**

DOVER

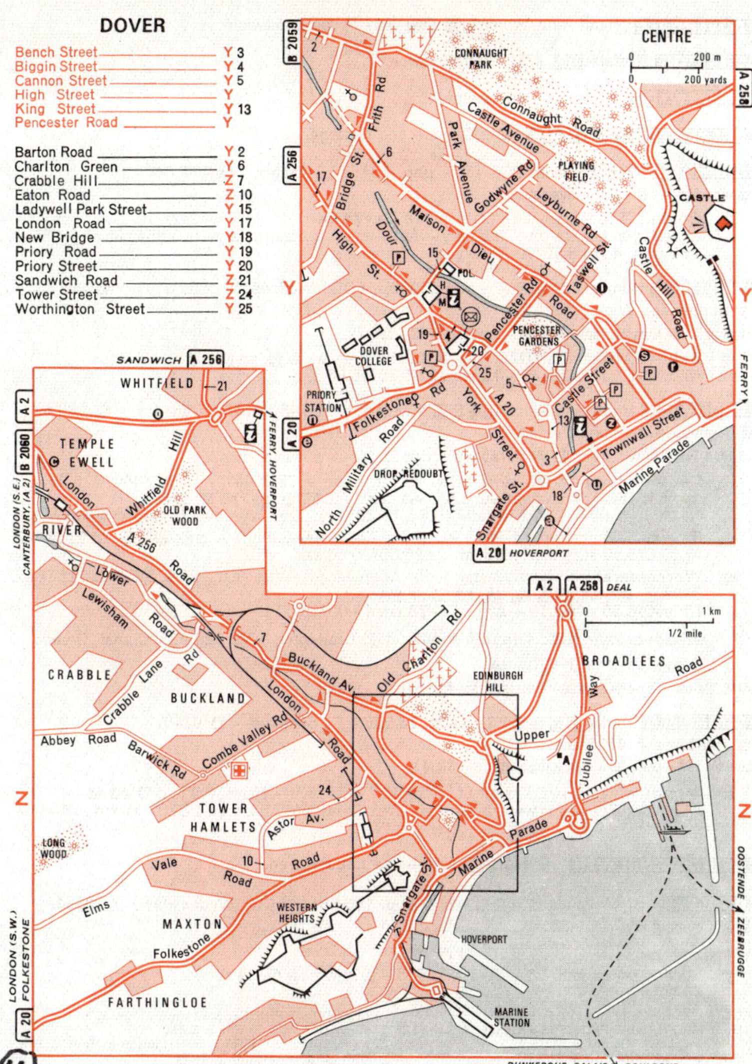

Hubert House, 9 Castle Hill Rd, CT16 1QW, ℡ 202253 – 🅿 ⛝   Y **s**
closed 28 September-13 October – **M** *(closed Saturday lunch and Sunday)* a la carte
3.60/6.65 ⅃ 1.75 – **8 rm** ⊆ 9.00/12.00 **t.**

St. Martins, 17 Castle Hill Rd, CT16 1QP, ℡ 205938 – TV   Y **r**
9 rm ⊆ 5.00/10.00 **st.**

at Whitfield N : 3 ½ m. by A 256 and A 2 – ✉ ☺ 0304 Dover :

Dover Motel, Sinledge Lane, CT16 3LF, ℡ 821222, Telex 965866 – TV 🅿 ⛝ AE ① VISA
M a la carte 3.45/6.55 **t.** ⅃ 2.00 – ⊆ 1.90 – **58 rm** 20.00/26.00 **st.**   Z **o**

at Temple Ewell NW : 2 m. on A 2060 – ✉ Dover – ☺ 030 47 Kearsney :

Kearsney, without rest., 124 London Rd, CT16 3BZ, ℡ 2002, ⇜ – 🅿 – **19 rm.**   Z **c**

AUSTIN-MORRIS-MG-ROVER-TRIUMPH 6/12 Folkestone Rd ℡ 201760
BMW, FORD Whitefield ℡ 821351
MERCEDES, VAUXHALL Combe Valley Rd ℡ 201851
RELIANT South Rd ℡ 206160
RENAULT London Rd, River ℡ 030 47 (Kearsney) 4155
TOYOTA Beaconsfield Rd ℡ 205646
VW, AUDI-NSU 1 Crabble Hill ℡ 206710

DOVERDALE Heref. and Worc. **403** **404** N 27 – see Droitwich.

DRAYTON Norfolk **404** X 25 – see Norwich.

DRENEWYDD Powys – see Newtown.

DRENEWYDD YN NOTAIS Mid Glam. – see Nottage.

DREWSTEIGNTON Devon **403** I31 – pop. 534 – ⊠ Exeter – ☎ 064 721.
London 214 – Exeter 13 – Plymouth 35.

    Old Inn, The Square, EX6 6QR, ☎ 276 – ⚑ AE ⓪
    closed mid January-mid February – **M** *(closed Sunday)* a la carte 5.85/7.85 **t.** 🍷 1.55 –
    ⊇ 2.00 – **4 rm** 5.00/10.00 **t.**

DRIFFIELD Humberside **986** ㉔ – pop. 7,040 – ECD: Wednesday – ⊠ York – ☎ 0377.
🛈 Sunderland Wick ☎ 43116.
London 201 – Kingston-upon-Hull 21 – Scarborough 22 – York 29.

    Bell, 46 Market Pl., YO25 7AN, ☎ 43342 – ⇱wc ☎ **P.** ⚑ AE **VISA**
    M 3.10/5.50 **st.** 🍷 1.75 – **13 rm** ⊇ 11.50/15.50 **t.**

DROITWICH Heref. and Worc. **403** **404** N 27 – pop. 12,748 – ECD: Thursday – ☎ 090 57.
🛈 Norbury House, Friar St. ☎ 2352.
London 129 – Birmingham 20 – Bristol 66 – Worcester 6.

    Château Impney ﹩, WR9 0BN, NE: 1 m. on A 38 ☎ 4411, Telex 336673, « Repro-
    duction 16C French château », ✗. ⇙, park – 📶 TV **P.** ⛳. ⚑ AE ⓪ **VISA**
    closed Christmas – **M** a la carte 10.95/16.30 **st.** 🍷 2.95 – ⊇ 4.95 – **67 rm** 35.90/39.90 **st.**

    Raven, St. Andrews Rd, WR9 8DU, ☎ 2224, Telex 339907 – 📶 TV **P.** ⛳. ⚑ AE ⓪ **VISA**
    M 5.50/6.50 **st.** 🍷 2.00 – **55 rm** ⊇ 20.50/30.00 **st.**

    Worcestershire (Best Western), St. Andrews Rd, WR9 8DL, on A 38 ☎ 2371, Telex
    338309, ⇙ – 📶 TV ♿ **P.** ⛳. ⚑ AE ⓪ **VISA**
    M 3.50/4.50 **s.** 🍷 2.10 – ⊇ 1.75 – **76 rm** 13.00/18.00 **s.**

    at Doverdale NW: 4 m. off A 442 – ⊠ Droitwich – ☎ 029 923 Cutnall Green:

    ✗ Ripperidge Inn, ☎ 620 – **P.**

AUSTIN-MORRIS-MG-ROVER-TRIUMPH St. Georges Sq. ☎ 3337

DRONFIELD Derbs. **403** **404** P 24 – pop. 13,980 – ⊠ Sheffield – ☎ 0246.
🛈 Hallowes ☎ 413149.
London 158 – Derby 30 – Nottingham 31 – Sheffield 6.

    ✗ **Manor** with rm, 10-15 High St., S18 6PY, ☎ 413971 – TV ⇱wc ♨wc **P.** ⚑ ⓪
    M *(closed Sunday dinner and Monday lunch)* a la carte 2.95/8.30 🍷 2.20 – **10 rm** ⊇ 16.00/
    25.00 **st.**

DRUIDSTON HAVEN Dyfed **403** E 28 – see Little Haven.

DUDLEY West Midlands **403** **404** N 26 – pop. 185,581 – ECD: Wednesday – ☎ 0384.
🛈 39 Churchill Precinct ☎ 50333.
London 133 – Birmingham 10 – Wolverhampton 7.

    Station, Castle Hill, DY1 4RA, ☎ 53418 – 📶 ⇱wc ☎ **P.** ⛳.
    29 rm.

AUSTIN-MORRIS Netherton ☎ 57841
AUSTIN-MORRIS-MG-PRINCESS-WOLSELEY 413/415
Himley Rd, Lower Gornal ☎ 54336
FIAT, LOTUS Stafford St. ☎ 213431
MAZDA, POLSKI-FIAT Queens Cross ☎ 59897

MORRIS-MG-PRINCESS 99 High St. ☎ 53791
RENAULT Castle Hill ☎ 52474
VAUXHALL, BEDFORD 221 Halesaren Rd, Old Hill,
0334 (Cradley Heath) ☎ 64026

DULOE Cornwall **403** G 32 – see Looe.

GREEN TOURIST GUIDES

Picturesque scenery, buildings
Attractive routes
Touring programmes
Plans of towns and buildings

15 guides available for your holidays.

DUNKIRK Avon **403** **404** N 29 – pop. 50 – ⊠ Badminton – ☎ 045 423 Didmarton.
London 118 – Bath 15 – Bristol 19 – Cirencester 18.

- XX Petty France, with rm, GL9 1AF, on A 46 ☏ 361, « Country house atmosphere », 🚗 –
  TV ⌷ ⓕwc ☎ wc Ⓟ
  16 rm.

DUNSOP BRIDGE Lancs. – pop. 201 – EDC : Wednesday – ⊠ Clitheroe – ☎ 020 08.
London 245 – Burnley 22 – Preston 28.

- 🏖 **Thorneyholme Hall** ⑤, BB7 3BB, ☏ 271, ≤, 🚗 – Ⓟ. △ **VISA**
  closed January – **M** *(closed Monday except Bank Holidays)* 3.50/6.50 **st.** ▯ 2.00 – **5 rm**
  ⌸ 7.50/15.00 **st.** – P 16.50/17.50 **st.**

DUNSTABLE Beds. **404** S 28 – pop. 31,828 – ECD : Thursday – ☎ 0582.
See : Priory Church of St. Peter (West front*). **Envir. :** Whipsnade Park* (zoo) ≤** *AC*, S : 3 m.
▣ Whipsnade ☏ 044 284 (Little Gaddesden) 2330, S : 4 m. – ▣ Dunstable Rd ☏ (052 521)
Hockcliffe 722, N : 2 m. on A 5.

🛈 Queensway Hall, Vernon Pl. ☏ 603326.

London 40 – Bedford 24 – Luton 4,5 – Northampton 35.

- 🏨 Highwayman, London Rd, LU6 3DX, SE : 1 m. on A 5 ☏ 61999 – TV ⌷wc ⓕwc ☎ Ⓟ
  26 rm.
- 🏨 **Cook's Motel,** 306 High St. North, LU6 1LW, ☏ 62341 – TV ⌷wc ⓕwc ☎ Ⓟ. △ ⓪ **VISA**
  M *(closed Saturday lunch and Sunday)* a la carte 4.70/6.55 **st.** – ⌸ 2.10 – **12 rm** 13.50/
  20.00 **st.**
- 🏨 Roxburgh, 42-46 Priory Rd, LU5 4HR, ☏ 64089 – Ⓟ
  20 rm.
- XX **Old Palace Lodge** with rm, Church St., LU5 4RT, ☏ 62201, 🚗 – ⌷wc ⓕwc ☎ Ⓟ. △
  AE ⓪ **VISA**
  closed 26 December – **M** a la carte 6.20/10.85 – ⌸ 2.25 – **16 rm** 12.50/16.50.

ALFA-ROMEO 3 Tring Rd ☏ 63231
AUSTIN-MORRIS-MG-ROVER-TRIUMPH London Rd
☏ 69111

FORD 55 London Rd ☏ 67811
PEUGEOT Common Rd, Kensworth ☏ 872182
VW, AUDI-NSU 104 Church St. ☏ 68796

Pour les 🏨, 🏨, 🏨, nous ne donnons pas
le détail de l'installation,
ces hôtels possédant, en général, tout le confort.

⌷wc ⓕwc

☎

DUNSTER Somerset **403** J 30 – pop. 815 – ECD : Wednesday – ⊠ Minehead – ☎ 064 382.
See : Dunster castle* 16C-19C – Yan Market*.
London 184 – Bristol 61 – Exeter 40 – Taunton 22.

- 🏨 **Luttrell Arms** (T.H.F.), 36 High St., TA24 6SG, ☏ 555, « 15C inn », 🚗 – TV ⌷wc ☎.
  △ AE ⓪ **VISA**
  M 3.00/5.00 **st.** ▯ 1.65 – **21 rm** ⌸ 13.50/28.00 **st.**
- 🏨 **Osborne House** (Best Western), 31 High St., TA24 6SF, ☏ 475 – △ AE
  March-October – **M** 6.50/8.25 **st.** ▯ 2.75 – **8 rm** ⌸ 12.75/24.00 **st.**

DURHAM Durham **986** ⑲ – pop. 24,776 – ECD : Wednesday – ☎ 0385.
See : Cathedral*** (Norman) (Chapel of the Nine Altars**) B **A** – University (Gulbenkian
Museum of Art and Archaeology** *AC*) by Elvet Hill Rd **A** – Castle* (Norman chapel*) *AC* **B**.
▣ Low Job's Hill, Crook ☏ 038 882 (Crook) 24, SW : 10 m. by A 690 **A** – ▣ South Moor
☏ 0207 (Stanley) 32848, NW : 8 m. by Framwelgate Peth A and B 6532.

🛈 13 Claypath ☏ 3720.

London 267 – Leeds 77 – Middlesbrough 23 – Sunderland 12.

Plan on next page

- 🏨 Royal County (Swallow), Old Elvet, DH1 3JN, ☏ 66821, Group Telex 53168 – 🛗 TV Ⓟ
  122 rm.   **B a**
- 🏨 Durham Crest Motel (Crest), DH1 3SP, ⊠ Croxdale ☏ 780524 – TV ⌷wc ☎ Ⓟ. △
  AE ⓪ **VISA**   S : 3 m. on A 167 **B**
  ⌸ 2.40 – **35 rm** 18.00/24.50 **st.**
- 🏨 Three Tuns (Swallow), New Elvet, DH1 3AQ, ☏ 64326, Group Telex 53168 – TV ⌷wc
  ☎ Ⓟ – **20 rm.**   **B e**
- X Travellers Rest, 72 Claypath, DH1 1QT, ☏ 65370.   **B c**

AUSTIN-MG-WOLSELEY 74 New Elvet ☏ 2278
CITROEN Croxdale ☏ 0388 (Spennymoor) 814671
DAIMLER-MORRIS-MG-ROVER-TRIUMPH-WOLSELEY
Gilesgate Moor ☏ 67231

DATSUN 81 New Elvet ☏ 2233
OPEL-VAUXHALL Claypath ☏ 2511
VW, AUDI-NSU 20 Alma Rd, Gilesgate Moor ☏ 67215

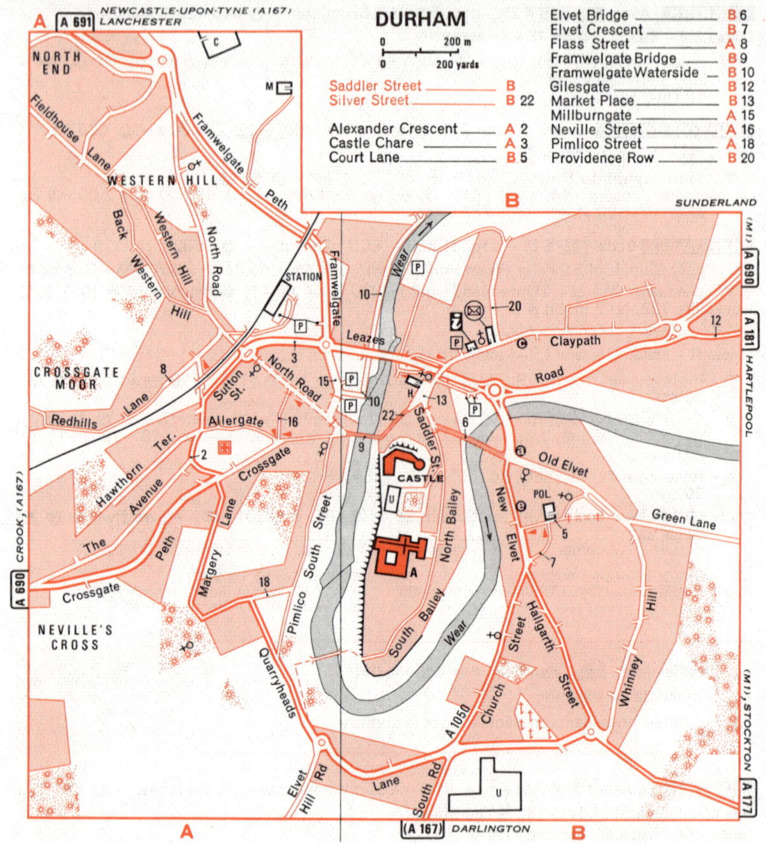

EAGLESCLIFFE Cleveland – see Stockton-on-Tees.

EASTBOURNE East Sussex **404** U 31 – pop. 70,921 – ECD: Wednesday – ☎ 0323.

See : Grand Parade* X. **Envir.** : Beachy Head* (cliff), ☀* SW : 3 m. Z – Seven Sisters* (cliffs) from Birling Gap, SW : 5 m. Z – Wilmington (the Long Man* : prehistoric giant figure) NW : 8 m. by A 27 Y – W : scenic road* from Eastdean by A 259 Z up to Wilmington by Westdean.

☍₁₈, ☍₉ Paradise Drive Z ☏ 30412.

🛈 3 Cornfield Ter. ☏ 27474 – Lower Promenade ☏ 27474 (summer only) – at Pevensey, Castle Car park, High St. ☏ 0323 (Eastbourne) 761441 (Weekends only in winter).

London 68 – Brighton 25 – Dover 61 – Maidstone 49.

Plan opposite

Grand (De Vere), King Edward's Par., BN21 4EQ, ☏ 22611, Telex 87332, ≤, ⅃ heated, ⇌ – 🛗 TV &. 🅿. ⚓. ☒ AE ⓪ VISA   Z x
M 7.00/8.00 st. ⅃ 1.90 – **164 rm** ☷ 28.00/56.00 st.

Cavendish (De Vere), 37-40 Grand Par., BN21 4DH, ☏ 27401, Telex 87579, ≤ – 🛗 TV &. 🅿. ⚓. ☒ AE ⓪ VISA   X r
M 6.50/7.50 st. ⅃ 1.90 – **115 rm** ☷ 20.00/45.00 st.

Queen's (De Vere), Marine Par., BN21 3DY, ☏ 22822, Telex 877736, ≤ – 🛗 TV 🅿. ⚓. ☒ AE ⓪ VISA   V e
M 5.75/6.00 st. ⅃ 1.90 – **104 rm** ☷ 17.00/34.00 st.

EASTBOURNE

A 2021
A 259
Lewes Road
Whitley
A 2021
Firle
Road
Seaside
Road
Enys Rd
St. Anne's Rd
The Avenue
Upper
Upper Av.
Road
Av.
Bourne
Cavendish
3
A 259
A 2040
Commercial
STATION
Grove Rd
South St.
Langney
Street
Rd
2
2
28
Terminus
25
16
Seaside
Rd
7
14
15
Rd
Seaside
5
27
V
Grange Rd
Compton St.
Grand Parade
Marine Par.
Royal Par.
6
Carlisle Rd
CENTRE
0   300 m
0   300 yards
POL
H
X

A 22 LONDON
A 27 LEWES
A 27 PEVENSEY
8
18
24
Pevensey Rd
13
Wannock Road
POLEGATE
Eastbourne
Road
B 2105
WILLINGDON
A 22
A 2021
Decoy Drive
HAMPDEN PARK
King's
Willingdon Road
A 22
Victoria Drive
Drive
Lottbridge
Seaside
Drove
B 2104
A 259 HASTINGS
Princes Road
21
Y
P
20
28
9
4
A
26
S
Road
Drive
Paradise
9, 18
Meads Rd
Dean
East
B 2103
BRIGHTON A 259
Head Carlisle Rd
Beachy
King Edward's Par.
BUILT UP AREA
0   1 km
0   1/2 mile

Burlington (Myddleton), Grand Par., BN21 3YN, ℡ 22724, Telex 87591, ⪡ – ▯ TV ⌷wc 🅿. ⌂. AE ⓓ VISA **V u**
M a la carte 6.50/10.00 st. – **124 rm** ⌷ 14.90/29.00 st.

Lansdowne (Best Western), King Edward's Par., BN21 4EE, ℡ 25174, ⪡ – ▯ ⌷wc ⌂. ⌂ **Z z**
closed 2 weeks January – M 4.25/4.90 st. ⌾ 1.90 – **141 rm** ⌷ 13.00/14.50 st. – P 18.00/24.00 st.

Mansion (T.F.H.), Grand Par., BN21 3YS, ℡ 27411, Group Telex 877288, ⪡ – ▯ TV ⌷wc ⌂. ⌂. AE ⓓ VISA **X i**
M 4.25/5.00 st. ⌾ 1.80 – **103 rm** ⌷ 13.00/25.50 st.

Wish Tower (T.H.F.), King Edward's Par., BN21 4EB, ℡ 22676, Group Telex 877288, ⪡ – ▯ TV ⌷wc ⌂. AE ⓓ VISA **Z r**
M 4.25/5.00 st. ⌾ 1.80 – **74 rm** ⌷ 13.00/25.50 st.

Chatsworth, Grand Par., BN21 3YR, ℡ 30327, ⪡ – ▯ TV ⌷wc ⌷wc ⌂ **X n**
closed 7 January-1 March – M 4.00/4.85 s. ⌾ 1.90 – **46 rm** ⌷ 12.25/23.20 s. – P 16.50/17.50 s.

Sandhurst, Grand Par., BN21 4DJ, ℡ 27868, ⪡ – ▯ ⌷wc ⌷wc ⌂. AE **X o**
M 3.95/4.50 ⌾ 1.75 – **65 rm** ⌷ 10.50/23.00 – P 14.50/18.50.

Eastbourne Motel, Pevensey Bay Rd, BN23 6JG, NE: 2 m. on A 259 ℡ 764188 – TV ⌷wc ⌷wc ⌂ ⌂ 🅿 on A 259 **Y**
82 rm.

Princes, 12-20 Lascelles Ter., BN21 4BL, ℡ 22056 – ▯ ⌷wc. ⌂ **X z**
March-November and Christmas – M 3.50/4.25 st. ⌾ 2.00 – **50 rm** ⌷ 12.00/28.60 st. – P 19.00/21.40 st.

Langham, 44-49 Royal Par., BN22 7AH, ℡ 31451, ⪡ – ▯ ⌷wc **V c**
Easter-mid October – M 3.80/5.25 st. ⌾ 2.15 – **87 rm** ⌷ 10.00/24.00 st. – P 16.20/17.90 st.

Farrar's, 3-5 Wilmington Gdns, BN21 4JN, ℡ 23737 – ▯ ⌷wc ⌷wc 🅿. ⌂ AE VISA **X s**
M 3.15/4.60 t. ⌾ 1.50 – **42 rm** ⌷ 10.50/23.00 t. – P 16.75/20.75 t.

Heatherleigh, 63-66 Royal Par., BN22 7AG, ℡ 21167, ⪡ – ▯ ⌷wc **Z n**
March-October – M 3.50/4.25 st. ⌾ 1.50 – **49 rm** ⌷ 8.50/18.50 st.

Orchard House, 10 Old Orchard Rd, BN21 4TR, ℡ 23682, ⌂ **V o**
8 rm ⌷ 11.00/13.00 s.

Edward, 16 Trinity Trees, BN21 3LE, ℡ 29222 – 🅿 **V v**
12 rm ⌷ 7.50/18.60 st.

Nirvana, 32 Redoubt Rd, BN22 7DL, ℡ 22603, ⌂ **V n**
closed 19 October-3 November and 1 week at Christmas – **8 rm** ⌷ 6.50/12.00 s.

Crimples Flemish Room, 42-44 Meads St., BN20 7GR, ℡ 26805 – ⌂ VISA **Z a**
closed Sunday dinner, Monday, 1 week spring, 2 weeks end October and 25-26 December – M a la carte 4.05/6.75 t. ⌾ 2.00.

Le Chantecler, 7 Bolton Rd, BN21 3JU, ℡ 30748. **V i**

Bistro Byron, 6 Crown St., BN21 1NX, ℡ 20171, Bistro – VISA **Z s**
closed Sunday and Bank Holidays – M (dinner only) a la carte 5.60/7.10 t. ⌾ 2.00.

La Taverna, 92 Seaside, BN22 7QP, ℡ 23240, Italian rest. – ⌂ ⓓ VISA **V a**
M a la carte 4.95/7.45 ⌾ 1.50.

at Willingdon N: 2 ¾ m. off A 22 – ✉ ☎ 0323 Eastbourne:

Chalk Farm ⌂ with rm, Coopers Hill, BN20 9JD, ℡ 53800, ⌂ – 🅿 **Y a**
closed Christmas and 1 January – M (closed Sunday dinner and Monday except Bank Holidays) 4.50/5.50 ⌾ 1.60 – **8 rm** ⌷ 8.80/16.40 – P 17.70/18.70.

at Stone Cross N: 3 ½ m. by A 259 – **Y** – and B 2104 – ✉ Eastbourne – ☎ 0323 Hailsham:

Glyndley Manor ⌂, Hailsham Rd, BN24 5BS, NW: 1 ½ m. on B 2104, ℡ 843737, ⌂, park – TV ⌷wc ⌷wc ⌂ 🅿
18 rm.

at Pevensey NE: 5 m. by A 259 – **Y** – on A 27 – ✉ ☎ 0323 Eastbourne:

Priory Court (Best Western), BN24 5LE, ℡ 763150, ⌂ – ⌷wc 🅿. ⌂ VISA
M (bar lunch Monday to Saturday) a la carte 7.15/12.45 t. – **9 rm** ⌷ 7.50/23.00 t.

at Jevington NW: 6 m. by A 259 – **Z** – on B 2105 – ✉ ☎ 032 12 Polegate:

Hungry Monk, Jevington Rd, BN20 0AG, ℡ 2178 – 🅿
closed 24 and 25 December – M (dinner only and Sunday lunch) 5.90/6.90 ⌾ 1.70.

EAST DEREHAM Norfolk 404 W 25 – pop. 8,060 – ☎ 0362 Dereham.
🛈 Quebec Rd ☏ 3122.
London 109 – Cambridge 57 – King's Lynn 27 – Norwich 16.

   🏨 **Phœnix** (T.H.F.), Church St., NR19 1DN, ☏ 2276 – 📺 🛏wc 📡 🅿. 🛉. 🔁 ᴁ ⓪ 𝘝𝘐𝘚𝘈
      M 5.00/5.75 st. 🍷 1.65 – **27 rm** 🍽 13.50/21.00 st.

   🏨 **King's Head,** Norwich St., NR19 1AD, ☏ 3842 – 📺 🛏wc 📡 🅿. 🔁 𝘝𝘐𝘚𝘈
      M 2.80/3.90 🍷 1.55 – **10 rm** 🍽 10.20/18.65 t.

AUSTIN-MG Two Oaks Garage Beetley ☏ 86219   FORD High St. ☏ 2281
AUSTIN-MORRIS-MG-ROVER-TRIUMPH Norwich Rd
☏ 2293

EAST GRINSTEAD West Sussex 404 T 30 – pop. 16,560 – ECD : Wednesday – ☎ 0342.
Envir : Hever Castle* (13C-20C) and gardens** *AC,* NE : 10 m.

🛈 East Court Mansion, College Lane ☏ 23636.

London 32 – Brighton 29 – Eastbourne 33 – Lewes 21 – Maidstone 32

   🏨 **Ye Olde Felbridge,** London Rd, RH19 2BH, ☏ 24424, Telex 95156, 🌊 heated, 🚗 – 📺
     🛏wc 📡 🅿. 🛉. 🔁 ᴁ ⓪ 𝘝𝘐𝘚𝘈
     M a la carte 5.85/9.25 t. 🍷 1.75 – 🍽 2.75 – **48 rm** 17.00/31.00 t.

    at Gravetye SW : 4½ m. off B 2110 – ✉ East Grinstead – ☎ 0342 Sharpthorne :

   🏰 ❀ **Gravetye Manor** 🦢, RH19 4LJ, ☏ 810567, ≼, « 16C manor house with beautiful
     gardens and grounds by William Robinson », 🌿, park – 📺 🅿
     M a la carte 7.95/13.75 t. 🍷 3.50 – 🍽 6.00 – **14 rm** 27.00/60.00 t.
     Spec. Crème topinambour (October-March), Escalope de saumon à l'oseille (February-October), Médaillons de
     chevreuil Grand Veneur (October-February).

BRITISH LEYLAND King St. ☏ 24666   TALBOT The Parade, North End ☏ 21456
FORD 220 London Rd ☏ 24344

EAST MOLESEY Surrey 404 S 29 – see Esher.

EASTON CROSS Devon 403 I 31 – see Chagford.

EASTON GREY Wilts. 403 404 N 29 – see Malmesbury.

EAST PRESTON West Sussex 404 S 31 – see Worthing.

EAST RETFORD Notts. 404 R 24 – pop. 18,413 – ✉ ☎ 0777 Retford.
🛈 Retford ☏ 3733.
London 135 – Leeds 47 – Lincoln 23 – Nottingham 31 – Sheffield 26.

   XXX **West Retford** with rm, 24 North Rd, DN22 7XG, ☏ 706333, 🚗 – 📺 🛏wc 📡 🅿. 🔁 ᴁ
     ⓪ 𝘝𝘐𝘚𝘈
     M a la carte 7.65/10.85 st. 🍷 2.00 – 🍽 2.40 – **30 rm** 18.00/25.00 st.

EATON SOCON Cambs. 404 T 27 – see St. Neots.

EBBERSTON North Yorks. – pop. 430 – ✉ ☎ 0723 Scarborough.
London 243 – Scarborough 9 – York 31.

   ⋔ **Foxholm,** YO13 9NJ, off A 170 ☏ 85550, 🚗 – 🛏wc 🅿
     March-October – **10 rm** 🍽 9.50/22.00 t.

EDWALTON Notts. 403 404 Q 25 – see Nottingham.

EGHAM Surrey 404 S 29 – pop. 30,609 – ECD Thursday – ☎ 078 43.
London 29 – Reading 21.

   🏨 **Runnymede,** Windsor Rd, TW20 0AG, on A 308 ☏ 6171, Telex 934900, ≼ – 🧳 📺
     🅿. 🛉. 🔁 ᴁ ⓪ 𝘝𝘐𝘚𝘈
     M approx. 5.50 t. 🍷 1.80 – **90 rm** 🍽 23.50/32.00 st.

   🏨 **Great Fosters,** Stroude Rd, TW20 9UR, S : 1 m. off B 388 ☏ 3822, ≼, « Elizabethan
     mansion with extensive gardens », 🎯, 🌊 heated, park – 🅿. 🛉. 🔁 ᴁ ⓪ 𝘝𝘐𝘚𝘈
     M 6.50/7.75 st. 🍷 2.10 – **38 rm** 🍽 21.00/34.00 st. – P 31.25/45.25 st.

   XXX Bailiwick, Wick Rd, Englefield Green, TW20 0HN, SW : 2 ½ m. off A 30 ☏ 2223 – 🅿.

BMW, FIAT Egham-by-pass ☏ 6431   DATSUN The Avenue ☏ 4743
BRITISH LEYLAND The Causeway ☏ 6191

EGLWYSFACH Dyfed 403 I 26 – see Machynlleth.

ELSTEAD Surrey 404 R 30 – pop. 2,548 – ✉ Godalming – ☎ 025 122.
London 43 – Guildford 9 – Southampton 44.

   X **Emmerich's,** Thursley Rd, GU8 6DH, ☏ 2323, Austrian rest. – 🅿. ⓪ 𝘝𝘐𝘚𝘈
     closed Sunday dinner and Monday – M a la carte 4.85/7.00 🍷 2.15

ELTERWATER Cumbria – see Ambleside.

ELY Cambs. 🗺️ U 26 – pop. 9,020 – ECD : Tuesday – ☎ 0353.
See : Cathedral** 11C-16C (Norman nave***, lantern***).
⛳ Cambridge Rd ☎ 2751.
🚗 ☎ 58800 ext 106.
🛈 24 St. Mary's St. ☎ 3311.
London 74 – Cambridge 16 – Norwich 60.

🏨 **Lamb** (County), 2 Lynn Rd, CB7 4ES, ☎ 3574 – 🛏️wc 🄿. 🅂 AE ⓪ VISA
  M 3.75/4.75 st. ₰ 1.55 – **29 rm** ☷ 15.00/21.00 s.

✗ **Old Fire Engine House**, 25 St. Mary's St., CB7 4ER, ☎ 2582, 🌳 – 🄶
  closed Sunday and 24 December for 2 weeks – **M** a la carte approx. 5.80 t.

AUSTIN-MG Lynn Rd ☎ 2981
FIAT 64 St. Mary's St. ☎ 2300
FORD Station Rd ☎ 2348

MORRIS-MG-ROVER-TRIUMPH St. Mary's St. ☎ 2952
VOLVO Witcham ☎ (0353) 778403

EMBOROUGH Somerset 🗺️ 🗺️ M 30 – pop. 165 – ✉ Bath (Avon) – ☎ 0761 Stratton-on-Fosse.
London 134 – Bath 15 – Bristol 16 – Taunton 35.

🏠 **Court**, Lynch Hill, BA3 4SA, E: ½ m. on B 3139 ☎ 232237, 🌳 – 📺 🛁wc 🄿
  M a la carte 4.50/7.25 t. ₰ 1.70 – **9 rm** ☷ 12.00/18.50 t.

EPPING Essex 🗺️ U 28 – pop. 10,830 – ECD : Wednesday – ☎ 0378.
See : Forest*. **Envir. :** Waltham Abbey (Abbey*) E: 6 m.
⛳ Forest Approach, Bury Rd ☎ 529 1039.
London 20 – Cambridge 40 – Chelmsford 18.

🏨 **Post House** (T.H.F.), High Rd, Bell Common, CM16 4DG, S: ¾ m. on B 1393 ☎ 73137,
  🌳 – 📺 🛏️wc ☎ 🄿. 🅂 AE ⓪ VISA
  M 4.25/5.10 st. ₰ 1.85 – **60 rm** 18.00/25.50 st.

🏨 **Epping Forest Motel** (County), 234 High St., CM16 4AL, ☎ 73134, Telex 25471 – 🛗
  📺 🛏️wc ☎ 🄿. 🛗. 🅂 AE ⓪ VISA
  M 4.10/4.50 st. ₰ 1.55 – **28 rm** ☷ 14.00/20.00 s.

RENAULT High Rd ☎ 72266

EPSOM Surrey 🗺️ T 29 – pop. 72,301 (inc. Ewell) – ECD : Wednesday – ☎ 037 27.
Envir. : Chessington Zoo* AC, NW : 3 ½ m.
⛳ ☎ 23363.
London 17 – Guildford 16.

🏨 **Drift Bridge** (Crest), Reigate Rd, KT17 3JZ, SE : 2¼ m. on A 240 by A 2022 ☎ 073 73
  (Burgh Heath) 52163 – 📺 🛏️wc ☎ 🄿. 🛗. 🅂 AE ⓪ VISA
  25 rm ☷ 15.90/25.20 st.

🏠 **Linden House**, 9 College Rd off Church Rd, KT17 4HF, ☎ 21447, 🌳 – 🛏️wc 🚗 🄿.
  🛗
  M *(closed Sunday and Bank Holidays)* a la carte 2.75/5.20 ₰ 1.60 – **22 rm** ☷ 10.15/20.25 st.

↑ **White House**, Downs Hill Rd, KT18 5HW, ☎ 22472, 🌳 – 🛏️wc 🄿
  closed 1 week at Christmas – **10 rm** ☷ 10.15/19.60 st.

BRITISH LEYLAND 4 Church St. ☎ 26611
4 Church St. ☎ 26611
FORD 28 Church St. ☎ 25101

PEUGEOT, TALBOT 28/38 Upper High St. ☎ 25611
RENAULT 1/3 Dorking Rd ☎ 28391
VAUXHALL 48 Upper High St. ☎ 25920

ERBISTOCK (ERBISTOG) Clwyd 🗺️ L 25 – pop. 350 – ✉ Wrexham – ☎ 097 873 Overton-on-Dee. – London 184 – Chester 18 – Shrewsbury 22.

✗ **Boat Inn**, LL13 0DL, ☎ 243, ≤, « Picturesque inn on the banks of the River Dee », 🌳 –
  🄿. 🅂 AE ⓪ VISA
  M a la carte 6.00/7.40 st.

ERMINGTON Devon 🗺️ I 32 – see Modbury.

ESHER Surrey 🗺️ S 29 – pop. 64,414 – ECD : Wednesday – ☎ 0372.
⛳ Portsmouth Rd ☎ 63533 – ⛳ More Lane ☎ 65921.
London 20 – Portsmouth 58.

at East Molesey NW : 2 m. off A 309 – ✉ East Molesey – ☎ 01 London :

✗✗ Vecchia Roma, 55-57 Bridge Rd, KT8 9EL, ☎ 979 5490, Italian rest.

✗✗ **Le Chien Qui Fume**, 107 Walton Rd, KT8 0DR, ☎ 979 7150 – 🅂 AE ⓪ VISA
  closed Saturday lunch, Sunday, first 2 weeks August and Bank Holidays – **M** a la carte 8.25/11.25 ₰ 1.50.

✗ **Lantern**, 20 Bridge Rd, KT8 9AH, ☎ 979 1531, French rest. – 🅂 AE ⓪ VISA
  closed Sunday – **M** (dinner only) a la carte 6.75/9.60 t. ₰ 1.80.

AUSTIN-DAIMLER-JAGUAR-MORRIS-MG-ROVER-TRIUMPH Kingston By-Pass, Hinchley Wood ☎ 01 (London) 398 0123

ESKDALE Cumbria – pop. 450 – ECD : Wednesday and Saturday – ✉ Holmrook – ☎ 094 03.
Envir. : Wast Water* NE : 6 m. – Wasdale Head (site*) NE : 7 m.
London 312 – Carlisle 59 – Kendal 60.

   Bower House Inn ⌂, Holmrook, CA19 1TD, W : ¾ m. ☎ 244, ⚞ – ⌷wc **P** – **12 rm.**

ETON Berks. **404** S 29 – see Windsor.

EVERCREECH Somerset **403** **404** M 30 – pop. 1,548 – ECD : Wednesday – ✉ Shepton Mallet
– ☎ 074 983 (3 fig.) or 0749 (6 fig.).
London 122 – Bristol 24 – Southampton 58 – Taunton 35.

   Glen ⌂, Queen's Rd, BA4 6JS, ☎ 830369, ≼, ⚞ – ⌷wc **P**. **🅰** **AE** **VISA**
   closed 25 and 26 December – **M** *(closed Sunday dinner to non-residents)* 3.25 **t.** – **17 rm**
   �㎡ 9.00/19.00 **t.**

AUSTIN-MORRIS-MG Weymouth Rd ☎ 393

EVESHAM Heref. and Worc. **403** **404** O 27 – pop. 13,855 – ECD : Wednesday – ☎ 0386.
London 99 – Birmingham 30 – Cheltenham 16 – **Coventry 32.**

   Evesham, Coopers Lane, off Waterside, WR11 6DA, ☎ 6344, Telex 339342 – **TV** ⌷wc
   🚿wc 🅮 **P**. 🅰. **🅰** **AE** **①** **VISA**
   M (buffet lunch) a la carte 5.80/7.10 **st.** 🍷 2.30 – **18 rm** �㎡ 17.75/31.00 **st.**

   Northwick Arms, Waterside, WR11 6BT, ☎ 6109 – ⌷wc **P**. **🅰** **VISA**
   closed Christmas – **M** *(closed Sunday lunch)* a la carte 3.60/6.30 **s.** 🍷 1.30 – **22 rm** �㎡
   10.50/28.00 **s.**

AUSTIN-JAGUAR-MORRIS-MG-ROVER-TRIUMPH-
Broadway Rd ☎ 6441
AUSTIN-MORRIS-MG-WOLSELEY Abbey Rd ☎ 6173
BEDFORD, VAUXHALL 70 High St. ☎ 2614
BMW, VW, AUDI Harvington ☎ 038 671 (Harving-
ton) 612

FIAT 3 Cheltenham Rd ☎ 2301
FORD Market Pl. ☎ 2525
PEUGEOT Riverside ☎ 2021
RENAULT 123 Pershore Rd, Hampton ☎ 2446
TALBOT Elm Rd ☎ 2773
TOYOTA Icknield St., Honeybourne ☎ 830350

EWEN Glos. **403** **404** O 28 – see Cirencester.

EXETER Devon **403** J 31 – pop. 95,729 – ☎ 0392.
See : Cathedral** 12C-14C (Tierceron ribbed vault***, West front*, Bishop's Throne*) **AZ A** –
St. Nicholas' Priory* 11C **AZ B** – Guildhall* 14C-15C **AZ D** – Maritime Museum* *AC* **AZ M¹**.
Downes Crediton ☎ 03632 (Crediton) 3991, NW : 7 ½ m. by A 377 **AY**.
Exeter Airport : ☎ 67433, Telex 42648, E : 3 m. by A 30 **BY** – **Terminal :** St. David's Station.
Civic Centre, Dix's Field ☎ 72434.
London 201 – Bournemouth 80 – Bristol 78 – Plymouth 46 – Southampton 106.

Plan on next page

   Rougemont (Mt. Charlotte), Queen St., EX4 3SP, ☎ 54982 – 🛗 **TV** **P**. 🅰. **🅰** **AE** **①** **VISA**
   M a la carte 5.55/7.75 **t.** 🍷 2.10 – **63 rm** �㎡ 19.00/30.00 **t.**   **AZ x**

   Imperial, New North Rd, EX4 4JX, ☎ 72750, ⚞ – **TV** ⌷wc 🅮 🚗 **P**. 🅰. **🅰** **AE** **VISA** **AZ v**
   M 3.45/4.60 **st.** 🍷 1.75 – **30 rm** �㎡ 15.50/27.50 **st.** – P 22.55/24.55 **st.**

   White Hart, 61 South St., EX1 1EE, ☎ 79897, « Part 14C inn » – **TV** ⌷wc 🚿wc 🅮
   P. 🅰. **🅰** **AE** **①** **VISA**   **AZ n**
   M *(closed dinner 25 and 26 December)* 3.75/5.55 **t.** 🍷 1.60 – **46 rm** �㎡ 17.70/19.50 **t.** –
   P 20.80/27.00 **t.**

   Buckerell Lodge (Crest), Topsham Rd, EX2 4SQ, SE : 1 m. on A 377 ☎ 52451, ⚞ – **TV**
   ⌷wc 🅮 **P**. **🅰** **AE** **①** **VISA**   **BY a**
   19 rm �㎡ 15.00/23.60 **st.**

   Countess Wear Lodge(County), 398 Topsham Rd, EX2 6HE, S : 2 ½ m. on A 377
   ☎ 039 287 (Topsham) 5441, Group Telex 25971 – **TV** ⌷wc 🅮 **P**. 🅰. **🅰** **AE**
   ① **VISA**   **BY o**
   M 4.30 **st.** 🍷 1.55 – **43 rm** �㎡ 18.50/22.50 **s.**

   Royal Clarence (Norfolk Cap.), Cathedral Yard, EX1 1HD, ☎ 58464, Group Telex
   23241 – 🛗 **TV** ⌷wc 🚿wc 🅮. **🅰** **AE** **①** **VISA**   **AZ z**
   M a la carte 5.20/7.25 **st.** 🍷 1.75 – **63 rm** �㎡ 18.15/28.05 **st.**

   Great Western (T.H.F.), St. David's Station App., EX4 4NU, ☎ 74039 – **TV** ⌷wc 🅮.
   🅰 **AE** **①** **VISA**   **AZ u**
   M 3.35/4.00 **st.** 🍷 1.65 – **44 rm** �㎡ 12.50/24.00 **st.**

   Edgerton Park, Pennsylvania Rd, EX4 6DH, ☎ 74029 – ⌷wc 🚿wc **P**. **🅰** **AE** **①** **VISA**
   M 4.00/6.00 **s.** 🍷 2.00 – **17 rm** �㎡ 11.50/19.00 **s.**   **AY c**

   Red House, Whipton Village Rd, EX4 8AR, ☎ 56104 – **P**. **🅰** **AE** **①** **VISA**   **BY r**
   M a la carte 3.65/5.25 **t.** 🍷 1.50 – **19 rm** �㎡ 9.50/15.50 **t.**

   St. Andrews, 28 Alphington Rd, EX2 8HN, ☎ 76784 – **P**. **🅰** **VISA**   **AY a**
   closed Christmas – **20 rm** �㎡ 10.95/17.85 **st.**

   Park View, 8 Howell Rd, EX4 4LG, ☎ 71772 – 🚿 **P**   **AZ i**
   13 rm �㎡ 5.20/11.50 **t.**

EXETER

Bedford Street	AZ 3	Edmund Street	AZ 9	Paris Street	BZ 28
Fore Street	AZ	East Wonford Hill	BY 10	Prince Charles Road	BY 30
High Street	AZ	Frog Street	AZ 12	Prince of Wales Road	AY 31
Shopping Precinct	AZ	Ladysmith Road	BZ 16	Richmond Road	AZ 32
		Little John's Cross Hill	AY 17	St. Andrew's Road	AY 33
Alphington Road	AZ 2	Magdalen Street	AZ 20	Southernhay East	ABZ 34
Blackall Road	AZ 4	Mount Pleasant Road	BY 21	Southernhay West	AZ 35
Butts Road	BY 5	New Bridge Street	AZ 22	Sweetbriar Lane	BY 36
Commins Road	BZ 8	North Street	AZ 23	Union Road	AY 37
		North Street HEAVITREE	BY 24	Western Way	AZ 38
		Okehampton Road	AZ 26	Whipton Lane	BY 39
		Old Tiverton Road	BZ 27	Wonford Street	BY 40

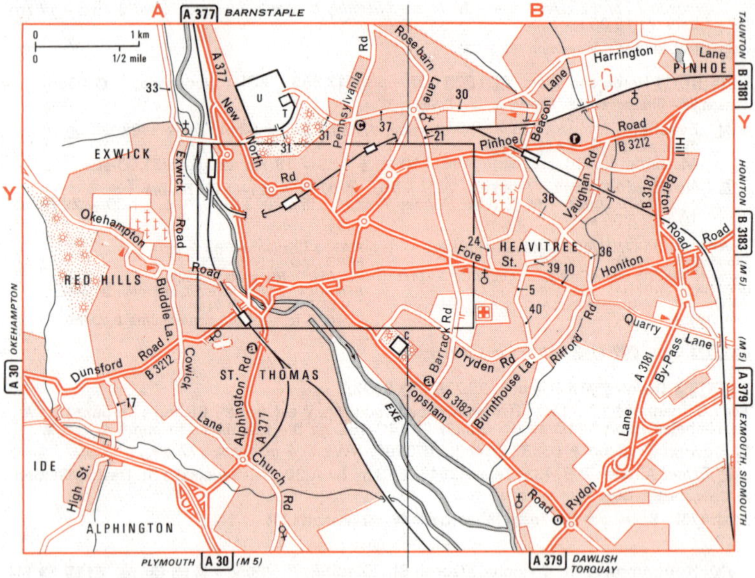

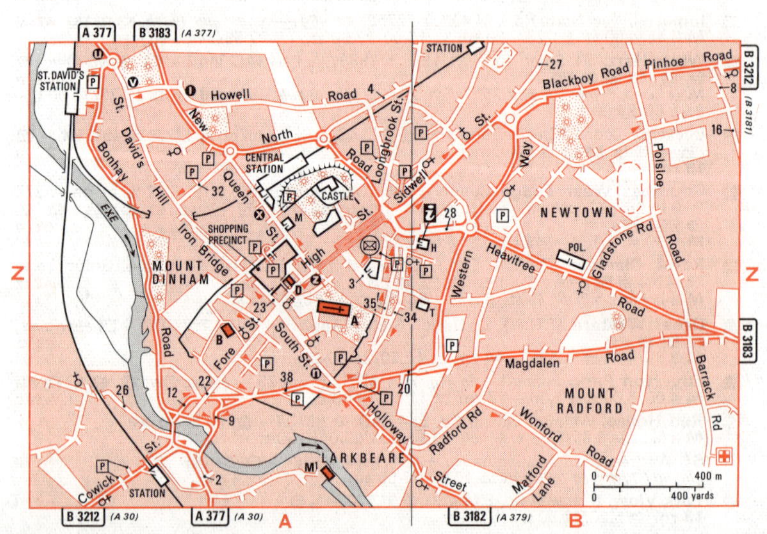

at Kennford S : 5 m. on A 38 by A 30 – AY – ⊠ ☎ 0392 Kennford :

🏨 Exeter Ladbroke Mercury Motor Inn, Exeter By-Pass, EX6 7UX, ☏ 832121 – 📺 ⇔wc 🕿 ᴋ 🅿 – **60 rm.**

♔ **Fairwinds,** EX6 7UD, ☏ 832911 – 📺 🅿
closed 19 December-12 January – ⨅ 2.20 – **7 rm** 11.00/17.00 **t.**

XX Haldon Thatch, Telegraph Hill, EX6 7XX, off A 38 ☏ 832273 – 🅿.

MICHELIN Branch, Kestrel Way, Sowton Industrial Estate, EX2 7LH, ☏ 77246.

ALFA-ROMEO Hennock Rd Marsh Barton ☏ 37337
AUSTIN-DAIMLER-JAGUAR-MORRIS-MG Alphington St. ☏ 58241
AUSTIN-MORRIS-MG 55 Sidwell St. ☏ 78342
AUSTIN-MORRIS 85/88 Sidwell St. ☏ 54923
AUSTIN-MORRIS-MG-ROVER-TRIUMPH, ROLLS ROYCE Marsh Barton Rd ☏ 74161
DAIMLER-JAGUAR, FERRARI Frog St., Inner By-Pass ☏ 75237
DATSUN Honiton Rd ☏ 37152

CITROEN, FIAT, MERCEDES-BENZ Trusham Rd, Marsh Barton ☏ 77311
FIAT 189 Pinhoe Rd, Polsloe Bridge ☏ 69351
FORD 9 Marsh Barton Rd ☏ 50141
PEUGEOT 11 Verney St. ☏ 55372
RENAULT Summerland St. ☏ 77225
MAZDA, SAAB Ladysmith Rd ☏ 73990
TOYOTA Howell Rd ☏ 34761
VOLVO Longbrook Terrace, Longbrook St. ☏ 35374
VW, AUDI Haven Rd ☏ 71645

EXFORD Somerset 🗺 J 30 – pop. 452 – ECD : Thursday – ⊠ Minehead – ☎ 064 383.
London 194 – Exeter 35 – Minehead 13 – Taunton 32.

🏠 **Crown,** TA24 7PP, ☏ 243 – ⇔wc 🅿
M (bar lunch) a la carte 3.50/7.00 **st.** ⦿ 2.00 – ⨅ 2.00 – **18 rm** 10.50/23.00 **t.**

EXMOUTH Devon 🗺 J 32 – pop. 21,030 – ECD Wednesday – ☎ 039 52.
🛈 Alexandra Ter. ☏ 3744 (summer only).
London 210 – Exeter 11.

🏨 **Imperial** (T.H.F.), The Esplanade, EX8 2SW, ☏ 74761, ≼, ⅀ heated, 🚗 – 🛗 📺 🅿. 🖳. 🔲 AE ⓪ VISA
M 3.65/4.90 **st.** ⦿ 1.65 – **40 rm** ⨅ 18.00/30.50 **st.**

🏨 **Devoncourt,** 16 Douglas Av., EX8 2EX, ☏ 72277, ≼, ℀, ⅀ heated, 🚗 – 🛗 🅿
M 2.50/3.50 ⦿ 1.30 – **65 rm** ⨅ 14.00/28.00 – P 18.50.

🏨 **Royal Beacon,** The Beacon, EX8 2AF, ☏ 4886, ≼ – 🛗 📺 ⇔wc 🅿. 🔲 AE ⓪ VISA
M 3.75/4.75 **st.** ⦿ 2.00 – **35 rm** ⨅ 11.00/24.00 **st.** – P 18.00/21.00 **st.**

🏠 **Balcombe House** ⌂, 7 Stevenstone Rd, EX8 2EP, NE: 1 m. off A 376 ☏ 6349, 🚗 – 🏯wc ᴋ 🅿
April-October – **M** (bar lunch) 4.00/5.50 **t.** ⦿ 1.50 – **12 rm** ⨅ 9.00/18.00 **t.** – P 13.00/17.00 **t.**

AUSTIN-MG 12 High St. ☏ 72048
BRITISH LEYLAND The Parade ☏ 72258
RENAULT 4 Church Rd ☏ 72921

TALBOT St. Andrews Rd ☏ 3045
VAUXHALL Salterton Rd ☏ 4366
VW, AUDI Belvedere Rd ☏ 4303

EYE Suffolk 🗺 X 27 – pop. 1,660 – ECD : Tuesday – ☎ 037 987.
London 93 – Ipswich 20 – Norwich 23.

at Brome NW : 2 m. on A 140 by B 1077 – ⊠ ☎ 037 987 Eye :

🏠 Grange Motel, IP23 8AP, ☏ 456 – 📺 ⇔wc 🕿 🅿
22 rm.

EYPE Dorset – 🗺 L 31 – see Bridport.

FAIRBOURNE Gwynedd 🗺 H 25 – pop. 400 – ECD : Wednesday – ☎ 034 16.
London 229 – Dolgellau 8 – Shrewsbury 65.

♔ Liety Heulog, 2-4 Alyn Rd, LL38 2LZ, ☏ 228 – 🅿
12 rm.

FAIRFORD Glos. 🗺 🗺 O 28 – pop. 1,840 – ECD : Saturday – ☎ 0285.
See : St. Mary's Church (stained glass windows** 15C-16C).
London 99 – Bristol 46 – Gloucester 28 – Oxford 27.

🏠 **Bull,** Market Pl., GL7 4AA, ☏ 712535, ⌇, 🚗 – ⇔wc 🅿. 🔲 AE
closed 22 to 27 December – **M** a la carte 4.70/7.70 **t.** ⦿ 2.00 – **16 rm** ⨅ 13.00/25.00 **t.**

X **Pink's,** London Rd, GL7 4AR, ☏ 712355 – 🅿. 🔲 AE VISA
closed Sunday dinner, Christmas Day and 2 weeks January – **M** a la carte 5.00/8.40 **t.** ⦿ 2.15.

FAIRY CROSS Devon 🗺 H 31 – see Horns Cross.

Red Lion

Wenn der Name eines Hotels dünn gedruckt ist,
dann hat uns der Hotelier Preise
und Öffnungszeiten nicht angegeben.

FAKENHAM Norfolk **404** W 25 — pop. 4,462 — ECD : Wednesday — ☎ 0328.
Envir. : Houghton Hall** (18C) *AC*, W: 8 m.
⌐₉ ☎ 2867.
London 112 — Cambridge 61 — King's Lynn 22 — **Norwich 26.**

   ⚑ Crown, Market Pl., NR21 9BG, ☎ 2010 — **Ⓟ**
   12 rm.

AUSTIN-MORRIS-MG-ROVER-TRIUMPH Holt Rd   OPEL Greenway Lane ☎ 2200
☎ 2277   TALBOT Norwich Rd ☎ 2251
DATSUN Norwich Rd ☎ 2266   VAUXHALL Hempton Rd ☎ 3331
FORD Oak St. ☎ 2317

FALFIELD Avon **403 404** M 29 — pop. 658 — ⊠ Gloucester (Glos.) — ☎ 045 48.
London 129 — Bristol 16 — Gloucester 18 — Newport 30.

   ⌂ Park, GL12 8DR, S: 1 m. on A 38 ☎ 550, 🚗 — 📺 ⇔wc 🗍wc ☎ **Ⓟ**. ◣ AE ⓪ VISA
   M *(closed Sunday)* 6.00/7.00 **st.** ▯ 2.00 — � 2.25 — **10 rm** 13.50/20.00 **st.**

FALLOWFIELD Greater Manchester **403 404** M 23 — see Manchester.

   ☞ *Keine bezahlte Reklame im Michelin-Führer.*

FALMOUTH Cornwall **403** E 33 — pop. 18,041 — ECD : Wednesday — ☎ 0326.
See : Pendennis Castle 16C (≤*) *AC*.
⌐₁₈ Swanpool Rd ☎ 311262 — ⌐₉ at Budock Vean ☎ 0326 (Mawnan Smith) 250288, SW: 7 m.
🛈 Catrick offices, The Moor ☎ 312300.
London 308 — Penzance 26 — Plymouth 65 — Truro 11.

   🏨 **Falmouth,** Cliff Rd, TR11 4NZ, ☎ 312671, Telex 45639, ≤, ⌁ heated, 🚗 — ⫴ 📺 **Ⓟ**. ◭.
   ◣ AE VISA
   M 4.80/6.00 **st.** ▯ 2.00 — **73 rm** � 14.00/35.80 **st.** — P 19.50/26.65 **st.**

   🏨 **Green Lawns,** Western Ter., TR11 4QJ, ☎ 312734, 🚗 — 📺 ⇔wc 🗍wc ☎ **Ⓟ**. ◭. ◣
   AE ⓪ VISA
   M approx. 4.50 ▯ 1.35 — **34 rm** � 9.50/16.00.

   🏨 **Bay,** Cliff Rd, TR11 4NU, ☎ 312094, ≤, 🚗 — ⫴ 📺 ⇔wc ☎ 🚗 **Ⓟ**. ◣ AE VISA
   closed Christmas — **M** approx. 5.75 **st.** — **39 rm** ⊒ 11.50/35.00 **st.** — P 16.50/23.50 **st.**

   🏨 Green Bank, Harbourside, TR11 2SR, ☎ 312440, ≤ harbour — ⫴ ⇔wc ☎ 🚗 **Ⓟ**
   42 rm.

   🏨 **St. Michaels,** Gyllyngvase Beach, Seafront, TR11 4NB, ☎ 312707, Telex 45617, ≤,
   « Gardens » — 📺 ⇔wc 🗍wc ☎ **Ⓟ**. ◣ AE VISA
   M 3.50/5.50 **s.** ▯ 2.00 — **55 rm** ⊒ 14.00/24.00 **s.** — P 19.50/23.00 **s.**

   🏨 **Trelawne** ⅏, Maenporth, TR11 5HS, SW: 4 m. ☎ 0326 (Mawnan Smith) 250226, ◪.
   🚗 — ⇔wc 🗍wc **Ⓟ**. ◣ AE ⓪ VISA
   March-October — **M** 3.50/6.50 **t.** ▯ 1.80 — **18 rm** ⊒ (dinner included) 15.00/33.00 **t.**

   ⌂ **Penmere Manor** ⅏, Mongleath Rd, TR11 5BY, ☎ 311356, ⌁ heated, 🚗 — ⇔wc **Ⓟ**.
   ◣ AE VISA
   March-October — **M** (bar lunch) approx. 5.80 **st.** — **31 rm** ⊒ 12.50/32.00 **st.**

   ⌂ **Crill House** ⅏, Golden Bank, TR11 5BL, ☎ 312994, ⌁ heated, 🚗 — ⇔wc **Ⓟ**
   April-mid October — **M** (bar lunch) approx. 5.00 **st.** ▯ 2.00 — **10 rm** ⊒ 14.00/28.00 **st.**

   ⌂ **Carthion,** Cliff Rd, TR11 4AP, ☎ 313669, ≤, 🚗 — ⇔wc 🗍 **Ⓟ**. ◣ ⓪ VISA
   closed January — **M** (bar lunch) 6.00 **t.** ▯ 1.60 — **20 rm** ⊒ 11.00/23.00 **t.** — P 16.00 **t.**

   ⌂ **Somerdale,** Sea View Rd, TR11 4EF, ☎ 312566, 🚗 — ⇔wc 🗍wc **Ⓟ**. ◣ VISA
   March-October — **M** 2.00/4.50 ▯ 1.75 — **19 rm** ⊒ 8.00/19.50.

   ⋔ **Gyllyngvase House,** Gyllyngvase Rd, TR11 4DJ, ☎ 312956, 🚗 — 🗍wc **Ⓟ**
   March-October — **17 rm** ⊒ 7.00/16.00.

   ⋔ **Cotswold House,** 49 Melvill Rd, TR11 4DF, ☎ 312077 — ⇔wc 🗍 **Ⓟ**
   closed 1 week at Christmas — **11 rm** ⊒ 8.30/17.70 **t.**

   ⋔ **Tresillian House,** 3 Stracey Rd, TR11 4DW, ☎ 312425 — ⇔wc 🗍wc **Ⓟ**
   March-October — **13 rm** ⊒ 10.25/22.25 **t.**

   ✗ **Continental,** 29 High St., TR11 2AD, ☎ 313003 — ⓪
   closed Sunday and 2 weeks November — **M** (dinner only) a la carte 4.50/7.20 **t.** ▯ 2.00.

   at Mawnan Smith SW : 5 m. off B 3291 — ⊠ Falmouth — ☎ 0326 Mawnan Smith :

   🏨 **Meudon** ⅏, TR11 5HT, E: ½ m. ☎ 250541, « ≤ Terraced gardens », park — 📺 **Ⓟ**. ◣ AE
   ⓪ VISA
   closed January — **M** 4.00/6.00 **st.** ▯ 2.50 — **38 rm** ⊒ 17.00/55.00 **st.**

   🏨 Nansidwell Country House ⅏, TR11 5HU, E: ¼ m. ☎ 250340, ≤, ✗, 🚗, park — ⇔wc **Ⓟ**
   season — **20 rm.**

   ✗ **Blanchards Cockleshell,** The Square, TR11 5EP, ☎ 250714 — **Ⓟ**. ◣ AE ⓪ VISA
   closed Sunday, Monday from October to April and first 2 weeks January — **M** (dinner only)
   a la carte 5.20/7.30 ▯ 1.90.

at Budock Vean SW : 7 m. via Mawnan Smith – ⊠ Falmouth – ☻ 0326 Mawnan Smith :

🏨 **Budock Vean** ⌂, TR11 5LG, ℡ 250288, ≼, ❀, ◻, ┣, ⌖, ▰, park – 🛗 🅿. ◪ Æ ⓪ **VISA**
closed mid January - early March – **M** 4.60/8.05 ⌕ 1.85 – **54 rm** ⌸ (dinner included) 21.00/51.00 – P 29.00.

BRITISH LEYLAND Dracaena Av. ℡ 312338
BRITISH LEYLAND The Moor ℡ 312316
DATSUN Dracaena Av. ℡ 311616
FORD Ponsharden ℡ 72011

RENAULT Falmouth Rd, Penryn ℡ 032 67 (Penryn) 2641
TOYOTA North Parade ℡ 313029
VW, AUDI-NSU Dracaena Av. ℡ 312283

FAREHAM Hants. 📵 📵 Q 31 – pop. 80,403 – ECD : Wednesday – ☻ 032 92.

┣ Southwick Park ℡ 07018 (Cosham) 80131, NE : 3 ½ m.

Envir. : Porchester castle* (ruins 3C-12C), Keep ≼* *AC*, SE : 2 ½ m.

London 77 – Portsmouth 9 – Southampton 13 – Winchester 19.

🏠 Red Lion, East St., PO16 0BP, ℡ 234113 – ⓟ
23 rm.

AUSTIN-MG-WOLSELEY 216 West St. ℡ 232488
FIAT, LANCIA Newgate Lane ℡ 282811

MORRIS-MG-ROVER-TRIUMPH East St. ℡ 231511

FARINGDON Oxon. 📵 📵 P 29 – pop. 3,898 – ECD : Thursday – ☻ 0367.

London 79 – Bristol 55 – Oxford 17 – Reading 34.

🏠 **Bell,** Market Pl., SN7 7HP, ℡ 20534 – ⓟ. ◪ Æ ⓪ **VISA**
M *(closed Sunday dinner)* 5.00/8.00 **st.** ⌕ 2.00 – ⌸ 2.00 – **9 rm** 8.25/21.50 **st.**

BMW Church St. ℡ 20614

PEUGEOT Marlborough St. ℡ 21212

FARNBOROUGH Hants. 📵 R 30 – pop. 41,474 – ECD : Thursday – ☻ 0252.

See : St. Michael's Abbey church* 19 C (Imperial crypt *AC*).

┣ Ively Rd ℡ 48700, W : 1 m.

🛈 Country Library, Pinehurst Av. ℡ 513838.

London 41 – Reading 17 – Southampton 44 – Winchester 33.

🏨 **Queens** (Anchor), Lynchford Rd, GU14 6AZ, S : 1 ½ m. on Farnborough Rd (A 325)
℡ 45051, Group Telex 857785 – 📺 ⌂wc ☎ ⓟ. ⌸. ◪ Æ ⓪ **VISA**
M a la carte approx. 6.00 **st.** – **79 rm** ⌸ 18.50/26.00 **st.**

at Frimley Bridges (Surrey) N : 1 ¼ m. on A 325 – ⊠ ☻ 0276 Camberley :

✕✕ **Auctioneer,** GU14 8DF, ℡ 23559 – ⓟ. ◪ ⓪ **VISA**
closed Saturday lunch, Sunday, 12 to 27 August and Bank Holidays – **M** (lunch only and Saturday dinner) a la carte 6.95/11.60 **t.** ⌕ 2.00.

ALFA-ROMEO 13 Cross St. ℡ 46291
AUSTIN-MORRIS-ROVER-TRIUMPH 116 Farnborough
Rd ℡ 41345

FORD Elles Rd ℡ 44344

FARNE ISLANDS Northumb.

See : Islands** (Sea Bird Sanctuary and grey seals, by boat from Seahouses *AC*).

Hotels see : Bamburgh.

FARNHAM Surrey 📵 R 30 – pop. 21,110 – ECD : Wednesday – ☻ 025 13.

See : Castle keep 12C (square tower*) *AC*. **Envir. :** Birdworld* (zoological bird gardens) *AC*, SW : 3 ½ m.

┣ Farnham Park ℡ 3319.

🛈 Locality Office, South St. ℡ 048 68 (Godalming) 4104 est 214/5.

London 45 – Reading 22 – Southampton 39 – Winchester 28.

🏨 Bush (Anchor), The Borough, GU9 7NN, ℡ 715237, Group Telex 858875, ▰ – 📺 ⌂wc
☎ ⓟ. ◪ Æ ⓪ **VISA**
51 rm ⌸ 13.75/28.00 **st.** .

✕✕ **Bishop's Table** with rm, 27 West St., GU9 7DR, ℡ 715545, ▰ – 📺 ⌂wc ⌂wc ☎.
◪ Æ ⓪ **VISA**
closed 25 December-1 January – **M** *(closed Sunday and Bank Holidays)* a la carte 4.55/9.15 ⌕ 1.50 – **12 rm** ⌸ 12.50/18.00.

at Seale E : 4 m. on A 31 – ⊠ Farnham – ☻ 025 18 Runfold :

🏠 **Hog's Back** (Embassy), GU10 1EX, ℡ 2345, ≼, ▰ – 📺 ⌂wc ☎ ⓟ. ⌸. ◪ Æ ⓪
VISA
closed Christmas – **M** 4.75/5.50 **st.** ⌕ 2.50 – **13 rm** ⌸ 14.00/24.00 **st.**

BRITISH LEYLAND East St. ℡ 716201
MAZDA, MERCEDES-BENZ 48/50 Shortheath Rd ℡
716266
SAAB Frensham ℡ 025 125 (Frensham) 2002

TALBOT Lower Bourne ℡ 715610
VW, AUDI, PORSCHE West St. and Crondall Lane ℡
715616

FARNLEY TYAS West Yorks. 📵 📵 O 23 – see Huddersfield.

FARNSFIELD Notts. 403 404 Q 24 – pop. 2,500 – ECD : Wednesday and Saturday – ⊠ Newark – ✆ 0623 Mansfield.
London 145 – Nottingham 13 – Sheffield 31.

  XX White Post Inn, Mansfield Rd, NG22 8HH, W 1 ¼ m. on A 614 ✆ 882215 – **P**.

FARRINGTON GURNEY Avon 403 404 M 30 – pop. 647 – ⊠ Bristol – ✆ 0761 Temple Cloud.
London 132 – Bath 13 – Bristol 12 – Wells 8.

  XX **Old Parsonage**, BS18 5UB, ✆ 52211, 🐎 – **P**
    closed Sunday dinner and Monday to non-residents – **M** a la carte 6.20/8.50 ⌀ 1.65.

FAUGH Cumbria – see Carlisle.

FAWLEY Bucks. 404 R 29 – pop. 398 – ECD : Wednesday – ⊠ Henley-on-Thames (Oxon.) – ✆ 049 163 Turville Heath.
London 45 – Oxford 25 – Reading 12.

  X Walnut Tree, Fawley Green, RG9 6JE, ✆ 360 – **P**.

FELINHELI Gwynedd – see Port Dinorwic.

FELIXSTOWE Suffolk 404 Y 28 – pop. 18,925 – ECD : Wednesday – ✆ 039 42.
🚢 Shipping connections with the Continent : to Göteborg (Tor Line) – to Rotterdam : Europoort (Townsend Thoresen) – to Zeebrugge (Townsend Thoresen) – to Swinoujscie via Copenhagen (Polish Baltic Shipping).
🛈 91 Undercliffe Rd West ✆ 2122 or 3303 (winter) – Tourist Information Caravan, No. 2 Gate, The Docks ✆ 78359 (summer only).
London 84 – Ipswich 11.

  🏨 **Orwell Moat House**, Hamilton Rd, IP11 7DX, ✆ 5511, 🐎 – 🛗 TV **P**. ⚙. ☒ AE ⓪ VISA
    M 4.50 st. ⌀ 1.90 – ☕ 2.25 – **65 rm** 17.50/24.50 st. – P 26.00/30.00 st.

  🏠 **De Novo**, Orwell Rd, IP11 4ZX, ✆ 78441 – ⇱wc 🕾 **P**. ☒ AE ⓪ VISA
    M 2.50/3.50 s. ⌀ 2.70 – **25 rm** ☕ 11.50/19.00 s.

AUSTIN-MORRIS-MG-ROVER-TRIUMPH-WOLSELEY   TALBOT Garrison Lane ✆ 5591
Crescent Rd ✆ 3221

FENSTANTON Cambs. 404 T 27 – see St. Ives.

FERNDOWN Dorset 403 404 O 31 – pop. 11,752 – ECD : Wednesday – ✆ 0202.
London 108 – Bournemouth 6 – Dorchester 27 – Salisbury 23.

  🏨 **Dormy** (De Vere) ⚶, New Rd, BH22 8ES, on A 347 ✆ 872121, Telex 22121, ≤, ✗,
    ⚊ heated, 🐎 – 🛗 TV ⅓ **P**. ⚙. ☒ AE ⓪ VISA
    M 5.25/6.00 st. ⌀ 1.90 – **90 rm** ☕ 22.00/44.00 st.

  🏨 **Coach House Motel**, Tricketts Cross, BH22 9NW, on A 31 ✆ 871222 – TV ⇱wc **P**.
    ☒ AE ⓪ VISA
    M 3.25/4.75 s. ⌀ 1.65 – ☕ 1.65 – **32 rm** 11.00/16.00 s.

COLT Victoria Rd ✆ 871131   TOYOTA Ringwood Rd ✆ 872201
ROVER-TRIUMPH 553 Ringwood Rd ✆ 872212   VAUXHALL Wimborne Rd East ✆ 872055

FILEY North Yorks. 986 ㉔ – pop. 5,336 – ECD : Wednesday – ✆ 0723 Scarborough.
🛈 John St. ✆ 512204.
London 251 – Kingston-upon-Hull 40 – Scarborough 7.5 – York 41.

  🏨 **White Lodge**, The Crescent, YO14 9JX, ✆ 512268, ≤, 🐎 – 🛗 ⇱wc. ☒ VISA
    M 3.30/5.60 ⌀ 2.00 – **22 rm** ☕ 10.50/21.00 – P 16.00/18.00.

FINDON West Sussex 404 S 31 – see Worthing.

FINGEST Bucks. 404 R 29 – pop. 3,080 (inc. Lane End) – ⊠ Henley-on-Thames (Oxon.) – ✆ 049 163 Turville Heath.
London 42 – High Wycombe 8 – Oxford 24 – Reading 16.

  X **Chequers Inn**, RG9 6QD ✆ 335, 🐎 – **P**. ⓪ VISA
    closed Sunday dinner, Monday and Bank Holidays – **M** a la carte 5.55/12.40 t. ⌀ 2.10.

FISHBOURNE I.O.W. 403 404 Q 31 – Shipping Services : see Wight (Isle of).

Außer den mit XXXXX ... X gekennzeichneten
Häusern haben auch sehr viele Hotels
ein gutes Restaurant.

FISHGUARD (ABERGWAUN) Dyfed **403** F 28 – pop. 2,810 – ECD : Wednesday – ☎ 0348.
Envir.: Porthgain (cliffs ❄***) SW : 10 m. – Goodwick (⩽**) NW : 1 ½ m. – Strumble Head
(⩽** from the lighthouse) NW : 5 m. – Trevine (⩽**) SW : 8 m. – Bryn Henllan (site*) NE : 5 m.

🚗 ☏ 01 (London) 723 7000 ext 3148.

⚓ to Rosslare (Sealink) 1-2 daily (Sundays : summer only) (3 h. 30 mn). – to Dun Laoghaire
(Sealink) 1 daily (5 h 30 mn).

🛈 Town Hall, ☏ 873484 (Easter-September).

London 267 – Cardiff 110 – Gloucester 157 – Holyhead 166 – Shrewsbury 134 – Swansea 72.

    🏛 **Cartref,** High St., SA65 9AW, ☏ 872430 – ▨ *VISA*
       M (buffet lunch) 2.25/4.00 **st.** 🍷 2.00 – **16 rm** ☷ 8.50/15.50 **st.** – P 14.75 **st.**

    ✗ **The Bistro** with rm, Main St., SA65 9HH, ☏ 873365 – **Ⓟ.** *VISA*
       Easter-October – **M** *(closed November and Monday in winter)* (dinner only) a la carte
       4.95/7.95 🍷 1.45 – ☷ 2.00 – **5 rm** 6.00/12.00 **t.**

       at Castle Morris (Casmorys) SW : 8 ¼ m. by A 487 on B 4331 – ✉ Haverfordwest
       – ☎ 034 84 Letterston :

    ✗✗ **Y Gwesty Bach,** SA62 5ER, ☏ 337 – **Ⓟ**
       *closed mid October-mid November, February, Sunday, Monday to Wednesday from
       November to Easter, Monday and Tuesday from Easter to Whitsun –* **M** (dinner only)
       8.00 **st.** 🍷 1.75.

       at Goodwick (Wdig) NW : 1 ½ m. – ✉ ☎ 0348 Fishguard :

    🏨 **Fishguard Bay,** Quay Rd, SA64 0BT, ☏ 873571, Telex 48503, ⌇ heated, 🌴, park – ▤
       ⇋wc 🗋 ⅄ **Ⓟ.** ⚐. ▨ AE ⓪ *VISA*
       M 4.50/5.50 **st.** – **62 rm** ☷ 14.00/28.00 **st.**

MORRIS-MG-ROVER-TRIUMPH West St. ☏ 872253

FITTLEWORTH West Sussex **404** S 31 – pop. 895 – ECD : Wednesday – ✉ Pulborough –
☎ 079 882.

London 52 – Brighton 28 – Chichester 15 – Worthing 17.

    🏛 Swan, Lower St., RH20 1EN, ☏ 429, 🌴 – ⇋wc **Ⓟ.** ▨ AE ⓪ *VISA*
       8 rm ☷ 9.00/20.00 **st.**

FLEET Hants. **404** R 30 – pop. 17,260 – ECD : Wednesday – ☎ 025 14.
🛈 Fleet Service Station, M3 Motorway, Hartley Wintney Basingstoke ☏ 21154.

London 46 – Guildford 14 – Reading 16 – Southampton 42.

    🏨 **Lismoyne,** Church Rd, GU13 8NA, ☏ 28555, 🌴 – ☐ ⇋wc 🗋wc ☎ **Ⓟ.** AE *VISA*
       M 2.80/3.60 **s.** 🍷 1.50 – **38 rm** ☷ 10.00/18.50 **s.**

    ✗✗ **Fleet Chantelle,** 33 Reading Rd South, GU13 9QP, ✉ Aldershot ☏ 3775 – **Ⓟ.** ▨
       ⓪ *VISA*
       *closed Saturday lunch, Sunday, 2 weeks August, 24 December for 2 weeks and Bank
       Holidays –* **M** a la carte 5.65/7.50 **t.** 🍷 1.55.

AUSTIN-MG-MORRIS-ROVER-TRIUMPH 66 Albert St.   VW, AUDI 42 Reading Rd South ☏ 3425
☏ 3303

FLEETWOOD Lancs. **986** ㉓ – pop. 28,599 – ECD : Wednesday – ☎ 039 17.
🛈 Princes Way ☏ 3114, W : from Promenade.

⚓ to the Isle of Man : Douglas (Isle of Man Steam Packet Co.) 2-5 weekly summer only
(4 h.).

🛈 Marine Hall, Esplanade ☏ 71141.

London 245 – Blackpool 10 – Lancaster 28 – Manchester 53.

    🏛 North Euston, Esplanade, FY7 6BN, ☏ 3375 – ▤ ⇋wc 🗋wc ☎ **Ⓟ**
       63 rm.

FLITTON Beds. **404** S 27 – pop. 717 – ✉ Ampthill – ☎ 0525 Silsoe.
London 48 – Bedford 11 – Luton 10.

    ✗✗ **White Hart Inn,** Brook Lane, MK45 5DY, ☏ 60403, Seafood – **Ⓟ**
       closed Sunday and Bank Holidays – **M** a la carte 7.20/8.90 **t.** 🍷 1.90.

FOLKESTONE Kent **404** X 30 – pop. 43,801 – ECD : Wednesday and Saturday – ☎ 0303.
See : Site*. **Envir. :** The Warren* (cliffs) E : 2 m. by A 20 ✗ – Acrise Place* *AC,* NW : 6 m.
by A 260 ✗.

🛈 Sene, ☏ 66726, N : 2 m. of Hythe on B 2065, W : by A 259 ✗.

⚓ Shipping connections with the Continent : to Boulogne, Calais and Oostende (Sealink) –
to Boulogne (P & O Ferries : Normandy Ferries).

🛈 Harbourg St. ☏ 58594 – The Precinct Sandgate Rd ☏ 53840 (summer only).

London 72 – Brighton 74 – Dover 7 – Maidstone 35.

FOLKESTONE

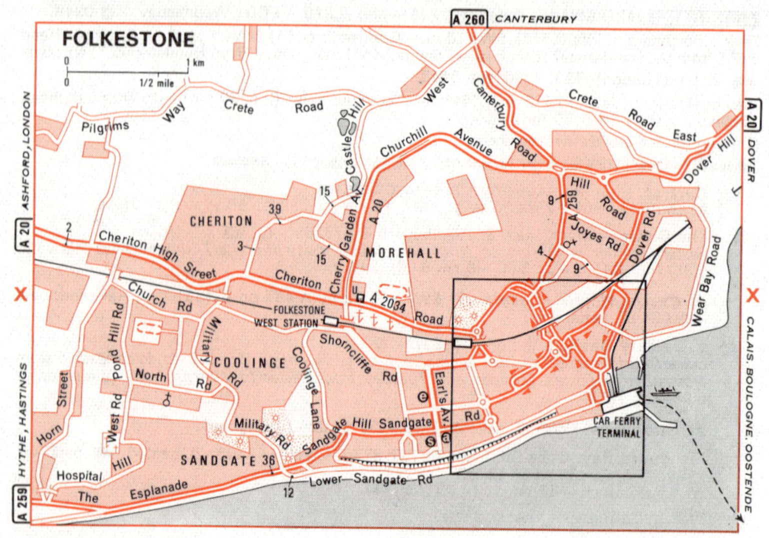

<table>
<tr><td>Guildhall Street</td><td>Y</td><td>22</td></tr>
<tr><td>Rendezvous Street</td><td>YZ</td><td></td></tr>
<tr><td>Sandgate Road</td><td>Z</td><td></td></tr>
<tr><td>Tontine Street</td><td>Y</td><td></td></tr>
</table>

Ashford Road	X	2
Ashley Avenue	X	3
Black Bull Road	X,Y	4
Bouverie Place	Z	6
Bouverie Road East	Z	7
Bradstone Road	Y	8
Canterbury Road	X	9
Castle Hill Av.	Z	10
Castle Road	X	12
Cheriton Place	Z	13
Cherry Garden Lane	X	15
Clifton Crescent	Z	16
Clifton Road	Z	17
Dunlocks (The)	Z	20
Grace Hill	Y	21
Harbour Street	Z	24
Harbour App. Road	Z	25
Langhorn Gardens	Z	27
Manor Road	Z	28
Marine Terrace	Z	29
Morrison Street	Y	31
North Street	Y	32
Radnor Bridge Road	Y	33
Remembrance (Road of)	Z	34
Ryland Place	Y	35
Sandgate Hill Street	X	36
Shorncliffe Road	Y	37
Tilekiln Lane	X	39
Trinity Gardens	Z	41
Victoria Grove	Y	43
Wear Bay Road	Y	44
West Terrace	Z	45

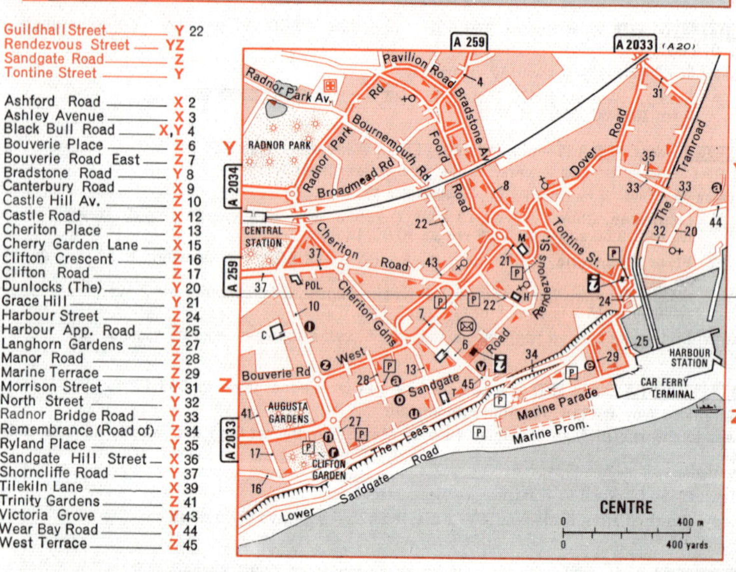

🏨 **Burlington** (Best Western), Earl's Av., CT20 2HR, ☎ 55301, Telex 96215, ≤, 🚗 – 🛗 TV P.   X s
🅰 AE ① VISA
M 3.50/4.50 t. 🍷 2.25 – **57 rm** ⛺ 16.50/26.50 t.

🏨 **Clifton** (T.H.F.), The Leas, CT20 2EB, ☎ 41231, ≤ – 🛗 TV 🛏 WC 🚿 ♨ 🅰 AE ① VISA   Z r
M 3.70/4.70 st. 🍷 1.65 – **59 rm** ⛺ 12.00/23.00 st.

🏨 **Banque** without rest., 4 Castle Hill Av., CT20 2RT, ☎ 53797 – TV 🛏 WC   Z z
10 rm ⛺ 10.00/20.00.

🏨 **Southcliff**, 25-26 The Leas, CT20 2DY, ☎ 56075, ≤, 🚗 – 🛗 🛏 WC P. ♨   Z u
M (dinner only and Sunday lunch) 2.00/3.00 s. 🍷 1.50 – **28 rm** ⛺ 7.25/16.50 – P 11.50.

🏨 **Chilworth Court**, 39-41 Earl's Av., CT20 2HB, ☎ 55673, 🚗 – TV 🛏 WC 🛏 WC P.   X e
🅰 AE ① VISA
M (buffet lunch) 4.50 st. 🍷 1.75 – **23 rm** ⛺ 13.00/22.00 st.

⋔ **Beaumont,** 5 Marine Ter., CT20 1PZ, ☎ 52740 – 🖭 AE ⓪ VISA   **Z e**
8 rm ☕ 6.00/11.00.

⋔ **Wearbay,** 25 Wear Bay Crescent, CT19 6AX, ☎ 52586, 🚗 – 🗢. 🖭   **Y a**
7 rm ☕ 6.95/13.40 **st.**

⋔ **Belmonte,** 30 Castle Hill Av., CT20 2RE, ☎ 54470 – 🖭 AE VISA   **Z i**
April-October – **14 rm** ☕ 5.95/11.90 **s.**

XX **Emilio's Portofino,** 124a Sandgate Rd, CT20 2BT, ☎ 55762, Italian rest. – 🖭 AE ⓪
VISA   **Z a**
closed Monday, Christmas Day and Bank Holidays – **M** a la carte 5.20/7.00 **t.** 🍷 1.70.

XX **La Tavernetta,** Leaside Court, Clifton Gdns, CT20 2EY, ☎ 54955, Italian rest. – 🖭 ⓪ VISA
closed Sunday and first 2 weeks February – **M** a la carte 5.50/8.20 **t.** 🍷 1.65.   **Z n**

XX **Nicola's l'Escargot,** 3 Trinity Crescent, CT20 2ES, ☎ 53864 – 🖭 AE ⓪ VISA   **X a**
closed Sunday – **M** a la carte 4.40/7.10 **t.** 🍷 1.75.

X **Paul's,** 3 West Terrace, CT20 1RR, ☎ 59697 – 🖭 ⓪   **Z v**
closed Sunday and Monday dinner – **M** a la carte 6.05/7.40 **st.** 🍷 1.85.

X New Delhi, 135 Sandgate Rd, CT20 2BL, ☎ 58884, Indian rest.   **Z o**

AUSTIN-MORRIS-MG-PRINCESS-ROVER-TRIUMPH
141/143 Sandgate Rd ☎ 55101
CITROEN, FIAT, ROLLS ROYCE, VAUXHALL Caesars
Way, Cheriton ☎ 76431
DAF, SKODA Hamstreet ☎ 2207

DATSUN Cheriton High St. ☎ 76995/75428
FORD 104 Ford Rd ☎ 41234
LANCIA Etchinghill ☎ 0303 (Lyminge) 862113
RENAULT 360 Cheriton Rd, Cheriton ☎ 75412
TALBOT 1/3 Park Rd ☎ 75114

FORDINGBRIDGE Hants. ⁴⁰³ ¹⁶⁴ O 31 – pop. 5,432 – ECD : Thursday – 🕿 0425.
See : St. Mary's Church* 13C. **Envir. :** Breamore House* (Elizabethan) *AC*, N : 2 m.
🛈 Avon Valley Travel Services, 52 High St. ☎ 54410.
London 101 – Bournemouth 17 – Salisbury 11 – Winchester 30.

XX **Shepherd's Spring,** Southampton Rd, SP6 2JP, E : ½ m. on B 3708 ☎ 52862 – 🅿.
🖭 VISA
closed Sunday dinner and Monday – **M** a la carte approx. 7.20 🍷 1.75.

X **Hour Glass,** Salisbury Rd, Burgate, SP6 1LX, N : 1 m. on A 338 ☎ 52348 – 🅿. 🖭 AE ⓪ VISA
*closed Sunday dinner, Monday, 25 and 26 December, 2 weeks September and 3 weeks
February* – **M** (dinner only and Sunday lunch) a la carte 6.15/9.75 **t.** 🍷 2.00.

FORDWICH Kent ⁴⁰⁴ X 30 – see Canterbury.

FOREST ROW East Sussex ⁴⁰⁴ U 30 – pop. 4,484 – ECD : Wednesday – 🕿 034 282.
🛈₁₈ ☎ 2018 – 🛈₁₈ Chapel Lane ☎ 2010 and 2751.
London 35 – Brighton 26 – Eastbourne 30 – Maidstone 32.

🏨 **Brambletye,** RH18 5EZ, ☎ 4144, Telex 95363, 🚗 – 📺 🛌wc 🕿 🅿. 🖭 AE ⓪ VISA
M 4.25/4.75 **t.** 🍷 1.80 – **13 rm** ☕ 16.50/23.50 **t.** – P 27.50/30.00 **t.**

at Wych Cross S : 2 ½ m. on A 22 – ✉ 🕿 034 282 Forest Row :

🏨 **Roebuck,** RH18 5JL, ☎ 3811, Telex 957088, 🚗 – 📺 🅿. 🏥. 🖭 AE ⓪ VISA
M 6.25/6.50 **st.** 🍷 2.10 – ☕ 3.00 – **33 rm** 19.50/30.00 **st.**

at Chelwood Gate S : 3 ½ m. on A 275 by A 22 – ✉ Hayward's Heath – 🕿 082 574
Chelwood Gate :

XX **Red Lion,** Lewes Rd, RH17 7DE, ☎ 265 – 🅿. 🖭 AE ⓪ VISA
closed Sunday in summer – **M** a la carte 6.15/9.25 **st.** 🍷 1.85.

CITROEN 92-93 Hartfield Rd ☎ 3055   LOTUS, MAZDA Wych Cross and Hartfield Rd ☎ 3864

FOSSEBRIDGE Glos. ⁴⁰³ ⁴⁰⁴ O 28 – ✉ Northleach – 🕿 028 572.
London 88 – Cirencester 7 – Gloucester 25 – Oxford 33.

🏠 **Fossebridge Inn,** GL54 3JS, ☎ 310, 🚗 – 🛌wc 🅿
closed 1 week at Christmas – **M** a la carte 2.70/4.60 **t.** 🍷 1.60 – **12 rm** ☕ 12.00/25.00 **t.**

FOWEY Cornwall ⁴⁰³ G 32 – pop. 2,369 – ECD : Wednesday – 🕿 072 683.
🛈 Toyne Carter, 1 Albert Quay ☎ 3320.
London 277 – Newquay 24 – Plymouth 34 – Truro 22.

🏨 **Fowey** ♨, The Esplanade, PL23 1HX, ☎ 2551, Telex 45640, ≼ Fowey estuary and Polruan,
🚗 – 🛗 📺 🛌wc 🗢wc 🕿 🅿. 🖭 AE ⓪ VISA
M 5.25/7.50 **t.** 🍷 1.75 – **35 rm** ☕ 16.00/32.00 **t.**

🏠 **Riverside,** 32 Passage St., PL23 1DF, ☎ 2275, ≼ – 🛌wc 🗢wc 🚙 🅿. 🖭 AE ⓪ VISA
Easter-October – **M** (bar lunch) approx. 6.00 – **13 rm** ☕ 8.00/18.00.

🏠 **Old Quay House,** 28 Fore St., PL23 1AQ, ☎ 3302 – 🛌wc 🗢wc
March-October – **M** (bar lunch) approx. 4.25 **st.** 🍷 1.25 – **14 rm** ☕ 8.00/19.00 **st.**

X **Cordon Bleu,** 3 Esplanade, PL23 1AY, ☎ 2359 – AE ⓪
closed Sunday and mid March-mid December – **M** (dinner only) a la carte 5.60/9.10 **t.**

at *Golant* N : 3 m. off B 3269 – ✉ ☎ 072 683 Fowey :

🏠 **Cormorant** ⌂, PL23 1LL, ☎ 3426, ≤ river Fowey, ☒, 🍴 – 🛏wc 🅿
M (buffet lunch) a la carte 4.05/6.05 ▯ 1.55 – **14 rm** ⊒ 11.00/22.00.

at *Bodinnick-by-Fowey* E : ¼ m. via car ferry – ✉ Fowey – ☎ 072 687 Polruan :

🏠 **Old Ferry Inn**, PL23 1LX, ☎ 237, ≤ Fowey Estuary and town, « Part 16C inn » – 🛏wc
🚗 🅿
April–October – M (bar lunch) approx. 5.60 ▯ 2.00 – **12 rm** ⊒ 9.00/20.00.

ALFA-ROMEO Polvillion Rd ☎ 3393

FOWLMERE Cambs. 404 U 27 – see Cambridge.

FRAMFIELD East Sussex 404 U 31 – see Uckfield.

FRAMLINGHAM Suffolk 404 Y 27 – pop. 2,258 – ECD : Wednesday – ✉ Woodbridge –
☎ 0728.
See : Castle ramparts* (Norman ruins) *AC*.
London 92 – Ipswich 19 – Norwich 42.

🏠 **Crown** (T.H.F.), Market Hill, IP13 9HN, ☎ 723521, « 16C inn » – 📺 🛏wc ☎ 🅿. ☒ AE
① VISA
M 4.25/8.50 st. ▯ 1.65 – **14 rm** ⊒ 13.50/22.00 st.

FORD Market Hill ☎ 723215

FRAMPTON ON SEVERN Glos. 403 404 M 28 – pop. 1,231 – ☎ 0452 Saul.
London 121 – Bristol 29 – Gloucester 11.

⌂ **Old Vicarage** ⌂, GL2 7EQ, ☎ 740562, 🍴 – 🛏wc 🛁wc 🅿
15 rm ⊒ 7.50/17.00 s.

FRESHWATER BAY I.O.W. – 403 404 P 32 – see Wight (Isle of).

FRESSINGFIELD Suffolk 404 X 26 – pop. 730 – ✉ Diss – ☎ 037 986.
London 103 – Ipswich 30 – Norwich 23.

🍴 **Fox and Goose**, IP21 5PB, ☎ 247 – 🅿
closed Tuesday and 21 to 28 December – M (booking essential) a la carte 7.45/11.50 t.
▯ 2.10.

FRILFORD Oxon. 403 404 P 28 – see Abingdon.

FRIMLEY BRIDGES Surrey 404 N 30 – see Farnborough.

FRINTON-ON-SEA Essex 404 X 28 – pop. 12,475 (inc. Walton) – ECD : Wednesday –
☎ 025 56.
London 72 – Chelmsford 39 – Colchester 17.

🏨 **Frinton Lodge**, Esplanade, CO13 9HL, ☎ 4391, ≤ – 🛊 📺 🛏wc ☎ 🅿. ☒ AE ① VISA
M 4.50/5.75 st. – **26 rm** ⊒ 16.00/29.00 st. – P 26.25/35.00 st.

🏨 Grand Esplanade, CO13 9DS, ☎ 4321, ≤ – 🛊 🛏wc ☎ 🅿 – **38 rm.**

🏠 **Maplin**, Esplanade, CO13 9EL, ☎ 3832, ≤, ⌓ heated – 📺 🛏wc ☎ 🅿. AE ①
closed January – M 4.75/6.25 st. ▯ 2.15 – **12 rm** ⊒ 11.00/26.00 st.

at *Kirby Cross* W : 1 ½ m. on B 1033 – ✉ ☎ 025 56 Frinton-on-Sea :

🏠 **Linnets**, 2 Thorpe Rd, CO13 0LD, ☎ 4910, 🍴 – 🛏wc 🛁 🅿
M (buffet lunch) approx. 6.00 st. ▯ 2.00 – **15 rm** ⊒ 8.00/17.50 s. – P 13.00/14.00 s.

AUSTIN-MORRIS-MG-WOLSELEY Connaught Av. ☎   TALBOT ☎ 4383
4311   TOYOTA Frinton Rd, Kirby Cross ☎ 4141
FIAT, VOLVO 132 Connaught Av. ☎ 4341

FROME Somerset 403 404 N 30 – pop. 12,310 – ECD : Thursday – ☎ 0373.
Envir. : Longleat House** (Elizabethan) *AC* and Lion Reserve** *AC*, SE : 7 m. – Nunney
Castle* (ruins 14C) SW : 3 ½ m. – Westbury Hill (White Horse*, ≤*) NE : 8 m.
London 115 – Bristol 28 – Southampton 51 – Taunton 43.

🏨 **Mendip Lodge**, Bath Rd, BA11 2HP, ☎ 3223, ≤, 🍴 – 📺 🛏wc ☎ 🅿. 🛁. ☒ AE ① VISA
M (buffet lunch) 3.75/6.45 st. – ⊒ 1.80 – **40 rm** 21.00/27.50 st.

🏠 **Portway**, Portway, Christchurch St. East, BA11 1QP, ☎ 3508, 🍴 – 🛏wc 🛁 ☎ 🅿. 🛁.
AE ① VISA
M 3.75/4.75 ▯ 1.75 – **22 rm** ⊒ 12.50/18.00.

🍴🍴 La Cambusa, 8 The Bridge, BA11 1AR, ☎ 3567, Italian rest.

RENAULT Manor Rd ☎ 5881   VAUXHALL Rodden Rd ☎ 3489
ROVER-TRIUMPH 33 Christchurch St. ☎ 2685

FUNTINGTON West Sussex **404** R 31 – see Chichester.

GAINSBOROUGH Lincs. **404** R 23 – pop. 18,110 – ☎ 0427.
See : Old Hall★★ (15C) *AC*.
London 150 – Lincoln 19 – Nottingham 42 – Sheffield 34.

Hotels and restaurants see : Bawtry NW : 12 m.
Scunthorpe NE : 17 m.

AUSTIN-MORRIS-ROVER-TRIUMPH North St. ☏ 3303
AUSTIN-MORRIS-MG North St. ☏ 4064

FORD Trinity St. ☏ 3146
TALBOT North St. ☏ 2505

GANLLWYD Gwynedd **403** I 25 – see Dolgellau.

GARFORTH West Yorks. – see Leeds.

GARGRAVE North Yorks. – pop. 1,426 – ⊠ Skipton – ☎ 075 678.
London 222 – Leeds 30 – Preston 37.

⌂ Anchor Inn, BD23 3NA, ☏ 666, 🛋 – 📺 🛏wc ℗
17 rm.

GATESHEAD Tyne and Wear **986** ⑲ – pop. 94,469 – ECD : Wednesday – ☎ 0632.
🏌 Mossheaps ☏ 876014 – 🏌 Hollinside Park, Wickam ☏ 7309, SW : 5 m.
🛈 Central Library, Prince Consort Rd ☏ 773478.
London 282 – Durham 16 – Middlesbrough 38 – Newcastle-upon-Tyne 1 – Sunderland 11.

Plan : see Newcastle-upon-Tyne

🏨 Five Bridges (Swallow), High West St., NE8 1PE, ☏ 771105, Telex 53534 – 🛗 📺 ℗. 🏋
106 rm. CZ r

🏨 Springfield (Embassy), Durham Rd, NE9 5BT, ☏ 774121 – 📺 🛏wc 📞 ℗. 🏋. 🔟 🆎
BX s
⓪ VISA
M 4.40/5.10 st. – 32 rm ⇋ 16.50/20.00 st.

✕ Italia, 580a Durham Rd, NE9 6HX, ☏ 879362, Italian rest. by A 6127 BX

AUDI, NSU, VN Bensham Rd ☏ 771291
BRITISH LEYLAND Durham Rd ☏ 870911
TOYOTA St. James Sq. ☏ 771135

VAUXHALL 106/108 Lobley Hill Rd ☏ 0632 (Dunston) 604691

GATWICK AIRPORT West Sussex **404** T 30 – see hotels at Crawley and Horley.

GERRARDS CROSS Bucks. **404** S 29 – pop. 6,524 – ECD : Wednesday – ☎ 028 13.
London 22 – Aylesbury 22 – Oxford 36.

🏨 Bull (De Vere) Oxford Rd, SL9 7PA, on A 40 ☏ 85995, Telex 22121, 🛋 – 📺 ℗. 🏋. 🔟
🆎 ⓪ VISA
M a la carte 5.00/10.00 st. 🍷 1.75 – 38 rm ⇋ 24.00/32.00 st.

BMW 44 Oak End Way ☏ 88321
MORRIS-MG-WOLSELEY, VOLVO Packhorse Rd ☏ 85555

PEUGEOT Market Pl. ☏ 86635
TALBOT Oxford Rd ☏ 82545

GISBURN Lancs. **986** ㉓ – pop. 433 – ECD : Wednesday – ⊠ Clitheroe – ☎ 020 05.
London 243 – Manchester 37 – Preston 25.

🏨 Stirk House, BB7 4LJ, SW : 1 m. on A 59 ☏ 581, 🔲, 🛋 – 📺 🛏wc 📞 ℗. 🏋. 🔟 🆎 ⓪
VISA
M 3.60/5.10 – 46 rm ⇋ 12.50/19.50.

GITTISHAM Devon **403** K 31 – pop. 220 – ECD : Thursday – ⊠ ☎ 0404 Honiton.
London 164 – Exeter 14 – Sidmouth 9 – Taunton 21.

✕✕✕ Combe House 🦢 with rm, EX14 0AD, ☏ 2756, ≤, « Country house atmosphere », 🛋,
park – 🛏wc 🚗 ℗. 🔟 🆎 ⓪ VISA
closed January and February – M (bar lunch Monday to Saturday) a la carte 6.55/11.55
🍷 2.00 – 13 rm ⇋ 13.00/30.00.

GLASTONBURY Somerset 403 404 L 30 – pop. 6,558 – ECD : Wednesday – ☎ 0458.

See : Abbey★ (ruins 12C) – Tribunal★ 15C.

🛈 7 Northload St. ☏ 32954 (summer only).

London 136 – Bristol 26 – Taunton 22.

   🏛 **George and Pilgrims,** 1 High St., BA6 9DP, ☏ 31146, « Part 15C inn » – ⌖wc. 🅝 🆎 ⓸ 𝗩𝗜𝗦𝗔
     M (Sunday dinner buffet only) 4.25/6.70 **t.** ⌕ 1.95 – **15 rm** ⊆ 13.00/25.00 **t.**

   XXX **N° 3,** 3 Magdalene St., BA6 9EW, ☏ 32129, 🜗 – 🅟
     closed Sunday dinner, Monday, May and November – **M** (dinner only and Sunday lunch)
     (booking essential) a la carte 8.50/12.50 ⌕ 1.85.

AUSTIN-MG-WOLSELEY Street Rd ☏ 32137   RENAULT Mill Lane ☏ 32741
FORD Magdalene St. ☏ 31622

GLEN PARVA Leics. 403 404 Q 26 – see Leicester.

GLENRIDDING Cumbria – see Ullswater.

*Questi prezzi, fissati alla fine dell'anno 1979,
possono venire modificati qualora il costo della vita
subisca notevoli variazoni.
Essi debbono comunque essere considerati come prezzi base.*

GLOUCESTER Glos. 403 404 N 28 – pop. 90,232 – ECD : Thursday – ☎ 0452.

See : Cathedral★★ 12C-14C (Great Cloister★★★ 14C) Y **A** – Bishop Hooper's Lodging (Folk Museum)★ 15C Y **M**.

🛈₈, 🛈₉ Matson Lane, S: 2 m. Z.

✈ Staverton Airport : ☏ 713351, NE : 5 m. by A 40 Z and near M 5 Motorway, intersection N° 11 – **Terminal :** Market Parade.

🛈 6 College St. ☏ 421188.

London 103 – Birmingham 51 – Bristol 33 – Cardiff 60 – Coventry 57 – Northampton 87 – Oxford 48 – Southampton 101 – Swansea 87 – Swindon 34.

Plan opposite

   🏨 **Tara,** Upton Hill, GL4 8DE, by Upton-St. Leonards S: 3 m. on B 4073 ☏ 67412, ⪡ Severn Valley, ⌇ heated, 🜗 – 📺 ⌖wc 🗍wc ☞ 🅟. 🜲. 🅝 🆎 ⓸ 𝗩𝗜𝗦𝗔 by B 4073 Z
     M *(closed Saturday lunch)* (bar lunch) a la carte 4.90/8.65 ⌕ 2.75 – **22 rm** ⊆ 15.00/29.00 **s.**

   🏛 **New County** (Norfolk Cap.), Southgate St., GL1 2DU, ☏ 24977, Group Telex 23241 – ⌖wc ☞. 🅝 🆎 ⓸ 𝗩𝗜𝗦𝗔   Y **c**
     M 3.75/4.50 **st.** ⌕ 1.75 – **36 rm** ⊆ 10.65/21.65 **st.**

   🏛 **New Wellington** (Embassy), Bruton Way, GL1 1DG, ☏ 20022 – 📺 ⌖wc – **23 rm.** Y **n**

   ⌂ **Stanley House,** 87 London Rd, GL1 3HH, ☏ 20140 – 🅟. 🅝 𝗩𝗜𝗦𝗔   Y **r**
     14 rm ⊆ 6.50/14.50 **st.**

   XX **Don Pasquale,** 19 Worcester St., GL1 3AJ, ☏ 25636, Italian rest. – 🅝 🆎 ⓸ 𝗩𝗜𝗦𝗔   Y **a**
     closed Sunday, Monday and first 3 weeks July – **M** a la carte 5.60/7.60 **s.** ⌕ 1.90.

   at Corse Lawn N : 11 m. on B 4211 by A 417 – Z – ✉ Gloucester – ☎ 045 278 Tirley :

   XXX **Corse Lawn House,** GL19 4LZ, ☏ 479 – 🅟. 🅝 🆎 ⓸ 𝗩𝗜𝗦𝗔
     closed Sunday dinner and Monday – **M** a la carte 4.60/7.40 **s.** ⌕ 2.00.

AUSTIN-DAIMLER-JAGUAR-LAND ROVER-MORRIS-   FORD Eastern Av. ☏ 21731
ROVER-TRIUMPH 207/211 Westgate St. ☏ 34581   PEUGEOT 72/76 Barton St. ☏ 32731
AUSTIN-MORRIS-MG Mercia Rd ☏ 29531   RENAULT St. Oswalds Rd ☏ 35051
BEDFORD, PANTHER LIMA, VAUXHALL Shepherd   TALBOT London Rd ☏ 24081
Rd, Cole Av. ☏ 26711   TOYOTA Southgate St. ☏ 26741
BMW London Rd ☏ 23456   VAUXHALL Barnwood ☏ 66621
CITROEN, FIAT 143 Westgate St. ☏ 23252   VAUXHALL Shepherd Rd, Cole Av. ☏ 26711
COLT 176 Barton St. ☏ 22922   VW, AUDI 98/106 Barton St. ☏ 25251
DAF-POLSKI South Gate St. ☏ 22353

GLYNGARTH Gwynedd 403 H 24 – see Menai Bridge.

GOATHLAND North Yorks. – pop. 458 – ECD : Wednesday and Saturday – ✉ Whitby – ☎ 094 786.

London 248 – Middlesbrough 36 – York 38.

   🏛 **Mallyan Spout** ⌖, YO22 5AN, ☏ 206, 🝨, 🜗 – 📺 ⌖wc 🗍wc 🅟. 🆎
     M (bar lunch) 3.75/6.00 **t.** ⌕ 2.00 – **23 rm** ⊆ 10.00/20.00 **t.**

   🏛 **Goathland Hydro** ⌖, YO22 5LZ, ☏ 296, 🜗 – ⌖wc 🅟
     Easter-mid October – **M** 2.95/3.70 **st.** ⌕ 2.10 – **32 rm** ⊆ 10.00/22.60 **st.**

   X **Goathland** with rm, YO22 5LY, ☏ 203 – 🗍wc 🅟
     M 3.25/6.00 **st.** ⌕ 1.75 – **9 rm** ⊆ 10.00/11.00 **st.** – P 15.50 **st.**

GLOUCESTER

Eastgate Shopping Centre	Y	
Eastgate Street	Y	10
Northgate Street	Y	16
Southgate Street	Y	
Barnwood By-Pass	Z	3
Bruton Way	Y	5
Commercial Road	Y	6
Cotteswold Road	Z	8
Derby Road	Z	9
Great Western Road	Y	12
Heathville Road	Y	13
King Edward's Avenue	Z	14
Lower Westgate Street	Y	15
Parkend Road	Z	17
Parliament Street	Y	18
Pitt Street	Y	19
Quay Street	Y	20
Royal Oak Road	Y	21
St. Aldate Street	Y	22
St. Johns Lane	Y	23
Southern Avenue	Z	24
Spa Road	Y	26
Stroud Road	Z	28
Tredworth Road	Z	30
Worcester Street	Y	31

Benutzen Sie auf Ihren Reisen in Europa die Michelin-Länderkarten 1 : 1 000 000.

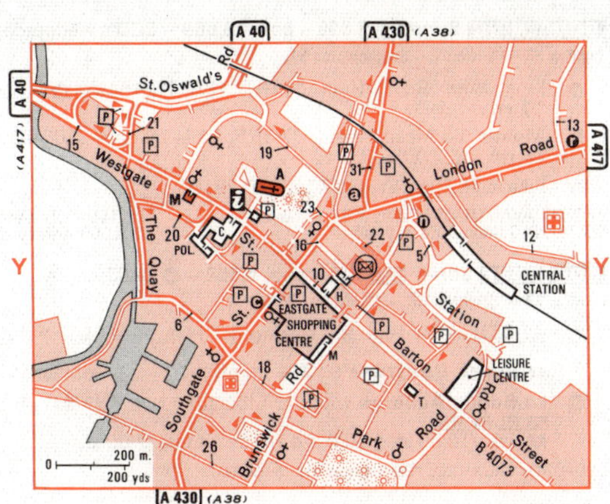

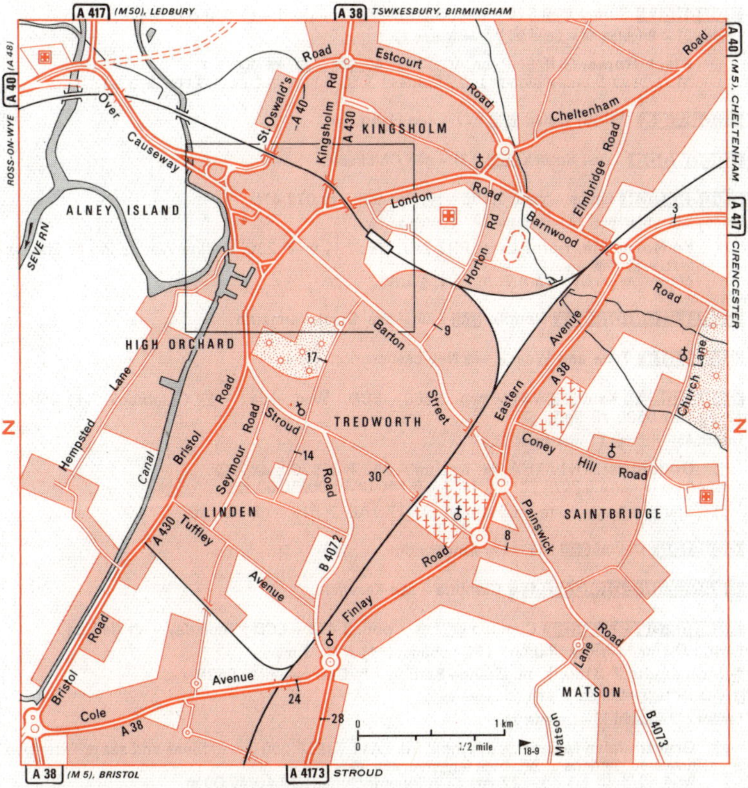

GODALMING Surrey 404 S 30 – pop. 18,669 – ECD : Wednesday – ☎ 048 68.
London 38 – Guildford 5 – Southampton 51.

- 🏨 King's Arms Royal, High St., GU7 1EB, ☏ 21545 – Ⓟ
  17 rm.
- 🏠 **Meads,** 65 Mead Row, GU7 3HS, N : ½ m. on A 3100 ☏ 21800 – 🚿wc 🛁wc Ⓟ
  15 rm 🍽 7.00/14.50 **s.**
- ✗✗ Pike's, 78 High St., GU7 1DU, ☏ 29191.

BEDFORD-VAUXHALL Ockford Rd ☏ 5666   DATSUN The Wharf ☏ 5201
CITROEN Guildford Rd ☏ 23555   TALBOT Farncombe ☏ 7743

GODSTONE Surrey 404 T 30 – pop. 5,568 – ☎ 0883.
London 22 – Brighton 36 – Maidstone 28.

- ✗✗ White Hart, 71 High St., Godstone Green, RH9 8DT, ☏ 842521 – Ⓟ.

  at South Godstone S : 2 ¼ m. off A 22 – ✉ Godstone – ☎ 034 285 South Godstone :
- ✗✗ **La Bonne Auberge** with rm, Tilburstow Hill, RH9 8JY, ☏ 3184, 🌳, 🌻, park – 🚿wc Ⓟ.
  ⬛ AE ⑩ VISA
  M 6.00/12.00 **st.** 🍷 2.60 – **4 rm** 🍽 14.00/22.00 **st.**

BEDFORD, VAUXHALL Eastbourne Rd ☏ 842000

GOLANT Cornwall 403 G 32 – see Fowey.

GOMSHALL Surrey 404 S 30 – pop. 3,705 – ✉ Guildford – ☎ 048 641 Shere.
London 31 – Brighton 44 – Guildford 7 – Maidstone 47.

- 🏯 **Black Horse,** GU5 9NP, on A 25 ☏ 2242, 🌻 – Ⓟ. ⑩ VISA
  M *(closed Sunday dinner and Monday)* 3.50/6.50 **t.** 🍷 1.85 – **6 rm** 🍽 8.50/17.00.

GOODWICK (WDIG) Dyfed 403 E 27 – see Fishguard.

GOODWOOD West Sussex 404 R 31 – see Chichester.

GOOSNARGH Lancs. – pop. 1,105 – ✉ Preston – ☎ 077 476.
London 228 – Blackpool 18 – Lancaster 20 – Preston 5.

- ✗ **Ye Horns Inn,** Horns Lane, PR3 2FJ, NE : 2 ½ m. ☏ 230, « Olde Worlde inn », English
  rest. – Ⓟ. ⑩
  closed Monday – **M** 4.75/6.75 **t.** 🍷 1.80.

GORLESTON-ON-SEA Norfolk 404 Z 26 – see Great Yarmouth.

GOSFORTH Tyne and Wear – see Newcastle-upon-Tyne.

GOUDHURST Kent 404 V 30 – pop. 2,950 – ECD : Wednesday – ✉ Cranbrook – ☎ 058 03
(3 fig.) or 0580 (6 fig.).
London 45 – Hastings 22 – Maidstone 13.

- 🏯 **Goudhurst,** TN17 1HA, W : 1 m. on A 262 ☏ 211200, 🌻 – Ⓟ
  M a la carte 5.30/6.65 **t.** 🍷 1.70 – **6 rm** 🍽 10.00/20.00 **t.**
- ✗✗ Star and Eagle, with rm, High St., TN17 1AL, ☏ 512 – Ⓟ – **6 rm.**

GOVETON Devon 403 I 33 – see Kingsbridge.

GRANGE-IN-BORROWDALE Cumbria – see Keswick.

GRANGE-OVER-SANDS Cumbria 986 ㉓ – pop. 3,474 – ECD : Thursday – ☎ 044 84.
Envir. : Cartmel (Priory Church* 12C : chancel**) NW : 3 m.
⛳ Meathop Rd ☏ 3180, ½ m. Grange Station – ⛳ Grange Fell ☏ 2536.
🅘 Victoria Hall, Main St. ☏ 4331 (summer only).
London 268 – Kendal 13 – Lancaster 24.

- 🏨🏨 **Graythwaite Manor** 🐾, Fernhill Rd, LA11 7JE, ☏ 2001, ≼ gardens and sea, « Extensive
  flowered gardens », 🎾, park – 🚿wc 🚗 Ⓟ
  M 4.50/6.25 🍷 1.85 – **27 rm** 🍽 (dinner included) 19.40/42.00 **st.**
- 🏨 **Netherwood** 🐾, Lindale Rd, LA11 6ET, ☏ 2552, ≼, 🌻 – 🚿wc 🛁wc 🚗 Ⓟ
  M 3.00/4.75 **st.** 🍷 1.55 – **23 rm** 🍽 8.50/22.40 **st.** – P 15.20/17.60 **st.**
- 🏨 **Grange** (Best Western) 🐾, Lindale Rd, LA11 6EJ, ☏ 3666, Telex 65294, ≼ – 🚿wc Ⓟ.
  ⬛ AE ⑩ VISA
  March-October and Christmas week – **M** a la carte 2.85/11.00 **st.** – **32 rm** 🍽 11.35/
  19.50 **st.**

⌂ **Somerset House,** Kents Bank Rd, LA11 7EY, ☏ 2631
8 rm.

⌂ **Elton,** Windermere Rd, LA11 6EQ, ☏ 2838 – 𝘝𝘐𝘚𝘈
closed October and Christmas – **9 rm** ⌑ 6.50/13.00 **t.**

XX **Hardcragg Hall** with rm, Grange Fell Rd, LA11 6BJ, ☏ 3353, « Renovated 16C manor », 🐎 – 🅿
M *(closed Sunday and Monday to non-residents)* (bar lunch) 5.00/8.50 – **7 rm** ⌑ 9.00/19.00.

at Kents Bank SW : 1 ¾ m. off B 5277 – ✉ ☎ 044 84 Grange-over-Sands :

⌂ **Kents Bank,** Kentsford Rd, LA11 7BB, ☏ 2054, ≼ – 🅿
10 rm ⌑ 7.00/14.00 **s.**

at Cartmel NW : 3 m. – ✉ Grange-over-Sands – ☎ 044 854 Cartmel :

🏨 **Aynsome Manor** ⤸, LA11 6HH, ☏ 276, « Country house atmosphere », 🐎 – ⊟wc
🏛wc 🅿. ◪
M *(closed Sunday dinner to non-residents)* (bar lunch for residents only except Sunday)
5.50/8.00 **t.** 🍷 2.50 – **16 rm** ⌑ (dinner included) 15.50/33.50 **t.**

AUSTIN-MORRIS-MG Station Sq. ☏ 2612	TALBOT, FORD Lindale Corner ☏ 2282
BMW Lindale Corner ☏ 2284	VW, AUDI Lindale ☏ 4242

If you write to a hotel abroad,
enclose an International Reply Coupon.
(available from Post Offices).

GRANTHAM Lincs. 404 S 25 – pop. 27,943 – ECD : Wednesday – ☎ 0476.
See : St. Wulfram's Church* 13C. **Envir. :** Belton House* (Renaissance) *AC*, NE : 2 m. – Belvoir Castle 19C (interior*) W : 8 m.

🏌 Belton Lane, Londonthorpe Rd ☏ 3355, N : 2 m. – 🏌 Great North Rd ☏ 045 683 (Great Ponton) 275, S : 6 m. on A 1.

🛈 Guildhall ☏ 5591.

London 113 – Leicester 31 – Lincoln 29 – Nottingham 24.

🏨 **Angel and Royal** (T.H.F.), 4 High St., NG31 6PN, ☏ 5816, « 13C stone walled restaurant and bar » – 📺 ⊟wc ☎ 🅿. ⛷. ◪ 𝖠𝖤 ⓞ 𝘝𝘐𝘚𝘈
M a la carte 3.75/4.50 **st.** 🍷 1.95 – **32 rm** ⌑ 13.50/21.00 **st.**

🏨 **George,** High St., NG31 6NN, ☏ 3286 – 📺 ⊟wc ☎ 🅿. ⛷. ◪ 𝖠𝖤 ⓞ 𝘝𝘐𝘚𝘈
closed Christmas Day – **M** 5.00/6.00 **st.** – **37 rm** ⌑ 17.00/21.50 **st.** – P 22.00/29.00 **st.**

🏨 **King's,** North Par., NG31 8AU, ☏ 5881 – 📺 ⊟wc 🏛wc ☎ 🚗 🅿. ◪ 𝖠𝖤 𝘝𝘐𝘚𝘈
M 2.95/3.60 **t.** 🍷 1.55 – **19 rm** ⌑ 9.55/18.10 **st.** – P approx. 16.05 **st.**

X **Hop Sing,** Tudor House, 21 Westgate, NG31 6LU, ☏ 2302, Chinese rest. – ◪ 𝖠𝖤 ⓞ 𝘝𝘐𝘚𝘈
M approx. 5.00 **s.** 🍷 2.00.

AUSTIN-MG-WOLSELEY 12 North St. ☏ 61066	RENAULT London Rd ☏ 61338
CITROEN Swinegate ☏ 3393	ROVER-TRIUMPH 50/58 London Rd ☏ 2651
DATSUN Barrowby High Rd ☏ 4443	TALBOT 66 London Rd ☏ 2595
FORD 30/40 London Rd ☏ 5195	VAUXHALL Watergate ☏ 3267
PEUGEOT Swinegate ☏ 68729	VOLVO Barrowby Rd ☏ 4114

GRAPPENHALL Cheshire 403 404 M 23 – see Warrington.

GRASMERE Cumbria 986 ⑲ – pop. 990 – ECD : Thursday – ☎ 096 65.
Envir. : W : Langdale Valley** by B 5343 **AY.**

🛈 Broadgate Newsagency ☏ 245.

London 282 – Carlisle 43 – Kendal 18.

Plan : see Ambleside

🏨 **Gold Rill** ⤸, Langdale Rd, LA22 9PU, ☏ 486, ≼, ▨ heated, 🐎 – ⊟wc ☎ 🅿   **BZ c**
March-November – **M** 4.95/7.95 **st.** – **23 rm** ⌑ (dinner included) 20.00/50.00 **st.**

🏨 **Grasmere Red Lion,** Red Lion Sq., LA22 9SS, ☏ 456, 🐎 – ▯ ⊟wc ☎ 🅿. ◪ 𝖠𝖤 ⓞ
𝘝𝘐𝘚𝘈   **BZ a**
season – **38 rm.**

🏨 **Michael's Nook** ⤸, LA22 9RP, ☏ 496, ≼ mountains and countryside, « Tastefully
furnished, fine gardens » – 📺 ⊟wc 🏛wc ☎ 🅿   **AY n**
M 7.25/11.25 **s.** – **10 rm** ⌑ (dinner included) 24.00/38.00 **s.**

🏨 **Swan** (T.H.F.), LA22 9RF, ☏ 551, ≼, 🐎 – ⊟wc ☎ 🅿. ◪ 𝖠𝖤 ⓞ 𝘝𝘐𝘚𝘈   **AY r**
M 4.50/6.00 **st.** 🍷 1.65 – **31 rm** ⌑ 15.00/25.50 **st.**

🏨 **Oak Bank,** Broadgate, LA22 9TA, ☏ 217, 🐎 – ⊟wc 🏛wc 🅿. ◪ 𝖠𝖤 ⓞ 𝘝𝘐𝘚𝘈   **BZ e**
Easter-October – **M** (bar lunch) 3.00/5.50 **st.** 🍷 2.00 – **13 rm** ⌑ 8.50/12.00 **st.**

P.T.O. →

GRASMERE

- 🕮 Rothay Bank, Broadgate, LA22 9RH, ℡ 334, ⇱ – 🛏wc 🅟   AY e
  15 rm.
- 🕮 **Moss Grove,** LA22 9SW, ℡ 251 – 🅟   BZ i
  March–October – **M** (dinner only) 5.50 **st.** 🍷 1.60 – **16 rm** � 9.25/21.50 **st.**
- 🏠 **Meadow Brow** 🦢, LA22 9RR, ℡ 275, ≼ mountains and valley, ✗, ⇱ – 🅟
  April–October – **5 rm** ⊏ 9.50 **t.**   by A 591 AY
- 🏠 **Bridge House** 🦢, Stock Lane, LA22 9SN, ℡ 425, ⇱ – 🚿wc 🅟   BZ n
  April–October – **12 rm** ⊏ 14.50/32.00 **t.**
- 🏠 **Ben Place** 🦢, LA22 9RL, ℡ 372, ⇱ – 🅟   AY s
  March–October – **13 rm** ⊏ (dinner included) 12.00/24.00 **t.**
- 🏠 **Rothay Lodge** 🦢, White Bridge, LA22 9RH, ℡ 341, ⇱ – 🅟   AY o
  closed 19 to 31 December – **7 rm** ⊏ (dinner included) 9.30/18.60 **t.**

GRAVESEND Kent 🆘 V 29 – pop. 54,106 – ECD : Wednesday – ☎ 0474.
London 25 – Dover 54 – Maidstone 16 – Margate 53.

- 🏨 **Europa Lodge Tollgate** (County), Watling St., DA13 9RA, S : 2 m. at junction A 2 and
  A 227 ℡ 52768, Telex 25971 – 📺 🚿wc ⅏ 🅟. 🔁 AE ⓪ VISA
  M a la carte 4.20/7.90 **st.** 🍷 1.55 – **114 rm** ⊏ 13.00/21.00 **s.**

AUSTIN-MG-MORRIS St. James St. ℡ 22111   RELIANT Rochester Rd ℡ 65211
CITROEN Rochester Rd ℡ 64155   RENAULT West St. ℡ 67801
DATSUN 50 Singlewell Rd ℡ 66148   TOYOTA 10/12 High St. ℡ 4550
FORD 1/3 Pelham Rd ℡ 64411   VAUXHALL Overcliffe ℡ 63566
MORRIS-MG-ROVER-TRIUMPH The Grove ℡ 22111   VW-AUDI Old West Rd ℡ 57926

GRAVETYE East Sussex 🆘 T 30 – see East Grinstead.

GREASBY Merseyside 🆘 K 23 – pop. 6,860 – ☎ 051 Liverpool.
London 223 – Chester 19 – Liverpool 7.

- ✗✗✗ Manor Farm, 91 Greasby Rd, Wirral, L49 3NF, ℡ 677 7034 – 🅟.

GREAT BARDFIELD Essex 🆘 V 28 – pop. 944 – ✉ Braintree – ☎ 0371 Great Dunmow.
London 49 – Cambridge 30 – Chelmsford 20 – Colchester 26.

- ✗ **Corn Dolly,** High St., CM7 4SP, ℡ 810554, English rest.
  closed Sunday, Monday, Tuesday and first 2 weeks January – **M** 5.00/9.00 **t.** 🍷 2.00.

GREAT BARR West Midlands 🆘 🆘 O 26 – see Birmingham.

GREAT BROUGHTON Cleveland – pop. 1,000 – ✉ Middlesbrough – ☎ 064 97 Wainstones.
London 250 – Middlesbrough 11 – Northallerton 17 – York 46.

- ✗ **Wainstones** with rm, Helmsley Rd, TS9 7EH, ℡ 268 – 🅟. 🔁 VISA
  M a la carte 5.50/8.90 🍷 1.90 – **8 rm** ⊏ 8.00/15.00 **t.**

GREAT CORNARD Suffolk 🆘 W 27 – see Sudbury.

GREAT DUNMOW Essex 🆘 V 28 – pop. 3,827 – ☎ 0371.
London 42 – Cambridge 27 – Chelmsford 13 – Colchester 24.

- 🏨 **Saracen's Head** (T.H.F.), High St., CM6 1AG, ℡ 3901 – 📺 🚿wc 🐾 🅟. 🖼. 🔁 AE ⓪
  VISA
  M 4.00/5.00 **st.** 🍷 1.65 – **14 rm** ⊏ 13.50/21.00 **st.**

BMW The Downs ℡ 2884

GREAT WALTHAM Essex 🆘 V 28 – see Chelmsford.

GREAT WITLEY Heref. and Worc. 🆘 🆘 M 27 – pop. 460 – ✉ Worcester – ☎ 029 921.
See : Witley Court (ruins) and the Parish Church of St. Michael and All Saints (Baroque
interior★★).

London 136 – Birmingham 26 – Worcester 12.

- ✗✗ Hundred House, WR6 6HS, on A 443 ℡ 215 – 🅟. 🔁 AE VISA
  closed Sunday and Monday dinner – **M** (buffet lunch) a la carte 7.25/9.65 **t.**

VW. AUDI, SAAB Worcester Rd ℡ 202

GREAT YARMOUTH Norfolk **404** Z 26 – pop. 50,236 – ECD : Thursday – **☎** 0493.
🏌 Warren Rd, Gorleston ☏ 61082.
🚢 Shipping connections with the Continent: to Scheveningen (Norfolk Line).
🛈 Town Hall, 14 Regent St. ☏ 4313/4 – Marine Parade ☏ 2195 (summer only).
London 126 – Cambridge 81 – Ipswich 53 – Norwich 20.

  🏨 **Carlton**, Kimberley Ter., Marine Par., NR30 3JE, ☏ 55234, Telex 97249 – ▮ 📺 ⇔ **P**.
  ⚱. ☒ AE ⓪ VISA
  M a la carte 6.70/9.30 t. ⓥ 2.15 – **94 rm** ⚏ 19.00/29.00 t.

  🏨 **Star** (County), Hall Quay, NR30 1HG, ☏ 2294, Telex 25971 – ▮ 📺 ⇔wc ⇔ **P**. ⚱.
  ☒ AE ⓪ VISA
  M 3.50/4.00 st. ⓥ 1.55 – **42 rm** ⚏ 12.50/21.00 s.

     at Gorleston-on-sea S : 3 m. on A 12 – ⊠ **☎** 0493 Great Yarmouth :

  🏛 **Cliff**, Cliff Hill, NR31 6DH, ☏ 62179 – ⇔wc **P**. ☒ AE VISA
  M 3.45/4.35 t. ⓥ 1.50 – **31 rm** ⚏ 11.50/22.00 s. – P 17.00/33.00.

     at Belton SW : 4½ m. off A 143 – ⊠ **☎** 0493 Great Yarmouth :

  ✗ **Norfolk Barn**, New Rd, NR31 9JL, ☏ 780750, « Converted 18C barn » – **P**. ☒ AE ⓪ VISA
  closed Sunday, Monday lunch and last 2 weeks September – **M** a la carte 5.15/7.65 **t.**
  ⓥ 1.25.

AUSTIN-MORRIS-ROVER-TRIUMPH Lowestoft Rd, Gorleston-on-sea ☏ 65316
AUSTIN-MORRIS-MG-ROVER-TRIUMPH 55 St. Nicholas Rd ☏ 55431
CITROEN Repps ☏ 069 27 (Potter Heigham) 271
DATSUN 81 Southtown Rd ☏ 56836

FORD South Gates Rd ☏ 4922
RENAULT, VOLVO Suffolk Rd ☏ 55142
TALBOT Drudge Rd ☏ 64158
TALBOT North Quay ☏ 4266
VAUXHALL Station Rd ☏ 3677
VW, AUDI-NSU South Denes Rd ☏ 57711

GREAT YELDHAM Essex **404** V 27 – pop. 1,290 – ⊠ Halstead – **☎** 0787.
Envir. : Hedingham Castle (Norman keep★) *AC*, SE: 2 ½ m.
London 56 – Cambridge 27 – Chelmsford 23 – Colchester 21.

  ✗✗ **White Hart**, Poole St., CO9 4HJ, ☏ 237250, « 15C timbered inn », 🚗 – ☒ AE ⓪ VISA
  M a la carte 5.65/9.25 ⓥ 1.60.

TALBOT ☏ 218

This Guide is not a comprehensive list of all hotels and restaurants,
nor even of all good hotels and restaurants in Great Britain and Ireland.

Since our aim is to be of service to all motorists,
we must show establishments in all categories and so we have made a
selection of some in each.

GRETA BRIDGE Durham – pop. 85 – ⊠ Barnard Castle – **☎** 0833 Teesdale.
London 253 – Carlisle 63 – Leeds 63 – Middlesbrough 32.

  🏨 **Morritt Arms**, DL12 9SE, ☏ 21232, ⚲ 🚗 – ⇔wc ⇔ **P**. ⚱. ☒ ⓪
  M 4.50/6.00 st. ⓥ 2.30 – **24 rm** ⚏ 13.50/24.50 st. – P 19.00/22.00 st.

GRIMLEY Heref. and Worc. **403 404** M 27 – pop. 574 – ⊠ Hallow – **☎** 0905 Worcester.
London 129 – Kidderminster 13 – Worcester 5.

  ✗ Wagon Wheel Inn, WR2 6LU, ☏ 640340 – **P**.

GRIMSBY Humberside **404** T 23 – pop. 95,540 – ECD : Thursday – **☎** 0472.
🛈 Central Library, Town Hall Sq. ☏ 53123.
London 172 – Boston 50 – Lincoln 36 – Sheffield 75.

Plan on next page

  🏨 Humber Royal (Crest), Littlecoates Rd, DN34 4LX, ☏ 50295 – ▮ 📺 ⇔wc ⇔ 🦽 **P**. ⚱.
  ☒ AE ⓪ VISA
  ⚏ 2.80 – **54 rm** 19.90/26.45 st.   **Y** c

  🏨 Grimsby Crest Motel (Crest), St. James Sq., DN31 1EP, ☏ 59771 – ▮ 📺 ⇔wc ⇔ 🦽 **P**.
  ⚱. ☒ AE ⓪ VISA
  ⚏ 2.40 – **132 rm** 18.50/25.20 st.   **AZ** n

ALFA-ROMEO, HONDA Alexandra Rd ☏ 58625
AUSTIN-DAIMLER-JAGUAR-MORRIS-MG Brighowgate ☏ 58851
AUSTIN-MG-WOLSELEY 166/168 Hainton Av. ☏ 52461
AUSTIN-MG-ROVER-TRIUMPH 415 Victoria St. ☏ 56161
BEDFORD, VAUXHALL Brighowgate ☏ 58486
DATSUN 210/212 Victoria St. ☏ 53572

FIAT Wellowgate ☏ 55951
FORD Corporation Rd ☏ 58941
MERCEDES-BENZ Bradley Cross Rd ☏ 79274
OPEL 123 Cromwell Rd ☏ 59371
PEUGEOT 33 Louth Rd ☏ 79207
RENAULT Chelmsford Av. ☏ 70111
SKODA Rendel St. ☏ 57362
TALBOT Victoria St. ☏ 57151

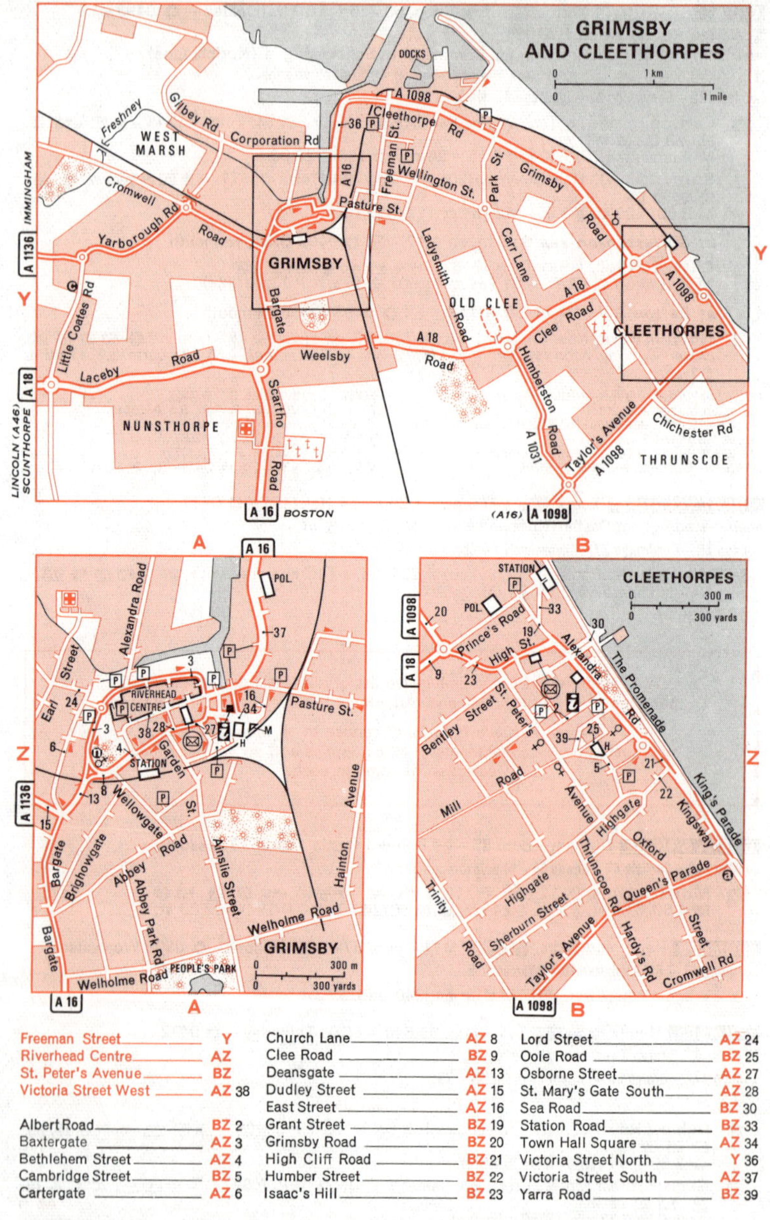

<table>
<tr><td>Freeman Street</td><td>Y</td></tr>
<tr><td>Riverhead Centre</td><td>AZ</td></tr>
<tr><td>St. Peter's Avenue</td><td>BZ</td></tr>
<tr><td>Victoria Street West</td><td>AZ 38</td></tr>
</table>

Albert Road	BZ 2	Church Lane	AZ 8	Lord Street	AZ 24
Baxtergate	AZ 3	Clee Road	BZ 9	Oole Road	BZ 25
Bethlehem Street	AZ 4	Deansgate	AZ 13	Osborne Street	AZ 27
Cambridge Street	BZ 5	Dudley Street	AZ 15	St. Mary's Gate South	AZ 28
Cartergate	AZ 6	East Street	AZ 16	Sea Road	BZ 30
		Grant Street	BZ 19	Station Road	BZ 33
		Grimsby Road	BZ 20	Town Hall Square	AZ 34
		High Cliff Road	BZ 21	Victoria Street North	Y 36
		Humber Street	BZ 22	Victoria Street South	AZ 37
		Isaac's Hill	BZ 23	Yarra Road	BZ 39

GRIMSTHORPE Lincs. 404 S 25 – pop. 313 – ✉ Bourne – ☎ 077 832 Edenham.
London 105 – Lincoln 43 – Nottingham 38.

XX **Black Horse Inn** with rm, PE10 0LY, ☎ 247, 🚗, English rest. – 🅿
closed Sunday, Christmas Day and Bank Holidays – **M** a la carte 5.30/8.00 – **4 rm** ☟
11.50/12.50.

GRINDLEFORD Derbs. **403** **404** OP 24 – pop. 1,200. – ⊠ Sheffield – ☎ 0433 Hope Valley.
London 165 – Derby 31 – Manchester 34 – Sheffield 10.

Maynard Arms, Maynard Rd, ☎ 30321, ⩽, 🐎 – 🛏WC 🚿WC **P.** ⚓. 🅰 **AE** ⓪ **VISA**
M 3.90/4.55 🍷 2.50 – **13 rm** ☕ 14.50/21.50 **t.**

GRIZEDALE Cumbria – see Hawkshead.

GUILDFORD Surrey **404** S 30 – pop. 57,213 – ECD : Wednesday – ☎ 0483.
See : Cathedral* (1961) **z A. Envir. :** Clandon Park** (Renaissance House) *AC*, E : 3 m. by
A 246 **z**. – 🏌 Puttenham ☎ 810 498, W : 4m. by A 31 **z**.
🛈 Civic Hall, London Rd ☎ 67314.
London 33 – Brighton 43 – Reading 27 – Southampton 49.

GUILDFORD

High Street	______	**Y**
North Street	______	**Y**
Tungsgate	______	**Y** 33
Bedford Road	______	**Y** 2
Bridge Street	______	**Y** 3
Castle Street	______	**Y** 5
Commercial Road	______	**Y** 8
Eastgate Gardens	______	**Y** 9
Friary Bridge	______	**Y** 12
Ladymead	______	**Z** 13
Leapale Lane	______	**Y** 15
Leapale Road	______	**Y** 16
Leas Road	______	**Y** 18
Mary Road	______	**Y** 19
Midleton Road	______	**Z** 20
Millbrook	______	**Y** 21
New Inn Lane	______	**Z** 22
One Tree Hill Road	______	**Z** 24
Onslow Street	______	**Y** 25
Park Street	______	**Y** 27
Quarry Street	______	**Y** 28
Stoughton Road	______	**Z** 30
Trood's Lane	______	**Z** 31
Warwick's Bench	______	**Y** 34
Woodbridge Hill	______	**Z** 36
Woodbridge Road	______	**Z** 37

📪 *Michelin n'accroche pas de panonceau aux hôtels et restaurants qu'il signale.*

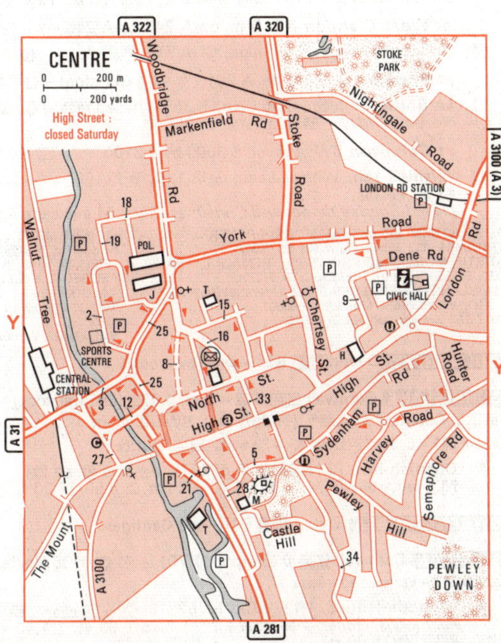

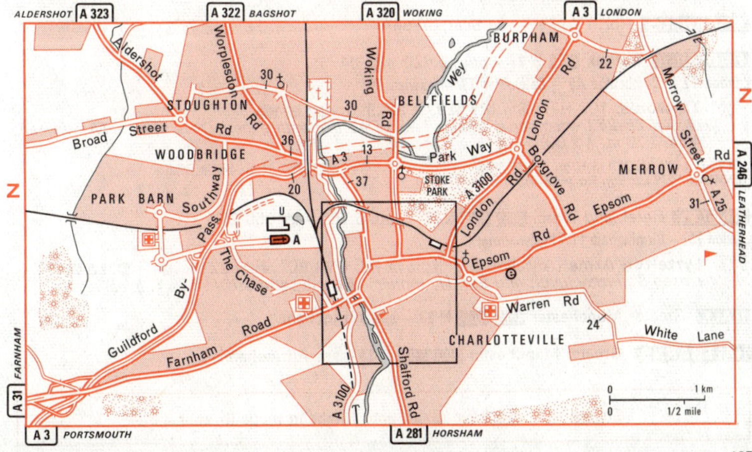

🏨 **Angel** (T.H.F.), High St., GU1 3DR, ☎ 64555 – 📺 ⬜wc ☎. ⬛ AE ⓞ *VISA*   **Y a**
M 4.50/4.95 st. ⌀ 1.65 – **24 rm** ☲ 17.00/24.00 st.

🏨 **White Horse** (Embassy), Upper High St., GU1 3JG, ☎ 64511 – 📺 ⬜wc ☎ 🅿. ⬛ AE
ⓞ *VISA*   **Y u**
M 5.00 st. ⌀ 1.40 – ☲ 2.50 – **38 rm** 16.50/22.00 st. – P 21.00/24.50 st.

♨ **Quinns**, Epsom Rd, GU1 2BX, ☎ 60422 – 🅿   **Z e**
M *(closed Sunday)* (dinner only) 5.50 s. ⌀ 2.30 – **12 rm** ☲ 9.90/19.80 s.

XX **Mad Hatter**, 1st floor, 5-6 Sydenham Rd, GU1 3RT, ☎ 63011 – ⬛ AE ⓞ *VISA*   **Y n**
closed Saturday lunch, Sunday, Monday and 3 weeks late June-early July – **M** a la carte
6.25/7.25 ⌀ 1.35.

XX **Swiss**, 14 Park St., GU1 4XB, ☎ 61458 – ⬛ AE ⓞ *VISA*   **Y c**
closed Sunday and Monday – **M** a la carte 4.85/7.15 t. ⌀ 2.50.

at West Clandon NE: 5 m. on A 247 by A 246 – **z** – ✉ ☎ 0483 Guildford:

XXX Onslow Arms Inn, The Street, GUA 7TE, ☎ 222447 – 🅿.

at Bramley S: 3 m. on A 281 – **z** – ✉ Guildford – ☎ 048 647 Bramley:

XX **La Baita**, High St., GU5 0HB, ☎ 3392, Italian rest. – 🅿. ⬛ AE ⓞ
closed Sunday – **M** a la carte 6.40/9.40.

at Compton SW: 4 m. on B 3000 by A 3100 – **z** – ✉ Guildford – ☎ 048 68 Godalming:

XX **Withies Inn**, Withies Lane, GU3 1JA, ☎ 21158, « Garden with shaded pergola » – 🅿.
⬛ AE ⓞ *VISA*
closed Sunday dinner and Christmas Day – **M** a la carte 4.05/8.70 ⌀ 2.00.

AUSTIN-DAIMLER-JAGUAR-MORRIS-ROVER-TRIUMPH 113 Portsmouth Rd ☎ 62907
AUSTIN-MORRIS-MG-PRINCESS, RENAULT, VAN-DEN PLAS Walnut Tree Close ☎ 77371
FIAT, LANCIA, MERCEDES-BENZ Aldershot Rd ☎ 60751
FORD Woodbridge Meadow ☎ 60601
MAZDA 224 London Rd ☎ 75326

MORRIS-MG-ROVER-TRIUMPH, ROLLS ROYCE Woodbridge Rd ☎ 69231
OPEL 26 High St. ☎ 048 647 (Bramley) 8159
PEUGEOT 8 North St. ☎ 65242
TALBOT By-Pass Rd ☎ 76931
TOYOTA Pitch Pl. Worplesdon ☎ 048 631 (Worplesdon) 4242
VAUXHALL Working Rd ☎ 37731

GULWORTHY Devon **403** H 32 – see Tavistock.

GUNNISLAKE Cornwall **403** H 32 – pop. 4,079 (inc. Calstock) – ECD: Wednesday – ☎ 0822.
Envir. : Cotehele House* (Tudor) *AC*, SW: 2 ½ m.
London 244 – Bude 37 – Exeter 43 – Plymouth 20 – Tavistock 5.

🏨 **Cornish Inn**, PL18 9BW, ☎ 832475 – ⬜wc 🅿. ⬛ *VISA*
M a la carte 2.05/4.20 t. ⌀ 1.40 – **8 rm** ☲ 8.50/17.50 t.

GWBERT-ON-SEA Dyfed **403** F 27 – see Cardigan.

GWITHIAN Cornwall **403** D 33 – pop. 1,701 – ✉ ☎ 0736 Hayle.
London 311 – Penzance 10 – Truro 17.

🏨 **Glencoe House**, TR27 5BX, ☎ 752216, ⬛ – 📺 ⬜wc 🅿. ⬛ *VISA*
February-October – **M** (bar lunch) 2.75/5.00 st. ⌀ 1.40 – **11 rm** ☲ 10.50/20.00 st. –
P 16.50/18.00 st.

HACKNESS North Yorks. – see Scarborough.

HADLEIGH Suffolk **404** W 27 – pop. 5,620 – ☎ 0473.
London 72 – Cambridge 49 – Colchester 17 – Ipswich 10.

X **Taviton's**, 103 High St., IP7 5EJ, ☎ 822820 – ⬛ AE *VISA*
closed 25-26 December and last week of each month except December – **M** a la carte
4.55/7.20 st. ⌀ 2.00.

BRITISH LEYLAND 115 High St. ☎ 3286
RENAULT 272 London Rd ☎ 554563

TALBOT 132 High St. ☎ 3525

HAGLEY Heref. and Worc. **403** **404** N 26 – pop. 5,760 – ☎ 056 286.
London 132 – Birmingham 11 – Kidderminster 6.

XX **Lyttelton Arms** (Ansells), Bromsgrove Rd, DY9 9LJ, ☎ 882213, 🍴 – 🅿. ⬛ AE
closed Saturday lunch and Sunday dinner – **M** a la carte 4.70/10.35 t. ⌀ 0.90.

HALE Greater Manchester **403** **404** M 23 – see Altrincham.

HALEBARNS Greater Manchester **403** **404** M 23 – see Altrincham.

HALESWORTH Suffolk **404** Y 26 – pop. 3,236 – ✆ 098 67.
London 103 – Ipswich 30 – Norwich 25.

   ✗   **Bassett's,** 84 London Rd, IP19 8LS, on A 144 ☎ 3154, ⇗
      closed Sunday, 24 to 27 December and 1 January – **M** (dinner only) 7.00 **t.** ≬ 1.60.
BRITISH LEYLAND, VANDEN PLAS ☎ 3213   MAZDA Hotton Rd ☎ 3129
BMW, HONDA Norwich Rd ☎ 3666   VAUXHALL London Rd ☎ 2138

HALIFAX West Yorks. **986** ㉓ – pop. 91,272 – ECD : Thursday – ✆ 0422.
⌇₁₈ Holywell Green ☎ 0422 (Elland) 74108 – ⌇₁₈ Highroad Well ☎ 53608, N : 3 m. –
⌇₉ Ryburn, Norland ☎ 31355, S : 3 m.
🛈 The Piece Hall ☎ 68725.

London 205 – Bradford 8 – Burnley 21 – Leeds 15 – Manchester 28.

   🏨   **White Swan** (T.H.F.), Princess St., HX1 1TS, ☎ 54227 – ▐$▌ 📺 ⊑wc ☏ 🅿. 🛆. 🔊 🆎 ⓪
      VISA
      M a la carte 4.60/6.35 **st.** ≬ 1.65 – **50 rm** ⌷ 14.00/21.50 **st.**

      at Holmfield N : 3 m. off A 629 – ✉ ✆ 0422 Halifax :

   🏫   **Holdsworth House,** HX2 9TQ, ☎ 244270 – 📺 🅿. 🛆. 🔊 🆎 ⓪ *VISA*
      closed Easter, Christmas Day and 1 January – **M** *(closed Saturday lunch and Sunday)* a la
      carte 7.60/12.00 **s.** ≬ 2.50 – **30 rm** ⌷ 17.60/30.00 **s.**
AUSTIN-DAIMLER-JAGUAR-ROVER-TRIUMPH Hud-   RENAULT Hope St. ☎ 52087
dersfield Rd ☎ 65944   ROLLS ROYCE, BENTLEY Haley Hill ☎ 65944
DAF Boothtown ☎ 67516   SAAB Saville Park Rd ☎ 59425
FIAT, CITROEN Queens Rd ☎ 67711   TALBOT Skircoat Rd ☎ 53701
FIAT, POLSKI Rochdale Rd ☎ 65036   VAUXHALL Northgate ☎ 62851
FORD Skircoat Rd ☎ 62951   VOLVO 354 Pellon Lane ☎ 61961
OPEL 7 Horton St. ☎ 65846   VW, AUDI-NSU Denholme Gate Rd, Hipperholme
PEUGEOT Wakefield Rd, Copley ☎ 67302   ☎ 201681

HALLAND East Sussex **404** U 31 – pop. 762 – ECD : Wednesday – ✉ Lewes – ✆ 082 584.
London 48 – Brighton 16 – Eastbourne 16 – Royal Tunbridge Wells 19.

   ✗✗   **Halland Motel and Old Forge Rest.** with rm, BN8 6PW, on A 22 ☎ 456, ⇗ – 📺
      ⊑wc ☏ 🅿. 🆎 ⓪
      closed Christmas – **M** a la carte 4.45/14.70 **t.** ≬ 2.00 – ⌷ 2.05 – **12 rm** 10.55/18.50 **t.**

HALSE TOWN Cornwall **403** D 33 – see St. Ives.

HALSTEAD Essex **404** V 28 – pop. 6,590 – ✆ 078 74.
London 51 – Cambridge 34 – Chelmsford 18 – Colchester 14.

   ✗✗   Fernando's, 26 High St., CO9 2AP, ☎ 2001.
CITROEN Sible Hedingham ☎ 0787 (Hedingham) 60538   VW, AUDI Gosfield ☎ 2131
SAAB Colchester Rd ☎ 2183

HALSTEAD Kent **404** U 30 – pop. 1,734 – ECD : Wednesday – ✉ Sevenoaks – ✆ 095 97
Badgers Mount.
London 20 – Maidstone 21.

   ✗✗   **Monte Carlo,** London Rd, Polhill, TN13 1BH, on A 21 ☎ 236, Italian rest. – 🅿. 🔊 🆎
      ⓪ *VISA*
      closed Saturday lunch, Sunday dinner, Monday and Bank Holidays – **M** a la carte 6.35/
      11.00 ≬ 2.90.

HAMBROOK Avon **403** **404** M 29 – see Bristol.

HAMPOLE South Yorks. **404** Q 23 – see Doncaster.

HAMSTEAD MARSHALL Berks. **403** **404** P 29 – pop. 199 – ✉ Newbury – ✆ 048 85 Kintbury.
London 72 – Newbury 5 – Southampton 39.

   ✗   **White Hart,** RG15 0HW, ☎ 762, ⇗ – 🅿
      closed Sunday dinner and Monday – **M** a la carte 4.80/7.70 **t.** ≬ 2.00.

HANDFORTH Cheshire **403** **404** N 23 – see Wilmslow.

HANLEY Staffs. **403** **404** N 24 – see Stoke-on-Trent.

HARBERTON Devon **403** I 32 – pop. 974 – ✉ Totnes – ✆ 080 423 Harbertonford.
London 226 – Exeter 26 – Plymouth 25 – Torquay 11.

   🏠   **Old Mill Country House** ⌂, TQ9 7SS, S : 2 m. ☎ 349, ✎, ⇗ – 🅿
      closed 2 weeks November and 1 week February – **M** *(closed Monday and Tuesday dinner
      to non-residents from November to April)* (bar lunch) a la carte 5.20/7.50 ≬ 2.00 – **8 rm**
      ⌷ 12.00/20.00

HARBERTONFORD Devon **408** I 32 – pop. 974 – ⊠ Totnes – ✆ 080 423.
London 228 – Exeter 28 – Plymouth 24 – Torquay 13.

   XX **Hungry Horse**, Old Rd, TQ9 7TA, ✆ 441 – **P**. AE
    closed Sunday and Monday – **M** (dinner only) a la carte 5.30/7.15 ₰ 1.80.

HAREWOOD West Yorks. **986** ㉓ – pop. 3,459 – ⊠ Leeds – ✆ 0532.
See : Harewood House** 18C : the Bird Garden* *AC.*
London 202 – Harrogate 7 – **Leeds 8.**

   ⌂ Harewood Arms, LS17 9LH, ✆ 886235, ⚏ – TV ➩wc ⇔ **P**
   11 rm.

HARLECH Gwynedd **408** H 25 – pop. 1,405 – ECD : Wednesday – ✆ 076 673.
See : Castle** (13C) *AC*, site and ⩽ from the castle*. **Envir. :** Llanbedr (Cwm Bychan*)
S : 3 ½ m. – Vale of Ffestinoig* NE : 9 m.
⌷₁₈ Royal St. David's ✆ 203.
🛈 Snowdonia National Park and Wales Tourist Centre, High St. ✆ 658 (Easter-September).
London 241 – Chester 72 – Dolgellau 21.

   🏰 **Maes-y-Neuadd** ⚐, LL47 6YA, NE: 3 m. off B 4573 ✆ 200, ⩽, « Part 14C country
   house », ⚏, park – TV ➩wc **P**
   Easter-September – **M** (dinner only) 7.50 **st.** ₰ 3.00 – ⇋ 2.50 – **13 rm** 11.80/23.60 **st.**

   🏰 **St. Davids**, LL46 2 PT, ✆ 366, ⩽ sea and golf courses, �🏊 heated, ⚏ – ▯ ➩wc ☏ & **P**. 🛌
   M 4.00/6.00 **t.** ₰ 1.95 – **80 rm** ⇋ 10.00/22.00 **t.** – P 17.00 **t.**

   ⌂ **Noddfa**, Lower Rd, LL46 2UB, ✆ 319, ⩽ – ➩wc **P**. 🛌
   M 3.50 ₰ 1.50 – **7 rm** ⇋ 12.00/18.00.

HARLOW Essex **404** U 28 – pop. 83,500 – ECD : Wednesday – ✆ 0279.
London 26 – Cambridge 34 – Chelmsford 20.

   🏰 **Saxon Inn Motor,** Southern Way, CM18 7BA, on A 414 ✆ 22441, Telex 63271 – TV
   ➩wc ☏ **P**. 🛌. 🛌 AE ⓞ VISA
   M 3.70/4.20 **s.** ₰ 2.00 – ⇋ 1.95 – **120 rm** 14.50/19.00 **s.**

   at Old Harlow :

   XX **Gables,** 1 Fore St., CM17 0AA, ✆ 27108 – 🛌 ⓞ
   closed Saturday lunch, Sunday, Monday lunch and 2 weeks mid summer – **M** a la carte
   5.25/9.65.

AUSTIN-JAGUAR-ROVER-TRIUMPH First Av., The   RENAULT Station Rd ✆ 39631
Stow ✆ 27541   TALBOT Harrolds Rd ✆ 32111
DATSUN, PEUGEOT Tillwicks Rd ✆ 22381   VAUXHALL Potter St. ✆ 22391
FORD Edinburgh Way ✆ 21166   VW, AUDI Wych Elm ✆ 21461

HARNHAM Wilts. **408 404** O 30 – see Salisbury.

HARPENDEN Herts. **404** S 28 – pop. 21,230 – ECD : Wednesday – ✆ 058 27.
London 32 – Luton 6.

   🏨 **Harpenden Moat House,** 18 Southdown Rd, AL5 1PE, ✆ 64111, ⚏ – TV **P**. 🛌 AE ⓞ VISA
   M a la carte 7.05/10.40 ₰ 2.20 – ⇋ 2.75 – **35 rm** 16.00/23.00 **s.**

   🏰 Glen Eagle, 1 Luton Rd, AL5 2PX, ✆ 60271, ⚏ – ▯ TV ➩wc ☏ & **P**. 🛌 – **43 rm.**

AUSTIN-MORRIS-MG 74 High St. ✆ 4545   VAUXHALL 17 Luton Rd ✆ 67776
RENAULT Southdown Rd ✆ 5217   VOLVO Station Rd ✆ 64311

HARROGATE North Yorks. **986** ㉓ – pop. 62,427 – ECD : Wednesday – ✆ 0423.
See : Harlow Car gardens** by B 6162 Z. **Envir. :** Fountains Abbey*** (ruins 12C-13C, floodlit
in summer), Studley Royal Gardens** and Fountains Hall* (17C) *AC*, NW: 9 m. by A 61 Y.
⌷₁₈ Starbeck, nr. Harrogate ✆ 863158, E : 2 m. by A 59 YZ – ⌷₁₈ Oakdale, off Kent Rd Y ✆ 502806 –
⌷₁₈ Pannal ✆ 871641, S : 2 ½ m. by A 61 Z.
🛈 Royal Baths Assembly Rooms, Crescent Rd ✆ 65912/65652 ext 23/28.
London 211 – Bradford 18 – **Leeds 15** – Newcastle-upon-Tyne 76 – York 22.

Plan opposite

   🏨 **Majestic** (T.H.F.), Ripon Rd, HG1 2HU, ✆ 68972, Telex 57918, ✗, �🏊 heated, ⚏ – ▯
   TV **P**. 🛌. 🛌 AE ⓞ VISA   Y c
   M 4.30/5.60 **st.** ₰ 1.65 – ⇋ 2.50 – **159 rm** 18.50/27.50 **st.**

   🏨 **Old Swan,** Swan Rd, HG1 2SR, ✆ 504051, Telex 57922, ✗, ⚏, park – ▯ & **P**. 🛌. 🛌
   AE ⓞ VISA   Y e
   M 6.25/7.25 **st.** ₰ 2.50 – **145 rm** ⇋ 25.00/42.00 **st.**

   🏨 **Crown** (T.H.F.), Crown Pl., HG1 2RZ, ✆ 67755, Telex 57652 – ▯ TV **P**. 🛌. 🛌 AE ⓞ VISA
   M 4.75/5.50 **st.** ₰ 1.65 – ⇋ 2.50 – **112 rm** 17.00/26.50 **st.**   Z i

   🏨 **Cairn** (Best Western), Ripon Rd, HG1 2JD, ✆ 504005, Telex 57992, ✗, ⚏ – ▯ **P**. 🛌.
   🛌 AE ⓞ VISA   Y n
   M 5.15/6.15 **st.** ₰ 2.70 – **139 rm** ⇋ 24.00/34.40 **st.**

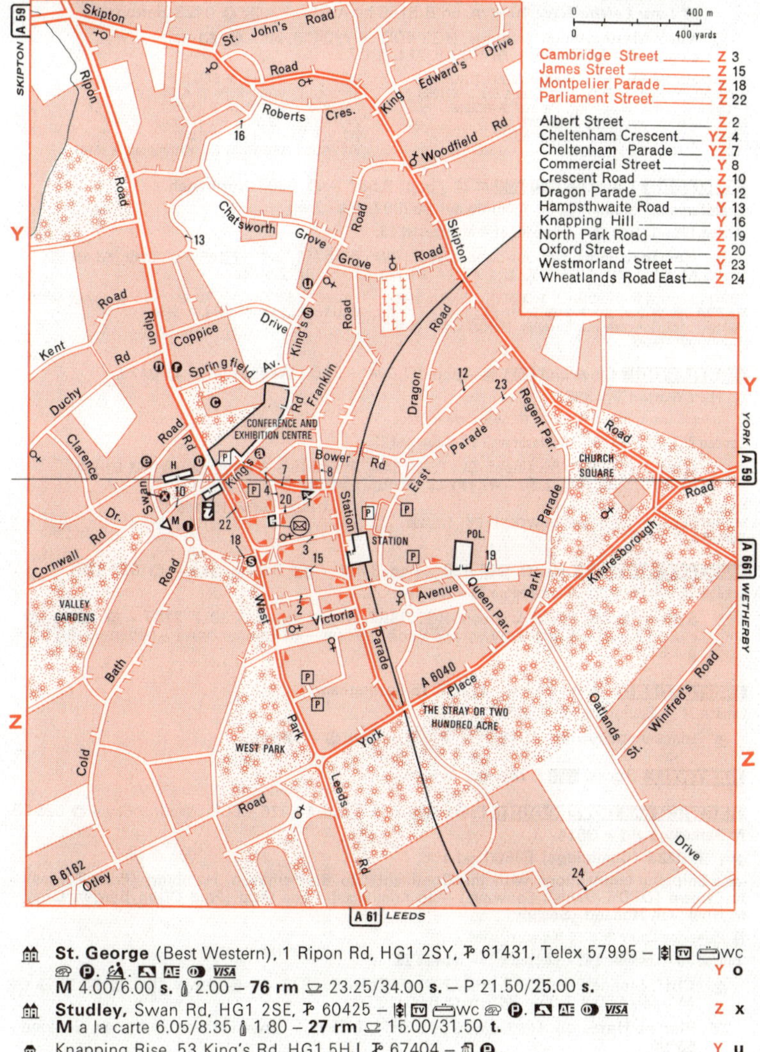

St. George (Best Western), 1 Ripon Rd, HG1 2SY, ℡ 61431, Telex 57995 – ▯ TV ▭ WC ☏ P. ⌂ ⌂ AE ① VISA — Y o
M 4.00/6.00 s. ⌂ 2.00 – **76 rm** ⌂ 23.25/34.00 s. – P 21.50/25.00 s.

Studley, Swan Rd, HG1 2SE, ℡ 60425 – ▯ TV ▭ WC ☏ P. ⌂ AE ① VISA — Z x
M a la carte 6.05/8.35 ⌂ 1.80 – **27 rm** ⌂ 15.00/31.50 t.

Knapping Rise, 53 King's Rd, HG1 5HJ, ℡ 67404 – ⌂ P — Y u
17 rm.

Gilmore, 98 King's Rd, HG1 5HH, ℡ 503699 – P — Y s
18 rm ⌂ 5.50/11.00 st.

Number Six, 6 Ripon Rd, HG1 2JB, ℡ 502908 — Y r
closed Monday, last week July, first 2 weeks August, Christmas Day and 1 January –
M (dinner only) 7.95/11.95.

Oliver, 24 King's Rd, HG1 5JW, ℡ 68600 – ⌂ AE — Y a
closed Sunday and Bank Holidays – **M** (dinner only) 9.50 t. ⌂ 2.20.

Drum and Monkey, 5 Montpelier Gardens, HG1 2TF, ℡ 502650, Seafood — Z s
closed Sunday and 24 December-2 January – **M** (buffet lunch) a la carte 6.75/10.40 t.

at Burn Bridge S : 4 m. off A 61 – **Z** – ✉ ☎ 0423 Harrogate :

Roman Court, 55 Burn Bridge Rd, HG3 1PB, ℡ 879933, Italian rest. – P
closed Sunday – **M** (dinner only) 7.25 t. ⌂ 2.25.

at Low Laithe NW: 10 ½ m. on B 6165 by A 61 – ɣ – ✉ ☎ 0423 Harrogate:

XXX **Knox Manor,** Summerbridge, HG3 4DQ, ☎ 780473, ⛟ – ℗. 🔄 *VISA*
closed Sunday dinner – **M** 5.00/9.00 **t.** ⌀ 1.75.

AUSTIN-DAIMLER-JAGUAR-MG-ROVER-TRIUMPH-WOLSELEY, ROLLS ROYCE 91 Leeds Rd ☎ 871263	PEUGEOT Pannal ☎ 879231
CITROEN, FIAT Leeds Rd, Pannal ☎ 879236	RENAULT West Park ☎ 61751
DAF, LANCIA Starbeck ☎ 886351	TALBOT West Park ☎ 504601
DATSUN Cheltenham Mount ☎ 66001	VAUXHALL 19 York Pl. ☎ 64511
FORD Station Par. ☎ 61061	VOLVO East Parade ☎ 64567
	VW, AUDI-NSU Otley Rd, Killinghall ☎ 55141

HARTFORD Cheshire **403 404** M 24 – pop. 3,587 – ☎ 0606 Northwich.
Delamere Forest ☎ 0606 (Sandiway) 882807, SW: 2 m.

London 188 – Chester 15 – Liverpool 31 – Manchester 25.

Hartford Hall, School Lane, CW8 1PW, ☎ 75711, ⛟ – TV ⌂wc ☎ ℗. 🔄 ① *VISA*
M a la carte 4.20/6.60 **t.** ⌀ 2.05 – **21 rm** ⌷ 15.50/22.50 **t.**

FORD Chesterway, Northwich ☎ 0606 (Northwich) 6141	TALBOT 322 Chester Rd ☎ 0606 (Sandiway) 888188
MAZDA 199 Witton St. ☎ 2485	VAUXHALL London Rd ☎ 3434
POLSKI 141 Runcorn Rd, Barnton, Northwich ☎ 0606 (Northwich) 74293	

HARTLEPOOL Cleveland **986** ⑲ – pop. 97,094 – ECD : Wednesday – ☎ 0429.
Hart Warren ☎ 4398.

🛈 Victor Square, Victoria Rd ☎ 68366 (summer only).

London 263 – Durham 19 – Middlesbrough 9 – Sunderland 21.

Grand (B.T.H.), Swainson St., TS24 8AA, ☎ 66345 – 🕴 TV ♿ ℗ ⛱. 🔄 AE *VISA*
M 3.75/5.30 **st.** ⌀ 2.30 – **47 rm** ⌷ 19.65/26.95 **st.**

FORD Stockton Rd ☎ 64311	VAUXHALL Oxford Rd ☎ 67719
MORRIS-MG-ROVER-TRIUMPH-WOLSELEY 128/130 York Rd ☎ 66393	VW, AUDI 52/54 Park Rd ☎ 69018

HARTLEY WINTNEY Hants. **404** R 30 – pop. 3,435 – ✉ Basingstoke – ☎ 025 126.
London 46 – Reading 12 – Southampton 40 – Winchester 28.

X **Stilton Dish,** Phoenix Green, RG27 8RT, SW: 1 m. on A 30 ☎ 2107 – ℗. 🔄 AE *VISA*
closed Sunday, Christmas Day and Bank Holidays – **M** (dinner only) a la carte 7.00/10.00 ⌀ 1.65.

HARTOFT END North Yorks. – ☎ 075 15 Lastingham.
London 243 – Scarborough 26 – York 32.

Blacksmith's Arms, YO18 8EN, ☎ 331 – ⌂wc ℗ – **12 rm.**

HARTWELL Bucks. **404** R 28 – see Aylesbury.

HARWICH and DOVERCOURT Essex **404** X 28 – pop. 14,926 – ECD : Wednesday – ☎ 025 55.
Parkeston Rd ☎ 3616.

🚗 ☎ 0223 (Cambridge) 58800 ext 106.

🚢 Shipping connections with the Continent : to Bremerhaven, Hamburg (Prins Ferries) – to Esbjerg (DFDS Danish Seaways) – to Kristiansand and Oslo (Fred Olsen-Bergen Line) – to Hoek van Holland (Sealink).

🛈 Parkeston Quay ☎ 6139 (summer only).

London 74 – Chelmsford 41 – Colchester 19 – Ipswich 23.

Cliff, Marine Par., CO12 3RD, ☎ 3345, Telex 987372, ≼ – TV ⌂wc ⌂wc ℗. 🔄 AE ① *VISA*
M 3.50/4.50 ⌀ 1.05 – **34 rm** ⌷ 8.00/19.00.

XX **Pier at Harwich,** The Quay, CO12 3HH, ☎ 3363, ≼ Orwell haven and quay, Seafood –
🔄 *VISA*
closed 1 week at Christmas – **M** a la carte 4.75/6.35 **t.** ⌀ 2.00.

HASLEMERE Surrey **404** R 30 – pop. 10,920 – ECD : Wednesday – ☎ 0428.
Envir.: Petworth House*** 17C (paintings*** and carved room***) *AC,* SE: 11 m.

London 47 – Brighton 46 – Southampton 44.

Lythe Hill ⚘, Petworth Rd, GU27 3BQ, E: 1 ½ m. on B 2131 ☎ 51251, Telex 858402,
≼, XX, ⚓, ⛟. park – TV ℗. ⛱. 🔄 AE ① *VISA*
M 6.00/8.50 **st.** ⌀ 2.75 – **34 rm** 19.00/31.00 **st.** – P approx. 32.00 **st.**

Georgian, High St., GU27 2JY, ☎ 51555, ⛟ – ⌂wc ☎ ℗. 🔄 AE ① *VISA*
M 4.00/5.50 **st.** ⌀ 1.75 – **22 rm** ⌷ 11.80/23.85 **st.**

XXX **Auberge de France,** Petworth Rd, GU27 3BQ, E: 1 ½ m. on B 2131 ☎ 4131, Telex
858402, ≼, French rest. – ℗. 🔄 AE ① *VISA*
closed Tuesday lunch, Monday and 26 December-1 March – **M** a la carte 9.50/11.80 **st.**
⌀ 2.75.

AUSTIN-MORRIS-MG-TRIUMPH, VANDEN PLAS Kings Rd ☎ 4222
AUSTIN-JAGUAR-MORRIS-ROVER-TRIUMPH Grayswood Rd ☎ 2303
FORD Farnham Lane ☎ 3222

PEUGEOT High St. ☎ 52552
TALBOT West St. ☎ 3333
VAUXHALL 101/107 Camelsdale Rd ☎ 3678
VW, AUDI Hindead Rd ☎ 3216

HASTINGS AND ST. LEONARDS

King's Road _______ **AZ** 22
London Road _______ **AZ**
Norman Road _______ **AZ**
Queen's Road _______ **BZ**
Robertson Street _______ **BZ** 27
Wellington Place _______ **BZ** 35

Bourne (The) _______ **BY** 4
Castle Street _______ **BZ** 7
Castle Hill Road _______ **BZ** 8
Cornwallis Gardens _______ **BZ** 9
Cornwallis Terrace _______ **BZ** 10
Dane Road _______ **AY** 12
Denmark Place _______ **BZ** 13
Dorset Place _______ **BZ** 15
Gensing Road _______ **AZ** 16
George Street _______ **BY** 18

Grosvenor Crescent _______ **AY** 19
Harold Place _______ **BZ** 20
High Street _______ **BY** 21
Priory Street _______ **BZ** 24
Rock-a-Nore Road _______ **BY** 30
St. Helen's Park Road _______ **BY** 32
Silchester Road _______ **AZ** 33
Warrior Square _______ **AZ** 34
Wellington Square _______ **BZ** 36
White Rock Road _______ **BZ** 38

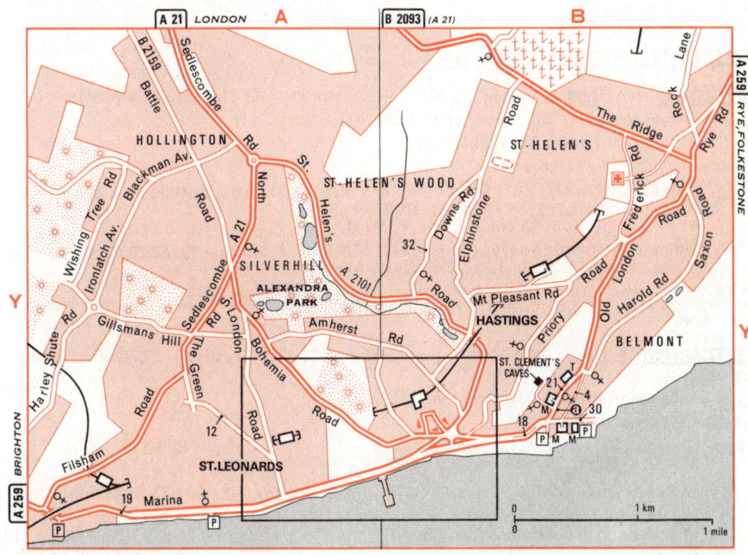

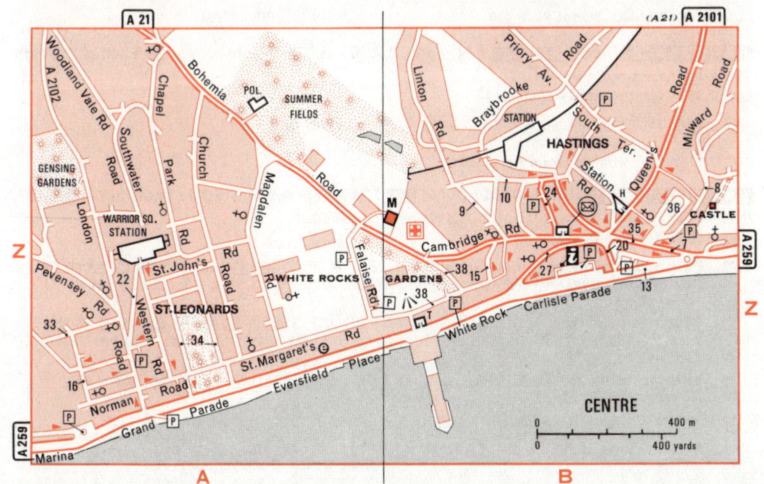

HASTINGS and ST. LEONARDS East Sussex 404 V 31 – pop. 72,410 – © 0424.

See : Norman Castle (ruins) ※** AC BZ – Alexandra Park* AY – White Rocks gardens ←* ABZ – Public Museum and Art Gallery (pottery*, Durbar Hall*) BZ M.

📇 Beauport Park, St. Leonards, ☏ 52977, NW : 3 m. by B 2159 AY.

🛈 4 Robertson Ter. ☏ 424242.

London 65 – Brighton 37 – Folkestone 37 – Maidstone 34.

Plan on preceding page

🏨 **Beauport Park** ⑤, Battle Rd, TN38 8EA, NW : 3 ½ m. on A 2100, ☏ 51222, « Formal garden », ⤵ heated, park – 📺 🅿. 🔄 🆎 ⑩ VISA   on B 2159 AY
  M 3.50/4.50 st. ░ 1.70 – **15 rm** ☲ 12.50/24.00 st. – P 15.50/20.00 st.

XX **Saraceno,** 64 Eversfield Pl. ☏ 432358, Italian rest.   AZ e

X **Mitre,** 56 High St., Old Town, TN34 3EN, ☏ 427000, French rest.   BY a

AUSTIN-MORRIS-MG-ROVER 5-9 Western Rd ☏ 37628
DAF Winchelsea Rd ☏ 424445
FIAT Bexhill Rd ☏ 433533
FORD Braybrooke Rd ☏ 422727
RENAULT 109/111 Sedlescombe Rd North ☏ 422727
VAUXHALL 36/39 Western Rd, St. Leonards ☏ 424545
VW, AUDI-NSU 111/113 Bexhill Rd ☏ 424146

HATCH BEAUCHAMP Somerset 403 K 30 – see Taunton.

HATFIELD Herts. 404 T 28 – pop. 26,000 – ECD : Monday and Thursday – © 070 72.

See : Hatfield House*** AC (gardens* and Old Palace*).

📇 Bedwell Park ☏ Potters Bar 42624, E : 3 m.

London 27 – Bedford 38 – Cambridge 39.

🏨 **Comet** (Embassy), 301 St. Albans Rd West, AL10 9RH, junction A 1 and A 414, ☏ 65411, 🍽 – 📺 🛏wc ☎ 🅿. 🔄. 🔄 🆎 ⑩ VISA
  M 4.60 st. ░ 1.45 – **45 rm** ☲ 16.50/22.00 st.

XXX **Salisbury,** The Broadway, Old Hatfield, AL9 5JB, ☏ 62220 – 🅿. 🔄 🆎 ⑩ VISA
  closed Sunday dinner and Bank Holidays – M a la carte 5.85/9.45 s.

ALFA-ROMEO, HONDA, TALBOT By-Pass ☏ 64521
AUSTIN-MORRIS-MG-ROVER-TRIUMPH 1 Great North Rd ☏ 64366
FIAT North Parade ☏ 62908
LANCIA, PEUGEOT 42 Beaconsfield Rd ☏ 71226

HATHERLEIGH Devon 403 H 31 – pop. 915 – ECD : Wednesday – ✉ Okehampton – © 083 781.

📇 at Okehampton ☏ 0837 (Okehampton) 2113, SE : 7 m.

London 230 – Exeter 29 – Plymouth 38.

🏠 **George,** Market St., EX20 3JN, ☏ 454, « 15C inn », ⤵ – 🛏wc 🅿. 🆎 ⑩
  M 4.50/5.50 ░ 1.20 – **13 rm** ☲ 9.50/19.00.

at Sheepwash NW : 4 ½ m. off A 3072 – ✉ Beaworthy – © 040 923 Black Torrington :

🏠 **Half Moon Inn** ⑤, EX21 5NE, ☏ 376, « 17C inn », ⤵ – 🛏wc 🅿. 🔄 VISA
  M (closed mid week from November to February) (bar lunch) 6.75 t. ░ 1.75 – **14 rm** ☲ 10.50/24.00 t.

AUSTIN-MORRIS-MG Market Pl. ☏ 210
AUSTIN-MORRIS ☏ 244

HATHERSAGE Derbs. 403 404 P 24 – pop. 1,458 – ECD : Wednesday – ✉ Sheffield (South Yorks.) – © 0433 Hope Valley.

London 165 – Manchester 33 – Sheffield 10.

🏠 **George,** Main Rd, S30 1BB, ☏ 50436, 🍽 – 🛏wc 🅿
  10 rm.

AUSTIN-ROVER-TRIUMPH Main Rd ☏ 50341

HAVERFORDWEST (HWLFFORDD) Dyfed 403 F 28 – pop. 9,104 – ECD : Thursday – © 0437.

🛈 Wales Tourist Board Centre, 40 High St. ☏ 3110 (Easter September).

London 250 – Fishguard 15 – Swansea 57.

🏨 **Pembroke House,** Spring Gdns, SA61 2EN, ☏ 3652 – 📺 🛏wc 📶wc ☎ 🅿. 🔄 🆎 ⑩ VISA
  closed Christmas Day – M (closed Sunday lunch) approx. 3.50 t. ░ 1.70 – **25 rm** ☲ 10.35/18.40 t.

🏨 **Mariners** (Embassy), Mariners Sq., SA61 2DU, ☏ 3353 – 📺 🛏wc 🅿. 🔄 🆎 ⑩ VISA
  closed Christmas – M (bar lunch Monday to Saturday) 4.60/5.25 st. – **29 rm** ☲ 10.50/21.00 st.

🏠 **Elliotts Hill** ⑤, SAG1 1NU, NW : 1 ½ m. on B 4330 ☏ 2383, ✖, 🍽 – 🅿
  22 rm ☲ 5.00/10.00.

AUSTIN-DAIMLER-JAGUAR-MG-ROVER-TRIUMPH
WOLSELEY Salutation Sq. ☏ 4511
BMW, DATSUN Rhos ☏ 251
FIAT Portfield ☏ 3414
FORD Dew St. ☏ 3772
RENAULT St. Thomas Green ☏ 5151
SAAB Johnston ☏ 0437 (Johnston) ☏ 890 377
TALBOT Old Hakin Rd ☏ 2468
VAUXHALL Bridgend Sq. ☏ 2717

HAWKCHURCH Devon **403** L 31 – pop. 431 – ⊠ Axminster – ☎ 029 77.
London 155 – Dorchester 27 – Exeter 31 – Taunton 24.

   🏨 **Fairwater Head** ⤳, EX13 5TX, ☏ 349, ≤ Axe Vale, ⇆ – ⌂wc ℗
    March-October – **M** 4.60/5.20 **st.** ↓ 1.75 – **14 rm** ⊒ 14.75/26.20 **st.** – P 20.70 **st.**

HAWKHURST Kent **404** V 30 – pop. 4,107 – ECD : Wednesday – ☎ 058 05.
Envir. : Bedgebury Pinetum* *AC*, NW : 2 m.
🛈 High St. ☏ 2396.
London 50 – Folkestone 34 – Hastings 15 – Maidstone 19.

   🏨 **Royal Oak**, Highgate, TN18 4EP, ☏ 2184, ⇆ – ⇔ ℗. 𝔸𝔼 ⓪ 𝘝𝘐𝘚𝘈
    M *(closed Sunday dinner and Monday lunch)* 4.00 **t.** ↓ 2.00 – **11 rm** ⊒ 8.00/15.00 **t.** –
    P 14.00/15.00 **t.**

   XX **Tudor Arms** with rm, Rye Rd, TN18 5DA, E : ½ m. on A 268 ☏ 2312, « ≤ over rose
    garden » – ⌂wc ℗. 𝔸 𝔸𝔼 ⓪ 𝘝𝘐𝘚𝘈
    M *(closed Sunday dinner to non-residents)* 3.50/4.50 **st.** ↓ 2.50 – ⊒ 1.50 – **10 rm** 11.00/
    30.00 **st.** – P 17.00/21.00 **st.**

OPEL Rye Rd ☏ 3251   ROVER-TRIUMPH Horns Rd ☏ 2020

HAWKRIDGE Somerset **403** J 30 – ⊠ Dulverton – ☎ 064 385 Winsford.
London 203 – Exeter 32 – Minehead 17 – Taunton 32.

   🏨 **Tarr Steps** ⤳, TA22 9PY, ☏ 293, ≤, « Country house atmosphere », ◗, ⇆, park –
    ⌂wc ℗
    April-November – **M** (bar lunch) approx. 6.60 **s.** ↓ 2.00 – **15 rm** ⊒ 10.30/22.50 **s.**

HAWKSHEAD Cumbria **986** ⑲ – pop. 684 – ECD : Thursday – ⊠ Ambleside – ☎ 096 66.
🛈 Main Car Park, Main St. ☏ 525 (summer only).
London 283 – Carlisle 52 – Kendal 19.

   🏨 **Tarn Hows** ⤳, LA22 0PR, NW : 1 ½ m., ☏ 330, ≤, ✗, ⤢ heated, ◗, ⇆, park – ⌂wc
    ☏ ℗. 𝔸 𝔸𝔼 𝘝𝘐𝘚𝘈
    March-November – **M** 4.75/8.50 **st.** ↓ 1.50 – **24 rm** ⊒ 17.50/26.00 **st.**
   ⋔ **Highfield House** ⤳, Hawkshead Hill, LA22 0PN, W : ½ m. on B 5285 ☏ 344, ≤, ⇆ – ℗
    March-October – **11 rm** ⊒ 8.00/16.00 **t.**

   at Near Sawrey SE : 1 ½ m. on B 5285 – ⊠ Ambleside – ☎ 096 66 Hawkshead :

   ⋔ **Sawrey House** ⤳, LA22 0LF, on B 5285 ☏ 387, ≤, ⇆ – ℗
    April-5 November – **11 rm** ⊒ 6.00/12.00 **s.**

   at Grizedale S : 2 ¾ m. – ⊠ Ambleside – ☎ 096 66 Hawshead :

   XX **Ormandy** ⤳ with rm, LA22 0QH, ☏ 532 – ⌂wc ℗
    closed January-mid February – **M** *(closed Wednesday)* a la carte 4.15/7.00 ↓ 1.90 –
    5 rm ⊒ 14.00/18.00.

HAYLING ISLAND Hants. **404** R 31 – pop. 10,560 – ECD : Wednesday – ☎ 070 16.
London 77 – Brighton 45 – Southampton 28.

   🏨 **Post House** (T. H. F.), Northney Rd, PO11 0NQ, ☏ 5011, Telex 86620, ⤢ heated – 📺
    ⌂wc ☏ ℗. 𝔸 𝔸 𝔸𝔼 ⓪ 𝘝𝘐𝘚𝘈
    M 4.75/5.75 **st.** ↓ 1.75 – ⊒ 2.25 – **96 rm** 19.00/28.00 **st.**

   X **Jeanne's Cuisine** with rm, 33 Station Rd, West Town, PO11 0EA, ☏ 3178, French Bistro –
    🛏. 𝔸 𝘝𝘐𝘚𝘈
    M *(closed Sunday)* (dinner only) a la carte 5.15/6.65 ↓ 1.45 – **4 rm** ⊒ 12.00 **s.**

   X **Three Musketeers**, 64 Station Rd, West Town, PO11 0EB, ☏ 3226 – ℗.

HAYWARDS HEATH West Sussex **404** T 30 – pop. 23,090 – ECD : Wednesday – ☎ 0444.
Envir. : Sheffield Park Gardens** *AC*, E : 5 m.
🛈 High Beech ☏ 044 47 (Lindfield) 2310, N : 2 m.
London 44 – Brighton 15 – Eastbourne 29 – Lewes 12.

   🏨 **Hilton Park** ⤳, Tylers Green, RH17 5EG, W : 1 m. on A 272 ☏ 54555, ⇆ – ⌂wc
    ⌂wc ℗. 𝔸 𝔸𝔼 ⓪ 𝘝𝘐𝘚𝘈
    M (buffet lunch) approx. 5.50 **s.** ↓ 1.50 – **14 rm** ⊒ 13.00/25.00 **s.**

AUSTIN-DAIMLER-JAGUAR-LAND ROVER-MORRIS-   FORD 22/24 Wivelsfield Rd ☏ 50222
RANGE ROVER-ROVER-TRIUMPH Mill Green Rd   MORRIS-MG-ROVER-TRIUMPH The Broadway ☏
☏ 50404   51511
BMW 275a Chelwood Gate ☏ 082 574 (Chelwood Gate)   ROLLS-ROYCE-BENTLEY Market Pl. ☏ 51511
456   VAUXHALL 104 Franklynn Rd ☏ 50115

HEALD GREEN Greater Manchester **403** **404** N 23 – see Manchester.

HECKFIELD Hants. **404** R 29 – pop. 340 – ⊠ Basingstoke – ☎ 073 583.
London 52 – Basingstoke 10 – Reading 9.

XXX **Andwells**, RG27 0LN, on A 33 ☏ 202 – **P.** **AE** **①** **VISA**
closed Sunday dinner in winter – **M** a la carte 9.80/15.50 **t.** ⌕ 2.75.

HEDDON'S MOUTH Devon **403** I 30 – ⊠ Barnstaple – ☎ 059 83 Parracombe.
London 209 – Exeter 57 – Minehead 23 – Taunton 48.

⌂ **Hunters Inn** ⌕, Parracombe, EX31 4PY, ☏ 230, ⌕, ⌕ – ⌕wc **P.** **AE** **VISA**
Easter-October – **M** (bar lunch) approx. 8.00 **st.** ⌕ 1.75 – **11 rm** ⌕ 9.50/20.00 **st.**

HELFORD Cornwall **403** E 33 – pop. 289 (inc. Manaccan) – ⊠ Helston – ☎ 032 623 Manaccan.
London 324 – Falmouth 15 – Penzance 22 – Truro 27.

XX **Riverside** with rm, TR12 6JU, ☏ 443, « Converted cottage »
April-October – **M** *(closed Sunday dinner and Monday to non-residents* (dinner only and
Sunday lunch) 9.50/10.50 **st.** ⌕ 2.25 – **3 rm** ⌕ 11.50/21.00 **st.**

HELMSLEY North Yorks. **986** ㉔ – pop. 1,278 – ECD : Wednesday – ☎ 043 92 (fig. 3)
or 0439 (5 and 6 fig.).
See : Castle* (ruins 12C) *AC.* **Envir. :** Rievaulx Abbey** (ruins 12C-13C) *AC,* NW : 2 ½ m. –
Byland Abbey* (ruins 12C) *AC,* SW : 6 m. by Ampleforth.
London 234 – Middlesbrough 29 – York 24.

⌂ **Black Swan** (T.H.F.), Market Pl., YO6 5BJ, ☏ 466, ⌕ – **TV** ⌕wc ☏ ⌕ **P.** **AE** **①**
VISA
M 3.70/5.30 **st.** ⌕ 1.65 – **38 rm** ⌕ 17.50/25.50 **st.**

⌂ **Feversham Arms** (Best Western), 1 High St., YO6 5AG, ☏ 70346 – ⌕wc **P**
closed Christmas – **M** 4.00/6.00 ⌕ 1.50 – **15 rm** ⌕ 18.00/22.00.

HEMEL HEMPSTEAD Herts. **404** S 28 – pop. 76,000 – ECD : Wednesday – ☎ 0442.
⛳ Little Hay ☏ 832674, off A 41 at Box Lane.
🛈 Pavilion, The Marlowes ☏ 64451.
London 30 – Aylesbury 16 – Luton 10 – Northampton 46.

⌂ **Post House** (T.H.F.), Breakspear Way, HP2 4UA, NE : 2 ½ m. on A 4147 ☏ 51122 ⌕ –
⌕ **TV** ⌕wc ☏ **P.** ⌕. **AE** **①** **VISA**
M 4.25/4.95 **st.** ⌕ 1.65 – ⌕ 2.25 – **91 rm** 18.00/25.50 **st.**

↑ **South Lea**, 8 Charles St., HP1 1JH, ☏ 3061 – **P**
11 rm 7.50/14.00 **s.**

X **Casanova**, 75 Waterhouse St., HP2 1AT, ☏ 47482, Italian rest. – **AE** **①** **VISA**
closed Saturday lunch, Sunday, Christmas Day and Bank Holidays – **M** a la carte 5.20/
9.95 **t.** ⌕ 2.20.

X **White Hart**, 30-32 High St., HP1 5AE, ☏ 42458, English rest. – **P.** **AE** **①**
closed Saturday, Sunday and Bank Holidays – **M** (lunch only) a la carte approx. 6.00 ⌕ 2.50.

X **Lautrec**, 95 High St., HP1 3TR, ☏ 55146, French rest. – **AE** **①** **VISA**
closed Saturday lunch, Sunday, last 2 weeks August and Bank Holidays – **M** a la carte
5.10/8.15 ⌕ 1.50.

X **Spinning Wheel**, 80 High St., HP1 3AQ, ☏ 64309 – **AE** **①** **VISA**
closed 25 and 26 December – **M** approx. 6.00 **st.** ⌕ 2.00.

AUSTIN-MORRIS-MG London Rd ☏ 51611
AUSTIN-MORRIS-MG-ROVER-TRIUMPH Redbourn Rd
☏ 63013
FIAT, VAUXHALL Two Waters Rd ☏ 51212

FORD London Rd ☏ 42841
TALBOT Frogmore Rd ☏ 51212
TOYOTA Leverstock Green ☏ 53522

HENLEY-IN-ARDEN Warw. **403** **404** O 27 – pop. 1,577 – ECD : Thursday – ☎ 056 42.
London 104 – Birmingham 15 – Stratford-upon-Avon 8 – Warwick 8.5.

XX **Beaudesert**, Birmingham Rd, B95 5QR, N : 1 m. on A 34 ☏ 2675 – **P.** **AE** **①** **VISA**
closed Sunday dinner, Monday and August – **M** (dinner only and Sunday lunch)
a la carte 8.80/10.50 **st.** ⌕ 1.90.

X **Le Filbert Cottage**, 64 High St., B95 5BX, ⊠ Solihull ☏ 2700, French rest.
closed Saturday, Sunday, 3 weeks July, 3 weeks at Christmas and Bank Holidays –
M (dinner only) a la carte 5.70/10.20 **t.** ⌕ 1.95.

AUSTIN-MORRIS 57 High St. ☏ 2543

HENLEY-ON-THAMES Oxon. **404** R 29 – pop. 11,431 – ECD : Wednesday – ☎ 049 12.
Envir.: Greys Court* *AC,* NW : 2 ½ m.
⛳ Huntercombe ☏ 049 18 (Nettlebed) 641 207, W : 6 m. on A 423.
🛈 West Hill House, 4 West St. ☏ 2626.
London 42 – Oxford 23 – Reading 9.

🏚 **Red Lion**, Hart St., RG9 2AR, ☎ 2161, ⇐ – 📺 🛏wc 🅿. 🆎 *VISA*
M a la carte 6.00/7.00 **t.** 🍾 1.65 – **28 rm** ⌷ 15.00/25.00 **st.**

✗✗ **The Rembrandt**, 58-60 Bell St., RG9 2BN, ☎ 4892 – 🔄 🆎 ⓪ *VISA*
M a la carte 6.65/10.50 **st.** 🍾 2.20.

✗ **Cherub**, 49-51 Market Pl., RG9 2AA, ☎ 3060 – 🆎 ⓪ *VISA*
closed Monday – **M** a la carte 5.25/8.95 **t.** 🍾 2.15.

AUSTIN-MORRIS-MG-ROVER-TRIUMPH-VOLSELEY
58 Reading Rd ☎ 77933
FIAT 66 Bell St. ☎ 3077

FORD 12 Station Rd ☎ 2955
PORSCHE 18 Reading Rd ☎ 4952
RENAULT 47 Station Rd ☎ 3555

HERBRANDSTON Dyfed **403** E 28 – see Milford Haven.

HEREFORD Heref. and Worc. **403 404** L 27 – pop. 46,503 – ECD : Thursday – ✆ 0432.
See : Cathedral✶✶ 12C-13C (the Mappa Mundi✶ 13C) **A A** – The Old House✶ 17C **A B. Envir. :**
Abbey Dore✶ (12C-17C) SW : 12 m. by A 465 **B**.

🛏18 Raven's Causeway, Wormsley ☎ 043271 (Canon Pyon) 219, NW : 6 m. by A 438 **B**.

ℤ Shirehall ☎ 68430.

London 133 – Birmingham 51 – Cardiff 56.

HEREFORD

Broad Street ————— **A** 7
Commercial Street ——— **A** 13
High Street —————— **A** 19
High Town —————— **A** 20

Bath Street ————— **A** 2
Belmont Road ———— **B** 5
Blue School Street —— **A** 6
Castle Street ———— **A** 9

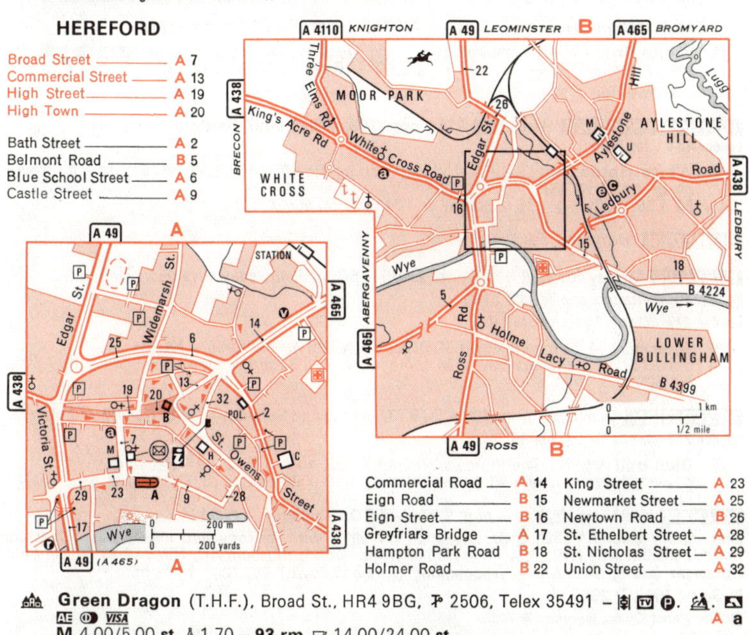

Commercial Road —— **A** 14
Eign Road —————— **B** 15
Eign Street————— **B** 16
Greyfriars Bridge —— **A** 17
Hampton Park Road **B** 18
Holmer Road———— **B** 22

King Street ————— **A** 23
Newmarket Street —— **A** 25
Newtown Road ——— **B** 26
St. Ethelbert Street — **A** 28
St. Nicholas Street — **A** 29
Union Street————— **A** 32

🏛 **Green Dragon** (T.H.F.), Broad St., HR4 9BG, ☎ 2506, Telex 35491 – ▮ 📺 🅿. ♨. 🔄
🆎 ⓪ *VISA*   **A a**
M 4.00/5.00 **st.** 🍾 1.70 – **93 rm** ⌷ 14.00/24.00 **st.**

🏛 **Oaklands**, 43 Bodenham Rd, HR1 2TP, ☎ 2775, 🚗 – 📺 🛏wc 🛁wc 🅿. *VISA*   **B c**
M (dinner only) 4.00 **t.** 🍾 1.25 – **20 rm** ⌷ 8.50/16.75.

🏛 **Merton**, 28 Commercial Rd, HR4 2BD, ☎ 65925 – 🛁wc 📞. 🔄   **A v**
M *(closed Sunday dinner)* 3.00/7.50 **t.** 🍾 1.80 – **10 rm** ⌷ 13.80/28.75 **t.**

🏛 **Litchfield Lodge**, Bodenham Rd, HR1 2TS, ☎ 3258 – 🛏wc 🅿   **B e**
M *(closed Sunday dinner)* 3.00/4.00 🍾 1.15 – **10 rm** ⌷ 5.50/15.00 – P 10.50.

🏠 **Alexander House**, 61 Whitecross Rd, HR4 0DQ, ☎ 4882 – 🅿   **B a**
8 rm ⌷ 8.25/15.00 **st.**

✗✗ **Greyfriars Garden**, 23 Greyfriars Av., HR4 0BE, ☎ 67274, 🚗 – 🅿. 🔄 🆎 ⓪ *VISA* **A r**
closed Sunday, Monday dinner and Bank Holidays – **M** a la carte 2.75/9.60 🍾 1.50.

AUSTIN-DAIMLER-JAGUAR-LAND ROVER-MORRIS-
MG-PRINCESS-ROVER-TRIUMPH 91/97 Widemarsh
St. ☎ 67611
AUSTIN-MORRIS-PRINCESS Callow G 92 ☎ 3074
AUSTIN-MORRIS-MG-ROVER-TRIUMPH, VANDEN
PLAS Commercial Rd ☎ 6456
BMW, TALBOT Blue School St. ☎ 2354
CITROEN 38 St. Martin St. ☎ 2545
DAF, LADA Kings Acre Rd ☎ 66974

DATSUN Muchgowarne ☎ 053186 (Bosbury) 605/606
/607
FIAT Bath St. ☎ 4134
FORD Commercial Rd ☎ 6494
HONDA, RELIANT Bridge St. ☎ 2341
LANCIA Whitestone ☎ 043 275 (Bartestree Cross) 464
PEUGEOT 101/105 St. Owen St. ☎ 6268
RENAULT White Cross Rd ☎ 2589
VAUXHALL Blackfriars St. ☎ 67441

HERNE BAY Kent **404** X 29 – pop. 24,350 – ECD : Thursday – ❸ 022 73.

Envir. : Reculver (Church twin towers★ *AC*) E : 3 m.

🖼 Council Offices, 1 Richmond St. ☎ 66031.

London 63 – Dover 24 – Maidstone 31 – Margate 12.

  🏠 St. George, Western Esplanade, CT6 8JA, ☎ 3776, ≼, 🚗 – 🛏 ❷ – **15 rm.**

  XX **La Chandelle,** 74 Charles St., CT6 5HW, ☎ 61126, French rest. – ❷. ⚏ *VISA*
    closed Sunday dinner and Monday – **M** a la carte 4.90/7.20 **t.** ⌐ 2.20.

AUSTIN-MORRIS-MG Kings Rd ☎ 3871

HERSTMONCEUX East Sussex **404** U 31 – pop. 2,036 – ❸ 032 181.

See : Castle 15C (home of the Royal Greenwich Observatory), site and grounds★★ *AC*.

Envir. : Michelham Priory (site★) *AC*, SW : 6 m.

London 63 – Eastbourne 12 – Hastings 14 – Lewes 16.

  XX ❀ **Sundial,** Gardner St., BN27 4LA, ☎ 2217, « Converted 16C cottage », French rest. –
    ❷. ① *VISA*
    closed Sunday dinner, Monday, last 2 weeks August, first 2 weeks September and January –
    M a la carte 7.20/9.50 ⌐ 1.95
    Spec. Petite bouillabaisse à la rouille, Suprême de saumon au Noilly, Cœur de filet d'agneau en feuilleté.

  at Boreham Street SE : 2 m. on A 271 – ✉ ❸ 032 81 Herstmonceux :

  🏠 **White Friars** (Best Western), BN27 4SE, ☎ 2355, 🚗 – 🛁wc 📺 ❷. ⚏ 🅰🅴 ① *VISA*
    closed January – **M** 4.25/5.25 **st.** ⌐ 2.40 – **15 rm** ⌿ 14.50/29.00 **st.**

HONDA Buckwell Hill ☎ 2211

HERTINGFORDBURY Herts. **404** T 28 – pop. 703 – ✉ ❸ 0992 Hertford.

London 26 – Luton 18.

  🏠 **White Horse Inn** (T.H.F.), Hertingfordbury Rd, SG14 2LB, ☎ 56791, 🚗 – 📺 🛁wc
    📶 ❷. ⚏ 🅰🅴 ① *VISA*
    M 4.25/5.50 **st.** ⌐ 1.65 – **30 rm** ⌿ 17.00/22.50 **st.**

HESLEDEN Durham – see Peterlee.

HESWALL Merseyside **403** K 24 – pop. 2,475 – ECD : Wednesday – ❸ 051 Liverpool.

🏌 Private Cottage Lane ☎ 342 2193.

London 210 – Chester 14 – Liverpool 10.

  XX **Squires,** 154 Telegraph Rd, L60 0AH, on A 540 ☎ 342 1966 – ⚏ *VISA*
    closed Sunday and Monday – **M** (dinner only and Saturday lunch) a la carte 4.90/7.50 **t.**
    ⌐ 1.30.

HEVERSHAM Cumbria – pop. 703 – ECD : Thursday and Saturday – ✉ ❸ 044 82 Milnthorpe.

London 259 – Kendal 6 – Lancaster 15.

  XX **Blue Bell** with rm, The Prince's Way, LA7 7EE, on A 6 ☎ 3159 – 🛁wc ❷
    closed Christmas Day – **M** 4.00/7.00 **st.** ⌐ 1.50 – **20 rm** ⌿ 13.00/19.50 **st.**

HEXHAM Northumb. **986** ⑲ – pop. 9,270 – ECD : Thursday – ❸ 0434.

See : Abbey Church★ 13C. **Envir. :** Hadrian's Wall★★ with its forts and milecastles (Chesters
Fort★, museum *AC*) NW : 5 ½ m. – Housesteads Fort★★, museum *AC*, NW : 14 m. – Derwent
Reservoir (site★) SE : 7 m. – Vindolanda★ (fort and town) *AC*, NW : 14 ½ m.

🏌 Spital Park ☎ 2057.

🖼 The Manor Office, Hallgates ☎ 5225.

London 304 – Carlisle 37 – Newcastle-upon-Tyne 21.

  🏠 Beaumont, Beaumont St., NE46 3LT, ☎ 2331 – 📺 🛁wc 📶wc. ⚏ ①
    20 rm ⌿ 10.00/20.00 **st.**

  at Wall N : 4 m. on B 6320 – ✉ Hexham – ❸ 043 481 Humshaugh :

  XX **Hadrian** with rm, NE46 4EE, ☎ 232, 🚗 – ❷
    M a la carte 6.00/8.10 ⌐ 3.00 – **8 rm** ⌿ 11.00/19.50 – P 16.00/17.50.

CITROEN ☎ 3615
DATSUN Haugh Lane ☎ 4527
FIAT Tyne Mills ☎ 3013
TALBOT West Rd ☎ 3861

VAUXHALL Parkwell ☎ 2411
VOLVO ☎ 2184
VW, AUDI-NSU Station Garage ☎ 2179

HEYSHAM Lancs. **986** ㉓ – pop. 41,908 (inc. Morecambe) – ECD : Wednesday – ❸ 0524.

🚢 to Isle of Man : Douglas (Manx Line) summer 1-3 daily ; winter : 9 weekly (3 h).

🏌 Trumacar Park ☎ 51011.

London 251 – Blackpool 33 – Carlisle 74 – Lancaster 8.

  Hotels and restaurant see : Lancaster E : 8 m.
                Morecambe NE : 3 m.

HIGHAM Derbs. 403 404 P 24 – pop. 4,909 (inc. Shirland) – ✉ ☎ 077 383 Alfreton. London 147 – Derby 16 – Nottingham 20 – Sheffield 20.

  XX **Higham Farm** with rm, Main Rd, Old Higham, DE5 6EH, ☏ 3812, ⌧, ⚲, ☇, park – TV ⊟WC ⋔WC ☎ P. ⊠ AE ⓪ VISA
    M a la carte 6.25/9.50 **s.** ⫲ 1.65 – **12 rm** ⊇ 11.55/22.55 **s.**

HIGH EASTER Essex 404 V 28 – see Chelmsford.

HIGH WYCOMBE Bucks. 404 R 29 – pop. 59,340 – ECD : Wednesday – ☎ 0494.
Envir. : Hughenden Manor* (site*, Disraeli Museum) *AC*, N : 1 m. – West Wycombe (Manor House* 18C, *AC*, St. Lawrence's Church : from the tower 74 steps, *AC*, ❋*) NW : 2 ½ m.
🛈 Council Offices, Queen Victoria Rd ☏ 26100.
London 34 – Aylesbury 17 – Oxford 26 – Reading 18.

  🏨 Falcon, High St., HP11 2AX, ☏ 22173 – P
    10 rm.

  ⋔ Clifton Lodge, 210 West Wycombe Rd, HP12 3AR, ☏ 29062, ☇ – P
    15 rm.

MICHELIN Branch, Unit E2, Knaves Beech Industrial Estate, Loudwater, HP 10 9QY, ☏ 06285 (Bourne End) 27472/5.

AUSTIN-DAIMLER-JAGUAR-MG-ROVER-TRIUMPH 111/121 London Rd ☏ 26180
CITROEN Naphill ☏ 024 024 (Naphill) 3270
DAF Lane End ☏ 881354
DATSUN, VAUXHALL London Rd ☏ 30021

FIAT-SAAB 125 Amersham Rd ☏ 23832
FORD Oxford Rd ☏ 23111
OPEL West Wycombe Rd ☏ 32545
RENAULT Desborough Av. ☏ 36331
TOYOTA Littleworth Rd, Downley ☏ 35811

HILLINGTON Norfolk 404 V 25 – pop. 230 – ✉ King's Lynn – ☎ 048 56.
London 112 – King's Lynn 7,5 – Norwich 39.

  ✗ **Ffolkes Arms,** Lynn Rd, PE31 6BJ, on A 148 ☏ 210 – P. ⊠ AE ⓪ VISA
    closed 25 and 26 December – **M** a la carte 5.90/9.35 **s.** ⫲ 2.40.

HILLMORTON Warw. 403 404 Q 26 – see Rugby.

HIMLEY Staffs. 403 404 N 26 – pop. 739 – ECD : Thursday – ✉ Dudley – ☎ 0902 Wombourne.
London 136 – Birmingham 15.

  🏨 **Himley House,** DY3 4LD, on A 449 ☏ 892468, ☇ – TV ⊟WC ⋔WC ☎ P. ⊠ AE ⓪ VISA
    M *(closed Sunday dinner)* 3.95/6.95 **t.** ⫲ 1.60 – **24 rm** ⊇ 11.00/22.25 **t.**

HINDON Wilts. 403 404 N 30 – pop. 534 – ECD : Saturday – ✉ Salisbury – ☎ 074 789.
London 107 – Bath 28 – Bournemouth 40 – Salisbury 15.

  🏨 **Lamb,** SP3 6DP, ☏ 225, ☇ – ⊟WC P. AE VISA
    closed 25 and 26 December – **M** 4.50/5.50 **t.** ⫲ 1.30 – **16 rm** ⊇ (dinner included) 12.50/30.00 **st.** – P 15.50/18.00 **st.**

HINTLESHAM Suffolk 404 X 27 – pop. 486 – ☎ 047 387.
London 73 – Colchester 18 – Ipswich 5.

  XXX ❀ **Hintlesham Hall,** IP8 3QP, ☏ 268, park – P. AE
    M 10.25/11.75 ⫲ 2.85
    Spec. Diplomate aux grenouilles, Aiguillettes de canard, Trio of fresh fruit sorbets.

HITCHIN Herts. 404 T 28 – pop. 25,610 – ECD : Wednesday – ☎ 0462.
🛈₈, 🛈₉ Beadlow Manor ☏ 0525 (Silsoe) 60800, NW : 9 m.
London 40 – Bedford 14 – Cambridge 26 – Luton 9.

  at Little Wymondley SE : 2 ½ m. by A 602 – ✉ Hitchin – ☎ 0438 Stevenage :

  🏨 **Blakemore,** SG4, 7JJ, ☏ 55821, Telex 825479, ⌧ heated, ☇ – ▯ TV P. ⌧. ⊠ AE ⓪ VISA
    M 6.50 **s.** ⫲ 2.00 – **70 rm** ⊇ 22.50/35.00 **s.** – P 35.50 **s.**

  🏨 **Redcoats Farmhouse** ⌖, SG4 7JL, ☏ 3500, QZ – ⊟WC ⋔WC P. AE VISA
    closed 1 week at Christmas – **M** *(closed Sunday and Monday)* a la carte 5.50/6.70 – **10 rm** ⊇ 12.00/17.10 **st.**

AUSTIN-DAIMLER-MG-ROVER-TRIOMPH Queen St. ☏ 50311
AUSTIN-MORRIS Walsworth Rd ☏ 4436

CITROEN High St., Graveley ☏ 0438 (Stevenage) 66177
SAAB The Heath, Breachwood Green ☏ 043 887 (Whitwell) 300

HOCKLEY HEATH West Midlands 403 404 O 26 – pop. 3,507 – ECD : Thursday – ✉ Solihull – ☎ 056 43 Lapworth.
London 108 – Birmingham 11 – Coventry 14 – Warwick 10.

  🏨 **Barn Motel,** Stratford Rd, B94 6NX, ☏ 2144 – TV ⊟WC ☎ P. ⊠ AE ⓪ VISA
    M approx. 4.50 **t.** – **36 rm** ⊇ 15.45/22.90 **t.**

HOGSTHORPE Lincs. 𝟦𝟢𝟦 U 24 – pop. 542 – ⊠ ☉ 0754 Skegness.
London 146 – Boston 30 – Grimsby 38 – Lincoln 48.

XX **Belmont** with rm, Thames St., PE25 5PT, ☏ 72288, 🚗 – 📺 🏢wc ℗
M *(closed Sunday dinner and Monday)* (dinner only Tuesday to Saturday) a la carte
5.70/9.00 ▯ 2.75 – ⊑ 1.25 – **4 rm** 10.00/14.00.

HOLFORD Somerset 𝟦𝟢𝟥 K 30 – pop. 283 – ⊠ Bridgwater – ☉ 027 874.
London 171 – Bristol 48 – Minehead 15 – Taunton 22.

🏨 **Alfoxton Park** ⑤. TA5 1SG, W: 1 ½ m., ☏ 211, ≤, 🍴, ⌇ heated, 🚗, park – 🛏wc
M 3.50/5.50 – **15 rm** ⊑ 14.25/24.25.

🏠 **Combe House** ⑤, TA5 1RZ, SW: 1 m. ☏ 382, « Country house atmosphere », 🍴, 🚗 –
🛏wc ℗. 🅰 ᴀᴇ 𝘝𝘐𝘚𝘈
M (bar lunch) approx. 6.00 t. ▯ 2.30 – **15 rm** ⊑ 10.50/21.00 t.

HOLKHAM Norfolk 𝟦𝟢𝟦 W 25 – pop. 272 – ⊠ ☉ 032 871 Wells-next-the-Sea.
See : Holkham Hall** (18C) *AC.*
London 124 – King's Lynn 32 – Norwich 38.

Hotels see : Blakeney E: 10 m.

HOLLAND-ON-SEA Essex 𝟦𝟢𝟦 X 28 – see Clacton-on-Sea.

HOLMBRIDGE West Yorks. 𝟦𝟢𝟥 𝟦𝟢𝟦 O 23 – pop. 1,083 – ⊠ Huddersfield – ☉ 048 489 Holm-
firth.
London 189 – Huddersfield 9 – Leeds 24 – Sheffield 24.

XX **Fernleigh House**, Bank Lane, HD7 1NG, ☏ 2603 – ℗
closed Saturday lunch, Sunday dinner, Monday and 20 July-11 August – **M** 3.25/4.75 t.
▯ 1.95.

HOLME UPON SPALDING MOOR Humberside – pop. 1,712 – ⊠ York – ☉ 0696 Market
Weighton.
London 205 – Doncaster 32 – Kingston-upon-Hull 22 – Leeds 36 – York 23.

✗ **Ye Olde Red Lion**, 25 Old Rd, YO4 4AD, ☏ 60220 – 📺 🏢wc ℗
closed Sunday dinner and Christmas Day – **M** (bar lunch) a la carte 4.65/7.10 st. ▯ 1.90.

HOLMFIELD West Yorks. – see Halifax.

HOLMROOK Cumbria – pop. 254 – ☉ 094 04.
London 311 – Kendal 59 – Workington 23.

♨ Lutwidge Arms, CA19 1UH, on A 595 ☏ 230, ⌇ – 🚗 ℗ – **10 rm.**

HOLNEST PARK Dorset 𝟦𝟢𝟥 𝟦𝟢𝟦 M 31 – see Sherborne.

HOLT Norfolk 𝟦𝟢𝟦 X 25 – pop. 2,532 – ECD : Thursday – ☉ 026 371.
London 124 – King's Lynn 34 – Norwich 22.

🏠 Feathers, 6 Market Pl., NR25 6BW, ☏ 2318 – 🛏wc ℗
23 rm.

↑ **Lawns**, 26 Station Rd, NR25 6BS, ☏ 3390, 🚗 – ℗
9 rm ⊑ 6.50/14.00 st.

HOLYHEAD (CAERGYBI) Gwynedd 𝟦𝟢𝟥 G 24 – pop. 11,530 – ECD : Tuesday – ☉ 0407.
Envir. : South Stack (cliffs*) W: 3 ½ m.
🚢 to Dun Laoghaire (Sealink) 1-4 daily (3 h 30 mn).
🛈 Tourist Information Centre, Marine Sq., Salt Island Approach ☏ 2622 (Easter-September).
London 270 – Birkenhead 94 – Cardiff 224 – Chester 83 – Shrewsbury 106 – Swansea 186.

Hotels and restaurant see : Rhosneigr SE : 13 m.
Trearddur Bay S : 2 ½ m.

HOLY ISLAND Northumb. – pop. 200 – ☉ 0289.
See : Castle (16C) ≤** *AC* – Priory* (ruins 12C) *AC.*
London 342 – Berwick-upon-Tweed 13 – Newcastle-upon-Tyne 59.

Hotels see : Berwick-upon-Tweed NW : 13 m.

HONITON Devon 𝟦𝟢𝟥 K 31 – pop. 5,072 – ECD : Thursday – ☉ 0404.
⛳ ☏ 3633, S : 1 m.
London 159 – Exeter 17 – Taunton 18.

🏠 **Monkton Court**, EX14 9QH, NE: 2 ¼ m. on A 30 ☏ 2309, 🚗 – 📺 🛏wc ℗. 🅰 ᴀᴇ ① 𝘝𝘐𝘚𝘈
M 5.00 t. ▯ 1.80 – ⊑ 0.80 – **8 rm** 9.70/21.40 t. – P 16.00/17.00 t.

HOPE Derbs. 403 404 O 23 – pop. 850 – ⊠ Sheffield (South Yorks.) – ✆ 0433 Hope Valley.
London 172 – Manchester 28 – Sheffield 15.

XX **House of Anton** with rm, 95 Castleton Rd, S30 2RD, on A 625 ℱ 20380 – ⇱wc **P.**
🄰 AE ⓄⒹ *VISA*
closed 1 January – **M** a la carte 7.50/12.75 **t.** ░ 2.50 – **5 rm** ⊇ 16.00/24.00 **t.**

HOPE COVE Devon 403 I 33 – see Salcombe.

HORLEY Surrey 404 T 30 – pop. 13,700 – ECD : Wednesday – ✆ 029 34.
London 27 – Brighton 26 – Royal Tunbridge Wells 22.

Plan of built up area see : Crawley

🏨 **Gatwick Park,** Povey Cross Rd, RH6 0BE, ℱ 5533, Telex 87440 – 🅿 TV **P.** 🏊 . 🄰 AE
Ⓓ *VISA*
See plan of Crawley   AY **a**
M 5.25/7.50 **st.** ░ 3.00 – ⊇ 3.00 – **176 rm** 20.00/25.25.

🏨 **Post House** (T.H.F.), Povey Cross Rd, RH6 0VA, ℱ 71621, Telex 877351, ⌁ heated –
🅿 TV ⇱wc ☏ ☖ **P.** 🏊 . 🄰
AE Ⓓ *VISA*
See plan of Crawley   AY **c**
M a la carte 6.90/9.70 **st.**
░ 1.65 – ⊇ 2.50 – **149 rm**
21.50/30.00.

🏨 **Europa Lodge** (County),
Longbridge Roundabout, RH6
0AB, ℱ 5599, Telex 877138 –
🅿 TV ⇱wc ☏ ☖ **P.** 🏊 . 🄰 AE
Ⓓ *VISA*
See plan of Crawley   AY **e**
M 4.80 **st.** ░ 1.55 – **110 rm**
⊇ 20.00/27.00 **t.**

🏨 **Chequers** (Thistle), Brighton
Rd, RH6 8PH, ℱ 6992, ⌁
heated – TV ⇱wc ☏ ☖ **P.** 🄰
AE Ⓓ *VISA*   **a**
M 4.50/6.05 **st.** ░ 1.65 – ⊇
3.00 – **78 rm** 21.00/27.00 **st.**
– P 29.75 **st.**

🏨 **Skylane,** Brighton Rd, RH6
8QG, ℱ 6971 – TV ⇱wc **P.**
🏊 . 🄰 AE Ⓓ *VISA*   See plan of
Crawley by A 23   AY
M 4.00 **t.** ░ 1.75 – ⊇ 2.50 –
59 rm 18.50/27.00 **st.**

🏠 **White House,** 24 Brighton
Rd, RH6 7HD, on A 23 ℱ
4322, 🚗 – TV **P.** 🄰 *VISA*   **c**
16 rm ⊇ 10.50/16.00 **s.**

AUSTIN-MORRIS-MG Massetts Rd ℱ
5176
PEUGEOT Keppers Corner Burstow
ℱ 0342 (Copthorne) 712017
RENAULT 61 Brighton Rd ℱ 72566

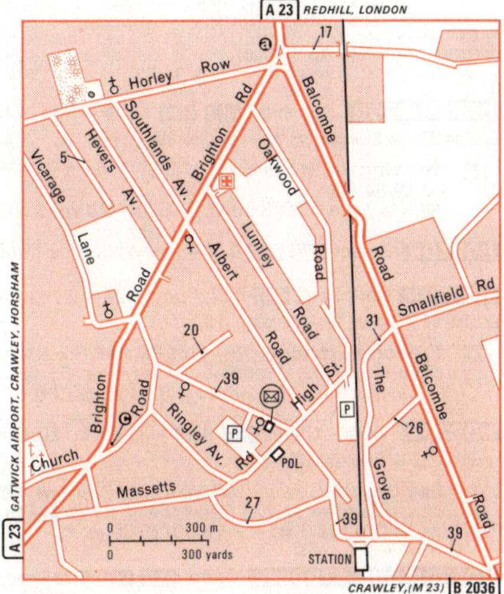

HORNBY Lancs. – pop. 695 – ⊠ Lancaster – ✆ 0468.
London 251 – Kendal 20 – Lancaster 8.

🏠 **Castle,** Main St., LA2 8JT, ℱ 21204 – TV ⇱wc **P.** 🄰 AE Ⓓ *VISA*
M *(closed Sunday dinner)* 4.00/9.50 **st.** – **12 rm** ⊇ 12.00/22.50 **st.**

HORNCASTLE Lincs. 404 T 24 – pop. 4,102 – ECD : Wednesday – ✆ 065 82.
🄸 Town Hall, Boston Rd ℱ 3513.
London 140 – Lincoln 21.

🏨 **Rodney,** North St., LN9 5DX, ℱ 3583 – TV **P.**
M *(closed Sunday dinner)* (bar lunch) approx. 3.50 **t.** ░ 1.50 – **15 rm** ⊇ 8.00/16.00 **t.**

MORRIS Fulletby ℱ 065 84 (Tetford) 217   RENAULT Lincoln Rd ℱ 2451
FORD Lincoln Rd ℱ 2203

HORNING Norfolk 404 Y 25 – pop. 975 – ⊠ Norwich – ✆ 0692.
London 122 – Great Yarmouth 17 – Norwich 11.

🏨 **Petersfield House** (Mt. Charlotte) 🦢, Lower St., NR12 8PF, ℱ 630741, 🚗 – TV
⇱wc ☏ **P.** 🄰 AE Ⓓ *VISA*
M 4.25/6.00 **t.** ░ 2.00 – ⊇ 2.65 – **16 rm** 15.80/23.10.

HORNS CROSS Devon **403** H 31 – pop. 170 – ECD : Wednesday – ✉ Bideford – ☎ 023 75.
London 237 – Barnstaple 15 – Exeter 48.

    Hoops Inn, EX39 5DL, W: ¾ m. on A 39 ☏ 222 – TV ⌂wc ☎ P
    closed November – **M** 3.85/5.75 **st.** ⌂ 1.90 – **14 rm** ⌂ 11.00/20.80 **st.** – P 15.55/
    20.20 **st.**

    Foxdown Manor , EX39 5PJ, S: 1 m. ☏ 325, ⩽, « Country house atmosphere »,
    , heated, , , park – ⌂wc P.
    Easter-mid November – **M** (bar lunch) approx. 6.50 ⌂ 1.30 – **6 rm** ⌂ 12.00/22.00 –
    P 17.15.

    at Fairy Cross E: 2½ m. off A 39 – ✉ Bideford – ☎ 023 75 Horns Cross:

    Portledge , EX39 5BX, ☏ 262, ⩽, « Part 13C and 17C manor house », , heated,
    , park – P
    Easter-October – **M** (buffet lunch) 2.95/7.95 **t.** ⌂ 1.35 – **35 rm** ⌂ 12.50/29.00 **t.**

HORSFORTH West Yorks. **986** ⑧ – see Leeds.

HORSHAM West Sussex **404** S 30 – pop. 25,800 – ECD : Monday and Thursday – ☎ 0403.
 Mannings Heath ☏ 65224, SE: 3 m. A 281.
London 39 – Brighton 23 – Guildford 20 – Lewes 25 – Worthing 20.

    Ye Olde King's Head, 35 Carfax, RH12 1EG, ☏ 3126 – TV ⌂wc ⌂wc ☎ P.
    VISA
    M a la carte 5.00/9.10 **t.** ⌂ 1.65 – **29 rm** ⌂ 13.00/21.50 **t.**

AUSTIN-MORRIS-MG Plummers Plain ☏ 76244
AUSTIN-MORRIS-MG-ROVER-TRIUMPH, VANDEN
PLAS Springfield Rd ☏ 4311
CITROEN Guildford Rd ☏ 61293
OPEL, VAUXHALL Broadbridge Heath ☏ 6101
PEUGEOT Lyons Corner, Slinfold ☏ 0403 (Slinfold)
790766
RENAULT 108 Crawley Rd ☏ 2274
ROVER-TRIUMPH North St. ☏ 3291
VOLVO 51 North Par. ☏ 60281

HORSINGTON Somerset **403** **404** M 30 – pop. 443 – ✉ ☎ 096 37 Templecombe.
London 123 – Bournemouth 41 – Bristol 39 – Yeovil 14.

    Horsington House , BA8 0EG, on A 357 ☏ 721, ⩽, , park – ⌂wc ⌂wc ☎ P.
    AE ⓪ VISA
    M a la carte 6.00/8.65 **st.** ⌂ 2.20 – **23 rm** ⌂ 15.00/24.00 **st.**

HORTON Dorset **403** **404** O 31 – see Wimborne Minster.

HORTON Northants. **404** R 27 – pop. 424 – ✉ ☎ 0604 Northampton.
London 66 – Bedford 18 – Northampton 6.

    French Partridge, Newport Pagnell Rd, NN7 2AP, ☏ 870033 – P
    closed Sunday, Monday, 10 days at Easter, 3 weeks July-August and 2 weeks at
    Christmas – **M** (dinner only) 8.50 **st.** ⌂ 1.60.

HORTON West. Glam. **403** H 29 – ☎ 044 120 Gower.
London 212 – Swansea 16.

    Sea Beach, Gower, SA3 1LJ, ☏ 252, ⩽, – ⌂wc ⌂ ☎ P
    closed October and 23 December-February – **M** (bar lunch) 2.00/5.00 **st.** ⌂ 1.50 – **21 rm**
    ⌂ 11.00/24.00 **st.** – P 16.00/20.00 **st.**

HORTON-CUM-STUDLEY Oxon. **403** **404** Q 28 – pop. 432 – ECD : Wednesday – ✉ Oxford –
☎ 086 735 Stanton St. John.
London 57 – Aylesbury 23 – Oxford 7.

    Studley Priory , OX9 1AZ, ☏ 203, Telex 847777, « Converted priory in park », – TV
    ⌂wc ⌂wc ☎ P. AE ⓪ VISA
    M a la carte 8.20/11.10 **st.** ⌂ 2.00 – **19 rm** ⌂ 21.65/41.95 **st.**

HOUGHTON CONQUEST Beds. **404** S 27 – see Bedford.

HOVE East Sussex **404** T 31 – see Brighton and Hove.

HOVINGHAM North Yorks. – pop. 305 – ECD : Thursday – ✉ York – ☎ 065 382.
London 235 – Middlesbrough 36 – York 25.

    Worsley Arms, YO6 4LA, ☏ 234, – ⌂wc ☎ P. VISA
    closed Christmas Day – **M** 6.50/7.50 **st.** ⌂ 2.00 – **14 rm** ⌂ 11.75/20.25 **st.**

HOWDEN Humberside **986** ㉔ – pop. 2,651 – ECD : Thursday – ☎ 0430.
See : St. Peter's Church* 12C-14C.
London 196 – Kingston-upon-Hull 23 – Leeds 37 – York 22.

    Bowmans, Bridgegate, DN14 7JG, ☏ 30805 – TV ⌂wc P
    M *(closed Sunday dinner to non-residents)* 4.20/5.20 **t.** – **13 rm** ⌂ 15.50/22.00.

HOYLAKE Merseyside 408 K 23 – pop. 25,700 – ECD : Wednesday – ☺ 051 Liverpool.
ⁱ₈ Carr Lane ☏ 632 2956.
London 226 – Chester 22 – Liverpool 10.

  🏛 **Stanley,** King's Gap, Wirral, L47 2AH, ☏ 632 3311 – 🛏wc 🏠 ☻
    M 3.20/4.30 **t.** 🍾 1.45 – **16 rm** 🍽 11.25/22.40 **t.**

HUDDERSFIELD West Yorks. 408 404 O 23 – pop. 131,190 – ECD : Wednesday – ☺ 0484.
ⁱ₈ Meltham ☏ 850227, W : 5 m. – ⁱ₈ Crosland Heath ☏ 653216, W : 3 m. – ⁱ₉ Maple St., off
Somerset Rd ☏ 22304.
ℹ High St. Buildings, Albion St. ☏ 23133.
London 191 – Bradford 11 – Leeds 15 – Manchester 25 – Sheffield 26.

  🏛 Pennine President, Ainley Top, HD3 3RH, NW : 2 ½ m. at junction A 629 and M 62,
    exit 24 ☏ 0422 (Elland) 75431, Telex 517346 – ⒮ 📺 🛏wc ☎ ♿ ☻. ⚓
    118 rm.

  🏛 **George** (T.H.F.), St. George's Sq., HD1 1JA, ☏ 25444 – ⒮ 📺 🛏wc ☎. ⚓. ⚡ AE ⓪
    VISA
    M 4.50/5.05 **st.** 🍾 1.65 – **62 rm** 🍽 14.00/23.50 **st.**

  XXX **Quo Vadis,** 4 St. Peter's St., HD1 1LJ, ☏ 35440, Italian rest. – ⚡ ⓪
    closed Sunday and Bank Holidays – **M** a la carte 4.80/8.20 **t.** 🍾 1.80.

    at Farnley Tyas S : 5 ½ m. off A 616 – ✉ ☺ 0484 Huddersfield :

  X **Golden Cock Inn,** HD4 6UN, ☏ 661979 – ☻
    closed Sunday dinner and Monday lunch – **M** a la carte 5.00/8.55 **t.** 🍾 2.50.

ALFA-ROMEO, PEUGEOT Northgate ☏ 20822
AUSTIN-MG-ROVER-TRIUMPH 100 Wakefield Rd ☏ 35341
AUSTIN-DAIMLER-JAGUAR-MORRIS-MG-TRIUMPH Southgate ☏ 29461
BEDFORD, VAUXHALL 386 Leeds Rd ☏ 23191
BMW Somerset Rd ☏ 25435
CITROEN Scar Lane ☏ 656164
DATSUN Northgate ☏ 35251

FORD Southgate ☏ 29675
LANCIA Lockwood Rd ☏ 29344
OPEL Northgate ☏ 20566
RENAULT 4 Queensgate ☏ 39351
ROVER-TRIUMPH 100 Wakefield Rd ☏ 35341
SAAB Kirkheaton ☏ 29754
TOYOTA Fartown ☏ 23201
VOLVO Northgate ☏ 31362
VW, AUDI-NSU Bradford Rd ☏ 42001

HULL Humberside 986 ㉔ – see Kingston-upon-Hull.

HUNGERFORD Berks. 408 404 P 29 – pop. 4,083 – ECD : Thursday – ☺ 048 86.
Envir. : Littlecote House* (Tudor) *AC*, NW : 3 ½ m.
ⁱ₈ Chaddleworth ☏ 048 82 (Chaddleworth) 574, N : 2 ½ m.
London 74 – Bristol 57 – Oxford 28 – Reading 26 – Southampton 46.

  🏛 **Bear at Hungerford,** Charnham St., RG17 0EL, on A 4 ☏ 2512, ⚔ – 📺 🛏wc 🏠wc ☎
    ☻. ⚓. ⚡ AE ⓪ *VISA*
    M 5.35/6.25 **st.** 🍾 1.80 – **25 rm** 🍽 15.00/26.00 **st.**

BMW Bath Rd ☏ 2772
FIAT Bath Rd ☏ 2033

FORD 17/19 Bridge St. ☏ 2279

HUNSTANTON Norfolk 404 V 25 – pop. 3,911 – ECD : Thursday – ☺ 048 53.
ℹ Le Strange Terrace ☏ 2610.
London 120 – Cambridge 60 – Norwich 45.

  🏛 Le Strange Arms, Golf Course Rd, PE36 6JJ, N : 1 m. off A 149 ☏ 2810, ≼, ⚔ – 🛏wc ☻
    29 rm.

AUSTIN-MORRIS-MG-ROVER-TRIUMPH 12 Kings Lynn Rd ☏ 33435

CITROEN, FORD Church St. ☏ 2508
VAUXHALL Westgate ☏ 2842

HUNSTRETE Avon 408 404 M 29 – see Bath.

HUNTINGDON Cambs. 404 T 26 – pop. 16,557 (inc. Godmanchester) – ECD : Wednesday – ☺ 0480.
See : Cromwell Museum – All Saints' Church (interior*). **Envir. :** Hinchingbrooke House* (Tudor mansion-school) W : 1 m. – Ramsey (Abbey Gatehouse* 15C) NE : 11 ½ m.
London 69 – Bedford 21 – Cambridge 16.

  🏛 **Old Bridge,** 1 High St., PE18 6TQ, ☏ 52681 – 📺 🛏wc ☎ ☻. ⚡ AE ⓪ *VISA*
    closed Christmas Day – **M** a la carte 6.35/8.60 **s.** – **25 rm** 🍽 17.00/24.75.

  🏛 **George** (T.H.F.), George St., PE18 6AB, ☏ 53096 – 📺 🛏wc ☎ ☻. ⚓. ⚡ AE ⓪ *VISA*
    M 4.50/5.25 **st.** 🍾 1.65 – **21 rm** 🍽 13.50/22.50 **st.**

AUSTIN-MORRIS-LAND ROVER-TRIUMPH 13 Hartford Rd ☏ 56441

BMW, VAUXHALL Brookside ☏ 52694

Do not use yesterday's maps for today's journey.

HURLEY-ON-THAMES Berks. **404** R 29 – pop. 2,203 – ⊠ Maidenhead – ✆ 062 882 Littlewick Green.
London 38 – Oxford 26 – Reading 12.

   XXX **Ye Olde Bell** with rm, High St., SL6 5LX, ✆ 4244, 🐎 – 📺 ➰wc ☎ 🚗 🅿. AE ① VISA
        M a la carte 12.00/13.75 **t.** – ☕ 3.00 – **11 rm** 21.00/35.00 **t.**

HURST GREEN Lancs. – pop. 1,100 – ECD : Wednesday – ⊠ Whalley – ✆ 025 486 Stonyhurst.
London 236 – Blackburn 12 – Burnley 13 – Preston 12.

    🏠 **Shireburn Arms** ⊰, BB6 9QJ, ✆ 208, « Tastefully furnished part 18C house », 🐎 – 📺
      ➰wc 🅿. VISA
      M (dinner only and Bank Holiday lunch) a la carte 4.45/7.60 **s.** 🍾 1.70 – **11 rm** ☕ 7.50/
      24.00 **s.**

HUSBANDS BOSWORTH Leics. **403** **404** Q 26 – pop. 820 – ⊠ Lutterworth – ✆ 0858 Market Harborough.
London 236 – Birmingham 40 – Leicester 14 – Northampton 17.

   XX **Fernie Lodge,** Berridges Lane, LE17 6LE, ✆ 880551 – 🅿
      closed Saturday lunch, Sunday, Monday and Bank Holidays – **M** 5.75/7.00 **t.**

HWLFFORDD Dyfed – see Haverfordwest.

HYTHE Kent **404** X 30 – pop. 11,959 – ECD : Wednesday – ✆ 0303.
See : St. Leonard's Church (≼* from the churchyard) – Canal.
🏌 Princes Parade ✆ 67441.
✈ Lydd Airport : ✆ 0679 (Lydd) 20401, SW : 13 m.
London 67 – Folkestone 4 – Hastings 33 – Maidstone 30.

   🏨 **Imperial** ⊰, Princes Par., CT21 6AE, ✆ 67441, ≼, 🍽, 🏊, 🏌, 🐎, park – 🛗 🅿. ⚘. 🔲
      AE ① VISA
      M 6.00/7.00 **t.** – **87 rm** ☕ 15.50/31.00 **t.** – P 23.00/26.50 **t.**

   🏨 **Stade Court,** West Par., CT21 6DT, ✆ 68263, ≼ – 🛗 ➰wc ☎ 🅿. 🔲 AE ① VISA
      M 5.00/5.75 **t.** 🍾 2.40 – **30 rm** ☕ 12.50/26.60 **t.** – P 15.45/19.30 **s.**

   XX Gambrinos, 74 High St., CT21 5AL, ✆ 60571.
AUSTIN-MORRIS High St. ✆ 69335   SAAB 215 Seabrook Rd ✆ 38467
PEUGEOT The Green ✆ 60511

IBSLEY Hants. **403** **404** O 31 – see Ringwood.

IDDESLEIGH Devon **403** H 31 – ⊠ Winkleigh – ✆ 083 781 Hatherleigh.
London 229 – Barnstaple 18 – Exeter 28 – Plymouth 40.

   ⚲ **Duke of York** ⊰, ✆ 253 – ➰wc 🚿wc 🅿. 🔲 AE
      M *(closed Sunday dinner)* (buffet lunch) 6.00 **s.** 🍾 1.25 – **8 rm** ☕ 5.00/14.00 **s.**

ILCHESTER Somerset **403** **404** L 30 – pop. 1,685 – ECD : Saturday – ⊠ Yeovil – ✆ 0935.
London 132 – Bristol 36 – Taunton 27 – Yeovil 5.

   🏠 **Northover Manor,** BA22 8LD, ✆ 840447, ⊰, 🐎 – ➰wc 🚗 🅿. 🔲 AE ① VISA
      closed Christmas – **M** *(closed Sunday)* a la carte 4.70/6.75 🍾 1.50 – **7 rm** ☕ 7.50/15.00.

ILFRACOMBE Devon **403** H 30 – pop. 8,360 – ECD : Thursday – ✆ 0271.
See : Tors Walks*, Capstone Hill ≼*.
🏌 Hele Bay ✆ 62176, E : 1 m. – ⛴ to Isle of Lundy (Lundy Co.) 1-3 weekly (2 h 30 mn).
🛈 The Promenade ✆ 63001.
London 223 – Exeter 54 – Taunton 61.

   🏠 Harleigh House, Wilder Rd, EX34 9AE, ✆ 63850 – ➰wc – **29 rm.**
   🏠 **St. Helier,** Hillsborough Rd, EX34 9QQ, ✆ 63862, 🐎 – 🚗 🅿
      May-October – **M** (bar lunch) approx. 3.80 **s.** 🍾 2.00 – **35 rm** ☕ 7.00/16.00 **s.** – P 12.80/
      13.80 **s.**

      at Berrynarbor E : 3 m. off A 399 – ⊠ Ilfracombe – ✆ 027 188 Combe Martin :

   🏡 Seacliffe Country, EX34 9SP, ✆ 3273, 🐎 – 🅿 – **10 rm.**

      at Lee W : 3 ¼ m. off B 3231 – ⊠ ✆ 0271 Ilfracombe :

   🏨 Lee Bay, EX34 8LR, ✆ 63503, ≼, 🏊 heated, 🐎, park – ➰wc 🅿 – **54 rm.**

RENAULT Northfield Rd ✆ 62075   TALBOT West Down ✆ 63104

ILKLEY West Yorks. 𝟵𝟴𝟲 ㉓ – pop. 10,930 – ECD : Wednesday – ☎ 0943.

ᴵ⁸ Myddleton ℙ 607277 and 600214 – ₉ Ben Rhydding, High Wood ℙ 608759.

London 210 – Bradford 13 – Harrogate 17 – **Leeds** 16 – Preston 46.

- **Craiglands** (T.H.F.), Cowpasture Rd. LS29 8RQ, ℙ 607676, Telex 51137, ✗, 🚗 – ▮ TV
  ⌸wc ☎ & 🅿. 🏊 🔼 AE ⓪ VISA
  M 3.75/5.15 **st.** ⌁ 1.65 – **73 rm** ⌷ 18.00/26.50 **st.**

- **Cow and Calf**, Moor Top, LS29 8BT, SE : 1 ½ m. ℙ 607335 – TV ⌸wc 🔥 🅿. 🔼 AE
  ⓪ VISA
  M (bar lunch *Monday to Saturday*) a la carte 2.25/7.65 **t.** ⌁ 1.90 – **9 rm** ⌷ 13.00/22.00 **t.**

- Crescent (Crest), Brook St., LS29 8DG, ℙ 600012 – ⌸wc ☎ 🅿
  21 rm.

- ✗✗✗ ✿✿ **Box Tree Cottage**, Church St., LS29 9DR, ℙ 608484, « Tasteful decor » – 🔼 AE ⓪
  VISA
  closed 2 weeks August, 1 week February and Bank Holidays – **M** (dinner only) 14.00
  Spec. Dariole de champignons et truffes, Noisette d'agneau Box Tree, Marquise au chocolat et cognac.

AUSTIN-DAIMLER-JAGUAR-ROVER-TRIUMPH,   TALBOT   Skipton Rd ℙ 608966
ROLLS ROYCE-BENTLEY   Ben Rydding ℙ 601515   VAUXHALL   Bradford Rd, Menston ℙ 0943 (Menston)
MORRIS   Skipton Rd ℙ 607606   75147

ILLOGAN Cornwall 𝟰𝟬𝟯 E 33 – pop. 10,304 – ✉ Redruth – ☎ 0209 Portreath.

- ✗✗ **Aviary Court**, Mary's Well, TR16 4QZ, ℙ 842256, 🚗 – 🅿
  closed Sunday dinner – **M** (dinner only and Sunday lunch) a la carte 4.15/7.80 **t.** ⌁ 1.75.

ROVER-TRIUMPH   Bridge ℙ 842 230   VAUXHALL   Highway ℙ 215502

IMMINGHAM Humberside 𝟰𝟬𝟰 T 23 – pop. 6,030 – ☎ 0469.

Envir. : Thornton Abbey (ruins 14C) : the Gatehouse★ *AC*, NW : 8 m. – Thornton Curtis (St. Lawrence's Church★ : Norman and Gothic) NW : 10 m.

⛴ Shipping connections with the Continent : to Gothenburg (Tor Line).

London 181 – Grimsby 9 – Lincoln 38 – Scunthorpe 22.

- Pelham, Washdyke Lane, DN40 2HL, ℙ 74191 – TV ⌸wc ☎ 🅿
  10 rm.

FORD   Stallingborough Rd ℙ 73677   VAUXHALL   Pelham Rd ℙ 76276

INGATESTONE Essex 𝟰𝟬𝟰 V 28 – pop. 5,420 – ECD : Wednesday – ☎ 027 75.

London 27 – Chelmsford 6.

at *Margaretting* NE : 2 ¼ m. off A 12 – ✉ ☎ 027 75 Ingatestone :

- ✗✗✗✗ **Furze Hill**, Ivy Barn Lane, CM4 0EW, ℙ 4755, « Tastefully converted Victorian house »,
  ⌿ heated, 🚗, Dancing (Friday and Saturday) – 🅿. 🔼 AE ⓪ VISA
  closed Sunday dinner and Bank Holidays – **M** a la carte 6.90/11.00 **t.** ⌁ 2.15.

INSTOW Devon 𝟰𝟬𝟯 H 30 – see Bideford.

IPSWICH Suffolk 𝟰𝟬𝟰 X 27 – pop. 123,312 – ECD : Monday and Wednesday – ☎ 0473.

See : St. Margaret's Church (the roof★) X A – Christchurch Mansion (museum★) X B – Ancient House★ 16C X D – Pykenham House★ 16C X E.

ᴵ⁸, ₉ Purdis Heath ℙ 78941, E : 3 m. by Bucklesham Rd Z – ᴵ⁸ Rushmere Heath ℙ 77109 Y.

🛈 Town Hall, Princes St. ℙ 55851.

London 73 – Norwich 42.

Plan on next page

- **Marlborough**, 73 Henley Rd, IP1 3SP, ℙ 57677, 🚗 – TV ⌸wc ☎ 🅿. 🔼 AE ⓪ VISA   Y e
  M 5.00 **t.** ⌁ 2.60 – **25 rm** ⌷ 15.25/28.00 **t.**

- **Post House** (T.H.F.), London Rd, IP2 0UA, SW : 2 ¼ m. on A 12 ℙ 212313, Telex 987150,
  ⌿ heated – TV ⌸wc ☎ 🅿. 🏊 🔼 AE ⓪ VISA   Z a
  M 4.50/5.15 **st.** ⌁ 1.50 – ⌷ 2.25 – **118 rm** 18.00/25.50.

- **Great White Horse** (T.H.F.), Tavern St., IP1 3AH, ℙ 56558 – TV ⌸wc ☎. 🏊. 🔼 AE
  ⓪ VISA   X n
  M (Carvery rest.) 4.75 **st.** ⌁ 1.65 – **55 rm** ⌷ 13.00/22.00 **st.**

- Gables, 17 Park Rd, IP1 3SX, ℙ 54252, 🚗 – 🅿   Y r
  12 rm ⌷ 6.00/12.00 **s.**

- ✗ **Rosie's Place**, 200 St. Helens St., IP4 2LH, ℙ 55236, Bistro – AE   YZ s
  closed 23 to end of each month – **M** (dinner only) a la carte 4.95/5.55 ⌁ 1.30.

at *Belstead* SW : 2 ½ m. – ✉ ☎ 0473 Ipswich :

- **Belstead Brook** 🐦, Belstead Rd, IP2 9HB, ℙ 216456, Telex 987674, 🚗, park – TV
  ⌸wc ☎ 🅿. 🏊. 🔼 AE ⓪ VISA   Z u
  M a la carte 4.60/12.00 – **24 rm** ⌷ 20.00/30.00 **s.**

P.T.O. →

IPSWICH

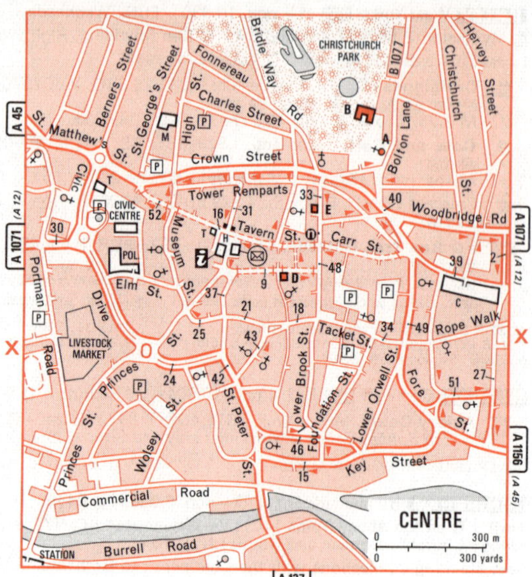

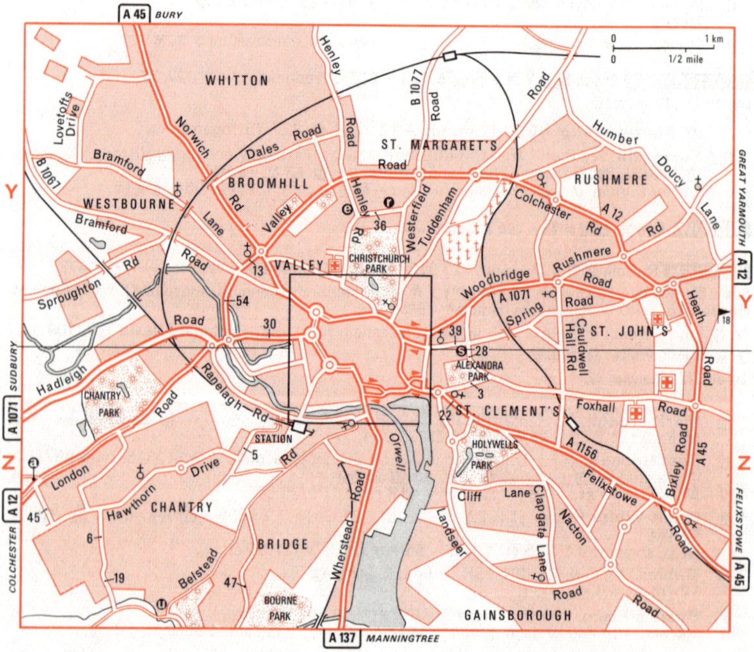

at Copdock SW: 4 m. on A 12 – z – ✉ Ipswich – ☎ 047 386 Copdock:

🏨 **Copdock House** (Best Western), London Rd, IP8 3JD, ☎ 444, 🚗 – 📺 ⛱WC

📞 **P.** 🏊 ⬛ AE ① **VISA**

closed 25 – 26 December – **M** 4.50/7.00 **s.** 🍷 1.65 – **47 rm** ⬚ 15.25/22.75 **s.**

AUSTIN-MG 935 Woodbridge Rd ☎ 76929
AUSTIN-MG-WOLSELEY Barrack Lane ☎ 54202
AUSTIN-DAIMLER-JAGUAR, ROLLS ROYCE-BENTLEY
Majors Corner ☎ 52271
CITROEN, VOLVO Derby Rd ☎ 70 101
DATSUN 176/182 Norwich Rd ☎ 53173
FIAT Burrel Road ☎ 210321
FORD Princes St. ☎ 55401
MAZDA, POLSKI Fuchsia Lane ☎ 74535

MORRIS-MG-WOLSELEY Felixstowe Rd ☎ 75431
PEUGEOT 162/166 London Rd ☎ 54461
RENAULT 301/305 Norwich Rd ☎ 43021
ROVER-TRIUMPH 88 Princes St. ☎ 214231
SAAB Dales Rd ☎ 42547
VAUXHALL St. Helens St. ☎ 56363
TOYOTA 301/5 Woodbridge Rd ☎ 76927
VW, AUDI Knightsdale Rd ☎ 43044
VW, AUDI St. Helen St. ☎ 50545

IVER HEATH Bucks. **404** S 29 – pop. 5,200 – ⊗ 028 16 Fulmer.
London 21 – Reading 25.

⤳ **Bridgettine Convent,** Fulmer Common Rd, SL0 0NR, NW: 1 ½ m. off A 412 ☎ 2645,
🚗 – **P.** 🅰 AE ⓪ VISA
18 rm ⌨ 5.50/11.00 **st.**

IVINGHOE Bucks. **404** S 28 – pop. 949 – ⊠ Leighton Buzzard – ⊗ 0296 Cheddington.
₁₈ ☎ 668881.
London 42 – Aylesbury 9 – Luton 11.

XXX King's Head (T.H.F.), Station Rd, LU7 9EB, ☎ 668388 – **P.**

JAMESTON Dyfed **403** F 29 – see Manorbier.

JEVINGTON East Sussex **404** U 31 – see Eastbourne.

KELLING Norfolk **404** X 25 – pop. 571 – ⊠ ⊗ 026 371 Holt.
London 127 – Cromer 8,5 – Norwich 25.

🏠 **Kelling Park** ⌖, Weybourne Rd, NR25 7ER, S: 1 ½ m. ☎ 2235, ≼, « Gardens and
aviary », park – ⌨wc **P.** 🅰 AE VISA
M a la carte 4.70/9.35 **t.** ⌁1.55 – **7 rm** ⌨ 9.00/18.90 **t.**

*Do not always take your holidays in **July** or **August**;*
some districts are more beautiful in other months.

KENDAL Cumbria **986** ⑲⑳ – pop. 21,596 – ECD : Thursday – ⊗ 0539.
See : Abbot Hall Art Gallery (Museum of Lakeland Life and Industry*) *AC.*
Envir. : Levens Hall* (Elizabethan) *AC* and Topiary Garden* *AC*, SW: 5 ½ m.
₁₈ The Heights ☎ 24079 – ₉ The Riggs, Sedbergh, E: 9 m.
🛈 Town Hall, ☎ 23649 ext 253.
London 264 – Bradford 64 – Burnley 62 – **Carlisle 49** – Lancaster 21 – **Leeds 71** – **Middlesbrough 80** – **Newcastle-
upon-Tyne 94** – Preston 44 – Sunderland 89.

🏨 Woolpack (Swallow), Stricklandgate, LA9 4ND, ☎ 23852, Group Telex 53168 – 📺
⌨wc 🛁wc ☎ ⅙ **P.** ⛵
67 rm.

🏨 **County** (Open House), Station Rd, LA9 6BT, ☎ 22461 – ⋕ 📺 ⌨wc ☎ **P.** 🅰 AE ⓪ VISA
closed 24 to 27 December – **M** *(closed Saturday lunch and Bank Holidays for lunch)*
3.10/5.00 ⌁1.60 – **31 rm** ⌨ 12.50/24.00 **st.**

🏠 **Shenstone Country** ⌖, LA8 8AA, S: 2 m. on A 6 ☎ 21023 🚗 – **P.** AE
closed Christmas – **M** *(closed lunch Monday to Friday)* approx. 3.75 **st.** ⌁ 1.50 – **13 rm**
⌨ 8.50/17.00 **st.**

at Meal Bank NE: 2 m. off A 685 – ⊠ ⊗ 0539 Kendal :

🏠 **High Laverock House** ⌖, LA8 9DJ, ☎ 23082, 🚗 – ⌨wc **P.**
M (bar lunch) a la carte 5.40/7.10 **t.** ⌁1.85 – **8 rm** ⌨ 12.00/19.50 **t.**

ALFA-ROMEO, MERCEDES-BENZ, VAUXHALL Ings
☎ 0539 (Staveley) 442
AUSTIN-MORRIS-MG Sandes Av. ☎ 21695
AUSTIN-DAIMLER-JAGUAR-MORRIS-MG-ROVER-
TRIUMPH 84/92 Highgate ☎ 23610

DATSUN, VAUXHALL Sandes Av. ☎ 24420
FIAT 113 Stricklandgate ☎ 20967
FORD Kendal ☎ 23534
PEUGEOT Mint Close ☎ 24396
VW, AUDI-NSU, PORSCHE Longpool ☎ 24331

KENILWORTH Warw. **403** **404** P 26 – pop. 19,670 – ECD : Monday – ⊗ 0926.
See : Castle* (12C) *AC.*
₁₈ Crew Lane ☎ 54296.
🛈 11 Smalley Pl. ☎ 52595.
London 102 – Birmingham 19 – Coventry 5 – Warwick 5.

🏩 **De Montfort** (De Vere), The Square, CV8 1ED, ☎ 55944, Telex 311012 – ⋕ 📺 **P.** ⛵
🅰 AE ⓪ VISA
M 5.00 **st.** ⌁1.75 – **97 rm** ⌨ 22.00/36.50 **st.**

🏠 **Clarendon House,** 6-8 High St., CV8 1LZ, ☎ 54694 – ⌨wc 🛁 **P.** 🅰 AE ⓪ VISA
M (lunch by arrangement) approx. 4.75 ⌁1.30 – **13 rm** ⌨ 9.00/17.00.

KENILWORTH

  XX **Bosquet,** 97a Warwick Rd, CV8 1HP, ☏ 52463
    closed Sunday, Monday, 1 week Easter, mid July-August and 1 week at Christmas –
    M (dinner only) a la carte 7.20/9.85 **t.** ⚱ 1.90.

  XX **Diment,** 121-123 Warwick Rd, CV8 1HP, ☏ 53763, French rest. – **P.** ⚡ AE ⓪
    closed Sunday – **M** (dinner only) a la carte 6.65/8.70 **s.** ⚱ 1.90.

JAGUAR-ROVER-TRIUMPH 82/90 Priory Rd ☏ 58343   LANCIA Station Rd ☏ 53073

KENNFORD Devon **403** J 31 – see Exeter.

KENNINGTON Kent **404** W 30 – see Ashford.

KENTS BANK Cumbria – see Grange-over-Sands.

KERESLEY West Midlands **403** **404** P 26 – see Coventry.

KERSEY Suffolk **404** W 27 – pop 385 – ✉ ☎ 0473 Hadleigh.
London 74 – Cambridge 44 – Colchester 19 – **Ipswich 12.**

  X **Quills,** The Street, IP7 6DY, ☏ 827161, « Timbered cottage »
    closed Sunday, Monday, 2 weeks May, 2 weeks October and 25 December-1 January –
    M a la carte 7.50/8.50 ⚱ 1.75.

KESSINGLAND Suffolk **404** Z 26 – see Lowestoft.

☛   *Utilizzate, per lunghe percorrenze, le* carte stradali Michelin *in scala 1/1 000 000.*

KESWICK Cumbria **986** ⑲ – pop. 5,183 – ECD : Wednesday – ☎ 0596.
See : Derwent Water⋆⋆ **Y. Envir. :** Castlerigg (stone circle) ⋇⋆ E : 2 m. **Y A.**
▯₉ Threlkeld Hall ☏ 059 683 (Threlkeld) 324, E : 4 m. by A 66 **Y.**
▯ The Moot Hall, Market Sq. ☏ 72645 (summer only) – Council Offices, 50 Main St. ☏ 72645 (winter only).
London 294 – Carlisle 31 – Kendal 30.

Plan opposite

  🏨 **Keswick** (T.H.F.) ⑤, Station Rd, CA12 4NQ, ☏ 72020, Telex 64200, ⚤ – ◧ TV ➾ **P.**
    ⚴. ⚡ AE ⓪ *VISA*   **z a**
    Mid March-mid November – **M** 4.70/5.90 **st.** ⚱ 1.80 – **76 rm** ⊊ 14.00/26.00 **st.**

  🏨 **Royal Oak** (T.H.F.), Station St., CA12 5HH, ☏ 72965 – ◧ TV ➱wc ➾ **P.** ⚴. ⚡ AE
    ⓪ *VISA*   **z i**
    M 4.70/5.10 **st.** ⚱ 1.65 – **66 rm** ⊊ 10.50/22.50 **st.**

  🏨 **Skiddaw,** 29-31 Main St., CA12 5BN, ☏ 72071 – ◧ TV ➱wc **P.** ⚡ AE ⓪ *VISA*   **z c**
    M 3.80/4.50 **st.** ⚱ 2.00 – **52 rm** ⊊ 11.75/30.60 **st.** – P 18.75 **st.**

  🏨 **Millfield,** Penrith Rd, CA12 4HB, ☏ 72099, ⚤ – ◧ ➱wc ➾ **P**   **z n**
    closed February and 2 weeks November – **M** (bar lunch) approx. 4.15 ⚱ 2.00 – **25 rm**
    ⊊ 10.20/22.00.

  🏨 **Lairbeck** ⑤, Vicarage Hill, CA12 5QB, ☏ 73373, ⚤ – ➱wc **P**   **Y a**
    M (bar lunch) 4.50/6.50 **t.** ⚱ 2.55 – **15 rm** ⊊ 7.30/16.75 **t.** – P 16.85/17.85 **t.**

  🏨 **Lyzzick Hall** ⑤, Under Skiddaw, CA12 4PY, NW : 2 ½ m. off A 591 ☏ 72277, ☒ heated,
    ⚤ – ◨ **P**   by A 591 **Y**
    April-October – **M** (bar lunch) 5.50 **t.** – **18 rm** ⊊ 9.00/18.00.

  🏠 **Gale** ⑤, Under Skiddaw, CA12 4PL, NW : 1 ¾ m. off A 591 on Ormathwaite Rd ☏ 72413,
    ≼ Derwent Valley and countryside, ⚤ – **P**   by A 59 **Y**
    March-October – **13 rm** ⊊ 6.00/12.00 **st.**

  🏠 **Cumbria,** 1 Derwentwater Pl., Ambleside Rd, CA12 4DR, ☏ 73171 – **P.** ⚡ AE   **z e**
    March-October – **9 rm** ⊊ 6.60/13.20 **st.**

  🏠 **Walpole,** 35 Station Rd, CA12 4NA, ☏ 72072 – ➱wc �fwc   **z o**
    18 rm ⊊ 6.60/14.80 **t.**

  🏠 **Highfield,** The Heads, CA12 5ER, ☏ 72508, ≼   **z r**
    Easter-October – **10 rm** ⊊ 7.20/12.25 **t.**

    at Borrowdale S : 3 ¼ m. on B 5289 – ✉ Keswick – ☎ 059 684 Borrowdale:

  🏨🏨 **Lodore Swiss** ⑤, CA12 5UX, ☏ 285, Group Telex 64305, ≼ Derwent water and mountains,
    XX, ☒, ☒ heated, ⚤, park – ◧ TV ➾ **P**   **Y n**
    March-October – **M** 4.75/6.70 **t.** – **72 rm** ⊊ 20.00/40.00 **t.** – P 28.00 **t.**

  🏨 **Borrowdale,** CA12 5UV, ☏ 224, ≼, ⚤ – ➱wc ⓯wc **P**   **Y o**
    closed January – **M** 3.60/5.80 **st.** ⚱ 1.50 – **37 rm** ⊊ 13.00/22.00 – P 16.50/17.00 **st.**

  🏨 **Leathes Head House** ⑤, CA12 5UY, ☏ 247, ≼, ⚤ – ➱wc **P**   **Y e**
    Easter-4 November – **M** (dinner only) 8.00 **st.** ⚱ 1.45 – **12 rm** ⊊ 12.00/26.00 **st.**

  🏨 **Mary Mount** ⑤, CA12 5UU, ☏ 223, ≼ Derwent water and mountains, « Country house
    atmosphere », ⚤, park – TV ➱wc ➾ **P**   **Y r**
    closed mid November-mid December – **M** (bar lunch) approx. 6.50 **t.** – **15 rm** ⊊ 17.00/
    26.00 **t.**

KESWICK

*North is at the top
on all town plans.*

*Les plans de villes
sont orientés
le Nord en haut.*

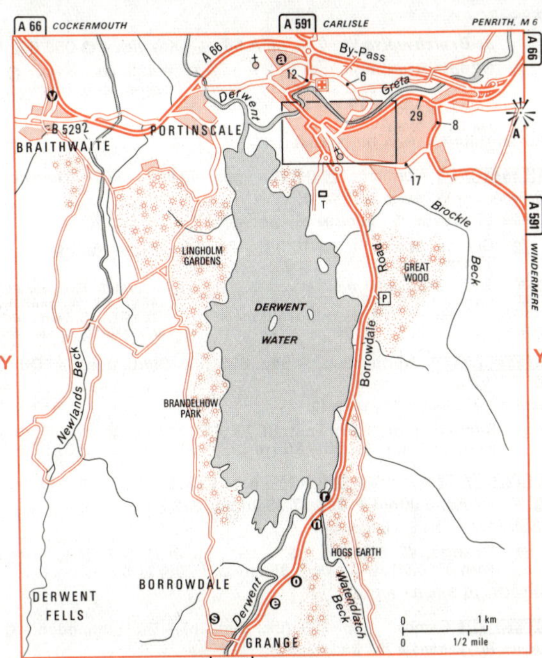

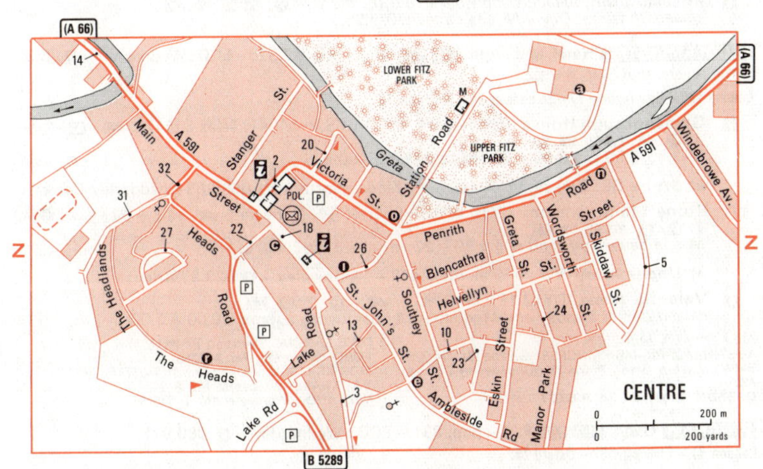

at Grange-in-Borrowdale S : 4 ¾ m. off B 5289 – ✉ Keswick – ☎ 059 684 Borrowdale:

Borrowdale Gates, CA12 5UQ, ☎ 204, ≼, 🚗 – wc **P**　　　　**Y** s
April–October – **M** (bar lunch) approx. 5.20 **st.** 1.40 – **15 rm** 9.50/21.00 **s.** –
P 13.00/15.00 **s.**

at Rosthwaite S : 6 m. on B 5289 – **Y** – ✉ Keswick – ☎ 059 684 Borrowdale:

Scafell, CA12 5BX, ☎ 208, 🚗 – wc **P** – **22 rm.**

Royal Oak, CA12 5XB, ☎ 214 – wc **P.**
closed 1 to 26 December – **12 rm** 8.00/17.00 **t.**

at Braithwaite W : 2 m. on A 66 – ✉ Keswick – ☎ 059 682 Braithwaite :

🏠 **Middle Ruddings,** CA12 5RY, on A 66 ℡ 436, 🍴 – 🛏wc 🅿   Y v
closed December and January except Christmas and 1 January – **M** (bar lunch) 3.00/5.00 t. 🍷 1.50 – **14 rm** 🍳 8.50/20.00 st.

FIAT Lake Rd ℡ 72064   TALBOT Keswick ℡ 72606
ROVER-TRIUMPH High Hill ℡ 72768

KETTERING Northants. **404** R 26 – pop. 42,668 – ECD : Thursday – ☎ 0536.
🛈 Public Library, Sheep St. ℡ 82143.

London 85 – Bedford 25 – **Leicester 26** – Northampton 14 – Stamford 22.

🏨 **George,** Sheep St., NN16 0AN, ℡ 2705 – 🛏wc 🅿. 🛁
50 rm.

DAF, VOLVO Stamford Rd ℡ 518351   RELIANT Ebenezer Pl., Silver St. ℡ 2196
FIAT Britannia Rd ℡ 3098   RENAULT Windmill Av. ℡ 2392
JENSEN, SCIMITAR, TVR 28-30 Queensberry Rd   TOYOTA Britannia Rd ℡ 3571
℡ 3351   VAUXHALL London Rd ℡ 85371

KETTLEWELL North Yorks. – pop. 333 (inc. Starbotton) – EDC : Tuesday – ✉ Skipton –
☎ 075 676.

London 237 – Bradford 33 – **Leeds 40.**

🏠 **Race-Horses,** Town Foot, BD23 5QZ, ℡ 233, 🍴 – 🛏wc 🅿. 🔥
M 4.50/6.50 t. 🍷 2.00 – **16 rm** 🍳 11.50/24.00 t. – P 31.00/33.00 t.

KEYNSHAM Avon **403** **404** M 29 – pop. 13,370 – ECD : Wednesday – ✉ Bristol – ☎ 027 56.
🏌 Manor Rd, Saltford ℡ 022 17 (Saltford) 3220, SE : 2 m.

London 127 – Bath 8 – **Bristol 4.**

🏠 **Grange,** 42 Bath Rd, BS18 1SN, on B 3116 ℡ 2130 – 🛏wc 🅿
M 4.00/4.50 st. 🍷 3.00 – **35 rm** 🍳 11.95/21.85 st.

TALBOT 20 Bath Rd ℡ 2908

KEYSTON Cambs. – pop. 259 (inc. Bythorn) – ✉ Huntingdon – ☎ 080 14 Bythorn.
London 75 – Cambridge 29 – Northampton 24.

XX **Pheasant Inn,** Village Loop Rd, PE18 0RE, ℡ 241 – 🅿. 🔥 AE ⓓ VISA
closed Christmas Day – **M** a la carte 5.70/8.95.

KIDDERMINSTER Heref. and Worc. **403** **404** N 26 – pop. 47,326 – ECD : Wednesday – ☎ 0562.
🛈 The Library, Market St. ℡ 62832.

London 139 – Birmingham 17 – Shrewsbury 34 – Worcester 15.

🏨 **Gainsborough House,** Bewdley Hill, DY11 6BS, ℡ 64041, Telex 336472, 🍴 – 📺 🛏wc
📷 🅿. 🛁. 🔥 AE ⓓ VISA
M 3.50/5.50 t. 🍷 2.00 – **42 rm** 🍳 16.50/24.50 st.

at Stone SE : 2 ½ m. on A 448 – ✉ Kidderminster – ☎ 056 283 Chaddesley Corbett :

XXX **Stone Manor** with rm, DY10 4PJ, ℡ 555, ≤, 🍴, 🏊 heated, 🍴, park – 📺 🛏wc 🚻wc
📷 🅿. 🛁. 🔥 AE ⓓ VISA
M a la carte 4.80/8.55 s. 🍷 1.90 – **22 rm** 🍳 23.00/29.50 s.

at Upper Arley NW : 6 ¼ m. off A 442 – ✉ Bewdley – ☎ 029 97 Arley :

XX **Valentia Arms,** DY12 1PP, ℡ 218, ≤, 🍴 – 🅿. AE ⓓ VISA
closed dinner Sunday and Monday – **M** (bar lunch) approx. 10.00 🍷 3.00.

ALFA-ROMEO Mill St. ℡ 3708   FIAT, LANCIA Stourport Rd ℡ 68211
AUSTIN-MORRIS-MG-PRINCESS George St. ℡ 2255   FORD Worcester Rd ℡ 62661
BMW Mustow Green ℡ 056 283 (Chaddesley Corbett) MORRIS-MG Worcester Rd ℡ 740777
435   VAUXHALL Worcester Rd ℡ 2202
DATSUN Stourport Rd ℡ 63024   VW, AUDI Worcester Rd ℡ 745056

KINGHAM Oxon. **403** **404** P 28 – pop. 831 – ECD : Wednesday – ☎ 060 871.
London 81 – Gloucester 32 – Oxford 25.

🏠 **Mill** 🦢, OX7 6UH, ℡ 255, 🍴 – 🅿. 🔥 ⓓ VISA
M 3.50/4.60 t. 🍷 1.95 – **11 rm** 🍳 10.35/18.75 t.

🏠 Langston Arms, OX7 6UP, on B 4450 ℡ 319, 🍴 – 📺 🛏wc 🅿 – **7 rm.**

KINGSBRIDGE Devon **408** I 33 – pop. 3,545 – ECD : Thursday – ☎ 0548.

☗ Bigbury ☏ 054 881 (Bigbury-on-Sea) 207, W : 7 ½ m.

🛈 The Quay ☏ 3195.

London 236 – Exeter 36 – Plymouth 20 – Torquay 21.

- 🏨 **Crabshell Motor Inn,** Embankment Rd, TQ7 1JZ, ☏ 3301 – 📺 ⌂wc **P**. ▲ AE ⓪
  M (bar lunch) a la carte 3.10/6.90 **st.** ⌕ 1.50 – ⌐ 2.30 – **30 rm** 14.50/17.50 **s.**

- 🏠 **Kingsbridge Motel** without rest., The Quay, TQ7 1HN, ☏ 2540, ⌿, ⚞ – 📺 ⌂wc **P**.
  AE ⓪
  ⌐ 2.00 – **20 rm** 9.50/13.50 **s.**

- ☯ **Harbour Lights,** 13 Ebrington St., TQ7 1DE, ☏ 2418
  Easter-September – **M** (dinner only) 4.95 **t.** – **6 rm** ⌐ approx. 14.50 **t.**

  at Goveton NE : 2 ½ m. off A 381 – ✉ ☎ 0548 Kingsbridge :

- 🏨 **Buckland-Tout-Saints** (Best Western) ⌾, TQ7 2DS, ☏ 2586, Telex 45562, ⬳, « Country house atmosphere, Queen Anne mansion gardens », ⌿, park – ⌂wc ⋔wc **P**. ▲ AE ⓪
  VISA
  April-October – **M** (bar lunch) approx. 10.00 **st.** ⌕ 2.50 – **14 rm** ⌐ (dinner included) 29.50 **st.**

  at Chillington SE : 5 m. by A 379 – ✉ Kingsbridge – ☎ 054 853 Frogmore :

- ☯ **Oddicombe House,** TQ7 2JD, ☏ 234, ⬳, ⌿ heated, ⚞ – ⌂wc **P**. ▲ **VISA**
  M (bar lunch) approx. 7.90 **st.** ⌕ 1.75 – **12 rm** ⌐ 9.00/18.50 **st.**

  at Thurlestone W : 4 m. off A 381 – ✉ Kingsbridge – ☎ 054 857 Thurlestone :

- 🏨 **Thurlestone** (Best Western) ⌾, TQ7 3NN, ☏ 386, Telex 45151, ⌘, ⬳, ⌿ heated, ⌿, ⚞
  park – ⧉ 📺 ⌂wc ⋔wc ☏ ⬳ **P**. ⌾. ▲ AE ⓪ **VISA**
  closed 10 days January – **M** 5.00/6.00 **t.** – **74 rm** ⌐ 17.00/34.00 **t.** – P 22.00/35.00 **t.**

AUSTIN-MORRIS-MG-ROVER-TRIUMPH   The Quay
☏ 2323
FORD Bridge St. ☏ 2305

RENAULT Aveton Gifford ☏ 054 855 (Loddiswell) 248
VAUXHALL Embankment Rd ☏ 2140

☛ *Inclusion in the **Michelin Guide**
cannot be achieved by
pulling strings or by offering favours.*

☛ *Pour être inscrit au **Guide Michelin**
- pas de piston,
- pas de pot-de-vin!*

KINGSGATE Kent **404** Y 29 – see Broadstairs.

KING'S HEATH West Midlands **408** **404** O 26 – see Birmingham.

KING'S LYNN Norfolk **404** V 25 – pop. 30,107 – ECD : Wednesday – ☎ 0553.

See : St. Margaret's Church* (17C, chancel 13C) – St. Nicholas' Chapel* (Gothic). **Envir. :** Sandringham House* and park** *AC*, NE : 6 m.

🛈 Town Hall, Saturday Market Pl. ☏ 61241.

London 103 – Cambridge 45 – Leicester 75 – Norwich 44.

- 🏨 **Duke's Head** (T.H.F.), Tuesday Market Pl., PE30 1JS, ☏ 4996, Telex 817349 – ⧉ 📺
  ⌂wc ☏ **P**. ⌾. ▲ AE ⓪ **VISA**
  M a la carte 6.00/9.90 **st.** ⌕ 1.65 – ⌐ 2.50 – **72 rm** 18.00/25.50 **st.**

AUSTIN-DAIMLER-JAGUAR-MORRIS-MG-ROVER-
TRIUMPH, ROLLS ROYCE-BENTLEY Church St. and
24 St. James St. ☏ 63133
FIAT, LANCIA St. Germans ☏ 055 385 (St. Germans)
296
FORD South Gates ☏ 64441
HONDA, OPEL, RELIANT Valingers Rd ☏ 23500

RENAULT Hardwick Rd ☏ 2644
TALBOT Lynn Rd, Heacham ☏ 0485 (Heacham) 70243
TALBOT, CITROEN Kings Lynn ☏ 4281
TOYOTA, Tottenhill ☏ 055 381 (Watlington) 306
VAUXHALL North St. ☏ 3861
VW, AUDI-NSU Beaulah St. ☏ 672875

KINGSTON-UPON-HULL Humberside **986** ㉔ – pop. 285,970 – ECD: Monday and Thursday – ☎ 0482 Hull.

Envir.: Burton Constable Hall* (16C) *AC*, NE : 8 m. by A 165 z.

☗ Kirk Ella ☏ 658919, W : 5 m. by A 164 z – ☗ Willerby Rd ☏ 656309, W : by Spring Bank West z – ☗ Salthouse Rd ☏ 74242, E : 3 m. z.

⚓ Shipping connections with the Continent: to Rotterdam : Europoort, to Zeebrugge (North Sea Ferries).

🛈 Central Library, Albion St. ☏ 223344 – King George Dock ☏ 702118.

London 188 – Leeds 60 – Nottingham 90 – Sheffield 66.

KINGSTON-UPON-HULL

Carr Lane	Y	
George Street	X	
Jameson Street	XY	
King Edward Street	Y	19
Paragon Street	Y	29
Prospect Street	X	
Whitefriargate	Y	49
Albion Street	X	2
Bond Street	X	3
Cannon Street	X	4
Caroline Street	X	6
Chapman Street	X	7
Commercial Road	Y	8
Dock Office Row	X	10
Dock Street	X	12
Great Union Street	X	13
Grimston Street	X	15
Humber Dock Street	Y	16
Jarrat Street	X	17
Lockwood Street	X	21
Lowgate	Y	23
Market Place	Y	24
Maybury Road	Z	25
Prince's Avenue	Z	31
Prince's Dock Street	Y	32
Queen's Road	Z	33
Queen's Street	Y	35
Queen's Dock Avenue	X	36
Reform Street	X	37
St. Luke's Street	Y	39
St. Mark's Street	X	40
Scott Street	X	42
Southcoates Avenue	Z	43
Southcoates Lane	Z	44
Waterhouse Lane	Y	47
Wellington Street	Y	48
Wilberforce Drive	X	50
Worship Street	X	52

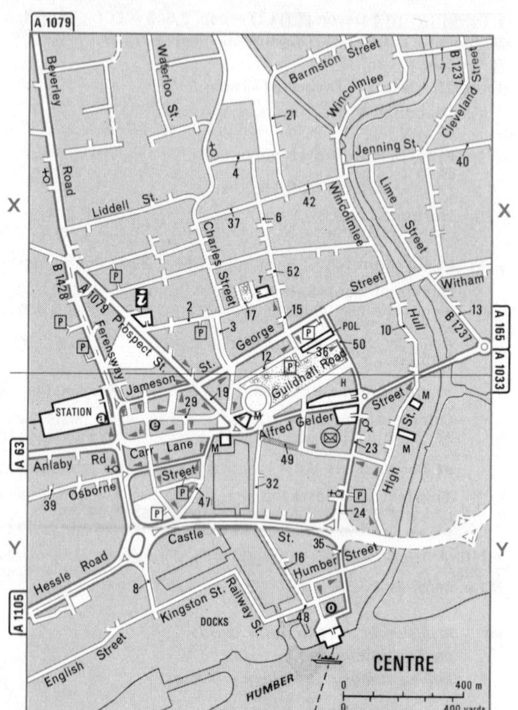

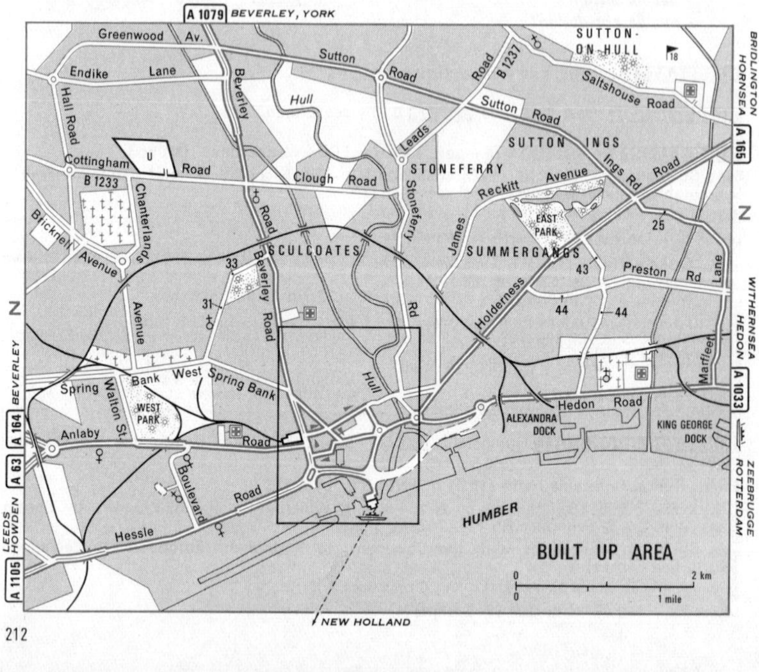

🏨 **Royal Station** (B.T.H.), 170 Ferensway, HU1 3UF, ☏ 25087, Telex 52450 – 📶 📺
🅿. 📶. 🆖 AE ⓘ VISA **Y a**
closed Christmas, 1 January and Bank Holidays – **M** *(closed Friday dinner, Saturday and Sunday)* a la carte 7.80/13.75 **st.** ⌂ 2.30 – **108 rm** ⌱ 23.45/35.15 **st.**

🏨 Hull Centre (Centre), Paragon St., HU1 3PJ, ☏ 26462, Telex 52431 – 📶 📺 🛏wc ☎
🚻. 📶. 🆖 AE ⓘ VISA **Y e**
⌱ 1.65 – **125 rm** 16.95/23.25 **st.**

XXX **Cerutti's**, 10 Nelson St., HU1 1XE, ☏ 28501, Seafood **Y o**
closed Saturday lunch, Sunday and Bank Holidays – **M** a la carte 5.05/8.50 **t.** ⌂ 2.00.

at Willerby NW: 5 m. on A 164 – **Z** – ✉ Willerby – ✆ 0482 Hull:

🏨 **Willerby Manor,** Well Lane, HU10 6ER, ☏ 652616, 🚗 – 📺 🛏wc ☎ 🅿. 📶. 🆖 AE
ⓘ VISA
M 4.00/5.25 **st.** ⌂ 1.00 – **37 rm** ⌱ 12.65/23.00 **st.**

at Little Weighton NW: 11 m. off A 164 – **Z** – ✉ ✆ 0482 Hull:

🏨 **Rowley Manor** 🦢, HU20 3XB, ☏ 848248, ≼, « *Tastefully converted house in well kept gardens* », park – 📺 🅿. 🆖 AE ⓘ VISA
M *(bar lunch Monday to Friday)* 4.95/8.50 **t.** ⌂ 2.15 – **15 rm** ⌱ 14.00/26.00 **t.**

at North Ferriby W: 7 m. off A 63 – **Z** – ✉ Kingston-upon-Hull – ✆ 0482 Hull:

🏨 Hull Crest Motel (Crest), Ferriby High Rd, HU14 3LG, ☏ 645212, Telex 52558 – 📺
🛏wc ☎ 🅿. 🆖 AE ⓘ VISA
⌱ 2.40 – **54 rm** 19.20/25.20 **st.**

MICHELIN Branch, Springfield Way, Anlaby, Hull, HU10 6RJ, ☏ 561191.

AUDI, MERCEDES-BENZ 169 George St. ☏ 20370
AUSTIN-MORRIS-MG-PRINCESS 132 Anlaby Rd ☏ 24373
BMW, PEUGEOT 54 Anlaby Rd ☏ 25071
DATSUN Whitham ☏ 24131
HONDA 61 Boothferry Rd ☏ 52078
FIAT 96 Boothferry Rd ☏ 506976
FORD 172 Anlaby Rd ☏ 25732
LADA, LOTUS 160 Hedon Rd ☏ 28752
MAZDA 300/2 Boothferry Rd, Hessle ☏ 645 283

OPEL Clarence St. ☏ 20061
RENAULT Holderness High Rd ☏ 74436
SAAB Osborne St. ☏ 23773
SKODA 245 Newland Av. ☏ 442235
TALBOT Anlaby Rd ☏ 23631
TOYOTA Clarence St. ☏ 20039
VAUXHALL 230/6 Anlaby Rd ☏ 23681
VOLVO Hessle Rd ☏ 52010
VW, AUDI 1/13 Boothferry Rd ☏ 649124

KINGSTOWN Cumbria – see Carlisle.

KINGSWEAR Devon 🗺 J 32 – see Dartmouth.

KINGSWINFORD West Midlands 🗺 🗺 N 26 – pop. 14,065 (inc. Wallheath) – ECD
Thursday – ✆ 038 44 (4 and 5 fig.) or 0384 (6 fig.).
London 135 – Birmingham 14 – Stafford 22 – Worcester 32.

🏨 **Summerhill House** (Ansells), Swindon Rd, DY6 9XA, ☏ 5254, 🚗 – 🛏 🅿. 📶. 🆖 AE
M 4.10/5.00 **t.** ⌂ 1.80 – **10 rm** ⌱ 14.70/17.35 **t.**

AUSTIN-MORRIS-ROVER-TRIUMPH 45 Dudley Rd ☏ 280404

KINTBURY Berks. 🗺 🗺 P 29 – pop. 2,060 – ✉ Newbury – ✆ 048 85.
London 73 – Newbury 6 – Reading 23.

XX **Dundas Arms** with rm, RG15 0UT, ☏ 263, ≼, 🍴 – 📺 🛏wc 🅿. 🆖 AE ⓘ VISA
closed Sunday, Monday, Christmas and Ascot week – **M** (dinner only) 9.00 ⌂ 2.00 – **5 rm**
⌱ 16.00/22.00.

KINVER West Midlands 🗺 🗺 N 26 – see Stourbridge.

KIRBY CROSS Essex 🗺 X 28 – see Frinton-on-Sea.

KIRKBY Merseyside 🗺 L 25 – pop. 58,360 – ECD: Wednesday – ✆ 051 Liverpool.
📍18 Ingoe Lane. – 🅙 Municipal Buildings ☏ 548 6555.
London 213 – Liverpool 6.

🏨 Golden Eagle (Embassy), Cherryfield Drive, L32 8SB, ☏ 546 4355 – 📶 📺 🛏wc ☎ 🅿
🆖 AE ⓘ VISA
closed 25 and 26 December – **74 rm.**

KIRKBY LONSDALE Cumbria 👁👁👁 ㉓ – pop. 1,506 – ECD : Wednesday – ✉ Carnforth – ☎ 0468.

🏌 Casterton Rd ☎ 71796, 1 m. on Sedbergh Rd.

🛈 18 Main St. ☎ 71603.

London 259 – Carlisle 62 – Kendal 13 – Lancaster 17 – **Leeds 58.**

   🏛 Royal, 2 Main St., LA6 2AE, ☎ 71217 – ⌷wc 🅿
   23 rm.

KIRKBYMOORSIDE North Yorks. 👁👁👁 ㉔ – pop. 1,880 – ECD : Thursday – ☎ 0751.

🏌 Manor Vale ☎ 31525.

London 244 – Scarborough 26 – York 33.

   🏛 **George and Dragon,** Market Pl., YO6 6AA, ☎ 31637 – ⌷wc 🛁wc 🅿
   closed 24 to 26 December – **M** a la carte 4.85/8.05 🍷 1.55 – **17 rm** 🍽 9.00/17.00.

DATSUN Pickering Rd ☎ 31551   VAUXHALL ☎ 31434

KIRKBY STEPHEN Cumbria 👁👁👁 ⑲ – pop. 1,539 – ECD : Thursday – ☎ 0930.

Envir.: Brough (Castle ruins 12C-14C : keep ❊* *AC*) N : 4 m.

London 285 – Carlisle 48 – Kendal 24.

   🏛 **King's Arms,** Market Sq., CA17 4NH, ☎ 71378, 🚗 – 🔄 AE ⓪ VISA
   M 3.50/7.50 **st.** 🍷 2.20 – **11 rm** 🍽 15.50/28.00 **st.** – P 23.00 **st.**

KISLINGBURY Northants. 👁👁👁 👁👁👁 Q 27 – pop. 1,046 – ECD : Wednesday – ✉ ☎ 0604
Northampton.

London 75 – Coventry 33 – Northampton 4.

   ✕✕ Cromwell Cottage (Gd Met.), NN7 4AG, ☎ 830288 – 🅿.

KNARESBOROUGH North Yorks. 👁👁👁 ㉓ – pop. 10,640 – ECD : Thursday – ☎ 0423 Harrogate.

🏌 Boroughbridge Rd ☎ 863219, N : 1 ¼ m.

🛈 Market Place (summer only) ☎ 866886.

London 217 – Bradford 21 – Harrogate 3 – **Leeds 18** – York 18.

   🏰 **Dower House,** Bond End, HG5 9AL, ☎ 863302, 🚗 – ⌷wc 🛁wc 🐾 🅿. VISA
   closed 25 and 26 December – **M** (dinner only and Sunday lunch) 4.55/7.25 **t.** 🍷 2.50 –
   19 rm 🍽 11.75/28.00 **st.**

FORD York Place ☎ 2291   OPEL-VAUXHALL Bond End ☎ 21919

KNIGHTON (TREFYCLAWDD) Powys 👁👁👁 K 26 – pop. 2.000 – ECD : Wednesday – ☎ 054 72
(fig 3.) or 0547 (4 fig.).

🏌 The Frydd, S : ½ m.

London 165 – Aberystwyth 57 – Birmingham 56 – Shrewsbury 33.

   🏛 Norton Arms, Broad St., LD7 1BT, ☎ 321, 🐾 – 🚿 ⌷wc 🐾 🅿
   11 rm.

AUSTIN-JAGUAR-MORRIS-MG-ROVER-TRIUMPH, FORD ☎ 528645

KNIGHTWICK Heref. and Worc. 👁👁👁 👁👁👁 M 27 – pop. 114 – ECD : Wednesday – ✉ Worcester – ☎ 088 62.

London 132 – Hereford 20 – Leominster 18 – Worcester 8.

   🏠 **Talbot,** WR6 5PJ, ☎ 235, 🐾 – ⌷wc 🛁wc 🅿
   closed 1 week at Christmas – **M** (bar lunch) approx. 8.00 **st.** 🍷 1.75 – **7 rm** 🍽 12.00/
   15.00 **st.**

KNOWLE West Midlands 👁👁👁 👁👁👁 O 26 – pop. 7,676 – ECD : Thursday – ✉ Solihull –
☎ 056 45.

London 108 – Birmingham 9 – Coventry 10 – Warwick 11.

   ✕✕ **Florentine,** 15 Kenilworth Rd, B93 0JB, ☎ 6449, Italian rest. – 🔄 AE ⓪ VISA
   closed Sunday, Monday lunch and Bank Holidays – **M** a la carte 4.05/6.85.

   at Chadwick End SE : 3 m. on A 41 – ✉ ☎ 056 45 Knowle :

   🏰 **Chadwick Manor** 🦢, B93 0AT, ☎ 2821, ≼, 🚗 – 📺 🅿. 🔄 AE ⓪ VISA
   closed 26 December – **M** (Sunday dinner by reservation) a la carte 8.90/11.00 **t.** 🍷 1.90
   – **13 rm** 🍽 22.00/35.00 **st.**

AUSTIN-MORRIS-MG-ROVER-TRIUMPH Grange Rd,   AUSTIN-MORRIS-PRINCESS, VANDEN PLAS 25
Dorridge ☎ 6131   Station Rd ☎ 4221

KNOWL HILL Berks. 👁👁👁 R 29 – pop. 495 – ✉ Twyford – ☎ 062 882 Littlewick Green.

London 38 – Maidenhead 5 – Reading 8.

   ✕✕ **Bird in Hand,** Bath Rd, RG10 9UP, ☎ 2781, 🚗 – 🅿. AE ⓪ VISA
   M a la carte 5.40/7.40 **t.** 🍷 2.00.

KNUTSFORD Cheshire 403 404 M 24 – pop. 10,050 – ECD : Wednesday – © 0565.
Envir. : Tatton Hall* (Georgian) and gardens** *AC*, N : 2 m. – Jodrell Bank (Concourse building-radiotelescope *AC*) SE : 8 ½ m.

🛈 Council Offices, Toft Rd ℡ 2611.

London 187 – Chester 25 – Liverpool 33 – Manchester 18 – Stoke-on-Trent 30.

🏨 **Royal George,** King St., WA16 6EE, ℡ 4151 – 📺 ⌂wc ☎ 🅿. ♨. 🅰 AE ⑩ VISA
M 5.35/5.95 t. – �* 2.00 – **25 rm** 14.00/22.00.

🏠 **Longview,** 55 Manchester Rd, WA16 0LX, ℡ 2119 – 🅿
closed Christmas, 1 January and Bank Holidays – **10 rm** �* 11.00/18.00 st.

%% **La Belle Epoque** with rm, 60 King St., WA16 6DX, ℡ 3060, « Art nouveau », 🍴 – 🅿.
🅰 AE ⑩ VISA
closed Sunday and Bank Holidays – **M** (dinner only) a la carte 5.65/7.75 🍷 1.65 – **5 rm**
�* 11.00/21.00 st.

% **David's Place,** 10 Princess St., WA16 6DD, ℡ 3356 – 🅰 AE ⑩
closed Monday lunch and Sunday – **M** a la carte 7.30/11.40 t. 🍷 1.65.

at Lower Peover S : 3 m. ½ by A 50 on B 5081 – ✉ Knutsford – © 056 581 Lower Peover :

% **Bells of Peover,** The Cobbles, ℡ 2269, « Attractive gardens » – 🅿. ⑩ VISA
closed Sunday dinner and Monday – **M** a la carte 6.40/9.00 t. 🍷 2.30.

at Bucklow Hill NW : 3 ½ m. junction A 556 and A 5034 – ✉ Knutsford – © 0565 Bucklow Hill :

🏨 **Swan,** Chester Rd, WA16 6RD, ℡ 830295, Telex 666911 – 📺 ⌂wc 🗼wc ☎ 🅿. 🅰 AE
⑩ VISA
M approx. 4.50 st. 🍷 2.30 – **56 rm** �* 23.00/29.50 st.

ALFA-ROMEO London Rd, Allostock ℡ 056 581 (Lower Peover) 2899
AUSTIN-MORRIS-MG   Bucklow Hill ℡ 830041

FORD Garden Rd ℡ 4141
RENAULT Toft Rd ℡ 4294

LACOCK Wilts. 403 404 N 29 – pop. 1,318 – ✉ Chippenham – © 024 973.
See : Abbey* (16C) *AC*.

London 109 – Bath 16 – Bristol 30 – Chippenham 3.

🏯 **Sign of the Angel,** 6 Church St., SN15 2LB, ℡ 230, « 14C inn in National Trust village »,
🍴
closed 22 December-1 January – **M** *(closed Sunday dinner)* 8.00/9.00 t. 🍷 3.00 – **6 rm**
�* 20.00/30.00 t.

LAKE VYRNWY Powys 403 J 25 – pop. 324 – ✉ Oswestry (Salop) – © 069 173 Llanwddyn.
London 204 – Chester 52 – Llanfyllin 10 – Shrewsbury 40.

🏨 **Lake Vyrnwy** 🦢, SY10 0LY, ℡ 244, ≤ lake Vyrnwy, 🍴, 🎣, 🍴, park – 📺 ⌂wc 🚗
🅿
closed 14 January-1 March – **M** (buffet lunch) 4.50/4.75 st. 🍷 1.60 – **30 rm** �* 12.00/28.00 st.

LAMBERHURST Kent 404 V 30 – pop. 1,297 – ✉ Royal Tunbridge Wells – © 089 278.
Envir. : Scotney Castle gardens (trees*, Bastion view*) *AC*, SE : 1 m.

London 43 – Hastings 21 – Maidstone 17.

%% **George and Dragon** with rm, TN3 8DQ, ℡ 605, 🍴 – ⌂wc 🗼wc 🅿. 🅰 VISA
M a la carte 7.30/11.15 t. 🍷 2.30 – �* 1.50 – **6 rm** 10.95/18.95 t.

LAMORNA COVE Cornwall 403 D 33 – ECD : Thursday – ✉ Penzance.
Envir. : Land's End** W : 7 ½ m.

London 323 – Penzance 5 – Truro 31.

🏨 **Lamorna Cove** 🦢, TR19 6XH, ℡ 073 673 (Mousehole) 411, ≤, 🏊 heated, 🍴 – 📺
⌂wc 🗼wc 🅿. 🅰 AE ⑩ VISA
M 4.75/7.00 t. – **23 rm** �* 18.70/37.40 t.

🏠 **Menwinnion** 🦢, TR19 6BJ, W : 1 m. off B 3315 ℡ 073 672 (St. Buryan) 233, « Country
house atmosphere », 🍴 – ⌂wc 🅿
March-October – **M** (bar lunch) 3.50/6.00 s. 🍷 2.50 – **8 rm** �* 11.00/26.00 s.

LAMPETER (LLANBEDR PONT STEFFAN) Dyfed 403 H 27 – pop. 2,189 – ECD : Wednesday –
© 0570.
🛈 ℡ 057 045 (Llangybi) 286, NE : 4 m. off A 485.

London 223 – Brecon 41 – Carmarthen 22 – Swansea 50.

🏠 **Black Lion Royal,** High St., SA48 7JP, ℡ 422172 – ⌂wc 🅿
18 rm.

AUSTIN-MORRIS-MG Cwmann ℡ 422366

LANCASTER Lancs. 𝟡𝟠𝟞 ㉓ – pop. 49,584 – ECD : Wednesday – ✆ 0524.

🏌 Ashton Hall ☎ 0524 (Galgate) 751247, S : 3 m. on A 588.

🛈 7 Dalton Sq. ☎ 2878.

London 244 – Blackpool 25 – Bradford 62 – Burnley 42 – **Leeds** 69 – Middlesbrough 96 – Preston 22.

    ✕ **Portofino,** 23 Castle Hill, LA1 1YN, ☎ 2388, Italian rest. – ◪ 𝔸𝔼 ⓪ 𝘝𝘐𝘚𝘈
        closed Sunday and Bank Holidays – **M** a la carte 3.80/6.00 **t.** ⌷ 1.90.

AUSTIN-DAIMLER-JAGUAR-MG-WOLSELEY 110 Penny St. ☎ 2233
BRITISH LEYLAND Willow Lane ☎ 2424
FORD Parliament St. ☎ 63553

MORRIS-MG Brookhouse ☎ 0524 (Caton) 770501
RENAULT Aldrens Lane ☎ 67221
TALBOT Bulk Rd ☎ 63373
VAUXHALL, CITROEN Penny St. ☎ 2442

LANERCOST Cumbria – pop. 655 – ✉ ✆ 069 77 Brampton.

See : Priory* (ruins 14C) *AC.*

Envir. : Bewcastle (churchyard Runic Cross* 8C) N : 8 ½ m.

London 320 – Carlisle 12 – Newcastle-upon-Tyne 48.

    🏠 **New Bridge,** ⊗, CA8 2HG, ☎ 2224 – ⊟wc ⋔wc ℗
        M (bar lunch) a la carte 4.55/6.50 **st.** ⌷ 2.40 – **11 rm** ⊇ 10.15/21.50 **st.**

LANGSTONE Gwent 𝟜𝟘𝟛 L 29 – see Newport.

LANGTHWAITE North Yorks. – ✉ Richmond – ✆ 074 884 Reeth.

London 257 – Leeds 67 – Middlesbrough 40 – Newcastle-upon-Tyne 58.

    🏠 **Scar House** ⊗, Arkengarthdale, DL8 6RG, ☎ 526, ≼, ⚲, 🚉, park – ⊟wc ℗
        Easter-September – **M** (dinner only) 5.50 **st.** ⌷ 2.00 – **12 rm** ⊇ 10.00/20.00.

LANREATH Cornwall 𝟜𝟘𝟛 G 32 – pop. 352 – ✉ Looe – ✆ 050 32.

London 269 – Plymouth 26 – Truro 34.

    🏠 **Punch Bowl Inn,** PL13 2NX, ☎ 218, 🚉 – 📺 ⊟wc ⋔ ℗
        April-October – **M** a la carte 5.00/10.25 **s.** ⌷ 1.45 – **18 rm** ⊇ 9.60/21.45 **s.**

LASTINGHAM North Yorks. – pop. 88 – ECD : Wednesday – ✉ York – ✆ 075 15.

London 244 – Scarborough 26 – York 32.

    🏠 Lastingham Grange ⊗, YO6 6TH, ☎ 345, « Country house atmosphere », 🚉 – ⊟wc ℗
        12 rm.

LAVENHAM Suffolk 𝟜𝟘𝟜 W 27 – pop. 1,480 – ECD : Wednesday – ✉ Sudbury – ✆ 0787.

See : SS. Peter and Paul's Church : the Spring Parclose* (Flemish).

London 66 – Cambridge 39 – Colchester 22 – Ipswich 19.

    🏘 **Swan** (T.H.F.), High St., CO10 9QA, ☎ 247477, « Part 14C timbered inn », 🚉 – 📺 ℗.
        🛋. ◪ 𝔸𝔼 ⓪ 𝘝𝘐𝘚𝘈
        M 5.00/6.00 **st.** ⌷ 1.75 – ⊇ 2.25 – **42 rm** 18.00/25.00 **st.**

PEUGEOT ☎ 247228

LEAMINGTON SPA Warw. 𝟜𝟘𝟛 𝟜𝟘𝟜 P 27 – see Royal Leamington Spa.

LECHLADE Glos. 𝟜𝟘𝟛 𝟜𝟘𝟜 O 28 – pop. 1,689 – ✆ 0367.

London 97 – Gloucester 32 – Oxford 23 – Swindon 11.

    ✕ **Trout Inn,** St. John's Bridge, Faringdon Rd, GL7 3HA, SE : ¾ m. on A 417 ☎ 52313,
        🚉 – ℗. ◪ 𝘝𝘐𝘚𝘈
        closed Monday except Bank Holidays, Tuesday, Wednesday and 25-26 December – **M** a la
        carte 5.20/7.35 **st.** ⌷ 1.95.

LEDBURY Heref. and Worc. 𝟜𝟘𝟛 𝟜𝟘𝟜 M 27 – pop. 3,911 – ECD : Wednesday – ✆ 0531.

See : Church Lane*. **Envir. :** Birtsmorton Court* (15C) *AC*, SE : 7 m.

🛈 St. Katherine's, High St. ☎ 2461 and 3429.

London 119 – Hereford 14 – Newport 46 – Worcester 16.

    🏠 **Feathers,** High St., HR8 1DS, ☎ 2600, « Heavily timbered 16C inn » – ℗. ◪ ⓪
        M 5.00/7.25 **st.** ⌷ 2.20 – **13 rm** ⊇ 12.50/22.00 **st.**

AUSTIN-MORRIS-MG-ROVER-TRIUMPH New St. ☎ 2233
TALBOT The Homend ☎ 2053

LEE Devon 𝟜𝟘𝟛 I 30 – see Ilfracombe.

Per viaggiare in Europa, utilizzate le Carte Michelin

Le Grandi Strade scala 1/1 000 000.

LEEDS West Yorks. **986** ㉓ – pop. 496,009 – ECD : Wednesday – ✆ 0532.
See: St. John's Church* 17C **DZ A. Envir.:** Temple Newsam House* 17C (interior**) *AC*, E:
4 m. **CX D** – Kirkstall Abbey* (ruins 12C) *AC*, NW: 3 m. **BV B.**

ⁱ⁸, ⁱ⁸ Temple Newsam Rd, Halton ☏ 645214, E: 3 m. **CX** – ⁱ⁸ Gotts Park, Armley Ridge Rd,
☏ 638232, W: 2 m. **BV** – ⁱ⁸ Layton Rise ☏ 586819, NW: 6 m. **BV** – ⁹ Town St., Middleton
☏ 700449, S: 3 m. **CX.**

✈ Leeds & Bradford Airport: ☏ (0532) 503431, NW: 8 m. by A 65 and A 658 **BV** – **Terminal:**
Vicar Lane, Bus Station, Leeds.

🄴 Central Library, Calverley St. ☏ 462453/4.

London 194 – Liverpool 70 – Manchester 42 – Newcastle-upon-Tyne 93 – Nottingham 67.

Plans on following pages

🏨 **Queen's** (B.T.H.), City Sq., LS1 1PL, ☏ 31323, Telex 55161 – 🛗 📺 ⴕ. 🏊. 🔼 AE ⑩ *VISA*
   M a la carte 4.50/12.00 **st.** – **193 rm** ⊇ 26.50/32.00 **st.**   **DZ e**

🏨 **Ladbroke Dragonara,** Neville St., LS1 4BX, ☏ 442000, Telex 557143 – 🛗 📺 ⴕ 🅿.
   🏊. 🔼 AE ⑩ *VISA*   **DZ r**
   M a la carte 6.55/9.00 **st.** 🍷 2.15 – ⊇ 3.20 – **231 rm** 22.00/32.00 **s.**

🏨 **Merrion,** Merrion Centre, Wade Lane, LS2 8NH, ☏ 39191, Telex 55459 – 🛗 📺. 🏊. 🔼
   AE ⑩ *VISA*   **DZ a**
   M a la carte 6.55/9.00 **t.** 🍷 1.95 – **120 rm** ⊇ 24.80/31.50 **t.**

🏨 **Metropole** (T.H.F.), King St., LS1 2HQ, ☏ 450841 – 🛗 📺 ⌷wc ☏ 🅿. 🏊. 🔼 AE ⑩
   VISA   **CZ o**
   M approx. 4.95 🍷 1.65 – **106 rm** ⊇ 14.50/23.50 **st.**

🏨 **Parkway** (Embassy), Otley Rd, LS16 8AG, NW: 6 m. on A 660 ☏ 672551, 🚗 – 📺 ⌷wc
   ☏ 🅿. 🏊. 🔼 AE ⑩ *VISA*   by A 660 **BV**
   M 4.15/5.40 **st.** 🍷 2.20 – **45 rm** ⊇ 13.50/22.50 **st.** – P 23.00/28.00 **st.**

🏨 Golden Lion, Lower Briggate, LS1 4AE, ☏ 36454 – 🛗 📺 ☏. 🏊   **DZ s**
   82 rm.

⋔ **Aragon** ⌄, 250 Stainbeck Lane, LS7 2PS, ☏ 759306, 🚗 – 🅿   **CV c**
   10 rm ⊇ 7.50/15.00 **s.**

⋔ **Highfield,** 79 Cardigan Rd, LS6 1EB, ☏ 752193 – 🅿   **AY x**
   10 rm ⊇ 7.00/13.00 **s.**

⋔ **Oak Villa,** 57 Cardigan Rd, LS6 1DW, ☏ 758439, 🚗 – 🅿   **AY a**
   closed Christmas – **10 rm** ⊇ 7.00/12.50 **s.**

✗✗✗ Terrazza, Minerva House, 16 Greek St., LS1 5RU, ☏ 32880, Italian rest., Dancing (Wednesday, Friday and Saturday only).   **CDZ n**

✗✗ **Embassy,** 333 Roundhay Rd, LS8 4HT, NE: 2 ½ m. off A 58 ☏ 490562 – 🅿. AE   **BY v**
   M (dinner only) 7.00 🍷 1.75.

✗✗ Shabab, 2 Eastgate, ☏ 468988, Indian rest.   **DZ v**

✗ **Rules,** 188 Selby Rd, LS15 0LF, ☏ 604564 – 🔼 AE ⑩ *VISA*   **CV u**
   closed Sunday, first 2 weeks August and Banks Holidays – **M** (dinner only) a la carte
   5.65/7.45 🍷 1.60.

✗ **Get Stuffed Dining Chambers,** 20 York Pl., LS1 2QH, ☏ 455965, Bistro – 🔼 AE ⑩
   VISA   **CZ i**
   closed Saturday lunch, Sunday lunch, Monday and Bank Holidays – **M** a la carte 5.00/
   7.25 **st.** 🍷 1.80.

at Seacroft NE: 5 ½ m. at junction of A 64 and A 6120 – ✉ ✆ 0532 Leeds:

🏨 **Windmill** (Stakis), Ring Rd, LS14 5QP, ☏ 732323, Telex 778704 – 🛗 📺 ⌷wc 🏠wc
   ☏ ⴕ 🅿. 🏊. 🔼 AE ⑩ *VISA*   **CV a**
   M a la carte 5.50/6.85 **st.** 🍷 1.75 – **40 rm** ⊇ 18.00/28.00 **st.**

at Garforth E: 6 m. at junction A 63 and A 642 – ✉ ✆ 0532 Leeds:

🏨 Ladbroke Mercury Motor Inn, Wakefield Rd, LS26 1LH, ☏ 866556 – 📺 ⌷wc ☏ ⴕ 🅿.
   🏊 – **120 rm.**   **CV e**

at Oulton SE: 6 ¼ m. at junction A 639 and A 642 – ✉ ✆ 0532 Leeds:

🏨 Leeds Crest Motel (Crest), The Grove, LS26 8EJ, ☏ 826201 – 📺 ⌷wc ☏ ⴕ 🅿. 🔼 AE
   ⑩ *VISA*   **CX z**
   ⊇ 2.40 – **40 rm** 18.50/25.20 **st.**

at Pudsey W: 4 ½ m. by A 647 – ✉ Leeds – ✆ 0274 Bradford:

✗ **Tiberio,** 68 Galloway Lane, LS28 8LE, W: 1 ½ m. on B 6154 ☏ 665895, Italian rest. –
   🔼 *VISA*   **BV o**
   closed Sunday – **M** (dinner only) a la carte 4.50/7.50 **s.** 🍷 1.80.

at Horsforth NW: 5 m. off A 6120 by A 65 – ✉ ✆ 0532 Leeds :

✗✗✗ **Low Hall,** Calverley Lane, LS18 4EF, ☏ 588221, « Elizabethan house » – 🅿. 🔼 *VISA* **BV a**
   *closed Saturday lunch, Sunday, 24 August-8 September, 25 to 30 December and Bank
   Holidays* – **M** approx. 9.85 **st.** 🍷 3.50.

✗✗ **Roman Garden,** Hall Park, LS18 5JY, ☏ 587962, ⬳, Italian rest. – 🅿   **BV i**
   closed Saturday lunch, Sunday and Monday – **M** 4.00/7.25 **t.** 🍷 2.25.

LEEDS AND BRADFORD
ENLARGED AREA
3 km
2 miles
LEEDS
See BRADFORD
A 64 YORK
SELBY A 63
KINGSTON - UPON - HULL M 62
A 58 WETHERBY
A 61 HARROGATE
A 660 OTLEY
HARROGATE
A 658
A 65 ILKLEY
A 650 KEIGHLEY
A 641 BRIGHOUSE
A 647 HALIFAX
A 62 HUDDERSFIELD
A 653 DEWSBURY
A 650 WAKEFIELD
M 1 SHEFFIELD
M 62 MANCHESTER
SEACROFT
HALTON
ROTHWELL
MORLEY
HORSFORTH
PUDSEY
SHIPLEY
SHELF
Ring Road
Ring Road
Harrogate Road
Scott Hall Road
Easterly Road
York Road
Otley Rd
Abbey Rd
Stanningley Rd
Stanningley
Ring Road
Tong Road
Whitehall Road
Tong Lane
Roker Lane
Tong Street
Pontefract Road
Wakefield Rd
Dewsbury Rd
Dewsbury Road
Elland Road
Gelderd Road
Bradford Rd
Dick Lane
Harrogate Rd
Leeds Rd
Canal Rd
Toller Lane
Thornton Road
Great Horton Road
Halifax Road
Manchester Road
Leeds Road
Whinhall Road
A 6120
A 64
A 63
A 61
M 1
A 642
A 639
A 654
A 61
M 62
A 653
A 650
A 652
A 643
A 651
A 638
A 6036
B 6380
B 6145
B 6144
A 650
A 657
A 6037
A 6120
A 65
A 657
B 6157
A 647
A 6110
B 6157
B 6154
A 647
A 58
A 62
M 621
M 62
M 606
A 58
A 638
By-Pass
5
6
16
41
59
67
69
17
18
18
18
80
9
9

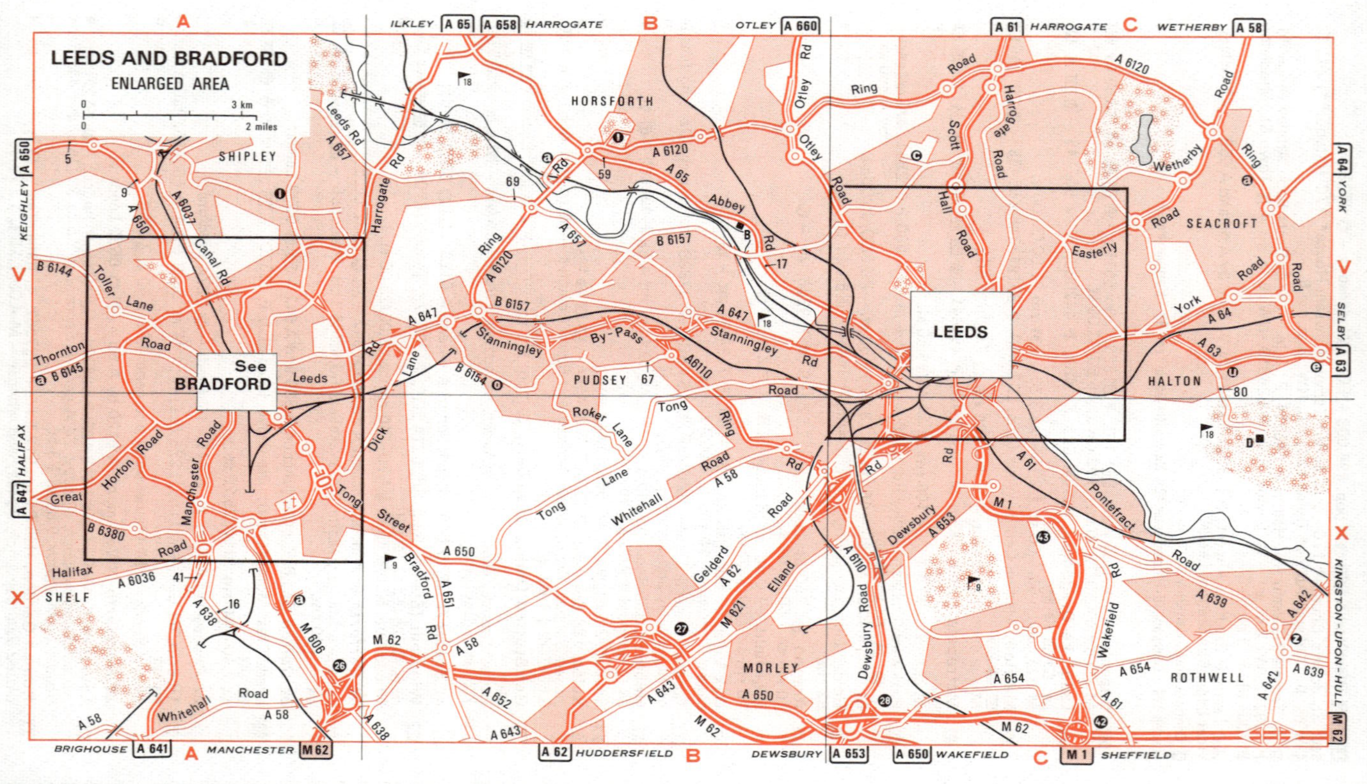

218

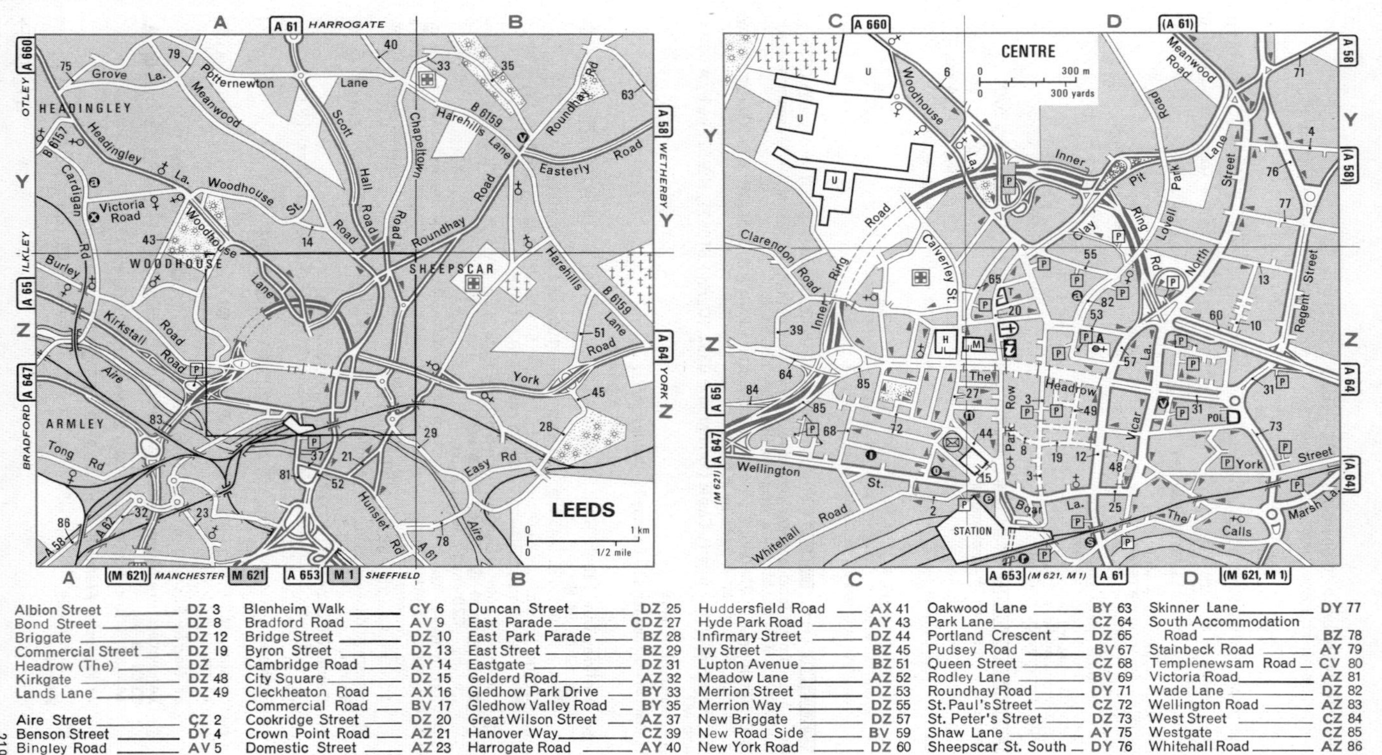

LEEDS
CENTRE

Albion Street — DZ 3
Bond Street — DZ 8
Briggate — DZ 12
Commercial Street — DZ 19
Headrow (The) — DZ
Kirkgate — DZ 48
Lands Lane — DZ 49

Aire Street — CZ 2
Benson Street — DY 4
Bingley Road — AV 5
Blenheim Walk — CY 6
Bradford Road — AV 9
Bridge Street — DZ 10
Byron Street — DZ 13
Cambridge Road — AY 14
City Square — DZ 15
Cleckheaton Road — AX 16
Commercial Road — BV 17
Cookridge Street — DZ 20
Crown Point Road — AZ 21
Domestic Street — AZ 23
Duncan Street — DZ 25
East Parade — CDZ 27
East Park Parade — BZ 28
East Street — BZ 29
Eastgate — DZ 31
Gelderd Road — AZ 32
Gledhow Park Drive — BY 33
Gledhow Valley Road — BY 35
Great Wilson Street — AZ 37
Hanover Way — CZ 39
Harrogate Road — AY 40
Huddersfield Road — AX 41
Hyde Park Road — AY 43
Infirmary Street — DZ 44
Ivy Street — BZ 45
Lupton Avenue — BZ 51
Meadow Lane — AZ 52
Merrion Street — DZ 53
Merrion Way — DZ 55
New Briggate — DZ 57
New Road Side — BV 59
New York Road — DZ 60
Oakwood Lane — BY 63
Park Lane — CZ 64
Portland Crescent — DZ 65
Pudsey Road — BV 67
Queen Street — CZ 68
Rodley Lane — BV 69
Roundhay Road — DY 71
St. Paul's Street — CZ 72
St. Peter's Street — DZ 73
Shaw Lane — AY 75
Sheepscar St. South — DY 76
Skinner Lane — DY 77
South Accommodation Road — BZ 78
Stainbeck Road — AY 79
Templenewsam Road — CV 80
Victoria Road — AZ 81
Wade Lane — DZ 82
Wellington Road — AZ 83
West Street — CZ 84
Westgate — CZ 85
Whitehall Road — AZ 86

HEADINGLEY
Grove La.
Headingley
Cardigan Rd
Victoria Road
Potternewton
Meanwood
Scott Lane
Hall Road
Chapeltown Road
Harehills Lane
B 6159
Roundhay Rd
Easterly Road
WOODHOUSE
Woodhouse St.
Woodhouse Lane
Kirkstall Road
Aire
ARMLEY
Tong Rd
SHEEPSCAR
Roundhay Road
York Road
Easy Rd
Hunslet Rd
OTLEY A 660
ILKLEY A 65
BRADFORD A 647
HARROGATE
WETHERBY
YORK
(M 621) MANCHESTER M 621
A 653 M 1 SHEFFIELD
A 58   A 61   A 64

CENTRE
Woodhouse La.
Clarendon Road
Inner Ring Road
Calverley St.
Meanwood Road
Lovell Park Rd
Clay Pit
North Street
Regent Street
Vicar La.
Park Row
Headrow
The Calls
York Street
Marsh La.
Boar La.
Wellington St.
Whitehall Road
STATION
POL
A 660   A 61   A 58   A 64   A 65   A 647
A 653 (M 621, M 1)

1 km   1/2 mile
300 m   300 yards

LEEDS

MICHELIN Branch, Gelderd Rd, LS12 6EU, ☎ 793911.

AUSTIN-MG-ROVER-TRIUMPH-WOLSELEY 27 Burley Rd ☎ 39291
AUSTIN-MORRIS-MG-WOLSELEY North St. ☎ 32731
AUSTIN-MORRIS-MG-WOLSELEY North Lane ☎ 51948
AUSTIN-MORRIS-MG-PRINCESS Church Lane, Crossgates ☎ 645151
BMW Bramhope ☎ 842238
BMW York Rd ☎ 643772
DAIMLER-JAGUAR, ROLLS ROYCE-BENTLEY Roseville Rd ☎ 32721
DATSUN Meadow Rd ☎ 444531
DATSUN Street Lane ☎ 661043
DATSUN, PORSCHE, SAAB Apperley Lane, Yeadon ☎ 0532 (Rawdon) 502231
FIAT, CITROEN Water Lane ☎ 38091
FORD 98 Roundhay Rd ☎ 629301
FORD Aberford Rd ☎ 863261
FORD Whitehall Rd ☎ 634222
LADA Domestic St. ☎ 468141
LANCIA 251 Whitehall Rd ☎ 634418
MERCEDES-BENZ 39/41 Lowell Park Rd ☎ 31153
MORRIS-MG-WOLSELEY Town St., Stanningley ☎ 097 35 (Pudsey) 3181
PEUGEOT 633 Roundhay Rd ☎ 656565
PEUGEOT South Milford ☎ 0977 (South Milford) 682714
RENAULT Regent St. ☎ 30837
ROVER-TRIUMPH, ASTON MARTIN Regent St. ☎ 38201
SAAB Wellington Rd ☎ 633331
TALBOT Regent St. ☎ 31914
TALBOT Crossgates ☎ 641573
TALBOT Armley Rd ☎ 34554
TALBOT Wike Ridge Lane ☎ 661129
TOYOTA ☎ 702341
TOYOTA Regent St. ☎ 444223
VAUXHALL 123 Hunslet Rd ☎ 39911
VAUXHALL Roseville Rd ☎ 41551
VOLVO Wellington Rd ☎ 36412
VW, AUDI-NSU Gelderd Rd ☎ 633431

LEE-ON-THE-SOLENT Hants. **403 404** Q 31 – pop. 6,266 – ECD : Thursday – ✆ 0705.
London 81 – Portsmouth 13 – Southampton 15 – Winchester 23.

🏠 Belle Vue, 39 Marine Par. East, PO13 9BW, ☎ 550258, ≼ – ⇔wc 🛏wc 🅿 – **34 rm.**

DATSUN High St. ☎ 551785

SAAB 178 Portsmouth Rd ☎ 550448

Si vous écrivez à un hôtel à l'étranger,
joignez à votre lettre un coupon-réponse international.
(disponible dans les bureaux de poste).

LEICESTER Leics. **403 404** Q 26 – pop. 284,208 – ECD : Monday and Thursday – ✆ 0533.
See : Museum of local archaeology, Jewry Wall and baths* AC BY **M¹** – Museum and Art Gallery* CY **M²** – St. Mary de Castro's Church* 12C BY **A.**

🏌 Evington Lane ☎ 736035, E : 2 m. AY – 🏌 Western Park ☎ 872339, W : 4 m. AY – 🏌 Oadby ☎ 700326, S : 2 m. on A 5096 by A 6 AY.

✈ East Midlands Airport : Castle Donington ☎ 0332 (Derby) 810621, NW : 22 m. by A 50 AX and M1.

🛈 12 Bishop St. ☎ 20644.

London 104 – Birmingham 43 – Coventry 26 – Nottingham 24.

Plans on following pages

🏨 **Holiday Inn,** 129 St. Nicholas Circle, LE1 5LX, ☎ 51161, Telex 341281, 🔲 – 🛗 TV 🔥 🅿.
🍴. 🔳 AE ⓞ VISA
BY c
M a la carte 6.35/10.45 t. 🍷 2.80 – 🍽 3.50 – **190 rm** 19.50/26.00 s.

🏨 **Grand** (Embassy), 73 Granby St., LE1 6ES, ☎ 56222 – 🛗 TV 🅿. 🍴. 🔳 AE ⓞ VISA
CY o
M 5.15/7.00 st. 🍷 2.20 – 🍽 2.00 – **93 rm** 18.00/24.00 st.

🏨 Leicester Centre (Centre), Humberstone Gate, LE5 3AT, ☎ 20471, Telex 341460 –
🛗 TV ⇔wc 🎧 🅿. 🍴. 🔳 AE ⓞ VISA
CX n
🍽 1.65 – **220 rm** 17.50/23.25 st.

🏨 **Eaton Bray,** Abbey St., LE1 3TE, ☎ 50666, Telex 342434, ≼ – 🛗 TV ⇔wc 🛏wc 🎧 🅿.
🍴. 🔳 AE ⓞ VISA
CX a
closed Christmas – **M** (closed Saturday lunch, Sunday and Bank Holidays) 5.00/7.00 st.
🍷 2.85 – 🍽 3.95 – **68 rm** 24.95/29.95 st.

🏨 Belmont (Best Western), De Montfort St., LE1 7GR, ☎ 544773 – 🛗 TV ⇔wc 🛏wc 🎧 🅿. 🍴.
55 rm.
CY c

🌴 **Daval,** 292 London Rd, LE2 2AG, ☎ 708234 – 🛏 🅿
AY a
closed 1 week at Christmas – **M** (closed Saturday and Sunday) (dinner only) 3.45 🍷 1.75 –
14 rm 🍽 8.50/14.00 t.

⌂ **Rowans,** 290 London Rd, LE2 2AG, ☎ 705364 – 🛏 🅿. 🔳 VISA
AY i
13 rm 🍽 7.00/13.00 s.

⌂ **Gables,** 368 London Rd, LE2 2PN, ☎ 706969 – 🅿
AY c
11 rm 🍽 6.50/11.00 s.

at Oadby SE : 3 ¼ m. on A 5096 by A 6 – AY – ✉ ✆ 0533 Leicester :

🏨 **Leicestershire Moat House,** Wigston Rd, LE2 5QE, ☎ 719441 – 🛗 TV ⇔wc 🎧 🅿. 🍴.
🔳 AE ⓞ VISA
M 4.80/5.00 t. 🍷 2.00 – 🍽 2.00 – **29 rm** 15.00/22.00 t.

at Wigston Fields S : 3 m. on A 50 – ✉ ✆ 0533 Leicester :

🏨 Wigston Stage Motel, Welford Rd, LE8 1JF, ☎ 886161 – TV ⇔wc 🛏wc 🎧 🅿. 🍴. AZ e
80 rm.

P.T.O. →

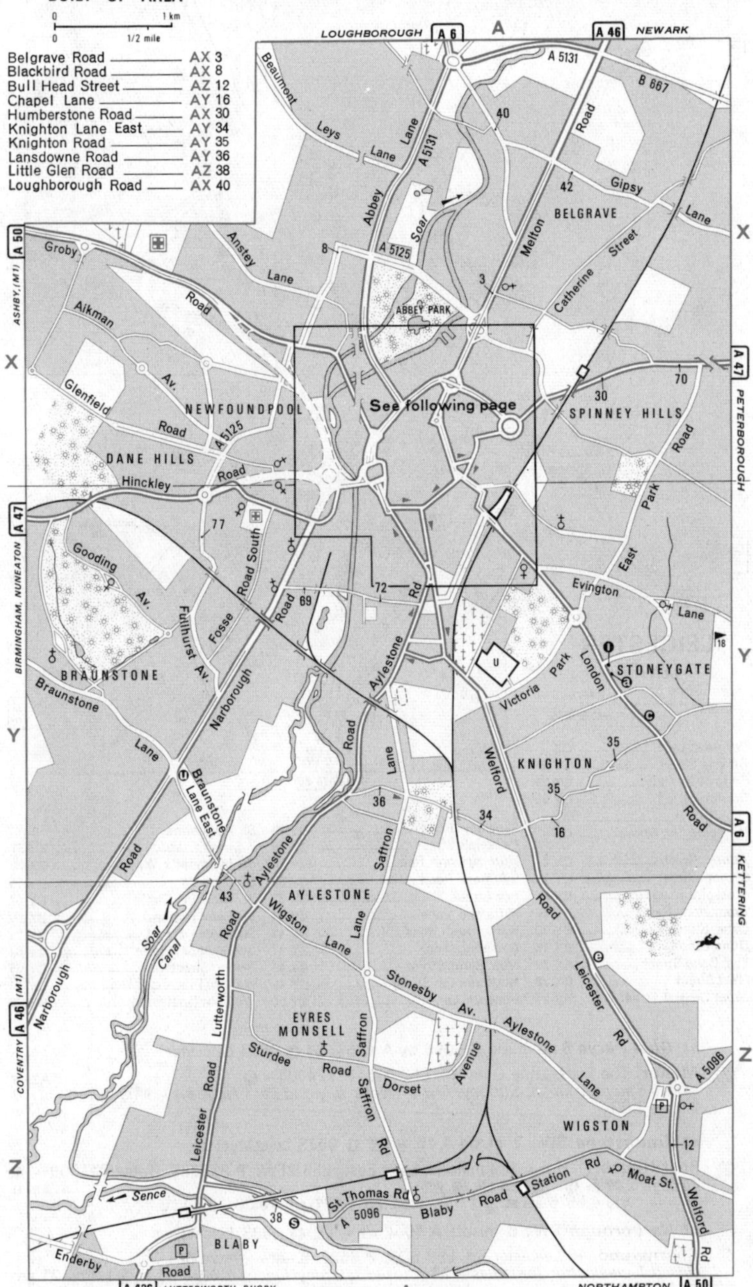

LEICESTER
BUILT UP AREA

0   1 km
0   1/2 mile

Belgrave Road — AX 3
Blackbird Road — AX 8
Bull Head Street — AZ 12
Chapel Lane — AY 16
Humberstone Road — AX 30
Knighton Lane East — AY 34
Knighton Road — AY 35
Lansdowne Road — AY 36
Little Glen Road — AZ 38
Loughborough Road — AX 40

Marfitt Street — AX 42
Middleton Street — AZ 43
Upperton Road — AY 69
Uppingham Road — AX 70
Walnut Street — AY 72
Wyngate Drive — AY 77

LOUGHBOROUGH A 6   A   A 46 NEWARK
A 5131
B 667
A 5131
40
42
Gipsy
Lane
BELGRAVE
Beaumont
Leys
Lane
Abbey
Lane
Soar
A 5125
8
Anstey
Lane
Road
Melton
Catherine
Street
3
ABBEY PARK
A 50
Groby
Aikman
Av.
Glenfield
Road
A 5125
NEWFOUNDPOOL
See following page
30
70
SPINNEY HILLS
A 47
PETERBOROUGH
DANE HILLS
Hinckley
Road
Road South
77
A 47
BIRMINGHAM, NUNEATON
ASHBY, (M1)
Gooding
Av.
Fulhurst Av.
Fosse
Road
69
72 Rd
East
Park
Road
Evington
Lane
18
BRAUNSTONE
Braunstone
Narborough
Aylestone
Road
Victoria
U
Park
London
Road
STONEYGATE
Lane
Braunstone
Lane East
Road
36
Saffron
Lane
34
Welford
KNIGHTON
35
35
16
A 6
KETTERING
43
AYLESTONE
Aylestone
Road
Wigston
Lane
Lane
Saffron
Road
Leicester
Rd
Soar
Canal
Narborough
COVENTRY A 46 (M1)
Lutterworth
Road
Leicester
Road
EYRES
MONSELL
Sturdee
Saffron
Road
Dorset
Stonesby
Av.
Saffron
Rd
Avenue
Aylestone
Lane
Leicester
Road
A 5096
WIGSTON
12
Station Rd
Moat St.
Welford
Rd
Sence
Blaby
Road
Station
St. Thomas Rd
A 5096
Blaby
38
BLABY
Enderby
Road
A 426 LUTTERWORTH, RUGBY   A   NORTHAMPTON A 50

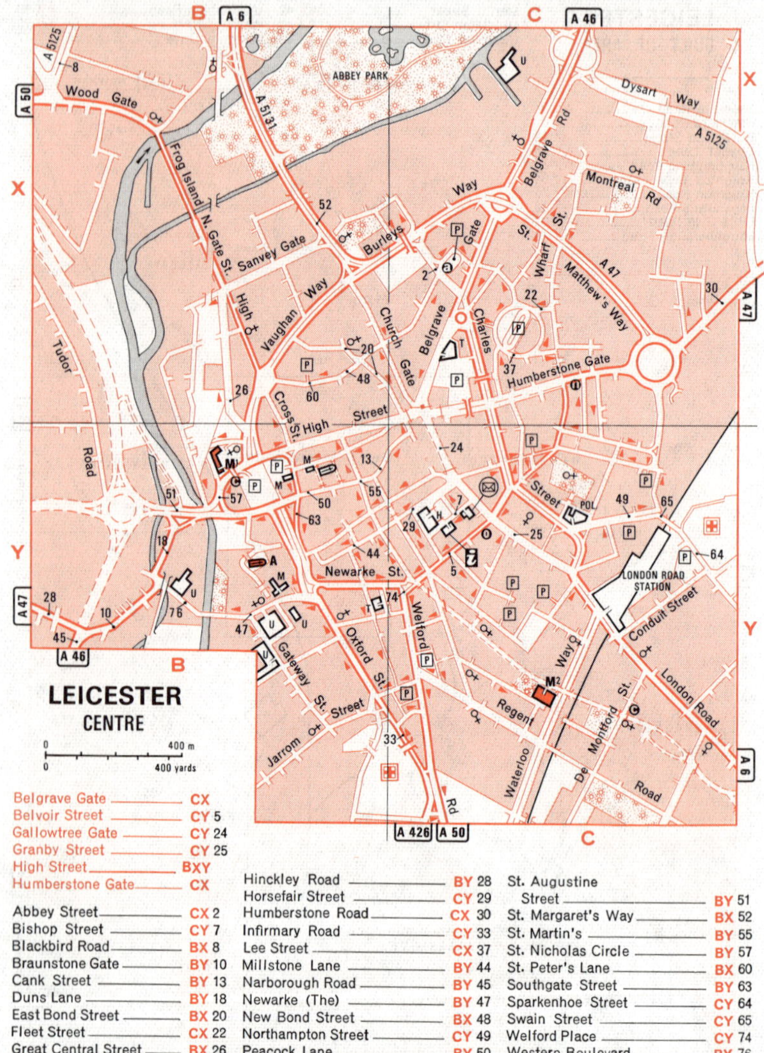

LEICESTER
CENTRE

0   400 m
0   400 yards

at Glen Parva S : 5 m. on A 5096 by A 426 – ✉ ☎ 0533 Leicester :

XXX **Manor,** The Ford, Little Glen Rd, LE2 9TL, ☎ 774604 – **P**   AZ **s**
closed Saturday lunch, Sunday, first 2 weeks July and Bank Holidays – **M** a la carte 5.70/ 8.60 ▯ 2.00.

at Braunstone SW : 2 m. on A 46 – ✉ ☎ 0533 Leicester :

Post House (T.H.F.), Braunstone Lane East, LE3 2FW, ☎ 896688, Telex 341009 –
📺 ☐ wc 🅿 🐕 ⚓ 🅿 🔥 🅰🅴 ⓪ 𝗩𝗜𝗦𝗔   AY **u**
M a la carte 4.55/6.70 **st.** ▯ 1.85 – ☐ 2.25 – **171 rm** 18.00/25.50 **st.**

at Narborough SW : 6 m. off A 46 – AZ – ✉ ☎ 0533 Leicester :

Charnwood, 48 Leicester Rd, LE9 5DF, ☎ 862218, 🚗 – ☐ wc **P**
closed 1 week after Christmas – **M** *(closed saturday lunch)* 2.00/4.20 **st.** ▯ 1.90 – **21 rm** ☐ 11.00/17.50 **st.**

at Leicester Forest East W : 3 m. on A 47 – AY – ✉ ☎ 0533 Leicester :

🏨 **Europa Lodge** (County), Hinckley Rd, LE3 3GH, ☏ 394661, Group Telex 25971 – 📺 🛏wc ☏ 🄿. 🛃. 🄰 AE ⓪ *VISA*
M approx. 4.50 st. ▮ 1.55 – **31 rm** ☲ 17.00/20.00 s.

MICHELIN Branch, 33 Blackbird Av., Blackbird Rd, LE4 0AD, ☏ 25596.

AUSTIN-MORRIS, TALBOT Leicester Rd ☏ 881601
AUSTIN-DAIMLER-JAGUAR-MORRIS-ROVER-TRIUMPH Dover St. ☏ 27252
AUSTIN-DAIMLER-MORRIS-MG-PRINCESS, ROVER-TRIUMPH, ROLLS ROYCE Welford Rd ☏ 548757
AUSTIN-MORRIS-PRINCESS-ROVER-TRIUMPH, VANDEN PLAS 203 Belgrave Gate ☏ 56631
AUSTIN-MORRIS Stoughton Drive North ☏ 736362
CITROEN ☏ 289/297 Melton Rd 63371
CITROEN Queens Rd ☏ 708947
COLT, SAAB Nelson St. ☏ 50928
DATSUN 56 Thurcaston Rd ☏ 666861
FIAT, LANCIA-RELIANT 459 Ayleston Rd ☏ 831052
FIAT Station St. ☏ 976 (Kegworth) 2523
FIAT 47 Blackbird Rd ☏ 53137

FORD Belgrave Gate ☏ 50501
FORD Welford Rd ☏ 706215
HONDA Thurlaston Rd ☏ 666861
MORRIS-PRINCESS Green Lane Rd ☏ 767551
OPEL-VAUXHALL Aylestone Rd ☏ 547515
PEUGEOT Mayfield Corner ☏ 543675
PORSCHE Coventry Rd at Narborongh ☏ 848270
RENAULT 60/62 Northgate St. ☏ 28612
TALBOT 91 Abbey Lane ☏ 61501
TOYOTA Catherine St. ☏ 62628
VAUXHALL Evington ☏ 730421
VW, AUDI 670/696 Melton Rd, Thurmaston ☏ 693731
VW, AUDI, MERCEDES-BENZ Church Gate ☏ 530413
VW, AUDI, MERCEDES-BENZ Church Gate ☏ 25841

LEIGH Greater Manchester 🗺 🗺 M 23 – pop. 46,181 – ECD : Wednesday – ☎ 0942.

🏌 Kenyon Hall, Culcheth ☏ 092 576 (Culcheth) 3130, S : by A 574.

London 205 – Liverpool 25 – Manchester 12 – Preston 25.

🏨 **Greyhound Motor** (Embassy), Warrington Rd, WN7 3XQ, S : 1 m. at junction A 580 and A 574 ☏ 671256 – 📶 📺 🛏wc ☏ 🄐 🚗 🄿. 🄰 AE ⓪ *VISA*
M a la carte 3.45/7.75 **st.** – ☲ 2.25 – **64 rm** 16.50/20.00 **st.**

DATSUN 39 Plank Lane ☏ 673334
OPEL Wigan Rd ☏ 671951

RENAULT, TOYOTA Wigan Rd ☏ 676236
VAUXHALL 196 Chapel St. ☏ 671326

LELANT Cornwall 🗺 D 33 – see St. Ives.

LENWADE-GREAT WITCHINGHAM Norfolk 🗺 X 25 – ECD : Wednesday – ✉ Norwich – ☎ 060 544 Great Witchingham.

London 121 – Fakenham 14 – Norwich 10.

🏠 **Lenwade House** ⚓, NR9 5QP, ☏ 288, ⚓, ✗, ☇ heated, ⚓, 🚗, park – 📺 🛏wc 🚽wc 🄿. 🄰 AE ⓪ *VISA*
M 3.75 ▮ 1.30 – **13 rm** ☲ 12.45/18.70.

LEOMINSTER Heref. and Worc. 🗺 L 27 – pop. 7,079 – ECD : Thursday – ☎ 0568.
See : Priory Church* 14C (the north aisle* 12C). **Envir. :** Berrington Hall* (Georgian) AC, N : 3 m. – Croft Castle* (15C) AC, NW : 6 m.

🛈 The Library. South St. ☏ 2384.

London 141 – Birmingham 47 – Hereford 13 – Worcester 26.

🏠 Talbot, West St., HR6 8EP, ☏ 2121 – 📺 🛏wc 🚽wc 🄿
31 rm.

AUSTIN-DAIMLER-JAGUAR-LAND ROVER-MORRIS-ROVER-TRIUMPH South St. ☏ 2545

COLT Broad St. ☏ 2787
TALBOT, OPEL The Bargates ☏ 2337

LETCHWORTH Herts. 🗺 T 28 – pop. 27,150 – ECD : Wednesday – ☎ 046 26.
London 40 – Bedford 22 – Cambridge 22 – Luton 14.

🏨 Broadway (Crest), The Broadway, SG6 3MZ, ☏ 5651 – 📶 📺 🛏wc ☏ 🄿. 🛃. 🄰 AE ⓪ *VISA*
32 rm ☲ 15.90/25.20 **st.**

🏨 Letchworth Hall ⚓, Letchworth Lane, SG6 3NP, S : 1 m. off A 505 ☏ 3747, ⚓, ✗, 🚗 – 📺 🛏wc ☏ 🄿
19 rm.

AUSTIN-MORRIS-MG-ROVER-TRIUMPH Works Rd ☏ 73161
FORD 18/24 Station Rd ☏ 3722

HONDA, OPEL Norton Way North ☏ 4850
RENAULT Norton Way North ☏ 6341

LEWDOWN Devon 🗺 H 32 – ECD : Wednesday – ✉ Okehampton – ☎ 056 683.
London 234 – Exeter 33.

🏨 **Coach House Motel** without rest., EX20 4DS, on A 30 ☏ 322, Telex 45388 – 📺 🛏wc 🚽wc 🄿. 🄰 AE ⓪ *VISA*
50 rm ☲ 14.50/24.00 **t.**

LEWES East Sussex **404** U 31 – pop. 14,159 – ECD : Wednesday – ✆ 079 16.

See : Norman Castle (ruins) site and ≼*, 45 steps, *AC* – Anne of Cleves' House* (1559) *AC*.
Envir.: Glynde Place (pictures*) *AC*, E : 3 ½ m. – Firle Place* (mansion 15C-16C) *AC*, SE :
4 ½ m. – Ditchling Beacon ≼* W : 7 ½ m. – Glyndebourne Opera Festival (May-August) *AC*,
E : 3 m.

Chapel Hill ✆ 3245, Opp. Junction Cliffe High/South St.

187 High St. ✆ 6151 ext 57.

London 53 – Brighton 8 – Hastings 29 – Maidstone 43.

- **The Shelleys**, High St., BN7 1XS, ✆ 2361, 🚗 – 📺 🛁wc 🚿wc 🅿 – **21 rm.**

- **White Hart** (Best Western), 55 High St., BN7 1XE, ✆ 4676 – 📺 🛁wc 🚿 🅿. 🔄 AE ⓪
VISA
M a la carte 4.70/6.55 ◊ 2.50 – **32 rm** ⌁ 13.00/25.00 **s.**

- **Trumps**, 19-20 Station St., BN7 2DB, ✆ 3906
closed Sunday, Monday and lunch Tuesday, Wednesday – **M** a la carte 7.35/9.00 **t.** ◊ 2.55.

- **Pelham Arms (Sussex Kitchen)**, High St., BN7 1XL, ✆ 6149 – 🅿
*closed Sunday, Monday, last week August, first week September, 5 November and Bank
Holidays* – **M** a la carte 4.05/4.90 **t.** ◊ 1.80.

- **La Cucina**, 13 Station St., BN7 2DA, ✆ 6707, Italian rest. – 🔄 **VISA**
closed Sunday and 23 December-2 January – **M** a la carte 4.70/7.20 ◊ 1.20.

- Nitchevo, 199 High St., BN7 2NS, ✆ 2343, Russian rest.

at Selmeston SE : 6 ½ m. off A 27 – ✉ Polegate – ✆ 032 183 Ripe :

- **Corin's**, Church Farm, BN26 6TZ, ✆ 343, « 17C farmhouse », 🚗 – 🅿. 🔄 **VISA**
closed Sunday dinner, Monday, Christmas Day and January – **M** (dinner only and Sunday
lunch) 3.30/6.50 **t.** ◊ 2.35.

AUSTIN-MORRIS-MG Western Rd ✆ 3221   FORD Station St. ✆ 4461
AUSTIN-MORRIS-MG Cliffe Bridge ✆ 2245   RENAULT 96/106 Malling St. ✆ 4136

LIBANUS Powys **403** J 28 – see Brecon.

LICHFIELD Staffs. **403** **404** O 25 – pop. 22,660 – ECD : Wednesday – ✆ 054 32.
See : Cathedral** 12C-14C.

Tamworth Rd ✆ 0543 (Whittington) 432 212, 2 ½ m. Lichfield Station.

9 Bread Market St. ✆ 52109.

London 128 – Birmingham 16 – Derby 23 – Stoke-on-Trent 30.

- **Little Barrow**, Beacon St., WS13 7AQ, ✆ 53311 – 📺 🛁wc 🚿 🅿. 🏊. 🔄 AE ⓪ **VISA**
M 4.00/6.00 **t.** ◊ 2.50 – ⌁ 2.60 – **26 rm** 12.00/16.20.

- **George**, Bird St., WS13 6PR, ✆ 23061 – 📺 🛁wc 🚿 🅿. 🏊. 🔄 AE ⓪ **VISA**
M 5.45 **st.** ◊ 2.55 – ⌁ 2.90 – **40 rm** 14.40/19.55 **st.**

- **Angel Croft**, Beacon St., WS13 7AA, ✆ 23147, 🚗 – 🚿wc 🅿. 🔄 ⓪ **VISA**
closed 25 and 26 December – **M** (closed Sunday dinner) 4.50/6.00 **st.** – **13 rm** ⌁ 11.00/
23.25 **st.**

AUSTIN-MORRIS-MG-ROVER-TRIUMPH St. John St.   FORD, RENAULT Birmingham Rd ✆ 53571
✆ 51451

LIFTON Devon **403** H 32 – pop. 820 – ECD : Tuesday – ✆ 056 684.
Envir.: Launceston (castle* : Norman ruins *AC*, St. Mary Magdalene's Church : carving outside
walls* 16C) E : 3 ½ m.

Laucenston ✆ 0566 (Launceston) 3442, W : 5 m.

London 238 – Bude 24 – Exeter 37 – Launceston 4 – Plymouth 32.

- **Arundell Arms** (Best Western), Fore St., PL16 0AA, on A 30 ✆ 244, 🎣, 🚗 – 🚿wc 🅿.
🔄 AE ⓪ **VISA**
closed 24 to 28 December – **M** a la carte 6.65/9.55 **st.** ◊ 2.40 – **27 rm** ⌁ 17.00/31.00 **st.**

LIMPSFIELD Surrey **404** T 30 – see Oxted.

See : Cathedral*** 11C-15C (Angel Choir**, Library: Magna Carta *AC*) Y **A** – Jew's House**
12C Y **B** – Castle* (11C) *AC* Y – Newport Arch* (Roman) Y **E** – Stonebow and Guildhall*
15C-16C z **S. Envir. :** Doddington Hall* (Elizabethan) *AC*, SW: 7 m. by A 15 z and A 46.

⌷₁₈ Lincoln ☏ 042 771 (Torksey) 210, W: 12 m. by A 57 z.

🄩 90 Bailgate ☏ 29828 – City Hall, Beaumont Fee ☏ 32151 ext 515/6.

London 143 – Bradford 79 – **Cambridge** 93 – Kingston-upon-Hull 37 – **Leeds** 70 – Leicester 49 – Norwich 104 –
Nottingham 36 – **Sheffield** 46 – York 80.

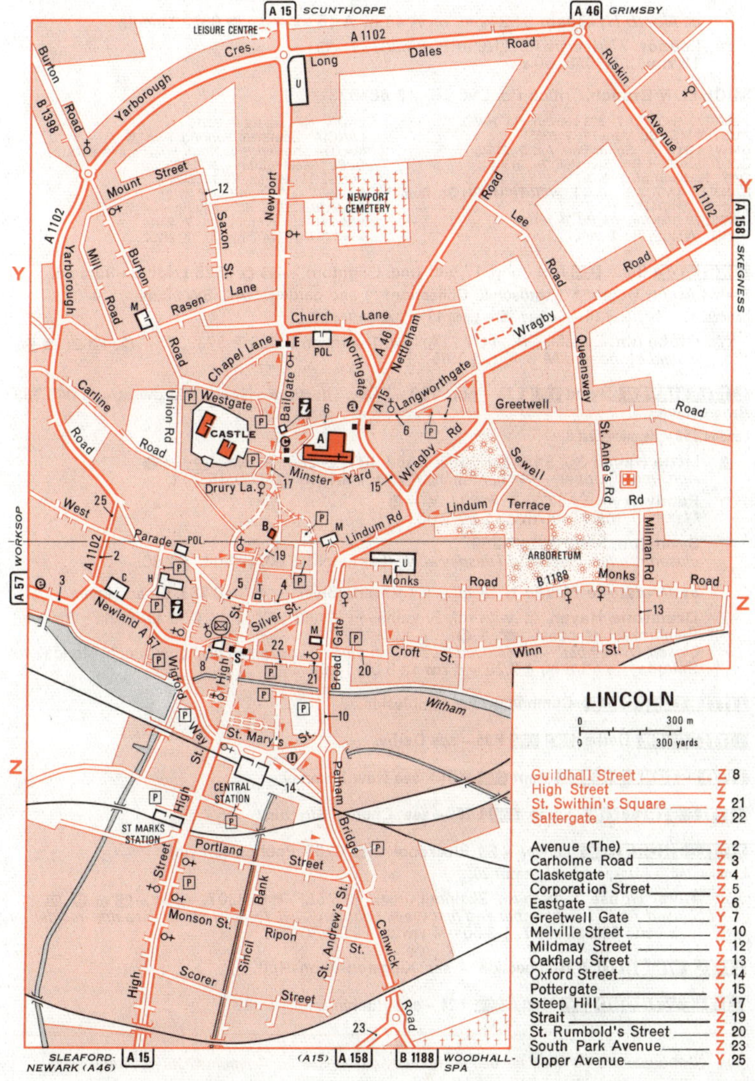

🏨 White Hart, Bailgate, LN1 3AR, ☏ 26222, Telex 56304, « Antique furniture » – 📶 📺
🚗 P. 🛁 – **62 rm.**   Y **c**

🏨 **Eastgate** (T.H.F.), Eastgate, LN2 1PN, ☏ 20341, Telex 56316 – 📶 📺 ♿ P. 🛁 🔲 AE
① VISA   Y **a**
M a la carte 4.80/7.30 **st.** 🍷 1.65 – 🍵 2.50 – **71 rm** 18.00/26.50 **st.**

🏠 **Grand,** St. Mary's St., LN5 7EP, ☎ 24211 – ⌷wc ☎ **P**. 🔌 ⓘ 𝗩𝗜𝗦𝗔   z u
   M 3.50/3.80 st. 🍷 1.40 – **51 rm** 🍽 15.00/27.00 st.

⌂ **Hollies,** 65 Carholme Rd, LN1 1RT, ☎ 22419 – **P**   z e
   10 rm 🍽 6.50/13.00 s.

   at Branston SE: 4 ½ m. on B 1188 – z – ✉ ☎ 0522 Lincoln :

🏠 **Moor Lodge,** 23 Sleaford Rd, LN4 1HU, ☎ 791366 – ⌷wc **P**. 🔌 AE ⓘ
   M 4.50 st. 🍷 1.50 – **33 rm** 🍽 12.00/28.00 st.

   at North Hykeham S: 3 ½ m. on A 46 by A 15 – z – ✉ ☎ 0522 Lincoln :

⌂ **Loudor,** 37 Newark Rd, LN6 8RB, ☎ 680333 – **P**
   12 rm 🍽 6.30/12.50 s.

MICHELIN Branch, Tritton Rd, LN6 7RX, ☎ 684023.

ALFA-ROMEO, FIAT 223 Newark Rd ☎ 22329
AUSTIN-MG St. Mary St. ☎ 33351
BMW, TOYOTA South Park Av. ☎ 21345
COLT Sleaford Rd, Branston ☎ 791384
DAF Portland St. ☎ 22097
DAIMLER-JAGUAR-LAND ROVER-TRIUMPH St. Rumbold St. ☎ 27117
DATSUN 148 Newark Rd ☎ 261223
FORD Wragby Rd ☎ 30101
LADA Newark Rd ☎ 20216
LANCIA Boultham Park Rd ☎ 31735
MAZDA Newark Rd, North Hykeham ☎ 681242
OPEL Skellingthorpe ☎ 62670
PEUGEOT Burton Rd ☎ 32424
TALBOT 477 High St. ☎ 29131
SABARU 53/55 St. Catherines ☎ 20201
VAUXHALL Wragby Rd ☎ 27127
VW, AUDI 134 High St. ☎ 21252

LINSLADE Beds. 🄜🄚🄚 R 28 – pop. 17,580 (inc. Leighton) – ✉ ☎ 0525 Leighton Buzzard.
Envir.: Ascott House✶✶ (Rothschild Collection✶✶) and gardens✶ *AC,* SW: 2 m.
London 49 – Aylesbury 10 – Bedford 19 – Luton 13 – Northampton 30.

XX **Globe Inn,** Bletchley Rd, LU7 7TA, NW: 1 ½ m. on B 488 ☎ 373338 – **P**. 🔌 AE ⓘ 𝗩𝗜𝗦𝗔
   closed Monday – **M** 6.45 t. 🍷 1.65.

LITTLE HAVEN Dyfed 🄜🄚🄛 E 28 – pop. 150 – ECD : Thursday – ✉ Haverfordwest – ☎ 043 783
Broad Haven.
London 258 – Haverfordwest 8.

🏠 **Little Haven** ⌘, Strawberry Hill, SA62 3UT, ☎ 285, ⩗, 🚗 – ⌷wc **P**
   April-mid October – **M** (bar lunch) 4.75 t. – **14 rm** 🍽 8.00/18.00 t.

⌂ **Pendyffryn,** SA62 3LA, ☎ 337, ⩗ – **P**
   March-October – **9 rm** 🍽 5.50/9.00.

X **Swan Inn,** SA62 3UL, ☎ 256
   closed dinner Sunday to Tuesday – **M** (bar lunch) 8.00/12.50 t. 🍷 1.80.

   at Druistone Haven N: 3 m. – ✉ Haverfordwest – ☎ 048 783 Broad Haven :

X **Druistone Haven** ⌘ with rm, Broadhaven, SA62 3TY, ☎ 221, ⩗ St. Bride's Bay and
   Pembrokeshire coast, 🚗 – **P**
   closed November – **M** *(closed Sunday dinner to non-residents)* (bar lunch Monday to
   Saturday) 5.50/6.50 🍷 2.20 – **8 rm** 🍽 8.00/16.00.

LITTLE LANGDALE Cumbria – see Ambleside.

LITTLEOVER Derbs. 🄜🄚🄛 🄜🄚🄚 P 25 – see Derby.

LITTLESTONE-ON-SEA Kent 🄜🄚🄚 W 31 – see New Romney.

LITTLE STRETTON Salop 🄜🄚🄛 L 26 – see Church Stretton.

LITTLE THORNTON Lancs. – ✉ Blackpool – ☎ 0253 Poulton-le-Fylde.
London 240 – Blackpool 5 – Lancaster 20.

XX **River House** ⌘ with rm, Skippool Creek, FY5 5LF, ☎ 883307, ⩗, 🚗 – 📺 ☎ **P**. AE
   closed 7 to 21 September and first week February – **M** *(closed Monday to non-residents)*
   a la carte 6.60/14.00 t. 🍷 3.00 – **4 rm** 🍽 15.00/30.00 t.

LITTLE WEIGHTON Humberside – see Kingston-upon-Hull.

LITTLE WYMONDLEY Herts. 🄜🄚🄚 T 28 – see Hitchin.

N'oubliez pas qu'il existe des limitations de vitesse au Royaume Uni en dehors de celles mentionnées sur les panneaux.

60 mph (= 96 km/h) sur route.

70 mph (= 112 km/h) sur route à chaussées séparées et autoroute.

LIVERPOOL Merseyside �403 L 23 – pop. 610,113 – ECD : Wednesday – ✪ 051.

See : Walker Art Gallery** CY M¹ – City of Liverpool Museums* CY M² – Anglican Cathedral* (1904) CZ A – Roman Catholic Cathedral* (1967) DZ B. **Envir. :** Knowsley Safari Park** AC, NE : 8 m. by A 57 BX – Speke Hall* (16C) AC, SE : 7 m. by A 561 BX.

⌗₁₈ Dunnings Bridge, Bootle ☏ 928 6196, N : 5 m. by A 5036 AV – ⌗₁₈ Allerton Park ☏ 428 1046, S : 5 m. by B 5180 BX – ⌗₁₈ Naylor's Rd, Gateacre ☏ 487 9982, E : 7 m. by B 5178 BX.

✈ ☏ 427 4101, SE : 6 m. by A 561 BX – **Terminal :** Pier Head and Lime St.

🛳 to Belfast (P & O Ferries : Irish Sea Services) 8 weekly (10 h) – to Dublin (B & I Line) 2-3 weekly (7 h) – to the Isle of Man : Douglas (Isle of Man Steam Packet Co.) 1-6 daily ; (4 h 30 mn).

🛈 187 St. John's Centre, Elliot St. ☏ 709 3631 or 8681.

London 215 – **Birmingham** 99 – **Leeds** 70 – **Manchester** 36.

Town plans : Liverpool pp. 2-5

🏨 **Atlantic Tower** (Thistle), 30 Chapel St., L3 9RE, ☏ 227 4444, Telex 627070, ⇐ – ▮ 📺 ♿ 🍴 . 🅰 AE ⓪ VISA CY r
M 4.75/6.25 **st.** 🍷 1.75 – ☕ 3.00 – **226 rm** 23.00/30.00 **st.**

🏨 **Adelphi** (B.T.H.), Ranelagh Pl., L3 5UL, ☏ 709 7200, Telex 629644, 🌊 – ▮ 📺 . 🍴 . 🅰 AE CZ o
M 3.50 **st.** 🍷 2.40 – **167 rm** ☕ 23.70/31.05 **st.**

🏨 **Holiday Inn,** Paradise St., L1 8JD, ☏ 709 0181, Telex 627270, 🌊 – ▮ 📺 ♿ 🅿 . 🍴 . 🅰 AE ⓪ VISA CZ n
M 4.90/5.90 **t.** 🍷 2.75 – ☕ 3.60 – **273 rm** 19.50/25.00 **s.** – P 35.90/40.60.

🏨 **St. George's** (T.H.F.), St. John's Precinct, Lime St., L1 1NQ, ☏ 709 7090, Telex 627630 – ▮ 📺 ♿ . 🍴 . 🅰 AE ⓪ VISA CY v
M 4.50/5.10 **st.** 🍷 1.65 – ☕ 2.50 – **155 rm** 21.50/27.50 **st.**

🏨 Liverpool Centre (Centre), Lord Nelson St., L3 5QB, ☏ 709 7050, Telex 627954 – ▮ 📺 🛏 wc 📞 🅿 . 🍴 . 🅰 AE ⓪ VISA CY i
☕ 1.65 – **170 rm** 15.80/19.80 **st.**

🏨 **Alexandra Court** 🌿 . Alexandra Drive, L17 8TE, SE : 3 m. by A 561 ☏ 727 2551, 🚗 – 🛏 wc 🅿 . 🅰 AE VISA BX n
closed Bank Holidays – **M** (closed Saturday and Sunday) (dinner only) 4.25 **st.** 🍷 2.00 – **24 rm** ☕ 15.15/21.40 **st.**

🏨 **Lord Nelson,** Lord Nelson St., L3 5PD, ☏ 709 4362 – ▮ 🛏 wc 📞 🚗 . 🅰 AE ⓪ VISA CY e
M 3.75/4.25 **t.** 🍷 2.50 – **63 rm** ☕ 13.50/19.50 **t.** – P 21.50/27.50 **t.**

🏨 **Shaftesbury,** Mount Pleasant, L3 5SA, ☏ 709 4421 – ▮ 🛏 wc 📞 . 🍴 . 🅰 AE ⓪ VISA CZ c
M (closed Sunday dinner) 3.50/4.75 **t.** 🍷 2.45 – **70 rm** ☕ 12.00/18.00 **t.**

🏨 **Green Park,** 4-6 Greenbank Drive, L17 1AN, SE : 2 ½ m. by A 562 ☏ 733 3382, 🚗 – 📺 🛏 🛏 wc 📞 ♿ 🅿 BX u
M (bar lunch) 4.00 **s.** 🍷 1.50 – **23 rm** ☕ 8.00/16.00 **s.** – P 14.00/18.00 **s.**

XXX Ristorante del Secolo, 40 Stanley St., L2 6LY, ☏ 236 4004, Italian rest. CY x

XXX **Oriel,** 16 Water St., L2 8TH, ☏ 236 4664 – 🅰 AE ⓪ VISA CY s
closed Saturday lunch, Sunday, Christmas and Bank Holidays – **M** a la carte 9.95/12.95 **st.** 🍷 3.20.

XX **Jenny's Seafood,** Old Ropery, Fenwick St., L2 7NT, ☏ 236 0332, Seafood – 🅰 AE ⓪ VISA CZ e
closed Saturday lunch, Sunday and Bank Holidays – **M** a la carte 6.50/10.65 **t.** 🍷 1.85.

X Seven Up, 15 Great George St., ☏ 709 8178, Chinese rest. CZ z

at Waterloo N : 5 ¾ m. off A 565 – ✉ ✪ 051 Liverpool :

🏨 **Royal,** 30 Bath St., L22 5PS, ☏ 928 2332 – 📺 🛏 wc 🛏 wc 📞 🅿 . AE ⓪ VISA AV a
M 4.40 **t.** 🍷 1.40 – **20 rm** ☕ 12.60/24.20 **t.** – P approx. 17.10 **t.**

at Netherton N : 6 m. off A 59 – AV – ✉ ✪ 051 Liverpool :

🏨 Park, Park Lane West, L30 3SU, ☏ 525 7555 – ▮ 📺 🛏 wc 🛏 wc 📞 ♿ 🅿 . 🍴 . 🅰 AE ⓪ VISA
61 rm ☕ 17.50/23.00 **st.**

at Blundellsands N : 6 ½ m. off A 565 – AV – ✉ ✪ 051 Liverpool :

🏨 Blundellsands, Agnes Rd, L23 6TN, ☏ 924 6515 – ▮ 📺 🛏 wc 📞 🅿 . 🍴
44 rm.

at Aigburth SE : 4 m. by A 561 – BX – ✉ ✪ 051 Liverpool :

🏨 **Grange,** 14 Holmefield Rd, L19 3PG, ☏ 427 2950, 🚗 – 🛏 wc 🅿
M (dinner only) 6.00 🍷 1.75 – **27 rm** ☕ 9.50/16.00.

P.T.O. →

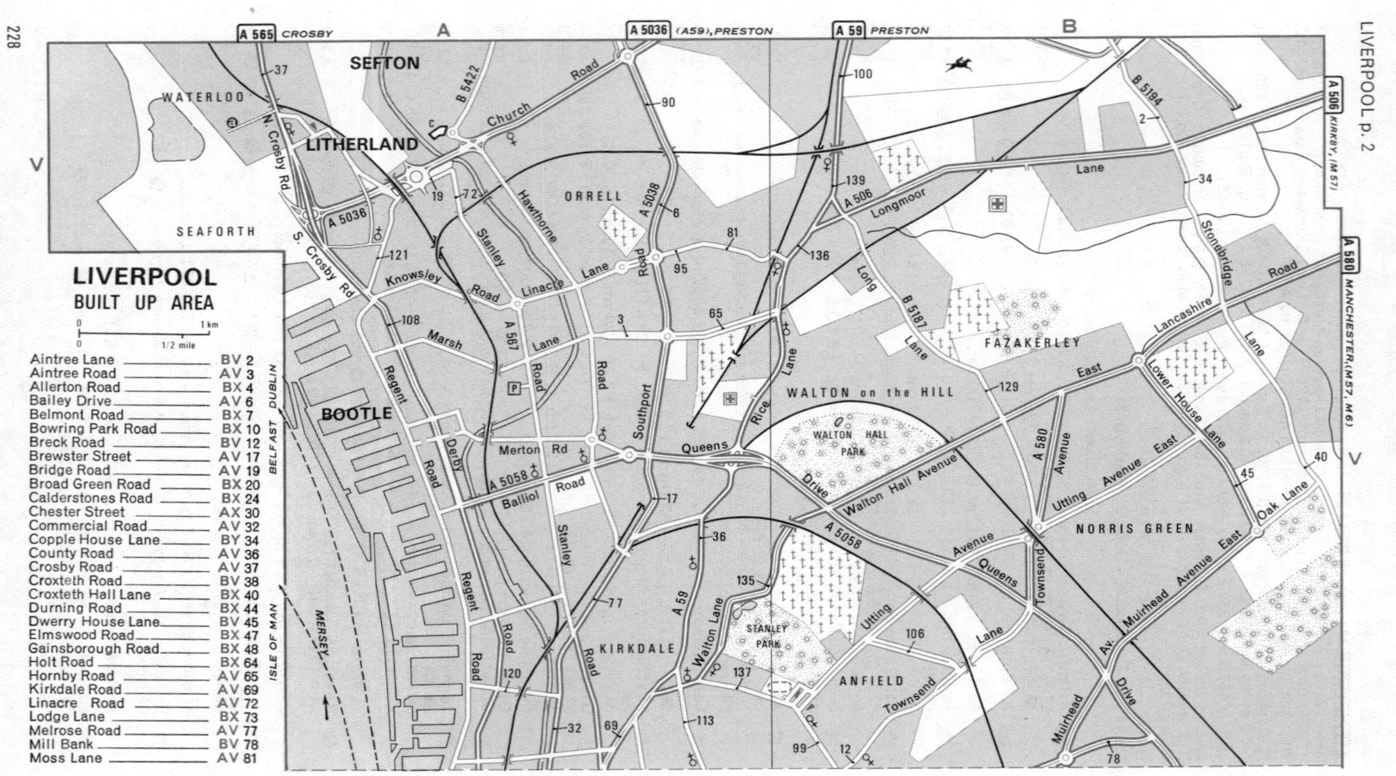

A 565 CROSBY
A 5036 (A59), PRESTON
A 59 PRESTON
A 506 KIRKBY, (M 57)
A 580 MANCHESTER,(M 57, M 6)
A 5036
A 5038
A 506
A 567
A 5058
B 5422
B 5194
B 5187
SEFTON
WATERLOO
LITHERLAND
SEAFORTH
BOOTLE
ORRELL
KIRKDALE
ANFIELD
NORRIS GREEN
FAZAKERLEY
WALTON on the HILL
WALTON HALL PARK
STANLEY PARK
BELFAST, DUBLIN
ISLE OF MAN
MERSEY
Church Road
B 5422
Hawthorne Road
Stanley Road
Linacre Lane
Knowsley Road
Marsh Lane
Regent Road
Derby Road
Balliol Road
Merton Rd
Southport Road
Rice Lane
Long Lane
Longmoor Lane
Lancashire Lane
Lower House Lane
Stonebridge Road
Walton Hall Avenue
Utting Avenue
Utting Avenue East
Muirhead Avenue East
Muirhead Drive
Townsend Avenue
Townsend Lane
Queens Avenue
Walton Lane
Oak Lane
N. Crosby Rd
S. Crosby Rd
Queens
Drive
East
37 100 90 2 34 139 6 81 136 129
121 72 19 95 65 3 108 40 45
36 17 135 106 137 77 113 69 32 120
99 12 78

LIVERPOOL
BUILT UP AREA
0   1 km
0   1/2 mile

Aintree Lane — BV 2
Aintree Road — AV 3
Allerton Road — BX 4
Bailey Drive — AV 6
Belmont Road — BX 7
Bowring Park Road — BX 10
Breck Road — BV 12
Brewster Street — AV 17
Bridge Road — AV 19
Broad Green Road — BX 20
Calderstones Road — BX 24
Chester Street — AX 30
Commercial Road — AV 32
Copple House Lane — BY 34
County Road — AV 36
Crosby Road — AV 37
Croxteth Road — BV 38
Croxteth Hall Lane — BX 40
Durning Road — BX 44
Dwerry House Lane — BV 45
Elmswood Road — BX 47
Gainsborough Road — BX 48
Holt Road — BX 64
Hornby Road — AV 65
Kirkdale Road — AV 69
Linacre Road — AV 72
Lodge Lane — BX 73
Melrose Road — AV 77
Mill Bank — BV 78
Moss Lane — AV 81

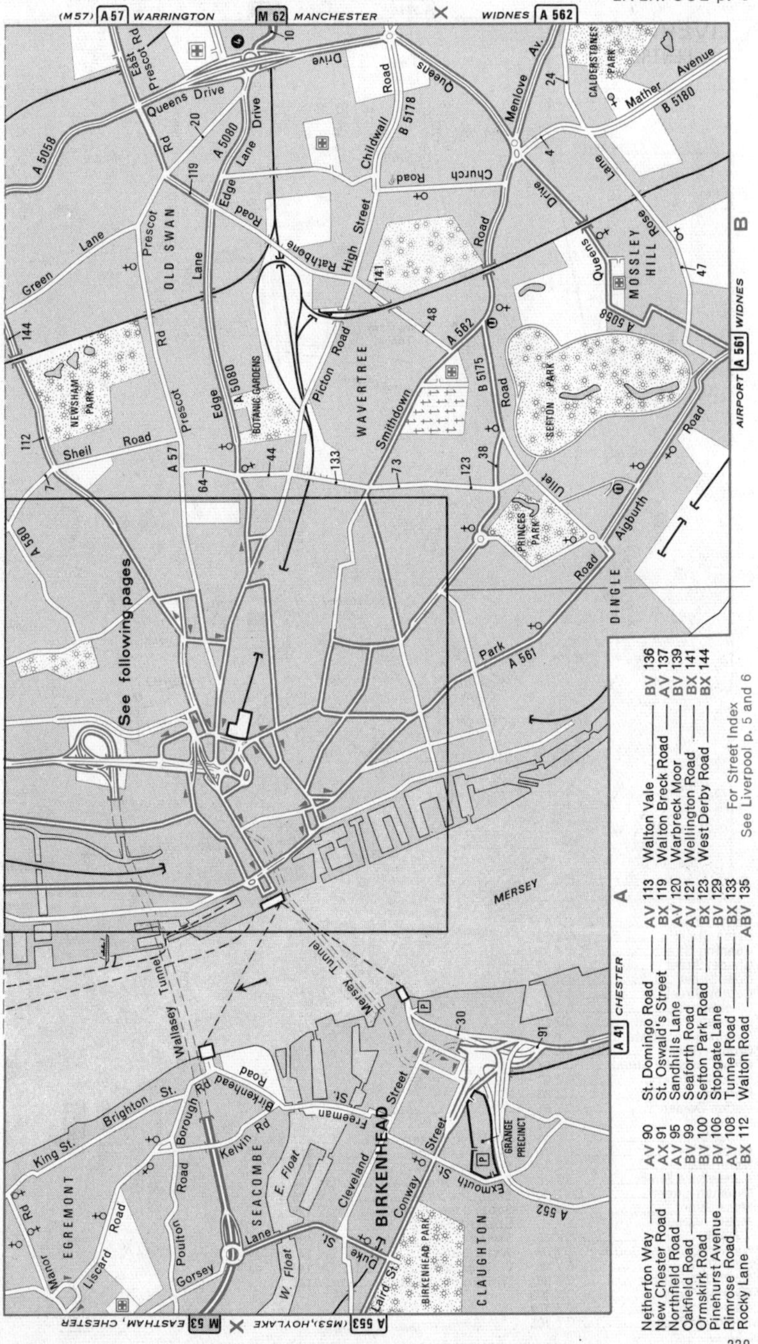
(M57) A 57 WARRINGTON
M 62 MANCHESTER
WIDNES A 562
CALDERSTONES PARK
Mather Avenue
B 5180
Menlove Av.
East Prescot Rd
Queens Drive
Drive
Queens
Road
Childwall
B 5178
Church
Church Road
Road
Queens Drive
Rd
Prescot
A 5080
Edge Lane Drive
Edge Lane
Road
Rathbone
High Street
Lane
A 5058
Green
Lane
OLD SWAN
Prescot
Rd
Lane
Edge
A 5080
BOTANIC GARDENS
Picton Road
WAVERTREE
Smithdown
Road
B 5175
A 562
SEFTON PARK
MOSSLEY HILL Road
Queens
A 5058
Drive
NEWSHAM PARK
Sheil
Road
A 57
Prescot
Road
Ullet
Road
PRINCES PARK
Dingle
Aigburth
Road
DINGLE
A 580
See following pages
Park
A 561
MERSEY
Wallasey Tunnel
Mersey Tunnel
P
P
GRANGE PRECINCT
BIRKENHEAD
Exmouth St.
Conway Street
Queens
Street
Freeman Street
CLAUGHTON
BIRKENHEAD PARK
A 552
SEACOMBE
E. Float
W. Float
Birkenhead Road
Borough Rd
Brighton St.
King St.
EGREMONT
Manor Rd
Liscard Road
Poulton Road
Gorsey Lane
Duke St.
Laird St.
Kelvin Rd
Cleveland Street
A 553 (M53) EASTHAM, HOYLAKE
M 53
A 41 CHESTER
A 561 WIDNES
AIRPORT
144
112
7
64
44
133
73
123
38
141
48
4
24
47
30
91
10
20
119
A
Netherton Way —— AV 90
New Chester Road —— AX 91
Northfield Road —— AV 95
Oakfield Road —— BV 99
Ormskirk Road —— BV 100
Pinehurst Avenue —— BV 106
Rimrose Road —— AV 108
Rocky Lane —— BX 112
St. Domingo Road —— AV 113
St. Oswald's Street —— BX 119
Sandhills Lane —— AV 120
Seaforth Road —— AV 121
Sefton Park Road —— BX 123
Stopgate Lane —— BV 129
Tunnel Road —— BX 133
Walton Road —— ABV 135
Walton Vale —— BV 136
Walton Breck Road —— AV 137
Warbreck Moor —— BV 139
Wellington Road —— BX 141
West Derby Road —— BX 144
For Street Index
See Liverpool p. 5 and 6

LIVERPOOL
CENTRE

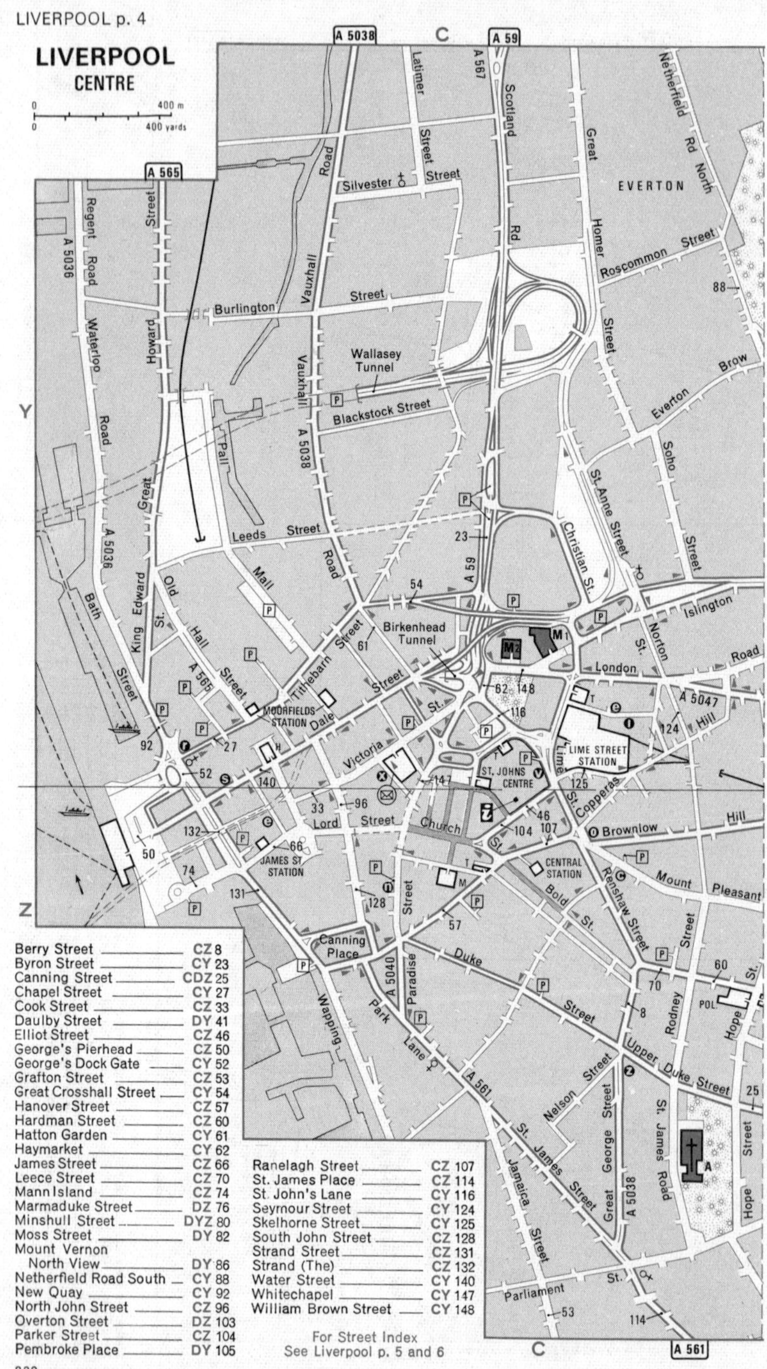

For Street Index
See Liverpool p. 5 and 6

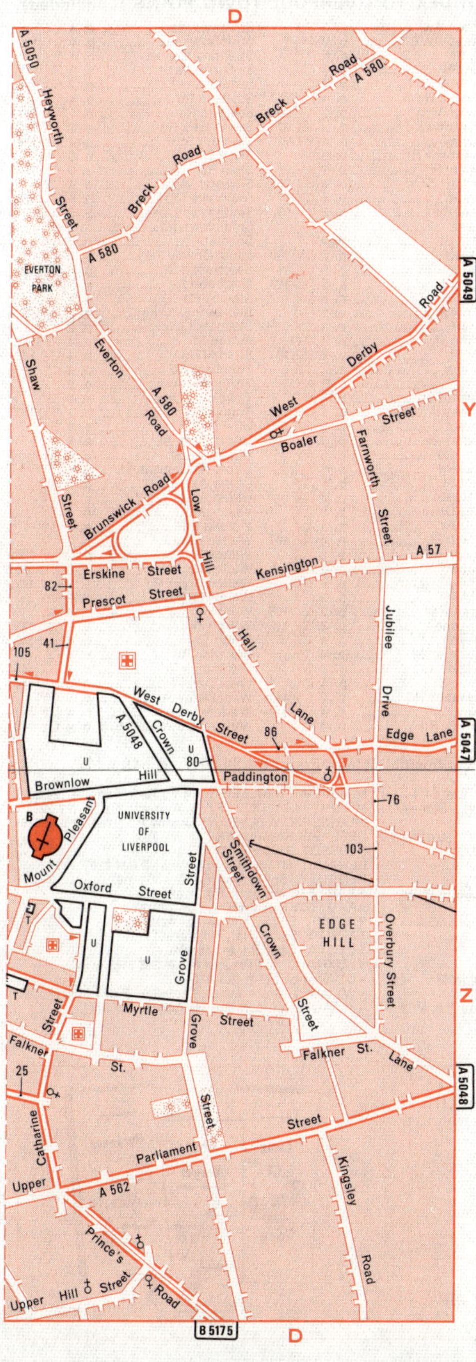

Concluded on next page

STREET INDEX TO LIVERPOOL TOWN PLANS (concluded)

MICHELIN Branch, Knowsley Park Industrial Estate, Prescot, L34 9HT, ☎ 548 6242.

AUSTIN-MORRIS 72/74 Coronation Rd ☎ 924 6411
AUSTIN-MG-WOLSELEY 782 Queens Drive, Stoneycroft ☎ 228 6464
AUSTIN-DAIMLER-JAGUAR-MG-WOLSELEY Hanover St. ☎ 709 9636
CITROEN Speke Hall Rd ☎ 427 6464
CITROEN 607 West Derby Rd ☎ 228 3670
DAIMLER-JAGUAR-ROVER-TRIUMPH, ROLLS ROYCE-BENTLEY 66/72 Mill Lane ☎ 228 0919
DATSUN 164 Allerton Rd ☎ 724 4699
FIAT East Prescott Rd ☎ 228 9151
FORD Linacre Lane ☎ 922 8201
FORD 35 Hardman St. ☎ 709 6622
MORRIS-MG-WOLSELEY 308/310 Kensington ☎ 263 0661
MORRIS-MG-WOLSELEY 175 Lower House Lane ☎ 546 5671

MORRIS-MG-WOLSELEY 84/88 Rose Lane ☎ 724 2377
MORRIS-MG-WOLSELEY 1 Aigburth Rd ☎ 727 2204
MORRIS-MG-WOLSELEY Crosby Rd North ☎ 928 6434
OPEL 215 Knowsley Rd ☎ 922 7585
PEUGEOT Ullet Rd ☎ 727 1413
RENAULT 47/49 Brook Rd West ☎ 924 2387
RENAULT Speke Hall Rd ☎ 486 8846
SAAB 574 Aigburth Rd ☎ 427 3500
SAAB 203 Queens Drive ☎ 228 3964
TALBOT Edge Lane ☎ 924 4210
TALBOT Speke Hall Rd 486 8511
TOYOTA Gale Rd ☎ 546 8228
VAUXHALL 143 Prescot Rd ☎ 263 3488
VOLVO Fox St. ☎ 207 4364
VW, AUDI Moor Lane, Thornton ☎ 924 9186
VW, AUDI Wilson Rd, Huyton ☎ 489 9771

LES GUIDES VERTS MICHELIN

Paysages, monuments
Routes touristiques
Géographie, Économie
Histoire, Art
Itinéraires de visite
Plans de villes et de monuments

Un choix de 31 guides pour vos vacances.

LIZARD Cornwall **403** E 34 – pop. 1,000 – ✆ 032 629 The Lizard.
See : Lizard Point★. **Envir.** : Kynance Cove★ *AC*, NW : 1 ½ m.
London 326 – Penzance 24 – Truro 29.

 🏨 **Housel Bay** ⑂, Housel Bay, TR12 7PG, ☎ 417, ⇐ Housel Cove, 🚗 – ⭤wc 🅿. 🔺
   M 4.40/6.80 st. – **27 rm** ⊆ 9.70/26.90 **s.**

LLANANDRAS Powys – see Presteigne.

LLANARMON DYFFRYN CEIRIOG Clwyd **403** K 25 – pop. 161 – ✉ Llangollen – ✆ 069 176.
London 196 – Chester 33 – Shrewsbury 32.

 🏨 **Hand** ⑂, LL20 7AD, ☎ 666, ⬍, 🚗 – ⭤wc 🅿. 💳 ⓓ
   closed February – **M** 4.50/6.00 **st.** ▯ 1.50 – **13 rm** ⊆ 10.00/20.00 **st.**
 🏨 **West Arms** ⑂, LL20 7LD, ☎ 665, ⬍, 🚗 – ⭤wc ⛲ 🅿. 💳
   M (buffet lunch) 3.00/5.20 **t.** ▯ 1.50 – **15 rm** ⭤ 10.00/23.20 **t.** – P 15.00/18.00 **t.**

LLANBEDR PONT STEFFAN Dyfed – see Lampeter.

LLANDDONA Gwynedd **403** H 24 – ✆ 0248 Beaumaris.
London 256 – Caernarfon 15 – Holyhead 24.

 XX **Le Patron,** Wern-y-Wylan, LL58 8TR, NW : 1 ½ m. ☎ 810209, 🚗 – 🅿. 💳 ⓓ
   closed Sunday, Monday, Tuesday from October to March, last 2 weeks October, 25-26 De-
   cember, 1 January and first 2 weeks February – **M** (dinner only) a la carte 6.15/9.00 **t.**
   ▯ 1.15.

LLANDEILO Dyfed **404** I 28 – pop. 1,799 – ECD : Thursday – ✆ 055 82.
Envir.: Talley (abbey and lakes★) N : 7 m.
🏌 Llandybie nr. Ammanford ☎ 026 975 (Llandybie) 472.
London 218 – Brecon 34 – Carmarthen 15 – Swansea 25.

 🏨 Cawdor Arms, Rhosmaen St., SA19 6EN, ☎ 3500 – 📺 ⭤wc ⛲wc ☎ 🅿 – **20 rm.**

   at Rhosmaen N : 1 m. on A 40 – ✉ ✆ 055 82 Llandeilo :

 X **Plough Inn,** SA19 6NP, ☎ 3431 – 🅿
   closed Sunday, first week November and Christmas Day – **M** a la carte 4.60/9.50 **t.**

AUSTIN-MORRIS-MG-TRIUMPH 28 Rhosmaen St. ☎ 2297

LLANDOGO Gwent **403** L 28 – pop. 290 – ECD : Thursday – ✉ Monmouth – ✆ 059 453
St. Briavels.
London 140 – Bristol 26 – Gloucester 43 – Newport 25.

 🏨 Old Farmhouse, NP5 4TL, on A 466 ☎ 303 – ⭤wc 🅿 – **28 rm.**

LLANDOVERY (LLANYMDDYFRI) Dyfed **403** I 28 – pop. 2,002 – ECD : Thursday – ✆ 0550.
🛈 Brecon Beacons National Park, Central Car Park, 8 Broad St. ☎ 20693 (Easter-September).
London 204 – Brecon 21 – Carmarthen 28 – Swansea 38.

 ⌂ **Dyfri,** Market Sq., SA20 5AI, ☎ 20297 – 🅿
   16 rm ⊆ 6.50/13.50 **st.**

LLANDRILLO-YN-RHOS Clwyd – see Colwyn Bay.

LLANDUDOCH Dyfed – see Cardigan.

LLANDUDNO Gwynedd **403** I 24 – pop. 15,890 – ECD : Wednesday except Summer –
✆ 0492.
See : Great Orme's Head (⇐★★ from the summit) by Ty-Gwyn Rd **A** – Tour of the Great
Orme's Head★★.
🏌 72 Bryniau Rd ☎ 75325 **A** – 🏌 Penryn Bay ☎ 49641 by A 546 **B**
⛴ to the Isle of Man : Douglas (Isle of Man Steam Packet Co.) **summer 2-4 weekly (3 h).**
🛈 Information Centre, 1-2 Chapel St. ☎ 76413 – Information Office, Arcadia Theatre ☎ 76143 ext 264 (summer only).
London 243 – Birkenhead 55 – Chester 47 – Holyhead 43.

Plan on next page

 🏨 **Empire,** 73 Church Walks, LL30 2HE, ☎ 77260, Telex 617161, 🔲 – ▮ 📺 🅿. 🔺 💳 ⓓ 💳VISA   **A e**
   closed 2 weeks at Christmas and 1 January – **M** 5.50/6.50 **st.** ▯ 1.25 – **51 rm** ⊆ 13.75/
   22.50 **st.** – P 19.00/28.00 **st.**
 🏨 Clarence, Gloddaeth Av., LL30 2DS, ☎ 76485 – ▮ – **74 rm.**   **A o**
 🏨 St. Tudno, North Par., LL30 2LP, ☎ 76309 – ▮ 📺 ⭤wc   **A c**
   Easter-October – **M** 3.50/4.65 ▯ 1.25 – **18 rm** ⊆ 9.90/22.30 – P 14.00/15.50.
 🏨 Headlands, Hill Terrace, LL30 2LS, ☎ 77485, ⇐ – ⭤wc 🅿   **AB a**
   Mid April-October – **M** (bar lunch) 4.25 **t.** ▯ 2.00 – **19 rm** ⊆ 8.50/20.00 **t.**

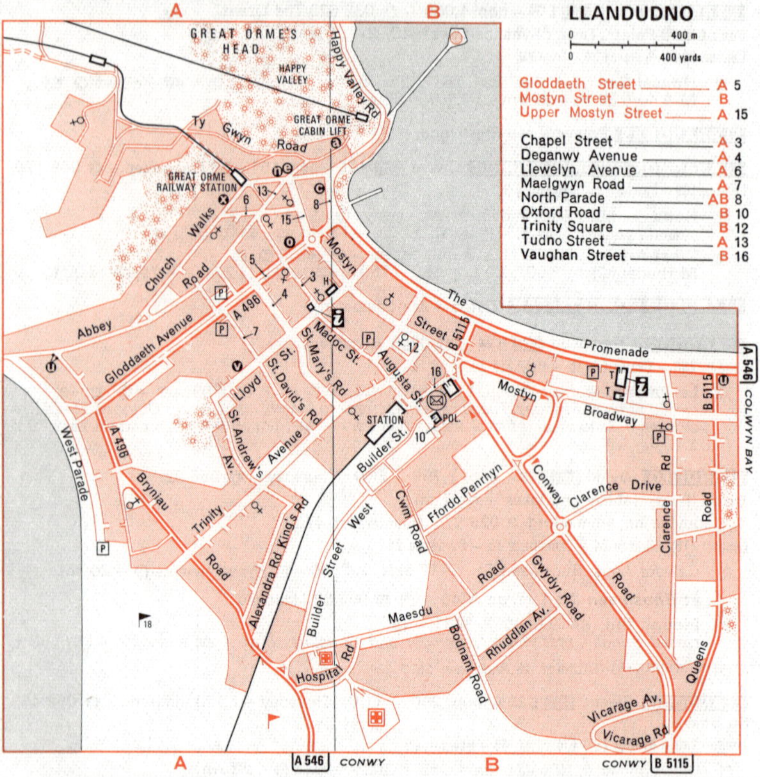

LLANDUDNO

Branksome, 62-64 Lloyd St., LL30 2YP, ℡ 75989 – ⌷wc 🛁wc Ⓟ   A v
24 rm ⊆ 6.00/14.00 **s.**

Bryn-y-Bia Lodge, Bryn-y-Bia Rd, Craigside, LL30 3AS, E: 1 m. on A 546 ℡ 49644, ⩻, 🐎 – ⌷wc 🛁wc Ⓟ   by A 546 B
18 rm ⊆ 8.00/18.00 **t.**

Clontarf, Great Ormes Rd, West Shore, LL30 2AS, ℡ 77621 – ⌷wc Ⓟ   A u
10 rm ⊆ 6.50/17.00 **s.**

Bromwell Court, 6 Craig-y-Don Par., Promenade, LL30 1BB, ℡ 78416 – 🛁wc   B u
closed December and January – **12 rm** ⊆ 7.55/16.30.

Cranleigh, Great Orme's Rd, West Shore, LL30 2AR, ℡ 77688 – 🛁wc Ⓟ   A u
Easter-October – **13 rm** ⊆ 6.95/15.90.

Bella Vista, 72 Church Walks, LL30 2HG, ℡ 76855 – 🛁 Ⓟ. ▨   A n
closed mid December-mid January – **12 rm** ⊆ 5.20/10.40 **st.**

Bron Orme, 54 Church Walks, LL30 2HO, ℡ 76735 – ▨ AE *VISA*   A x
closed January and February – **11 rm** ⊆ 5.50/11.00.

at Deganwy S: 2½ m. by A 546 – **A** – ✉ Conwy – ☏ 0492 Deganwy :

🏰 **Deganwy Castle**, LL31 9DA, ℡ 83358, ⩻, 🐎 – 📺 ⌷wc 🕾 Ⓟ. ▨ AE *VISA*
M (bar lunch Monday to Saturday) 4.00/5.50 **t.** – **30 rm** ⊆ 12.00/26.00 **t.** – P 14.00/16.00 **t.**

CITROEN Herkomer Rd ℡ 77607   TALBOT Conwy Rd ℡ 77461

In this guide
a symbol or a character, printed in red or black, in bold or light type, does not have the same meaning.
Please read the explanatory pages (p. 13 to 16) carefully.

LLANELLI Dyfed **403** H 28 – pop. 26,383 – ECD : Tuesday – ☎ 055 42.
Envir. : Kidwelly (Castle★★ 12 C) *AC*, NW : 9 m.
London 206 – Carmarthen 20 – Swansea 11.

- **Stradey Park** (T.H.F.), Furnace, SA15 4HA, N : ¾ m. on B 4309 ☎ 58171, Telex 48521 –
  ▯ TV ☐wc ☎ ❷. ☒ ☒ AE ⓪ VISA
  M 4.30/5.30 **st.** ▯ 1.65 – **80 rm** ☑ 15.00/22.00 **st.**

- Stepney (Crest), Park St., SA15 3YE, ☎ 2155 – ☎ ❷
  30 rm.

AUSTIN-MORRIS-ROVER-TRIUMPH Vauxhall St. ☎ 3371
FORD Sandy Rd ☎ 3285

MORRIS-MG-WOLSELEY Pwll ☎ 3666
VAUXHALL Sandy Rd ☎ 59284

LLANELWY Clwyd – see St. Asaph.

LLANFYLLIN Powys **403** K 25 – pop. 1,118 – ECD : Friday – ☎ 069 184.
London 188 – Chester 42 – Shrewsbury 24 – Welshpool 11

- **Bodfach Hall** ⚘, SY22 5HS, NW : 1 m. on B 4391 ☎ 272, ≤, « Country house in extensive
  gardens », park – ☐wc ❷
  March-October – **M** (lunch by arrangement) 3.90/5.30 **t.** – **9 rm** ☑ 10.00/22.40 **t.**

LLANGADOG Dyfed **403** I 28 – pop. 1,186 – ☎ 055 03.
London 218 – Carmarthen 15 – **Swansea 29.**

- **Plas Glansevin** ⚘, SA19 9HY, E : 1 ½ m. on Myddfai Rd ☎ 238, ≤, « Country house
  atmosphere », ☞ – ☐wc ❷. ☒ AE ⓪ VISA – **M** (dinner only) 6.85 **st.** ▯ 2.45 – **7 rm** ☑
  12.90/20.80 **st.**

*Dans le guide Vert Michelin " **Londres** " (édition en français)*

vous trouverez :

- *des descriptions détaillées des principales curiosités*

- *de nombreux renseignements pratiques*

- *des itinéraires de visite dans les secteurs sélectionnés*

- *des plans de quartiers et de monuments.*

LLANGAMMARCH WELLS Powys **404** J 27 – ECD : Wednesday – ☎ 059 12.
London 200 – Brecon 17 – Builth Wells 8.

- **Lake** ⚘, LD4 4BS, E : ¾ m. ☎ 202, ≤, ⚒, 🏳9, ⚓, ☞, park – ☐wc ☎ ❷
  April-October – **M** 4.00/6.00 ▯ 1.10 – **27 rm** ☑ 8.00/17.00 – P 13.00/16.00.

LLANGOLLEN Clwyd **403** K 25 – pop. 3,080 – ECD : Thursday – ☎ 0978.
See : Plas Newydd★★ (the house of the Ladies of Llangollen) *AC.* **Envir. :** Horseshoe Pass★
NW : 4 ½ m.
☐₁₈ ☎ 860040, E : 1 ½ m.
🛈 Wales Tourist Office, Town Hall ☎ 860828.
London 194 – Chester 23 – Holyhead 76 – Shrewsbury 30.

- Bryn Howel ⚘, LL20 7UW, E : 2 ¾ m. on A 539 ☎ 860331, ≤, ⚓, ☞ – TV ☐wc ☎ ❷.
  ⚐
  38 rm.

- **Royal** (T.H.F.), Bridge St., LL20 8PG, ☎ 860202, ≤, ⚓ – TV ☐wc ☎ ❷. ⚐. ☒ AE ⓪
  VISA
  M 3.65/4.25 **st.** ▯ 1.65 – **39 rm** ☑ 13.50/22.00 **st.**

- Chain Bridge, LL20 8BS, W : 2 m. by A 5 ☎ 860215, ≤ river Dee – ☐wc ☐wc ☎ ❷
  34 rm.

AUSTIN-MORRIS-MG-WOLSELEY Berwyn St. ☎ 860270   TALBOT Regent St. ☎ 860276

LLANILLTUD FAWR South Glam. – see Llantwit Major.

LLANRHAEADR Clwyd **403** J 24 – pop. 891 – ✉ Denbigh – ☎ 074 578 Llanynys.
London 214 – Chester 28 – Shrewsbury 50.

- Bryn Morfydd ⚘, LL16 4NP, ☎ 280, ≤ Vale of Clwyd, ⚒, ⚊ heated, ☞, park – TV
  ☐wc ☐wc ☎ ❷. ⚐
  21 rm.

  Annex : Llanrhaeadr Hall 🏛 ⚘, on A 525, ≤, ☞ – ☐wc ❷
  13 rm.

AUSTIN-MG-WOLSELEY ☎ 227

LLANRWST Gwynedd **403** I 24 – pop. 2,610 – ECD : Thursday – ☎ 0492.
See : Gwydir Castle*. **Envir.:** Capel Garmon (Burial Chamber*) SE : 6 m.
🅸 Snowdonia National Park Countryside Centre, Glan-y-Borth ☏ 640604.
London 230 – Holyhead 50 – Shrewsbury 66.

🏨 **Gwesty Plas Maenan** ≫, LL26 0YR, N : 4 m. on A 470 ☏ 049 269 (Dolgarrog) 232, ≼,
🚗, park – TV ➱wc ☏ ℗. 🛦
M 3.50/5.50 **st.** 🍷 1.70 – **15 rm** ☲ 15.60/22.60 **st.**

XX **Meadowsweet** with rm, Station Rd, LL26 0DS, ☏ 640732, ≼ – TV 🍴wc ℗. 🆂 AE VISA
closed January – **M** *(closed lunch from November to Easter, except Christmas Day)* a
la carte 5.25/8.50 **t.** 🍷 1.45 – **10 rm** ☲ 9.00/20.00 **t.**

MORRIS-MG-ROVER-TRIUMPH ☏ 640381

LLANTWIT MAJOR (LLANILLTUD FAWR) South Glam. **403** J 29 – pop. 8,740 – ☎ 044 65.
London 175 – Cardiff 18 – Swansea 33.

🏠 **West House**, West St., CF6 9TR, ☏ 2406, 🚗 – ➱wc ℗. 🆂 VISA
M a la carte approx. 4.50 – **19 rm** ☲ 13.50/27.00 **st.**

XX **Quaintways**, Colhugh St., CF6 9RE, ☏ 2321 – ℗
closed Sunday – **M** (dinner only) a la carte 4.85/9.80 **t.** 🍷 2.00.

TOYOTA 2 Colhugh St. ☏ 3466

LLANWNDA Gwynedd **403** H 24 – see Caernarfon.

LLANWRTYD WELLS Powys **403** J 27 – pop. 488 – ECD : Wednesday – ☎ 059 13.
See : Cambrian Mountains : road** from Llanwrtyd to Tregaron. **Envir.:** Rhandir-mwyn (≼* of
Afon Tywi Valley) SW : 12 m.
London 214 – Brecon 32 – Carmarthen 39.

🏨 **Abernant Lake** (Mt. Charlotte), Station Rd, LD5 4RR, ☏ 250, XX, ⅃ heated, ≫, 🚗,
park – 🛗 ➱wc ℗. 🆂 AE ⓞ VISA
closed Christmas – **M** 4.25/5.00 **t.** – **60 rm** ☲ 12.00/29.00.

at Abergwesyn NW : 4 ½ m. – ✉ Builth Wells – ☎ 059 13 Llanwrtyd Wells :

🏠 **Llwynderw** ≫, LD5 4TW, ☏ 238, ≼ countryside and hills, 🚗 – ➱wc ℗
March-October – **M** (dinner only) 12.00 **st.** – 🍷 3.00 – **10 rm** ☲ (dinner included) 28.00/
35.00 **t.**

LLANYMDDYFRI Dyfed – see Llandovery.

LLWYNMAWR Clwyd **403** K 25 – pop. 740 – ✉ Llangollen – ☎ 069 172 Glynceiriog.
London 192 – Shrewsbury 28 – Wrexham 15.

🏠 **Golden Pheasant** ≫, LL20 7BB, ☏ 281, ≼, ≫, 🚗 – ➱wc ℗. 🆂 AE
M a la carte 5.25/6.60 **st.** 🍷 1.50 – **14 rm** ☲ 12.50/25.00 **st.** – P 21.00/23.00 **st.**

LOFTUS Cleveland **986** ⑳ – pop. 6,850 – ECD : Wednesday – ✉ Saltburn by the Sea –
☎ 0287.
London 264 – Leeds 73 – Middlesbrough 17 – Scarborough 36.

🏨 **Grinkle Park** ≫, Easington, TS13 4UB, SE : 2 m off A 174, ☏ 40515, ≼, « Country house
atmosphere », 🚗, park – TV ➱wc ☏ ℗
20 rm.

London

LONDON (Greater) 404 STU 29 – pop. 7,452,346 – ✆ 01.

✈ Heathrow, ☏ 759 4321, Telex 934892 p. 8 **AY**.

✈ Gatwick, ☏ 0293 (Crawley) 28822 and ☏ 01 (London) 668 4211, p. 8 : by A 23 **DZ** and M 23.

BA Air Terminal : Buckingham Palace Rd, Victoria, SW1, ☏ 834 2323, p. 26 **AX**.

British Caledonian Airways, Victoria Air Terminal : Victoria Station, SW1, ☏ 833 9411, p. 26 **BX**.

⛴ Shipping connections with the Continent : to Ostend (P & O Jet Ferries).

🚗 Euston ☏ 387 9400 ext 4461 – Kensington Olympia ☏ 603 4555 – King's Cross ☏ 837 4200 ext 4700 – Paddington ☏ 723 7000 ext 3148.

🛈 London Tourist Board, Head Office : 26 Grosvenor Gardens, SW1W 0DU, ☏ 730 0791, Telex 919041. Victoria Station (adjacent to Platform 15), Buckingham Palace Rd, SW1, ☏ 739 0202. British Tourist Authority, 64 St. James's St., SW1, ☏ 499 9325/6, Telex 21231.

The maps in this section of the Guide are based upon the Ordnance Survey of Great Britain with the permission of the Controller of Her Majesty's Stationery Office. Crown Copyright reserved.

Remember the speed limits that apply in the United Kingdom, unless otherwise signposted.

    — 60 mph on single carriageway roads
    — 70 mph on dual carriageway roads and Motorways

11

SIGHTS

CURIOSITÉS
LE CURIOSITÀ
SEHENSWÜRDIGKEITEN

◼ HISTORIC BUILDINGS AND MONUMENTS

Palace of Westminster*** (Houses of Parliament) p. 19 NX – Tower of London*** p. 20 QU.
Banqueting House** p. 19 NV – Buckingham Palace** p. 26 BV – Kensington Palace** p. 18
JV – Lincoln's Inn** p. 27 FV – Royal Hospital Chelsea** p. 25 FU – St. James's Palace** p. 23
EP – South Bank Arts Centre** p. 19 NV – The Temple** p. 15 NU – Tower Bridge** p. 20 QV.
Albert Memorial* p. 24 CQ – Apsley House* p. 22 BP – Bloomsbury* p. 15 NT – Burlington
House* p. 23 EM – Charterhouse* p. 16 PT – Commonwealth Institute* p. 17 HX – County Hall*
p. 19 NX – Design Centre* p. 23 FM – HMS Discovery* p. 27 FX – George Inn*, Southwark
p. 20 QV – Gray's Inn* p. 15 NT – Guildhall* (Lord Mayor's Show**) p. 16 PT – Dr Johnson's
House* p. 16 PTU A – Lancaster House* p. 23 EP – Leigthon House* p. 17 GX – London
Bridge* p. 20 QV – Mansion House* p. 16 QU P – The Monument* (❈*) p. 16 QU G – Old
Admiralty* p. 19 MV – Post Office Tower* p. 15 LT D – Royal Exchange* p. 16 QU V – Royal Opera
House* (Covent Garden) p. 27 EV – Somerset House* p. 27 EV – Staple Inn* p. 15 NT Y –
Stock Exchange* p. 16 QTU – Westminster Bridge* (≤***) p. 19 NX.

◼ CHURCHES

St. Paul's Cathedral*** (Dome ❈***) p. 16 PU – Westminster Abbey*** p. 19 MX.
St. Bartholomew the Great** p. 16 PT K – St. Dunstan-in-the-East** p. 16 QU F – St. Mary-at-
Hill** p. 16 QU B – Southwark Cathedral** p. 20 QV.
Christ Church* p. 16 PT E – Queen's Chapel* p. 23 EP – St. Bride* p. 16 PU J – St. Clement
Danes* p. 27 FV – St. Giles Cripplegate* p. 16 PT N – St. Helen* (Bishopsgate) p. 16 QTU R –
St. James* p. 23 EM – St. Margaret Lothbury* p. 16 QT S – St. Martin-in-the-Fields* p. 27 DX –
St. Mary Abchurch* p. 16 QU X – St. Olave* p. 16 QU Y – St. Paul* (Covent Garden) p. 27 DV –
St. Stephen Walbrook* p. 16 QU Z.

◼ PARKS

Regent's Park*** (London Zoo***) p. 14 KS.
Hyde Park** p. 18 JU – St. James's Park** p. 19 MV.
Kensington Gardens* p. 18 JV.

◼ STREETS AND SQUARES

The City*** p. 16 PU.
Bedford Square** p. 15 MT – Belgrave Square** p. 26 AV – Burlington Arcade** p. 23 DM –
The Mall** p. 23 FP – Nash Terraces**, Regent's Park p. 14 KS – Piccadilly** p. 23 EM – The
Thames** pp. 18-20 – Trafalgar Square** p. 27 DX – Whitehall** (Horse Guards : changing of
the Guard**) p. 19 MV.
Barbican* p. 16 PT – Bond Street* pp. 22-23 CK-DM – Carlton House Terrace* p. 23 GN –
Carnaby Street* p. 23 EKL – Charing Cross* p. 27 DX – Cheyne Walk* p. 18 JZ – Downing
Street* p. 19 NV – Fitzroy Square* p. 15 LT – Jermyn Street* p. 23 EN – Portman Square* p. 22
AJ – Portobello Road* p. 13 GU – Queen Anne's Gate* p. 19 MX – Regent Street* p. 23 EM –
St. James's Square* p. 23 FN – St. James's Street* p. 23 EN – Shepherd Market* p. 22 CN –
Soho Square* p. 23 FJ – Strand* p. 27 DX – Victoria Embankment* p. 27 EX – Waterloo Place*
p. 23 FN.

■ MUSEUMS

British Museum*** p. 15 MT – National Gallery*** p. 23 GM – Science Museum*** p. 24 CR – Victoria and Albert Museum*** p. 25 DR – Wallace Collection*** p. 22 AH.

Courtauld Institute Galleries** p. 15 MT M – Museum of London** p. 16 PT M – National Portrait Gallery** p. 23 GM – Natural History Museum** p. 24 CS – Queen's Gallery** p. 26 BV – Tate Gallery** p. 19 MY.

Clock Museum* (Guildhall) p. 16 PT – Geological Museum* p. 24 CR – Imperial War Museum* p. 20 PX – Madame Tussaud's* p. 14 KT M – Museum of Mankind* (treasure**) p. 23 DM – National Army Museum* p. 25 FU – Percival David Foundation of Chinese Art* p. 15 MS M – Sir John Soane's Museum* p. 15 NT M – Wellington Museum* p. 22 BP.

■ OUTER LONDON

Hampton Court (Hampton Court***) p. 8 BZ – **Kew** p. 8 (Royal Botanic Gardens*** BY **A**, Kew Palace* BY **B**) – Windsor (Castle***) by A 4, M 4 AX.

Brentford (Syon Park** p. 8 BY **D**) – **Chiswick** p. 8 (Chiswick House** BCY **E**, Chiswick Mall** CY, Hogarth's House* CXY **F**) – **Greenwich** p. 9 EY **G** (Cutty Sark**, National Maritime Museum**, Royal Naval College**, Royal Observatory*, Ranger's House*) – **Hampstead** (Kenwood House** p. 8 DV **N**, Fenton House*: porcelain collection** p. 13 GR) – **Hendon** (Royal Air Force Museum**) p. 8 CV **M** – **Hounslow** (Osterley Park**) p. 8 BY **P** – **Richmond** p. 8 (Richmond Park** BY, Richmond Bridge** BY **R**, Richmond Green** BY **R**, Ham House** BY **K**).

Dulwich (Dulwich College Picture Gallery*) p. 9 EY **S** – **Shoreditch** (Geffrye Museum*) p. 9 EX **M** – **Sydenham** (Crystal Palace Park*) p. 9 EZ **V** – **Tower Hamlets** (St. Katharine Dock*) p. 9 EX **X** – **Twickenham** (Marble Hill House*) p. 8 BY **Y**.

ALPHABETICAL LIST OF HOTELS AND RESTAURANTS
LISTE ALPHABÉTIQUE DES HOTELS ET RESTAURANTS
ELENCO ALFABETICO DEGLI ALBERGHI E RISTORANTI
ALPHABETISCHES HOTEL- UND RESTAURANTVERZEICHNIS

GREEN TOURIST GUIDES

Picturesque scenery, buildings
Attractive routes
Touring programmes
Plans of towns and buildings

15 guides available for your holidays.

Town plans : *roads most used by traffic and those on which guide listed hotels and restaurants stand are fully drawn; the beginning only of lesser roads is indicated.*

Plans de villes : *Les rues sont sélectionnées en fonction de leur importance pour la circulation et le repérage des établissements cités. Les rues secondaires ne sont qu'amorcées.*

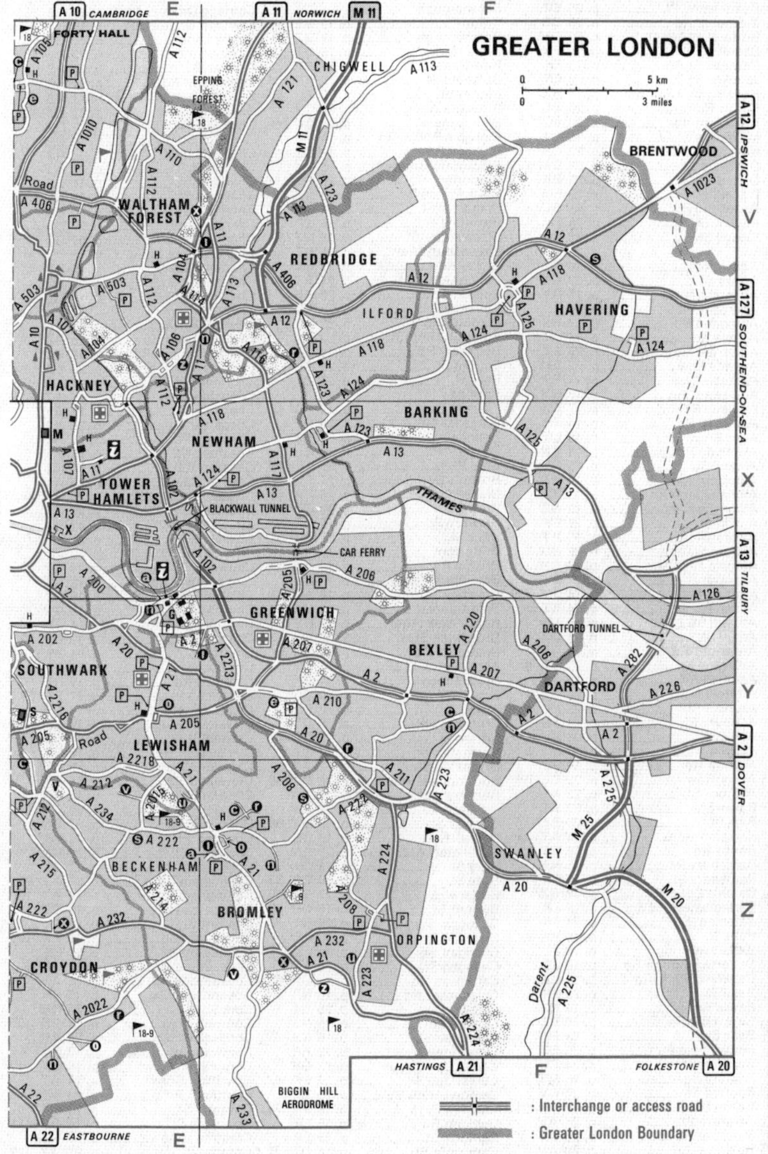

Piante di città : le vie sono selezionate in funzione della loro importanza
per la circolazione e l'ubicazione degli edifici citati.
Non indichiamo che l'inizio delle vie secondarie.

Stadtpläne: Die Auswahl der Straßen wurde unter Berücksichtigung
des Verkehrs und der Zufahrt zu den erwähnten Häusern getroffen.
Die weniger wichtigen Straßen werden nur angedeutet.

Continued on next page

Concluded p. 21

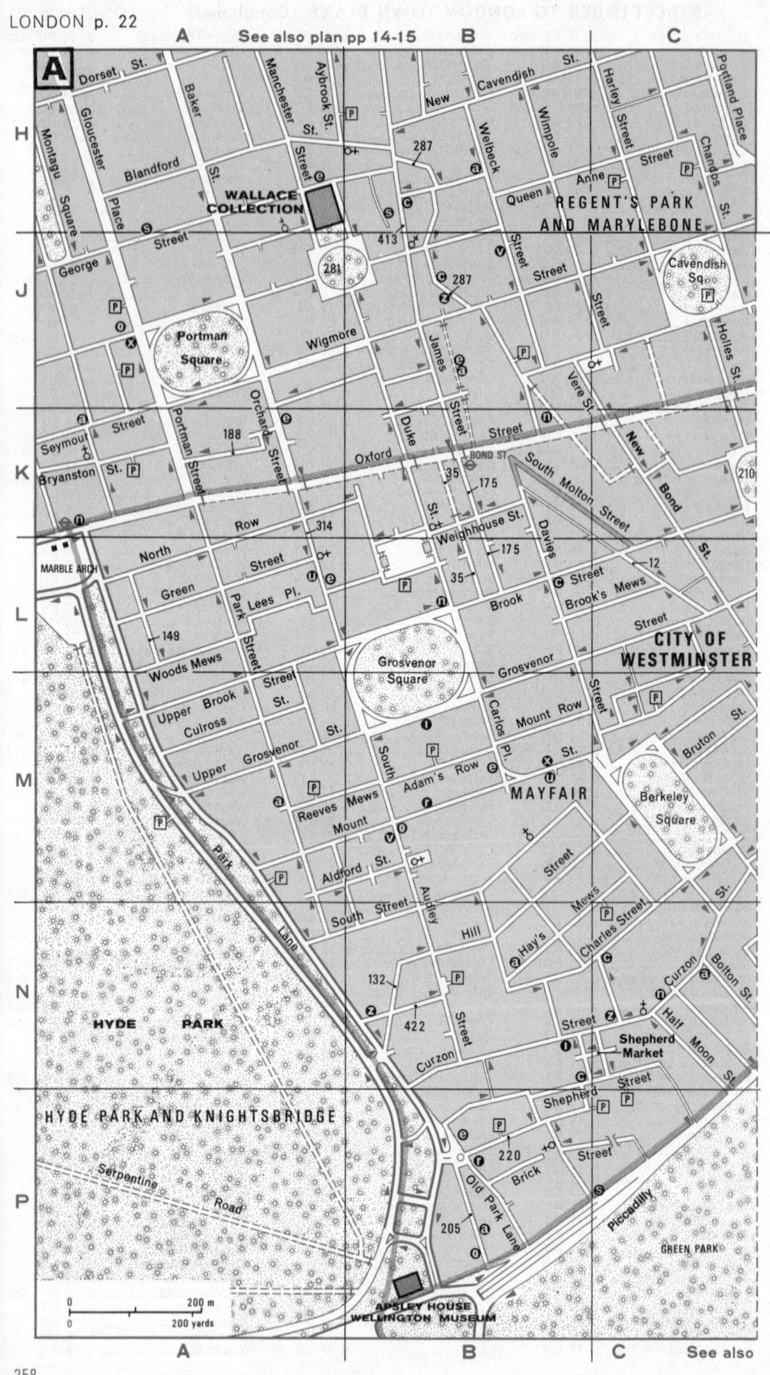

A
See also plan pp 14-15
A   B   C
WALLACE COLLECTION
Dorset St.
Baker
Manchester
Aybrook St.
New
Cavendish
St.
Harley
Portland Place
Blandford
St.
Street
Welbeck
Wimpole
Street
Chandos
REGENT'S PARK
AND MARYLEBONE
Montagu Square
Gloucester Place
Queen
Anne
Street
Cavendish Sq.
George
Street
281
287
413
287
Portman Square
Wigmore
Street
Vere St.
Holles St.
210
Street
James
Street
Seymour
Street
Portman Street
Orchard Street
Duke
Street
Street
New
Bond
Bryanston St.
188
Oxford
Bond St.
South Molton Street
St.
35
175
Row
314
Weighhouse St.
175
12
North
Street
35
Davies
Street
Brook's Mews
MARBLE ARCH
Green
Lees Pl.
Brook
Street
Street
149
Park Street
CITY OF WESTMINSTER
Woods Mews
Grosvenor Square
Grosvenor
Upper Brook Street St.
Culross
Carlos Pl.
Mount Row
Street
Bruton St.
Upper Grosvenor
South
Adam's Row
MAYFAIR
Berkeley Square
Reeves Mews
Mount
Aldford St.
Street
Audley
Hill
Street
Hay's
Mews
Charles Street
Curzon
Bolton St.
South Street
132
422
Street
Curzon
Street
Shepherd Market
Half Moon St.
HYDE PARK
PARK
Lane
Curzon
Shepherd
Street
HYDE PARK AND KNIGHTSBRIDGE
Shepherd
Serpentine
Road
220
Brick
Street
Old Park Lane
205
Piccadilly
GREEN PARK
0   200 m
0   200 yards
APSLEY HOUSE
WELLINGTON MUSEUM
A   B   C
See also

258

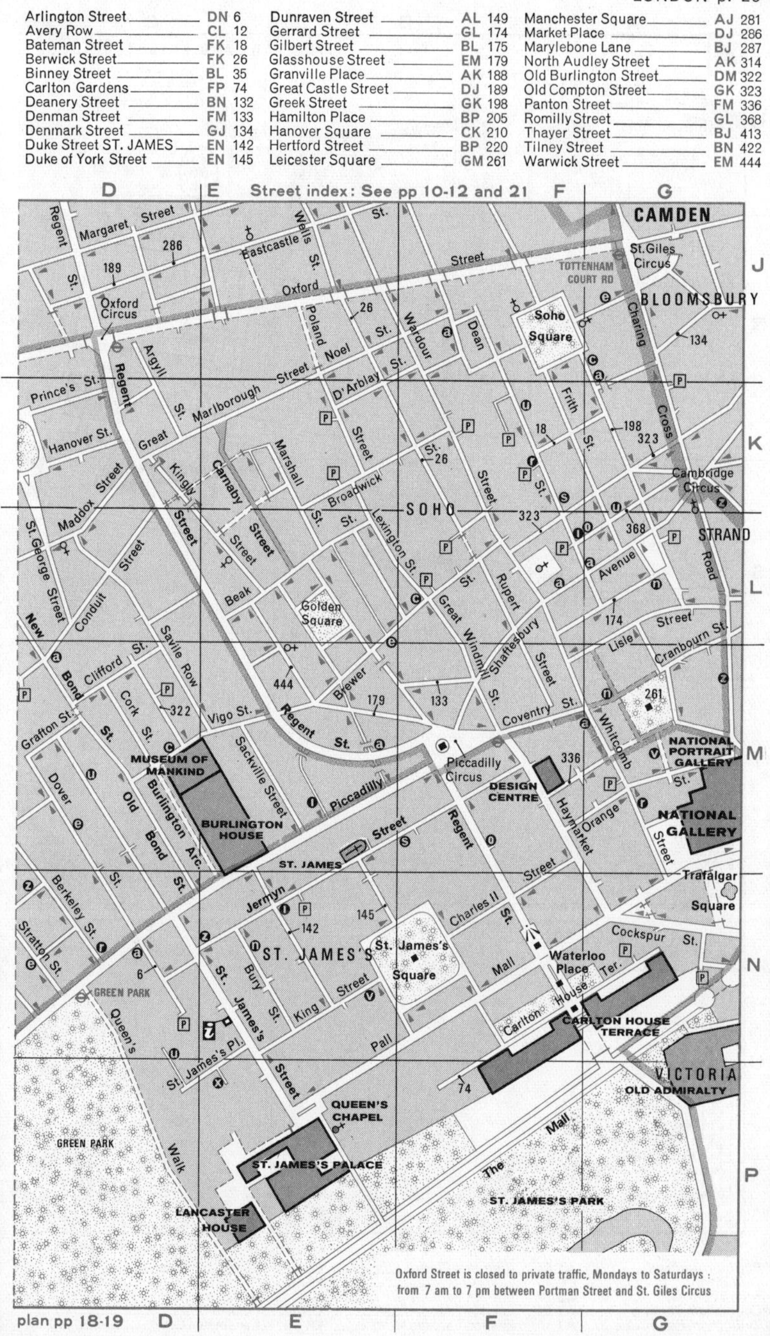

Street index: See pp 10-12 and 21
CAMDEN
St.Giles Circus
TOTTENHAM COURT RD
BLOOMSBURY
Margaret Street
Eastcastle
Wells St.
Street
286
189
Oxford
Oxford Circus
Poland
Noel
Prince's St.
D'Arblay
Marlborough
Street
Wardour
Dean
Soho Square
Charing
134
Hanover St.
Great
Argyll
St.
Marshall
Broadwick
18
Frith
198
323
Maddox Street
Carnaby
Street
St.
SOHO
Street
Cambridge Circus
St.George Street
Kingly
Street
St.
26
323
STRAND
Conduit
Beak
Golden Square
Lexington St.
Great Windmill
Rupert
368
Avenue
New
Clifford
Street
Shaftesbury
174
Lisle
Street
Bond
Cork St.
322
444
Brewer
133
Cranbourn St.
Grafton St.
Vigo St.
179
Coventry St.
261
St.
Regent
Whitcomb
NATIONAL PORTRAIT GALLERY
MUSEUM OF MANKIND
Sackville Street
Piccadilly
336
NATIONAL GALLERY
Dover
Burlington Arc.
BURLINGTON HOUSE
Piccadilly Circus
DESIGN CENTRE
Haymarket
Orange
Berkeley St.
Old Bond
St.
Piccadilly
Street
ST. JAMES
Regent
Street
Trafalgar Square
Stratton St.
Jermyn
142
145
Charles II
St.
Cockspur
St.
6
ST. JAMES'S
Bury
St.James's Square
Mall
Waterloo Place
Green Park
King
Street
VICTORIA
St.James's
Queen's
James's Pl.
Pall
74
CARLTON HOUSE TERRACE
OLD ADMIRALTY
QUEEN'S CHAPEL
Walk
The Mall
GREEN PARK
ST. JAMES'S PALACE
ST. JAMES'S PARK
LANCASTER HOUSE
Oxford Street is closed to private traffic, Mondays to Saturdays :
from 7 am to 7 pm between Portman Street and St. Giles Circus
plan pp 18-19

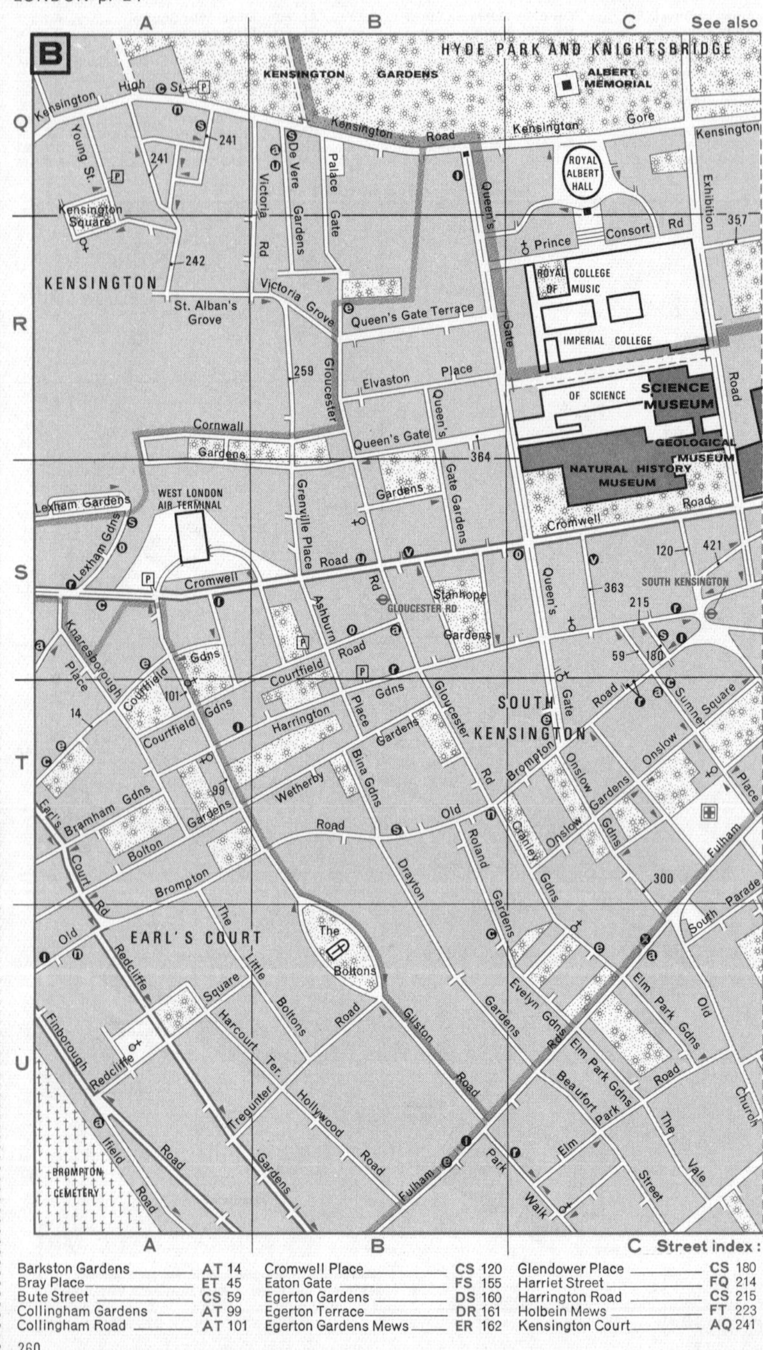
B
See also
HYDE PARK AND KNIGHTSBRIDGE
KENSINGTON GARDENS
ALBERT MEMORIAL
Q
Kensington
High St.
241
241
242
Young St.
Kensington Square
KENSINGTON
St. Alban's Grove
Victoria Rd
De Vere Gardens
Palace Gate
Kensington Road
Kensington Gore
Kensington
ROYAL ALBERT HALL
Prince Consort Rd
Exhibition
357
ROYAL COLLEGE OF MUSIC
IMPERIAL COLLEGE
R
Victoria Grove
259
Gloucester
Queen's Gate Terrace
Elvaston Place
Queen's Gate
Queen's Gate Gardens
364
Gardens
OF SCIENCE
SCIENCE MUSEUM
Road
GEOLOGICAL MUSEUM
NATURAL HISTORY MUSEUM
Cornwall
Gardens
Grenville Place
Gardens
Cromwell
Road
S
Lexham Gardens
WEST LONDON AIR TERMINAL
Lexham Gdns
Cromwell
Road
Rd
Stanhope Gardens
GLOUCESTER RD
120
421
363
SOUTH KENSINGTON
215
59
180
Knaresborough Place
Courtfield
Gdns
101
Courtfield Gdns
Courtfield
14
Harrington
Road
Place
Gdns
Gloucester
Gdns
Wetherby
Bina Gdns
Road
Gardens
Old
SOUTH KENSINGTON
Sumner Square
Onslow
Onslow Gardens
Onslow Gdns
Gate
Road
Brompton
Cranley Gdns
Roland Gardens
Drayton
Gardens
300
Eulham
T
Earl's
Bramham Gdns
Bolton
Brompton
Court Rd
Old
Redcliffe
Square
EARL'S COURT
Little Boltons
The Boltons
Road
Gilston Road
Evelyn Gdns
Elm Park Gardens
South Parade
Elm Park Gdns
Old
Road
U
Finborough
Redcliffe
Ifield Road
BROMPTON CEMETERY
Harcourt Ter.
Tregunter
Gardens
Hollywood Road
Fulham
Park
Road
Elm
Beaufort
Elm Park Gdns
Road
Church
The Vale
Street
Walk
A
B
C
Street index:

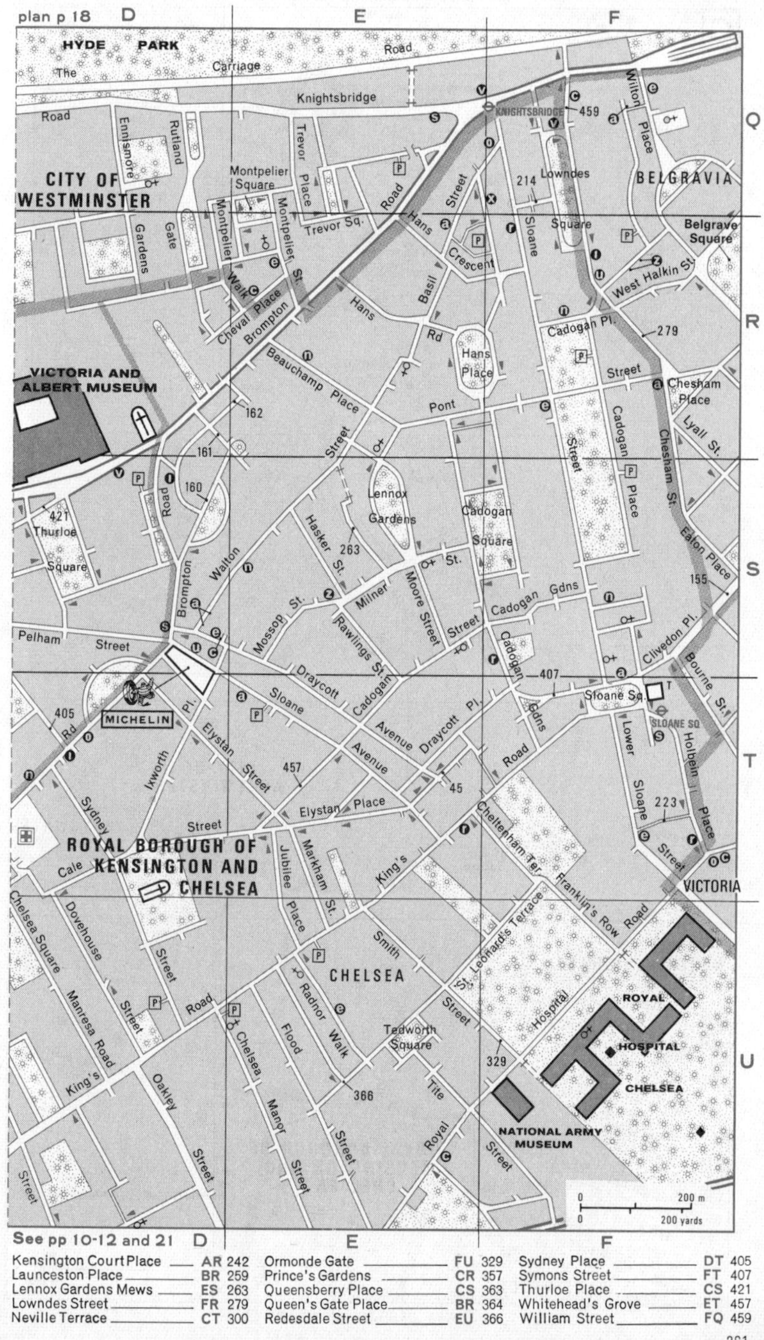
plan p 18
D
E
F
HYDE PARK
The
Carriage
Road
Knightsbridge
KNIGHTSBRIDGE
459
Q
Road
Ennismore
Rutland
Trevor Place
214
Lowndes
BELGRAVIA
CITY OF WESTMINSTER
Montpelier Square
Montpelier St.
Trevor Sq.
Hans Road
Sloane
Square
Belgrave Square
Gardens
Gate
Montpelier Walk
Basil
Crescent
West Halkin St.
Cheval Place
Brompton
Hans
Rd
Sloane
Cadogan Pl.
279
R
VICTORIA AND ALBERT MUSEUM
Beauchamp Place
Hans Place
Street
Chesham
Place
162
Pont
Street
Cadogan Place
Chesham St.
Lyall St.
161
Street
Lennox Gardens
Cadogan
160
Hasker St.
263
Square
Street
Eaton Place
421
Thurloe
Walton
Milner
Moore Street
Cadogan Gdns
155
S
Square
Street
Cadogan
Clivedon Pl.
Pelham
Brompton
Mossop St.
Rawlings St.
Street
Cadogan
407
Bourne St.
405 Rd
MICHELIN
Elystan
Draycott
Cadogan
Sloane Sq.
SLOANE SQ
T
Sloane
Avenue Draycott Pl.
Gdns
Holbein Place
Ixworth
Elystan Street
457
Avenue
45
Road
Lower Sloane
223
Street
Sydney
Elystan Place
Cheltenham Ter.
VICTORIA
ROYAL BOROUGH OF KENSINGTON AND CHELSEA
Cale Street
Jubilee Place
Markham St.
King's
Franklin's Row
Chelsea Square
Dovehouse
Smith
Leonard's Terrace
ROYAL
Manresa Road
Street
Radnor Walk
CHELSEA
Street
Hospital
HOSPITAL
King's
Oakley
Chelsea Road
Flood
Tedworth Square
329
CHELSEA
Manor
Tite
Royal
NATIONAL ARMY MUSEUM
366
Street
Street
U
0   200 m
0   200 yards

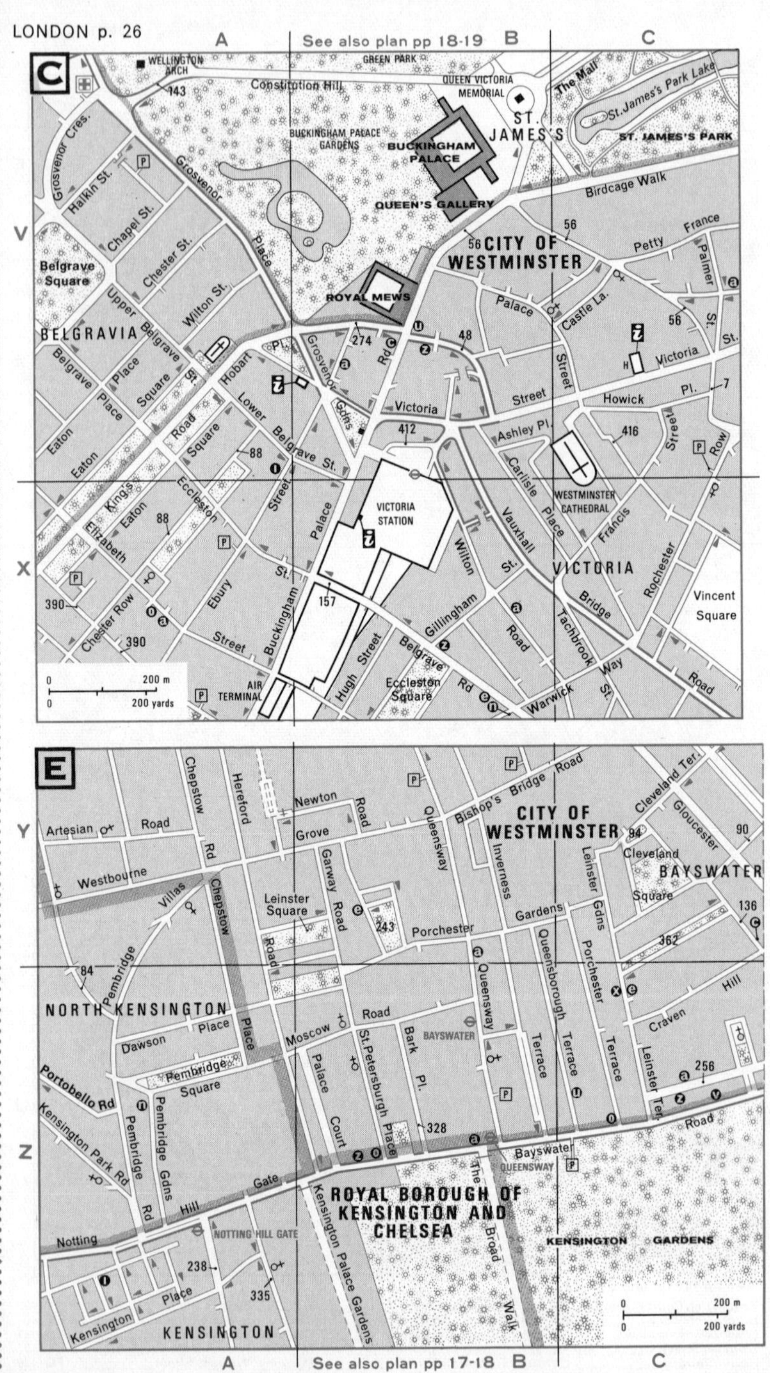
See also plan pp 18-19
C
WELLINGTON ARCH
143
Constitution Hill
GREEN PARK
QUEEN VICTORIA MEMORIAL
The Mall
St. James's Park Lake
ST. JAMES'S
St. James's Park
BUCKINGHAM PALACE GARDENS
BUCKINGHAM PALACE
QUEEN'S GALLERY
Birdcage Walk
Grosvenor Cres.
Halkin St.
Chapel St.
Chester St.
Grosvenor
Place
56
CITY OF WESTMINSTER
56
Petty
France
Palmer
Belgrave Square
Upper
Belgrave
Wilton St.
ROYAL MEWS
Palace
Castle La.
Street
56
St.
St.
BELGRAVIA
Belgrave
Place
Square
St.
Hobart
Pl.
Lower
Belgrave St.
Grosvenor Gdns
274
Rd
48
Street
Victoria
H
Victoria
Belgrave
Place
Road
Square
Street
Victoria
412
Ashley Pl.
Street
Howick
Pl.
7
Eaton
Eaton
88
Palace
Carlisle
Place
416
Row
King's
Eaton
Eccleston
88
Street
VICTORIA STATION
Wilton
Vauxhall
WESTMINSTER CATHEDRAL
Francis
Rochester
Elizabeth
Eaton
St.
St.
VICTORIA
Bridge
390
Ebury
157
Gillingham
St.
Tachbrook
Vincent Square
Chester Row
390
Street
Buckingham
Hugh
Street
Belgrave
Rd
Way
Road
0   200 m
0   200 yards
AIR TERMINAL
Eccleston Square
Warwick
Road

E
Chepstow
Hereford
Newton
Road
Bishop's
Bridge
Road
Cleveland Ter.
Gloucester
90
Artesian
Road
Grove
Queensway
CITY OF WESTMINSTER
94
Cleveland
BAYSWATER
Westbourne
Garway
Road
Inverness
Leinster Gdns
Square
136
Chepstow Rd
Villas
Leinster Square
243
Porchester
Gardens
Queensborough
Porchester
362
Chepstow Road
84
Moscow
Road
Queensway
Terrace
Terrace
Hill
NORTH KENSINGTON
Pembridge
Dawson
Place
Bark
Pl.
BAYSWATER
Craven
Pembridge
Square
Palace
Court
St.Petersburgh
Place
Terrace
Leinster Ter.
256
Portobello Rd
Pembridge Gdns
328
Bayswater
Road
Kensington Park Rd
Pembridge
Rd
Gate
The
Broad
Walk
Bayswater
QUEENSWAY
Hill
Notting
NOTTING HILL GATE
ROYAL BOROUGH OF KENSINGTON AND CHELSEA
KENSINGTON GARDENS
238
Kensington Palace Gardens
335
Place
KENSINGTON
0   200 m
0   200 yards
See also plan pp 17-18

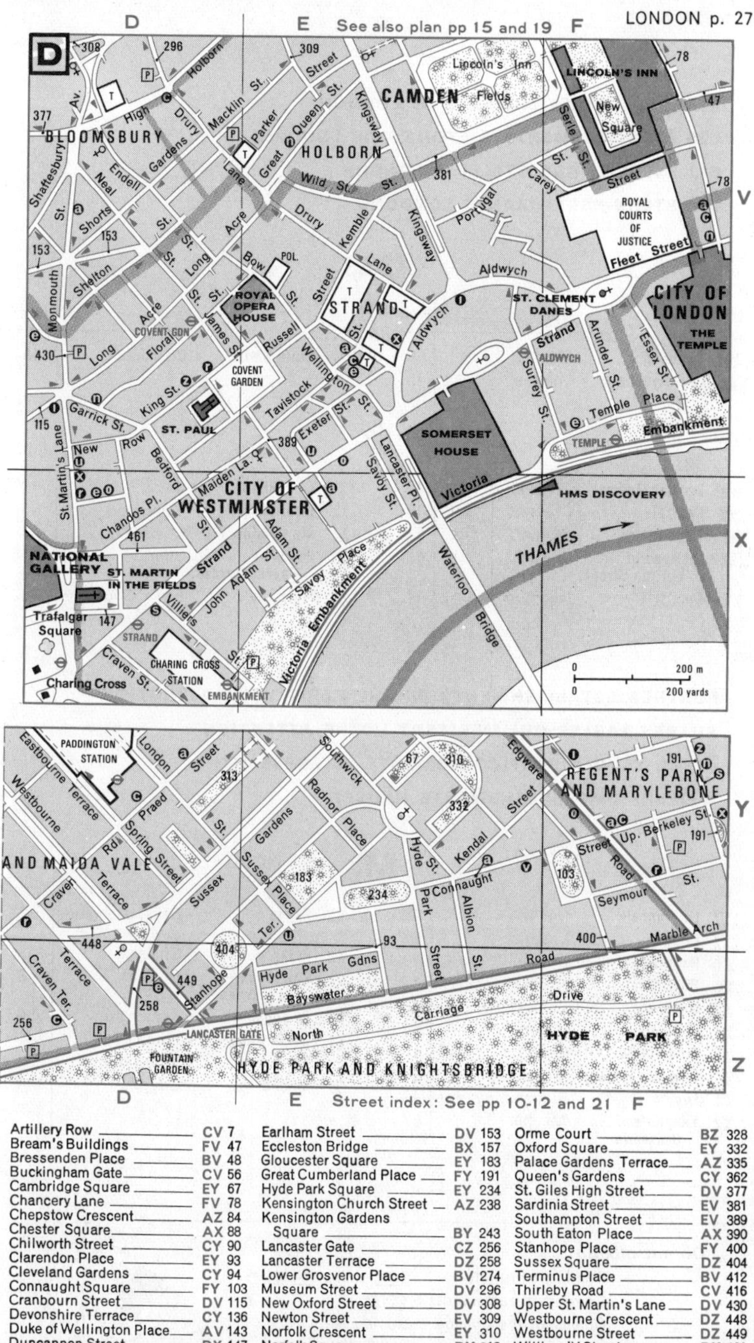

Street index

STARRED ESTABLISHMENTS IN LONDON

LES ÉTABLISSEMENTS A ÉTOILES DE LONDRES

GLI ESERCIZI CON STELLE A LONDRA

DIE STERN-RESTAURANTS LONDONS

	Area	Page			Area	Page
Connaught	Mayfair	56		Tante Claire	Chelsea	48
Le Gavroche	Chelsea	48				

	Area	Page			Area	Page
Carlton Tower	Chelsea	47		Le Poulbot	City	43
Capital	Chelsea	48		Lichfield's	Richmond	53
Inigo Jones	Strand	61		Ma Cuisine	Chelsea	48
Waltons of Walton Street	Chelsea	48		Poons of Covent Garden	Strand	61
Carrier's	Islington	47		Tiger Lee	Earl's Court	49

FURTHER ESTABLISHMENTS WHICH MERIT YOUR ATTENTION

AUTRES TABLES QUI MÉRITENT VOTRE ATTENTION

ALTRE TAVOLE PARTICOLARMENTE INTERESSANTI

WEITERE EMPFEHLENSWERTE HÄUSER

M

		Page				Page
Le Français	Chelsea	48		Pangs	Bayswater and Maida Vale	55
Kundan	Victoria	62				
Bagatelle	Chelsea	49		Parke's	Chelsea	48
Chez Moi	North Kensington	51		Poissonnerie de l'Avenue	Chelsea	48
Daphne's	Chelsea	48				
Eatons	Victoria	62		La Toque Blanche	Kensington	50
Frederick's	Islington	47		Uncle Pang	Finchley	40
Kew Rendezvous	Richmond	53		The Ark	Kensington	50
Lacy's	Bloomsbury	42		Bubb's	City	44
Langan's Brasserie	Mayfair	57				

Do not mix up :	
Comfort of hotels	: ...
Comfort of restaurants	: .....
Quality of the cuisine	: ✿✿, ✿, **M**

RESTAURANTS CLASSIFIED ACCORDING TO TYPE

RESTAURANTS CLASSÉS SUIVANT LEUR GENRE

RISTORANTI CLASSIFICATI SECONDO IL LORO GENERE

RESTAURANTS NACH ART UND EINRICHTUNG GEORDNET

Borough	Area	Restaurant		Page
BISTRO				
Barnet	Finchley	✕	**Aubergade (L')**	40
Camden	Hampstead	✕	**Chateaubriand**	43
City of London	City of London	✕	**Bistingo (Le)**	44
Hammersmith	Fulham	✕	**Red Onion Bistro**	45
—	—	✕	**Trencherman Bistro**	45
Islington	Islington	✕	**M'sieur Frog**	47
Kensington & Chelsea (Royal Borough of)	South Kensington	✕	**Bistingo (Le)**	52
Kingston-upon-Thames	Kingston	✕	**Stonewalls**	52
Lewisham	Blackheath	✕	**Goulue (La)**	52
Wandsworth	Battersea	✕	**Jacks Place**	54
—	Putney	✕	**Cassis**	54
Westminster (City of)	Bayswater & Maida Vale	✕	**Bistingo (Le)**	59
—	—	✕	**Chef (Le)**	56
—	Victoria	✕	**Bumbles**	62
—	—	✕	**Pimlico**	62
—	—	✕	**Poule au Pot (La)**	62
DANCING				
Hammersmith	Fulham	✕✕	**Barbarella**	45
Westminster (City of)	Bayswater & Maida Vale	✕✕	**Concordia Notte**	56
—	Mayfair	✕✕✕	**Tiberio**	57
—	Strand	✕✕✕	**Bussola (La)**	61

<table>
<tr><td colspan="2">Ne confondez pas :</td></tr>
<tr><td>Confort des hôtels</td><td>: 🏨🏨🏨 .., 🏨, 🏛, 仚</td></tr>
<tr><td>Confort des restaurants</td><td>: ✕✕✕✕✕ . . . . . ✕</td></tr>
<tr><td>Qualité de la table</td><td>: ✿✿, ✿, M</td></tr>
</table>

Borough	Area		Restaurant	Page
			SEAFOOD	
Camden	Bloomsbury	XX	**Wheeler's Antoine**	42
—	—	X	**Trattoria dei Pescatori**	42
City of London	City of London	XXX	**Piscean**	43
—	—	XXX	**Wheeler's Fenchurch**	43
—	—	XX	**Bill Bentley's**	43
—	—	XX	**Wheeler's City**	44
Croydon	Croydon	XX	**Hook, Line and Sinker**	44
Kensington & Chelsea (Royal Borough of)	Chelsea	XX	**Poissonnerie de l'Avenue**	48
—	—	XX	**Suquet (Le)**	49
—	Earl's Court	XX	**Croisette (La)**	49
—	Kensington	XX	**Wheeler's Alcove**	50
Westminster (City of)	Belgravia	XX	**Wheeler's Carafe**	56
—	Mayfair	XXXX	**Scott's**	57
—	—	XX	**Golden Carp**	57
—	Regent's Park & Marylebone	XX	**Bill Bentley's**	59
—	—	XX	**Fisherman's Wharf**	59
			AUSTRIAN	
Westminster (City of)	Regent's Park & Marylebone	XX	**Kerzenstüberl**	59
			CHINESE	
Barnet	Finchley	XX	**Uncle Pang**	40
City of London	City of London	X	**City Friends**	44
Kensington & Chelsea (Royal Borough of)	Earl's Court	XX	❀ **Tiger Lee**	49
	Kensington	XX	**Sailing Junk**	50
—	—	X	**Lee Yuan**	50
Richmond-upon-Thames	Richmond	XX	**Kew Rendezvous**	53
—	—	X	**Richmond Rendezvous**	53
—	—	X	**Richmond Rendezvous (Annexe)**	53
Westminster (City of)	Bayswater & Maida Vale	XX	**Lotus House**	55
—	—	XX	**Pangs**	55
—	Hyde Park & Knightsbridge	XX	**Mr. Chow**	56
—	Mayfair	XX	**Mr Kai**	57
—	Regent's Park & Marylebone	XX	**Lords Rendezvous**	59
—	Soho	XX	**Soho Rendezvous**	60
—	—	X	**Village (The)**	60
—	Strand	X	❀ **Poons of Covent Garden**	61
			ENGLISH	
Camden	Hampstead	X	**Turpin's**	43
City of London	City of London	XXX	**Baron of Beef**	43
Kensington & Chelsea (Royal Borough of)	Chelsea	XX	**English House**	48
—	—	X	**Hungry Horse**	49
Westminster (City of)	Belgravia	X	**Upper Crust in Belgravia**	56
—	St. James's	XXX	**Hunting Lodge**	60
—	Strand	XXX	**Simpson's-in-the-Strand**	61
—	Victoria	XX	**Lockets**	62
—	—	X	**Tate Gallery Rest.**	62

Borough	Area	Restaurant	Page

FRENCH

Borough	Area	Restaurant	Page
Bromley	Orpington	XXX Oven d'Or	41
Camden	Bloomsbury	XXX Etoile (L')	42
—	—	XXX Savarin (Au)	42
—	—	X Brasserie du Coin	42
—	—	X Mon Plaisir	42
—	Hampstead	XXX Keats	43
—	—	X Cellier du Midi (Le)	43
City of London	City of London	XXX ❀ Poulbot (Le) (basement)	43
—	—	XX Gaulois (Le)	44
—	—	X Bubb's	44
—	—	X Gamin (Le)	44
—	—	X Germainerie (La)	44
Harrow	Central Harrow	XX Old Etonian	46
Kensington & Chelsea (Royal Borough of)	Chelsea	XXXX ❀❀ Gavroche (Le)	48
—	—	XXX Français (Le)	48
—	—	XXX ❀❀ Tante Claire	48
—	—	XX Bagatelle	49
—	—	XX ❀ Ma Cuisine	48
—	—	X Brasserie (La)	49
—	Kensington	XXX Bressan (Le)	50
—	—	XX Pomme d'Amour (La)	50
—	—	XX Toque Blanche (La)	50
—	—	X Ark (The)	50
—	—	X Jardinière (La)	50
—	North Kensington	XX Chez Moi	51
Merton	Merton	X Les Amoureux	52
Richmond-upon-Thames	Hampton Court	XX Bastians	53
Wandsworth	Battersea	X Lavender Hill	54
Westminster (City of)	Belgravia	X Arcades Brasserie (Les)	56
—	Mayfair	XXX Napoule (La)	57
—	—	XXX Snooty Fox	57
—	Regent's Park & Marylebone	XX Petit Montmartre (Le)	59
—	St. James's	XXXX Ecu de France (A l')	60
—	Soho	XXXXX Café Royal Grill	60
—	—	XXXXX Relais du Café Royal (Le)	60
—	—	XX Jardin des Gourmets (Au)	60
—	Strand	XX Chez Solange	61
—	—	X Cellier de Medici	61

GREEK

Borough	Area	Restaurant	Page
Camden	Bloomsbury	XXX White Tower	42
Westminster (City of)	Bayswater & Maida Vale	XX Kalamaras Taverna	56
—	Regent's Park & Marylebone	X Hellenic	59

Borough	Area	Restaurant	Page

HUNGARIAN

Borough	Area		Restaurant	Page
Westminster (City of)	Soho	XX	Gay Hussar	60

INDIAN & PAKISTANI

Borough	Area		Restaurant	Page
Hammersmith	Hammersmith	XX	Anarkali	46
—	—	XX	Aziz	46
Kensington & Chelsea (Royal Borough of)	Chelsea	XX	Tandoori	49
	Earl's Court	XX	Naraine	50
—	South Kensington	X	Jamshid's	52
—	—	X	Star of India	52
Merton	Wimbledon	XX	Rawalpindi	53
Redbridge	South Woodford	X	Meghna Grill	53
Waltham Forest	Leytonstone	XX	Golden Curry Tandoori	54
Westminster (City of)	Belgravia	XXX	Salloos	56
—	Hyde Park & Knightsbridge	XX	Shezan	56
—	Mayfair	XXX	Tandoori	57
—	—	XX	Gaylord	57
—	Regent's Park & Marylebone	XX	Gaylord	59
—	—	XX	Viceroy of India	59
—	Victoria	XXX	Kundan	62

ITALIAN

Borough	Area		Restaurant	Page
Barnet	Finchley	XX	Luigi's " Belmont "	40
—	—	X	Otello	40
Bexley	Sidcup	X	Botte (La)	40
Bromley	Beckenham	X	Gran Sasso	40
—	Bromley	XX	Chariot Wheel	41
—	Keston	XX	Giannino's	41
Camden	Bloomsbury	X	Belmonte	42
—	—	X	Conca d'Oro	42
—	Finchley Road	XX	Trattoria del Buonamico	42
—	Hampstead	XX	Baita (La)	43
—	—	X	Villa Bianca	43
City of London	City of London	XXX	City Tiberio	43
—	—	XX	Terrazza-Est	43
Croydon	Sanderstead	X	Elio	44
—	South Croydon	X	Trattoria Bella Venezia	44
Ealing	Ealing	XX	Gino's	44
Hammersmith	Fulham	XX	Barbarella	45
Haringey	Highgate	XX	San Carlo	46
Hillingdon	Eastcote	X	Trombino	46
Islington	Islington	XX	Ristorante Portofino	47
Kensington & Chelsea (Royal Borough of)	Chelsea	XXX	Claudius	48
—	—	XX	Don Luigi	48
—	—	XX	Eleven Park Walk	49
—	—	XX	Famiglia (La)	49
—	—	XX	Girasole (Il)	49

Borough	Area	Restaurant		Page
ITALIAN (continued)				
Kensington & Chelsea (Royal Borough of)	—	XX	Meridiana	49
—	—	XX	Sale e Pepe	49
—	—	XX	San Frediano	49
—	—	XX	Santa Croce	49
—	Chelsea	X	Como Lario	49
—	—	X	Leonardo Ristorante	49
—	—	X	San Quintino	49
—	Earl's Court	XX	Pontevecchio	49
—	—	X	Palio di Siena (II)	50
—	Kensington	XX	Franco Ovest	50
—	—	XX	Gatamelata	50
—	—	XX	Gondoliere	50
—	—	XX	Trattoo	50
—	—	X	Paesana (La)	50
—	South Kensington	XX	Giorno e la Notte (II)	52
—	—	XX	Pulcinella	52
Merton	Wimbledon	XX	San Lorenzo Fuoriporta	53
Redbridge	Ilford	XX	Marios'	53
Richmond-upon-Thames	Richmond	XX	Franco's	53
—	—	XX	Gino's	53
—	—	XX	Veranda (La)	53
Southwark	Dulwich Village	XX	Manzoni's	54
Sutton	Sutton	XX	Trattoria Toscana	54
Waltham Forest	Leytonstone	X	Trattoria Parmigiana	54
Wandsworth	Putney	XX	Forchetta (La)	54
Westminster (City of)	Bayswater & Maida Vale	XX	Canaletto	55
—	—	XX	Lupa (La)	55
—	—	XX	San Marino	55
—	—	XX	Trat-West	55
—	—	X	Concordia	56
—	Hyde Park & Knightsbridge	XX	Montpeliano	56
—	Mayfair	XXX	Cecconi's	57
—	—	XXX	Tiberio	57
—	—	XX	Genova (La)	57
—	—	X	Trattoria Fiori	57
—	Regent's Park & Marylebone	XX	Loggia (La)	59
—	—	XX	Rossetti	59
—	—	XX	Sandro	59
—	—	XX	Tonino	59
—	—	X	Barbino (II)	59
—	—	X	Biagi's	59
—	—	X	Vecchio Parioli	59
—	St. James's	XX	Frank's	60
—	Soho	XXX	Gennaro's	60
—	—	XXX	Leonis Quo Vadis	60
—	—	XX	Paparazzi (I)	60
—	—	XX	Peter Mario	60
—	—	XX	Romeo e Giulietta	60
—	—	XX	Rugantino	60
—	—	XX	Terrazza (La)	60
—	—	XX	Venezia	60

Borough	Area	Restaurant		Page
ITALIAN *(continued)*				
Westminster (City of)	—	✗	Hostaria Romana	60
—	—	✗	Trattoria Imperia	60
—	Strand	✗✗✗	Bussola (La)	61
—	—	✗✗	San Martino	61
—	—	✗	Colosseo	61
—	—	✗	Laguna 50	61
—	—	✗	Luigi's	61
—	Victoria	✗✗	Gran Paradiso	62
—	—	✗✗	La Fontana	62
—	—	✗	Mimmo d'Ischia	62
JAPANESE				
City of London	City of London	✗✗	Aykoku Kaku	43
—	—	✗	Ginnan	44
Westminster (City of)	Mayfair	✗	Tokyo	57
—	Regent's Park & Marylebone	✗✗	Masako	59
—	—	✗✗	Mikado	59
—	Soho	✗✗	Fuji	60
—	—	✗	Hokkai	60
—	Strand	✗✗	Azami	61
MALAYSIAN				
Westminster (City of)	Regent's Park & Marylebone	✗	Singapore	59
POLYNESIAN				
Westminster (City of)	Mayfair	✗✗✗	Trader Vics (at Hilton)	57
SWISS				
Westminster (City of)	Soho	✗✗	Chesa (Swiss Centre)	60
—	—	✗	Rendezvous (Swiss Centre)	60

Verwechseln Sie nicht:

Komfort der Hotels	: 🏨 ... 🏠, 🏡, 🛖
Komfort der Restaurants	: ✗✗✗✗✗ . . . . ✗
Gute Küche	: ❀❀, ❀, **M**

RESTAURANTS OPEN ON SUNDAY (L : lunch - D : dinner) AND RESTAURANTS TAKING LAST ORDERS AFTER 11.30 p.m.

RESTAURANTS OUVERTS LE DIMANCHE (L : déjeuner - D : dîner) ET RESTAURANTS PRENANT LES DERNIÈRES COMMANDES APRÈS 23 h 30

RISTORANTI APERTI LA DOMENICA (L : colazione - D : pranzo) E RISTORANTI CHE ACCETTANO ORDINAZIONI DOPO LE 23. 30

RESTAURANTS, DIE SONNTAGS GEÖFFNET SIND (L : Mittagessen - D : Abendessen), BZW. BESTELLUNGEN AUCH NACH 23.30 UHR ANNEHMEN

Borough	Area	Restaurant		Sunday	11.30 p. m.	Page
Barnet	Finchley	XX	Luigi's « Belmont »	L D		40
—	—	XX	Uncle Pang	L D	x	40
—	—	X	Otello	L D		40
Bexley	Bexley	XX	King's Head	L		40
Bromley	Farnborough	XXX	New Fantail	L		41
—	—	X	George at Farnborough (The)	L D		41
Camden	Bloomsbury	XX	Wheeler's Antoine	L D		42
—	—	X	Trattoria dei Pescatori		x	42
—	Finchley Road	XX	Capability Brown	L D		42
—	—	XX	Trattoria del Buonamico	L D		42
—	Hampstead	XXX	Keats		x	43
—	—	XX	Baita (La)		x	43
—	—	X	Cellier du Midi (Le)		x	43
—	—	X	Chateaubriand		x	43
—	—	X	Turpin's	L D		43
—	—	X	Villa Bianca	L D	x	43
—	Holborn	XXX	Opera (L') (12.00)		x	43
—	Swiss Cottage	XX	Peter's	L D	x	43
City of London	City of London	X	Bistingo (Le) (12.00)		x	44
—	—	X	City Friends (12.00)		x	44
Croydon	South Croydon	X	Trattoria Bella Venezia		x	44
Ealing	Ealing	XX	Gino's		x	44
Greenwich	Greenwich	X	Meantime	L		45
Hammersmith	Fulham	XX	Barbarella (12.00)		x	45
—	—	XX	Newton's		x	45
—	Hammersmith	XX	Anarkali (11.45)	L D	x	46
—	—	XX	Aziz		x	46
Haringey	Highgate	XX	San Carlo	L D	x	46

Borough	Area		Restaurant	Sunday	11.30 p. m.	Page
Harrow	Pinner	✗	Giralda (La)	L D		46
—	—	✗	Old Oak	L D		46
Hillingdon	Eastcote	✗	Sambuca		x	46
Islington	Islington	✗✗✗	❀ Carrier's		x	47
—	—	✗✗	Frederick's		x	47
—	—	✗✗	Julius's		x	47
—	—	✗	M'sieur Frog		x	47
Kensington & Chelsea (Royal Borough of)	Chelsea	✗✗✗✗	❀❀ Gavroche (Le) (11.45)		x	48
		✗✗✗✗	❀ Waltons of Walton Street	L	x	48
—	—	✗✗✗	Claudius	L D		48
—	—	✗✗	Bewick's		x	48
—	—	✗✗	Daphne's		x	48
—	—	✗✗	Don Luigi	L D	x	48
—	—	✗✗	Eleven Park Walk		x	49
—	—	✗✗	English House	L D	x	48
—	—	✗✗	Famiglia (La)		x	49
—	—	✗✗	Girasole (Il) (11.45)		x	49
—	—	✗✗	Meridiana (12.00)		x	49
—	—	✗✗	Parke's		x	48
—	—	✗✗	Poissonnerie de l'Avenue		x	48
—	—	✗✗	Salamis (11.45)		x	49
—	—	✗✗	Sale e Pepe		x	49
—	—	✗✗	San Frediano (11.45)		x	49
—	—	✗✗	Santa Croce		x	49
—	—	✗✗	Suquet (Le)	L D		49
—	—	✗✗	Tandoori	L D	x	49
—	—	✗	Brasserie (La)	L D	x	49
—	—	✗	Como Lario		x	49
—	—	✗	Hungry Horse	L D	x	49
—	—	✗	San Quintino		x	49
—	Earl's Court	✗✗	Croisette (La)	L D		49
—	—	✗✗	Naraine (12.00)		x	49
—	—	✗✗	Pontevecchio	L D	x	49
—	—	✗✗	❀ Tiger Lee	D	x	49
—	—	✗	Palio di Siena (Il) (11.45)	L D	x	50
—	Kensington	✗✗	Franco Ovest		x	50
—	—	✗✗	Sailing Junk	D	x	50
—	—	✗✗	Trattoo	L D	x	50
—	—	✗	Ark (The)	D		50
—	—	✗	Lee Yuan (11.45)	L D	x	50
—	—	✗	Paesana (La) (11.50)		x	50
—	North Kensington	✗✗✗	Leith's	D	x	51
—	—	✗✗	Chez Moi		x	51
—	South Kensington	✗✗	Giorno e la Notte (11.45)		x	52
—	—	✗✗	Pulcinella		x	52
—	—	✗	Bistingo (Le) (11.45)	L D	x	52
—	—	✗	Jamshid's	L D	x	52
—	—	✗	Star of India (11.45)		x	52
Kingston-upon-Thames	Kingston	✗	Stonewalls	L D		52

Borough	Area		Restaurant	Sunday	11.30 p. m.	Page
Lambeth	Waterloo	XX	National Theatre Rest.		x	52
Lewisham	Blackheath	X	La Goulue	D		52
—	Catford	XX	Casa Cominetti	L		52
Merton	Wimbledon	XX	San Lorenzo Fuoriporta		x	53
—	—	X	Lemon Tree	L D		53
Richmond-upon-Thames	Barnes	XX	Autres Granges (Les)		x	53
—	Richmond	XX	Franco's (12.00)	L D		53
—	—	XX	Gino's		x	53
—	—	XX	Kew Rendezvous	L D		53
—	—	X	Richmond Rendezvous (Annexe)	L D		53
—	—	X	Richmond Rendezvous	L D	x	53
Waltham Forest	Leytonstone	XX	Golden Curry Tandoori	L D	x	54
—	—	X	Trattoria Parmigiana		x	54
Wandsworth	Battersea	XX	Alonso's		x	54
Westminster (City of)	Bayswater & Maida Vale	XX	Concordia Notte (12.30)		x	56
		XX	Kalamaras Taverna		x	56
—	—	XX	Lotus House	L D	x	55
—	—	XX	Lupa (La)			55
—	—	XX	Pangs	L D	x	55
—	—	XX	San Marino		x	55
—	—	XX	Trat-West	L D	x	55
—	—	X	Chef (Le)		x	56
—	—	X	Concordia		x	56
—	Belgravia	XXX	Salloos		x	56
—	—	XX	Wheeler's Carafe	L D		56
—	—	X	Arcades Brasserie (Les)	L D	x	56
—	—	X	Upper Crust in Belgravia	L D		56
—	Hyde Park & Knightsbridge	XX	Mr. Chow	L D	x	56
—	—	XX	Montpeliano		x	56
—	—	XX	Shezan		x	56
—	Mayfair	(hotel)	Inn on the Park (Four Seasons)	L D	x	56
—	—	XXXXX	Mirabelle		x	57
—	—	XXXX	Scott's	D		57
—	—	XXX	Snooty Fox (11.45)		x	57
—	—	XXX	Tandoori (12.30)		x	57
—	—	XXX	Tiberio (1.30)		x	57
—	—	XXX	Trader Vics (at Hilton)		x	57
—	—	XX	Gaylord	L D	x	57
—	—	XX	Golden Carp		x	57
—	—	XX	Mr Kai		x	57
—	—	X	Tokyo	L D		57
—	Regent's Park & Marylebone	XX	Gaylord	L D	x	59
—	—	XX	Loggia (La)		x	59
—	—	XX	Lords Rendezvous	L D	x	59
—	—	XX	Petit Montmartre (Le)		x	59
—	—	XX	Rossetti (11.45)	L D	x	59

Borough	Area		Restaurant	Sunday	11.30 p. m.	Page
Westminster (City of)	Regent's Park & Marylebone	XX	Sandro		x	59
—		XX	Viceroy of India	L D		59
—	—	X	Barbino (Il)		x	59
—	—	X	Biagi's	L D		59
—	St. James's	XXXX	Ecu de France (A l')	D	x	60
—	Soho	XXXXX	Café Royal Grill		x	60
—	—	XXXXX	Relais du Café Royal (Le)		x	60
—	—	XXX	Gennaro's		x	60
—	—	XXX	Leonis Quo Vadis (11.45)	D		60
—	—	XX	Chesa (Swiss Centre)	L D	x	60
—	—	XX	Fuji	D		60
—	—	XX	Gay Hussar		x	60
—	—	XX	Jardin des Gourmets (Au)		x	60
—	—	XX	Paparazzi (I)	L D	x	60
—	—	XX	Peter Mario		x	60
—	—	XX	Rugantino		x	60
—	—	XX	Soho Rendezvous (11.45)	L D	x	60
—	—	XX	Terrazza (La)	L D	x	60
—	—	XX	Venezia		x	60
—	—	X	Hokkai	D		60
—	—	X	Hostaria Romana	L D	x	60
—	—	X	Rendezvous (Swiss Centre) (12.00)	L D	x	60
—	—	X	Trattoria Imperia		x	60
—	—	X	Village (The) (12.00)	L D	x	60
—	Strand	XXXX	❀ Inigo Jones (11.45)		x	61
—	—	XXX	Bussola (La) (12.00)		x	61
—	—	XX	Chez Solange		x	61
—	—	XX	Grange (11.45)		x	61
—	—	XX	San Martino (11.45)		x	61
—		X	Cellier de Medici		x	61
—	—	X	Colosseo		x	61
—	—	X	Laguna 50		x	61
—	—	X	Luigi's		x	61
—	—	X	❀ Poons of Covent Garden (11.45)		x	61
—	Victoria	XXX	Kundan		x	62
—	—	XX	Gran Paradiso		x	62
—		XX	La Fontana		x	62
—	—	X	Mimmo d'Ischia		x	62
—	—	X	Pimlico	L D	x	62

Non confondete:

Confort degli alberghi : 🏨 ... 🏠, 🏤, ⌂

Confort dei ristoranti : XXXXX X

Qualità della tavola : ❀❀❀, ❀, **M**

LICENSING HOURS: WHEN DRINKING ALCOHOLIC BEVERAGES IS PERMITTED IN PUBS AND BARS AND OTHER LICENSED PREMISES
(The general rule).

HEURES PERMISES POUR LA CONSOMMATION DES BOISSONS ALCOOLISÉES (Règle générale).

ORARI CONSENTITI PER LA CONSUMAZIONE DI BEVANDE ALCOLICHE (Regola Generale).

AUSSCHANKZEITEN FÜR ALKOHOLISCHE GETRÄNKE (Allgemeine Regelung).

	from / de	to / à	from / de	to / à	
Weekdays (other than Good Friday and Christmas Day) **Jours de Semaine** (autres que Vendredi-Saint et Jour de Noël)	**11.00**	**15.00**	**18.00**	**22.30**	**Giorni della Settimana** (esclusi Venerdì Santo e Natale) **Wochentags** (außer Karfreitag und Weihnachten)
Sundays, Good Friday, Christmas Day **Dimanches, Vendredi-Saint, Jour de Noël**	**12.00**	**14.00**	**19.00**	**22.30**	**Domeniche, Venerdì Santo, Natale** Sonntags, Karfreitag und Weihnachten
	dalle / von	alle / bis	dalle / von	alle / bis	

Children under 14 are not allowed in the bars of licensed premises (Public Houses, Hotels and Restaurants) where alcoholic drinks may be bought and consumed. The sale of alcoholic drink to minors under the age of 18 is illegal.

Unlicensed hotels and restaurants are not permitted to sell alcoholic beverages, including beer, at any time.

L'accès dans les bars des lieux autorisés à la vente des boissons alcoolisées (Public Houses, Hôtels, Restaurants) est interdit aux enfants de moins de 14 ans. La vente de boissons alcoolisées est interdite aux personnes de moins de 18 ans.

Les établissements sans licence (unlicensed) ne peuvent vendre, à aucun moment, aucune boisson alcoolisée.

E'vietato ai ragazzi minori di 14 anni l'ingresso ai bars dei locali autorizzati alla vendita di bevande alcoliche (Public Houses, Alberghi, Ristoranti).

E' vietata la vendita di bevande alcoliche ai minori di 18 anni. Gli esercizi senza licenza (unlicensed) non possono vendere bevande alcoliche in nessun momento.

Kindern unter 14 Jahren ist der Besuch von Lokalen (Bars) mit Alkoholausschank (Public houses, Hotels, Restaurants) untersagt. Der Verkauf von alkoholischen Getränken an Jugendliche unter 18 Jahren ist verboten.

Betriebe ohne Konzession (unlicensed) dürfen grundsätzlich keinen Alkohol verkaufen.

BOROUGHS and AREAS

Greater London is divided, for administrative purposes, into 32 boroughs plus the City; these sub-divide naturally into minor areas, usually grouped around former villages or quarters, which often maintain a distinctive character.

✆ of Greater London : 01 except special cases.

BARNET pp. 8 and 9.

Finchley – ✉ N3/N12/NW11.

XX **Luigi's " Belmont ",** 2-4 Belmont Parade, Finchley Rd, NW11 6XP, at Temple Fortune, ☏ 455 0210, Italian rest. – 🗚 AE ⓪ VISA   **CV x**
closed Monday – **M** a la carte 5.90/9.80 **s.** 🍷 3.00.

XX **Uncle Pang,** 30 Temple Fortune Par., NW11, ☏ 455 9444, Chinese rest. – AE ⓪ VISA   **CV z**
M a la carte 8.00/10.00 **st.** 🍷 2.80.

X **Otello,** 241 Regents Park Rd, N3 3LA, ☏ 346 5232, Italian rest. – 🗚 ⓪   **CV o**
a la carte 4.50/14.05 🍷 1.50.

X **L'Aubergade,** 816 Finchley Rd, NW11 6XL, at Temple Fortune ☏ 445 8853, French Bistro – VISA   **CV v**
closed Saturday lunch and Sunday – **M** a la carte 8.15/9.60 **st.** 🍷 2.30.

Golders Green – ✉ NW11.

↑ **Croft Court,** 44-46 Ravenscroft Av., NW11 8AY, ☏ 458 3331, 🚗 – 🛏wc ☎   **CV n**
19 rm 🍽 10.50/21.50 **st.**

Hendon – ✉ NW4/NW7. – ⛳ off Sanders Lane ☏ 346 7810.

🏨 **Hendon Hall,** Ashley Lane, NW4 1HF, ☏ 203 3341, 🚗 – 🛗 TV ⓟ. 🛁. 🗚 AE ⓪ VISA   **CV e**
M 4.70 **t.** – **52 rm** 🍽 23.50/28.75 **t.**

🏨 **TraveLodge** (T.H.F.) without rest., at Scratchwood Service Area on M1, NW7 3HB, ☏ 906 0611 – TV 🛏wc ☎ 🦽 ⓟ. 🛁. 🗚 AE ⓪ VISA   **BV n**
100 rm 🍽 14.50/21.50 **st.**

Totteridge – ✉ N 20.

↑ **Totteridge,** Totteridge Village, N20 8AE, ☏ 445 3666 – ⓟ – **11 rm.**   **CV r**

BEXLEY pp. 8 and 9.
🛈 Town Hall at Erith ✉ Kent, CA8 1TL, ☏ 303 7777.

Bexley – ✉ Kent – ✆ 0322 Crayford.

XX **King's Head,** 65 High St., DA5 1AA, ☏ 526112 – ⓟ. 🗚 ⓪ VISA   **FY c**
closed Sunday dinner and Christmas Day – **M** a la carte 5.05/8.50 **t.** 🍷 2.30.

XX **Le Boulot,** 80 High St., DA5 1LB, ☏ 529905 – 🗚 AE ⓪ VISA   **FY n**
closed Saturday lunch and Sunday – **M** a la carte 5.00/8.25 **st.** 🍷 2.00.

Sidcup – ✉ Kent.

X **La Botte,** 9 Marechal Neil Par., Main Rd, DA14 6QF, ☏ 300 5233, Italian rest. – 🗚 AE ⓪ VISA   **FY r**
closed Saturday lunch, Sunday and Christmas Day – **M** a la carte 4.70/7.50 **t.** 🍷 1.60.

BRENT pp. 8 and 9.

Wembley – ✉ Middx.
⛳ Bridgewater Rd ☏ 902 0218 – ⛳ Whitton Av. ☏ 902 4555.

🏨 **Wembley Eurocrest** (Crest), Empire Way, HA9 8DS, ☏ 903 8839, Telex 24837 – 🛗 TV 🦽 ⓟ. 🛁. 🗚 AE ⓪ VISA   **BV o**
🍽 2.80 – **320 rm** 25.20/37.00 **st.**

BROMLEY pp. 8 and 9.
🛈 Town Hall, Widmore Rd ☏ 464 3333.

Beckenham – ✉ Kent. – ⛳, ⛳ ☏ 650 2292.

↑ **Four Chimneys,** 18 Brackley Rd, BR3 1RQ, ☏ 650 5225, 🚗 – 🛏wc ⓟ   **EZ v**
14 rm 🍽 5.00/11.00.

X **Gran Sasso** 189b High St., BR3 1AH, ☏ 658 3614, Italian rest. – 🗚 AE ⓪ VISA   **EZ s**
closed Saturday lunch, Sunday and Bank Holidays – **M** a la carte 5.85/9.40 **t.** 🍷 1.55.

Bickley – ⊠ Kent.

↟ **Glendevon House,** 80 Southborough Rd, BR1 2EN, ☎ 467 2183 – ℗   FZ n
9 rm ☲ 8.50/18.00 **t.**

Bromley – ⊠ Kent.

Ⓟ Magpie Hall Lane ☎ **462 7014.**

↟ **Holly House,** Holwood Rd, BR1 3EB, ☎ 460 7037 – ℗   FZ o
13 rm ☲ 7.00/12.50 **s.**

↟ **Grianan,** 23 Orchard Rd, BR1 2PR, ☎ 460 1795 – ℗   FZ r
10 rm ☲ 8.05/16.10 **st.**

↟ **Bromley Continental,** 56 Plaistow Lane, BR1 3JE, ☎ 464 2415, 🚗 – ℗   FZ c
13 rm ☲ 8.00/18.00 **st.**

XX **Chariot Wheel,** 21-22 Westmoreland Pl., Bromley South Shopping Centre, BR2 0TE,
☎ 460 8477, Italian rest. – 🄝 AE ⓪ VISA   FZ i
closed Sunday, Monday, 2 weeks August and Bank Holidays – **M** a la carte 5.50/12.15 **t.**
🍾 1.80.

X **Capisano,** 9 Simpsons Rd, BR2 9AP, ☎ 464 8036 – 🄝 AE ⓪ VISA   EZ a
closed Sunday, Monday lunch and Bank Holidays – **M** a la carte 4.25/6.60 **t.** 🍾 1.80.

Chislehurst – ⊠ Kent.

X London Steak House, 7a High St. BR7 5AA, ☎ 467 0278.   FZ s

Farnborough – ⊠ Kent – ☎ 0689 Farnborough.

Ⓟ High Elms Rd 58175, off A 21 via Shire Lane.

XXX **New Fantail,** Locksbottom, BR6 8NF, ☎ 54848 – ℗. 🄝 AE ⓪ VISA   FZ x
closed Sunday dinner, Monday, 19 August-4 September and Bank Holidays – **M** a la carte
4.40/9.00 **t.** 🍾 1.50.

X **The George at Farnborough,** High St., BR6 7BA, ☎ 52005 – ℗. 🄝 ⓪ VISA   FZ z
closed Tuesday – **M** a la carte 3.50/6.50 **t.** 🍾 1.30.

Keston – ⊠ Kent – ☎ 0689 Farnborough.

XX Giannino's, 6 Commonside ☎ 56410, Italian rest.   FZ v

Orpington – ⊠ Kent – ☎ 0689 Orpington.

Ⓟ Cray Valley ☎ 37909.

XXX **Oven d'Or,** 4a Crescent Way, BR5 2GT, ☎ 52170, French rest. – 🄝 AE ⓪ VISA   FZ u
closed Saturday lunch, Sunday, Monday, 3 to 27 August, 1 to 7 January and Bank Holidays
– **M** a la carte 6.00/13.50 **t.**

X **Le Troquet,** 4 Crescent Way ☎ 52170 – 🄝 AE ⓪ VISA   FZ u
closed Sunday, 3 to 27 August, 1 to 7 January and Bank Holidays – **M** a la carte 2.80/
5.65 **t.** 🍾 2.00.

__Le Grand Londres__ (GREATER LONDON) est composé de la City et de 32 arrondissements administratifs (Borough) eux-mêmes divisés en quartiers ou villages ayant conservé leur caractère propre (Area).

CAMDEN Except where otherwise stated see pp. 13-16.

🛈 Town Hall, Euston Rd, NW1 2RU, ☎ 278 4444.

Bloomsbury – ⊠ NW1/W1/WC1.

🏨 **Drury Lane** (Gd. Met.), 10 Drury Lane, High Holborn, WC2B 5RE, ☎ 836 6666, Telex
8811395 – 🛗 📺 ♿ 🛀. 🄝 AE ⓪ VISA   p. 27 DV c
M 7.50/8.50 **st.** – **129 rm** 29.00/40.00 **s.**

🏨 **Russell** (T.H.F.), Russell Sq., WC1B 5BE, ☎ 837 6470, Telex 24615 – 🛗 📺. 🛀. 🄝 AE
⓪ VISA   NT o
M (Carvery Rest.) 5.80 **st.** 🍾 2.10 – ☲ 3.00 – **318 rm** 26.00/35.25 **st.**

🏨 **Cora,** Upper Woburn Pl., WC1H 0HT, ☎ 387 5111, Telex 261591 – 🛗 📺 🛏wc 📞. 🛀.
🄝 AE ⓪ VISA   MS z
M 7.00 **st.** 🍾 1.85 – **150 rm** ☲ 21.00/31.40 **st.**

🏨 **Bonnington,** 92 Southampton Row, WC1B 4BH, ☎ 242 2828, Telex 261591 – 🛗 📺
🛏wc 📞. 🛀. 🄝 AE ⓪ VISA   NT s
M a la carte 4.70/8.15 **st.** 🍾 2.00 – **250 rm** ☲ 24.00/35.00 **st.**

🏨 Bloomsbury Centre (Centre), Coram St., WC1N 1HT, ☎ 837 1200, Telex 22113 – 🛗 📺
🛏wc 📞 ♿ ℗. 🛀. 🄝 AE ⓪ VISA   MNS c
☲ 1.65 – **250 rm** 21.55/29.60 **st.**

P.T.O. →

🏨 **Kingsley** (T.H.F.), Bloomsbury Way, WC1A 2SD, ℡ 242 5881, Telex 21157 – ▯ TV ⌁wc
🕾. ⛴.   **NT** r
173 rm.

↑ Crichton, 36 Bedford Pl., WC18 5JR, ℡ 637 3955, Telex 263250 – 🝙 🕾   **NT** x
62 rm.

↑ **Crescent,** 49-50 Cartwright Gdns, WC1H 9EL, ℡ 387 1515   **MS** a
28 rm ⌑ 8.00/15.00 **st.**

↑ **Harlingford,** 61-63 Cartwright Gdns, WC1H 9EL, ℡ 387 1551   **MS** n
43 rm ⌑ 10.00/15.00 **st.**

↑ Wansbeck, 5-6 Bedford Pl., WC1B 5JD, ℡ 636 6232   **NT** a
34 rm.

↑ **Staunton,** 13-15 Gower St., WC1E 6HE, ℡ 580 2740   **MT** c
20 rm ⌑ 6.00/12.00.

XXX **L'Etoile,** 30 Charlotte St., W1P 1HJ, ℡ 636 7189, French rest. – AE ⓪   **LT** e
closed Saturday, Sunday, 27 July-21 August and Bank Holidays – **M** a la carte 8.70/12.00 **t.**
🍶 1.95.

XXX **White Tower,** 1 Percy St., W1P 0ET, ℡ 636 8141, Greek rest. – ▧ AE ⓪   **MT** u
closed Saturday, Sunday, 3 weeks August and Bank Holidays – **M** a la carte 7.90/13.40 **t.**
🍶 2.00.

XXX **Au Savarin,** 8 Charlotte St., W1P 1HE, ℡ 636 7134, French rest. – ▧ AE ⓪ *VISA*   **LT** e
closed Sunday, first 3 weeks August and Bank Holidays – **M** a la carte 14.70/40.90 🍶 3.50.

XX **Lacy's,** 26-28 Whitfield St., W1P 5RD, ℡ 636 2323 – ▧ AE ⓪ *VISA*   **MT** a
closed Saturday lunch, Sunday and Bank Holidays – **M** a la carte 9.35/13.00.

XX **Wheeler's Antoine,** 40 Charlotte St., W1P 1HP, ℡ 636 2817, Seafood – ▧ AE ⓪ *VISA*
closed Saturday and Bank Holidays – **M** a la carte 10.00/14.20 **st.** 🍶 1.75.   **LT** e

X **Trattoria dei Pescatori,** 55-57 Charlotte St., W1P 1LA, ℡ 580 3289, Italian Seafood
closed Sunday and Bank Holidays – **M** a la carte 5.70/9.50 **t.** 🍶 1.95.   **LT** v

X **Conca d'Oro,** 54 Red Lion St., WC1 4PD, ℡ 242 6964, Italian rest. – ⓪ *VISA*   **NT** c
closed Saturday lunch, Sunday and 3 weeks August – **M** a la carte 4.85/6.00 **t.** 🍶 1.60.

X **Mon Plaisir,** 21 Monmouth St., WC2H 9DD, ℡ 836 7243, French rest.   p. 27   **DV** a
closed Saturday, Sunday, August and Bank Holidays – **M** a la carte 5.60/7.80 🍶 1.75.

X **Brasserie du Coin,** 54 Lambs Conduit St., WC1N 3LN, ℡ 405 1717, French rest. – ▧
AE ⓪   **NT** z
closed Saturday, Sunday and Bank Holidays – **M** a la carte 3.50/8.15 **t.** 🍶 2.75.

X Belmonte, 31 Rathbone Pl., W1, ℡ 636 8965, Italian rest.   **MT** s

Euston – ✉ NW1.

🏨 **Kennedy** (Gd. Met.), 43 Cardington St., NW1 2LP, ℡ 387 4400, Telex 28250 – ▯
TV ⌁wc 🕾 ⛴ P. ⛴. ▧ AE ⓪ *VISA*   **LS** r
M 6.00 **st.** – **319 rm** 22.50/31.00 **s.**

Finchley Road – ✉ NW1/NW3.

🝙 Nether Court, Frith Lane ℡ 346 2436.

🏨 **Charles Bernard,** 5 Frognal, NW3 6AL, ℡ 794 0101, Telex 23560 – ▯ TV ⌁wc
🕾 P. ▧ AE ⓪ *VISA*   **GR** s
M 6.50 **s.** 🍶 1.75 – **57 rm** ⌑ 20.00/28.00 **s.**

↑ **Dawson House,** 72 Canfield Gdns, NW6 3ED, ℡ 624 0079, 🚗   **HR** a
15 rm ⌑ 7.00/14.00 **st.**

XX **Capability Brown,** 351 West End Lane, NW6, ℡ 794 3234   pp. 8 and 9   **CV** i
closed 2 weeks August, 1 week at Christmas and Bank Holidays – **M** (dinner only and
Sunday lunch) a la carte 7.75/11.90 **t.** 🍶 2.10.

XX **Trattoria del Buonamico,** 122a Finchley Rd, NW3 5HT, ℡ 794 5784, Italian rest. – ▧
AE ⓪ *VISA*   **JR** o
M a la carte 5.10/8.10 **t.** 🍶 1.65.

Hampstead – ✉ NW3.

🏨 **Clive,** Primrose Hill Rd, NW3 3NA, ℡ 586 2233, Telex 22759 – ▯ TV P. ⛴. ▧ AE ⓪ *VISA*
M 6.00/7.00 **t.** 🍶 1.80 – ⌑ 3.30 – **84 rm** 25.00/29.00.   **KR** a

🏨 **Swiss Cottage,** 4 Adamson Rd, NW3 3HX, ℡ 722 2281, Telex 27950, « Antique furniture collection » – ▯ TV ⌁wc 🝙wc 🕾. ▧ AE ⓪ *VISA*   **JR** n
M 6.30/7.30 **st.** – **64 rm** ⌑ 16.00/30.00 **s.**

🏨 **Post House** (T.H.F.), 215 Haverstock Hill, NW3 4RB, ℡ 794 8121, Telex 262494 – ▯
TV ⌁wc 🕾 P. ⛴. ▧ AE ⓪ *VISA*   **GR** r
M a la carte 5.15/8.30 **st.** 🍶 1.65 – ⌑ 2.50 – **140 rm** 19.00/28.00 **st.**

↑ **Sandringham** ⑧, 3 Holford Rd, NW3 1AD, ℡ 435 1569, 🚗 – P   **GR** u
closed Christmas and 1 January – **13 rm** ⌑ 7.00/14.00.

↑ Frognal Lodge, 14 Frognal Gdns, NW3 6UX, ℡ 435 8238 – ▯ ⌁wc 🕾   **GR** v
17 rm.

XXX **Keats,** 3-4 Downshire Hill, NW3 1NR, ☎ 435 1499, French rest. – ⬛ AE ⓪ *VISA*   **GR i**
closed Sunday, 3 weeks August and Bank Holidays – **M** (dinner only) a la carte 9.75/ 13.60 **t.** ₰ 3.20.

XX La Baita, 200 Haverstock Hill, NW3 2AG, ☎ 794 4126, Italian rest.   **GR e**

X **Villa Bianca,** 1 Perrin's Court, NW3 1QR, ☎ 435 3131, Italian rest. – ⬛ AE ⓪ *VISA*   **GR c**
closed August – **M** a la carte 6.30/9.55 **t.** ₰ 1.60.

X **Turpin's,** 118 Heath St., NW3 1DR, ☎ 435 3791, English rest. – ⬛ AE ⓪ *VISA*   **GR a**
M a la carte 6.65/8.30 **t.** ₰ 1.75.

X **Le Cellier du Midi,** 28 Church Row, NW3 6UP, ☎ 435 9998, French rest. – ⬛ AE ⓪ *VISA*   **GR x**
closed Sunday, Easter, Christmas and Bank Holidays – **M** (dinner only) 7.95 **t.** ₰ 1.80.

X **Chateaubriand,** 48 Belsize Lane, NW3 5AR, ☎ 435 4882, Bistro – ⬛ AE ⓪ *VISA*   **GR n**
closed Sunday, 24 to 26 December and 1 January – **M** (dinner only) a la carte 6.30/ 10.60 **t.** ₰ 2.50.

Holborn – ✉ WC2.

XXX **L'Opera,** 32 Great Queen St., WC2B 5AA, ☎ 405 9020 – ⬛ AE ⓪ *VISA*   p. 27 **EV n**
closed Saturday lunch and Sunday – **M** a la carte 7.00/9.90 **t.** ₰ 1.80.

King's Cross – ✉ N1.

🏨 **Great Northern** (B.T.H.), N1 9AN, ☎ 837 5454, Telex 299041 – 🛗 TV ⇌wc ☎. ♨.   **MNS s**
⬛ AE ⓪ *VISA*
M a la carte 5.25/10.50 **st.** ₰ 2.40 – **66 rm** � 22.65/35.15 **st.**

Regent's Park – ✉ NW1.

🏨 **White House** (Rank), Albany St., NW1 3UP, ☎ 387 1200, Telex 24111 – 🛗 TV ♿. ♨.   **LS o**
⬛ AE ⓪ *VISA*
M *(closed Saturday lunch, Sunday and Bank Holidays)* a la carte approx. 11.05 **st.** –
⊏ 3.05 – **587 rm** 27.00/36.00 **st.**

Swiss Cottage – ✉ NW3.

🏨 **Holiday Inn,** 128 King Henry's Rd, NW3 3ST, ☎ 722 7711, Telex 267396, ⬛ – 🛗 TV ♿   **JR a**
℗. ♨. ⬛ AE ⓪ *VISA*
M 6.50/12.50 **t.** ₰ 2.50 – ⊏ 3.50 – **297 rm** 30.50/37.50 **s.**

XX **Peter's,** 65 Fairfax Rd, NW6 4EE, ☎ 624 5804 – ⓪ *VISA*   **JR i**
closed Saturday lunch, Christmas Day and 1 January – **M** a la carte 6.25/8.65 **t.** ₰ 1.75.

CITY OF LONDON Except where otherwise stated see p. 16.

🛈 St. Paul's Churchyard, EC4, ☎ 606 3030.

🏨 **Great Eastern** (B.T.H.), Liverpool St., EC2M 7QN, ☎ 283 4363, Telex 886812 – 🛗 TV
♿. ♨. ⬛ AE ⓪ *VISA*   **QT r**
M approx. 7.00 **st.** ₰ 2.40 – **156 rm** ⊏ 18.00/40.00 **st.**

XXX ❀ **Le Poulbot** (basement), 45 Cheapside, EC2V 6AR, ☎ 236 4379, French rest.   **PU i**
closed Saturday, Sunday and Bank Holidays – **M** (lunch only) a la carte 12.00/18.00 **st.**
Spéc. Mousseline de volaille à l'estragon, Filets de sole Leonora, Piccatta de veau à ma façon.

XXX **Piscean,** 12-13 Lime St., EC3M 7AA, ☎ 623 1843, Seafood – ⬛ AE ⓪ *VISA*   **QU r**
closed Saturday, Sunday and Bank Holidays – **M** (lunch only) a la carte 7.85/11.40 **t.**
₰ 2.30.

XXX City Tiberio, 8-11 Lime St., EC3, ☎ 623 3616, Italian rest.   **QU i**

XXX **Baron of Beef,** Gutter Lane, Gresham St., EC2V 6BR, ☎ 606 9415, English rest. – ⬛
AE ⓪ *VISA*   **PT r**
closed Saturday and Sunday – **M** a la carte 6.10/13.10 **t.** ₰ 2.50.

XXX City Yacht (T.H.F.), 1 Addle St., EC2V 7EU, ☎ 606 8536.   **PT c**

XXX **Wheeler's Fenchurch,** 9-13 Fenchurch Buildings, EC3P 3HY, ☎ 488 4848, Seafood –
⬛ AE ⓪ *VISA*   **QU n**
closed Saturday, Sunday and Bank Holidays – **M** (lunch only) a la carte 10.00/14.20 **st.**
₰ 1.75.

XXX Cotillion Room, Bucklersbury House, 18 Walbrook, EC4N 8EL, ☎ 248 4735.   **PU s**

XXX Essex Rib Roast, Dunster House, Mark Lane, EC3R 7DP, ☎ 626 5513.   **QU o**

XX **Bill Bentley's,** Swedeland Court, 202-204 Bishopsgate, EC2M 4NR, ☎ 283 1763, Seafood – ⬛ AE ⓪ *VISA*   **QT e**
closed Saturday, Sunday and Bank Holidays – **M** (lunch only) a la carte 6.75/11.70 **t.**
₰ 1.80.

XX **Terrazza-Est,** 125 Chancery Lane, WC2A 1PP, ☎ 242 2601, Italian rest. – ⬛ AE ⓪
VISA   p. 27 **FV n**
closed Saturday and Sunday – **M** a la carte 6.70/10.80 **t.** ₰ 1.70.

XX Aykoku-Kaku, 9 Walbrook, EC4, ☎ 236 9020, Japanese rest.   **QU u**

XX **Wheeler's City,** 19-21 Great Tower St., EC3R 5AQ, ☎ 626 3685, Seafood – 🔲 AE ⓪ VISA
QU e
closed Saturday, Sunday and Bank Holidays – **M** (lunch only) a la carte 10.00/14.20 st. 🍷 1.75.

XX **Le Gaulois,** 119 Chancery Lane, WC2A 1PP, ☎ 405 7769, French rest. – 🔲 VISA
closed Saturday, Sunday, Easter, Christmas week and Bank Holidays – **M** a la carte 5.40/6.80 🍷 1.70.
p. 27 FV c

XX **La Bastille,** 116 Newgate St., EC1A 7AE, ☎ 600 1134 – 🔲 AE ⓪ VISA
PT n
closed Saturday, Sunday and Bank Holidays – **M** (lunch only) a la carte 7.60/8.70 t. 🍷 1.80.

X **Le Gamin,** 32 Old Bailey, EC4M 7HS, ☎ 236 7931, French rest. – 🔲 AE ⓪ VISA
PU a
closed Saturday, Sunday and Bank Holidays – **M** (lunch only) a la carte 4.85/8.45 st.

X **Bubb's,** 329 Central Markets, Farringdon St., EC1A 9NB, ☎ 236 2435, French rest. –
🔲 ⓪ VISA
PT a
closed Saturday, Sunday, August and Bank Holidays – **M** a la carte 5.50/7.95 🍷 1.60.

X **Ginnan,** 5 Cathedral Pl., St. Paul's, EC4M 7EA, ☎ 236 4120, Japanese rest. – 🔲 AE ⓪ VISA
closed Saturday, Sunday, 1 to 3 January and Bank Holidays – **M** 6.50/8.50 t. 🍷 1.10. PT e

X Mincing Lane Grill Room, Plantation House, Mincing Lane, EC3M 3OX, ☎ 626 4479.
QU c

X **La Germainerie,** 120 Chancery Lane, WC2A 1PP, ☎ 405 0290, French rest. p. 27 FV a
closed Saturday, Sunday, Easter, 1 May, 25-26 and 31 December – **M** (lunch only) a la carte 4.20/5.20 🍷 1.70.

X George and Vulture (T.H.F.), George Yard, Lombard St., EC3 9DL, ☎ 626 9710. QU a

X City Friends, 34 Old Bailey, EC4, ☎ 248 5189, Chinese rest. PU c

X Le Bistingo, 65 Fleet St., EC4, ☎ 353 4436, Bistro. PU e

CROYDON pp. 8 and 9.

🏌 Woodcote Park ☎ 660 0176, 2 m. of Purley.

Croydon – ✉ Surrey.

🏌 🏌 Featherbed Lane ☎ 657 0281, E: 3 m. – 🏌 Coulsdon ☎ 660 0468, S: 5 m.

🏨 **Aerodrome** (Anchor), Purley Way, CR9 4LT, ☎ 688 5185, Group Telex 858875, 🚗 – 📺
🛏wc ☎ 🅿. 🛁. 🔲 AE ⓪ VISA
DZ c
M approx. 4.50 st. – **62 rm** 🍽 14.50/27.00 st.

XX **Hook, Line and Sinker,** 3 George St., CR10 1LA, ☎ 688 8604, Seafood – 🔲 AE ⓪
VISA
DZ s
closed Sunday, Monday dinner and Bank Holidays – **M** a la carte 6.15/10.75 t. 🍷 1.90.

Sanderstead – ✉ Surrey.

🏨 **Selsdon Park,** Addington Rd, CR2 8YA, ☎ 657 8811, Telex 945003, ≤, 🎾, 🏊 heated,
🏌, 🚗, park – 📶 📺 🕭 🅿. 🛁. 🔲 AE ⓪ VISA
EZ o
M a la carte 7.75/12.00 s. 🍷 3.75 – **160 rm** 🍽 25.00/36.00 s.

X Elio, 17 Limpsfield Rd, CR2 9LA, ☎ 657 2953, Italian rest. EZ n

South Croydon – ✉ Surrey.

↑ **Briarley,** 8-10 Outram Rd, CR0 6XE, ☎ 654 1000, 🚗 – 🛆wc 🅿. 🔲 EZ x
19 rm 🍽 14.00/19.00 st.

XX **Pastori's Farmhouse,** 88 Selsdon Park Rd, Addington, CR2 8JT, ☎ 657 2576 – 🅿. 🔲
AE ⓪ VISA
EZ r
closed Sunday, Monday, 25-26 December and Bank Holidays – **M** a la carte 6.70/8.75 🍷 2.50.

X Trattoria Bella Venezia, 248 Brighton Rd, CR2 6AH, ☎ 686 2680, Italian rest. DZ a

EALING pp. 8 and 9.

Ealing – ✉ W5.

🏌 Church Rd, Hanwell ☎ 567 4230. – 🅹 Town Hall, New Broadway, W5, ☎ 579 2424.

🏨 **Carnarvon,** Ealing Common, W5 3HN, ☎ 993 1809, Telex 935114 – 📶 📺 🛆wc ☎ 🅿.
🛁. 🔲 AE ⓪ VISA
BX s
M a la carte 5.00/6.35 st. 🍷 2.40 – **150 rm** 🍽 22.50/31.50 st.

🏛 **Kenton House,** 5 Hillcrest Rd, Hanger Hill, W5 2JL, ☎ 997 8436 – 📺 🛆wc 🛏wc ☎ 🅿.
🔲 AE ⓪ VISA
BX e
M a la carte 5.25/6.50 st. – **51 rm** 🍽 27.00/36.50 st.

XX Gino's, 4 The Mall, Uxbridge Rd, W5, ☎ 567 3681, Italian rest. BX a

ENFIELD pp. 8 and 9.

Enfield – ⊠ Middx.
See : Forty Hall (park★).
🛆 Enfield Municipal GC., Whitewebbs Park ☎ 363 4458, N : 1 m.

🏨 **Royal Chace**, 162 The Ridgeway, EN2 3AR, ☎ 366 6500, ≤, ✕, 🏊 heated, 🐎 – 📺 ♿   **DV a**
🅿. 🅰. 🔊 AE ⓪ VISA
M a la carte 7.35/12.35 **t.** – � 2.00 – **50 rm** 18.00/28.50 **t.**

🏨 **Holtwhites**, 92 Chase Side, EN2 0QN, ☎ 363 0124, Telex 299670 – 📺 ☁wc ♨wc ☎   **EV c**
🅿. 🔊 AE ⓪ VISA
M *(closed Saturday, Sunday and Bank Holidays)* a la carte 5.35/8.35 🍷 3.00 – **26 rm** ⊻
15.50/26.50 **t.**

✕✕✕ **Norfolk**, 80 London Rd, EN2 6AP, ☎ 363 0979 – 🔊 AE ⓪ VISA   **EV e**
closed Sunday, Monday dinner, 21 July-9 August and Bank Holidays – **M** a la carte 5.05/
9.45 🍷 2.00.

Hadley Wood – ⊠ Herts.
🏨 **West Lodge Park** 🦢, off Cockfosters Rd, ⊠ Barnet, EN4 0PY, ☎ 440 8311, ≤,
🐎, park – 🛗 📺 ♿ 🅿. 🅰. 🔊 AE ⓪ VISA   **DV s**
M a la carte 5.35/9.05 **st.** 🍷 1.90 – **54 rm** ⊻ 23.00/36.00 **st.**

Palmers Green – ⊠ N13.
✕✕ Pilgrims Rest, 16-18 Hazelwood Lane, N13 5EX, ☎ 886 2454.   **DV o**

MICHELIN Branch, Eley's Estate, Angel Rd, N18 3DQ, ☎ 803 7341/2/3/4.

GREENWICH pp. 8 and 9.

Eltham – ⊠ SE9.
✕✕ **La Reine** (King's Arms), 60 Eltham High St., SE9 1BT, ☎ 859 0606 – 🔊 ⓪ VISA   **FY e**
closed Sunday and Monday dinner – **M** a la carte 8.45/10.95 **t.** 🍷 2.50.

Greenwich – ⊠ SE10.
🄸 King William Walk, Cutty Sark Gardens, SE10, ☎ 854 888 (summer only).
✕ **Le Papillon,** 57 Greenwich Church St., SE10 9BL, ☎ 858 2668   **EY n**
closed Saturday lunch and Sunday – **M** a la carte 6.55/8.40 **t.** 🍷 1.80.

✕ **Meantime,** 47-49 Greenwich Church St., SE10 9BL, ☎ 858 8705 – 🔊 AE ⓪ VISA   **EX a**
closed Sunday dinner and Monday – **M** a la carte 6.85/8.90 **t.** 🍷 1.50.

HAMMERSMITH Except where otherwise stated see pp. 17-20.

Fulham – ⊠ SW6.
🏨 Lindsay, without rest., 422-430 Fulham Rd, SW6 1DU, ☎ 385 8561 – 🛗 📺 ☁wc ☎ 🅿
57 rm.   **HZ s**

✕✕ Newton's, 576 King's Rd, SW6 2DY, ☎ 736 1804.   **JZ a**

✕✕ **Barbarella,** 428 Fulham Rd, SW6 1DU, ☎ 385 9434, Italian rest. Dancing – 🔊 AE ⓪
VISA   **HZ x**
closed Sunday – **M** (dinner only) a la carte 6.50/7.80 🍷 3.30.

✕ Red Onion Bistro, 636 Fulham Rd, SW6, ☎ 736 0920, Bistro.   pp. 8 and 9 **CY e**

✕ **Trencherman Bistro,** 271 New King's Rd, SW6 4RD, ☎ 736 4988, Bistro – 🔊 AE
⓪ VISA   pp. 8 and 9 **CY s**
closed Saturday lunch, Sunday, Good Friday and 5 days at Christmas – **M** a la carte 7.25/
10.00 **t.** 🍷 1.55.

*La Grande Londra (GREATER LONDON) e' composta dalla City e da 32 distretti
amministrativi (Borough) divisi a loro volta in quartieri o villaggi che hanno conser-
vato il loro proprio carattere (Area).*

Hammersmith - ⊠ W6/W12/W14.
🛈 Town Hall, King St., W6, ☏ 748 3020.

🏨 Cunard International, 1 Shortlands, W6 8DR, ☏ 741 1555, Telex 934539 – 📶 TV ♿ Ⓟ.
☒ – **640 rm.**
GY a

XX Aziz, 116 King St., W6, ☏ 748 1826, Indian rest.
pp. 8 and 9 CX c

XX **Anarkali**, 303-305 King St., W6 9NH, ☏ 748 1760, Indian rest. – 🔺 AE ⓪ VISA
M a la carte 6.25/12.50 🍷 2.40.
pp. 8 and 9 CX c

West Kensington – ⊠ SW6/W14.

🏨 West Centre (Centre), Lillie Rd., SW6 1UQ, ☏ 385 1255, Telex 917728 – 📶 TV ⊟wc
☎ Ⓟ. ☒. 🔺 AE ⓪ VISA
☒ 1.65 – **510 rm** 20.40/25.55 **st.**
HZ e

🏨 Lily, 23-33 Lillie Rd, SW6 1UG, ☏ 381 1881, Telex 918922 – 📶 TV ⊟wc ☎ Ⓟ. 🔺 AE
⓪ VISA
M (dinner only) 4.00 **st.** – **99 rm** ☒ 17.00/22.00 **s.**
HZ o

HARINGEY pp. 8 and 9.

Highgate – ⊠ N6.

XX **San Carlo,** 2 High St., N6 5JL, ☏ 340 5823, Italian rest. – 🔺 AE ⓪ VISA
closed Monday and Bank Holidays – **M** a la carte 5.50/10.10 **t.** 🍷 1.75.
DV e

HARROW pp. 8 and 9.

Central Harrow – ⊠ Middx.

🏨 **Cumberland,** 1 St. John's Rd, HA1 2EF, ☏ 863 4111, 🚿 – TV ⊟wc 🛏wc ☎ Ⓟ
M 1.95/3.45 🍷 1.50 – **63 rm** ☒ 15.00/19.00.
BV u

XX **Old Etonian,** 38 High St., Harrow Hill, HA1 3LL, ☏ 422 8482, French rest. – 🔺 AE
⓪ VISA
closed Saturday lunch, Sunday and Bank Holidays – **M** a la carte 5.10/6.30 **t.** 🍷 1.60.
BV c

XX London Steak House, 51 High St., Harrow Hill, HA1 3MX, ☏ 422 8473.
BV r

Pinner – ⊠ Middx.

XX **The Ember,** 141 Marsh Rd, HA5 5PB, ☏ 866 9764 – 🔺 AE ⓪ VISA
closed Saturday lunch, Sunday and Bank Holidays – **M** a la carte 4.60/7.55 🍷 1.90.
AV r

X **La Giralda,** 66 Pinner Green, HA5 2AB, ☏ 868 3429 – 🔺 AE ⓪ VISA
M 3.00/5.00 **t.** 🍷 1.25.
AV o

X **Old Oak,** 11 High St., HA5 5PJ, ☏ 866 0286 – 🔺 AE ⓪ VISA
closed 25 and 26 December – **M** 2.15/8.45 **st.** 🍷 2.00.
AV s

HAVERING pp. 8 and 9.

Hornchurch – ⊠ Essex – ☎ 040 23 Ingrebourne.

🏨 Fairlane Motor Inn, Southend Arterial Rd (A 127), RM11 3UJ, ☏ 46789, Telex 887315 –
TV ⊟wc ☎ Ⓟ. ☒ – **145 rm.**
FV s

HILLINGDON pp. 8 and 9.

Eastcote – ⊠ Middx.

X Trombino, 4 Black Horse Parade, Eastcote High Rd ☏ 868 5599, Italian rest.
AV v

X Sambuca, 113 Field End Rd, HA5 1QG, ☏ 866 7500.
AV a

Heathrow Airport – ⊠ Middx.

🏨 **Sheraton Skyline,** Bath Rd, Harlington, Hayes, UB3 5BP, ☏ 759 2535, Telex 934254,
« Exotic indoor garden with 🔲 » – 📶 TV ♿ Ⓟ. ☒. 🔺 AE ⓪ VISA
M a la carte 10.05/15.25 **st.** 🍷 2.50 – ☒ 3.30 – **353 rm** 37.00/41.00 **s.**
AXY x

🏨 **Holiday Inn,** Stockley Rd, West Drayton, UB7 9NA, ☏ 089 54 (West Drayton) 45555,
Telex 934518, ✂, 🔲, 🏌 – 📶 TV ♿ Ⓟ. ☒. 🔺 AE ⓪ VISA
M a la carte 7.50/23.15 **t.** 🍷 2.45 – ☒ 3.25 – **281 rm** 27.00/34.50 **st.**
AX c

🏨 **Excelsior** (T.H.F.), Bath Rd, West Drayton, UB7 0DU, ☏ 759 6611, Telex 24525, ⤢
heated – 📶 TV ♿ Ⓟ. ☒. 🔺 AE ⓪ VISA
M a la carte 9.50/12.35 **st.** 🍷 1.75 – ☒ 3.00 – **662 rm** 28.50/36.50 **st.**
AY s

The Heathrow, Bath Rd, Hounslow, TW6 2AQ, ☏ 897 6363, Telex 934660, ⩽, ☒ – 🛗 ▮▮ ☒ ⬤ ☒ ⬤ ☒. ▮▮. ☒ AE ⓪ VISA — **AY n**
M approx. 7.45 **st.** ⓵ 2.50 – ☕ 3.75 – **670 rm** 34.00/38.00 **s.**

Sheraton Heathrow, Colnbrook by-pass, West Drayton, UB7 0HJ, ☏ 759 2424, Telex 934331, ☒ – 🛗 ☒ ▮▮ ⬤ ☒. ▮▮. ☒ AE ⓪ VISA — **AY i**
M a la carte 5.60/10.45 **t.** ⓵ 2.90 – **440 rm** 24.75/30.40.

Post House (T.H.F.), Sipson Rd, West Drayton, UB7 0JU, ☏ 759 2323, Telex 934280 – 🛗 ☒ ▮▮ ⬤ ☒. ▮▮. ☒ AE ⓪ VISA — **AXY e**
M a la carte 6.40/8.00 **st.** ⓵ 1.65 – ☕ 2.50 – **594 rm** 21.50/30.00 **st.**

Skyway (T.H.F), 140 Bath Rd, Hayes, UB3 5AW, ☏ 759 6311, Telex 23935, ☒ heated – 🛗 ☒ ▮▮ ⬤ ☒. ▮▮. ☒ AE ⓪ VISA — **AXY v**
M a la carte 7.75/10.25 **st.** ⓵ 1.85 – ☕ 2.75 – **440 rm** 22.50/29.50 **st.**

Ariel (T.H.F.), Harlington Corner, Bath Rd, Hayes, UB3 5AJ, ☏ 759 2552, Telex 21777 – 🛗 ☒ ⊟wc ☎ ▮▮ ⬤. ▮▮ – **178 rm.** — **AXY z**

Arlington (Norfolk Cap.), Shepiston Lane, Hayes, UB3 1LP, ☏ 573 6162, Group Telex 23241 – ☒ ⊟wc ⊪wc ⬤. ▮▮. ☒ AE ⓪ VISA — **AX r**
M 5.50/6.50 **st.** ⓵ 1.75 – ☕ 2.20 – **80 rm** 21.30/27.20 **st.**

Hillingdon – ✉ Middx – ✿ Uxbridge. – 🛈 Civic Centre, High St., Uxbridge ☏ 50600.

Master Brewer Motel, Western Av., Hillingdon Circus, UB10 9BR. ☏ 51199 – ☒ ⊟wc ☎ ⬤ ▮▮ ⬤. ▮▮. ☒ AE ⓪ VISA — **AVX c**
M a la carte 2.85/6.65 **t.** ⓵ 1.65 – ☕ 1.75 – **64 rm** 19.00/24.00 **st.**

Ruislip – ✉ Middx – ✿ Ruislip.
🛈₁₈ Ickenham Rd ☏ 32004.

Barn, West End Rd, HA4 6JD, ☏ 36057, 🚗 – ☒ ⊟wc ☎ ⬤ — **AV n**
M (dinner only Monday to Thursday) 4.00 **s.** – **50 rm** ☕ 12.75/20.00.

HOUNSLOW pp. 8 and 9.

Cranford – ✉ Middx.

Berkeley Arms (Embassy), Bath Rd, TW5 9QE, ☏ 897 2121, Telex 34533, 🚗 – 🛗 ☒ ⬤. ☒ AE ⓪ VISA — **AY o**
closed 24 to 27 December – M a la carte 7.90/12.00 **st.** – ☕ 2.65 – **42 rm** 21.00/29.00 **st.**

Hounslow – ✉ Middx.

Master Robert Motel, 366 Great West Rd, TW5 0BD, ☏ 570 6261, 🚗 – ☒ ⊟wc ⊪wc ☎ ⬤. ☒ AE ⓪ VISA — **AY a**
M 4.70 **t.** ⓵ 1.55 – ☕ 1.50 – **63 rm** 19.00/23.00.

ISLINGTON pp. 13-16.

Finsbury – ✉ WC1/EC1.

Royal Scot (Thistle), 100 King's Cross Rd, WC1X 9DT, ☏ 278 2434, Telex 27657 – 🛗 ☒ ⊟wc ☎ ⬤. ▮▮ – **349 rm.** — **NS n**

London Ryan, Gwynne Pl., King's Cross Rd, WC1X 9QN, ☏ 278 2480, Telex 27728 – 🛗 ☒ ⊟wc ☎ ⬤. ☒ AE ⓪ VISA — **NS a**
M 4.50/6.00 **st.** ⓵ 1.55 – ☕ 1.75 – **213 rm** 25.00/35.00 **st.**

Islington – ✉ N1.
🛈 Central Library, Fieldway Crescent, N5, ☏ 607 8940.

✿ **Carrier's,** 2 Camden Passage, N1 8ED, ☏ 226 5353 – AE — **PR e**
closed Sunday, Easter Saturday and Bank Holidays – M 12.00/14.00
Spec. Cervelas chaud de canard, Calf's liver with avocado, Œufs à la neige au caramel.

Frederick's, Camden Passage, N1 8EG, ☏ 359 2888, « Conservatory and walled garden » – ☒ AE ⓪ VISA — **PR a**
closed Sunday, 25-26 December and Bank Holidays – M a la carte 7.05/12.05 ⓵ 2.35.

Ristorante Portofino, 39 Camden Passage, N1, ☏ 226 0884, Italian rest. — **PR o**

Julius's, 39 Upper St., N1 0PN, ☏ 226 4380. — **PR i**

M'sieur Frog, 31a Essex Rd, N1 2SE, ☏ 226 3495, Bistro — **PR n**
closed Sunday and 3 weeks August – M (dinner only) a la carte 6.20/8.25 **t.** ⓵ 1.50.

KENSINGTON and CHELSEA (Royal Borough of).

Chelsea – ✉ SW1/SW3/SW10 – Except where otherwise stated see pp. **24** and **25.**

✿ **Carlton Tower,** 2 Cadogan Pl., SW1X 9PY, ☏ 235 5411, Telex 21944 – 🛗 ☒ ⬤. ▮▮. ☒ AE ⓪ VISA — **FR n**
M Chelsea Room (closed 26 to 28 December) a la carte 14.90/19.00 **st.** ⓵ 3.50 – **Rib Room** (closed 1 to 3 January) a la carte 12.40/17.55 **st.** ⓵ 3.50 – ☕ 5.00 – **244 rm** 68.00/79.00 **s.**
Spec. Salade nouvelle, Fricassée de turbot et homard aux concombres, Filets d'agneau au basilic et tomate.

Sheraton Park Tower, 101 Knightsbridge, SW1X 7RN, ☎ 235 8050, Telex 917222 – AE VISA
M a la carte 12.20/14.20 **st.** – 4.25 – **295 rm** 64.00/74.00 **s.** FQ v

Capital, 22-24 Basil St., SW3 1AT, ☎ 589 5171, Telex 919042 – AE VISA
M a la carte 9.50/15.50 – 3.50 – **56 rm** 35.00/50.00 ER a
Spec. Mousseline de coquilles St-Jacques à la crème d'oursins, Carré d'agneau persillé aux herbes de Provence, Sorbet à la Fine Champagne.

Holiday Inn, 17-25 Sloane St., SW1X 9NU, ☎ 235 4377, Telex 919111, – AE VISA
M a la carte 5.55/11.25 **st.** 3.00 – 3.50 – **217 rm** 47.00/56.00 **st.** FR r

Ladbroke Belgravia, 20 Chesham Pl., SW1X 8HQ, ☎ 235 9916, Telex 919020 – AE VISA
M a la carte 5.95/14.85 **s.** – 4.05 – **110 rm** 39.00/49.00 **s.** FR a

Basil Street, 8 Basil St., SW3 1AH, ☎ 581 3311, Telex 28379 – AE VISA
M 5.75/7.05 **t.** 2.45 – 1.85 – **109 rm** 20.50/46.00 **t.** FQ o

Cadogan (Thistle), 75 Sloane St., SW1X 9SG, ☎ 235 7141, Telex 267893 – AE VISA
M 4.75/5.50 **t.** 1.75 – 3.75 – **72 rm** 29.50/53.50 **t.** FR e

Wilbraham, 1-5 Wilbraham Pl., Sloane St., SW1X 9AE, ☎ 730 8296 – wc. AE VISA
M *(closed Sunday)* 2.50/4.25 **s.** 2.35 – 1.80 – **50 rm** 13.50/26.00 **s.** FS n

Royal Court (Norfolk Cap.), Sloane Sq., SW1W 8EG, ☎ 730 9191, Group Telex 23241 – wc. AE VISA
M 5.50/6.50 **st.** 1.75 – 2.20 – **96 rm** 26.40/38.50 **st.** FST a

Fenja without rest., 69 Cadogan Gdns, SW3 2RB, ☎ 589 1183 – wc. AE VISA
18 rm 19.20/32.65 **s.** FS r

Park House, without rest., 47 Egerton Gdns, SW3, ☎ 589 0715 – wc
16 rm. DS i

Willett without rest., 32 Sloane Gardens, Sloane Sq., SW1W 8DJ, ☎ 730 0634 – wc
17 rm 15.00/17.50 **st.** FT s

XXXX **Le Gavroche,** 61-63 Lower Sloane St., SW1W 8DH, ☎ 730 2820, French rest. – AE FT e
closed Sunday, 24 December-3 January and Bank Holidays – **M** (dinner only) a la carte 15.80/25.20 **st.**
Spec. Bressole de barbue Sylvano, Mousseline de homard au Champagne, Sablé aux fraises.

XXXX **Waltons of Walton Street,** 121 Walton St., SW3 2HP, ☎ 584 0204 – AE VISA
closed Sunday dinner and Bank Holidays – **M** 14.00/17.00 DS a
Spec. Waltons layered fish pâté, Poached salmon trout, Noisettes of Welsh lamb.

XXX **Tante Claire,** 68 Royal Hospital Rd, SW3 2HP, ☎ 352 6045, French rest. – AE EU c
closed Saturday, Sunday, Easter, 4 weeks August-September, Christmas, 1 January and Bank Holidays – **M** a la carte 11.00/14.75 **st.** 3.40
Spec. Andouillette de la mer au vinaigre de cassis, Caneton aux épices, Biscuit glacé aux noisettes.

XXX **Claudius,** Chelsea Cloisters, Sloane Av., SW3 3DN, ☎ 584 8608, Italian rest. – AE VISA
M a la carte 7.10/9.50 **t.** ET a

XXX **Le Français,** 257-259 Fulham Rd, SW3 6HY, ☎ 352 4748, French rest. – AE CU a
closed Sunday – **M** a la carte 7.70/11.20 **t.** 3.10.

XX **Bewick's,** 87-89 Walton St., SW3 2HP, ☎ 584 6711 – AE VISA ES n
closed Saturday lunch, Sunday, 24 December-3 January and Bank Holidays – **M** a la carte 8.45/11.75 3.20.

XX **Daphne's,** 112 Draycott Av., SW3 3AE, ☎ 589 4257 – AE VISA DS e
closed Sunday and Bank Holidays – **M** (dinner only) a la carte 7.90/11.50 1.85.

XX **Ma Cuisine,** 113 Walton St., SW3 2JY, ☎ 584 7585, French rest. – AE DS a
closed Saturday, Sunday, 1 week Easter, 1 month July-August, 2 weeks at Christmas and Bank Holidays – **M** a la carte 7.80/10.45 **t.** 3.50
Spec. Œuf Vert Galant, Noisette d'agneau pastourelle, Mousse brûlée.

XX **English House,** 3 Milner St., SW3 2QA, ☎ 584 3002, English rest. – AE VISA ES z
closed 3 weeks August and Bank Holidays – **M** a la carte 7.00/10.75 1.85.

XX **Parke's,** 4-5 Beauchamp Pl., SW3 1NG, ☎ 589 1390 – AE VISA ER n
closed Saturday lunch, Sunday, 4 days at Easter and 4 days at Christmas – **M** 15.00.

XX **Don Luigi,** 33c King's Rd, SW3 4LX, ☎ 730 3023, Italian rest. – AE VISA ET r
M a la carte 7.50/9.00 **t.**

XX **Poissonnerie de l'Avenue,** 82 Sloane Av., SW3 3DZ, ☎ 589 2457, Seafood – AE VISA DS u
closed Sunday and Bank Holidays – **M** a la carte 6.60/10.45 **t.** 2.00.

XX **Bagatelle,** 5 Langton St., SW10 0JL, ☎ 351 4185, French rest. – 🔲 AE ⑩ VISA
closed Sunday, Easter Day and 25-26 December – **M** a la carte 7.80/11.00 t.
🍾 2.20.   pp. 17-20 JZ u

XX **Le Suquet,** 104 Draycott Av., SW3 3AE, ☎ 581 1785, French rest. Seafood – AE DS c
closed Monday and Tuesday lunch – **M** a la carte 9.50/13.80 **t.**

XX Sale e Pepe, 13-15 Pavillion Rd, SW1, ☎ 235 0098, Italian rest.   FQ x

XX **Salamis,** 204 Fulham Rd, SW10 9PJ, ☎ 352 9827 – 🔲 AE ⑩ VISA   BU e
closed Sunday and Bank Holidays – **M** a la carte 4.90/7.55 t. 🍾 1.40.

XX **Eleven Park Walk,** 11 Park Walk, SW10, ☎ 352 3449, Italian rest. – AE CU r
closed Sunday, Christmas and Bank Holidays – **M** a la carte approx. 10.00 t. 🍾 1.50.

XX La Famiglia, 7 Langton St., SW10 0JL, ☎ 351 0761, Italian rest. – 🔲 AE ⑩ VISA.
                                                                                pp. 17-20 JZ r

XX **Meridiana,** 169 Fulham Rd, SW3 6SP, ☎ 589 8815, Italian rest. – 🔲 AE ⑩ VISA DT i
closed Sunday and Bank Holidays – **M** a la carte 6.80/8.10 🍾 1.60.

XX San Frediano, 62-64 Fulham Rd, SW3 6HH, ☎ 584 8375, Italian rest.   DT n

XX **Santa Croce,** 112 Cheyne Walk, Chelsea Embankment, SW10 0DJ, ☎ 352 7534, Italian
rest. – 🔲 AE ⑩ VISA   pp. 17-20 JZ n
closed Sunday and Bank Holidays – **M** a la carte 5.90/7.50 **t.**

XX Il Girasole, 126 Fulham Rd, SW3, ☎ 370 6656, Italian rest.   CU x

XX **Tandoori,** 153 Fulham Rd, SW3 6SN, ☎ 589 7749, Indian and Pakistani rest. – 🔲 AE
⑩ VISA   DT o
M (dinner only and Sunday lunch) a la carte 5.80/7.70 🍾 2.30.

X San Quintino, 45-47 Radnor Walk, SW3 4BP, ☎ 352 2698, Italian rest.   EU e

X Leonardo Ristorante, 397 Kings Rd, SW10, ☎ 352 4146, Italian rest.   pp. 17-20 JZ v

X Como Lario, 22 Holbein Pl., Pimlico Rd, SW1N 8NL, ☎ 730 2954, Italian rest. FT r

X **Hungry Horse,** 196 Fulham Rd, SW10 9PN, ☎ 352 7757, English rest.   BU i
closed 25 and 26 December – **M** (dinner only and Sunday lunch) a la carte 5.30/7.70
🍾 1.25.

X **La Brasserie,** 272 Brompton Rd, SW3 2AW, ☎ 584 1668, French rest. – AE ⑩ VISA DS s
M a la carte 6.65/7.15 t. 🍾 1.65.

Earl's Court – ✉ SW5/SW10 – Except where otherwise stated see pp. 24 and 25.

🏨 **Barkston** (T.H.F.), Barkston Gdns, SW5 0ER, ☎ 373 7851 – 📶 TV 🍴wc ☏. 🛁. 🔲 AE
⑩ VISA   AT c
M 5.00/6.50 st. – ☕ 2.00 – **71 rm** 21.00/25.00 st.

🏨 **Hogarth,** 27-35 Hogarth Rd, SW5 0QQ, ☎ 370 6831, Telex 916684 – 📶 TV 🍴wc ☏ 🅿.
🔲 AE ⑩   AS a
closed 23 to 26 December – **M** (dinner only) a la carte approx. 6.20 st. 🍾 1.10 – ☕ 1.80 –
66 rm 19.00/26.50 st.

🏨 **Town House,** 44-48 West Cromwell Rd, SW5 9QL, ☎ 373 4546, Telex 918554, « Taste-
ful decor » – TV 🍴wc ☏. 🔲 AE ⑩ VISA   pp. 17-20 HY o
M (bar lunch) 6.00 s. – ☕ 1.50 – **45 rm** 16.00/22.00 s.

🏨 **Kensington Court** without rest., 33-35 Nevern Pl., SW5 9NP, ☎ 370 5151, Telex
8814451 – 📶 TV 🍴wc ☏. 🔲 AE ⑩ VISA   pp. 17-20 HY n
☕ 2.50 – **35 rm** 18.00/23.00 s.

🏨 Burns, 18-26 Barkston Gdns, SW5 0EN, ☎ 373 3151, Telex 27885 – 📶 TV 🍴wc ☏ AT e
108 rm.

🏨 **George,** 5-11 Templeton Pl., SW5 9NB, ☎ 370 1092, Telex 8814825, � – 📶 TV 🍴wc
🍴wc ☏ 🅿. 🔲 AE ⑩ VISA   pp. 17-20 HY r
M a la carte 4.40/5.30 t. 🍾 2.00 – ☕ 1.50 – **130 rm** 16.00/25.00 st.

🏨 **Oliver** without rest., 198 Cromwell Rd, SW5 0SN, ☎ 370 6881 – 📶 TV 🍴wc 🍴wc ☏.
🔲 AE ⑩ VISA   pp. 17-20 HY a
48 rm ☕ 13.00/20.00 s.

🏨 Manor Court, without rest., 33-35 Courtfield Gdns, SW5, ☎ 373 8585, Telex 885230 –
🍴wc ☏ – **78 rm.**   AS e

🏠 **Beaver,** 57-59 Philbeach Gdns, SW5 9ED, ☎ 373 4553 – 🍴wc ☏. VISA pp. 17-20 HY e
50 rm ☕ 9.50/18.00 t.

🏠 **Terstan,** 29-31 Nevern Sq., SW5 9PE, ☎ 373 5368 – 📶 🍴wc 🍴wc – 🔲 VISA
57 rm ☕ 12.50/18.50 st.   pp. 17-20 HY v

XX ❀ **Tiger Lee,** 251 Old Brompton Rd, SW5 9HP, ☎ 398 5102, Chinese rest., Seafood –
AE ⑩   AU n
M (dinner only) a la carte 8.30/15.50
Spec. Special shark fin soup, Stuffed fish, Yam basket.

XX **La Croisette,** 168 Ifield Rd, SW10 9AF, ☎ 373 3694, French rest., Seafood – AE AU a
closed Tuesday lunch and Monday – **M** 11.00 **t.**

XX **Pontevecchio,** 256 Old Brompton Rd, SW5 9HR, ☎ 373 9082, Italian rest. – 🔲 AE ⑩
VISA   AU i
closed Bank Holidays – **M** a la carte 5.60/7.80 🍾 1.40.

XX   Naraine, 10 Kenway Rd., SW5 0RR, ☎ 370 3853, Indian rest.   pp. 17-20   HY i

X   **Il Palio di Siena**, 133 Earl's Court Rd., SW5 9HR, ☎ 373 8060, Italian rest. – ⧄ AE ⓪ VISA
     pp. 17-20   HY c
     closed Easter Sunday and Christmas Day – **M** a la carte 5.20/7.95 ⌀ 1.80.

Kensington – ✉ SW7/W8/W11/W14 – Except where otherwise stated see pp. **17-20**.

🏨 **Royal Garden** (Rank), Kensington High St., W8 4PT, ☎ 937 8000, Telex 263151,
    ⇆ – 🛗 TV ⌖ 🅿 . ⧄ AE ⓪ VISA   pp. 24 and 25   AQ c
    M a la carte 9.25/21.50 **st.** ⌀ 3.25 – ⨋ 4.25 – **434 rm** 45.75/59.75 **st.**

🏨 **Kensington Close** (T.H.F.), Wrights Lane, W8 5SP, ☎ 937 8170, Telex 23914, ⧄ – 🛗
    TV . ⧄ AE ⓪ VISA   HX c
    M (Carvery Rest.) 6.00 **st.** ⌀ 2.05 – ⨋ 3.00 – **530 rm** 23.50/31.00 **st.**

🏨 Kensington Palace (Thistle), De Vere Gdns, W8 5AF, ☎ 937 8121, Telex 262422 – 🛗
    TV . ⧄   pp. 24 and 25   BQ a
    318 rm.

🏨 **Hilton International,** 179-199 Holland Park Av., W11 4UL, ☎ 603 3355, Telex 919763 –
    🛗 TV ⌖ 🅿 . ⧄ AE ⓪ VISA   GV s
    M a la carte 6.70/10.15 **t.** ⌀ 1.50 – ⨋ 3.85 – **611 rm** 28.25/36.60.

🏨 **De Vere** (De Vere), 60 Hyde Park Gate, W8 5AS, ☎ 584 0051, Telex 8953644 – 🛗 TV
    ⌖ . ⧄ AE ⓪ VISA   pp. 24 and 25   BQ s
    M approx. 5.00 **st.** ⌀ 1.75 – ⨋ 3.00 – **83 rm** 26.00/40.00 **st.**

🏨 **Tara,** Scarsdale Pl., W8 5SR, ☎ 937 7211, Telex 918834 – 🛗 TV ⌖ 🅿 . ⧄ AE ⓪ VISA
    M 6.00/9.00 **t.** ⌀ 1.95 – ⨋ 2.60 – **843 rm** 23.00/28.50 **s.**   HX u

🏨 **Royal Kensington,** 380 Kensington High St., W14 8NL, ☎ 603 3333, Telex 22229 –
    🛗 TV ⧄ AE ⓪ VISA   GX o
    M a la carte 6.00/11.00 **st.** ⌀ 2.60 – ⨋ 3.75 – **409 rm** 26.00/30.00 **st.**

🏨 Prince of Wales, 16-26 De Vere Gdns, W8 5AG, ☎ 937 8080 – 🛗 TV ⨦wc ☎.
    ⧄   pp. 24 and 25   BQ u
    315 rm.

XXX **Le Bressan,** 14 Wrights Lane, W8 6TF, ☎ 937 8525, French rest. – ⧄ AE ⓪ VISA   HX a
     closed Saturday, Sunday, last 2 weeks August, first week September and Bank Holidays –
     M a la carte 10.80/15.00 ⌀ 3.20.

XX   **Wheeler's Alcove,** 17 Kensington High St., W8 5NP, ☎ 937 1443, Seafood – ⧄ AE ⓪
     VISA   pp. 24 and 25   AQ n
     closed Sunday and Bank Holidays – **M** a la carte 10.00/14.20 **st.** ⌀ 1.75.

XX   **La Toque Blanche,** 21 Abingdon Rd, W8 6AH, ☎ 937 5832, French rest. – AE ⓪   HX n
     closed Saturday, Sunday, Easter, August, Christmas and Bank Holidays – **M** a la carte
     6.20/10.25 **t.** ⌀ 2.20.

XX   **Trattoo,** 2 Abingdon Rd, W8 6AF, ☎ 937 4448, Italian rest. – ⧄ AE ⓪ VISA   HX e
     M a la carte 6.70/10.00 **t.**

XX   **La Pomme d'Amour,** 128 Holland Park Av., W11 4UE, ☎ 229 8532, French rest. – AE
     ⓪ VISA   GV e
     closed Saturday lunch, Sunday and Bank Holidays – **M** a la carte 5.55/7.85 ⌀ 1.50.

XX   **Gondoliere,** 3 Gloucester Rd, SW7 4PP, ☎ 584 8062, Italian rest. – ⧄ AE VISA
     pp. 24 and 25   BR e
     closed Saturday lunch, Sunday and Bank Holidays – **M** a la carte 6.40/7.65 **t.** ⌀ 1.85.

XX   **Gatamelata,** 343 Kensington High St., W8 6NW, ☎ 603 3613, Italian rest.   GHX s
     closed Saturday lunch and Sunday – **M** a la carte 5.50/8.50 ⌀ 1.75.

XX   **Franco Ovest,** 3 Russell Gardens, W14 8EZ, ☎ 602 1242, Italian rest. – ⧄ AE ⓪ VISA
     closed Saturday lunch, Sunday, Good Friday, Easter Monday and Bank Holidays – **M** a la
     carte 6.80/8.00 ⌀ 2.50.   GX u

XX   **Sailing Junk,** 59 Marloes Rd, W8 6LE, ☎ 937 5833, Chinese rest. – ⧄ AE ⓪ VISA
     M (dinner only) 5.55 ⌀ 1.60.   HX x

X   **Lee Yuan,** 40 Earl's Court Rd, W8 6EJ, ☎ 937 7047, Chinese rest. – ⧄ AE ⓪ VISA
     closed 25 and 26 December – **M** a la carte approx. 9.00 **t.** ⌀ 2.60.   HX r

X   **The Ark,** 35 Kensington High St., W8 5BA, ☎ 937 4294, French rest. – ⧄ AE ⓪ VISA
     closed Sunday lunch, 4 days at Easter and 4 days at Christmas – **M** a la carte 5.75/7.50 **t.**
     ⌀ 1.90.   pp. 24 and 25   AQ s

X   La Jardinière, 148 Holland Park Av., W11, ☎ 221 6090, French rest.   GV z

X   La Paesana, 30 Uxbridge St., W8 7TA, ☎ 229 4332, Italian rest.   pp. 26 and 27   AZ i

North Kensington – ✉ W2/W10/W11 – Except where otherwise stated see pp. **13-16**.

🏨 Portobello, 22 Stanley Gdns, W11 2NG, ☎ 727 2777, Telex 21879 – 🛗 TV ⨦wc ☎   GU n
    25 rm.

🏨 **Pembridge Court,** 34 Pembridge Gdns, W2 4DX, ☎ 229 9977, Telex 298363 –
    TV ⨦wc ⨦wc ☎ – ⧄ AE ⓪ VISA   pp. 26 and 27   AZ n
    M *(closed Sunday)* (dinner only) a la carte 5.55/8.80 **t.** ⌀ 1.95 – **36 rm** ⨋ 18.50/
    23.50 **s.**

XXX **Leith's**, 92 Kensington Park Rd, W11 2PN, ℡ 229 4481 – ⟋ AE ⓪ VISA   GU e
closed 4 days at Christmas – **M** (dinner only) 14.00 st.

XX **Chez Moi**, 3 Addison Av., Holland Park, W11 4QS, ℡ 603 8267, French rest.
*closed Sunday, last 3 weeks August, last week December, first 2 weeks January and
Bank Holidays* – **M** (dinner only) a la carte 6.85/11.00 ⦷ 2.15.   pp. 17-20 GV n

South Kensington – ⊠ SW5/SW7/W8 – pp. 24 and 25.

Gloucester (Rank), 4-18 Harrington Gdns, SW7 4LH, ℡ 373 6030, Telex 917505 –
⧼ TV ⧽ ⓟ. ⦛. ⟋ AE ⓪ VISA   BS r
M a la carte 3.95/10.20 st. ⦷ 2.10 – ⟺ 3.70 – **550 rm** 43.50/50.50 st.

Elizabetta, 162 Cromwell Rd, SW5 0TT, ℡ 370 4282, Telex 918978 – ⧼ TV   AS r
84 rm.

Penta (Gd Met.), 97 Cromwell Rd, SW7 4ED, ℡ 370 5757, Telex 919663 – ⧼ TV ⧽ ⓟ.
⦛. ⟋ AE ⓪ VISA   BS o
M 10.00 st. ⦷ 3.50 – **914 rm** 24.00/34.00 s.

John Howard, 4 Queen's Gate, SW7 5EH, ℡ 581 3011, Telex 8813397 – ⧼ TV ⓟ. ⟋
AE ⓪ VISA   BQ i
M 14.00 st. ⦷ 1.80 – ⟺ 2.50 – **32 rm** 35.00/59.00 st.

Blakes, 33-35 Roland Gdns, SW7 3PF, ℡ 370 6701, Telex 21879 – ⧼ TV ⌷wc ☏. ⟋ AE
⓪ VISA   BU c
M (dinner only) a la carte 5.80/10.00 t. ⦷ 2.50 – ⟺ 5.00 – **50 rm** 35.00/48.00 st.

Eden Plaza, 68-69 Queen's Gate, SW7 5JT, ℡ 370 6111, Telex 916228 – ⧼ TV ⌷wc
⌷wc ☏. ⟋ AE ⓪ VISA   CS o
M 3.50/6.50 t. ⦷ 1.50 – **62 rm** ⟺ 21.85/31.05 st.

Rembrandt (Gd. Met.), Thurloe St., SW7 2RS, ℡ 589 8100, Telex 917575 – ⧼ TV ⌷wc
M (Carvery rest.) 4.95 st. ⦷ 1.80 – **184 rm** 20.50/28.00 s.   DS v

Bailey's, Gloucester Rd, SW7, ℡ 373 8131 – ⌷wc ☏. ⦛   BS a
150 rm.

Adelphi without rest., 127-129 Cromwell Rd, SW7 4DT, ℡ 373 7177, Telex 8813164 –
⧼ TV ⌷wc ☏. ⟋ AE ⓪ VISA   AS i
57 rm ⟺ 18.90/26.90 st.

Regency, 100-105 Queen's Gate, SW7 5AG, ℡ 370 4595, Telex 267594 – ⧼ TV ⌷wc
⌷wc ☏. ⦛   CT e
200 rm.

Vanderbilt, 76 Cromwell Rd, SW7 5BT, ℡ 584 0491, Telex 919867 – ⧼ TV ⌷wc ☏   BS v
105 rm.

Norfolk (Norfolk Cap.), 2-10 Harrington Rd, SW7 3ER, ℡ 589 8191, Group Telex
23241 – ⧼ TV ⌷wc ☏. ⟋ AE ⓪ VISA   CS r
M 5.50/6.50 st. ⦷ 1.75 – ⟺ 2.20 – **70 rm** 22.65/32.45 st.

Cranley Gardens, 6-12 Cranley Gdns, SW7 3DB, ℡ 373 3232, Telex 267465 – ⧼ TV ⌷wc
⌷wc ☏   BT n
87 rm.

Edwardian, 40-44 Harrington Gdns, SW7 4LT, ℡ 370 4444 – ⧼ TV ⌷wc ⌷wc ☏   AT i
83 rm.

Alexander without rest., 9 Sumner Pl., SW7 3EE, ℡ 581 1591 – ⌷wc ☏. ⟋ AE ⓪
VISA   CT a
⟺ 2.00 – **40 rm** 16.00/30.00 st.

Number Sixteen without rest., 16 Sumner Pl., SW7 3EG, ℡ 589 5332 – ⌷wc ⌷wc
☏. AE ⓪   CT c
⟺ 1.50 – **24 rm** 18.00/32.00 s.

Richwood, 25 Cranley Gdns, SW7 3BD, ℡ 589 5281, Telex 8951330, ⟅ – ⧼ TV ⌷wc
⌷wc ☏. ⟋ AE ⓪ VISA   CU e
⟺ 1.00 – **57 rm** 11.00/21.00 st.

Apollo, 18-22 Lexham Gdns, W8 5JE, ℡ 373 3236, Telex 264189 – ⧼ ⌷wc ☏. ⟋
AE ⓪ VISA   AS o
M (dinner only) 3.50 st. – ⟺ 1.50 – **58 rm** 9.25/16.00 st.

⋔ **Queensberry Court** without rest., 7-11 Queensberry Pl., SW7 2EA, ☏ 589 3693 – ▯
🛏wc ⋔wc ☎. ◪ 🆎 ⓪ *VISA*
42 rm ⊑ 12.80/23.50 **st.**   **CS v**

⋔ **Buckingham**, 94-102 Cromwell Rd, SW7 4ER, ☏ 373 7131, Telex 8951330 – ▯ 🛏wc
⋔wc ☎. ◪ 🆎 ⓪ *VISA*
M *(closed Sunday)* (dinner only) a la carte 4.50/7.00 **st.** 🍶 2.00 – **98 rm** ⊑ 12.50/24.00 **st.**   **BS u**

⋔ **Atlas** without rest., 24-30 Lexham Gdns. W8 5JE, ☏ 373 7873, Telex 264189 – ▯
🛏wc ☎. ◪ 🆎 ⓪ *VISA*
⊑ 1.50 – **70 rm** 9.25/16.00 **st.**   **AS s**

⌂ **Concord**, 155-157 Cromwell Rd, SW5 0TQ, ☏ 370 4151 – 🛏wc ⋔ ☎. 🆎   **AS c**
40 rm ⊑ 8.80/18.70 **s.**

✕✕ **Il Giorno e la Notte**, 60 Old Brompton Rd, SW7 3DY, ☏ 584 4028, Italian rest. – ◪
🆎 ⓪ *VISA*
closed Sunday, Easter and Christmas Day – **M** a la carte 4.75/8.10 🍶 1.80.   **CT r**

✕✕ **Pulcinella**, 30 Old Brompton Rd, SW7 3DL, ☏ 589 0529, Italian rest. – ◪ 🆎 ⓪ *VISA*   **CS i**
closed Sunday and Bank Holidays – **M** a la carte 4.30/6.05 🍶 1.40.

✕ **Jamshid's**, 6 Glendower Pl., SW7 3DP, ☏ 584 2309, Indian and Pakistani rest. – ◪ 🆎
⓪ *VISA*   **CS s**
closed Christmas Day – **M** a la carte 3.85/4.90 🍶 1.40.

✕ Star of India, 154 Old Brompton Rd, SW5 0BE, ☏ 373 2901, Indian rest.   **BT s**

✕ **Le Bistingo**, 56 Old Brompton Rd, SW7 3DY, ☏ 589 1929, Bistro – ◪ 🆎 ⓪ *VISA*   **CT r**
M a la carte 4.50/6.00 **t.** 🍶 1.55.

KINGSTON-UPON-THAMES – ✉ Surrey – pp. 8 and 9.
🏌 Hampton Wick ☏ 977 6645, W: 2 ½ m.

Kingston – ✉ Surrey.

✕ **Stonewalls**, 14 Kingston Hill, KT2 5HR, ☏ 549 5984, Bistro – ◪ ⓪   **BZ c**
closed 25 to 29 December and 1 January – **M** a la carte 4.70/6.60 **t.** 🍶 1.50.

LAMBETH pp. 17-20.

Waterloo – ✉ SE1.

✕✕ **National Theatre Rest.**, National Theatre, South Bank, SE1 9PX, ☏ 928 2033 – Ⓟ – ◪
🆎 ⓪ *VISA*   **NV c**
closed Sunday, Good Friday and Christmas Day – **M** (dinner only and Saturday lunch)
4.65/6.95 **st.** 🍶 1.70.

LEWISHAM pp. 8 and 9.

Blackheath – ✉ SE3.

✕ La Goulue, 17 Montpelier Vale, SE3 0TJ, ☏ 852 9226, Bistro.   **EFY i**

Bromley – ✉ SE3.

🏨 **Bromley Court** ⑤, Bromley Hill, BR1 4JD, ☏ 464 5011, Telex 896310, ≼, 🎠 – ▯ 📺
Ⓟ ⚕. ◪ 🆎 ⓪ *VISA*   **EZ u**
M approx. 7.50 **t.** 🍶 2.00 – **130 rm** ⊑ 21.00/29.00 **t.**

Catford – ✉ SE6.

✕✕ **Casa Cominetti**, 129 Rushey Green, SE6 4AA, ☏ 697 2314   **EY o**
closed Sunday dinner, 25 to 27 December, 1 January and Good Friday lunch – **M** a la carte
5.70/8.10 **t.** 🍶 1.75.

MERTON pp. 8 and 9.

Merton – ✉ SW19.

✕ **Les Amoureux**, 156 Merton Hall Rd, SW19 3PZ, ☏ 543 0567, French rest. – ◪ 🆎
VISA   **CZ a**
closed Sunday, 3 weeks August and January – **M** a la carte 5.05/7.00 🍶 2.50.

__Groß-London__ (GREATER LONDON) besteht aus der City und 32 Verwaltungs-
bezirken (Borough) : diese sind wiederum in kleinere Bezirke (Area) unterteilt, deren
Mittelpunkt ehemalige Dörfer oder Stadtviertel sind, die oft ihren eigenen Charakter
bewahrt haben.

Wimbledon – ✉ SW19.
🛈 Town Hall, Broadway, SW 19, ☏ 946 8070.

⩑ **Hatherley,** 87 Worple Rd, SW19 4JH, ☏ 946 5917 – 🔌 AE VISA   CZ e
9 rm ヱ 10.50/15.75 **t.**

⩑ **Wimbledon,** 78 Worple Rd, SW19 4HZ, ☏ 946 9265 – **P.** 🔌 AE VISA   CZ a
9 rm ヱ 10.50/15.75 **st.**

XX San Lorenzo Fuoriporta, Worple Rd Mews, SW19 4DB, ☏ 946 8463, Italian rest.   CZ e

XX Rawalpindi, 26 High St., SW19, ☏ 946 2798, Indian rest.   CZ r

X **Lemon Tree,** 8 High St., SW19, ☏ 947 6477 – 🔌 ⓪   CZ i
closed Monday and 25-26 December – **M** a la carte 5.50/7.00 **t.**

MICHELIN Branch, Deer Park Rd, SW19, ☏ 540 9034/7.

REDBRIDGE pp. 8 and 9.

Ilford – ✉ Essex.
🛂 Wanstead Park Rd ☏ **554 5174.**
🛈 Town Hall, High Rd, IG1 1DD, ☏ 478 3020.

XX Marios', 251 Cranbrook Rd, IG1 4TG, ☏ 554 2921, Italian rest., Dancing (Friday and
Saturday only).   FV r

South Woodford – Essex.

X Meghna Grill, 219 High Rd, E18 2PB, ☏ 504 0923, Indian rest.   EFV i

RICHMOND-UPON-THAMES pp. 8 and 9.

Barnes – ✉ SW13.

XX **Les Autres Granges,** 8-9 Rocks Lane, SW13 0DB, ☏ 876 2554 – 🔌 AE ⓪ VISA   CY a
closed Sunday – **M** (dinner only) a la carte 5.30/7.65 🍷 2.05.

Hampton Court – ✉ Middx.
🛆 Twickenham ☏ 941 2206, NW: 2 m.

🏨 **Greyhound** (T.H.F.), Hampton Court Rd, East Molesey, KT8 9BZ, ☏ 977 8121 – TV
🛏WC ☎ **P.** 🔌 AE ⓪ VISA   BZ i
M a la carte 5.00/5.50 **st.** 🍷 1.95 – **29 rm** ヱ 12.00/21.50.

XX **Bastians,** Hampton Court Rd, East Molesey, KT8 9BY, ☏ 977 6074, French rest. – 🔌 AE
⓪ VISA   BZ e
closed Saturday lunch, Sunday and Bank Holidays – **M** a la carte 6.05/7.15.

Kew – ✉ Surrey.

X **Jasper's Bun in the Oven,** 9-13 Kew Green ☏ 940 3987 – 🔌 AE ⓪ VISA   BY n
closed Sunday, Christmas, Easter and Bank Holidays – **M** a la carte 5.15/6.95 **t.** 🍷 1.65.

Richmond – ✉ Surrey.
🛆, 🛆 Richmond Park ☏ 876 3205.
🛈 Old Richmond Town Hall, Hill St., TW1 3LT, ☏ 892 0032.

🏨 **Richmond Gate,** Richmond Hill, TW10 6RP, ☏ 940 0061, Telex 928556, 🍴 – TV
🛏WC ☎ **P.** ⛴   BY z
M (see **Petershan H.**) – **52 rm** ヱ 20.00/28.00 **s.**

🏨 **Petersham,** Richmond Hill, TW10 6RP, ☏ 940 7471, Telex 928556 – 🛗 TV 🛏WC ☎ **P.**
⛴   BY z
M *(closed Saturday lunch and Sunday)* a la carte 7.20/11.35 🍷 2.00 – **60 rm** ヱ 20.00/
28.00 **s.**

XX 🕸 **Lichfield's,** 13 Lichfield Ter., Sheen Rd, ☏ 940 5236 – 🔌 AE VISA   BY o
closed Sunday and Monday – **M** a la carte 7.60/10.80 **t.** 🍷 1.75
Spec. Crêpes soufflées au fromage, Roast breast of duck with lime compote, St. Emilion au chocolat.

XX Gino's, 15-17 Hill Rise, ☏ 940 3002, Italian rest.   BY i

XX **Kew Rendezvous,** 110 Kew Rd, TW9 2PQ, ☏ 948 4343, Chinese rest. – 🔌 AE ⓪ VISA
closed 25-26 December and Bank Holidays – **M** a la carte 5.00/7.50 🍷 1.40.   BY x

XX La Veranda, 102 Kew Rd, TW9 1RZ, ☏ 940 9044, Italian rest.   BY x

XX **Franco's,** 5 Petersham Rd, TW9 1EN, ☏ 940 9051, Italian rest. – 🔌 AE ⓪ VISA   BY i
M a la carte 5.55/7.10 **t.** 🍷 1.50.

X **Richmond Rendezvous,** 1 Paradise Rd, TW9 1RX, ☏ 940 5114, Chinese rest. – 🔌
AE ⓪ VISA   BY a
closed Monday and 26 December – **M** a la carte 5.00/6.50 🍷 1.40.

X **Richmond Rendezvous** (Annexe), 1 Wakefield Rd, TW9 1RX, ☏ 940 6869, Chinese
rest. – 🔌 AE ⓪ VISA   BY a
closed 25 and 26 December – **M** a la carte 5.00/6.50 🍷 1.40.

SOUTHWARK pp. 8 and 9.

Dulwich Village – ⊠ SE21.

XX   Manzoni's, 129 Gipsy Hill, SE9 1QS, ☏ 670 1396, Italian rest.   EZ **c**

SUTTON pp. 8 and 9.

⛳ Woodmansterne Rd, Carshalton ☏ 642 9608.

Sutton – ⊠ Surrey.

⋔   **The Dene,** 39 Cheam Rd, SM1 2AT, ☏ 642 3170, ☼ – ▭ ⌷wc ℗   CZ **n**
     17 rm ⌷ 9.50/20.00 **s.**

XX   **Trattoria Toscana,** 6-7 Station Par., Brighton Rd, SM2 5AD, ☏ 642 3341, Italian rest. –
     🔲 AE ⓪ VISA   DZ **e**
     closed Sunday and Bank Holidays – **M** a la carte 4.40/6.35 **t.** ▯ 1.75.

TOWER HAMLETS   Except where otherwise stated see pp. 8 and 9.

Tower Hamlets – ⊠ E1.

🛈 Information Centre, 88 Roman Rd, E2 0PG, ☏ 980 3749.

🏰   **Tower,** St. Katharine's Way, E1 9LD, ☏ 481 2575, Telex 885934, ⇐ Tower Bridge and
     river Thames – 🛗 ▭ ⅃ ℗. 🛆. 🔲 AE ⓪ VISA   pp. 17-20 QV **r**
     M 6.50 **t.** ▯ 2.40 – ⌷ 2.25 – **826 rm** 42.00/52.00 **st.**

WALTHAM FOREST pp. 8 and 9.

⛳ at Chingford 158 Station Rd ☏ Silverstorne 529 2107.

Leytonstone – ⊠ E11.

XX   **Golden Curry Tandoori,** 734 High Rd, E11 3AW, ☏ 539 5429, Indian rest. – 🔲 AE ⓪ VISA
     M a la carte approx. 4.20 ▯ 1.70.   EFV **n**

X   **Trattoria Parmigiana,** 715 High Rd, E11 4RD, ☏ 539 1700, Italian rest. – 🔲 AE ⓪
     VISA   EV **z**
     closed Sunday – **M** a la carte 5.55/9.80 **t.** ▯ 2.95.

Woodford Green – ⊠ Essex.

🏠   **Waltham Forest,** 30 Oak Hill, IG8 9NY, ☏ 505 4511 – 🛗 ▭ ⌷wc ⌷wc ☎ ℗. 🛆.
     🔲 AE ⓪ VISA   EV **x**
     M *(closed Saturday lunch)* 4.10 **t.** ▯ 2.20 – **50 rm** ⌷ 20.00/26.00 **st.**

WANDSWORTH pp. 8 and 9.

🛈 Municipal Buildings, SW18, ☏ 874 6464.

Battersea – ⊠ SW8/SW11.

XX   Alonso's, 32 Queenstown Rd, SW8 3RX, ☏ 720 5986 – AE ⓪   DY **e**
     closed Saturday lunch, Sunday and Bank Holidays.

X   **Lavender Hill,** 245 Lavender Hill, SW11 1JW, ☏ 223 4129, French rest. – 🔲 AE ⓪
     VISA   DY **u**
     closed Sunday and Monday – **M** (dinner only) 10.50 **s.** ▯ 1.60.

X   **Jacks Place,** 12 York Rd, SW11 3PX, ☏ 228 8519, Bistro – 🔲   DY **v**
     closed Sunday, Monday and 2 weeks August – **M** (dinner only) a la carte 5.35/8.55
     ▯ 1.30.

Clapham – ⊠ SW11.

XX   Hathaways, 13 Battersea Rise, SW11 1HG, ☏ 228 3384 – 🔲 AE ⓪ VISA   DY **i**
     closed Sunday, last 2 weeks August, 4 days at Christmas and Bank Holidays – **M** (dinner
     only) a la carte 5.50/6.20 **t.** ▯ 1.55.

Putney – ⊠ SW15.

XX   La Forchetta, 3 Putney Hill, SW15 6BA, ☏ 785 6749, Italian rest. – 🔲 AE ⓪ VISA CY **o**
     closed Sunday and Bank Holidays – **M** a la carte 4.60/6.00 ▯ 1.30.

X   Cassis, 30 Putney High St., SW15 1SQ, ☏ 788 8668, French Bistro   CY **c**
     closed Saturday lunch, Sunday and Bank Holidays – **M** a la carte 5.20/7.90 **t.** ▯ 1.50.

WESTMINSTER (City of)

🛈 Westminster City Hall, Victoria St., SW1E 6QW, 🕾 828 8070.

Bayswater and Maida Vale – ✉ W2/W9 – Except where otherwise stated see pp. 26 and 27.

Royal Lancaster (Rank), Lancaster Ter., W2 2TY, 🕾 262 6737, Telex 24822, ≼ – 🛗 📺 &. 🅿. 🏖. 🔼 AE ① VISA
M a la carte 10.45/12.90 **st.** 🍷 2.40 – 🍵 3.55 – **433 rm** 45.00/58.00 **st.**   DZ **e**

Great Western Royal (B.T.H.), Praed St., W2 6JS, 🕾 723 8064, Telex 263972 – 🛗 📺 &. 🏖. 🔼 AE ① VISA
M a la carte 4.35/10.75 **st.** 🍷 2.40 – **170 rm** 🍵 29.00/38.00 **st.**   DY **c**

Metropole, Edgware Rd, W2 1JU, 🕾 402 4141, Telex 23711, ≼ – 🛗 📺 🅿. 🏖. 🔼 AE ①
VISA   pp. 13-16   JT **c**
M a la carte 4.90/8.75 🍷 1.40 – 🍵 3.25 – **552 rm** 35.00/42.00.

Post House (T.H.F.), 104 Bayswater Rd, W2 3HL, 🕾 262 4461, Telex 22667, ≼ – 🛗 📺 ⇌wc ☎ 🅿. 🔼 AE ① VISA
M a la carte 6.60/8.10 **st.** 🍷 1.85 – 🍵 2.25 – **175 rm** 21.50/30.00 **st.**   CZ **o**

London Embassy (Embassy), 150 Bayswater Rd, W2 4RT, 🕾 229 1212, Telex 27727 – 🛗 📺 ⇌wc ☎ &. 🅿. 🏖. 🔼 AE ① VISA
M 6.50/7.00 **st.** 🍷 3.00 – 🍵 2.75 – **194 rm** 29.00/39.00 **st.**   BZ **o**

White's (T.H.F.), Bayswater Rd, 90-92 Lancaster Gate, W2 3NN, 🕾 262 2711, Group Telex 23922 – 🛗 📺 ⇌wc ☎ 🅿. 🔼 AE ① VISA
M a la carte 5.85/9.45 **st.** 🍷 2.20 – **59 rm** 🍵 24.00/35.25 **st.**   CZ **v**

Leinster Towers, 25-31 Leinster Gdns, W2 2AU, 🕾 262 4591, Group Telex 27120 – 🛗 📺 ⇌wc 🚿wc – **164 rm.**   CZ **x**

Park Court (T.H.F.), 75 Lancaster Gate, W2 3NN, 🕾 402 4272, Group Telex 23922, 🚗 – 🛗 📺 ⇌wc ☎. 🏖. 🔼 AE ① VISA
M a la carte 5.30/9.45 **st.** 🍷 2.20 – **442 rm** 🍵 19.25/29.00 **st.**   CZ **z**

Clarendon Court (Best Western), Edgware Rd, W9 1AG, 🕾 286 8080, Telex 27374 – 🛗 📺 ⇌wc 🚿wc ☎. 🏖. 🔼 AE ① VISA   pp. 13-16   JS **a**
M 6.00 **st.** 🍷 2.20 – 🍵 2.00 – **155 rm** 26.60/37.70 **st.**

Coburg, 129 Bayswater Rd, W2 4RJ, 🕾 229 3654, Telex 268235 – 🛗 📺 ⇌wc ☎. 🏖. 🔼 AE ① VISA   BZ **a**
M 5.00/6.00 **st.** 🍷 1.80 – **120 rm** 🍵 16.00/37.50 **st.**

Grosvenor Court (Gd. Met.), 144 Praed St., W2 1HU, 🕾 262 3464, Group Telex 25971 – 🛗 📺 ⇌wc ☎. 🔼 AE ① VISA   DY **a**
M (coffee shop only) a la carte 1.95/5.95 **st.** 🍷 1.55 – **93 rm** 15.00/22.00 **s.**

Westland, 154 Bayswater Rd, W2 4HP, 🕾 229 9191 – 🛗 📺 ⇌wc ☎ 🅿. 🔼 AE VISA   BZ **z**
M (dinner only) a la carte 3.15/5.45 🍷 1.30 – **30 rm** 🍵 20.95/25.90.

Windsor (T.H.F.), 56-60 Lancaster Gate, W2 3NG, 🕾 262 4501. Group Telex 23922 – 🛗 📺 ⇌wc 🚿wc ☎. 🔼 AE ① VISA   CZ **a**
M a la carte 4.45/5.30 🍷 1.90 – **92 rm** 🍵 13.50/23.50 **st.**

Averard without rest., 10-11 Lancaster Gate, W2 3EL, 🕾 723 8877 – 🛗 ⇌wc 🚿wc ☎. AE 🔼 ① VISA   DZ **c**
🍵 1.00 – **60 rm** 15.00/20.00 **s.**

Allandale, 3 Devonshire Ter., Lancaster Gate, W2 3DN, 🕾 723 8311 – ⇌wc 🚿wc   CY **a**
18 rm 🍵 13.00/18.00.

Caring, 24 Craven Hill Gdns, Leinster Ter., W2 3EA, 🕾 262 8708 – 📺 ⇌wc 🚿   CZ **e**
26 rm 🍵 9.50/14.00 **s.**

Garden Court, 30-31 Kensington Gardens Sq., W2 4BG, 🕾 229 2553 – ⇌wc 🚿wc   BY **e**
40 rm 🍵 9.50/18.50 **s.**

Trevose, 68-70 Queensborough Ter., W2 3SH, 🕾 229 5974   CZ **u**
33 rm 🍵 11.00/17.00 **st.**

✗✗ **Pangs,** 215 Sutherland Av., W9 ,🕾 289 2562, Chinese rest. – 🔼 AE ① VISA pp. 13-16   JS **r**
closed Monday, Good Friday and 25-26 December – **M** a la carte 8.85/14.30 **st.**

✗✗ **Trat-West,** 143 Edgware Rd, W2 2HR, 🕾 723 8203, Italian rest. – 🔼 AE ① VISA
M a la carte 6.75/8.75 **t.** 🍷 1.70.   pp. 13-16   KT **i**

✗✗ **San Marino,** 26 Sussex Pl., W2 2TH, 🕾 723 8395, Italian rest. – 🔼 AE ① VISA   EY **u**
closed Sunday and Bank Holidays – **M** a la carte 6.25/10.20 **t.**

✗✗ **Lotus House,** 61-69 Edgware Rd, W2 2HZ, 🕾 262 4341, Chinese rest., Dancing – 🔼 AE ① VISA   FY **o**
M a la carte approx. 6.50 🍷 1.80.

✗✗ **La Lupa,** 23 Connaught St., W2 2AY, 🕾 723 0540, Italian rest. – 🔼 AE ① VISA   EY **v**
closed Saturday lunch and Sunday – **M** a la carte 4.45/8.00 **t.**

✗✗ **Canaletto,** 451 Edgware Rd, W2 1TH, 🕾 262 7027, Italian rest. – 🔼 AE ① VISA   pp. 13-16   JT **v**
closed Saturday lunch, Sunday and Bank Holidays – **M** a la carte 5.40/8.00 **t.** 🍷 1.75.

P.T.O. ⟶

XX **Concordia Notte,** 29-31 Craven Rd, W2 3BX, ⌾ 402 4985, Italian rest., Dancing – ⌧
⌧ ⌧ *VISA*   **DY r**
closed Sunday – **M** a la carte 10.00/15.00 ⌾ 1.75.

XX **Kalamaras Taverna,** 76-78 Inverness Mews, W2 3JQ, ⌾ 727 9122, Greek rest. – ⌧ ⌧
closed Sunday and Bank Holidays – **M** (dinner only) a la carte 5.85/8.25 ⌾ 1.80. **BY a**

X **Concordia,** 29-31 Craven Rd, W2 3BX, ⌾ 402 4985, Italian rest. – ⌧ ⌧ ⌧ *VISA* **DY r**
closed Sunday – **M** a la carte 7.00/10.00 t. ⌾ 2.20.

X Le Chef, 41 Connaught St., W2 2AY, ⌾ 262 5945, French Bistro.   **EY a**

▮Belgravia▮ – ✉ SW1 – Except where otherwise stated see pp. 24 and 25.

🏨 Berkeley, Wilton Pl., SW1X 7RL, ⌾ 235 6000, Telex 919252, ⌧ – ⌧⌧ 🚗 . ⌧ – ⌧
M Restaurant (*closed Saturday*) – **Le Perroquet** (*closed Sunday*) – **152 rm.**   **FQ e**

🏨 Lowndes (Thistle), 21 Lowndes St., SW1 9ES ⌾ 235 6020, Telex 919065 – ⌧⌧   **FR i**
80 rm.

XXX **Salloos,** 62-64 Kinnerton St., SW1 8ER, ⌾ 235 4444, Pakistani rest. – ⌧ ⌧ ⌧ *VISA* **FQ a**
closed Sunday and Bank Holidays – **M** a la carte 5.50/7.50 ⌾ 1.50.

XX **Motcombs,** 26 Motcomb St., SW1X 8JU, ⌾ 235 6382 – ⌧ ⌧ ⌧ *VISA*   **FR z**
closed Saturday, Sunday and Bank Holidays – **M** a la carte 6.80/11.60 t. ⌾ 2.20.

XX **Wheeler's Carafe,** 15-16 Lowndes St., SW1X 9EY, ⌾ 235 2525, Seafood – ⌧ ⌧ ⌧
VISA   **FR u**
closed Monday and Bank Holidays – **M** a la carte 10.00/14.20 st. ⌾ 1.75.

X **Les Arcades Brasserie** 27, Motcomb St., SW1X 8JU, ⌾ 235 1668, French rest. – ⌧
⌧ *VISA*   **FR z**
M a la carte 4.95/8.15 t. ⌾ 1.65.

X **Upper Crust in Belgravia,** 9 William St., SW1X 9HL, ⌾ 235 8444, English rest. – ⌧
⌧ ⌧ *VISA*   **FQ c**
M a la carte 5.35/6.45 t.

▮Hyde Park and Knightsbridge▮ – ✉ SW1/SW7 – pp. 24 and 25.

🏨 **Hyde Park** (T.H.F.), 66 Knightsbridge, SW1Y 7LA, ⌾ 235 2000, Telex 262057, ⌧ – ⌧
⌧ . ⌧ ⌧ ⌧ *VISA*   **EQ v**
M a la carte 7.75/15.60 st. ⌾ 2.65 – ⌧ 4.50 – **201 rm** 55.50/69.50 **st.**

XX **Shezan,** 16-22 Cheval Pl., Montpelier St., SW7 1ES, ⌾ 589 7918, Indian and Pakistani
rest. – ⌧ ⌧ ⌧ *VISA*   **ER c**
closed Sunday, Good Friday, Easter Monday and Bank Holidays – **M** a la carte 7.70/8.70
⌾ 3.00.

XX **Mr Chow,** 151 Knightsbridge, SW1X 7PA, ⌾ 589 7347, Chinese rest. – ⌧ ⌧ ⌧ *VISA*
closed 25 and 26 December – **M** a la carte 7.55/9.25 ⌾ 2.00.   **EQ s**

XX **Montpeliano,** 13 Montpelier St., SW7 1HQ, ⌾ 589 0032, Italian rest.   **ER e**
closed Sunday and Bank Holidays – **M** a la carte 6.40/9.70 ⌾ 1.50.

▮Mayfair▮ – ✉ W1 – pp. 22 and 23.

🏨 **Dorchester,** Park Lane, W1A 2HJ, ⌾ 629 8888, Telex 887704 – ⌧⌧ ⌧ ⌧ . ⌧ . ⌧ ⌧
⌧ *VISA*   **BN z**
M The Terrace (*closed Sunday*) a la carte 15.40/19.00 st. ⌾ 1.80 – **Grill** (*closed Saturday*)
a la carte 10.50/20.50 st. ⌾ 1.80 – ⌧ 3.40 – **286 rm** 66.00/74.80 **st.**

🏨 Claridge's, Brook St., W1A 2JQ, ⌾ 629 8860, Telex 21872 – ⌧⌧ ⌧ . ⌧ . ⌧   **BL c**
205 rm.

🏨 **Inn on the Park,** Hamilton Pl., Park Lane, W1A 1AZ, ⌾ 499 0888, Telex 22771, ⌧ – ⌧
⌧ ⌧ ⌧ . ⌧ . ⌧ ⌧ ⌧ *VISA*   **BP a**
M Four Seasons a la carte 10.80/18.00 st. ⌾ 2.75 – **Vintage Room** (Dancing) 16.00/
21.50 st. (wine included) – ⌧ 3.60 – **228 rm** 59.00/69.00 **s.**

🏨 **Grosvenor House** (T.H.F.), Park Lane, W1A 3AA, ⌾ 499 6363, Telex 24871, ⌧ – ⌧
⌧ ⌧ ⌧ . ⌧ . ⌧ ⌧ ⌧ *VISA*   **AM a**
M a la carte 11.00/18.25 st. ⌾ 2.35 – ⌧ 4.50 – **478 rm** 51.00/67.00 **st.**

🏨 ✿✿ **Connaught,** 16 Carlos Pl., W1Y 6AL, ⌾ 499 7070 – ⌧⌧ . ⌧   **BM e**
M 14.50/19.00 t. ⌾ 1.90 – ⌧ a la carte approx. 5.60 – **89 rm** 34.00/53.00 **t.**
Spec. Pâté de turbot froid au homard sauce pudeur, Sole " Jubilé ", Noisettes d'agneau en chevreuil à ma façon.

🏨 **Inter-Continental,** 1 Hamilton Pl., Hyde Park Corner, W1R 0LU, ⌾ 409 3131, Telex
25853 – ⌧⌧ ⌧ ⌧ . ⌧ . ⌧ ⌧ ⌧ *VISA*   **BP o**
M a la carte 9.15/17.80 t. ⌾ 3.70 – ⌧ 4.70 – **497 rm** 64.00/73.00.

🏨🏨 **Hilton,** 22 Park Lane, W1A 2HH, ☎ 493 8000, Telex 24873, ⪡ London — ⧉ 📺 ♿ Ⓟ ☂.
🄳 AE ⓪ VISA — **BP e**
M a la carte 7.70/13.60 **t.** 🍷 3.00 — ☕ 4.50 — **509 rm** 56.00/64.00 **t.**

🏨🏨 **Athenaeum** (Rank), 116 Piccadilly, W1V 0BJ, ☎ 499 3464, Telex 261589 — ⧉ 📺 ☂.
🄳 AE ⓪ VISA — **CP s**
M a la carte 10.50/14.40 **st.** 🍷 3.90 — ☕ 4.60 — **112 rm** 51.00/65.00 **st.**

🏨🏨 **May Fair** (Gd. Met.), Berkeley St., W1A 2AW, ☎ 629 7777, Telex 262526 — ⧉ 📺. ☂.
🄳 AE ⓪ VISA — **DN z**
390 rm 39.00/53.00 **s.**

🏨🏨 **Brown's** (T.H.F.), 21-24 Dover St., W1A 4SW, ☎ 493 6020, Telex 28686 — ⧉ 📺. ☂. 🄳
AE ⓪ VISA — **DM e**
M a la carte 9.70/22.85 **st.** 🍷 2.35 — ☕ 3.50 — **127 rm** 43.70/58.60 **st.**

🏨🏨 **Westbury** (T.H.F.), New Bond St., W1Y 0PD, ☎ 629 7755, Telex 24378 — ⧉ 📺 ♿ Ⓟ.
☂. 🄳 AE ⓪ VISA — **DM a**
M 9.60/14.35 **t.** 🍷 2.75 — ☕ 3.50 — **270 rm** 40.00/64.00 **st.**

🏨🏨 **Britannia** (Gd. Met.), 42 Grosvenor Sq., W1X 0DX, ☎ 629 9400, Telex 23941 — ⧉ 📺
Ⓟ. ☂. 🄳 AE ⓪ VISA — **BM i**
M a la carte 7.00/13.00 🍷 1.80 — **434 rm** 41.50/55.00 **s.**

🏨🏨 **Bristol,** 3 Berkeley St., W1X 6NE, ☎ 493 8282, Telex 24561 — ⧉ 📺 ♿ Ⓟ. ☂. 🄳 AE ⓪
VISA — **DN r**
M a la carte 8.55/17.50 **st.** 🍷 2.75 — ☕ 4.35 — **189 rm** 45.00/52.00.

🏨🏨 **Chesterfield** (Gd. Met.), 34-36 Charles St., W1X 8LX, ☎ 491 2622, Telex 269394 —
⧉ 📺. 🄳 AE ⓪ VISA — **CN c**
M a la carte 9.40/13.90 **st.** 🍷 2.00 — **87 rm** 31.00/42.00 **s.**

🏨🏨 **Europa** (Gd. Met.), Grosvenor Sq., W1A 4AW, ☎ 493 1232, Telex 268101 — ⧉ 📺 ♿ Ⓟ.
☂. 🄳 AE ⓪ VISA — **BL n**
M a la carte 8.85/23.25 **st.** 🍷 1.80 — **275 rm** 39.00/53.00 **s.**

🏨🏨 Londonderry, 19 Park Lane, W1Y 8AP, ☎ 493 7292, Telex 263292, ⪡ — ⧉ 📺 Ⓟ — **BP r**
140 rm.

🏨 **Washington** (Gd. Met.), Curzon St., W1Y 8DT, ☎ 499 7030, Telex 24540 — ⧉ 📺 🛏WC
☎. ☂. 🄳 AE ⓪ VISA — **CN n**
M a la carte 5.35/8.00 🍷 1.80 — **160 rm** 26.50/34.00 **s.**

XXXXX **Mirabelle** (De Vere), 56 Curzon St., W1Y 8DL, ☎ 499 4636, 🚗 — 🄳 AE ⓪ VISA — **CN a**
closed Sunday and Bank Holidays — **M** a la carte 15.00/25.00 **t.**

XXXX **Scott's,** 20 Mount St., W1Y 5RB, ☎ 629 5248, Seafood — 🄳 AE ⓪ VISA — **BM r**
closed Sunday lunch and Bank Holidays — **M** a la carte 10.20/18.80 🍷 2.10.

XXX **Cecconi's,** 5a Burlington Gardens, W1Y 5DT, ☎ 434 1500, Italian rest. — 🄳 AE — **DM c**
closed Saturday lunch and Sunday - **M** a la carte 13.30/15.40 **t.** 🍷 3.00.

XXX **Tiberio,** 22 Queen St., W1X 7PJ, ☎ 629 3561, Italian rest., Dancing — 🄳 AE ⓪ VISA — **CN z**
closed Saturday lunch and Sunday — **M** a la carte 10.85/16.35 🍷 1.90.

XXX **Snooty Fox,** 51-52 Hertford St., W1Y 7HJ, ☎ 629 1786, French rest. — AE ⓪ VISA — **BN c**
closed Saturday lunch, Sunday and Bank Holidays — **M** 8.00/8.75 🍷 2.10.

XXX Trader Vics (at Hilton), 22 Park Lane, W1A 2AA, ☎ 493 7586, Polynesian rest. — **BP e**

XXX **La Napoule,** 8-10 North Audley St., W1Y 1WK, ☎ 629 4178, French rest. — 🄳 AE ⓪
VISA — **AL e**
closed Saturday lunch, Sunday and Bank Holidays — **M** a la carte 9.50/12.50 **t.** 🍷 3.00.

XXX **Tandoori,** 37a Curzon St., W1Y 7AF, ☎ 629 0600, Indian and Pakistani rest. — 🄳 AE
⓪ VISA — **BN i**
closed Sunday and 25-26 December — **M** a la carte 7.15/9.20 🍷 1.95.

XX **Greenhouse,** 27a Hay's Mews, W1X 7RJ, ☎ 499 3331 — 🄳 AE ⓪ VISA — **BN a**
closed Sunday and Bank Holidays — **M** a la carte 6.80/8.95 **t.**

XX Mr. Kai, 65 South Audley St., W1, ☎ 493 8988, Chinese rest. — **BM v**

XX **Marquis,** 121a Mount St., W1Y 5HB, ☎ 499 1256 — 🄳 AE ⓪ VISA — **BM u**
closed Sunday and Bank Holidays — **M** a la carte 5.95/9.45 **t.** 🍷 2.50.

XX **La Genova,** 32 North Audley St., W1Y 1WG, ☎ 629 5916, Italian rest. — 🄳 AE ⓪ VISA — **AL u**
closed Sunday and Bank Holidays — **M** a la carte 4.90/10.00 🍷 1.60.

XX **Langan's Brasserie,** Stratton St., W1X 5FD, ☎ 493 6437 — AE ⓪ — **DN e**
closed Saturday lunch, Sunday and Bank Holidays — **M** a la carte 7.50/11.00 **t.** 🍷 2.30.

XX **Golden Carp,** 8a Mount St., W1Y 5AD, ☎ 499 3385, Seafood — 🄳 AE ⓪ VISA — **BM x**
closed Saturday lunch, Sunday and 12 to 31 August — **M** a la carte 5.50/9.75 **t.** 🍷 2.50.

XX **Gaylord,** 16 Albemarle St., W1 3HA, ☎ 629 8542, Indian rest. — 🄳 AE ⓪ VISA — **DM u**
M a la carte approx. 5.50 🍷 2.40.

X **Trattoria Fiori,** 87-88 Mount St., W1Y 5HG, ☎ 499 1447, Italian rest. — 🄳 AE ⓪
VISA — **BM o**
closed Sunday, 25 and 26 December and Bank Holidays — **M** a la carte 5.95/9.10 **t.**
🍷 1.90.

X **Tokyo,** 7 Swallow St., W1R 7HD, ☎ 734 2269, Japanese rest. — 🄳 AE ⓪ VISA — **EM i**
M a la carte 10.95/15.45 **s.** 🍷 1.50.

Regent's Park and Marylebone – ✉ NW1/NW6/NW8/W1 – Except where otherwise stated see pp. 22 and 23.

Churchill, 30 Portman Sq., W1H 0AJ, ☎ 486 5800, Telex 264831 – 劇 ⊡ ఈ ❷. 🏊. 🔊 AE ⓪ VISA — AJ x
M a la carte 11.50/16.50 **st.** 🍷 2.00 – ☕ 4.60 – **489 rm** 47.00/55.00.

Selfridge, 400 Orchard St., W1H 0JS, ☎ 408 2080, Telex 22361 – 劇 ⊡ ఈ ❷. 🏊. 🔊 AE ⓪ VISA — AK e
M a la carte 12.15/14.05 **t.** 🍷 2.90 – ☕ 4.40 – **298 rm** 47.00/60.00 **t.**

Portman, 22 Portman Sq., W1H 9FL, ☎ 486 5844, Telex 261526 – 劇 ⊡ ఈ ❷. 🏊. 🔊 AE ⓪ VISA — AJ o
M a la carte 11.00/16.00 **t.** 🍷 2.25 – ☕ 4.60 – **275 rm** 50.00/55.00.

Montcalm, Great Cumberland Pl., W1A 2LF, ☎ 402 4288, Telex 28710 – 劇 ⊡. 🏊. 🔊 AE ⓪ VISA — pp. 26 and 27 FY x
M 8.50/10.50 **st.** 🍷 2.00 – ☕ 4.50 – **112 rm.**

Holiday Inn, 134 George St., W1M 6DN, ☎ 723 1277, Telex 27983, 🔊 – 劇 ⊡ ఈ ❷. 🔊 AE ⓪ VISA — pp. 26 and 27 FY i
M a la carte 6.80/12.05 **st.** 🍷 2.05 – ☕ 3.50 – **243 rm** 41.50/51.50 **s.**

St. George's (T.H.F.), Langham Pl., W1N 8QS, ☎ 580 0111, Telex 27274, ≼ – 劇 ⊡. 🔊 AE ⓪ VISA — pp. 13-16 LT a
M a la carte 6.15/11.95 **st.** 🍷 2.10 – ☕ 3.50 – **85 rm** 35.20/49.00 **st.**

Cumberland (T.H.F.), Marble Arch, W1A 4RF, ☎ 262 1234, Telex 22215 – 劇 ⊡ ఈ ❷. 🏊. 🔊 AE ⓪ VISA — AK n
M a la carte 6.35/10.80 **t.** 🍷 2.20 – **894 rm** 35.15/47.90 **st.**

Westmoreland at Lords, 18 Lodge Rd, NW8 7JT, ☎ 722 7722, Telex 23101 – 劇 ⊡ ❷. 🏊. 🔊 AE ⓪ VISA — pp. 13-16 JS v
M a la carte approx. 6.50 **st.** 🍷 2.20 – ☕ 2.00 – **335 rm** 26.00/35.00 **s.**

Durrants, 26-32 George St., W1H 6BJ, ☎ 935 8131 – 劇 ⊡ ⊖wc ☎. 🏊. ⓪ — AH e
M a la carte 6.75/9.75 🍷 1.75 – **86 rm** ☕ 16.00/28.50 **s.**

Clifton Ford (Gd. Met.), 47 Welbeck St., W1M 8HS, ☎ 486 6600, Group Telex 22569 – 劇 ⊡ ⊖wc ☎. 🏊. 🔊 AE ⓪ VISA — BH a
M a la carte 4.95/10.70 **st.** 🍷 1.80 – **220 rm** 26.50/34.00 **s.**

Londoner (Gd. Met.), 57 Welbeck St., W1M 8HS, ☎ 935 4442, Group Telex 22569 – 劇 ⊡ ⊖wc ☎. 🔊 AE ⓪ VISA — BJ v
M a la carte 3.60/8.10 **st.** 🍷 1.80 – **142 rm** 26.50/34.00 **s.**

Harewood, Harewood Row, NW1 6SE, ☎ 262 2707, Telex 267465 – 劇 ⊡ ⊖wc 🚿wc ☎. 🔊 AE ⓪ VISA — pp. 13-16 KT x
M a la carte 2.30/5.55 **st.** 🍷 1.40 – ☕ 2.25 – **93 rm** 20.75/29.25 **st.**

Stratford Court (Gd. Met.), 350 Oxford St., W1N 0BY, ☎ 629 7474, Telex 22270 – 劇 ⊡ ⊖wc ☎. 🔊 AE ⓪ VISA — BK n
M a la carte 3.10/5.75 **st.** 🍷 1.80 – **137 rm** 19.50/29.00 **s.**

Regent Centre (Centre), Carburton St., W1P 8EE, ☎ 388 2300, Telex 22453 – 劇 ⊡ ⊖wc ☎ ❷. 🏊. 🔊 AE ⓪ VISA — pp. 13-16 LT i
☕ 1.65 – **350 rm** 23.55/30.45 **st.**

Bryanston Court without rest., 56-60 Great Cumberland Pl., W14 7FD, ☎ 262 3141, Telex 21120 – 劇 ⊡ ⊖wc 🚿wc ☎. 🔊 AE ⓪ VISA — pp. 26 and 27 FY z
closed Sunday – M 6.00/7.00 **t.** 🍷 1.50 – ☕ 1.20 – **57 rm** 18.00/24.00 **s.**

Concorde without rest., 50 Great Cumberland Pl., W1H 7FD, ☎ 402 6169 – 劇 ⊖wc 🚿wc ☎. 🔊 AE ⓪ VISA — pp. 26 and 27 FY n
☕ 1.20 – **28 rm** 17.00/23.00 **s.**

Rose Court without rest., 35 Great Cumberland Pl., W1H 8DJ, ☎ 262 7241 – 劇 ⊖wc 🚿wc ☎. 🔊 AE ⓪ — pp. 26 and 27 FY s
45 rm 17.00/22.00 **s.**

Hallam, without rest., 12 Hallam St., W1N 5LJ, ☎ 580 1166 – ⊖wc 🚿wc ☎ — pp. 13-16 LT r
27 rm.

Somerset House, 6 Dorset Sq., Baker St., NW1 6QA, ☎ 723 0741 – ⊡ ⊖wc 🚿 ☎ — pp. 13-16 KT u
28 rm.

Portman Court, 30 Seymour St., W1H 5WD, ☎ 402 5401 – ⊖wc 🚿 ☎. 🔊 VISA — AK a
☕ 0.75 – **30 rm** 12.00/22.80 **t.**

XXX Geneviève, 13-14 Thayer St., W1M 5LD, ☏ 486 2244. BH s

XXX **Oslo Court,** Prince Albert Rd, Regent's Park, NW8, ☏ 722 8795 pp. 13-16 JKS s
closed Saturday lunch, Sunday, Monday, 2 weeks Easter, last 2 weeks August, first week September and Christmas – **M** a la carte 7.45/10.65 **t.** 🍷 2.15.

XXX **Odins,** 27 Devonshire St., W1N 1RJ, ☏ 935 7296 pp. 13-16 KT n
closed Saturday lunch, Sunday and Bank Holidays – **M** a la carte 10.30/14.80 **t.**

XX Le Petit Montmartre, 15-17 Marylebone Lane, W1M 5FE, ☏ 935 9226, French rest. BJ z

XX **La Loggia,** 68 Edgware Rd., W2 2EG, ☏ 723 0554, Italian rest. – 🖼 AE ⓪ VISA
closed Sunday and Bank Holidays – **M** a la carte 6.50/10.50 🍷 1.65. pp. 26 and 27 FY a

XX Fisherman's Wharf, 73 Baker St., W1M 1AH, ☏ 935 0471, Seafood. pp. 13-16 KT e

XX **Bill Bentley's,** 239 Baker St., NW1 6XE, ☏ 935 3130, Seafood – 🖼 AE ⓪ VISA
pp. 13-16 KST a
closed Sunday and Bank Holidays – **M** a la carte 6.35/8.80 **t.** 🍷 1.60.

XX **Tonino,** Berkeley Court, 12 Glentworth St., NW1 5PG, ☏ 935 4220, Italian rest. – AE ⓪
VISA
pp. 13-16 KT c
closed Sunday – **M** a la carte 5.95/9.95 **s.** 🍷 2.05.

XX **Viceroy of India,** 3-5 Glentworth St., NW1, ☏ 486 3401, Indian rest. – 🖼 AE ⓪ VISA
closed Easter Sunday, Easter Monday and 25-26 December – **M** a la carte 6.75/14.10 **t.**
🍷 2.15.
pp. 13-16 KT o

XX **Lords Rendezvous,** 24 Finchley Rd, NW8 6ES, ☏ 586 4280, Chinese rest. – 🖼 AE
⓪
pp. 13-16 JR r
M 6.50/11.00.

XX **Rossetti,** 23 Queens Grove, St. John's Wood, NW8 6PR, ☏ 722 7141, Italian rest. – 🖼
AE ⓪ VISA
pp. 13-16 JR c
closed Bank Holidays – **M** a la carte 4.75/8.45 **t.** 🍷 1.85.

XX **Kerzenstüberl,** 9 St. Christopher's Pl., W1M 6DU, ☏ 486 3196, Austrian rest. – 🖼 AE
⓪ VISA
BJ a
closed Saturday lunch, Sunday, mid August - mid September and Bank Holidays – **M** a
la carte 5.80/8.80 🍷 1.95.

XX **Gaylord,** 79-81 Mortimer St., W1N 7TB, ☏ 636 0808, Indian and Pakistani rest. – 🖼 AE
⓪ VISA
pp. 13-16 LT c
M a la carte approx. 6.50 🍷 2.45.

XX Masako, 6-8 St. Christopher's Pl., W1M 5HB, ☏ 935 1579, Japanese rest. BJ e

XX **Sandro,** 114 Crawford St., W1H 1AG, ☏ 935 5736, Italian rest. – 🖼 AE ⓪ VISA
pp. 13-16 KT r
closed Saturday lunch, Sunday and Bank Holidays – **M** a la carte 5.95/9.95 **s.** 🍷 2.05.

XX **Mikado,** 110 George St., W1H 6DJ, ☏ 935 8320, Japanese rest. – AE ⓪ VISA
AH s
closed Saturday lunch, Sunday, 1 week August-September and Bank Holidays – **M** a la
carte 8.50/14.00.

X **Biagi's,** 39 Upper Berkeley St., W1H 7PG, ☏ 723 0394, Italian rest. – 🖼 AE ⓪ VISA
closed Bank Holidays – **M** a la carte 4.75/7.55. 🍷 1.65. pp. 26 and 27 FY c

X **Il Barbino,** 64 Seymour St., W1H 5AF, ☏ 402 6866, Italian rest. – 🖼 AE ⓪ VISA
closed Saturday lunch, Sunday, 25-26 December and Bank Holidays for lunch – **M** a la
carte 5.40/7.70 **t.** 🍷 1.50.
pp. 26 and 27 FY r

X **Vecchio Parioli,** 129 Crawford St., W1H 1AA, ☏ 935 3791, Italian rest. – 🖼 AE
closed Saturday lunch, Sunday, 25-26 December and Bank Holidays – **M** a la carte
5.60/7.90 **t.** 🍷 1.50.
pp. 13-16 KT s

X **Hellenic,** 30 Thayer St., W1M 5LJ, ☏ 935 1257, Greek rest. BH c
closed Saturday lunch, Sunday and Bank Holidays – **M** a la carte 3.95/6.00 🍷 1.70.

X Singapore, 62 Marylebone Lane, W1M 5FF, ☏ 486 2004, Malaysian rest. BJ c

St. James's W1/SW1/WC2 – pp. 22 and 23.

🏨🏨🏨 **Ritz,** Piccadilly, W1A 2JS, ☏ 493 8181, Telex 267200 – 📶 📺 🖼 AE ⓪ VISA DN a
M a la carte 10.70/17.95 **st.** 🍷 2.40 – 🍵 5.00 – **142 rm** 50.00/80.00.

🏨🏨 **Dukes** ⌛, 35 St. James's Pl., SW1A 1NY, ☏ 491 4840, Telex 28283 – 📶 📺 🖼 AE ⓪
VISA
EP x
M a la carte 10.40/14.70 **s.** 🍷 2.00 – 🍵 3.90 – **54 rm** 40.00/51.00 **s.**

🏨🏨 Stafford ⌛, 16 St. James's Pl., SW1A 1NJ, ☏ 493 0111, Telex 28602 – 📶 📺 ♿ DN u
62 rm.

🏨🏨 **Cavendish** (T.H.F.), Jermyn St., SW1Y 6JF, ☏ 930 2111, Telex 263187 – 📶 📺 ♿ 🅿 ♿.
🖼 AE ⓪ VISA
EN i
M a la carte 9.55/14.00 **st.** – **255 rm** 42.75/59.00 **st.**

🏨🏨 **Quaglino's** (T.H.F), 16 Bury St., SW1Y 6AJ, ☏ 930 6767 – 📶 📺. ♿. 🖼 AE ⓪ VISA
M 10.50/15.50 **st.** 🍷 2.20 – 🍵 3.50 – **41 rm** 36.50/47.00 **st.**
EN n

🏨 Royal Trafalgar, Whitcomb St., WC2H 7HG, ☏ 930 4477, Group Telex 24616 – 📶 📺
🚿wc ☎ – **108 rm.**
GM r

🏨 Royal Angus, 39 Coventry St., W1V 8EL, ☏ 930 4033, Group Telex 24616 – 📶 📺 🚿wc ☎
92 rm.
FGM a

🏨 **Pastoria** (Gd. Met.), St. Martin's St., WC2H 7HL, ☏ 930 8641, Telex 25971 – 🛗 📺 ⬛WC
⌂. 🅿 AE ⓞ VISA — **GM v**
M 5.50/6.25 **st.** 🍷 1.80 – **52 rm** 16.50/28.00 **s.**

XXXX **A l'Ecu de France**, 111 Jermyn St., SW1Y 6HB, ☏ 930 2837, French rest. – 🅿 AE ⓞ
VISA — **FM s**
closed lunch Saturday and Sunday – **M** a la carte 10.25/15.45 **t.** 🍷 2.90.

XXX Hunting Lodge (T.H.F.), 16-18 Lower Regent St., SW1Y 4PH, ☏ 930 4222, English
rest. — **FM o**

XXX Lafayette, 32 King St., SW1 6RJ, ☏ 930 1131. — **EN v**

XX **Frank's**, 63 Jermyn St., SW1Y 6LX, ☏ 493 3646, Italian rest. – 🅿 AE ⓞ VISA — **EN z**
closed Sunday – **M** a la carte approx. 6.15 🍷 1.60.

Soho – ✉ W1/WC2 – pp. 22 and 23.

XXXXX Le Relais du Café Royal (T.H.F.), 68 Regent St., W1R 6EL, ☏ 437 9090, French rest. **EM a**

XXXXX Café Royal Grill (T.H.F.), 68 Regent St., W1R 6EL, ☏ 437 9090, French rest. **EM a**

XXX Gennaro's (T.H.F.), 44-45 Dean St., W1V 5AP, ☏ 437 3950, Italian rest. **FK s**

XXX **Leonis Quo Vadis**, 26-29 Dean St., W1V 7PH, ☏ 437 9585, Italian rest. – 🅿 AE ⓞ VISA
closed Sunday lunch, Good Friday and Easter Sunday – **M** a la carte 8.45/11.20 **t.**
🍷 1.75. — **FK u**

XX **La Terrazza**, 19 Romilly St., W1T 5TG, ☏ 734 2504, Italian rest. – 🅿 AE ⓞ VISA **FL i**
M a la carte approx. 10.60 **t.**

XX **Au Jardin des Gourmets**, 5 Greek St., Soho Sq., W1V 5LA, ☏ 437 1816, French rest. –
🅿 AE ⓞ VISA — **GJ a**
closed Saturday lunch and Sunday – **M** a la carte 7.85/11.10 **t.** 🍷 1.75.

XX **Venezia**, 21 Great Chapel St., W1V 5HA, ☏ 437 6506, Italian rest. – 🅿 AE ⓞ VISA **FJ a**
closed Saturday lunch, Sunday and Bank Holidays – **M** a la carte 4.75/8.50 🍷 1.50.

XX Romeo e Giulietta, 11 Sutton Row, W1V 5FE, ☏ 734 4914, Italian rest. **GJ e**

XX **I Paparazzi**, 52-54 Dean St., W1V 5HJ, ☏ 437 3916, Italian rest. – 🅿 AE ⓞ VISA **GL a**
closed 25-26 December and Bank Holidays – **M** a la carte 2.65/5.05 🍷 1.60.

XX **Peter Mario**, 47 Gerrard St., W1V 7LP, ☏ 437 4170, Italian rest. – 🅿 AE ⓞ VISA **GL n**
closed Sunday, Good Friday, Easter Monday and Bank Holidays – **M** a la carte 4.75/
7.05 **t.** 🍷 1.45.

XX **Rugantino**, 26 Romilly St., W1V 5TQ, ☏ 437 5302, Italian rest. – 🅿 AE ⓞ VISA **GK u**
closed Saturday lunch, Sunday and Bank Holidays – **M** a la carte 4.55/5.75 **t.** 🍷 1.65.

XX **Gay Hussar**, 2 Greek St., W1V 6NB, ☏ 437 0973, Hungarian rest. **GJ c**
closed Sunday and Bank Holidays – **M** a la carte 6.05/8.75 **t.** 🍷 2.30.

XX **Fuji**, 36-40 Brewer St., W1R 3HP, ☏ 734 0957, Japanese rest. – 🅿 AE ⓞ VISA **FL c**
closed Saturday lunch, Sunday lunch, Monday, 1 week Easter and 2 weeks Christmas –
M a la carte 5.80/12.90 🍷 3.00.

XX **Chesa (Swiss Centre)**, 2 New Coventry St., W1V 3HG, ☏ 734 1291, Swiss rest. –
🅿 AE ⓞ VISA — **GM n**
closed Christmas Day – **M** a la carte 6.90/10.00 **st.**

XX **Soho Rendezvous**, 21 Romilly St., W1V 5TG, ☏ 437 1486, Chinese rest. – 🅿 AE ⓞ VISA
M a la carte 5.10/7.40. — **GL o**

X **Hostaria Romana**, 70 Dean St., W1V 5HB, ☏ 734 2869, Italian rest. – 🅿 AE ⓞ VISA **FK r**
M a la carte 5.20/6.60 **t.** 🍷 1.50.

X **Trattoria Imperia**, 19 Charing Cross Rd, WC2H 0ES, ☏ 930 8364, Italian rest. – 🅿 AE
ⓞ VISA — **GM z**
closed Sunday and Bank Holidays – **M** a la carte 4.15/6.90 🍷 1.35.

X **Hokkai**, 59-61 Brewer St., W1R 3FB, ☏ 734 5826, Japanese rest. – 🅿 AE ⓞ VISA **ELM e**
closed Sunday lunch and 25-26 December – **M** 7.50/9.80.

X **The Village**, 61-63 Shaftesbury Av., W1V 7AA, ☏ 437 5021, Chinese rest. – 🅿 AE
ⓞ VISA — **FL a**
M a la carte 3.70/6.60 🍷 1.50.

X Rendezvous (Swiss Centre), 2 New Coventry St., W1V 3HG, ☏ 734 1291, Swiss rest. –
🅿. 🅿 AE ⓞ VISA — **GM n**
closed Christmas Day.

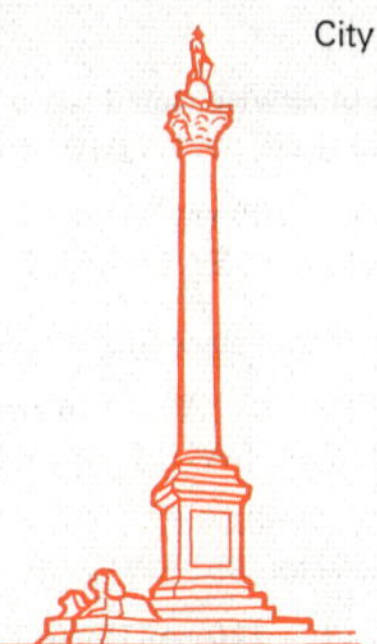

Strand – ✉ WC2 – p. 27.

🏨🏨🏨🏨 **Savoy**, Strand, WC2R 0BP, ☎ 836 4343, Telex 24234 – 🛗 TV 🅿️ 🏊 — **337 rm.**   EX a

🏨🏨🏨 **Waldorf** (T.H.F.), Aldwych, WC2B 4DD, ☎ 836 2400, Telex 24574 – 🛗 TV 🏊 · 🔙 AE ① VISA   EV x
M a la carte 7.00/11.50 **st.** ⛀ 2.50 – ☕ 3.50 – **310 rm** 40.00/50.00 **st.**

🏨🏨🏨 **Charing Cross** (B.T.H.), Strand, WC2N 5HX, ☎ 839 7282, Telex 261101 – 🛗 TV ♿ 🏊 · 🔙 AE ① VISA   DX s
M a la carte 10.55/14.45 **st.** ⛀ 2.40 – ☕ 3.75 – **210 rm** 30.25/48.25 **st.**

🏨🏨🏨 **Howard**, 12 Temple Pl., WC2R 2PR, ☎ 836 3555, Telex 268047 – 🛗 TV ♿ 🚗 🏊 · 🔙 AE ① VISA   FV e
M a la carte 8.00/15.00 – ☕ 4.25 – **141 rm** 50.00/60.00 **s.**

🏨🏨🏨 **Strand Palace** (T.H.F.), Strand, WC2R 0JJ, ☎ 836 8080, Telex 24208 – 🛗 TV 🏊 · 🔙 AE ① VISA   EV u
M 6.50 **t.** ⛀ 2.20 – **786 rm** 25.50/38.00 **st.**

XXXX ❀ **Inigo Jones**, 14 Garrick St., WC2E 9BJ, ☎ 836 6456, « Converted Mission house »   DV n
closed Saturday lunch, Sunday and Bank Holidays – **M** a la carte 10.90/14.10 ⛀ 2.00
Spec. Blinis au saumon fumé d'Ecosse, Carré d'agneau en croûte sauce à la menthe, Lou Magret aux deux purées.

XXXX **Ivy**, 1-5 West St., WC2H 9NE, ☎ 836 4751 – 🔙 AE ① VISA   DV e
closed Saturday lunch, Sunday, Easter, 25-26 December and Bank Holidays for lunch –
M a la carte 8.20/12.70 ⛀ 2.00.

XXX **Simpson's-in-the-Strand**, 100 Strand, WC2R 0EW, ☎ 836 9112, English rest.   EV o

XXX **La Bussola**, 42-49 St. Martin's Lane, WC2N 4EJ, ☎ 240 1148, Italian rest., Dancing.   DX r

XXX **Thomas de Quincey's**, 36 Tavistock St., WC2E 7EB, ☎ 240 3972 – 🔙 AE ① VISA   EV c
closed Saturday lunch, Sunday, last 3 weeks August and Bank Holidays – **M** a la carte
8.30/10.10 **t** ⛀ 2.25.

XX **San Martino**, 46 St. Martin's Lane, WC2N 4EJ, ☎ 240 2336, Italian rest. – 🔙 AE ① VISA   DX x
closed Saturday lunch, Sunday and Bank Holidays for lunch – **M** a la carte 5.15/7.55 ⛀ 1.50.

XX **Grange**, 39 King St., WC2E 8JS, ☎ 240 2939 – AE   DV z
closed Saturday lunch, Sunday and Bank Holidays – **M** 10.65 **t.** ⛀ 2.10.

XX **Chez Solange**, 35 Cranbourn St., WC2H 7AD, ☎ 836 5886, French rest.   DV i

XX **Azami**, 13-15 West St., WC2H 9BL, ☎ 240 0634, Japanese rest.   pp. 22 and 23 GK z

XX **Forum**, Bush House, Aldwych, WC2B 4PA, ☎ 836 9828.   EV i

XX **Friends**, 30 Wellington St., WC2E 6BD, ☎ 836 5520 – 🔙 AE ① VISA   EV e
closed Saturday lunch, Sunday, 18 August-8 September and Bank Holidays – **M** a la carte
7.05/9.25 ⛀ 2.00.

X **Luigi's**, 15 Tavistock St., WC2E 7PA, ☎ 240 1795, Italian rest. – ① VISA   EV a
closed Sunday and Bank Holidays – **M** a la carte 5.40/7.40 **t.** ⛀ 1.80.

X ❀ **Poons of Covent Garden**, 41 King St., WC2E 8JS, ☎ 240 1743, Chinese rest. – AE ①   DV r
closed Sunday – **M** a la carte 4.80/6.80 ⛀ 2.70
Spec. Baked lobster or crab with fresh ginger, Wind-dried food (September-February).

X **Laguna 50**, 50 St. Martin's Lane, WC2N 4EA, ☎ 836 0960, Italian rest. – 🔙 AE ① VISA   DV u
closed Sunday – **M** a la carte 3.35/7.15 **t.** ⛀ 1.65.

X **Colosseo**, 12 May's Court, St. Martin's Lane, WC2N 4BS, ☎ 836 6140, Italian rest. – 🔙 AE ① VISA   DX e
closed Saturday lunch and Sunday – **M** a la carte 5.20/7.25 **t.** ⛀ 1.65.

X **Cellier de Medici**, 8 May's Court, St. Martin's Lane, WC2N 4BS, ☎ 836 9180, French rest. – AE ① VISA   DX o
closed Saturday lunch, Sunday and Bank Holidays – **M** a la carte 6.80/8.00 **t.** ⛀ 1.60.

Victoria – ✉ SW1 – Except otherwise stated see p. 26.

Goring, Beeston Pl., Grosvenor Gdns, SW1W 0JW, ☏ 834 8211, Telex 919166 – 🛗 📺 ⚖.
🍴 ㏂ ⑩ 𝘝𝘐𝘚𝘈   BV **a**
M 8.00/9.00 t. ⚱ 3.00 – ☲ 3.50 – **100 rm** 34.00/43.00 **st.** – P 48.00 **st.**

Royal Horseguards, 2 Whitehall Court, SW1A 2EJ, ☏ 839 3400, Telex 917096 – 🛗 📺 ♿.
🍴 – **280 rm.**   pp. 17-20 NV **a**

Royal Westminster, Buckingham Palace Rd, SW1W 0QT, ☏ 834 1302, Telex 916821 –
🛗 📺 🍴. ㏂ ⑩ 𝘝𝘐𝘚𝘈   BV **z**
M a la carte 7.90/10.40 t. ⚱ 2.10 – ☲ 3.15 – **136 rm** ☲ 37.25/47.90 t.

St. Ermin's (Gd. Met.), Caxton St., SW1H 0QW, ☏ 222 7888, Telex 917731 – 🛗 📺 ⒫.
🍴. ㏂ ⑩ 𝘝𝘐𝘚𝘈   CV **a**
M 5.80 **st.** ⚱ 1.80 – **241 rm** 29.00/40.00 **s.**

Eccleston (Norfolk Cap.), Eccleston Sq., SW1V 1PS, ☏ 834 8042, Group Telex 23241 –
🛗 📺 🚿wc 📞. 🍴. ㏂ ⑩ 𝘝𝘐𝘚𝘈   BX **z**
M 4.00/5.00 **st.** ⚱ 1.75 – ☲ 2.20 – **120 rm** 15.70/33.00 **st.**

Rubens (Gd. Met.), 39 Buckingham Palace Rd, SW1W 0PS, ☏ 834 6600, Telex 916577 –
🛗 📺 🚿wc 📞. 🍴. ㏂ ⑩ 𝘝𝘐𝘚𝘈   BV **u**
M 5.20 **st.** ⚱ 1.80 – **146 rm** 14.50/23.00 **s.**

Ebury Court, 26 Ebury St., SW1W 0LU, ☏ 730 8147 – 🛗 🚿wc 📞   AV **i**
M a la carte 3.25/7.40 **st.** ⚱ 1.25 – **37 rm** ☲ 16.00/35.50 **st.**

Hamilton House, 60 Warwick Way, SW1V 1SA, ☏ 821 7113 – 📺 🚿wc 📞. ㏂ ⑩
𝘝𝘐𝘚𝘈   BX **n**
M a la carte 2.60/4.75 t. ⚱ 1.45 – **40 rm** ☲ 15.00/25.00 t.

Elizabeth, 37 Eccleston Sq., SW1V 1PB, ☏ 828 6812   BX **c**
24 rm ☲ 13.00/22.00 **st.**

Belgrave House, 30-32 Belgrave Rd, SW1V 1RG, ☏ 834 8620 – **40 rm.**   BX **e**

XXX **Kundan,** 3 Horseferry Rd, SW1P 2AN, ☏ 834 3434, Indian and Pakistani rest. – ㏂ ㏂
⑩ 𝘝𝘐𝘚𝘈   pp. 17-20 NXY **a**
closed Sunday, Good Friday, Easter Monday, 26 December and Bank Holidays – **M** a la
carte 5.20/10.00 ⚱ 2.50.

XX **Pomegranates,** 94 Grosvenor Rd, SW1V 3LG, ☏ 828 6560 – ㏂ ㏂ ⑩ 𝘝𝘐𝘚𝘈
                                                                               pp 17-20 LMZ **a**
closed Saturday lunch, Sunday and Bank Holidays – **M** a la carte 8.00/11.75 ⚱ 2.50.

XX **Lockets,** Marsham Court, Marsham St., SW1P 4JY, ☏ 834 9552, English rest. – ㏂ ㏂ ⑩
𝘝𝘐𝘚𝘈   pp. 17-20 MY **z**
closed Saturday, Sunday and Bank Holidays – **M** a la carte 7.45/11.15 **t.** ⚱ 1.75.

XX **Eatons,** 49 Elizabeth St., SW1W 9PP, ☏ 730 0074 – ㏂ ㏂ ⑩   AX **a**
closed Saturday, Sunday and Bank Holidays – **M** a la carte 4.95/6.50 **s.** ⚱ 1.75.

XX **Gran Paradiso,** 52 Wilton Rd, SW1V 1DE, ☏ 828 5818, Italian rest. – ㏂ ㏂ ⑩ 𝘝𝘐𝘚𝘈 BX **a**
closed Saturday lunch, Sunday, Easter, Christmas and Bank Holidays – **M** a la carte 5.05/
7.05 **t.** ⚱ 1.25.

XX **La Fontana,** 101 Pimlico Rd, SW1W 8PH, ☏ 730 6630, Italian rest. – ㏂ ⑩
closed Saturday lunch and Sunday – **M** a la carte 6.00/8.40 ⚱ 1.80.   pp. 24 and 25 FT **o**

X **Tate Gallery Rest.,** Tate Gallery, Millbank, SW1P 4RG, ☏ 834 6754, « Rex Whistler
murals », English rest.   pp. 17-20 NY **c**
closed Sunday, Good Friday, 24 to 26 December and 31 December-1 January – **M** (lunch
only) a la carte 6.25/10.70 **t.** ⚱ 2.55.

X **Mimmo d'Ischia,** 61 Elizabeth St., SW1W 9PP, ☏ 730 5406, Italian rest. – ㏂ ㏂ ⑩ 𝘝𝘐𝘚𝘈
closed Sunday and Bank Holidays – **M** 10.00 ⚱ 1.40.   AX **o**

X **Pimlico,** 89 Pimlico Rd, SW1W 9PH, ☏ 730 5323, Italian Bistro – ㏂ ⑩
                                                                            pp. 24 and 25 FT **c**
closed Tuesday lunch and Monday – **M** a la carte 5.10/7.10 **t.** ⚱ 1.75.

X **La Poule au Pot,** 231 Ebury St., SW1W 8UT, ☏ 730 7763, French Bistro – ㏂ 𝘝𝘐𝘚𝘈
closed Sunday and Bank Holidays – **M** a la carte 5.15/7.40 ⚱ 3.00   pp. 17-20 KY **n**

X **Bumbles,** 16 Buckingham Palace Rd, SW1W 0QP, ☏ 828 2903, Bistro – ㏂ ㏂ ⑩ 𝘝𝘐𝘚𝘈
closed Saturday lunch, Sunday and Bank Holidays – **M** a la carte 4.60/6.35 **t.** BV **c**

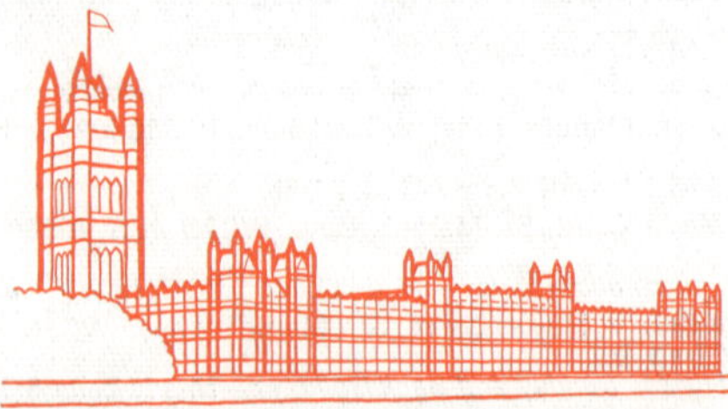

CAR DEALERS AND REPAIRERS

GARAGISTES RÉPARATEURS

OFFICINE MECCANICHE

REPARATURWERKSTÄTTEN

BOROUGH

BARNET

ALFA ROMEO, VOLVO
205 Regents Park Rd
☏ 346 6616
DAIMLER, JAGUAR, ROVER
Lyttleton Rd
☏ 458 7111

PEUGEOT
Hendon Way
☏ 202 6105
RENAULT
Finchley Lane
☏ 203 1145

BRENT

AUSTIN-MORRIS
28/30 Watford Rd
☏ 904 4567
BRITISH LEYLAND, FORD
Neasden Lane
☏ 450 8000

CITROEN
Abbey Rd, Park Royal
☏ 965 7757
TALBOT
Watford Rd
☏ 904 0971

BROMLEY

CITROEN, LANCIA, MERCEDES-BENZ
Bromley Hill
☏ 460 1194
FORD
Masons Hill
☏ 460 9101

VW, AUDI
10 Masons Hill
☏ 460 4693

CAMDEN

CITROEN
265 Finchley Rd
☏ 435 8532
CITROEN
133B Upper St., Islington
☏ 226 3437
DATSUN
617 Finchley Rd
☏ 435 2254

FIAT, ALFA-ROMEO
Randolph St.
☏ 485 8716
FORD
591 Commercial Rd
☏ 790 1851
PEUGEOT
93/103 Drummond St.
☏ 388 5303

CROYDON

FORD
15/19 Brighton Rd
☏ 686 8888
MERCEDES-BENZ, VW, AUDI
375/379 Brighton Rd
☏ 681 3881

PEUGEOT
468/472 Purley Way
☏ 681 2600
RENAULT
117 Whitehorse Rd
☏ 684 5591

EALING

CITROEN, PEUGEOT
Western Av.
☏ 992 5181
DAF
Woodstock Av.
☏ 840 1661

RENAULT
Western Av.
☏ 998 1515
TALBOT, HILLMAN, HUMBER, SUNBEAM
Hastings Rd
☏ 567 1475

ENFIELD

DAF, LADA, RELIANT, SUBARU
Cornwall Rd
☏ 428 1985

PEUGEOT
70/76 London Rd
☏ 363 3950

GREENWICH

PEUGEOT
Footscray Rd
☏ 850 2889

RENAULT
2/12 Dorset Rd
☏ 857 2231

HAMMERSMITH

COLT MITSUBISHI, VOLVO
181-183 Warwick Rd
☏ 370 3152

HARINGEY

BEDFORD, VAUXHALL
Tottenham Lane
☏ 340 8051

HARROW

BRITISH LEYLAND
Marsh Rd
☏ 866 2111

FORD
364/372 High Rd
☏ 427 4377

BOROUGH

HAVERING

CITROEN
132 Hornchurch Rd
℡ Hornchurch 54212
FORD
Jutsums Lane
℡ Romford 45091

VAUXHALL, OPEL
134 London Rd, Romford
℡ Romford 22311

HILLINGDON

ALFA-ROMEO, RENAULT
36 George St., Staines
℡ Staines 61976

FORD
215/218 High St.
℡ Uxbridge 33444

HOUNSLOW

DAF, OPEL, RELIANT
644 Hanworth Rd
℡ 894 1951

PORSCHE
400 London Rd
℡ 560 1011

KENSINGTON & CHELSEA

AUSTIN-MORRIS-MG-ROVER-
TRIUMPH
107/109 Old Brompton Rd
℡ 589 3621
FORD, TALBOT
7/17 Ansdell St.
℡ 937 7207

FORD
133 Old Brompton Rd
℡ 373 3333
PORSCHE
250 Brompton Rd
℡ 581 1234

KINGSTON-UPON-THAMES

VAUXHALL
High St.
℡ 546 7193

LAMBETH

CITROEN, FIAT
64 Wandsworth Rd
℡ 622 0042

VAUXHALL, BEDFORD
80 Clapham Rd
℡ 735 4211

LEWISHAM

BEDFORD, VAUXHALL
2/22 Burnt Ash Rd, Lee Green
℡ 852 1202

MERTON

CITROEN
256 Wimbledon Park Rd
℡ 788 4577
COLT
151 Hartfield Rd
℡ 540 1615
FIAT
213/217 The Broadway
℡ 540 9991

PEUGEOT
165/177 The Broadway
℡ 543 1131
RENAULT
14 Morden Rd
℡ 542 2454

NEWHAM

VAUXHALL
125/131 High St.
℡ 534 6699

RICHMOND-UPON-THAMES

AUSTIN-DAIMLER-JAGUAR-MG-
MORRIS-ROVER-TRIUMPH
174/176 Sheen Rd
℡ 940 6441

TALBOT
1/6 North Rd
℡ 878 0271

SOUTHWARK

BEDFORD, VAUXHALL
100 Enid St.
℡ 237 4661

VW, AUDI
434/450 Old Kent Rd
℡ 231 0031

SUTTON

DAF, VOLVO
56/58 Cheam Rd
℡ 642 2206

TOWER HAMLETS

VAUXHALL
343 Mile End Rd
℡ 980 3633

WALTHAM FOREST

TALBOT
Nightingale Lane
℡ 989 5155

VAUXHALL
400 Hoe St.
℡ 520 8241

WANDSWORTH

AUSTIN-MORRIS-MG-PRINCESS-
ROVER-TRIUMPH, VANDEN PLAS,
VAUXHALL
23/25 East Hill
℡ 870 8711

DAIMLER-JAGUAR-MORRIS-MG-
ROVER-TRIUMPH, ROLLS ROYCE
BENTLEY
100 York Rd
℡ 228 6444

WESTMINSTER

PORSCHE
6 Hall Rd, St. John's Wood
℡ 289 2211

VAUXHALL, BEDFORD
466/490 Edgware Rd
℡ 723 0024

LONG EATON Derbs. 403 404 Q 25 – see Nottingham.

LONGFORD West Midlands 403 404 P 26 – see Coventry.

LONG MELFORD Suffolk 404 W 27 – pop. 2,870 – ECD : Thursday – ☎ 078 725.
See : Holy Trinity Church* 15C.
London 62 – Cambridge 34 – Colchester 18 – Ipswich 24.

- **Bull** (T.H.F.), Hall St., CO10 9JG, ☎ 494, « Part 15C coaching inn » – TV Ⓟ. AE ⓓ VISA
  M 4.00/5.10 **st.** 1.65 – **25 rm** 17.00/25.00 **st.**

LONGNOR Staffs. 403 404 O 24 – pop. 352 – ✉ Buxton – ☎ 029 883.
London 161 – Derby 29 – Manchester 31 – Stoke-on-Trent 22.

- ✕ **Ye Olde Cheshire Cheese,** High St., SK17 0NS, ☎ 218 – Ⓟ. AE ⓓ VISA
  M a la carte 10.00/12.00 **s.** 2.00.

LONG SUTTON Somerset 403 L 30 – pop. 704 – ✉ Langport – ☎ 045 824.
London 136 – Ilchester 6 – Taunton 16.

- ✕✕ Devonshire Arms (Best Western) with rm, TA10 9LP, on B 3165, ☎ 271, – TV Ⓟ
  6 rm.

LOOE Cornwall 403 G 32 – pop. 4,090 – ECD : Thursday – ☎ 050 36.
18 ☎ 050 34 (Widegates) 247, E : 3 m.
The Guildhall, Fore St. ☎ 2072 (summer only).
London 264 – Plymouth 21 – Truro 39.

- **Hannafore Point,** Marine Drive, PL13 2DG, ☎ 3273, ← Looe Bay – Ⓟ. AE ⓓ VISA
  closed first 3 weeks January – **M** (bar lunch) 3.75/5.85 **t.** 1.85 – **40 rm** 15.00/30.00 **t.**
- **Rock Towers,** Hannafore Rd, PL13 2DQ, ☎ 2140, ← Looe Bay – wc Ⓟ. VISA
  M 3.50/5.00 0.80 – **25 rm** 7.00/25.00.
- **Klymiarven,** Barbican Hill, PL13 1BH, ☎ 2333, ← Looe and harbour, heated, –
  wc Ⓟ
  closed January and February – **M** 3.80/5.00 **st.** 1.70 – **15 rm** 8.50/20.60 **st.**
- **Commonwood Manor,** St. Martins Rd, PL13 1LP, ☎ 2929, ←, – Ⓟ. VISA
  March-October – **16 rm** 9.00/20.00 **st.**

  at Sandplace N : 2 ¼ m. on A 387 – ✉ ☎ 050 36 Looe :

- **Polraen Country House,** PL13 1PJ, ☎ 3956, – wc Ⓟ
  closed December and January – **M** (bar lunch) 7.50 **t.** 2.00 – **7 rm** 10.80/16.00 **t.**

  at Duloe N : 3 ½ m. on B 3254 by A 387 – ✉ ☎ 050 36 Looe :

- **Duloe Manor** , PL14 4PW, ☎ 2795, « Country house atmosphere », , heated,
  , park – wc Ⓟ
  3 April-11 October – **M** (bar lunch) 6.50 **s.** 1.80 – **11 rm** 12.50/27.00 **s.**

  at Talland Bay SW : 4 m. off A 387 – ✉ Looe – ☎ 0503 Polperro :

- **Talland Bay** , PL13 2JB, ☎ 72667, Telex 45388, ←, « Country house atmosphere »,
  heated, – TV wc Ⓟ. AE ⓓ
  closed December and January – **M** 5.00/7.25 **t.** 1.75 – **20 rm** 15.00/49.00 **t.**

  at Pelynt W : 4 ¼ m. by A 387 on B 3359 – ✉ Looe – ☎ 050 32 Lanreath :

- Jubilee Inn, PL13 2JZ, ☎ 312, – wc Ⓟ – **9 rm.**

LOSTWITHIEL Cornwall 403 G 32 – pop. 1,905 – ECD : Wednesday – ☎ 0208.
Envir.: Restormel Castle* (ruins 12C-13C) *AC,* N : **1** m.
London 273 – Plymouth 30 – Truro 23.

- **Carotel Motel,** Castle Hill, PL22 0DD, on A 390 ☎ 872223 – TV wc wc Ⓟ. AE
  ⓓ VISA
  M *(closed lunch November to March)* a la carte 3.15/5.15 **s.** 1.70 – 1.60 – **32 rm**
  11.00/16.00 **s.**
- **Royal Talbot,** Liddicoat Rd, PL22 0DG, on A 390 ☎ 872498 – Ⓟ
  M a la carte 5.25/6.50 **t.** 2.00 – **8 rm** 8.50/17.00 **s.**

> Pleasant hotels and restaurants
> are shown in the Guide by a red sign.
>
> Please send us the names
> of anywhere you have enjoyed your stay.
>
> Your Michelin Guide 1981 will be even better.

LOUGHBOROUGH Leics. 403 404 Q 25 – pop. 45,875 – ECD : Wednesday – ✆ 0509.

ʰ₉ Joe Moores Lane ☏ 0509 (Woodhouse Eaves) 890035, S : 6 m.

🛈 John Storer House, Wards End ☏ 30131.

London 117 – Birmingham 41 – Leicester 11 – Nottingham 15.

- 🏨 **King's Head** (Embassy), High St., LE11 2QL, ☏ 214893 – 📶 TV 🅿. 🏊. 🔌 AE ⓘ VISA
  M 4.25/4.70 **st.** – **80 rm** ☲ 12.00/22.00 **st.**

- 🏨 **Cedars**, Cedar Rd, LE11 2AB, ☏ 214459, 🏊 heated, 🚘 – TV ⌷wc 🚻wc 🅿
  closed 26 to 28 December – **M** (dinner only and Sunday lunch) 4.00 **t.** 🍷 2.40 – **34 rm**
  ☲ 11.00/18.00 **t.**

- ⌂ **Sunnyside**, 5 The Coneries, LE11 1D7, ☏ 216217 – 🅿
  11 rm ☲ 5.00/10.00.

- ✗ **Harlequin**, 11 Swan St., LE11 0BJ, ☏ 215235, Italian rest. – AE ⓘ VISA
  closed Sunday and 15 July-1 August – **M** a la carte 5.10/8.30 **s.** 🍷 1.75.

AUSTIN-JAGUAR-MORRIS-ROVER-TRIUMPH Wood-gate ☏ 66771
FORD Derby Rd ☏ 67721

PEUGEOT Nottingham Rd ☏ 67657
RENAULT The Coneries ☏ 214854
VW, AUDI 28 Market St. ☏ 217080

LOUTH Lincs. 404 U 23 – pop. 11,170 – ✆ 0507.

See : St. James' Church* 15C.

ʰ₁₈ Crowtree Lane ☏ 2554.

🛈 Town Hall, Eastgate ☏ 2391.

London 155 – Boston 33 – Grimsby 17 – Lincoln 26.

- 🏨 **King's Head,** Mercer Row, LN11 9JG, ☏ 602965 – 🅿. 🔌 AE ⓘ VISA
  closed 25 and 26 December – **M** (closed Sunday dinner) a la carte 3.40/7.80 **st.** 🍷 1.20 –
  17 rm ☲ 8.60/16.10 **st.**

LOWER BENTHAM North Yorks. – pop. 2,731 (inc. High Bentham) – ✉ Lancaster – ✆ 0468 Bentham.

ʰ₉ Robin Lane ☏ 61018.

London 255 – Kendal 20 – Lancaster 14 – **Leeds** 53.

- ✗ **Stonegate House,** LA2 7DS, ☏ 61362, 🚘 – 🅿. VISA
  closed Tuesday – **M** (dinner only) a la carte 4.15/7.75.

LOWER LIMPLEY STOKE Avon 403 404 M 29 – see Bath.

LOWER PEOVER Cheshire 403 404 M 24 – see Knutsford.

LOWER SLAUGHTER Glos. – see Stow-on-the-Wold.

LOWER SWELL Glos. 403 404 O 28 – see Stow-on-the-Wold.

LOWESTOFT Suffolk 404 Z 26 – pop. 52,267 – ECD : Thursday – ✆ 0502.

🛈 The Esplanade ☏ 65989 – Town Hall, High St. ☏ 62111.

London 116 – Ipswich 43 – Norwich 30.

- 🏨 Victoria, Kirkley Cliff, NR33 0BZ, ☏ 4433, ≼, 🏊 heated – 📶 TV ⌷wc 📱 ♿ 🅿. 🏊
  52 rm.

- 🏨 Royal George, The Esplanade, NR33 0QP, ☏ 65337, ≼, 🏊 heated – 📶 TV ⌷wc 🚻wc 📱
  🅿
  38 rm.

- ⌸ **Windsor,** Kirkley Cliff Rd, NR33 0BY, ☏ 65138, ≼ – ⌷wc 🚻wc
  closed 23 December-2 January – **M** (closed Saturday lunch and Sunday) 4.00 **s.** 🍷 1.70 –
  12 rm ☲ 10.00/20.00 **s.** – P 16.00/24.00 **s.**

  at Kessingland S : 4 m. on A 12 – ✉ ✆ 0502 Lowestoft :

- ✗✗ **Grove Park,** 2 Whites Lane, N33 7TF, ☏ 740063 – 🅿. 🔌 AE ⓘ VISA
  closed Sunday dinner – **M** a la carte 5.25/12.40 **t.** 🍷 1.85.

AUSTIN-DAIMLER-JAGUAR-MORRIS-MG-ROVER-TRIUMPH 97/99 London Rd South ☏ 61711
DATSUN High St. ☏ 65301
FIAT Beccles Rd, Oulton Broad ☏ 63622
FORD Whapload Rd ☏ 3553

MAZDA 2/8 Bridge Rd, Oulton Broad ☏ 3797
RENAULT 9 London Rd ☏ 2783
VAUXHALL London Rd South ☏ 3512
VW, AUDI Cooke Rd, South Lowestoft Industrial Estate ☏ 2583

LOWESWATER Cumbria – pop. 202 – ECD : Thursday – ✉ Cockermouth – ✆ 090 085 Lorton.

London 305 – Carlisle 33 – Keswick 12.

- 🏨 **Scale Hill** ⌂, CA13 9UX, ☏ 232, ≼, 🚘 – ⌷wc 🅿
  22 March-12 November – **M** 4.25/7.50 **st.** 🍷 1.95 – **13 rm** ☲ 12.50/25.00 **st.** –
  P 22.50/25.00 **st.**

LOWFIELD HEATH West Sussex 404 T 30 – see Crawley.

LOWICK GREEN Cumbria – see Ulverston.

LOW LAITHE North Yorks. – see Harrogate.

LUDLOW Salop **403** L 26 – pop. 6,780 – ECD : Thursday – ✆ 0584.
See : Castle* (ruins 11C-16C) *AC* – Parish Church* 13C – Feathers Hotel* early 17C – Broad Street* 17C. **Envir :** Stokesay Castle* (13C) *AC*, NW : 6 ½ m.

📁 Bromfield ☎ 058 477 (Bromfield) 285, N : 2 m on A 49.

🛈 County Museum, 13 Castle St. ☎ 3857 (summer only).

London 162 – Birmingham 39 – Hereford 24 – Shrewsbury 29.

🏨 **Feathers**, Bull Ring, SY8 1AA, ☎ 2919, « Part Elizabethan house » – 📺 ⌂wc ☎ 🅿. 🔲 AE ① VISA
M a la carte 4.85/7.25 **st.** ▯ 1.75 – **31 rm** ⌸ 15.00/34.00 **st.** – P 25.00/35.00 **st.**

🏨 **Angel**, Broad St., SY8 1NG, ☎ 2531 – ⌂wc 🅿. 🔲 ① VISA
M *(closed Sunday dinner)* 3.00/5.00 **t.** ▯ 1.50 – **17 rm** ⌸ 9.00/22.50 **t.**

🏨 **Overton Grange**, SY8 4AD, S : 1 ½ m. on A 49 ☎ 3500, 🐎 – ⌂wc 🅿
closed mid January-February – **M** (bar lunch) a la carte 3.30/5.90 **st.** ▯ 2.00 – **17 rm** ⌸ 10.00/20.50 **st.**

🏠 **The Croft**, Dinham, SY8 1EJ, ☎ 2076
8 rm ⌸ 9.00/11.00 **t.**

🏠 **Cecil**, Sheet Rd, SY8 1LH, ☎ 2442, 🐎 – 🛗 🅿. 🔲 VISA
10 rm ⌸ 6.00/12.00 **st.**

🏠 **The Cliff**, Dinham, SY8 2JE, ☎ 2063, 🐎 – 🍴 🅿. VISA
15 rm ⌸ 8.50/18.00 **s.**

AUSTIN-DAIMLER-JAGUAR-LAND ROVER-MORRIS-MG-ROVER-TRIUMPH Corve St. ☎ 2301

LUNDY (Isle of) Devon **403** FG 30.

🚢 to Ilfracombe (Lundy Co.) 1-3 weekly (2 h 30 mn).

Hotels see : Ilfracombe.

LUSTLEIGH Devon **403** I 32 – see Moretonhampstead.

LUTON Beds. **404** S 28 – pop. 161,405 – ECD : Wednesday – ✆ 0582.
See : Luton Hoo* (Wernher Collection**) and park* *AC*.

📁 Stockwood Park, London Rd ☎ 31421, S : 1 m. on A 6.

📁 South Beds, Warden Hills ☎ 55201, N : 2 m.

✈ Luton International Airport ☎ 36061 ext 66, E : 1 ½ m.

🛈 Central Library, St. George's Sq. ☎ 32629, 25 George St. ☎ 413237.

London 36 – Cambridge 35 – Ipswich 86 – Oxford 43 – Southend-on-Sea 70.

🏨 **Strathmore** (Thistle), Arndale Centre, LU1 2TR, ☎ 34199, Telex 825763 – 🛗 📺 ⅙ 🛎.
🔲 AE ① VISA
M *(closed Saturday lunch)* 7.10/7.55 **st.** ▯ 1.75 – ⌸ 3.00 – **151 rm** 23.00/30.00 **st.** – P 23.10/35.00 **st.**

🏨 Luton Eurocrest (Crest), Dunstable Rd, Waller Av., LU4 9RU, NW : 2 m. on A 505
☎ 55911, Telex 825048 – 🛗 📺 ⌂wc ☎ ⅙ 🅿. 🛎. 🔲 AE ① VISA
⌸ 2.80 – **99 rm** 21.00/27.90 **st.**

🏨 Luton Crest Motel (Crest), 641 Dunstable Rd, LU4 8RQ, NW : 2 ¾ m. on A 505
☎ 55955 – 🛗 📺 ⌂wc ☎ 🅿. 🛎. 🔲 AE ① VISA
⌸ 2.40 – **139 rm** 19.20/25.90.

AUSTIN-DAIMLER-JAGUAR-MORRIS-MG-ROVER-TRIUMPH-WOLSELEY 691 Dunstable Rd ☎ 51408
AUSTIN-DAIMLER-JAGUAR-MORRIS-ROVER-TRIUMPH Park St. West ☎ 411311
BMW 82/88 Marsh Rd ☎ 56622
BRITISH LEYLAND Leagrave Rd ☎ 51221

DATSUN 619 Hitchin Rd ☎ 35332
FORD 326/340 Dunstable Rd ☎ 31133
RENAULT Castle St. ☎ 28461
VAUXHALL 15 Hitchin Rd ☎ 22268
VAUXHALL Memorial Rd ☎ 52577
VAUXHALL 540/550 Dunstable Rd ☎ 55944

LUTTERWORTH Leics. **403 404** Q 26 – pop. 5,965 – ECD : Wednesday – ✉ Leicester – ✆ 045 55.

📁 Ullesthorpe ☎ 0455 (Leire) 209021, NW : 3 m.

London 92 – Birmingham 34 – Leicester 15 – Northampton 24.

🏨 **Denbigh Arms**, 24 High St., LE17 4AD, ☎ 3537 – 📺 ⌂wc 🅿
closed 5 days at Christmas – M 3.90/4.35 – ⌸ 2.00 – **25 rm** 7.80/20.50.

TALBOT Bitteswell Rd ☎ 2177

LYDFORD Devon **403** H 32 – pop. 2,241 – ECD : Thursday – ✉ Okehampton – ✆ 082 282.
Envir. : Gorge* *AC*, SW : 1 ½ m.

London 232 – Exeter 31 – Plymouth 22.

🏨 **Castle Inn**, EX20 4BH, ☎ 242 – 🅿
closed Christmas Day – M (buffet lunch) a la carte 3.50/6.80 **t.** ▯ 1.35 – **5 rm** ⌸ 8.00/15.00 **st.**

LYDNEY Glos. **403** **404** M 28 – pop. 5,990 – ECD : Thursday – ✉ Gloucester – ☎ 059 44.
ⓝ ☎ 2614.
London 140 – Bristol 26 – Gloucester 19 – Newport 25.

🏛 Feathers, High St., GL15 5DL, ☎ 2826 – 🛏wc Ⓟ – **16 rm.**

AUSTIN-MG-ROVER-TRIUMPH Newerne St. ☎ 2446　　RENAULT Gloucester Rd ☎ 2364
AUSTIN-MORRIS-MG High St. ☎ 2481　　TOYOTA Swan Rd ☎ 2131

LYME REGIS Dorset **403** L 31 – pop. 3,403 – ECD : Thursday – ☎ 029 74.
ⓝ Timber Hill ☎ 2043.
🛈 The Guildhall, Bridge St. ☎ 2138.

London 160 – Dorchester 25 – Exeter 31 – Taunton 27.

🏛 **Alexandra,** Pound St., DT7 3HZ, ☎ 2010, ⩽, 🚗 – 🛏wc 🛁wc Ⓟ. ⚑ AE ⓪ VISA
February-October – **M** 3.40/5.20 **st.** – **23 rm** ⌑ 15.00/34.00 **st.**

🏛 **High Cliff** ⑤, Sidmouth Rd, DT7 3EH, ☎ 2300, ⩽ sea and coastline, 🚗 – 🛏wc 🛁wc
🚙 Ⓟ
April-November – **M** 4.50/5.50 **t.** ▯ 1.50 – **12 rm** ⌑ 15.90/33.00 **st.**

🏛 **Mariners,** Silver St., DT7 3HS, ☎ 2753, 🚗 – 🛏wc 🛁wc Ⓟ. ⚑ AE ⓪ VISA
closed 27 December-7 March – **M** 3.45/6.15 **st.** ▯ 1.75 – **16 rm** ⌑ (dinner included)
18.60/37.60 **st.**

↑ **Kersbrook,** Pound Rd, DT7 3HX, ☎ 2596, 🚗 – Ⓟ
March-mid November – **9 rm** ⌑ 6.85/16.70.

✗ **Toni's,** 14-15 Monmouth St., DT7 3PX, ☎ 2079, Italian rest. – ⓪ VISA
Easter-September – **M** *(closed Sunday)* (dinner only) a la carte 5.55/8.60 **t.** ▯ 2.00.

at Rousdon (Devon) W : 3 m. on A 3052 – ✉ ☎ 029 74 Lyme Regis :

🏛 **Orchard Country,** DT7 3XW, ☎ 2974, 🚗 – 🛏wc 🛁wc Ⓟ. AE ⓪
closed November – **M** (lunch by arrangement) 3.20/4.25 **t.** ▯ 1.65 – **15 rm** ⌑ 7.20/
16.40 **t.**

at Uplyme (Devon) NW : 1 ¼ m. on A 3070 – ✉ ☎ 029 74 Lyme Regis :

🏛 **Devon,** DT7 3TQ, ☎ 3231, ⌇ heated, 🚗, park – 🛏wc Ⓟ. AE VISA
Mid March-October – **M** 4.60/5.75 **st.** ▯ 2.00 – **21 rm** ⌑ 16.50/33.00 **st.**

LYMINGTON Hants. **403** **404** P 31 – pop. 35,733 – ECD : Wednesday – ☎ 0590.
⛴ to the Isle of Wight : Yarmouth (Sealink) Monday-Thursday 15 daily ; Friday, Saturday-
Sunday 7-28 daily (30 mn).
London 104 – Bournemouth 18 – Southampton 19 – Winchester 32.

🏛 **Stanwell House,** 15 High St., SO4 9AA, ☎ 77123 – 📺 🛏wc 📞. ⚑ AE ⓪ VISA
closed 26 to 29 December – **M** (rest. see **Railings**) – **18 rm** ⌑ 12.00/22.50 **st.**

↑ **Farino,** 53 New St., SO4 9BP, ☎ 77140 – Ⓟ
8 rm ⌑ 7.50/15.00 **t.**

✗✗ **Railings** (at Stanwell House H.), 15 High St., SO4 9AA, ☎ 77124 – ⚑ AE ⓪ VISA
closed 26 to 29 December – **M** a la carte 8.80/10.40 **st.** ▯ 2.50.

✗ **Limpets,** 9 Gosport St., SO4 9BG, ☎ 75595, French rest.
closed Sunday dinner in winter, Monday and November – **M** (dinner only and Sunday
lunch in winter) a la carte 6.00/8.10 **t.** ▯ 2.20.

✗ **Flounders,** 5 Quay St., SO4 8LS, ☎ 77364, Bistro
closed Monday – **M** (dinner only) a la carte 5.00/7.75 **t.** ▯ 2.00.

at Mount Pleasant NW : 2 m. off A 337 – ✉ Lymington – ☎ 0590 Sway :

🏛 **Passford House** ⑤, SO4 0FX, ☎ 682398, ✗⚲, ⌇ heated, 🚗, park – 📺 🛏wc 📞 Ⓟ. AE
M 3.50/5.50 ▯ 1.20 – **51 rm** ⌑ 17.00/30.00 – P 23.00/26.00.

at Sway NW : 4 m. off A 337 on B 3055 – ✉ Lymington – ☎ 059 068 (4 fig.) or 0590
(6 fig.) Sway :

🏛 **White Rose,** Station Rd, SO4 0BA, ☎ 2754, ⌇ heated, 🚗, park – 📶 📺 🛏wc Ⓟ. ⚑
VISA
M 3.25/4.60 **t.** ▯ 1.75 – **13 rm** ⌑ 11.00/23.00 **t.**

🏛 **Pine Trees** ⑤, Mead End Rd, SO4 0EE, ☎ 682288, 🚗 – 🛁wc Ⓟ. AE VISA
closed 25 and 26 December – **M** (dinner only) 8.50 **st.** ▯ 1.65 – ⌑ 1.00 – **7 rm** 16.50/
25.00 **st.**

AUSTIN-MORRIS-MG-WOLSELEY 76 High St. ☎ 2378　　VAUXHALL Bath Rd ☎ 3981
FIAT Sway ☎ 2212

LYMM Cheshire **403** **404** M 23 – pop. 8,450 – ECD : Wednesday – ☎ 092 575.
ⓝ Whitbarrow Rd ☎ 2177.
London 193 – Chester 24 – Liverpool 23 – Manchester 15.

🏛 **Dingle,** 26 Rectory Lane, WA13 0AH, ☎ 2297, 🚗 – 📺 🛏wc 🛁wc 📞 Ⓟ. ⚑ AE ⓪ VISA
M *(closed Saturday lunch and Sunday)* 5.25/5.50 **t.** ▯ 3.00 – **31 rm** ⌑ 17.80/22.70 **t.**

LYNDHURST Hants. 403 404 P 31 – pop. 2,948 – ECD : Wednesday – ☎ 042 128.
See : New Forest★.

🏌 New Forest ☎ 2450.

🛈 Main Car Park ☎ 2269 (summer only).

London 95 – Bournemouth 20 – Southampton 10 – Winchester 23.

🏨 **Crown,** 9 High St., SO4 7NF, ☎ 2722, 🚗 – 🛗 TV ℗. 🛆. 🔄 AE ⓞ VISA
M 6.15/7.40 t. ⋅ 1.80 – **38 rm** ⊇ 16.00/28.25 t. – P 26.65/28.50 t.

🏨 **Parkhill** ⌇, Beaulieu Rd, SO4 7FZ, SE : 1 ¼ m. off B 3056, ☎ 2944, ≼, « Tastefully
furnished country house », ⌇ heated, ⌇, 🚗, park – TV 🛏wc ☎ ℗. 🔄 AE ⓞ VISA
closed January – M 5.00/8.00 t. ⋅ 2.50 – **18 rm** ⊇ 22.85/45.70 t. – P 27.50/32.85 t.

🏨 **Lyndhurst Park** (Best Western), High St., SO4 7BG, ☎ 2824, ⌇ heated, 🚗 – 🛗 TV
🛏wc ☎ ℗. 🛆. 🔄 AE ⓞ VISA
M (buffet lunch) 5.60 t. ⋅ 2.10 – ⊇ 1.35 – **63 rm** 13.00/24.00 t.

🏨 **David Bell's Forest Lodge,** Pike's Hill, Romsey Rd, SO4 7AS, ☎ 2365, ⌇ heated,
🚗 – TV 🛏wc 🛏wc ℗. 🔄 ⓞ VISA
M (bar lunch) 4.50/6.50 st. – **13 rm** ⊇ 12.00/26.00 t.

🏠 **Evergreens,** Romsey Rd, SO4 7AR, ☎ 2175, ⌇ heated, 🚗 – 🛏wc ℗
closed 24 December-3 January – M 3.75/5.00 st. ⋅ 1.75 – **18 rm** ⊇ 9.25/22.00 st.

🏠 **Ormonde House,** Southampton Rd, SO4 7BN, ☎ 2806 – 🛏wc ℗
17 rm ⊇ 7.00/19.00 st.

AUSTIN-MORRIS-MG-WOLSELEY High St. ☎ 2861   OPEL Romsey Rd ☎ 2609

LYNMOUTH Devon 403 I 30 – see Lynton.

LYNTON Devon 403 I 30 – pop. 1,981 – ECD : Thursday – ☎ 059 85.
See : Lynmouth (site★).

🛈 Lee Rd ☎ 2225.

London 206 – Exeter 59 – Taunton 44.

🏨 **Lynton Cottage** ⌇, North Walk, EX35 6ED, ☎ 2342, ≼, 🚗 – 🛏wc 🛏wc ℗
April-September – M (bar lunch) 3.00/5.60 st. ⋅ 1.45 – **22 rm** ⊇ 10.60/20.50 s. –
P 16.50/18.20 s.

🏠 **Crown,** Sinai Hill, EX35 6AR, ☎ 2253 – 🛏wc ℗. 🔄 ⓞ VISA
M a la carte 4.10/7.40 st. ⋅ 1.75 – **19 rm** ⊇ 10.85/32.10 st.

🏠 **Seawood** ⌇, North Walk, EX35 6HJ, ☎ 2272, ≼ – 🛏wc ℗
29 March-5 October – **12 rm** ⊇ 9.00/18.00.

🏠 **Chough's Nest** ⌇, North Walk, EX35 6HJ, ☎ 3315, ≼ – 🛏wc
Easter-mid October – **11 rm** ⊇ (dinner included) 10.00/20.00 s.

🏠 **The Hoe** ⌇, North Walk, EX35 6HJ, ☎ 2293, ≼ Lynmouth Bay – 🛏wc ℗
Easter-mid October – **11 rm** ⊇ 7.00/16.00 s.

🏠 **Pine Lodge** ⌇, Lynway, EX35 6AX, ☎ 3230, ≼ – ℗
10 rm ⊇ 7.00/14.00 s.

at Lynmouth – ✉ Lynmouth – ☎ 059 85 Lynton :

🏨 **Tors** ⌇, EX35 6NA, ☎ 3236, ≼ Bay, ⌇ heated – 🛗 🛏wc ℗
39 rm.

🏠 **Bath,** EX35 6EL, ☎ 2238 – 🛏wc ℗. 🔄 AE ⓞ
April-October – M 3.00/5.00 st. ⋅ 2.30 – **25 rm** ⊇ 6.70/22.70 t.

LYTHAM ST. ANNE'S Lancs. 986 ㉓ – pop. 40,299 – ECD : Wednesday – ☎ 0253 St. Anne's.
🏌 Lytham Hall Park, ☎ 736741, E : 2 m. – 🏌 Ballam Rd ☎ 734782.

🛈 St. Anne's Sq. ☎ 721222/725610.

London 237 – Blackpool 7 – Liverpool 44 – Preston 13.

🏨 Grand (Crest), 77 South Promenade, FY8 1NB, ☎ 722155 – 🛗 🛏wc ℗. 🔄 AE ⓞ VISA
37 rm ⊇ 13.00/22.60 st.

at Lytham SE : 3 m. – ✉ ☎ 0253 Lytham :

🏨 **Clifton Arms** (Best Western) West Beach, FY8 5QJ, ☎ 739898 – 🛗 TV ℗. 🛆. 🔄 AE
VISA
M 4.60/5.80 t. – **43 rm** ⊇ 19.00/36.00 t. – P 25.00/27.00 st.

AUSTIN-DAIMLER-MG-WOLSELEY Kings Rd ☎ 728051   BRITISH LEYLAND Henry St. ☎ 736670

MACCLESFIELD Cheshire 403 404 N 24 – pop. 28,210 – ☎ 0625.
🛈 Town Hall, Market Pl. ☎ 21955 ext. 114/5.

London 186 – Chester 38 – Manchester 18 – Stoke on trent 21.

✕ **Oliver's French Bistro,** 101 Chestergate, SK11 6DU, ☎ 32003, Bistro
closed Sunday and Monday – M a la carte 6.15/8.70 t. ⋅ 1.75.

MACHYNLLETH Powys **403** I 26 – pop. 2,030 – ECD: Thursday – ☎ 0654.
Envir.: NW: Cader Idris (road★★ to Cader Idris: Cregenneu lakes) – SE: Llyfnant Valley★ via Glaspwll.

ⁱₛ Maes-y-Gollen ⍶ 2000 N: 1 m. off A 489.

ℹ Wales Tourist Office, Owain Glyndwr ⍶ 2401.

London 220 – Shrewsbury 56 – Welshpool 37.

🏨 **Wynnstay** (T.H.F.), Maengwyn St., SY80 8AE, ⍶ 2003 – 📺 ⌷wc 🅿. 🔼 AE ⓪ VISA
M 3.75/4.25 st. ⋀ 1.65 – **26 rm** ⌷ 13.50/22.00 st.

at Eglwysfach SW: 6 m. off A 487 – ✉ Machynlleth – ☎ 065 474 Glandyfi:

🏨 **Ynyshir Hall** ⋙, SY20 8TA, ⍶ 209, ⋖, « Country house in large gardens », park –
⌷wc 🛁wc 🅿. 🔼 AE ⓪ VISA
M (bar lunch) 5.50/7.50 ⋀ 1.65 – **10 rm** ⌷ 13.50/26.50.

at Pennal (Gwynedd) W: 4 ½ m. on A 493 – ✉ Machynlleth (Powys) – ☎ 065 475 Pennal:

🏠 **Llugwy** ⋙, SY20 9JX, ⍶ 228, ⋖, ⋏, 🚗 – 📺 ⌷wc 🅿. 🔼 AE ⓪ VISA
M (bar lunch) a la carte 6.25/8.25 ⋀ 1.45 – **10 rm** ⌷ 13.00/26.00 – P approx. 17.50.

🔅 **Riverside**, SY20 9DW, ⍶ 285, 🚗 – 🅿. 🔼 VISA
M (bar lunch Monday to Saturday) a la carte approx. 7.10 – **7 rm** ⌷ 12.50/17.50.

AUSTIN-MORRIS-MG-PRINCESS-ROVER-TRIUMPH ⍶ 21008

MADINGLEY Cambs. **404** U 27 – see Cambridge.

MAENORBYR Dyfed – see Manorbier.

MAIDENCOMBE Devon **403** J 32 – see Torquay.

MAIDENHEAD Berks. **404** R 29 – pop. 45,288 – ECD: Thursday – ☎ 0628.
ℹ Central Library, St. Ives Rd ⍶ 25657.

London 35 – Oxford 32 – Reading 13.

🏨 **Maidenhead Eurocrest** (Crest), Shoppenhangers Rd, SL6 2RA, ⍶ 23444, Telex 847502,
🚗 – ⎸ 📺 ⌷wc ☎ ♿ 🅿. ⚱. 🔼 AE ⓪ VISA
M (see rest. Shoppenhangers Manor) – ⌷ 2.80 – **193 rm** 22.60/29.00.

🏠 **Bear** (Anchor), 8-10 High St., SL6 1QJ, ⍶ 25183, Group Telex 858875 – 🛁. 🔼 AE ⓪ VISA
M 3.50 – **12 rm** ⌷ 15.50/21.00 st.

XXX Shoppenhangers Manor (Crest) (at Maidenhead Eurocrest), Manor Lane, SL6 2RA,
⍶ 23444. 🚗 – 🅿. 🔼 AE ⓪ VISA.

XX **La Riva**, Ray Mead Rd, SL6 8NJ, ⍶ 33522 – 🅿. 🔼 AE ⓪ VISA
closed Sunday – M a la carte 7.20/10.70 t.

XX **Chez Michel et Valérie**, 7 Glynwood House, Bridge Av., SL6 1RS, ⍶ 22450, French rest.
closed Sunday, Monday, Good Friday and last 3 weeks August – M a la carte 5.10/7.75 t. ⋀ 3.00.

AUSTIN-MORRIS-MG-WOLSELEY Braywick Rd ⍶ 25321
BMW Altwood Rd ⍶ 37611
FIAT Woodlands Park ⍶ 062 882 (Littlewick Green) 3211
FORD Bath Rd, Taplow ⍶ 29711
PEUGEOT Furze Platt ⍶ 27524
RENAULT 7 Bath Rd ⍶ 21331
ROLLS ROYCE 128 Bridge Rd ⍶ 33188

MAIDSTONE Kent **404** V 30 – pop. 70,987 – ECD: Wednesday – ☎ 0622.
See: All Saints' Church★ – Carriage Museum★ *AC* – Chillington Manor (Museum and Art Gallery★). Envir.: Leeds Castle★ *AC*, SE: 4 ½ m. – Aylesford (The Friars carmelite priory: great courtyard★) NW: 3 ½ m.

ⁱₛ Leeds Castle ⍶ 062 780 (Hollingbourne) 467, E: 5 m.

ℹ The Gatehouse, Old Palace Gardens ⍶ 671361.

London 38 – Brighton 51 – Cambridge 86 – Colchester 73 – Croydon 32 – Dover 43 – Southend-on-Sea 47.

🏨 **Royal Star** (Embassy), 15 High St., ME14 1JA, ⍶ 55721 – 📺 ⌷wc 🛁wc ☎ 🅿. ⚱. 🔼
AE ⓪ VISA
M 5.05 st. ⋀ 1.60 – **37 rm** ⌷ 16.50/22.00 st. – P 26.60 st.

XX Dino's, 14 London Rd, ME16 8QL, ⍶ 52460, Italian rest. – 🅿.

MICHELIN Branch, St. Michaels Close, Forstal Trading Estate, Aylesford, ME20 7HR, ⍶ 76228.

AUSTIN-DAIMLER-JAGUAR-MORRIS-MG-ROVER-TRIUMPH Bircholt Rd ⍶ 65461
AUSTIN-MORRIS-MG-ROVER Ashford Rd ⍶ 54744
FIAT 29 Union St. ⍶ 52071
FORD Ashford Rd ⍶ 56781
MERCEDES-BENZ 215/233 Sutton Rd ⍶ 55531
OPEL-VAUXHALL Park Wood, Sutton Rd ⍶ 55531
RENAULT Sutton Rd ⍶ 50881
TALBOT Mill St. ⍶ 53333
VAUXHALL London Rd, Ditton ⍶ 0732 (West Malling) 843227

MALDON Essex **404** W 28 – pop. 13,891 – ECD: Wednesday – ✆ 0621.

London 42 – Chelmsford 9 – Colchester 17.

   🏨 **Blue Boar** (T.H.F.), Silver St., CM9 7QE, ✆ 52681 – 📺 🛏wc ☎ **P**. 🔼 AE ⓪ 𝐕𝐈𝐒𝐀
       M 4.25/4.80 **st.** ⬗ 1.85 – **25 rm** ⬚ 16.50/21.00 **st.**

   ✕ **Francine's,** 1a High St., CM9 7PB, ✆ 56605 – **P**. 🔼 𝐕𝐈𝐒𝐀
       closed Saturday lunch, Sunday, Monday and 25-26 December – **M** a la carte approx. 4.95
       ⬗ 1.50.

ALFA ROMEO Forstal Rd, Aylesford ✆ 43382
AUSTIN-MORRIS-MG-ROVER-TRIUMPH- WOLSELEY
Heybridge ✆ 52468
BMW, FIAT Spital Rd ✆ 52131
CITROEN Bow Rd, ✆ 812358
FORD 1 Spital Rd ✆ 2345

PEUGEOT A 20 Parkfield ✆ 0732 (West Malling)
840000
RELIANT Knightrider St. ✆ 58663
VAUXHALL 127/131 High St. ✆ 52424
VOLVO Looe Rd ✆ 43382
VW, AUDI Upper Stone St. ✆ 50821

MALLWYD Gwynedd **403** I 25 – pop. 459 – ✉ Machynlleth (Powys) – ✆ 065 04 Dinas Mawddwy.

Envir. : N: Road* from Dinas Mawddwy to Pandy – Aberangell Clipiau (site*) SE : 3 m. – NW : Road* from Dinas Mawddwy to Cross Foxes Hotel.

London 209 – Aberystwyth 29 – Dolgellau 12 – Shrewsbury 45.

   🏠 **Brigands Inn,** SY20 9HJ, ✆ 208, ⚲, 🚗 – 🛏wc **P**. 🔼
       closed November – **M** (bar lunch) 5.50 **t.** – **12 rm** ⬚ 8.75/18.50 **t.**

MALMESBURY Wilts. **403** **404** N 29 – pop. 2,527 – ECD: Thursday – ✆ 066 62.
See : Abbey Church* 12C-14C (porch**). **Envir. :** Badminton House* (17C) *AC*, SW: 10 m. – Dodington House* (18C) *AC*, SW: 15 m.

London 108 – Bristol 28 – Gloucester 24 – Swindon 19.

   🏨 **Old Bell,** Abbey Row, SN16 0BW, ✆ 2344, 🚗 – 📺 🛏wc **P**. 🏊. 🔼 AE ⓪ 𝐕𝐈𝐒𝐀
       M a la carte 6.00/8.00 **t.** ⬗ 2.00 – **19 rm** ⬚ 14.50/28.00 **t.**

   ✕ **Suffolk Arms,** Tetbury Hill, SN16 9JW, on B 4014 ✆ 2271 – **P**. 🔼 𝐕𝐈𝐒𝐀
       closed Sunday dinner, Christmas Day and Bank Holidays – **M** a la carte 5.35/8.75 **st.** ⬗ 1.75.

   at Easton Grey W: 2 m. on B 4040 – ✉ ✆ 066 62 Malmesbury:

   🏨 **Whatley Manor** ⚶, SN16 0RB, ✆ 2888, ≼, « Tasteful decor and furnishings », ⯊ heated,
       ⚲, 🚗, park – 📺 🛏wc ☎ **P**. 🔼 AE
       closed 3 weeks January – **M** *(closed Sunday dinner to non-residents)* (lunch by arrange-
       ment) 5.50/7.00 **t.** ⬗ 1.40 – **12 rm** ⬚ 30.00/45.00 **t.**

BRITISH LEYLAND Bristol Rd ✆ 2211
                                            PEUGEOT Gloucester Rd ✆ 3434

MALTON North Yorks. **986** ㉔ – pop. 3,986 – ECD: Thursday – ✆ 0653.
Envir. : Castle Howard** (18C) *AC*, SW: 6 m. – Flamingo Park Zoo* *AC*, N : 4 ½ m.

🏌 Welham Park ✆ 2959.

London 229 – Kingston-upon-Hull 36 – Scarborough 24 – York 17.

   🏠 **Talbot** (T.H.F.), Yorkersgate, YO17 0AJ, ✆ 4031 – 📺 🛏wc ☎ ⬳ **P**. 🔼 AE ⓪ 𝐕𝐈𝐒𝐀
       M 3.70/5.30 **st.** ⬗ 1.65 – **24 rm** ⬚ 13.50/21.00 **st.**

AUSTIN-MORRIS-MG Wintringham ✆ 09442 (Rilling-
ton) 242
AUSTIN-MORRIS-MG-ROVER-TRIUMPH 4 Welham
Rd ✆ 2165

BMW Church St., Norton ✆ 2252
FORD Scarborough Rd ✆ 2331
VAUXHALL York Rd ✆ 2176
VOLVO Horse Market Rd ✆ 3019

MALVERN Heref. and Worc. **403** **404** N 27 – pop. 30,340 – ECD: Wednesday – ✆ 068 45.
See : Great Malvern (Priory Church* 11C). – 🏌 Wood Farm, Malvern Wells ✆ 3905 **A**.

🛈 Winter Gardens, Grange Rd ✆ 4700.

London 127 – Birmingham 34 – Cardiff 66 – Gloucester 24.

Plan on next page

   🏠 Gold Hill, Avenue Rd, WR14 3AL, ✆ 4000, 🚗 – 🛗 🛏wc 🚽wc **P** – **21 rm.**   **B a**

   ⌂ **Walmer Lodge,** 49 Abbey Rd, WR14 3HH, ✆ 4139, ≼, 🚗 – 🛏wc 🚽wc **P**   **A n**
       closed 3 weeks October and 26 December-2 January – **M** (dinner only) a la carte 4.40/
       5.95 ⬗ 1.75 – **10 rm** ⬚ 6.00/16.00.

   ⌂ **Thornbury,** 16 Avenue Rd, WR14 3AR, ✆ 2278, 🚗 – **P**   **B c**
       M (bar lunch) 3.50/5.00 ⬗ 2.00 – **20 rm** ⬚ 7.60/14.15 **st.** – P 13.40/14.90 **st.**

   ⌂ **Cotford,** Graham Rd, WR14 2JW, ✆ 2427, 🚗 – 🛏wc 🚽wc **P**   **B o**
       closed November – **14 rm** ⬚ 8.00/17.00 **st.**

   ⌂ **Bredon House,** 34 Worcester Rd, WR14 4AA, ✆ 5323, ≼ – **P**   **B n**
       8 rm ⬚ 6.50/13.00 **st.**

   ⌂ **Long Mynd,** 23 Avenue Rd, WR14 3AY, ✆ 5922 – **P**. 𝐕𝐈𝐒𝐀   **B e**
       8 rm ⬚ 7.00/14.00 **st.**

   ✕✕ **Charlie's,** 15 Worcester Rd, WR14 4QY, ✆ 5064 – 🔼 AE ⓪ 𝐕𝐈𝐒𝐀   **B i**
       closed Sunday, Monday and 25 to 31 December – **M** a la carte 5.40/8.70 **st.** ⬗ 2.05.

P.T.O. ⟶

MALVERN

Church Street — **B** (red)
Wells Road
GREAT MALVERN — **B**

Albert Road North — B 2
Albert Road South — B 3
Blackmoor
Park Road — A 5
Clerkenwell Crescent — B 6
Cockshot Road — B 8
Court Road — B 12
Croft Bank — A 13
Happy Valley
off St.Ann's Road — B 15
Imperial Road — B 16
Jubilee Drive — A 17
Lygon Bank — B 18
Madresfield Road — B 20
Moorlands Road — B 22
North Malvern Road — B 23
Orchard Road — B 24
Richmond Road — B 26
Upper Welland Road — A 27
Walwyn Road — A 29
Wells Road — A 30

Town plans roads most used by traffic and those on which guide listed hotels and restaurants stand are fully drawn; the beginning only of lesser roads is indicated.

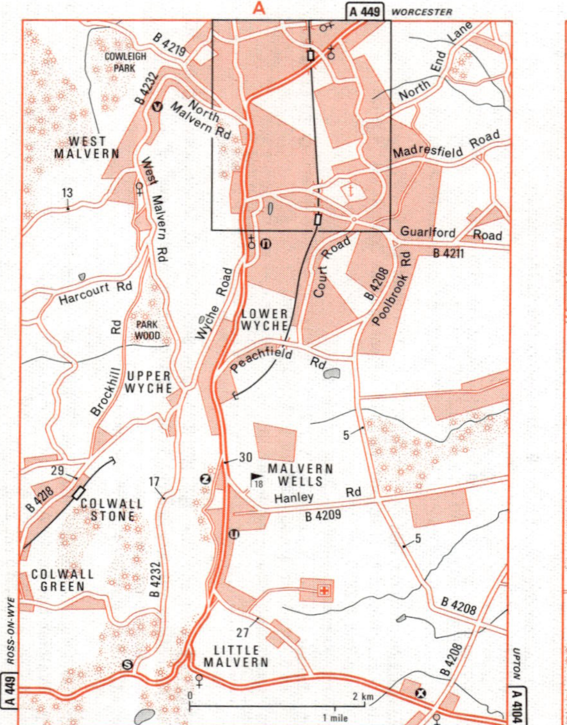

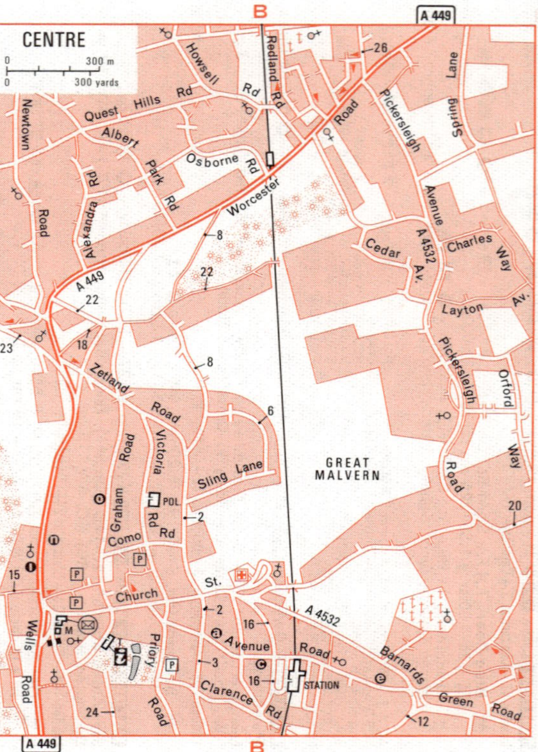

at Welland SE : 4 ½ m. on A 4104 – ✉ Malvern – ✆ 068 43 Hanley Swan :

↟ **Holdfast Cottage** ॐ, WR13 6NA, W : ¾ m. ☎ 288, ☞ – **P** **A x**
8 rm ☲ 7.50/15.00 **s.**

at Malvern Wells S : 2 m. on A 449 – ✉ ✆ 068 45 Malvern :

🏰 **Cottage in the Wood** ॐ, Holywell Rd, WR14 4LG, ☎ 3487, ≼ Severn and Evesham
Vales, ☞ – 📺 ⌂wc ☏ **P**. ◪ 🅰🅴 ⓞ 𝘝𝘐𝘚𝘈 **A z**
closed 22 to 29 December – **M** 6.00/8.00 **st.** 🍾 2.25 – ☲ 2.75 – **20 rm** 14.00/
31.00 **st.**

XX **Croque-en-Bouche,** 221 Wells Rd, WR14 4LD, ☎ 65612 – **P**. ◪ 🅰🅴 ⓞ 𝘝𝘐𝘚𝘈 **A u**
closed Monday and Tuesday – **M** (dinner only and Sunday lunch) 8.25 **t.** 🍾 1.80.

at Wynds Point S : 4 m. on A 449 – ✉ Malvern ✆ 0684 Colwall :

🏛 **Malvern Hills,** WR13 6DW, ☎ 40237 – ⌂wc **P**. ◪ ⓞ **A s**
M 4.00/5.50 **s.** 🍾 2.00 – **15 rm** ☲ 18.00/25.00 **st.**

at West Malvern W : 2 m. on B 4232 – ✉ ✆ 068 45 Malvern :

⌘ **Broomhill,** West Malvern Rd, WR14 4AY, ☎ 64367, ≼ hills and countryside, ☞ – **P** **A v**
March-October – **M** (bar lunch) 4.50 – **11 rm** ☲ 7.50/13.50 – P 15.00.

AUSTIN-MORRIS-DAIMLER-JAGUAR-LAND ROVER- CITROEN 62 Court Rd ☎ 3393
ROVER-TRIUMPH Worcester Rd ☎ 3301 VOLVO Pickersleigh Rd ☎ 61498

MANCHESTER Greater Manchester �403 �404 N 23 – pop. 543,650 – ECD : Wednesday – ✆ 061.
See : Town Hall* 19C **DZ** H – City Art Gallery* **DZ** M – Whitworth Art Gallery* **BY** M – Cathedral
15C (chancel*) **DZ** B – John Ryland's Library (manuscripts*) **CZ** A. **Envir. :** Heaton Hall* (18C)
AC, N : 5 m. **AX** M.

🛇 Heaton Park, ☎ 061 773 (Prestwich) 1085, N : by A576 **ABX** – 🛇 Ford Lane, Northenden
☎ 998 2743, S : by A 34 **BY** – 🛇 Booth Rd, Audenshaw ☎ 370 1641, E : by A 635 **BY** –
🛇 Brookdale, Woodhouses ☎ 681 4534, N : 5 m. **BX**.

✈ ☎ (061) 437 5233, S : 10 m. by A 5103 **AY** and M 56 – **Terminal :** Victoria Station.

🛈 Magnum House, Portland St. Piccadilly ☎ 247 3694/3712/3713 – Town Hall ☎ 236 3377 ext 432/433/516.

London 202 – Birmingham 86 – Glasgow 213 – Leeds 42 – Liverpool 36 – Nottingham 69.

Plans on following pages

🏨 **Piccadilly** (Embassy), Piccadilly Plaza, M60 1QR, ☎ 236 8414, Telex 668765, ≼ – ≣ 📺
🕭 **P**. 🏊. ◪ 🅰🅴 ⓞ 𝘝𝘐𝘚𝘈 **DZ s**
M a la carte 8.10/15.20 **st.** – ☲ 3.40 – **250 rm** 26.00/34.00 **st.**

🏨 **Midland** (B.T.H.), Peter St., M60 2DS, ☎ 236 3333, Telex 667797 – ≣ 📺. 🏊. ◪ 🅰🅴 ⓞ
𝘝𝘐𝘚𝘈 **CDZ n**
M a la carte 8.05/11.20 **st.** 🍾 2.40 (see also **French Restaurant**) – **301 rm** ☲ 30.00/
41.00 **st.**

🏨 **Portland** (Thistle), 3-5 Portland St., M1 6DP, ☎ 228 3400, Telex 669157 – ≣ 📺.
🏊. ◪ 🅰🅴 ⓞ 𝘝𝘐𝘚𝘈 **DZ v**
M 4.00/5.95 **st.** 🍾 1.75 – ☲ 3.00 – **221 rm** 25.00/32.00 **st.**

🏨 **Grand** (T.H.F.), Aytoun St., M1 3DR, ☎ 236 9559, Telex 667580 – ≣ 📺. 🏊. ◪ 🅰🅴 ⓞ 𝘝𝘐𝘚𝘈
M 4.50/5.00 **st.** 🍾 1.65 – ☲ 2.75 – **146 rm** 23.50/32.00 **st.** **DZ u**

XXXX **French Restaurant** (at Midland H.) (B.T.H.), Peter St., M60 2DS, ☎ 236 3333,
Telex 667797 – ◪ 🅰🅴 ⓞ 𝘝𝘐𝘚𝘈 **CDZ n**
*closed Saturday lunch, Sunday, mid July-early August, 24-25 December and Bank
Holidays* – **M** a la carte 9.15/13.00 **st.**

XXX **L'Elysée,** 44 Princess St., M1 6DE, ☎ 236 1652, French rest. – 🅰🅴 𝘝𝘐𝘚𝘈 **DZ x**
closed Saturday lunch and Sunday – **M** a la carte 7.80/21.80 🍾 1.85.

XXX **Via Veneto,** 35 George St., M1 4HQ, ☎ 236 4887, Italian rest. – ◪ 🅰🅴 ⓞ 𝘝𝘐𝘚𝘈 **DZ z**
closed Saturday lunch, Sunday, Good Friday, Christmas Day and Bank Holidays –
M a la carte 6.65/8.00 **t.** 🍾 1.70.

XXX **La Terrazza,** 14 Nicholas St., M1 4FE, ☎ 236 4033, Italian rest. – ◪ 🅰🅴 ⓞ 𝘝𝘐𝘚𝘈 **DZ r**
closed Saturday lunch and Sunday – **M** a la carte approx. 12.00 **t.** 🍾 1.70.

XX **Isola Bella,** 6a Booth St., M2 4AW, ☎ 236 6417, Italian rest. – 🅰🅴 ⓞ 𝘝𝘐𝘚𝘈 **DZ e**
closed Sunday – **M** a la carte 5.70/9.50 **s.** 🍾 1.20.

XX Rajdoot, St. James' House, South King St., ☎ 834 2176, Indian rest. **CZ c**

XX Casa España, 100 Wilmslow Rd, M14 5AJ, S : 2 m. on A 34 ☎ 224 6826, Spanish rest. **BY v**

X **Woo Sang,** 1st floor, 19-21 George St., M1 4AG, ☎ 236 3697, Chinese rest. – ◪ 🅰🅴
ⓞ 𝘝𝘐𝘚𝘈 **DZ a**
closed 25 and 26 December – **M** a la carte 4.15/7.35 🍾 2.10.

X **Danish Food Centre** (Copenhagen Room), Cross St., M2 7BY, ☎ 832 9924,
Smorrebrod – ◪ 🅰🅴 ⓞ 𝘝𝘐𝘚𝘈 **DZ n**
closed Sunday and Bank Holidays – **M** a la carte 5.45/9.60 **st.**

P.T.O. ⟶

LEEDS M 62 A A 56 (M 62, M 66), BURY
BOLTON
A 666
M 62 (M 61)
Manchester Road
15
X
PRESTON A 6
LIVERPOOL (M 61-M 62) A 580
M 602 (M 62), (M 63)
WARRINGTON, (M 63) A 57
LIVERPOOL, (M 61-M 62) M 63
Y
BURY
PRESTWICH
HEATON PARK
A 665
Bury Old Road
Scholes Lane
A 6044
Sheepfoot Lane
Middleton Road
A 576
M
New Lane
Hilton Lane
80
Bury Road
Leicester Road
Old Road
PENDLEBURY
Agecroft
A 6044
Station Road
Bolton Road
Chorley Road
Partington La.
H
Hospital Rd
A 6
Worsley Road
Manchester Road
East Lancashire Road
SALFORD
Old Claremont Rd
Road
U
U
M
93
A 6
A 576
45
A 6010
85
47
Great Clowes St.
New Road A 56
25
15
Langworthy Road
A 5186
Broad St.
U
M
88
2
See following page
Eccles
A 576
22
81
Eccles
New Road
Cross Lane
A 5063
A 6
POL
24
Regent Road
A 57
71
Road
TRAFFORD PARK
Trafford Road
Ordsall Lane
Chester Road
A 56
Choriton Road
A 5103
Ashburton Road East
A 5081
Trafford Park Road
Way
Barton
Mosley Road
Road
Dock Road
Park
Stretford
TRAFFORD
Barton
Road
H
POL
A 5067
Stretford Road
STRETFORD
Talbot Road
Seymour Grove
Upper Choriton Road
68
a
ALEXANDRA PARK
Princess Road
73
Chester Road
53
A 5145
Stretford Road
Urmston La.
Sandy Lane
Edge Lane
LONGFORD PARK
Wilbraham
56
50
A 5145
A 6010
Mauldeth Road West
URMSTON
Eccles By-Pass
7
10
CHESTER, (M 6) A 56 M 63 STOCKPORT A
BIRMINGHAM, AIRPORT, (M 63, M 56, M 6) A 5103

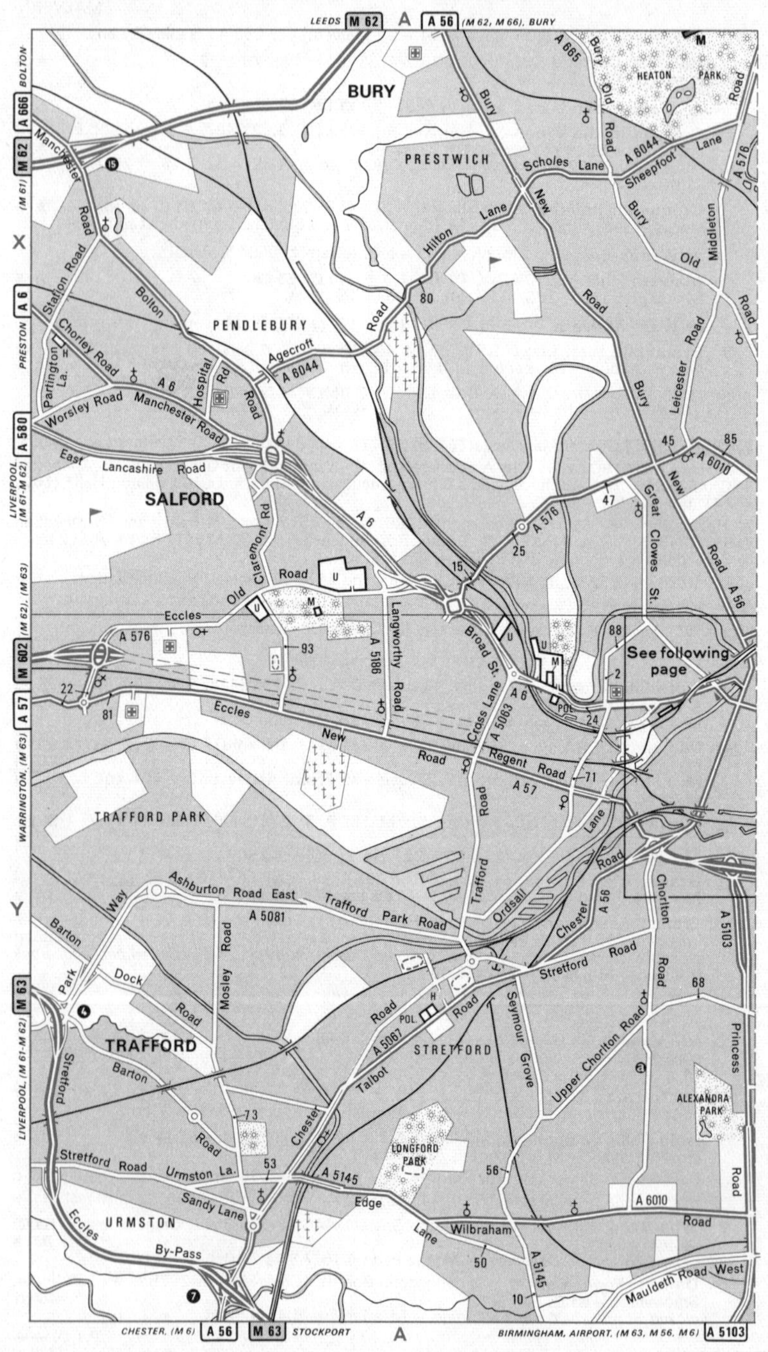

310

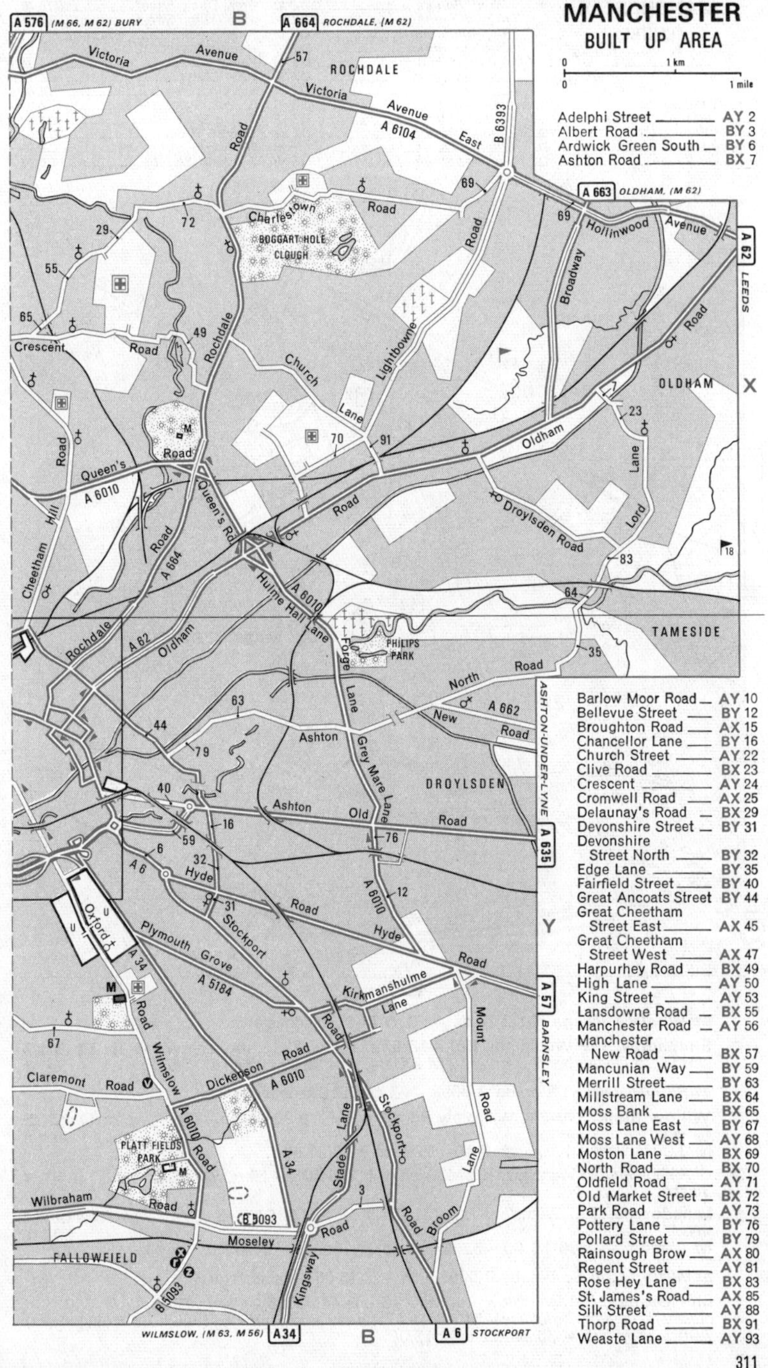

Barlow Moor Road __ AY 10
Bellevue Street _____ BY 12
Broughton Road _____ AX 15
Chancellor Lane _____ BY 16
Church Street _______ AY 22
Clive Road _________ BX 23
Crescent __________ AY 24
Cromwell Road _____ AX 25
Delaunay's Road __ BX 29
Devonshire Street _ BY 31
Devonshire
   Street North _____ BY 32
Edge Lane ________ BY 35
Fairfield Street ____ BY 40
Great Ancoats Street BY 44
Great Cheetham
   Street East _______ AX 45
Great Cheetham
   Street West _____ AX 47
Harpurhey Road ___ BX 49
High Lane ________ AY 50
King Street _______ AY 53
Lansdowne Road _ BX 55
Manchester Road _ AY 56
Manchester
   New Road ______ BX 57
Mancunian Way __ BY 59
Merrill Street _____ BY 63
Millstream Lane __ BX 64
Moss Bank ______ BX 65
Moss Lane East __ BY 67
Moss Lane West __ AY 68
Moston Lane ______ BX 69
North Road_______ BX 70
Oldfield Road _____ AY 71
Old Market Street _ BX 72
Park Road ________ AY 73
Pottery Lane _____ BY 76
Pollard Street ____ BY 79
Rainsough Brow __ AX 80
Regent Street ____ AY 81
Rose Hey Lane __ BX 83
St. James's Road _ AX 85
Silk Street _______ AY 88
Thorp Road ______ BX 91
Weaste Lane _____ AY 93

311

MANCHESTER
CENTRE

0 ——— 400 m
0 ——— 400 yards

Deansgate ——— **CZ**
Lower Mosley Street ——— **DZ**
Market Place, Market Street ——— **DZ**
Mosley Street ——— **DZ**
Princess Street ——— **DZ**

Albert Square	**CDZ** 4	Great Ducie Street	**CZ** 48
Aytoun Street	**DZ** 8	John Dalton Street	**CZ** 51
Blackfriars Street	**CZ** 13	King Street	**DZ** 52
Charlotte Street	**DZ** 17	Medlock Street	**CZ** 61
Cheetham Hill Road	**DZ** 19	Parker Street	**DZ** 75
Chorlton Street	**DZ** 20	Peter Street	**CZ** 77
Church Street	**DZ** 21	St. Ann's Street	**CZ** 84
Dale Street	**DZ** 27	St. Peter's Square	**DZ** 87
Dawson Street	**CZ** 28	Spring Gardens	**DZ** 89
Ducie Street	**DZ** 33	Viaduct Street	**CZ** 92
Egerton Street	**CZ** 36	Whitworth Street West	**CZ** 95
Fairfield Street	**DZ** 39	Windmill Street	**CZ** 96

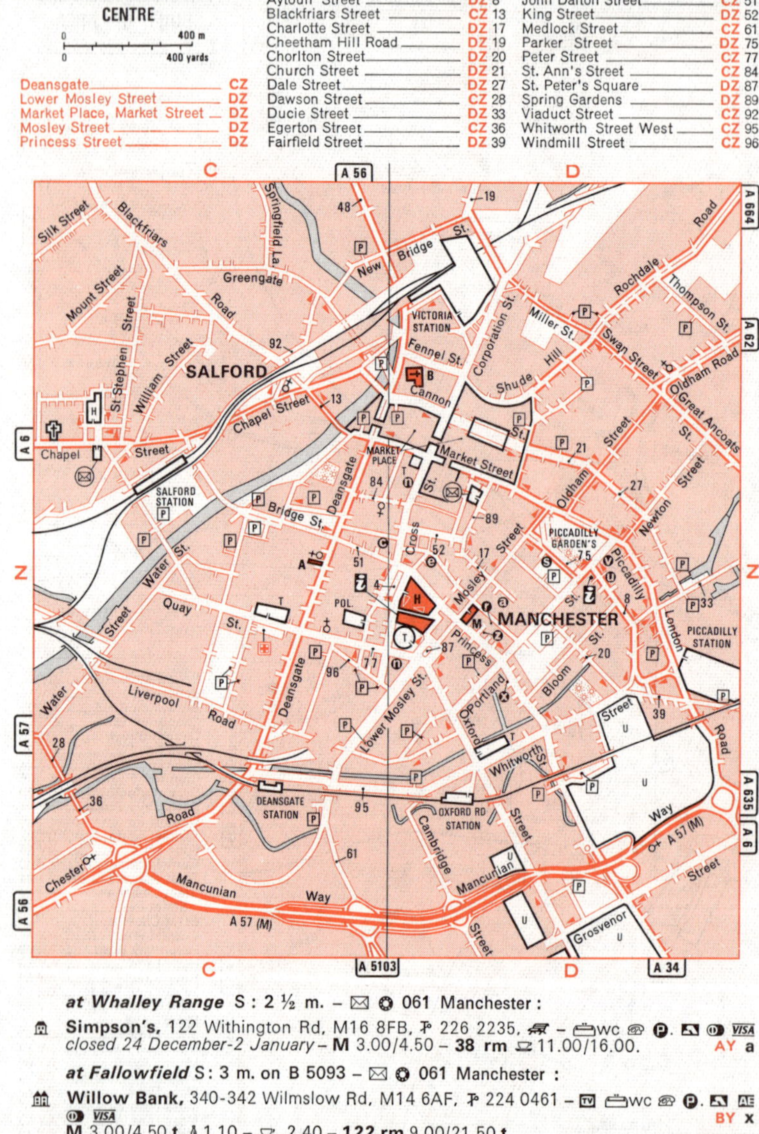

at **Whalley Range** S : 2 ½ m. – ✉ ☎ 061 Manchester :

Simpson's, 122 Withington Rd, M16 8FB, ☏ 226 2235, 🚗 – 🛁wc ☎ **P**. 🔟 ⓪ *VISA*
closed 24 December-2 January – **M** 3.00/4.50 – **38 rm** ⛱ 11.00/16.00. **AY a**

at **Fallowfield** S : 3 m. on B 5093 – ✉ ☎ 061 Manchester :

Willow Bank, 340-342 Wilmslow Rd, M14 6AF, ☏ 224 0461 – 📺 🛁wc ☎ **P**. 🔟 **AE**
⓪ *VISA* **BY x**
M 3.00/4.50 **t.** 🍷 1.10 – ⛱ 2.40 – **122 rm** 9.00/21.50 **t.**

Brookhouse, 393 Wilmslow Rd, M20 9WA, ☏ 224 2015 – 📺 🛁wc ☎ **P** **BY z**
38 rm.

Lansdowne, 346 Wilmslow Rd, M14 6AB, ☏ 224 6244 – 🔔 🛁wc 🛁wc ☎ **P**. 🔟
VISA **BY r**
M (bar lunch) 7.00 🍷 1.00 – **52 rm** ⛱ 15.00/19.50 **s.** – P 17.50/22.50 **s.**

at **Withington** S : 4 m. by B 5093 – **BY** – ✉ ☎ 061 Manchester:

Elm Grange, 561 Wilmslow Rd, M20 9GJ, ☏ 445 3336 – 🛁wc ☎ **P**
closed 8 days at Christmas – **M** *(closed Saturday and Sunday)* (lunch by arrangement)
2.00/3.15 🍷 1.25 – **30 rm** ⛱ 6.00/13.00.

at West Didsbury S: 5 ½ m. by B 5093 – BY – ⊠ ✪ 061 Manchester:

XX George's Armenian Rest., 125 Palatine Rd, M20 9YA, ☏ 434 1122, Armenian rest. – ℗.

at Northenden S: 6 ½ m. by A 5103 – AY – and M 56 – ⊠ ✪ 061 Manchester:

🏨 **Post House** (T.H.F.), Palatine Rd, M22 4FH, ☏ 998 7090, Telex 669248 – 📶 📺 🛏 wc
☎ ⅊ ℗. ☝. 🗠 AE ⓘ VISA
M 4.50/6.50 **st.** ⚬ 1.65 – ⊑ 2.25 – **201 rm** 19.00/28.00 **st.**

at Manchester Airport S: 9 m. by A 5103 – AY – and M 56 – ⊠ ✪ 061 Manchester:

🏨 **Excelsior** (T.H.F.), M22 5NS, ☏ 437 5811, Telex 668721, ⚌, ⛱ heated – 📶 📺 ⅊ ℗.
☝. 🗠 AE ⓘ VISA
M a la carte 7.15/8.80 **st.** ⚬ 1.65 – ⊑ 2.75 – **255 rm** 23.00/29.50 **st.**

XXX **Moss Nook,** Ringway Rd, M22 5NA, ☏ 437 4778 – ℗. 🗠 AE
closed Monday lunch, Sunday, 25 to 31 December and Bank Holidays – **M** a la carte
15.00/30.00 **t.**

at Heald Green S: 10 m. by A 5103 – AY – and M 56 – ⊠ ✪ 061 Manchester:

XX **La Bonne Auberge,** 224 Finney Lane, SK8 3QA, ☏ 437 5701, French rest. – ℗. AE
ⓘ
closed Monday dinner, Sunday and Bank Holidays – **M** a la carte 5.10/6.90 ⚬ 0.90.

MICHELIN Branch, Ferris St., off Louisa St., Openshaw, M11 1BS, ☏ 223 2010 and 3274.

ALFA-ROMEO 250 Plymouth Grove ☏ 225 3434
AUSTIN-MORRIS-MG-PRINCESS 156 Barlow Moor Rd
☏ 434 1133
AUSTIN-MORRIS-MG-ROVER-TRIUMPH-WOLSELEY
261 Wilmslow Rd ☏ 224 2894
AUSTIN-MG-WOLSELEY 186 Bury New Rd ☏ 792 2261
AUSTIN-MORRIS-MG Gill St. ☏ 205 2792
BMW, Gt Bridgewater St. ☏ 832 8781
CITROEN 66 Port St. ☏ 236 1341
COLT 81/85 Barlow Moor Rd ☏ 445 7818
DATSUN 770 Chester Rd ☏ 865 1151
DATSUN Victoria Rd ☏ 330 3840
DATSUN 845 Manchester Rd ☏ 766 3089
FORD 292 Bury New Rd ☏ 792 6161
FORD 391 Palatine Rd ☏ 998 3427
FORD Oxford Rd ☏ 224 7301
FORD 660 Chester Rd ☏ 872 7711
FORD 3/5 New Wakefield St. ☏ 236 4168

OPEL Middleton Rd ☏ 740 2812
PEUGEOT 22 Rochdale Rd ☏ 833 0752
PORSCHE Bury New Rd at Whitefield ☏ 796 7414
RENAULT Blackfriars Rd ☏ 832 6121
RENAULT 412 Ashton Old Rd ☏ 273 2101
ROLLS ROYCE-BENTLEY Carnavon St. ☏ 833 0548
ROVER-TRIUMPH 208 Bury New Rd ☏ 792 4343
TALBOT Chester Rd ☏ 834 6677
TALBOT 119 Wilmslow Rd ☏ 224 7282
TOYOTA Moseley Rd ☏ 224 6265
VAUXHALL 141 Waterloo Rd ☏ 792 4321
VAUXHALL Blackfriars Rd ☏ 834 8200
VAUXHALL 80/90 Port St., Gt Ancoats St. ☏ 236 4311
VAUXHALL 94 Whithington Rd ☏ 226 1122
VAUXHALL 799 Chester Rd ☏ 872 2141
VAUXHALL Manchester Rd, Denton ☏ 336 3911
VOLVO Rowsley St. ☏ 223 7272

MANORBIER (MAENORBYR) Dyfed **403** F 29 – pop. 1,168 – ECD: Saturday – ✪ 083 482.

See: Castle* (13C) *AC.*

London 253 – Carmarthen 33 – Haverfordwest 18.

🏠 **Castle Mead** ⅗, Tenby, SA70 7TA, ☏ 358, ≼ Manorbier Bay, ⛵ – 🛏 wc ℗
Easter-October – **M** (bar lunch) 4.25 **st.** ⚬ 1.60 – **11 rm** ⊑ 10.00/20.00 **st.** – P 13.00/
15.00 **st.**

at Jameston W: 2 m. on A 4139 – ⊠ ✪ 083 482 Manorbier:

🏠 **Tudor Lodge** ⅗, SA70 7SS, ☏ 320, ⛵ – ℗
M 5.00/7.00 **st.** ⚬ 1.70 – **9 rm** ⊑ 10.00/20.00 **s.**

MARAZION Cornwall **403** D 33 – pop. 1,475 – ECD: Wednesday – ⊠ Penzance – ✪ 0736.

See: St. Michael's Mount** *AC.*

London 318 – Penzance 3 – Truro 26.

🏠 **Mount Haven,** TR17 0DD, on A 394 ☏ 710249 – 🛏 wc ℗. 🗠 VISA
M a la carte 3.40/6.75 **s.** ⚬ 1.75 – **19 rm** ⊑ 9.50/18.00.

MARGAM Mid Glam. **403** I 29 – see Port Talbot.

MARGARETTING Essex **404** V 28 – see Ingatestone.

MARGATE Kent **404** Y 29 – pop. 50,347 – ECD: Thursday – ✪ 0843 Thanet.

🛈 Marine Terrace ☏ 20241 and 20242.

London 74 – Dover 22 – Maidstone 42 – Southend-on-Sea 84.

⌂ **Tyrella,** 19 Canterbury Rd, CT9 5AW, ☏ 22746 – 🗍
9 rm ⊑ 5.50/10.00.

at Cliftonville E: 1 m. by B 2052 – ⊠ Cliftonville – ✪ 0843 Thanet:

⌂ Ye Olde Charles Inn, 382-384 Northdown Rd ☏ 21817, ⛵ – 🗍 ℗
12 rm.

P.T.O. ⟶

MARGATE

at Westgate-on-Sea W : 2 m. off A 28 – ⊠ Westgate-on-Sea – ☎ 0843 Thanet :

⋔ Westgate Lodge, 36 Westgate Bay Av., CT8 8TA, ☏ 31278, 🚗 – 🅿
12 rm.

XX **Angelo's Blue Room,** 18 Cuthbert Rd, CT8 8NR, ☏ 31646, Italian rest. – 🔼 ⑩ *VISA*
closed Sunday dinner and Monday – **M** a la carte 7.50/13.75 **t.** 🍷 2.00.

OPEL 1 Cuthbert Rd ☏ 32060   RENAULT 412 Northdown Rd ☏ 20919

MARKET DEEPING Lincs. 🔟🔟🔟 T 25 – pop. 2,816 – ☎ 0778.
London 94 – Cambridge 44 – Leicester 41 – Lincoln 42.

☖ **Deeping Stage,** Market Pl., PE6 8EA, ☏ 343234 – 🅿. *VISA*
M *(closed Sunday dinner, Monday lunch and Bank Holidays)* 3.50 **t.** 🍷 1.85 – **8 rm**
⛌ 8.50/17.00 **st.**

MARKET DRAYTON Salop 🔟🔟🔟 🔟🔟🔟 M 25 – pop. 5,890 – ECD : Thursday – ☎ 0630.
London 161 – Birmingham 44 – Chester 33 – Shrewsbury 19 – Stoke-on-Trent 16.

🏛 **Corbet Arms,** High St., TF9 1PY, ☏ 2037 – 📺 ⇔wc 🅿. 🔼 *VISA*
M a la carte 2.60/7.80 **t.** 🍷 1.40 – **8 rm** ⛌ 11.45/18.50 **t.**

AUSTIN-DAIMLER-LAND ROVER-MORRIS-MG-   TALBOT, MAZDA Shrewsbury Rd ☏ 2027
PRINCESS-ROVER-TRIUMPH Cheshire St. ☏ 2444   VOLVO, FORD, SCIMITAR Queen St. ☏ 2462
PEUGEOT Shrewsbury Rd ☏ 4257

MARKET HARBOROUGH Leics. 🔟🔟🔟 R 26 – pop. 13,130 – ECD : Wednesday – ☎ 0858.
🛈 Public Library, 53 The Square ☏ 62649.

London 88 – Birmingham 47 – Leicester 15 – Northampton 17.

🏨 **Three Swans,** 21 High St., LE16 7NJ, ☏ 66664 – ⇔wc 🛁wc ☎ 🅿. AE ⑩
M 4.20/7.50 **t.** 🍷 1.85 – **18 rm** ⛌ 14.00/19.00 **t.**

at Marston Trussell W : 3 ¼ m. by A 427 – ⊠ ☎ 0858 Market Harborough :

🏛 **Sun Inn** 🦢, LE16 9TY, ☏ 65531 – ⇔wc ☎ 🅿. 🔼 ⑩
closed 25 to 29 December – **M** a la carte 5.90/9.20 **st.** 🍷 2.75 – **10 rm** ⛌ 16.00/19.50 **st.**

DAIMLER-JAGUAR-ROVER-TRIUMPH Northampton   FORD Leicester Rd ☏ 66682
Rd ☏ 65511

MARKET RASEN Lincs. 🔟🔟🔟 T 23 – pop. 2,433 – ECD : Thursday – ☎ 067 32.
London 159 – Grimsby 20 – Lincoln 16.

🏛 **Limes,** Gainsborough Rd, LN8 3JW, ☏ 2357, ✗ – ⇔wc 🛁wc ☎ 🅿. 🔼
M a la carte 3.90/6.70 🍷 2.00 – **14 rm** ⛌ 12.00/19.00 **t.**

MARKET WEIGHTON Humberside 🔟🔟🔟 ㉔ – pop. 2,584 – ⊠ York – ☎ 069 62.
London 208 – Kingston-upon-Hull 18 – Leeds 40 – York 19.

☖ Londesborough Arms, High St., YO43 3AH, ☏ 2219 – 🅿 – **10 rm.**

MARKS TEY Essex 🔟🔟🔟 W 28 – see Colchester.

MARLBOROUGH Wilts. 🔟🔟🔟 🔟🔟🔟 O 29 – pop. 6,108 – ECD : Wednesday – ☎ 067 25.
See : Marlborough College* 17C. Envir. : Avebury (stone circles**) W : 6 m.
🏌 The Common ☏ 52147, N : 1 m.
🛈 St. Peter's Church, High St. ☏ 53989 (summer only).

London 84 – Bristol 47 – Southampton 40 – Swindon 12.

🏛 **Ailesbury Arms,** High St., SN8 1AB, ☏ 3451, 🚗 – 📺 ⇔wc 🛁wc ☎ 🚘 🅿. 🔼 AE ⑩ *VISA*
M 4.00/5.50 **t.** 🍷 2.50 – ⛌ 2.00 – **30 rm** 10.20/21.20 **t.**

🏛 **Castle and Ball** (T.H.F.), High St., SN8 1DZ, ☏ 2002 – 📺 ⇔wc ☎ 🅿. 🔼 AE ⑩ *VISA*
M 3.35/4.90 **st.** 🍷 1.65 – **30 rm** ⛌ 13.50/22.00 **st.**

at Savernake SE : 5 ½ m. off A 346 – ⊠ Marlborough – ☎ 0672 Burbage :

🏛 **Savernake Forest** (Best Western) 🦢, SN8 3AY, ☏ 810206, ✎ 🚗 – ⇔wc 🅿. 🔼 AE
⑩ *VISA*
M a la carte 3.15/5.80 **t.** 🍷 1.25 – **14 rm** ⛌ 11.00/23.00 **t.**

AUSTIN-JAGUAR-MG-ROVER-TRIUMPH London Rd   MORRIS-MG 80/83 High St. ☏ 2076
☏ 2381   RENAULT London Rd ☏ 2564

MARLOW Bucks. 🔟🔟🔟 R 29 – pop. 10,350 – ECD : Wednesday – ☎ 062 84.
London 35 – Aylesbury 22 – Oxford 29 – Reading 14.

🏨 **Compleat Angler,** Marlow Bridge, SL7 1RG, ☏ 4444, Telex 848644, ≤ river Thames,
« Riverside setting and gardens », ✗, ✎ – 📺 🅿. 🏊. 🔼 AE ⑩ *VISA*
M 12.00 **st.** 🍷 2.50 – ⛌ 3.50 – **42 rm** 30.00/40.00 **st.**

X Dino's, 5 High St. ☏ 4919, Italian rest.

at Bisham SW: 1 m. on B 482 – ✉ ☎ 062 84 Marlow:

XX **Bull**, Marlow Rd, SL7 1RR, ☎ 4734 – **P**. 🔲 ⓞ 𝘝𝘐𝘚𝘈
  M a la carte 7.50/11.00 🍾 1.80.

AUSTIN-MORRIS-MG-WOLSELEY West St. ☎ 2215

MARPLE Greater Manchester 🆘🅾🆘 N 23 – pop. 17,170 – ✉ Stockport – ☎ 061 Manchester.
London 202 – Manchester 11 – Sheffield 37.

  🏠 **West Towers**, 194 Church Lane, SK6 7LB, ☎ 427 2968 – 📺 🛏wc 🚾wc **P**. 🔲 AE ⓞ 𝘝𝘐𝘚𝘈
  M 3.50/5.25 🍾 2.00 – **38 rm** ⌒ 12.75/20.70 **t.**

MARSTON TRUSSELL Leics. 🆘🅾🆘 R 26 – see Market Harborough.

MARTOCK Somerset 🆘🅾 L 31 – pop. 2,703 – ☎ 093 582.
London 139 – Taunton 22 – Yeovil 9.

  🏠 **White Hart**, Market Sq., TA12 6JQ, ☎ 2246 – 📺 **P**
  M (bar lunch) 3.50/4.50 **s.** – **8 rm** ⌒ 6.50/13.00.

AUSTIN-MG-WOLSELEY ☎ 2547

MARTON Cleveland – see Middlesbrough.

MATLOCK Derbs. 🆘🅾🆘 P 24 – pop. 19,588 – ECD: Thursday – ☎ 0629.
See: Site*. Envir.: Riber Castle (ruins) ⋖* (Fauna Reserve and Wildlife Park *AC*) SE: 2 ½ m.
🅱 The Pavilion ☎ 55082.
London 153 – Derby 17 – Manchester 46 – Nottingham 24 – Sheffield 24.

  🏛 **Riber Hall** ⅋, Riber, DE4 5JU, SE: 3 m. off A 615 ☎ 2795, ⋖, « Elizabethan manor
  house », 🚘 – 📺 🛏wc ☎ **P**. 🔲 AE ⓞ 𝘝𝘐𝘚𝘈
  M (dinner only and Sunday lunch) 4.50/7.50 🍾 2.00 – ⌒ 2.75 – **8 rm** 20.00/25.00.

  at Matlock Bath S : 1 ½ m. on A 6 – ✉ ☎ 0629 Matlock:

  🏛 **New Bath** (T.H.F.) New Bath Rd, DE4 3PX, ☎ 3275, ✂, 🔲, ⅃ heated, 🚘 – 📺
  🛏wc ☎ **P**. ♿. 🔲 AE ⓞ 𝘝𝘐𝘚𝘈
  M 4.50/6.00 **st.** 🍾 1.80 – **57 rm** ⌒ 19.00/25.00 **st.**

AUSTIN-MORRIS-MG-ROVER-TRIUMPH-WOLSELEY   FORD 41 Causeway Lane ☎ 2231
Bakewell Rd ☎ 3291

MATLOCK BATH Derbs. 🆘🅾🆘 P 24 – see Matlock.

MAWGAN PORTH Cornwall 🆘🅾 E 32 – pop. 530 – ECD : Wednesday – ✉ Newquay –
☎ 063 74 St. Mawgan.
London 293 – Newquay 7 – Truro 20.

  🏠 **Tredragon**, TTR8 4DQ, ☎ 213, ⋖ Mawgan Porth, 🚘 – 🛏wc 🚾wc **P**
  Easter-October – **M** (bar lunch) 4.50 **t.** 🍾 1.90 – **30 rm** ⌒ 9.50/20.00 **t.**

MAWNAN SMITH Cornwall 🆘🅾 E 33 – see Falmouth.

MAYFIELD East Sussex 🅾🆘 U 30 – pop. 3,847 – ECD : Wednesday – ☎ 043 55.
London 46 – Brighton 25 – Eastbourne 22 – Lewes 17 – Royal Tunbridge Wells 9.

  XX **Middle House** with rm, High St., TN20 6AB, ☎ 2146, Telex 95338, « 16C buildings »,
  🚘 – 🛏wc 🏠 **P**. 🔲 AE ⓞ 𝘝𝘐𝘚𝘈
  M *(closed Sunday dinner and Monday)* a la carte 6.15/9.75 **st.** 🍾 1.50 – **10 rm** ⌒ 9.00/
  22.00 **st.**

AUSTIN-MORRIS-MG High St. ☎ 3386

MEAL BANK Cumbria – see Kendal.

MEASHAM Leics. 🆘🅾🆘 P 25 – pop. 3,620 – ECD : Wednesday – ☎ 0530.
London 119 – Birmingham 26 – Derby 18 – Leicester 18 – Nottingham 25.

  🏛 **Measham Inn**, Tamworth Rd, DE12 7DY, ☎ 70095 – 📺 🛏wc ☎ **P**. ♿. 🔲 AE ⓞ 𝘝𝘐𝘚𝘈
  M *(closed Saturday lunch and Sunday dinner)* 3.05/4.70 **st.** 🍾 1.40 – **32 rm** ⌒ 13.75/
  20.90 **st.**

BRITISH-LEYLAND High St. ☎ 70545

MELBOURN Cambs. 🅾🆘 U 27 – pop. 2,851 – ✉ ☎ 0763 Royston (Herts.).
🅱 Baldock Rd, Royston ☎ 42177, SW: 3 m.
London 44 – Cambridge 10.

  XX **Pink Geranium**, 25 Station Rd, SG8 6DX, ☎ 60215 – **P**
  closed Sunday, Monday and last 2 weeks August – **M** (dinner only) (booking essential)
  a la carte 5.35/6.85.

MELMERBY North Yorks. – see Ripon.

MELTON MOWBRAY Leics. 404 R 25 – pop. 17,810 – ECD : Thursday – ☎ 0664.
☔ Thorpe Arnold ☏ 2118, NE : 2 m.
🛈 Carnegie Museum, Thorpe End ☏ 69946.

London 113 – Leicester 15 – Northampton 45 – Nottingham 18.

🏨 **Harboro** (Anchor), Burton St., NG24 1XB, ☏ 68598, Group Telex 858875 – 📺 🛏wc
🕾 🅿. AE ⓪ VISA
M 3.50 – **17 rm** ⚏ 12.50/25.00 **st.**

🏨 **George**, High St., LE13 0TR, ☏ 2112 – 📺 🛏wc 🅿. 🔲 AE ⓪ VISA
M a la carte 5.80/7.95 **st.** ⬥ 1.85 – **17 rm** ⚏ 10.50/22.75 **st.**

🏨 **King's Head**, Nottingham St., LE13 1NW, ☏ 2110 – 🛏wc 🚿wc 🚗 🅿. ⚐
M 3.15/3.80 ⬥ 1.50 – **15 rm** ⚏ 11.50/25.00 **st.**

🏠 **Westbourne House**, 11a Nottingham Rd, LE13 0NP, ☏ 3556 – 🅿. VISA
18 rm ⚏ 6.00/12.00 **st.**

FIAT Mill St. ☏ 62559
MORRIS-MG-ROVER-TRIUMPH 16 Burton St. ☏ 63394
SKODA Albert St. ☏ 62235
TALBOT King St., Scalford ☏ 62872
VOLVO 56 Scalford Rd ☏ 63241

MENAI BRIDGE (PORTHAETHWY) Gwynedd 404 H 24 – pop. 2,340 – ECD : Wednesday –
☎ 0248.
See : Menai Strait * (channel), Menai Suspension Bridge ⪡ *. **Envir. :** Bryn Celli Du (burial
chamber*) SW : 3 ½ m.
🛈 Wales Tourist Information Centre, Coed Cyrnol ☏ 712626.

London 249 – Birkenhead 70 – Holyhead 21 – Shrewsbury 85

🏛 **Anglesey Arms**, LL59 5EA, on A 5 ☏ 712305, 🍴 – 🛏wc 🅿
17 rm.

at Glyngarth NE : 2 m. on A 545 – ✉ ☎ 0248 Menai Bridge :

🏛 **Gazelle**, LL59 5PD, ☏ 713364, ⪡ Menai Straits and hills, 🍴 – 🅿
14 rm.

MENTMORE Bucks. 404 R 28 – pop. 208 – ✉ Leighton Buzzard – ☎ 0296 Cheddington.
London 46 – Aylesbury 10 – Luton 15.

✕✕ **Stag Inn**, The Green, LU7 0QF, ☏ 668423 – 🅿. 🔲 AE ⓪ VISA
closed Monday – **M** a la carte 7.40/12.40 **t.** ⬥ 1.70.

MERE Wilts. 403 404 R 30 – pop. 2,085 – ECD : Wednesday – ☎ 074 786.
Envir. : Stourhead House* (18C) *AC* and park** *AC*, NW : 2 m.
🛈 The Square ☏ 341.

London 113 – Exeter 65 – Salisbury 26 – Taunton 40.

🏛 **Old Ship**, Castle St., BA12 6JE, ☏ 258 – 📺 🛏wc 🕾 🅿. 🔲 AE ⓪ VISA
M 3.25/4.95 **st.** ⬥ 1.80 – **22 rm** ⚏ 13.90/21.90 **st.**

BRITISH LEYLAND Salisbury St. ☏ 244
CITROEN Castle St. ☏ 404

MERE BROW Lancs. – pop. 400 – ☎ 077 473 Hesketh Bank.
London 221 – Liverpool 22 – Preston 11 – Southport 6.

✕ Crab and Lobster, behind the Leigh Arms, PR4 6LA, ☏ 2734, Seafood – 🅿.

MERIDEN West Midlands 403 404 P 26 – see Coventry.

MERTHYR TYDFIL Mid Glam. 403 J 28 – pop. 55,317 – ECD : Thursday – ☎ 0685.
☔ Cilsanws Mountain ☏ 3308 – ☔ Tredegar ☏ 0685 (Rhymney) 840732, NE : 6 m.
🛈 Sports and Leisure Centre (enquiries) ☏ 71491.

London 181 – Brecon 17 – Cardiff 24 – Swansea 30.

🏨 Baverstock's, Heads of the Valleys Rd, CF47 8DE, W : 3 m. on A 465 by A 4102
☏ 6221 – 📺 🛏wc 🚿wc 🕾 🅿. ⚐
26 rm.

AUSTIN-MORRIS-MG-ROVER-TRIUMPH High St.
☏ 2611
FORD Pentrebach Rd ☏ 74111

MESSING Essex 404 W 28 – pop. 372 – ✉ Colchester – ☎ 0621 Tiptree.
London 48 – Chelmsford 15 – Colchester 8 – Ipswich 27.

✕ **Old Crown Inn**, CO5 9TZ, ☏ 815575 – 🅿
closed Monday dinner, Sunday and Bank Holidays – **M** a la carte 5.20/8.00 ⬥ 1.80.

MICKLETON Glos. 403 404 O 27 – see Chipping Campden.

🏰 Brass Castle Lane ☏ 36430, S : 3 m. by A 172 **BZ**.

✈ Tees-side Airport : ☏ 032 573 (Dinsdale) 2811, SW : 13 m. by A 66 **AZ** and A 19 on A 67.

🛈 125 Albert Rd ☏ 245750/245432 ext 3580.

London 251 – Kingston-upon-Hull 85 – Leeds 61 – Newcastle-upon-Tyne 39.

MIDDLESBROUGH

Corporation Road	**BY**	8
Dundas Street	**ABY**	12
Grange Road	**ABY**	
Linthorpe Road	**AY**	
Newport Road	**AY**	
Albert Road	**BY**	2
Ayresome Green Lane	**AZ**	3
Bridge Street West	**AY**	4
Bright Street	**BY**	5
Clairville Road	**BZ**	6
Cleveland Street	**BY**	7
Devonshire Road	**AZ**	10
Eastbourne Road	**AZ**	14
Ferry Road	**BY**	15

Finsbury Street	**AZ**	16	Smeaton Street	**BY**	30
Gresham Road	**AZ**	18	South Bank Road	**BY**	31
Hartington Road	**AY**	19	Tees Bridge		
Longford Street	**AZ**	22	Approach Road	**AZ**	34
Ormesby Road	**BZ**	24	West Terrace Ormesby	**BZ**	35
Princes Road	**AZ**	26	Westbourne Gro. Ormesby	**BZ**	36
St. Barnabas Road	**AZ**	27	Wilson Street	**AY**	38
Saltersgill Avenue	**BZ**	28	Zetland Street	**ABY**	39

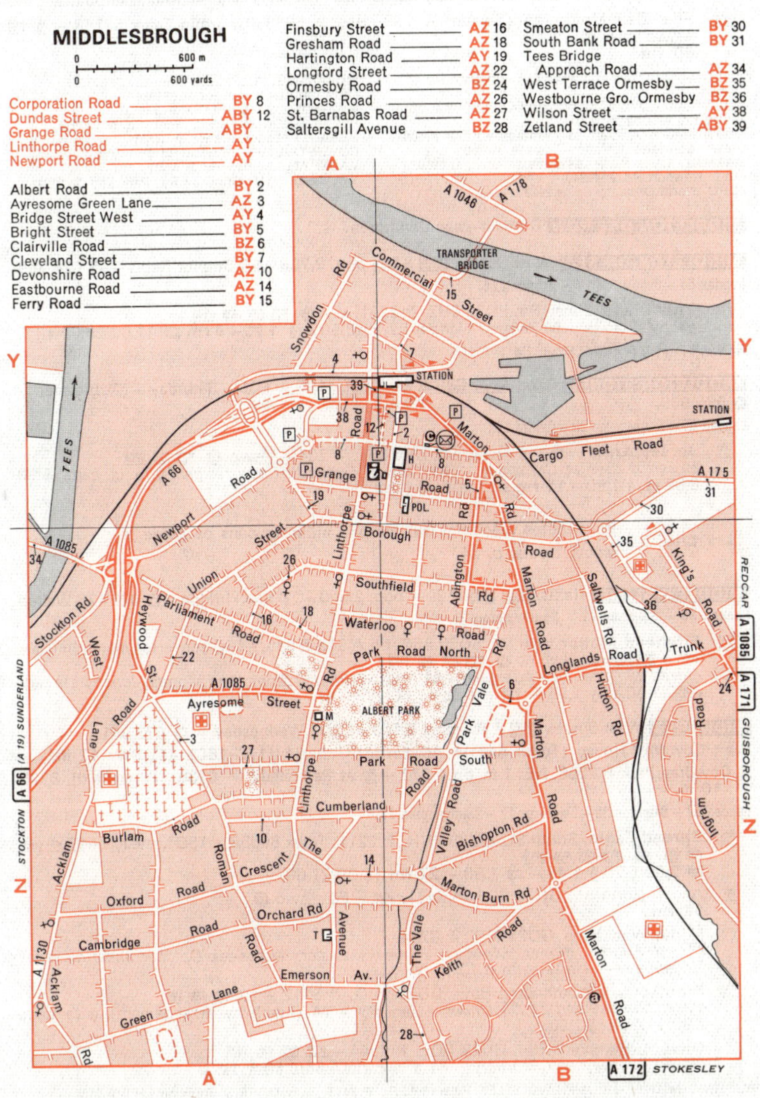

🏨 Ladbroke Dragonara, Fry St., TS1 1JH, ☏ 248133, Telex 58266 – 🛗 📺 ♿ 🅿 🎱 **BY** c
210 rm.

🏨 Middlesbrough Crest Motel (Crest), Marton Way, TS4 3BS, S : 2 m. on A 172
☏ 87651 – 📺 🚾 ⌚ ♿ 🅿 🎱 🚗 **AE** ① **VISA** **BZ** a
🍴 2.40 – **53 rm** 17.25/23.80 **st.**

P.T.O. →

MIDDLESBROUGH

at Marton SE: 4 m. on A 172 – BZ – ✉ ☎ 0642 Middlesbrough:

🏨 **Marton Hotel and Country Club**, Stokesley Rd, TS7 8DS, ☏ 317141 – 📺 ⇌wc ☎ 🅿.
⚎. VISA
M 3.00/4.00 t. �🍷 0.90 – **54 rm** � 14.50/20.00 t. – P 16.50/34.00 t.

at Acklam SW: 2 m. on A 174 by Acklam Rd – AZ – ✉ ☎ 0642 Middlesbrough:

🏨 Blue Bell Motor Inn (Swallow), TS5 7HL, ☏ 593939, Group Telex 53168 – 🛗 📺
⇌wc ☎ ⚐ 🅿
60 rm.

AUSTIN-MG-ROVER-WOLSELEY Eastbourne Rd
☏ 86658
AUSTIN-MG-ROVER-TRIUMPH-WOLSELEY 336 Sto-
kesley Rd, Marton ☏ 317171
AUSTIN-MG-WOLSELEY 339 Linthorpe Rd ☏ 87606
BMW, Stokesley 1 Manor Close ☏ 710566
DATSUN Trunk Rd ☏ 06495 (Eston Grange) 69303
FIAT Newport Rd ☏ 49346
FORD North Ormesby Rd ☏ 2452

MORRIS-MG-WOLSELEY Ormesby ☏ 317227
OPEL 370 Linthorpe Rd ☏ 822884
PEUGEOT 132 Park Lane ☏ 246031
RELIANT-HONDA South Bank Rd ☏ 247934
RENAULT Longlands Rd ☏ 44651
ROVER-TRIUMPH Marton Rd ☏ 246065
VAUXHALL Marton Rd ☏ 43415
VW, AUDI-NSU Ormesby Rd, Park End ☏ 37971

MIDDLETON ONE ROW Durham – see Darlington.

MIDDLETON-ON-SEA West Sussex 404 S 31 – pop. 2,708 – ✉ Bognor Regis – ☎ 024 369.
London 65 – Bognor Regis 4 – Brighton 26.

🏖 **Villa Plage**, Elmer Rd, PO22 6HZ, ☏ 2251, ≼ – 🅿. ☒ AE ① VISA
Easter-October – **M** *(closed Monday)* 2.95/3.50 t. ⍾ 1.25 – **6 rm** ⊂ 11.00/20.00 t.

RENAULT Harefield Rd, Elmer Rd ☏ 3557

MIDDLETON STONEY Oxon. 403 404 Q 28 – pop. 196 – ECD: Saturday – ✉ Bicester –
☎ 086 989.

London 66 – Northampton 30 – Oxford 12.

XX **Jersey Arms** with rm, Ardley Rd, OX6 8SE, ☏ 234 – ⇌wc 🅿. ☒ AE VISA
closed 4 days at Christmas – **M** *(closed Sunday to non-residents)* a la carte 5.30/
8.65 st. ⍾ 1.90 – **11 rm** ⊂ 10.00/20.00 st.

Les prix	Pour toutes précisions sur les prix indiqués dans ce guide, reportez-vous p. 24.

MIDDLE WALLOP Hants. 403 404 P 30 – pop. 2,800 – ✉ Stockbridge – ☎ 026 478 Wallop.
London 80 – Salisbury 11 – Southampton 21.

XX **Fifehead Manor** with rm, SO20 8EG, on A 343 ☏ 566, « 16C converted manor house »,
🚗 – 📺 ⇌wc 🅱wc ☎ 🅿. ☒ AE ① VISA
closed 23 December-7 January – **M** *(closed Sunday dinner and Monday lunch)* a la carte
4.60/7.90 t. ⍾ 1.65 – **12 rm** ⊂ 17.00/28.00 st.

MIDHURST West Sussex 404 R 31 – pop. 2,169 – ECD: Wednesday – ☎ 073 081.
See : Cowdray House (Tudor ruins)* *AC.* Envir. : Uppark* (17C-18C) *AC*, SW: 12 m.
🏌 Cowdray Park ☏ 2088, NE: 1 m. on A 272 – 🏌 at Petersfield ☏ 0730 (Petersfield) 3725,
W: 10 m.

London 57 – Brighton 38 – Chichester 12 – Southampton 41.

🏨 **Spread Eagle**, South St., GU29 9NH, ☏ 2211, Telex 86853, « 15C hostelry » – 📺 ⇌wc
☎ 🅿. ⚎. ☒ AE ① VISA
M 3.60/5.20 ⍾ 1.45 – ⊂ 1.30 – **27 rm** 16.00/27.00.

🏠 Angel, North St., GU29 9DJ, ☏ 2421, 🚗 – 📺 ⇌wc 🅿
18 rm.

XX **Mida**, Wool Lane, GU29 9BX, ☏ 3284
*closed Sunday dinner, Monday, 2 weeks Easter, last week October and first week
November* – **M** a la carte 6.70/10.00.

XX **Knockers**, Knockhundred Row, GU29 9DQ, ☏ 3712 – ☒ AE ① VISA
closed Sunday and 24 December–2 January – **M** *(lunch by arrangement)* a la carte
7.90/11.25 t. ⍾ 1.60.

X **Olivers**, Rumbolds Hill, GU29 0QE, ☏ 2544 – ☒ AE ① VISA
closed Tuesday and February – **M** a la carte 4.55/8.60 ⍾ 1.30.

AUSTIN-MG-ROVER-TRIUMPH-WOLSELEY Petersfield Rd ☏ 2443   MORRIS Rumbolds Hill ☏ 2162

MILDENHALL Suffolk 404 V 26 – pop. 6,780 – ECD: Thursday – ☎ 0638.
🏌 Worlington ☏ 712216.

London 73 – Cambridge 22 – Ipswich 38 – Norwich 41.

🏠 Bell, High St., IP28 7EA, ☏ 712134 – ⇌wc 🅿. ☒ AE ① VISA
M 3.50/3.75 st. ⍾ 1.50 – **19 rm** ⊂ 11.00/19.50 st. – P 17.25/18.25 st.

MILFORD HAVEN MILFFWRD Dyfed **403** **404** P 31 – pop. 13,960 – ECD : Thursday – ☎ 064 62.
Envir. : Martin's Haven ❄★★ W : **11** m. – St. Ann's Head ★★ by Dale (≼★) W : 14 m.
London 257 – Carmarthen 37 – Fishguard 22.

- 🏠 **Lord Nelson**, Hamilton Ter., SA73 3AW, ☎ 3265, 🚗 – 🛏wc 🅿. 🔼 🅰🅴 ⓪ 𝗩𝗜𝗦𝗔
  M a la carte 4.15/6.00 **st.** ⬧ 1.20 – **27 rm** ⊡ 9.50/22.50 **st.**

  at Herbrandston NW : 3 m. – ✉ ☎ 064 62 Milford Haven :

- 🏠 **Sir Benfro**, SA73 3TD, ☎ 4242, ⬧ heated – 📺 🛏wc ☏ 🅿
  M *(closed Sunday)* 4.00/5.50 **t.** ⬧ 2.00 – **12 rm** ⊡ 10.50/20.00 **s.**

MILFORD-ON-SEA Hants. **403** **404** P 31 – pop. 3,625 – ECD : Wednesday – ✉ Lymington – ☎ 059 069.
London 109 – Bournemouth 15 – Southampton 24 – Winchester 37.

- 🏨 **South Lawn**, Lymington Rd, SO4 0RF, ☎ 3261, 🚗 – 📺 🛏wc 🅿
  closed 25 December-first week February – **M** (dinner only and Sunday lunch) 5.75 **t.**
  ⬧ 2.10 – **17 rm** ⊡ 16.25/32.50 **t.**

- ✕✕ **Westover Hall**, with rm, Park Lane, SO4 0PT, ☎ 3044, ≼ Solent and the Needles, « Restored Victorian mansion » – 🅿
  3 rm.

- ✕ **Mill House**, 1 High St., SO4 0QF, ☎ 2611 – 🔼 🅰🅴 ⓪
  closed Sunday dinner, Monday and 27 October-10 November – **M** a la carte 5.90/7.25 **t.** ⬧ 1.30.

AUSTIN-MORRIS-MG-ROVER-TRIUMPH-WOLSELEY High St. ☎ 2161   AUSTIN-MORRIS-MG-WOLSELEY High St. ☎ 2378

MILNROW Greater Manchester **404** N 23 – pop. 10,346 – ✉ Rochdale (Lancs.) – ☎ 045 77 Saddleworth.
London 222 – Manchester 14 – Rochdale 2.

  at Ogden SE : 3 m. on A 640 – ✉ Rochdale – ☎ 045 77 Saddleworth :

- ✕✕✕ **Moorcock**, Huddesfield Rd, OL16 3TJ, ☎ 2659 – 🅿. 🔼 🅰🅴 ⓪ 𝗩𝗜𝗦𝗔
  closed Sunday and Monday – **M** a la carte 6.15/19.05 ⬧ 2.85.

MILTON ABBAS Dorset **403** **404** N 31– pop. 788 – ✉ Blandford – ☎ 0258.
See : Village★ 18C.
London 127 – Bournemouth 23 – Weymouth 19.

- 🏠 **Milton Manor** ⅋, DT11 0AZ, ☎ 880254, ≼, « Country house atmosphere », 🚗 – 🅿
  March-October – **M** 3.20/4.50 **st.** ⬧ 1.50 – **12 rm** ⊡ 10.50/21.00 **st.** – P 18.20 **st.**

MILTON COMMON Oxon. **403** **404** Q 28 – ✉ Oxford – ☎ 084 46 Great Milton.
London 50 – Oxford 9.

- 🏨 **Belfry**, Brimpton Grange, OX9 2JW, M 40 exit 7 NW off A 329 ☎ 381, ⬧ – 📺 🛏wc
  ☏ 🅿. ⬧ 🔼 🅰🅴 ⓪ 𝗩𝗜𝗦𝗔
  M 4.00/5.00 **st.** ⬧ 2.00 – ⊡ 1.50 – **32 rm** 12.00/24.00 **st.**

MILTON DAMEREL Devon **403** H 31 – pop. 409 – ✉ Holsworthy – ☎ 040 926.
London 249 – Barnstaple 21 – Plymouth 48.

- 🏨 **Woodford Bridge**, EX22 7LL, N : 1 m. on A 388 ☎ 252, ⬧, 🚗 – 🛏wc 🛁wc 🅿
  M (buffet lunch Monday to Saturday) a la carte 7.15/10.80 **s.** ⬧ 1.10 – **16 rm** ⊡ 11.75/26.65 **t.**

MILTON ERNEST Beds. **404** S 27 – see Bedford.

MILTON ON STOUR Dorset **403** **404** N 30 – pop. 4,050 (inc. Gillingham) – ECD : Thursday – ☎ 074 76 Gillingham.
London 115 – Shaftesbury 6 – Taunton 42.

- 🏨 **Milton Lodge** ⅋, SP8 5QD, ☎ 2262, ⬧ heated, 🚗 – 🛏wc ☏ 🅿. 🅰🅴
  closed 1 week at Christmas – **M** 3.00/7.00 **t.** ⬧ 2.50 – **10 rm** ⊡ 12.50/25.00 **t.** – P 20.00/25.00 **t.**

Ne confondez pas:

Confort des hôtels	: 🏨🏨🏨 ... 🏠, 🏡, 🏠
Confort des restaurants	: ✕✕✕✕✕ ..... ✕
Qualité de la table	: ✿✿, ✿, **M**

MINEHEAD Somerset 403 J 30 – pop. 7,370 – ECD : Wednesday – ☎ 0643.
Warren Rd ℡ 2057.
Market House, ℡ 2624.
London 187 – Bristol 64 – Exeter 43 – Taunton 25.

Beach (T.H.F.), The Avenue, TA24 5AP, ℡ 2193, heated – TV WC ☎ P. AE ① VISA
M 3.50/4.20 **st.** 1.65 – **41 rm** 13.50/27.00 **st.**

Northfield , Northfield Rd, TA24 5PU, ℡ 5155, « gardens » – WC P. AE ① VISA
M 3.50/5.20 1.50 – **23 rm** (dinner included) 19.20/39.65 **t.**

Benares , Northfield Rd, TA24 5PT, ℡ 2340, – WC P
closed Christmas – **M** (bar lunch) 5.00 – **22 rm** 10.65/21.30.

York, 48 The Avenue, TA24 5AN, ℡ 2037 – WC P. AE VISA
M a la carte 3.75/6.45 **t.** 2.00 – **24 rm** 7.50/9.50 – P 13.00/15.00.

Remuera, Northfield Rd, TA24 5QH, ℡ 2611, – WC P. VISA
March-October – **11 rm** 9.00/21.00.

AUSTIN-MORRIS-MG North Rd ℡ 2336   RENAULT Blue Anchor ℡ 064 382 (Dunster) 571
FIAT, VAUXHALL Townsend Rd ℡ 3379   VW, AUDI-NSU Mart Rd ℡ 2108

MINSTER LOVELL Oxon. 403 404 P 28 – pop. 1,085 – ✉ Witney – ☎ 099 387 Asthall Leigh.
London 72 – Gloucester 36 – Oxford 16.

Old Swan (Embassy) with rm, OX8 5RN, ℡ 614, – P. AE
M a la carte 6.55/9.75 **t.** 3.00 – **6 rm** 11.00/20.00 **t.**

MITHIAN Cornwall 403 E 33 – see St. Agnes.

MODBURY Devon 403 I 32 – pop. 1,131 – ECD : Wednesday – ☎ 054 883.
London 237 – Exeter 37 – Plymouth 12.

Exeter Inn, Church St., PL21 0QR, ℡ 239, « 15C inn » – AE ①
M (bar lunch) 8.25 **t.**

at Ermington NW : 2 ½ m. by A 379 on B 3210 – ✉ Ivy Bridge – ☎ 054 883 Modbury :

Ermewood House, PL21 9NS, ℡ 741, – WC WC ☎ P. AE VISA
M (closed Monday in winter) 4.25/5.25 **t.** 1.20 – **12 rm** 11.00/24.00 **t.** –
P 18.00/19.50 **t.**

MONK FRYSTON North Yorks. – pop. 539 – ✉ Lumby – ☎ 0977 South Milford.
London 190 – Kingston-upon-Hull 42 – Leeds 13 – York 20.

Selby Fork (Anchor), LS25 5LF, W : 2 ¼ m. by A 63 on A 1 ℡ 682711, Group
Telex 858875, – TV P. AE ① VISA
M a la carte approx. 6.00 **st.** – 2.50 – **115 rm** 19.50/25.00 **st.**

Monk Fryston Hall, LS25 5DU, ℡ 682369, « Italian garden », park – TV WC ☎ P.
M 3.95/5.50 **t.** 1.50 – **24 rm** 17.50/24.50 **t.**

MONKSPATH STREET West Midlands 403 404 O 26 – see Solihull.

MONMOUTH Gwent 403 L 28 – pop. 6,570 – ECD : Thursday – ☎ 0600.
Envir. : SE : Wye Valley* – Raglan (castle* 15C) SW : 7 m. – Skenfrith (castle and church*)
NW : 6 m.
Leasebrook Lane ℡ 2212.
Wales Tourist Information Centre, c/o Nelson Museum ℡ 3899 (Easter-September).
London 147 – Gloucester 26 – Newport 24 – Swansea 64.

King's Head, Agincourt Sq., NP5 3DY, ℡ 2177, Telex 497294 – TV WC ☎ P.
AE ① VISA
M a la carte 6.65/10.10 **t.** 2.45 – **28 rm** 13.50/28.20 **t.**

Beaufort Arms (T.H.F.), Agincourt Sq., NP5 3BT, ℡ 2411 – TV WC P. AE ① VISA
M 3.45/4.75 **st.** 1.80 – **26 rm** 13.00/22.00 **st.**

at Whitebrook S : 8 ½ m. off A 466 – ✉ Monmouth – ☎ 060 082 Trelleck :

Crown Inn with rm, NP5 4TX, ℡ 254, , French rest. – WC WC P.
closed mid January-February – **M** a la carte 8.05/12.65 **st.** – **8 rm** 12.50/25.00 **st.**

AUSTIN-DAIMLER-JAGUAR-LAND ROVER-MORRIS-   FORD 77/79 Monnow St. ℡ 2366
ROVER-TRIUMPH St. James Sq. ℡ 2773   VAUXHALL, BEDFORD Wonastow Rd ℡ 2896

MONTACUTE Somerset 403 L 31 – see Yeovil.

MORECAMBE Lancs. 𝟵𝟴𝟲 ㉓ – pop. 41,908 (inc. Heysham) – ECD : Wednesday – ✆ 0524.

See : Marineland★ *AC*.

☗ Clubhouse ☏ 418050, on sea front.

🛈 Marine Rd Central ☏ 414110 and 417120.

London 248 – Blackpool 29 – Carlisle 66 – Lancaster 4.

  🏨 **The Elms**, Bare, LA4 6DD, ☏ 411501, 🚗 – ▯ ⇌wc ⇔ 🅿. ◪ *VISA*
     M 3.45/5.20 **st.** ▯ 1.50 – **41 rm** ⊐ 12.65/27.30 **st.** – P approx. 21.15 **st.**

  🏨 **Midland,** Marine Rd, LA4 4BZ, ☏ 417180, ≼ – ▯ 📺 ⇌wc �wc ☎ 🅿. ◪. ◪ AE ⓪ *VISA*
     M 3.95/4.95 **st.** – **42 rm** ⊐ 14.75/28.00 **st.**

  🏨 **Strathmore,** Marine Rd East, LA4 5AP, ☏ 411314 – ▯ ⇌wc ⇔ 🅿. ◪ AE ⓪ *VISA*
     M a la carte 5.25/6.25 **st.** – **67 rm** ⊐ 12.50/27.00 **st.** – P 17.00/18.00 **st.**

  ⌂ **Prospect,** 363 Marine Rd, East Promenade, LA4 5AQ, ☏ 417819 – ⇌wc
     April-October – **13 rm** ⊐ 4.50/10.50 **s.**

AUSTIN-MG-WOLSELEY Marine Rd Central ☏ 410134   TOYOTA West Gate ☏ 415636
FORD Clarke St. ☏ 415061   VAUXHALL Bare Lane ☏ 410205
LADA Thornton Rd ☏ 414141   VW, AUDI Heysham Rd ☏ 415833
SAAB, VOLVO Marlborough Rd ☏ 417437

MORETONHAMPSTEAD Devon 𝟰𝟬𝟯 I 32 – pop. 1,440 – ECD : Thursday – ✆ 064 74.

🛈 ☏ 355.

London 213 – Exeter 12 – Plymouth 38.

  🏨 **Manor House** (B.T.H.) ⅋, TQ13 8RE, SW : 2 m. on B 3212 ☏ 355, Telex 42794, ≼,
     ✕, 🛈, 🢑, 🚗, park – ▯ 📺 ♿ 🅿. ◪. ◪ AE ⓪ *VISA*
     M 6.50/8.75 **st.** ▯ 2.40 – **67 rm** ⊐ 28.50/48.70 **st.**

     at Lustleigh SE : 4 m. on A 382 – ✉ ✆ 064 77 Lustleigh :

  ✕ **Moorwood Cottage,** TQ13 9SN, NW : 1 ½ m. on A 382 ☏ 341 – 🅿
     closed Sunday – **M** (dinner only) a la carte 4.35/6.25 **t.** ▯ 2.00.

     at North Bovey SW : 2 m. – ✉ ✆ 064 74 Moretonhampstead :

  🏠 Glebe House ⅋, TQ13 8RA, ☏ 544, ≼, 🚗 – ⇌wc filwc 🅿
     10 rm.

  ⌂ **Blackaller House** ⅋, TQ13 8QY, ☏ 322, ≼, 🢑, 🚗 – 🅿
     closed January and February – **M** (bar lunch) 6.00 **t.** ▯ 2.25 – **6 rm** ⊐ 8.50/17.00 **t.**

MORETON-IN-MARSH Glos. 𝟰𝟬𝟯 𝟰𝟬𝟰 0 26 – pop. 2,477 – ECD : Wednesday – ✆ 0608.

Envir. : Chastleton House★★ (Elizabethan) *AC*, SE : 3 ½ m.

🛈 Council Offices, High St. ☏ 50881.

London 86 – Birmingham 40 – Gloucester 31 – Oxford 29.

  🏨 **Manor House** (Best Western), High St., GL56 0LJ, ☏ 50501, Telex 837151, « Gar-
     dens » – ▯ 📺 ⇌wc ☎ 🅿. ◪. ◪ AE ⓪ *VISA*
     closed first week January – **M** a la carte 5.25/7.00 **st.** ▯ 2.90 – **34 rm** ⊐ 15.00/
     36.50 **st.**

  🏠 **White Hart Royal** (T.H.F.), High St., GL56 0BA, ☏ 50731, 🚗 – 📺 ⇌wc ☎ 🅿. ◪.
     ◪ AE ⓪ *VISA*
     M 4.25/4.75 **st.** ▯ 1.80 – **27 rm** ⊐ 13.50/22.50 **st.**

  ✕✕ **Lamb's,** High St., GL56 0AZ, ☏ 50251, « Tasteful decor » – ◪ *VISA*
     closed Sunday dinner, Tuesday lunch and Monday – **M** a la carte 4.25/12.30 **t.** ▯ 1.80.

  ✕✕ Redesdale Arms (Crest) with rm, High St., GL56 0AW, ☏ 50308 – ⇌wc 🅿. ◪ AE ⓪
     VISA
     15 rm ⊐ 13.30/23.70 **st.**

ALFA-ROMEO Oddington Service Station ☏ 0451   BMW ☏ 50323
(Stow-on-the-Wold) 30132   RENAULT Little Compton ☏ 74202
AUSTIN-MORRIS-MG-ROVER-TRIUMPH London Rd
☏ 50585

MORPETH Northumb. 𝟵𝟴𝟲 ⑲ – pop. 14,054 – ECD : Thursday – ✆ 0670.

Envir.: Brinkburn Priory (site★, church★ : Gothic) *AC*, NW : 10 m.

☗ The Common ☏ 2065, S : 1 m. on A 197 – ☗ Acorn Bank ☏ 0670 (Bedlington) 822457,
SE : 4 m.

London 301 – Edinburgh 93 – Newcastle-upon-Tyne 15.

  ✕✕ **Gourmet,** 59 Bridge St., NE61 1PQ, ☏ 56200 – ◪ AE ⓪ *VISA*
     closed Sunday, Monday, 3 weeks February and Bank Holidays – **M** a la carte 4.85/8.50 **t.**
     ▯ 1.90.

AUSTIN-MORRIS-MG-ROVER-TRIUMPH Oldgate ☏   FORD 53/55 Bridge St. ☏ 2323
3286   RENAULT Cliton ☏ 2538
FIAT Queen St. Amble ☏ 0665 (Amble) 710247   VAUXHALL Bridge End ☏ 2115
FIAT ☏ 3655   VW-AUDI ☏ 3777

MORTEHOE Devon 📖 H 30 – see Woolacombe.

MOULTON Northants. 📖 R 27 – see Northampton.

MOULTON North Yorks. – pop. 198 – ⊠ Richmond – ✆ 032 577 Barton.
London 243 – Leeds 53 – Middlesbrough 25 – Newcastle-upon-Tyne 43.

XX **Black Bull Inn**, DL10 6QJ, ☏ 289, « Victoriana decor and Brighton Belle Pullman coach » – P
    closed Sunday and 24 to 31 December – **M** a la carte 6.45/11.00 **st.**

MOUNT PLEASANT Hants. 📖 📖 P 31 – see Lymington.

MOUSEHOLE Cornwall 📖 D 33 – pop 1,079 – ✆ 073 673.
London 321 – Penzance 3 – Truro 29.

🏠 **Lobster Pot**, TR19 6PT, ☏ 251, ≼ – ⊷wc 🛏wc
    Mid February-mid November – **M** 4.00/6.00 ⌀ 1.70 – **31 rm** �涎 9.00/22.00.

MUDEFORD Dorset 📖 📖 O 31 – see Christchurch.

MULLION Cornwall 📖 E 33 – pop. 1,346 – ECD : Wednesday – ⊠ Helston – ✆ 0326.
See : Mullion Cove (site★).
🏌 Cury ☏ 240276, N : 3 m.
London 323 – Falmouth 21 – Penzance 21 – Truro 26.

🏠 **Polurrian** ⤳, TR12 7EN, SW : ½ m. ☏ 240421, ≼ Mounts Bay, ✽, ⌷ heated, 🚗 – ⊷wc P
    May-September – **M** 4.00/5.40 **st.** ⌀ 1.75 – **45 rm** �涎 12.75/40.20 **st.**

🏠 **Mullion Cove** ⤳, TR12 7EP, SW : 1 ¼ m. ☏ 240328, ≼ Mullion Cove and Mounts Bay, ✽, ⌷ heated, 🚗 – ⊷wc P
    M (bar lunch) 5.00 **st.** – **45 rm** �涎 10.00/26.00 **st.** – P 14.00/15.00 **st.**

MUMBLES West Glam. 📖 I 29 – pop. 13,712 – ECD : Wednesday – ⊠ ✆ 0792 Swansea.
See: Mumbles Head★. Envir.: Cefn Bryn (✽★★★ from the reservoir) W : 12 m – Rhosili (site and ≼ ★★★) W : 18 m.
London 202 – Swansea 6.

🏠 **Osborne** (Embassy), Rotherslade Rd, Langland Bay, SA3 4QL, W : ¾ m. ☏ 66274, ≼, 🚗 – 🍴 TV ⊷wc ☎ P. 🔲 AE ⓪ VISA
    closed Christmas – **M** *(closed Sunday dinner)* 4.60/4.95 **st.** – **42 rm** �涎 12.00/22.00 **st.** – P 20.80/45.10 **st.**

🏠 **Langland Court** ⤳, 31 Langland Court Rd, Langland Bay, SA3 4TD, W : 1 m. ☏ 68505, 🚗 – TV ⊷wc 🛏 ⤻ P. 🅿 AE
    M 4.00/5.00 ⌀ 2.00 – �涎 2.50 – **20 rm** 13.50/25.00 – P 21.50/23.00.

🏠 **St. Annes**, Western Lane, SA3 4EY, ☏ 69147, ≼ – TV ⊷wc ☎ P
    closed 1 week at Christmas – **M** (bar lunch Monday to Saturday) 3.00 **s.** ⌀ 2.00 – **21 rm** �涎 7.00/15.00 **s.**

🏠 **Brynfield** ⤳, Brynfield Rd, Langland Bay, SA3 4SX, W : 1 m. ☏ 66208, ≼, 🚗 – ⊷wc P
    17 rm.

⌂ **Carlton**, 654-656 Mumbles Rd, Southend, SA3 4EA, ☏ 60450 – 🛏
    closed Saturday and Sunday in winter and 21 December-5 January – **19 rm** ⊿ 8.50/18.00 **t.**

XXX **Norton House** with rm, 17 Norton Rd, SA3 5TQ, ☏ 66174 – P. 🔲
    closed 25-26 December and 1 January – **M** *(closed Sunday)* (dinner only) a la carte 6.20/13.40 **t.** – ⊿ 2.30 – **4 rm** 16.00/20.00 **t.**

X Quo Vadis, 614-616 Mumbles Rd, Southend, SA3 4EF, ☏ 60706, Italian rest.

X **La Gondola**, 590 Mumbles Rd, SA3 4DL, ☏ 62338, Italian rest. – 🔲
    closed Monday – **M** a la carte 4.50/6.05 **st.** ⌀ 1.40.

NANNERCH Clwyd 📖 K 24 – pop. 262 – ⊠ Mold – ✆ 035 283 Hendre.
London 213 – Birkenhead 26 – Chester 18 – Shrewsbury 46.

X **Rising Sun Inn**, CH7 5HG, on A 541 ☏ 205 – P. 🔲 VISA
    closed Sunday dinner – **M** a la carte 3.80/8.10 **t.**

Switch to Michelin for longer life.

Michelin radial tyres

XZX

The XZX follows the classic Michelin steel-braced radial configuration combined with a specially designed tread and is suitable for fitment to cars capable of speeds up to 180 km/h (113 mph).

- Exceptional adhesion particularly in the wet due to the tread design
- Tread life is well up to the high standards set by Michelin
- Excellent comfort and low noise levels
- Reduces fuel consumption

TRX

An entirely new generation of radials with a unique super low profile allied to a new wheel and rim combination.

- Outstanding road holding and vehicle control
- Exceptional adhesion, wet or dry
- Exceptional passenger and vehicle protection
- Maintains the high mileage characteristic of Michelin radials

XAS

The XAS is an asymmetric radial tyre designed to deal with problems associated with speeds up to 130 mph. The unique disposition of steel cord stabilising plies beneath the tread, contribute to exceptional straight line stability and cornering precision.

- HR category, for speeds up to 130 mph
- Exceptional grip wet or dry
- Remarkable comfort
- Reduces fuel consumption

XVS

The XVS is an asymmetric tyre complementary to the XAS and suitable for fitment to cars with a maximum speed capability of up to 210 km/h (130 mph) and able to sustain speeds at or near that figure.

- Designed for sustained high speed performance
- Exceptional adhesion on wet and dry surfaces
- Reduces fuel consumption
- Remarkable comfort

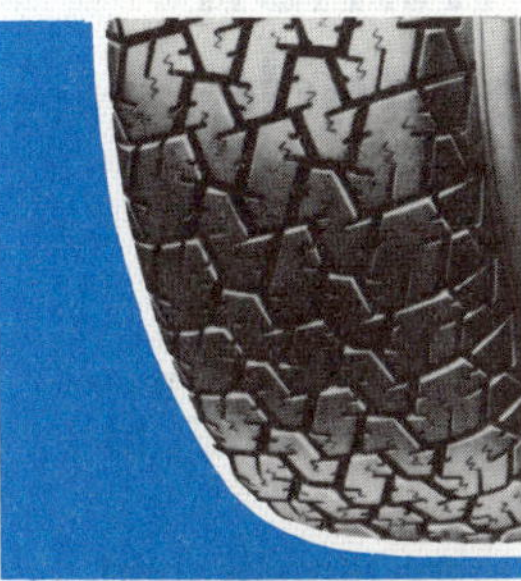

XDX

The XDX is designed to meet the requirements of cars capable of speeds in excess of 210 km/h (130 mph) but having a maximum of 227 km/h (142 mph)

- Excellent road holding and stability
- Exceptional ride comfort for a VR tyre
- Quiet running not normally associated with tyres in the VR category
- Low power absorption (leading to fuel economy)

XWX

The XWX is designed for high performance cars with a speed capability well in excess of 210 km/h (130 mph)

- Provides excellent stability at very high speeds
- Exceptional grip and road holding

R CATEGORY

XM+S tyres

Designed to give exceptional adhesion and traction in adverse conditions. Suitable for speeds up to 160 km/h (100 mph) or 150 km/h (90 mph) if studded

- Radial winter tyre
- Suitable for normal road use
- Extra adhesion in snow, mud or adverse conditions
- Moulded holes for studs
- Reduces fuel consumption

XM+S88/89

The XM+S88/89 are improved winter radials suitable for speeds up to 160 km/h (100 mph) or 150 km/h (90 mph) if studded

- Excellent grip on snow, ice and muddy conditions
- Extremely good stability
- Moulded holes for studs
- Reduces fuel consumption

Michelin tyre fitment and pressure guide

Alignment: with Michelin radial tyres all round the best alignment is parallel. Where the vehicle manufacturer recommends a TOE-IN setting PARALLEL to $\frac{1}{16}''$ TOE-IN should be used. Where a TOE-OUT alignment is recommended PARALLEL to $\frac{1}{16}''$ TOE-OUT setting should be used.

Pressures: the pressures shown in the fitment chart are in pounds per square inch (lb/in^2). Where additional pressure is required for full load conditions or sustained high speed or both this is indicated by (L), for full load and (S) for speed or (LS) for a combination of full load and sustained high speed.

Towing: An increase in pressure in the rear tyres of the car is recommended when towing unless an increase in the rear tyre pressures is already being used i.e. (L), (S) or (LS) in which case no further increase is necessary.

XRN*, XM+S, XM+S8, XM+S89. These tyres may replace XZX/ZX tyres on cars shown in the fitment tables.

XRN*. Use XZX/ZX pressures.

XM+S, XM+S88, XM+S89. It is recommended that these tyres are fitted in complete sets. If fitted, increase XZX/ZX pressures by 3 lb/in^2 except for Minis and derivatives where standard XZX/ZX pressures should be used.

Fitting of Michelin radial tubeless tyres

Most sizes of Michelin radial tyres are available in tubeless versions, but they may only be fitted as such providing certain conditions are fulfilled. Please consult your tyre specialists for full information.

XAS, XVS, XDX, XWX. It is preferred that these tyres are fitted in complete sets only. If it is necessary to mix these tyres, consult Michelin.

TRX. These tyres must be fitted in complete sets only.

** XRN tyres are no longer produced.*

Car Make and Model	Michelin Radial Fitment	Pressure Front	Rear
ALFA ROMEO			
Alfasud 5M, SE, 5M (1186cc)	145 SR 13XZX	28	22
Alfetta 1·8, 1·6	165 SR 14XZX	26	29
2000GTV	165 HR 14XAS	26	26
AUDI			
Audi 80, 80L, S, LS	155 SR 13XZX	25,26(L)	25,32(L)
80GTE	175/70 HR 13XVS	25,26(L)	25,32(L)
Audi 100, 100S, 100GL, 100LS	165 SR 14XZX	29,32(L)	29,32(L)
Audi 100GL 5E, L 5E, SE	185/70 HR 14XVS	28,30(L)	28,30(L)
AUSTIN–see Leyland			
BMW			
2002 Tii (Sept 73 onwards)	165 HR 13XAS	29,29(L)	29,32(L)
316, 318	165 SR 13XZX	26,28(L)	26,29(L)
320/6	185/70 HR 14XVS	29,30(L)	29,34(L)
320i	185/70 HR 13XVS	28,29(L)	28,30(L)
518	175 SR 14XZX	28,30(L)	28,34(L)
520, 520A, 520i	195/70 HR 14XVS	28,30(L)	28,34(L)
525, 525 Auto	175 HR 14XAS	30,32(L)	30,36(L)
528	195/70 HR 14XVS	30,32(L)	30,35(L)
2500 (Sept 73 onwards)	175 HR 14XAS	30,32(L)	30,34(L)
2800 (Sept 73 onwards)	195/70 HR 14XVS	30,32(L)	28,34(L)
2800CS	195/70 HR 14XVS	32	32
3.0L	195/70 HR 14XVS	32,32(L)	32,36(L)
3.0Si, 3.3Li	195/70 VR 14XDX	32,32(L)	32,36(L)
3.0CS, CSi, CSA	195/70 VR 14XDX	29,32(L)	29,32(L)
3.0CSL	195/70 VR 14XDX	30,34(L)	30,35(L)
3.3L	195/70 VR 14XDX	29,33(L)	30,35(L)
630CS 633CSi	195/70 VR 14XWX	34,35(L)	30,35(L)
728	195/70 HR 14XVS	32,34(L)	32,38(L)
733i	205/70 VR 14XDX	32,34(L)	32,38(L)
CHRYSLER–see Talbot			
CITROEN			
2CV, Dyane 4 and 6, 2CV6	125–15X	20	26
Ami 8	125–15X	26	26
Ami Super and Super Estate	135 SR 15XZX	26	28
GS 1015 and 1220 All Models	145 SR 15XZX	26	28
CX2000/2200 Manual steering	185 SR 14XZX(Front) 175 SR 14XZX(Rear)	28	30
CX2000/2200 Power assisted steering	185 HR 14XVS(Front) 175 HR 14XVS(Rear)	28	30
CX2200 Diesel Saloon Manual steering	185 SR 14XZX(Front) 175 SR 14XZX(Rear)	30	30
CX2200 Diesel Safari	185 SR 14XZX	30	32
CX2400 Super CX2400 Pallas	185 HR 14XVS(Front) 175 HR 14XVS(Rear)	28	30
CX2400 G.T.I.	185 HR 14XVS	30	32
CX2400 Prestige	185 HR 14XVS	32	32
SM 2·6i, 2·9 Auto	205/70VR 14XWX	34	30
COLT			
Lancer 1400, 1600 Saloons	155 SR 13XZX	23	24
Celeste 1600ST, 1600GS, 2000	165 SR 13XZX	26	28
Galant 1600 Estate	165 SR 13XZX	24,26(L)	24,33(L)
Galant GTO 2000GSR	185/70 HR 13XVS	24	30
Sigma 2000, 1600	165 SR 13XZX	27	27
DAF–see Volvo			

*(L) (S) (LS) See notes at head of table

Car Make and Model	Michelin Radial Fitment	Pressure Front	Rear
DAIMLER			
Sovereign 2·8, 3·4, 4·2			
Sovereign Series II & III	205/70VR15XDX	25,31(LS)	26,36(LS)
Vanden Plas 4·2 Saloon			
Double Six			
Double Six Vanden Plas	205/70VR15XDX	26,34(LS)	26,36(LS)
DATSUN			
100A Cherry, B110/1200			
Saloon and Coupé	155 SR12XZX	21	21
120A Coupé	155 SR12XZX	21	21
120Y MkII Saloon & Coupé	155 SR13XZX	24	24
120Y MkII Estate	155 SR13XZX	24,24(L)	24,28(L)
140J, 160J, 160J SSS	165 SR13XZX	24,28(L)	24,28(L)
160B, 180B	165 SR13XZX	24,28(L)	24,28(L)
2000 Estate	175 SR14XZX	21,26(LS)	21,36(LS)
200L & GL Laurel Saloon & Coupé	165 SR14XZX	24	24
240C Saloon	175 SR14XZX	26,30(LS)	26,30(LS)
240K GT	175 HR14XAS	24,28(LS)	26,30(LS)
260C Saloon & Coupé	175 HR14XAS	26,30(LS)	26,30(LS)
FIAT			
124, 124S, 124 Special T	155 SR13XZX	24	26
124 Sports Coupé 1400	165 SR13XZX	26	29
124 Sports Coupé 1·6, 1·8	165 SR13XZX	29	29
124 Estate	165 SR13XZX	23,23(L)	29,32(L)
126	135 SR12XZX	20	29
127L (2 door) & Special	135 SR13XZX	24	27
127CL, 1050CL (3 door)	135 SR13XZX	24,24(L)	27,31(L)
128, 128S, Coupé Rally	145 SR13XZX	26	24
X1·9	165/70 13ZX	26	28
130B (3·2 litre)	205/70 HR14XVS	29	32
130BC Coupé (3·2 litre)	205/70 VR14XDX	32	32
131 1300 & 1600	155 SR13XZX	26	28
131 1300, 1600 Estates	165 SR13XZX	26	32
132 Special, GLS 1600, 1800	185/70 SR13ZX	26	28
132 (2000)	175/70 SR14ZX	26	28
Option	180/65 HR 390TRX		
Mirafiori 1300L, 1600CL	155 SR13XZX / 175/70 SR13ZX	26	26
Super Mirafiori	165 SR13XZX	26	29
	175/70 SR13ZX	26	26
FORD			
Fiesta L, S, Ghia	145 SR12XZX	23,26(L)	26,29(L)
Escort MkI 1100, 1300	155 SR12XZX	22	28
Escort MkI Estates 1100 & 1300	155 SR12XZX	22,22(L)	28,32(L)
Escort MkI 1300GT	155 SR12XZX	24	28
Escort MkI Sport & Executive	165 SR13XZX	20,23(L)	23,30(L)
Escort MkII 1100	155 SR12XZX	22,25(LS)	28,36(LS)
	155 SR13XZX	22,25(LS)	25,36(LS)
Escort MkII 1100 Estate	155 SR12XZX	22,25(LS)	28,36(LS)
Heavy-Duty	155 SR12XZX Reinf.	22,25(LS)	28,36(LS)
Escort MkII Popular 'Base'			
1100 & 1300	155 SR12XZX	22,25(LS)	28,36(LS)
1100 Popular 'Plus'	155 SR13XZX	22,25(LS)	25,36(LS)
1300 Popular 'Plus'	155 SR12XZX	22,25(LS)	28,36(LS
Escort MkII 1300, L, GL,			
Ghia 1300, 1300 Estate	155 SR13XZX	22,25(LS)	25,36(LS)
1300 Estate Heavy-Duty	155 SR13XZX Reinf.	22,25(LS)	25,36(LS)
Escort MkII 1300, 1600 Sport	175/70SR13ZX	22,23(LS)	25,36(LS)
Escort MkII 1600	155 SR13XZX	22,25(LS)	25,36(LS)
Escort MkII RS 1800, RS 2000	175/70 HR13XVS	24,26(L)	27,28(L)

*(L) (S) (LS) See notes at head of table

Car Make and Model	Michelin Radial Fitment	Pressure Front	Rear
FORD			
Escort Mexico	175/70 HR 13 XVS	24,26(L)	27,28(L)
Cortina MkIII Saloons until September 73	165 SR 13 XZX	23,26(L)	23,28(L)
September 73 until 76	165 SR 13 XZX	26,26(L)	26,30(L)
Cortina MkIII Family Estates (until 76)	165 SR 13 XZX	23,26)(L)	23,36(L)
Cortina MkIII Saloons (76 onwards)	165 SR 13 XZX	26,28(L)	26,36(L)
Cortina MkIII Estates (76 onwards)	165 SR 13 XZX	26,26(L)	26,40(L)
Cortina MkIV Saloons	165 SR 13 XZX	26,28(L)	26,36(L)
Cortina MkIV Estates	165 SR 13 XZX	26,28(L)	26,40)(L)
Cortina MkIV Estates Heavy-Duty	175 SR 13 ZX Reinf.	21,25(L)	24,40(L)
Capri 1300 and GT 1600 and GT, 2000GT	165 SR 13 XZX	24	27
Capri 3000, E, GT, GXL	185/70 HR 13 XVS	26	26
Capri II 1300, 1600, 2000	165 SR 13 XZX	21,27(LS)	27,31(LS)
Capri II 3000	185/70 HR 13 XVS	28,28(LS)	28,34(LS)
Granada 2 litre, Consul 2 litre	175 SR 14 XZX	21,24(L)	23,27(L)
	185 SR 14 XZX	20,23(L)	21,26(L)
Granada 2·5 litre	175 SR 14 XZX	24,26(L)	24,30(L)
Consul, Granada 2·5 Estate	185 SR 14 XZX	23,27(L)	23,28(L)
Granada 3·0 Estate Auto	185 SR 14 XZX	24,27(L)	24,33(L)
Manual	185 HR 14 XVS		
	185 SR 14 XZX	23,24(L)	23,27(L)
Granada 3 litre Automatic Ghia and Coupé	175 SR 14 XZX / 185 SR 14 XZX	24,26(L) / 23,24(L)	24,30(L) / 23,27(L)
Granada 3 litre Manual Ghia and Coupé	175 HR 14 XAS / 185 HR 14 XVS	24,26(L) / 23,24(L)	24,30(L) / 23,27(L)
Granada 3000 S	195/70 HR 14 XVS	24,27(L)	24,33)(L)
Granada II Estates 2·0L, 2·3L Estates	185 SR 14 XZX	25,27(L)	25,36(L)
2·8GL Auto Estate 'S' option	185 SR 14 XZX / 190/65 HR 390TRX	25,27(L)	25,36(L)
2·8i GL 'S' Estate option	190/65 HR 390TRX / 185/70 HR 14 XVS	25,27(L)	27,36(L)
Granada II Saloons 2·0L, 2·3L 2·1 diesel	175 SR 14 XZX / 185 SR 14 XZX	24,27(L)	24,27(L)
2·3GL 2·8GL Auto	175 SR 14 XZX / 185 SR 14 XZX	24,27(L)	24,27(L)
'S' option	190/65 HR 390TRX	25,28(L)	25,36(L)
2·8iGL 'S', 2·8i Ghia	190/65 HR 390TRX	25,28(L)	25,36(L)
option	185 HR 14 XVS	24,27(L)	24,33(L)
2·8 Ghia Auto	185 SR 14 XZX	24,27(L)	24,27(L)
'S' option	190/65 HR 390TRX	25,28(L)	25,36(L)
2·8i 'S' option	190/65 HR 390TRX / 195/70 HR 14 XVS	24,27(L)	24,36(L)
HILLMAN–see Talbot			
HONDA			
Civic 1500 & 1200	155 SR 12 XZX	24	24
Accord	155 SR 13 XZX	24	24
JAGUAR			
XJ6, XJ6L, XJ6C, 2·8, 3·4, 4·2	205/70VR15XDX	25,31(LS)	26,36(LS)
XJ12, XJ12L, XJ12C	205/70 VR 15 XDX	26,34(LS)	26,36(LS)
E Type V12	205/70 VR 15 XWX	24,38(S)	28,40(S)
XJS	205/70 VR 15 XWX	26 <120 mph / 32 >120 mph	26 / 32

*(L) (S) (LS) See notes at head of table

Car Make and Model	Michelin Radial Fitment	Pressure Front	Rear
LADA			
1200 Saloon	155 SR 13XZX	25	
1200 Estate	165 SR 13XZX	22,22(L)	29,32(L)
LANCIA			
Beta 1300, 1400	155 SR 14ZX	25,28(LS)	25,28(LS)
Beta 1600, 1800, 2000			
Beta 1800 ES, 2000 ES	175/70 SR 14ZX	25,28(LS)	25,28(LS)
Beta 1600 Coupé			
Beta 1800, 2000 Coupé	175/70 HR 14XVS	25,28(LS)	25,28(LS)
Beta HPE 1600/1800/2000	175/70 SR 14ZX	25,28(LS)	25,28(LS)
Fulvia 1·3S Coupé	165 SR 14XZX	26	26
LEYLAND			
Mini, Mini Cooper			
Mini Countryman	145 SR 10XZX	28	26
Mini Clubman & Estate			
Mini Cooper 'S' 1275 GT (until 74)	145 SR 10XAS	26	26
1100, 1300, 1100 Princess 1300GT	155 SR 12XZX	23	26
1100, 1300 Countryman	155 SR 12XZX	23,23(L)	26,29(L)
Allegro 1100, 1300 MkI	145 SR 13XZX	26	30
Allegro 1500, 1750 MkI & Vanden Plas MkI	155 SR 13XZX	26	30
Allegro 1100, 1300, 1500 MkII	145 SR 13XZX	26	24
Vanden Plas MkII, 1750 MkII	155 SR 13XZX		
Allegro Estate 1300 MkII	145 SR 13XZX	26,26(L)	24,29(L)
1500 MkII	155 SR 13XZX		
Marina 1·3, 1·8	145 SR 13XZX	26	28
Marina 1·8TC, 2-1·8, 1·8S HL, GT	155 SR 13XZX	26	28
Marina, Marina 2-Estate	155 SR 13XZX	26,26(L)	28,32(L)
Maxi 1500, 1750	155 SR 13XZX	26	24
1750HL	165 SR 13XZX		
1800 MkII, 1800, 2200 MkIII	165 SR 14XZX	30	24
MAZDA			
1000, DL	155 SR 13XZX	26	26
323 1300	155 SR 13XZX	26	26
818 Saloon & Coupé, RX3	155 SR 13XZX	26	26
616	165 SR 13XZX	26	26
929 Saloon & Coupé	175 SR 13XZX	24	24
MERCEDES BENZ			
200/8, 220/8, 200D/8 220D/8, 230/8 (until 76)	175 SR 14ZX-P	29	34
200, 200D, 220D, 240D, 230.4, 230.6, 250 (76 onwards)	175 SR 14ZX-P	29 <100 mph 32 >100 mph	34 36
230SL	185 HR 14XVS-P	26	32
280, 280C, 280E, 280CE (76 onwards)	195/70 HR 14XVS-P	29 <100 mph 32 >100 mph	34 36
280S, 280SE (Post 1972)	185 HR 14XVS-P	30,34(L)	34,36(L)
280SL, SLC	185 HR 14XVS-P	32	36
280SE 3·5 and 300SEL 3·5	205/70 VR 14XDX 205/70 VR 14XWX	32	36
350SE 3·5 litre	205/70 HR 14XVS	30,34(L)	34,36(L)
350SL, 350SLC, 450SL, 450SLC	205/70 VR 14XDX 205/70 VR 14XWX	32	36

*(L) (S) (LS) See notes at head of table

Car Make and Model	Michelin Radial Fitment	Pressure Front	Rear
MERCEDES BENZ			
350SE 4·5 Litre, 450SE	205/70 VR 14XDX	30,34(L)	34,36(L)
450SEL 4·5	205/70 VR 14XWX		
450SEL 6·9 Litre	215/70 VR 14XWX	32,35(L)	32,35(L)
MG			
1100 & 1300	155 SR 12XZX	23	26
Midget MkI, II, III & 1500	145 SR 13XZX	22,22(L)	24,26(L)
MGB Tourer, GT	165 SR 14XZX	21,21(L)	24,26(L)
MGB GT V8	175 HR 14XAS	21,26(L)	25,32(L)
MORRIS – see Leyland			
OPEL			
Kadett Economy	155 SR 12XZX	19,22(L)	24,30(L)
Kadett DL, Special, Coupé, City DL, City Special	155 SR 13XZX	20,22(L)	25,29(L)
Kadett Estate	155 SR 13XZX	22,23(L)	29,35(L)
Kadett 1·2 Coupé Rallye	175/70 SR 13ZX	19,20(L)	22,26(L)
Kadett GTE Coupé	175/70 HR 13XVS	25,28(L)	25,32(L)
Ascona 1·6 & 1·9 (75 onwards)	165 SR 13XZX	25,29(L)	25,29(L)
Ascona Estate 1·6, 1·6S & 1·9S	165 SR 13XZX	26,26(L)	29,38(L)
Manta 1·6 & 1·9 (75 onwards)	165 SR 13XZX	25,29(L)	25,29(L)
Manta Berlinetta 1·6 & 1·9 (75 onwards)	185/70 SR 13ZX	23,26(L)	23,26(L)
1·9SH & Coupés	175 SR 14XZX	26,26(L)	26,29(L)
Rekord II 2,000 S Saloon	175 SR 14XZX	26,26(L)	26,29(L)
Commodore GS, 2·5H	165 HR 14XAS	26,29(S)	26,30(S)
Commodore GS, 2·5E, 2·8H & Coupés	165 HR 14XAS	29,32(S)	30,35(S)
PEUGEOT			
104 GL	135 SR 13XZX	28	32
104 SL	135 SR 13XZX	26	29
104 Coupé	135 HR 13XAS	26	32
204	135 SR 14ZX	25	29
204 Estate	145 SR 14ZX	25,25(L)	30,38(L)
304 GL, SLS (Sept 73 onwards)	145 SR 14XZX	26	30
304 GL Estate, SL Estate (Sept 73 onwards)	145 SR 14XZX	26	39
305 GL, GR, SR	145 SR 14XZX-P	26	30
504 L Petrol	165 SR 14XZX	26	30
504 L Estate, GL Estate, Family Estate Petrol	185 SR 14XZX Reinf.	23	46
504 L Diesel	165 SR 14XZX	25	29
504 L, Family Diesel Estates	185 SR 14XZX Reinf.	25	46
504 GL, GL Diesel	175 SR 14XZX	26	30
504 Ti	175 HR 14XAS	22	26
504 V6 (L.H.D.)	190/65 HR 390TRX	20	26
604 SLS V6, SL, Ti	175 HR 14XAS-P	26,30(L) or (S)	30,35(L) or (S)
	190/65 HR 390TRX	22	30
PRINCESS			
18-22 Series (all models) 2200 HLS	185/70 SR 14ZX	26	24
RENAULT			
R4, R4L, R4TL	135 SR 13XZX	20	23
R5, R5L, R5TL, R5GTL	145 SR 13XZX	23,26(LS)	26,29(LS)
R5TS	145 SR 13XZX	23,25(LS)	28,29(LS)
R6, R6L	135 SR 13XZX	22,25(LS)	25,28(LS)

*(L) (S) (LS) See notes at head of table

Car Make and Model	Michelin Radial Fitment	Pressure Front	Rear
R6TL (4 seat)	135 SR 13 XZX	22,23(LS)	26,29(LS)
(5 seat)	145 SR 13 XZX	20,22(LS)	25,26(LS)
R12L, R12TL	145 SR 13 XZX	23,26(LS)	26,29(LS)
R12TS	145 SR 13 XZX	23,26(LS)	26,29(LS)
R12 Estate	155 SR 13 XZX	23,25(LS)	26,29(LS)
R14TL	145 SR 13 XZX	25	28
R15TL, R15TS	155 SR 13 XZX	26,29(LS)	28,30(LS)
R15GTL Manual	145 SR 13 XZX	26	28
R16, R16TL	145 SR 14 ZX	23,25(LS)	29,32(LS)
R16TS, R16TX	155 SR 14 ZX	26,25(LS)	26,32(LS)
R17TL	155 SR 13 XZX	26,29(LS)	28,30(LS)
R17TS, R17 Gordini	165 HR 13 XAS	28,30(LS)	30,32(LS)
R20TL (Manual)	165 SR 13 XZX	28,30(L)	28,30(L)
R20TL (Auto)	165 SR 13 XZX	29,32(L)	28,30(L)
30TS (Manual)	175 HR 14 XAS	26,29(LS)	28,32(LS)
30TS (Automatic)	175 HR 14 XAS	28,30(LS)	29,32(LS)

ROVER

Car Make and Model	Michelin Radial Fitment	Pressure Front	Rear
2000 & TC, 2200 & TC	165 SR 14 XZX	30	28
3500, 3500S	185 HR 14 XVS	28,30(L)	30,34(L)
2300, 2600 SD1	175 HR 14 XVS	29,30(L)	30,32(L)
3,500 SD1	185 HR 14 XVS	26,26(L)	26,30(L)
Range Rover	205 R 16 XM+S	25,25(L)	25,35(L)

SAAB

Car Make and Model	Michelin Radial Fitment	Pressure Front	Rear
96 V4	155 SR 15 XZX	25,28(L)	25,28(L)
99 (1·85, 2·0 litre)	155 SR 15 XZX	28,30(L)	28,30(L)
99 GL, GLE, GLS	165 SR 15 XZX	28,30(L)	28,30(L)
99 EMS (Aug 75 on)	165 HR 15 XAS	28,30(L)	28,30(L)

SIMCA

Car Make and Model	Michelin Radial Fitment	Pressure Front	Rear
1000 S, SR, GLS, 1000 LS Rally and Rally1	145 SR 13 XZX	16,19(LS)	26,29(LS)
1100, LE, LX, GLX, ES, GLS	145 SR 13 XZX	25,26(LS)	26,29(LS)
1100 Estate GLS	155 SR 13 XZX	23,23(L)	26,32(L)
1300, 1301, 1301 Special 1500, 1501, 1501 Special	165 SR 13 XZX	23,26(LS)	25,28(LS)
1301, 1501 Estates 1501, 1301 Special Estates	175 SR 13 ZX	23,23(L)	26,32(L)

SINGER – for Chamois and Chamois Sports models – see Talbot (Hillman Imp)

SKODA

Car Make and Model	Michelin Radial Fitment	Pressure Front	Rear
S100, S110	155 SR 14 XZX	20	25
Estelle 105, 120	155 SR 14 XZX	20	26

TALBOT

Car Make and Model	Michelin Radial Fitment	Pressure Front	Rear
Rapier 1967 +	165 SR 14 XZX	26	26
Avenger 1300, 1600, DL, S & Estates, 1600GT, 1600GLS	155 SR 13 XZX	24,24(L)	24,30(L)
Avenger Heavy-Duty Estate	155 SR 13 XZX	24,24(L)	24,36(L)
180	175 SR 14 XZX	22,23(LS)	26,28(LS)
2 litre 1973 +	175 SR 14 XZX	22,23(LS)	26,28(LS)
Alpine GL, S, GLS	155 SR 13 XZX	26,28(L) or (S)	26,29(L) or (S)
Horizon 1·1GL, LS, 1·3GL, LS, GLS	145 SR 13 XZX	26,30(LS)	26,30(LS)
Sunbeam 1·0	145 SR 13 XZX / 155 SR 13 XZX	21,22(L)	25,32(L)
Sunbeam 1·3, 1·6	155 SR 13 XZX	22,22(L)	22,28(L)
Imp (all Models)	155 SR 12 XZX	18	30
Hunter, DL, S, GT	155 SR 13 XZX	24	24
Hunter Estate	165 SR 13 XZX	24	26

*(L) (S) (LS) See notes at head of table

Car Make and Model	Michelin Radial Fitment	Pressure Front	Rear
TOYOTA			
Corolla 1100	155 SR 12XZX	20	22
Corolla 1200 Saloon & Coupé	155 SR 12XZX	22	24
Corolla 1200 Estate	155 SR 12XZX Reinf.	24,24(L)	26,30(L)
Corolla 30 Saloon & Coupé	155 SR 13XZX	24,24(L)	24,26(L)
Corolla 30 Estate	155 SR 13XZX	24,24(L)	24,28(L)
Corona 1900	165 SR 13XZX	24	26
Carina & Celica 1600 (until 76)	165 SR 13XZX	24	26
Celica 1600 ST	165 SR 13XZX	24	27
Celica 2000 GT Liftback	185/70 HR 14XVS	24	27
Carina (76 onwards)	165 SR 13XZX 185/70 SR 13ZX	24,26(L)	26,30(L)
Cressida	175 SR 14XZX	24	26
Publica 1000 Saloon, Coupé	155 SR 12XZX	24,26(L)	24,28(L)
Crown 2600 Saloon & Coupé	175 SR 14XZX	26,26(L)	26,28(L)
TRIUMPH			
1300,1500	155 SR 13XZX	22	22
Spitfire Mk I, II, III, IV	145 SR 13XZX	22	28
Toledo	155 SR 13XZX	24	28
Dolomite 1300,1500,1850	155 SR 13XZX	26	30
Dolomite Sprint	155 HR 13XAS	26	30
2000 Mk I, II	175 SR 13ZX	26	26
2000 Estate Mk I, II	175 SR 13ZX	26,26(L)	26,34(L)
2000TC	175 SR 13ZX	26	30
2·5 Pi Mk I, II	175 SR 13ZX	26	30
2500 S	175 HR 14XAS	26	30
TR5, TR6	165 HR 15XAS	22	26
TR7	175/70 SR 13ZX	24	28
Stag	185 HR 14XVS	26	30
VAUXHALL			
Cresta PC	175 SR 14XZX	24	27
Viva HC (All models)	155 SR 13XZX 165 SR 13XZX 175/70 SR 13ZX	24,26(L)	24,30(L)
Ventora FD	165 SR 13XZX	24,28(LS)	24,28(LS)
Magnum Saloons & Coupés	155 SR 13XZX 175/70 SR 13ZX	24,26(L)	24,30(L)
Magnum/Viva HC Estates	155 SR 13XZX 165 SR 13XZX	24,30(L)	24,30(L)
Firenza DL, SL and Sport	165 SR 13XZX	24,24(L)	24,26(L)
Cavalier, 1600, 1900 Saloons	165 SR 13XZX	24,29(L)*	24,32(L)
Cavalier 1300	165 SR 13XZX	24,29(L)	24,32(L)
Chevettes except GLS & 2300HS	155 SR 13XZX until Sept. 76	21,25(L)	24,28(L)
	175/70 SR 13ZX Sept. 76 onwards	21,25(L)	25,29(L)
Chevette Estate	155 SR 13XZX 175/70 SR 13ZX	21,24(L)	25,34(L)
Victor 1800 FE Ventora FE VX 1800 1976 +	175 SR 14XZX	24,28(LS)	24,28(LS)
VX4/90 FE Ventora FE Victor 3300 Estate FE	185/70 SR 14ZX	24,28(LS)	24,28(LS)
Cavalier 1600, 1900	165 SR 13XZX	24,29(L)	24,29(L)
Cavalier 1900 Coupé	185/70 SR 13ZX	23,26(L)	23,26(L)
VX 1800, 2300 Saloons & Estates	175 SR 13ZX	24,28(LS)	24,28(LS)
VX 2300 GLS, VX4/90 E Saloons & Estates	185/70 SR 14ZX	24,28(LS)	24,28(LS)

*(L) (S) (LS) See notes at head of table

Car Make and Model	Michelin Radial Fitment	Pressure Front	Rear
VOLKSWAGEN			
1200, 1300, 1500 Beetle	155 SR 15XZX	19	28
1600 Super (1302)	155 SR 15XZX	19	28
1303, 1303S, 1303 LS	155 SR 15XZX	19	28
412 (all models)	155 SR 15XZX	20,23(L)	26,32(L)
Passat L, S, LS (until Nov 78)	155 SR 13XZX	26	26
Passat L, S, LS (Nov 78 onwards)	155 SR 13XZX	25,26(L)	25,32(L)
Passat GLS (until Nov 78)	175/70 SR 13ZX	26	26
Passat GLS (Nov 78 onwards)	175/70 SR 13ZX	25,26(L)	25,32(L)
Scirocco 1100L, 1500S, LS	155 SR 13XZX	25,26(L)	25,32(L)
Scirocco 1500 TS	175/70 SR 13ZX	25,26(L)	25,32(L)
Scirocco GTI, GLS	175/70 HR 13XVS	25,26(L)	25,32(L)
Golf 1·1 L, GL, N & 1500 LD	155 SR 13XZX	25,26(L)	25,32(L)
Golf S & LS 1500 & 1600	175/70 SR 13ZX	25,26(L)	25,32(L)
Golf GLS	155 SR 13XZX	25,26(L)	25,32(L)
Polo, L & N (until Nov 78)	135 SR 13XZX	22,25(L)	22,28(L)
Polo, L & N (Nov 78 onwards)	135 SR 13XZX	23,26(L)	23,29(L)
Polo LS	145 SR 13XZX	22,25(L)	22,28(L)
VOLVO			
66, 66 Coupé & Estate	135 SR 14XZX	23	26
	155 SR 13XZX	20	23
66 Marathon, Coupé & Estate	155 SR 13XZX	20	23
145 Estate	165 SR 15XZX Reinf.	26,28(L)	28,40(L)
164	165 SR 15XZX	28,29(L)	28,35(L)
164 (Aug 72 onwards)	175 SR 15ZX	25,26(L)	26,30(L)
164 E	175 HR 15XAS	25,26(L)	26,30(L)
343 DL	155 SR 13XZX	27,28(L)	27,34(L)
244 L	165 SR 14XZX	26,28(L)	28,34(L)
244 DL	175 SR 14XZX	26,26(L)	28,32(L)
244 GL	185/70 SR 14ZX	28,28(L)	28,33(L)
245 L & DL & E Estate	185 SR 14XZX	28,29(L)	28,35(L)
264 DL (Carburetter)	175 SR 14XZX	27,27(L)	27,32(L)
264 L, DL (Fuel Injection)	185 SR 14XZX	28,28(L)	28,34(L)
264 GL & GLE	185 HR 14XVS	28,28(L)	28,35(L)

WOLSLEY –for Hornet, 1100, 1300, 18-22 Series, 18/85 and Six–See
equivalent Austin models under Leyland

*(L) (S) (LS) See notes at head of table

🅷 Beam St. ☎ 63914.

London 176 – Chester 20 – Liverpool 45 – Stoke-on-Trent 17.

XXX **Rookery Hall** ⏃ with rm, Worleston, CW5 6DJ, N : 2 ½ m. on B 5074 by A 51 ☎ 626866, ⦉, « Country house », ✕, 🚗, park – 🛗 📺 🚿wc 🕿 🅿
closed Sunday, Monday, 21 July-4 August and Bank Holidays – **M** (dinner only) a la carte 9.95/13.75 **st.** ⑂ 2.95 – **7 rm** ⇌ 21.50/42.35 **st.**

XX **Churche's Mansion,** 150 Hospital St., CW5 0RY, ☎ 65933, « 16C half-timbered house », 🚗 – 🅿
closed Sunday dinner and 25 to 28 December – **M** 4.50/7.50 **st.** ⑂ 2.40.

BEDFORD, VAUXHALL Station Rd ☎ 64027   BRITISH LEYLAND London Rd ☎ 63151

NARBERTH (ARBERTH) Dyfed 🄫🄫🄫 F 28 – pop. 937 – ◎ 0834.

London 240 – Fishguard 25 – Swansea 47.

🛖 **Plas Hyfryd,** Moorfield Rd, SA67 8BR, ☎ 860653, ⏄ heated, 🚗 – 🅿
closed 1 to 18 February – **7 rm** ⇌ 9.60/15.30 **t.**

XX **Robeston House** ⏃ with rm, Robeston Wathen, SA67 8AU, NW : 1 ¾ m. by B 4314 on A 40 ☎ 860392, ⏃, 🚗, park – 🚿wc �car 🅿. 🄫
closed 25 and 26 December – **M** (booking essential) 6.50 ⑂ 2.50 – **6 rm** ⇌ 10.00/19.00.

NARBOROUGH Leics. 🄫🄫🄫 🄫🄫🄫🄫 Q 26 – see Leicester.

NATIONAL EXHIBITION CENTRE West Midlands 🄫🄫🄫 🄫🄫🄫🄫 O 26 – see Birmingham.

NAYLAND Suffolk 🄫🄫🄫🄫 W 28 – see Colchester (Essex).

NEAR SAWREY Cumbria – see Hawkshead.

NEATH (CASTELL-NEDD) West Glam. 🄫🄫🄫 I 29 – pop. 28,619 – ECD : Thursday – ◎ 0639.
🅃🅸🅶 Cadoxton ☎ 3615 – 🅟🅶 Glynneath ☎ 720452, N : 10 m.

London 194 – Cardiff 35 – Swansea 9.

🏨 **Cimla Court Motel,** 77 Upper Cimla Rd, SA11 3TT, ☎ 3771 – 🚿wc 🅿
closed Christmas Day – **M** 2.60 ⑂ 2.00 – **30 rm** ⇌ 8.50/18.00.

🏨 Castle, The Parade, SA11 1RE, ☎ 3581 – 🏛wc 🕿
35 rm.

AUSTIN-MG-ROVER-TRIUMPH-WOLSELEY Gnoll Park   FORD 17/22 Alfred St. ☎ 2601
Rd ☎ 3911   RENAULT 57 Windsor Rd ☎ 2708

NEATISHEAD Norfolk 🄫🄫🄫🄫 Y 25 – ◎ 0692 Horning.

London 122 – North Walsham 8,5 – Norwich 11.

⚓ **Barton Angler** ⏃, Irstead, NR12 8XP, E : ¾ m. ☎ 630740, 🚗 – 🅿
Mid March-mid October – **M** (bar lunch Monday to Saturday) a la carte 6.10/7.50 **t.** ⑂ 1.80 – **8 rm** ⇌ 8.50/17.00.

NEFYN Gwynedd 🄫🄫🄫 G 25 – pop. 2,086 – ECD : Wednesday – ◎ 075 882.

See : Site*

🅃🅸🅶 ☎ 218, N : 2 m.

London 265 – Caernarfon 20.

🏨 Nanhoron Arms, St. Davids Rd, LL53 6EA, ☎ 203 – 🚿wc 🅿
20 rm.

⚓ Caeau Capel ⏃, Rhodfa'r Mor, LL53 6EB, ☎ 240, ✕, 🚗 – 🚿wc 🅿
Easter-September – **M** (bar lunch) 4.00 ⑂ 0.90 – **21 rm** ⇌ 6.00/14.50.

AUSTIN-MORRIS-MG Church St. ☎ 206

NETHERTON Merseyside 🄫🄫🄫 L 23 – see Liverpool.

NEWARK-ON-TRENT Notts. 🄫🄫🄫🄫 R 24 – pop. 24,646 – ECD : Thursday – ◎ 0636.
🅃🅸🅶 ☎ 063 684 (Fenton Claypole) 241, E : 4 m.
🅷 The Ossington, Beast Market Hill ☎ 78962 (summer only).

London 127 – Lincoln 16 – Nottingham 20 – Sheffield 42.

🏨🏨 **Robin Hood** (Anchor), Lombard St., NG24 1XB, ☎ 3858, Group Telex 858875 – 📺
🚿wc 🕿 🅿. 🄫. 🄫 AE ⓘ VISA
M 3.50 **st.** – **19 rm** ⇌ 17.50/25.50 **st.**

🏨 Ram, Castle Gate, NG24 1AZ, ☎ 2255 – 🄫
M 3.15/3.80 ⑂ 1.35 – **21 rm** ⇌ 12.50/27.00 **st.**

NEWARK-ON-TRENT

AUSTIN-MG-WOLSELEY 18 Balderton Gate ☎ 73888
FIAT Sleaford Rd ☎ 3405
FORD Farndon Rd ☎ 4131
JAGUAR-MORRIS-MG-ROVER-TRIUMPH-WOLSELEY
Castle Gate ☎ 4456
OPEL 116 Farndon Rd ☎ 5431

RENAULT 36/40 Albert St. ☎ 4619
SAAB North Muskham ☎ 3232
TALBOT 23/25 London Rd ☎ 5335
VAUXHALL 69 Northgate ☎ 3413
VW-AUDI-NSU Northern Rd ☎ 4484

NEWBURY Berks. **403 404** Q 29 – pop. 23,634 – ECD : Wednesday – ✆ 0635.

🛈 Council Offices, Wharf Rd ☎ 42400.

London 67 – Bristol 66 – Oxford 28 – Reading 17 – Southampton 38.

🏨 **Chequers** (T.H.F.), 6-8 Oxford St., RG13 1JB, ☎ 43666, 🚗 – 📺 🛏 wc ☎ 🅿. ♨. 🔺
AE ① VISA
M 4.75/5.00 **st.** 🍷 1.75 – **69 rm** � 12.00/23.50 **st.**

🏛 **Bacon Arms**, 10 Oxford St., RG13 1JK, ☎ 40408 – 🅿. 🔺 AE ① VISA
M *(closed Sunday dinner)* a la carte 4.75/6.00 **t.** 🍷 1.50 – **11 rm** � 8.50/17.50 **st.**

🏠 **Guest House**, 133 Andover Rd, RG14 6JJ, ☎ 41359, 🚗 – 🅿
11 rm � 5.00/9.00 **st.**

✕ **La Riviera**, 26 The Broadway, RG13 1AU, ☎ 47499 – ① VISA
closed Wednesday, first 3 weeks April, 25-26 December and Bank Holidays – **M** a la
carte 4.50/5.75 🍷 1.75.

✕ **Sapient Pig**, 29 Oxford St., RG13 1JG, ☎ 44867, Bistro – 🔺 VISA.

CITROEN Newtown Rd ☎ 41911
DAIMLER-JAGUAR-MORRIS-MG-ROVER-TRIUMPH
123 London Rd ☎ 43181
RENAULT London Rd ☎ 41020

TALBOT Kings Rd ☎ 49444
VOLVO 45 Bartholomew St. ☎ 40168
VW, AUDI The Broadway ☎ 40678

NEWBY BRIDGE Cumbria – pop. 200 – ✉ Ulverston – ✆ 0448.

London 270 – Kendal 16 – Lancaster 27.

🏨 **Swan**, LA12 8NB, ☎ 31681, ≼, ⌇, 🚗 – 🛏 wc ☎ 🅿. AE ① VISA
closed first 3 weeks January – **M** (buffet lunch Monday to Saturday) 4.15/8.00 **t.**
🍷 2.30 – **36 rm** � 15.50/28.00 **t.**

NEWCASTLE EMLYN (CASTELLNEWYDD EMLYN) Dyfed **403** G 27 – pop. 651 – ECD : Wednesday – ✆ 0239.

Envir. : Cenarth Falls* W : 3 m. – Cilgerran (castle* 13C) *AC*, W : 9 m. – New Quay
(site*) NE : 12 ½ m. **Exc. :** E : Teifi Valley*.

London 240 – Carmarthen 20 – Fishguard 29.

🏨 **Emlyn Arms**, Bridge St., SA38 9DU, ☎ 710317 – 📺 🛏 wc ☎ 🅿. 🔺 AE ① VISA
M 3.50/4.50 **t.** 🍷 1.80 –
38 rm � 14.00/23.00 **t.**

FORD New Rd ☎ 710245

NEWCASTLE-UNDER-LYME
Staffs. **403 404** N 24 – pop. 77,126 –
ECD : Thursday – ✆ 0782 Stoke-
on-Trent.

🛪 ☎ 078271 (Keele Park) 582
by A 525 **v** – 🛪 Trentham Park
☎ 657315, S : 4 m. **v**.

🛈 Library, The Ironmarket ☎ 618125.

**London 161 – Birmingham 46 – Liverpool
56 – Manchester 43.**

**Plan of Built up Area :
see Stoke-on-Trent**

🏨 **Clayton Lodge** (Embassy),
Clayton Rd, Clayton, ST5
4AF, S : 1 ¼ m. on A 519 ☎
613093 – 📺 🛏 wc ☎ 🅿.
♨. 🔺 AE ① VISA   **v e**
M 4.45/5.20 **st.** – **51 rm**
� 16.50/22.50 **st.**

🏨 **Post House** (T.H.F.), Clay-
ton Rd, Clayton, ST5 4DL,
S : 2 m. on A 519 ☎ 625151,
Telex 36531 – 📺 🛏 wc ☎
🅿. ♨. 🔺 AE ① VISA   **v n**
M 4.50/5.00 **st.** 🍷 2.00 –
� 2.25 – **106 rm** 18.00/
25.50 **st.**

**NEWCASTLE-
UNDER-LYME
CENTRE**

High Street

Albert Street	2
Blackfriars Road	4
Church Street	6
Iron Market	8
Merrial Street	10
Vessey Terrace	12

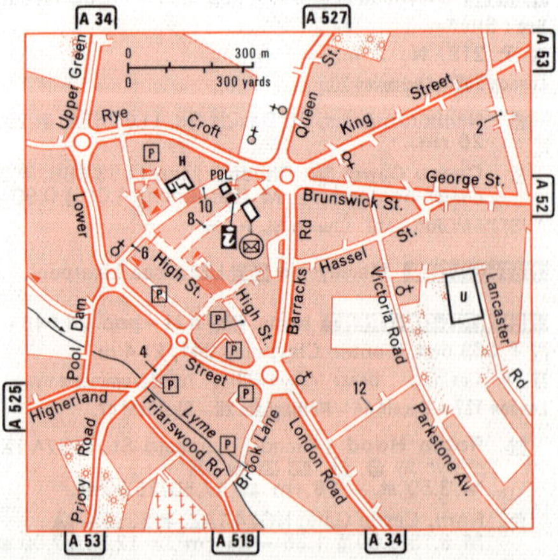

See : Cathedral* 14C **CZ A.**

📍 Three Mile Bridge, Gosforth ✆ 851775, N : 3 m. by A 6125 **AV** – 📍 Broadway East, Gosforth, ✆ 856710, N : 3 m. by Kenton Rd **AV** – 📍 Whorlton Grange, Westerhope, ✆ 869125, W : 5 m. by B 6324 **AV** – 📍 Portobello Rd, Birtley ✆ 402207, S : 6 m. by A 696 **BX.**

✈ Newcastle Airport, ✆ 860966, NW : 5 m. by A 696 **AV** – **Terminal :** Bus Assembly : Central Station Forecourt.

🚗 ✆ 611234 ext 2621 – ✆ 0904 (York) 53022 ext 2631.

🛳 Shipping connections with the Continent : to Bergen, Stavanger, Kristiansand and Oslo, (Fred Olsen-Bergen Line) – to Esbjerg (DFDS Danish Seaways) – to Göteborg (DFDS Danish Seaways/Tor Line) NE : by A 1058 **BV.**

🅘 Central Library, Princess Sq. ✆ 610691 – Prudential Building, 140-150 Pilgrim St. ✆ 28795.

London 283 – Edinburgh 108 – Leeds 93.

Plans on following pages

🏨 Royal Station (B.T.H.), Neville St., NE99 1DW. ✆ 20781, Telex 53681 – 🛗 📺 🅿. ⚒.
🅰 AE ⓪ VISA
CZ i
closed 25 and 26 December – **113 rm** 🍽 23.95/33.00 **st.**

🏨 Swallow (Swallow), Newgate St., NE1 5SX, ✆ 25025, Group Telex 53168 – 🛗 📺 🅿.
⚒.
CZ o
96 rm.

🏨 Newcastle Centre (Centre), Newbridge St., NE1 8BS, ✆ 26191, Telex 53467 – 🛗 📺
🛏wc 📞 ♿ 🅿. ⚒. 🅰 AE ⓪ VISA
CY n
🍽 1.65 – **180 rm** 19.25/24.70 **st.**

🏨 County (Thistle), Neville St., NE99 1AH, ✆ 22471, Telex 537873 – 🛗 📺 🛏wc 📞 🅿.
⚒. 🅰 AE ⓪ VISA
CZ a
105 rm.

🏨 Royal Turks Head (Open House), 3 Grey St., NE1 6EL, ✆ 26111 – 🛗 📺 🛏wc 📞. ⚒
67 rm.
CY r

🏨 Imperial (Swallow), Jesmond Rd, NE2 1PR, ✆ 815511, Group Telex 53168, 🍽 – 🛗 📺
🛏wc 📞 🅿. ⚒
CY c
135 rm.

🍴 **Fisherman's Wharf,** 15 The Side, NE1 3JE, ✆ 21057, Seafood – 🅰 AE ⓪ VISA **CZ v**
closed Saturday lunch, Sunday, 23 December-2 January and Bank Holidays – **M** a la carte 5.80/13.40 🍷 1.80.

🍴 Black Gate, Side, LE1 1LF, ✆ 26661.
CZ n

🍴 **Parigi,** 27 Sandhill, NE1 3VF, ✆ 20377, Italian – rest. 🅰 AE ⓪ VISA **CZ x**
M (dinner only) a la carte 5.00/12.30 **s.** 🍷 1.55.

🍴 Mario, 59 Westgate Rd ✆ 20708, Italian rest.
CZ u

at Gosforth N : 4 ¾ m. on A 6125 – **AV** – ✉ Newcastle-upon-T. – ✆ 089 426 Wideopen :

🏨 **Gosforth Park** (Thistle), High Gosforth Park, NE3 5HN, on B 1318 ✆ 4111, Telex 53655,
≼, 🍽, 🎾, park – 🛗 📺 🅿. ⚒. 🅰 AE ⓪ VISA
M 6.35/8.15 **st.** 🍷 2.50 – ☕ 3.50 – **178 rm** 27.50/35.00 **st.**

at Seaton Burn N : 8 m. on A 6125 – **AV** – ✉ Newcastle-upon-T. – ✆ 089 426 Wideopen :

🏨 Holiday Inn, NE13 6BP, N : ¾ m. ✆ 5432, Telex 53271, 🍽 – 📺 ♿ 🅿. ⚒
151 rm.

at Wallsend E : 4 m. on A 1058 – **BV** – ✉ ✆ 0632 Newcastle-upon-Tyne :

🏨 **Europa Lodge** (County), Coast Rd, NE28 9HP, junction of A 1058 and A 1 ✆ 628989,
Telex 53583 – 🛗 📺 🅿. ⚒. 🅰 AE ⓪ VISA
M 4.50/5.50 **st.** 🍷 1.55 – **182 rm** 🍽 19.00/23.00 **s.**

at Newcastle Airport NW : 6 m. on A 696 – **AV** – ✉ Woolsington – ✆ 0661 Ponteland :

🏨 Airport (Stakis), NE13 8DJ, ✆ 24911 – 🛗 📺 🛏wc 📞 🅿. ⚒. 🅰 AE ⓪ VISA – **100 rm.**

MICHELIN Branch, Benton Sq., Industrial Trading Estate, NE12 9TP, ✆ 666266.

ALFA-ROMEO Diana St. ✆ 22314
AUSTIN Westgate Rd ✆ 37901
AUSTIN-MG 87 Osborne Rd ✆ 811677
AUSTIN-MG-ROVER-TRIUMPH-WOLSELEY Warwick St. ✆ 24367
CITROEN Westgate Rd ✆ 737821
DAF, POLSKI Four Lane Ends ✆ 666331
DAIMLER-JAGUAR-MORRIS-MG-ROVER-TRIUMPH, ROLLS ROYCE Forth St. ✆ 28981
DATSUN 62 Westmorland Rd ✆ 28281
DATSUN Benfield Rd ✆ 659171
FIAT Railway St. ✆ 732131
FORD Main St. ✆ 0661 (Ponteland) 4261

FORD Market St. ✆ 611471
FORD Scotswood Rd ✆ 739161
LANCIA George St. ✆ 734591
MORRIS-MG-ROVER-TRIUMPH Etherstone Av. ✆ 663311
RENAULT Shiremoor ✆ 532318
RENAULT Scotswood Rd ✆ 30101
SAAB, SUBURU Whitley Rd, Longbenton ✆ 668223
TALBOT Benton Rd ✆ 666361
VAUXHALL Dunn St. ✆ 735201
VAUXHALL Two Ball Lonnen ✆ 39211
VAUXHALL Great North Rd ✆ 089 426 (Wideopen) 3176
VW, AUDI Fossway ✆ 657121

NEWCASTLE-
UPON-TYNE

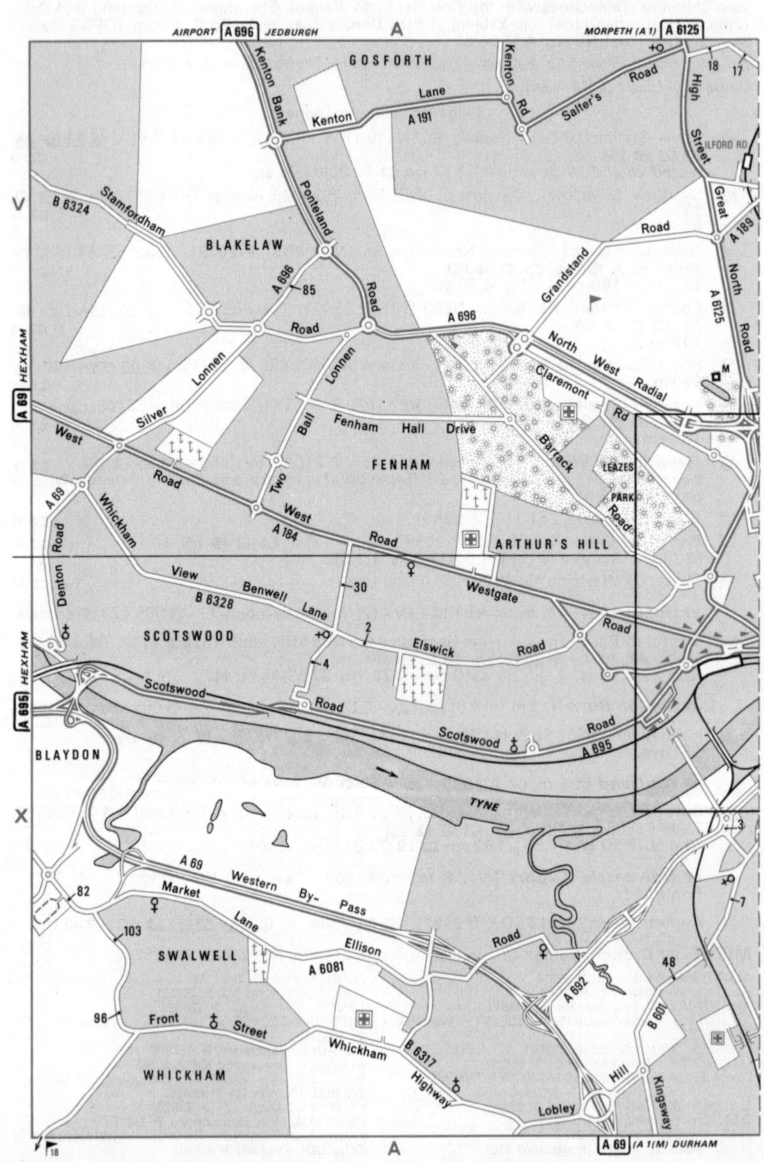

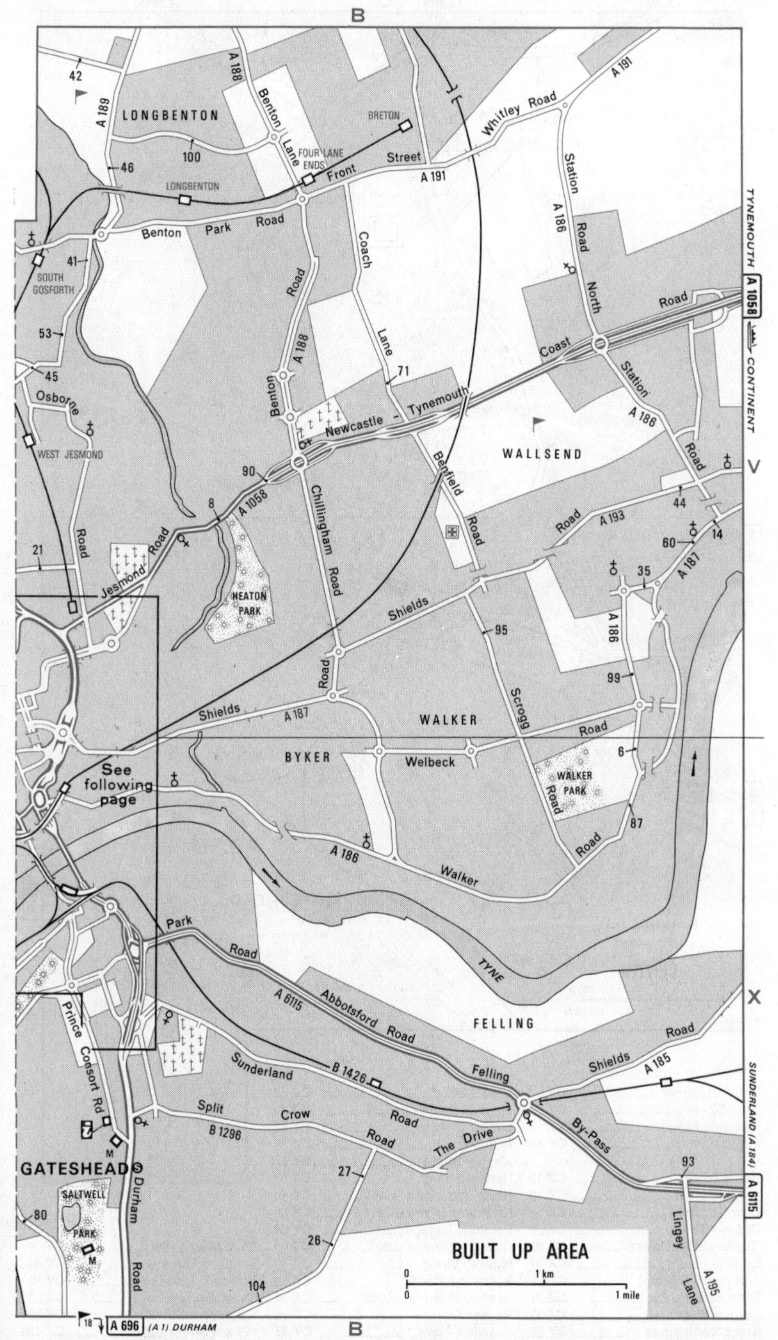

B
42
A 189
LONGBENTON
A 188
BRETON
46
100
FOUR LANE ENDS
LONGBENTON
Front
Street
Benton Lane
A 191
Benton Park Road
Whitley Road
A 191
Coach
Station Road
A 186
SOUTH GOSFORTH
41
53
45
Osborne
Road
Road
Benton
A 188
Lane
71
Coast
Road
North
Station Road
Station
A 186
WEST JESMOND
Newcastle — Tynemouth
WALLSEND
Road
A 186
90
Benfield Road
Road
A 193
44
14
8
A 1058
Chillingham Road
60
A 181
35
21
Jesmond Road
HEATON PARK
Shields
95
A 186
99
Road
Scrogg
Road
6
See following page
Shields
A 187
WALKER
Road
BYKER
Welbeck
WALKER PARK
87
Road
A 186
Walker
Road
Park
Road
TYNE
Road
Abbotsford Road
A 6115
FELLING
Shields
X
Road
A 185
Sunderland
B 1426
Felling
Prince Consort Rd
Split
Crow
Road
The Drive
By-Pass
SUNDERLAND (A 184)
A 6115
B 1296
Road
93
GATESHEAD
M
27
Lingey Lane
SALTWELL
Durham Road
80
PARK
26
M
A 195
BUILT UP AREA
0   1 km
0   1 mile
18   A 696 (A 1) DURHAM
B
TYNEMOUTH A 1058 CONTINENT

A 696
B 6338
A 6125
C
A 1058
EXHIBITION PARK
Claremont
JESMOND
Jesmond Rd
Central
Sandyford
67
Portland
Richardson
Victoria
Road
Barras Bridge
Motorway
A 696
East
Street
Shield
Street
Road
77
LEEZES PARK
Queen
Road
U
H
92
T
79
Y
Y
HAYMARKET
84
Falconer
Clarense St.
Percy
St.
64
Strawberry Pl.
65
Barrack
MONUMENT
M
New
Bridge
Street
A 187
Rd
101
Blackett St.
52
St.
Gibson St.
St. JAMES
Grey
POL
Crawhall
Road
Gallowgate
Newgate
Street
66
Melbourne
Corporation
52
MANORS STATION
A 186
Road
Bath St.
A 184
Westgate
Clayton
St.
24
City
55
City
Lane
Grainger
Rd
40
57
A 186
Street
23
62
29
A
Side
Road
Quayside
Westmorland
Road
CENTRAL STATION
Close
Tyne Bridge
George St.
Blenheim
Road
Forth Banks
The
98
Hawks
Road
Z
70
Z
34
Burn
43
12
20
37
Scotswood
70
Rd.
TYNE
GATESHEAD STATION
10
A 695
Skinner
74
Road
GATESHEAD
West
High
A 6115
NEWCASTLE-UPON-TYNE
CENTRE
72
Askew
A 692
105
St.
13
Park
0   400 m
0   400 yards
Bensham Rd
76
69
High
POL
Prince
West
B 1426
C
Consort
Rd
A 696

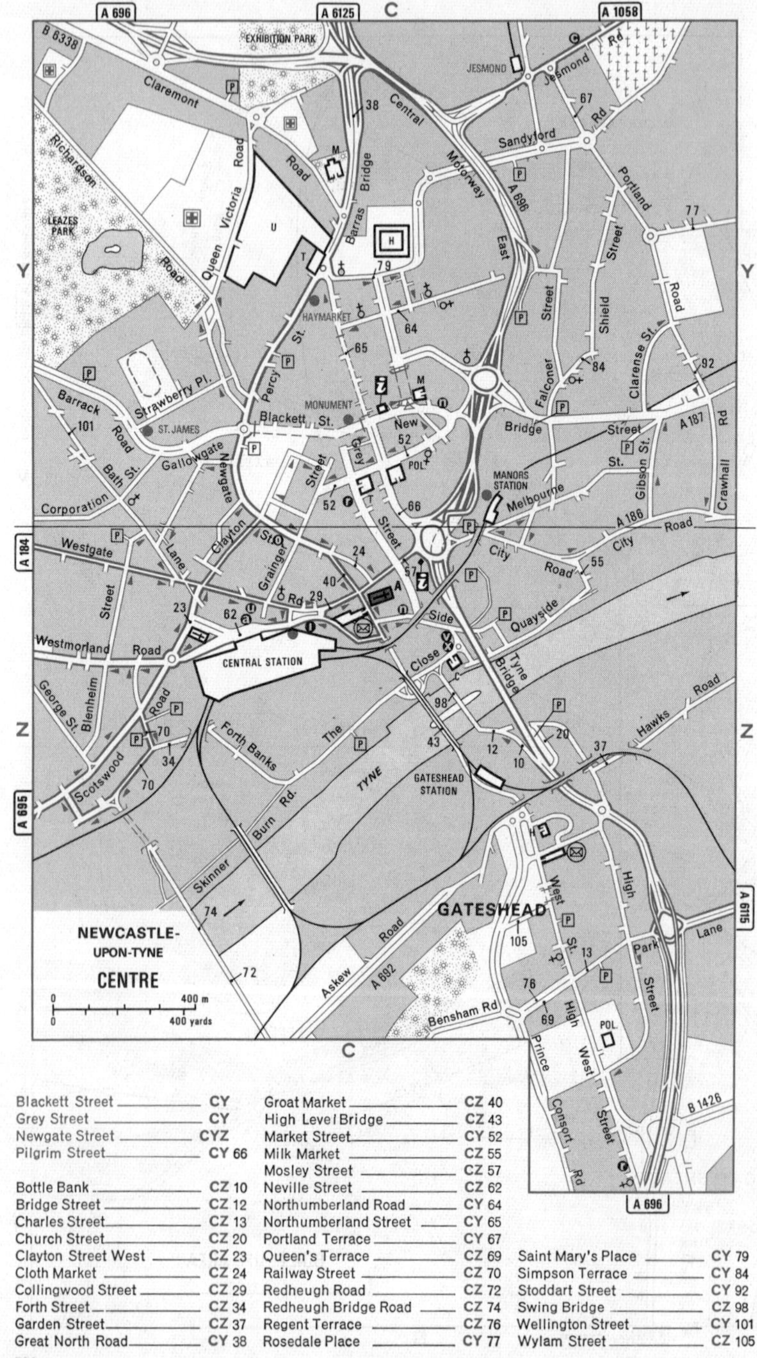

328

NEW DENHAM Bucks. 404 S 29 – pop. 7,543 – ⊠ ✆ 0895 Uxbridge.

London 20 – Aylesbury 25 – Oxford 40.

XXX **Giovanni's,** at Denham Lodge, Oxford Rd, UB9 4AA, on A 4020 ✆ 31568, Italian rest. –
P. ⬛ AE ⓘ VISA
closed Saturday lunch, Sunday and Bank Holidays – **M** a la carte 4.80/11.85 **t.** ₪ 1.90.

NEWDIGATE Surrey 404 T 30 – pop. 1,404 – ✆ 030 677.

London 32 – Brighton 32 – Guildford 18.

XX **The Forge,** Parkgate Rd, RH5 5DZ, N : 1 m. ✆ 582 – P. ⬛ AE ⓘ VISA
closed Sunday, Monday, first 2 weeks August and first 2 weeks January – **M** a la carte
10.25/12.80 **st.** ₪ 3.50.

NEWHAVEN East Sussex 404 U 31 – pop. 9,710 – ECD : Wednesday – ✆ 079 12.

ₙ₉ Brighton Rd ✆ 4049.

⛴ Shipping connections with the Continent : to Dieppe (Sealink).

🚗 Car Ferry Terminal Car Park ✆ 7450 (summer only).

London 63 – Brighton 9 – Eastbourne 14 – Lewes 7.

🏨 Newhaven Mercury Motor Inn, Bishopstone Rd, BN25 2RB. SE : 1 ½ m. on A 259
✆ 891055, Telex 628064 – TV ⌴wc ☎ P. ⚶ – **70 rm.**

FORD Drove Rd ✆ 5303

NEWLYN Cornwall 403 D 33 – see Penzance.

NEWMARKET Suffolk 404 V 27 – pop. 9,900 – ECD : Wednesday – ✆ 0638.

ₙ₁₈ Cambridge Rd ✆ 2131, SW : 1 m.

London 64 – Cambridge 13 – Ipswich 40 – Norwich 48.

🏨 **White Hart** (T.H.F.), High St., CB8 8JP, ✆ 3051 – TV ⌴wc ☎ P. ⚶. ⬛ AE ⓘ VISA
M 4.50/5.00 **st.** ₪ 2.00 – **21 rm** ⟷ 13.50/21.00 **st.**

🏨 **Bedford Lodge,** Bury Rd, CB8 7BX, NE : ½ m. on A 1304 ✆ 3175, 🐎 – TV ⌴wc
🛏wc ☎ P. ⬛ AE ⓘ VISA
M a la carte 5.50/10.50 **t.** ₪ 1.65 – **11 rm** ⟷ 11.75/24.00 **t.**

TOYOTA Bury Rd ✆ 2130　　　　　　　　　　VOLVO Dullingham ✆ 063876 (Stetchworth) 244
VAUXHALL All Saints Rd ✆ 4982

NEW MILTON Hants. 403 404 P 31 – pop. 4,373 – ECD : Wednesday – ⊠ Bournemouth
(Dorset) – ✆ 0425.

London 106 – Bournemouth 12 – Southampton 21 – Winchester 34.

🏨 ❄ **Chewton Glen** 🦅, Christchurch Rd, BH25 6QS, E : ¾ m. on A 337 ✆ 5341, Telex
41456, ≤ gardens, ✂, ⬛ heated, park – TV P. ⚶. ⬛ AE ⓘ VISA
M 7.50/12.00 **st.** ₪ 3.00 – ⟷ 3.50 – **47 rm** 35.00/54.00 **st.**
Spec. Coquilles St-Jacques au gingembre, Loup de mer Mouginoise, Côte de bœuf d'Ecosse au Fleurie.

AUSTIN-MORRIS Christchurch Rd ✆ 611198　　　MORRIS-MG-WOLSELEY Old Milton Rd ✆ 614665
DATSUN 25 Station Rd ✆ 610034　　　　　　　RENAULT 56 Old Milton Rd ✆ 612296
FORD Fernhill Lane ✆ 612121

NEWNHAM Glos. 403 404 M 28 – pop. 1,201 – ✆ 059 47.

London 115 – Bristol 33 – Gloucester 12 – Newport 32.

🏠 **Victoria,** High St., GL14 1AD, ✆ 221, 🐎 – 🚗 P
M *(closed Sunday)* (buffet lunch) a la carte 5.40/6.85 **t.** ₪ 1.60 – **11 rm** ⟷ 10.55/20.00 **t.**
– P 18.00/24.00 **t.**

NEWPORT Glos. 403 404 M 28 – see Berkeley.

NEWPORT I.O.W. 403 404 Q 31 – see Wight (Isle of).

NEWPORT Gwent 403 L 29 – pop. 112,286 – ECD : Thursday – ✆ 0633.

ₙ₁₈ Great Oak, ✆ 063 343 (Rhiwderin) 2683 and 4496, W : 3 m. on A 467 – ₙ₁₈ ✆ 063 341
(Llanwern) 2380, E : 3 m.

London 145 – Bristol 31 – Cardiff 12 – Gloucester 48.

🏨 **Gateway Motor Motel,** The Coldra, Chepstow Rd, NP6 2YG, E : 3 m. on A 48
✆ 412777 – TV ⌴wc ☎ & P. ⚶. ⬛ AE ⓘ VISA
M 4.25/4.75 **st.** ₪ 1.50 – **120 rm** ⟷ 18.35/26.40 **st.**

🏨 **Westgate** (T.H.F.), Commercial St., NP1 1TT, ✆ 66244, Telex 49173 – 🛗 TV ⌴wc
☎. ⚶. ⬛ AE ⓘ VISA
M 4.50 **st.** ₪ 1.65 – **68 rm** ⟷ 13.00/21.00 **st.**

🏨 **Queen's** (Anchor), 19 Bridge St., NPT 4RN, ✆ 62992, Group Telex 858875 – TV ⌴wc
☎. ⚶. ⬛ AE ⓘ VISA
M (buffet lunch) 3.50 **st.** – **42 rm** ⟷ 13.00/23.00 **st.**

XX Conti's Grill, 1st floor, 40-41 Llanarth St., NPT 1HR ,✆ 63684 – ⬛ AE ⓘ VISA

at Langstone E: 4 ½ m. on A 48 – ✉ Newport – ☎ 063 341 Llanwern :

🏨 **New Inn Motel** (Ansells), Chepstow Rd., NP6 2JN, ☎ 2426 – 📺 🛏wc 📞 🅿. 🔲 AE
M 3.40/3.75 t. 🍷 1.80 – **30 rm** 🛏 14.65/19.00 t.

AUSTIN-MORRIS-MG-WOLSELEY Shaftsbury St. ☎ 58451
AUSTIN-DAIMLER-JAGUAR-MORRIS -MG-WOLSELEY Corporation Rd ☎ 72381
AUSTIN-MORRIS-MG-WOLSELEY Cardiff Rd ☎ 63847
CITROEN Chepstow Rd ☎ 71955
DATSUN Spytty Rd ☎ 74891

FIAT, VAUXHALL Turner St. ☎ 59771
FORD Agincourt St. ☎ 52233
MORRIS-MG-WOLSELEY Bassaleg Rd ☎ 63717
RENAULT Queens Hill ☎ 51317
ROVER-TRIUMPH Bassaleg Rd ☎ 53771
VW, AUDI-NSU Maeglas Industrial Estate ☎ 211

NEWPORT (TREFDRAETH) Dyfed **408** F 27 – pop. 1,062 – ECD : Wednesday – ☎ 0239.
See : Site*. **Envir. :** Pentre Ifan (burial chamber*) SE : 4 ½ m.

🏌 Newport Sands ☎ 244.

London 258 – Fishguard 7.

XX **Pantry**, Market St., SA42 0PH, ☎ 820420
closed Sunday, Monday, 25-26 and 31 December – **M** (dinner only) a la carte 7.00/
10.30 t. 🍷 1.90.

NEWPORT Salop **408** **404** M 25 – pop. 5,230 – ECD : Thursday – ☎ 0952.
🏌 Abbey Rd ☎ 095 284 (Lilleshall) 4365, SW : 3 m.

London 150 – Birmingham 33 – Shrewsbury 18 – Stoke-on-Trent 21.

🏨 Royal Victoria, St. Mary's St., TF10 7AB, ☎ 810831 – 🛏wc 🛏wc 📞 🅿 – **21 rm.**
TALBOT 23 High St. ☎ 811076

NEWPORT PAGNELL Bucks. **404** R 27 – pop. 5,120 – ECD : Thursday – ☎ 0908.
London 57 – Bedford 13 – Luton 21 – Northampton 15.

🏨 **TraveLodge** (T.H.F.) without rest., M 1 Service Area 3, MK16 8DS, W : 1 ½ m. off A
422 on M 1 ☎ 610878 – 📺 🛏wc 📞 🅿. 🔲 AE ① VISA
100 rm 🛏 14.50/20.00 st.

🏨 **Swan Revived**, High St., MK16 9JS, ☎ 610565 – 📶 📺 🛏wc 🛏wc 📞 🅿. 🔲 AE ① VISA
M 3.85 t. 🍷 1.85 – **31 rm** 🛏 20.85/28.15 st.

XX **Glovers**, 18-20 St. John St., MK16 8HJ, ☎ 090 862 (Goldcrest) 6398 – 🅿. 🔲 AE ①
VISA
*closed Saturday lunch, Sunday, Monday, first 2 weeks August, 1 week at Christmas
and Bank Holidays* – **M** a la carte 5.95/9.45 t. 🍷 1.65.

AUDI, VW Tickford St. ☎ 611642   PEUGEOT High St. ☎ 611715

NEWQUAY Cornwall **408** E 32 – pop. 12,240 – ECD : Wednesday – ☎ 063 73.
🏌 Perranporth ☎ 087 257 (Perranporth) 2454, SW : 6 m. by A 3075 Y.
🛈 Cliff Rd ☎ 2119/2716/2822/4558.

London 291 – Exeter 83 – Penzance 34 – Plymouth 48 – Truro 14.

Plan opposite

🏨 **Bristol**, Narrowcliff, TR7 2PQ, ☎ 5181, ⬉, 🔲 – 📶 📺 🅿. AE   **Z r**
closed 3 weeks October – **M** 4.50/6.00 st. 🍷 1.80 – **104 rm** 🛏 13.50/35.00 st. – P 24.00/
27.00 st.

🏨 **Riviera** (Best Western), Lusty Glaze Rd., TR7 3AA, ☎ 4251, ⬉, 🏊 heated, 🐎 – 📶 📺
🅿   **Z o**
closed 25 to 27 December – **M** (buffet lunch) 4.50/7.50 t. 🍷 1.65 – **54 rm** 🛏 14.00/
30.50 t. – P 22.80/24.00 t.

🏨 **Kilbirnie**, Narrowcliff, TR7 2RS, ☎ 5155, 🔲 – 🛏wc 🅿   **Z e**
closed 3 to 26 November and 22 to 28 December – **M** 3.50/5.50 t. 🍷 2.40 – **72 rm**
🛏 9.00/24.00 t. – P 13.50/20.00 t.

🏨 **Windsor**, Mount Wise, TR7 2AY, ☎ 5188, 🔲, 🏊 heated, 🐎 – 📺 🛏wc 🅿   **Z n**
Easter-October – **M** (bar lunch) 5.00 t. – **51 rm** 🛏 10.00/24.00 t.

🏨 **Trebarwith**, Trebarwith Crescent, TR7 1BZ, ☎ 2288, ⬉ bay, 🔲, 🐎 – 🛏wc 🅿   **Z a**
6 May-7 October – **M** (bar lunch) 6.00 st. 🍷 2.00 – **48 rm** 🛏 16.00/32.00 st.

🏨 **Edgcumbe**, Narrowcliff, TR7 2RR, ☎ 2061, 🔲, 🏊 heated – 📶 📺 🛏wc 🛏wc 🅿   **Z u**
Mid March-November – **M** 3.90/5.50 t. 🍷 1.70 – **88 rm** 🛏 16.00/32.00 t.

🏨 **Barrowfield**, Hillgrove Rd., TR7, ☎ 2560 🔲, 🏊 heated – 📺 🛏wc 🅿   **Z i**
Easter-October – **M** 2.90/4.00 🍷 1.95 – **61 rm** 🛏 9.00/21.00 s.

🏨 Water's Edge, Esplanade Rd., TR7 1QA, ☎ 2048, ⬉ Fistral Bay, 🐎 – 🛏wc 🛏wc 🅿
22 rm.   **Y u**

🏨 **Mordros**, Pentire Av., TR7 1PB, ☎ 6700, 🏊 heated – 🛏wc 🅿   **Y x**
Easter-mid October – **M** (closed Saturday lunch) 2.30/6.00 🍷 1.25 – **30 rm** 🛏 (dinner
included) 12.00/15.60.

🏨 **Bewdley**, Pentire Rd., TR7 1NX, ☎ 2883, 🏊 heated – 🛏wc 🅿   **Y s**
M 3.00/4.50 🍷 2.50 – **36 rm** 🛏 9.50/17.00 s. – P 13.25/15.75 s.

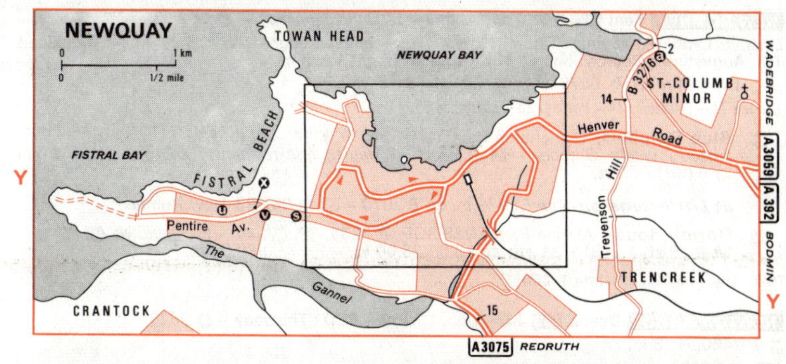

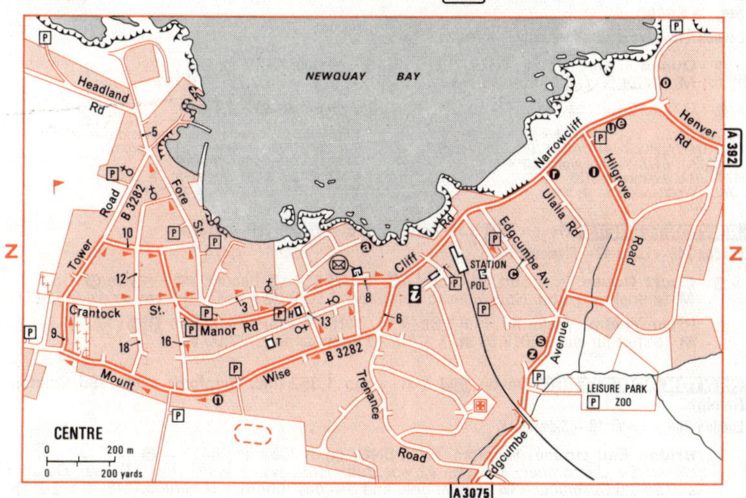

Bank Street	Z 3	Beacon Road	Z 5	Marcus Hill	Z 13
East Street	Z 8	Berry Road	Z 6	Porth Way	Y 14
Fore Street	Z	Higher Tower Road	Z 9	Trevemper Road	Y 15
		Hope Terrace	Z 10	St. Georges Road	Z 16
Alexander Road	Y 2	Jubilee Street	Z 12	St. John's Road	Z 18

Hepworth, 27 Edgcumbe Av., TR7 4NJ, ℡ 3686, 𝕊 – 🛁wc 🅿   Z c
Easter-September – **13 rm** ☕ 14.00/29.00.

Wheal Treasure, 72 Edgcumbe Av., TR7 2NN, ℡ 4136 – 🅿   Z z
May-October – **11 rm** ☕ 8.00/16.00 **s.**

Copper Beech, 70 Edgcumbe Av., TR7 2NN, ℡ 3376 – 🅿. *VISA*   Z s
Easter-October – **16 rm** ☕ 7.75/15.50.

Pendeen, 7 Alexandra Rd, Porth, TR7 3ND, ℡ 3521 – 🅿   Y a
Easter-October – **12 rm** ☕ 12.00/18.00 **s.**

Cherington, 7 Pentire Av., TR7 1NZ, ℡ 3363 – 🅿   Y v
Easter-September – **28 rm** ☕ 6.00/12.00.

at Crantock SW: 4 m. off A 3075 – Y – ✉ Newquay – ☎ 063 77 Crantock:

Crantock Bay ⟳, West Pentire, TR8 5SE, W: ¾ m. ℡ 229, ⟨ Crantock Bay, 𝕊 –
🛁wc 🅿. *VISA*
Easter-October – **M** 3.50/3.85 **t.** 🍷 1.70 – **31 rm** ☕ 10.45/20.90.

Fairbank, West Pentire Rd, TR8 5SA, ℡ 424, ⟨, 𝕊 – 🛁wc 🅿. *VISA*
May-October – **20 rm** ☕ 10.25/21.00.

Glynn Heath, West Pentire Rd, TR8 5SA, ℡ 830373, ⟨, 𝕊 – 🅿
7 April-20 October – **11 rm** ☕ (dinner included) 16.00/26.00 **st.**

AUSTIN-DAIMLER-JAGUAR-MORRIS-MG-TRIUMPH-   COLT, VOLVO Sommercourt ℡708251 (Mitchell) 386
WOLSELEY Quintrell Downs ℡ 2410   DAF Newlyn East ℡ 087 251 (Mitchell) 347

NEW ROMNEY Kent ▨▨ W 31 – pop. 3,447 – ECD : Wednesday – ✆ 067 93.

Envir. : Lydd (All Saints' Church tower : groined vaulting*) SW : 3 ½ m. – Brookland (St. Augustine's Church : belfry* 15C, Norman font*) W : 6 m.

✈ Lydd Airport ☏ 0679 (Lydd) 20401, S : 5 m.

London 71 – Folkestone 14 – Hastings 23 – Maidstone 33.

☎ **Blue Dolphins,** Dymchurch Rd, TN28 8BE, ☏ 3224 – 🕮 🅿. 🔲
closed 2 weeks October – **M** *(closed Sunday to non-residents)* approx. 3.80 – **8 rm** ☲ 9.00/17.00 **st.**

    at Littlestone-on-Sea E : 1 ½ m. on B 2070 – ✉ ✆ 067 93 New Romney :

🏨 **Dormy House,** Marine Par., TN28 8QF, ☏ 3233, ✗, 🔲, 🚗 – 📺 🛏wc 📞 🅿. 🆎 ⓪
    M 5.20 **st.** 🍷 2.50 – **31 rm** ☲ 13.00/25.00 **st.** – P 37.00/50.00 **st.**

FIAT The Avenue, Littlestone ☏ 2184

NEWTON ABBOT Devon ▨▨ J 32 – pop. 19,130 – ECD : Thursday – ✆ 0626.

⛳ ☏ 2460, N : 3 m.

🚗 ☏ 66490.

London 216 – Exeter 16 – Plymouth 31 – Torquay 7.

🏛 **Queen's,** Queen's St., TQ12 2EZ, ☏ 5216 – 🛏wc. 🔲 🆎 ⓪ 𝗩𝗜𝗦𝗔
    M 4.00/4.50 **t.** 🍷 1.65 – **33 rm** ☲ 12.25/21.50 **t.** – P 20.75/24.00 **t.**

🏛 Globe, Courtenay St., TQ12 2QH, ☏ 4106 – 🛏wc 📞 🅿 – **24 rm.**

ALFA-ROMEO, VOLVO Wolborough St. ☏ 2545
AUSTIN-DAIMLER-JAGUAR-MORRIS-MG-ROVER-
TRIUMPH 64/72 Wolborough St. ☏ 4141
FIAT The Avenue ☏ 2526
FORD Wolborough St. ☏ 5081

RENAULT 174 Exeter Rd, Kingsteignton ☏ 3545
TALBOT 177/187 Queen St. ☏ 3838
TOYOTA Highweek ☏ 4702
VAUXHALL 83/85 Queen St. ☏ 2653
VW, AUDI The Avenue ☏ 2641

NEWTON FERRERS Devon ▨▨ H 33 – pop. 1,815 – ✆ 0752 Plymouth.

London 242 – Exeter 42 – Plymouth 11.

🏛 **Court House** 🦢, Court Rd, PL8 1AQ, ☏ 872324, 🏊 heated, 🚗 – 🛏wc 🅿
    M (dinner only from November to February) 4.50/6.00 🍷 2.00 – **11 rm** ☲ 14.00/24.00.

🏛 **River Yealm,** Yealm Rd, PL8 1BL, ☏ 872419, ≼ estuary – 🛏wc 🕮 🅿
    M (buffet lunch) 2.50/5.50 **st.** 🍷 1.65 – **19 rm** ☲ 9.50/23.00 **st.**

NEWTON POPPLEFORD Devon ▨▨ K 31 – pop. 1,352 (inc. Harpford) – ✆ 0395 Colaton Raleigh.

London 208 – Exeter 10 – Sidmouth 4.

✗ **Bridge End House,** Harpford, EX10 0NG, on A 3052 ☏ 68411 – 🅿
    closed Sunday dinner, Monday except Bank Holidays, 1 week April, 1 week October and 25-26 December – **M** (dinner only and Sunday lunch) a la carte 5.15/8.70 **t.** 🍷 2.15.

NEWTON SOLNEY Derbs. ▨▨ ▨▨ P 25 – pop. 528 – ✉ ✆ 0283 Burton-upon-Trent (Staffs.).

London 131 – Burton-upon-Trent 3 – Derby 11.

🏨 **Newton Park** (Embassy) 🦢, DE15 0SS, ☏ 703568, ≼, 🚗, park – 📺 🅿. ⛺. 🔲 🆎 ⓪
    𝗩𝗜𝗦𝗔
    closed 23 to 27 December – **M** *(closed Saturday lunch and Sunday dinner to non-residents)* 6.00/6.60 **st.** 🍷 1.80 – **27 rm** ☲ 20.00/27.00 **st.**

NEWTOWN (DRENEWYDD) Powys ▨▨ K 26 – pop. 5,450 – ECD : Thursday – ✆ 0686.

🛈 Wales Tourist Office, Central Car Park ☏ 25580 (Easter-September).

London 196 – Aberystwyth 44 – Chester 56 – Shrewsbury 32.

🏨 **The Bear,** Broad St., SY16 2LU, ☏ 26964 – 📺 🛏wc 🕮wc 📞 🅿. 🔲 🆎 ⓪ 𝗩𝗜𝗦𝗔
    M 4.00/5.00 **st.** – **40 rm** ☲ 13.50/22.60 **st.**

    at Abermule NE : 4 ½ m. on A 483 – ✉ ✆ 068 686 Abermule :

☎ **Dolforwyn Hall** 🦢, SY15 6JG, N : ½ m. on A 483 ☏ 221 – 🛏wc 🅿
    closed 24 to 31 December – **M** *(closed Sunday)* 5.30 **t.** 🍷 2.15 – **7 rm** ☲ 9.50/20.50 **t.**

AUSTIN-MORRIS-MG-ROVER-TRIUMPH-WOLSELEY
Pool Rd ☏ 25942

DAF Powys ☏ 05516 (Trefeglwys) 202
FORD Pool Rd ☏ 25514

NEWTOWN LINFORD Leics. ▨▨ ▨▨ Q 25 – pop. 1,046 – ✆ 053 05 Markfield.

London 112 – Birmingham 51 – Derby 27 – Leicester 6 – Nottingham 27.

✗✗ **Grey Lady,** Sharpley Hill, LE6 0AA, N : ¾ m. ☏ 3558 – 🅿. 🆎
    M *(closed Sunday and Monday)* (dinner only) a la carte 5.45/6.60 **t.** 🍷 2.00.

NINFIELD East Sussex 👁️👁️ V 31 – pop. 1,096 – ✉️ Battle – ☎ 0424.
London 62 – Brighton 28 – Hastings 9 – Lewes 20.

🏨 **Moor Hall** ⊗, High St., TN33 9JT, ☎ 892330, ✕, ⤵ heated, ⟍, 🚗 – 🛏️wc 🛁wc 🅿️.
♨️. 🔲 AE VISA
M 4.00/5.00 **st.** ⚗ 1.75 – **32 rm** ☲ 13.50/27.00 **st.** – P 19.50/22.50 **st.**

NITON I.O.W. 👁️👁️ 👁️👁️ Q 32 – see Wight (Isle of).

NORTHALLERTON North Yorks. 👁️👁️ ⑲ – pop. 9,300 – ECD : Thursday – ☎ 0609.
Envir. : Bedale (Parish church* 13C-14C) SW : 7 ½ m.

🏌 at Bedale ☎ 067 72 (Bedale) 2568, SW : 7 ½ m.

London 238 – Leeds 48 – Middlesbrough 24 – York 33.

🏨 **Golden Lion** (T.H.F.), High St., DL7 8PP, ☎ 2404 – 📺 🛏️wc ☎ 🅿️. ♨️. 🔲 AE ① VISA
M 3.50/4.85 **st.** ⚗ 1.80 – **29 rm** ☲ 13.50/21.00 **st.**

✕✕ **McCoys at the Tontine,** Staddlebridge, DL6 1JB, NE : 8 ½ m. by A 684 on A 19
☎ 060 982 (East Harlsey) 207, « 1930's decor » – 🅿️. VISA
closed Sunday – **M** (bar lunch) a la carte 8.60/12.75 **t.** ⚗ 2.30.

✕✕ **Romanby Court,** High St., DL7 8EG, ☎ 4918, Italian rest.
closed Sunday, Monday and 3 weeks August – **M** (dinner only) 9.00 **t.** ⚗ 2.00.

AUSTIN-MG Brompton Rd ☎ 3891
HONDA, SAAB East Rd ☎ 3921
MORRIS-ROVER-TRIUMPH 84 High St. ☎ 2372
RENAULT Leeming Bar ☎ 2388

NORTHAMPTON Northants. 👁️👁️ R 27 – pop. 151,000 – ECD : Thursday – ☎ 0604.
See : Church of the Holy Sepulchre* 12C – Central Museum and Art Gallery (collection of footwear*). **Envir.**: Brixworth (All Saints Church* 7C Saxon) N : 7 m. – Earls Barton (All Saints Church : 10C Saxon tower*) NE : 5 m.

🏌 Delapre, Eagle Drive ☎ 64036, 1 ½ m. from junction 15 on M 1.

🛈 21 St. Giles St. ☎ 34881 ext 404/537 (Monday to Friday).

London 71 – Cambridge 51 – Coventry 31 – Leicester 36 – Luton 35 – Oxford 45.

🏨 **Saxon Inn,** Silver St., NN1 2TA, ☎ 22441, Telex 311142 – 🛗 📺 🅿️. ♨️. 🔲 AE ① VISA
M 3.70/4.20 **s.** ⚗ 2.20 – ☲ 1.95 – **134 rm** 15.00/20.00.

🏨 **Grand,** Gold St., NN1 1RE, ☎ 34416 – 🛗 🛏️wc 🅿️. ♨️. 🔲 ① VISA
M (Carvery rest.) – **52 rm.**

🏨 **Angel** (County), Bridge St., NN1 1NA, ☎ 21661, Group Telex 25971 – 🛏️wc 🅿️. 🔲
AE ① VISA
M a la carte 6.20/9.70 **st.** ⚗ 1.55 – **47 rm** ☲ 13.50/20.00 **s.**

✕ **Ca d'Oro,** 334 Wellingborough Rd, NN1 ES4, ☎ 32660, Italian rest.
closed Sunday – **M** (dinner only) a la carte 6.15/10.50 **s.**

✕ **Vineyard,** 7 Derngate, NN1 1TU, ☎ 33978 – 🔲 ① VISA
closed Saturday lunch, Sunday, Monday, last week July and 2 weeks after Christmas –
M a la carte 3.50/8.30 **t.** ⚗ 2.00.

✕ **Napoleon's Bistro,** 9-11 Welford Rd, Kingsthorpe, NN2 8TG, N : 1 ¾ m. by A 508 on
A 50 ☎ 713899 – 🔲 ① VISA
closed Saturday lunch, Sunday, Monday, 11 to 25 August, 25-26 December and Bank Holidays – **M** a la carte 4.85/7.95 **t.** ⚗ 1.75.

at Weston Favell NE : 3 ½ m. by A 45 – ✉️ ☎ 0604 Northampton :

🏨 **Westone** (County) ⊗, Ashley Way, NW3 3EA, ☎ 406262, Group Telex 25971, 🚗 – 🛗
📺 🛏️wc ☎ ⅙ 🅿️. ♨️. 🔲 AE ① VISA
M 4.40/4.85 **st.** ⚗ 1.55 – **65 rm** ☲ 19.50/23.00 **s.**

at Moulton NE : 4 ¼ m. off A 43 – ✉️ ☎ 0604 Northampton :

🏠 **Poplars,** 33 Cross St., NN3 1RZ, ☎ 43983 – 🛁wc 🅿️
21 rm ☲ 6.25/15.00 **s.**

ALFA ROMEO 78 St. Michaels Rd ☎ 38411
AUSTIN-DAIMLER-MORRIS-JAGUAR-MG-ROVER,
TRIUMPH, ROLLS ROYCE Bedford Rd ☎ 39645
AUSTIN-DAIMLER-JAGUAR-LAND ROVER-MORRIS -
ROVER-TRIUMPH 22 Wellingborough Rd ☎ 401141
CITROEN 194/200 Kingsthorpe Rd ☎ 713202
DATSUN 159/185 Abington Av. ☎ 714303
FIAT 91/93 Harborough Rd, Kingsthorpe ☎ 711333
HONDA 13/15 Sheep St. ☎ 36758
MORRIS-MG-ROVER-TRIUMPH Weedon Rd ☎ 54041
RENAULT 74 Kingsthorpe Rd ☎ 714555
ROVER-TRIUMPH 46/50 Sheep St. ☎ 35471
TOYOTA 348 Wellingborough Rd ☎ 31086
VOLVO Bedford Rd ☎ 21363
VW, AUDI, MERCEDES-BENZ 42/50 Harborough Rd
☎ 716716

NORTH BADDESLEY Hants. 👁️👁️ 👁️👁️ P 3 – see Southampton.

Für die 🏨🏨🏨, 🏨🏨, 🏨 geben wir keine Einzelheiten
über die Einrichtung an,
da diese Hotels im allgemeinen jeden Komfort besitzen.

🛏️wc 🛁wc

☎

NORTH BOVEY Devon **403** I 32 – see Moretonhampstead.

NORTHENDEN Greater Manchester **403** **404** N 23 – see Manchester.

NORTH FERRIBY Humberside – see Kingston-upon-Hull.

NORTHFIELD West Midlands **403** **404** O 26 – see Birmingham.

NORTH HYKEHAM Lincs. **404** S 24 – see Lincoln.

NORTH NEWBALD Humberside – pop. 681 – ⊠ York – ☎ 069 65.
London 209 – Kingston-upon-Hull 16 – Leeds 50 – York 23.

XX **Tiger Inn,** The Green, YO4 3SA, ☎ 252 – Ⓟ
closed Monday dinner – **M** (bar lunch) a la carte 5.10/6.60 t. ⓦ 1.50.

NORTHREPPS Norfolk **404** Y 25 – see Cromer.

NORTH STIFFORD Essex **404** U 29 – ⊠ Grays – ☎ 0375 Grays Thurrock.
London 22 – Chelmsford 24 – Southend-on-Sea 20.

🏨 **Europa Lodge** (County), Cuckoo Lane, BM16 1OE, ☎ 71451, Group Telex 25971, ⚒,
🛏 – ⚟ ⌷wc ☎ Ⓟ. ⚿. ⬛ AE ⓞ VISA
M 4.70/5.10 st. ⓦ 1.55 – **64 rm** ⌷ 19.00/23.00 **s.**

NORTH TAWTON Devon **403** I 31 – pop. 1,132 – ECD : Wednesday – ☎ 083 782.
London 220 – Exeter 19 – Plymouth 38.

🏠 **Kayden House,** High St., EX20 2HF, ☎ 242 – ⚟ ⌷wc. ⬛ VISA
M a la carte 3.55/5.85 st. ⓦ 1.25 – **8 rm** ⌷ 8.50/19.00 st.

AUSTIN-MORRIS-MG The Square ☎ 232

NORTH WARNBOROUGH Hants. **404** R 30 – see Odiham.

NORWICH Norfolk **404** X 26 – pop. 122,083 – ☎ 0603.
See: Cathedral** 11C-12C (bosses** of nave vaulting) **Y A** – Castle (museum**) *AC* **z M** – St.
Peter Mancroft's Church* (Perpendicular) **z B** – Sainsbury Centre for Visual Arts* (University
of East Anglia) *AC*, by B 1108 **X. Envir.** : Wymondham (Abbey Church* : Perpendicular) SW :
9 m. by A 11 **X** – Norfolk Wildlife Park* *AC*, NW : 12 m. by A 1067 **V.**

18 Barnham Broom ☎ 545437, W : 7 m. off A 47 **V.**

✈ ☎ 411923, N : 3 ½ m by A 140 **V.**

🛈 Augustine Steward House, 14 Tombland ☎ 20679 or 23445.

London 111 – Kingston-upon-Hull 149 – Leicester 117 – Nottingham 124.

Plan opposite

🏨 **Norwich** (Best Western), 121-131 Boundary Rd, NR3 2BA, on A 1047 ☎ 410431,
Telex 975337 – ⚟ ⌷wc ☎ ⚐ Ⓟ. ⚿. ⬛ AE ⓞ VISA **V r**
M approx. 5.00 st. ⓦ 2.00 – ⌷ 2.25 – **85 rm** 17.50/21.00 st.

🏨 **Post House** (T.H.F.), Ipswich Rd, NR4 6EP, S : 2 ¼ m. on A 140 ☎ 56431, Telex 975106,
⚊ heated – ⚟ ⌷wc ☎ ⚐ Ⓟ. ⚿. ⬛ AE ⓞ VISA on A 140 **X**
M 4.60/5.80 st. ⓦ 1.65 – ⌷ 2.25 – **120 rm** 18.00/25.50 st.

🏨 **Nelson,** Prince of Wales Rd, NR1 1DX, ☎ 28612, Telex 975203, ⬐ – 📶 ⚟ ⌷wc ☎ Ⓟ.
⚿. ⬛ AE ⓞ VISA **z a**
M 5.00 st. ⓦ 1.95 – ⌷ 2.25 – **94 rm** 18.50/22.50 st.

🏨 **Castle** (De Vere), Castle Meadow, NR1 3PZ, ☎ 611511, Telex 22121 – 📶 ⚟ ⌷wc ☎.
⚿. ⬛ AE ⓞ VISA **z n**
M 4.25/4.75 st. ⓦ 1.75 – **78 rm** ⌷ 16.50/21.00 st.

🏨 **Maid's Head,** Tombland, NR3 1LB, ☎ 28821, Telex 975080 – 📶 ⚟ ⌷wc ⌷wc ☎
Ⓟ. ⬛ AE ⓞ VISA **Y u**
M 4.50/5.00 t. ⓦ 2.05 – ⌷ 2.60 – **82 rm** 18.00/23.00 t. – P 27.00 t.

🏨 **Lansdowne,** 116 Thorpe Rd, NR1 1RU, ☎ 20302 – 📶 ⚟ ⌷wc Ⓟ. ⬛ AE ⓞ VISA **X i**
M (*closed Saturday lunch*) 4.15/4.75 st. ⓦ 2.90 – **44 rm** ⌷ 16.00/22.00 st.

XX **Marco's,** 17 Pottergate, NR2 1DS, ☎ 24044, Italian rest. – ⬛ AE ⓞ VISA **YZ e**
closed Sunday, Monday and Bank Holidays – **M** a la carte 5.60/11.20 ⓦ 2.50.

XX Parson Woodfoorde (1st floor), Old Post Office Yard, 19-21 Bedford St., ☎ 24280,
« Former 17C Warehouse ». **YZ x**

XX **Smedleys,** 15-17 Prince's St., NR3 1AF, ☎ 23193 – ⬛ AE ⓞ VISA **Y v**
closed Sunday and Bank Holidays – **M** a la carte 4.40/7.40 st. ⓦ 1.50.

XX **Belmonte,** 60 Prince of Wales Rd, NR1 1LT, ☎ 22533, Italian rest. – ⬛ AE **Z c**
closed Sunday, Monday and Bank Holidays except Christmas Day lunch – **M** a la carte
5.50/11.65 t. ⓦ 2.05.

X **Hobbs,** 19 Fye Bridge St., NR3 1LJ, ☎ 21825, Italian rest. – ⬛ AE ⓞ VISA **Y o**
closed Sunday – **M** a la carte 5.80/9.05 t. ⓦ 1.55.

P.T.O. ⟶

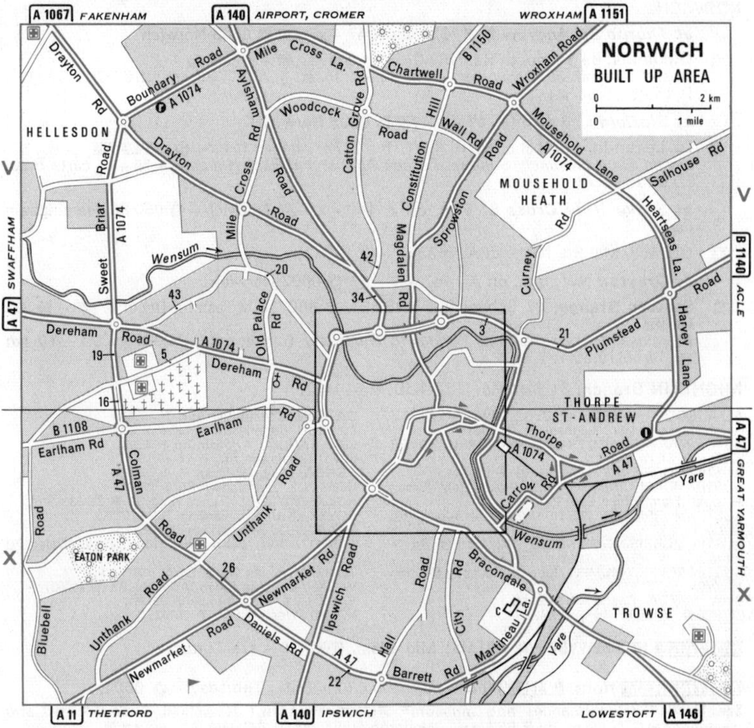

NORWICH
BUILT UP AREA
0   2 km
0   1 mile

A 1067 FAKENHAM
A 140 AIRPORT, CROMER
WROXHAM A 1151
A 1074
B 1150
Drayton Road
Mile Cross La.
Chartwell
Wroxham Road
Mousehold Lane
Salhouse Rd
Boundary Road
Aylsham Rd
Woodcock Road
Wall Rd
A 1074
Heartseas La.
HELLESDON
Drayton Road
Mile Cross Road
Catton Grove Rd
Constitution Hill
MOUSEHOLD HEATH
SWAFFHAM
Briar Road
A 1074
Mile Cross Road
Magdalen Rd
Sprowston Road
Curney Rd
Harvey Lane
Road
B 1140 ACLE
A 47
Sweet
Wensum
20
42
34
Plumstead Road
A 47 GREAT YARMOUTH
43
Old Palace Rd
3
21
Dereham Road
A 1074
Dereham Rd
THORPE ST-ANDREW
19
5
Thorpe Road
Yare
16
Rd
A 1074
B 1108
Earlham Rd
Earlham Road
Carrow Rd
Wensum
Earlham Road
Colman
A 47
Unthank Road
EATON PARK
Newmarket Rd
Ipswich Road
Road
Rd
Bracondale
Martineau La.
TROWSE
26
Road
City Rd
Yare
Road
Bluebell
Unthank Road
Daniels Rd
A 47
Hall Rd
Barrett Rd
22
Newmarket Road
A 11 THETFORD
A 140 IPSWICH
LOWESTOFT A 146

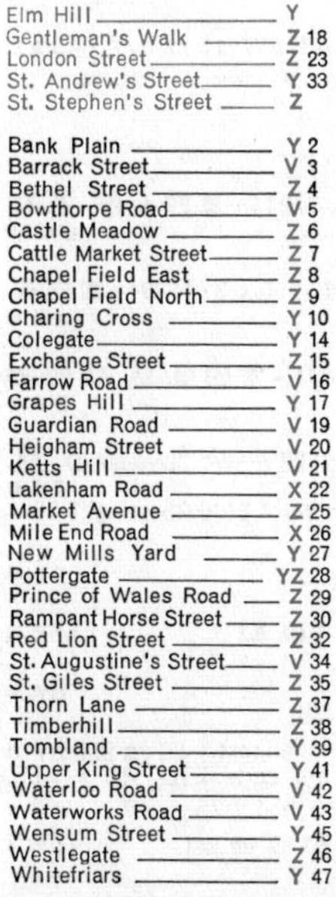

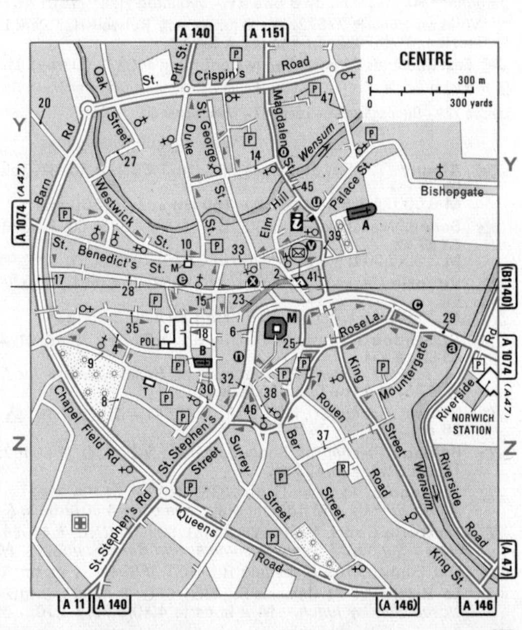

CENTRE
0   300 m
0   300 yards
A 140
A 1151
A 1074 (A 47)
Oak Rd
Pitt St.
St. Crispin's Road
Magdalen St.
Wensum
47
Barn Rd
Duke Street
St. George's St.
14
Westwick St.
Elm Hill
45
Palace St.
Bishopgate
St. Benedict's St.
10
33
39
A
(B 1140)
17
28
2
41
C
15
23
Rose La.
29
35
18
6
M
25
POL.
B
Mountergate
A 1074 (A 47)
9
32
38
King Street
Rouen Road
NORWICH STATION
30
8
46
7
37
Ber Street
Surrey Street
Wensum
Riverside Road
Chapel Field Rd
St. Stephen's Street
St. Stephen's Rd
Queens Road
King St.
A 11
A 140
(A 146)
A 146
(A 47)

at Thorpe St. Andrew E: 2 ¼ m. on A 47 – X – ✉ ☉ 0603 Norwich:

🏛 **Oaklands**, 89 Yarmouth Rd, NR7 0HH, ☏ 34471, ☞ – 🚁wc **P** — *closed 24 and 25 December* – **M** 3.25/4.35 **st.** 🍷 2.25 – **37 rm** ⇄ 9.00/17.00 **st.** – P 15.45/16.95 **st.**

at Blofield E: 8 m. off A 47 – X – ✉ ☉ 0603 Norwich:

XX **La Locanda**, Fox Lane, NR13 4LW, ☏ 713787, Italian rest. – **P.** 🔲 AE VISA — *closed Saturday lunch, Sunday, 1 week August and Bank Holidays* – **M** a la carte 5.20/10.00 **t.** 🍷 1.75.

at Stoke Holy Cross S: 5 m. off A 140 – X – ✉ Norwich – ☉ 050 86 Framingham Earl:

XX Old Mill, Mill Rd, NR14 8PA, ☏ 3337 – **P.**

at Drayton NW: 5 m. on A 1067 – V – ✉ ☉ 0603 Norwich:

🏛 **Stower Grange**, 42 School Rd, NB8 6EF, ☏ 860210, « Tasteful Decor », ☞ – **P.** 🔲 ⓞ VISA — **M** *(closed to non-residents Sunday to Thursday)* (dinner only) 9.00 **t.** 🍷 2.00 – **10 rm** ⇄ 14.65/19.55 **t.**

MICHELIN Branch, 81 Barn Rd, NR2 4UB, ☏ 614427.

ALFA ROMEO, MERCEDES-BENZ, VW, AUDI-NSU Heigham Causeway, Heigham St. ☏ 61211
ASTON MARTIN-DAIMLER-JAGUAR-MORRIS-ROVER 37 Surrey St. ☏ 29011
AUSTIN-MORRIS-MG Melrose Rd ☏ 52534
AUSTIN-MORRIS Norwich Rd, Stoke Holy Cross ☏ 05086 (Framingham Earl) 2218
AUSTIN-MORRIS-MG 106/110 Prince of Wales Rd ☏ 28271
AUSTIN-MORRIS-MG-PRINCESS 162 Cromer Rd ☏ 46946
AUSTIN-ROVER-TRIUMPH Ipswich Rd, Long Stratton ☏ 30491
BMW, MAZDA Castle Hill ☏ 21471
CITROEN Whiffler Rd ☏ 43643

DATSUN Constitution Hill ☏ 43944
DATSUN 79 Mile Cross Lane ☏ 410661
FIAT, LANCIA Aylsham Rd ☏ 45345
FORD 39 Palace St. ☏ 24144
HONDA, OPEL 36 Duke St. ☏ 29825
RENAULT 22 Heigham St. ☏ 28911
ROLLS ROYCE-BENTLEY King St. ☏ 28383
ROVER-TRIUMPH Earlham Rd ☏ 21393
SAAB 32/36 Harvey Lane ☏ 33536
TALBOT, VW, AUDI-NSU 116 Prince of Wales Rd ☏ 28811
TOYOTA Rouen Rd ☏ 21629
VAUXHALL Mile Cross, Aylsham Rd ☏ 410861
VAUXHALL Mountergate ☏ 23111
VOLVO Westwick St. ☏ 26192

NOTTAGE (DRENEWYDD YN NOTAIS) Mid Glam. ⁴⁰³ I 29 – see Porthcawl.

NOTTINGHAM Notts. ⁴⁰³ ⁴⁰⁴ Q 25 – pop. 300,630 – ECD: Thursday – ☉ 0602.

See: Castle* (Renaissance) and museum* AC CZ **M. Envir.**: Newstead Abbey** 16C and gardens** AC, N: 9 m. by B 683 AY – Wollaton Hall* (16C) AC, W: 3 ½ m. AZ **M.**

🏌 Wollaton Park ☏ 77572, W: 2 m. AZ – 🏌 Bulwell Hall Park Links ☏ 278021, N: 5 m. AY – 🏌 Beeston, ☏ 257062, S: 4 m. by A 52 AZ.

✈ East Midlands Airport: Castle Donington ☏ 0332 (Derby) 810621, SW: 15 m. by A 648 AZ.

🛈 18 Milton St. ☏ 40661 – at Long Eaton: Central Library, Tamworth Rd ☏ 060 76 (Long Eaton) 5426.

London 124 – Birmingham 50 – Leeds 67 – Manchester 69.

Plans on following pages

🏨 **Albany** (T.H.F.), St. James's St., NG1 6BN, ☏ 40131, Telex 37211 – 📶 TV ♿ **P.** 🛗 🔲 AE ⓞ VISA **CYZ a** — **M** 6.00 **t.** 🍷 1.85 – ⇄ 2.50 – **160 rm** 26.50/37.00 **st.**

🏨 **Savoy**, Mansfield Rd, NG5 2BT, N: 1 m. on A 60 ☏ 602621, Telex 377429 – 📶 TV **P.** 🔲 AE ⓞ **BY u** — **M** 3.80/5.00 **t.** 🍷 1.50 – **125 rm** ⇄ 19.50/26.00 **t.**

🏨 **Victoria** (Stakis), Milton St., NG1 3PZ, ☏ 49561, Telex 37401 – 📶 TV **P.** 🛗 🔲 AE ⓞ VISA **DY a** — **M** 3.50/5.25 **t.** 🍷 1.70 – **167 rm** ⇄ 19.50/24.50 **t.**

🏨 **Strathdon** (Thistle), 44 Derby Rd, NG1 5FT, ☏ 48501 – 📶 TV 🚁wc 🚿wc 📞 **P.** 🛗 🔲 AE ⓞ VISA **CY c** — **M** *(closed Saturday, Sunday and Bank Holidays for lunch)* 4.25/6.25 **st.** 🍷 1.65 – ⇄ 3.25 – **64 rm** 19.50/26.00 **st.**

🏨 George, George St., NG1 3BP, ☏ 45641 – 📶 🚁wc 📞 🛗 **DY e** — **66 rm.**

🏠 **Pelham**, Pelham Rd, Sherwood Rise, NG7 6JQ, ☏ 604829 – **P.** 🔲 **ABY a** — **10 rm** ⇄ 6.00/10.00 **st.**

XX **Rhinegold**, Fletcher Gate, NG5 1NB, ☏ 51294 – AE **DY v** — *closed Sunday* – **M** (dinner only) a la carte 4.90/8.50 **s.** 🍷 1.45.

XX **Trattoria Conti**, 14-16 Wheeler Gate, NG1 2NB, ☏ 44056, Italian rest. – AE ⓞ VISA **CY n** — *closed Sunday, 3 weeks in summer and Bank Holidays* – **M** a la carte 4.70/7.10 🍷 1.50.

X Old English, 189 Mansfield Rd, NG1 3FS, N: ½ m. on A 60 ☏ 42025. **CY s**

X **Le Bistro**, 20 St. James's St., NG1 6FG, ☏ 42993, Bistro – 🔲 AE ⓞ VISA **CY i** — *closed Sunday lunch* – **M** a la carte 4.40/6.75 🍷 1.70.

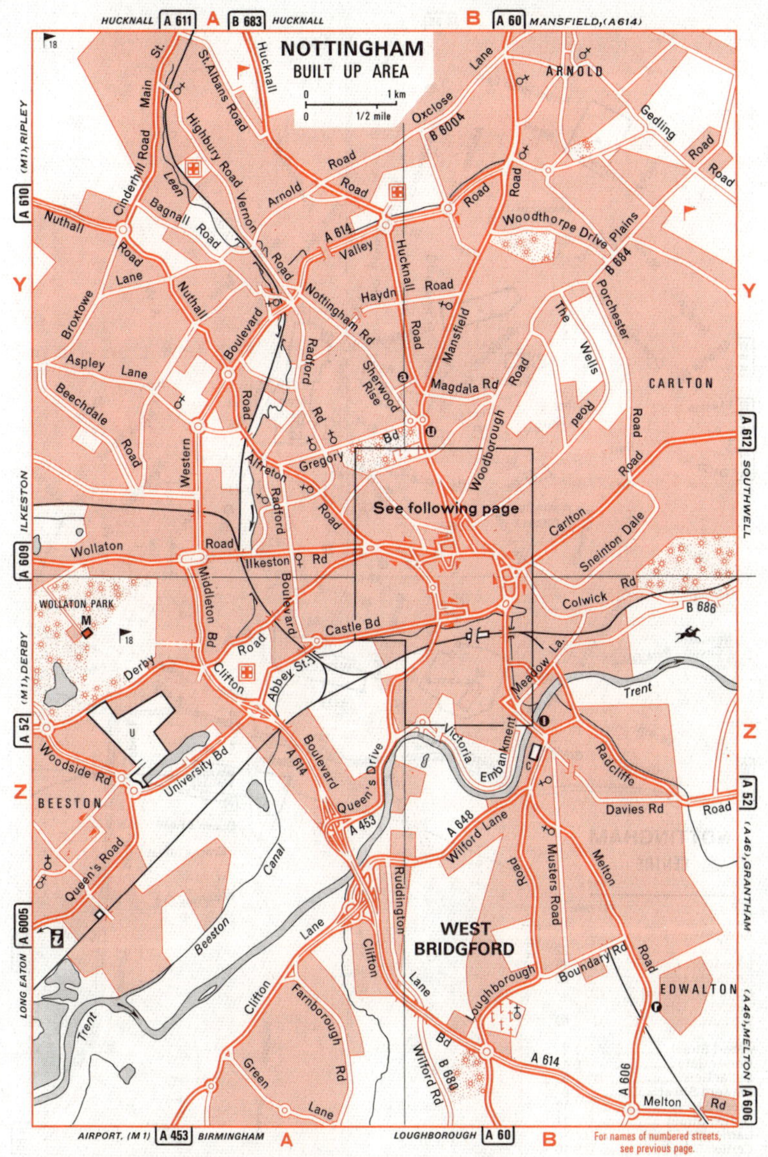

at Trent Bridge S : 2 m. on A 52 – ✉ ☎ 0602 Nottingham :

Bridgford, Pavilion Rd. NG2 5FD, ☎ 868661, ≤ – 📺 🅿 🛁 AE ⓪   **BZ i**
M 3.75 s. 🍷 1.25 – **90 rm** ☴ 16.50/19.50 s.

at Edwalton S : 3 m. on A 606 – ✉ ☎ 0602 Nottingham :

Edwalton Hall, NG12 4AE, ☎ 231116, 🍽 – ☎ 🅿   **BZ r**
closed 25 and 26 December – M *(closed Sunday dinner and Monday to non-residents)*
3.50/4.50 🍷 1.40 – **13 rm** ☴ 9.50/16.50.

P.T.O. ⟶

337

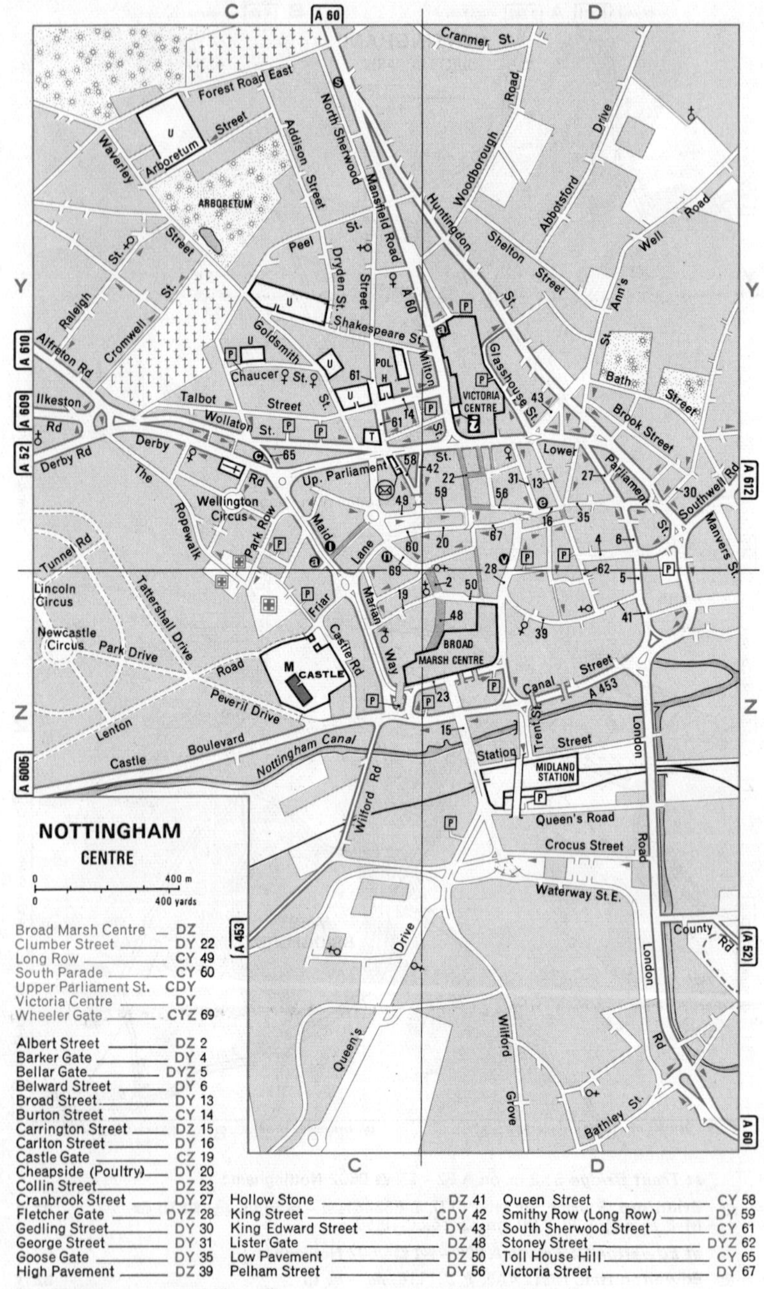

NOTTINGHAM

CENTRE

0 _____________ 400 m
0 _____________ 400 yards

I prezzi

Per ogni chiarimento sui prezzi qui riportati, consultate le spiegazioni a p. 32.

at Toton S: 6 ½ m. on A 6005 by A 453 – AZ – ⊠ Nottingham – ☎ 060 76 Long Eaton :

⋔ **Manor,** Nottingham Rd, NG9 6EF, ☏ 3487 – ℗
closed Christmas – **17 rm** ⊐ 7.50/13.00.

XX Grange Farm, Nottingham Rd, NG9 6EJ, ☏ 69426 – ℗.

at Long Eaton (Derbs.) SW: 8 m. on B 6002 by A 52 – AZ – ⊠ Nottingham –
☎ 060 76 Long Eaton :

🏨 **Novotel,** Bostock Lane, NG10 4EP, ☏ 60106, Telex 377585, ⌁ heated, ☞ – ▯ ▯
⌂wc ☎ ᴴ ℗. ⌂. ⌱ AE ⓪ VISA
M 4.20 **st.** ⌁ 2.45 – ⊐ 2.10 – **112 rm** 17.75/24.00 **st.**

at Sandiacre W: 8 m. on A 52 – AZ – ⊠ ☎ 0602 Nottingham :

🏨 **Post House** (T.H.F.), Bostocks Lane, NG10 5NJ, ☏ 397800, Telex 377378 – ▯ ⌂wc
☎ ᴴ ℗. ⌂. ⌱ AE ⓪ VISA
M 4.30/6.00 **st.** ⌁ 1.75 – **106 rm** 18.00/25.00 **st.**

ALFA-ROMEO, CITROEN 333 Mansfield Rd ☏ 606666
AUSTIN-MORRIS-MG Clifton Bridge Roundabout, Lenton Lane ☏ 866501
AUSTIN-MORRIS-MG-ROVER-TRIUMPH Talbot St. ☏ 56051
AUSTIN-MORRIS-MG 136 Burton Rd, Carlton ☏ 248808
AUSTIN-MORRIS-MG Church St. ☏ 77781
AUSTIN-MORRIS-MG-ROVER-TRIUMPH Hucknall Rd, Bulwell ☏ 272915
BRITISH LEYLAND Melton Rd, West Bridgford ☏ 811386
COLT 61a Mansfield Rd ☏ 45635
DAIMLER-JAGUAR-MG-ROVER-TRIUMPH, ROLLS ROYCE-BENTLEY Derby Rd ☏ 77701
DATSUN Woodborough Rd ☏ 623324
DATSUN Main St., Bulwell ☏ 272226

FIAT 375/381 Mansfield Rd ☏ 623251
FORD Lower Parliament St. ☏ 56282
MERCEDES Loughborough Rd ☏ 862121
OPEL Beechdale Rd ☏ 293023
RENAULT Ilkestone Rd ☏ 781938
RENAULT Sawley, Long Eaton ☏ 060 76 (Long Eaton) 3121
SAAB 499/509 Woodborough Rd ☏ 606674
TALBOT Lenton Lane ☏ 863301
TALBOT, DODGE 134/138 Loughborough Rd ☏ 814320
VAUXHALL Clifton Lane, Clifton ☏ 211228
VAUXHALL 5 Haywood Rd, Mapperley ☏ 603231
VAUXHALL Main St., Bulwell ☏ 279216
VOLVO 50 Plains Rd ☏ 266336
VW, AUDI-NSU 180 Loughborough Rd ☏ 813813

NUNEATON Warw. 🗺403 🗺404 P 26 – pop. 67,027 – ECD : Thursday – ☎ 0682.

Envir.: Arbury Hall★ (Gothic house 18C) *AC,* SW: 4 m.

🛈 Nuneaton Library, Church St. ☏ 384027.

London 107 – Birmingham 25 – Coventry 10 – Leicester.

🏨 **Nuneaton Crest Motel** (Crest), Watling St., CV11 6JH, NE: 2 ½ m. at junction A 47 and A 5 ☏ 329711 – ▯ ⌂wc ☎ ℗. ⌂. ⌱ AE ⓪ VISA
⊐ 2.40 – **47 rm** 17.30/23.80 **st.**

🏨 **Chase** (Ansells), Higham Lane, CV11 6AG, NE: 1 m. off A 47 ☏ 383406 – ▯ ⌂wc ℗.
⌱ AE
M 4.00/4.60 **t.** ⌁ 1.80 – **28 rm** ⊐ 17.30/21.95 **t.**

at Bulkington SE: 4 m. by B 4114 on B 4112 – ⊠ Nuneaton – ☎ 0203 Bedworth :

⋔ Weston Hall, Weston Lane, CV12 9RU, ☏ 315475 – ⌂wc ℗
32 rm.

AUSTIN-JAGUAR-MORRIS-MG Weddington Rd ☏ 383471
DATSUN Heath End Rd ☏ 382387
FIAT Haunchwood Rd ☏ 382807
RENAULT Nuneaton Rd, Bulkington ☏ 383344

SAAB Lutterworth Rd ☏ 382093
TALBOT 208/214 Edward St. ☏ 383339
TOYOTA 45 Attleborough Rd ☏ 382241
VAUXHALL Arbury Rd, Stockingford ☏ 384833
VOLVO Watling St. ☏ 385757

OADBY Leics. 🗺403 🗺404 Q 26 – see Leicester.

OAKHAM Leics. 🗺404 R 25 – pop. 6,414 – ECD : Thursday – ☎ 0572.

🛈 Public Library, Catmos St. ☏ 2918.

London 103 – Leicester 26 – Northampton 35 – Nottingham 28.

🏨 **Crown** (Best Western), 16 High St., LE15 6AP, ☏ 3631 – ▯ ⌂wc ☎ ℗. ⌂. ⌱ AE ⓪ VISA
closed 25 and 26 December – **M** 3.80/5.40 **st.** ⌁ 3.00 – **25 rm** ⊐ 14.50/19.50 **t.**

🏨 **George,** Market Pl., LE15 6DT, ☏ 56971 – ⌂wc ☎ ℗. ⌱ AE VISA
M (buffet lunch) a la carte 6.25/7.30 **t.** ⌁ 2.50 – **18 rm** ⊐ 11.00/14.00 **st.**

AUSTIN-LAND ROVER-MORRIS-MG-ROVER-TRIUMPH Burley Rd ☏ 2657

OAKLEY Hants. 🗺403 Q 30 – see Basingstoke.

OBORNE Dorset 🗺403 🗺404 M 31 – see Sherborne.

OCKHAM Surrey 🗺404 S 30 – pop. 447 – ⊠ ☎ 048 643 Ripley.

London 29 – Guildford 8.

XXX **Hautboy Inn** with rm, Alms Heath, GU23 6NP, ☏ 3553, ☞ – ⌂wc ℗. ⌱ AE ⓪ VISA
M a la carte 6.05/8.05 ⌁ 1.40 – **5 rm** ⊐ 12.50/15.00.

ODIHAM Hants. 404 R 30 – pop. 4,310 – ECD : Wednesday – ☎ 025 671.
London 51 – Reading 16 – Winchester 25.

    at Well SE : 3 ½ m. – ✉ Basingstoke – ☎ 025 681 Long Sutton :

  ✗ **Chequers Inn,** Long Sutton ☏ 605, French rest. – **P.** AE VISA
    closed Sunday, Monday and first 2 weeks February – **M** a la carte 4.55/6.80 **st.** ᐁ 1.65.

    at North Warnborough NW : 1 m. by A 287 on A 32 – ✉ ☎ 025 671 Odiham :

  ✗✗ **Mill House,** RG25 1ET, ☏ 2953, ≼, « Riverside terrace and gardens » – **P.** ⚅ ① VISA
    closed Sunday, Monday and 26 December-mid January – **M** a la carte 6.75/10.10 **t.**
    ᐁ 1.75.
MERCEDES-BENZ The Square ☏ 2294

ODSTOCK Wilts. 403 404 O 30 – see Salisbury.

OGDEN Greater Manchester 404 N 23 – see Milnrow.

OLD BOSHAM West Sussex 404 R 31 – see Chichester.

OLDHAM Greater Manchester 404 M 23 – pop. 105,913 – ECD : Tuesday – ☎ 061 Manchester.
⌞₁₈ Lees New Rd ☏ 624 4986 – ⌞₁₈ High Barn ☏ 624 2154.
🅣 Local Interest Centre, Greaves St. ☏ 620 8930.

London 212 – Leeds 36 – Manchester 7 – Sheffield 38.

  🏨 The Bower, Hollinwood Av., OL9 8DE, SW : 2 ½ m. by A 62 on A 6104 ☏ 682 7254 –
    TV ⇔wc ⑁wc ☎ **P.** ⚿. ⚅ AE ① VISA
    closed Bank Holidays – **M** *(closed Saturday lunch)* – **49 rm** ⚏ 16.00/21.30 **st.**

  🏨 Belgrade, Manchester St., OL8 1UZ, ☏ 624 0555, Telex 667782 – ⃦⃞ TV ⇔wc ☎ **P.** ⚿.
    130 rm.
RENAULT Manchester Rd, Hollinwood ☏ 624 1979

OLD HARLOW Essex 404 U 28 – see Harlow.

OLLERTON Notts. 403 404 Q 24 – pop. 9,170 – ECD : Thursday – ✉ Newark – ☎ 0623
Mansfield.
⌞₁₈ Eakring Rd, Mansfield ☏ 0623 (Mansfield) 23327, SW : 7 m. – ⌞₉ Woodhouse ☏ 0623
(Mansfield) 33362, SW : 7 m.

London 151 – Leeds 53 – Lincoln 25 – Nottingham 19 – Sheffield 27.

  ⚜ **Hop Pole,** Church St., NG22 9AD, ☏ 822573 – **P**
    M *(closed Sunday dinner)* 4.00/7.00 ᐁ 1.90 – **10 rm** ⚏ 9.00/14.50 **t.**

OLNEY Bucks. 404 R 27 – pop. 2,750 – ☎ 0234 Bedford.
London 62 – Bedford 11 – Oxford 45.

  ✗✗ **Four Pillars,** 60 High St., MK46 4BE, ☏ 711563, ⇌ – ⚅ ① VISA
    M 4.00/7.00 **s.** ᐁ 1.70.

OMBERSLEY Heref. and Worc. 403 404 N 27 – pop. 2,209 – ✉ Droitwich – ☎ 0905 Worcester.
London 130 – Birmingham 24 – Kidderminster 4 – Worcester 5.

  ✗✗ **Venture In,** WR9 0EW, ☏ 620552 – **P.** ⚅ ① VISA
    closed Sunday, Monday and 3 weeks August – **M** a la carte 8.30/13.30 **t.**

ORFORD Suffolk 404 Y 27 – pop. 673 – ECD : Wednesday – ✉ Woodbridge – ☎ 039 45.
London 93 – Ipswich 20 – Norwich 48.

  🏛 **Crown and Castle** (T.H.F.), IP12 2LJ, ☏ 205, ⇌ – TV ⇔wc ☎ **P.** ⚅ AE ① VISA
    M 5.30 **st.** ᐁ 1.65 – **20 rm** ⚏ 13.50/21.00 **st.**

  ✗ **Butley-Orford Oysterage,** Market Hill, IP12 2LF, ☏ 277, Seafood
    closed 25 and 26 December – **M** *(lunch only in winter)* a la carte 2.55/4.50 **t.**

OSWESTRY Salop 403 L 25 – pop. 13,000 – ECD : Thursday – ☎ 0691.
⌞₁₈ at Llanymynech ☏ 830542, S : 5 m.
🅣 Babbinswood, Whittington ☏ 069 187 (Whittington Castle) 488 (summer only).

London 182 – Chester 28 – Shrewsbury 18.

  🏨 **Wynnstay** (T.H.F.), 43 Church St., SY11 2SZ, ☏ 5261, ⇌ – TV ⇔wc ☎ **P.** ⚅ AE ①
    VISA
    M 3.75/4.25 **st.** ᐁ 1.65 – **31 rm** ⚏ 13.50/22.00 **st.**

  ⌂ **Ashfield,** Llwyn-y-Maen, Trefonen, SY10 9DD, SW : 1 ½ m. ☏ 5200, ≼, ⇌ – **P**
    March-October – **9 rm** ⚏ 7.50/15.00.

AUSTIN-MG-WOLSELEY Lower Brook St. ☏ 2285   OPEL ☏ 3491
BMW Victoria Rd ☏ 2413   TALBOT Willow St. ☏ 2301
DATSUN Salop Rd ☏ 3237   VAUXHALL Smithfield St. ☏ 2235
FORD Salop Rd ☏ 4141

OTFORD Kent 404 U 30 – see Sevenoaks.

OTTERBURN Northumb. 986 ⑮ – pop. 564 – ECD : Thursday – ☎ 083 02 (3 fig.) or 0830 (5 fig.).
London 314 – Carlisle 54 – Edinburgh 74 – Newcastle-upon-Tyne 31.

    Percy Arms (Swallow), NE19 1NR, ☏ 20261, Group Telex 53168, 🎣, 🐎 – ⬜wc ☎ 🅿.
    32 rm.

    Otterburn Tower (S & N) 🦢, NE19 1HP, ☏ 20673, 🎣, 🐎 – ⬜wc 🅿. 🔺 AE ⓞ VISA
    M a la carte 3.65/6.00 **t.** 🍷 1.45 – **15 rm.**

OTTERY ST. MARY Devon 403 K 31 – pop. 5,834 – ECD : Wednesday – ☎ 040 481.
See : St. Mary's Church* 13C-16C.
London 167 – Exeter 12 – Taunton 24.

    XX **The Lodge,** Silver St., EX11 1DB, ☏ 2356
    closed Sunday dinner, Monday, 1 week November, 3 weeks January-February and Bank Holidays – **M** a la carte 5.90/9.20 **t.** 🍷 1.60.

OULTON West Yorks. 986 ⑫ – see Leeds.

OUNDLE Northants. 404 S 26 – pop. 3,739 – ECD : Wednesday – ✉ Peterborough – ☎ 083 22.
London 89 – Leicester 37 – Northampton 30.

    Talbot (Anchor), New St., PE8 4EA, ☏ 3621, Group Telex 858875, 🐎 – 📺 ⬜wc ☎
    🅿. 🔺 AE ⓞ VISA
    M 4.00/4.50 **st.** – **23 rm** ⛶ 12.50/30.00 **st.**

    X **Tyrells,** 68 New St., ☏ 2347 – 🔺 VISA
    closed Sunday dinner and Monday – **M** a la carte 4.10/8.15 **t.** 🍷 2.20.

AUSTIN-MORRIS-MG, FORD 1 Station Rd ☏ 3542   AUSTIN-MORRIS 1 Benefield Rd ☏ 3519

OVERCOMBE Dorset 403 404 M 32 – see Weymouth.

OVERCOTE FERRY Cambs. 404 U 27 – see St. Ives.

OWLSWICK Bucks. 404 R 28 – ✉ Aylesbury – ☎ 084 44 Princes Risborough.
London 47 – Oxford 20.

    Shoulder of Mutton 🦢, HP17 9RH, ☏ 4304, 🐎 – 📺 ⬜wc ☎ 🅿. 🔺 AE ⓞ VISA
    M *(closed Sunday dinner)* (lunch by arrangement) 6.00 **s.** – **10 rm** ⛶ 12.00/20.00 **s.**

OXFORD Oxon. 403 404 Q 28 – pop. 108,805 – ECD : Thursday – ☎ 0865.
See: Colleges Quarter*** : Merton College* (Old Library***, hall*, quadrangle*, chapel windows and glass*) BZ L – Christ Church College* (hall**, cathedral*, quadrangle*, tower*) BZ D – Bodleian Old Library** (painted ceiling**) BZ M² – Divinity School (carved vaulting**) BZ M² – Magdalen College** (cloister**, chapel*) BZ K – New College (cloister*, chapel*) BZ Y – All Souls College (chapel*) BZ A – University College (gateway*) BZ V – Corpus Christi College (quadrangle and sundial*) BZ E – Radcliffe Camera* BZ O – Sheldonian Theatre* BZ M³ – High Street* BZ 9 – Ashmolean Museum** BY M¹.

🏌 Banbury Rd ☏ 54415, N : by A 423 AY.

🛈 St. Aldates ☏ 48707 or 49811 (Monday to Friday) 40170.

London 58 – Birmingham 63 – Brighton 99 – Bristol 69 – Cardiff 101 – Coventry 50 – Southampton 66.

Plans on following pages

    Randolph (T.H.F.), Beaumont St., OX1 2LN, ☏ 47481, Telex 83446 – 🛗 📺 🅿. 🏌. 🔺
    AE ⓞ VISA   **BZ n**
    M 5.25/5.95 **st.** 🍷 1.80 – ⛶ 2.50 – **109 rm** 21.50/29.00 **st.**

    Linton Lodge (Myddleton), 9-13 Linton Rd off Banbury Rd, OX2 6UJ, ☏ 53461, 🐎 –
    🛗 📺 ⬜wc ☎ 🦽 🅿. 🏌   **AY e**
    72 rm.

    Cotswold Lodge, 66A Banbury Rd, OX2 2NR, ☏ 512121 – 📺 ⬜wc 🏛 ☎ 🅿. 🏌.
    🔺 AE ⓞ VISA   **BY i**
    M 3.50/6.00 **s.** – **46 rm** ⛶ 18.00/27.00 **st.**

    TraveLodge (T.H.F.) without rest., Pear Tree Hill Roundabout, Woodstock Rd, OX2
    8JZ, ☏ 54301, Telex 83202, ⅃ heated – 📺 ⬜wc ☎ 🦽 🅿. 🏌. 🔺 AE ⓞ VISA   **AY n**
    101 rm ⛶ 14.50/21.50 **st.**

    Oxford Europa Lodge (County), Wolvercote Roundabout, OX2 8HL, N : 2 ½ m. at
    junction A 40 and A 4144 ☏ 59933, Group Telex 25971 – 📺 ⬜wc ☎ 🦽 🅿. 🏌. 🔺
    AE ⓞ VISA   **AY s**
    M 4.00/5.50 **st.** 🍷 1.55 – **89 rm** ⛶ 20.00/26.00 **s.**

    Royal Oxford (Embassy), Park End St., OX1 1HR, ☏ 48432 – 📺 ⬜wc ☎ 🅿. 🏌. 🔺
    AE ⓞ VISA   **BZ v**
    M 3.95/4.75 **st.** – **23 rm** ⛶ 16.50/22.00 **st.**

P.T.O. ⟶

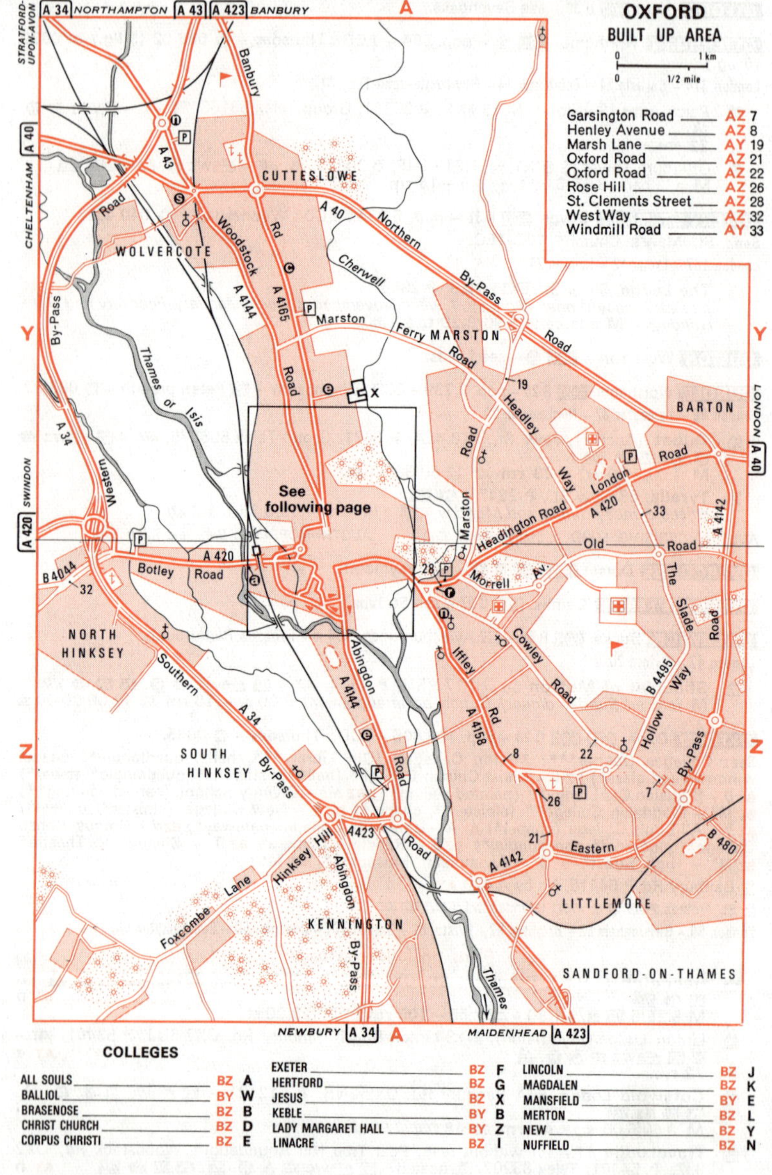

COLLEGES

ALL SOULS	BZ A	EXETER	BZ F	LINCOLN	BZ J
BALLIOL	BY W	HERTFORD	BZ G	MAGDALEN	BZ K
BRASENOSE	BZ B	JESUS	BZ X	MANSFIELD	BY E
CHRIST CHURCH	BZ D	KEBLE	BY B	MERTON	BZ L
CORPUS CHRISTI	BZ E	LADY MARGARET HALL	BY Z	NEW	BZ Y
		LINACRE	BZ I	NUFFIELD	BZ N

Eastgate (Anchor), The High, OX1 4BE, ☎ 48244, Group Telex 858875 – 📶 TV ▭ wc ☎ P. 🖼. 🅰 AE ① VISA — **BZ z**
M 4.00/4.50 st. – 45 rm ☕ 13.50/30.00 st.

Old Parsonage, 1-3 Banbury Rd, OX2 6NN, ☎ 54843, ⇔ – P. 🖼 VISA — **BY u**
closed 1 week at Christmas – **M** (dinner only and Sunday lunch) a la carte 5.15/6.35 t.
🍷 1.60 – 34 rm ☕ 9.50/18.00 t.

Isis, 45-53 Iffley Rd, OX4 1ED, ☎ 48894 – ▭ wc P. 🖼 VISA — **AZ n**
M 2.30/5.50 t. 🍷 1.65 – 38 rm ☕ 12.20/23.35 t.

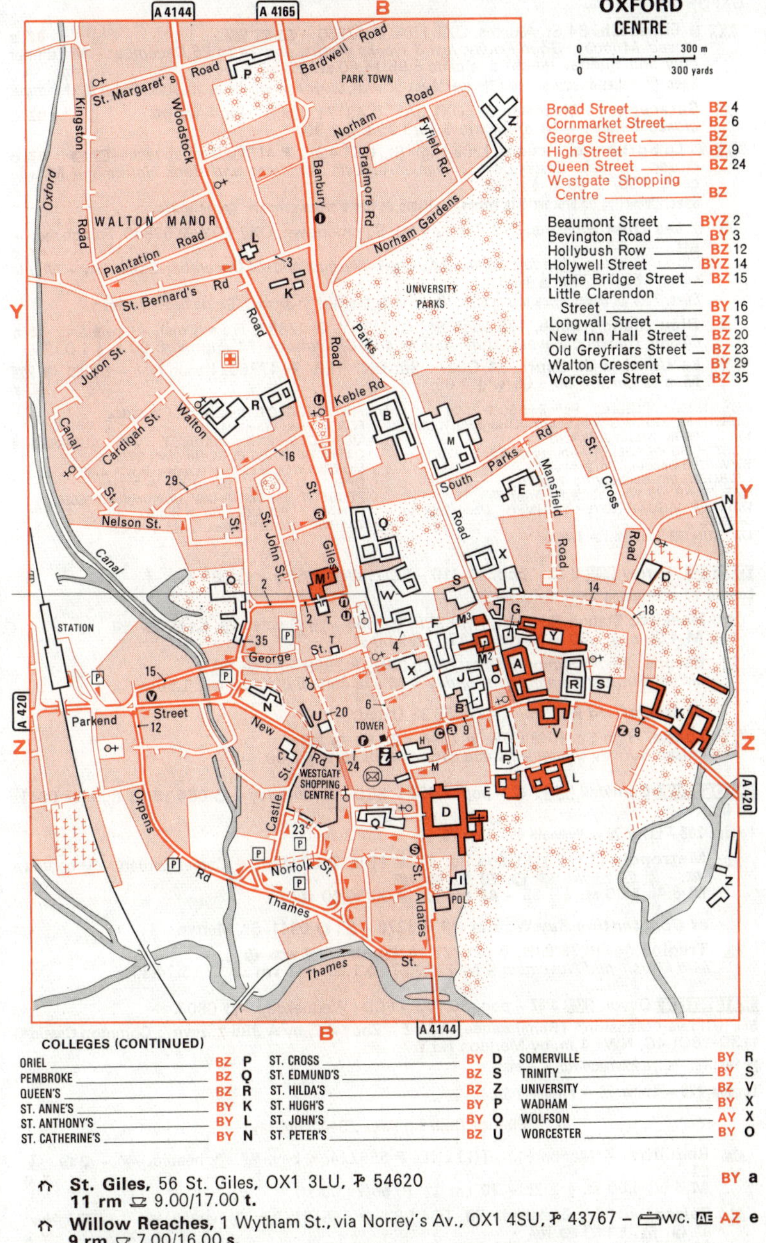

St. Giles, 56 St. Giles, OX1 3LU, ☎ 54620 — BY a
11 rm ⌷ 9.00/17.00 **t.**

Willow Reaches, 1 Wytham St., via Norrey's Av., OX1 4SU, ☎ 43767 – wc. AE — AZ e
9 rm ⌷ 7.00/16.00 **s.**

Old Black Horse, 102 St. Clements St., OX4 1AR, ☎ 44691 – P — AZ r
closed Christmas and 1 January – **20 rm** ⌷ 8.55/15.00 **t.**

River, 17 Botley Rd, OX2 0AA, ☎ 43475 – wc P — AZ a
closed Christmas and 1 January – **29 rm** ⌷ 9.00/17.00 **t.**

P.T.O. →

XXX ❀ **Elizabeth,** 84 St. Aldates, OX1 1RA, ☎ 42230 – ◪ AE *VISA*　　　　**BZ s**
closed Monday, Good Friday, last 3 weeks August and 24 to 26 December – **M** (dinner only and Sunday lunch) a la carte 8.95/14.60 **st.** ⌕ 3.50
Spec. Quenelles de saumon sauce Nantua (March-October), Suprême de volaille au vin blanc, Sorbet au champagne.

XX **Saraceno,** 15 Magdalen St., OX1 3AE, ☎ 49171, Italian rest. – ◑ *VISA*　　**BZ u**
closed Sunday – **M** a la carte 6.45/9.05 **t.** ⌕ 1.90.

XX ❀ **La Sorbonne,** 1st floor, 130a High St., OX1 4DH, ☎ 41320, French rest. – AE ◑　**BZ c**
closed Sunday, Easter, last 2 weeks August, Christmas and Bank Holidays – **M** a la carte 7.00/10.80 **t.** ⌕ 1.20
Spec. Quenelles de brochet à la lyonnaise, Râble de lièvre sauce poivrade, Crème brûlée.

XX ❀ **Les Quat'Saisons,** 272 Banbury Rd, Summertown, OX2 7DY, ☎ 53540, French rest. –
VISA　　　　　　　　　　　　　　　　　　　　　　　　　　　　　　**AY c**
closed Sunday, Monday, Easter, 14 July-14 August and 24 December-2 January – **M** a la carte 7.50/10.75 **s.** ⌕ 1.05
Spec. Pâté de turbot sauce beurre blanc, Feuilleté de Coquilles St-Jacques, Gâteau de topinambours.

X **Bleu Blanc Rouge,** 129 High St., OX1 3HY, ☎ 42883, French rest. – AE ◑　**BZ a**
closed Tuesday, 2 weeks July-August and Christmas – **M** approx. 5.90 **t.** ⌕ 1.00.

X **La Cantina di Capri,** 34 Queen St., OX1 1ER, ☎ 47760, Italian rest. – ◪ AE ◑ *VISA*
M a la carte 3.80/9.05 **t.** ⌕ 1.65.　　　　　　　　　　　　　　　　　　**BZ r**

AUSTIN-MG-WOLSELEY Park End St. ☎ 21421
AUSTIN-MORRIS-MG-WOLSELEY Oxford Rd, Kidlington ☎ 086 75 (Kidlington) 4363
AUSTIN-MG-WOLSELEY Abingdon Rd ☎ 42241
BMW 280 Banbury Rd ☎ 511461
CITROEN 281 Banbury Rd ☎ 54521
DAF, SAAB 75 Woodstock Rd ☎ 57028
DAIMLER-JAGUAR-ROVER-TRIUMPH Woodstock Rd ☎ 59955
DATSUN 72 Rose Hill ☎ 774696

FIAT, PEUGEOT Banbury Rd ☎ 59944
FORD West Way ☎ 4996
MERCEDES-BENZ, PEUGEOT, VW, AUDI-NSU 2 Oxford Rd ☎ 086 75 (Kidlington) 3732
MORRIS-WOLSELEY Magdalen Rd ☎ 47307
OPEL, VAUXHALL Botley Rd ☎ 722455
PEUGEOT Benson ☎ 0491 (Wallingford) 35656
RENAULT 265 Iffley Rd ☎ 40101
TALBOT 311/321 Banbury Rd ☎ 53232

OXTED Surrey **404** U 30 – pop. 12,410 – ECD : Wednesday – ✆ 088 33.
London 23 – Brighton 38 – Maidstone 26.

🏠 **Hoskins,** Station Rd West, RH8 9EF, ☎ 2338 – TV ⓦwc ☎ P. ◪ AE ◑ *VISA*
M 4.00 **s.** ⌕ 1.30 – **10 rm** ⌂ 17.50/25.00 **st.**

XX **Barons,** 28-30 Station Rd East, RH8 0PG, ☎ 3988 – ◪ AE *VISA*
closed Sunday dinner and Monday – **M** a la carte 5.60/7.25 **t.** ⌕ 1.50.

at Limpsfield E : 1 m – ✉ ✆ 088 33 Oxted :

XX **Lodge,** High St., RH8 0DR, ☎ 2996 – P. ◪ ◑ *VISA*
closed Sunday dinner – **M** a la carte 5.55/9.75 **t.** ⌕ 2.00.

PADSTOW Cornwall **403** F 32 – pop. 2,802 – ECD : Wednesday – ✆ 084 13 (3 fig.) or 0841 (6 fig.).
London 288 – Exeter 78 – Plymouth 45 – Truro 23.

🏨 **Metropole** (T.H.F.), Station Rd, PL28 8DB, ☎ 532486, ← Camel Estuary, ⌇ heated, 🚗 – ▤ TV ⌅wc ☎ P. ◪ AE ◑ *VISA*
M 3.45/4.80 **st.** ⌕ 1.65 – **42 rm** ⌂ 14.00/30.00 **st.**

at Constantine Bay W : 3 m. off B 3276 – ✉ ✆ 0841 St. Merryn :

🏨 **Treglos** ⌇, PL28 8JH, ☎ 520727, ←, ◪, 🚗 – TV 🚐 P
Mid March-mid November – **M** 4.25/5.75 ⌕ 1.60 – **41 rm** ⌂ 12.15/24.30.

PAIGNTON Devon **403** J 32 – pop. 35,100 – ECD : Wednesday – ✆ 0803.
See : Oldway Mansion* (Renaissance) *AC* **Y** E – Zoo* *AC*, by A 385 **Z**. Envir. : Compton Castle* (13C-16C) *AC*, NW : 4 m. by Marldon Rd **Y**.
🛈 Festival Hall, Esplanade Rd ☎ 558383.
London 226 – Exeter 26 – Plymouth 29.

Plan of Built up Area : See Torquay

🏨 **Redcliffe,** 4 Marine Par., TQ3 2NL, ☎ 556224, ← bay, ⌇, ⌇ heated, 🚗 – ▤ P. ⛱.
AE　　　　　　　　　　　　　　　　　　　　　　　　　　　　　　　**Y n**
M 4.50/6.00 **st.** ⌕ 2.25 – **70 rm** ⌂ 10.50/24.00 **st.**

🏨 **Palace** (T.H.F.), Esplanade Rd, TQ4 6BJ, ☎ 555121, ⌇, ⌇ heated, 🚗 – ▤ TV ⌅wc ☎ P. ⛱. ◪ AE ◑ *VISA*　　　　　　　　　　　　　　　　　　　　　**Y e**
M 3.75/5.00 **st.** ⌕ 1.85 – **55 rm** ⌂ 13.50/29.50 **st.**

🏠 **St. Ann's,** 6 Alta Vista Rd, TQ4 6BZ, ☎ 557360, ←, ⌇ heated, 🚗 – ⌅wc P　**Z o**
Easter-October – **M** (dinner only) 8.00 **st.** ⌕ 1.65 – **26 rm** ⌂ 11.45/25.80 **st.**

🏠 **Erleigh Court,** 1 Elmsleigh Rd, TQ4 5AX, ☎ 551565 – P　　　　　　　**Z s**
16 rm ⌂ 7.00/17.00 **st.**

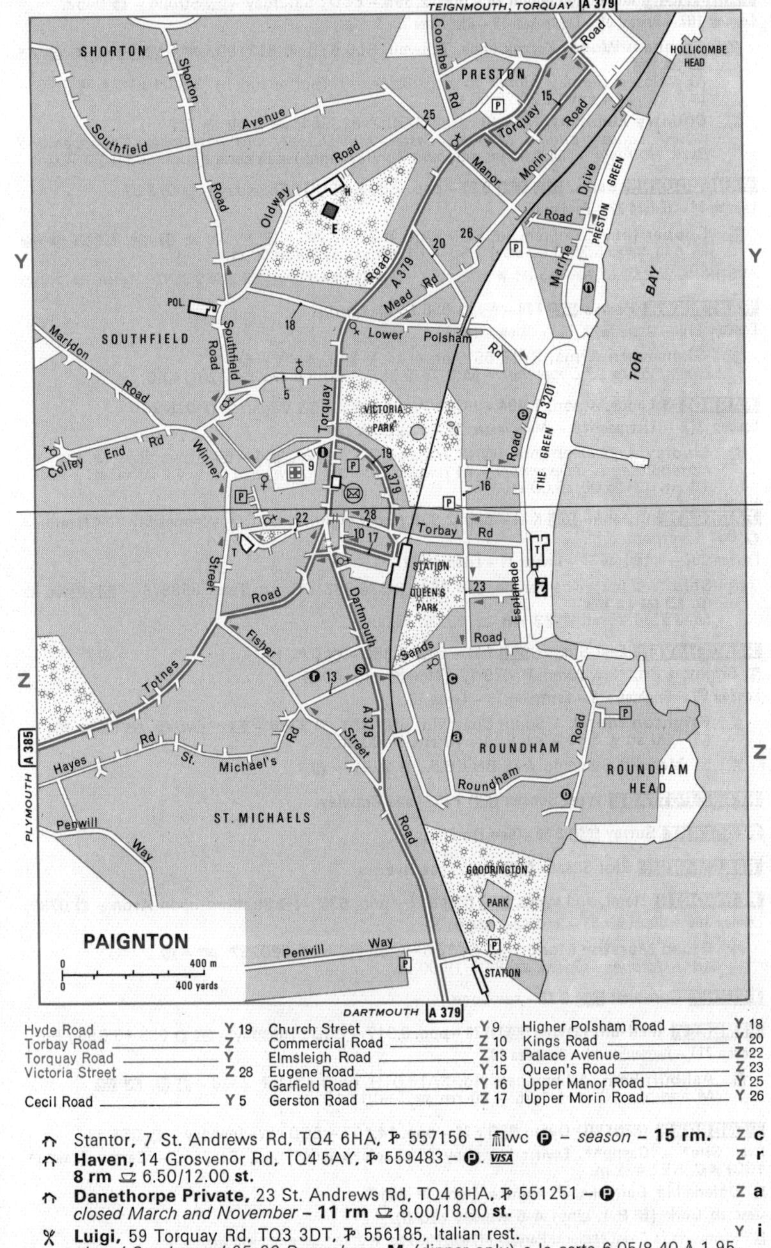

↑ Stantor, 7 St. Andrews Rd, TQ4 6HA, ☎ 557156 – ▥wc ℗ – *season* – **15 rm.** Z c

↑ **Haven,** 14 Grosvenor Rd, TQ4 5AY, ☎ 559483 – ℗. *VISA* Z r
8 rm ⊡ 6.50/12.00 st.

↑ **Danethorpe Private,** 23 St. Andrews Rd, TQ4 6HA, ☎ 551251 – ℗ Z a
closed March and November – **11 rm** ⊡ 8.00/18.00 st.

✕ **Luigi,** 59 Torquay Rd, TQ3 3DT, ☎ 556185, Italian rest. Y i
closed Sunday and 25-26 December – **M** (dinner only) a la carte 6.05/8.40 ▯ 1.95.

ALFA-ROMEO, BMW, SAAB Collaton St. Mary ☎ 558567
AUDI Bishop's Pl. ☎ 556234
AUSTIN-MORRIS-ROVER-TRIUMPH 69 Torquay Rd ☎ 551818

FIAT Totnes Rd ☎ 554484
FORD 338 Torquay Rd ☎ 62021
TALBOT 375 Torquay Rd ☎ 523555
TOYOTA Dartmouth Rd ☎ 554721
VAUXHALL Steartfield Rd ☎ 559122

PAINSWICK Glos. **403** **404** N 28 – pop. 2,895 – ECD : Saturday – ⊠ Stroud – ☎ 0452.
London 107 – Bristol 35 – Cheltenham 10 – Gloucester 7.

- **Cranham Wood,** Kemps Lane, Tibiwell, GL6 6YB, ℡ 812160, ⇌ – 🖵 ⊟wc ☎ ℗. ⛆ AE ⓘ VISA
  M *(closed Sunday dinner to non-residents)* (buffet lunch) 3.00/10.00 **t.** ⬧ 1.50 –
  ⊒ 1.25 – **14 rm** 13.25/26.50 **t.**

- **Country Elephant,** New St., GL6 6XH, ℡ 813564, ⇌ – AE ⓘ VISA
  *closed Sunday dinner, Monday, Easter, mid October-mid November, Christmas and
  Bank Holidays* – **M** (dinner only and Sunday lunch) a la carte approx. 6.80 ⬧ 1.70.

PANGBOURNE Berks. **403** **404** Q 29 – pop. 2,503 – ECD : Thursday – ☎ 073 57.
London 56 – Oxford 22 – Reading 6.

- **Copper Inn,** 2 Church Rd, RG8 7AR, ℡ 2244, ⇌ – 🖵 ⊟wc ☎ ℗. ⛆. ⛆ AE ⓘ VISA
  M a la carte 5.30/8.90 **st.** ⬧ 1.50 – **14 rm** ⊒ 20.00/26.00 **st.**

AUSTIN-MG-WOLSELEY Reading Rd ℡ 2376   JENSEN, LANCIA, MERCEDES-BENZ Station Rd ℡ 3322

PANT MAWR Powys **403** I 26 – ⊠ ☎ 055 15 Llangurig.
London 219 – Aberystwyth 21 – Shrewsbury 55.

- **Glansevern Arms,** SY18 6SY, on A 44 ℡ 240, ⇌, ⤚ – ℗
  closed 20 to 28 December – **M** 3.75/5.25 ⬧ 1.60 – **6 rm** ⊒ 7.25/14.50.

PARBOLD Lancs. – pop. 1,994 – ECD : Wednesday – ⊠ Wigan – ☎ 025 76.
London 212 – Liverpool 18 – Manchester 33 – Preston 18.

- **Lindley,** Lancaster Lane, WN8 7AB, on B 5246 ℡ 2804 – 🖵 ⊟wc �🖵wc ℗. VISA
  closed 25 and 26 December – **M** *(closed Saturday lunch)* a la carte 4.95/8.60 **st.** ⬧ 1.60 –
  10 rm ⊒ 15.00/20.00 **st.**

PARKGATE Cheshire **403** K 24 – pop. 2,939 (inc. Leighton) – ECD : Wednesday – ⊠ Neston –
☎ 051 Liverpool.

London 207 – Birkenhead 10 – Chester 11 – Liverpool 12.

- **Ship** (Anchor), The Parade, L64 6SA, ℡ 336 3931, Group Telex 858875 – 🖵 ⊟wc ☎
  ℗. ⛆ AE ⓘ VISA
  M 3.75/4.25 **st.** – **23 rm** ⊒ 13.00/25.00 **st.**

PEACEHAVEN East Sussex **404** T 31 – pop. 8,350 – ☎ 079 14.
🈂 Brighton Rd, Newhaven ℡ 079 12 (Newhaven) 4049.
London 60 – Brighton 6.5 – Eastbourne 16 – Lewes 10.

- **Brighton Motel,** 1 South Coast Rd, BN9 8SY, ℡ 3736 – 🖵 ⊟wc ℗. ⛆ AE ⓘ VISA
  M 7.00 **st.** ⬧ 1.00 – ⊒ 2.00 – **19 rm** 19.00 **st.**

- **✗** La Mer, 20 Steyning Av., BN9 8JL, ℡ 2291 – ℗.

PEASE POTTAGE West Sussex **404** T 30 – see Crawley.

PEASLAKE Surrey **404** S 30 – see Dorking.

PEASMARSH East Sussex **404** W 31 – see Rye.

PEBWORTH Heref. and Worc. **403** **404** O 27 – pop. 636 – ⊠ Stratford-upon-Avon – ☎ 0789.
London 106 – Gloucester 33 – Stratford-upon-Avon 10.

- **Broad Marston Manor** ⤴, CV37 8XY, SE : ½ m. ℡ 720252, ⇌ – ℗
  April-October – **7 rm** ⊒ 8.00/16.00 **st.**

PELYNT Cornwall **403** G 32 – see Looe.

PEMBREY (PEN-BRE) Dyfed **403** H 28 – pop. 6,317 – ECD : Tuesday – ⊠ ☎ 055 46 Burry Port.
London 211 – Carmarthen 14 – Swansea 16.

- **Ashburnham,** Ashburnham Rd, SA16 0TH, on B 4311 ℡ 2328 – �🖵 ℗. ⛆ VISA
  M approx. 4.00 **t.** ⬧ 1.25 – **10 rm** ⊒ 7.50/17.10 **st.**

PEMBROKE (PENFRO) Dyfed **403** F 28 – pop. 14,197 – ECD : Wednesday – ☎ 064 63.
See : Site* – Castle**. Envir.: Lamphey (Bishop's palace*) *AC*, E : 2 m. – Carew (castle*
13C) *AC*, NE : 4 ½ m.
🈂 Defensible Barracks, Pembroke Dock ℡ 3817.
⚓ to Cork (B & I. Line) 4-6 weekly (10 h).
🅸 Pembrokeshire Coast National Park, Drill Hall, Main St. ℡ 2148 (Easter-September).

London 252 – Carmarthen 32 – Fishguard 26.

- **Old Kings Arms,** 13 Main St., SA71 4JS, ℡ 3611, Telex 48598 – 🖵 ⊟wc ☎ ℗. ⛆ VISA
  closed 2 weeks at Christmas – **M** 10.00/12.00 **st.** – **21 rm** ⊒ 13.75/24.00 **st.**

AUSTIN-JAGUAR-MORRIS-MG-ROVER-TRIUMPH Main St. ℡ 3169

PEMBROKESHIRE (Coast) ** Dyfed **403** E 28.

See : From Cemaes Head to Strumble Head** : Newport (site*) – Bryn Henllan (site*) –
Goodwick ≤** – Strumble Head (≤** from the lighthouse). From Strumble Head to Solva** :
Trevine ≤** – Porthgain (cliffs ✾***) – Abereiddy (site*) – St. David's Head** – Whitesand
Bay** – Solva (site*).

From Solva to Dale** : Newgale ≤** – Martin's Haven ✾** – St. Ann's Head ≤** – Dale ≤*.

From Dale to Freshwater West* : Freshwater West (site*).

From Freshwater West to Pendine Sands** (Stack Rocks**) – St. Govan's Chapel (site*) –
Freshwater East (site*) – Manorbier (castle*) – Tenby (site**) – Amroth (site*) – Pendine
Sands*.

PENARTH South Glam. **403** K 29 – pop. 22,570 – ECD : Wednesday – ☯ 0222.

📍8 Lavernock Rd ☏ 707048.

🛈 Information Office, West House ☏ 707201 (Easter-September).

London 161 – Cardiff 4.

  XXX **Caprice**, 1st floor, 1 Beach Cliff, The Esplanade, CF6 2AS, ☏ 702424, ≤ – 🅰 AE ⓪
    VISA
    closed Sunday and Bank Holidays – **M** a la carte 7.65/11.95 **t.** 🍷 2.15.

    at Swanbridge S : 2 ½ m. off B 4267 – ✉ Penarth – ☯ 0222 Sully :

  XXX **Sully House** ⚓ with rm, Lavernock Beach Rd, CF6 2XR, ☏ 530448, 🚗 – 📺 🛁wc ℗.
    🅰 VISA
    M *(closed Saturday lunch, Sunday and Bank Holidays)* a la carte 8.00/11.15 **t.** 🍷 2.60 –
    4 rm ☲ 19.00/26.00 **t.**

PEN-BRE Dyfed – see Pembrey.

PENCRAIG Heref. and Worc. **403** **404** M 27 – see Ross-on-Wye.

PENDOGGETT Cornwall **403** F 32 – pop. 60 – ✉ Bodmin – ☯ 020 888 Port Isaac.
London 264 – Newquay 22 – Truro 30.

  XX **Cornish Arms** with rm, St. Kew, PL30 3HH, ☏ 263, 🚗 – ℗. 🅰 AE ⓪ VISA
    closed 3 days at Christmas – **M** (buffet lunch Monday to Saturday) a la carte 4.35/
    9.00 **t.** 🍷 1.60 – **6 rm** ☲ 18.35/24.05 **st.**

PENFRO Dyfed – see Pembroke.

PENGETHLEY Heref. and Worc. **403** **404** M 28 – see Ross-on-Wye.

PENMAENHEAD Clwyd **403** I 24 – see Colwyn Bay.

PENMAENMAWR Gwynedd **403** I 24 – pop. 3,991 – ECD : Wednesday – ✉ ☯ 049 265.
📍9 ☏ 3330.
London 241 – Chester 50 – Holyhead 34.

  ↑ **Red Gables**, Bangor Rd, on A55 ☏ 3722
    7 rm ☲ 6.00/7.00 **s.**

PENMAENPOOL Gwynedd **403** I 25 – see Dolgellau.

PENMORFA Gwynedd **403** H 25 – see Portmadoc.

PENNAL Gwynedd **403** I 25 – see Machynlleth (Powys).

PENRITH Cumbria **986** ⑲ – pop. 10,590 – ECD : Wednesday – ☯ 0768.
Envir. : Lowther (Wildlife Park* *AC*) S : 5 m.
📍18 ☏ 2217 and 5429, E : ½ m. on Salkeld Rd.
🛈 Robinson's School, Middlegate ☏ 4671 ext 33.
London 290 – Carlisle 24 – Kendal 31 – Lancaster 48.

  🏠 **George**, Devonshire St., CA11 7SU, ☏ 62696 – 🛁wc 🚿wc ℗. 🎱
    M 3.50/5.50 **st.** 🍷 2.00 – **30 rm** ☲ 9.00/20.00 **st.**

AUDI-NSU, CITROEN Ullswater Rd ☏ 4545
AUSTIN-MORRIS-MG 18/19 King St. ☏ 3312
AUSTIN-MORRIS-MG-ROVER-TRIUMPH Victoria Rd
☏ 3666
FIAT King St. ☏ 4691

FORD Old London Rd ☏ 2307
RENAULT 11 King St. ☏ 2371
TALBOT Roper St. ☏ 3641
TOYOTA 15 Victoria Rd ☏ 4555
VAUXHALL Scotland Rd ☏ 3756

See : Penshurst Place* (and Tudor Gardens** 14C) *AC*. Envir. : Chiddingstone (castle : Egyptian and Japanese collections* *AC*) NW : 5 m. – Hever Castle* (13C) *AC*, W : 6 m.

London 38 – Maidstone 19 – Royal Tunbridge Wells 6.

🏨 **Leicester Arms,** High St., TN11 8BT, ☎ 551, ≼, 🚗 – TV 📶 wc 🄿. 🄰 AE ⑪ VISA
closed 24 to 26 December – M *(closed Sunday dinner and Monday to non-residents)* 4.50/
7.50 **t.** 🍷 1.60 – **7 rm** ⊇ 13.50/22.50 **t.**

    at Chiddingstone NW : 5 m. – ✉ Edenbridge – ✆ 0892 Penshurst :

XX **Castle Inn,** TN8 7AE, ☎ 870247, 🚗 – 🄰 AE ⑪
closed Wednesday lunch, Tuesday and January – **M** a la carte 9.65/10.75 **st.** 🍷 2.05.

PEN-Y-BONT Mid Glam. – see Bridgend.

PENZANCE Cornwall 403 D 33 – pop. 19,415 – ECD : Wednesday – ✆ 0736.

Envir. : St. Michael's Mount** *AC*, E : 3 m. by A 30 **Y** – Land's End** SW : 10 m. by A 30 **Z** –
Porthcuno (Minack Theatre) site * *AC*, SW : 8 m. by B 3315 **Z**.
Access to the Isles of Scilly by helicopter.

🚗 ☎ 5831. – ⚓ to the Isles of Scilly : St. Mary's (Isles of Scilly Steamship Co.) summer
Monday to Saturday 1 daily ; winter 3 weekly (2 h 30 mn).

🛈 Alverton St. ☎ 2207.

London 318 – Exeter 114 – **Plymouth 75** – Taunton 149.

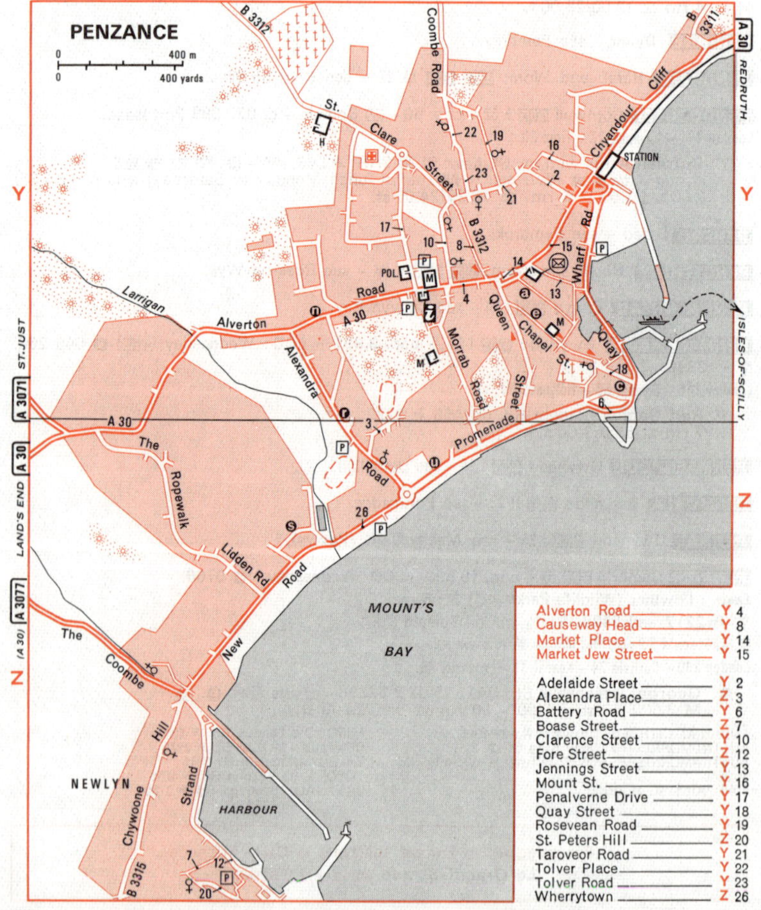

Alverton Road — Y 4
Causeway Head — Y 8
Market Place — Y 14
Market Jew Street — Y 15

Adelaide Street — Y 2
Alexandra Place — Z 3
Battery Road — Y 6
Boase Street — Z 7
Clarence Street — Y 10
Fore Street — Z 12
Jennings Street — Y 13
Mount St. — Y 16
Penalverne Drive — Y 17
Quay Street — Y 18
Rosevean Road — Y 19
St. Peters Hill — Z 20
Taroveor Road — Y 21
Tolver Place — Y 22
Tolver Road — Y 23
Wherrytown — Z 26

🏠 **Queens,** Promenade, TR18 4HG, ☏ 2371, ⬉ – 🛗 🛏wc **P**. ◪ AE ⓓ *VISA* **Z u**
M 4.00/5.50 **t.** ⬧ 2.10 – **69 rm** ⊐ 13.00/30.00 **t.**

🏠 **Union,** Chapel St., TR18 4AE, ☏ 2319 – 🛏wc 🛏wc 🚗 . ◪ AE *VISA* **Y e**
M (buffet lunch) 5.25 **t.** ⬧ 1.75 – **27 rm** ⊐ 9.50/10.75 **st.**

🏠 **Alverton Court,** Alverton Rd, TR18 4TJ, ☏ 2306, 🚗 – 🛏wc 🛏wc **P** **Y n**
April-September – **M** (bar lunch) approx. 6.00 **st.** ⬧ 1.35 – **15 rm** ⊐ 7.50/15.00 **s.**

🏠 **Trevaylor** ⊱, Newmill Rd, Gulval, TR20 8UR, NE : 1¾ m. off B 3311 ☏ 2882, ⬉,
« Country house atmosphere », 🚗 – 🛏wc 🛏wc **P** by B 3311 **Y**
Easter-October – **M** (dinner only) a la carte approx. 4.70 **t.** ⬧ 1.05 – **8 rm** ⊐ 7.50/15.00 **t.**

⋔ **Sea and Horses,** 6 Alexandra Ter., TR18 4NX, ☏ 61961 – 🛏 **P**. ◪ ⓓ **Z s**
March-October – **11 rm** ⊐ 5.75/11.50 **st.**

⋔ **Dunedin,** Alexandra Rd, TR18 4LZ, ☏ 2652 – ◪ **Y r**
March-November – **9 rm** ⊐ 6.00/12.00 **t.**

✕✕ **Le Tarot,** 19 Quay St., TR18 4BD, ☏ 3118 – ◪ AE ⓓ *VISA* **Y c**
closed Sunday and January – **M** (dinner only) a la carte 5.20/7.80 **t.** ⬧ 1.95.

✕ **Bistro One,** 46 New St., TR18 2LZ, ☏ 4408 – AE *VISA* **Y a**
closed Sunday – **M** (dinner only) a la carte 6.20/9.85 **t.** ⬧ 2.10.

   at Newlyn SW : 2 m. on B 3315 – **Z** – ✉ ☎ 0736 Penzance :

🏠 **Higher Faugan** ⊱, TR18 5NS, ☏ 2076, ✎, ⊿ heated, 🚗, park – 🛏wc 🛏wc **P**. ◪ AE
ⓓ
M (bar lunch) 6.90 **st.** ⬧ 1.80 – **16 rm** ⊐ 10.35/20.70 **t.**

BRITISH LEYLAND Coinage Hall St. ☏ 2307 TALBOT Newlyn ☏ 2038
PEUGEOT Hayle Terr. ☏ 753143

PERSHORE Heref. and Worc. **403** **404** N 27 – pop. 5,530 – ECD : Thursday – ☎ 038 65.
🛈 37 High St. ☏ 2442.

London 106 – Birmingham 32 – Cheltenham 22 – Stratford-upon-Avon 21 – Worcester 9.

🏠 **Angel,** 9 High St., WR10 1AF, ☏ 2046, ⬎, 🚗 – 🛏wc 🛏wc **P**. ◪ AE ⓓ *VISA*
M 4.50/5.50 **t.** ⬧ 1.50 – **18 rm** ⊐ 11.75/21.00 **t.**

✕ **Zhivago's,** 22 Bridge St., WR10 1AT, ☏ 3828 – ◪ AE ⓓ *VISA*
closed Sunday and Bank Holidays – **M** a la carte 5.00/8.85 **t.** ⬧ 1.80.

AUSTIN-MORRIS-MG-ROVER-TRIUMPH High St. ☏ 2255

PETERBOROUGH Cambs. **404** T 26 – pop. 102,500 – ECD : Monday and Thursday – ☎ 0733.
See : Cathedral★★ 12C-13C (nave : painted roof★★★). Envir. : Crowland : Abbey Church★ (8C
ruins), Triangular Bridge★ 13C, NE : 8 m.
🛈 Nene Parkway ☏ 267701, W : 3 m. on A 47 – 🛈 Ramsey ☏ 0487 (Ramsey) 813573, SE : 12 m.
🛈 Central Library, Broadway ☏ 69105 ext 4 – Town Hall, Bridge St. ☏ 63141.

London 85 – Cambridge 35 – Leicester 41 – Lincoln 51.

🏠 **Great Northern** (B.T.H.), Station Rd, PE1 1QL, ☏ 52331, 🚗 – 📺 🛏wc 📞 **P**. ⚗. ◪
AE ⓓ *VISA*
closed 22 to 28 December – **M** a la carte 5.15/8.40 **st.** – **49 rm** ⊐ 20.25/27.45 **st.**

🏠 **Bull,** Westgate, PE1 1RB, ☏ 61364 – 🛏wc 📞 **P**. ⚗. ◪ AE ⓓ *VISA*
M approx. 4.80 **s.** ⬧ 2.10 – **125 rm** ⊐ 14.50/20.50 **s.**

   at Whittlesey SE : 7 m. on A 605 – ✉ ☎ 0733 Peterborough :

✕✕ **Falcon,** London St., PE7 1BH, ☏ 203247 – **P**. ◪ AE ⓓ *VISA*
closed Christmas Day – **M** a la carte 5.25/7.45 **s.** ⬧ 1.95.

   at Wansford W : 8 m. off A 47 – ✉ Peterborough – ☎ 0780 Stamford :

🏠 **Haycock Inn,** Great North Rd, Bridge End, PE8 6JA, ☏ 782223, 🚗 – 📺 🛏wc 📞 **P**.
◪ AE ⓓ *VISA*
M a la carte 6.60/7.90 **s.** ⬧ 2.50 – **20 rm** ⊐ 13.00/24.75 **st.**

ALFA-ROMEO, DAF, MAZDA 659 Lincoln Rd ☏ 52141 LANCIA Midland Rd ☏ 53146
AUSTIN-MG-WOLSELEY, ROLLS ROYCE-BENTLEY MERCEDES-BENZ, PEUGEOT High St., Eye ☏ 222363
7 Oundle Rd ☏ 66011 RENAULT Thorney Rd, Newborough ☏ 073 123
BMW, SKODA Cowgate ☏ 66173 (Newborough) 625
DAIMLER-JAGUAR-ROVER-TRIUMPH Broadway ☏ TALBOT Lincoln Rd ☏ 71739
61201 TALBOT 343 Eastfield Rd ☏ 64566
DATSUN 50/64 Burghley Rd ☏ 65787 VAUXHALL Sturrock Way ☏ 264981
FIAT Oxney Rd ☏ 67201 VW, AUDI Oxney Rd ☏ 65857
FORD 27/39 New Rd ☏ 65271

PETERLEE Durham **986** ⑲ – pop. 26,500 – ECD : Wednesday – ☎ 0783.
🛈 Castle Eden ☏ 042 981 (Castle Eden) 220, S : 2 m.
🛈 Arts and Information Centre, The Upper Chare ☏ 864450.

London 270 – Durham 13 – Middlesbrough 19 – Sunderland 11.

at Hesleden S : 3 ½ m. by A 1088 and B 1281 – ✉ Hartlepool (Cleveland) – ✆ 042 981 Castle Eden :

XX **Golden Calf** with rm, Front St., TS27 4PH, ☏ 493 – 🅿. ⬛ ⓘ *VISA*
M *(closed Sunday dinner and Monday)* (bar lunch) a la carte 4.80/7.65 **t.** ₰ 1.70 – **4 rm**
⌑ 7.50/13.50 **t.**

PETT BOTTOM Kent 🔲🔲🔲 X 30 – see Canterbury.

PETWORTH West Sussex 🔲🔲🔲 S 31 – pop. 2,506 – ECD : Wednesday – ✆ 0798.
See : Petworth House*** 17C (paintings*** and carved room***) *AC.*

London 54 – Brighton 31 – Portsmouth 33.

XX **Paddington's Table,** East St., GU28 0AB, ☏ 43149 – ⬛ *VISA*
closed Sunday, Wednesday, October and 25 to 28 December – **M** (bar lunch) a la carte
5.95/7.45 **t.** ₰ 1.75.

PEVENSEY East Sussex 🔲🔲🔲 V 31 – see Eastbourne.

PICKERING North Yorks. 🔲🔲🔲 ㉔ – pop. 4,545 – ECD : Wednesday – ✆ 0751.
See : SS. Peter and Paul's Church (wall paintings* 15C) – Norman castle* (ruins) : ≼* *AC.*
🗗 North York Moors Railway, The Station ☏ 73791.

London 237 – Middlesbrough 43 – Scarborough 19 – York 25.

🏛 **Forest and Vale,** 2 Hungate, YO18 7DL, ☏ 72722, 🚗 – 📥wc 🅿. ⬛ *VISA*
M 4.00/5.50 **st.** ₰ 3.50 – **15 rm** ⌑ 10.50/24.00 **st.** – P 20.00 **st.**

FORD, MERCEDES-BENZ Eastgate ☏ 72251   TALBOT Middleton ☏ 72557

PIDDLETRENTHIDE Dorset 🔲🔲🔲 🔲🔲🔲 M 31 – pop. 501 – ✆ 030 04.
Envir. : Athelhampton Hall* (15C) *AC*, SE : 6 m.

London 135 – Bournemouth 27 – Dorchester 7 – Sherborne 13.

🏛 **Old Bakehouse,** DT2 7QR, S : 1 m. on B 3143 ☏ 305, 🌊 heated – 📥wc 🅿
M (dinner only) 4.25 ₰ 1.45 – **9 rm** ⌑ 10.00/19.50.

✕ **Poachers Inn** with rm, DT2 7RB, on B 3143 ☏ 358, 🚗 – 🅿
M 4.00/7.50 ₰ 1.75 – **5 rm** ⌑ 10.00/14.00.

PILLATON Cornwall 🔲🔲🔲 H 32 – pop. 334 – ✉ Saltash – ✆ 0579 St. Dominick.
London 254 – Plymouth 11.

🏛 **Weary Friar,** PL12 6QS, ☏ 50238, « Part 12C inn » – 📺 📥wc 🅿. ⬛ AE *VISA*
M 4.05/5.75 **st.** ₰ 1.60 – **13 rm** ⌑ 13.25/26.50 **t.**

PLAYDEN East Sussex 🔲🔲🔲 W 31 – see Rye.

🚙 *There is no paid publicity in this Guide.*

PLYMOUTH Devon 🔲🔲🔲 H 32 – pop. 239,452 – ECD : Wednesday – ✆ 0752.
See : The Hoe** **BZ** – Municipal Museum and Art Gallery* **BZ M. Envir. :** Buckland Abbey*
(13C) *AC*, N : 7 m. by A 386 **ABY** – Antony House* (Renaissance) *AC*, W : 5 m. by A 374 **AY.**
🗗 Elfordleigh, Plympton ☏ 336428, E : 6 m. by A 374 **BY** – 🗗 Staddon Heights, Plymstock ☏ 42475,
SW : by Stamborough Rd **BY** – 🗗 at Yelverton ☏ 082 285 (Yelverton) 3618, N : 8 m. by
A 386 **ABY.**
🚗 ☏ 21300.
⛴ Shipping connections with the Continent : to Roscoff (Brittany Ferries) – to St-Malo
(Brittany Ferries) – to Santander (Brittany Ferries).
🗗 Civic Centre and Ferry Terminal, Millbay Docks ☏ 68000-12 – The Barbican ☏ 23806 (summer only).

London 243 – Bristol 120 – Southampton 148.

Plans on following pages

🏨 Holiday Inn, Armada Way, PL1 2HJ, ☏ 62866, Telex 45637, ≼ city and sea, ⬛ – 📶 📺
    ₲. 🅿. ⛴   **BZ e**
    222 rm.

🏨 **Mayflower Post House** (T.H.F.), Cliff Rd, The Hoe, PL1 3DL, ☏ 62828, ≼ Plymouth
    Sound, 🌊 heated – 📶 📺 📥wc 🅿 ₲. 🅿. ⛴. ⬛ AE ⓘ *VISA*   **AZ c**
    M 5.50/6.50 **st.** – ⌑ 2.25 – **104 rm** 18.50/27.00 **st.**

🏨 **Duke of Cornwall** (Best Western), Millbay Rd, PL1 3LG, ☏ 266256, Telex 45424 –
    📶 📺 📥wc 🝙 🅿. ⛴. ⬛ AE ⓘ *VISA*   **AZ a**
    closed 22 to 29 December – **M** 4.00/6.00 **t.** ₰ 1.75 – **70 rm** ⌑ 14.85/26.00 **t.**

🏨 **Strathmore House,** Elliott St., The Hoe, PL1 2SP, ☏ 62101 – 📶 📺 📥wc 🝙wc 🅿.
    ⬛ AE *VISA*   **BZ s**
    M 2.50/4.00 **st.** ₰ 1.75 – **57 rm** ⌑ 9.95/20.00 **st.** – P 15.00/21.45 **st.**

P.T.O. ⟶

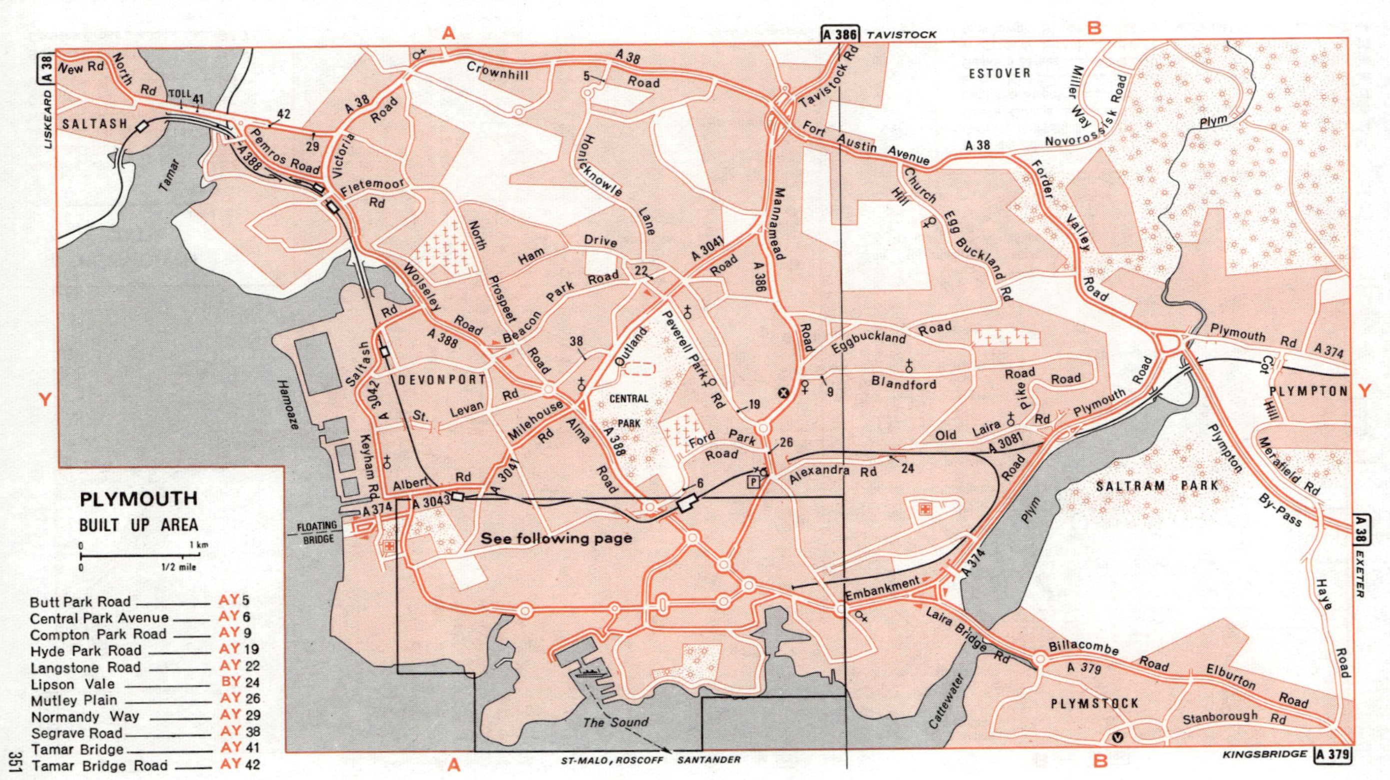

PLYMOUTH
BUILT UP AREA

A 386 TAVISTOCK
A 38 EXETER
A 379 KINGSBRIDGE
LISKEARD A 38
A 38
New Rd
North Rd
TOLL 41
SALTASH
Tamar
42
29
Pemros Road
A 388
Victoria Road
Fletemoor Rd
Crownhill
A 38
Road
5
Road
ESTOVER
Miller Way
Novorossisk Road
Plym
A 38
Tavistock Rd
Fort Austin Avenue
Church Hill
Egg Buckland Rd
Forder Valley Road
Honicknowle Lane
North Prospect
Ham
Drive
Park Road
22
A 3041
Road
Mannamead
A 386
Road
Eggbuckland
Road
Blandford
Road
Road
Plymouth Rd
A 374
Cot Hill
Merafield Rd
PLYMPTON
By-Pass
Wolseley Road
A 388
Beacon
Road
38
Outland
Peverell Park Rd
19
9
DEVONPORT
A 3042
Saltash Rd
St. Levan Rd
Milehouse Rd
Alma Road
A 388
CENTRAL PARK
Ford Park Road
26
Old Laira Rd
A 3081
Pike Rd
Plymouth Road
Plym
SALTRAM PARK
Keyham Rd
Albert Rd
A 3041
6
P
Alexandra Rd
24
Embankment
A 374
Laira Bridge Rd
Cattewater
Billacombe Road
A 379
Elburton Road
Stanborough Rd
PLYMSTOCK
Hamoaze
A 374
A 3043
FLOATING BRIDGE
See following page
The Sound
ST-MALO, ROSCOFF SANTANDER
Haye Road
Y
A
B
351
1 km
0
1/2 mile
0

Butt Park Road ———— AY 5
Central Park Avenue ———— AY 6
Compton Park Road ———— AY 9
Hyde Park Road ———— AY 19
Langstone Road ———— AY 22
Lipson Vale ———— BY 24
Mutley Plain ———— AY 26
Normandy Way ———— AY 29
Segrave Road ———— AY 38
Tamar Bridge ———— AY 41
Tamar Bridge Road ———— AY 42

PLYMOUTH
CENTRE
0   400 m
0   400 yards
N
A 3042
A 374
A 388
A 386
A 379
PLYMOUTH STATION
DEVONPORT PARK
VICTORIA PARK
GREAT WESTERN DOCKS
SUTTON HARBOUR
ROYAL CITADEL
THE HOE
THE SOUND
ST-MALO, ROSCOFF
SANTANDER
Ferry Rd
Avenue
Devonport Road
Molesworth Rd
Stuart Rd
Fitzroy Rd
Wilton Street
Stuart Street
Clifton Pl.
East Road
North Hill
Armada St
Greenbank Rd
Lipson
Tothill Road
Beaumont Road
Exeter St.
Park Avenue
Fore Street
Paradise
Place
North Road
Cecil Street
West Approach
Saltash Road
North Road
Cobourg St.
Regent Street
Ebrington
Exeter St.
Breton Side
Sutton Rd
Chapel Street
King's Road
Stoke Rd
Clarence Pl.
King St.
Western
Cornwall St.
Drake Circus Centre
POL.
Duke St.
George St.
James St.
Cumberland Rd
Devonport Hill
High St.
Union Street
A 374
Manor St.
Phoenix St.
Martin St.
Millbay Rd
Union St.
Royal Parade
Notte St.
Barbican Road
Teats Hill Rd
Richmond Walk
Durnford Street
Caroline Place
West Hoe Rd
Great Western Rd
The Crescent
Citadel Road
Elliott St.
Lockyer St.
Grand Parade
The Promenade
Madeira Road
Hoe Road
B 3240
DRAKE CIRCUS CENTRE
M
H

Armada Way —— BZ 2
Cornwall Street —— BZ
Drake Circus Centre —— BZ
New George Street —— BZ 27
Old Town Street —— BZ 32
Royal Parade —— BZ
Buckwell Street —— BZ 5
Charles Cross —— BZ 7
Charles Street —— BZ 8
Derry's Cross —— BZ 10
Drake Circus —— BZ 12
Eastlake Street —— BZ 13
Eldad Hill —— AZ 15
Gasking Street —— BZ 16
Kinterbury Street —— BZ 21
Mayflower Street —— BZ 25
North Cross —— BZ 31
Providence Place —— AZ 34
Quay Road —— BZ 35
St. Andrew's Cross —— BZ 37
St. Judes Road —— BZ 38
Southside Street —— BZ 39
Stonehouse Bridge —— AZ 40
Vauxhall Street —— BZ 44

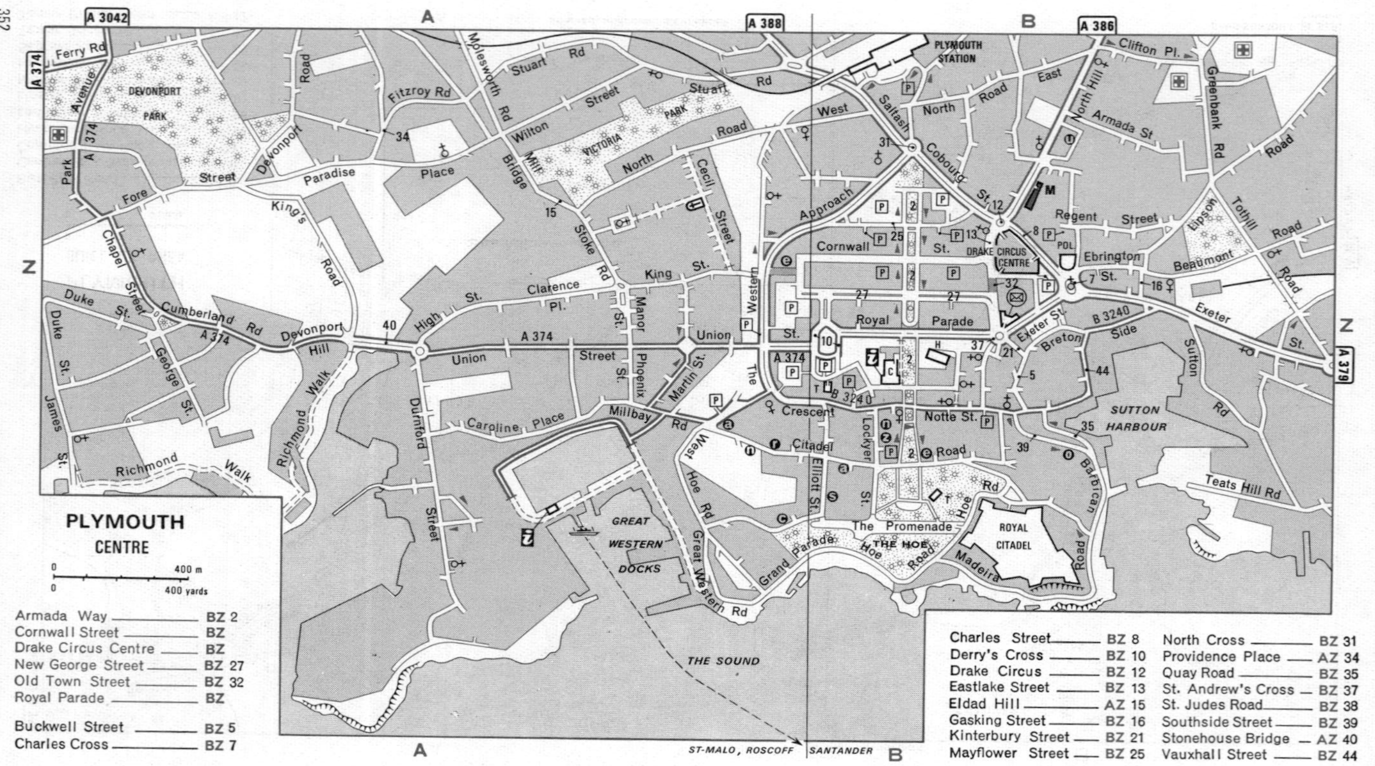

352

🏛 **Merlin,** 2 Windsor Villas, Lockyer St., The Hoe, PLI 2QD, ☏ 28133 – 🅟. ◿ AE ⓪ VISA   **BZ z**
closed Christmas and 1 January – **M** (closed Sunday) 2.50/3.50 **st.** ⌁ 1.95 – **18 rm**
☒ 8.00/16.00 **st.** – P 14.00/16.00 **st.**

🏛 **Imperial,** 3 Windsor Villas, Lockyer St., The Hoe, PL1 2QD, ☏ 27311 – ⫟wc 🅟   **BZ n**
closed 21 December-1 January – **M** (dinner only) 3.30 **s.** ⌁ 1.80 – **24 rm** ☒ 8.00/18.00 **s.**

🏛 **Merchantman,** Addison Rd, North Hill, PL4 8LL, ☏ 69870 – ⌁wc ⫟   **BZ u**
M (buffet lunch) 2.75/6.25 **t.** ⌁ 1.65 – **13 rm** ☒ 10.00/16.50 – P 13.00/19.00.

🏛 **Georgian House,** 51 Citadel Rd, The Hoe, PL1 3AL, ☏ 63237 – ⫟. ◿ VISA   **AZ r**
M (closed Sunday dinner) (bar lunch residents only) a la carte 5.30/7.05 **st.** ⌁ 1.95 –
10 rm ☒ 8.00/15.00 **st.**

⋔ **Mooreton,** 71 Mannahead Rd, PL3 4ST, ☏ 266566 – 🅟   **AY x**
9 rm ☒ 6.00/11.00 **s.**

⋔ **Chichester,** 280 Citadel Rd, The Hoe, PL1 2PZ, ☏ 62746 – VISA   **BZ a**
10 rm ☒ 5.00/9.50 **s.**

⋔ **Carnegie,** 172 Citadel Rd, The Hoe, PL1 3BD, ☏ 25158 – ⫟   **AZ n**
10 rm ☒ 7.95/16.90 **st.**

✕✕ **Bella Napoli,** 41-42 Southside St., Barbican, PL1 2LW, ☏ 67772, Italian rest. – ◿ AE
⓪ VISA   **BZ o**
closed Sunday, 25-26 December and 1 January – **M** a la carte 5.80/8.95 **t.** ⌁ 2.20.

✕ **Chez Nous,** 13 Frankfort Gate, PL1 1QA, ☏ 266793, French rest. – ◿ AE VISA   **AZ e**
closed Sunday, 1 January and February – **M** (dinner only) a la carte 6.50/14.30 **t.** ⌁ 2.50.

at Yelverton N : 9 ½ m. on A 386 – **ABY** – ✉ ☎ 082 285 Yelverton :

🏛🏛 **Moorland Links** ⌂, PL20 6DA, S: 1 ¼ m. on A 386 ☏ 2245, ⪡, ✕, ⌁, ☰, park – 📺
🅟. ⌂. ◿ AE ⓪ VISA
M 7.00/10.75 **st.** ⌁ 2.30 – ☒ 3.45 – **27 rm** 20.15/26.45 **st.**

⋔ **Retreat Country House,** Tavistock Rd, PL20 6ED, ☏ 2099, ☰ – 🅟
10 rm ☒ 8.50/14.50 **s.**

at Plympton E: 6¼ m. off A 374 – **BY** – ✉ ☎ 0752 Plymouth :

🏛 **Elfordleigh** ⌂, PL7 5EB, ☏ 336428, ⪡, ✕, ⌁ heated, ▷9, ☰, park – ⌁wc ⫟wc 🅟
closed Christmas – **M** (bar lunch) 2.50/5.60 **t.** ⌁ 1.20 – **16 rm** ☒ 13.50/20.00.

at Plymstock SE: 3 m. on A 379 – ✉ ☎ 0752 Plymouth :

🏛 Highlands, Dean Cross Rd, PL9 7AZ, ☏ 43643, ⌁ – 📺 ⌁wc ⫟wc 🅟. AE   **BY v**
14 rm.

AUSTIN-MORRIS-MG Derry's Cross ☏ 23451
BRITISH LEYLAND 301 Hamdrive, Peverell ☏ 771392
BRITISH LEYLAND Roborough ☏ 772767
BRITISH LEYLAND Pridham Lane, Peverell ☏ 771493
CITROEN Colebrook Rd ☏ 336606
CITROEN, COLT 87 Crownhill Rd ☏ 772345
DATSUN Newnham Rd ☏ 336462
DATSUN The Crescent ☏ 68332
FIAT, VOLVO Valley Rd, Plympton ☏ 338306
FORD Millbay ☏ 68040

HONDA Albert Rd ☏ 51810
LANCIA Budshead Rd ☏ 771123
MERCEDES-BENZ, PEUGEOT 58/64 Embankment Rd
☏ 63003
RENAULT 23 Wolsley Rd, Milehouse ☏ 53484
TALBOT BMW, Union St. ☏ 69202
TOYOTA Elm Rd, Mannamead ☏ 21594
VAUXHALL Bretonside ☏ 67111
VAUXHALL Cattledown Rd ☏ 68886
VW, AUDI Durnford St., Stonehouse ☏ 68351

PLYMPTON Devon 🔢 H 32 – see Plymouth.

PLYMSTOCK Devon 🔢 H 32 – see Plymouth.

POCKLINGTON Humberside – pop. 4,176 – ✉ York – ☎ 075 92.
London 213 – Kingston-upon-Hull 25 – York 13.

🏛 **Feathers** (S & N), 56 Market Pl., YO4 2QF, ☏ 3155 – ⌁wc 🅟. ◿ VISA
M a la carte approx. 4.50 **st.** – **14 rm** ☒ 8.10/17.95 **st.**

AUSTIN-MORRIS-MG, TALBOT, VAUXHALL Station
Rd ☏ 2021

FORD ☏ 2768

POLKERRIS Cornwall 🔢 F 32 – pop. 75 – ✉ ☎ 072 681 Par.
London 277 – Newquay 22 – Plymouth 34 – Truro 20.

✕✕ **Rashleigh Inn,** PL24 2TL, ☏ 3991, ⪡ – 🅟
closed Sunday dinner and December-February – **M** (buffet lunch) (booking essential)
approx. 5.25 ⌁ 1.60.

POLPERRO Cornwall 🔢 G 33 – pop. 1,600 – ✉ Looe – ☎ 0503.
See : Village *.
London 271 – Plymouth 28.

⋔ **Claremont,** PL13 2RG, ☏ 72241 – ⫟wc 🅟
Easter-October – **10 rm** ☒ 7.50/18.50 **t.**

✕ **Captain's Cabin,** Lansallos St., PL13 2QU, ☏ 72292
April-October – **M** (closed Sunday) a la carte 7.00/10.00 **t.** ⌁ 1.80.

PONTARFYNACH Dyfed – see Devil's Bridge.

PONT-AR-GOTHI Dyfed **403** H 28 – ⊠ Carmarthen – ✆ 026 788 Nantgaredig.
London 218 – Carmarthen 6 – Swansea 25.

  🏛 **Cothi Bridge**, SA32 7NG, ⍾ 251, ⇦ – 🛏wc 🛁wc ℗. 🔄 AE ① VISA
  M (bar lunch Monday to Saturday) 4.50 **st.** 🍷 2.00 – **16 rm** � 8.50/17.00 **st.** – P 10.75/
  12.75 **st.**

PONTERWYD Dyfed **403** I 26 – pop. 280 – ⊠ Aberystwyth – ✆ 097 085.
🛈 Tourist Information Centre, c/o Llywernog Silver Lead Mine ⍾ 620 (Easter-September).
London 228 – Aberystwyth 12 – Chester 88 – Shrewsbury 64.

  🏛 Dyffryn Castell, Dyffryn Castell, SY23 3LB, E: 2 m. on A 44 ⍾ 237, ⇦ – ℗
  6 rm.

PONTLYFNI Gwynedd **403** G 24 – pop. 375 – ⊠ Caernarfon – ✆ 028 686 Clynnog Fawr.
London 257 – Caernarfon 8.

  🏛 **Bron Dirion** 🦢, LL54 5EU, SE : ¾ m. off A 499 ⍾ 346, ⇦, 🍴 – ℗
  March-October – **M** (dinner only) 4.00 **s.** 🍷 1.50 – **9 rm** ⊐ 6.50/13.00 **s.**

POOLE Dorset **403** **404** O 31 – pop. 107,161 – ECD : Wednesday – ✆ 020 13 (4 and 5 fig.)
or 0202 (6 fig.).
See : Compton Acres Gardens* *AC* AX.
🛈 Civic Centre ⍾ 5151 - Arndale Centre ⍾ 3322.
London 116 – Bournemouth 4 – Dorchester 23 – Weymouth 28.

Plan : see Bournemouth

  🏨 Dolphin, 180 High St., BH15 1DU, ⍾ 3612 – 🕻 📺 🛏wc 🛁wc 🐾 🛁   by A 35 AX
  74 rm.

  ⌂ **Dene** 🦢, 16 Pinewood Rd, Branksome Park, BH13 6JS, ⍾ 0202 (Bournemouth) 761143 –
  🛁wc ℗. 🔄
  15 rm ⊐ 11.50/23.00 **st.**   BX **c**

  ⌂ **Avalon** 🦢, 14 Pinewood Rd, Branksome Park, BH13 6JS, ⍾ 0202 (Bournemouth)
  760917 – 🛏wc ℗
  14 rm ⊐ 8.50/21.00.   BX **e**

  ✕✕ **Grovefield** 🦢 with rm, 18 Pinewood Rd, Branksome Park, BH13 6JS, ⍾ 0202 (Bournemouth) 766798 – 🛏wc ℗. AE ① VISA   BX **i**
  M *(closed Sunday dinner and Monday)* 4.50/5.50 **t.** 🍷 2.00 – **8 rm** ⊐ 11.50/19.50 **t.**

  ✕ **John B's**, 20 High St., BH15 1BP, ⍾ 2440 – 🔄 AE   by A 35 AX
  closed Saturday, Sunday and 25 to 28 December – **M** a la carte 8.95/9.00 **t.** 🍷 1.95.

  ✕ **Isabel's**, 32 Station Rd, Lower Parkstone, BH14 8UD, ⍾ 0202 (Bournemouth) 747885 –
  VISA   AX **a**
  closed Sunday and October – **M** (dinner only) a la carte 5.55/10.00 **t.** 🍷 1.80.

  ✕ **Edelweiss**, 232 Ashley Rd, Upper Parkstone, BH14 9BZ, ⍾ 0202 (Parkstone) 747703,
  Austrian rest. – 🔄 AE ① VISA   AX **e**
  closed Tuesday, 25-26 December and 1 January – **M** (dinner only) a la carte 3.90/
  7.45 **t.** 🍷 1.70.

  ✕ **Piccolo Mondo**, 22 High St., BH15 1BP, ⍾ 70181, Italian rest. – 🔄 ① VISA
  closed Sunday dinner, Monday and 2 weeks from 4 November – **M** a la carte 4.50/8.00
  🍷 1.80.   by A 35 AX

  at Broadstone N : 4 m. off A 349 by A 35 – AX – ⊠ ✆ 0202 :

  ⌂ **Fairlight**, 1 Golf Links Rd, BH18 8BE, ⍾ 694316, 🍴 – ℗
  8 rm ⊐ 7.50/15.00 **st.**

AUSTIN-MG-WOLSELEY The Quay ⍾ 4187
CITROEN 490 Blandford Rd ⍾ 020 122 (Lychett
Minster) 3636
CITROEN Broadstone ⍾ 020 124 (Broadstone) 693501
MORRIS-ROVER-TRIUMPH West Quay Rd ⍾ 77511
PEUGEOT Station Rd ⍾ 745000

RENAULT Haven Rd ⍾ 707387
VAUXHALL Poole Rd, Branksome ⍾ 0202 (Bournemouth) 763361
VW, AUDI-NSU 3 Commercial Rd ⍾ 0202 (Parkstone)
740850

POOLEY BRIDGE Cumbria – see Ullswater.

POOL-IN-WHARFEDALE West Yorks. – pop. 1,672 – ⊠ Otley – ✆ 0532 Arthington.
London 204 – Bradford 10 – Harrogate 8 – Leeds 10.

  ✕✕ **Pool Court**, Pool Bank, LS21 1EH, ⍾ 842288 – ℗. ① VISA
  closed Sunday, Monday, 27 July-11 August and 25 December-7 January – **M** (dinner
  only) a la carte 5.35/9.25 🍷 1.80.

AUSTIN-MORRIS-MG-WOLSELEY Main St. ⍾ 842318

☛ *Benutzen Sie für weite Fahrten*
die Michelin-Länderkarten im Maßstab 1 : 1 000 000.

PORLOCK WEIR Somerset **403** J 30 – pop. 95 – ECD : Wednesday – ✉ Minehead – ☎ 0643 Porlock.

London 193 – Bristol 70 – Exeter 49 – Taunton 31.

- 🏨 **Anchor,** TA24 8PB, ☎ 862636, ≼, 🚗 – 🛏wc ☎ Ⓟ
  M 4.00/6.00 🍷 1.80 – **17 rm** ☶ 9.00/20.00.

- 🏠 **West Porlock House** ⌂, West Porlock, TA24 8NX, SE : 1 m. ☎ 862492, ≼, « Gardens » – Ⓟ
  Mid March-mid October – **M** (buffet lunch) 3.20/5.75 🍷 1.75 – **7 rm** ☶ 11.50/19.00 **s.**

- ✕✕ **Ship Inn** with rm, TA24 8PB, ☎ 862753 – 🛏wc ☎ Ⓟ
  M (bar lunch) approx. 6.50 🍷 1.80 – **6 rm** ☶ 9.00/20.00.

PORT DINORWIC (FELINHELI) Gwynedd **403** H 24 – ☎ 0248.

London 249 – Caernarfon 4 – Holyhead 23.

- ✕ **Seahorse,** 20 Snowdon St., LL56 4HQ, ☎ 670546 – 🅰 *VISA*
  closed Sunday, October and 25-26 December – **M** (dinner only) a la carte 4.95/5.70 🍷 1.70.

PORT GAVERNE Cornwall **403** F 32 – see Port Isaac.

PORTHAETHWY Gwynedd – see Menai Bridge.

PORTHCAWL Mid Glam. **403** I 29 – pop. 12,520 – ECD : Wednesday – ☎ 065 671.

🛈 Wales Tourist Office, The Old Police Station, John St. ☎ 6639 (Easter-September).

London 183 – Cardiff 28 – Swansea 18.

- 🏨 **Seabank** (Best Western), West Drive, CF36 3LU, ☎ 2261, ≼, ☐ heated – 📶 📺 Ⓟ. 🏖.
  🅰 🅰🅴 ⑩ *VISA*
  M 4.00/4.50 **t.** 🍷 2.25 – **80 rm** ☶ 15.30/32.95 **t.**

- 🏨 **Atlantic,** West Drive, Sea Front, CF36 3LT, ☎ 5011, ≼, 🚗 – 📶 📺 🛏wc ☎ Ⓟ
  16 rm.

- 🏠 **Fairways,** West Drive, Sea Front, CF36 3LS, ☎ 2085, ≼ – 📶 🛏wc Ⓟ
  M (bar lunch) 4.50 🍷 1.80 – **25 rm** ☶ 9.50/21.75.

- ♠ **Seaways,** 26-28 Mary St., CF36 3YA, ☎ 3510
  12 rm ☶ 10.00/16.00 **st.**

  at Nottage N : ¾ m. – ✉ ☎ 065 671 Porthcawl :

- 🏠 Rose and Crown, ☎ 4850 – 🛏wc Ⓟ
  8 rm.

FORD Lias Rd ☎ 6221

PORTHMADOG Gwynedd – see Portmadoc.

PORT ISAAC Cornwall **403** F 32 – pop. 966 – ☎ 020 888.

London 266 – Newquay 24 – Tintagel 14 – Truro 32.

- 🏠 Slipway, PL29 3RH, ☎ 264 – 🛏wc
  11 rm.

  at Port Gaverne S : ½ m. – ✉ ☎ 020 888 Port Isaac :

- 🏨 **Port Gaverne,** PL29 3FQ, ☎ 244 – 🛏wc Ⓟ
  closed 20 January-1 March – **M** (bar lunch) approx. 5.95 **st.** 🍷 1.90 – **20 rm** ☶ 11.00/24.50 **st.**

PORTLAND Dorset **403** **404** M 32 – pop. 9,990 – ECD : Wednesday – ☎ 0305.

London 149 – Dorchester 14 – Weymouth 6.

- 🏠 **Pennsylvania Castle** ⌂, Pennsylvania St., Wakeham, DT5 1HT, ☎ 820561, ≼, ✕, 🚗 – 🛏wc 🛏wc ☎ Ⓟ. 🅰 🅰🅴 ⑩ *VISA*
  M 5.75 **st.** 🍷 1.40 – **13 rm** ☶ 13.50/19.50 **st.**

PORTLOE Cornwall **403** F 33 – pop. 200 – ✉ Truro – ☎ 087 250 Veryan.

London 296 – St. Austell 15 – Truro 15.

- 🏨 **Lugger,** TR2 5RD, ☎ 322, ≼ – 🛏wc Ⓟ. 🅰 🅰🅴 ⑩ *VISA*
  Mid February-mid November – **M** (bar lunch Monday to Saturday) 4.00/7.00 **t.** 🍷 1.10 – **20 rm** ☶ 13.00/31.00 **s.** – P 18.50/21.00 **t.**

PORTMADOC (PORTHMADOG) Gwynedd **403** H 25 – pop. 3,840 – ECD : Wednesday – ☎ 0766.

🛈 Morfa Bychan ☎ 2037, W : 2 m.

🛈 Wales Tourist Office, Festiniog Railway Station ☎ 2981 (summer only).

London 245 – Caernarfon 20 – Chester 70 – Shrewsbury 81.

- 🏠 **Royal Sportsman** (T.H.F.), High St., LL49 9HA, ☎ 2015 – 📺 🛏wc ☎ Ⓟ. 🅰 🅰🅴 ⑩ *VISA*
  M 4.00/5.00 **st.** 🍷 1.65 – **21 rm** ☶ 13.00/22.50 **st.**

P.T.O. ⟶

PORTMADOC

at Penmorfa NW: 1 ¾ m. on A 487 – ⊠ ✆ 0766 Portmadoc:

Bwlch-y-Fedwen Country House, LL49 9RY, ☏ 2975, « Tastefully renovated 17 C inn », – ⇱wc ℗
Mid March-October – M *(closed October-mid November and mid February-mid March)* (dinner only) 6.75 **st.** � 1.30 – **6 rm** � 12.75/20.50 **st.**

PORTMEIRION Gwynedd **403** H 25 – pop. 200 – ⊠ ✆ 076 674 Penrhyndeudraeth.
London 244 – Chester 69 – Dolgellau 23 – Holyhead 52.

Portmeirion ⟿, LL48 6ER, ☏ 228, ≼ village and estuary, « Picturesque private village », ⟰ heated, ⟲, park – 🆃🆅 ℗. ⟰. 🅂 AE ⓞ VISA
April-October – M 5.50/10.00 **t.** � 2.30 – **50 rm** ⊑ 26.00/48.00 **st.**

PORTSCATHO Cornwall **403** F 33 – pop. 800 – ECD : Wednesday and Saturday – ⊠ Truro – ✆ 087 258.
London 298 – Plymouth 55 – Truro 16.

Rosevine ⟿, TR2 5EW, N : 2 m. off A 3078 ☏ 206, ≼, ⟲ – ⇱wc ▥ ℗. VISA
Easter-September – M 7.50 **t.** � 2.90 – **18 rm.**

Gerrans Bay, Gerrans, TR2 5ED, ☏ 338, ⟲ – ⇱wc ℗. 🅂 AE VISA
May-9 October – M *(closed Sunday dinner to non-residents)* (dinner only and Sunday lunch) 4.20/6.30 **s.** � 1.80 – **15 rm** ⊑ 11.00/24.00 **s.**

Roseland House ⟿, Rosevine, TR2 5EW, N : 2 m. off A 3078 ☏ 320, ≼ Gerrans Bay, ⟲, park – ⇱wc ℗
Easter-mid October – M (dinner only) a la carte 5.10/7.80 **st.** � 1.50 – **18 rm** ⊑ 9.00/18.00 **st.**

PORTSMOUTH and SOUTHSEA Hants. **403** **404** Q 31 – pop. 197,431 – ECD : Monday, Wednesday and Thursday – ✆ 0705.

See : H.M.S. Victory★★★ and Victory Museum★ *AC* **BY** A – Royal Marines' Museum★, at Eastney **AZ** M¹.

▥ Great Salterns ☏ 64549 **AY** – ▥ Crookhorn Lane, ☏ 070 18 (Cosham) 72210 N : 1 m. off B 2177 **AY**.

⚓ Shipping connections with the Continent : to Cherbourg, Le Havre (Townsend Thoresen) – to St-Malo (Brittany Ferries) – to the Isle of Wight : Fishbourne (Sealink) Monday/Thursday 20-29 daily ; Friday/Saturday/Sunday 11-35 daily (45 mn) – to Jersey (Sealink) summer : 1 daily ; winter : 4-5 weekly (9 h 30 mn) – to Guernsey (Sealink) summer : 1 daily ; winter : 4-5 weekly (7 h).

⚓ to the Isle of Wight : Ryde (Sealink) 9-22 daily (25 to 60 mn) – from Southsea to the Isle of Wight : Ryde (Hovertravel) summer 12-24 daily ; winter 8-12 daily (7 mn).

🛈 Guildhall Sq. ☏ 834092 – Castle Building, Clarence Esplanade Southsea ☏ 26722/3/4 – Ferry Terminal, Mile End Quay ☏ 819688 (summer only).

London 77 – Southampton 20.

Plans on following pages

Pendragon (T.H.F.), Clarence Par., Southsea, PO5 2HY, ☏ 23201, Telex 86376 – ⫿ 🆅 ⇱wc ☎ ℗. ⟰. 🅂 AE ⓞ VISA   **BZ c**
M a la carte 6.20/8.10 **st.** � 1.70 – **56 rm** ⊑ 13.00/23.50 **st.**

Portsmouth Centre (Centre), Pembroke Rd, PO1 2NS, ☏ 27651, Telex 86397 – ⫿ 🆅 ⇱wc ☎ ℗. ⟰. 🅂 AE ⓞ VISA   **BZ o**
⊑ 1.65 – **118 rm** 17.80/23.00 **st.**

Royal Beach (Mt. Charlotte), South Parade, Southsea, PO4 0RN, ☏ 731281, Telex 86719, ≼ – ⫿ 🆅 ⇱wc ☎ ℗. ⟰. 🅂 AE ⓞ VISA   **BZ r**
M approx. 5.00 **s.** – **120 rm** ⊑ 13.00/22.00 **s.**

Keppels Head (Anchor), 24-26 The Hard, PO1 3DT, ☏ 21954, Group Telex 858875 – ⫿ 🆅 ⇱wc ℗. 🅂 AE ⓞ VISA   **BY a**
M 4.00/4.50 **st.** – **20 rm** ⊑ 14.00/27.00 **st.**

Tudor Court, 1 Queen's Grove, Southsea, PO5 3HH, ☏ 20174, ⟲ – ℗   **BZ n**
9 rm ⊑ 8.50/12.50 **st.**

Chequers, Salisbury Rd, Southsea, PO4 9RH, ☏ 735277 – ℗. VISA   **AZ c**
24 rm ⊑ 7.00/14.00 **s.**

Salisbury, 57-59 Festing Rd, Southsea, PO4 0NQ, ☏ 23606 – ℗   **AZ n**
23 rm ⊑ 6.00/12.00 **s.**

Murray's, 27a South Par., Southsea, PO5 2JF, ☏ 732322 – 🅂 AE ⓞ VISA   **BZ s**
closed Sunday and 25-26 December – M a la carte 4.50/7.50 � 1.90.

AUSTIN-DAIMLER-JAGUAR-MORRIS-MG-ROVER-TRIUMPH Granada Rd, Southsea ☏ 7335311
AUSTIN-MG-WOLSELEY 1 Stubbington Av. ☏ 62216
AUSTIN-MORRIS-MG-ROVER-TRIUMPH Hambledon Rd ☏ 070 14 (Waterlooville) 2641
DAIMLER-ROVER-TRIUMPH, ROLLS ROYCE 41 Castle Rd, Southsea ☏ 27261
DATSUN 135/153 Fratton Rd ☏ 27551
FIAT 117 Copnor Rd ☏ 691621

FORD Southampton Rd ☏ 070 18 (Cosham) 70944
MERCEDES-BENZ 76 Castle Rd, Southsea ☏ 812951
MORRIS-MG-WOLSELEY Havant Rd, Drayton ☏ 74041
RENAULT 28 Milton Rd ☏ 815151
TALBOT Grove Rd South, Southsea ☏ 23261
TOYOTA Gamble Rd ☏ 60734
VAUXHALL London Rd, Hilsea ☏ 61321
VOLVO 23 Bedhampton Rd ☏ 070 12 (Havant) 472953
VW, AUDI-NSU 41/53 Highland Rd ☏ 815111

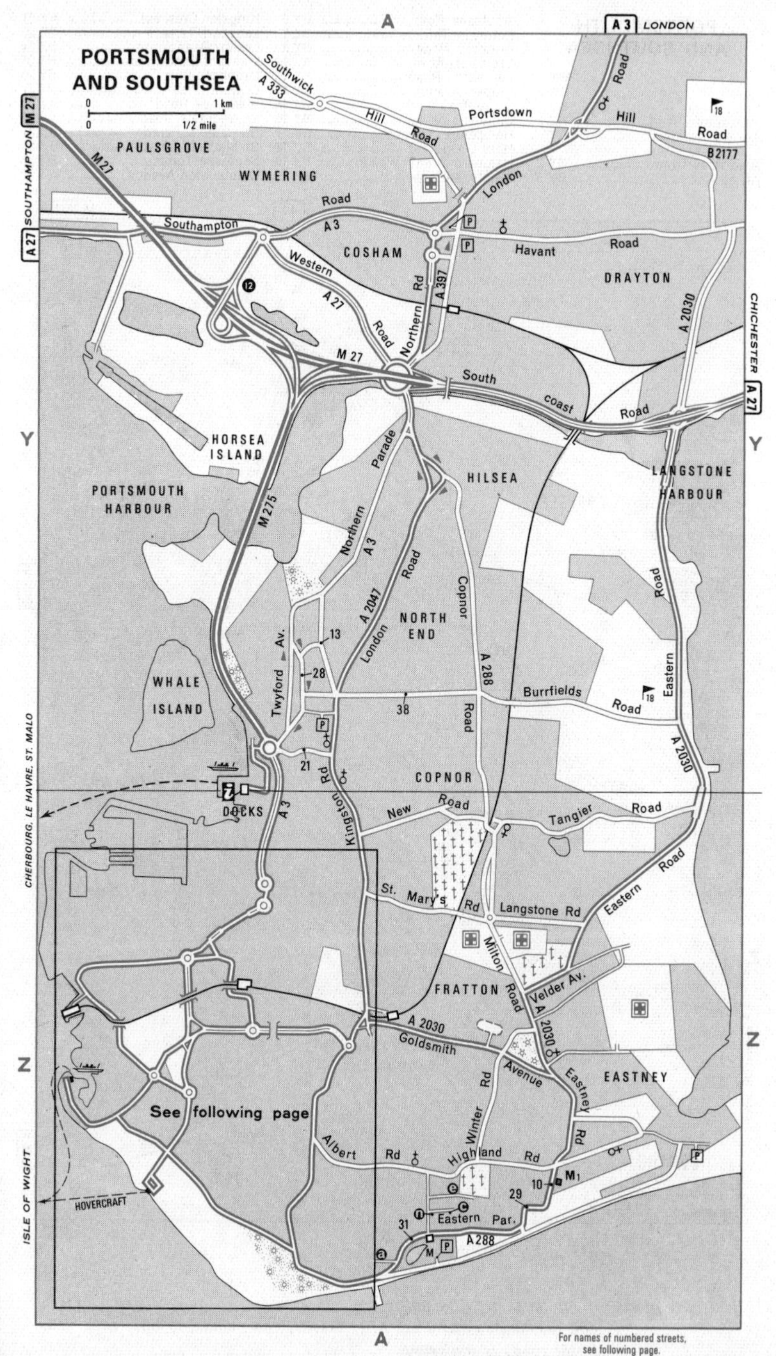

PORTSMOUTH AND SOUTHSEA
A 3 LONDON
A
SOUTHAMPTON M 27
A 27
Southwick
A 333
Hill
Road
Portsdown
Road
Hill
18
Road
B 2177
PAULSGROVE
WYMERING
M 27
London
CHICHESTER A 27
Southampton
Road
A 3
COSHAM
Western
A 27
12
Northern Rd
A 397
Havant
Road
DRAYTON
M 27
South
coast
Road
A 2030
HORSEA ISLAND
Parade
HILSEA
Y
LANGSTONE HARBOUR
PORTSMOUTH HARBOUR
M 275
Northern
A 3
Road
Copnor
NORTH END
Road
Eastern
WHALE ISLAND
Twyford Av.
A 2047
London Road
A 288
Burrfields
Road
18
A 2030
13
28
38
Road
P
21
COPNOR
Rd
Tangier
Road
DOCKS
A 3
Kingston
New
Road
CHERBOURG, LE HAVRE, ST. MALO
St. Mary's Rd
Langstone Rd
Eastern
Road
Milton Road
FRATTON
Velder Av.
A 2030
See following page
Goldsmith
A 2030
Avenue
Eastney Rd
EASTNEY
Z
Winter Rd
Highland Rd
P
Albert Rd
ISLE OF WIGHT
HOVERCRAFT
10
M 1
29
31
i
Eastern Par.
A 288
M
P
A
For names of numbered streets,
see following page.

PORTSMOUTH AND SOUTHSEA

Arundel Street	BY	Anglesea Road	BY 6	Kingston Crescent	AY 21
Charlotte Street	BY 9	Bellevue Terrace	BZ 7	Landport Terrace	BZ 22
Commercial Road	BY	Bradford Road	BY 8	Lennox Road South	BZ 24
Palmerston Road	BZ	Cromwell Road	AZ 10	Museum Road	BZ 25
Tricorn Centre	BY	Edinburgh Road	BY 12	Ordnance Row	BY 26
		Gladys Avenue	AY 13	Outram Road	BZ 27
Alec Rose Lane	BY 2	Grove Road South	BZ 15	Stamshaw Road	AY 28
Alfred Road	BY 5	Guildhall Walk	BY 16	St. George's Road	AZ 29
		Hampshire Terrace	BZ 17	St. Helen's Parade	AZ 31
		Hard (The)	BY 18	St. Michael's Road	BY 33
		Isambard Brunel Road	BY 19	Southsea Terrace	BZ 36
		King's Terrace	BZ 20	Stubbington Avenue	AY 38

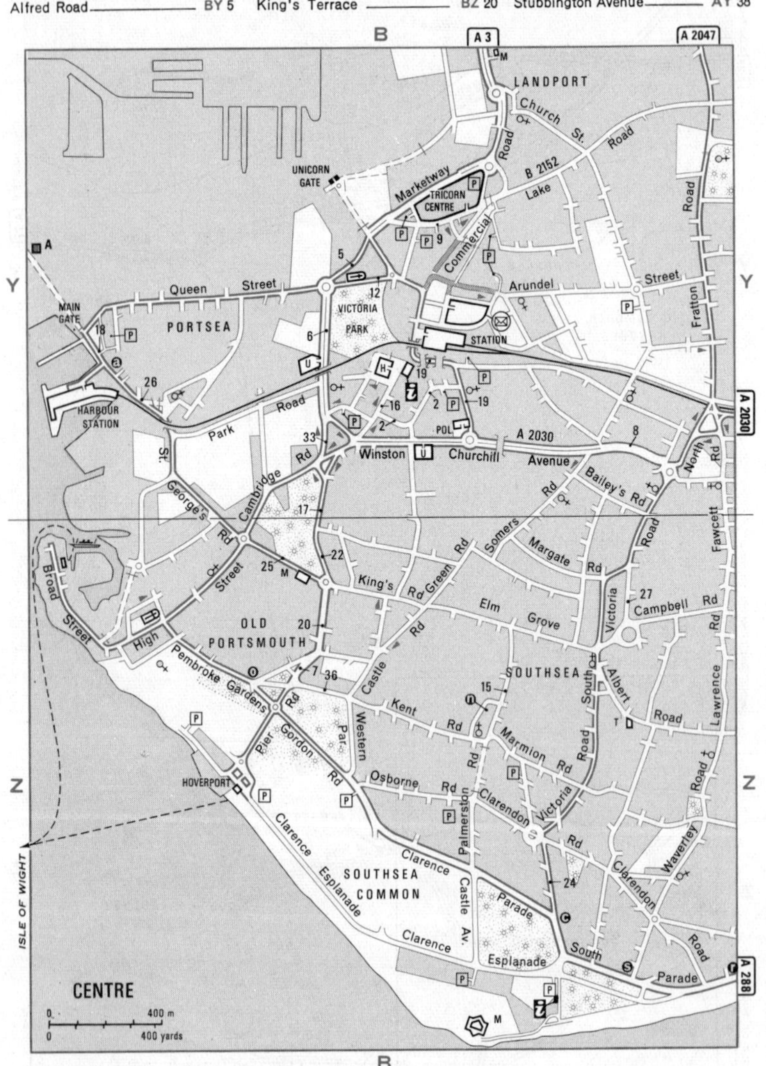

Town plans: roads most used by traffic and those on which guide listed hotels and restaurants stand are fully drawn; the beginning only of lesser roads is indicated.

PORT TALBOT West Glam. 408 I 29 – pop. 50,729 – ECD: Thursday – ✆ 063 96.
London 187 – Cardiff 32 – Swansea 9.

🏨 **Executive**, Princess Margaret Way, Aberavon Beach, SA12 6QP, ☎ 4949 – 📶 📺 ⌨wc
⌨wc 📞 🅿. 🏋. 🔺 AE ① VISA
M 3.50 ⟐ 2.55 – **69 rm** ⌑ 16.00/23.00 – P 23.50.

at Margam SE: 2 m. on A 48 – ✆ 063 96 Port Talbot:

🏨 Twelve Knights, Margam Rd, SA13 2DB, ☎ 2381 – 📺 ⌨wc 📞 🅿 🏋
11 rm.

AUSTIN-MORRIS-MG Baglan ☎ 813247   FORD Acacia Av. ☎ 2112

POSTBRIDGE Devon 408 I 32 – ✉ Yelverton – ✆ 0822.
London 225 – Exeter 24 – Plymouth 21.

🏛 **Lydgate House** ⑤, PL20 6JJ, ☎ 88209, ⟐, 🚗 – 🅿
closed Christmas – **M** *(closed Monday lunch)* a la carte approx. 5.90 **st.** – **8 rm**
⌑ (dinner included) 10.00/21.00 **s.**

POUND HILL West Sussex 404 T 30 – see Crawley.

POUNDISFORD PARK Somerset 408 K 30 – see Taunton.

POYNINGS East Sussex 404 T 31 – see Brighton and Hove.

PRAA SANDS Cornwall 408 D 33 – pop. 300 – ✉ Penzance – ✆ 073 676 Germoe.
London 321 – Penzance 8 – Truro 24.

🏨 **Lesceave Cliff** ⑤, TR20 9TX, ☎ 2325, ⟨ Mounts Bay, 🚗 – ⌨wc 🅿. 🔺 AE ① VISA
M (bar lunch) 4.00/5.00 **st.** ⟐ 2.00 – **26 rm** ⌑ 12.00/23.00 **st.**

🏠 **Praa Sands,** Chy-an-Dour Rd, TR20 9SY, ☎ 2438, ⟨, ✗, 🚗 – ⌨wc 🅿
April-September – **M** 3.50/5.00 **t.** ⟐ 2.00 – **25 rm** ⌑ 9.00/20.00.

PRESTBURY Cheshire 408 404 N 24 – pop. 2,891 – ✆ 0625.
Envir.: Adlington Hall* (15C) *AC,* N : 3 ½ m.

London 184 – Liverpool 43 – Manchester 17 – Stoke-on-Trent 25.

🏰 **Mottram Hall** ⑤, Mottram St. Andrew, SK10 4QT, NW: 2 ½ m. on A 538 ☎ 828135,
Telex 668181, « Tastefully renovated 18C mansion in park », ✗, ⟐, 🚗, park – 📺 🅿.
🏋. 🔺 AE ① VISA
M 4.25/7.00 **t.** ⟐ 2.00 – **41 rm** ⌑ 23.00/29.50 **t.** – P approx. 35.50 **t.**

✗✗ Legh Arms, Main St., SK10 4DG, ☎ 829130 – 🅿.

PRESTBURY Glos. 408 404 N 28 – see Cheltenham.

PRESTEIGNE (LLANANDRAS) Powys 408 K 27 – pop. 1,213 – ECD: Thursday – ✆ 054 44.
See: Church (Flemish Tapestry*). Envir.: Old Radnor (church*) SW: 7 ½ m.
🏌 at Kington ☎ 054 43 (Kington) 340, S: 7 m.
London 159 – Llandrindod Wells 20 – Shrewsbury 39.

🏨 **Radnorshire Arms** (T.H.F.), High St., LD8 2BE, ☎ 406, 🚗 – 📺 ⌨wc 📞 🚗 🅿. 🔺 AE
① VISA
M 4.00/5.00 **st.** ⟐ 1.65 – **17 rm** ⌑ 15.00/22.50 **st.**

PRESTON Lancs. 986 ㉓ – pop. 98,088 – ECD: Thursday – ✆ 0772.
Envir.: Samlesbury Old Hall* (14C) *AC,* E : 2 ½ m.
🏌 Lea ☎ 726480, W : 3 m. – 🏌 Blundell Lane ☎ 43207, W : 1 ½ m. – 🏌 Fishwick Hall,
Farringdon Park ☎ 51390.
🛈 Town Hall, Lancaster Rd ☎ 53731/54881 ext 211.
London 224 – Blackpool 17 – Burnley 22 – Liverpool 31 – Manchester 32 – Stoke-on-Trent 67.

🏨 Preston Eurocrest (Crest), The Ringway, PR1 3AU, ☎ 59411, Telex 677147 – 📶 📺
⌨wc 📞 ♿ 🅿. 🏋. 🔺 AE ① VISA
⌑ 2.80 – **133 rm** 19.20/25.20 **st.**

🏠 Whitburn, 111 Garstang Rd, PR2 3EB, ☎ 717973 – 🅿. AE
13 rm ⌑ 6.00/12.00 **st.**

at Samlesbury E: 2 ½ m. at junction M 6 and A 59 – ✉ Preston – ✆ 077 477 Samlesbury:

🏨 **Tickled Trout,** Preston New Rd, PR5 0UJ, ☎ 671, ⟨, ⟐, 🚗 – ⌨wc 📞 ♿ 🅿. 🏋.
🔺 AE ① VISA
M 3.35/5.00 **st.** ⟐ 1.85 – **66 rm** ⌑ 18.40/25.30 **st.**

✗✗ **Samuel Whitbread,** Cuerdale Lane, PR5 0DH, on B 6230 ☎ 641 – 🅿
closed Saturday lunch – **M** a la carte 3.90/5.90 **t.** ⟐ 1.45.

PRESTON

MICHELIN Branch, 39-41 Rough Hey Rd, Grimsargh, PR2 5AR, ℡ 797990.

BMW Garstang Rd ℡ 0772 (Broughton) 863922
CITROEN Garstang Rd ℡ 718852
DAF, VOLVO Emmanuel St. ℡ 21581
DAIMLER-JAGUAR-MORRIS-MG-ROVER-TRIUMPH,
ROLLS ROYCE-BENTLEY Corporation St. ℡ 54242
DATSUN Chorley Rd ℡ 53911
FIAT 306/310 Ribbleton Lane ℡ 21326

FORD Penwortham ℡ 44471
FORD Marsh Lane ℡ 54083
PEUGEOT 314/318 Ribbleton Lane ℡ 709060
RENAULT Manchester Rd ℡ 58389
TOYOTA 350 Blackpool Rd ℡ 719841
VOLVO Strand Rd ℡ 50501
VW, AUDI-NSU Blackpool Rd, Ashton ℡ 724391

PUDDINGTON Cheshire **403** K 24 – pop. 348 – ✉ Wirral – ☎ 051 Liverpool.
London 204 – Birkenhead 12 – Chester 8.

 Craxton Wood 🦢, Parkgate Rd, South Wirral, L66 9PB, (A 540) ℡ 339 4717,
« ← picturesque grounds and gardens », 🍴, park – 🛏wc 🅿. ☒ AE ⓪
closed last 2 weeks August – **M** *(closed Sunday and Bank Holidays)* a la carte 5.50/
7.25 ↥ 1.65 – **12 rm** ☲ 15.50/21.00.

PUDSEY West Yorks. **986** ⑫ – see Leeds.

PULBOROUGH West Sussex **404** S 31 – pop. 3,316 – ECD: Wednesday – ☎ 079 82.
Envir. : Hardham (church: wall paintings* 12C) S: 1 m.
London 49 – Brighton 25 – Guildford 25 – Portsmouth 35.

 XX **Stane Street Hollow,** Codmore Hill, RH20 1BG, NE: 1 m. on A 29 ℡ 2819 – 🅿
closed Saturday lunch, Sunday, Monday, 2 weeks May and 3 weeks October – **M** a la
carte 4.55/7.15 **t.** ↥ 2.00.

AUSTIN-MORRIS-MG-ROVER-TRIUMPH London Rd   SAAB, HONDA London Rd ℡ 079 881 (Bury) 691
℡ 2407

PURFLEET Essex **404** U 29 – pop. 430 – ECD: Wednesday – ☎ 040 26.
London 17 – Chelmsford 25.

 🏠 **Royal** (T.H.F.), High St., RM16 1QA, ℡ 5432, ← – 📺 🛏wc 🅿. ☒ AE ⓪ VISA
M a la carte 5.00/5.50 **st.** ↥ 1.95 – **28 rm** ☲ 13.50/22.50 **st.**

PUTSBOROUGH Devon **403** H 30 – pop. 1,342 – ✉ Braunton – ☎ 027 189 (3 fig.) or 0271
(6 fig.) Croyde.
London 233 – Barnstaple 11 – Exeter 51 – Ilfracombe 9.

 Putsborough Sands, EX33 1LB, ℡ 890555, ←, ☒ – 🛏wc 🅿. ☒ VISA
April-September – **M** 3.25/5.20 **st.** ↥ 1.70 – **62 rm** ☲ 9.10/18.20 **st.**

RADLETT Herts. **404** T 28 – pop. 8,180 – ECD: Wednesday – ☎ 092 76.
🏌 at Aldenham ℡ 7775, SW: 3 m.
London 21 – Luton 15.

 🏠 **Red Lion** (T.H.F.), Watling St., WD7 7NP, ℡ 5341 – 📺 🛏wc 🅿. ☒ AE ⓪ VISA
M a la carte approx. 5.50 **st.** ↥ 1.95 – **17 rm** ☲ 13.50/22.50 **st.**

AUSTIN-MORRIS-MG-ROVER-TRIUMPH, SHERPA 411   FORD 203/205 Watling St. ℡ 4851
Watling St. ℡ 5681   MAZDA Station Rd ℡ 6711
BMW 74/6 Watling St. ℡ 4802

RAKE West Sussex **404** R 30 – pop. 523 – ✉ Petersfield (Hants.) – ☎ 073 082 Liss.
London 54 – Guildford 21 – Petersfield 5.

 XX **Les Gourmets,** London Rd, GU33 7PH, on A 3 ℡ 2377, 🍴, French rest. – 🅿. AE ⓪
VISA
closed Sunday, Monday, 1 week end October-November and 2 weeks February – **M** a la
carte 6.75/8.55 **t.** ↥ 2.40.

RAMSBURY Wilts. **403** **404** P 29 – pop. 1,390 – ECD: Wednesday and Saturday – ✉ Marlborough – ☎ 067 22.
London 79 – Southampton 51 – Swindon 13.

 XX **Bell Inn,** The Square, SN8 2PE, ℡ 230 – 🅿. AE ⓪
closed Sunday dinner, Monday and last 2 weeks August – **M** a la carte 8.75/11.50 t.
↥ 1.85.

Non confondete :
   Confort degli alberghi: 🏰🏰🏰 ... 🏠, 🏠 , 🏠
   Confort dei ristoranti : XXXXX X
   Qualità della tavola   : 🕸🕸, 🕸, **M**

RAMSGATE Kent **404** Y 30 – pop 39,561 – ECD : Thursday – ✆ 0843 Thanet.

See : St. Augustine's Abbey Church (interior*). **Envir.** : Minster-in-Thanet (abbey : remains* 7C-12C) W : 4 ½ m.

⚓ Shipping connections with the Continent : to Calais (Hoverlloyd by hovercraft).

🛈 International Hoverport ☏ 57115 – Council Offices, Queen St. ☏ 51086.

London 77 – Dover 20 – Maidstone 44 – Margate 4.

🏨 **Savoy**, 43 Grange Rd, CT11 9NA, ☏ 52637 – 📺 ⛲wc 🚿wc ☎ **🅿**. 🔳 **AE** ⓪ **VISA**
   closed February – **M** *(closed Sunday in winter)* a la carte 3.05/9.70 **st.** ⌀ 1.75 – **25 rm** ⊊ 8.50/20.00 **st.**

🏠 **Court Stairs Hotel and Country Club** ⅌, Pegwell Rd, CT11 0JE, ☏ 51850, ≼,
   ✕. 🚗 – ⛲wc 🚿 **🅿**. 🔳 ⓪ **VISA**
   M (bar lunch) a la carte 4.25/8.00 ⌀ 1.65 – ⊊ 1.25 – **14 rm** 13.80/25.30 **t.**

⋔ **Abbeygail**, 17 Penshurt Rd, East Cliff, CT11 8EG, ☏ 54154
   closed Christmas – **10 rm** ⊊ 5.50/11.00 **st.**

✕ **Mallets**, 52 Queen St., CT11 8GF, ☏ 52854 – 🔳 **VISA**
   closed Sunday, Monday and January – **M** a la carte 6.25/7.25 **t.** ⌀ 1.55.

AUSTIN-MORRIS-MG-ROVER-TRIUMPH Grange Rd ☏ 51476
FORD Boundary Rd ☏ 53784
LADA Wilsons Rd ☏ 53465
VAUXHALL West Cliff Rd ☏ 53877
VW, AUDI-NSU St. Lawrence ☏ 52333

RAMSGILL North Yorks. – ✉ ✆ 0423 Harrogate.

London 229 – Leeds 33 – York 37.

🏠 **Yorke Arms**, HG3 5RL, ☏ 75243 – ⛲wc **🅿**. **AE** ⓪
   16 rm.

RANTON Staffs. **403** **404** N 25 – see Stafford.

RAVENSCAR North Yorks. – see Scarborough.

RAVENSTONEDALE Cumbria – ECD : Thursday – ✉ Kirkby Stephen – ✆ 058 73 Newbiggin-on-Lune.

London 280 – Carlisle 43 – Kendal 19 – Kirkby Stephen 5.

⚲ **Black Swan** ⅌, CA17 4NG, ☏ 204, 🚗 – **🅿**. **VISA**
   M 5.00/5.50 ⌀ 1.75 – **6 rm** ⊊ 9.00/18.00 **t.** – P 19.00/20.00.

This Guide is not a comprehensive list of all hotels and restaurants, nor even of all good hotels and restaurants in Great Britain and Ireland.

Since our aim is to be of service to all motorists, we must show establishments in all categories and so we have made a selection of some in each.

READING Berks. **403** **404** R 29 – pop. 132,939 – ✆ 0734.

Envir. : Stratfield Saye Park* *AC*, S : 7 m. by A 33 **X** – Mapledurham House* *AC*, NW : 3 ½ m. by A 329 **X**.

⛳ Black Swan ☏ 0734 (Twyford) 345116, NE : 5 m. by A 4 **X**.

🚗 ☏ 01 (London) 603 4555.

🛈 Civic Offices, Civic Centre ☏ 55911.

London 4 – Brighton 71 – Bristol 77 – Croydon 47 – Luton 52 – Oxford 28 – Portsmouth 55 – Southampton 48.

Plans on next page

🏨 **Post House** (T.H.F.), Basingstoke Rd, RG2 0SL, S : 2 ½ m. on A 33 ☏ 85485, Telex 849160, ⚊ heated – 📺 ⛲wc ☎ **🅿**. ⚱. 🔳 **AE** ⓪ **VISA**   **X a**
   M 4.15/5.00 **st.** ⌀ 1.65 – ⊊ 2.25 – **121 rm** 19.00/28.00 **st.**

🏠 Ship (Anchor), 4-8 Duke St., RG1 4RU, ☏ 583455, Group Telex 858875 – 📺 ⛲wc
   ☎ **🅿**. 🔳 **AE** ⓪ **VISA**   **Z e**
   34 rm ⊊ 13.50/25.00 **st.**

ALFA-ROMEO 108 Bath Rd ☏ 586425
AUSTIN-DAIMLER-JAGUAR-MG-ROVER-TRIUMPH 38 Portman Rd ☏ 585011
BMW, DAF 291 Oxford Rd ☏ 54204
CITROEN Chatham St. ☏ 57008
DAF Earley ☏ 61402
DATSUN 67 Caversham Rd ☏ 50432
DATSUN 209/211 Shinfield Rd ☏ 81620
FIAT Wolsey Rd, Caversham ☏ 582521
FORD 160 Basingstoke Rd ☏ 85333
MORRIS-MG-WOLSELEY 660 Wokingham Rd ☏ 61602
OPEL 705 London Rd ☏ 55501
RENAULT Chatham St. ☏ 583322
TALBOT Christchurch Rd ☏ 85242
TOYOTA 814 Oxford Rd ☏ 57368
TOYOTA 569/575 Basingstoke Rd ☏ 81278
VOLVO 406/412 London Rd ☏ 67321
VW, AUDI-NSU Erleigh Rd ☏ 666111
VW, AUDI-NSU Oxford Rd ☏ 413434

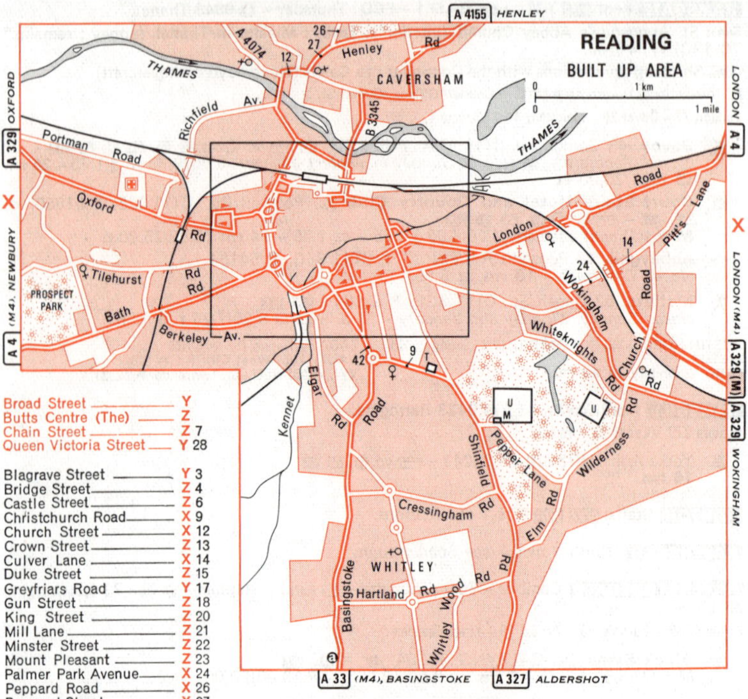

Broad Street — Y
Butts Centre (The) — Z
Chain Street — Z 7
Queen Victoria Street — Y 28

Blagrave Street — Y 3
Bridge Street — Z 4
Castle Street — Z 6
Christchurch Road — X 9
Church Street — X 12
Crown Street — Z 13
Culver Lane — X 14
Duke Street — Z 15
Greyfriars Road — Y 17
Gun Street — Z 18
King Street — Z 20
Mill Lane — Z 21
Minster Street — Z 22
Mount Pleasant — Z 23
Palmer Park Avenue — X 24
Peppard Road — X 26
Prospect Street — X 27
St. Mary's Butts — Z 29
Station Hill — Y 30
Station Road — Y 31

Tilehurst Road — Z 33
Tudor Road — Y 34
Valpy Street — Y 37

Watlington Street — Z 40
West Street — Y 41
Whitley Street — X 42

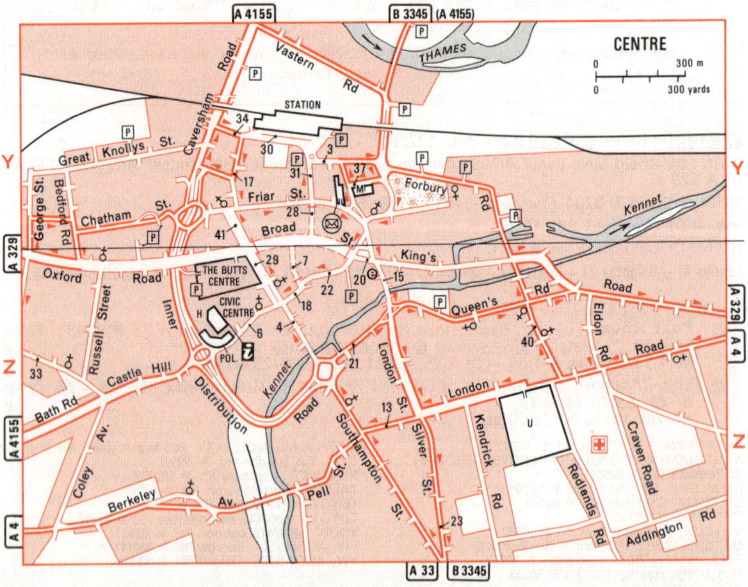

REDBOURN Herts. 404 S 28 – pop. 4,853 – ECD : Wednesday – ⊠ St. Albans – ☎ 058 285.
🏌 🏌 Luton Lane ℡ 3493.
London 31 – Luton 6 – Northampton 42.

🏨 **Aubrey Park** (Best Western), Hemel Hempstead Rd, AL3 7AF, SW : 1 m. on B 487 ℡ 2105, Telex 847777, ⌇ heated, ☞ – 📺 ⌂wc ☏ ℗. ♨. ⚡ AE ⓪ VISA
M 3.75/5.75 s. ⱷ 1.75 – ⌸ 2.50 – **57 rm** 16.00/24.00 s.

REDBOURNE Humberside – pop. 348 – ⊠ Gainsborough – ☎ 065 24 Kirton Lindsey.
London 162 – Lincoln 19 – Scunthorpe 10.

🕍 **Red Lion**, Main St., DN21 4QR, ℡ 648302 – 📺 ℗
M *(closed Saturday lunch and Sunday dinner)* a la carte 3.80/5.30 t. ⱷ 1.20 – **12 rm** ⌸ 8.50/17.00 t.

REDCAR Cleveland 986 ⑲ ⑳ – pop. 12,270 – ECD : Wednesday – ☎ 064 93.
🏌 Cleveland ℡ 3693.
🛈 Zetland Shipping Museum, The Esplanade ℡ 71921.
London 263 – Leeds 70 – Middlesbrough 9 – York 57.

🏨 Swan (Crest), High St., TS10 3DE, ℡ 3678 – 📺 ⌂wc ☏. ⚡ AE ⓪ VISA
37 rm ⌸ 13.30/20.30 st.

ALFA-ROMEO Redcar Rd, Marske ℡ 71054
FORD Corporation Rd ℡ 72601
MORRIS-MG-WOLSELEY Longbeck Estate, Marske ℡ 2943
TALBOT Redcar Rd, Marske ℡ 6386
TOYOTA Redcar Lane ℡ 73231
VAUXHALL Trunk Rd ℡ 71792
VOLVO Queen St. ℡ 3589

REDDITCH Heref. and Worc. 403 404 O 27 – pop. 51,800 – ECD : Wednesday – ☎ 0527.
🏌 Plymouth Rd ℡ 60140.
🛈 Royal Square ℡ 60806.
London 111 – Birmingham 15 – Cheltenham 33 – Stratford-upon-Avon 15.

🏨 **Southcrest** ⌇, Mount Pleasant, B97 4JG, ℡ 41511, Telex 338455, park – 📺 ⌂wc 🏯wc ☏ ℗. ♨. ⚡ AE ⓪ VISA
M *(closed Sunday dinner and Bank Holidays)* 4.80/5.50 t. ⱷ 2.70 – ⌸ 2.40 – **31 rm** 17.00/21.00 st.

at Astwood Bank S : 4 m. on A 441 – ⊠ Redditch – ☎ 052 789 Astwood Bank :

✗ Nevill Arms, B96 6NB, S : 1 m. on A 441 ℡ 2603 – ℗.

BRITISH LEYLAND Washford Drive ℡ 25055
CITROEN Birmingham Rd ℡ 63636
JAGUAR-ROVER-TRIUMPH 530 Evesham Rd ℡ 43261
TALBOT Hewell Rd Garage ℡ 65341
VW, AUDI George St. ℡ 62417

REDHILL Surrey 404 T 30 – pop. 56,223 (inc. Reigate) – ECD : Wednesday – ☎ 0737.
Envir. : Box Hill ⩙** W : 9 m.
London 22 – Brighton 31 – Guildford 20 – Maidstone 34.

🏠 **Ashleigh House**, 39 Redstone Hill, RH1 4BG, ℡ 64763, ⌇ heated, ☞ – ℗
9 rm ⌸ 9.50/15.00 s.

AUSTIN-MORRIS Allingham Rd, Reigate ℡ 073 72 (Reigate) 43805
AUSTIN-ROVER-TRIUMPH 22/36 Bell St., Reigate ℡ 073 72 (Reigate) 43333
DAIMLER-MORRIS-MG-WOLSELEY, ROLLS ROYCE London Rd, Reigate ℡ 073 72 (Reigate) 46881
FORD Sidlow Bridge, Reigate ℡ 073 72 (Reigate) 45749
RENAULT 50/64 Church St., Reigate ℡ 073 72 (Reigate) 45482
VOLVO Lesbourne Rd, Reigate ℡ 073 72 (Reigate) 44781

REDLYNCH Wilts. 403 404 O 30 – see Salisbury.

RHIWABON Clwyd – see Ruabon.

RHOSMAEN Dyfed 403 I 28 – see Llandeilo.

RHOSNEIGR Gwynedd 403 G 24 – pop. 1.200 – ☎ 0407.
See : Site*.
🏌 ℡ 810219.
London 267 – Holyhead 13.

✗ **Dolphin**, Morfa Hill, LL64 5JD, ℡ 810302 – ⚡
closed Sunday all year, Monday and Tuesday from October to Easter – **M** (dinner only) a la carte 4.65/6.65 t. ⱷ 1.25.

RHOS-ON-SEA (LLANDRILLO-YN-RHOS) Clwyd 403 I 24 – see Colwyn Bay.

RHUTHUN Clwyd – see Ruthin.

RHYDGALED Dyfed – see Aberystwyth.

RHYDYMAIN Gwynedd 403 I 25 – see Dolgellau.

RHYL Clwyd **403** J 24 – pop. 34,150 (inc. Prestatyn) – ECD: Thursday except summer –
✆ 0745.
Envir. : Rhuddlan (castle* 13C) *AC, S* : 3 m.
🖈 Rhuddlan ☎ 590217, S : 3 m – 🖈 Coast Rd ☎ 53171.
🛈 Wales Tourist Office, Promenade, ☎ 55068 (Easter-September) – Town Hall Information Bureau ☎ 31515
(summer only).

London 230 – Birkenhead 42 – Chester 34 – Holyhead 53.

🏨 **Westminster,** 10-12 East Parade, LL18 3AH, ☎ 2241 – 🛗 📺 🛏wc ☎ 🅿. ⚓. 🔺 AE
ⓞ *VISA*
M 4.00/5.00 **st.** 🍷 2.10 – **53 rm** ⟷ 13.75/21.75 **st.** – P 22.00/24.00 **st.**

AUSTIN-MORRIS-MG-ROVER-TRIUMPH-WOLSELEY   PEUGEOT Foel Rd ☎ 570307
Elwy St. ☎ 2301   VW Fforddlas Rd ☎ 4011
FORD Vale Rd ☎ 4436

RICHMOND North Yorks. **986** ⑲ – pop. 7,245 – ECD: Wednesday – ✆ 0748.
See : Castle* (Norman ruins) *AC.* **Envir** : Bolton Castle* (15C) *AC,* ≼ *, SW: 13 m.
🖈 Bend Hagg ☎ 2457.
🛈 Friary Gardens, Queen's Rd ☎ 3525 (summer only).

London 243 – Leeds 53 – Middlesbrough 26 – Newcastle-upon-Tyne 44.

🏨 King's Head (Swallow), Market Sq., DL10 4LNS, ☎ 2311, Group Telex 53168 – 📺
🛏wc ☎. 🔺
23 rm.

🏠 **Frenchgate,** 59-61 Frenchgate, DL10 7AE, ☎ 2087, 🚗 – 📺 🛏wc 🛁wc ☎ 🅿
closed Christmas – **M** *(closed Sunday to non-residents)* 5.50/6.00 **t.** 🍷 2.00 – **12 rm**
⟷ 14.00/25.85 **st.** – P 18.50/19.00 **st.**

at Dalton NW: 7 m. – ✉ Richmond – ✆ 083 321 Barningham :

✕ **Traveller's Rest,** DL11 7HU, ☎ 225 – 🅿
closed Sunday, Christmas Day and 1 January – **M** (dinner only) a la carte 4.75/6.75 **t.**
🍷 1.95.

AUSTIN-MORRIS-MG Victoria Rd ☎ 2539   MERCEDES-BENZ Brompton on Swale ☎ 811306
DATSUN Dundas St. ☎ 3956   TALBOT Catterick Village ☎ 811334

RICKMANSWORTH Herts. **404** S 29 – pop. 19,320 – ECD: Wednesday – ✆ 092 37 (5 fig.)
or 0923 (6 fig.).
🖈 Moor Lane ☎ 73163 – 🖈 ☎ Chorleywood 2009, NW: 2 m.
🛈 17-23 High St. ☎ 76611.

London 27 – Watford 5.

🏨 **Victoria,** Victoria Close, WD3 4EQ, junction A 404 and A 412 ☎ 75211 – 📺 🛏wc ☎ 🅿.
🔺 AE *VISA*
M *(closed Sunday dinner)* a la carte 4.75/6.85 **t.** 🍷 2.15 – **24 rm** ⟷ 12.00/23.00 **st.**

AUSTIN-JAGUAR-MORRIS-MG-ROVER-TRIUMPH 10   RENAULT Moneyhill Par. ☎ 73621
High St. ☎ 73110

RINGWOOD Hants. **403 404** O 31 – pop. 7,850 – ECD : Monday and Thursday – ✆ 042 54.
🖈 Ringwood ☎ 042 53 (Burley) 2431, NE: 4 m.
London 102 – Bournemouth 11 – Salisbury 17 – Southampton 20.

🏠 **Little Moortown House,** 244 Christchurch Rd, BH24 3AS, S: ½ m. ☎ 3325, 🚗 –
🛁wc 🅿. 🔺 AE *VISA*
closed December and January – **M** (lunch by arrangement) 5.00 – **6 rm** ⟷ 8.50/15.50.

at Ibsley N: 2 ½ m. on A 338 – ✉ ✆ 042 54 Ringwood :

✕ **Old Beams,** BH24 3PP, ☎ 3387, « 14C Thatched cottage » – 🅿
M a la carte 4.25/7.70 **t.** 🍷 1.70.

at St. Leonards SW: 2 ½ m. on A 31 – ✉ Ringwood – ✆ 0202 Ferndown :

⚘ **Avon Forest,** Ringwood Rd, BH24 2NR, ☎ 877764 – ♿ 🅿
closed January – **10 rm** ⟷ 6.75/13.50 **st.**

RIPLEY Surrey **404** S 30 – pop. 2,110 – ECD : Wednesday – ✆ 048 643.
Envir. : Wisley gardens** *AC,* NE : 1 m.
London 28 – Guildford 6.

✕✕✕ Clock House, High St., GU23 6AF, ☎ 2777, 🚗.

✕✕ **Talbot,** High St., GU23 6BB, ☎ 3188, 🚗 – 🅿. 🔺 AE ⓞ *VISA*
M a la carte 9.00/10.80 **st.** 🍷 2.25.

RIPON North Yorks. ⑨⑧⑥ ㉓ – pop. 10,989 – ECD : Wednesday – ☎ 0765.
See : Cathedral* 12C-15C. Envir. : Fountains Abbey*** (ruins 12C-13C, floodlit in summer),
Studley Royal Gardens** and Fountains Hall* (17C) *AC*, SW : 3 m. – Newby Hall* (18C) *AC*
(the tapestry room** and gardens* *AC*) SE : 3 ½ m. – Brimham Rocks* SW : 8 ½ m.

☞ Palace Rd ☏ 3640, N : 1 m. on A 6108.

🛈 Wakemans House, Market Pl. ☏ 4625 (summer only).

London 222 – Leeds 26 – Middlesbrough 35 – York 23.

🏨 **Ripon Spa** (Best Western), Park St., HG4 2BU, ☏ 2172, ≼, 🚗 – 🛗 📺 ⛌wc 🐾 🅿. ☒
   AE VISA
   M approx. 5.00 🍷 2.15 – **40 rm** ⚏ 11.70/37.50 **t.** – P 17.50/25.00 **t.**

✕ **Old Deanery**, Minster Rd, HG4 1QS, ☏ 3518 – 🅿
   closed Sunday – **M** a la carte 3.70/9.20 **st.** 🍷 2.20.

✕ **Hornblower**, Duck Hill, HG4 1BL, ☏ 4841 – VISA
   closed Sunday, Monday, 1 week May and 1 week October – **M** (dinner only) approx.
   12.00 **t.** 🍷 1.75.

   at Melmerby NE : 4 ½ m. off A 61 – ✉ Ripon – ☎ 076 584 Melmerby :

⋔ **Melmerby Hall**, HG4 5HA, ☏ 329, 🚗 – 📺 ⛌wc 🅿. ☒ VISA
   April-October – **10 rm** ⚏ 11.00/18.00 **s.**

RIPPONDEN West Yorks. – pop. 4,799 – ✉ ☎ 042 289.
London 210 – Halifax 5 – Huddersfield 9 – Leeds 21.

✕✕ **Over the Bridge**, Millfold, off A 58 ☏ 3722, « Tasteful Decor » – AE
   closed Sunday and Bank Holidays – **M** (dinner only) 8.50 🍷 3.00.

AUSTIN-DAIMLER-JAGUAR-MORRIS-MG-ROVER-   FORD North St. ☏ 2324
TRIUMPH Borrage Bridge ☏ 2371   VOLVO Palace Rd ☏ 2461
FIAT, MERCEDES-BENZ, VAUXHALL Kirkby Rd ☏ 4491

RIVENHALL END Essex ④⓪④ VW 28 – see Witham.

ROCHESTER Kent ④⓪④ V 29 – pop. 55,519 – ECD : Wednesday – ☎ 0634 Medway.
See : Castle*, ❋** (142 steps) *AC* – Cathedral* (interior**) – Eastgate House* 1590 – Fort
Pitt Hill ≼* – to Brompton : Royal Engineers' Museum*. Envir. : Cobham Hall (Gilt Hall*)
AC, W : 4 m.

☞ at Hoo ☏ 0634 (Medway) 251180, NE : 4 m.

🛈 85 High St. ☏ 0634 (Medway) 43666.

London 30 – Dover 47 – Maidstone 8 – Margate 46.

Hotels and restaurant see : Gravesend NW : 6 ½ m.
Maidstone S : 8 m.

FIAT Pier Rd, Gillingham ☏ 52333   SKODA High St., Rochester ☏ 75571
FORD Pier Rd, Gillingham ☏ 575151   TALBOT High St. ☏ 42231
HONDA-SAAB Dock Rd, Chatham ☏ 408361   TOYOTA Maidstone Rd ☏ 41906
JAGUAR-ROVER-TRIUMPH Chatham ☏ 41122   VAUXHALL Station Rd, Strood ☏ 79661
RENAULT High St., Rainham ☏ 362868   VOLVO Wood St., Gillingham ☏ 0634 (Medway) 402777

ROCHFORD Essex ④⓪④, W 29 – pop. 6,520 – ECD : Wednesday – ✉ ☎ 0702 Southend-
on-Sea.
London 43 – Southend-on-Sea 4.

✕✕ **Renouf's**, 1 South St., SS1 2YS, ☏ 544393 – 🅿. ☒ AE VISA
   closed Sunday and Monday – **M** a la carte 7.45/9.30 **t.** 🍷 2.00.

ROCK Cornwall ④⓪③ F 32 – pop. 350 – ECD : Wednesday ✉ Wadebridge – ☎ 020 886 Trebetherick.

☞, ☞ St. Enodoc ☏ 3216.

London 288 – Newquay 22 – Plymouth 45 – Truro 30.

⚿ **St. Enodoc** 🦐, PL27 6LA, ☏ 2311, 🚗 – ⛌wc 🅿
   closed mid January-February – **M** (bar lunch Monday to Saturday) 5.00 🍷 2.00 –
   13 rm.

   at Trebetherick N : 2 ¼ m. – ✉ Wadebridge – ☎ 020 886 :

⚿ **Bodare** 🦐, Daymer Bay, PL27 6SA, ☏ 3210, 🚗 – ⛌wc 🚿wc 🅿
   April-September – |**M** (bar lunch Monday to Saturday) 3.75/5.50 **s.** 🍷 1.50 – **20 rm**
   ⚏ 7.70/21.00 **s.**

RODBOROUGH Glos. ④⓪③ ④⓪④ N 28 – see Stroud.

ROKE Oxon. ④⓪③ ④⓪④ Q 29 – see Benson.

ROLLESTON ON DOVE Staffs. ④⓪③ ④⓪④ P 25 – see Burton-upon-Trent.

See : Abbey Church* 12C-13C (interior**).

ⁱ₈ Shootash Hill ✆ 0794 (Lockerley) 40459, SE : 3 m. on A 27 – ⁱ₈ Ampfield Par Three ✆ 68480, NE: on A 31.

🅱 King John's House, Church St. ✆ 512200.

London 82 – Bournemouth 28 – Salisbury 16 – Southampton 8 – Winchester 10.

🏨 **White Horse** (T.H.F.), Market Pl., SO5 8ZJ, ✆ 512431 – 📺 ⌷wc ☎ & ℗. ◨ 🄰🄴 ⑩ VISA
   M 3.85/4.60 **st.** ⌗ 1.65 – **33 rm** ⌷ 16.00/23.00 **st.**

AUSTIN-MORRIS-MG-ROVER-TRIUMPH-WOLSELEY Winchester Rd ✆ 512850

PEUGEOT 45/55 Winchester Hill ✆ 513185
VAUXHALL 24 Middlebridge St. ✆ 513806

Envir. : Goodrich (Castle* : ruins 12C-14C) *AC*, SW: 3 ½ m.

ⁱ₈ ✆ 098 982 (Gorsley) 267, E: 5 m.

🅱 20 Broad St. ✆ 2768.

London 118 – Gloucester 15 – Hereford 15 – Newport 35.

🏨 **Chase**, Gloucester Rd, HR9 5LH, on A 40 ✆ 3161, 🚗 – 📺 ⌷wc ☎ ℗. 🄰. ◨ 🄰🄴 ⑩ VISA
   M a la carte 6.15/9.80 **st.** ⌗ 2.00 – **40 rm** ⌷ 20.00/35.00 **st.**

🏨 **Royal** (T.H.F.), Palace Pound, Royal Parade, HR9 5HZ, ✆ 2769, 🚗 – 📺 ⌷wc ℗. ◨ 🄰🄴 ⑩ VISA
   M 3.25/4 45 **st.** ⌗ 1.70 – **32 rm** ⌷ 13.50/23.00 **st.**

🏠 **Swan**, Edde Cross St., HR9 7BZ, ✆ 2169 – 📺 ⌷wc ⌷wc ℗. ◨ 🄰🄴 ⑩ VISA
   M 3.45/4.60 **st.** ⌗ 1.50 – **19 rm** ⌷ 15.20/23.00 **st.**

🏠 **Chasedale** ⌂, Walford Rd, HR9 5PQ, ✆ 2423, 🚗 – ⌷wc ℗
   April-October – **M** 3.25 ⌗ 1.90 – **17 rm** ⌷ 7.00/15.00 – P 14.00/15.00.

🏠 Orles Barn, Wilton, HR9 6AE, ✆ 2155, ⛲ heated, 🚗 – ℗. VISA
   6 rm.

   at Weston-under-Penyard E : 2 m. on A 40 – ✉ ☼ 0989 Ross-on-Wye :

🏨 **Wye**, HR9 7NT, ✆ 3541, 🚗, park – 📺 ⌷wc ☎ ℗. 🄰. ◨ 🄰🄴 ⑩ VISA
   M 4.75/5.25 **t.** ⌗ 2.05 – **46 rm** ⌷ 14.00/24.00 **t.**

🏠 **Sandiway**, Gloucester Rd, HR9 7PE, ✆ 2748, 🚗 – ⌷wc ℗
   M (bar lunch) 4.00 ⌗ 1.75 – **13 rm** ⌷ 7.50/16.50.

   at Pencraig SW: 3 ¾ m. on A 40 – ✉ Ross-on-Wye – ☼ 098 984 Llangarron :

🏠 **Pencraig Court**, HR9 6HR, ✆ 306, 🚗 – ⌷wc ℗. ◨ VISA
   April-October – **M** (bar lunch) 6.00 **s.** ⌗ 1.35 – **12 rm** ⌷ 10.00/19.00 **s.**

   at Pengethley W: 4 m. on A 49 – ✉ Ross-on-Wye – ☼ 098 987 Harewood End :

🏨 **Pengethley** ⌂, HR9 6LL, ✆ 211, ⟨, ⛲ heated, 🚗, park – 📺 ⌷wc ☎ ℗. 🄰🄴 ⑩
   M 6.50/6.75 **s.** ⌗ 2.00 – **14 rm** ⌷ 20.00/26.00 **s.**

AUSTIN-MORRIS-ROVER-TRIUMPH Cantilupe Rd ✆ 2400   RENAULT Overross St. ✆ 3666

London 321 – Penzance 6 – Truro 24.

🏠 **Courtlands**, TR20 9PN, on A 394 ✆ 710476, 🚗 – ⌷wc ℗. ◨ VISA
   closed December except Christmas – **M** (lunch by arrangement) 2.75/4.15 **st.** ⌗ 1.10 –
   16 rm ⌷ 12.10/25.20 **st.**

ⁱ₈ Rothley Park ✆ 302019.
London 109 – Leicester 5 – Loughborough 6.

🏨 **Rothley Court**, Westfield Lane, LE7 7LG, W: ½ m. on B 5328 ✆ 374141, ⟨, 🚗 – 📺 ⌷wc ☎ ℗. 🄰. ◨ 🄰🄴 ⑩ VISA
   closed 25 and 26 December – **M** *(closed Saturday lunch, Sunday dinner and Bank Holidays)* 5.00/6.00 **s.** ⌗ 2.50 – **38 rm** ⌷ 21.50/27.50.

🏠 **Rothley**, 35 Mount Sorrel Lane, LE7 7PS, ✆ 302531 – ℗
   8 rm ⌷ 7.20/13.80.

London 58 – Brighton 4 – Lewes 9 – Newhaven 5.

🏠 White Horse, Marine Drive, BN2 7HR, ✆ 31955, ⟨ – 📱 📺 ⌷wc ☎ ℗
   16 rm.

ROUSDON Devon **403** L 31 – see Lyme Regis.

ROWLEY REGIS West Midlands **403** **404** N 26 – pop. 12,753 – ECD: Thursday – ✉ ✆ 021 Birmingham.
London 132 – Birmingham 9 – Wolverhampton 10.

↑ **Highfield House,** Waterfall Lane, B65 0BH, ℡ 559 1066 – ℗
12 rm ⊡ 6.00/12.00 **st.**

ROWSLEY Derbs. **403** **404** P 24 – pop. 221 – ECD: Thursday – ✉ Matlock – ✆ 062 983 Darley Dale.
Envir. : Haddon Hall★★ (14C-16C) *AC*, W: 1 ½ m.
London 157 – Derby 23 – Manchester 40 – Nottingham 30.

🏨 **Peacock** (Embassy), DE4 2EB, ℡ 3518, « 17C stone house, with antiques », ⚓, 🚣 –
⊡ 🛏 wc ☎ ℗. ⚠ AE ① *VISA*
M 5.00/8.25 **st.** – **20 rm** ⊡ 12.50/26.00 **st.** – P 22.00/38.25 **st.**

ROYAL LEAMINGTON SPA Warw. **403** **404** P 27 – pop. 45,064 – ECD: Monday and Thursday – ✆ 0926.

⛳ Whitnash ℡ 20298, S: 1 ½ m. by A 452 – ⛳ Newbold Terrace East ℡ 21157, off Willes Rd.
🛈 Jephson Lodge, The Parade ℡ 311470 and 27072 ext 216.

London 99 – Birmingham 23 – Coventry 9 – Warwick 3.

🏨 **Manor House** (De Vere), Avenue Rd, CV31 3NJ, ℡ 23251, Telex 22121 – ⌽ ⊡ ℗. ⚠ AE ① *VISA* i
M 4.00/5.00 **st.** 1.90 – **55 rm** ⊡ 17.00/26.00 **st.**

🏨 **Clarendon** (T.H.F.), The Parade, CV32 4DJ, ℡ 22201 – ⌽ ⊡ 🛏 wc ☎ ℗. ⚠ AE ① *VISA* o
M 3.70/4.75 **st.** 1.65 – **54 rm** ⊡ 13.50/22.50 **st.**

🏨 **Regent** (Best Western), 77 The Parade, CV32 4AX, ℡ 27231 – ⌽ 🛏 wc ☎ ℗. ⚠ AE ① *VISA* r
M 4.40/6.00 **t.** – **80 rm** ⊡ 19.75/29.50 **t.**

🏨 **Falstaff,** 20 Warwick New Rd, CV32 5JG, ℡ 21219 – ⌽ ⊡ 🛏 wc 🚿 wc ☎ ℗. ⚠ AE *VISA*
see plan of Warwick z u
closed 1 week at Christmas – **M** (*closed Sunday dinner*) (*bar lunch Monday to Friday*) 4.00 1.10 – **34 rm** ⊡ 11.00/20.00.

🏨 **Amersham,** 34 Kenilworth Rd, CV32 6JE, ℡ 21637, 🚣 – ℗
13 rm. see plan of Warwick z c

🏨 **Angel,** 143 Regent St., CV32 4NZ, ℡ 23683 – ⊡ 🛏 wc 🚿 ℗. ⚠ AE ① *VISA*
M (*closed Sunday*) 3.25/3.50 **st.** 1.20 – ⊡ 1.50 – **13 rm** 8.25/14.00.

🏨 **Abba Court,** 40 Kenilworth Rd, CU32 5TJ, ℡ 311188, 🚣 – ⊡ 🛏 wc 🚿 wc ℗
see plan of Warwick z r
M (*buffet lunch*) a la carte 3.75/5.40 – **18 rm** ⊡ 10.50/15.50 **s.**

🏨 **Park,** 17 Avenue Rd, CV31 3PG, ℡ 28376 – 🛏 wc 🚿 wc ℗ x
M (*bar lunch*) approx. 4.50 0.90 – **16 rm** ⊡ 8.25/16.50.

ROYAL LEAMINGTON SPA CENTRE

Parade	Clarendon Place ____ 15
Regent Street	Hamilton Terrace ____ 17
Warwick Street	High Street ____ 18
	Kenilworth Road ____ 22
Avenue Road ____ 2	Lower Avenue ____ 26
Bath Street ____ 3	Priory Terrace ____ 37
Beauchamp Hill ____ 4	Regent Grove ____ 40
Binswood Street ____ 5	Spencer Street ____ 45
Brandon Parade ____ 7	Tachbrook Road ____ 47
Church Hill ____ 14	Victoria Terrace ____ 49

P.T.O. ⟶

ROYAL LEAMINGTON SPA

- **Chesford House**, 12 Clarendon St., CV32 5ST, ☏ 20924 – ▭wc ⋔wc **P**. 座 e
  ☲ 1.50 – **10 rm** 7.00/16.00 **s**.

- Veleta, 42 Warwick New Rd, ☏ 21380 – **P** – **12 rm.**   see plan of Warwick by A 452 z

- XXX ❀ **Mallory Court** ☞ with rm, Harbury Lane, Bishops Tachbrook, CV33 9QB, S : 2 m. by
  A 452 ☏ 30214, ≤, ⬭, 🚲, park – 📺 ▭wc **P**. 座 座 ⓪ *VISA*   see plan of Warwick z a
  closed 4 days at Christmas and last 2 weeks February – **M** *(closed lunch and Sunday
  dinner to non-residents)* approx. 11.50 **s**. – ☲ 2.75 – **6 rm** 15.00/32.00 **s**.
  Spec. Mousse de truite Périgueux, Selle d'agneau en feuilletage (March-October), Tartes fines chaudes aux pommes.

- XX **The Vaults** (at Regent Hotel), The Parade, CV32 4AX, ☏ 32860 – **P**. 座 座 ⓪ *VISA*
  closed Sunday and Bank Holidays – **M** a la carte 6.15/12.25 **t**.

- X Quo Vadis, 50 Clarendon St., CV32 4PE, ☏ 24471, Italian rest.   a

AUSTIN-MG-MORRIS-ROVER-TRIUMPH Dormer Pl.
☏ 36511
AUSTIN-MG Fenny Compton Wharf ☏ 77244
AUSTIN-LAND ROVER-MORRIS-MG Old Milverton Rd
☏ 35533
AUSTIN-JAGUAR-MORRIS-ROVER-RANGE ROVER-
TRIUMPH The Parade ☏ 27156
CITROEN Warwick St. ☏ 35659

FORD Sydenham Drive ☏ 29411
HONDA-SAAB Lime Av. ☏ 23221
PEUGEOT Clarendon Av. ☏ 22311
TALBOT Spencer St. ☏ 30115
TOYOTA Wood St. ☏ 24681
VAUXHALL Old Warwick Rd ☏ 20861
VOLVO High St. ☏ 21381

ROYAL TUNBRIDGE WELLS Kent 𝟜𝟎𝟜 U 30 – pop. 44,612 – ECD : Wednesday – ✆ 0892.

See : The Pantiles* (promenade 18C) B – Town Hall Museum (wood-mosaic articles*) B M.

🛈 Town Hall ☏ 26121.

London 37 – Brighton 33 – Folkestone 48 – Hastings 29 – Maidstone 18.

ROYAL TUNBRIDGE WELLS

High Street — B 14	Clarence Road — B 8	Mount Ephraim — A 23
Mount Pleasant	Crescent Road — B 9	Mount Ephraim Road — B 24
Road — B 25	Fir Tree Road — A 10	Prospect Road — A 27
Pantiles (The) — B 26	Grosvenor Road — B 12	Rusthall Road — A 28
	Hall's Hole Road — A 13	St. John's Road — B 29
Benhall Mill Road — A 3	High Rocks Lane — A 16	Tea Garden Lane — A 30
Bishop's Down — A 4	Hungershall Park Road — A 17	Upper Grosvenor Road — B 31
Calverley Park Gardens — B 7	Lansdowne Road — B 18	Vale Road — B 33
	Lower Green Road — A 20	Victoria Road — B 34
	Major York's Road — A 22	Warwick Park — B 35

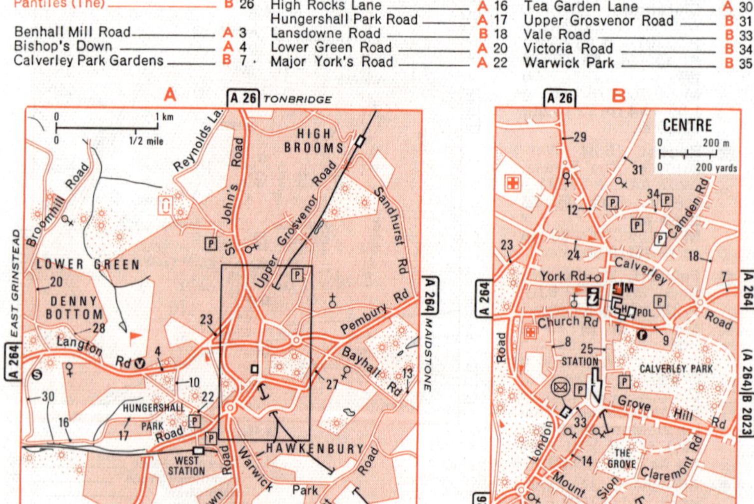

- **Spa** (Best Western), Mount Ephraim, TN4 8XJ, ☏ 20331, Telex 957188, ≤, 🚲, park – ⧫
  📺 **P**. ⬭ 座 ⓪ *VISA*   A v
  M 5.25/6.00 **st**. ⋔ 2.00 – ☲ 2.50 – **76 rm** 22.00/34.00 **st**.

- **Calverley**, Crescent Rd, TN1 2LY, ☏ 26455, ≤, 🚲 – ⧫ ▭wc ⬭ ♿ **P**. 座 座 ⓪ *VISA*   B r
  M 3.25/4.05 **t**. ⋔ 1.60 – **39 rm** ☲ 11.50/23.00 **t**.

- **Beacon** ☞, Tea Garden Lane, TN3 9JH, W : 1 m. by A 26 ☏ 24252, ≤, 🚲 – ▭wc
  ⋔wc **P**. 座 *VISA*   A s
  M (bar lunch) 4.00 **t**. – **9 rm** ☲ 12.50/20.45 **st**.

XX **High Rocks Inn,** by High Rocks Lane, TN3 9JJ, W: 2 m. ℡ 26074, « Garden » – **P**.
⟦🅰 AE ⓪ VISA⟧   by High Rocks Lane A
closed Sunday dinner and Monday – **M** a la carte 4.65/8.70 **t.** ⦙ 1.70.

     at *Southborough* N : 2 m. on A 26 – A – ✉ ☏ 0892 Royal Tunbridge Wells :

XXX **Weavers,** London Rd, TN4 0PU, ℡ 29896 – **P**. 🅰 ⓪ VISA
closed Sunday dinner, Monday, Good Friday, 25 to 30 December and 1 week February –
M a la carte 6.20/9.30 **t.** ⦙ 2.60.

     at *Wallcrouch* SE : 9 ¼ m. by A 267 – A – on B 2099 – ✉ Wadhurst (East Sussex) –
☏ 0580 Ticehurst :

🏠 **Spindlewood** 🦌, TNS 7JG, ℡ 200430, 🍽, 🚗 – ⟦wc **P**
closed Christmas – **M** *(closed Sunday and Monday to non-residents)* (dinner only) a
la carte 6.95/9.25 **st.** ⦙ 1.75 – **10 rm** ⟦ 9.50/23.00 **st.**

     at *Speldhurst* NW : 3 ½ m. off A 26 – A – ✉ Royal T. Wells – ☏ 089 286 Langton :

XX **George and Dragon Inn,** TN3 0NN, ℡ 3125, « Part 13C inn » – **P**. 🅰 AE ⓪ VISA
closed Saturday lunch, Sunday and Bank Holidays – **M** a la carte 9.35/12.50 **t.** ⦙ 2.00.

AUSTIN-MORRIS-MG 41/43 St. Johns Rd ℡ 24131	FORD Mount Ephraim ℡ 20323
CITROEN, FIAT, LANCIA 321 St. Johns Rd ℡ 35111	MORRIS-MG-WOLSELEY 41/43 St. Johns Rd ℡ 24131
COLT, RELIANT Calverley Rd ℡ 27174	OPEL, SAAB St. James Rd ℡ 31345
DAIMLER-JAGUAR-ROVER-TRIUMPH Mount Sion ℡ 26463	PEUGEOT London Rd ℡ 33035
	TALBOT 49 Mount Pleasant ℡ 27202
DATSUN 13/17 London Rd ℡ 29292	VAUXHALL 39 St. Johns Rd ℡ 20211
FORD 34 Hastings Rd, Pembury ℡ 089282 (Pembury) 2294	

RUABON (RHIWABON) Clwyd ⟦403⟧ K 25 – pop. 3,290 – ✉ ☏ 0978 Wrexham.
London 190 – **Chester** 17 – **Shrewsbury** 26 – **Stoke-on-Trent** 30.

🏠 **Wynnstay Arms,** High St., LL14 6BL, ℡ 822187 – TV **P**. 🛁 🅰
M a la carte 3.95/7.00 **t.** ⦙ 1.60 – **9 rm** ⟦ 11.50/23.00 **st.**

RUAN-HIGH-LANES Cornwall ⟦403⟧ F 33 – see Veryan.

RUGBY Warw. ⟦403⟧ ⟦404⟧ Q 26 – pop. 59,396 – ECD : Wednesday – ☏ 0788.
Envir. : Stanford-on-Avon (castle 17C : park* *AC*) NE : 5 m.
🛈 Borough Library, St. Matthews St. ℡ 2687.
London 88 – **Birmingham** 33 – **Leicester** 21 – **Northampton** 20 – **Warwick** 17.

🏨 **Three Horse Shoes,** Sheep St., CV21 3BX, ℡ 4585 – TV ⟦wc ⟦wc 🐾. 🅰 AE ⓪ VISA
M 3.95/6.25 ⦙ 1.85 – ⟦ 2.75 – **33 rm** 16.00/32.00.

XX **Andalucia,** 10 Henry St., CV21 2QA, ℡ 76404, Spanish rest. – 🅰 AE ⓪ VISA
M a la carte 6.50/11.50 ⦙ 2.00.

     at *Clifton-upon-Dunsmore* NE : 2 ¾ m. off B 5414 – ✉ ☏ 0788 Rugby :

🏨 **Clifton Court** 🦌, Lilbourne Rd, CV23 0BB, ℡ 65033, 🚗 – TV ⟦wc ⟦wc 🐾 **P**. 🛁. 🅰
closed last week July, first week August and 24 to 31 December – **M** *(closed Sunday
to non-residents)* 4.00/5.00 **s.** ⦙ 2.00 – **14 rm** ⟦ 18.00/25.00 **s.**

     at *Hillmorton* SE : 2 m. on A 428 – ✉ ☏ 0788 Rugby :

🏠 **Hillmorton Manor,** 78 High St., CV21 4EE, ℡ 76512 – ⟦wc **P**. AE ⓪ VISA
M approx. 3.80 **t.** ⦙ 1.85 – **20 rm** ⟦ 11.50/24.00 **t.**

     at *Crick* SE : 6 m. on A 428 – ✉ ☏ 0788 Rugby :

🏨 **Post House** (T.H.F.), NN6 7XR, W: ½ m. on A 428 ℡ 822101, Telex 311107 – TV
⟦wc 🐾 **P**. 🛁. 🅰 AE ⓪ VISA
M a la carte 5.80/9.50 **st.** ⦙ 1.70 – ⟦ 2.35 – **96 rm** 19.00/28.00 **st.**

AUSTIN-JAGUAR-MORRIS-MG-ROVER-TRIUMPH Railway Terrace ℡ 3477	DATSUN Temple St. ℡ 3094
	RENAULT 100 Railway Terrace ℡ 2660
DAF, HONDA Leicester Rd ℡ 2685	VAUXHALL Bilton Rd ℡ 2063

RUGELEY Staffs. ⟦403⟧ ⟦404⟧ O 25 – pop. 17,240 – ECD : Wednesday – ☏ 088 94
Envir. : Blithfield Hall* (Elizabethan) *AC*, N : 5 m.
London 135 – **Birmingham** 23 – **Stafford** 9 – **Stoke-on-Trent** 23.

🏠 **Cedar Tree,** 118 Main Rd, Brereton, WS15 1DY, S: ¾ m. on A 51 ℡ 4241 – ⟦wc
⟦wc **P**. AE
M *(closed Sunday dinner)* 3.25/3.75 **t.** ⦙ 2.00 – **20 rm** ⟦ 11.00/24.00 **st.**

🏠 Eaton Lodge, 118 Wolseley Rd, WS15 2ET, ℡ 3454 – **P** – **7 rm.**

     at *Armitage* SE : 3 m. on A 513 – ✉ Rugeley – ☏ 0543 Armitage :

XX **Old Farmhouse,** WS15 4AT, ℡ 490353, 🚗 – **P**. 🅰
*closed Monday lunch, Saturday, Sunday, 26 to 31 May, 28 July-9 August, 6-7 October
and 22 to 27 December –* **M** 5.75/8.45 **t.** ⦙ 2.00.

AUSTIN-MORRIS-MG 6 Market St. ℡ 3385	SAAB, HONDA Market St. ℡ 2347

RUNCORN Cheshire **403** L 23 – pop. 51,698 – ECD : Wednesday – ☎ 092 85 (5 fig.) or 0928 (6 fig.).

☍ Highfield Rd Widnes ℡ 051 (Widnes) 424 2440, N : 4 m. – ☍ Clifton Rd ℡ 72093.

🛈 57/61 Church St. ℡ 76776 or 69656.

London 202 – Liverpool 14 – Manchester 29.

🏨 Runcorn Eurocrest (Crest), Wood Lane, Beechwood, WA7 3HA, SE : ¼ m. off junction 12 ℡ 714000, Telex 627426 – 📶 📺 ☕wc ☎ ⅋. 🅿. ⌕. ☒ Æ ⓸ 𝘝𝘐𝘚𝘈
      ☞ 2.80 – **141 rm** 18.50/25.20 **st.**

AUSTIN-MORRIS-MG Balfour St. ℡ 72271   MAZDA 51 Halton Rd ℡ 63099
FORD Victoria Rd ℡ 74333

RUSHLAKE GREEN East Sussex **404** U 31 – pop. 1,195 (inc. Warbleton) – ✉ Heathfield – ☎ 043 56.

London 57 – Eastbourne 14 – Hastings 15 – Royal Tunbridge Wells 21.

🏨 **Priory** ⌕, TN21 9QJ, N : 1 m. ℡ 553, ≼, « Former Priory with country house atmosphere », ⌕, 🖾, park – 📺 ☕wc ☎ 🅿. ☒ ⓸ 𝘝𝘐𝘚𝘈
      closed 24 December-17 January – **M** (lunch booking essential) 5.75/9.00 **t.** 🍷 2.25 –
      10 rm ☞ 29.20/34.50 **t.**

RUSHYFORD Durham – pop. 339 – ✉ Ferryhill – ☎ 0388.

London 260 – Durham 10 – **Leeds 70 – Middlesbrough 18.**

🏨 Eden Arms (Swallow), DL17 0LL, ℡ 720 541, Group Telex 53168, 🖾 – 📺 ☕wc ☎
      🅿. ⌕ – **41 rm.**

RUSTINGTON West Sussex **404** S 31 – pop. 8,904 – ECD : Wednesday – ✉ Littlehampton – ☎ 090 62.

☍ Ham Manor ℡ 3288 – ☍ Littlehampton ℡ 7170, W : bank river Arun.

London 63 – Brighton 16 – Southampton 47.

🏩 Broadmark, Broadmark Lane, BN16 2JN, ℡ 4281, ≼ – ☕wc ☎ 🅿 – **17 rm.**

AUSTIN-DAIMLER-JAGUAR-ROVER-TRIUMPH   Ash Lane ℡ 72222   FIAT   Sea Lane ℡ 2052

RUTHIN (RHUTHUN) Clwyd **403** K 24 – pop. 4,338 – ECD : Thursday – ☎ 082 42.
See : Church*.

☍ at Pantmywyn ℡ 035 284 (Pantmywyn) 318, NE : 8 m. – ☍ Pwllglas ℡ 2296, S : 2 ½ m.

London 210 – Birkenhead 31 – Chester 23 – Shrewsbury 46.

🏨 **Ruthin Castle** ⌕, Corwen Rd, LL15 2NU, ℡ 2664, Telex 61169, ≼, ⌕, 🖾, park – 📶
      ☕wc ☎ 🅿. ⌕. Æ 𝘝𝘐𝘚𝘈
      M 4.50/7.00 **t.** – **59 rm** ☞ 18.00/33.00 **t.** – P 25.00/27.00 **t.**

🏨 Castle, St. Peter's Sq., LL15 1AA, ℡ 2479 – 📺 ☕wc ⋔wc ☎ 🅿. ⌕
      26 rm.

AUSTIN-MG-MORRIS-WOLSELEY   Llanfair D.C. ℡ 2969   OPEL   Well St. ℡ 2645

RYDAL Cumbria – see Ambleside.

RYDE I.O.W. **403 404** Q 31 – see Wight (Isle of).

RYE East Sussex **404** W 31 – pop. 4,449 – ECD : Tuesday – ☎ 079 73.
See : Old Town* (chiefly : Mermaid Street) – Ypres Tower ≼*. **Envir. :** Winchelsea (Church of St. Thomas the Martyr* 1283 : tombs** 12C) SW : 3 m. – Small Hythe (Ellen Terry's House* AC) N : 7 ½ m.

🛈 The Regent, Cinque Ports St. ℡ 2480.

London 65 – Brighton 48 – Folkestone 26 – Maidstone 32.

🏨 **Mermaid,** Mermaid St., TN31 7EY, ℡ 3065, Telex 957141, « 15C inn » – ☕wc
      ⋔wc 🅿. Æ ⓸ 𝘝𝘐𝘚𝘈
      M 4.10/5.50 **t.** 🍷 1.65 – **28 rm** ☞ 10.00/21.00 **t.**

🏨 George (T.H.F.), High St., TN31 7JT, ℡ 2114 – 📺 ☕wc ⋔wc 🅿. ☒ Æ ⓸ 𝘝𝘐𝘚𝘈
      M 3.75/4.25 **st.** 🍷 1.65 – **22 rm** ☞ 15.00/23.00 **st.**

🏨 Hope Anchor, Watchbell St., TN31 7HA, ℡ 2216, ≼ – ☕wc. ☒ Æ ⓸ 𝘝𝘐𝘚𝘈
      M *(closed Monday lunch)* 3.75/6.50 🍷 1.65 – **13 rm** ☞ 7.50/25.00.

🏩 **Mariners** without rest., High St., TN31 7JF, ℡ 3480, 🖾 – ☕wc. ☒ Æ ⓸ 𝘝𝘐𝘚𝘈
      15 rm ☞ 8.50/18.00 **st.**

🏩 Saltings, Hilders Cliff, High St., TN31 7EP, ℡ 3838 – ☕wc ⋔wc 🅿. ☒ Æ ⓸ 𝘝𝘐𝘚𝘈
      M a la carte 5.45/11.50 **t.** 🍷 1.75 – **18 rm** ☞ 7.95/21.95 **t.**

🏩 Ship Inn, Strand Quay, TN31 7TJ, ℡ 2233, Telex 957141 – 📺. Æ ⓸ 𝘝𝘐𝘚𝘈
      M (buffet lunch Monday to Saturday) 3.00/4.25 **t.** 🍷 1.50 – **12 rm** ☞ 8.50/17.00 **t.**

↑ **Old Borough Arms,** The Strand, TN31 7DB, ℡ 2128 – 📺 ⋔wc
      April-December – **9 rm** ☞ 8.50/15.00 **s.**

XX **Flushing Inn,** Market St., TN31 7LA, ℡ 3292, « 14C Inn with period mural ». ⑤ ⑩
VISA
*closed Monday dinner, Tuesday, 1 week after Easter, last week September-mid October
and 26 December-mid January* – **M** a la carte 5.80/13.50 **t.** ⌕ 2.50.

XX **Monastery** with rm, 6 High St., TN31 7LA, ℡ 3272, 🚗
closed November – **M** *(closed Monday and Tuesday from December to March)* a la
carte 6.10/7.15 **t.** – **7 rm** ⌑ 9.00/18.00 **st.**

X **Old Forge,** 24 Wish St., TN31 7DA, ℡ 3227 – ⑤
*closed Sunday, Monday in winter, Tuesday lunch, 2 weeks autumn and 2 weeks
January-February* – **M** a la carte 3.80/8.75 **t.** ⌕ 2.00.

at Playden N : 1 m. on A 268 – ✉ ⊙ 079 73 Rye :

🏠 **Playden Oasts,** TN31 7UL, ℡ 3502, 🚗 – 🛁wc ⑫. ⑤ *VISA*
closed Sunday and Monday – **M** (dinner only) a la carte approx. 6.00 **s.** ⌕ 1.45 – **6 rm**
⌑ 10.00/18.00 **s.**

at Rye Foreign N : 2 ½ m. on A 268 – ✉ Rye – ⊙ 079 721 Peasmarsh :

🏠 **Rumpel's Motel,** London Rd, TN31 7SY, ℡ 494, 🚗 – 📺 🛁wc ☎ ⑫
12 rm.

at Peasmarsh NW : 4 m. on A 268 – ✉ Rye – ⊙ 079 721 Peasmarsh :

🏠 **Flackley Ash,** London Rd, TN31 6YH, ℡ 381, 🚗 – 🛁wc ⑫. *VISA*
closed 28 December-12 January – **M** *(closed Tuesday, Wednesday and Thursday)*
(dinner only) 6.00 **t.** ⌕ 1.95 – **17 rm** ⌑ 13.50/23.00 **t.**

AUSTIN-JAGUAR-LAND ROVER-MORRIS-MG-ROVER-TRIUMPH Bedford Pl. ℡ 3334

SAFFRON WALDEN Essex ⁴⁰⁴ U 27 – pop. 9,971 – ECD : Thursday – ⊙ 0799.
See : Parish church* (Perpendicular) – Audley End House* (Jacobean : interior**) *AC.*
🛈 Corn Exchange, Market Sq. ℡ 23178.
London 46 – Cambridge 15 – Chelmsford 25.

🏠 **Saffron,** 8-10 High St., CB10 1AY, ℡ 22676 – 🛁wc ☎
closed 25 December-1 January – **M** *(closed Saturday lunch and Sunday)* approx.
9.00 **st.** ⌕ 1.50 – ⌑ 2.50 – **20 rm** 14.00/24.00 **st.**

AUSTIN-MORRIS-MG High St. ℡ 27909   ROVER-TRIUMPH 66 High St. ℡ 23597
RENAULT 13/15 Station St. ℡ 23238

ST. AGNES Cornwall ⁴⁰³ E 33 – pop. 4,747 – ECD : Wednesday – ⊙ 087 255.
See : The Beacon ✳**.
London 302 – Newquay 12 – Penzance 26 – Truro 9.

♨ Driftwood Spars, Quay Rd, Trevaunance Cove, TR5 0RZ, ℡ 2428 – 📺 🕍 ⑫
12 rm.

♨ Trevaunance Point 🦢, Quay Rd, Trevaunance Cove, TR5 0RR, ℡ 3235, ≼ bay and
cliffs, 🚗 – ⑫
13 rm.

at Mithian E : 2 m. by B 3285 – ✉ ⊙ 087 255 St. Agnes :

🏠 **Rose-in-Vale** 🦢, TR5 0QD, ℡ 2202, ≼, « Country house atmosphere », ⛱ heated
🚗 – 🛁wc 🕍wc ⑫
Easter-October – **M** (bar lunch) 4.25 **st.** ⌕ 1.70 – **15 rm** ⌑ 9.20/19.50 **st.**

ST. ALBANS Herts. ⁴⁰⁴ ST 28 – pop. 52,174 – ECD : Thursday – ⊙ 0727.
See : Site** – Cathedral and Abbey Church* (Norman Tower*). **Envir. :** Verulamium (Roman
remains* and museum) *AC,* W : 2 m.
🏌₁₈ Batchwood Hall ℡ 52100.
🛈 Town Hall, 37 Chequer St. ℡ 64511/2.
London 27 – Cambridge 41 – Luton 10.

🏨 **St. Michael's Manor** 🦢, Fishpool St., AL3 4RY, ℡ 64444, « Manor house, lake,
≼ garden », 🚗, park – 📺 🛁wc ☎ ⑫. ⛱. ⑤ Æ *VISA*
M 4.75/5.75 ⌕ 2.10 – **22 rm** ⌑ 12.50/19.50.

🏨 **Sopwell House** (Best Western) 🦢, Cotton Mill Lane, AL1 2HQ, SE : 1 ½ m. off A 6
by Milehouse Lane ℡ 64477, 🚗, park – 📺 🛁wc ☎ ⑫. ⛱. ⑤ Æ ⑩ *VISA*
M 3.75/4.75 ⌕ 1.90 – ⌑ 1.75 – **18 rm** 15.00/23.00.

🏨 Noke (Thistle), Watford Rd, AL2 3DS, SW : 2 ½ m. at junction A 405 and A 412
℡ 54252 – 📺 🛁wc ☎ ⑫. ⛱ – **56 rm.**

♨ **Black Lion,** 198 Fishpool St., St. Michael's Village, AL3 4SB, ℡ 51786 – ⑫. ⑤ Æ
⑩ *VISA*
M *(closed Sunday dinner)* approx. 7.00 ⌕ 2.00 – ⌑ 1.50 – **11 rm** 9.00/16.50.

⌂ **Melford House,** 24 Woodstock Rd North, AL1 4QQ, ℡ 53642 – ⑫
12 rm ⌑ 6.50/13.00 **s.**

ST. ALBANS

AUSTIN-DAIMLER-JAGUAR-MG-ROVER-TRIUMPH,
ROLLS ROYCE-BENTLEY   Acrewood Way, Hatfield Rd
☎ 66522
AUSTIN-MORRIS-ROVER-TRIUMPH Park St., Frog-
more ☎ 72626
AUSTIN-JAGUAR-MG-WOLSELEY, ROLLS ROYCE
Catherine St. ☎ 54342
CITROEN 66-70 High St., Potters Bar ☎ (Potters Bar)
42391

DAF, MAZDA 2/4 Grange St. ☎ 57208
FORD London Rd ☎ 59155
OPEL, SCIMITAR 101 Holywell Hill ☎ 65756
RENAULT 99/111 London Rd ☎ 52345
TALBOT 220 London Rd ☎ 63377
VAUXHALL 100 London Rd ☎ 50601
VW, AUDI 260/264 Hatfield Rd ☎ 60536

ST. ASAPH (LLANELWY) Clwyd **403** J 24 – pop. 2,910 – ECD : Thursday – ☼ 0745.
� ☎ 074 571 (Denbigh) 4159, S : 6 m.

London 225 – Chester 29 – Shrewsbury 59.

  🏨 **Oriel House,** Upper Denbigh Rd, LL17 0LW, S : ¾ m. on A 525 ☎ 582716, –
  📺 ⊟wc 🚿wc ☎ 🅿. 🏊. 🅾 *VISA*
  M a la carte 6.25/10.05 **st.** ⵌ 2.00 – **19 rm** ⚏ 15.00/19.00 **st.**

AUSTIN-JAGUAR-MORRIS-MG-ROVER-TRIUMPH Bod Ewr Corner ☎ 582345

ST. AUSTELL Cornwall **403** F 32 – pop. 25,158 – ECD : Thursday – ☼ 0726.
☍18 Carlyon Bay ☎ 072 681 (Par) 4250, E : 2 m. – 🚗 ☎ 5671/2.

London 281 – Newquay 16 – Plymouth 38 – Truro 14.

  🏛 **White Hart,** Church St., PL25 4AT, ☎ 2100 – 📺 ⊟wc 🚿
  closed 25 and 26 December – **M** 2.50/4.00 ⵌ 1.60 – **20 rm** ⚏ 8.80/17.60.

  at Tregrehan E : 2 ½ m. off A 390 – ✉ St. Austell – ☼ 072 681 Par :

  %% **Boscundle Manor** ⑤ with rm, PL25 3RL, ☎ 3557, 🚗 – 📺 🅿
  closed 3 weeks February – **M** *(closed Saturday lunch and Sunday to non-residents)*
  a la carte 5.55/7.30 **t.** ⵌ 1.50 – **5 rm** ⚏ 12.50/22.50 **st.**

  at Carlyon Bay E : 2 ½ m. off A 3601 – ✉ St. Austell – ☼ 072 681 Par :

  🏰 Carlyon Bay ⑤, PL25 3RD, ☎ 2304, ⩕ Carlyon Bay, « Extensive gardens », %%, ⌿
  heated, ☍18, park – ▯ 🅿. 🏊 – **74 rm.**

  🏨 **Porth Avallen** ⑤, Sea Rd, PL25 3SG, ☎ 2802, ⩕ Carlyon Bay, 🚗 – ⊟wc 🅿. 🅾 *AE*
  closed mid December-mid January – **M** 4.50/5.50 **s.** ⵌ 1.60 – **25 rm** ⚏ 11.60/24.80 **s.**

BRITISH LEYLAND Carlyon Bay ☎ 072 681 (Par) 2451
BRITISH LEYLAND Gover Rd ☎ 5571
CITROEN 77 Fore St. ☎ 0726 (Stenalees) 850 241
FIAT Bucklers Lane ☎ 5667
FORD Slades Rd ☎ 2333

PEUGEOT Gwendra, St.Stephen ☎ 0726 (Nanpean)
822566
RENAULT Woodland Rd ☎ 5551
VW, AUDI East Hill ☎ 5624

ST. DAVID'S (TYDDEWI) Dyfed **403** E 28 – pop. 1,638 – ECD : Wednesday – ☼ 043 788.
See : Cathedral★★ 12C (site★) – Bishop's palace★ *AC.* **Envir.** : Porthgain (cliffs★★★) NE : 7 m. –
Whitesand Bay★★ and St. David's Head★★ NW : 2 m. – Newgale (⩕★★) by Solva (site★) E : 7 m. –
Abereiddy (site★) NE : 5 m.

� ☎ 425, W : 2 m.

🛈 Grove Car Park, High St. ☎ 747 (Easter-September) – National Park Centre, City Hall ☎ 392 (Easter-September).

London 266 – Carmarthen 46 – Fishguard 16.

  🏨 **Warpool Court** ⑤, SA62 6BN, ☎ 300, ⩕ sea and countryside, ⊠, ⧖, 🚗 – 📺 ⊟wc
  🚿wc 🅿. 🅾 *AE*
  closed January – **M** 3.60/6.30 **st.** ⵌ 2.80 – **25 rm** ⚏ 14.40/26.80 **st.** – P 20.50 **st.**

  🏨 **St. Non's,** Catherine St., SA62 6RJ, ☎ 239, 🚗 – ⊟wc 🅿. 🅾 ① *VISA*
  M (bar lunch) a la carte 5.90/7.35 **t.** ⵌ 1.75 – **20 rm** ⚏ 17.25/22.30 **t.** – P 38.00 **t.**

  🏠 **Old Cross,** Cross Sq., SA62 6SP, ☎ 387, 🚗 – ⊟wc 🅿. 🅾 *AE VISA*
  15 March-October – **M** (bar lunch) approx. 5.80 **st.** ⵌ 1.00 – **18 rm** ⚏ 15.00/22.00 **st.**

  at Whitesand Bay NW : 2 m. on B 4583 – ✉ ☼ 043 788 St. David's :

  🏨 **Whitesands Bay** ⑤, SA62 6PT, ☎ 403, ⩕ Whitesand Bay, ⌿ heated, 🚗, park – 📺
  ⊟wc 🅿. 🅾 *VISA*
  Mid April-mid October – **M** 6.00/8.50 **st.** ⵌ 2.30 – **30 rm** ⚏ 18.00/45.00.

ST. DOGMAELS (LLANDUDOCH) Dyfed **403** F 27 – see Cardigan.

ST. HELENS Merseyside **986** ⑤ and ㉓ ㉗ – pop. 104,341 – ECD : Thursday – ☼ 0744.
Envir. : Knowsley Safari Park★★ *AC*, W : 6 m.
� Sherdley Park ☎ 813149, E : 2 m. on A 570.

London 204 – Liverpool 14 – Manchester 21 – Preston 25.

  🏨 **Fleece,** 15 Church St., WA10 1BA, ☎ 26546 – ▯ 📺 ⊟wc ☎ 🅿. 🏊. 🅾 *AE* ① *VISA*
  M *(closed Sunday lunch)* (bar lunch Monday to Saturday) 6.35/6.80 **st.** ⵌ 1.70 – **76 rm**
  ⚏ 18.50/24.00 **st.**

AUSTIN-MG-WOLSELEY Knowsley Rd ☎ 34441
AUSTIN-MORRIS, VAUXHALL Knowsley Rd ☎ 35221
DAIMLER-JAGUAR-MORRIS-MG-ROVER-TRIUMPH-
WOLSELEY 18 Dentons Green Lane ☎ 20934
DATSUN Jackson St. ☎ 26681

FORD City Rd ☎ 26381
PEUGEOT East Lancashire Rd ☎ 27373
ROVER-TRIUMPH Elephants Lane ☎ 811565
TALBOT Knowsley Rd ☎ 32411

ST. IVES Cornwall **403** D 33 – pop. 9,839 – ECD : Thursday – ☼ 073 670.

See : Parish church* 15C.

🛈 The Guildhall, Street-an-Pol ☏ 6297.

London 319 – Penzance 10 – Truro 25.

🏨 Tregenna Castle (B.T.H.) ⌘, TR26 2DE, ☏ 5254, Telex 45128, ≤, ⚒, ⅃ heated, 🛦, 🚗,
park – 🛗 TV ♿ ℗. 🅿 AE ⓪ **VISA**
83 rm ⛋ 22.00/43.00 **st.** – P 30.00/48.00 **st.**

🏨 **Porthminster,** The Terrace, TR26 2BN, ☏ 5221, ≤, ⅃ heated, 🛦 – 🛗 TV ⌷wc 🛁wc
🚗 ℗. 🅿 AE ⓪ **VISA**
M 3.50/4.50 **st.** ⅄ 1.50 – **52 rm** ⛋ 13.50/27.00 **st.** – P 16.65/20.85 **st.**

🏨 **Garrack** ⌘, Burthallan Lane, Higher Ayr, TR26 3AA, ☏ 6199, ≤, 🛦 – ⌷wc ℗. 🅿
AE ⓪
Easter-September – **M** a la carte 5.45/9.10 **st.** ⅄ 2.60 – **20 rm** ⛋ 10.30/30.00 **st.**

🏨 **Trecarrell** ⌘, Carthew Terrace, Ayr, TR26 1EB, ☏ 5707, 🛦 – 🛁wc ☏ ℗. 🅿 AE **VISA**
Easter-5 October – **M** *(closed Saturday and Sunday lunch)* (bar lunch) 2.75/4.25 **s.**
⅄ 2.00 – **14 rm** ⛋ 10.75/26.50 **s.** – P 15.70/18.25 **s.**

🏨 **Chy-an-Drea,** The Terrace, TR26 2BP, ☏ 5076, ≤ – ⌷wc ℗. 🅿 AE ⓪ **VISA**
March-October – **M** 2.75/5.00 **t.** ⅄ 2.00 – **36 rm** ⛋ 10.00/25.00 **t.** – P 15.00/21.00 **t.**

🏨 **Pedn-Olva,** Porthminster Beach, TR26 2EL, ☏ 6222, ≤ coastline – ⌷wc ℗
Easter-October – **M** 3.00/4.75 **st.** ⅄ 2.65 – **29 rm** ⛋ 12.00/25.00 **st.**

🏨 **Chy-an-Dour,** Trelyon Av., TR26 2AD, ☏ 6436, ≤, 🛦 – 🛗 🛁wc ℗. 🅿 **VISA**
M (bar lunch) 4.00 **t.** ⅄ 1.95 – **29 rm** ⛋ 10.50/24.00 **t.**

🏠 **Old Vicarage** ⌘, Parc-an-Creet, TR26 2ET, ☏ 6124, 🛦 – ℗
Easter-October – **8 rm** ⛋ 6.00/14.00 **s.**

✗ **Outrigger,** Street-an-Pol, TR26 2DS, ☏ 5936
closed Monday and December – **M** (dinner only) a la carte 4.70/8.25 **t.** ⅄ 2.10.

✗ **Chopping Block,** Tregenna Hill, TR26 2BN, ☏ 5161 – 🅿 AE ⓪ **VISA**
closed Sunday in winter and 3 weeks from 1 November – **M** (dinner only) a la carte
4.00/10.50 **t.** ⅄ 1.90.

at Carbis Bay S : 1 ½ m. on A 3074 – ✉ ☼ 073 670 St. Ives :

🏨 **Carbis Bay,** TR26 2NP, ☏ 5311, ≤, ⅃ heated, 🛦 – ⌷wc ℗. 🅿 AE ⓪ **VISA**
Easter-October – **M** a la carte 6.25/10.75 **st.** ⅄ 1.95 – **28 rm** ⛋ 15.90/35.45 **st.** –
P 22.45/25.40 **st.**

🏨 **Boskerris** ⌘, Boskerris Rd, TR26 2NQ, ☏ 5295, ≤, 🛦 – ⌷wc ℗
Easter-early October – **M** 3.00/4.50 **st.** ⅄ 2.25 – **23 rm** ⛋ 9.50/20.00 **st.** – P 13.50/
16.50 **st.**

🏨 **Hendras,** Porthrepta Rd, TR26 2NZ, ☏ 5030, 🛦 – ⌷wc 🚗 ℗
Mid May-September – **M** 4.00/5.00 **st.** – **37 rm** ⛋ 10.00/22.00 **t.** – P 14.00/15.00 **t.**

🏨 **St. Uny,** TR26 2NQ, ☏ 5011, 🛦 – ⌷wc 🛁 ℗
May-September – **M** (bar lunch) 3.00/5.00 **s.** ⅄ 1.60 – **36 rm** ⛋ (dinner included)
10.50/26.00.

at Lelant S : 3 ¼ m. on A 3074 – ✉ St. Ives – ☼ 0736 Hayle :

🏠 **Ar-Lyn** ⌘, Vicarage Lane, TR26 3JZ, ☏ 754269, 🛦 – ℗
11 rm ⛋ 8.00/16.00 **st.**

CITROEN ☏ 5442

ST. IVES Cambs. **404** T 27 – pop. 7,148 – ECD : Thursday – ☼ 0480.

See : Bridge* 15C.

🚗 High Leys ☏ 64459.

London 75 – Cambridge 14 – Huntingdon 6.

🏨 **Golden Lion,** Market Hill, PE17 4AL, ☏ 63159 – TV ⌷wc. 🅿 **VISA**
M 4.00/9.00 **st.** ⅄ 2.25 – **20 rm** ⛋ 12.50/25.00 **st.**

🏨 **St. Ives Motel,** London Rd, PE17 4EX, S : ½ m. on A 1096 ☏ 63857, 🛦 – TV ⌷wc ☏ ℗.
🅿 AE ⓪. **VISA**
M *(closed 25 and 26 December)* a la carte 4.00/6.80 ⅄ 2.00 – ⛋ 1.85 – **16 rm** 13.80/
18.30 **t.**

✗✗✗ **Slepe Hall** with rm, Ramsey Rd, PE17 4RB, ☏ 63122 – TV ⌷wc ☏ ℗. 🛁. 🅿 AE ⓪ **VISA**
closed 25 and 26 December – **M** a la carte 6.05/10.40 ⅄ 1.95 – **15 rm** ⛋ 14.50/25.50 –
P 21.00/30.00.

at Overcote Ferry E : 3 ½ m. off A 1123 – ✉ ☼ 0480 St. Ives :

🚗 Pike and Eel, Overcote Lane, PE17 3TW, ☏ 63336, ≤, ⚓, 🛦 – ℗ – **10 rm.**

at Fenstanton S : 2 m. by A 1096 on A 604 – ✉ ☼ 0480 St. Ives :

🏨 Tudor Inn, High St., PE18 9LN, ☏ 62532, 🛦 – TV ⌷wc ℗ – **10 rm.**

AUSTIN-MORRIS-MG The Quadrant ☏ 62871
AUSTIN-MORRIS-MG-PRINCESS Station Rd ☏ 63322

FIAT, LANCIA Station Rd ☏ 62641
FORD Ramsey Rd ☏ 63184

ST. LEONARDS Dorset 403 403 0 31 – see Ringwood.

ST. MARGARET'S BAY Kent 404 Y 30 – pop. 2,185 – ✉ ☎ 0304 Dover.
London 79 – Dover 4 – Ramsgate 19.

🏠 **Granville** 🍴, Granville Rd, CT15 6DT, ☏ 852212, ≤ sea and coastline, 🚗 – ⌂wc ☏.
🅂 AE ⓪ VISA
M 4.00/4.50 ⌂ 1.70 – ⌂ 1.60 – **21 rm** 7.60/19.00 – P 15.00/18.00.

ST. MARY'S Cornwall 403 B 34 – see Scilly (Isles of).

ST. MAWES Cornwall 403 E 33 – pop. 870 – ✉ Truro – ☎ 032 66.
See : Castle 16C (≤*) AC.
London 299 – Plymouth 56 – Truro 18.

🏨 **Tresanton** 🍴, TR2 5DR, ☏ 544, ≤ estuary, 🚗 – ⌂wc 🚗
Mid February-mid November and Christmas – M 6.50/8.85 ⌂ 1.75 – **30 rm** ⌂ (dinner included) 22.00/30.00.

🏨 **Rising Sun,** The Square, TR2 5DJ, ☏ 233 – ⌂wc
closed December – M a la carte 6.20/8.90 – **20 rm** 13.50/30.00.

🏨 **Idle Rocks,** Tredenham Rd, TR2 5AN, ☏ 771, ≤ harbour and estuary – ⌂wc. 🅂 AE ⓪ VISA
April-October – M (bar lunch) approx. 7.00 t. ⌂ 1.10 – **22 rm** ⌂ 13.00/31.00 t. – P 18.50/21.00 t.

🏠 **Pen Eglos** 🍴, Riviera Lane, TR2 5BG, ☏ 302, ≤ estuary, 🚗 – ⌂wc ℗
March-October – M (buffet lunch) 3.00/7.50 st. ⌂ 1.50 – **11 rm** (full board only) – P 22.00 st.

🏠 Manor House, 11 The Square, TR2 5AG, ☏ 392, ≤ – ⌂wc ℗ – *season* – **19 rm.**

🏨 **St. Mawes,** 2 Marine Parade, TR2 5DW, ☏ 266, ≤ – TV ⌂wc. 🅂 AE VISA
M 3.75/4.75 ⌂ 1.70 – **8 rm** ⌂ 9.50/21.00.

✗✗ **Green Lantern** with rm, Marine Parade, TR2 5DW, ☏ 502, ≤ – ⌂wc ⌂wc. AE ⓪ VISA
closed mid December - mid February – M (dinner only and Sunday lunch) 3.50/6.50 s.
⌂ 1.75 – **11 rm** ⌂ 8.50/17.00.

BRITISH LEYLAND ☏ 200

ST. MICHAEL'S-ON-WYRE Lancs. – pop. 529 – ECD : Wednesday – ✉ Preston – ☎ 099 58.
London 234 – Blackpool 11 – Lancaster 14 – Preston 11.

✗✗ **Rivermede** 🍴 with rm, PR3 0UB, ☏ 267, 🍴, 🚗 – TV ⌂wc 🚗 ℗. 🅂 AE
closed 25 December-January – M *(closed Tuesday)* (dinner only) 9.00 t. ⌂ 2.00 – **3 rm** ⌂ 16.50/27.75 t.

ST. NEOTS Cambs. 404 T 27 – pop. 10,110 – ☎ 0480 Huntingdon.
See : St. Mary's Church* 15C. – 🔃 Cross Hall Rd ☏ 75617, W : 1 m.
London 60 – Bedford 11 – Cambridge 17 – Huntingdon 9.

✗✗ **Chequers Inn,** St. Mary's St., PE19 2TA, Eynesbury S : ½ m. on B 1043 ☏ 72116 – ℗.
🅂 AE ⓪ VISA
closed Christmas Day – M a la carte 5.75/7.15 s. ⌂ 2.00.

at Eaton Socon SW : 1 ½ m. on A 428 – ✉ St. Neots – ☎ 0480 Huntingdon :

✗ **Old Plough,** 99 Great North Rd, PE19 2TR, on A 428 ☏ 72815 – ℗. 🅂 AE ⓪ VISA
closed Tuesday lunch and 25 and 26 December – M a la carte 4.50/9.15 ⌂ 1.70.

AUSTIN-MORRIS-MG 11 New St. ☏ 73237   ROVER-TRIUMPH 42 Huntingdon St. ☏ 73578
FORD Cambridge St. ☏ 73321

ST. WENN Cornwall 403 F 32 – pop. 300 – ✉ Bodmin – ☎ 072 689 Roche.
London 284 – Newquay 11 – Plymouth 42 – Truro 20.

🏠 **Wenn Manor** 🍴, PL30 5PS, ☏ 240, « Country house atmosphere », 🚗, park – ⌂wc
℗. 🅂 VISA
M (buffet lunch) approx. 4.00 t. ⌂ 1.60 – **8 rm** ⌂ 8.00/18.00 t.

SALCOMBE Devon 403 I 33 – pop. 2,496 – ECD : Thursday – ☎ 054 884.
🛈 Market St. ☏ 2736.
London 243 – Exeter 43 – Plymouth 27 – Torquay 28.

🏨 Marine, Cliff Rd, TQ8 8JH, ☏ 2251, Telex 45185, ≤ estuary, 🅂, 🅂 heated, 🚗 – 🛗 TV ⌂
℗. 🅂 AE ⓪ VISA
March-November – **51 rm.**

🏨 **Tides Reach,** South Sands, TQ8 8LJ, ☏ 2888, ≤ estuary, 🚗 – 🛗 TV ⌂wc ℗. 🅂 AE ⓪
VISA
March-October – M 3.00/6.00 st. ⌂ 1.50 – **40 rm** ⌂ 16.00/40.00 s. – P 17.50/22.50 s.

🏨 **Bolt Head** 🍴, South Sands, TQ8 8LW, ☏ 2780, ≤ estuary, 🅂 heated – ⌂wc ℗. 🅂
AE ⓪ VISA
March-November – M (bar lunch) 2.10/5.00 ⌂ 1.95 – **20 rm** ⌂ 16.90/18.80 st.

🏛 **Castle Point** ⌖, Sandhills Rd, TQ8 8JP, ☏ 2167, ≼ estuary, 🚗 – 🛏wc 🅿
Easter-mid October – **M** (bar lunch) approx. 5.25 **s.** ⌕ 1.75 – **20 rm** ⌷ (dinner included) 18.00/36.00 **s.**

🏛 **Knowle**, Onslow Rd, TQ8 8HY, ☏ 2846, 🚗 – 🛏wc 🅿. 🔲
Easter-October – **M** (bar lunch) 4.50 **s.** ⌕ 1.55 – **17 rm** ⌷ 9.50/22.00 **s.**

🏛 **St. Elmo** ⌖, Sandhills Rd, TQ8 8JR, ☏ 2233, 🚗 – 🛏wc 🅿
Easter week and May-October – **M** (buffet lunch) 3.50/6.75 **s.** – **27 rm** ⌷ 15.50/31.00 **s.**

🏛 **Grafton Towers** ⌖, Moult Rd, TQ8 8LG, ☏ 2882, ≼, 🚗 – 🛏wc 🚿wc 🅿
May-September – **M** (buffet lunch) 2.50/5.00 ⌕ 1.25 – **14 rm** ⌷ 12.00/26.00.

🏛 **Penn Torr**, Herbert Rd, TQ8 8HN, ☏ 2234 – 🚿wc 🅿
Easter-September – **M** (bar lunch) 3.50 ⌕ 2.00 – **10 rm** ⌷ 6.50/14.20 – P 10.50.

🏛 **Sunny Cliff**, Cliff Rd, TQ8 8JU, ☏ 2207, ≼ estuary, ⌇ heated, 🚗 – 🛏wc 🚿wc 🅿
Late March-October – **M** (bar lunch) approx. 5.00 **st.** ⌕ 2.25 – ⌷ 1.50 – **17 rm** 8.25/16.50 **st.** – P 11.50/14.50 **st.**

🏠 **Bay View**, Bennett Rd, TQ8 8JJ, ☏ 2238, ≼ estuary – 🅿
Easter-September – **11 rm** ⌷ 9.50/21.00 **t.**

🏠 **Woodgrange**, Devon Rd, TQ8 8HJ, ☏ 2439, 🚗 – 🛏wc 🅿
Easter-September – **11 rm** ⌷ 7.00/16.00 **st.**

XX **Galley**, 5 Fore St., TQ8 8BY, ☏ 2828, ≼ – 🔲 AE ⓪ VISA
closed November – **M** (Saturday dinner only from December to March) a la carte 3.10/9.00 **t.** ⌕ 2.25.

at Hope Cove W: 4 m. – ✉ Kingsbridge – ☎ 054 854 Galmpton:

🏰 **Lantern Lodge** ⌖, TQ7 3HE, ☏ 280, ≼ Bigbury Bay, « Antique furnishings », 🚗 – 🛏wc 🚿wc 🅿
Easter-September – **M** (bar lunch) approx. 6.00 **st.** ⌕ 2.10 – **15 rm** ⌷ 13.50/18.00 **st.**

🏰 **Cottage** ⌖, TQ7 3HJ, ☏ 555, ≼ Bolt Tail and Bigbury Bay, 🚗 – 🛏wc 🅿
closed January – **M** 4.90/6.30 **s.** ⌕ 2.80 – **37 rm** ⌷ 13.95/20.15 **s.**

SALFORDS Surrey 🔳 T 30 – ✉ ☎ 0737 Redhill.
London 24 – Brighton 29.

🏛 **Mill House**, Brighton Rd, RH1 5BT, ☏ 67277, 🚗 – 🛏wc 🚿wc 📺 🅿. 🔲 AE ⓪ VISA
closed 26 December – **M** *(closed Saturday lunch)* 5.00 ⌕ 1.35 – ⌷ 1.50 – **31 rm** 8.00/15.00.

SALISBURY Wilts. 🔳 🔳 0 30 – pop. 35,302 – ECD : Wednesday – ☎ 0722.
See : Cathedral*** 13C (cloister***, chapter house***, Library : Magna Carta* *AC*) **Z** A.
Envir.: Stonehenge (Megalithic monument)*** *AC*, NW: 10 m. by A 345 **Y** – Old Sarum (excavations 12C-13C)* *AC*, N : 2 m. by A 345 **Y** – Longford Castle* (16C) *AC*, SE : 2 ½ m. by A 338 **z** – Wilton House** 17C-19C (The Double cube**) *AC*, W: 2 ½ m. by A 30 **Y**.
🖙, 🖙 Netherhampton ☏ 072 274 (Wilton) 2131, by A 3094 **z** – 🖙 Great Durnford ☏ 072 273 (Middle Woodford) 231 · N : 4 m. by A 345 **Y**.
🛈 10 Endless St. ☏ 4956 – Fisherton St. ☏ 27676/4432.

London 91 – Bournemouth 28 – Bristol 53 – Southampton 23.

Plan on next page

🏰 **White Hart** (T.H.F.), 1 St. John's St., SP1 2SD, ☏ 27476 – 📺 🛏wc 📺 🅿. 🏊 . 🔲 AE ⓪ VISA   **Z s**
M 4.25/5.25 **st.** ⌕ 1.80 – ⌷ 2.50 – **72 rm** 12.50/23.50 **st.**

🏛 **Cathedral**, 7 Milford St., SP1 2AJ, ☏ 20144 – 📶 🛏wc. VISA   **Y a**
M (bar lunch) approx. 4.50 **st.** ⌕ 1.50 – **32 rm** ⌷ 14.70/26.90 **st.**

🏛 **Kings Arms**, St. John's St., SP1 2SB, ☏ 27629, « Part 13C and part 15C inn » – 🛏wc. 🔲 VISA   **Z r**
M a la carte 4.00/6.20 **t.** ⌕ 2.00 – **17 rm** ⌷ 12.50/23.30 **st.**

🏠 **Byways House**, 31 Fowlers Rd, off Milford Hill, SP1 2QP, ☏ 28364, 🚗   **Z e**
10 rm ⌷ 6.00/12.00 **st.**

🏠 **Glen Lyn**, Milford Hill, SP1 2QZ, ☏ 27880, 🚗   **Y n**
8 rm ⌷ 6.00/12.00 **st.**

XX **Crane's**, 90-92 Crane St., SP1 2QD, ☏ 3471, French rest., 🚗 – 🔲 AE ⓪ VISA   **Z a**
closed Sunday, Monday, last week September, 2 weeks October and 25 December – 14 January – **M** a la carte 7.80/11.00 **st.** ⌕ 1.50.

XX **The Haunch of Venison**, Minster St., SP1 1TF, ☏ 22024, « 14C timbered inn », English rest. – 🔲 AE ⓪   **Y e**
closed Sunday, Monday, 2 weeks July and 2 weeks February – **M** a la carte 6.35/9.10 **t.** ⌕ 2.20.

XX **Provençal**, 14 Ox Row, Market Pl., SP1 1EU, ☏ 28923, French rest. – 🔲 AE ⓪ VISA   **Y c**
closed Saturday lunch, Sunday and 5 days at Christmas – **M** a la carte 6.20/8.70 **t.** ⌕ 1.50.

XX **Dutch Mill**, 58 A Fisherton St., SP2 7RB, ☏ 23447. 🔲 AE   **Y i**
M a la carte 5.55/7.65 **t.**

P.T.O. ⟶

at Redlynch SE: 8 ½ m. by A 338 – z – off B 3080 – ✉ Salisbury – ✆ 079 439 Earldoms :

XX **Langley Wood** 🦢 with rm, Timberley Lane, SP5 2PA, SE: 1 ½ m. ☏ 348, 🍴 – 🅿
closed Sunday, 25-26 December, 2 weeks October and 1 January – **M** (dinner only)
(booking essential) a la carte 6.15/8.10 **t.** 🍷 1.65 – **3 rm** 🛏 8.00.

at Odstock S: 2 ½ m. off A 338 – z – ✉ ✆ 0722 Salisbury :

X **Yew Tree Inn**, SP5 4JE, ☏ 29786 – 🅿. 🔲 AE ⓸ *VISA*
closed Sunday, Monday and Bank Holidays – **M** a la carte 4.60/8.15 🍷 1.95.

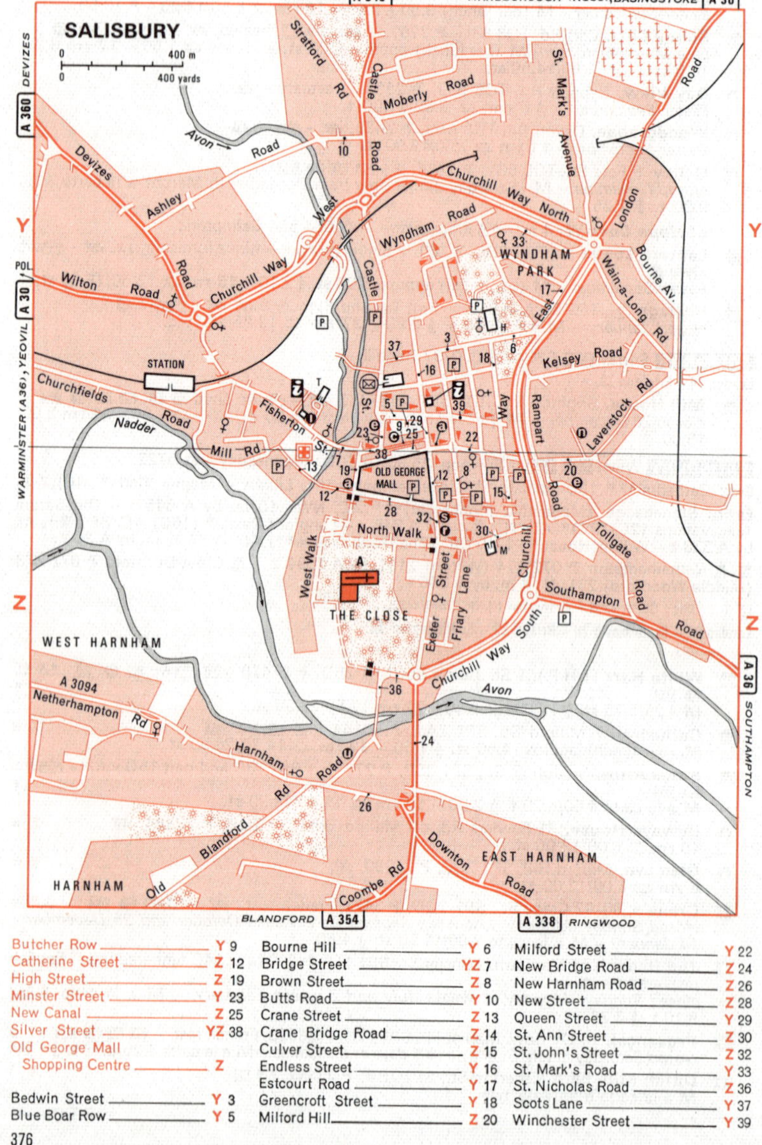

at Harnham SW: 1 ½ m. off A 3094 – ⊠ ✆ 0722 Salisbury:

🏠 **Rose and Crown** (County), Harnham Rd, SP2 8JQ, ✆ 27908, Telex 25971, ⇐, «Garden on riverside » – 📺 ⛱ wc ☎ ⅙ Ⓟ. 🔆 Ⓐ𝔼 ⑩ 𝑽𝑰𝑺𝑨 z u
M 4.25/4.75 **st.** ⚱ 1.55 – **30 rm** ⚏ 22.00/27.00 **s.**

at Barford St. Martin W: 6 m. on A 30 – Y – ⊠ ✆ 072 274 Wilton:

✕✕ **Chez Maurice,** SP3 4AB, ✆ 2240, French rest. – Ⓟ. ⑩ 𝑽𝑰𝑺𝑨
closed Sunday, 26 December, 1 January and Easter Monday – M *(closed dinner Christmas Day)* a la carte 9.00/10.95 **t.** ⚱ 2.20.

at Wilton NW: 3 m. on A 30 – z – ⊠ Salisbury – ✆ 072 274 Wilton:

🏠 **Pembroke Arms,** Minster St., SP2 0BH, ✆ 3127 – Ⓟ. 🔆
M a la carte 3.70/5.55 **t.** ⚱ 1.90 – **8 rm** ⚏ 8.85/15.95 **st.**

AUSTIN-MG-WOLSELEY 41/45 Winchester St. ✆ 6681
CITROEN Stephenson Rd ✆ 24136
DAF Downton Rd ✆ 4886
DAIMLER-JAGUAR-ROVER-TRIUMPH Brunell Rd ✆ 23131
FIAT Castle St. ✆ 5668
FORD Castle St. ✆ 28443
MORRIS-MG, ROLLS ROYCE Southampton Rd ✆ 5251
PEUGEOT Southampton Rd ✆ 5268
RENAULT 114/120 Wilton Rd ✆ 28328
SAAB Downton Rd, Redlynch ✆ 20340
TALBOT Scamels Rd ✆ 28321
VAUXHALL Brunell Rd ✆ 23522
VOLVO Telford Rd ✆ 3650
VW, AUDI-NSU 16 Lower Rd, Churchfields ✆ 27162

SALTBURN BY THE SEA Cleveland 📖 ⑳ – pop. 6,160 – ECD: Tuesday – ✆ 028 72.
📗 Hob Hill ✆ 2812.

London 264 – Leeds 74 – Middlesbrough 13 – York 61.

🏠 Zetland, Marine Par., TS12 1AR, ✆ 2961, ⇐ – 🛗 ⛱ wc ☎ Ⓟ. 🏊
45 rm.

🏠 Queen, Station St., TS12 1AE, ✆ 3371 – 📺 ⛱ wc 🗌 wc ☎. 🏊 – **18 rm.**

SAMLESBURY Lancs. – see Preston.

SANDIACRE Notts. 📖 📖 O 25 – see Nottingham.

SANDOWN I.O.W. 📖 📖 Q 32 – see Wight (Isle of).

SANDPLACE Cornwall 📖 G 32 – see Looe.

SANDWICH Kent 📖 Y 30 – pop. 4,490 – ECD: Wednesday – ✆ 030 46.
📗, 📗, 📗 Sandwich Bay ✆ 2247.

London 71 – Canterbury 12 – **Dover 13** – Maidstone 39 – Margate 9.

🏠 **Bell,** 2 Upper Strand St., CT13 9EF, ✆ 2836 – 📺 ⛱ wc ☎ Ⓟ. 🔆 Ⓐ𝔼 ⑩ 𝑽𝑰𝑺𝑨
M 4.50/6.00 **st.** – **28 rm** ⚏ 16.00/29.00 **st.**

✕✕ **The Cave,** 15 Harnet St., CT13 9ES, ✆ 2274 – ⑩
closed Sunday lunch, Monday except Bank Holidays and 25 and 26 December – M *(buffet lunch)* a la carte 5.80/8.70 **t.** ⚱ 1.75.

AUSTIN-MG-MORRIS Market Hall ✆ 3066

SANDYPARK Devon 📖 I 31 – see Chagford.

SAUNDERSFOOT Dyfed 📖 F 28 – pop. 3,150 – ECD: Wednesday – ✆ 0834.
London 245 – Carmarthen 25 – Fishguard 34 – Tenby 3.

🏠 **St. Brides,** St. Brides Hill, SA69 9NH, ✆ 812304, Telex 48350, ⇐ Saundersfoot Bay, 🏊 heated, 🚗 – 📺 ⛱ wc 🗌 wc ☎ Ⓟ. 🏊. 🔆 Ⓐ𝔼 ⑩ 𝑽𝑰𝑺𝑨
M 4.50/6.25 **st.** ⚱ 2.00 – **50 rm** ⚏ 18.00/30.00 **st.**

🏠 **Glen Beach,** Swallow Tree Woods, SA69 9DE, ✆ 813430, 🚗 – 🗌 wc Ⓟ. 🔆
M *(buffet lunch)* 5.00 – **14 rm** ⚏ 10.00/20.00 **st.**

🏠 Merlewood, St. Brides Hill, SA69 9NP, ✆ 812421, 🏊 heated, 🚗 – 🗌 wc Ⓟ. 𝑽𝑰𝑺𝑨
closed November and December – **34 rm** ⚏ *(dinner included)* 11.50/24.50 **s.**

SAUNDERTON Bucks. 📖 R 28 – pop. 256 – ⊠ Aylesbury – ✆ 084 44 Princes Risborough.
London 42 – Aylesbury 9 – Oxford 20.

🏠 **Rose and Crown,** Wycombe Rd, HP17 9NP, S : on A 4010 ✆ 5299 – Ⓟ. Ⓐ𝔼 ⑩ 𝑽𝑰𝑺𝑨
closed 1 week at Christmas – M *(closed Sunday)* a la carte 4.65/7.10 ⚱ 1.85 – **9 rm** ⚏ 15.00/23.00 **t.**

SAUNTON Devon 📖 H 30 – pop. 200 – ⊠ Braunton – ✆ 027 189 (3 fig.) or 0271 (6 fig.)
Croyde. – 📗, 📗 ✆ 812436.
London 230 – Barnstaple 8 – Exeter 48.

🏠 **Saunton Sands,** EX33 1LQ, ✆ 890212, ⇐ Saunton Sands, ✕, 🔆, 🚗 – 🛗 Ⓟ. 🔆 Ⓐ𝔼 ⑩ 𝑽𝑰𝑺𝑨
M 3.95/6.00 **t.** ⚱ 2.10 – ⚏ 1.00 – **160 rm** 10.00/32.00.

🏠 **Preston House,** EX33 1LG, ✆ 890472, ⇐ Saunton Sands, 🚗 – ⛱ wc 🗌 wc Ⓟ
March-October – M *(bar lunch)* 6.20 **st.** ⚱ 1.95 – **11 rm** ⚏ 10.30/20.60 **s.**

SAVERNAKE Wilts. ⁴⁰³ ⁴⁰⁴ O 29 – see Marlborough.

SAWLEY Lancs. – see Clitheroe.

SCALBY North Yorks. 986 ㉔ – see Scarborough.

SCARBOROUGH North Yorks. 986 ㉔ – pop. 44,440 – ECD : Monday and Wednesday –
⊛ 0723.

See : Castle 12C (⊰*) *AC* Y.

🏌 North Cliff Av. ☎ 60786, NW : 2 m. by A 165 Y – 🏌 Deepdale Av., off Filey Rd ☎ 60522,
S : 1 m. by A 165 z.

🛈 St. Nicholas Cliff ☎ 72261.

London 253 – Kingston-upon-Hull 47 – Leeds 67 – Middlesbrough 52.

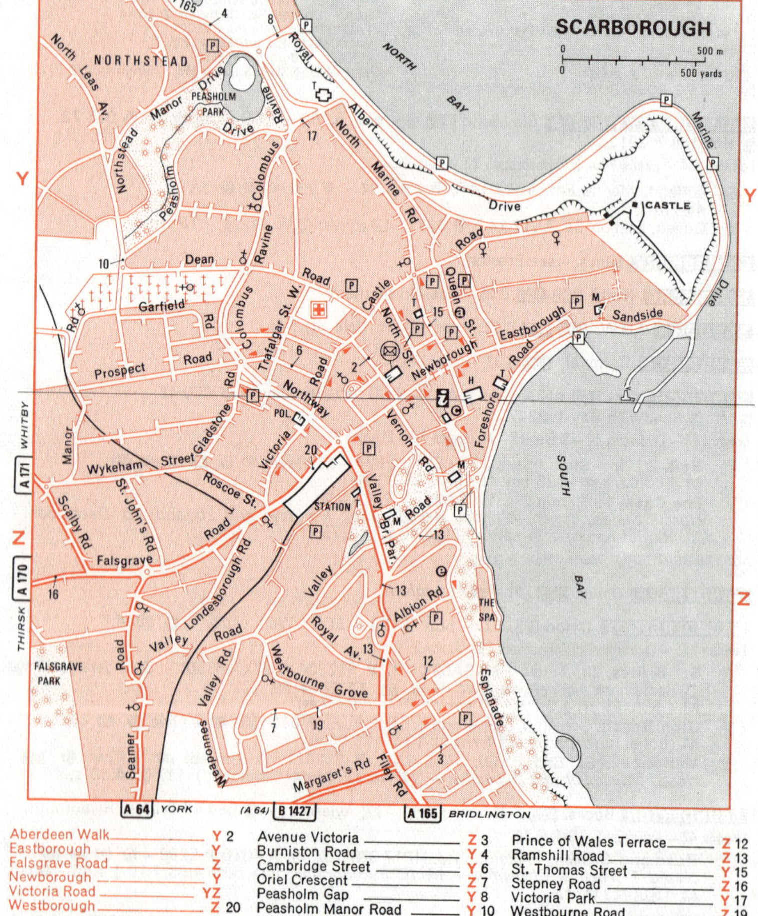

Aberdeen Walk	Y 2	Avenue Victoria	Z 3	Prince of Wales Terrace	Z 12		
Eastborough	Y	Burniston Road	Y 4	Ramshill Road	Z 13		
Falsgrave Road	Z	Cambridge Street	Y 6	St. Thomas Street	Y 15		
Newborough	Y	Oriel Crescent	Z 7	Stepney Road	Z 16		
Victoria Road	YZ	Peasholm Gap	Y 8	Victoria Park	Y 17		
Westborough	Z 20	Peasholm Manor Road	Y 10	Westbourne Road	Z 19		

🏨 Crown, Esplanade, YO11 2AG, ☎ 73491, Telex 52580 – 📶 TV 🛁. 🔲 AE ⓪ VISA Z e
80 rm.

🏨 **Royal,** St. Nicholas St., YO11 2HE, ☎ 64333, Telex 52472 – 📶. 🛁. 🔲 AE ⓪ VISA Z c
M 4.50/6.00 t. 🍴 1.50 – **128 rm** ⬜ 16.00/32.00 st. – P 26.00/30.00 st.

🏨 Holbeck Hall ⊰, Seacliff Rd, YO11 2XX, ☎ 74374, ⊰, « Country house atmosphere »,
🚌 – ⬛wc 📺 🅿 – by A 165 z
closed January and February – **30 rm** ⬜ 17.10/34.20 **st.**

XX **Lanterna,** 33 Queen St., YO11 1HQ, ℡ 63616, Italian rest. – *VISA*   **Y a**
closed Sunday, Monday and Easter – **M** a la carte 5.10/6.60 🍷 1.50.

at Ravenscar N : 10 m. off A 171 – **Z** – ✉ ☎ 0723 Scarborough :

🏨 Raven Hall ⌖, YO13 0ET, ℡ 870353, ≼ Robin Hoods Bay, « Country house atmosphere »,
XX, ⌸, 🎱, ⌖, 🚗, park – 🛏wc ℗
Easter-November – **M** 4.00/6.00 **t.** 🍷 2.50 – **60 rm.**

at Scalby NW : 3 m. on A 171 – **Z** – ✉ ☎ 0723 Scarborough :

X **Gatehouse,** 17-19 High St., YO13 0PT, ℡ 62840 – ℗
closed Sunday dinner, Monday, Tuesday, 2 weeks Easter and 2 weeks September –
M (dinner only and Sunday lunch) a la carte 4.60/7.80 **t.** 🍷 2.10.

at Hackness NW : 7 m. by A 171 – **Z** – ✉ ☎ 0723 Scarborough :

🏨 **Hackness Grange** ⌖, YO13 0JW, ℡ 69966, ≼, « Country house atmosphere », XX,
⌸, 🎱, 🚗, park – ℗. ⚡ AE ① *VISA*
M 5.50/9.00 **t.** 🍷 2.20 – **30 rm** ⊏ 18.00/36.00 **st.** – P 24.50/28.00 **st.**

AUSTIN-MORRIS-MG Valley Bridge Rd ℡ 60221	OPEL Main St. ℡ 862242
CITROEN, HONDA Main St. ℡ 863421	RENAULT Clifton St. ℡ 60791
FORD Vine St. 75581	TALBOT, DATSUN Northway ℡ 63533
MAZDA Falconers Rd ℡ 60322	VAUXHALL Seamer Rd ℡ 60335

SCILLY (Isles of) Cornwall 🔠 AB 34 – pop. 2,020.

See : Archipelago★★.

St. Mary's – pop. 1,958 – ✉ St. Mary's – ☎ 0720 Scillonia.
See : Hugh Town (the Garrison ≼★).
Access to Penzance by helicopter.
🚢 to Penzance (Isles of Scilly Steamship Co.) summer : Monday to Saturday 1 daily ;
winter : 3 weekly (2 h 30 mn).
🛈 Town Hall, ℡ 22536.

🏨 **Tregarthen's** ⌖, TR21 0PP, ℡ 22540, ≼ Harbour and islands – 🛏wc ☎. ⚡ *VISA*
April-mid October – **M** 4.50/7.00 **t.** 🍷 2.00 – **33 rm** ⊏ 15.00/34.00 **st.** – P 18.00/25.00 **st.**

🏨 **Godolphin,** Church St., TR21 0JR, ℡ 22316 – 📺 🛏wc. AE
Mid March-mid October – **M** 4.80/6.30 **s.** 🍷 1.50 – **29 rm** ⊏ (dinner included)
19.55/39.10 **st.**

🏠 **Bell Rock,** Church St., TR21 0JS, ℡ 22575, ⌸ heated – 🛏wc 🛁wc
March-October – **M** 4.00/4.75 – **17 rm** ⊏ 14.00/28.00.

🏠 **Atlantic,** Hugh St., TR21 0PL ℡ 22417, ≼ St. Mary's harbour – 🛏wc
February-28 October – **M** (bar lunch) 3.50/4.75 **s.** 🍷 1.50 – **28 rm** ⊏ 10.50/23.00.

🏠 **Star Castle** ⌖, TR21 0JA, ℡ 22317, « Elizabethan fortress », XX, ⌸ heated, 🚗 –
🛁wc
April-October – **M** 3.00/5.00 – **24 rm** ⊏ 8.00/16.00 – P 12.50/14.50.

Tresco – pop. 246 – ✉ Tresco – ☎ 0720 Scillonia.
See : Tresco Gardens★★ *AC.*

🏨 **Island** ⌖, TR24 0PU, ℡ 22883, ≼ Islands, ⌸ heated, 🚗, park – 📺 🛏wc ☎. ⚡ AE ① *VISA*
March-mid October – **M** 5.75/9.50 **st.** 🍷 1.40 – **37 rm** ⊏ 12.85/29.50 **st.** – P 29.40/
33.40 **st.**

🏠 **New Inn** ⌖, TR24 0QQ, ℡ 22844, ≼ Islands, ⌸ heated – 🛏wc
April-October – **M** 4.00/7.50 **st.** 🍷 1.10 – **16 rm** ⊏ 12.00/24.00 **st.** – P 21.00 **st.**

SCOTCH CORNER North Yorks. 🔠 ⑲ – ✉ ☎ 0748 Richmond.
London 243 – Leeds 53 – Middlesbrough 22 – Newcastle-upon-Tyne 40.

🕭 **Vintage,** DL10 6NP, ℡ 2961 – ℗
closed 25 and 26 December – **M** (*closed Sunday dinner*) 3.75/6.50 **t.** 🍷 1.95 – **5 rm**
⊏ 8.50/17.00 **t.** – P 18.00/18.50 **t.**

SCUNTHORPE Humberside 🔠 R 23 – pop. 70,907 – ECD : Wednesday – ☎ 0724.
Envir. : Normanby Hall★ (Regency) : Wildlife park★ *AC,* N : 4 m. – Barton-upon-Humber
(St. Mary's Church★ 12C, Old St. Peter's Church★ 10C-11C) NE : 13 ½ m.
🎱 Kingsway ℡ 68117.
🛈 Central Library, Carlton St. ℡ 60161.
London 167 – Leeds 54 – Lincoln 30 – Sheffield 45.

🏨 **Royal** (Anchor), Doncaster Rd, DN15 7DE, ℡ 68181, Group Telex 858875 – 📺 🛏wc
☎ ℗. 🛁. ⚡ AE ① *VISA*
M a la carte approx. 6.00 **st.** – **28 rm** ⊏ 18.00/25.50.

X **Town House,** 62 Mary St., DN15 6LD, ℡ 63692 – ⚡ AE ① *VISA*
closed Saturday lunch, Monday dinner and Sunday – **M** a la carte 4.00/6.50 🍷 1.90.

P.T.O. ⟶

at Althorpe E: 4 ½ m. off. A 18 – ⊠ ☎ 0724 Scunthorpe:

XX **Lansdowne House** with rm, DN17 3HJ, ☎ 783369, 🚗 – 📺 🛏WC P. 🅿 AE ⓪ VISA
M (closed Sunday) approx. 7.75 **st.** ▯ 1.90 – **5 rm** ⊆ 14.50/19.00 **st.**

AUSTIN-MORRIS-MG Normandy Rd ☎ 4534
BMW Normandy Rd ☎ 64251
CITROEN 136/144 Ashby High St. ☎ 67474
DATSUN Old Crosby ☎ 4542
FIAT 187 Ashby Rd ☎ 61191
FORD Station Rd ☎ 61144
OPEL Winterton Rd ☎ 61083

RENAULT Robert St. ☎ 2616
ROVER-TRIUMPH 76 Doncaster Rd ☎ 67101
TALBOT Smith St. ☎ 69323
TOYOTA High St. East ☎ 2011
VAUXHALL Ferry Rd ☎ 3284
VW, AUDI 14/16 Collum Lane ☎ 3716

SEACROFT West Yorks. – see Leeds.

SEAFORD East Sussex 404 U 31 – pop. 12,470 – ECD: Wednesday – ☎ 0323.
Envir.: Charleston Manor* *AC*, NE: 4 m.
🛇 Southdown Rd ☎ 890139.
🛈 The Downs, Sutton Rd ☎ 892224 ext 48.
London 67 – Brighton 13 – Eastbourne 10 – Lewes 11.

⌂ **Clearview**, 36-38 Claremont Rd, BN25 2BD, ☎ 890138 – 🛏WC P
14 rm ⊆ 8.00/15.50 **st.**

AUSTIN-MORRIS-MG-ROVER-TRIUMPH Sutton Park Rd ☎ 890864

SEAL Kent 404 U 30 – see Sevenoaks.

SEALE Surrey 404 R 30 – see Farnham.

SEATON Devon 404 K 31 – pop. 4,139 – ECD: Thursday – ☎ 0297.
🛇 Axe Cliff ☎ 20499.
🛈 Sea Front ☎ 21660 (summer only).
London 162 – Dorchester 32 – Exeter 23 – Taunton 28.

⌂ **Netherhayes**, Fore St., EX12 2LE, ☎ 21646, 🚗 – P
Easter-October – **10 rm** ⊆ 6.50/13.00.

XX **Copperfields**, Fore St., EX12 2LE, ☎ 22294 – P. AE VISA
closed Sunday dinner – **M** a la carte 4.30/7.05 ▯ 1.75.

SEATON BURN Tyne and Wear – see Newcastle-upon-Tyne.

SEATON CAREW Cleveland – pop. 7,332 – ⊠ ☎ 0429 Hartlepool.
🛇 Tees Rd ☎ 66249.
London 263 – Durham 21 – Middlesbrough 7 – Sunderland 23.

🏨 **Staincliffe** (Swallow), The Cliff, TS25 1AB, ☎ 64301, Telex 53168, ≼, XX – 📺 🛏WC
☎ P. 🅿 – **22 rm.**

SEAVINGTON ST. MARY Somerset 403 L 31 – pop. 212 – ⊠ Ilminster – ☎ 0460 South Petherton.
London 142 – Taunton 14 – Yeovil 11.

XX **Pheasant** ⌘ with rm, TA19 0QH, ☎ 40502, 🚗 – 🛏WC ☎ P
closed last 2 weeks September, 25-26 December and last 2 weeks February – **M** (Sunday
dinner residents only) a la carte 4.80/6.80 **t.** – **11 rm** ⊆ 10.70/18.10 **t.**

SEDGEFIELD Durham 986 ⑲ – pop. 5,337 – ⊠ Stockton-on-Tees (Cleveland) – ☎ 0740.
London 261 – Hartlepool 14 – Middlesbrough 13 – Newcastle-upon-Tyne 28.

🏨 **Hardwick Hall** ⌘, TS21 2EH, NW: 1½ m. on A 177 ☎ 20253, ≼, 🚗, park – 📺 🛏WC
☎ P. 🅿 AE ⓪ VISA
M 6.50/8.25 **t.** ▯ 1.85 – **17 rm** ⊆ 20.50/22.75 **t.**

SEDLESCOMBE East Sussex 404 V 31 – pop. 1,318 – ⊠ Battle – ☎ 042 487.
London 56 – Hastings 7 – Lewes 26 – Maidstone 27.

🏦 **Brickwall**, The Green, TN33 0QA, ☎ 253, ⌇ heated, 🚗 – 🛏WC P. 🅿 AE ⓪
closed January – **M** 4.25/4.95 **t.** ▯ 1.95 – **16 rm** ⊆ 9.60/20.30 **t.** – P 15.00/16.00 **t.**

X **Holmes House**, The Green, TN33 0QA, ☎ 450 – 🅿 AE ⓪ VISA
closed Sunday dinner and Monday – **M** a la carte 3.60/8.00 **t.** ▯ 1.60.

SELBY North Yorks. 📖 ㉓㉔ – pop. 13,200 – ECD : Thursday – ☎ 0757.
See : Abbey Church★★ 12C-16C. Envir. : Carlton Towers★ (19C) *AC*, S : 6 m.
📇 Mill Lane ☏ 075 782 (Gateforth) 234, SW : 3 m.
London 197 – Kingston-upon-Hull 34 – Leeds 21 – York 14.

⌂ **Londesborough Arms,** Market Pl., YO8 0NS. ☏ 707355 – ◻wc 🏚 **P**. ⛛. 🔊 **VISA**
  M 3.50/4.50 **st.** ⚗ 1.90 – **37 rm** ⊐ 11.25/23.00 **st.**

AUSTIN-MORRIS-MG-ROVER-TRIUMPH Gowthorpe   SKODA Chapel Haddlesey ☏ 075 787 (Burn) 638
☏ 3023   VAUXHALL Brook St. ☏ 3258

SELMESTON East Sussex 📗 U 31 – see Lewes.

SELSEY West Sussex 📗 R 31 – pop. 5,650 – ☎ 024 361.
📇 ☏ 2203.
London 78 – Brighton 40 – Chichester 9.

⚐ **Thatched House** ⚘, 23 Warner Rd, off Clayton Rd, PO20 9DD, ☏ 2207, 🍴 – ◻
  P. 🔊 ⓪ **VISA**
  M (bar lunch) 4.25/6.50 ⚗ 1.65 – ⊐ 2.15 – **8 rm** 7.50/14.00.

⚐ **Conifers** ⚘, Seal Sq., Seal Rd, PO20 0HP, ☏ 2436, 🍴 – ◻wc **P**. 🔊
  closed 15 January-28 February – **M** *(lunch by arrangement)* 4.50/5.50 **st.** ⚗ 1.50 –
  ⊐ 1.50 – **9 rm** 8.00/19.00 **st.** – P 14.00/15.00 **st.**

SENNEN Cornwall 📕 C 33 – pop. 704 – ✉ Penzance – ☎ 073 687.
London 328 – Penzance 10 – Truro 36.

⌂ **Tregiffian** ⚘, TR19 7BE, NE : 2 ¼ m. off A 30 ☏ 408, 🍴 – ◻wc **P**. 🔊 **VISA**
  Easter-October – **M** (bar lunch) 1.80/4.00 **s.** ⚗ 1.30 – **9 rm** ⊐ 9.50/24.00 **s.**

⌂ **Old Success Inn,** Sennen Cove TR19 7DG. ✉ Land's End ☏ 232. ⋖ – ◻wc **P**
  closed 3 weeks October-November and 1 week at Christmas – **M** (bar lunch) 5.00
  ⚗ 2.00 – **20 rm** ⊐ 7.00/16.00 – P 10.60/12.15.

SETTLE North Yorks. 📖 ㉓ – pop. 2,171 – ECD : Wednesday – ☎ 072 92.
📇 Giggleswick ☏ 3580, off A 65.
🅸 Town Hall Market Pl. ☏ 3617 (summer only).
London 238 – Bradford 34 – Kendal 30 – Leeds 41.

⌂ **Royal Oak,** Market Pl., BD24 9ED, ☏ 2561 – 🏚wc 🚗 **P**
  M 3.75/7.50 **st.** ⚗ 2.00 – **6 rm** ⊐ 11.50/20.50 **st.** – P 22.50/25.00 **st.**

AUSTIN-MORRIS-MG-ROVER-TRIUMPH-WOLSELEY Station Rd ☏ 2323

SEVENOAKS Kent 📗 U 30 – pop. 24,750 – ECD : Wednesday – ☎ 0732.
See : Knole★★ (15C-17C) *AC*. Envir.: Lullingstone (Roman Villa : mosaic panels★) *AC*, N : 6 m.
📇 Darenth Valley ☏ 095 92 (Otford) 2922, N : 3 m.
London 26 – Guildford 40 – Maidstone 17.

⌂ **Moorings** without rest., 97 Hitchen Hatch Lane, TN13 3BE, ☏ 52589, 🍴 – 📺 🏚wc **P**
  10 rm ⊐ 13.80/19.55 **st.**

⌂ **Sevenoaks Park,** Seal Hollow Rd, TN13 3RX, ☏ 54245, 🍴 – 📺 ◻wc 🏚wc **P**. 🔊
  🆎 ⓪ **VISA**
  M 4.00/6.00 ⚗ 1.95 – **11 rm** ⊐ 13.25/21.20 **st.**

XX **Al Mottarone,** 7 Tubs Hill Par., TN13 1DH, ☏ 54385, Italian rest. – ⓪ **VISA**
  closed Sunday – **M** a la carte 4.70/5.80 ⚗ 1.40.

X **Le Chantecler,** 43 High St., TN13 1JF, ☏ 54662 – 🔊 🆎 ⓪ **VISA**
  closed Sunday, 2 weeks August, 1 week September and Bank Holidays – **M** a la carte 5.90/
  9.65 ⚗ 1.80.

at Otford N : 3 m. on A 225 – ✉ Sevenoaks – ☎ 095 92 Otford :

XX **Forge House,** TN14 5PQ, ☏ 2463 – 🔊 🆎 ⓪ **VISA**
  closed Sunday dinner and Monday – **M** a la carte 7.25/13.00 **t.** ⚗ 2.50.

at Seal NE : 2 m. on A 25 – ✉ ☎ 0732 Sevenoaks :

XX **Copper Kettle,** 67 High St., TN15 0AW, ☏ 61481 – **P**. 🔊 🆎 ⓪ **VISA**
  M *(closed Saturday lunch, Sunday dinner, Monday, 25 December-1 January and 2 days
  at Bank Holidays)* a la carte 5.10/9.85 **t.** ⚗ 1.65.

AUSTIN-MORRIS-MG, ROLLS ROYCE-BENTLEY 166   ROVER-TRIUMPH 71 St. Johns Hill ☏ 55174
High St. ☏ 52371   SAAB Station Approach ☏ 0732 (Borough Green)
CITROEN Tonbridge Rd ☏ 53328   883044
FIAT London Rd ☏ 57177   TOYOTA Badgers Mount ☏ 095 97 (Badgers Mount)
FORD The Vines ☏ 59911   218
PEUGEOT London Rd, Dunton Green ☏ 073 273   VAUXHALL 128 Seal Rd ☏ 51337
(Dunton Green) 292

 Dorset **403** **404** N 30 – pop. 3,976 – ECD : Wednesday and Saturday – ☎ 0747.
Envir. : Old Wardour castle* (ruins 14C) *AC*, site*, NE : 5 m.
London 115 – Bournemouth 31 – Bristol 47 – Dorchester 29 – Salisbury 20.

> 🏨 **Grosvenor** (T.H.F), The Commons, SP7 8JA, ☎ 2282 – 📺 ⛱wc ⊛. ᕕ. 🅢 🅰🅴 ⑩ 𝘝𝘐𝘚𝘈
> M 3.45/4.55 **st.** ⬧ 1.65 – **48 rm** ⥊ 13.00/25.00 **st.**

> 🏚 **Royal Chase** (Best Western), Royal Chase Roundabout, SP7 8DB, Junction of
> A 30 and A 350 ☎ 3355, Telex 417294, ⇄ – ⛱wc 🛁wc ☎ 🅿. 🅢 🅰🅴 ⑩ 𝘝𝘐𝘚𝘈
> M a la carte 5.15/6.95 **st.** – **19 rm** ⥊ 13.60/29.50 **st.**

AUSTIN-MORRIS-MG Salisbury Rd ☎ 2295   PEUGEOT ☎ 2939
FIAT New Rd ☎ 2117

 I.O.W. **403** **404** N 30 – see Wight (Isle of).

 Derbs. **403** **404** P 25 – pop. 906 (inc. Great Wilne) – ✉ ☎ 0332 Derby.
London 124 – Derby 6 – Leicester 23 – Nottingham 13.

> ✕✕ **Lady in Grey** with rm, 5 Wilne Lane, DE7 2HA, ☎ 792331, ⇄ – 📺 ⛱wc 🛁wc 🅿. 🅢
> 🅰🅴 ⑩ 𝘝𝘐𝘚𝘈
> *closed 25-26 December and Bank Holidays* – **M** *(closed Sunday dinner)* a la carte 7.85/
> 11.50 **st.** ⬧ 2.00 – **15 rm** ⥊ 15.00/26.00 **st.**

 Wilts. **403** **404** N 29 – pop. 800 – ✉ ☎ 0225 Melksham.
London 112 – Bristol 23 – Salisbury 35.

> ⌂ **Shaw Farm**, SN12 8EF, on A 365 ☎ 702836, ⌇ heated, ⇄ – 🅿
> *closed Christmas-1 January* – **10 rm** ⥊ 9.50/22.00 **t.**

 Hants. **403** **404** Q 31 – pop. 2,730 – ✉ Southampton – ☎ 0329 Wickham.
London 75 – Portsmouth 13 – Southampton 10.

> 🏨 **Meon Valley Golf and Country Club**, Sandy Lane, SO3 2HQ, off A 334, ☎ 833455, ⪡,
> ✂, 🅢, ⟨18⟩, park – 📺 ⛱wc ⊛ 🅿. ᕕ. 🅢 🅰🅴 𝘝𝘐𝘚𝘈
> M 5.00/5.75 **st.** ⬧ 1.75 – **49 rm** ⥊ 19.50/25.50 **st.**

 Devon **403** H 31 – see Hatherleigh.

 Kent **404** W 29 – pop. 13,860 – ☎ 079 56.
See : ⪡* from the pier.
Envir.: Minster (abbey: brasses*, effigied tombs*) SE : 2 ½ m.
🛳 Shipping connections with the Continent: to Vlissingen (Olau-Line).
🅱 Bridge Rd, Car Park ☎ 5324 – Council Office, Sea front ☎ 2395 ext 59 (summer only).

London 52 – Canterbury 24 – Maidstone 20.

> ***Hotels and restaurants see: Maidstone*** SW : 20 m.

COLT New Rd ☎ 4329   VAUXHALL Queenborough Corner ☎ 3133
RENAULT Queenborough Rd ☎ 2782

 South Yorks. **403** **404** P 23 – pop. 520,327 – ECD : Thursday – ☎ 0742.
See: Abbeydale Industrial Hamlet* (steel and scythe works) *AC*, SW : by A 621 AZ.
⟨18⟩ Hemsworth Rd ☎ 54402, S : 3 ½ m. AZ – ⟨18⟩ Beauchief ☎ 360648, SW : by B 6068 AZ –
⟨18⟩ Tinsley Park ☎ 442237, E : by A 57 BZ – ⟨18⟩ Birley Lane ☎ 390099, S : 4 m. on A 616 BZ.
🚗 ☎ 20002 ext 2254.
🅱 Central Library, Surrey St. ☎ 734760/1/4.

London 169 – Leeds 34 – Liverpool 79 – Manchester 40 – Nottingham 42.

Plans on following pages

> 🏨 **Hallam Tower** (T.H.F.), Manchester Rd (A 57), S10 5DX, ☎ 686031, Telex 547293,
> ⪡, ⇄ – 📶 📺 🅿. ᕕ. 🅢 🅰🅴 ⑩ 𝘝𝘐𝘚𝘈   AZ o
> M 5.00/5.50 **st.** ⬧ 1.65 – ⥊ 2.50 – **135 rm** 22.50/31.00 **st.**

> 🏨 **Grosvenor House** (T.H.F.), Charter Sq., S1 3EH, ☎ 20041, Telex 54312 – 📶 📺 ᕕ 🅿. ᕕ.
> 🅢 🅰🅴 ⑩ 𝘝𝘐𝘚𝘈   CZ a
> M 5.10/5.60 **st.** ⬧ 1.75 – ⥊ 2.50 – **133 rm** 22.50/31.00 **st.**

> 🏨 Royal Victoria (B.T.H.), Victoria Station Rd, S4 7YE, ☎ 78822 – 📶 📺 🅿. ᕕ. 🅢 🅰🅴 ⑩
> 𝘝𝘐𝘚𝘈   DY c
> M (Saturday and Sunday lunch by arrangement) a la carte 6.75/9.85 **st.** ⬧ 2.30 – **63 rm.**

> 🏨 St. George ⧖, Kenwood Rd, S7 1NG, ☎ 583811, Telex 547030, ⪡, ⌇, ⇄, park –
> 📶 📺 ⛱wc ⊛ ᕕ 🅿. ᕕ   AZ r
> **76 rm.**

> 🏨 **Rutland**, 452 Glossop Rd, S10 2PY, ☎ 665215 – 📶 ⛱wc ⊛ 🅿. ᕕ. 🅢 𝘝𝘐𝘚𝘈   AZ e
> M 3.50/5.50 **st.** ⬧ 2.15 – **95 rm** ⥊ 15.50/28.70 **st.**

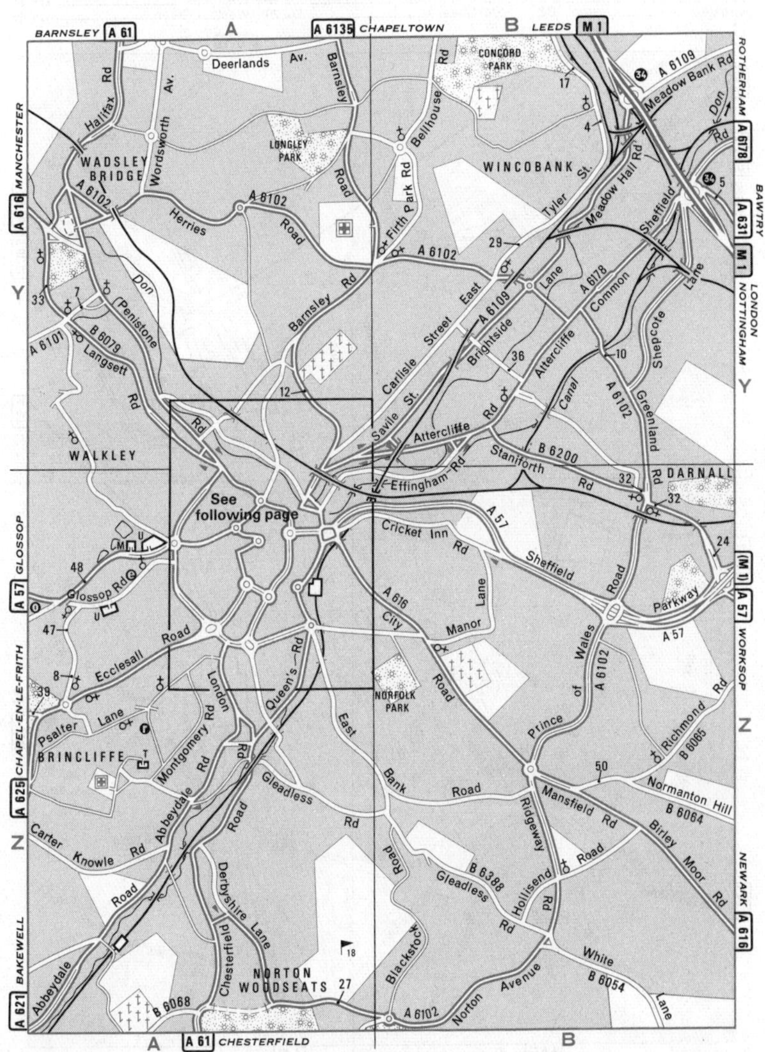

✗ **Stirrings,** 141 Oakbrook Rd, S11 7EB, ☎ 305540   by Rustlings Rd AZ
closed Sunday, 1 week at Christmas and Bank Holidays – **M** (dinner only) a la carte 6.70/
8.75 🍷 1.75.

at Dore SW : 5 m. off A 621 – AZ – ⌷ ◉ 0742 Sheffield :

✗✗ **Dore Grill,** 38 Church Lane, S17 3GS, ☎ 365948 – **P.** ▨ AE ⓪
closed Sunday dinner – **M** a la carte 5.65/11.50 **t.** 🍷 1.85.

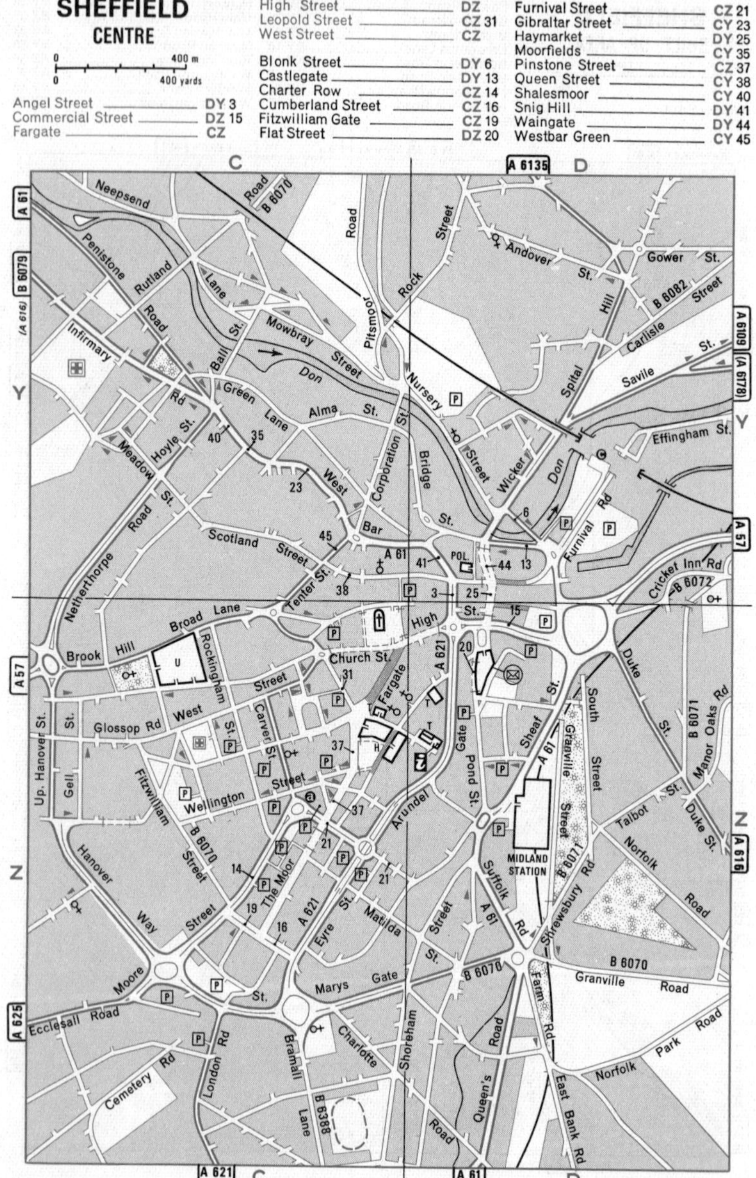

SHEFFIELD
CENTRE

400 m
400 yards

High Street — DZ
Leopold Street — CZ 31
West Street — CZ
Blonk Street — DY 6
Castlegate — DY 13
Charter Row — CZ 14
Cumberland Street — CZ 16
Fitzwilliam Gate — CZ 19
Flat Street — DZ 20
Furnival Street — CZ 21
Gibraltar Street — CY 23
Haymarket — DY 25
Moorfields — CY 35
Pinstone Street — CZ 37
Queen Street — CY 38
Shalesmoor — CY 40
Snig Hill — DY 41
Waingate — DY 44
Westbar Green — CY 45

Angel Street — DY 3
Commercial Street — DZ 15
Fargate — CZ

Neepsend
Penistone Road
Rutland Lane
Mowbray Street
Don
Alma St.
Green Lane
Ball St.
Hoyle St.
Meadow St.
Netherthorpe Road
Scotland Street
West Bar
Infirmary
Pitsmoor
Rock Street
Nursery St.
Corporation St.
Bridge St.
Wicker
Don
Furnival Rd
Andover St.
Gower St.
Carlisle Street
Spital Hill
Savile St.
Effingham St.
Cricket Inn Rd
Brook Hill
Rockingham Street
Glossop Rd
West Street
Carver St.
Wellington
Fitzwilliam Street
Up. Hanover St.
Gell St.
Hanover Way
Moore St.
Ecclesall Road
Cemetery Rd
London Rd
Bramall Lane
Charlotte
Shoreham Street
Church St.
Fargate
High St.
Pond St.
Arundel Gate
Sheaf St.
Granville Street
South Street
Duke St.
Talbot St.
Norfolk Road
Manor Oaks Rd
Duke St.
MIDLAND STATION
Suffolk Road
Shrewsbury Rd
Granville Road
Norfolk Park Road
East Bank Rd
Farm Rd
Queen's Road
Matilda St.
Eyre St.
The Moor
A 621
Marys
Marys Gate
POL.
U
H
T
E
A 61
A 57
A 625
A 6135
A 6082
A 6109
A 6178
B 6070
B 6079
B 6071
B 6072
B 6388
B 6070

LOTUS Broad Lane ☏ 25048
MERCEDES-BENZ 115 Ecclesall Rd South ☏ 368161
MORRIS-MG 113/115 Abbeydale Rd ☏ 50685
MORRIS-MG 168 Penistone Rd ☏ 348801
MORRIS-MG-WOLSELEY 286 Sandygate Rd ☏ 302021
MORRIS-MG-WOLSELEY Broadfield Rd ☏ 52404
RENAULT London Rd ☏ 581041
RENAULT 885 Chesterfield Rd ☏ 585423
RENAULT 30/46 Suffolk Rd ☏ 21378

ROLLS ROYCE-BENTLEY Peel St., Bromhill ☏ 71141
ROVER-TRIUMPH 75 Herries Rd ☏ 387155
TALBOT, VAUXHALL Ecclesall Rd ☏ 664471
TALBOT Bradfield Rd ☏ 344256
TOYOTA Ellin St. ☏ 78717
VAUXHALL 44/46 Savile St. ☏ 29281
VOLVO 43/67 Ecclesall Rd ☏ 78705
VOLVO Netherthorpe Rd ☏ 78739
VW, AUDI-NSU 1 Ecclesall Rd South ☏ 668441

SHELDON Warw. 403 404 O 26 – see Birmingham.

SHELTON LOCK Derbs. 403 404 P 25 – see Derby.

SHEPPERTON Middx. 404 S 29 – pop. 10,765 – ◉ 093 22 Walton-on-Thames.
London 25.

🏨 **Elizabethan** ⚓, Felix Lane, TW17 8NP, E: 1 ¼ m. on B 375 ☏ 41404, Telex 928170 –
⌕ 📺 🛏wc 🕿 🅿. 🔁. ⌂ AE ⓞ VISA
M 4.15/5.20 t. ⌕ 1.60 – ⌕ 2.50 – **181 rm** 21.50/29.50 st.

🏨 **Warren Lodge,** Church Sq., TW17 9JZ, ☏ 42972, ≼, ⌦ – 📺 🛏wc ⍥wc 🕿 🅿. ⌂ AE
ⓞ VISA
M (closed Monday lunch and Sunday) a la carte 4.55/8.80 – **45 rm** ⌕ 15.00/24.00.

✗✗ **Thames Court,** Tow Path, Ferry Lane, TW17 9LJ, W: 1 ¼ m. off B 375, ☏ 21957, ≼
river Thames, ⌦ – 🅿. ⌂ AE ⓞ VISA
closed Sunday dinner, Monday and February – **M** a la carte 4.95/8.40 t. ⌕ 1.50.

at Upper Halliford NE: 1 m. off A 244 – ✉ Weybridge – ◉ 093 27 Sunbury-on-
Thames:

✗✗ Goat, 47 Upper Halliford Rd, TW17 8RX, ☏ 82415 – 🅿.

DATSUN Walton Bridge Rd ☏ 26784
FORD Station Approach ☏ 24811

HONDA High St. ☏ 40121

SHEPTON MALLET Somerset 403 404 M 30 – pop. 5,030 – ECD: Wednesday – ◉ 0749.
See : SS. Peter and Paul's Church (carved barrel roof* 15C).

⛳ Gurney Slade ☏ 074 984 (Oakhill) 205, N : 3 m. (A 37).

London 127 – Bristol 20 – Southampton 63 – Taunton 31.

✗✗ **Charlton House** with rm, Frome Rd, BA4 4PR, E: 1 m. on A 361 ☏ 2008, ≼, ⚓ heated,
⌦, park – 📺 🛏wc ⍥wc 🅿. ⌂ AE ⓞ VISA
M (closed Saturday lunch, Sunday and Monday lunch) 3.95/6.75 s. ⌕ 1.95 – **10 rm**
⌕ 11.00/22.00 s. – P 19.50/22.00 s.

✗✗ **Bowlish House** with rm, Coombe Lane, BA4 5JD, W: ½ m. on A 371, ☏ 2022, ⌦ –
🛏wc 🅿
M (closed Sunday lunch) (booking essential) a la carte 6.85/8.35 ⌕ 1.50 – ⌕ 1.00 –
5 rm 6.00/10.50 st.

HONDA, VOLVO Townsend Rd ☏ 2864
VAUXHALL Paul St. ☏ 2030

VW, AUDI High St. ☏ 2976

SHERBORNE Dorset 403 404 M 31 – pop. 7,272 – ECD: Wednesday – ◉ 093 581.
See : Abbey Church* 15C (choir: fan vaulting**).

⛳ Clatcombe, ☏ 2475, N : 1 m.

London 128 – Bournemouth 39 – Dorchester 19 – Salisbury 36 – Taunton 31.

🏨 **Post House** (T.H.F.), Horsecastles Lane, DT9 6BB, W: 1 m. on A 30 ☏ 3191, ⌦ – 📺
🛏wc 🕿 ⅙ 🅿. 🔁. ⌂ AE ⓞ VISA
M 4.25/5.25 st. ⌕ 1.65 – ⌕ 2.25 – **60 rm** 18.00/25.50 st.

🏨 **Eastbury,** Long St., DT9 3BY, ☏ 3387, ⌦ – 🛏wc
M 2.70/4.15 st. ⌕ 1.70 – **16 rm** ⌕ 9.35/17.20 st. – P 15.45/16.20 st.

🏠 **Saffron House,** The Avenue, DT9 3AH, ☏ 2734, ⌦ – 🅿
closed Christmas – **M** 4.50/5.00 st. ⌕ 1.40 – **6 rm** ⌕ 9.10/18.20 st.

at Oborne NE: 2 m. off A 30 – ✉ ◉ 093 581 Sherborne:

✗✗ **The Grange,** DT9 3RU, ☏ 3463, ≼, ⌦ – 🅿
closed Sunday dinner and Monday – **M** (dinner only and Sunday lunch) a la carte
7.10/10.20 t. ⌕ 2.50.

at Holnest Park SE: 5 ½ m. by A 352 – ✉ Sherborne – ◉ 096 321 Holnest:

🏠 **Manor Farm Country House** ⚓, DT9 6HA, ☏ 474, ≼, ⌦ – 🅿
March-October – **M** (closed Tuesday dinner) 3.20 – **10 rm** ⌕ 7.00/14.00.

MERCEDES-BENZ Yeovil Rd ☏ 3350
LANCIA Long St. ☏ 3262

VOLVO Digby Rd ☏ 2436

SHERFIELD ON LODDON Hants. 403 404 Q 30 – see Basingstoke.

SHIFNAL Salop **403** **404** M 25 – pop. 5,070 – ECD : Thursday – ✉ ✆ 0952 Telford.
See : St. Andrew's Church★ 12C-16C. **Envir.** : Weston Park★ 17C (paintings★★) *AC*, NE : 5 m.
London 150 – Birmingham 28 – Shrewsbury 16.

    Park House, Park St., TF11 9BA, ✆ 460128, ⌇ heated, ⇘ – �📺 ⌹wc ⌺wc ☏ ℗ ♿.
    AE ◻ ⑩ *VISA*
    M 4.50/6.50 **s.** ⌾ 1.70 – **21 rm** ⌸ 18.50/28.00 **s.**

AUSTIN-MORRIS Chepside ✆ 460412   MORRIS Western Heath ✆ 095 270 (Great Chatwell) 252

SHIPDHAM Norfolk **404** W 26 – pop. 1,520 – ✉ ✆ 0362 Dereham.
London 138 – East Dereham 5 – Norwich 21 – Watton 6.

    Shipdham Place, Church Close, IPX25 7LX, on A 1075 ✆ 820303, ⇘ – ⌹wc ☏ ℗
    Easter-Christmas – **M** *(closed Sunday to non-residents and Monday)* (dinner only
    Tuesday to Friday) 4.50/7.25 **t.** ⌾ 1.60 – **6 rm** ⌸ 17.00/27.00 **t.**

SHIPLEY Salop **403** **404** N 26 – see Wolverhampton.

SHIPSTON-ON-STOUR Warw. **403** **404** P 27 – pop. 2,773 – ✆ 0608.
Envir. : Compton Wynyates★ (Tudor mansion 15C-16C) *AC*, NE : 4 ½ m.
London 85 – Birmingham 34 – Oxford 29.

    George, Market Sq., CV36 4AJ, ✆ 61453 – ⌹wc ℗
    17 rm.

    Old Mill, with rm, Mill Rd, CV36 4AW, on B 4035 ✆ 61880, ⌇, ⇘ – ℗
    5 rm.

AUSTIN-MORRIS-MG Church St. ✆ 61430

SHIPTON Glos. **403** **404** O 28 – see Cheltenham.

SHIPTON-UNDER-WYCHWOOD Oxon. **403** **404** P 28 – pop. 860 – ECD : Wednesday – ✆ 0993.
London 81 – Birmingham 50 – Gloucester 37 – Oxford 25.

    Shaven Crown, High St., OX7 6BA, ✆ 830330, « 13C monk's hostel » – ⌹wc ℗. ◻
    ⑩ *VISA*
    M 3.50/7.00 **t.** ⌾ 1.80 – **10 rm** ⌸ 11.00/24.00 **t.**

    Lamb Inn with rm, High St., OX7 6DQ, ✆ 830465, ⇘ – ⌹wc ℗ AE ⑩ *VISA*
    M *(closed Sunday dinner)* (buffet lunch Monday to Saturday) 4.25/7.00 ⌾ 1.50 – ⌸ 1.75 –
    3 rm 8.50/16.00.

SHORNE Kent **404** V 29 – pop. 2,622 – ✉ Gravesend – ✆ 047 482.
London 27 – Gravesend 4 – Maidstone 12 – Rochester 4.

    Inn on the Lake, DA12 3HB, on A 2 ✆ 3333, ≤, ⌇, ⇘, park – 📺 ⌹wc ☏ ♿ ℗. ♿
    ◻ AE ⑩ *VISA*
    M a la carte 7.50/11.00 **st.** ⌾ 2.50 – **78 rm** ⌸ 21.00/29.00 **st.**

SHOTTISHAM Suffolk **404** Y 27 – pop. 164 – ECD : Wednesday – ✉ Woodbridge – ✆ 039 441.
London 87 – Ipswich 14 – Woodbridge 6.

    Wood Hall ⌲, IP12 9XX, on B 1083 ✆ 283, ≤ ⇘ – ⌹wc ℗
    18 rm.

SHREWSBURY Salop **403** L 25 – pop. 56,188 – ECD : Thursday – ✆ 0743.
See : Abbey church★ 11C-14C **D** – St. Mary's Church★ (Jesse Tree window★) **A** – Grope Lane★
15C. **Envir.** : Wroxeter★ (Roman city and baths) *AC*, SE : 6 m. by A 458 and A 5 – Condover
Hall★ (15C) *AC*, S : 5 m. by A 49.
⛳ ✆ 64050, junction A 5/A 49, Meole Brace S : by A 49.
🛈 The Square ✆ 52019.

London 164 – Birmingham 45 – Cardiff 109 – Chester 42 – Derby 67 – Gloucester 77 – Manchester 71 – Stoke-on-
Trent 35 – Swansea 118.

Plan opposite

    Lion (T.H.F.), Wyle Cop, SY1 1UY, ✆ 53107 – ▯ 📺 ⌹wc ☏ ℗. ♿. ◻ AE ⑩ *VISA*   **c**
    M 4.20/4.50 **st.** ⌾ 1.65 – **64 rm** ⌸ 13.00/24.50 **st.**

    Prince Rupert, Butcher Row, SY1 1UQ, ✆ 52461 – ▯ 📺 ⌹wc ☏. ◻ AE ⑩ *VISA*   **n**
    M 4.50/5.50 **t.** ⌾ 1.90 – **66 rm** ⌸ 14.50/24.50 **t.** – P 26.00/27.00 **t.**

    Lord Hill, 131 Abbey Foregate, SY2 6AX, ✆ 52601 – 📺 ⌹wc ⌺wc ☏ ℗. ♿   **e**
    26 rm.

    Beauchamp (S & N), 100 The Mount, SY3 8PG, ✆ 3230, ⇘ – 📺 ⌹wc ⌺wc ℗. ◻ AE
    ⑩ *VISA*   **a**
    M *(closed Sunday dinner)* 2.95/4.00 **st.** ⌾ 1.85 – **25 rm** ⌸ 12.00/22.00 **st.**

    Ainsworth's Radbrook Hall, Radbrook Rd, SY3 9BQ, W : 1 m. on A 488 ✆ 4861, ⇘ –
    📺 ⌹wc ⌺wc ☏ ℗. ♿. ◻ AE ⑩
    M 4.85 **s.** ⌾ 2.25 – **36 rm** ⌸ 10.50/22.00 **st.**

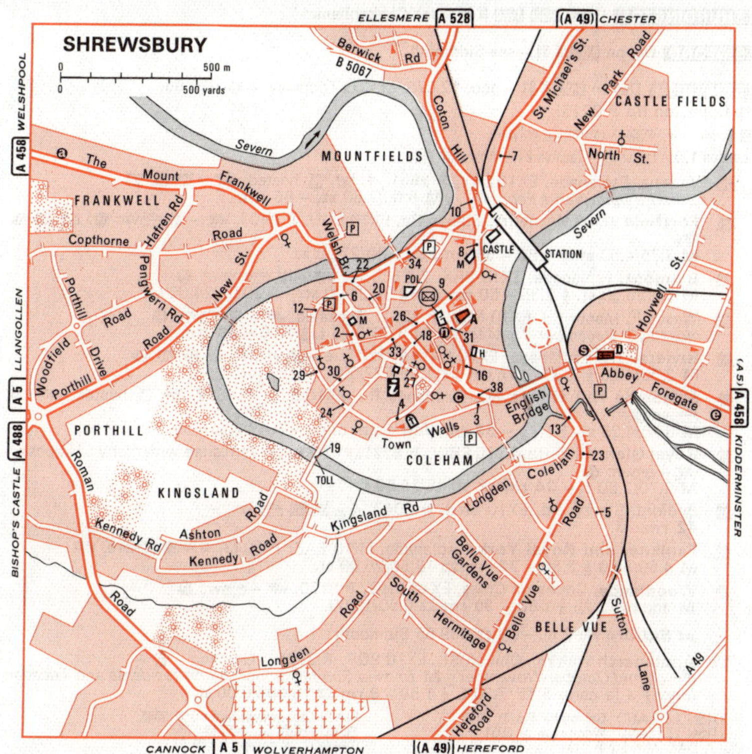

Street	No.	Street	No.	Street	No.
High Street	18	Castle Foregate	7	Mardol Quay	22
Pride Hill	26	Castle Gates	8	Moreton Crescent	23
Shoplatch	33	Castle Street	9	Murivance	24
		Chester Street	10	Princess Street	27
Barker Street	2	Claremont Bank	12	St. Chad's Terrace	29
Beeches Lane	3	Coleham Head	13	St. John's Hill	30
Belmont	4	Dogpole	16	St. Mary's Street	31
Betton Street	5	Kingsland Bridge	19	Smithfield Road	34
Bridge Street	6	Mardol	20	Wyle Cop	38

Shelton Hall, SY3 8BH, NW: 2 m. at junction of A 5 and A 458 ☎ 3982, – wc wc ℗
15 rm ⇆ 7.50/16.00 – P 13.00/18.00.

Penny Farthing, 23 Abbey Foregate, SY1 1BA, ☎ 56119 – **⬛ ⓞ**　　　　　**s**
closed Sunday, Monday, 2 weeks June and 2 weeks January – **M** a la carte 6.45/8.10
⬗ 2.15.

at Albrighton N: 3 m. on A 528 – ✉ Shrewsbury – ☏ 0939 Bomere Heath:

Albright Hussey, SY4 3AF, ☎ 290523, « 15C timbered manor house with garden » –
℗. **⬛ AE ⓞ VISA**
closed Sunday dinner, Monday and August – **M** a la carte 5.70/7.95 ⬗ 1.50.

at Cressage SE: 8 ½ m. on A 458 – ✉ Shrewsbury – ☏ 095 289 Cressage:

Old Hall, with rm, SY5 6AD, ☎ 298, ⬉, – ℗ – **5 rm.**

at Dorrington S: 7 m. on A 49 – ✉ Shrewsbury – ☏ 074 373 Dorrington:

Olde Hall, Hereford Rd, SY5 5JD, ☎ 465 – ℗. **⬛ ⓞ VISA**
closed Sunday dinner and Monday – **M** a la carte 4.70/5.55 ⬗ 1.50.

AUSTIN-MG-MORRIS-PRINCESS-ROVER-TRIUMPH-
WOLSELEY Chester St. ☎ 57231
BMW Castle Foregate ☎ 3250
CITROEN New St. ☎ 4039
DATSUN Harlescott Ind. Est ☎ 64951
FORD Coton Hill ☎ 3631

OPEL-VAUXHALL St. Julian's Friars ☎ 52321
RENAULT 159 Abbey Foregate ☎ 57711
TALBOT 170 Abbey Foregate ☎ 56326
VOLVO Featherbed Lane ☎ 51251
VW, AUDI, FIAT Wyle Cop ☎ 52471

SHURDINGTON Glos. 🔢 🔢 N 28 – see Cheltenham.

SIDFORD Devon 🔢 K 31 – see Sidmouth.

SIDMOUTH Devon 🔢 K 31 – pop. 12,076 – ECD: Thursday – ☼ 039 55.

🔢 Cotmaton Rd ☎ 3023.

🔢 Esplanade, ☎ 6441 (summer only).

London 170 – Exeter 14 – Taunton 27 – Weymouth 45.

🏨 Victoria, Esplanade, EX10 8RY, ☎ 2651, ≤, ✗, ⌕ heated, 🚗 – 🛗 ℗. AE
closed January and February – **M** 5.00/7.50 st. – **65 rm.**

🏨 **Fortfield** (Best Western), Station Rd, EX10 8NU, ☎ 2403, 🚗 – 🛗 ⌂wc ℗. 🔲 AE ⓪
VISA
M 3.75/4.50 st. ⌂ 1.80 – **59 rm** ⫶ 19.00/37.50 st.

🏨 **Belmont,** Esplanade, EX10 8RX, ☎ 2555, ≤, 🚗 – 🛗 ⌂wc ☎ ℗
M 5.50/6.50 st. ⌂ 2.35 – **50 rm** ⫶ 18.00/36.00 st. – P 20.00/24.00 st.

🏨 Westcliff, Manor Rd, EX10 8RU, ☎ 3252, ⌕ heated, 🚗 – 🛗 ⌂wc ℗
closed 23 December-15 March – **M** 3.75/5.25 t. ⌂ 2.00 – **38 rm.**

🏨 **Riviera,** The Esplanade, EX10 8AY, ☎ 5201, ≤ – 🛗 ⌂wc ☎ ℗. AE ⓪
M 3.50/4.25 ⌂ 1.30 – **37 rm** ⫶ 13.50/27.00.

🏨 **Salcombe Hill House** ⌘, Beatlands Rd, EX10 8JQ, ☎ 4697, ✗, ⌕ heated, 🚗 – 🛗
⌂wc ℗
M 3.75/4.25 st. ⌂ 1.45 – **33 rm** (full board only) – P 12.00/16.50.

🏨 **Royal Glen,** Glen Rd, EX10 8RW, ☎ 3221, « 17C house furnished with many antiques »,
🚗 – ⌂wc ℗
M 2.70/2.80 t. – **34 rm** ⫶ 10.45/25.50 t.

🏨 Bedford, Station Rd, EX10 8NR, ☎ 3047, ≤ – 🛗 TV ⌂wc
42 rm.

🏨 **Faulkner and Royal York,** Esplanade, EX10 8AZ, ☎ 3043, ≤ – 🛗 ⌂wc. **VISA**
M 4.50/5.50 ⌂ 2.50 – **72 rm** ⫶ 12.50/25.00 st.

🏨 **Woodlands,** Cotmaton Cross, EX10 8HG, ☎ 3120, 🚗 – ⌂wc ℗
M approx. 2.25 ⌂ 1.60 – **30 rm** ⫶ 9.50/19.00.

at Sidford N : 2 m. – ✉ ☼ 039 55 Sidmouth :

✗✗ **Applegarth** with rm, Church St., EX10 9QP, ☎ 3174, « Garden » – ℗
closed mid October-November – **M** (*closed Sunday dinner to non-residents and Tuesday
lunch*) a la carte 5.15/7.30 t. ⌂ 1.50 – **8 rm** ⫶ 10.00/20.00 st.

BRITISH LEYLAND Salcombe Rd ☎ 2522
BRITISH LEYLAND Woolbrook ☎ 2931
COLT, DAF Mill St. ☎ 3433
DATSUN Sidford ☎ 3334

FIAT Crossways, Sidford ☎ 3595
FORD High St. ☎ 5725
TALBOT Vicarage Rd ☎ 2433

SILCHESTER Hants. 🔢 🔢 Q 29 – pop. 766 – ✉ Reading (Berks.) – ☼ 0734.

London 62 – Basingstoke 8 – Reading 14 – Winchester 26.

🏨 **Romans** ⌘, Little London Rd, RG7 2PN, ☎ 700421, ✗, ⌕ heated, 🚗 – ⌂wc ℗. ⓪
VISA
closed last 2 weeks August and 25 to 28 December – **M** (*closed Saturday lunch, Sunday
dinner and Bank Holidays*) 7.00/8.50 ⌂ 1.75 – **22 rm** ⫶ 18.00/24.00.

SILLOTH Cumbria 🔢 ⑲ – pop. 2,662 – ECD: Wednesday – ✉ Carlisle – ☼ 0965.

🔢 ☎ 31304.

🔢 Central Garage, Waver St. ☎ 31276.

London 331 – Carlisle 22.

at Skinburness NE : 2 m. off B 5302 – ✉ Carlisle – ☼ 0965 Silloth :

🏨 **Skinburness,** CA5 4QY, ☎ 31468, 🚗 – ⌂wc ℗. 🔲
M 3.20/6.60 t. ⌂ 1.90 – **23 rm** ⫶ 10.30/18.50 t.

AUSTIN-MG Solway St. ☎ 351

FORD West End ☎ 449

SIMONSBATH Somerset 🔢 I 30 – pop. 181 – ✉ Minehead – ☼ 064 383 Exford.

London 200 – Exeter 40 – Minehead 19 – Taunton 38.

🏨 **Simonsbath** ⌘, TA24 7SH, ☎ 259, ≤, « Tastefully converted 17C country house »,
🚗 – TV ⌂wc ℗. 🔲 AE ⓪ **VISA**
M a la carte 6.40/8.10 t. ⌂ 1.60 – **9 rm** ⫶ 13.10/28.30 t. – P 22.80/26.85 t.

SITTINGBOURNE Kent **404** W 29 – pop. 26,450 – ECD : Wednesday – ☎ 0795.
London 44 – Canterbury 15 – Maidstone 12.

  Coniston, 70 London Rd, ME10 1NT, ℡ 23927 – ☒ 🛏wc 🅿. ♨. 🖭 🄰🄴 ⑩
  M 4.00 ▯ 2.00 – **50 rm** ヱ 14.00/21.00.

  ✕ **Nina's** with rm, 43 High St., ME10 4AW, ℡ 24670 – ☒ ⋔. *VISA*
  closed Good Friday, Easter Sunday and Christmas Day – **M** *(closed Sunday and Monday dinner)* a la carte 5.00/8.20 ▯ 1.25 – **5 rm** ヱ 10.45/15.45.

AUSTIN-MORRIS-MG Bapchild ℡ 23085   RENAULT Bapchild ℡ 76222
FORD Crown Quay Lane ℡ 70711   VAUXHALL 52 West St. ℡ 23333
RELIANT St. Michael's Rd ℡ 23421

SKEGNESS Lincs. **404** V 24 – pop. 12,680 – ECD : Thursday – ☎ 0754.
◫ Seacroft ℡ 3020, S : 1 ½ m. – ◫ North Shore ℡ 3298.
🛈 Foreshore Offices, Town Hall, North Parade ℡ 4761 – Tower Esplanade ℡ 4821 (summer).
London 145 – Lincoln 41.

  County, North Par., PE25 2UB, ℡ 2461, ⇐ – 🛗 🛏wc ☎ 🅿. ♨. 🄰🄴 ⑩
  M 4.10 ▯ 2.50 – **48 rm** ヱ 10.00/20.00 – P 13.50/15.50.

  Crown, Drummond Rd, Seacroft, PE25 3AB, ℡ 3084 – 🛏wc 🅿 – **27 rm.**

AUSTIN-MORRIS-MG Roman Bank ℡ 3671   OPEL Clifton Grove ℡ 3589
FIAT, ALFA-ROMEO Beresford Av. ℡ 67131 TALBOT Beacon Way ℡ 2556
FORD Wainfleet Rd ℡ 66019

SKELMERSDALE Lancs. **986** ⑤ – pop. 40,700 – ECD : Thursday – ☎ 0695.
London 210 – Liverpool 19 – Manchester 27 – Preston 22.

  Balcony Farm Inn, Prescot Rd, East Pimbo SE : 2 m. by A 506 ℡ 20401 – 🛏wc 🅿
  12 rm.

FORD Digmoor Rd ℡ 23434

☛ *Michelin puts no plaque or sign*
on the hotels and restaurants mentioned in this Guide.

SKELWITH BRIDGE Cumbria – see Ambleside.

SKINBURNESS Cumbria – see Silloth.

SKIPTON North Yorks. **986** ㉓ – pop. 13,220 – ECD : Tuesday – ✉ Bradford – ☎ 0756.
See : Castle* (14C) *AC.*
◪ Short Lee Lane, off Grassington Rd ℡ 3257, NW : 1 m.
🛈 High St. Car Park (summer only).
London 217 – Kendal 45 – **Leeds** 26 – Preston 36 – York 43.

  ⌂ **Highfield**, 58 Keighley Rd, BD23 2NB, ℡ 3182
  closed 1 week at Christmas and 1 January – **10 rm** ヱ 7.00/14.00 **st.**

  ✕✕ Oats, Chapel Hill, BD23 1NL, ℡ 3604 – 🅿.

SLEAFORD Lincs. **404** S 24 – pop. 7,880 – ECD : Thursday – ☎ 0529.
See : St. Denis' Church* 12C-15C.
◫ South Rauceby ℡ 052 98 (South Rauceby) 273 W : 1 m. on A 153.
London 119 – Leicester 45 – Lincoln 17 – Nottingham 39.

  ⚓ **Lion**, 7 Northgate, NG34 7BH, ℡ 302127 – 🅿
  M a la carte 2.25/4.00 **st.** ▯ 1.25 – **10 rm** ヱ 10.00/13.50 **st.** – P 16.00 **st.**

  ⚓ **White Hart**, 32 Southgate, NG34 7RY, ℡ 303120 – 🛏wc 🅿. 🖭 🄰🄴 ⑩ *VISA*
  M 3.25 **s.** ▯ 1.40 – **17 rm** ヱ 8.00/14.00.

AUSTIN-MORRIS-MG-ROVER-TRIUMPH Carre St. ℡ SAAB-LOTUS North Gate ℡ 302728
303034   TALBOT Boston Rd ℡ 302518
COLT Holdingham ℡ 302545   VAUXHALL 50 Westgate ℡ 2919
FORD London Rd ℡ 302921

SLOUGH Berks. **404** S 29 – pop. 87,075 – ECD : Wednesday – ☎ 0753.
Envir. : Eton (college**) S : 2 m.
◪ Wexham Park, ℡ Fulmer 3271, N : 2 m.
London 29 – Oxford 39 – Reading 19.

  Holiday Inn, Ditton Rd, Langley, SL3 8PT, SE : 2 ½ m. on A 4 ℡ 44244, Telex 267396,
  ✕, 🖭 – 🛗 ☒ 🕭 🅿. ♨. 🖭 🄰🄴 ⑩ *VISA*
  M 6.00/10.00 **st.** ▯ 1.80 – ヱ 3.00 – **239 rm** 23.50/29.00 **s.**

AUSTIN-MORRIS-MG-WOLSELEY Petersfield Av. ℡ 23031 FORD Petersfield Av. ℡ 36111
AUSTIN-MORRIS-MG-ROVER-TRIUMPH 57 Farnham Rd VAUXHALL 134 Bath Rd ℡ 24581
℡ 24001   VW, AUDI-NSU Colnbrook-By-Pass ℡ 028 12
DAF Beaconsfield Rd ℡ 028 14 (Farnham Common) 2301 (Colnbrook) 2708

SMALL DOLE West Sussex 404 T 31 – pop. 3,903 – ✉ Henfield – ◔ 0903 Steyning.
London 49 – Brighton 13 – Horsham 13 – Worthing 11.

  XX Golding Barn, Henfield Rd, BN5 9XH; S : 1 m. on A 2037, ☏ 813344. 🛉 – 🅿.

SMETHWICK West Midlands 403 404 O 26 – see Birmingham.

SNAINTON North Yorks. – pop. 652 – ECD : Wednesday – ✉ ◔ 0723 Scarborough.
London 240 – Scarborough 10 – York 29.

  🏠 Coachman Inn, YO13 9PL, ☏ 85231 – 🛏wc 🛗wc 🅿. 🔳 VISA
    M 5.00/7.50 t. 🍶 1.75 – **12 rm** ⇌ 13.00/27.00 t.

SNOWDON (YR WYDDFA) Gwynedd 403 H 24.
See: Ascent and ❊*** (1 h 15 mn from Llanberis (Pass**) by Snowdon Mountain Railway *AC*),

    Hotels see : S : Beddgelert
          Caernarfon NW: 9 m.

SOLIHULL West Midlands 403 404 O 26 – pop. 107,095 – ECD : Wednesday – ◔ 021
Birmingham.
🛈 Stratford Rd ☏ 744 6001.
🎫 Library Theatre Box Office, Homer Rd ☏ 705 0060.
London 109 – Birmingham 7 – Coventry 13 – Warwick 13.

  🏨 George (Embassy), The Square, B91 3RF, ☏ 704 1241 – 📺 🅿. 🛗. 🔳 AE ⓘ VISA
    closed 24 December-1 January – **M** 4.75/5.75 st. 🍶 1.65 – **47 rm** ⇌ 13.00/22.00 st.

  🏨 St. Johns, 651 Warwick Rd, B91 1AT, ☏ 705 6777, Telex 339352 – 🛗 📺 🛏wc 🕿 🅿.
    🛗. 🔳 AE ⓘ VISA
    M 3.70/5.25 st. – **218 rm** ⇌ 21.50/27.00 st. – P 19.00/22.00 st.

    at Monkspath Street SW: 2 m. on A 34 – ✉ Solihull – ◔ 021 Birmingham :

  X La Villa Bianca, 1036 Stratford Rd, B90 4EE, ☏ 744 7232, Italian rest. – 🅿.

AUSTIN-DAIMLER-JAGUAR-MORRIS-MG-ROVER-
TRIUMPH Stratford Rd, Shirley ☏ 744 4405
AUSTIN-MORRIS-MG-WOLSELEY 707 Warwick Rd ☏
705 3028
BMW Shirley ☏ 744 4488

FORD 361/369 Stratford Rd ☏ 744 4456
HONDA Station Lane ☏ 056 43 (Lapworth) 2933
RENAULT Stratford Rd, Hockley Heath ☏ 056 43 (Lap-
worth) 2244
TALBOT 386 Warwick Rd ☏ 704 1427

Questa guida non è un repertorio di tutti gli alberghi e ristoranti,
nè comprende tutti i buoni alberghi e ristoranti di Gran Bretagna ed Irlanda.

Nell'intento di tornare utili a tutti i turisti,
siamo indotti ad indicare esercizi
di tutte le classi ed a citarne soltanto un certo numero di ognuna.

SOMERTON Somerset 403 L 30 – pop. 3,267 – ◔ 0458.
London 137 – Exeter 52 – Southampton 74 – Taunton 17.

  🏨 Red Lion, Broad St., TA11 7NJ, ☏ 72339, Telex 46240 – 📺 🛏wc 🕿 🅿. 🛗. 🔳 AE
    ⓘ VISA
    M 2.50/5.50 🍶 1.50 – ⇌ 1.50 – **16 rm** 15.00/21.00 st.

SOMPTING West Sussex 404 S 31 – see Worthing.

SONNING-ON-THAMES Berks. 404 R 29 – pop. 1,469 – ECD : Wednesday – ◔ 0734 Reading.
London 48 – Reading 4.

  🏨 White Hart, Thames St., RG4 0UT, ☏ 692277, ≼ « Rose gardens on river bank » –
    🛏wc 🕿 🅿. 🔳 AE ⓘ VISA
    M a la carte 9.75/12.40 st. 🍶 3.50 – **17 rm** ⇌ 26.75/40.00 st.

  XXX French Horn with rm, RG4 0TN, ☏ 692204, ≼ river Thames and gardens, 🛉 – 📺
    🛏wc 🅿. AE ⓘ
    closed Good Friday and 26 December – **M** a la carte 10.00/18.40 st. – **5 rm** ⇌ 40.00 st.

SOURTON Devon 403 H 31 – pop. 348 – ✉ Okehampton – ◔ 083 786 Bridestowe.
London 228 – Exeter 27 – Plymouth 26.

  X Bearslake Farm, EX24 2HQ, S: ¾ m. on A 386, ☏ 334 – 🅿.

SOUTHAM Glos. 403 404 N 28 – see Cheltenham.

See : Docks* – Tudor House Museum* (16C) *AC* AZ M[1] – God's House Tower* 12C (Museum of Archaeologia) AZ M[2]. **Envir. :** Netley (abbey* ruins 13C) *AC*, SE: 3 m. BZ A.

📍 Stoneham ☏ 768151, N: 2m. BY – 📍 West Side Basset Av. ☏ 68407 AY. – 📍 Fleming Park ☏ 0703 (Eastleigh) 612797, N: 6 m. by A 33 AY.

✈ Southampton Airport: ☏ 0703 (Eastleigh) 612341, N: 4 m. BY.

⛴ Shipping connections with the Continent: to Cherbourg (Townsend Thoresen) – to Le Havre (Townsend Thoresen and P & O Ferries: Normandy Ferries) – to the Isle of Wight: Cowes (Red Funnel Services) Monday/Saturday 14-16 daily; Sunday 7-11 daily (55 mn to 1 h 10 mn).

⛴ to the Isle of Wight: Cowes (Red Funnel Services: hydrofoil) Monday/Saturday 10-12 daily; Sunday 5-11 daily (20 mn) and (Solent Seaspeed) frequent services (20 mn).

🛈 Canute Rd (opposite Dock Gate 3) ☏ 20438 – The Precinct, Above Bar St. ☏ 23855.

London 84 – Bristol 76 – Plymouth 148.

Plans on following pages

🏨 **Polygon** (T.H.F.), Cumberland Pl., SO9 4GD, ☏ 26401, Telex 47175 – 🛗 📺 🅿. ⚗. 🔊. AE ⓪ *VISA*   AZ **n**
M 5.25/5.95 **st.** ◊ 1.80 – ⬕ 2.50 – **120 rm** 20.50/27.50 **st.**

🏨 **Dolphin** (T.H.F.), 35 High St., SO9 2DS, ☏ 26178 – 🛗 📺 🛏wc 🕾 🅿. ⚗. 🔊 AE ⓪ *VISA*   AZ **i**
M 4.25/4.75 **st.** ◊ 1.80 – ⬕ 2.25 – **72 rm** 17.00/23.50 **st.**

🏨 **Post House** (T.H.F.), Herbert Walker Av., SO1 0HJ, ☏ 28081, Telex 477368, ⤝, 🏊 heated – 🛗 📺 🛏wc 🕾 ♿ 🅿. ⚗. 🔊 AE ⓪ *VISA*   AZ **o**
M 4.00/4.70 **st.** ◊ 1.85 – ⬕ 2.25 – **132 rm** 18.00/25.50 **st.**

🏨 **Cotswold** ·(Best Western), 119 Highfield Lane, Portswood Junction, SO9 1YQ, ☏ 559555, Telex 477476 – 🛗 📺 🛏wc 🕾 🅿. ⚗. 🔊 AE ⓪ *VISA*   BY **e**
closed 25 and 26 December – M 5.60/5.80 **st.** ◊ 2.60 – **80 rm** ⬕ 17.75/27.50 **st.**

🏨 **Royal**, Cumberland Pl., SO9 4NY, ☏ 23467, Telex 47388 – 🛗 🛏wc. ⚗. 🔊 AE *VISA*   AZ **c**
M 3.10/4.40 **st.** ◊ 2.00 – **100 rm** ⬕ 12.75/24.50 **st.**

🏨 **Wessex**, 66-68 Northlands Rd, SO1 2LH, ☏ 31744, ⇌ – 🕾 🅿. 🔊   AY **r**
M 2.00/2.50 ◊ 1.65 – **38 rm** ⬕ 11.00/17.60 **t.**

🏠 **Earley House**, 46 Pear Tree Av., Bitterne, SO2 7JP, ☏ 448117 – 🅿   BY **v**
9 rm ⬕ 8.00/16.00 **t.**

🏠 **Elizabeth House**, 43-44 The Avenue, SO1 2SX, ☏ 24327 – 🅿   AY **e**
closed 20 October-10 December and 23 to 28 December – **17 rm** ⬕ 8.50/17.00 **st.**

🏠 **Rosida**, 25-27 Hill Lane, SO1 5AB, ☏ 28501, 🏊 heated – 🅿   AZ **s**
36 rm ⬕ 8.00/14.00 **t.**

✗✗ **Olliver's**, 23 Ordnance Rd, off London Rd, SO1 2BA, ☏ 24789 – 🅿. 🔊 AE ⓪ *VISA*   AZ **e**
closed Saturday lunch and Sunday – M 4.75/5.95 ◊ 1.75.

✗✗ **London Steak House**, Civic Centre Rd, SO1 0FL, ☏ 24394 – 🔊 AE ⓪ *VISA*   AZ **u**
closed 25-26 December and 1 January – M a la carte 4.85/8.55 **t.** ◊ 1.80.

at North Baddesley N: 5 ¼ m. on A 27 – AY – ✉ North Baddesley – ☎ 0703 Southampton :

✗✗ **Hugo's**, 72 Botley Rd, SO2 5XB, ☏ 732377 – 🅿. 🔊 AE ⓪ *VISA*
closed Sunday and Monday – M a la carte 5.70/18.70 **t.** ◊ 2.55.

MICHELIN Branch, Solent Industrial Estate, Shamblehurst Lane, Hedge End, SO3 2FQ, ☏ 048 92 (Botley) 2381.

AUSTIN-MG The Causeway ☏ 042 16 (Totton) 5021
AUSTIN-MG-WOLSELEY 170 Portsmouth Rd ☏ 447761
AUSTIN-MORRIS-MG-WOLSELEY The Avenue ☏ 28801
AUSTIN-MG-WOLSELEY 102 High Rd ☏ 554346
AUSTIN-DAIMLER-JAGUAR-MORRIS-MG-WOLSELEY, ROLLS ROYCE The Avenue ☏ 28811
BMW Dorset St. ☏ 29003
CITROEN Northam Bridge ☏ 26907
COLT, DAF, SKODA 30/38 Bellemoor Rd ☏ 773088
DAIMLER-JAGUAR-ROVER-TRIUMPH Marsh Lane ☏ 30911
DATSUN, JENSEN 234 Winchester Rd ☏ 778316
DATSUN 21/23 St. Denys Rd ☏ 559533

FIAT 115/125 Lodge Rd ☏ 25518
FORD 362/364 Shirley Rd ☏ 775331
FORD Palmerston Rd ☏ 28331
MERCEDES-BENZ 110/112 Lodge Rd ☏ 22828
MORRIS-MG-WOLSELEY High St., West End ☏ 042 18 (West End) 3773
OPEL 14 Park St. ☏ 771929
PEUGEOT Winchester Rd, Shirley ☏ 771899
RENAULT 8/18 Cobden Av., Bitterne Park ☏ 555771
TALBOT Southampton Rd ☏ 042 127 (Cadnam) 2250
TALBOT Portswood Rd ☏ 559902
TOYOTA 159 Bitterne Rd ☏ 25466
VAUXHALL Portsmouth Rd, Sholing ☏ 449232
VOLVO Millbrook Roundabout ☏ 777616

SOUTHBOROUGH Kent 404 U 30 – see Royal Tunbridge Wells.

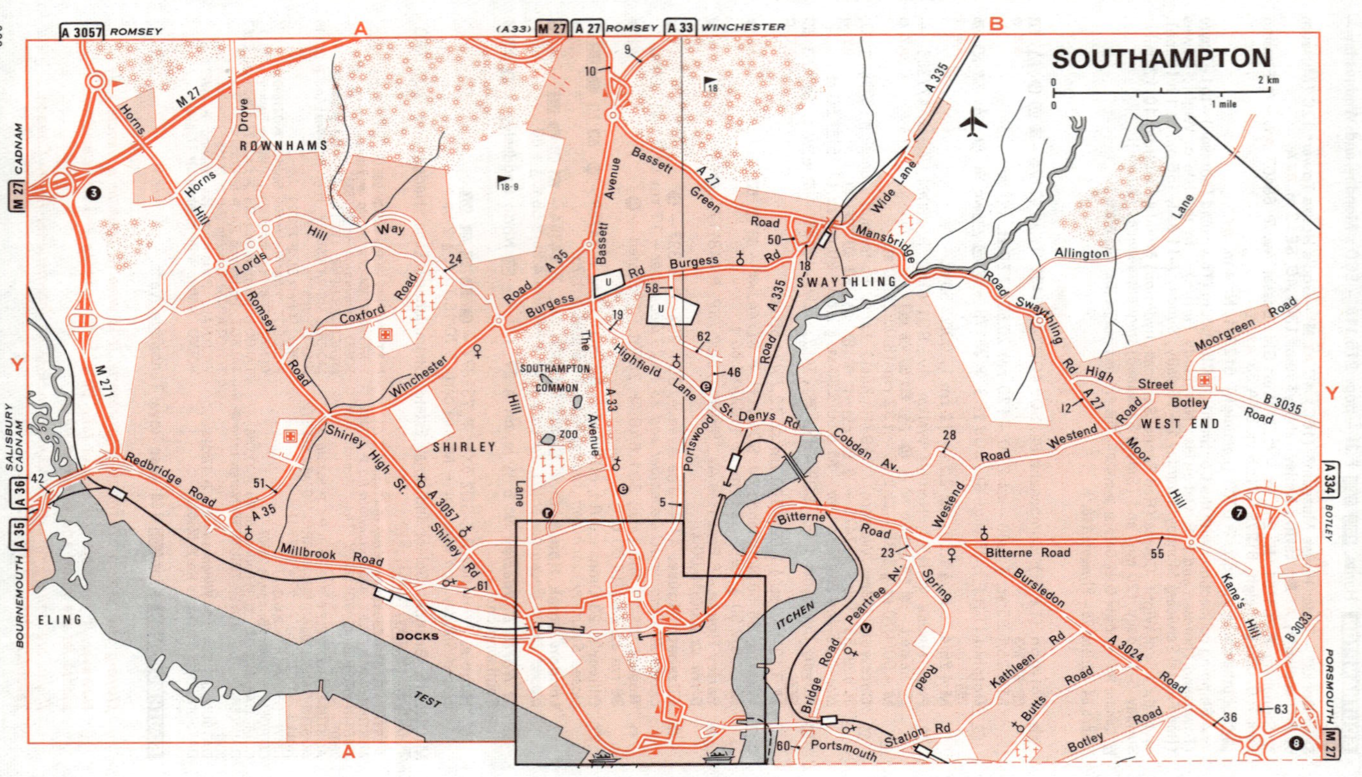
SOUTHAMPTON
2 km
1 mile
A 3057 ROMSEY
(A33) M 27 A 27 ROMSEY A 33 WINCHESTER
A 334 BOTLEY
PORSMOUTH M 27
B 3035
B 3033
A 335
M 27
CADNAM
M 27
Horns
M 271
Horns Hill
Drove
ROWNHAMS
18·9
18
9
10
Hill
Way
Lords
Coxford Road
Winchester Road
Romsey Road
Bassett Avenue
A 27
Bassett Green
Road
50
Burgess Rd
U Rd
58
U
19
62
46
Bassett
A 35
The Avenue
A 33
Highfield Lane
Burgess Road
SOUTHAMPTON COMMON
ZOO
Hill
Lane
Portswood
St. Denys Rd
A 335
Road
18
SWAYTHLING
Mansbridge
Wide Lane
Allington Lane
Swaythling Rd High
12
A 27
Street
Botley
WEST END
Moor
Moorgreen Road
Hill
Cobden Av.
28
Westend Road
Westend Road
Bitterne
Bitterne Road
23
Peartree Av.
Spring Road
Bridge Road
Kathleen Rd
Butts Road
Botley Road
A 3024 Road
Bursledon
Kane's Hill
55
7
36
63
8
SHIRLEY
Shirley High St.
A 3057
51
Shirley Rd
61
Millbrook Road
A 35
Redbridge Road
42
A 36
A 35
SALISBURY CADNAM
BOURNEMOUTH
Y
ELING
DOCKS
TEST
ITCHEN
Station Rd
60 Portsmouth
5
392

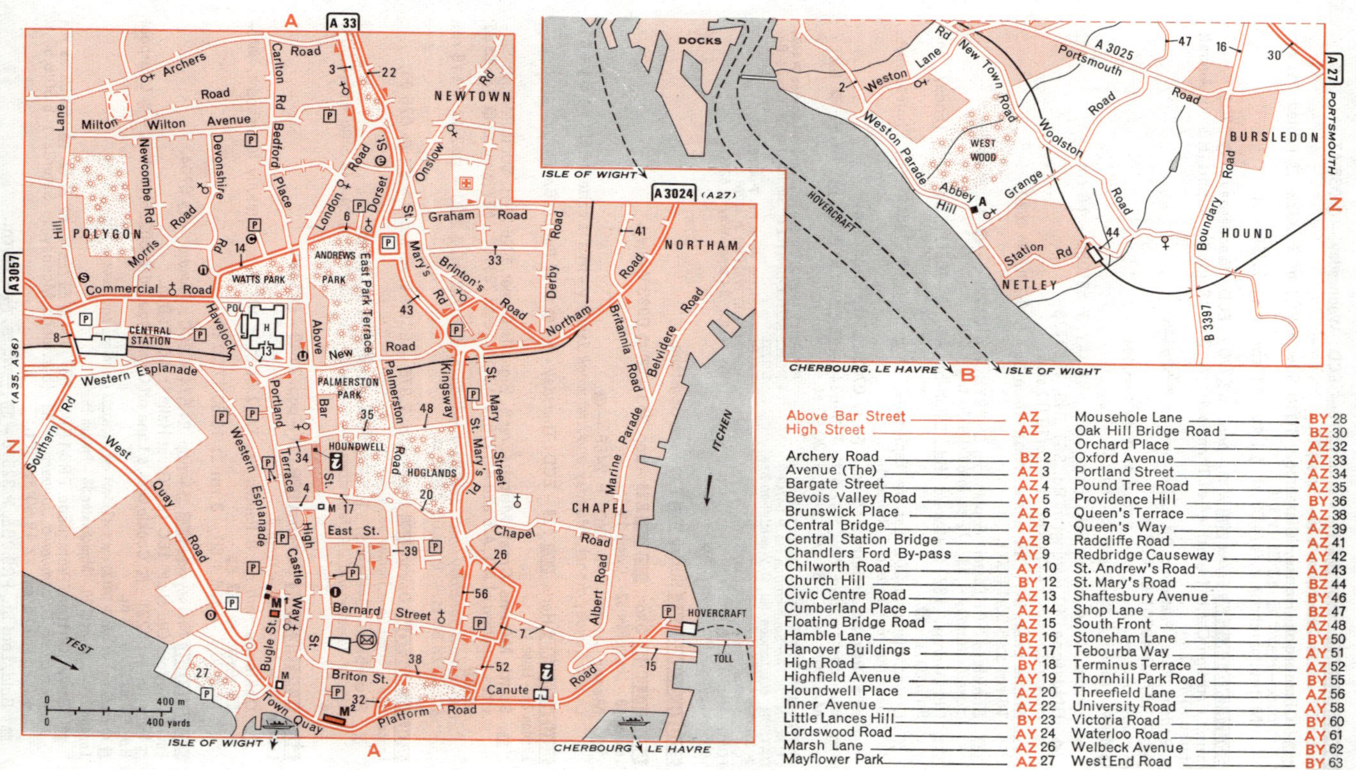

A 33
NEWTOWN
Archers Road
Carlton Rd
Milton Lane
Wilton Avenue
Newcombe Rd
Devonshire Rd
Bedford Place
Morris Road
POLYGON
Hill
Onslow St.
Dorset St.
Graham Road
Brinton's Rd
Derby Road
NORTHAM
London Road
ANDREWS PARK
East Park Terrace
St. Mary's Rd
Northam Road
Britannia Road
Marine Parade
Belvidere Road
A 3024 (A27)
DOCKS
ISLE OF WIGHT
A 27
PORTSMOUTH
A 3025
Weston Lane
Rd New Town Road
WEST WOOD
Weston Parade
Abbey Hill
Grange
Woolston Road
Station Rd
NETLEY
BURSLEDON
HOUND
Boundary Road
B 3397
HOVERCRAFT
CHERBOURG, LE HAVRE
ISLE OF WIGHT
B
A 3057
Commercial Road
WATTS PARK
Havelock
CENTRAL STATION
POL
Western Esplanade
Southern Rd
West Quay Road
TEST
400 m
400 yards
Palmerston Park
Above Bar
New Road
Portland Terrace
Western Esplanade
HOUNDWELL
High St.
Castle Way
Bugle St.
Town Quay
ISLE OF WIGHT
Bernard Street
Briton St.
Platform Road
Palmerston Road
Kingsway
St. Mary's Pl.
St. Mary Street
HOGLANDS
CHAPEL
Chapel Road
Albert Road
Canute Road
ITCHEN
HOVERCRAFT
TOLL
CHERBOURG LE HAVRE
393

Above Bar Street ____________ AZ
High Street ____________ AZ

Archery Road ____________ BZ 2
Avenue (The) ____________ AZ 3
Bargate Street ____________ AZ 4
Bevois Valley Road ____________ AY 5
Brunswick Place ____________ AZ 6
Central Bridge ____________ AZ 7
Central Station Bridge ____________ AZ 8
Chandlers Ford By-pass ____________ AY 9
Chilworth Road ____________ AY 10
Church Hill ____________ BY 12
Civic Centre Road ____________ AZ 13
Cumberland Place ____________ AZ 14
Floating Bridge Road ____________ AZ 15
Hamble Lane ____________ BZ 16
Hanover Buildings ____________ AZ 17
High Road ____________ BY 18
Highfield Avenue ____________ AY 19
Houndwell Place ____________ AZ 20
Inner Avenue ____________ AZ 22
Little Lances Hill ____________ BY 23
Lordswood Road ____________ AY 24
Marsh Lane ____________ AZ 26
Mayflower Park ____________ AZ 27

Mousehole Lane ____________ BY 28
Oak Hill Bridge Road ____________ BZ 30
Orchard Place ____________ AZ 32
Oxford Avenue ____________ AZ 33
Portland Street ____________ AZ 34
Pound Tree Road ____________ AZ 35
Providence Hill ____________ BY 36
Queen's Terrace ____________ AZ 38
Queen's Way ____________ AZ 39
Radcliffe Road ____________ AZ 41
Redbridge Causeway ____________ AY 42
St. Andrew's Road ____________ AZ 43
St. Mary's Road ____________ BZ 44
Shaftesbury Avenue ____________ BY 46
Shop Lane ____________ BZ 47
South Front ____________ AZ 48
Stoneham Lane ____________ BY 50
Tebourba Way ____________ AY 51
Terminus Terrace ____________ AZ 52
Thornhill Park Road ____________ BY 55
Threefield Lane ____________ AZ 56
University Road ____________ AY 58
Victoria Road ____________ BY 60
Waterloo Road ____________ AY 61
Welbeck Avenue ____________ BY 62
West End Road ____________ BY 63

SOUTH BRENT Devon 4️⃣0️⃣3️⃣ I 32 – pop. 1,876 – ECD: Wednesday – ✆ 036 47.
London 228 – Exeter 28 – Plymouth 16 – Torquay 17.

- 🏠 **Glazebrook House,** Glazebrook, TQ10 9JE, SW: 1 m. ☎ 3322, ⌇ heated, 🐟, 🐎,
  park – ⊟ wc 🅿. 🔲 AE ⓪ VISA
  M (buffet lunch) 2.75/4.00 **st.** ⌾ 1.45 – **11 rm** ⊏ 11.50/23.00 **t.**

SOUTHEND-ON-SEA Essex 4️⃣0️⃣4️⃣ W 29 – pop. 162,770 – ECD: Wednesday – ✆ 0702.
Envir.: Hadleigh Castle (ruins) ≼* of Thames *AC*, W: 3 m. – Southend Airport (Historic Aircraft
museum) N: 2 m.
☇ Belfairs Park, Eastwood Rd, Leigh-on-Sea ☎ 525345.
✈ ☎ (0702) 40201/6, N: 2 m.
🚉 Pier Hill ☎ 44091 – Civic Centre, Victoria Av. ☎ 49451 ext. 228.
London 41 – Cambridge 65 – Croydon 46 – **Dover 85.**

- 🏠 Haven, 32-34 Burges Rd, Thorpe Bay, SS1 3AY, ☎ 585085 – **16 rm.**
- 🏠 **Gladstone,** 40 Hartington Rd, SS1 2HS, ☎ 62776
  closed Christmas – **11 rm** ⊏ 6.75/13.00 **st.**
- 🏠 **Maple Leaf,** 9-11 Trinity Av., Westcliff-on-Sea, SS0 7PU, ☎ 46904
  16 rm ⊏ 8.00/14.60 **t.**
- ✕✕ **Schulers,** 161 Eastern Esplanade, SS1 2YB, ☎ 610172, ≼ – 🅿. 🔲 AE ⓪ VISA
  closed Monday – **M** a la carte 6.00/9.70 **t.** ⌾ 1.40.
- ✕✕ Old Vienna, 162 Eastwood Rd, Leigh-on-Sea, ☎ 76568, Dancing (Friday and
  Saturday) – 🅿.
- ✕ Chrysanthemum, 202 Eastern Esplanade, Thorpe Bay, ☎ 588162, ≼, Chinese rest.,
  Dancing (Friday and Saturday).

  at Southend Airport N: 2 m. – ✉ ✆ 0702 Southend-on-Sea:

- 🏨 **Airport,** Aviation Way, SS2 6UL, ☎ 546344 – 📺 ⊟ wc ☎ ⚕ 🅿. 🛗. 🔲 AE ⓪ VISA
  M 5.00/8.00 **t.** – **65 rm** ⊏ 22.00/30.00 **st.**

AUSTIN-MORRIS-MG Priory Crescent ☎ 67766
CITROEN 759/765 Southchurch Rd ☎ 64749
DATSUN 661 London Rd at Westcliff-on-Sea
☎ 35147
FIAT 22 Belle Vue Pl. ☎ 610482
FORD Arterial Rd ☎ 524501
LANCIA Station Rd, Thorpe Bay ☎ 588200
RENAULT 499/505 London Rd, Westcliff-on-Sea ☎ 4494
ROLLS ROYCE-BENTLEY Station Rd ☎ Thorpe Bay
582233
TALBOT 139/155 West Rd ☎ 47861
TOYOTA 57 West Rd ☎ 46288
VW, AUDI 2 Comet Way ☎ 526411

SOUTH GODSTONE Surrey 4️⃣0️⃣4️⃣ T 30 – see Godstone.

SOUTH LEIGH Oxon. 4️⃣0️⃣3️⃣ 4️⃣0️⃣4️⃣ P 28 – pop. 353 – ✉ ✆ 0993 Witney.
London 69 – Cheltenham 32 – Oxford 13.

- ✕✕ **Mason Arms,** OX8 6XQ, ☎ 2485 – 🅿
  closed Sunday dinner, Monday and first week January – **M** a la carte 4.05/9.70 **t.** ⌾ 1.65.

SOUTH MIMMS Herts. 4️⃣0️⃣4️⃣ T 28 – ECD: Thursday – ✉ ✆ 0707 Potters Bar.
London 21 – Luton 17.

- 🏨 **South Mimms Crest Motel** (Crest), Bignalls Corner, EN6 3NH, South Mimms Services, junction of A 1, A 6 and A 1178, ☎ 43311, Telex 299162 – 📺 ⊟ wc ☎ 🅿. 🛗. 🔲 AE
  ⓪ VISA
  M *(closed Saturday lunch and Bank Holidays)* 5.00/7.00 **st.** ⌾ 2.30 – ⊏ 2.40 – **115 rm**
  21.30/28.80 **st.** – P 27.00/32.00 **st.**

SOUTH MOLTON Devon 4️⃣0️⃣3️⃣ I 30 – pop. 2,875 – ECD: Wednesday – ✉ ✆ 076 95.
London 210 – Exeter 35 – Taunton 39.

- ✕ **Stumbles,** 134 East St., ☎ 3683, French rest. – 🅿. 🔲 AE VISA
  closed Sunday and 24 December for 4 weeks – **M** (buffet lunch) a la carte 4.65/6.50 **t.**
  ⌾ 1.50.

SOUTH PETHERTON Somerset 4️⃣0️⃣3️⃣ L 31 – pop. 2,549 – ✆ 0460.
London 138 – Taunton 21 – Yeovil 8.

- ✕✕ **Oaklands** with rm, 8 Palmer St., TA13 5DB, ☎ 40272, « Tastefully furnished », 🐎 –
  📺 ⊟ wc 🅿. AE ⓪
  M 5.20/7.70 **t.** ⌾ 1.80 – **3 rm** ⊏ 10.50/17.00 **t.**

SOUTHPORT Merseyside 9️⃣8️⃣6️⃣ ㉓ – pop. 84,574 – ECD: Tuesday – ✆ 0704.
Envir.: Rufford Old Hall* 15C (the Great Hall**) *AC*, E: 9 m.
☇ Park Rd ☎ 56221 – ☇ Cockle Dick's Lane off Cambridge Rd ☎ 30226, N: 1 m. – ☇ Liverpool
Rd ☎ 78092, S: 3 m.
🚉 Cambridge Arcade ☎ 33133 ext 154/40404 ext 44, 33333 (evenings and week ends).
London 221 – Liverpool 20 – Manchester 38 – Preston 19.

- 🏨 **Royal Clifton,** Promenade, PR8 1RB, ☎ 33771 – 📶 📺 ⊟ wc ☎ ⚕ 🅿. 🛗. 🔲 AE ⓪ VISA
  closed 23 December-6 January – **M** (bar lunch Monday to Saturday) 5.50/6.50 **t.**
  ⌾ 2.25 – **115 rm** ⊏ 19.50/33.00 **t.**

- 🏨 Bold, Lord St., PR9 0BE, ☎ 32578 – 📺 ⊟ wc ☎. 🛗 – **26 rm.**

🏨 Red Rum, 86-88 Lord St., PR8 1QB, ☏ 35111 – 📶 📺 🛏wc 🚿wc ☎ Ⓟ
25 rm.

XXX **Squires,** 78 King St., PR8 1LG, ☏ 30046 – 🔌 AE ⓪ VISA
closed Sunday and 2 weeks after Christmas – **M** (dinner only) a la carte 5.20/6.45 🍷 2.25.

ALFA-ROMEO, SAAB 609 Liverpool Rd ☏ 79080
AUSTIN-MG-ROVER-TRIUMPH-WOLSELEY 6/16 Roe
Lane ☏ 33555
MORRIS-MG-ROVER-TRIUMPH Regents Court Lord
St. ☏ 40616
OPEL 89/91 Bath St. North ☏ 35535

RENAULT 33 Liverpool Rd ☏ 66161
TOYOTA 205 Liverpool Rd ☏ 68515
VAUXHALL King St. ☏ 32286
VOLVO 51 Weld Rd ☏ 66613
VW, AUDI-NSU Zetland St. ☏ 31091

SOUTHSEA Hants. 403 404 Q 31 – see Portsmouth and Southsea.

SOUTH SHIELDS Tyne and Wear 986 ⑲ – pop. 100,659 – ECD: Wednesday – ☎ 0632.
🏌 Cleadon Hill ☏ 560475, Hillcrest, off the Lonnen.
🛈 South Foreshore, Sea Rd ☏ 557411 (summer only).
London 284 – Newcastle-upon-Tyne 9 – Sunderland 6.

🏨 Sea (Swallow), Sea Rd, NE33 2LD, ☏ 566227, Group Telex 53168 – 📺 🛏wc 🚿wc ☎
Ⓟ. ⚓
25 rm.

AUSTIN-MG-ROVER-TRIUMPH Burrow St. ☏ 62451
TALBOT, DAF St. Hilda St. ☏ 553234

VAUXHALL Ineary St. ☏ 568827

SOUTH WALSHAM Norfolk 404 X 26 – ✉ Norwich – ☎ 060 549.
London 120 – Great Yarmouth 11 – Norwich 9.

🏨 **South Walsham Hall H. and Country Club** ⏎, The Street, NR13 6DQ, ☏ 378, ⬉,
🏊 heated, 🌳, park – 📺 🛏wc 🚿 Ⓟ. 🔌 AE VISA
M *(closed 3 weeks from mid October)* (dinner only and Sunday lunch) a la carte 5.50/
9.30 **t.** 🍷 1.85 – **8 rm** ☕ 22.50/32.00 **st.**

SOUTHWELL Notts. 403 404 R 24 – pop. 5,129 – ECD: Thursday – ☎ 0636.
See: Minster* 12C-13C (Chapter house: foliage carving** 13C).
🏌 at Oxton ☏ 060 744 (Woodborough) 3545, SW: 4 m.
London 135 – Lincoln 24 – Nottingham 14 – Sheffield 34.

🏨 Saracen's Head (Anchor), Market Pl., NG25 0HE, ☏ 812701, Group Telex 858875 – 📺
🛏wc ☎ Ⓟ. ⚓. 🔌 AE ⓪ VISA
23 rm ☕ 18.50/27.00 **st.**

AUSTIN-MG King St. ☏ 812146

SOUTHWOLD Suffolk 404 Z 27 – pop. 1,998 – ECD: Wednesday – ☎ 0502.
🛈 Town Hall, Market Pl. ☏ 722366.
London 108 – Great Yarmouth 24 – Ipswich 35 – Norwich 34.

🏨 Swan, Market Pl., IP18 6EG, ☏ 722186, 🌳 – 📶 📺 🛏wc ☎ Ⓟ. 🔌 AE ⓪ – **52 rm.**
🏨 **Crown,** High St., IP18 6DP, ☏ 722275 – 🛏wc Ⓟ
M 4.30/5.15 **t.** 🍷 2.30 – **24 rm** ☕ 10.40/22.90 **t.** – P 16.90/19.10 **t.**
🏨 Pier Avenue, Station Rd, IP18 6AY, ☏ 722632 – 📺 🛏wc 🚿wc Ⓟ
12 rm.

✗ **Dutch Barn,** Ferry Rd, IP18 6HQ, ☏ 723172 – Ⓟ. 🔌 AE
closed Sunday dinner and Monday – **M** a la carte 6.35/8.30 🍷 1.15.

PEUGEOT Station Rd ☏ 722125

SOUTH ZEAL Devon 403 I 31 – ECD: Thursday – ✉ Okehampton – ☎ 083 784 Sticklepath.
London 218 – Exeter 17 – Plymouth 36 – Torquay 27.

🏨 **Oxenham Arms,** EX20 2JT, ☏ 244, « 12C inn », 🌳 – 🛏wc Ⓟ. 🔌 AE ⓪
M 4.50/6.50 **t.** 🍷 1.95 – **9 rm** ☕ 11.70/20.00 **t.**

SPALDING Lincs. 404 T 25 – pop. 15,850 – ECD: Thursday – ☎ 0775.
See: Parish church* 13C – Ayscoughfee Hall* 15C.
🏌 Surfleet ☏ 077 585 (Surfleet) 386, N: 4 m. off A 16.
🛈 Ayscoughfee Hall, Churchgate ☏ 5468.
London 106 – Leicester 51 – Lincoln 44 – Nottingham 54.

🏨 **White Hart** (T.H.F.), Market Pl., PE11 1SU, ☏ 5668 – 📺 🛏wc ☎ Ⓟ. ⚓. 🔌 AE ⓪ VISA
M 3.70/4.80 **st.** 🍷 1.65 – **28 rm** ☕ 13.50/21.00 **st.**

XX Cley Hall, 22 High St., PE11 1TX, ☏ 5157, 🌳 – Ⓟ.
✗ **Isobel's Pantry,** 4 Church Gate, PE11 2PB, ☏ 2193 – Ⓟ. 🔌 ⓪ VISA
closed Sunday, Monday and 1 to 14 August – **M** a la carte 3.70/6.35 🍷 1.30.

SPALDING

AUSTIN-MORRIS-MG Whaplode Drive ℡ 265
AUSTIN-MORRIS-MG-ROVER-TRIUMPH-WOLSELEY
Pinchbeck Rd ℡ 3651
DAF, VOLVO High Rd ℡ 040 66 (Moulton) 307
FIAT Albion St. ℡ 4445

FORD St. Johns Rd ℡ 3671
PEUGEOT ℡ 3033
RENAULT 24/40 Commercial Rd ℡ 3991
TALBOT Swan St. ℡ 2893
VAUXHALL Pinchbeck Rd ℡ 3391

SPELDHURST Kent **404** U 30 – see Royal Tunbridge Wells.

SPROTBROUGH South Yorks. **403** **404** Q 23 – see Doncaster.

STAFFORD Staffs. **403** **404** N 25 – pop. 55,001 – ECD: Wednesday – ☎ 0785.
See: High House* 16C – St. Mary's Church (Norman font*). **Envir.** : Eccleshall (Parish church*
12C) NW: 7 m.
🛈 Civic offices, Riverside ℡ 3181.

London 142 – Birmingham 26 – Derby 32 – Shrewsbury 31 – **Stoke-on-Trent 17.**

  🏨 **Tillington Hall,** Eccleshall Rd, ST16 1JJ, NW: 1 ½ m. on A 5013 ℡ 53531, Telex 36566 –
     🕃 📺 ⛱wc ☎ ♿ 🅿. ⛱. 🔲 AE ⓪ VISA
     M 4.00/4.50 **st.** 🍷 1.55 – **76 rm** ⚏ 20.25/25.50 **st.** – P 28.75 **st.**

  🏠 Vine, Salter St., ST16 2JU, ℡ 51071 – 🅿 – **24 rm.**

  🏠 Swan, 46 Greengate St., ST16 2JA, ℡ 58142 – 🅿 – **30 rm.**

  ♁ **Romaline,** 73 Wolverhampton Rd, ST17 4AW, ℡ 54100 – 🅿. 🔲 ⓪
     closed 25 and 26 December – **14 rm** ⚏ 8.00/15.95 **st.**

     at Ranton W: 7 ¼ m. by A 518 – ✉ Ranton – ☎ 078 575 Seighford:

  XX **Yew Tree,** Long Compton, ST18 9JT, S: 1 m. ℡ 278, ≼, 🐎 – 🅿. 🔲 AE ⓪ VISA
     closed Sunday dinner – **M** a la carte 3.70/6.75 🍷 1.85.

AUSTIN-DAIMLER-JAGUAR-MG-ROVER-TRIUMPH
Lichfield Rd ℡ 51366
BMW, VAUXHALL Walton-on-the-Hill ℡ 661293
DATSUN Wolverhampton Rd ℡ 42407
FORD Eccleshall Rd ℡ 51331
MORRIS-MG-PRINCESS Friars Terrace ℡ 3131

MORRIS-MG-ROVER-TRIUMPH Silkmore Lane ℡ 56111
OPEL Sandon Rd ℡ 51641
PEUGEOT Newport Rd ℡ 51084
RENAULT Wolverhampton Rd ℡ 52118
SAAB Yarlet Bank Sce Sta. ℡ 088 97 (Sandon) 248
TALBOT Milford ℡ 661226

STAINES Surrey **404** S 29 – pop. 56,712 – ECD: Thursday – ☎ 0784.
🛉18 Laleham Reach, Chertsey ℡ 093 28 (Chertsey) 62188, S: 2 m.

London 26 – Reading 25.

  🏠 Pack Horse (Anchor), Thames St., TW18 4SF, ℡ 54221, Group Telex 858875, ≼ – 📺 ☎
     🅿. ⛱ – **14 rm.**

  XX **Swan** with rm, The Hythe, TW18 3JB, ℡ 52494, ≼ – 🅿. 🔲 AE ⓪ VISA
     M *(closed Saturday lunch and Sunday dinner)* a la carte 4.95/8.85 **t.** – **7 rm** ⚏ 11.50/
     14.65 **st.**

AUSTIN-DAIMLER-MORRIS-MG-ROVER-TRIUMPH-
WOLSELEY, TALBOT 48-54 London Rd ℡ 55301

BRITISH LEYLAND 30-38 Church St. ℡ 55281

STAINTON Cumbria – pop. 500 – ✉ ☎ 0768 Penrith.
London 291 – Carlisle 25 – Keswick 16.

  ♁ **Limes Country** ⑤, Redhills, CA11 0DT, S: 1 m. off A 592 ℡ 63343, ≼, 🐎 – 🅿
     closed 1 week November – **8 rm** ⚏ 7.00/11.50.

STALISFIELD GREEN Kent **404** W 30 – see Ashford.

STAMFORD Lincs. **404** S 26 – pop. 14,662 – ECD: Thursday – ☎ 0780.
See: Burghley House** 16C (paintings : Heaven Room***) *AC.*
🛉18 Luffenham ℡ 720 205, W: 5 m.
🛈 Council Offices, St. Mary's Hill ℡ 4444.

London 92 – Leicester 31 – Lincoln 50 – **Nottingham 45.**

  🏨 **George,** 71 St. Martins, PE9 2LB, ℡ 2101, « 17C coaching inn with walled monastic
     garden » – 📺 🅿. ⛱. 🔲 AE ⓪ VISA
     M a la carte 7.20/9.60 **s.** 🍷 2.60 – **47 rm** ⚏ 15.00/26.00 **st.**

  🏠 **Crown,** All Saints Sq., PE9 2AG, ℡ 3136 – 📺 ⛱wc 🛁wc 🅿. 🔲 AE VISA
     M 3.75/5.00 **s.** 🍷 1.50 – **19 rm** ⚏ 11.00/18.00 **s.**

  XX **Candlesticks,** 1 Church Lane, PE9 3PQ, ℡ 4033 – 🔲 VISA
     closed Monday – **M** 5.60 🍷 1.50.

  XX **Royal,** 8 St. Paul's St., PE9 2BE, ℡ 52505 – ⓪ VISA
     closed Saturday lunch, Sunday, Christmas and Bank Holidays – **M** a la carte 4.80/8.35
     🍷 2.25.

     at Collyweston SW: 3 ¾ m. on A 43 – ✉ Stamford – ☎ 078 083 Duddington:

  ♔ **Cavalier,** Main St., PE9 3PQ, ℡ 288 – 📺 🅿
     M a la carte 4.70/8.60 – **6 rm** ⚏ 8.05/13.80.

AUSTIN-MORRIS-MG 36/40 St. Pauls St. ☏ 3174
FORD, ROVER-TRIUMPH Wharf Rd ☏ 2561
PEUGEOT 53/56 Scotgate ☏ 4003

TALBOT 69 Scotgate ☏ 3323
TOYOTA Collyweston ☏ 078 083 (Duddington) 271
VAUXHALL Rock House, Scotgate ☏ 51826

STANDISH Lancs. 🅶🅸🅸 ⑤ – pop. 11,174 – ECD : Wednesday – ✉ Wigan – ☎ 0257.
London 210 – Liverpool 22 – Manchester 21 – Preston 15.

🏨 **Cassinelli's Almond Brook Motor Inn,** Almond Brook Rd, WN6 0SR, W : 1 m. on
B 5239 ☏ 421504 – 📺 🚿wc 🛁wc ☎ 🚗 Ⓟ. 🏊. 🔼 ⒶⒺ ⑩ *VISA*
M 3.00/5.50 **st.** ⓧ 1.60 – **37 rm** 🍽 15.50/22.50 **st.** – P 24.00/30.00 **st.**

STANFORD LE HOPE Essex 🅐🅞🅐 V 29 – pop. 15,447 – ECD : Wednesday – ☎ 037 56.
London 27 – Southend-on-Sea 14 – Tilbury 7.

↑ Homesteads, 216 Southend Rd, SS17 7AQ, ☏ 2372
9 rm.

STANTON WICK Avon 🅐🅞🅐 🅐🅞🅐 M 29 – pop. 700 – ✉ Pensford – ☎ 076 18 Compton Dando.
London 129 – Bath 10 – Bristol 8 – Taunton 41.

✗ **Carpenters Arms,** BS18 4BX, off A 368 ☏ 202 – Ⓟ. 🔼 ⒶⒺ ⑩ *VISA*
M a la carte 5.50/10.00 **t.** ⓧ 2.00.

STAVERTON Devon 🅐🅞🅐 I 32 – pop. 551 – ✉ Totnes – ☎ 080 426.
London 226 – Exeter 26 – Plymouth 24 – Torquay 13.

♨ **Sea Trout Inn,** TQ9 6PA, ☏ 274, 🚗 – Ⓟ. 🔼 ⑩ *VISA*
M 4.50/9.00 ⓧ 1.75 – **6 rm** 🍽 10.50/25.00 **st.**

STEETON North Yorks. – ✉ Keighley – ☎ 0535.
London 217 – Bradford 13 – Skipton 6.5.

✗✗ **Currergate** with rm, Skipton Rd, BD20 6PE, ☏ 53204, Italian rest., 🚗 – 🚿wc 🛁wc ☎
Ⓟ. 🔼 ⑩ *VISA*
M *(closed Saturday lunch, Sunday lunch and Monday)* a la carte 7.55/9.65 **s.** ⓧ 1.70 –
14 rm 🍽 13.50/22.00 **s.**

STEPPINGLEY Beds. 🅐🅞🅐 S 27 – pop. 214 – ✉ ☎ 052 57 Flitwick.
London 48 – Bedford 12 – Luton 13.

✗✗ **French Horn,** MK45 5AU, ☏ 2051 – Ⓟ. 🔼 ⒶⒺ ⑩ *VISA*
closed Sunday dinner and Monday – **M** a la carte 5.85/8.20 **t.** ⓧ 1.60.

STEVENAGE Herts. 🅐🅞🅐 T 28 – pop. 76,000 – ECD : Monday and Wednesday – ☎ 0438.
Envir. : Knebworth House (furniture*) S : 3 m.
London 36 – Bedford 25 – Cambridge 27.

🏨 Cromwell, High St., Old Town, SG1 3AZ, ☏ 59111, 🚗 – 📺 🚿wc ☎ 🚗 Ⓟ. 🏊
57 rm.

🏨 **Grampian,** The Forum, SG1 1EJ, ☏ 50661, Telex 825697 – 🛗 📺 🚿wc ☎. 🏊. 🔼 ⒶⒺ
⑩ *VISA*
M 2.25/4.50 **t.** ⓧ 1.95 – **100 rm** 🍽 19.00/23.50 **t.** – P 26.00/28.00 **t.**

at Broadwater S : 1 ½ m. on B 197 – ✉ ☎ 0438 Stevenage :

🏨 **Roebuck Inn** (T.H.F.), Old London Rd, SG2 8DS, ☏ 65444 – 📺 🚿wc ☎ Ⓟ. 🔼 ⒶⒺ ⑩
VISA
M 5.25 **st.** ⓧ 1.65 – **54 rm** 🍽 16.50/22.00 **st.**

ALFA-ROMEO, BMW, HONDA Hertford Rd, Broadwater ☏ 51565
AUSTIN-JAGUAR-MORRIS-MG-ROVER-TRIUMPH
146 High St. ☏ 2400

DATSUN Broadwater Crescent ☏ 53642
TALBOT, VW, AUDI 137 High St. ☏ 54691
VAUXHALL 124/6 High St. ☏ 51113

STEYNING West Sussex 🅐🅞🅐 T 31 – pop. 7,060 – ECD : Thursday – ☎ 0903.
See : St. Andrew's Church (the nave* 12C).
London 52 – Brighton 12 – Worthing 10.

✗✗ **Springwells** with rm, High St., BN4 3GG, ☏ 812446, 🚗 – 📺 🚿wc 🚗. ⒶⒺ ⑩ *VISA*
closed 3 weeks January – **M** a la carte 7.00/9.20 **t.** ⓧ 2.00 – **10 rm** 🍽 10.00/21.00 **st.**

AUSTIN-LAND ROVER-MORRIS-MG-RANGE ROVER-ROVER-TRIUMPH 66 High St. ☏ 812202

STINCHCOMBE Glos. 🅐🅞🅐 🅐🅞🅐 N 28 – pop. 385 – ✉ ☎ 0453 Dursley.
London 135 – Bristol 22 – Gloucester 15.

🏨 **Stinchcombe Manor** 🍃, GL11 6BQ, ☏ 2538, Telex 437193, ≼, 🚗 – 📺 🚿wc ☎ Ⓟ.
🔼 ⒶⒺ ⑩ *VISA*
M 5.00 **s.** ⓧ 1.20 – **10 rm** 🍽 12.00/22.00 **s.** – P 20.00/28.00 **s.**

STOCK Essex 404 V 29 – pop. 1,798 – ✉ Ingatestone – ☎ 0277.

London 30 – Chelmsford 6 – Southend-on-Sea 20.

XX Stockpot, 61-63 Mill Rd, CM4 9NL, ☎ 840278, 🚗 – Ⓟ.

STOCKBRIDGE Hants. 403 404 P 30 – pop. 431 – ECD: Wednesday – ☎ 026 481.

London 75 – Salisbury 14 – Winchester 9.

Carbery, Salisbury Hill, SO20 6EZ, on A 30 ☎ 771, 🏊, 🚗 – Ⓟ
closed 2 weeks at Christmas – **11 rm** 6.50/12.00 **s.**

MORRIS-MG High St. ☎ 711

SAAB Middle Wallop ☎ 026 478 (Middle Wallop) 460

STOCKPORT Greater Manchester 403 404 N 23 – pop. 139,644 – ☎ 061 Manchester.

Envir.: Lyme Park* (16C-18C) *AC*, SE: 4 ½ m.

18 Heaton Mersey ☎ 432 2134 – 18 Club House, Hazel Grove ☎ 483 3217, S: 3 m. – 18 Offerton Rd ☎ 427 2001.

ℹ 9 Princes's St. ☎ 480 0315.

London 201 – Liverpool 42 – Manchester 6 – Sheffield 37 – Stoke-on-Trent 34.

Alma Lodge (Embassy), 149 Buxton Rd, SK2 6EL, ☎ 483 4431 – TV wc ☎ Ⓟ. AE VISA
M 4.25/5.60 **st.** 2.05 – **72 rm** 17.00/22.00 **st.**

AUSTIN-MORRIS-MG-WOLSELEY 35 Buxton Rd ☎ 480 4244
AUSTIN-MORRIS-MG-PRINCESS-ROVER-TRIUMPH 91 Heaton Moor Rd ☎ 4329416
AUSTIN-MORRIS-DAIMLER-JAGUAR-ROVER-TRIUMPH Town Hall Sq. ☎ 480 7966
AUSTIN-MORRIS-MG-PRINCESS-ROVER-TRIUMPH Wellington Rd North ☎ 432 6201
BMW, HONDA, SAAB 31/33 Buxton Rd ☎ 483 6271
CITROEN 309 Manchester Rd ☎ 432 6403
DATSUN Lancashire Hill ☎ 480 4423
FIAT Heaton Lane ☎ 480 6661
FORD Adswood Rd ☎ 480 0211
RENAULT 79 Lancashire Hill ☎ 480 9528
RENAULT 57 London Rd ☎ 483 0621
TALBOT 110 Buxton Rd ☎ 480 0831
VAUXHALL Wellington Rd South ☎ 480 6146
VAUXHALL 398 Wellington Rd North ☎ 432 3232

STOCKTON-ON-TEES Cleveland 986 ⑲ – pop. 81,274 – ECD: Thursday – ☎ 0642.

18 Yarm Rd, Eaglescliffe ☎ 780098, S: 3 m.

London 251 – Leeds 61 – Middlesbrough 4.

Swallow (Swallow), 10 John Walker Sq., TS18 1AQ, ☎ 69721, Group Telex 53168 – TV ♿ Ⓟ. – **126 rm.**

at Eaglescliffe S: 3 ½ m. on A 19 – ✉ ☎ 0642 Stockton-on-Tees:

Parkmore, 636 Yarm Rd, TS16 0DH, ☎ 780324, 🚗 – wc wc Ⓟ. VISA
M *(closed lunch Saturday and Sunday)* (buffet lunch Monday to Friday) 3.50/5.50 2.20 – **32 rm** 11.00/16.50 – P 15.00/20.00.

ALFA-ROMEO Norton Av. ☎ 531127
AUSTIN-MG Bishop St. ☎ 65351
AUSTIN-JAGUAR, MORRIS-MG-ROVER-TRIUMPH 102 Yarm Lane ☎ 63161
DATSUN Yarm Lane ☎ 63421
FORD 87 Oxbridge Lane ☎ 65471
LANCIA Billingham Rd ☎ 551541
MERCEDES-BENZ 45 Norton Rd ☎ 6536
MORRIS-MG 502/6 Yarm Rd, Eaglescliffe ☎ 63513
OPEL 318 Bishopton Rd West ☎ 65007
PEUGEOT 47 Yarm Lane ☎ 62643
RENAULT Skinner St. ☎ 66681
SAAB, SUBARU Chapel St. ☎ 69781
TALBOT Church Rd ☎ 612621
TOYOTA 336 Norton Rd ☎ 553003
VAUXHALL Boathouse Lane ☎ 67804
VOLVO Prince Regent St. ☎ 63251
VW, AUDI Church Rd ☎ 65601

STOKE GABRIEL Devon 403 J 32 – see Totnes.

STOKE HOLY CROSS Norfolk 404 X 26 – see Norwich.

STOKEINTEIGNHEAD Devon 403 J 32 – see Torquay.

STOKE MANDEVILLE Bucks. 404 R 28 – see Aylesbury.

STOKE-ON-TRENT Staffs. 403 404 N 24 – pop. 265,258 – ECD: Thursday – ☎ 0782.

See: Gladstone Pottery Museum* *AC*. V **M**. **Envir.**: Little Moreton Hall** (16C) *AC*, NW: 8 m. on A 34 U.

18 Trentham Park, ☎ 657315, S: 3 m. V – 9 Biddulph Hall, Congleton ☎ 026 02 (Congleton) 3540, N: 10 m. by A 527 U.

ℹ Central Library, Bethesda St., Hanley ☎ 21242/23122.

London 161 – Birmingham 45 – Leicester 57 – Liverpool 58 – Manchester 38 – Nottingham 50 – Sheffield 60.

Plans on following pages

North Stafford (T.H.F.), Station Rd, ST4 2AE, ☎ 48501, Telex 36287 – TV Ⓟ. AE VISA X a
M 4.80/5.55 **st.** 1.65 – 2.50 – **70 rm** 18.00/24.00 **st.**

at Hanley NW: 2 m. on A 5006 – ✉ ☎ 0782 Stoke-on-Trent:

Grand, 66 Trinity St., ST1 5NB, ☎ 22361 – TV wc ☎ Ⓟ. AE VISA Y c
M 4.45/4.90 **st.** 1.65 – **96 rm** 13.00/22.00 **st.**

MICHELIN Branch, Jamage Rd, Industrial Estate, Talke Pite, ST7 1QF, ☎ 078 16 (Kidsgrove) 71211/2/3/4.

AUSTIN-MORRIS 292 Waterloo Rd, Cobridge ☎ 22210
AUSTIN-MORRIS-MG-DAIMLER-JAGUAR-ROVER-TRIUMPH, ROLLS ROYCE Victoria Rd, Fenton ☎ 48111
AUSTIN-MORRIS-MG-ROVER-TRIUMPH Clough St. ☎ 23841
AUSTIN-MORRIS-MG-ROVER-TRIUMPH Broad St. ☎ 25523
AUSTIN-MORRIS-PRINCESS 35 Lawton Rd ☎ 093 63 (Alsager) 2146
AUSTIN-MG-MORRIS Lee New Rd, Hanley ☎ 29985
AUSTIN-MORRIS-MG-PRINCESS Trentham ☎ 657348
AUSTIN-MORRIS-MG Victoria Rd ☎ 45551
BMW, FERRARI, PEUGEOT Duke St., Fenton ☎ 315119
CITROEN Uttoxeter Rd ☎ 312235

DATSUN Providence Sq. ☎ 263764
FIAT Victoria Rd, Hanley ☎ 22875
FIAT Lightwood Rd, Longton ☎ 319212
FIAT Tunstall Rd ☎ 516622
FORD Clough St. ☎ 29591
LANCIA Leek Rd, Hanley ☎ 20244
OPEL Trent Vale ☎ 613061
RENAULT Werrington Rd, Bucknall ☎ 25406
SAAB High Lane, Tunstall ☎ 84527
TALBOT Lightwood Rd ☎ 317124
TALBOT Leek Rd ☎ 24371
TALBOT Newcastle Rd ☎ 614621
TOYOTA, LADA Leek Rd, Hanley ☎ 264888
VAUXHALL, VW Victoria Rd, Fenton ☎ 46431
VW, AUDI-NSU Botteslow St., Hanley ☎ 29966

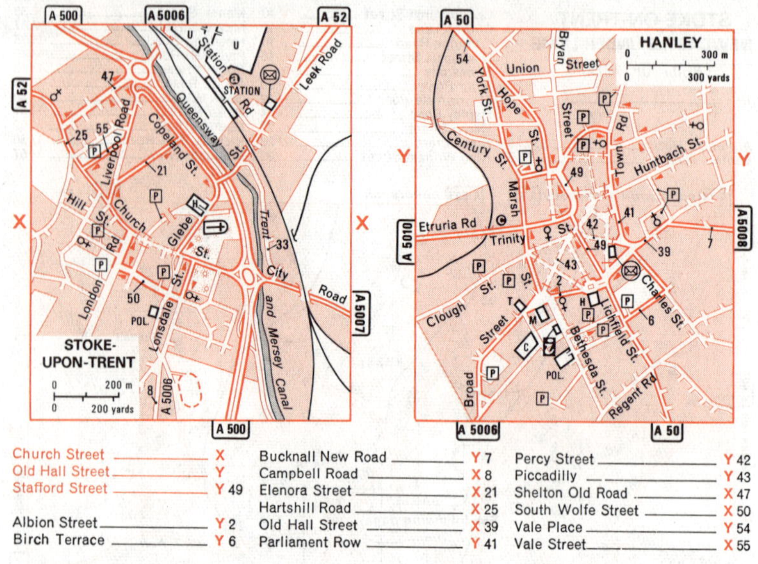

STOKESLEY Cleveland 📖 ⑲ – pop. 3,007 – ECD : Wednesday – ☎ 0642.
London 247 – Leeds 57 – Middlesbrough 9 – York 44.

  ✗ Golden Lion Inn, with rm, 27 High St. ☏ 710265 – ⇌wc ℗
15 rm.

STONE Glos. 403 404 M 29 – pop. 555 (inc. Ham) – ✉ Berkeley – ☎ 0454 Falfield.
London 130 – Bristol 17 – Gloucester 18.

  ⌂ **Elms,** GL13 9JX, ☏ 260279 – ℗
10 rm ☲ 7.00/14.00 **st.**

STONE Heref. and Worc. 403 404 N 26 – see Kidderminster.

STONE Staffs. 403 404 N 25 – pop. 11,003 – ECD : Wednesday – ☎ 078 583.
London 150 – Birmingham 36 – Stoke-on-Trent 9.

  🏨 **Crown,** High St., ST15 8AS, ☏ 3535 – 📺 ⇌wc ☏ ℗
M a la carte 6.70/8.50 **t.** –**13 rm** ☲ 15.00/26.00 **t.**

STONE CROSS East Sussex 404 U 31 – see Eastbourne.

STONEDGE Derbs. 403 404 P 24 – see Chesterfield.

STONEY CROSS Hants. 403 404 P 31 – pop. 146 – ✉ Lyndhurst – ☎ 042 127 Cadnam.
London 94 – Bournemouth 19 – Southampton 12.

  🏨 **Compton Arms,** Ringwood Rd, SO4 7GN, on A 31 ☏ 2134, ≤, 🚗 – ⇌wc ☏ ℗.
🅂 AE ⓘ VISA
M 5.00 **st.** ⌕ 2.20 – **12 rm** ☲ 12.00/21.00 **st.**

STONY STRATFORD Bucks. 404 R 27 – pop. 4.335 (inc. Calverton) – ECD : Thursday – ✉
☎ 0908 Milton Keynes.
🅸🅸 Abbey Hill ☏ 562482, S : 2 m.
London 63 – Bedford 19 – Northampton 17 – Oxford 33.

  ⚘ **Cock,** 72 High St., MK11 1AH, ☏ 562109 – ℗. 🅂 AE ⓘ VISA
closed 24 to 26 December – **M** (*closed Sunday dinner*) 6.00 **t.** ⌕ 2.00 – **15 rm** ☲ 13.00/
21.00 **st.**

  ✗✗ **Old George,** 41 High St., MK11 1AA, ☏ 562181 – 🅂 ⓘ VISA
M a la carte 5.45/8.50 **t.** ⌕ 1.50.

STORRINGTON West Sussex **404** S 31 – pop. 3,277 – ECD: Wednesday – ⊙ 090 66.
Envir. : Parham House* (Elizabethan) *AC*, W: 1 ½ m.
London 54 – Brighton 20 – Portsmouth 36 – Worthing 9.

  XX **Manley's,** Manleys Hill, RH20 4BT, ℡ 2331 – **P**. ⚑ **AE**
      closed Sunday dinner, Monday, 2 weeks from 26 December and Bank Holidays – **M** a la
      carte 7.40/10.50 **t.** ⌀ 2.25.

AUSTIN-MORRIS-MG The Square ℡ 3282

STOURBRIDGE West Midlands **403 404** N 26 – pop. 54,344 – ECD: Thursday – ⊙ 038 43.
London 147 – Birmingham 14 – Wolverhampton 10 – Worcester 21.

  🏛 Talbot, High St., DY8 1DW, ℡ 4350 – ⌱wc **P**
      21 rm.
  🏛 Bell, Market St., DY8 1DW, ℡ 5641 – ⌱ **P**
      20 rm.
  ⌂ Limes, 260 Hagley Rd, Pedmore, DY9 0RW, SE: 1 ½ m. on A 491 ℡ 056 288 (Hagley)
      2689, ⛃ – **P**
      10 rm ⚏ 9.00/15.00 **st.**

    at Kinver W: 5 ½ m. by A 458 and A 449 – ✉ Stourbridge – ⊙ 038 483 Kinver:

  XX **Whittington Inn,** DY7 6NY, E: 1 ½ m. on A 449 ℡ 2110, « Part 14C manor house »,
      ⛃ – **P**. **AE** ⓪
      closed Sunday, Monday and 2 weeks August – **M** a la carte 6.40/8.70 ⌀ 2.60.

ALFA-ROMEO, BEDFORD, VAUXHALL 131/135 Hagley
Rd, Oldswinford ℡ 3031
BRITISH LEYLAND Stourbridge Rd, Lye ℡ 038 482
(Lye) 2788
CITROEN Enville St. ℡ 77272

FORD Hagley Rd ℡ 3131
OPEL The Hayes, Lye ℡ 038 482 (Lye) 3001
PEUGEOT High St., Amblecote ℡ 3158
PORSCHE Grange Lane, Lye ℡ 038 482 (Lye) 3047/8/9
RENAULT Norton Rd ℡ 6655

STOURPORT-ON-SEVERN Heref. and Worc. **403 404** N 26 – pop. 14,230 – ECD: Wednesday –
⊙ 029 93.
🛈 The Library, Country Buildings ℡ 2866.
London 137 – Birmingham 21 – Worcester 12.

  🏛 Swan (Ansells), High St., DY13 8BX, ℡ 2050 – ⌱wc **P**. ⚑ **AE**
      M *(closed Saturday lunch and Sunday dinner)* 5.35/5.90 **t.** ⌀ 1.80 – **34 rm** ⚏ 14.45/
      18.90 **t.** – P 16.60/18.55 **t.**

FORD Vale Rd ℡ 2304

☛ *For the most up to date information*
use this year's guide.

STOW-ON-THE-WOLD Glos. **403 404** O 28 – pop. 1,737 – ECD: Wednesday – ⊙ 0451.
Envir.: Chastleton House** (Elizabethan) *AC*, NE: 8 m.
London 86 – Birmingham 44 – Gloucester 27 – Oxford 30.

  🏛🏛 **Stow Lodge,** The Square, GL54 1AB, ℡ 30485, ⛃ – 📺 ⌱wc **P**. **AE** ⓪
      March-November – **M** (bar lunch Monday to Saturday) 6.50/8.00 **st.** – **17 rm** ⚏ 32.00 **st.**
  🏛 Unicorn (Crest), Sheep St., GL54 1HQ, ℡ 30257 – ⌱wc **P**. ⚑ **AE** ⓪ **VISA**
      19 rm ⚏ 13.30/23.70 **st.**
  🏛 Talbot (Crest), The Square, GL54 1BQ, ℡ 30631 – ⌱wc **P**
      36 rm.
  🏛 Royalist, Digbeth St., GL54 1BN, ℡ 30670 – ⌱wc ⌱wc **P**. ⚑ **VISA**
      M (bar lunch) 4.50 ⌀ 1.50 – **13 rm** ⚏ 9.00/13.00.
  ♔ **King's Arms,** The Square, GL54 1AF, ℡ 30602 – **P**. ⚑ **AE** ⓪ **VISA**
      M a la carte 5.00/7.00 **t.** – **9 rm** ⚏ 10.00/20.00 **t.**
  XX **Fosse Manor** with rm, Fosse Way, GL54 1JX, S: 1 ¼ m. on A 429 ℡ 30354, ⛃ –
      ⌱wc ⌱wc **P**. **AE** ⓪ **VISA**
      M a la carte 5.00/7.55 ⌀ 2.20 – **21 rm** ⚏ 11.00/18.00.
  X **Rafters,** Park St., GL54 1AG, ℡ 30200 – ⚑ **AE** ⓪ **VISA**
      closed Sunday dinner, Monday and 3 weeks January – **M** a la carte 4.95/7.50 **st.** ⌀ 1.65.

    at Lower Slaughter SW: 3 m. off A 429 – ✉ ⊙ 0451 Bourton-on-the-Water:

  🏛🏛 Lower Slaughter Manor ⤸, ℡ 20456, « Country house atmosphere », ⚒, ⚑, ⚘, ⛃,
      park – ⌱wc **P**
      11 rm.

    at Upper Slaughter SW: 3 ¼ m. off A 436 – ✉ ⊙ 0451 Bourton-on-the-Water:

  🏛🏛 Lords of the Manor ⤸, GL54 2JD, ℡ 20243, « Country house, tasteful decor », ⚘,
      ⛃, park – ⌱wc ⚙ **P**. ⚑ **AE** ⓪ **VISA**
      M a la carte 7.35/8.70 **t.** ⌀ 2.50 – **11 rm** ⚏ 18.50/41.00 **st.**

P.T.O. ⟶

at Lower Swell W: 1 ¼ m. on A 436 – ✉ ☎ 0451 Stow-on-the-Wold:

✗ **Old Farmhouse** with rm, GL54 1LF, ☏ 30232, 🚗 – **🅿**. 🔲
closed 24 December-mid January – **M** *(closed Sunday dinner to non-residents)* (buffet lunch Monday to Friday) 6.85 **st.** 🍷 1.65 – **5 rm** 🛏 12.35/22.50 **st.**

SAAB Shepherd Way ☏ 30226

STRATFORD-UPON-AVON Warw. **403** **404** O 27 – pop. 19,452 – ECD: Thursday – ☎ 0789.
See : Shakespeare's birthplace* (16C) *AC* A **A** – Hall's Croft* (16C) *AC* A **B** – Anne Hathaway's cottage* *AC*, W: by Shottery Road **A** – Holy Trinity Church* 14C-15C **A** **D. Envir. :** Charlecote Park (castle 16C: interior*) *AC*, NE: 5 m. by B 4086 **B**.

🏌 Tiddington Rd ☏ 2669, E: by B 4086 **B**.

🛈 Judith Shakespeare House, 1 High St. ☏ 293127.

London 96 – Birmingham 23 – Coventry 18 – Oxford 40.

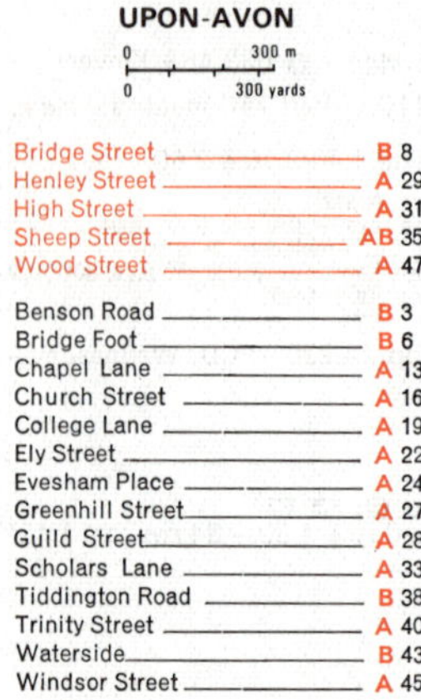

STRATFORD-UPON-AVON

Bridge Street	**B**	8
Henley Street	**A**	29
High Street	**A**	31
Sheep Street	**AB**	35
Wood Street	**A**	47
Benson Road	**B**	3
Bridge Foot	**B**	6
Chapel Lane	**A**	13
Church Street	**A**	16
College Lane	**A**	19
Ely Street	**A**	22
Evesham Place	**A**	24
Greenhill Street	**A**	27
Guild Street	**A**	28
Scholars Lane	**A**	33
Tiddington Road	**B**	38
Trinity Street	**A**	40
Waterside	**B**	43
Windsor Street	**A**	45

For maximum information from town plans : Consult the conventional signs key, p. 19.

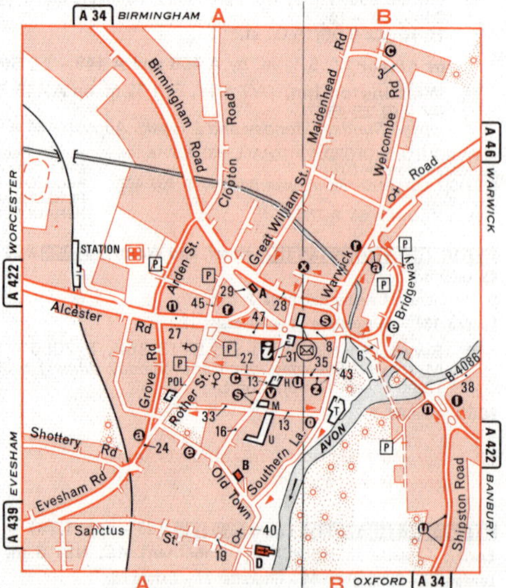

🏨 **Stratford-upon-Avon Hilton**, Bridgefoot, CV37 6YR, ☏ 67511, Telex 31127, 🚗 –
📶 📺 ♿ **🅿**. 🏊 🔲 AE ① VISA
B e
M approx. 4.65 **t.** 🍷 2.00 – 🛏 3.20 – **253 rm** 21.45/26.85 **t.**

🏨 **Welcombe** (B.T.H.) ♨, Warwick Rd, CV37 0NR, NE : 1 ½ m. on A 46 ☏ 295252,
Telex 31347, ⬅, « 19 C mansion in own grounds », 🏌, 🚗, park – 📺 ♿ **🅿**. 🏊 🔲 AE
① VISA
on A 46 **B**
M 6.50/7.50 **st.** 🍷 2.40 – **85 rm** 🛏 31.00/49.00 **st.**

🏨 **Shakespeare** (T.H.F.), Chapel St., CV37 6ER, ☏ 294771, Telex 311181 – 📶 📺 **🅿**. 🏊
🔲 AE ① VISA
A v
M 4.50/5.50 **st.** 🍷 1.85 – 🛏 2.50 – **66 rm** 20.50/28.50 **st.**

🏨 **Alveston Manor** (T.H.F.), Clopton Bridge, CV37 7HP, ☏ 4581, Telex 31324, 🚗 – 📺 **🅿**.
🏊 🔲 AE ① VISA
B i
M 4.80/5.60 **st.** 🍷 1.65 – 🛏 2.50 – **112 rm** 19.00/27.50 **st.**

🏨 **Falcon** (County), Chapel St., CV37 6HA, ☏ 5777, Group Telex 25971, 🚗 – 📶 📺 **🅿**. 🏊
🔲 AE ① VISA
A s
M 4.90/6.00 **st.** 🍷 1.55 – **68 rm** 22.00/28.50 **s.**

🏨 **Swan's Nest** (T.H.F.), Bridgefoot, CV37 7LT, ☏ 66761, Telex 31419, 🚗 – 📺 ⊖wc
🛁wc ☎ **🅿**. 🏊 🔲 AE ① VISA
B n
M 4.85/5.50 **st.** 🍷 1.60 – **69 rm** 🛏 15.50/29.50 **st.**

🏨 **White Swan** (T.H.F.), Rother St., CV37 6NH, ☏ 297022 – 📺 ⊖wc ☎. 🔲 AE ① VISA **A r**
M 3.50/4.50 **st.** 🍷 1.65 – **55 rm** 🛏 14.00/25.50 **st.**

🏨 **Stratford House** without rest., Sheep St., CV37 6EF, ☏ 68288 – 📺 ⊖wc **🅿**. 🔲 AE ① VISA
10 rm 🛏 16.00/26.50 **t.**
A u

🏨 **Arden**, 44 Waterside, CV37 6BA, ☏ 294949, 🚗 – 📺 ⊖wc ☎ **🅿**. 🔲 AE ① VISA **B o**
M (buffet lunch) 5.30 **t.** 🍷 1.75 – **60 rm** 🛏 11.00/22.50 **st.**

🏨 **Grosvenor House** (Best Western), 12 Warwick Rd, CV37 6YT, ☏ 69213, Telex 311699, **B r**
🚗 – TV ⌁wc ⌁wc ☏ **P**. ♨. ⊠ AE ⓪ VISA
closed 24 to 28 December – **M** 4.20/5.20 **st.** – **59 rm** ☌ 13.00/27.00 **st.** – P 13.75/16.50 **st.**

🏨 **Haytor** ⚜, Avenue Rd, CV37 6UX, ☏ 297799, 🚗 – ⌁wc ⌁wc **P**. AE **B c**
M (bar lunch) 3.50 **s.** ♦ 1.40 – **20 rm** ☌ 9.90/23.00 **s.**

🏨 **Red Horse** (Norfolk Cap.), Bridge St., CV37 6AE, ☏ 293211, Group Telex 23241 – **B s**
⌁wc ☏ **P**. ♨. ⊠ AE ⓪ VISA
M 3.75/4.50 **st.** ♦ 2.30 – **64 rm** ☌ 11.70/26.95 **st.**

🏨 **Bancroft Garden,** Waterside, CV37 6EF, ☏ 69196, Seafood rest. – ⌁wc ☏. ⊠ AE ⓪
VISA **B a**
closed 24 to 26 December – **M** 3.50/10.00 **s.** ♦ 2.40 – **17 rm** ☌ 10.95/18.50.

⌂ **Stratheden,** 5 Chapel St., CV37 6EP, ☏ 297119 – ⌁wc **A s**
closed last 2 weeks November, 1 week at Christmas and 2 weeks February – **10 rm**
☌ 9.50/13.00 **s.**

⌂ **Woodburn,** 89 Shipston Rd, CV37 7LW, S: ½ m. on A 34 ☏ 4453 – **P** **B u**
closed 24 December-2 January – **6 rm** ☌ 6.90/13.80 **st.**

⌂ **Marlyn,** 3 Chestnut Walk, CV37 6HG, ☏ 293752 **A e**
closed Christmas – **8 rm** ☌ 7.30/14.60 **st.**

⌂ **Hylands,** Warwick Rd, CV37 6YW, ☏ 297962, 🚗 – ⌁wc **P** **B a**
closed February – **12 rm** ☌ 14.80/19.00 **st.**

⌂ **The Fold,** 6 Payton St., CV37 6UA, ☏ 292493, 🚗 – **P** **AB x**
closed 6 January-mid March – **27 rm** ☌ 6.50/13.00 **s.**

⌂ **Grosvenor Villa,** 9 Evesham Pl., CV37 6HT, ☏ 66192 **A a**
8 rm ☌ 5.50/10.00 **st.**

XX **Giovanni,** 8 Ely St., CV37 6LW, ☏ 297999, Italian rest. **A c**
closed Sunday – **M** a la carte 4.50/8.00 ♦ 1.80.

XX **Le Provençal** with rm, 121 Shipston Rd, CV37 7LW, S: ¾ m. on A 34 ☏ 297567,
French rest. – ⌁wc **P**. AE **B u**
March-November – **M** *(closed Sunday and Monday)* (dinner only) a la carte 4.50/9.00 **t.**
♦ 1.75 – **11 rm** ☌ 6.00/16.00 **t.**

X **Christophi's,** 21-23 Sheep St., CV37 6EF, ☏ 293546, Greek rest., Dinner dancing –
⊠ AE ⓪ VISA **B z**
closed Sunday, 25-26 December and 1 January – **M** (dinner only) 5.80 ♦ 2.80.

X **Buccaneer** (Wayside Hotel), 11 Warwick Rd, CV37 6YW, ☏ 292550 – ⊠ AE ⓪ VISA
closed Monday and February – **M** (dinner only) a la carte 5.70/8.80 **t.** ♦ 1.90. **B a**

X **Marianne,** 3 Greenhill St., CV37 6LF, ☏ 293563, French rest. – AE ⓪ **A n**
closed Sunday and Bank Holidays – **M** a la carte 5.20/6.65 ♦ 1.65.

ALFA-ROMEO, VOLVO Western Rd ☏ 292468
AUSTIN-DAIMLER-JAGUAR-MORRIS-MG-ROVER-
TRIUMPH Birmingham Rd ☏ 2968121
FIAT Western Rd ☏ 3532

PEUGEOT Eversley Garage, Alderminster ☏ 078 987
(Alderminster) 331
RENAULT Western Rd ☏ 67911
VAUXHALL Rother St. ☏ 66254

STRATTON Glos. 403 404 O 28 – see Cirencester.

STRATTON ST. MARGARET Wilts. 403 404 O 29 – see Swindon.

STREET Somerset 403 L 30 – pop. 7,550 – ECD: Wednesday – ☎ 0458.
London 138 – Bristol 28 – Taunton 20.

🏨 **Wessex,** High St., BA16 0EK, ☏ 43383 – ⬧ TV ⌁wc ⌁wc ☏ **P**. ♨. ⊠ AE ⓪ VISA
M a la carte 2.40/5.15 **t.** ♦ 1.55 – **50 rm** ☌ 14.85/21.85.

MORRIS-MG-ROVER-TRIUMPH Creeches Lane, Walton ☏ 42735

STREETLY West Midlands 403 404 O 26 – see Birmingham.

STRETTON Cheshire 403 404 M 23 – see Warrington.

STROUD Glos. 403 404 N 28 – pop. 25,580 – ECD: Thursday – ☎ 045 36.
Envir. : Severn Wildfowl Trust* *AC,* W: 11 m.
⛳, ⛳ Michinhampton ☏ 045 383 (Nailsworth) 2642.
🛈 Council Offices, High St. ☏ 4252.
London 113 – Bristol 30 – Gloucester 9.

⌂ **Downfield,** 134 Cainscross Rd, GL5 4HN, ☏ 4496 – ⌁wc **P**. VISA
closed 22 December-5 January – **15 rm** ☌ 7.00/15.00 **st.**

X **Mr. Baillie's,** 203 Slad Rd, GL5 1RL, NE: 1 m. on B 4070 ☏ 5331, 🚗 – **P**. ⓪
*closed Sunday dinner, Monday except Bank Holidays, Tuesday after Bank Holidays
and 2 to 23 January* – **M** 4.90/9.00 **st.** ♦ 2.35.

P.T.O. →

STROUD

at Brimscombe SE: 2 ¼ m. on A 419 – ⊠ Stroud – ☎ 045 388 Brimscombe:

🏛 **Burleigh Court** ⤳, Burleigh Hill, GL5 2PF, SW: ½ m. off Burleigh Rd ☏ 3804, ≼, 🚗 – 🛗 🅿
  M (bar lunch) a la carte 5.00/7.00 **s.** 🍷 1.20 – **11 rm** ☕ 12.50/20.50 **s.**

at Rodborough S: ¾ m. by A 46 – ⊠ Stroud – ☎ 045 387 Amberley:

🏛 **Bear**, Rodborough Common, GL5 5DE, E: 1 ½ m. ☏ 3522, 🚗 – 📺 🛏wc ☎ 🅿. 🔺 AE ⓪ VISA
  M (closed Saturday lunch) a la carte 6.50/9.25 **t.** 🍷 1.95 – **32 rm** ☕ 15.30/32.00 **t.**

AUSTIN-MORRIS-MG-ROVER-TRIUMPH Caincross Rd ☏ 3671
CITROEN London Rd ☏ 2861
DATSUN Westword Rd, Ebley ☏ 4919

FORD London Rd ☏ 4311
RENAULT London Rd ☏ 4203
TALBOT Stonehouse ☏ 045 382 (Stonehouse) 2139

STUDLAND Dorset 408 404 O 32 – pop. 620 – ECD: Thursday – ⊠ Swanage – ☎ 092 944. 🏌, 🏌 ☏ 210.

London 130 – Bournemouth 22 – Dorchester 26.

🏛 **Manor House** ⤳, Studland Bay, BH19 3AU, ☏ 288, ≼ Old Harry rocks and Poole Bay, « Gothic style country house atmosphere », 🚗, park – 🛏wc 🛗wc 🅿. 🔺
  Easter-late October – **M** (bar lunch) 5.50 **t.** 🍷 1.70 – **18 rm** ☕ 9.00/24.00 **s.**

🏛 **Knoll House**, BH19 3AH, ☏ 251, ✗, 🏊 heated, 🏌, 🚗, park – 🛏wc ☎ 🅿
  3 April-19 October – **M** 6.25 **t.** 🍷 2.10 – **110 rm** ☕ 12.00/27.40 **s.**

STURMINSTER NEWTON Dorset 408 404 M 31 – pop. 2,111 – ☎ 0258.

London 123 – Bournemouth 30 – Bristol 49 – Salisbury 28 – Taunton 41.

✗✗ **Plumber Manor** ⤳ with rm, Hazelbury Bryan Rd, DT10 2AF, SW: 1 ¾ m. ☏ 72507, ≼, « Tastefully furnished country house », ✗, 🚗, park – 🛏wc 🅿
  closed February and first 2 weeks November – **M** (closed Sunday dinner to non-residents and Monday) (dinner only) 8.50 **t.** 🍷 1.85 – **6 rm** ☕ 14.00/22.00 **st.**

MAZDA, LADA Station Rd ☏ 72155

SUDBURY Derbs. 408 404 O 25 – pop. 868 – ⊠ Derby – ☎ 028 372 Marchington.
See : Sudbury Hall✶✶ (17C) AC.

London 138 – Birmingham 33 – Derby 13 – Stoke-on-Trent 23.

🏛 **Boar's Head Motel**, Lichfield Rd, DE6 5GX, S: 1 m. on A 515 ☏ 344 – 📺 🛏wc 🅿. 🔺 AE ⓪ VISA
  M (closed Sunday dinner) a la carte 4.75/7.45 **s.** 🍷 2.25 – ☕ 1.50 – **12 rm** 9.50/14.00 **s.**

SUDBURY Suffolk 404 W 27 – pop. 8,166 – ECD: Wednesday – ☎ 078 73.
🛈 Sudbury Library, Market Hill ☏ 72092/76029.

London 59 – Cambridge 37 – Colchester 15 – Ipswich 21.

🏛 **Mill**, Walnut Tree Lane, CO10 0BD, ☏ 75544, Telex 919161, ≼ – 📺 🛏wc ☎ 🅿. 🧖
  🔺 AE ⓪ VISA
  M 4.25/5.50 **t.** 🍷 1.80 – **50 rm** ☕ 16.50/24.95 **t.**

🏛 **Four Swans**, 10 North St., CO10 6RB, ☏ 72793 – 🛏wc ☎ 🅿. AE ⓪
  M (Carvery and grill rest.) 3.05 **st.** 🍷 1.40 – ☕ 1.65 – **17 rm** 8.75/17.50 **st.**

at Great Cornard SE: 1 m. on B 1508 – ⊠ ☎ 078 73 Sudbury:

⌂ **Oriel Lodge**, 21 Kings Hill, CO10 6XB, ☏ 72456 – 🅿. 🔺 AE ⓪ VISA
  11 rm ☕ 7.50/13.80 **t.**

MORRIS-MG-WOLSELEY Station Rd ☏ 72321
SAAB Lavenham ☏ 228

TALBOT Acton Sq. ☏ 72745
VAUXHALL Cornard Rd ☏ 72301

SUNBURY-ON-THAMES Surrey 404 S 29 – pop. 40,186 – ☎ 093 27.
London 23 – Reading 29.

✗✗ **Castle**, 21 Thames St., TW16 5QF, ☏ 83647 – 🅿. 🔺 VISA
  M 6.00/8.00 **t.** 🍷 2.45.

SUNDERLAND Tyne and Wear 986 ⑲ – pop. 217,079 – ECD: Wednesday – ☎ 0783.
🏌 Coxgreen ☏ 078 324 (Hylton) 2518, W: 2 m. by A 183 A – 🏌 Lizard Lane ☏ 0783 (Whitburn) 292144, N: 2 m. by A 183 A.

London 278 – Leeds 88 – Middlesbrough 29 – Newcastle-upon-Tyne 12.

Plans opposite

🏛 Seaburn (Swallow), Queen's Par., SR6 8DB, N: 2 ½ m. on A 183 ☏ 292041, Group Telex 53168, ≼ – 🛗 📺 🛏wc ☎ 🅿. 🧖
  60 rm.   A c

🏛 Mowbray Park (Thistle), Borough Rd, SR1 1PR, ☏ 78221 – 🛗 🛏wc ☎. 🧖   B a
  62 rm.

404

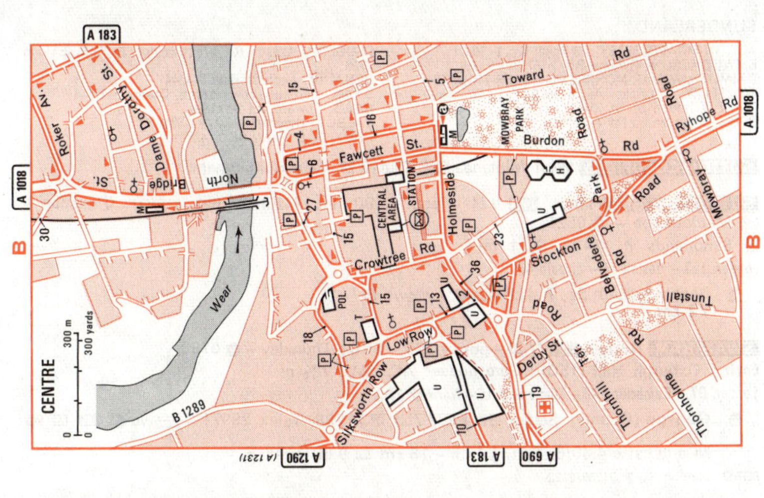

SUNDERLAND

Central Area	B	
Fawcett Street	B	
High Street West	B	15
Holmeside	B	
John Street	B	16
Albion Place	B	2
Barnes Park Road	A	3
Bedford Street	B	4
Borough Road	B	5
Bridge Street	B	6
Charlton Road	A	8
Chester Road	B	10
Fulwell Road	A	12
Green Terrace	B	13
Harbour View	A	14
Kayll Road	A	17
Livingstone Road	B	18
New Durham Road	B	19
Northern Way	A	20
Ormonde Street	A	21
Pallion Road	A	22
Park Lane	B	23
Roker Terrace	A	24
St. Luke's Terrace	A	26
St. Mary's Way	B	27
Shields Road	A	29
Southwick Road	B	30
Station Road	A	32
Sunderland Road	A	33
Trimdon Street	A	35
Vine Place	B	36
Wessington Way	A	38

Plans de villes :
Les noms des principales voies commerçantes sont inscrits en rouge au début des légendes rues.

BUILT UP AREA
0 1 km
0 1/2 mile
NEWCASTLE-UPON-TYNE
A 184
A
A 1018
SOUTH SHIELDS
A 183
WHITBURN
WASHINGTON
A 1231
CHESTER-LE-STREET
A 183
A 690
(A 1 : M), DURHAM
MIDDLESBROUGH
A 1018
MONKWEARMOUTH
SOUTHWICK
Newcastle
Sea Road
Whitburn Road
North Hylton Rd
Thompson Rd
Southwick Rd
Roker Av.
Dorothy St.
Dame
Wear
Pallion
New Rd
A 1290
St. Luke's Rd
Road
Hylton
Front Rd
Holborn Rd
The Broadway
Chester Rd
Springwell Rd
Durham
Queen
Tunstall Rd
Alexandra
Lane
Premier Rd
Durham Rd
Silksworth
Leechmere Road
Ryhope
Rd
Gray Rd
Hendon Rd
High St. East
Commercial Rd
Ocean Rd
Road

CENTRE
0 300 m
0 300 yards
B
A 1018
A 183
A 1290 (A 1231)
A 183
A 690
B 1289
Wear
Roker Av.
St.
Dame Dorothy St.
Bridge
North
Silksworth Row
Low Row
Crowtree Rd
CENTRAL AREA
STATION
Fawcett St.
Holmeside
MOWBRAY PARK
Toward
Burdon Road
Derby St.
Road
Stockton
Park
Belvedere Rd
Thornhill Ter.
Thornholme Rd
Tunstall
Road
Mowbray
Ryhope Rd
Rd
POL.

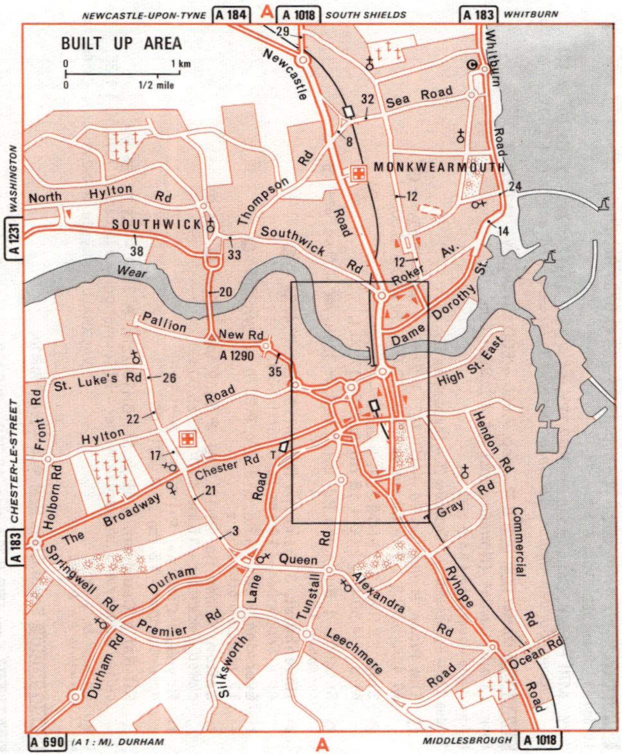

SUNDERLAND

AUSTIN-MG-WOLSELEY 23 Roker Av. ☏ 70881
BMW, DATSUN Ryhope Rd ☏ 57631
DAIMLER-JAGUAR-MORRIS-MG-ROVER-TRIUMPH-
WOLSELEY 190 Roker Av. ☏ 56221
FORD Trimdon St. ☏ 70491
OPEL Roker Baths Rd ☏ 74996

PEUGEOT Allison Rd, West Boldon ☏ 07833 (Boldon)
2726
RENAULT High St. East ☏ 43441
SAAB Harbour View Garage, Doker ☏ 77538
SAAB Toward Rd ☏ 77538
TALBOT Newcastle Rd ☏ 78811
VAUXHALL Paley St. ☏ 42841

SUTTON COLDFIELD West Midlands **403** **404** O 26 – see Birmingham.

SUTTON-ON-SEA Lincs. **404** U 24 – pop. 6,180 (inc. Mablethorpe) – ECD : Thursday – ✉ Mablethorpe – ✆ 0521.

☖ Sandilands ☏ 41432, S: 1 m.

London 153 – Boston 31 – Lincoln 43.

🏠 Bacchus, High St., ☏ 41204, 🚗 – 🛏wc 🅿
22 rm.

SWAFFHAM Norfolk **404** W 26 – pop. 4,280 – ECD : Thursday – ✆ 0760.
Envir. : Oxburgh Hall (15C) : Gate house* *AC*, SW: 7 ½ m.

London 97 – Cambridge 46 – King's Lynn 16 – Norwich 27.

🏠 **George** (County), Station St., PE37 7LJ, ☏ 21238, Telex 25971 – 🛏wc 🅿. 🔧 AE ⓪
VISA
M a la carte 4.40/6.70 **st.** ░ 1.55 – **18 rm** ⊡ 9.50/19.00 **s.**

FORD London St. ☏ 21239/2122

SWALLOWFIELD Berks. **404** R 29 – pop. 1,864 – ✉ ✆ 0734 Reading.
London 49 – Reading 6.

XX **Mill House**, Basingstoke Rd, RG7 1PY, on A 33 ☏ 883124, 🚗 – 🅿. 🔧 AE ⓪ *VISA*
closed Sunday dinner, 26 December and 1 January – **M** a la carte 4.85/10.25 ░ 1.50.

SWANAGE Dorset **403** **404** O 32 – pop. 7,860 – ECD : Thursday – ✆ 092 92.
Envir. : Corfe Castle* (Norman ruins) ≤* *AC*, NW : 6 m.

🛈 The White House, Shore Rd ☏ 2885.

London 130 – Bournemouth 22 – Dorchester 26 – Southampton 52.

🏨 **The Pines**, Burlington Rd, BH19 1LT, ☏ 2166, ≤. 🚗 – 🛗 🛏wc 🅿
M 4.00/5.00 ░ 1.50 – **50 rm** ⊡ 11.00/22.00 – P 16.00/18.00.

🏠 **Ship**, 23 High St., BH19 2LR, ☏ 2078 – 🔧 *VISA*
M 3.00/4.50 **t.** ░ 2.00 – **18 rm** ⊡ 8.50/17.00 **t.**

⌂ Suncliffe, 1 Burlington Rd, BH19 1LR, ☏ 3299, 🚗 – 🛁wc 🚙 🅿
season – **15 rm.**

⌂ **Havenhurst**, 3 Cranborne Rd, BH19 1EA, ☏ 4224 – 🅿
April-September – **16 rm** ⊡ 8.25/15.50 **t.**

⌂ **Eversden**, 5 Victoria Rd, B19 1LY, ☏ 3276 – 🛏wc 🛁wc 🅿
12 rm ⊡ 6.50/14.50 **s.**

⌂ **Sefton**, Gilbert Rd, BH19 1DU, ☏ 3469, 🚗 – 🛁wc 🅿. 🔧 AE
closed December – **15 rm** ⊡ 10.20/23.00 **t.**

⌂ **Boyne**, 1 Cliffe Av., BH19 1LX, ☏ 2939
April-October – **15 rm** ⊡ 8.00/16.00.

X **Rif-Raf's Cauldron**, 5 High St., BH19 2LN, ☏ 2671 – 🔧 AE ⓪ *VISA*
closed Sunday and Monday in winter – **M** (dinner only) a la carte 2.75/5.50 ░ 1.35.

FORD 281 High St. ☏ 2877
MAZDA Victoria Av. ☏ 2888
VAUXHALL Valley Rd ☏ 092 93 (Corfe Castle) 215

SWANBRIDGE South Glam. **403** K 29 – see Penarth.

SWANLEY Kent **404** U 29 – pop. 15,210 – ✆ 0322.
London 17 – Maidstone 19.

XX Bull, London Rd, Birchwood, BR8 7QB, ☏ 62086 – 🅿.

SWANSEA (ABERTAWE) West Glam. **403** I 29 – pop. 173,413 – ECD : Thursday – ✆ 0792.
Envir.: Cefn Bryn (※*** from the reservoir) W : 12 m. by A 4118 A – Exc. : Rhosili (site and
≤***) W : 18 m. by A 4118 A.

☖ Morriston ☏ 71079, N : 4 m. by A 48 A – ☖ Langland Bay ☏ 66023, W : 6 m. by A 4067 A –
☖ Jersey Marine ☏ 0792 (Skewen) 812198, E : 3 ½ m. by A 483 A.

🛈 Tourist Information Centre, Crumlin Burrows, Jersey Marine ☏ 462403/462498 (Easter-September) – Guildhall
Kiosk ☏ 50821 – Oystermouth Square, The Mumbles ☏ 61302 (Easter-September).

London 196 – Bristol 82 – Birmingham 133 – Cardiff 41 – Liverpool 228 – Stoke-on-Trent 174.

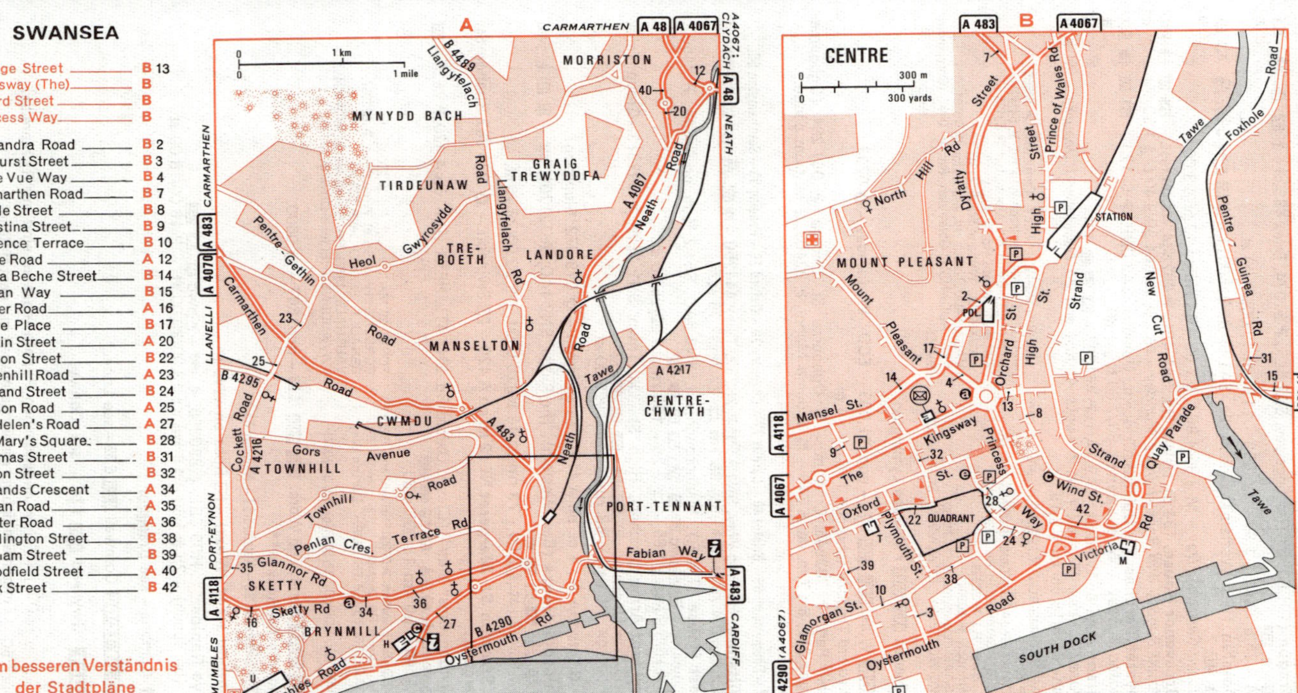

SWANSEA

College Street — B 13
Kingsway (The) — B
Oxford Street — B
Princess Way — B

Alexandra Road — B 2
Bathurst Street — B 3
Belle Vue Way — B 4
Carmarthen Road — B 7
Castle Street — B 8
Christina Street — B 9
Clarence Terrace — B 10
Clase Road — A 12
De La Beche Street — B 14
Fabian Way — B 15
Gower Road — A 16
Grove Place — B 17
Martin Street — A 20
Nelson Street — B 22
Ravenhill Road — A 23
Rutland Street — B 24
Station Road — A 25
St. Helen's Road — A 27
St. Mary's Square — B 28
Thomas Street — B 31
Union Street — B 32
Uplands Crescent — A 34
Vivian Road — A 35
Walter Road — A 36
Wellington Street — B 38
William Street — B 39
Woodfield Street — A 40
York Street — B 42

Zum besseren Verständnis
der Stadtpläne
lesen Sie bitte
die Zeichenerklärung
auf Seite 43.

407

A
CARMARTHEN   A 48   A 4067
A 4067: CLYDACH   A 48   NEATH
MORRISTON
12
40
20
1 km
1 mile
B 4489
Llangyfelach
MYNYDD BACH
GRAIG TREWYDDFA
CARMARTHEN
A 483   CARMARTHEN
TIRDEUNAW
Road
Liangyfelach Rd
Neath   A 4067   Road
LANDORE
LLANELLI
A 4070
Pentre - Gethin
Heol   Gwyrosydd
TRE-BOETH
Carmarthen
23
25
B 4295
Road
MANSELTON
Road
Tawe
A 4217
PENTRE-CHWYTH
Cockett Road
A 4216
CWMDU
Gors   Avenue
A 483
Neath
TOWNHILL
PORT-EYNON
Townhill   Road
Penlan Cres.   Terrace Rd
PORT-TENNANT
Fabian Way
A 483   CARDIFF
35   Glanmor Rd
SKETTY
Sketty Rd   34
36
A 4118   MUMBLES
16
BRYNMILL
27
B 4290   Oystermouth Rd
A 4067
Mumbles Road
Oystermouth
SWANSEA BAY
A

CENTRE
A 483   B   A 4067
300 m
300 yards
7
North Hill Rd
Dyfatty
Street
High St.
Prince of Wales Rd
STATION
Tawe
Foxhole Road
MOUNT PLEASANT
Mount Pleasant
2   POL.
17
Orchard St.
High St.
Strand
New Cut Road
Pentre - Guinea Rd
14   4
13   8
31
15   A 483
A 4118
Mansel St.
9
The
Kingsway
32   St.
Oxford
Wind St.
Strand
Quay Parade
A 4067
22   QUADRANT
Princess   Way
28
42
Plymouth St.
24
Victoria   M
39
38
Tawe
Glamorgan St.
10
3
Road
B 4290 (A 4067)
Oystermouth
SOUTH DOCK
B

🏨 **Dragon** (T.H.F.), 39 The Kingsway, SA1 5LS, 🕿 51074, Telex 48309 – 🛗 📺 🅿. ♨. 🔄 AE ⓘ VISA
B a
M 4.25/5.75 **st.** 🍷 1.85 – ⌑ 2.50 – **118 rm** 19.00/27.00 **st.**

🏨 **Dolphin** (Best Western), Whitewalls, SA1 3AB, 🕿 50011 – 🛗 📺 🛁wc 🕿. ♨. 🔄 AE ⓘ VISA
B e
closed Christmas Day – **M** 3.85/4.85 **t.** 🍷 1.60 – **64 rm** ⌑ 17.50/23.00 **t.**

XX **Grosvenor House**, 134 St. Helens Rd, SA1 4BL, 🕿 462884, Italian rest. – 🔄 AE ⓘ VISA
A c
closed Sunday and Bank Holiday Monday – **M** a la carte 4.90/9.40 **t.** 🍷 1.90.

XX **Oyster Perches**, 45 Uplands Crescent, Uplands, SA2 0NP, 🕿 59173 – 🔄 AE ⓘ VISA
A a
closed Sunday – **M** a la carte 4.80/7.90 **t.** 🍷 1.80.

XX **Drangway**, 66 Wind St., SA9 1AH, 🕿 461397 – 🔄 AE ⓘ VISA
B c
closed Sunday, Monday, first 2 weeks August and 25 December-1 January – **M** a la carte 8.25/18.65 **st.** 🍷 2.15.

AUSTIN, MORRIS-MG-ROVER-TRIUMPH 375 Carmarthen Rd 🕿 52941
AUSTIN-DAIMLER-JAGUAR-MORRIS-MG-ROVER-TRIUMPH 511 Carmarthen Rd 🕿 34141
DATSUN Sway Rd 🕿 75271
FORD Garngoch 🕿 893041
HONDA, SAAB Llangyfelach 🕿 71960
MORRIS-MG-WOLSELEY 10 Wyndham St. 🕿 53232

MORRIS-MG-WOLSELEY Cwmbwria 🕿 53885
PEUGEOT 1/24 Pentrechwyth Rd 🕿 54147
RENAULT Eaton Rd, Manselton 🕿 53125
TALBOT Neath Rd 🕿 73391
VAUXHALL William St. 🕿 41311
VAUXHALL Neath Rd, Morriston 🕿 75101
VW, AUDI-NSU Gorseinon Rd 🕿 0792 (Gorseinon) 894951

SWAY Hants. 403 404 P 31 – see Lymington.

SWINDON Wilts. 403 404 O 29 – pop. 91,033 – ECD: Wednesday – ✆ 0793.
Envir. : Lydiard Tregoze (church* 15C) W : 4 m.
🏌 Bremhill Park, 🕿 782946, E: 4 m. – 🏌 Ogbourne St. George, 🕿 067 284 (Ogbourne St. George) 217, S : 7 m. on A 345 – 🏌 Broome Manor 🕿 32403, 2 m. from centre.
🛈 32 The Arcade, Brunel Centre 🕿 26161 ext 518 and 30328.

London 87 – Bournemouth 69 – Bristol 40 – Cardiff 72 – Coventry 70 – Oxford 29 – Reading 39 – Southampton 66.

🏨 **Wiltshire**, Fleming Way, SN1 1TN, 🕿 28282, Telex 444250 – 🛗 📺. ♨. 🔄 AE ⓘ VISA
M approx. 4.75 **st.** 🍷 1.95 – **85 rm** ⌑ 22.75/32.75 **st.**

🏨 **Post House** (T.H.F.), Marlborough Rd, SN3 6AQ, SE: 2 ¾ m. on A 345 🕿 24601,
🏊 heated – 📺 🛁wc 🕿 🅿. ♨. 🔄 AE ⓘ VISA
M 4.15/5.30 **st.** 🍷 1.65 – ⌑ 2.25 – **103 rm** 18.00/25.50 **st.**

🏨 **Goddard Arms** (Anchor), High St., Old Town, SN1 3EW, 🕿 692313, Group Telex 858875 – 📺 🛁wc 🕿 🅿. ♨. 🔄 AE ⓘ VISA
M approx. 6.00 **st.** – **68 rm** ⌑ 13.00/26.00 **st.**

at Blunsdon N: 4 m. on A 419 – ✉ Swindon – ✆ 079 372 Blunsdon :

🏨 **Blunsdon House** (Best Western), The Ridge, SN2 4AD, 🕿 721701, ⇌ – 🛗 📺 🛁wc 🕿 🅿. ♨. 🔄 AE ⓘ VISA
M 4.50/5.25 **st.** 🍷 2.00 – **73 rm** ⌑ 19.50/26.50 **st.** – P 23.00/29.75 **st.**

at Stratton St. Margaret NE: 2 m. on A 420 – ✉ Swindon – ✆ 079 382 Stratton St. Margaret :

🏨 **Swindon Crest Motel** (Crest), Oxford Rd, SN3 4TL, NE: 1 ½ m. on A 420 🕿 2921 – 📺 🛁wc 🕿 ♿ 🅿. ♨. 🔄 AE ⓘ VISA
⌑ 2.40 – **50 rm** 18.00/24.50.

ALFA-ROMEO Shrivenham 🕿 0793 (Shrivenham) 782721
AUSTIN-MG Drove Rd 🕿 34035
DAIMLER-JAGUAR-ROVER-TRIUMPH Dorcan Way 🕿 5283
FIAT, VAUXHALL, VOLVO 32/36 High St. 🕿 20971

FORD 30 Marlborough Rd 🕿 20002
PORSCHE High St. at Wroughton 🕿 812387.
RENAULT Elgin Drive 🕿 693841
VAUXHALL 13/21 The Street, Moredon 🕿 23457
VW, AUDI-NSU Eldene Drive 🕿 31333

SYMONDS YAT Heref. and Worc. 403 404 M 28 – pop. 807 – ✆ 0600.
See : Symond's Yat Rock ⇐**.

London 126 – Gloucester 23 – Hereford 17 – Newport 31.

Symond's Yat (West) – ✉ Ross-on-Wye :

🏛 **Wye Rapids** 🦢, HR9 6BL, 🕿 890366, ⇐, ⇌ – 🛁wc 🅿. 🔄 VISA
M (bar lunch) 4.25 🍷 1.60 – **16 rm** ⌑ 13.00/30.00 **st.** – P 16.00/18.00 **st.**

TALKIN Cumbria – see Brampton.

TALLAND-BY-LOOE Cornwall 403 G 32 – see Looe.

TAL-Y-BONT Gwynedd 403 I 24 – see Conwy.

P 20.00/27.50   Die im Führer angegebenen **Pensionspreise** sind nur Richtpreise. Einigen Sie sich vor einem Aufenthalt mit dem Hotelier über den endgültigen Pensionspreis.

TAL-Y-CAFN Gwynedd **403** I 24 – ⊠ Colwyn Bay – ◯ 049 267 Tynygroes.
Envir.: Bodnant Gardens** *AC*, NE: 1 m.

London 238 – Colwyn Bay 7.

  🏠 **Ferry,** LL28 5RT, ☏ 202, ≼, ◗, 🚗 – 🛏wc ℗
     M 3.60/5.50 🍷 2.00 – **14 rm** ヱ 7.50/16.50.

TAL-Y-LLYN Gwynedd **403** I 25 – pop. 620 – ⊠ Towyn – ◯ 065 477 Abergynolwyn.
See : Lake**.

London 224 – Dolgellau 9 – Shrewsbury 60.

  🏰 **Tynycornel,** LL36 9AJ, on B 4405 ☏ 282, ≼ lake and mountains, ◗, 🚗 – 🛏wc ☏
     ℗. 🔊 *VISA*
     weekends only from November to April – **M** *(closed Sunday dinner to non-residents)*
     (bar lunch Monday to Saturday) 7.60 **t.** 🍷 1.30 – **17 rm** ヱ 12.80/25.40 **t.**

  🏡 **Minfford,** LL36 9AJ, N : 2 ¾ m. on A 487 ☏ 665, ≼, 🚗 – 🍽 ℗
     Easter-October and week-ends in winter – **M** (dinner only) 6.25 **st.** 🍷 2.25 – **7 rm**
     ヱ 10.90/23.00 **st.**

TANKERTON Kent **404** X 29 – see Whitstable.

TARPORLEY Cheshire **403** **404** M 24 – pop. 1,722 – ECD : Wednesday – ⊠ ◯ 082 93.
London 186 – Chester 11 – Liverpool 36 – Stoke on Trent 27.

  🏡 **Swan,** 50 High St., CW6 0AG, ☏ 2411 – 📺 ℗. 🔊 AE ⊙ *VISA*
     M 3.80/4.85 **t.** 🍷 2.05 – **9 rm** ヱ 10.00/16.50 **t.**

TAUNTON Somerset **403** K 30 – pop. 37,444 – ECD : Thursday – ◯ 0823.
See : St. Mary Magdalene's Church* 15C. **Envir.:** Trull (Parish church : carved woodwork*
16C) SW : 2 m.

📗 Corfe ☏ 082 342 (Blagdon Hill) 240, S : 5 m. on B 3170.

🎫 The Library, Corporation St. ☏ 84077/53424.

London 171 – Bournemouth 68 – Bristol 48 – Exeter 32 – **Plymouth 74** – Southampton 89 – Weymouth 49.

  🏰 **Castle,** Castle Green, TA1 1NF, ☏ 2671, Telex 46488, « Part 11C castle with Norman
     garden » – 🛗 📺 ⅛ 🚙 ℗. 🏊. 🔊 AE ⊙ *VISA*
     M 6.50/8.00 **st.** – ヱ 3.50 – **45 rm** 23.00/38.50 **st.**

  🏠 **County** (T.H.F.), East St., TA1 3LT, ☏ 87651 – 🛗 📺 🛏wc ☏ ℗. 🏊. 🔊 AE ⊙ *VISA*
     M 5.00/5.60 **st.** 🍷 1.65 – **75 rm** ヱ 14.00/26.00 **st.**

  🏠 **Corner House,** Park St., TA1 4DQ, ☏ 84683 – ℗
     closed Christmas – **M** 3.25/4.15 🍷 1.75 – **23 rm** ヱ 11.80/19.20 **st.** – P 17.00/18.00.

  at Hatch Beauchamp SE : 6 m. on A 358 – ⊠ Taunton – ◯ 0823 Hatch Beauchamp :

  XXX **Farthings** with rm, TA3 6SG, ☏ 480664, 🚗 – 📺 🛏wc ☏ ℗. 🔊 AE *VISA*
     closed 1 week October-November and 3 weeks January-February – **M** *(closed Sunday,*
     Monday and lunch to non-residents) (buffet lunch) a la carte approx. 8.60 🍷 1.85 –
     ヱ 1.50 – **5 rm** 15.00/26.00.

  at Poundisford Park S : 3 ¾ m. off B 3170 – ⊠ Taunton – ◯ 082 342 Blagdon Hill :

  XX **Well House,** TA3 7AF, ☏ 566, 🚗, park – ℗
     closed Sunday dinner, Monday and 2 weeks January – **M** (lunch by arrangement)
     a la carte 6.90/8.60.

  at Bishop's Hull W : 1 ¾ m. off A 38 – ⊠ ◯ 0823 Taunton :

  🏠 **Meryan House,** Bishops Hull Rd, TA1 5EG, ☏ 87445, 🚗 – ℗. *VISA*
     8 rm ヱ 7.00/13.00 **s.**

  at Bishop's Lydeard NW : 5 m. by A 358 – ⊠ Taunton – ◯ 0823 Bishop's Lydeard :

  X **Rose Cottage Inn,** TA4 3LR, SE : 1 m. on A 358 ☏ 432394 – ℗
     closed Sunday, Monday and 3 weeks from 24 December – **M** (bar lunch) a la carte
     5.20/7.60 **t.** 🍷 2.50.

AUDI-NSU, MERCEDES-BENZ Silver St. ☏ 88371
AUSTIN-DAIMLER-JAGUAR-ROVER-TRIUMPH South
St. ☏ 88991
CITROEN, FIAT 43/45 East St. ☏ 2607
FORD 151/6 East Reach ☏ 85481
LADA 16 Kingston Rd ☏ 88288

OPEL Priory Av. ☏ 87611
PEUGEOT 30 Wellington Rd ☏ 81081
RENAULT 138 Bridgwater Rd, Bathpool ☏ 412559
SAAB 60 East Reach ☏ 88351
TALBOT 30/33a East Reach ☏ 87871

TAVISTOCK Devon **403** H 32 – pop. 6,720 – ECD : Wednesday – ◯ 0822.
📗 Down Rd ☏ 2049, SW : 1 m.

London 239 – Exeter 38 – **Plymouth 15.**

  🏠 **Bedford** (T.H.F.), 1 Plymouth Rd, PL19 8BB, ☏ 3221 – 📺 🛏wc ☏ 🚙. 🔊 AE ⊙ *VISA*
     M 3.75/4.75 **st.** 🍷 1.65 – **35 rm** ヱ 12.50/24.50 **st.**

P.T.O. ⟶

at Gulworthy W : 3 m. on A 390 – ✉ Tavistock – ☎ 0822 Gunnislake :

XX ✿ **Horn of Plenty,** PL19 8JD, ☎ 832528, ≤ Tamar Valley and Bodmin Moor, 🌳 – Ⓟ
closed Friday lunch and Thursday – **M** a la carte 7.65/11.95 🍷 2.70
Spec. Quenelles de saumon frais à la crème (April or May-September), Agneau en croûte sauce paloise, Venison (November-March).

BRITISH LEYLAND Plymouth Rd ☎ 2301 FORD Vigo Bridge ☎ 3735

TEBAY Cumbria – pop. 636 – ✉ ☎ 058 74 Orton.

London 272 – Carlisle 41 – Kendal 12.

Tebay Mountain Lodge Motel without rest., M 6 Motorway Service Area, CA10 3SS, N : 1 m. on M 6 ☎ 351 – TV 🛁wc ☎ Ⓟ. AE VISA
☕ 1.00 – **31 rm** 13.25/17.85 **t.**

TEDBURN ST. MARY Devon 403 I 31 – pop. 586 – ECD : Thursday – ✉ Exeter – ☎ 064 76.

London 209 – Exeter 8.5 – Plymouth 51.

King's Arms Inn, EX6 6AL, on A 30 ☎ 224, 🌳 – Ⓟ
M a la carte 4.30/6.50 **t.** 🍷 1.50 – **6 rm** ☕ 8.00/15.00 **t.**

TEESSIDE AIRPORT Durham – see Darlington.

TEIGNMOUTH Devon 403 J 32 – pop. 12,575 – ECD : Thursday – ☎ 062 67.

ℹ The Den ☎ 6271 ext 207 (summer only).

London 216 – Exeter 16 – Torquay 8.

London, 24 Bank St., TQ14 8AW, ☎ 2776, heated – 🛗 🛁wc Ⓟ. VISA
M 3.00/5.00 **t.** 🍷 1.90 – **26 rm** ☕ 12.00/20.00 **t.** – P 19.00/21.00 **t.**

Belvedere, Barnpark Rd, TQ14 8PJ, ☎ 4561 – Ⓟ. VISA
13 rm ☕ 7.00/16.00 **st.**

Inglewood, Third Drive, Landscore Rd, TQ14 9JT, ☎ 4572, heated, 🌳 – Ⓟ
16 rm.

Overstowey, Dawlish Rd, TQ14 8TQ, on A 379 ☎ 4251, 🌳 – Ⓟ. AE VISA
10 rm ☕ 6.15/12.30 **t.**

XX **Churchill's,** 6-8 Den Rd, TQ14 8AP, ☎ 4311 – VISA
closed Saturday lunch, Sunday dinner Monday and 2 weeks October – **M** a la carte 4.95/7.15 🍷 1.40.

X **Venn Farm Country House** with rm, Higher Exeter Rd, TQ14 9PB, ☎ 2196, 🌳 – 🛁wc Ⓟ. VISA
closed January – **M** *(closed Sunday dinner and Monday from October to April)* a la carte 5.15/7.65 🍷 2.50 – **10 rm** ☕ 11.00/20.00.

DATSUN 106 Bitton Park Rd ☎ 2501
RENAULT Bridge Rd, Shaldon ☎ 062687 (Shaldon) 2369
TOYOTA The Triangle ☎ 2171

TELFORD Salop 403 404 M 25 – pop. 96,700 – ☎ 0952.

Envir. : Ironbridge Gorge Museum* (Iron Bridge**) *AC*, S : 5 m. – Buildwas Abbey* (ruins 12C) S : 7 m.

⛳18 Wrekin ☎ 44032 – ⛳18 Sutton Hill ☎ 586052.

ℹ The Iron Bridge Tollhouse ☎ 882753.

London 152 – Birmingham 33 – Shrewsbury 12 – Stoke-on-Trent 29.

Buckatree Hall 🐴, Ercall Lane, The Wrekin, TF6 5AL, off Holyhead Rd S : 1 ½ m. ☎ 51821, 🐴, 🌳, park – TV ♿ Ⓟ. VISA
M 3.75/4.25 🍷 2.75 – **25 rm** ☕ 18.00/24.50.

Charlton Arms, Church St., Wellington, TF1 1DG, ☎ 51351 – 🛁wc ☎ Ⓟ. 🏛. AE VISA
M *(closed Sunday dinner)* 4.50/5.00 **t.** – **27 rm** ☕ 12.25/20.50.

AUSTIN-MORRIS-MG VANDEN PLAS Market St., Wellington ☎ 44896
DATSUN Church St., Wellington ☎ 42671
RENAULT Watling St., Wellington ☎ 44162

TEMPLE EWELL Kent 404 X 30 – see Dover.

TEMPLE SOWERBY Cumbria – pop. 279 – ✉ Penrith – ☎ 093 06 Kirkby Thore.

London 297 – Carlisle 31 – Kendal 38.

Temple Sowerby House, CA10 1RZ, ☎ 578, 🌳 – 🛁wc ♿ Ⓟ. VISA
closed January and February – **M** *(closed Monday)* (dinner only) 8.00 **t.** – **12 rm** ☕ 15.00/24.00 **t.**

King's Arms, ☎ 211, 🌳 – Ⓟ – **12 rm.**

☛ *Michelin n'accroche pas de panonceau aux hôtels et restaurants qu'il signale.*

TENBURY WELLS Heref. and Worc. **403** **404** M 27 – pop. 2,151 – ECD : Thursday – ☎ 0584.
🛈 Teme St. ☏ 810465.

London 146 – Birmingham 35 – Hereford 22 – Shrewsbury 37.

 ☖ **Royal Oak,** Market St., WR15 8BQ, ☏ 810417 – **P.** ⓞ
 closed 24 to 26 December – **M** *(closed Sunday dinner to non-residents)* 3.00/4.80 **s.**
 🍷 1.50 – **6 rm** ☕ 9.50/15.00 **s.**

TENBY (DINBYCH-Y-PYSGOD) Dyfed **403** F 28 – pop. 4,994 – ECD : Wednesday – ☎ 0834.
See : Site★★.
🛅 The Burrows ☏ 2787.
🛈 Guildhall, The Norton ☏ 2402 (South Pembs.) and ☏ 3510 (Nat. Park).

London 247 – Carmarthen 27 – Fishguard 36.

 🏨 Imperial (Best Western), The Paragon, SA70 7HR, ☏ 3737, Telex 48444, ≤ sea and bay
 – 📶 TV ⛱wc 🛁wc ☎ 🚗 **P**
 48 rm.

 🏨 **Royal Lion,** 1 High St., SA70 7EX, ☏ 2127 – 📶 TV ⛱wc **P.** 🅂 VISA
 April-October – **M** 3.50/4.75 **t.** 🍷 1.80 – **36 rm** ☕ 10.50/20.00 **st.** – P 14.00/16.00 **st.**

 🏨 **Cobourg,** High St., SA70 7EU, ☏ 2009 – 📶 ⛱wc **P.** VISA
 May-September – **M** 4.00/5.00 **st.** 🍷 1.50 – **30 rm** ☕ 7.50/24.00 **st.** – P 16.00 **st.**

 ☖ **Heywood Lodge,** Heywood Lane, SA70 8BN, ☏ 2684, 🛋 – **P**
 Easter-October – **14 rm** ☕ 7.50/14.50 **s.**

AUSTIN-MORRIS-MG-TRIUMPH-WOLSELEY Warren   VAUXHALL Greenhill Rd ☏ 2459
St. ☏ 2202

TERNHILL Salop **403** **404** M 25 – ✉ Market Drayton – ☎ 063 083.
London 161 – Birmingham 44 – Chester 30 – Shrewsbury 16 – Stoke on Trent 19.

 🏨 **Ternhill Hall,** TF9 3PU, SW: ¼ m. on A 53 ☏ 310, ≤, 🛋 – ⛱wc **P.** 🅂 AE ⓞ VISA
 M a la carte 3.95/5.30 🍷 1.50 – **10 rm** ☕ 8.00/16.00.

TETBURY Glos. **403** **404** N 28 – pop. 3,461 – ECD : Thursday – ☎ 0666.
Envir.: Westonbirt Arboretum★ *AC*, SW: 3 ½ m.
🛅 ☏ 066 66 (Westonbirt) 242, S: 3 m.

London 113 – Bristol 27 – Gloucester 19 – Swindon 24.

 🏨 **White Hart,** Market Pl., GL8 8ES, ☏ 52436 – TV. 🅂 AE ⓞ VISA
 M 4.80/7.50 **t.** 🍷 3.00 – **10 rm** ☕ 17.50/26.00 **st.**

 XXX **The Close** with rm, 8 Long St., GL8 8AQ, ☏ 52272, « Tastefully furnished », 🛋 – TV
 ⛱wc 🛁wc ☎ **P.** 🅂 AE ⓞ VISA
 M a la carte 8.50/10.50 **st.** 🍷 2.30 – ☕ 2.00 – **12 rm** 14.00/34.50 **st.**

 at Westonbirt SW: 2 ½ m. on A 433 – ✉ Tetbury – ☎ 066 66 Westonbirt:

 🏨 **Hare and Hounds** (Best Western), GL8 8QL, ☏ 233, ✕, 🛋, park – ⛱wc ☎ 🚗 **P.**
 🅂 VISA
 M 4.50/6.00 **st.** 🍷 1.85 – **24 rm** ☕ 12.50/29.00 **st.** – P 20.00/23.50 **st.**

 FIAT Hampton St. ☏ 52340   VW, AUDI London Rd ☏ 52473

TEWKESBURY Glos. **403** **404** N 28 – pop. 8,749 – ECD : Thursday – ☎ 0684.
See : Abbey Church★ 12C-14C.
🛅 Lincoln Green ☏ 295405, S: ½ m.
🛈 The Crescent, Church St. ☏ 295027 (summer only).

London 108 – Birmingham 39 – Gloucester 11.

 🏨 **Tewkesbury Park Golf and Country Club** 🦢, Lincoln Green Lane, GL20 7DN,
 S: 1 ¼ m. off A 38 ☏ 295405, ≤ golf course and countryside, 🅂, 🛅, park – TV ⛱wc
 ☎ **P.** 🅂. 🅂 AE VISA
 M 4.50/5.90 **st.** 🍷 1.65 – **30 rm** ☕ 26.25/32.40 **st.** – P 31.00/39.25 **st.**

 🏨 Royal Hop Pole (Crest), Church St., GL20 5RT, ☏ 293236, 🔧, 🛋 – TV ⛱wc ☎ **P.**
 🅂. 🅂 AE ⓞ VISA
 25 rm ☕ 12.65/23.70 **st.**

 X Luigi's, 69-70 Church St., GL20 5RX, ☏ 294353, Italian rest.

AUSTIN-MORRIS-ROVER-TRIUMPH Gloucester Rd   FORD, VAUXHALL Ashchurch Rd ☏ 292398
☏ 293122   TALBOT, SCIMITAR Bredon Rd ☏ 293071

THAKEHAM West Sussex **404** S 31 – pop. 1,103 – ✉ Storrington – ☎ 079 83 West Chiltington.
London 53 – Brighton 22 – Worthing 12.

 🏨 **Abingworth Hall** 🦢, RH20 3EF, on B 2139 ☏ 2257, ≤, ✕, 🅉 heated, 🔧, 🛋, park –
 ⛱wc **P.** 🅂. 🅂
 M 3.25/4.50 🍷 2.00 – **26 rm** ☕ 12.00/36.00 **s.** – P 19.00/20.40 **s.**

THAME Oxon. **404** R 28 – pop. 5,948 – ECD : Wednesday – ✪ 084 421.
See : St. Mary's Church★ 13C. **Envir. :** Rycote Chapel★ (15C) *AC,* W : 3 ½ m.
🛈 Town Hall ☏ 2036/2834.
London 48 – Aylesbury 9 – Oxford 13.

   🏨 Spread Eagle (Best Western), 16 Cornmarket, OX9 2BR, ☏ 3661 – 🛏wc ☏ 🅿. ♨
       29 rm.

   ⌂ Jolly Sailor, Wellington St. ☏ 2682 – 🅿
       12 rm.

AUSTIN-MG-ROVER-TRIUMPH-WOLSELEY Queens   TALBOT North St. ☏ 2921
Rd ☏ 2726   VAUXHALL Park St. ☏ 2505
MORRIS-MG 44 Upper High St. ☏ 2011

THETFORD Norfolk **404** W 26 – pop. 13.727 – ECD : Wednesday – ✪ 0842.
🏌 Brandon Rd ☏ 2258.
🛈 Ancient House Museum, White Hart St. ☏ 2599.
London 83 – Cambridge 32 – Ipswich 33 – King's Lynn 30 – Norwich 29.

   🏨 Bell (T.H.F.), King St., IP24 2AZ, ☏ 4455 – 📺 🛏wc ☏ 🅿. ♨. 🔊 AE ① VISA
       M 4.25/5.00 **st.** ⬧ 1.80 – **42 rm** ⌿ 18.00/24.50 **st.**

   🏨 Anchor (Gd Met.), Bridge St., IP24 3AE, ☏ 3329 – 🛏wc 🅿. ♨
       20 rm.

AUSTIN-LAND ROVER-MORRIS-MG-ROVER-TRIUMPH-WOLSELEY Guildhall St. ☏ 4427

THIRLSPOT Cumbria – pop. 100 – ✉ ✪ 0596 Keswick.
London 288 – Kendal 24 – Keswick 6.

   🏨 King's Head, CA12 4TN, ☏ 72393, ≼ – 🛏wc 🅿
       15 rm.

THIRSK North Yorks. **986** ㉓ – pop. 5,820 – ECD : Wednesday – ✪ 0845.
See : St. Mary's Church★ (Gothic). **Envir. :** Sutton Bank (≼★★) E : 6 m. on A 170.
🛈 Museum, 16 Kirkgate ☏ 22755 (summer only).
London 227 – Leeds 37 – Middlesbrough 24 – York 24.

   🏨 Golden Fleece (T.H.F.), Market Pl., YO7 1LL, ☏ 23108 – 📺 🛏wc ☏ 🅿. ♨. 🔊 AE ①
       VISA
       M 3.50/4.50 **st.** ⬧ 1.65 – **20 rm** ⌿ 13.50/21.00 **st.**

AUSTIN-MORRIS Stockton Rd ☏ 22057   PEUGEOT Station Rd ☏ 22370
OPEL Long St. ☏ 23152

THORNABY-ON-TEES Cleveland **986** ⑲ – pop. 4,025 – ✉ Middlesbrough.
London 250 – Leeds 62 – Middlesbrough 3 – York 49.

   🏨 Post House (T.H.F.), Low Lane, TS17 9LW, SE : 3 m. by A 1045 on A 1044
       ☏ 0642 (Middlesbrough) 591213, Telex 58426 – 📺 🛏wc ☏ ♿ 🅿. ♨. 🔊 AE ① VISA
       M 4.75/6.00 **st.** ⬧ 1.65 – ⌿ 2.25 – **140 rm** 17.00/24.50 **st.**

   🏨 Golden Eagle (Thistle), Trenchard Av., TS17 0DA, ☏ 0642 (Stockton-on-Tees) 62511 –
       💲 📺 🛏wc ☏ ♿ 🅿. ♨
       57 rm.

VAUXHALL Acklam Rd ☏ 593333

THORNBURY Avon **403** **404** M 29 – pop. 9,900 – ECD : Thursday – ✉ Bristol – ✪ 0454.
Envir. : Severn Bridge★ W : 4 m.
London 128 – Bristol 12 – Gloucester 23 – Swindon 43.

   XXX ❀ **Thornbury Castle,** Castle St., BS12 1HH, ☏ 412647, « 15C castle » – 🅿. 🔊 AE VISA
       closed Monday and 5 days at Christmas – **M** (dinner only and Sunday lunch) a la
       carte 10.50/13.00 ⬧ 2.00
       Spec. Mousseline of sole, Breast of chicken flamed in Pernod, Raspberry sorbet.

THORNTON West. Yorks. – see Bradford.

THORNTON HOUGH Merseyside **403** K 24 – ✉ Neston – ✪ 051 Liverpool.
London 208 – Chester 12 – Liverpool 13.

   🏨 Thornton Hall, Neston Rd, Wirral, L63 1JS, ☏ 336 3938, ☞ – 📺 🛏wc ☏ 🅿
       33 rm.

THORPE Derbs. 403 404 O 24 – pop. 161 – ✉ Ashbourne – ☏ 033 529 Thorpe Cloud.
Envir. : N: Dovedale (valley)** – Ashbourne (St. Oswald's Church* 13C) SE: 3 m.
ਸ at Ashbourne ☏ 033 55 (Ashbourne) 2078, SE: 5 m.
London 151 – Derby 16 – Sheffield 33 – Stoke-on-Trent 26.

- **Izaak Walton** ⌂, Dovedale, DE6 2AY, W: 1 m. ☏ 261, ≼ Dovedale, ⚓, 🚗 – 🛏wc ☎
  🅿. ⚐
  M 3.70/5.30 t. ⚗ 2.10 – **26 rm** �より 15.95/23.45 t. – P 24.95 t.
- **Peveril of the Peak** (T.H.F.) ⌂, DE6 2AW, ☏ 333, ≼, ✕, 🚗 – 🛏wc ☎ 🅿. ⚐. ⚑ AE
  ⓪ VISA
  M 4.75/6.50 st. ⚗ 1.95 – **29 rm** ⊒ 13.50/22.00 st.

THORPE ST. ANDREW Norfolk 404 Y 26 – see Norwich.

THORVERTON Devon 403 J 31 – pop. 709 – ✉ Exeter – ☏ 039 286 Silverton.
London 200 – Exeter 9 – Taunton 33.

- **Berribridge House** ⌂, EX5 5JR, S : ½ m. ☏ 259, ⚓, 🚗 – 🅿
  M (dinner only) a la carte 2.90/6.80 t. – **6 rm** ⊒ 8.75/15.00 t.

THRAPSTON Northants. 404 S 26 – pop. 1,984 – ✉ Kettering – ☏ 080 12.
London 81 – Cambridge 33 – Leicester 35 – Northampton 20 – Peterborough 21.

- **Bridge,** Bridge St., LE21 2SV, ☏ 2128 – 🛏wc ☎ 🅿. AE ⓪
  M (closed Sunday dinner) a la carte 3.80/6.70 t. ⚗ 2.00 – **18 rm** ⊒ 9.00/19.00 t.

THRESHFIELD North Yorks. – pop. 465 – ✉ ☏ 0756 Grassington.
London 231 – Bradford 27 – Burnley 26 – Leeds 34.

- **Wilson Arms,** Station Rd, BD23 5EL, on B 6265 ☏ 752666, 🚗 – 🛏wc ☎ 🚗 🅿
  M 5.00/7.75 st. ⚗ 2.50 – **23 rm** ⊒ 20.50/35.00 st.

THURLESTONE Devon 403 I 33 – see Kingsbridge.

*If you are looking for a quiet hotel do not only use the maps on pages 50 to 60
but also look at the text of the establishments with the sign* ⌂.

THURSTASTON Merseyside 403 K 23 – pop. 237 – ✉ West Kirby – ☏ 051 Liverpool.
London 211 – Birkenhead 7.5 – Chester 15.

- ✕✕ **Cottage Loaf,** Telegraph Rd, L48 0RB, on A 540 ☏ 648 1635 – 🅿
  closed Monday and Christmas Day – **M** a la carte 5.45/7.50 t. ⚗ 2.20.

TILBURY Essex 404 V 29 – pop. 11,130 – ☏ 037 52.
⛴ Shipping connections with the Continent: to Helsinki and Leningrad (Baltic Shipping Co.)
– to Gdynia via Rotterdam (Polish Ocean Lines).
London 24 – Southend-on-Sea 20.

Hotels and restaurants see : London W: 24 m.

TINTAGEL Cornwall 403 F 32 – pop. 1,372 – ECD: Wednesday except summer – ☏ 084 04.
See : Castle (ruins 12C) : site*, ≼** AC – Old Post Office* (14C) AC.
London 264 – Exeter 63 – Plymouth 49 – Truro 41.

- **Bossiney House,** Bossiney, PL34 0AX, ☏ 240, 🚗 – 🛏wc ⋔wc 🅿
  Easter-mid October – **M** (bar lunch) 4.70 st. ⚗ 2.15 – **19 rm** ⊒ 9.25/20.50 s.

TINTERN (TYNDYRN) Gwent 403 L 28 – pop. 647 – ECD: Wednesday – ✉ Chepstow –
☏ 029 18.
See : Abbey** (ruins) AC.
🛈 Tourist Information Centre, Tintern Abbey Car Park ☏ 431.
London 137 – Bristol 23 – Gloucester 40 – Newport 22.

- **Beaufort** (Embassy), NP6 6SF, on A 466 ☏ 202, 🚗 – 📺 🛏wc ⋔wc ☎ 🅿
  27 rm.
- **Royal George** (T.H.F.), Tintern Chepstow, NP6 6SF, ☏ 205, 🚗 – 📺 🛏wc ☎ 🅿. ⚑ AE
  ⓪ VISA
  M 4.50/4.75 st. ⚗ 1.65 – **18 rm** ⊒ 13.50/22.00 st.
- **Wye Valley,** High St., NP6 6SF, ☏ 441 – ⋔ 🅿. ⚑ VISA
  M a la carte 3.75/5.65 t. ⚗ 1.70 – **10 rm** ⊒ 8.50/14.50 t.

TITCHWELL Norfolk – pop. 131 – ✉ Kings Lynn – ☏ 048 521 Brancaster.
London 124 – Cambridge 66 – Norwich 41.

- **Manor House,** PE31 8BB, on A 149 ☏ 221, 🚗 – 🛏wc 🅿. ⚑ AE
  M a la carte 3.85/8.55 t. ⚗ 1.95 – **9 rm** ⊒ 11.50/22.50 t.

TIVERTON Devon – pop. 15,566 – ECD : Thursday – ☼ 088 42.

Envir. : Cullompton (St. Andrew's Church* 15C) SE : 9 m.

London 190 – Exeter 14 – Taunton 23.

🏨 **Tiverton Motel,** Blundells Rd, EX16 4DB, E : ½ m. on A 373 ℡ 3427 – 📺 ⛱wc 🛁wc 📞 ♿ 🅿. ⚒. 🔲 AE ⓪ VISA
M (grill rest.) a la carte 4.00/7.50 **st.** ▯ 1.50 – 🖂 2.25 – **30 rm** 14.00/22.00 **st.**

XX **Lowman,** 45 Gold St., EX16 6QB, ℡ 57311, 🚗
closed Wednesday dinner, Thursday, 2 weeks in Spring, 2 weeks in Autumn, Christmas Day dinner, 26 December and 1 January – **M** a la carte 2.60/5.55 **t.** ▯ 1.80.

X **Hendersons,** 18 Newport St. ℡ 4256 – 🅿. 🔲
closed Sunday and Monday – **M** a la carte 3.75/6.10 **t.** ▯ 1.20.

at Bolham N : 1 ¼ m. on A 396 – 🖂 ☼ 088 42 Tiverton :

🏨 **Hartnoll Country House,** Bolham Rd, EX16 7RA, ℡ 2777, ⇐, 🎣, 🚗 – ⛱wc 🅿. ⓪ VISA
M a la carte 5.10/7.00 **st.** ▯ 1.20 – 🖂 2.00 – **12 rm** 10.15/19.00 **st.**

AUSTIN-MORRIS-MG-ROVER-TRIUMPH, VANDEN PLAS Blundells Rd ℡ 56851

MAZDA, SKODA Normansland ℡ 088481 (Witheridge) 538
TALBOT 31 Leat St. ℡ 2170

TONBRIDGE Kent **404** U 30 – pop. 32,890 – ECD : Wednesday – ☼ 0732.

See : Tonbridge School* (1553). **Envir. :** Ightham Mote* (Manor House 14C-15C) *AC,* site* N : 7 m.

🏌 Poult Wood ℡ 64039.

London 33 – Brighton 37 – Hastings 31 – Maidstone 14.

🏨 **Rose and Crown** (T.H.F.), High St., TN9 1DD, ℡ 357966 – 📺 ⛱wc 📞 🅿. ⚒. 🔲 AE ⓪ VISA
M a la carte 4.05/6.40 **st.** ▯ 1.65 – **46 rm** 🖂 18.00/23.50 **st.**

DAIMLER-JAGUAR-ROVER-TRIUMPH Cannon Lane ℡ 364444

FORD Avebury Av. ℡ 356301
VW, AUDI-NSU, MERCEDES-BENZ Vale Rd ℡ 355822

TORCROSS Devon **403** J 33 – pop. 150 – ECD : Saturday – 🖂 Kingsbridge – ☼ 054 858.

London 242 – Dartmouth 9 – Exeter 42 – Plymouth 26.

🏚 **Torcross,** TQ7 2TQ, ℡ 206, ⇐, 🚗 – ⛱wc 🅿
March-October – **M** (bar lunch) 4.00 **t.** ▯ 1.80 – **20 rm** 🖂 10.00/20.00 **t.**

SAAB ℡ 205

TORQUAY Devon **403** J 32 – pop. 109,257 (inc. Brixham and Paignton) – ECD : Wednesday and Saturday – ☼ 0803.

See : Kent's Cavern** *AC* CX A – Museum* *AC* CX M – Torbay Road* BCZ – Ilsham Marine Drive* CX.

🛈 Vaughan Parade ℡ 27428.

London 223 – Exeter 23 – Plymouth 32.

Plans on following pages

🏨 **Imperial** (T.H.F.), Park Hill Rd, TQ1 2DG, ℡ 24301, Telex 42849, ⇐ Torbay. XX, ⅀ heated, 🔲, 🚗 – ▮ 📺 ♿ 🚙 🅿. ⚒. 🔲 AE ⓪ VISA
M 6.50/8.00 **st.** ▯ 3.50 – 🖂 3.50 – **168 rm** 30.00/42.00 **st.**
CZ **a**

🏨 **New Grand,** Promenade, TQ2 6NT, ℡ 25234, Telex 42891, ⇐, XX, ⅀ heated, 🚗 – ▮ 📺 🚙 🅿. ⚒. 🔲 AE ⓪ VISA
M a la carte 5.30/11.00 **t.** ▯ 1.75 – **110 rm** 🖂 23.00/46.00 **t.** – P 30.00/33.00 **t.**
BZ **r**

🏨 **Palace,** Babbacombe Rd, TQ1 3TG, ℡ 22271, Telex 42606, XX, ⅀ heated, 🔲, 🎾, 🚗, park – ▮ ♿ 🚙 🅿. ⚒. 🔲 AE ⓪ VISA
M 4.00/7.00 – **138 rm** 🖂 19.00/42.00 – P 25.00/39.50.
CX **u**

🏨 **Livermead House** (Best Western), Sea Front, TQ2 6QJ, ℡ 24361, Telex 42918, ⇐, XX, ⅀ heated, 🚗 – ▮ ♿ 🅿. ⚒
M 3.85/5.15 **s.** ▯ 1.95 – **76 rm** 🖂 9.50/24.85 **s.** – P 16.90/20.40 **s.**
BZ **e**

🏨 **Livermead Cliff** (Best Western), Sea Front, TQ2 6RQ, ℡ 22881, Telex 42918, ⇐, ⅀ heated, 🚗 – ▮ 🅿. ⚒
M 3.95/5.45 **s.** ▯ 1.95 – **62 rm** 🖂 9.50/25.10 **s.** – P 17.10/21.10 **s.**
BX **r**

🏨 **Toorak,** Chestnut Av., TQ2 5JS, ℡ 27135, XX, ⅀ heated, 🚗 – 🅿. ⚒
closed January – **M** 4.75/7.00 **st.** ▯ 1.65 – **80 rm** 🖂 16.00/35.20 **st.** – P 26.00/35.00 **st.**
BY **v**

🏨 **Osborne** 🕊, Meadfoot Beach, TQ1 2LL, ℡ 213311, ⇐, XX, ⅀ heated, 🚗 – ▮ 📺 🅿. ⚒. 🔲 AE ⓪ VISA – **85 rm.**
CX **c**

🏨 **Gleneagles,** Asheldon Rd, Wellswood, TQ1 2QS, ℡ 23637, ⇐, ⅀ heated, 🚗 – ⛱wc 🅿
April-October – **M** 3.75/5.00 ▯ 1.95 – **40 rm** 🖂 9.50/18.00.
CX **n**

🏨 **Kistor,** Belgrave Rd, TQ2 5HF, ℡ 23219, 🔲, 🚗 – ▮ ⛱wc 🅿. 🔲 AE VISA
M 4.00/5.00 **st.** ▯ 1.65 – **45 rm** 🖂 13.50/27.00 **st.**
CY **r**

🏨 Palm Court, Sea Front, TQ2 5HD, ℡ 24881, Telex 42987 – 🛗 📺 ⛱wc ☎ Ⓟ   **CZ z**
73 rm.

🏨 **Rainbow House and San Remo,** Belgrade Rd, TQ2 5HP, ℡ 21161, Telex 42468, ⌇
heated, ⌇, 🚗 – 🛗 ⛱wc Ⓟ. ⬛ AE ① VISA   **CY s**
M (buffet lunch June-August) 3.25/5.00 **st.** – **97 rm** ⫶ 12.80/23.55 **st.** – P 21.80/
23.80 **st.**

🏨 Belgrave, Belgrave Rd, TQ2 5HE, ℡ 28566, ⌇ heated – 🛗 ⛱wc 🚿wc ☎ Ⓟ. ⛲   **CZ c**
64 rm.

🏨 **Nepaul,** 27 Croft Rd, TQ2 5UD, ℡ 22745, ≼, 🚗 – 🛗 ⛱wc ☎ Ⓟ   **CY v**
M 3.00/4.50 **t.** 🍷 1.50 – **38 rm** ⫶ 9.50/19.00 – P 18.50/23.50 **t.**

🏨 Manor House, Seaway Lane, TQ2 6PS, ℡ 65164, Telex 42759, 🚗 – ⛱wc Ⓟ   **BZ a**
26 rm.

🏨 Alpine, Warren Rd, TQ2 5TP, ℡ 27612, ≼ Torbay and harbour, 🚗 – 🛗 ⛱wc 🚿wc   **CZ e**
18 rm.

🏨 Devonshire, Park Hill Rd, TQ1 2DY, ℡ 24850, Telex 42712, ✗, ⌇ heated, 🚗 – ⛱wc   **CZ s**
Ⓟ. ⬛ AE VISA
M 3.75/5.00 **t.** 🍷 1.75 – **58 rm** ⫶ 15.00/33.40 **t.**

🏨 Queens, Victoria Par., TQ1 2AY, ℡ 24324, Telex 42906 – 🛗 ⛱wc ☎. ⬛ AE ① VISA   **CZ r**
M 3.70/4.60 **t.** 🍷 2.00 – **73 rm** ⫶ 13.00/28.30 **t.** – P 17.90/19.90 **t.**

🏤 **Roslin Hall,** 1 Belgrave Rd, TQ2 5HG, ℡ 24373, ⌇ heated, 🚗 – ⛱wc Ⓟ. VISA   **CY u**
M 3.20/4.25 **st.** 🍷 1.70 – **52 rm** ⫶ 8.70/19.00 **st.** – P 13.10/17.70 **st.**

🏤 **Cavendish,** Belgrave Rd, TQ2 5HN, ℡ 23682, ⌇ heated – ⛱wc 🚿wc Ⓟ   **BY c**
March-mid October – **M** 4.30/5.30 **t.** 🍷 2.00 – **59 rm** ⫶ 15.00/35.90 **t.** – P 21.80 **t.**

🏤 **Nethway,** Falkland Rd, TQ2 5JR, ℡ 27630, 🚗 – ⛱wc 🚿wc Ⓟ   **BY u**
Easter-October and Christmas – **M** (bar lunch) 3.80 **t.** 🍷 1.90 – **24 rm** ⫶ 9.50/
17.45 **t.**

🏤 **Coppice,** Barrington Rd, Wellswood, TQ1 2QJ, ℡ 27786, ⌇ heated, 🚗 – ⛱wc 🚿wc   **CX i**
Ⓟ
Easter-mid October – **M** (buffet lunch) 3.00/5.00 **s.** 🍷 1.50 – **18 rm** ⫶ 8.00/18.00 **s.**

🏤 Alvanley, Croft Rd, TQ2 5UD, ℡ 22466, 🚗 – ⛱wc Ⓟ   **CY c**
April-October and Christmas – **20 rm** ⫶ 8.00/18.00 **t.**

🏠 Clevedon, Meadfoot Sea Rd, TQ1 2LQ, ℡ 24260, 🚗 – Ⓟ   **CX v**
May-September – **15 rm** ⫶ 10.50/21.00 **t.**

🏠 **The Skerries,** 25 Morgan Av., TQ2 5RR, ℡ 23618 – Ⓟ   **CY a**
13 rm ⫶ 5.00/7.00 **st.**

🏠 Mount Nessing, St. Lukes Rd North, TQ2 5PD, ℡ 22970   **CZ i**
April-October – **14 rm** ⫶ 7.90/15.80 **t.**

🏠 Concorde, 26 Newton Rd, TQ2 5BZ, ℡ 22330, 🚗 – Ⓟ   **BY e**
17 rm.

🏠 **Audrey Court,** Lower Warbery Rd, TQ1 1QS, ℡ 24563, 🚗 – Ⓟ   **CX s**
March-October and Christmas – **20 rm** ⫶ 8.00/16.10 **st.**

✗✗ **Fanny's Dining Room,** 53 Abbey Rd, TQ2 5NQ, ℡ 28605   **CY o**
closed Sunday and 1 to 15 November – **M** (dinner only) a la carte 8.30/12.50 **t.** 🍷 2.45.

✗✗ **John Dory,** 7 Lisburne Sq., TQ2 2PT, ℡ 25217, Seafood – ⬛   **CX x**
closed Sunday and Monday – **M** (dinner only) 8.20 **st.** 🍷 2.25.

✗ **Mattie's Eating House,** 172 Union St., Castle Circus, TQ2 5QP, ℡ 27471 – AE ①
VISA   **CY n**
closed Sunday and Bank Holidays lunch – **M** (bar lunch) a la carte 2.80/6.00 **st.** 🍷 2.20.

*at **Maidencombe** N: 3 ½ m. on A 379* – **BX** – ✉ ☎ 0803 Torquay:

🏨 **Maidencombe House,** Teignmouth Rd, TQ1 4SF, ℡ 36611, ≼, ⌇ heated, 🚗 – ⛱wc
Ⓟ. ⬛ ①
M (bar lunch) 5.00 **st.** – **32 rm** ⫶ 10.65/21.30 **st.**

*at **Stokeinteignhead** N: 5 m. off A 379* – **BX** – ✉ Torquay – ☎ 062 687 Shaldon:

✗✗ Harvest Barn, Stoke Rd, TQ12 4QS, ℡ 3670 – Ⓟ.

*at **Babbacombe** NE: 1 ½ m.* – ✉ ☎ 0803 Torquay:

🏤 **Norcliffe,** Babbacombe Downs Rd, TQ1 3LF, ℡ 38456, ≼, 🚗 – ⛱wc Ⓟ   **CX r**
Easter-October – **M** (bar lunch) 2.50/4.50 **st.** 🍷 1.00 – **22 rm** ⫶ 12.50/25.00 **st.**

🚗 *Pas de publicité payée dans ce guide.*

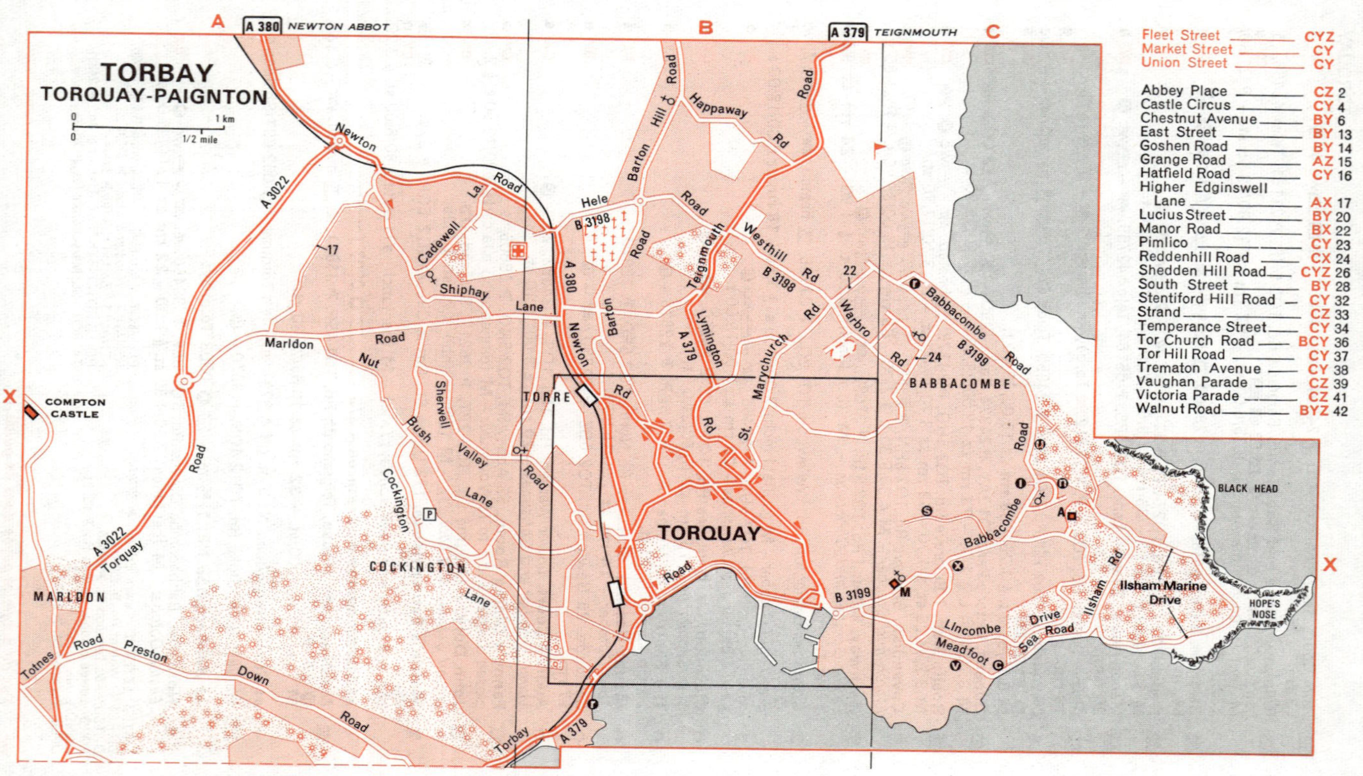

TORBAY
TORQUAY-PAIGNTON

0   1 km
0   1/2 mile

A 380 NEWTON ABBOT
A 379 TEIGNMOUTH
A
B
C
X

Fleet Street — CYZ
Market Street — CY
Union Street — CY

Abbey Place — CZ 2
Castle Circus — CY 4
Chestnut Avenue — BY 6
East Street — BY 13
Goshen Road — BY 14
Grange Road — AZ 15
Hatfield Road — CY 16
Higher Edginswell Lane — AX 17
Lucius Street — BY 20
Manor Road — BX 22
Pimlico — CY 23
Reddenhill Road — CX 24
Shedden Hill Road — CYZ 26
South Street — BY 28
Stentiford Hill Road — CY 32
Strand — CZ 33
Temperance Street — CY 34
Tor Church Road — BCY 36
Tor Hill Road — CY 37
Trematon Avenue — CY 38
Vaughan Parade — CZ 39
Victoria Parade — CZ 41
Walnut Road — BYZ 42

TORQUAY
TORRE
BABBACOMBE
COCKINGTON
MARLDON
COMPTON CASTLE
BLACK HEAD
HOPE'S NOSE
Ilsham Marine Drive

Newton
Road
La
A 3022
Cadewell
Shiphay
Lane
17
B 3198
Hele
Barton Hill Road
Happaway
Road
Teignmouth
Westhill Rd
B 3198
Warbro
22
24
B 3199
A 380
Barton
Newton
A 379
Lymington
Marychurch
Rd
St.
Marldon
Nut
Sherwell
Bush
Valley Lane
Cockington
Lane
Road
Road
Torquay
A 3022
Totnes
Preston
Down
Road
Torbay
A 379
B 3199
Babbacombe Road
Lincombe
Drive
Meadfoot
Sea Road
Ilsham Rd
M
A

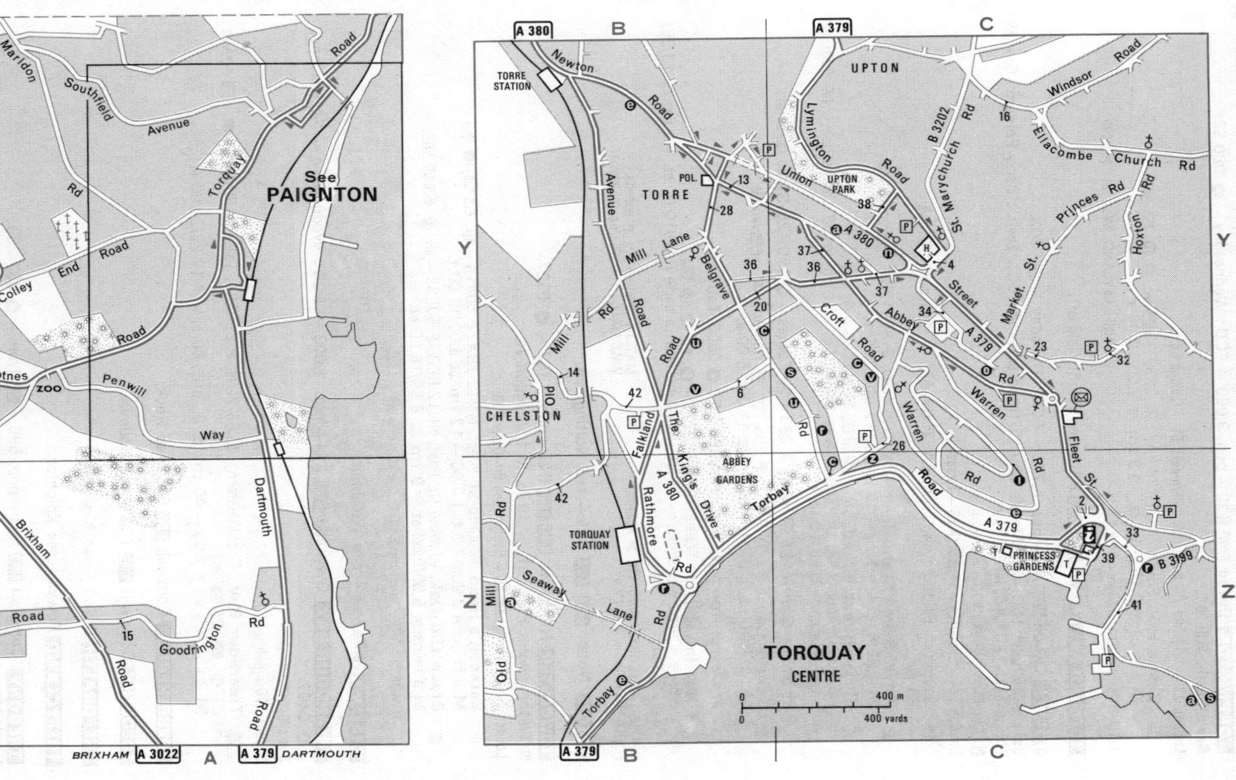

TORQUAY
CENTRE
See
PAIGNTON
A 380
A 379
A 385 PLYMOUTH
BRIXHAM A 3022
A 379 DARTMOUTH
TORRE STATION
Newton
Torre
TORQUAY STATION
UPTON
UPTON PARK
Union
Lymington Road
B 3202
St. Marychurch Rd
Windsor Road
Ellacombe
Church Rd
Princes Rd
Hoxton Rd
Market St.
Warren Rd
Warren Rd
Abbey
Croft Road
Belgrave
Mill Lane
Mill Rd
Avenue
Road
The King's Drive
Abbey Gardens
Torbay
Falkland Rd
Rathmore Rd
Torquay Road
Seaway Lane
Old Mill
Torbay Rd
Chelston
Old
Fleet St.
Street
A 379
Road
Princess Gardens
B 3199
POL.
ZOO
Marldon
Southfield
Avenue
King's
Ash Road
A 3022
Colley End Road
Totnes
Penwill Way
Road
Dartmouth
Brixham Road
Long Road
Goodrington Rd
400 m
400 yards

TORRINGTON Devon **403** H 31 – pop. 3,050 – ECD : Wednesday – ☎ 080 52.
See : Castle Hill ⩙★.
London 225 – Bideford 7 – Exeter 36 – Plymouth 51 – Taunton 54.

⚓ **Castle Hill,** South St., EX38 8AA, ☏ 2339 – ⛟wc 🏛 **P.** 🔃 **VISA**
M a la carte 3.15/6.10 **st.** – **13 rm** ☲ 9.50/16.00 **s.**

ALFA-ROMEO The Square ☏ 2555   BRITISH LEYLAND Well St. ☏ 2229

TOTLAND BAY I.O.W. **403 404** P 31 – see Wight (Isle of).

TOTNES Devon **403** I 32 – pop. 5,772 – ECD : Thursday – ☎ 0803.
See : Guildhall★ 16C – St. Mary's Church (rood screen★ 15C). **Envir. :** Berry Pomeroy Castle★
(ruins 13C-17C) AC, NE : 2 ½ m.
🛈 The Plains ☏ 863168 (summer only).
London 224 – Exeter 24 – Plymouth 23 – Torquay 9.

🏨 **Seymour,** Bridgetown, TQ9 5AA, ☏ 864686 – ⛟wc ☏ **P.** 🔁
30 rm.

🏨 **Royal Seven Stars,** The Plains, TQ9 5DD, ☏ 862125 – ⛟wc **P.** ⓞ
M 4.25/6.50 **t.** 🍷 1.75 – **18 rm** ☲ 12.00/22.00 **t.**

✗ **Elbow Room,** 6 North St., TQ9 5NZ, ☏ 863480 – **AE VISA**
closed Sunday, Monday, last 2 weeks October and 26 to 28 December – **M** (dinner
only) a la carte 6.85/10.15 **t.**

at Stoke Gabriel SE : 4 m. by A 385 – ✉ Totnes – ☎ 080 428 Stoke Gabriel :

🏨 **Gabriel Court** ⚘, TQ9 6SF, ☏ 206, ✎, 🏊 heated, 🛱 – ⛟wc **P**
M 5.00/7.00 **s.** 🍷 2.00 – **25 rm** ☲ 11.00/25.00 **s.**

at Dartington NW : 2 m. off A 385 – ✉ ☎ 0803 Totnes :

✗ **Cott Inn** with rm, TQ9 6HE, ☏ 863777 – **P.** 🔃 **AE ⓞ VISA**
closed Christmas dinner – **M** (buffet lunch) a la carte 8.50/10.00 **st.** – **6 rm** ☲ 13.25/
26.50 **st.**

BRITISH LEYLAND North St. ☏ 862466   MAZDA Station Rd ☏ 862404
FORD The Plains ☏ 862196   VAUXHALL The Plains ☏ 862247

TOTON Notts. **403 404** Q 25 – see Nottingham.

TOWCESTER Northants. **403 404** R 27 – pop. 3,768 – ☎ 0327.
🏌 Farthingstone ☏ 36291, W : 6 m. M 1 Junction 16.
London 70 – Birmingham 50 – Northampton 9 – Oxford 36.

🏨 **Saracen's Head,** Watling St. West, NN12 7BX, ☏ 50414 – **P.** 🔃 **AE ⓞ VISA**
M a la carte 3.90/6.50 **t.** 🍷 2.00 – **12 rm** ☲ 9.00/16.00 **t.**

🏨 **Brave Old Oak,** Watling St. East, NN12 8LB, ☏ 50533 – ☏ **P.** 🔃 **AE VISA**
M a la carte 5.00/9.00 **st.** – **9 rm** ☲ 8.50/18.50 **st.**

AUSTIN-MORRIS-MG Quinbury End ☏ 032 732 (Blakesley) 208

TRALLWNG Powys – see Welshpool.

TREARDDUR BAY Gwynedd **403** G 24 – pop. 1,000 – ECD : Wednesday – ✉ Holyhead
– ☎ 0407.
See : Site★.
London 270 – Holyhead 2.

🏨 **Trearddur Bay** (Best Western), LL65 2UN, ☏ 860301, Telex 61609, 🔃, 🛱 – 📺 ⛟wc
☏ **P.** 🔃 **AE ⓞ VISA**
M 3.45/5.20 **st.** 🍷 1.60 – **40 rm** ☲ 9.75/25.00 **s.** – P 17.25/20.00 **s.**

TREBETHERICK Cornwall **403** F 32 – see Rock.

TREDETHY Cornwall **403** F 32 – see Bodmin.

TREFDRAETH Dyfed – see Newport.

TREFYCLAWD Powys – see Knighton.

TREGONY Cornwall **403** F 33 – pop. 595 – ✉ Truro – ☎ 087 253.
London 290 – Exeter 84 – Plymouth 47 – Truro 9.

✗ **Kea House,** ☏ 642 – 🔃
closed Sunday dinner, 3 weeks October-November, 25 December and 1 January –
M (dinner only) a la carte approx. 5.30 **t.** 🍷 1.70.

TREGREHAN Cornwall **403** F 32 – see St. Austell.

TRENT BRIDGE Notts. 403 404 Q 25 – see Nottingham.

TRESCO Cornwall 403 B 34 – see Scilly (Isles of).

TREYARNON BAY Cornwall 403 E 32 – pop. 100 – ⊠ Padstow – ✆ 0841 St. Merryn.
London 292 – Newquay 9 – Truro 23.

- 🏨 **Waterbeach** ⚓, PL28 8JW, ☏ 520292, ≼, ✿, 🚗 – 🛏wc 🛆 🚘 🅿
  March–September – **M** (bar lunch) 5.00/7.00 **t.** – **18 rm** ⚏ 18.00/38.00 **st.**

TRING Herts. 404 R 28 – pop. 7,790 – ECD: Wednesday – ✆ 044 282.
See : Church of St. Peter and St. Paul (interior: stone corbels*).
London 38 – Aylesbury 7 – Luton 14.

- 🏨 **Rose and Crown** (T.H.F.), High St., HP23 5AH, ☏ 4071 – TV 🛏wc ☎ 🅿. 🛆. 🔾 AE ⓘ
  VISA
  M 3.80/4.80 **st.** 🍷 1.75 – **16 rm** ⚏ 13.50/21.00 **st.**

AUSTIN-DAIMLER-JAGUAR-MORRIS-ROVER-TRIUMPH Brook St. ☏ 2455

HONDA, RELIANT 110 Western Rd ☏ 4144
RENAULT 22 Western Rd ☏ 3027

TROUTBECK Cumbria – see Windermere.

TRUMPINGTON Cambs. 404 U 27 – see Cambridge.

TRURO Cornwall 403 E 33 – pop. 14,849 – ECD: Thursday – ✆ 0872.
See : Country Museum*. Envir. : Trelissick gardens* *AC*, S: 4 ½ m.
🏌₁₈ Treliske ☏ 2640, W: 2 m. on A 390.
🅱 Municipal Buildings, Boscawen St. ☏ 74555.
London 295 – Exeter 87 – Penzance 26 – Plymouth 52.

- 🏨 **Brookdale**, Tregolls Rd, TR1 1JZ, ☏ 3513 – TV 🛏wc 🛆wc ☎ 🅿. 🔾 AE ⓘ VISA
  M 2.50/4.75 **s.** – **52 rm** ⚏ 9.50/24.00 **s.** – P 16.20/18.50 **s.**

- 🏨 **Carlton**, 46 Falmouth Rd, TR1 2HL, ☏ 2450 – 🛏wc 🛆wc 🅿. 🔾
  closed 1 to 23 October and 22 December-1 January – **M** (dinner only) a la carte 4.00/5.50 🍷 1.60 – ⚏ 2.20 – **25 rm** 8.70/17.00 **s.**

BRITISH LEYLAND Newquay Rd ☏ 2581
DAF Calenick St. ☏ 2995
FORD Lemon Quay ☏ 3933
RENAULT Lemon Quay ☏ 74321

TALBOT Bissoe ☏ 0872 (Devoran) 863073
VAUXHALL Faimantle St. ☏ 76231
VW, AUDI Three Milestone ☏ 79301

TUDDENHAM Suffolk 404 V 27 – pop. 327 – ⊠ Bury St. Edmunds – ✆ 0638 Mildenhall.
London 73 – Cambridge 22 – Ipswich 37.

- ✗✗ Tuddenham Mill, IP28 6SQ, ☏ 713552, « Restored 18C water mill » – 🅿.

TUDWEILIOG Gwynedd 403 G 25 – ⊠ Pwllheli – ✆ 075 887.
London 267 – Caernarfon 25.

- ✗ **Dive Inn**, LL53 7PB, W: 2 m. off B 4417 ☏ 246 – 🅿
  closed Sunday dinner and Monday to Friday from November to Easter – **M** (bar lunch) 2.50/8.35 **t.** 🍷 1.80.

TUNBRIDGE WELLS Kent 404 U 30 – see Royal Tunbridge Wells.

TURVEY Beds. 404 S 27 – see Bedford.

TUTBURY Staffs. – pop. 3,025 – ECD: Wednesday – ⊠ ✆ 0283 Burton-upon-Trent.
London 132 – Birmingham 33 – Derby 11 – Stoke-on-Trent 27.

- ✗✗ **Ye Olde Dog and Partridge Inn** with rm, High St., DE13 9LS, ☏ 813030, « 15C timbered inn », 🚗 – TV 🛏wc ☎ 🅿. 🔾 AE ⓘ VISA
  closed 25-26 December and 1 January – **M** *(closed Saturday lunch, Sunday and Monday)* a la carte 5.65/9.90 **t.** – **17 rm** ⚏ 19.00/25.00 **t.**

TUXFORD Notts. 404 R 24 – pop. 2,145 – ECD: Wednesday – ⊠ Newark – ✆ 0777.
London 141 – Leeds 53 – Lincoln 18 – Nottingham 26 – Sheffield 29.

- 🏨 **Newcastle Arms**, NG22 0LA, ☏ 870208 – TV 🛏wc 🛆 ☎ 🅿. 🔾 AE ⓘ VISA
  M *(closed Sunday dinner)* 7.10/8.40 🍷 1.75 – **14 rm** ⚏ 15.00/22.00.

TWO BRIDGES Devon 403 I 32 – pop. 30 – ⊠ Yelverton – ✆ 0822 Postbridge.
London 226 – Exeter 25 – Plymouth 17.

- 🏠 **Cherrybrook** ⚓, PL20 6SP, NE: 1 m. on B 3212 ☏ 88260, ≼, 🚗 – 🅿
  closed Christmas and 1 January – **8 rm** ⚏ 7.15/14.30 **st.**

TYDDEWI Dyfed – see St. David's.

TYNDYRN Gwent – see Tintern.

TYNEMOUTH Tyne and Wear 🅱️🅱️🅱️ ⑲ – pop. 69,338 – ECD: Wednesday – ☎ 089 45 North Shields.

See : Priory and castle : ruins* (11C) *AC.*

🅱️ Grand Parade, North Shields ☏ 70251.

London 290 – Newcastle-upon-Tyne 8 – Sunderland 7.

 🏨 **Grand,** Grand Parade, NE30 3ER, ☏ 72106, ≼ – ▐ TV ⌷wc ☏ **P.** 🅰️. 🔄 AE ① VISA
  M 3.50/4.25 ▮ 1.75 – **38 rm** ⌷ 14.50/26.00 – P 18.60/21.50.

 🏨 **Park** (Open House), Grand Parade, NE30 4JQ, ☏ 71406, ≼ – TV ⌷wc ☏ **P.** 🅰️. 🔄
  AE ① VISA
  closed Christmas Day – **M** 3.95/5.25 **t.** ▮ 1.70 – **28 rm** ⌷ 14.00/25.00 **t.**

FIAT 5/7 Tynemouth Rd ☏ 71830   VAUXHALL Tynemouth Rd ☏ 70346
RENAULT Preston North Rd, Preston Grange ☏ 70352

UCKFIELD East Sussex 🅱️🅱️🅱️ U 31 – pop. 5,973 – ECD: Wednesday – ☎ 0825.
London 45 – Brighton 17 – Eastbourne 20 – Maidstone 34.

 ✕ **Sussex Barn,** Ringles Cross, TN22 1HB, N : 1 m. on A 22 ☏ 3827 – **P.** AE VISA
  closed Sunday dinner and Monday – **M** a la carte 6.05/7.75 **t.** ▮ 2.00.

 at Framfield SE : 1¾ m. on B 2102 – ✉ Uckfield – ☎ 082 582 Framfield :

 ✕ **Coach House,** The Street, TN22 5NL, ☏ 636 – **P**
  closed Sunday dinner, Monday, first week May, 25 October-9 November, 25-26 December
  and Bank Holidays – **M** a la carte 6.05/9.05 **t.** ▮ 2.20.

AUSTIN-MORRIS-MG-ROVER-TRIUMPH 84/86 High OPEL London Rd, Maresfield ☏ 2477
St. ☏ 4255   VAUXHALL 143/145 High St. ☏ 2786

ULLSWATER Cumbria 🅱️🅱️🅱️ ⑲ – ✉ Penrith – ☎ 085 36 Pooley Bridge.
See : Lake*.

🅱️ Beckside Car Park, Glenridding ☏ 085 32 (Glenridding) 414 (summer only).

London 296 – Carlisle 25 – Kendal 31 – Penrith 6.

 at Pooley Bridge on B 5320 – ✉ Penrith – ☎ 08536 Pooley Bridge :

 🏨 **Sharrow Bay Country House** 🦢, CA10 2LZ, S : 2 m. on Howtown Rd ☏ 301, ≼
  lake and hills, « Lake-side setting, tasteful decor », 🚗 – TV ♿ **P**
  March-November – **M** 9.75/11.75 **st.** – **26 rm** ⌷ (dinner included) 34.50/80.50 **st.**

 at Watermillock on A 592 – ✉ Penrith – ☎ 085 36 Pooley Bridge :

 🏨 **Leeming House** 🦢, CA11 0JJ, on A 592 ☏ 444, ≼ lake, hills and gardens, « Elegant
  installation and finely laid out gardens », park – **P.** 🔄 AE ① VISA
  16 February-5 November – **M** a la carte 5.50/7.15 **s.** ▮ 1.25 – ⌷ 1.75 – **24 rm** 15.00/
  30.00 **s.** – P 29.00/36.00 **s.**

 at Glenridding on A 592 – ✉ Penrith – ☎ 085 32 Glenridding :

 🏨 **Ullswater,** CA11 0PA, ☏ 444, Telex 64357, ≼, 🚗 – ▐ ♿ **P.** 🅰️. 🔄 AE ① VISA
  M approx. 9.50 **t.** ▮ 2.40 – **48 rm** ⌷ 15.00/30.00 **t.**

 🏨 **Glenridding,** CA11 0PB, on A 592 ☏ 228, ≼, 🚗 – ⌷wc **P.** 🔄 AE ① VISA
  M (bar lunch) 2.00/5.00 **st.** ▮ 2.10 – **33 rm** ⌷ 11.50/21.00 **st.** – P 15.00/16.00 **st.**

ULVERSTON Cumbria 🅱️🅱️🅱️ ㉓ – pop. 10,710 – ECD: Wednesday – ☎ 0229.
Envir. : Furness Abbey* (ruins 13C - 15C) *AC,* SW : 6 ½ m.

🛬 Hawcoat ☏ 0229 (Barrow-in-Furness) 25444, SW : 7 m. – 🛬 Askam-in-Furness ☏ 0229
(Barrow-in-Furness) 62675.

🅱️ The Renaissance Centre, 17 Foutain St. ☏ 52299.

London 278 – Kendal 25 – Lancaster 36.

 🏨 **Lonsdale House,** Daltongate, LA12 7BD, ☏ 52598, 🚗 – TV ⌷wc ☏. AE
  closed 1 week at Christmas – **M** (dinner only) a la carte 6.00/7.95 ▮ 2.00 – **19 rm**
  ⌷ 9.00/18.00.

 at Lowick Green NE : 5 m. on A 5092 by A 590 – ✉ Ulverston – ☎ 022 986 Greenodd :

 🏨 **Farmers Arms,** LA12 8DT, ☏ 277 – **P.** 🔄 VISA
  M (bar lunch) a la carte 4.10/6.70 **t.** ▮ 2.00 – **13 rm** ⌷ 7.70/16.50 **t.**

UNDERBARROW Cumbria – pop. 362 (inc. Bradleyfield) – ✉ Kendal – ☎ 044 88 Crosthwaite.
London 267 – Blackpool 49 – Carlisle 52 – Kendal 3.5.

 ✕✕ **Greenriggs Country House** 🦢 with rm, LA8 8HF, E : ½ m. ☏ 387, ≼, « Country
  house atmosphere », 🚗 – ⌷wc **P**
  closed January – **M** *(closed Sunday dinner)* (dinner only) 7.50 **t.** ▮ 1.50 – **12 rm**
  ⌷ 12.00/26.00 **t.**

UPLYME Devon **403** L 31 – see Lyme Regis.

UPPER ARLEY Heref. and Worc. **403** **404** M 26 – see Kidderminster.

UPPER HALLIFORD Surrey **404** S 29 – see Shepperton.

UPPER SLAUGHTER Glos. **403** **404** O 28 – see Stow-on-the-Wold.

UPPINGHAM Leics. **404** R 26 – pop. 3,250 – ECD : Thursday – ✆ 057 282.
London 101 – Leicester 19 – Northampton 28 – Nottingham 35.

     Falcon, Market Pl., LE15 9PY, ☎ 3535 – ⊟wc ⋔wc ☏ **P**. **AE** ⓪ **VISA**
     M a la carte approx. 5.75 ⋔ 1.90 – **22 rm** ⊇ 14.00/23.65.

     Central, 16 High St. West, LE15 9QD, ☎ 2352, 🚗 – 🔼 **AE** **VISA**
     closed 24 December-6 January – **M** 2.70/3.50 **st.** ⋔ 2.10 – **13 rm** ⊇ 8.00/15.00 **st.**

UPTON UPON SEVERN Heref. and Worc. **403** **404** N 27 – pop. 2,048 – ECD : Thursday –
✆ 068 46.
🛈 Church Lodge, 69 Old St. ☎ 2318.
London 116 – Hereford 25 – Stratford-upon-Avon 29 – Worcester 11.

     White Lion, High St., WR8 0PA, ☎ 2551 – ⊟wc **P**. 🔼
     M a la carte 3.65/5.25 ⋔ 2.10 – **14 rm** ⊇ 10.50/22.00 **t.**

     Pool House, Hanley Rd, WR8 0PA, NW : ½ m. on B 4211 ☎ 2151, ≤, ⚲, 🚗 – **P**
     May-September – **12 rm** ⊇ 6.50/13.00 **s.**

USK (BRYNBUGA) Gwent **403** L 28 – pop. 2,060 – ECD : Wednesday – ✆ 029 13.
See : Valley★.
🛈₁₈ at Pontypool ☎ 049 55 (Pontypool) 3655, W : 7 m.
London 144 – Bristol 30 – Gloucester 39 – Newport 10.

     Three Salmons, Bridge St., NP5 1BQ, ☎ 2133, 🚗 – 📺 ⊟wc ☏ **P**. 🔼 **VISA**
     closed 24 to 26 December – **M** *(closed Sunday dinner to non-residents)* a la carte 6.55/
     9.85 **t.** ⋔ 2.20 – **30 rm** ⊇ 13.00/23.00 **t.**

     Glen-yr-Afon House, Pontypool Rd, NP5 1SY, ☎ 2302, 🚗 – ⋔wc **P**
     M 3.75/4.25 **t.** ⋔ 1.75 – **15 rm** ⊇ 10.45/13.80 **t.** – P 12.95/13.95 **t.**

AUSTIN-MG-WOLSELEY ☎ 2136   MORRIS-MG-WOLSELEY ☎ 2014

UTTOXETER Staffs. **403** **404** O 25 – pop. 8,430 – ECD : Thursday – ✆ 088 93 – 🛈₉.
London 145 – Birmingham 33 – Derby 19 – Stafford 13 – Stoke-on-Trent 16.

     White Hart (Ansells), Carter St., ST14 8EU. ☎ 2437 – ⊟wc ⋔wc ☏ **P**. 🔼 **AE**
     M 5.35/6.40 **t.** ⋔ 1.80 – **16 rm** ⊇ 15.95/20.80 **t.**

AUSTIN-JAGUAR-MG-ROVER-TRIUMPH 20/24 Carter   FORD, VAUXHALL Derby Rd ☎ 2301
St. ☎ 2255   TALBOT Market St. ☎ 2858

VENN OTTERY Devon **403** K 31 – pop. 120 – ✉ ✆ 040 481 Ottery St. Mary.
London 209 – Exeter 11 – Sidmouth 5.

     Venn Ottery Barton 🦢, EX11 1RZ, ☎ 2733, 🚗 – ⊟wc **P**
     15 March-5 November – **10 rm** ⊇ 7.15/14.30 **t.**

VENTNOR I.O.W. **403** **404** Q 32 – see Wight (Isle of).

VERYAN Cornwall **403** F 33 – pop. 876 – ✉ Truro – ✆ 087 250.
London 291 – St. Austell 13 – Truro 13.

     Nare 🦢, TR2 5PF, SW : 1 ¼ m. ☎ 279, ≤ Gerrans Bay, ✗, ⌁ heated, 🚗 – ⊟wc ⋔wc
     P. ⚓. 🔼 **AE** ⓪
     Easter-October – **M** (buffet lunch) 3.05/6.90 **t.** ⋔ 2.45 – **43 rm** ⊇ 8.80/36.00 **t.** – P 17.00/
     23.00 **t.**

     Elerkey House, TR2 5QA, ☎ 261, 🚗 – ⊟wc ⋔ **P**
     April-September – **M** (bar lunch) approx. 4.75 **s.** ⋔ 1.50 – **9 rm** ⊇ 6.50/14.60.

     at Ruan High Lanes W : 1 ¼ m. on A 3078 – ✉ Truro – ✆ 087 250 Veryan :

     Polsue Manor 🦢, TR2 5LU, ☎ 270, ≤, 🚗 – ⊟wc **P**
     Easter-September – **M** (dinner only) 5.60 **s.** ⋔ 1.75 – **13 rm** ⊇ 10.50/24.00 **s.**

WADDESDON Bucks. **404** R 28 – pop. 1,939 – ECD : Thursday – ✆ 029 665.
See : Waddesdon Manor (Rothschild Collection★★★) *AC.*
London 52 – Aylesbury 6 – Birmingham 66 – Oxford 25.

     Hotels and restaurant see : **Aylesbury** E : 5 m

WADDINGTON Lancs. – pop. 885 – ✉ ✪ 0200 Clitheroe.
London 237 – Blackpool 36 – Leeds 45 – Liverpool 50.

🏠 Moorcock Inn, BB7 3AA, N : 2 m. on B 6478 ⌀ 22333, ≼, ⇗ – 📺 ⌷wc ☎ 🅿
5 rm.

WADEBRIDGE Cornwall 🔢 F 32 – pop. 3,553 – ECD : Wednesday – ✪ 020 881.
London 280 – Exeter 70 – Plymouth 37 – Truro 23.

🏠 **Molesworth Arms,** Molesworth St., PL27 7DP, ⌀ 2055 – ⌷wc 🅿. 🅿 VISA
M 3.50/4.50 st. ♦ 1.75 – **13 rm** ⌷ 9.00/20.00 st. – P 14.00/18.00 st.

BRITISH LEYLAND Egloshayle Rd ⌀ 2121   ROVER-TRIUMPH Brooklyn Garage ⌀ 2758

WAKEFIELD West Yorks. 🔢 ⑫ and ㉓ – pop. 59,590 – ECD : Wednesday – ✪ 0924.
Envir. : Pontefract (castle* : ruins 12C-13C) AC, E : 9 m.

🏌 Flushdyke, Osset ⌀ 092 43 (Osset) 3275, N : 2 m. – 🏌 Woodthorpe ⌀ 255104, S : 3 m. –
🏌 Lupset Park, Horbury Rd ⌀ 74316 – 🏌 Painthorpe Lane ⌀ 255083, near junction 39 on M 1.

🅸 Town Hall, Wood St. ⌀ 70700/70789.

London 188 – Leeds 9 – Manchester 38 – Sheffield 23.

🏨 **Post House** (T.H.F.), Queen's Drive, Osset, WF5 9BE, W : 2 ½ m. on A 638 ⌀ 276388,
Telex 55407, ⇗ – 🛗 📺 ⌷wc ☎ ᴕ 🅿. 🛎. 🅿 AE ⓞ VISA
M 5.00/6.00 st. ♦ 1.65 – ⌷ 2.25 – **96 rm** 18.00/25.50 st.

🏨 Swallow (Swallow), Queen St., WF1 1JR, ⌀ 72111 – 🛗 📺 ⌷wc ☎. 🛎 – **64 rm.**

AUSTIN-MORRIS-MG-ROVER-TRIUMPH-WOLSELEY   OPEL Westgate ⌀ 66261
Ings Rd ⌀ 70100   RENAULT 129 New Rd, Middlestown ⌀ 272087
AUSTIN-MG 160 Westgate ⌀ 74222   TALBOT, FIAT, CITROEN Ings Rd ⌀ 76771
BMW Ings Rd ⌀ 63796   TOYOTA Stanley Rd ⌀ 73493
DATSUN Barnsley Rd ⌀ 255904   VAUXHALL 106/118 Horbury Rd ⌀ 75588
FORD Barnsley Rd ⌀ 70551   VAUXHALL 68 Ings Rd ⌀ 72812
JAGUAR-ROVER-TRIUMPH Doncaster Rd ⌀ 77261   VOLVO Barnsley Rd ⌀ 255126
MORRIS-MG-WOLSELEY Robin Hood ⌀ 0532 (Leeds)   VW, AUDI Chapelthorpe ⌀ 250336
822254

WALBERSWICK Suffolk 🔢 Y 27 – pop. 423 – ECD : Wednesday – ✉ ✪ 050 272 (4 fig.)
or 0502 (6 fig.) Southwold. – London 106 – Great Yarmouth 28 – Ipswich 33 – Norwich 32.

🏠 Anchor, Main St., IP18 6UA, ⌀ 722112, ⇗ – ⌷wc 🅿. 🅿 AE ⓞ VISA – **14 rm.**

WALBERTON West Sussex 🔢 S 31 – see Arundel.

WALL Northumb. – see Hexham.

WALLCROUCH Kent U 30 – see Royal Tunbridge Wells.

WALLINGFORD Oxon. 🔢 🔢 Q 29 – pop. 6,182 – ECD : Wednesday – ✪ 0491.
🅸 Stone Hall, High St. ⌀ 36969 ext. 25.

London 54 – Oxford 12 – Reading 16.

🏨 **George,** High St., OX10 0BS, ⌀ 36665 – 📺 ⌷wc ☎ 🅿. 🛎. 🅿 AE ⓞ VISA
M 4.50 t. ♦ 2.00 – **18 rm** ⌷ 17.00/31.50 t.

🏨 **Shillingford Bridge,** OX10 8LZ, N : 2 m. on A 329 ⌀ 086 732 (Warborough) 8567,
≼, ⫩ heated, ⇖, ⇗ – ⌷wc ⌷wc ☎ 🅿. 🛎. 🅿 AE ⓞ VISA
M 6.00 t. ♦ 1.50 – **21 rm** ⌷ 16.00/24.00 t.

WALLSEND Tyne and Wear – see Newcastle-upon-Tyne.

WALMLEY West Midlands 🔢 🔢 O 26 – see Birmingham.

WALSALL West Midlands 🔢 🔢 O 26 – pop. 184,734 – ECD : Thursday – ✪ 0922.
London 126 – Birmingham 9 – Coventry 29 – Shrewsbury 36.

Plan of Enlarged Area : See Birmingham p. 2-3

🏨 Walsall Crest Motel (Crest), Birmingham Rd, WS5 3AB, SE : 1 m. on A 34 ⌀ 33555 –
📺 ⌷wc ☎ ᴕ 🅿. 🅿 AE ⓞ VISA   CT e
⌷ 2.40 – **106 rm** 18.50/25.20 st.

🏨 **County,** 45 Birmingham Rd, WS1 2NG, ⌀ 32323 – 📺 ⌷wc 🍴 ☎ 🅿. 🅿 AE ⓞ VISA CT u
M (closed Saturday lunch) 4.25/4.75 st. ♦ 1.70 – **47 rm** ⌷ 12.50/18.10 st.

at Walsall Wood NE : 3 ½ m. on A 461 – CT – ✉ Walsall – ✪ 054 33 Brownhills :

🏨 **Barons Court,** Walsall Rd, WS9 9AH, ⌀ 6543, Telex 338212 – 🛗 📺 🅿. 🛎. 🅿 AE ⓞ VISA
M 4.50/5.50 t. ♦ 1.50 – **75 rm** ⌷ 19.00/30.00 t.

AUSTIN-DAIMLER-JAGUAR-LAND ROVER-MORRIS-   FORD Wolverhampton St. ⌀ 21212
ROVER-TRIUMPH Hatherton Rd ⌀ 612243   RENAULT Day St. ⌀ 613232
AUSTIN-MORRIS-MG Hatherton Rd ⌀ 32911   SAAB West Bromwich Rd ⌀ 22695
AUSTIN-MORRIS-DAIMLER-JAGUAR-ROVER-   TALBOT, SCIMITAR Charlotte St. ⌀ 21723
TRIUMPH Wolverhampton St. ⌀ 26567   VAUXHALL 126 Lichfield St. ⌀ 25111
FIAT Stafford St. ⌀ 612555   VW, AUDI-NSU Pleck Rd ⌀ 25562

WALSGRAVE-ON-SOWE West Midlands 🔢 🔢 P 26 – see Coventry.

WALSHFORD North Yorks. – see Wetherby.

WALTON-ON-THAMES Surrey **404** S 29 – pop. 51,134 (inc. Weybridge) – ✆ 093 22.
🛈 Town Hall, New-Zealand Av. ℡ 28844.
London 22 – Portsmouth 60.

   ✗ **Angelo's,** 70 Terrace Rd, KT12 2SF, NE: 1¼ m. on A 3050 ℡ 41964, Italian rest. – AE
       ① VISA
       closed Sunday and Bank Holidays – **M** a la carte 7.20/9.60 ⌂ 1.70.
BRITISH LEYLAND New Zealand Av. ℡ 20404   RENAULT Station Av. ℡ 23736

WANSFORD Cambs. **404** S 26 – see Peterborough.

WANTAGE Oxon. **403** **404** P 29 – pop. 7,200 – ECD: Thursday – ✆ 023 57.
Envir. : White Horse ≤*.
London 75 – Bristol 58 – Oxford 15 – Reading 25.

   🏠 **Bear,** Market Pl., OX12 8AB, ℡ 66366 – TV ⊟wc **P**. 🅪 VISA
       M 3.95/4.25 **st.** ⌂ 1.85 – **18 rm** ⊇ 12.50/21.00 **st.**
AUSTIN-MG Wallingford St. ℡ 3355   SAAB East Hanney ℡ 023587 (West Hanney) 257
MORRIS Main St. Grove ℡ 3534   VW, AUDI-NSU, TALBOT Grove Rd ℡ 65511

WARE Herts. **404** T 28 – pop. 13,740 – ECD: Thursday – ✆ 0920.
London 24 – Cambridge 30 – Luton 22.

   🏨 **Cannons,** Baldock St., SG12 9DR, N: ½ m. on A 1170 ℡ 5011 – ▮ TV ⊟wc ☎ **P**. ⩗
       50 rm.

WAREHAM Dorset **403** **404** N 31 – pop. 4,368 – ECD: Wednesday – ✆ 092 95.
See : St. Martin's Church* (Norman), St. Mary's Church (font* 12C). **Envir. :** Bere Regis
(Parish Church: nave roof* 15C) NW: 7 ½ m.
🛆 Lakey Hill, Norgreth Heath ℡ 092 97 (Bere Regis) 776.
London 123 – Bournemouth 13 – Weymouth 19.

   🏨 **Priory** ⌖, Church Green, BH20 4ND, ℡ 2772, « Tastefully renovated part 16C priory
       with gardens » – ⊟wc ⋔wc ⌖ **P** – **12 rm.**
   ✗ **Olivers,** 46 West St., BH20 4JZ, ℡ 6164 – VISA
       closed Monday, Sunday from October to May, 2 weeks March and 25 to 29 December –
       M (dinner only) a la carte 5.40/7.25 **st.** ⌂ 1.70.

WARK Northumb. – pop. 689 – ECD: Thursday – ✉ Hexham – ✆ 0660.
London 310 – Carlisle 42 – Newcastle-upon-Tyne 27.

   🕯 **Battlesteads,** NE48 3LS, ℡ 30209, 🚗 – **P**
       closed Christmas Day and 1 January – **M** *(closed Sunday dinner and Monday lunch)*
       a la carte 4.45/7.75 **t.** ⌂ 1.75 – **7 rm** ⊇ 8.00/13.50 **t.**

WARMINSTER Wilts. **403** **404** N 30 – pop. 16,000 – ECD: Wednesday – ✆ 098 52 (4 fig.)
or 0985 (6 fig.).
London 111 – Bristol 29 – Exeter 74 – Southampton 47.

   🏯 **Bishopstrow House** ⌖, Boreham Rd, BA12 9HH, SE: 1½ m. on A 36 ℡ 212312, ≤,
       « Tastefully furnished country house », ⌖, 🚗, park – TV **P**. 🅪 VISA
       closed mid December-mid January – **M** 10.50 ⌂ 2.50 – ⊇ 1.85 – **9 rm** 20.00/25.00.

WARRINGTON Cheshire **403** **404** M 23 – pop. 133,400 – ECD: Thursday – ✆ 0925.
See : St. Elphin's Church (chancel* 14C).
🛆 Hill Warren ℡ 61620, S: 3 m. – 🛆 Walton Hall, Warrington Rd ℡ 66775, S: 2 m.
🛈 80 Sankey St. ℡ 36501.
London 195 – Chester 20 – Liverpool 18 – Manchester 21 – Preston 28.

   🏨 **Patten Arms,** Parker St. (Bank Quay Station), WA1 1LT, ℡ 36602 – TV ⊟wc ⋔wc ☎
       P. 🅪 AE ① VISA
       closed 25 and 26 December – **M** 3.75/5.50 **st.** ⌂ 2.25 – **46 rm** ⊇ 14.50/25.00 **st.**
   🏠 **Hill Cliffe Hydro,** London Rd, WA4 5BS, S: 2 ¼ m. on A 49 ℡ 63638, 🚗 – ⊟wc
       ⋔wc **P**. VISA
       M *(closed Sunday dinner)* 4.50/5.50 **t.** ⌂ 1.95 – **12 rm** ⊇ 11.50/19.00 **t.**
   🏠 **Birchdale** ⌖, Birchdale Rd, Stockton Heath, WA4 5AW, S: 1 ¾ m. off A 49 ℡ 63662,
       🚗 – **P**
       M *(closed Saturday and Sunday)* (bar lunch) 3.00/4.50 **st.** ⌂ 2.00 – **22 rm** ⊇ 9.50/15.00 **st.**

   at Grappenhall SE: 2 m. off A 50 – ✉ ✆ 0925 Warrington :

   🏨 **Fir Grove Inn,** Knutsford Old Rd, WA4 2LD, ℡ 67471 – TV ⊟wc ⋔wc ☎ **P**. ⩗. 🅪
       AE ① VISA
       M *(closed Saturday lunch and Sunday)* 5.25/5.50 **t.** – **38 rm** ⊇ 17.85/22.70 **t.**

P.T.O. ⟶

WARRINGTON

at Stretton S: 3 ½ m. by A 49 on B 5356 – ⊠ Warrington – ☺ 092 573 Norcott Brook :

🏠 **Old Vicarage,** Stretton Rd, WA4 4NS, ☏ 238, ✗, 🛏 – 🛗 🛏wc 🅿
closed Bank Holidays – **M** 3.50/4.75 **s.** 🍷 2.10 – **37 rm** 🛏 10.50/20.00 **s.**

AUSTIN-LAND ROVER-MORRIS-MG-PRINCESS-
ROVER-TRIUMPH Castle St. ☏ 0606 (Northwich) 75333
AUSTIN-DAIMLER-JAGUAR-MORRIS-MG-PRINCESS-
ROVER-TRIUMPH Warrington Rd, Penketh ☏ 725611

AUSTIN-MORRIS-MG-PRINCESS-ROVER-TRIUMPH
Padgate Lane ☏ 50011
FORD Winwick Rd ☏ 51111
RENAULT Farrell St. ☏ 30448
VW, AUDI-NSU, COLT 101 Knutsford Rd ☏ 65265

WARWICK Warw. 🔳🔳🔳🔳 P 27 – pop. 18,296 – ECD : Thursday – ☺ 0926.

See : Castle** (14C) *AC* **Y** – St. Mary's Church* 12C-18C **Y A** – Lord Leycester's Hospital* **Y B**.
🏌 Warwick Golf Centre ☏ 44316 **Y**.

🛈 Court House, Jury St. ☏ 42212.

London 96 – Birmingham 20 – Coventry 11 – Oxford 43.

WARWICK
ROYAL
LEAMINGTON SPA

High Street________________ **Y** 19
Jury Street _______________ **Y**
Market Place ______________ **Y** 27
Smith Street ______________ **Y**
Swan Street _______________ **Y** 46

Birmingham Road __________ **Z** 6
Bowling Green Street ______ **Y** 7
Brook Street ______________ **Y** 9
Butts (The) _______________ **Y** 12
Castle Hill _______________ **Y** 13
Church Street _____________ **Y** 15
Lakin Road________________ **Y** 23
Linen Street ______________ **Y** 25
North Rock________________ **Y** 33
Old Square________________ **Y** 34
Old Warwick Road _________ **Z** 36
Radford Road _____________ **Z** 38
St. John's Road ___________ **Y** 42
St. Nicholas Church Street ___ **Y** 44
Theatre Street_____________ **Y** 48
West Street _______________ **Y** 50

*Les plans de villes
sont orientés le Nord en haut.*

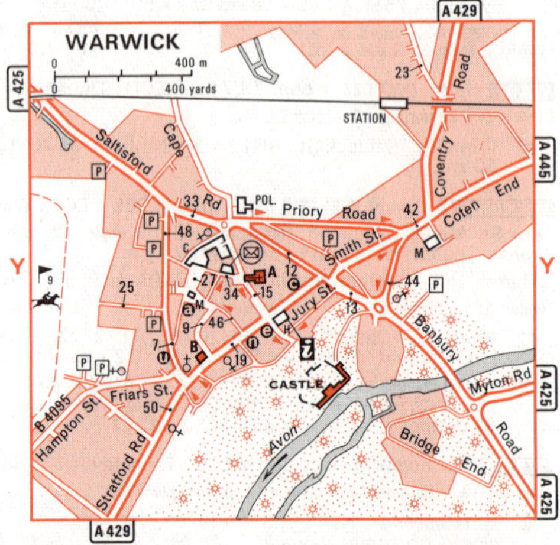

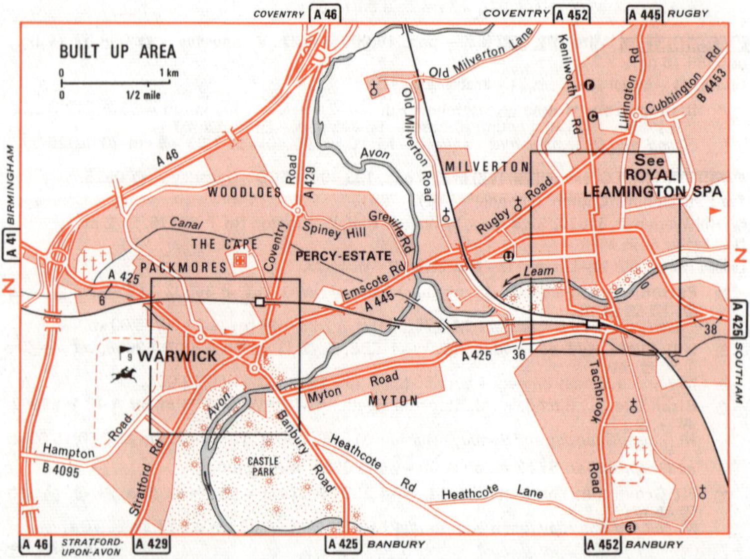

🏨 Woolpack (Crest), Market Pl., CV34 4SD, ☎ 41684 – 🛁wc. 🖴. 🅂 AE ⓪ VISA   **Y a**
26 rm 🍽 13.30/21.90 **st.**

🏨 **Lord Leycester** (Norfolk Cap.), Jury St., CV34 4EJ, ☎ 41481, Group Telex 23241 –
🛁wc 🕾 🅟. 🖴. 🅂 AE ⓪ VISA   **Y c**
M 3.75/4.50 **st.** 🍶 1.75 – **43 rm** 🍽 11.70/23.45 **st.**

🏨 **Warwick Arms,** 17 High St., CV34 4AT, ☎ 42759 – 🛁wc 🍴 🅟. 🖴. 🅂 AE ⓪ VISA   **Y n**
M *(closed Sunday dinner)* 2.25/4.00 **t.** 🍶 1.75 – **33 rm** 🍽 10.50/21.00 **st.** – P 17.50 **st.**

XXX **Westgate Arms,** Old Bowling Green St., CV34 4DD, ☎ 42362, 🚗 – 🅟. 🖴. 🅂 AE ⓪ VISA   **Y u**
closed Sunday and Bank Holiday Mondays – **M** a la carte 4.95/8.85.

XX **Aylesford,** 1 High St., CV34 4AP, ☎ 42799, Italian rest. – 🅂 AE ⓪ VISA   **Y e**
closed Sunday, last 3 weeks July, Christmas Day and Bank Holidays – **M** a la carte
7.15/15.20 **st.**

BMW, LADA, RENAULT Coten End ☎ 41235   VOLVO Millers Rd ☎ 41377
FIAT Wharf St. ☎ 46231   VW, AUDI Birmingham Rd ☎ 41731

WASHINGTON Tyne and Wear 🗺 ⑲ – pop. 41,000 – ECD: Wednesday – ✉ Tyneside –
☎ 0632.

London 278 – Durham 13 – Middlesbrough 32 – Newcastle-upon-Tyne 7.

🏨 **Post House** (T.H.F.), 5 Emerson District, NE37 1LB, via interchange A 1231 on
A 1 (M) off A 1231, ☎ 462264, Telex 537574 – 🛗 📺 🛁wc 🕾 🅟. 🖴. 🅂 AE ⓪ VISA
M 4.00/6.75 **st.** 🍶 1.65 – 🍽 2.75 – **145 rm** 18.00/25.50 **st.**

AUSTIN-MG Village Lane ☎ 460607

WASHINGTON West Sussex 404 S 31 – see Ashington.

WATCHET Somerset 403 J 30 – pop. 2,900 – ECD: Wednesday – ☎ 0984.
Envir.: Cleeve Abbey* (ruins 13C) SW: 2 m.
London 180 – Bristol 57 – Taunton 18.

🏨 **Downfield,** 16 St. Decumans Rd, TA23 0HR, ☎ 31267, 🚗 – 🅟
M (dinner only) 7.60 🍶 1.20 – **8 rm** 🍽 7.50/15.00.

WATERGATE BAY Cornwall 403 E 32 – ✉ Newquay – ☎ 063 74 St. Mawgan.
London 293 – Newquay 2 – Padstow 8.

🏨 **Tregurrian,** TR8 4AB, ☎ 280, 🏊 heated – 🍴wc 🅟
Early May-September – **M** (bar lunch) 3.50 🍶 1.80 – **28 rm** 🍽 6.75/20.00.

WATERHEAD Cumbria – see Ambleside.

WATERLOO Merseyside 403 K 23 – see Liverpool.

WATERLOOVILLE Hants. 403 404 Q 31 – pop. 10,109 – ECD: Wesnesday – ✉ Portsmouth
– ☎ 070 14.
🏌 Links Lane, ☎ 070 541 (Rowland's Castle) 2216, E: 5 m.
London 68 – Brighton 44 – Portsmouth 9 – Southampton 21.

🏠 **Far End** 🦢, 31 Queen's Rd, PO7 7SB, NE: 1 ½ m. off A 3 ☎ 3242, 🚗 – 🅟
8 rm 🍽 9.50/20.00 **s.**

WATERMILLOCK Cumbria – see Ullswater.

WATFORD Herts. 404 S 28 – pop. 78,465 – ECD: Wednesday – ☎ 0923.
London 21 – Aylesbury 23.

🏨 Ladbroke Mercury Motor Inn ,Elton Way, WDE 8HA, Watford By-Pass N: 3 ½ m. on A 41
at junction A 4008 ☎ 35881, Telex 923422 – 📺 🛁wc 🕾 🅓 🅟. 🖴
116 rm.

🏨 **Caledonian,** St. Albans Rd, WD1 1RN, on A 512 ☎ 29212 – 🛗 📺 🛁wc 🕾. 🖴. 🅂 AE
⓪ VISA
M 4.20/4.70 **t.** 🍶 1.85 – **85 rm** 🍽 19.50/22.50 **t.** – P 28.50/30.00 **t.**

AUSTIN-DAIMLER-JAGUAR-MORRIS-MG-ROVER-   HONDA, MERCEDES-BENZ, RELIANT, SCIMITAR
SHERPA-TRIUMPH 425/445 St. Albans Rd ☎ 22311   High Rd at Bushey ☎ 950 3311
AUSTIN-DAIMLER-MORRIS-ROVER 16 St. Albans Rd   PEUGEOT Aldenham ☎ 092 76 (Radlett) 2177
☎ 25283   SAAB Sutton Rd ☎ 26596
AUSTIN-MORRIS Pinner Rd ☎ 28680   VAUXHALL, VOLVO 329 St. Albans Rd ☎ 31716
FORD, OPEL 6/10 High Rd at Bushey Heath ☎ 950 7512

WATLINGTON Oxon. 403 404 Q 29 – pop. 2,055 – ☎ 049 161.
London 45 – Oxford 14 – Reading 14.

X **Martha's Kitchen,** 27 Couching St., PE33 0HR, ☎ 2673, Bistro
closed Sunday, Monday lunch, Good Friday and 24 December-3 January – **M** a la carte
4.40/6.25 **t.** 🍶 1.25.

WAUN Clwyd – see Chirk.

WDIG Dyfed – see Fishguard.

WEDMORE Somerset **403** L 30 – pop. 2,400 – ECD : Wednesday and Saturday – ✆ 0934.
London 140 – Bristol 24 – Taunton 25.

   ✿ George, Church St., BS28 4AB, ☏ 712124 – ⋔ **℗**
     10 rm.

VW, AUDI-NSU Latcham ☏ 712170

WELL Hants. **404** R 30 – see Odiham.

WELLAND Heref. and Worc. **403** **404** N 27 – see Malvern.

WELLESBOURNE Warw. **403** **404** P 27 – pop. 3,215 – ✆ 0789 Stratford-upon-Avon.
London 96 – Birmingham 26 – Stratford-upon-Avon 6 – Warwick 7.

   ✿ **King's Head,** CV35 9LT, ☏ 840206 – ⊟wc ⋔wc **℗**. AE ⟋ⅤⅠ VISA
     M (buffet lunch) 4.50/7.50 **st.** 🍷 2.25 – **9 rm** ⌑ 10.00/20.90 **st.**

FORD Warwick Rd ☏ 840208

WELLINGBOROUGH Northants. **404** R 27 – pop. 27,540 – ✆ 0933.
Envir. : Higham Ferrers (St. Mary's Church★ 13C-14C) E : 5 ½ m.

London 73 – Cambridge 43 – Leicester 34 – Northampton 10.

   🏨 Hind (Gd Met.), Sheep St., NN8 1BL, ☏ 222827, Group Telex 25971 – TV ⊟wc ☎
     ℗. 🛆
     27 rm.

AUSTIN-JAGUAR-MG-MORRIS-LAND ROVER-ROVER-
TRIUMPH St. John's St. ☏ 224918
COLT Alma St. ☏ 76173

FIAT, SKODA Broad Green ☏ 223924
RENAULT, VAUXHALL Oxford St. ☏ 223252
TALBOT Finedon Rd ☏ 76651

WELLINGTON Somerset **403** K 31 – pop. 7,620 – ECD : Thursday – ✆ 0823 Greenham.
🛈 Bowermans Travel, 6 South St. ☏ 2716.

London 178 – Exeter 27 – Taunton 7.

   ✕✕ **Beam Bridge** with rm, TA21 0HB, SW : 2 ½ m. on A 38 ☏ 672223 – **℗**. ⟋ⅤⅠ AE ⓪ VISA
     M *(closed Sunday dinner and Monday)* 3.25/4.75 **st.** 🍷 1.50 – **7 rm** ⌑ 8.25/15.00 **st.**

WELLS Somerset **403** **404** M 30 – pop. 8,604 – ECD : Wednesday – ✆ 0749.
See : Cathedral★★★ 13C-15C (West front★★★, Chapter House★★★, Retro-choir★★) – Vicar's
Close★ 14C – Deanery★ 15C – Bishop's Palace★ 13C – St. Cuthbert's Church★. **Envir. :**
Cheddar (Cheddar Gorge★★★ – Gough's Caves★★ *AC*) NW : 8 m. – Croscombe (Church : Jaco-
bean panelling★) E : 3 m. – Wookey Hole Caves★ *AC,* NW : 2 m.

🏌 ☏ 72868, E : Horrington Rd.
🛈 Town Hall, Market Place ☏ 72552 (summer only).

London 132 – Bristol 20 – Southampton 68 – Taunton 28.

   🏨 Swan (Best Western), Sadler St., BA5 2RX, ☏ 78877, Group Telex 449658 – TV ⊟wc
     ⋔wc ☎ **℗**. 🛆. ⟋ⅤⅠ AE VISA
     M 6.00/7.50 **t.** 🍷 2.50 – **26 rm** ⌑ 18.00/32.00 **t.**
   🏨 Star, High St., BA5 2SQ, ☏ 73055 – TV ⊟wc. ⟋ⅤⅠ AE ⓪ VISA
     M a la carte 3.65/5.50 **t.** 🍷 1.75 – **16 rm** ⌑ 12.75/25.00 **t.**
   🏨 Crown, Market Pl., BA5 2RP, ☏ 73457 – TV ⊟wc ☎ **℗**. ⟋ⅤⅠ AE ⓪ VISA
     M 3.70/5.10 **st.** 🍷 1.95 – **14 rm** ⌑ 12.50/24.00 **st.**
   🏨 Red Lion (Best Western), Market Pl., BA5 2RP, ☏ 72616, Group Telex 449658 – ⊟wc
     ⋔wc ☎ **℗**. 🛆. ⟋ⅤⅠ AE VISA
     M (dinner only) 6.00 🍷 2.00 – **33 rm** ⌑ 12.50/25.00 **t.**
   ✿ White Hart, 19 Sadler St., BA5 2RR, ☏ 72056 – ⊟wc 🚗 **℗**. 🛆. ⟋ⅤⅠ VISA
     M a la carte 3.70/5.75 🍷 1.50 – **14 rm** ⌑ 10.00/19.50.

AUSTIN-DAIMLER-JAGUAR-MORRIS-MG-ROVER-
TRIUMPH Glastonbury Rd ☏ 72626
COLT Chamberlain St. ☏ 72040

TALBOT Priory Rd ☏ 73834
VAUXHALL New St. ☏ 72099

WELSHPOOL (TRALLWNG) Powys **403** K 25 – pop. 7,030 – ECD : Thursday – ✆ 0938.
🏌 Golfa Hill ☏ 093 883 (Castle Caereinion) 249, W : 4 ½ m.
🛈 Wales Tourist Office, Vicarage Garden Car Park ☏ 2043.

London 182 – Birmingham 64 – Chester 45 – Shrewsbury 19.

   🏨 Royal Oak, The Cross, SY21 7RF, ☏ 2217 – ⊟wc **℗**. ⟋ⅤⅠ AE ⓪ VISA
     M 4.25/4.50 **s.** 🍷 1.85 – **23 rm** ⌑ 8.25/19.50 **s.**

Prévenez immédiatement l'hôtelier si vous ne pouvez pas occuper
la chambre que vous avez retenue.

WELWYN Herts. 404 T 28 – pop. 6,890 – ECD: Wednesday – ☎ 043 871.
London 30 – Bedford 31 – Cambridge 32.

Heath Lodge Motel ⛐, Danesbury Park Rd, AL6 9SL, NE: 1 ¼ m. off B 197 ☎ 5101, – TV ⇔wc ⋒wc ☎ P. AE ①
closed 23 December-2 January and Bank Holidays – **M** *(closed Sunday dinner)* a la carte 4.50/8.50 **st.** – **21 rm** ⊒ 10.75/24.00 **st.**

FORD By Pass Rd ☎ 5185 — VW, AUDI 54 Great North Rd ☎ 5911

WELWYN GARDEN CITY Herts. 404 T 28 – pop. 40,000 – ECD: Wednesday – ☎ 070 73 Welwyn Garden.
18 Panshanger ☎ 33350.
Council Offices, The Campus ☎ 31222.
London 28 – Bedford 34 – Cambridge 34.

Homestead Court, Homestead Lane, AL7 4LX, P.O. Box 115 ☎ 24336, Telex 25102, – |$| TV ⇔wc ⋒wc ☎ P. 🏊. AE VISA
closed Christmas – **M** 5.50/7.50 **st.** 2.80 – **58 rm** ⊒ 21.00/29.00 **st.** – P 30.00/35.00 **st.**

AUSTIN-DAIMLER-JAGUAR-MORRIS-MG-ROVER-TRIUMPH Stanborough Rd ☎ 26367 — RENAULT Great North Rd ☎ Hatfield 64567

WENTBRIDGE West Yorks. 404 Q 23 – pop. 130 – ✉ Pontefract – ☎ 097 764.
London 183 – Leeds 19 – Nottingham 55 – Sheffield 28.

Wentbridge House, WF8 3JJ, ☎ 444, – TV ⇔wc ⋒wc ☎ P. 🏊. AE ① VISA
closed 24 and 25 December – **M** a la carte 9.40/12.50 **st.** 2.40 – ⊒ 3.75 – **20 rm** 16.00/45.00 **st.**

at Barnsdale Bar S: 2 m. on A 1 – ✉ Pontefract – ☎ 097 764 Wentbridge:

TraveLodge (T.H.F.) without rest., Trunk Rd, WF8 3JB, on A 1 ☎ 711 – TV ⇔wc ☎ P. AE ① VISA
71 rm ⊒ 14.50/20.00 **st.**

WEOBLEY Heref. and Worc. 403 L 27 – pop. 881 – ECD: Wednesday – ☎ 054 45.
London 145 – Brecon 30 – Hereford 12 – Leominster 9.

XX **Red Lion** with rm, Broad St., HR4 8SE, ☎ 220 – TV ⇔wc ⋒wc ☎ P. AE ①
M a la carte 4.90/7.00 **st.** 1.25 – **7 rm** ⊒ 16.00/20.50 **st.**

WEST BAY Dorset 403 L 31 – see Bridport.

WEST BROMWICH West Midlands 403 404 O 26 – see Birmingham.

WEST CHILTINGTON West Sussex 404 S 31 – pop. 1,765 – ✉ Pulborough – ☎ 079 83.
London 50 – Brighton 22 – Worthing 12.

Roundabout (Best Western), Monkmead Lane, RH20 2PF, S: 1 ¼ m. ☎ 3123, – ⇔wc ⋒wc P. ① VISA
closed 1 to 24 January – **M** *(closed Monday lunch)* (Sunday and Monday dinner residents only) 5.30/6.70 **st.** 1.75 – **17 rm** ⊒ 17.00/27.00 **st.**

WEST CLANDON Surrey – see Guildford.

WEST COKER Somerset 403 404 M 31 – see Yeovil.

WEST DIDSBURY Greater Manchester 403 404 N 23 – see Manchester.

WESTERHAM Kent – pop. 4,641 – ECD: Wednesday – ☎ 0959.
Envir.: Chartwell* (Sir Winston Churchill's country home, Museum) *AC*, S: 2 m.
London 24 – Brighton 45 – Maidstone 22.

King's Arms (Embassy), Market Sq., TN16 1AN, ☎ 63246 – TV ⇔wc P – **16 rm.**

XX **Crown at Westerham,** London Rd, TN16 1DF, ☎ 63030 – P. ① VISA
closed Monday – **M** a la carte 4.80/6.55 **t.** 2.20.

AUSTIN-MORRIS-MG High St. ☎ 62212 — VW, AUDI London Rd ☎ 64333

WESTGATE-ON-SEA Kent 404 X 29 – see Margate.

WEST HUNTSPILL Somerset 403 L 30 – see Bridgwater.

WEST LULWORTH Dorset 403 404 N 32 – pop. 1,003 – ECD: Wednesday – ✉ Wareham – ☎ 092 941.
See: Lulworth Cove*. **Envir.**: Durdle Door** W: 1 m.
London 129 – Bournemouth 21 – Dorchester 17 – Weymouth 19.

Lulworth Cove, BH20 5RQ, ☎ 333, – TV ⇔wc ⋒wc P. AE ① VISA
M a la carte 4.05/8.40 **st.** 1.95 – **14 rm** ⊒ 8.00/19.00 **st.**

P.T.O. →

WEST LULWORTH

⌂ **Bishop's Cottage**, BH20 5RQ, ℡ 261, 🛁 – 🛏wc 🔺 *VISA*
April-October – **13 rm** ⌧ 6.00/12.00.

⌂ **Mill House**, BH20 5RH, ℡ 404, 🛁 – 🛏wc. 🔺 AE ⓪ *VISA*
6 rm ⌧ 8.50/19.20 **st.**

⌂ **Gatton House**, BH20 5RU, ℡ 252, 🛁 – Ⓟ
closed 20 December-20 January – **10 rm** ⌧ 6.00/12.00.

✗ Castle Inn, with rm, BH20 5RN, ℡ 311 – TV 🛏wc Ⓟ – **12 rm.**

WEST MALVERN Heref. and Worc. ⁨403⁩ ⁨404⁩ M 27 – see Malvern.

WESTON Devon ⁨403⁩ K 31 – ✉ ✲ 0404 Honiton.
London 164 – Exeter 15 – Sidmouth 10.

🏨 **Deer Park** ⟫, EX14 0PG, ℡ 2064, ≤, ✗✗, ⟋ heated, ⟍, 🛁, park – TV 🛏wc Ⓟ. 🔺 AE ⓪ *VISA*
M 4.45/6.00 **st.** ▯ 1.45 – **31 rm** ⌧ 14.00/40.00 **st.**

WESTONBIRT Glos. ⁨403⁩ ⁨404⁩ N 28 – see Tetbury.

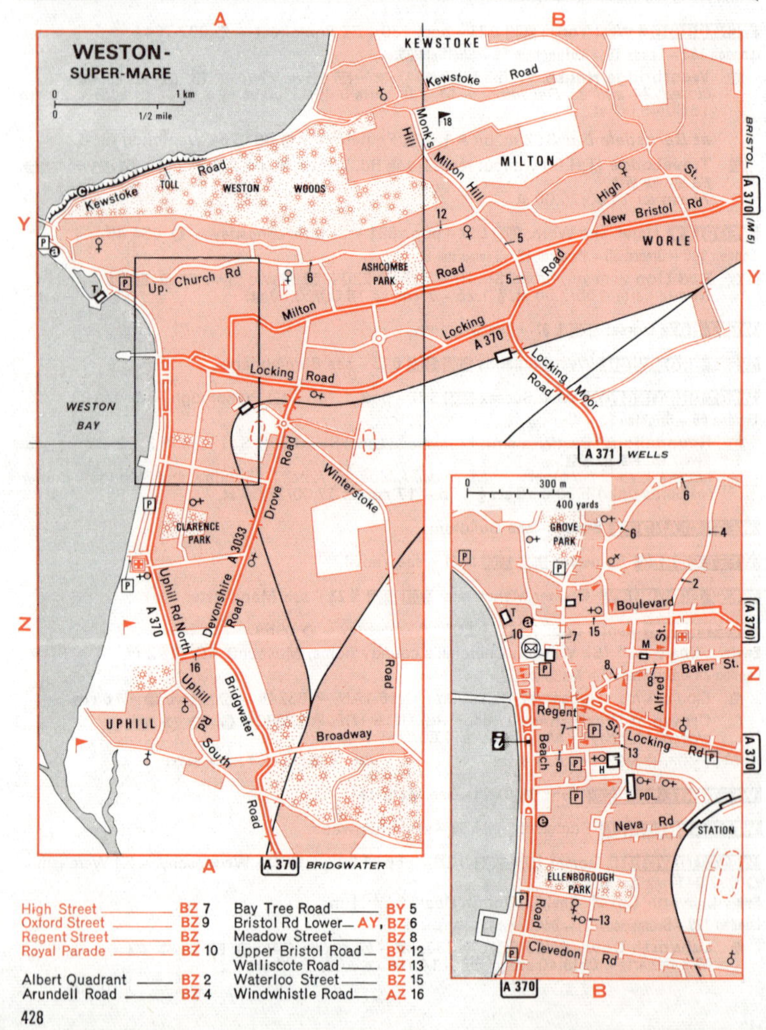

WESTON FAVELL Northants. 404 R 27 – see Northampton.

WESTON-SUPER-MARE Avon 403 K 29 – pop. 50,894 – ECD : Thursday – ☎ 0934.
See : Sea front ≼*.
📐 Worlebury ☎ 23214, 2 m. from station BY.
🛈 Beach Lawns ☎ 26838.

London 147 – Bristol 24 – Taunton 32.

Plan opposite

🏨 **Grand Atlantic** (T.H.F.), Beach Rd, BS23 1BA, ☎ 26543, ≼, ※, ⤴, ☞ – ≣ TV ℗.
🛆. ☒ AE ⓪ VISA
M 4.50/5.00 **st.** ⌀ 1.65 – **79 rm** ⇌ 18.00/31.00 **st.**   BZ **e**

🏨 **Royal** (Norfolk Cap.), South Par., BS23 1JP, ☎ 23601, Group Telex 23241, ☞ – ≣
⌂wc ⋔wc ☏ ℗. 🛆. ☒ AE ⓪ VISA   BZ **a**
M 3.75/4.50 **st.** ⌀ 1.75 – **36 rm** ⇌ 13.50/28.70 **st.** – P 17.25/19.00 **st.**

🏨 **Royal Pier,** Birnbeck Rd, BS23 2EF, ☎ 26644, ≼ – ≣ ⌂wc ☏ ℗. ☒ VISA   AY **a**
Mid March-October – M 3.25/3.75 **s.** ⌀ 1.80 – **47 rm** ⇌ 12.00/25.50 **s.**

※ **Cosa Nostra,** Kewstoke Rd, BS22 9JF, ☎ 32549, ≼, Italian rest. – ☒ AE ⓪ VISA   AY **c**
M a la carte 4.15/13.55 **t.** ⌀ 1.90.

AUSTIN-MG Drove Rd ☎ 75282
AUSTIN-MG 55 Upper Church Rd ☎ 21161
CITROEN Baker St. ☎ 23995
DAF, MAZDA 264 Milton Rd ☎ 25707
DAIMLER-JAGUAR-MORRIS-MG-ROVER-TRIUMPH-
Alfred St. ☎ 21451

FIAT 108/110 Milton Rd ☎ 26428
FORD Locking Rd ☎ 28291
PEUGEOT Broadway ☎ Bleadon 812479
RENAULT Locking Rd ☎ 25242
SAAB Main Rd ☎ 0934 (Bleadon) 812546
VAUXHALL 13 Langford Rd ☎ 23904

WESTON-UNDER-PENYARD Heref. and Worc. 403 404 M 28 – see Ross-on-Wye.

WESTON-UNDER-REDCASTLE Salop – 403 404 M 25 – pop. 245 – ✉ Shrewsbury –
☎ 093 924 Lee Brockhurst.
📐, 📐 Hawkstone Park ☎ 223.

London 165 – Chester 31 – Birmingham 48 – Shrewsbury 12 – Stoke-on-Trent 25.

🏨 **Hawkstone Park** ⑤, SY4 5UY, ☎ 611 ≼, ⤴ heated, 📐, ⚐, ☞, park – ⌂wc ☏ ℗. 🛆.
☒ AE ⓪ VISA
M 4.20/5.70 **st.** ⌀ 1.60 – **53 rm** ⇌ 13.80/28.75 **st.** – P 19.55/28.75 **st.**

WEST RUNTON Norfolk 404 X 25 – pop. 1,467 – ECD : Wednesday – ✉ Cromer – ☎ 026 375.
London 135 – King's Lynn 42 – Norwich 24.

🏨 **Links Country Park,** NR27 9QH, ☎ 691, 📐, ☞ – ≣ TV ⌂wc ⋔wc ☏ ℗. 🛆. ☒ AE
⓪ VISA
M (buffet lunch Monday to Friday) 4.00/6.00 ⌀ 2.00 – **34 rm** ⇌ 14.00/28.00.

※※ **Mirabelle,** Station Rd, NR27 9QD, ☎ 396 – ℗. AE
closed Monday, Sunday dinner from November to May and first 3 weeks November – M a
la carte 5.45/8.40 ⌀ 1.40.

WESTWARD HO Devon 403 H 30 – pop. 2,203 – ECD : Tuesday – ✉ ☎ 023 72 Bideford.
London 235 – Bideford 4 – Exeter 47 – Plymouth 62.

🏨 **Buckleigh Grange,** Buckleigh Rd, EX39 3PU, ☎ 4468, ※, ☞ – ⋔ ℗
March-October – M (bar lunch) 3.85 **t.** ⌀ 2.00 – **14 rm** ⇌ 9.60/20.40 **t.** – P 13.20/13.80 **t.**

WETHERAL Cumbria – pop. 4,081 – ✉ Carlisle – ☎ 0228.
London 308 – Carlisle 6 – Newcastle-upon-Tyne 56.

🏨 **Crown** ⑤, CA4 8ES, ☎ 60208, ☞
M 3.60/5.50 **t.** – **20 rm** ⇌ 11.00/20.00 **t.**

🏠 **Killoran Country House,** The Green, CA4 8ET, ☎ 60200, ☞ – ℗. ☒ VISA
M 5.75 **st.** – **8 rm** ⇌ 10.00/20.00 **st.** – P 18.50 **st.**

※※ **Fantails,** The Green, CA4 8EG, ☎ 60239 – ℗. ☒ AE ⓪ VISA
closed February – M (dinner only from November to March) a la carte 4.20/6.60 **t.**
⌀ 1.50.

WETHERBY West Yorks. 986 ㉓ – pop. 5,900 – ECD : Wednesday – ☎ 0937.
📐 Linton Lane ☎ 62527, 1 m. centre.
🛈 Council Offices, 24 Westgate ☎ 627069.

London 208 – Harrogate 8 – Leeds 13 – York 14.

🏨 **Wetherby Turnpike Motor Inn,** Leeds Rd, Wetherby Roundabout, LS22 5HE, junction
A 661 and A 1 ☎ 63881 – TV ⌂wc ☏ ℗. 🛆 – **73 rm.**

※※※ **Linton Spring,** Sicklinghall Rd, LS22 9XX, W : 1 ¾ m. ☎ 65353, ☞ – ℗. ☒ AE ⓪
closed Saturday lunch – M a la carte 8.65/11.05 **t.** ⌀ 2.20.

※※ **Cardinal,** 16 Bank St., LS22 4NQ, ☎ 63613 – ☒ AE ⓪ VISA
closed Monday, last week July and first week August – M (dinner only) 10.50 **t.** ⌀ 1.80.

P.T.O. ⟶

at Walshford N : 4 m. on A 1 – ⊠ ☎ 0937 Wetherby :

XXX **Bridge Inn,** LS22 5HS, ☏ 62345 – **P.** 🔊 AE ⓪ VISA
closed Sunday dinner, Monday, last week July, first week August and first week January –
M 8.95/10.95 **s.** ⓵ 2.10.

AUSTIN-MORRIS-MG-TRIUMPH-WOLSELEY North St. ☏ 62623   FORD 62/66 North St. ☏ 62029

WEYBOURNE Norfolk 𝟰𝟬𝟰 X 25 – pop. 430 – ⊠ Holt – ☎ 026 370.

London 128 – Cromer 7.5 – Norwich 26.

🏨 **Maltings,** NR25 7SY, on A 149 ☏ 275 – TV 🛏wc **P.** 🔊 VISA
M 4.00/5.00 **st.** ⓵ 2.00 – **16 rm** ⊊ 10.60/22.30 **st.**

XX **Gasché's Swiss,** High St., NR25 7SY, on A 149 ☏ 220 – **P.** AE
closed Sunday dinner and Monday – **M** a la carte 6.50/8.65 **t.** ⓵ 1.25.

WEYBRIDGE Surrey 𝟰𝟬𝟰 S 29 – pop. 51,134 (inc. Walton-on-Thames) – ECD : Wednesday –
☎ 0932.

🛈 Town Hall, New Zealand Av. Walton-on-Thames ☏ 28844.

London 23.

🏨 Ship (Thistle), Monument Green, KT13 8BQ, ☏ 48364 – TV 🛏wc 🗑wc ☎ **P.** 🛝. 🔊
AE ⓪ VISA – **39 rm.**

XX **Casa Romana,** 2 Temple Hall, Monument Hill, KT13 8RH, ☏ 43470, Italian rest. – **P**
closed Saturday lunch, Monday, Easter Sunday dinner, 25-26 December and 1 January –
M a la carte 7.65/11.80 **t.** ⓵ 1.80.

XX **London Steak House,** 7 Temple Market, KT13 9DL, ☏ 42826
M a la carte 5.40/11.20 **t.** ⓵ 1.85.

X **Phillip Lowe,** 43 High St., KT13 8DR, ☏ 46563, Chinese rest. – **P.** 🔊 AE ⓪ VISA
closed Sunday lunch – **M** a la carte 4.20/6.10 ⓵ 3.00.

AUSTIN-MORRIS-MG-PRINCESS Woodham Lane,   DATSUN 170 Oatlands Drive ☏ 42318
New Haw ☏ 093 23 (Byfleet) 42870   FIAT, LANCIA Brooklands Rd ☏ 093 23 (Byfleet) 49521
AUSTIN-MG-TRIUMPH-WOLSELEY 30 Queens Rd ☏   FORD Monument Hill ☏ 46231
42233   RENAULT 51/59 Baker St. ☏ 48247

WEYMOUTH Dorset 𝟰𝟬𝟯 𝟰𝟬𝟰 M 32 – pop. 42,349 (inc. Melcombe Regis) – ECD : Wednesday
– ☎ 030 57 (4 and 5 fig.) or 0305 (6 fig.).
Envir. : Abbotsbury (the Swannery* *AC,* the gardens* *AC*) NW : 8 ½ m.
⛴ Shipping connections with the Continent: to Cherbourg (Sealink) – to Guernsey
(Sealink) summer 2 daily; winter 3-5 weekly (4 h 45 m to 6 h 30 mn) – to Jersey (Sealink)
summer 2 daily; winter 3-5 weekly (6 h 30 mn to 9 h).
🛈 Publicity Office, 12 The Esplanade ☏ 72444 and 5747 (summer only).

London 143 – Bournemouth 35 – Bristol 69 – Exeter 57 – Swindon 88.

🏠 **Ingleton,** 7 Greenhill, DT4 7SW, ☏ 785804, 🚗 – 🛏wc 🗑wc **P**
closed 23 December-12 January – **M** 4.50/5.50 ⓵ 1.85 – **13 rm** ⊊ 11.00/15.00.

at Overcombe NE : 2 m. on A 353 – ⊠ Weymouth – ☎ 0305 Preston :

⋔ **Sunningdale,** Preston Rd, DT3 6QD, NE : 2 m. on A 353 ☏ 832179, ⌇ heated, 🚗 –
🛏wc 🗑 **P**
March-15 December – **20 rm** ⊊ 11.50/25.00 **t.**

AUSTIN-MG-PRINCESS-ROVER-TRIUMPH Victoria St.   RENAULT 148/162 Dorchester Rd ☏ 2222
☏ 5454   TALBOT 172 Dorchester Rd ☏ 6311
FORD Dorchester Rd ☏ 2284   VAUXHALL Chickerell Rd ☏ 3384

WHALLEY RANGE Greater Manchester 𝟰𝟬𝟯 𝟰𝟬𝟰 N 23 – see Manchester.

WHIPPINGHAM I.O.W. 𝟰𝟬𝟯 𝟰𝟬𝟰 Q 31 – see Wight (Isle of).

WHITBY North Yorks. 𝟵𝟴𝟲 ⑳ – pop. 12,150 – ECD : Wednesday – ☎ 0947.
See : Abbey ruins* (13C) *AC,* Old St. Mary's Church* 12C, East Terrace ≼*.
⛳ Low Straggleton ☏ 2768. – 🛈 New Quay Rd ☏ 2674.

London 257 – Middlesbrough 31 – Scarborough 21 – York 45.

XX **Stakesby Manor** with rm, High Stakesby, YO21 1HL, ☏ 2773, 🚗 – TV 🛏wc 🗑wc **P**
M 5.00/7.00 ⓵ 2.00 – **9 rm** ⊊ 12.00/18.00 – P 21.00/24.00.

AUSTIN-MORRIS-MG-DAIMLER-JAGUAR-ROVER-   DATSUN Castle Park ☏ 2841
TRIUMPH Castleton ☏ 028 76 (Castleton) 203   FORD Silver St. ☏ 2237
AUSTIN-MORRIS-MG-DAIMLER-JAGUAR-ROVER-   RENAULT 18 Silver St. ☏ 2093
TRIUMPH 6 Upgang Lane ☏ 3321

WHITCHURCH Bucks. 𝟰𝟬𝟰 R 28 – pop. 729 – ⊠ Aylesbury – ☎ 029 664.
London 51 – Bedford 28 – Oxford 30.

🏠 **Priory,** High St., HP22 4JS, ☏ 239, 🚗 – 🗑 **P**
M *(closed Sunday lunch)* a la carte 3.75/11.25 **st.** ⓵ 1.60 – **9 rm** ⊊ 12.50/21.00 **s.**

WHITCHURCH Salop **403** **404** L 25 – pop. 7,360 – ECD : Wednesday – ✪ 0948.

ϝ18, ϝ9 Terrick Rd ℡ 3584, N : 1 m.

London 171 – Birmingham 54 – Chester 22 – Manchester 43 – Shrewsbury 20.

- Redbrook Hunting Lodge, Wrexham Rd, Redbrook, SY13 3ET, W: 2 ½ m. on A 525 ℡ 094 873 (Redbrook Maelor) 204, 🚗 – 🛏wc 🅿
  14 rm.
- **Dodington Lodge,** SY13 1EW, ℡ 2539 – 🛏wc 🅿. ◪ 𝖠𝖤 𝖵𝖨𝖲𝖠
  M a la carte 4.50/7.00 **t.** ⌂ 2.40 – **9 rm** ⌷ 9.50/19.00 **t.**

AUSTIN-MG-MORRIS Brownlow St. ℡ 2826   MORRIS-MG-ROVER-TRIUMPH-LAND ROVER Newport Rd ℡ 3333

WHITEBROOK Gwent **403** L 28 – see Monmouth.

WHITESAND BAY Dyfed **403** E 28 – see St. David's.

WHITEWELL Lancs. – pop. 200 – ✉ Clitheroe – ✪ 020 08 Dunsop Bridge.

London 244 – Burnley 17 – Lancaster 16.

- ✕✕ Inn at Whitewell, with rm ⌂, BBY 3AT, ℡ 222, ≼, « Country house atmosphere », 🚗 – 🛏wc 🅿
  9 rm.

WHITFIELD Kent **404** X 30 – see Dover.

WHITLEY BAY Tyne and Wear **986** ⑲ – pop. 37,817 – ECD : Wednesday – ✪ 0632.

Envir. : Seaton Delaval Hall* (18C) *AC*, NW : 6 m.

🛈 Promenade ℡ 524494 (summer only).

London 293 – Newcastle-upon-Tyne 10 – Sunderland 10.

- **Ambassador,** 38-42 South Par., NE26 2RQ, ℡ 531218 – 📺 🛏wc 🅿. ◪ 𝖠𝖤 𝖵𝖨𝖲𝖠
  M 3.50/5.80 **t.** ⌂ 2.20 – **28 rm** ⌷ 17.50/24.50 **t.**

AUSTIN-DAIMLER-MORRIS-MG-ROVER-TRIUMPH-WOLSELEY Cauldwell Lane ℡ 522231   FORD Whitley Rd ℡ 522225
CITROEN Claremont Rd ℡ 525909   MAZDA Fox Hunters Rd ℡ 528282
DATSUN Claremont Rd ℡ 523347   VAUXHALL Earsdon Rd West Monkseaton ℡ 523355
    VW, AUDI-NSU Hillheads Rd ℡ 528225

☞ *Use this year's Guide.*

WHITLEY BRIDGE North Yorks. – pop. 361 – ECD : Wednesday – ✉ Goole – ✪ 0977.
London 190 – Kingston-upon-Hull 40 – Leeds 20 – York 22.

- **Maine Motor Inn,** Weeland Rd, Eggborough, DN14 0RY, ℡ 661395 – 📺 🏠 ☎ 🅿. ◪ 𝖵𝖨𝖲𝖠
  M *(closed Sunday dinner)* 4.00/5.00 **st.** ⌂ 1.35 – **15 rm** ⌷ 15.00/24.00 **st.**

WHITSTABLE Kent **404** X 29 – pop. 21,950 – ECD : Wednesday – ✪ 0227.

🛈 1 Tankerton Rd ℡ 272233.

London 58 – Dover 22 – Maidstone 26 – Margate 19.

- **Windmill Motel,** 35 Borstal Hill, CT5 4ND, ℡ 272866 – 📺 🛏wc 🏠wc 🅿. ◪ 𝖠𝖤 ⓞ 𝖵𝖨𝖲𝖠
  M *(closed Sunday)* a la carte 5.65/9.70 **t.** ⌂ 2.50 – **12 rm** 11.00/16.00 **st.**
- ✕✕ **Giovanni's,** 49-51 Canterbury Rd, CT5 4HH, ℡ 273034, Italian rest. – 🅿. ◪ 𝖠𝖤 ⓞ 𝖵𝖨𝖲𝖠
  M a la carte 6.50/9.80 **t.** ⌂ 1.75.

  at Tankerton E : ¾ m. on B 2205 – ✉ ✪ 0227 Whitstable :

- **Marine,** 33 Marine Par., CT5 2BE, ℡ 272672, ≼, 🚗 – 🛏wc 🅿. ◪ 𝖵𝖨𝖲𝖠
  closed 24 to 27 December – **M** 3.50/5.00 **t.** ⌂ 2.60 – **30 rm** ⌷ 12.25/28.00 **t.**
- ✕ Le Pousse Bedaine, 101 Tankerton Rd, CT5 2AJ, ℡ 272056, French bistro.

AUSTIN-MORRIS-MG Tankerton Rd ℡ 272244   RENAULT Tower Parade ℡ 261477

WHITTLESEY Cambs. **404** T 26 – see Peterborough.

WHITWELL ON THE HILL North Yorks. – ✉ York – ✪ 065 381.
London 223 – Malton 5 – York 12.

- **Whitwell Hall Country House** ⌂, YO6 7JJ, ℡ 551, ≼, « Country house atmosphere »,
  ✕, 🚗, park – 🛏wc 🏠wc ☎ 🅿. ◪ 𝖠𝖤 ⓞ 𝖵𝖨𝖲𝖠
  M 5.00/7.50 **t.** ⌂ 1.50 – **20 rm** ⌷ 13.00/26.00 **t.** – P 23.00 **t.**

WICKEN Northants. **404** R 27 – pop. 376 – ✉ Milton Keynes (Bucks.) – ✪ 090 857.
London 65 – Bedford 21 – Northampton 15 – Oxford 31.

- **Wicken Country** ⌂, Cross Tree Rd, MK19 6BX, ℡ 239, ✕, ⌿ heated, 🚗 – 📺 🛏wc
  🏠wc 🚘 🅿. ◪ 𝖠𝖤 ⓞ 𝖵𝖨𝖲𝖠
  M *(closed Sunday dinner)* a la carte 5.75/8.80 **s.** ⌂ 2.20 – ⌷ 1.50 – **12 rm** 14.00/21.00 **st.**

WICKHAM Hants. 403 404 Q 31 – pop. 3,896 – ECD : Wednesday – ✪ 0329.
London 74 – Portsmouth 12 – Southampton 11 – Winchester 16.

🏠 **Old House,** The Square, PO17 5JG, ☎ 833049, « Tastefully renovated Elizabethan house »,
🍴 – 🚻wc 🅿. 🔼 *VISA*
closed 2 weeks Easter, 2 weeks July-August and 1 week at Christmas – **M** *(closed Sunday)*
(dinner only) a la carte approx. 8.15 **s.** ⌾ 2.25 – **10 rm** ⌸ 18.00/28.00 **s.**

WICKHAM MARKET Suffolk 404 Y 27 – pop. 1,436 – ECD : Wednesday – ✪ 0728.
London 85 – Great Yarmouth 41 – Ipswich 12 – Norwich 43.

XX **White Hart** (Best Western) with rm, High St., IP13 0RB, ☎ 746203 – 🅿. 🔼 AE ① *VISA*
M a la carte 6.10/7.90 **t.** ⌾ 1.60 – **10 rm** ⌸ 14.50/29.00 **t.** – P 16.70 **t.**

MORRIS-MG-WOLSELEY 18 High St. ☎ 6161

WIDEMOUTH BAY Cornwall 403 G 31 – see Bude.

WIGAN Greater Manchester 404 M 23 – pop. 81,147 – ECD : Wednesday – ✪ 0942.
⛳ Haigh, Hall Park ☎ 42050, NW : 3 m. – ⛳ Arley Hall, Haigh ☎ 0257 (Standish) 421360,
N : 4 m.

London 206 – Liverpool 19 – Manchester 18 – Preston 18.

🏠 **Brocket Arms** (Embassy), Mesnes Rd, WN1 2DD, ☎ 46283 – 📺 🚻wc ☎ 🅿. 🔼. 🔼 AE
① *VISA*
closed 25 and 26 December – **M** 4.15/9.50 **st.** ⌾ 2.75 – **24 rm** ⌸ 12.50/18.50 **st.**

CITROEN Crompton St. ☎ 42281
DAIMLER-JAGUAR-MORRIS-MG-ROVER-TRIUMPH-
WOLSELEY Wallgate ☎ 44977
DATSUN Woodhouse Lane ☎ 34141
FORD Wallgate ☎ 41393

TALBOT Nicol Rd, Bryn ☎ 0942 (Ashton in Maker-
field) 78588
VAUXHALL Chapel St., Pemberton ☎ 214028
VAUXHALL Mesnes St. ☎ 43271
VW, AUDI-NSU 32 Whelly ☎ 41493

WIGHT (Isle of) 403 404 PQ 31 32 – pop. 109,512.
🚢 from Cowes to Southampton (Red Funnel Services) Monday/Saturday 14-16 daily ;
Sunday 7-11 daily (55 mn to 1 h 10 mn) – from Yarmouth to Lymington (Sealink) Monday/
Thursday 15 daily ; Friday/Saturday/Sunday 7-28 daily (30 mn) – from Fishbourne to Portsmouth (Sealink) Monday/Thursday 20-29 daily ; Friday/Saturday/Sunday 11-35 daily (45 mn).
🚤 from Cowes to Southampton (Solent Seaspeed Hovercraft) 3-12 daily (20 mn) and
(Red Funnel Services : hydrofoil) Monday/Saturday 10-12 daily ; Sunday 5-10 daily (20 mn) –
from Ryde to Southsea (Hovertravel) Summer 11-24 daily ; Winter 8-12 daily (7 mn) – from
Ryde to Portsmouth (Sealink) 9-23 daily (25 to 30 mn).

Bembridge – pop. 3,272 – ✉ ✪ 098 387 Bembridge.
Newport 14.

🏠 **Highbury,** Lane End Rd, PO35 5SU, ☎ 2838, 🏊 heated, 🍴 – 📺 🚻wc ☎ 🅿. 🔼 AE
① *VISA*
closed 24 to 28 December – **M** 3.45/6.90 **t.** ⌾ 2.95 – **9 rm** ⌸ 12.00/24.00 **st.**

🏠 **Elms Country** 🐾, Swaines Rd, PO35 5XS, ☎ 2248, 🍴 – 📺 🚻wc 🛁wc 🅿
March-mid October – **M** 3.50 ⌾ 1.80 – **14 rm** ⌸ 8.50/19.00.

PEUGEOT High St. ☎ 2121

Carisbrooke – pop. 3,217 – ECD : Thursday – ✉ ✪ 0983 Newport.
Newport 1.5.

⬆ **Clatterford House** 🐾, Clatterford Shute, PO30 1PD, ☎ 523969, 🍴 – 🛁 🅿. 🔼 *VISA*
6 rm ⌸ 7.50/15.00 **st.**

Chale – pop. 537 – ECD : Thursday – ✉ Ventnor – ✪ 0983 Niton.
Newport 9.

🌿 **Clarendon,** PO38 2HA, ☎ 730431, 🍴 – 🚻wc 🛁wc 🅿
M approx. 6.50 **st.** ⌾ 1.50 – **10 rm** ⌸ (dinner included) 10.00/24.00 **s.** – P 15.00/29.00 **s.**

Colwell Bay – ✉ Totland – ✪ 098 383 Freshwater.
Newport 12.

⬆ **Sandy Lane,** Colwell Common Rd, PO39 0DD, ☎ 3330
9 rm ⌸ 4.90/9.80 **s.**

Cowes – pop. 17,260 – ECD : Wednesday – ✉ ✪ 098 382 Cowes.
Envir. : Osborne House* (19C) *AC,* E : 1 m.
⛳ Baring Rd ☎ 3529.
Newport 4.

🏠 Holmwood, Egypt Point, 65 Queens Rd, PO31 8BW, ☎ 2508, ≤ Solent – 🚻wc 🛁wc
☎ 🅿 – **17 rm.**

Freshwater Bay – pop. 5,570 – ECD : Thursday – ✉ ☎ 098 383 Freshwater.
⛳₁₈ ☏ 2955.
Newport 13.

🏨 **Farringford** ⚜, Bedbury Lane, PO40 9PE, ☏ 2500, Telex 86726, ≼, ✗, ⌲ heated, ☜,
park – 📺 ⛲wc ☏ 🅿. ◪ Æ ⑥ *VISA*
M 4.00/6.50 **t.** ᐧ 2.00 – ⌲ 2.70 – **40 rm** ⌲ 11.00/30.00 **t.**

🏨 **Albion,** PO40 9RA, ☏ 3631, ≼ – ⛲wc ☏ 🅿
April-October – **M** 3.20/5.30 **st.** – **42 rm** ⌲ 7.75/21.00 **st.**

⌂ **Saunders,** Coastguard Lane, PO40 9QX, ☏ 2322, ☜ – 🅿
April-October – **13 rm** ⌲ 5.75/11.50 **t.**

DAF Avenue Rd ☏ 2179

Newport – pop. 22,309 – ECD : Thursday – ✉ ☎ 098 381 (4 fig.) or 0983 (6 fig.)
Newport.
Envir. : Carisbrooke Castle** 12C-16C (keep ≼*) *AC* – Shorwell (St. Peter's Church*
15C) SW: 5 m.
⛳₉ St. George's Down, Shide ☏ 5076, SE: 1 m.
🛈 21 High St. ☏ 524343.

🏨 **Bugle,** 117 High St., PO30 1TP, ☏ 522800 – ⛲wc 🏛 🅿. ◪ *VISA*
M 3.50/4.00 **t.** ᐧ 1.95 – **24 rm** ⌲ 9.85/18.45 **st.**

AUDI-NSU, MERCEDES-BENZ Medina Avenue ☏ 3232   BMW Blackwater ☏ 3684
AUSTIN - DAIMLER - JAGUAR - MORRIS - MG - ROVER-
TRIUMPH-WOLSELEY River Way ☏ 3555

Niton – pop. 1,742 – ✉ ☎ 0983 Niton.
Newport 12.

⌂ **Windcliffe House** ⚜, Sandrock Rd, PO38 2NG, ☏ 730215, ⌲ heated – 🅿
Easter-October – **12 rm** ⌲ 7.10/14.20 **s.**

Ryde – pop. 23,204 – ECD : Thursday – ✉ ☎ 0983 Ryde.
⛳₉ Ryde House Park ☏ 2088.
🛈 Western Gardens, Esplanade Pavilion ☏ 62905 (summer only).
Newport 7.5.

🏨 **Yelf's** (T.H.F.), Union St., PO33 2LG, ☏ 64062 – 📺 ⛲wc ☏. ⚶. ◪ Æ ⑥ *VISA*
M 3.60/5.00 **st.** ᐧ 1.65 – **32 rm** ⌲ 11.50/22.00 **st.**

ALFA-ROMEO Brading Rd ☏ 4166   TALBOT 186 High St. ☏ 2281
AUSTIN-MG-WOLSELEY Elmfield ☏ 2717   VW, AUDI-NSU Fishbourne Lane ☏ 0983 (Wootton
OPEL Havenstreet ☏ 0983 (Wootton Bridge) ☏ 882455   Bridge) 882465
ROVER-TRIUMPH Victoria St. ☏ 3661

Sandown – pop. 4,593 – ECD : Wednesday – ✉ ☎ 098 384 (4 fig.) or 0983 (6 fig.)
Sandown. – ⛳₁₈ ☏ 3170.
🛈 Esplanade ☏ 3886 or 4641.
Newport 9.

⚓ **St. Catherine's,** 1 Winchester Park Rd, PO36 8HJ, ☏ 402392 – ⛲wc 🏛. ◪ *VISA*
closed 16 to 30 September and 19 December-1 January – **M** (dinner only) 5.00 **st.** ᐧ 1.25 –
18 rm ⌲ 9.00/22.50 **st.**

Shanklin – pop. 7,240 – ECD : Wednesday – ✉ ☎ 098 386 Shanklin.
See : Old Village (thatched cottages)* – The Chine* *AC*. **Envir. :** Brading (Roman Villa :
mosaics* *AC*) N: 3 ½ m.
🛈 67 High St. ☏ 2942 or 4334.
Newport 9.

🏨 **Cliff Tops,** 1-5 Park Rd, PO37 6BB, ☏ 3262, Telex 86125, ≼, ⌲ heated, ☜ – 🛗 🅿. ◪
Æ *VISA*
M 3.80/5.75 **st.** ᐧ 1.50 – **98 rm** ⌲ 12.80/25.60 **st.**

🏨 **Shanklin,** Clarendon Rd, PO37 6DL, ☏ 2286, ≼ – 🛗 📺 ⛲wc ♿ 🅿. Æ
M (dinner only from October to April) 3.85/5.95 ᐧ 1.75 – **89 rm** ⌲ 13.00/33.00 – P 19.35/
21.35.

🏨 **Luccombe Hall,** Luccombe Rd, PO37 6RL, ☏ 2719, ≼, ✗, ⌲ heated, ☜ – ⛲wc 🏛wc
♿ 🅿
closed mid December-mid January – **M** (dinner only from November to March) 4.25/
5.50 **t.** – **33 rm** ⌲ 7.45/15.00 **t.**

🏨 **Auckland,** 10 Queens Rd, PO37 6AN, ☏ 2960 – 📺 ⛲wc 🅿. ◪ Æ ⑥ *VISA*
closed Christmas – **M** (dinner only) 6.50 **st.** – **29 rm** ⌲ 10.00/12.50 **st.**

🏨 Bourne Hall ⚜, Luccombe Rd, PO37 6RR, ☏ 2820, ⌲ heated, ☜ – ⛲wc 🅿
March-October – **27 rm** ⌲ 10.50/17.00 **st.**

P.T.O. →

⋔ **Delphi Cliff,** 7 St. Boniface Cliff Rd, PO37 6ET, ☏ 2179, ≼, 絲 – ⌂wc 🅿
17 May-September – **11 rm** ⊇ 6.00/14.00.

⋔ **Queensmead,** 12 Queens Rd, PO37 6DG, ☏ 2342, ⊒ heated, 絲 – ⌂wc 🇲wc 🅿
Easter-October – **26 rm** ⊇ 8.00/19.00 **s.**

⋔ **Overstrand** ॐ, Howard Rd, PO37 6HD, ☏ 2100, ✻, 絲 – ⌂wc 🅿
Easter-September – **15 rm** ⊇ 9.00/13.00.

Totland Bay – pop. 1,724 – ECD : Wednesday – ✉ ☎ 098 383 Freshwater.
Envir.: Alum Bay (coloured sands★) and the Needles★ SW : 1 m.
Newport 13.

🏛 **Sentry Mead,** Madeira Rd, PO39 0BJ, ☏ 3212, 絲 – ⌂wc 🅿
April-October and 5 days at Christmas – **M** 3.50/4.50 **s.** ᛁ 1.45 – **14 rm** ⊇ 9.50/20.50 **s.** –
P 16.00/18.00 **s.**

⋔ **Randolph,** Granville Rd, PO39 0AX, ☏ 2411, 絲 – 🅿
January-September – **8 rm** ⊇ 5.50/11.00 **s.**

⋔ **Brandelhow,** Ward Rd, PO39 0BD, ☏ 2238 – 🅿
April-October – **9 rm** ⊇ 5.00/10.00 **st.**

Ventnor – pop. 6,931 – ECD : Wednesday – ✉ ☎ 0983 Ventnor.
Envir. : St. Catherine's Point (≼★ from the car-park) W : 5 m.
🏌 Steephill Down Rd ☏ 853326.
🛈 34 High St. ☏ 853625 (summer only).
Newport 10.

🏰 **Royal** (T.H.F.), Belgrave Rd, PO38 1JJ, ☏ 852186, ⊒ heated, 絲 – 🛗 📺 ⌂wc ☎ 🅿.
🔼 AE ⓘ VISA
M 3.75/4.55 **st.** ᛁ 1.65 – **66 rm** ⊇ 12.50/25.00 **st.**

🏰 **Ventnor Towers,** 54 Madeira Rd, PO38 1QT, ☏ 852277, ≼, ✻, ⊒ heated, 絲 –
⌂wc 🅿
M 3.50/5.00 ᛁ 1.40 – **32 rm** ⊇ 9.80/21.70 **st.** – P 17.85/20.80 **st.**

🏰 **Metropole,** Sea Front, PO38 1JS, ☏ 852181, ≼ – 🛗 ⌂wc 🇲 🅿. 🔼 VISA
March-October and Christmas – **M** 3.50/4.75 **st.** ᛁ 1.90 – **42 rm** ⊇ 9.00/24.00 **st.** –
P 15.50/18.50 **st.**

⋔ **Madeira Hall** ॐ, Trinity Rd, PO38 1NS, ☏ 852624, ⊒ heated, 絲 – 🅿
Mid March-mid October – **12 rm** ⊇ 7.70/13.90 **st.**

⋔ **Richmond,** Esplanade, PO38 1JX, ☏ 852496 – 🇲wc 🅿
April-September – **12 rm** ⊇ 6.50/13.00 **s.**

⋔ **Skelmorlie** ॐ, Spring Gdns, PO38 1QX, ☏ 852283, 絲 – 🅿
11 rm ⊇ 5.50/17.00 **st.**

at Bonchurch – ✉ ☎ 0983 Ventnor.

🏰 **Winterbourne** ॐ, PO38 1RQ, ☏ 852535, ≼ gardens, « Country house atmosphere »,
絲 – 📺 ⌂wc 🅿. 🔼 AE ⓘ
Mid January-mid November – **M** 4.70/8.00 **st.** – **19 rm** ⊇ 21.00/42.00 **st.**

🏰 **Peacock Vane** ॐ, PO38 1RG, ☏ 852019, ≼, « Unique decor, country house atmosphere », ⊒ heated, 絲, park – ⌂wc 🅿. 🔼 AE ⓘ VISA
closed January-16 February – **M** *(closed Monday and Tuesday lunch to non-residents)*
6.00/8.00 ᛁ 1.60 – **11 rm** ⊇ 10.00/27.00 **s.** – P 25.00/30.00 **st.**

🏩 **Lake** ॐ, Shore Rd, PO38 1RF, ☏ 852613, 絲 – 🅿
Easter-September – **M** 3.00/5.00 **t.** ᛁ 1.50 – **23 rm** ⊇ 6.75/12.25 **t.** – P 10.15/12.00 **t.**

✕✕ **Bonchurch Manor** ॐ with rm, Bonchurch Shute, PO38 1NU, ☏ 852868, ≼, « Country
house atmosphere », 絲 – ⌂wc 🅿. 🔼 AE ⓘ VISA
M 4.20/5.50 **st.** ᛁ 1.50 – **10 rm** ⊇ 12.50/18.60 **st.** – P 15.50/21.50.

AUSTIN-MORRIS-MG-WOLSELEY Victoria St. ☏ 852650

Whippingham – ✉ ☎ 0983 Cowes. – Newport 3,5.

🏰 **Padmore House** ॐ, Beatrice Av., PO32 6LP, ☏ 293210, « Country house atmosphere »,
⊒ heated, 絲 – 📺 ⌂wc 🇲 ☎ 🅿. 🔼 AE ⓘ VISA
M 4.50/7.50 ᛁ 2.00 – **11 rm** ⊇ 11.75/28.00 **t.**

Yarmouth – pop. 984 – ECD : Wednesday – ✉ ☎ 0983 Yarmouth.
🛈 The Quay ☏ 760015 (summer only).
Newport 10.

🏛 **George,** Quay St., PO41 0PE, ☏ 760331, 絲 – ⌂wc ☎ ♿. 🔼 AE ⓘ VISA
M 3.75/5.95 ᛁ 1.75 – **20 rm** ⊇ 7.95/19.90.

⋔ **Jireh House,** St. James Sq., PO41 0QQ, ☏ 760513
9 rm ⊇ 8.05/16.10 **st.**

SAAB Mill Rd ☏ 760436

WIGSTON FIELDS Leics. 🚧403🚧 🚧404🚧 Q 26 – see Leicester.

WILLENHALL West Midlands – see Coventry.

WILLERBY Humberside – see Kingston-upon-Hull.

WILLINGDON East Sussex 🚧404🚧 U 31 – see Eastbourne.

WILLITON Somerset 🚧403🚧 K 30 – pop. 2,948 – ECD: Saturday – ✆ 0984.
London 177 – Minehead 8 – Taunton 16.

🏠 **White House,** 11 Long St., TA4 4QW, ✆ 32306 – ⊟wc ℗
June-September – **M** (dinner only) 6.90 t. ⦙ 1.50 – **14 rm** ⊠ 11.00/21.50 t.

BRITISH LEYLAND West Quantoxhead ✆ 32437   PEUGEOT 2 High St. ✆ 32761
OPEL Fore St. ✆ 32817

WILMCOTE Warw. 🚧403🚧 🚧404🚧 O 27 – pop. 1,005 – ✉ ✆ 0789 Stratford-upon-Avon.
See: Mary Arden's House* (16C) *AC.*
London 101 – Birmingham 20 – Stratford-upon-Avon 5 – Warwick 10.

🏠 **Swan House,** The Green, CV37 9XJ, ✆ 67030, 🍴 – ℗. **VISA**
closed Christmas Day – **M** *(closed Sunday dinner)* (bar lunch) 7.50 t. ⦙ 1.30 – **7 rm** ⊠ 10.05/22.60 **st.**

WILMINGTON Devon 🚧403🚧 K 31 – pop. 202 – ECD: Thursday – ✉ Honiton – ✆ 040 483.
London 162 – Dorchester 33 – Exeter 20 – Taunton 28.

XX **Home Farm** with rm, EX14 9JR, on A 35 ✆ 278, « Converted 17C thatched farm house », 🍴 – ⊟wc ℗
closed January and February – **M** *(closed Sunday dinner to non-residents)* 6.00/8.50 **st.**
12 rm ⊠ 14.75/30.00 **st.**

WILMINGTON East Sussex 🚧403🚧 U 31 – pop. 225 – ✉ ✆ 032 12 Polegate.
London 62 – Brighton 17 – Eastbourne 7 – Hastings 20.

↑ **Crossways,** BN26 5SG, on A 27 ✆ 2455, 🍴 – ℗
8 rm ⊠ 6.50/14.00 **st.**

WILMSLOW Cheshire 🚧403🚧 🚧404🚧 N 24 – pop. 27,220 – ECD: Wednesday – ✆ 099 64 (5 fig.) or 0625 (6 fig.).
🏌18 Great Warford ✆ 056 587 (Mobberley) 2579, SW: 1 ½ m.
London 189 – Liverpool 38 – Manchester 12 – Stoke-on-Trent 27.

🏨 **Valley Lodge,** Altrincham Rd, SK9 4LR, NW: 2 ¾ m. on A 538 ✆ 529201 – ⧈ TV ⊟wc
📺 ℗. 🏊. AE ⓪ ⦙ **M** 4.00/4.50 **st.** ⦙ 1.85 – ⊠ 2.50 – **66 rm** 16.00/23.00 **st.**

🏨 **Stanneylands,** Stanneylands Rd, SK9 4EY, N: 1 m. off A34 ✆ 525225, 🍴 – TV ⊟wc
⊟wc 📺 ℗. 🏊. 🅰 AE ⓪ **VISA**
M *(closed dinner Sunday and Christmas Day)* a la carte 6.25/10.80 **s.** ⦙ 1.80 – ⊠ 2.00 –
26 rm 11.50/21.00 **s.**

XX Pino's Quo Vadis, Water Lane ✆ 26766, Italian rest.

at Handforth N: 3 m. on A 34 – ✉ Wilmslow:

🏨 **Belfry,** Stanley Rd, SK9 3LD, ✆ 061 (Manchester) 437 0511, Telex 666358 – ⧈ TV ♿
℗. 🏊. 🅰 AE ⓪ **VISA**
M a la carte 5.85/10.85 **st.** ⦙ 2.05 – ⊠ 2.90 – **96 rm** 20.15/27.60 **st.**

🏨 **Pinewood,** 180 Wilmslow Rd, SK9 3LG, ✆ 0625 (Wilmslow) 529211, 🏊 heated, 🍴 –
⧈ TV ℗. 🏊. 🅰 AE ⓪ **VISA**
M a la carte 5.30/7.80 **s.** ⦙ 1.50 – ⊠ 2.50 – **64 rm** 17.75/26.00 **s.** – P 24.00/30.00 **s.**

LANCIA Station Rd ✆ 27356   VAUXHALL Water Lane ✆ 27311
RENAULT Knutsford Rd ✆ 23669

WILSHAMSTEAD Beds. 🚧404🚧 S 27 – see Bedford.

WILTON Wilts. 🚧403🚧 🚧404🚧 O 30 – see Salisbury.

WIMBORNE MINSTER Dorset 🚧403🚧 🚧404🚧 O 31 – pop. 7,400 – ECD: Wednesday – ✆ 0202 Wimborne. – See: Minster* 12C-15C.
🏌9 Ashley Wood ✆ 025 82 (Blandford) 52253, NW: 8 m.
London 112 – Bournemouth 10 – Dorchester 23 – Salisbury 27 – Southampton 30.

🏨 **King's Head** (T.H.F.), The Square, BH21 1JA, ✆ 880101 – ⧈ TV ⊟wc 📺 ℗. 🅰 AE ⓪
VISA
M 3.50/4.50 **st.** ⦙ 1.65 – **28 rm** ⊠ 12.50/25.00 **st.**

at Horton N: 6 m. on B 3078 – ✉ Wimborne Minster – ✆ 025 884 Witchampton:

🏠 Horton Inn, BH21 5AD, ✆ 252 – ⊟wc 📺 ℗. 🅰 AE ⓪ **VISA**
M a la carte 6.20/8.40 **t.** ⦙ 2.00 – **5 rm** ⊠ 15.00/23.50 **st.**

WIMBORNE MINSTER

AUSTIN-MG-WOLSELEY 41 Leigh Rd ☎ 883537
FORD Poole Rd ☎ 886211
JAGUAR-ROVER-TRIUMPH Wimborne Rd ☎ 884211
MORRIS-MG-WOLSELEY West St. ☎ 882261

MORRIS-MG-WOLSELEY 133 Wareham Rd ☎ 020 124
(Broadstone) 693681
VAUXHALL 11 Wimborne Rd, Colehill ☎ 2154

WINCANTON Somerset 403 404 M 30 – pop. 2,576 – ECD : Thursday – ☎ 0963.
Tower Hill ☎ 074 981 (Bruton) 3233, N : 5 m. on A 359.
County Library, 7 Carrington Way ☎ 32173. – **London 119** – Bristol 37 – Taunton 34 – Yeovil 16.

Holbrook House (Best Western) ⏴, Castle Cary Rd, BA9 8BS, W : 1 ½ m. on A 371
☎ 32377, ⏴, « Country mansion », ⏴, ⏴ heated, ⏴, park – ⏴wc ⏴wc ⏴ ⏴. ⏴ AE VISA
M 4.50/5.25 st. 1.75 – **20 rm** ⏴ 12.50/28.00 st.

AUSTIN-MORRIS-MG-ROVER-TRIUMPH Station Rd ☎ 2021

WINCHCOMBE Glos. 403 404 O 28 – pop. 4,070 – ECD : Thursday – ☎ 0242.
Envir.: Sudeley Castle* (12C-15C) *AC*, SE : 1 m.

London 107 – Cheltenham 8 – Gloucester 17 – Stratford-upon-Avon 23.

George, High St., GL54 5LJ, ☎ 602331, ⏴ – ⏴wc ⏴. AE VISA
M 3.50/5.25 – **16 rm** ⏴ 9.50/10.50 st.

WINCHESTER Hants. 403 404 Q 30 – pop. 31,107 – ECD : Thursday – ☎ 0962.
See : Cathedral*** 11C-13C **B A** – Winchester College** 14C **B B** – Pilgrim's Hall* 14C **B E** –
St. Cross Hospital* 12C-15C **A D. Envir. :** Marwell Zoological Park** *AC*, SE : 5 m. on A 333 **A**.
Guildhall, The Broadway ☎ 68166 and 65406 (Sats and Suns).

London 72 – Bristol 76 – Oxford 52 – Southampton 12.

WINCHESTER

High Street		B	Petersfield Road	A	28
			Quarry Road	A	29
Alresford Road	A	2	St. George's Street	B	32
Andover Road	B	3	St. Paul's Hill	B	33
Bereweeke Road	A	5	St. Peter Street	B	34
Bridge Street	B	6	Southgate Street	B	35
Broadway	B	8	Stoney Lane	A	36
Chilbolton Avenue	A	9	Stockbridge Road	B	37

City Road	B	10	Sussex Street	B	38
Clifton Terrace	B	12	Union Street	B	39
East Hill	B	15	Upper High Street	B	40
Eastgate Street	B	16			
Easton Lane	A	18			
Friarsgate	B	19			
Garnier Road	A	20			
Kingsgate Road	A	22			
Magdalen Hill	B	23			
Middle Brook Street	B	25			
Park Road	A	26			

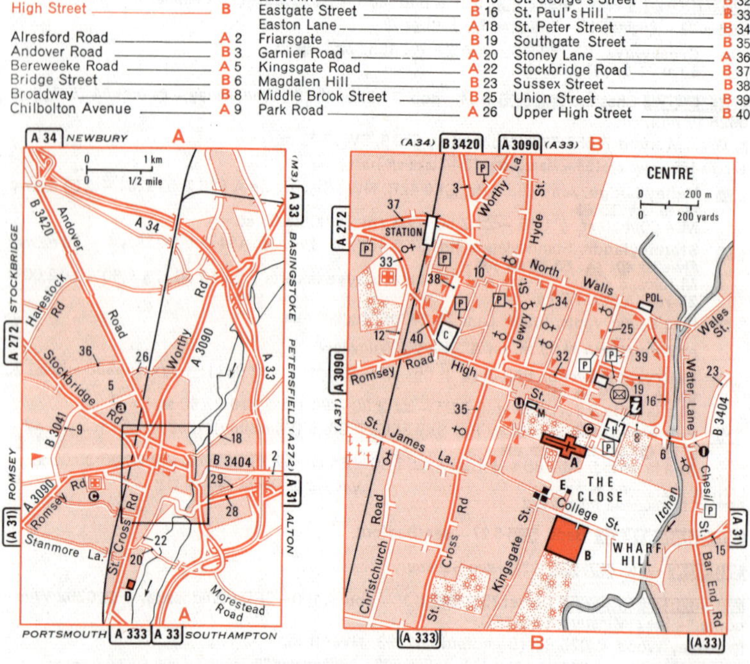

Wessex (T.H.F.), Paternoster Row, SO23 9LQ, ☎ 61611, ⏴ – ⏴ TV ⏴. ⏴. ⏴ AE ⏴ VISA
M 4.75/5.50 st. 1.80 – ⏴ 2.50 – **93 rm** 22.50/29.00 st.
B c

Chantry Mead, 22 Bereweeke Rd, SO22 6AJ, ☎ 2767, ⏴, ⏴ – ⏴wc ⏴ ⏴. ⏴
A a
closed 24 December-1 January – **M** (dinner only and Sunday lunch) a la carte approx.
4.50 1.65 – **21 rm** ⏴ 8.60/25.55 t.

Westacre, Sleepers Hill, SO22 4NE, ☎ 68403, ⏴ – ⏴wc ⏴ ⏴
A c
M a la carte 4.25/8.55 t. 2.00 – **17 rm** ⏴ 10.00/20.00 st.

XX **Old Chesil Rectory**, 1 Chesil St., SO23 8HU, ℡ 3177, « Converted 15C rectory » **B i**
Italian rest. – ⒶⒺ
closed Monday, Easter Sunday, 25 and 26 December – **M** a la carte 6.55/9.45 **t.** 🍶 1.80.

X Splinters, 9 Great Minster St., SO23 9HA, ℡ 64004. **B u**

ASTON-MARTIN Hursley ℡ 75218
AUSTIN-MG-WOLSELEY St. Swithun St. ℡ 68461
BMW Kingsworthy ℡ 881414
DATSUN Stockbridge Rd ℡ 2255
FIAT, TOYOTA Station Hill ℡ 62175
FORD Bar-End Rd ℡ 62211

MORRIS-MG-WOLSELEY Easton Lane, The By-pass ℡ 69182
MORRIS-MG-WOLSELEY St. Cross Rd ℡ 61555
TALBOT 2/4 St. Cross Rd ℡ 61855
VAUXHALL Gordon Rd ℡ 69544
VW, AUDI-NSU St. Cross Rd ℡ 66331

WINDERMERE Cumbria 𝟵𝟴𝟲 ⑲ – pop. 7,140 – ECD : Thursday – ✆ 096 62.
See : Lake✱. **Envir. :** Kirkstone Pass (on Windermere ⩽✱) N : 7 m by A 592 **Y**.
⛳ Cleabarrow ℡ 3123, by A 5074 **z** and B 5284.
🛈 Victoria St. ℡ 4561 (summer only) – Bowness Bay ℡ 2244 ext 43 and 2895.
London 274 – Blackpool 55 – Carlisle 46 – Kendal 10.

Plan on next page

🏨 **Langdale Chase** ⑤, LA23 1LW, N : 3 m. on A 591 ℡ 096 63 (Ambleside) 2201, ⩽ lake
Windermere and mountains, « Extensive grounds with lake frontage », ※, ⚓, 🚗, park –
on A 591 **Y**
📺 🅿. 🔲 ⓪ **VISA**
M 4.75/8.00 **st.** 🍶 2.20 – **36 rm** ⊆ 15.00/41.00 **st.** – P 25.00/32.50.

🏨 **Wild Boar**, Crook Rd, LA23 3NF, SE : 4 m. on B 5284 by A 5074 ℡ 3178, 🚗 – 🛏wc
by A 5074 **z**
🚻wc 🅿. 🔲 ⒶⒺ ⓪ **VISA**
M 5.20/8.50 **st.** 🍶 1.40 – **40 rm** ⊆ 15.00/20.00 **st.** – P 26.90/29.00 **st.**

🏨 **Miller Howe**, Rayrigg Rd, LA23 1EY, ℡ 2536, ⩽ lake Windermere and mountains, 🚗 –
Y s
🛏wc 🚻wc 🅿. ⒶⒺ ⓪
April-December – **M** (dinner only) 11.50 **t.** 🍶 2.50 – **13 rm** ⊆ (dinner included) 28.00/
45.00 **st.**

🏛 **Holbeck Ghyll Country House** ⑤, Holbeck Lane, LA23 1LU, NW : 3 ½ m. off
A 591 ℡ 096 63 (Ambleside) 2375, ⩽, « Country house atmosphere », 🚗 – 🛏wc 🅿
March-Oct. – **M** (dinner only) 5.50 **st.** 🍶 1.00 – **12 rm** ⊆ 16.20/35.10 **st.** by A 591 **Y**

🏛 **Birthwaite Edge Country House** ⑤, Birthwaite Rd, LA23 1BS, ℡ 2861, ⚓, 🚗 –
Y r
🛏wc 🚻wc 🅿. ⓪
closed January – **M** (dinner only) a la carte approx. 6.50 **t.** 🍶 1.20 – **14 rm** ⊆ 10.50/
20.00 **t.**

🏛 **Hide a Way**, Phoenix Way, LA23 1DB, ℡ 3070, 🚗 – 🛏wc 🚻wc 🅿 **Y c**
M (bar lunch) 3.00/6.00 **st.** 🍶 2.00 – **12 rm** ⊆ 8.00/16.00 **st.** – P 13.00/15.00 **st.**

⌂ **Willowsmere**, Ambleside Rd, LA23 1ES, ℡ 3575, 🚗 – 🛏wc 🚹. 🅿. 🔲 ⒶⒺ ⓪ **VISA** **Y a**
Easter-October – **15 rm** ⊆ 8.00/20.00 **t.**

XX **Postern Gate**, Broad St. CA23 2AB, ℡ 3344 – 🔲 ⒶⒺ ⓪ **VISA** **Y v**
closed Sunday and December – **M** (dinner only and Saturday lunch) a la carte 4.75/6.80 **t.**

at Bowness-on-Windermere S : 1 m. – ✉ ✆ 096 62 Windermere :

🏨 **Old England** (T.H.F.), LA23 3DF, ℡ 2444, Telex 65194, ⩽ lake Windermere and
mountains, ※, ⊒ heated, ⚓, 🚗 – 📧 📺 🅿. 🚹. 🔲 ⒶⒺ ⓪ **VISA** **Z e**
M 5.20/7.25 **st.** 🍶 2.00 – ⊆ 2.50 – **84 rm** 22.50/32.00.

🏨 **Belsfield** (T.H.F.), Kendal Rd, LA23 3EL, ℡ 2448, Telex 65238, ⩽ lake Windermere and
mountains, 🔲, 🚗 – 📧 📺 🅿. 🚹. 🔲 ⒶⒺ ⓪ **VISA** **Z i**
M 4.70/5.90 **st.** 🍶 1.80 – **73 rm** ⊆ 17.00/30.50 **st.**

🏨 **Windermere Hydro**, Helm Rd, LA23 3BA, ℡ 4455, Telex 65196, ⩽, 🚗 – 📧 📺 🛏wc
Z o
🚻wc ☎ 🅿. 🚹. 🔲 ⒶⒺ ⓪ **VISA**
M 5.00/8.00 **st.** – **97 rm** ⊆ 16.00/32.00 **s.**

🏨 **Linthwaite Country House** ⑤, Crook Rd, LA23 3JA, by A 5074 on B 5284 ℡ 3688,
⩽ Belle Isle, lake Windermere and mountains, « Extensive grounds and private lake », ⚓,
🚗, park – 📺 🛏wc 🅿
by A 5074 **z**
Easter-October – **M** (dinner only) 5.50 **s.** 🍶 1.75 – **13 rm** ⊆ (dinner included) 19.00/
38.00 **st.**

🏨 **Burnside** (T.H.F.), Kendal Rd, LA23 3EP, ℡ 2211, ⩽, 🚗 – 📺 🛏wc 🚻wc ☎ 🅿. 🚹.
🔲 ⒶⒺ ⓪ **VISA** **Z c**
M 4.75/5.50 **st.** 🍶 1.65 – **31 rm** ⊆ 15.00/28.00 **st.**

🏛 **Cranleigh**, Kendal Rd, LA23 3EW, ℡ 3293 – 🛏wc 🚻 🅿 **Z a**
16 March-10 November and Christmas – **M** (bar lunch) 5.00 **st.** 🍶 1.95 – **11 rm** ⊆
(dinner included) 12.00/28.00 **st.**

🏛 **St. Martin's**, Lake Rd, LA23 3DE, ℡ 3731 – 🅿 **Z x**
15 March-October – **M** (bar lunch) 3.50/5.50 **st.** 🍶 2.00 – **15 rm** ⊆ 8.80/20.00 **st.** –
P 14.75 **st.**

🏛 **Burn How Motel** ⑤, Back Belsfield Rd, LA23 3EW, ℡ 4486, 🚗 – 📺 🛏wc 🅿. ⒶⒺ ⓪
closed January and February – **M** (bar lunch) a la carte 4.65/6.45 **st.** 🍶 1.95 – ⊆ 1.75 –
18 rm 15.00/26.00 **st.** **Z r**

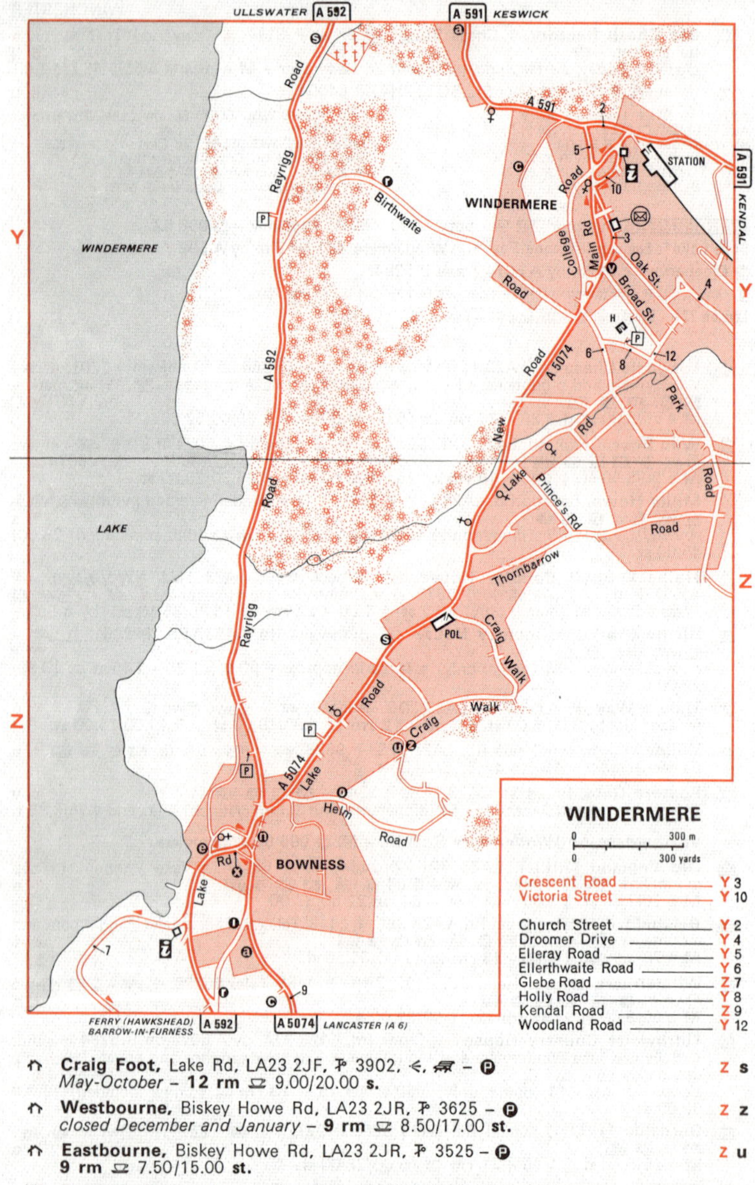

Craig Foot, Lake Rd, LA23 2JF, ☎ 3902, ≤, ⇔ – Ⓟ   Z s
May-October – **12 rm** ⇌ 9.00/20.00 s.

Westbourne, Biskey Howe Rd, LA23 2JR, ☎ 3625 – Ⓟ   Z z
closed December and January – **9 rm** ⇌ 8.50/17.00 st.

Eastbourne, Biskey Howe Rd, LA23 2JR, ☎ 3525 – Ⓟ   Z u
9 rm ⇌ 7.50/15.00 st.

Porthole Eating House, 3 Ash St., LA23 3EB, ☎ 2793, Italian rest.   Z n
closed Tuesday and December-mid February – **M** (dinner only) a la carte 6.30/10.00 t.
🍷 2.00.

at Troutbeck N: 4 m. off A 592 – Y – ⊠ Windermere – ☎ 096 63 Ambleside:

Mortal Man ⇘, LA23 1PL, ☎ 3193, ≤, ⇔ – Ⓟ
Mid February-mid November – **M** (dinner only and Sunday lunch) 5.00/7.00 st. 🍷 1.50 –
11 rm ⇌ 10.00/20.00 st.

AUSTIN-MORRIS-MG-ROVER-TRIUMPH College Rd ☎ 2451   TALBOT Main Rd ☎ 2441

WINDSOR

High Street — Z 13
Peascod Street — Z
St. Leonard's Road — Z
Thames Street — Z 24

Bexley Street — Z 2
Bolton Road — Y 3
Castle Hill — Z 4
Claremont Road — Z 6
Clarence Crescent — Z 7
Clewer Crescent Road — Z 9
Grove Road — Z 10
High Street (DATCHET) — Y 12
Horton Road — Y 14
Keats Lane — Z 16
Ragstone Road — Y 17
River Street — Z 19
Stovell Road — Z 20
Thames Avenue — Z 22
Trinity Place — Z 25
Windsor Bridge — Z 26
Windsor Road — Y 28

North is at the top on all town plans.

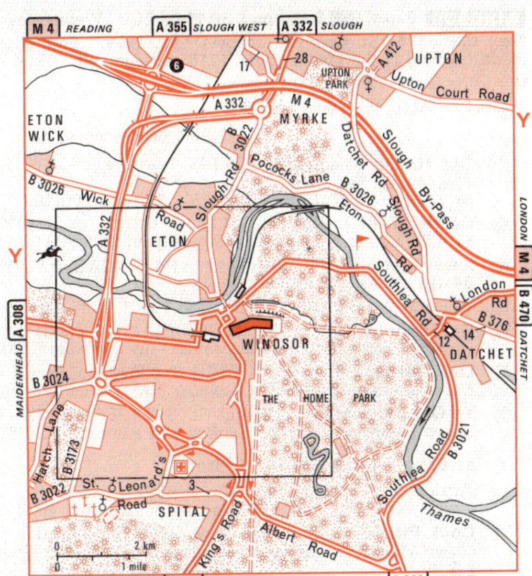

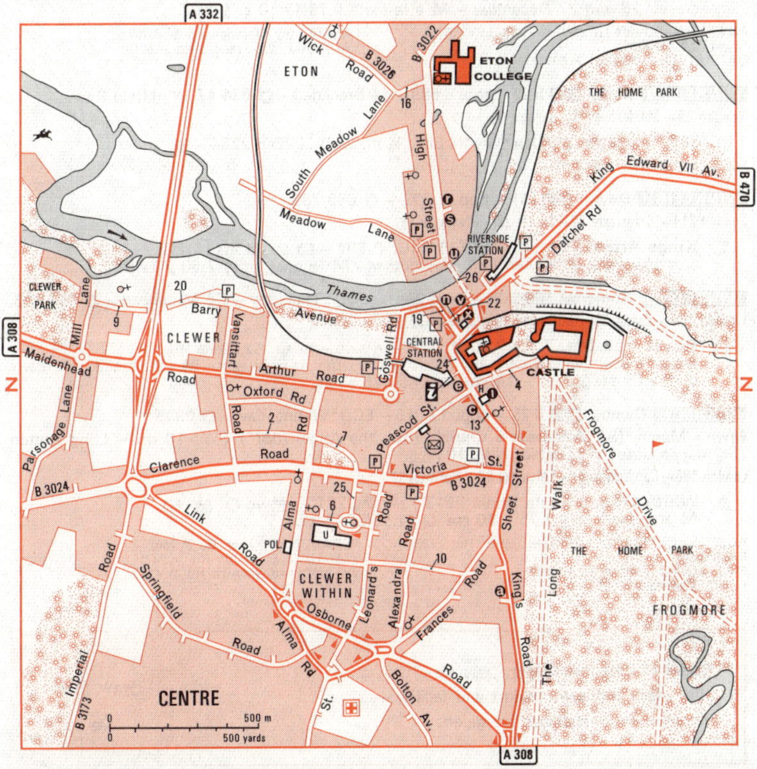

WINDSOR Berks. **404** S 29 – pop. 30,114 – ECD : Wednesday – ✆ 075 35.
See : Castle*** (St. George's Chapel***) **z. Envir. :** Eton (College**) N : 1 m. **z** – Runnymede (signing of the Magna Carta, 1215, museum) AC, SE : 4 m. by A 308 **Y.**
ℹ Windsor Central Station ℡ 52010 (summer only).
London 28 – Reading 19 – Southampton 59.

Plan on preceding page

  Old House, Thames St., SL4 1PX, ℡ 61354, ≼, « Former residence of Sir Christopher Wren » – **P.** ⓓ   **z v**
  M a la carte 5.80/13.90 – ☲ 2.75 – **39 rm** 20.00/28.50.

  Castle (T.H.F.), High St., SL4 1LJ, ℡ 51011, Telex 849220 – ⋕ 📺 **P.** ♨. ⚊ AE ⓓ VISA   **z c**
  M 4.90/5.20 **st.** � 1.65 – ☲ 2.50 – **63 rm** 20.50/28.00 **st.**

  Royal Adelaide (Crest), 42-46 Kings Rd, SL4 2AG, ℡ 63916 – ⊟wc **P.** ⚊ AE ⓓ VISA   **z a**
  34 rm ☲ 13.70/23.30 **st.**

  Ye Harte and Garter, 21 High St., SL4 1PH, ℡ 63426 – ⋕ 📺 ⊟wc – **45 rm.**   **z e**

  Don Peppino, 28-30 Thames St., SL4 1PU, ℡ 60081, Italian rest. – ⚊ AE ⓓ VISA   **z x**
  closed Sunday and 25-26 December – **M** a la carte 5.05/10.95 � 1.75.

  La Taverna, 2 River St., SL4 1OU, ℡ 63020, Italian rest. – ⚊ AE ⓓ VISA   **z n**
  closed Sunday and 25-26 December – **M** a la carte 4.95/9.10 � 1.75.

  Ye Old Kings Head, 7 Church St., SL4 1PE, ℡ 68952 – ⚊ AE ⓓ   **z i**
  closed Saturday lunch and Sunday – **M** a la carte 6.10/8.70 **t.** � 1.75.

  at Eton – ✉ ✆ 075 35 Windsor:

  Antico, 42 High St., SL4 6AX, ℡ 63977, Italian rest. – ⚊ AE ⓓ VISA   **z s**
  closed Saturday lunch – **M** a la carte 5.50/9.40 � 1.40.

  Cock Pit, 47-49 Eton High St. ℡ 60944, Italian rest.   **z r**
  closed Monday, last 2 weeks August and 1 week at Christmas – **M** a la carte 8.95/18.75 **t.** � 2.75.

  House on the Bridge, 71 High St., Windsor Bridge, SL4 6AA, ℡ 60914, ≼ – **P.**
  ⚊ AE ⓓ VISA   **z u**
  closed 26 and 27 December – **M** a la carte 5.70/17.10 **s.** � 2.00.

AUSTIN-MG-ROVER-TRIUMPH-WOLSELEY 37/39 Sheet St. ℡ 68131
DATSUN Dedworth Rd ℡ 69191
LANCIA 195 Clarence Rd ℡ 60707
VAUXHALL 2/6 Frances Rd ℡ 60131

WINKFIELD Berks. **404** R 29 – pop. 8,689 – ✉ Bracknell – ✆ 034 47 Winkfield Row.
London 36 – Maidenhead 9 – Reading 16.

  Jolly Gardener, Maidens Green, SW : ¾ m. on B 3022 ℡ 2284 – **P.**

FORD Hatchet Lane ℡ 2591

WINKLEIGH Devon **403** I 31 – pop. 1,093 – ✆ 083 783.
London 214 – Barnstaple 20 – Exeter 22 – Plymouth 41.

  Kings Arms, The Square, EX19 8HQ, ℡ 384 – ⚊ AE ⓓ VISA
  closed Sunday dinner and Monday dinner – **M** (dinner only) 7.50 � 1.65.

WINSFORD Somerset **403** J 30 – pop. 294 – ECD : Thursday – ✉ Minehead – ✆ 064 385.
London 194 – Exeter 31 – Minehead 10 – Taunton 32.

  Royal Oak Inn, TA24 7JE, ℡ 232 – ⊟wc ⇔ **P.** ⚊ AE ⓓ VISA
  closed December-January and Monday to Friday in February – **M** (bar lunch) a la carte 5.70/9.05 **st.** � 2.00 – **14 rm** ☲ 14.50/26.50 **st.**

WISBECH Cambs. **404** U 25 – pop. 17,016 – ECD : Wednesday – ✆ 0945.
Envir. : March (St. Wendreda's Church 15C : the Angel roof*) SW : 10 m. – Long Sutton (St. Mary's Church* : Gothic) NW : 10 m.
London 106 – Cambridge 47 – Leicester 62 – Norwich 57.

  White Lion, 5 South Brink, PE13 1JA, ℡ 3221 – ⊟wc **P.** ♨. ⚊
  M approx. 4.75 � 1.75 – **20 rm** ☲ 11.95/22.25 **st.**

AUSTIN-MORRIS-MG-ROVER-TRIUMPH Harecroft Rd ℡ 2771
FIAT, VOLVO Sutton Rd ℡ 3082
FORD Elm Rd ℡ 2681
RENAULT Old Lynn Rd ℡ 2662
VAUXHALL Elm High Rd ℡ 2471
VW-AUDI 46 Norwich Rd ℡ 4342

Hotels in categories 🏰🏰🏰, 🏰🏰, 🏰
offer every modern comfort and facility –
therefore no particulars are given.

⊟wc ⋔wc

☎

WITHAM Essex **404** V 28 – pop. 8,060 – ECD : Wednesday – ☎ 0376.
London 42 – Cambridge 46 – Chelmsford 9 – Colchester 13.

　　🏨　White Hart, 39 Newland St., CM8 2AF, ☏ 512245 – ⇱wc ℗. ⚲
　　　　13 rm.

　　　　at Rivenhall End NE : 1 ¾ m. by B 1389 on A 12 – ✉ ☎ 0376 Witham :

　　🏨　Rivenhall Motor Inn, CM8 3HF, on A 12 ☏ 516969 – 📺 �📶wc 🕿 ℗
　　　　26 rm.

AUSTIN-MORRIS-MG Newland St. ☏ 513272
DATSUN London Rd ☏ 515575
FORD Colchester Rd ☏ 513496
VAUXHALL Maldon Rd ☏ 513326

WITHERIDGE Devon **403** I 31 – pop. 768 – ✉ Tiverton – ☎ 088 481.
🏌 Bournebridge, ☏ 394, 1 m. S. of Meshaw.
London 200 – Exeter 24 – Taunton 33.

　　🕯　Mitre, 2 The Square, ☏ 741 – ⇱wc ℗
　　　　10 rm.

WITHINGTON Glos. **403** **404** O 28 – see Cheltenham.

WITHINGTON Greater Manchester **403** **404** N 23 – see Manchester.

WIVENHOE Essex **404** W 28 – see Colchester.

WOBURN Beds. **404** S 27 – pop. 796 – ECD : Wednesday – ✉ Milton Keynes – ☎ 052 525.
See : Woburn Abbey*** (18C) *AC*, Wild Animal Kingdom** *AC*.
London 49 – Bedford 13 – Luton 13 – Northampton 24.

　　🏨　**Bedford Arms,** 1 George St., MK17 9PX, ☏ 441 – 📺 ⇱wc 🕿 ⇦ ℗. ⚲. ◰ AE ① VISA
　　　　M 4.50 **t.** ⓵ 1.95 – **41 rm** �Ⓩ 17.00/28.00 **t.** – P 23.00/31.00 **t.**

WOKING Surrey **404** S 30 – pop. 75,952 – ECD : Monday and Wednesday – ☎ 048 62.
Envir. : Clandon Park** (Renaissance House) *AC*, SE : 6 m. – Wisley gardens** *AC*, E : 5 m.
🛈 Council Offices, Guildford Rd ☏ 5931.
London 31 – Southampton 55.

　　%%　**Mayford Manor** with rm, Guildford Rd, Mayford, GU22 0SQ, S : 2 ½ m. on A 320
　　　　☏ 66166, 🚗 – 📺 ⇱wc 🕿 ℗.
　　　　M *(closed Sunday dinner)* a la carte 6.80/10.50 **s.** ⓵ 2.00 – **6 rm** �Ⓩ 12.65/22.00 **s.**

AUSTIN-DAIMLER-MORRIS-MG-ROVER-TRIUMPH
82 Goldsworth Rd ☏ 61444
AUSTIN-MORRIS-JAGUAR-ROVER-TRIUMPH 2 White
Rose Lane ☏ 4515
DAF, RELIANT, SCIMITAR TVR Albert Drive ☏ 61517
DATSUN Guildford Rd ☏ 048 67 (Brookwood) 4988
DATSUN 67 High St. ☏ 61725
POLSKI, FIAT Vicarage Rd ☏ 099 05 (Chobham) 8031
TOYOTA St. John's Rd ☏ 64641
VAUXHALL 24/26 Guildford Rd ☏ 66572
VW, AUDI Portsmouth Rd ☏ 048 643 (Ripley) 2361

WOLF'S CASTLE (CAS-BLAIDD) Dyfed **403** F 28 – ✉ Haverfordwest – ☎ 043 787 Treffgarne.
London 258 – Fishguard 7 – Haverfordwest 8.

　　%%　**Wolfscastle Country** with rm, on A 40 ☏ 225, 🚗 – 📺 ⇱wc ℗. ◰ VISA
　　　　M (bar lunch Monday to Saturday) a la carte 5.25/6.80 ⓵ 1.75 – **12 rm** �Ⓩ 8.00/14.00 –
　　　　P 11.50/18.80.

WOLVERHAMPTON West Midlands **403** **404** N 26 – pop. 269,112 – ECD : Thursday – ☎ 0902.
See : St. Peter's Church* 15C B A.
🏌 Oxley Park, Bushbury ☏ 20506, N : 1 ½ m. A.
🏌 Blackhill Wood ☏ 772279, S : 5 m. by A 449 A.
London 132 – Birmingham 15 – Liverpool 89 – Shrewsbury 30.

Plans on following pages
Plan of Enlarged Area : See Birmingham p. 2-3

　　🏨　**Mount** (Embassy) 🦢, Mount Rd, Tettenhall Wood, WV6 8HL, W : 2 ½ m. off A 454　　　　　　A a
　　　　☏ 752055, 🚗, park – 📺 ℗. ⚲. ◰ AE ① VISA
　　　　closed 24 to 26 December – **M** 4.90/5.25 **st.** – **63 rm** �Ⓩ 17.00/22.50 **st.**

　　🏨　Park Hall (Embassy) 🦢, Park Drive, off Ednam Rd, Goldthorn Park, WV4 5AJ,　　　　　　A c
　　　　S : 2 m. by A 449 ☏ 31121, 🚗 – 📺 ⇱wc 🕿 ℗. ⚲
　　　　57 rm.

　　🏨　**Goldthorn,** 126 Penn Rd, WV3 0DX, ☏ 29216 – 📺 ⇱wc �📶wc ℗. ⚲. ◰　　　　　　B i
　　　　M *(Saturday lunch and Sunday dinner residents only)* 5.00 **t.** ⓵ 1.65 – **68 rm** �Ⓩ 10.65/
　　　　19.70 **t.**

　　🏨　Connaught, 44-50 Tettenhall Rd, WV1 4SW, ☏ 24433, Telex 338490 – 🛗 📺 ⇱wc �📶wc 🕿
　　　　℗.　　　　　　　　　　　　　　　　　　　　　　　　　　　　　　　　　　　　　　　B s
　　　　61 rm.

P.T.O. ⟶

WOLVERHAMPTON

Darlington Street	B	Alfred Squire Road	A 2	Market Street	B 14		
Mander Centre	B	Birmingham New Road	A 3	Princess Street	B 15		
Victoria Street	B 24	Bridgnorth Road	A 6	Queen Square	B 17		
Wulfrun Centre	B	Cleveland Street	B 7	Railway Drive	B 20		
		Garrick Street	B 8	Salop Street	B 22		
		Lichfield Road	A 10	Thompson Avenue	A 23		
		Lichfield Street	B 12	Wolverhampton Road	A 26		

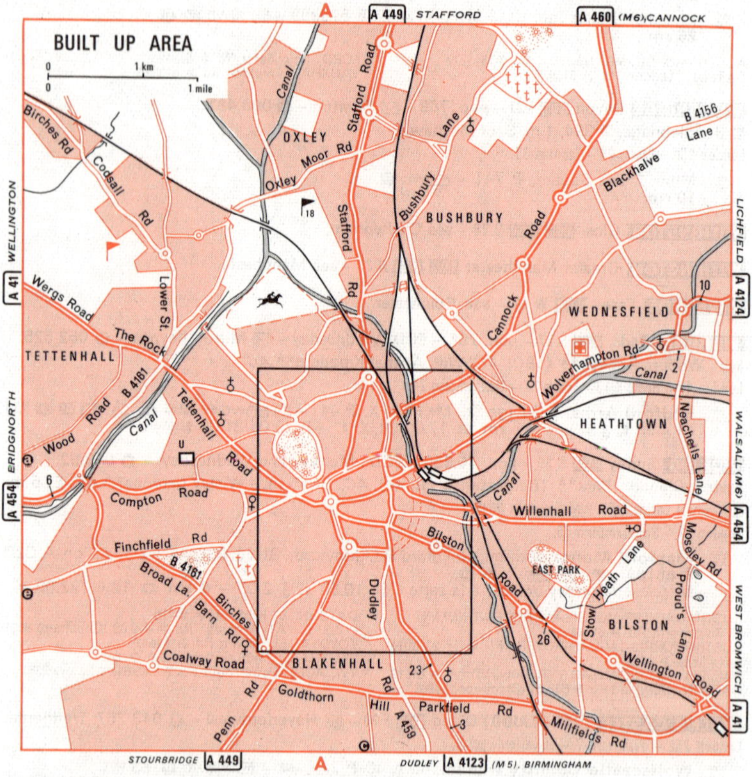

🏨 **Castlecroft** (Ansells), Castlecroft Rd, WV3 8NA, W : 3 ¼ m. off A 454 ☎ 761264, – TV – wc wc P. AE **A e**
M 3.60/4.30 **t.** 🍷 1.80 – **25 rm** ☕ 13.10/16.90 **t.**

🏨 Fox, 118 School St., WV3 0NR, ☎ 21680 – TV wc P – **29 rm.** **B n**

🏨 Ravensholt, Summerfield Rd, WV1 4PR, ☎ 24140 – wc wc P **B r**
29 rm.

XX **Tandoor,** 46 Queen St., WV1 3BJ, ☎ 20747, Indian rest. – AE VISA **B o**
closed 25 and 26 December – **M** (dinner only Sunday and Bank Holidays) a la carte 4.10/6.15 🍷 1.80.

at Shipley **(Salop) W: 7 m. on A 454 – A – ✉ 0902 Pattingham:**

XXX **Thornescroft,** Bridgnorth Rd, WV6 7EQ, ☎ 700253 – P. AE
closed Sunday, Monday, 25 December-2 January and Tuesday after Bank Holidays – **M** a la carte 5.85/8.40 **st.** 🍷 2.25.

ALFA-ROMEO Merridale Lane ☎ 23295
AUSTIN-DAIMLER-JAGUAR-MORRIS-MG-ROVER TRIUMPH Stafford St. ☎ 29122
AUSTIN-MORRIS-MG-ROVER-TRIUMPH Chapel Ash ☎ 26781
AUSTIN-MORRIS-PRINCESS Wolverhampton Rd, Wednesfield ☎ 731372
CITROEN Stafford St. ☎ 771295
FIAT, SAAB Warstones Rd ☎ 37488
FORD Bilston Rd ☎ 51515
LADA 372 Penn Rd, Penn ☎ 35570
LANCIA, MERCEDES-BENZ Penn Rd ☎ 27897
MORRIS-MG-WOLSELEY, VAUXHALL Finchfield ☎ 761171
OPEL Dudley Rd ☎ 25821
PEUGEOT Parkfield Rd, Ettingshall, ☎ 0902 (Bilston) 41735
RENAULT Bilston Rd ☎ 53111
ROVER-TRIUMPH 1 Evans St. ☎ 20362
TALBOT Cleveland Rd ☎ 25961
TALBOT 67/71 Bilston Rd ☎ 52611
VAUXHALL Raglan St. ☎ 27897
VOLVO 657 Parkfield Rd ☎ 333211

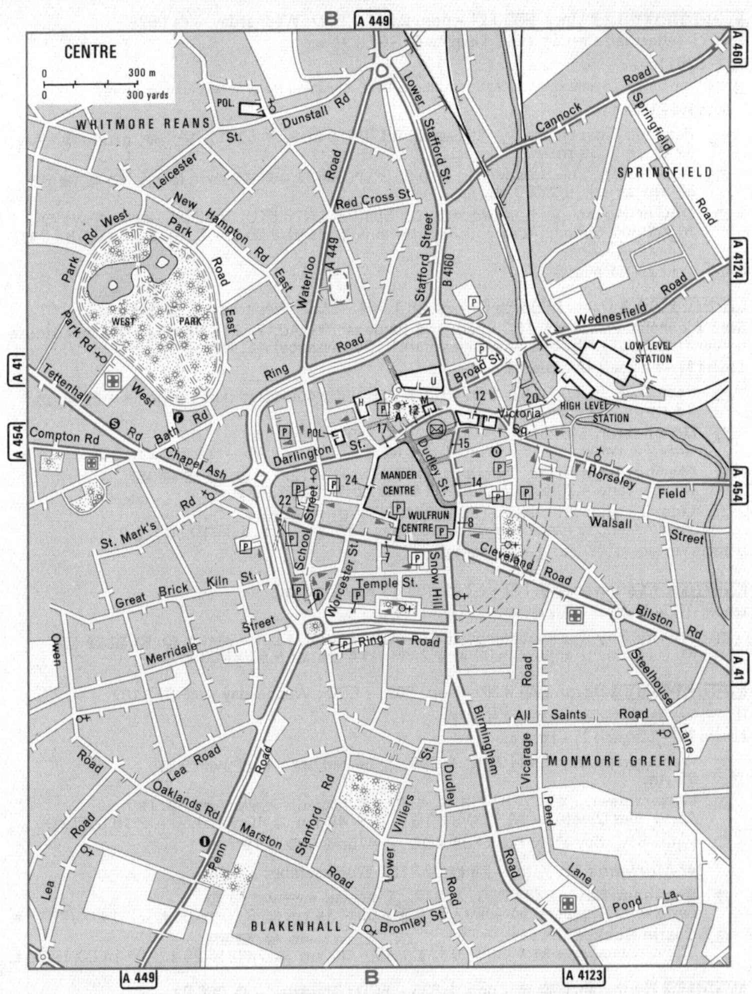

Pour parcourir l'Europe,
utilisez les cartes Michelin **Grandes Routes** à 1/1 000 000.

WOODBRIDGE Suffolk 404 X 27 – pop. 8,660 – ECD : Wednesday – 039 43.

18. 9 Bromeswell Heath, 2038, E : 2 m.

London 81 – Great Yarmouth 45 – Ipswich 8 – Norwich 47.

- **Seckford Hall** , IP13 6NU, SW : 1 ¼ m. off A 12 5678, , « Part Tudor country house », , , park – wc P. AE VISA
  M a la carte 5.45/7.30 1.70 – **24 rm** 13.80/27.50 **st.**

- **Crown** (T.H.F.), Thorofare, IP12 1AD, 4242 – TV wc P. AE VISA
  M 3.75/4.25 **st.** 1.65 – **25 rm** 13.50/21.00 **st.**

- **Captain's Table**, 3 Quay St., IP12 1BX, 4491 – P. AE VISA
  closed 25-26 December and 1 to 14 February – **M** a la carte 4.35/7.25 **t.** 1.50.

AUSTIN-MG-MORRIS-ROVER-TRIUMPH-WOLSELEY Melton Rd 3456
FORD 96 Thorough Fare 3333

FORD Bawsey 039 441 (Shottisham) 368
SAAB Hollesey 039 441 (Shottisham) 687

WOODHALL SPA Lincs. 404 T 24 – pop. 2,261 – ECD : Wednesday – ✆ 0526.
Envir. : Tattershall Castle* (15C keep) *AC*, SE: 3 ½ m.
18 ₱ 52511.
🛈 Council Offices, Stanhope Av. ₱ 52461 – Jubilee Park, Stixwould Rd ₱ 52448 (summer only).
London 138 – Lincoln 18.

- Petwood Moat House ⌂, Stixwould Rd, LN10 6QF, ₱ 52411, ✗, ☞, park – 🛉 ⌂wc ☎ Ⓟ. ♿ – **35 rm.**
- Golf (Crest), The Broadway, LN10 6SG, ₱ 52434, ☞ – ⌂wc Ⓟ. ♿. 🄰 AE ⓪ VISA **57 rm** ☲ 13.30/21.90 **st.**
- Dower House ⌂, Spa Grounds, off Spa Rd, LN10 6TU, ₱ 52588, ☞ – ⌂wc Ⓟ **M** *(closed Sunday lunch)* (lunch by arrangement) 9.00 **t.** – **7 rm** ☲ 10.00/18.50 **t.** – P 21.00/25.00 **t.**

SAAB Whitham Rd ₱ 52157

WOODSTOCK Oxon. 403 404 P 28 – pop. 1,961 – ECD : Wednesday – ✆ 0993.
See : Blenheim Palace*** 18C (park and gardens***) *AC*. Envir. : Rousham (Manor House gardens : statues*) NE: 5 m. – Ditchley Park* (Renaissance) *AC*, NW: 6 m.
London 65 – Gloucester 47 – Oxford 8.

- Bear, Park St., OX7 1SZ, ₱ 811511, « Tastefully converted part 16C inn » – TV Ⓟ. ♿ **33 rm.**
- Dorchester, Market St., OX7 1SX, ₱ 812291 – ⌂wc ⬛ *closed 1 week from 27 December* – **M** 3.00/3.90 ▮ 1.05 – **19 rm** ☲ 10.75/26.55 **st.**
- Marlborough Arms, Oxford St., OX7 1TS, ₱ 811227 – Ⓟ. 🄰 AE ⓪ VISA **M** a la carte 4.20/5.30 ▮ 2.00 – **14 rm** ☲ 11.50/22.90 **st.**
- Luis, 19 High St., OX7 1TE, ₱ 811017 – AE ⓪ VISA *closed Monday lunch and Bank Holidays* – **M** a la carte 6.35/10.50 **t.** ▮ 2.20.

MORRIS-MG-WOLSELEY 2 Oxford St. ₱ 811286

WOODY BAY Devon 403 I 30 – ✉ ✆ 059 83 Parracombe.
London 211 – Exeter 57 – Minehead 25 – Taunton 48.

- Woody Bay ⌂, Parracombe, EX31 4QY, ₱ 264, ≤ bay – ⌂wc Ⓟ. 🄰 AE ⓪ VISA **M** (bar lunch) approx. 5.00 **s.** ▮ 2.50 – **14 rm** ☲ 9.50/21.00 **s.**

WOOLACOMBE Devon 403 H 30 – pop. 809 – ECD : Wednesday – ✆ 027 187.
🛈 Hall 70, Beach Rd ₱ 553 (summer only).
London 237 – Barnstaple 15 – Exeter 55.

- Woolacombe Bay, EX34 7BN, ₱ 388, ⌁ heated, ☞ – 🛉 ⌂wc ☎ Ⓟ **65 rm.**
- Watersmeet, EX34 7FB, ₱ 333, ≤, ✗, ⌁ heated – ⌂wc ⇔ Ⓟ. ⓪ *Easter-mid October* – **M** 7.00/9.00 ▮ 1.70 – **40 rm** ☲ 10.50/23.00 – P 16.00/18.00.
- Whin Bay, Bay View Rd, EX34 7DQ, ₱ 475, ≤ – Ⓟ – **19 rm.**

  at Mortehoe N : ½ m. – ✉ ✆ 027 187 Woolacombe :

- Rockham Bay, EX34 7EG, ₱ 347, ⌁ heated – ⌂wc ☎ Ⓟ *Easter-mid October* – **M** 4.50/7.50 **t.** ▮ 2.00 – **34 rm** ☲ 8.00/16.00 **t.** – P 14.00/22.15 **t.**
- Castle Rock, EX34 7EB, ₱ 465, ≤, ☞ – ⌂wc ⇔ Ⓟ. 🄰 VISA *May-September* – **M** 4.00/6.00 **t.** ▮ 1.45 – **30 rm** ☲ 7.60/15.20 **t.** – P 14.00/15.80 **t.**

WOOLER Northumb. 986 ⑮ – pop. 1,833 – ECD : Thursday – ✆ 066 82.
🛈 High St. Car Park ₱ 602 (summer only).
London 332 – Edinburgh 62 – Newcastle-upon-Tyne 46.

- Tankerville Arms, Cottage Rd, NE71 6AD, on A 697 ₱ 581, ☞ – ⌂wc Ⓟ **M** 3.50/5.00 **t.** ▮ 1.80 – **15 rm** ☲ 10.50/20.75 **t.**

FORD ₱ 316   JAGUAR-MORRIS-MG-ROVER-TRIUMPH-WOLSELEY South Rd ₱ 267

WOOLVERTON Somerset 403 404 M 29 – see Bath.

WORCESTER Heref. and Worc. 403 404 N 27 – pop. 73,452 – ECD : Thursday – ✆ 0905.
See : Cathedral** 13C-15C (crypt** 11C) **A** – The Commandery* (15C) *AC* **B**.
🚗 ₱ 27171 ext 33.
🛈 Guildhall ₱ 23471.
London 124 – Birmingham 26 – Bristol 61 – Cardiff 74.

Plan opposite

- Giffard (T.H.F.), High St., WR1 2QR, ₱ 27155, Telex 338869 – 🛉 TV ⌂wc ☎ ♿. 🄰 AE ⓪ VISA **r**
  M 4.00/500 **st.** ▮ 1.65 – ☲ 2.50 – **99 rm** 18.00/24.00 **st.**

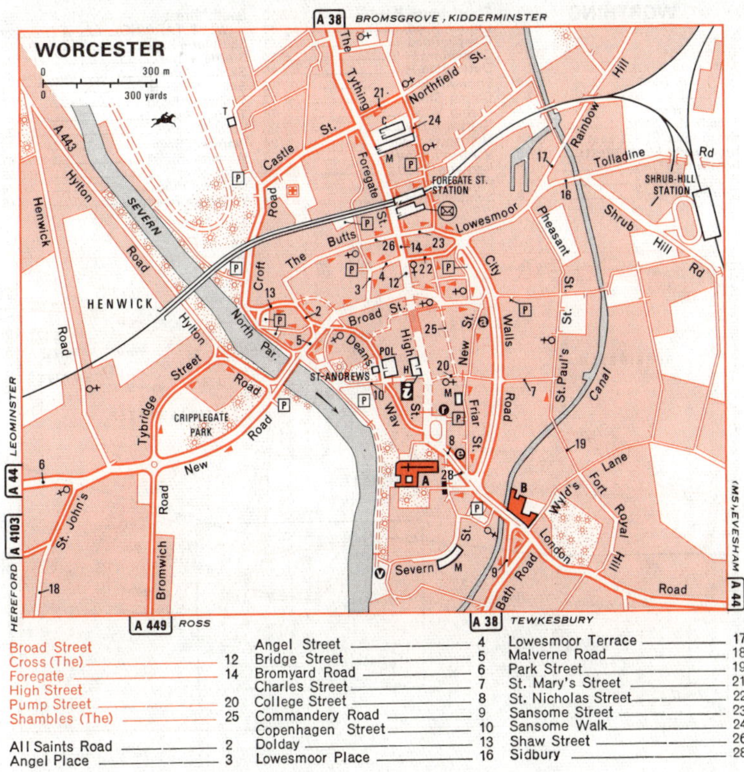

Ye Olde Talbot, College St., WR1 2NA, ☎ 23573 – 🍽 m̂. ☒ *VISA* **e**
M *(closed Sunday dinner)* a la carte 3.50/5.40 **st.** ⌀ 1.40 – **12 rm** ☲ 10.00/19.40 **st.**

Diglis, Riverside, Severn St., WR1 2NF, ☎ 353518, ≼, 🚗 – 🍽wc m̂. ℗ **v**
closed Christmas – **M** *(closed Sunday dinner and Monday)* a la carte 3.40/6.70
⌀ 2.00 – **15 rm** ☲ 8.25/18.00.

King Charles II, 29 New St., WR1 2DP, ☎ 22449, « 16C heavily timbered building »,
Italian rest. – ☒ *AE* *VISA* **a**
closed Sunday, last 3 weeks July, 25-26 December, 1 January and Bank Holidays –
M a la carte 6.50/12.20 **t.** ⌀ 1.75.

MICHELIN Branch, Blackpole Trading Estate, WR3 8TJ, ☎ 55626.

AUSTIN-DAIMLER-JAGUAR-MG-MORRIS-WOLSELEY
Castle St. ☎ 27100
FIAT, LANCIA Spetchley Rd ☎ 351821
MERCEDES, PEUGEOT 21 Barbourne Rd ☎ 28461

ROVER-TRIUMPH 26/30 Sidbury ☎ 26988
VOLVO Farrier St. ☎ 23338
VW, AUDI Hallow Rd ☎ 640512

WORKINGTON Cumbria 986 ⑲ – pop. 28,431 – ECD : Thursday – ☉ 0900.

🛈 Finkle St. ☎ 2122.

London 314 – Carlisle 33 – Keswick 21.

Westland, Branthwaite Rd, CA14 4SS, S : 2 m. off A 596 ☎ 4544 – 📺 🍽wc ☎ ℗
36 rm.

OPEL Annie Pitt Lane ☎ 3915
RENAULT Clay Flatts Estate ☎ 4542

VAUXHALL Harrington Rd ☎ 2159

WORSLEY Greater Manchester 403 404 M 23 – pop. 49,651 – ☉ 061 Manchester.

🛈 Ellesmere, Old Clough Lane, ☎ 790 2122.

London 207 – Liverpool 29 – Manchester 7.

Casserole, 2 Worsley Rd, M28 4NL, junction 13 on M 63 ☎ 794 2660 – ℗. ⓜ
closed Sunday, Monday and Christmas – **M** a la carte 7.50/8.50 **st.** ⌀ 1.70.

CITROEN Manchester Rd ☎ 790 4448

WORTHING

Chapel Road _______ BZ
Montague Street _______ BZ
Liverpool Terrace _______ BZ 21
South Street (WORTHING) - BZ

Broadwater Road _______ BZ 3
Broadwater Street East _______ BY 4
Broadwater Street West _______ BY 5
Broadway (The) _______ BZ 6
Brougham Road _______ BY 7
Brunswick Road _______ AZ 8

Christchurch Road _______ BZ 10
Church Road _______ AY 12
Cowper Road _______ AZ 13
Crockhurst Hill _______ AY 14
Durrington Hill _______ AY 15
Eriswell Road _______ ABZ 16
Goring Street _______ AY 17
Goring Way _______ AY 18
Grafton Road _______ BZ 20
Montague Place _______ BZ 24
Mulberry Lane _______ AY 25
Portland Road _______ BZ 26
Reigate Road _______ AY 27
Sompting Road _______ BY 28

South Street
(WEST TARRING) _______ AY, AZ 29
Southfarm Road _______ ABZ 30
Steyne (The) _______ BZ 32
Steyne Garden _______ BZ 33
Stoke Abbot Road _______ BZ 34
Tennyson Road _______ AZ 36
Thorne Road _______ AZ 37
Union Place _______ BZ 38
Warwick Road _______ BZ 40
Warwick Street _______ BZ 41
West Street _______ BZ 42
Western Place _______ BZ 44
Wykeham Road _______ AZ 45

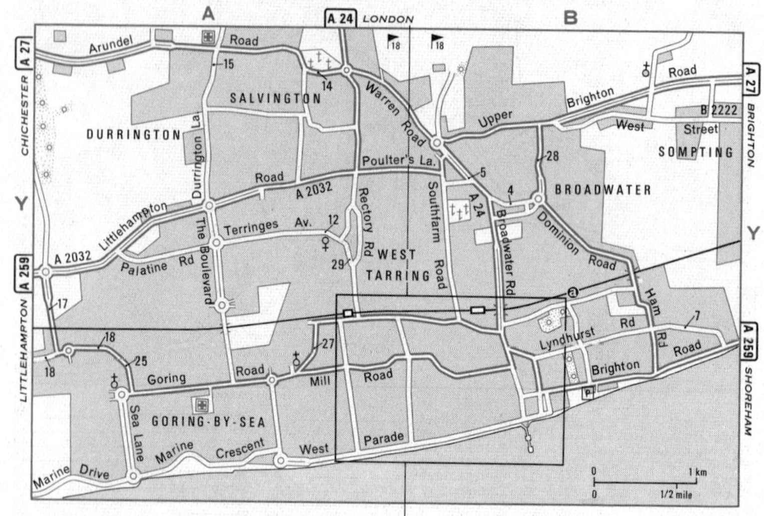

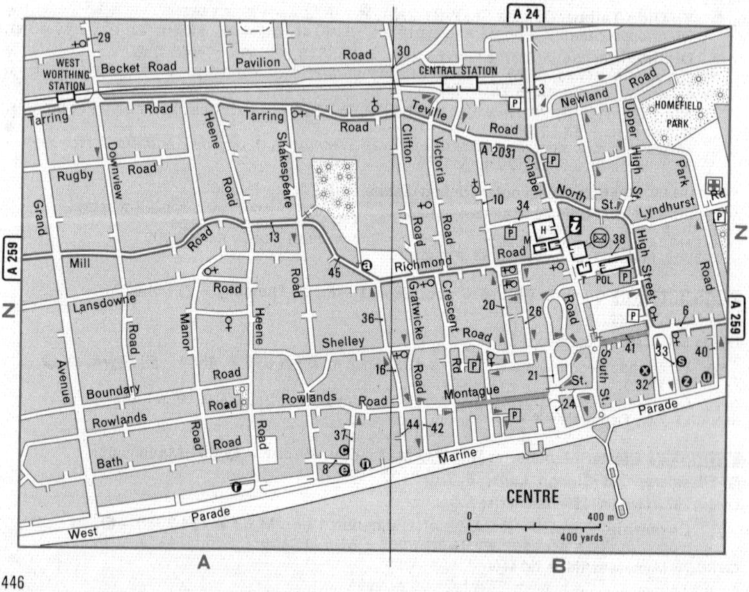

Envir. : Shoreham-by-Sea (St. Mary of Haura's Church* 12C-13C – St. Nichola's Church : carved arches* 12C) E : 5 m. by A 259 **BY**.

🏌, 🏌 Links Rd ☏ 60801 **AY** – 🏌 Hill Barn Lane ☏ 37301 **BY**.

🛈 Town Hall, Chapel Rd ☏ 204226.

London 59 – Brighton 11 – Southampton 50.

Plan opposite

🏨 **Beach,** Marine Par., BN11 3QJ, ☏ 34001, ≼ – ⃞ 📺 **P**. 🛁. 🔧 AE VISA   **AZ e**
M 4.50/5.75 st. 🍷 1.60 – **97 rm** ⊇ 11.50/24.40 st. – P 18.00/23.00 st.

🏨 **Chatsworth,** The Steyne, BN11 3DU, ☏ 36103 – ⃞ 📺 ⃔wc ☏. 🛁. 🔧 AE VISA   **BZ x**
M 5.50 t. 🍷 1.70 – **90 rm** ⊇ 14.50/24.00 t.

🏨 **Warnes,** Marine Par., BN11 3PR, ☏ 35222, ≼ – ⃞ 📺 ⃔wc ☏ **P**. 🛁. 🔧 AE ① VISA
M 4.25/6.00 t. 🍷 2.30 – ⊇ 1.50 – **70 rm** 12.00/27.00 t.   **BZ z**

🏨 **Eardley,** 3-10 Marine Par., BN11 3PW, ☏ 34444, ≼ – ⃞ 📺 ⃔wc ☏ **P**. 🛁. 🔧 AE VISA
M 3.75/4.80 t. 🍷 2.00 – **86 rm** ⊇ 10.50/18.00 t. – P 17.00/20.25 t.   **BZ u**

🏨 **Ardington,** Steyne Gdns, BN11 3DZ, ☏ 30451 – ⃔wc ⃔wc. 🛁   **BZ s**
M 4.00/4.50 t. 🍷 2.65 – **64 rm** ⊇ 10.00/22.00.

🏨 **Kingsway,** 117 Marine Par., BN11 3QA, ☏ 37542 – ⃞ 📺 ⃔wc. AE ① VISA   **AZ n**
M 2.95/4.25 t. 🍷 1.60 – **33 rm** ⊇ 10.40/23.35 t.

🏨 **Beechwood Hall,** Wykeham Rd, BN11 4AH, ☏ 32872, 🚘 – ⃔wc **P**   **AZ a**
M 3.50/4.50 s. 🍷 1.50 – **15 rm** ⊇ 8.50/20.00.

🛖 **Ainslea Court,** Abbey Rd, BN11 3RW, ☏ 30442 – 🔧 AE VISA   **AZ r**
closed January – **8 rm** ⊇ approx. 6.00.

🛖 **Wansfell,** 49 Chesswood Rd, BN11 2AA, ☏ 30612, 🚘 – 📺. AE   **BY a**
11 rm ⊇ 6.50/13.00 st.

XX **Paragon,** 9-10 Brunswick Rd, BN11 3NG, ☏ 33367 – AE VISA   **AZ c**
closed Sunday, Tuesday, 3 weeks June and Bank Holidays – **M** a la carte 6.25/9.85 t.
🍷 2.00.

at Findon N : 4 m. off A 24 – **AY** – ✉ Worthing – ☎ 090 671 Findon :

XX **Findon Manor** with rm, BN14 0TA, ☏ 2269, 🚘 – ⃔wc **P**
closed dinner Sunday and Bank Holidays – **M** (bar lunch) (Sunday lunch by arrangement)
a la carte 6.75/8.50 🍷 1.75 – **5 rm** ⊇ 10.50/21.00.

at Sompting NE : 2 ½ m. on B 2222 by A 27 – **BY** – ✉ ☎ 0903 Worthing :

X **Smugglers,** West St., BN15 0AP, ☏ 36072 – **P**
closed Sunday, Monday and Bank Holidays – **M** a la carte 4.50/9.05 t. 🍷 1.70.

at East Preston W : 4 m. by A 259 – **AY** – and B 2140 – ✉ Littlehampton – ☎ 090 62
Rustington :

XX **Old Forge,** The Street, BN16 1JJ, ☏ 2040 – **P**. 🔧 AE ① VISA
closed Sunday dinner and Monday – **M** a la carte 4.65/12.45 🍷 1.55.

at Angmering on Sea W : 4 ½ m. by A 259 – **AY** – off B 2140 – ✉ Littlehampton –
☎ 090 62 Rustington :

🏕 **South Strand,** BN16 1NY, ☏ 5086 – ⃔wc **P**
M 5.60 st. 🍷 1.70 – **12 rm** ⊇ 9.60/21.85 st.

WOTTON Surrey **404** S 30 – see Dorking.

WOTTON-UNDER-EDGE Glos. **403** **404** M 29 – pop. 4,318 – ECD : Wednesday – ☎ 045 385.

🏌 Dursley ☏ 0453 (Dursley) 2015, N : 5 m.

London 125 – Bristol 21 – Gloucester 18 – Swindon 34.

🏨 **Swan,** Market St., GL12 7AE, ☏ 2329 – 📺 ⃔wc ☏. 🔧 AE ① VISA
M 6.00/7.00 st. 🍷 2.00 – ⊇ 2.50 – **22 rm** 15.00/20.50 st.

WRAFTON Devon 🞐 H 30 – ✉ ☏ 0271 Braunton.
London 227 – Barnstaple 5 – Exeter 45 – Ilfracombe 9.

  XXX **Poyers Farm**, EX33 2DN, ☏ 812149 – **P**. ⒶⒺ
    closed Sunday dinner, 25-26 December and 1 week February – **M** 4.80/11.70 **st.**

WREXHAM (WRECSAM) Clwyd 🞐 L 24 – pop. 39,052 – ECD: Wednesday – ☏ 0978.
See: St. Giles' Church (tower★). **Envir**: Erddig★ (17C-18C) *AC*, SW: 2 m.
🏌 Holt Rd ☏ 4268 and 2189, NE: 2 m.
🅱 Guildhall Car Park, Town Centre ☏ 57845 (Easter-September).
London 192 – Chester 12 – Shrewsbury 28.

  🏨 Wrexham Crest Motel (Crest), 20 High St., LL13 8HP, ☏ 53431 – 📶 📺 🛏wc 📞 **P**. ⛱.
    🅰 ⒶⒺ ⓪ 𝘝𝘐𝘚𝘈
    ⊡ 2.40 – **80 rm** 18.00/24.50 **st.**

AUSTIN-MG-MORRIS 15/17 Hill St. ☏ 4024   RENAULT Regent St. ☏ 56822
FORD 67/73 Regent St. ☏ 51001   TALBOT Hightown Rd ☏ 4151

WROTHAM Kent 🞑 U 30 – pop. 1,785 – ECD: Wednesday – ✉ Sevenoaks – ☏ 0732
Borough Green.
Envir.: NE: Coldrum Long Barrow (prehistoric stones) site★: from Trottiscliffe 1 m. NE, plus
5 mn walk.
London 27 – Maidstone 10.

  XX **Moat** with rm, London Rd, TN15 7RP, SE: ½ m. on A 20 ☏ 882263 – **P**. 🅰 ⒶⒺ
    M a la carte 4.95/7.75 **st.** ⌗ 3.30 – **8 rm** ⊡ 11.00/24.00 **st.**

WROXHAM Norfolk 🞑 Y 25 – pop. 1,254 – ECD: Wednesday – ✉ Hoveton – ☏ 060 53.
London 118 – Great Yarmouth 21 – Norwich 7.

  🏠 **Wroxham**, Broads Centre, NR12 8UR, ☏ 2061, ⇐ – 📺 🛏wc **P**. 🅰 ⒶⒺ ⓪ 𝘝𝘐𝘚𝘈
    M 4.00 **st.** ⌗ 2.00 – **18 rm** ⊡ 13.00/28.00 **st.** – P 20.00/32.00 **st.**

TOYOTA Norwich Rd ☏ 2961

WROXTON Oxon. 🞐 🞑 P 27 – see Banbury.

WYCH CROSS East Sussex 🞑 U 30 – see Forest Row.

WYE Kent 🞑 W 30 – pop. 2,028 – ECD: Wednesday – ✉ Ashford – ☏ 0233.
London 61 – Folkestone 21 – Maidstone 24 – Margate 28.

  ♨ Kings Head, Church St., TN25 5BN, ☏ 812418 – **P**
    8 rm.

  XX **Wife of Bath**, 4 Upper Bridge St., TN25 5AW, ☏ 812540 – **P**
    closed Sunday, Monday and 23 December-1 January – **M** a la carte 5.75/7.05 **t.**

AUSTIN-MORRIS-MG Bridge St. ☏ 812331

WYNDS POINT Heref. and Worc. 🞐 🞑 M 27 – see Malvern.

YARMOUTH I.O.W. 🞐 🞑 P 31 – see Wight (Isle of).

YATELEY Hants. 🞑 R 29 – pop. 8,300 – ECD: Wednesday – ✉ Camberley – ☏ 0252.
London 42 – Reading 11 – Southampton 50.

  XX Casa dei Cesari, Handford Lane, Cricket Hill, GU17 7BA, off A 327 ☏ 873275, 🚗,
    Italian rest. – **P**.

YATTENDON Berks. 🞐 🞑 Q 29 – pop. 240 – ECD: Saturday – ✉ Newbury – ☏ 0635
Hermitage.
London 62 – Newbury 8 – Reading 12.

  X **Royal Oak** with rm, The Square, RG16 0UF, ☏ 201325 – 📺 🛏wc **P**. 🅰 ⒶⒺ ⓪ 𝘝𝘐𝘚𝘈
    M a la carte 5.85/12.20 **t.** ⌗ 2.60 – **5 rm** ⊡ 22.30/33.35 **t.**

YELVERTON Devon 🞐 H 32 – see Plymouth.

In addition to establishments indicated by
XXXXX ··· X,
many hotels possess
good class restaurants.

YEOVIL Somerset **403** **404** M 31 – pop. 25,503 – ECD: Monday and Thursday – ☎ 0935.
Envir. : Montacute House* (Elizabethan) *AC*, W: 4 m. – Cricket St-Thomas House (Wildlife Park*) *AC*, SW: 12 m.

� Sherborne Rd ☏ 5949.

London 136 – Exeter 48 – Southampton 72 – Taunton 26.

 🏨 Manor (Crest), BA20 1TG, on A 30, ☏ 23116, 🛋 – 📺 📠wc ☎ ❷. 🅟 AE ⓪ VISA
  21 rm ⌸ 19.90/29.00.

 🏨 **Mermaid,** High St., BA20 1RE, ☏ 23151 – 📺 📠wc ❷. 🅟 AE ⓪ VISA
  M *(closed Sunday dinner to non-residents)* a la carte 3.10/6.20 **t.** 🍷 1.10 – **16 rm**
  ⌸ 11.00/23.00 **t.**

 ↑ **Pickett Witch,** 100 Ilchester Rd, BA21 3BL, ☏ 4317, 🛋 – 📠wc ❷
  closed Christmas – **17 rm** ⌸ 7.35/13.45 **t.**

 ✕ The Maestro, 51 Princes St., BA20 1EG, ☏ 6960, Bistro.

 at Barwick S: 2 m. by A 30 off A 37 – ✉ ☎ 0935 Yeovil:

 ✕ **Little Barwick House** 🛏 with rm, BA22 9TD, ☏ 23902, 🛋 – ❷. 🅟 AE ⓪ VISA
  closed 26 December – **M** *(closed Sunday dinner to non-residents)* a la carte 4.60/6.75 **t.**
  🍷 1.75 – **4 rm** ⌸ 13.00/20.00 **t.**

 at West Coker SW: 3 m. on A 30 – ✉ Yeovil – ☎ 093 586:

 🏨 **Coker Motel,** BA22 9AJ, ☏ 2555, 🛋 – 📺 📠wc 🎿 ☎ 🛗 ❷. 🅟 AE ⓪ VISA
  M a la carte 2.05/6.00 **t.** 🍷 1.20 – ⌸ 1.50 – **22 rm** 12.00/18.00 **t.**

 at Montacute W: 4 m. on A 3088 – ✉ Yeovil – ☎ 093 582 Martock:

 ✕✕ **Milk House,** 17 The Borough, TA15 6XB, ☏ 3823 – 🅟 AE VISA
  closed Sunday, 2 weeks October and 2 weeks January – **M** (dinner only) a la carte
  6.35/8.40 **st.** 🍷 1.50.

AUSTIN-DAIMLER-JAGUAR-MORRIS-MG-ROVER-
TRIUMPH Princes St. ☏ 5242
BMW, PEUGEOT Sherborne Rd ☏ 23581
FORD Clarence St. ☏ 4770
HONDA, SAAB 12 Oxford Rd ☏ 6284

RENAULT Mudford ☏ 093577 (Marston Magna) 386
TALBOT Reckleford ☏ 4911
VAUXHALL Addlewell Lane ☏ 4842
VW, AUDI-NSU Vale Rd ☏ 22158

Y-FENNI Gwent – see Abergavenny.

YORK North Yorks. **986** ㉓㉔ – pop. 104,782 – ECD: Wednesday – ☎ 0904.
See : Minster*** 13C-15C (Chapter House***, ❊** from tower, *AC*, 275 steps) **CDY A** –
National Railway Museum*** **CY** M[1] – Castle Museum** *AC* **DZ** M[2] – Clifford's Tower*
(13C) *AC* **DYZ B** – Art Gallery* **CX** M[3] – Treasurer's House* (14C) *AC* **DX E** –City Walls*
14C – The Shambles* **DY.**

� Heslington Lane ☏ 55212, S : 2 m. **BZ** – � Strensall ☏ 490304, NE : 6 m. by Huntington
Rd **BY.**

🚗 ☏ 53022 ext 2631.

🛈 De Grey Rooms, Exhibition Sq. ☏ 21756/7.

London 211 – Kingston-upon-Hull 37 – Leeds 24 – Middlesbrough 48 – Nottingham 84 – Sheffield 60.

Plan on next page

 🏨 **Viking** (County), North St., YO1 1JF, ☏ 59822, Telex 57937, ≼ – ▤ 📺 ❷. 🎿. 🅟 AE
  ⓪ VISA   **CY n**
  M 4.40/5.50 **st.** 🍷 1.55 – **110 rm** ⌸ 25.50/32.50 **s.**

 🏨 Royal Station (B.T.H.), Station Rd, YO2 2AA, ☏ 53681, Telex 57912, 🛋 – ▤ 📺 ❷. 🎿.
  🅟 AE ⓪ VISA   **CY e**
  M 4.70/7.80 **st.** 🍷 2.30 – **129 rm.**

 🏨 **Post House** (T.H.F.), Tadcaster Rd, YO2 2QF, SW: 1 ¾ m. on A 64 ☏ 707921, Telex
  57798, 🛋 – ▤ 📺 📠wc ☎ 🛗 ❷. 🎿. 🅟 AE ⓪ VISA   **AZ r**
  M a la carte 5.15/7.70 **st.** 🍷 1.65 – ⌸ 2.25 – **104 rm** 19.00/25.00 **st.**

 🏨 **Chase,** Tadcaster Rd, YO2 2QQ, SW: 1 ½ m. on A 64 ☏ 707171, ≼, 🛋 – ▤ 📺
  📠wc ☎ ❷. 🎿. 🅟 AE ⓪ VISA   **AZ e**
  closed 25 and 26 December – **M** 3.15/5.00 – ⌸ 2.25 – **80 rm** 12.60/23.00.

 🏨 **Abbey Park** (Myddleton), 77-79 The Mount, YO2 2BN, ☏ 25481 – ▤ 📺 📠wc ☎ ❷.
  🎿. 🅟 AE ⓪ VISA   **CZ c**
  M 4.15/5.45 **st.** 🍷 1.75 – ⌸ 2.70 – **83 rm** 19.55/26.45 **s.**

 🏨 **Dean Court,** Duncombe Pl., YO1 2EF, ☏ 25082 – ▤ 📺 📠wc ☎ – 🅟 AE ⓪ VISA **CY a**
  M 4.50/6.50 **st.** 🍷 1.65 – **36 rm** ⌸ 18.50/37.00 **st.**

 🏨 **Sheppard,** 63 The Mount, YO2 2BD, ☏ 20500 – 📠wc ❷. 🅟 AE   **CZ i**
  M (bar lunch) 4.00 **s.** 🍷 1.85 – **19 rm** ⌸ 8.00/15.00 **s.**

 ↑ **Priory,** 126 Fulford Rd, YO1 4BE, ☏ 25280, 🛋 – ❷   **DZ r**
  closed Christmas – **12 rm** ⌸ 12.00/15.00 **s.**

 ↑ **Bootham Bar,** 4 High Petergate, YO1 2EH, ☏ 58516 – ▤   **CX a**
  8 rm ⌸ 6.90/13.80 **st.**

P.T.O. ⟶

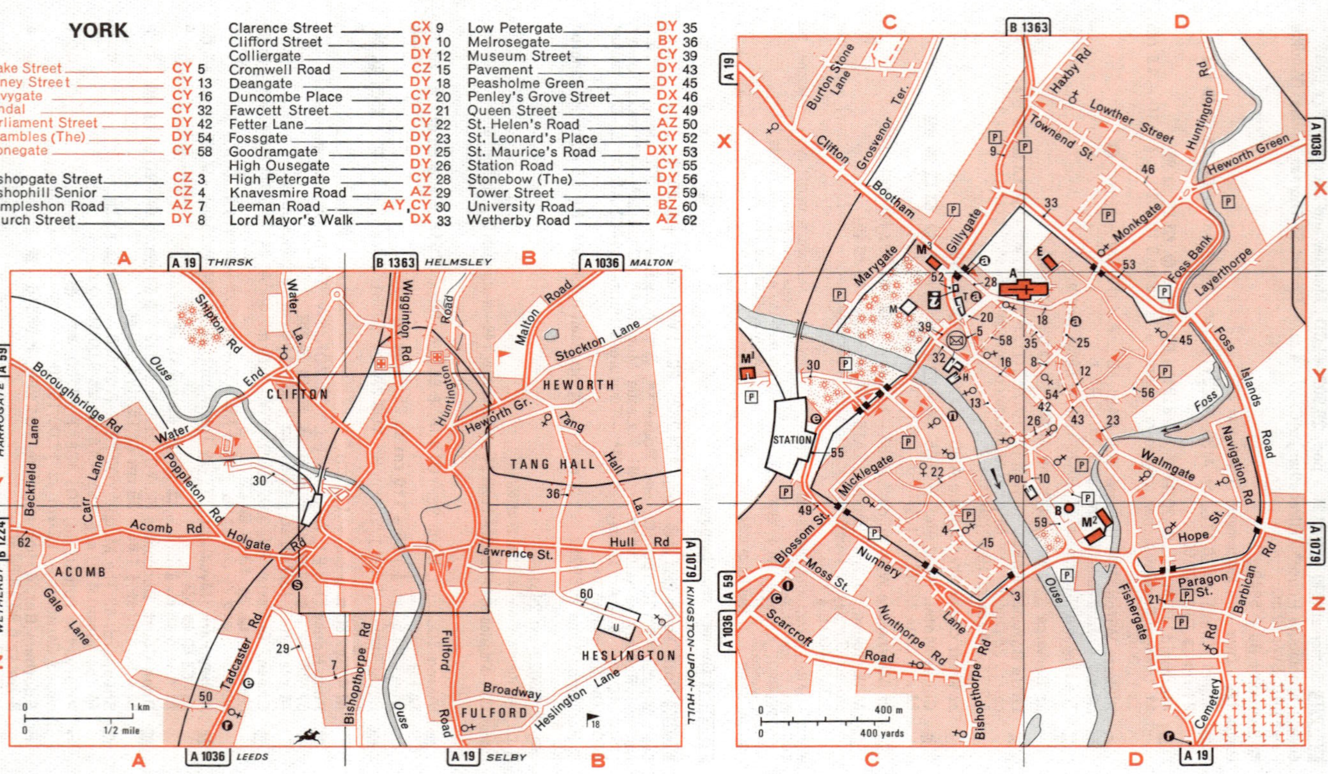

450
YORK
Blake Street — CY 5
Coney Street — CY 13
Davygate — CY 16
Lendal — CY 32
Parliament Street — DY 42
Shambles (The) — DY 54
Stonegate — CY 58
Bishopgate Street — CZ 3
Bishophill Senior — CZ 4
Campleshon Road — AZ 7
Church Street — DY 8
Clarence Street — CX 9
Clifford Street — DY 10
Colliergate — DY 12
Cromwell Road — CZ 15
Deangate — DY 18
Duncombe Place — CY 20
Fawcett Street — DZ 21
Fetter Lane — CY 22
Fossgate — DY 23
Goodramgate — DY 25
High Ousegate — DY 26
High Petergate — CY 28
Knavesmire Road — AZ 29
Leeman Road — AY, CY 30
Lord Mayor's Walk — DX 33
Low Petergate — DY 35
Melrosegate — BY 36
Museum Street — CY 39
Pavement — DY 43
Peasholme Green — DY 45
Penley's Grove Street — DX 46
Queen Street — CZ 49
St. Helen's Road — AZ 50
St. Leonard's Place — CY 52
St. Maurice's Road — DXY 53
Station Road — CY 55
Stonebow (The) — DY 56
Tower Street — DZ 59
University Road — BZ 60
Wetherby Road — AZ 62
A 19 THIRSK
B 1363 HELMSLEY
A 1036 MALTON
A 59 HARROGATE
B 1224 WETHERBY
A 1036 LEEDS
A 19 SELBY
A 1079 KINGSTON-UPON-HULL
Shipton Rd
Water La.
Ouse
Wigginton Rd
Malton Road
Stockton Lane
CLIFTON
HEWORTH
Heworth Gr.
Tang
TANG HALL
Hall
La.
Water End
Boroughbridge Rd
Beckfield Lane
Carr Lane
Poppleton Rd
Acomb Rd
Holgate Rd
ACOMB
Gale Lane
Tadcaster Rd
Bishopthorpe Rd
Ouse
Fulford Road
Lawrence St.
Hull Rd
Broadway
Heslington Lane
FULFORD
HESLINGTON
U
30
36
60
29
7
50
18
62
0 1 km
0 1/2 mile
B 1363
A 19
Burton Stone Lane
Clifton
Grosvenor Ter.
Haxby Rd
Lowther Street
Huntington Rd
Townend St.
Heworth Green
Bootham
Gillygate
Monkgate
Foss Bank
Layerthorpe
Marygate
Foss Islands Road
Walmgate
Navigation Road
Micklegate
STATION
Blossom St.
Moss St.
Nunnery Lane
Nunthorpe Rd
Bishopthorpe Rd
Scarcroft Road
Fishergate
Hope St.
Paragon St.
Barbican Rd
Cemetery
Ouse
POL
A 59
A 1036
A 19
A 1079
9
52
28
53
33
46
20
18
25
45
5
58
35
39
32
16
8
12
56
54
42
13
26
43
23
55
22
10
49
4
15
59
3
21
30
M1
M2
M3
B
0 400 m
0 400 yards

XXX **Mount Royale** with rm, 119 The Mount, YO2 2DA, ℡ 56261, ☒ heated, 🚗 – 📺 🛄 wc
🏛 wc 🅿. 🖾 AE ⓪ *VISA*   **AZ** s
closed 24 December-15 January – **M** *(closed Sunday)* (dinner only) 10.00 🍶 3.00 –
11 rm ☕ 15.50/22.00.

XX **Tanglewood**, Malton Rd, YO3 9TW, NE : 6 ½ m. on A 64 ℡ 090 486 (Flaxton Moor)
318 – 🅿. 🖾 AE ⓪ *VISA*   by A1036 **BY**
*closed Sunday dinner, Monday, 1 week late October-early November, Bank Holidays
except Good Friday and 26 December* – **M** a la carte 6.15/8.25 t. 🍶 1.85.

X **Trattoria Giovanni,** 55 Goodramgate, YO1 2LS, ℡ 23413, Italian rest. – 🖾 ⓪ *VISA* **DY** a
closed Sunday lunch, Monday and 25-26 December – **M** a la carte 2.70/7.50 t. 🍶 2.00.

at Bishopthorpe S : 3 ¼ m. by Bishopthorpe Rd – **BZ** – ✉ ☎ 0904 York :

X **L'Octogone,** Ferry Lane off Acaster Lane, YO2 1SB, ℡ 707878, ⋖, 🚗 – 🅿. 🖾
closed Sunday and Monday – **M** a la carte 4.45/8.95 t. 🍶 2.60.

ALFA-ROMEO Leeman Rd ℡ 22772
AUSTIN-MORRIS-MG Gladstone St. ℡ 58781
CITROEN Lowther St. ℡ 22064
DAIMLER-JAGUAR-ROVER-TRIUMPH Layerthorpe ℡ 58252
DATSUN 21/27 Layerthorpe ℡ 58809
FIAT Front St., Haxby ℡ 768344
FORD, LAND ROVER-MORRIS-MG-WOLSELEY, VAUXHALL Long St. ℡ 0347 (Easingwold) 21694

HONDA, SAAB 223 Malton Rd ℡ 55787
OPEL 100 Layerthorpe ℡ 56671
PEUGEOT Boroughbridge Rd ℡ 798388
RENAULT Clifton ℡ 58647
TALBOT, MAZDA The Stonebow ℡ 55118
TOYOTA 172 Fulford Rd ℡ 52947
VAUXHALL Rougier St. ℡ 25444
VOLVO 88/96 Walmgate ℡ 53798
VW, AUDI Clarence St. ℡ 23220

YR WYDDFA Gwynedd – see Snowdon.

Scotland

**HEURES PERMISES POUR LA CONSOMMATION DES BOISSONS
ALCOOLISÉES (Règle Générale).**

**ORARI CONSENTITI PER LA CONSUMAZIONE DI BEVANDE ALCOOLICHE
(Regola Generale).**

**AUSSCHANKZEITEN FÜR ALKOHOLISCHE GETRÄNKE
(Allgemeine Regelung).**

	from / de / dalle / von	to / à / alle / bis	from / de / dalle / von	to / à / alle / bis	
Weekdays / Jours de semaine	11.00	14.30	17.00	23.00	Giorni della settimana / Wochentags
Sundays, Dimanches, — Hotels Restaurants	12.30	14.30	18.30	23.00	Alberghi Ristoranti / Hotels Restaurants — Domeniche, Sonntags,
Pubs	Closed - Fermés - Chiusi - Geschlossen				Pubs

Wines and beverages may be taken with meals on licensed premises until 16.00 hours in the afternoon and until 01.00 hours in the morning.

Boissons avec un repas : service dans les lieux autorisés jusqu'à 16 h (déjeuner) et 1 h du matin (diner).

Bevande con il pasto: servite nei locali autorizzati, fino alle 16 (colazione) e fino all'una (cena).

Getränke zu den Mahlzeiten: in den lizensierten Betrieben bis 16 Uhr (Mittagessen) bzw. bis 1 Uhr morgens (Abendessen).

Place with at least :
one hotel or restaurant .... ● Tongue
one pleasant hotel .... 🏠 , ✗ with rm.
one quiet, secluded hotel .... ⊰
one restaurant with .... ✿, ✿✿, M
See this town for establishments
  located in its vicinity .... ABERDEEN

La località possiede come minimo :
una risorsa alberghiera .... ● Tongue
un albergo ameno .... 🏠 , ✗ with rm.
un albergo molto tranquillo, isolato .... ⊰
un'ottima tavola con .... ✿, ✿✿, M
La località raggruppa nel suo testo
  le risorse dei dintorni .... ABERDEEN

Localité offrant au moins :
une ressource hôtelière .... ● Tongue
un hôtel agréable .... 🏠 , ✗ with rm.
un hôtel très tranquille, isolé .... ⊰
une bonne table à .... ✿, ✿✿, M
Localité groupant dans le texte
  les ressources de ses environs .... ABERDEEN

Ort mit mindestens :
einem Hotel oder Restaurant .... ● Tongue
einem angenehmen Hotel .... 🏠 , ✗ with rm.
einem sehr ruhigen und abgelegenen Hotel ...... ⊰
einem Restaurant mit .... ✿, ✿✿, M
Ort mit Angaben über Hotels und Restaurants
  in seiner Umgebung .... ABERDEEN

Kinlochbervie
Scourie
ISLE
OF
LEWIS
Stornoway
Lochinver
Inchnadamph
Altnacealgach
Achiltibuie
Tarbert
Ullapool
Leckmelm
Laide
Dundonnell
ISLE OF HARRIS
Gairloch
Talladale
NORTH
UIST
Lochmaddy
Uig
Achnasheen
Skeabost
Dunvegan
Portree
Lochcarron
SOUTH
UIST
ISLE
OF
SKYE
Kyle of
Lochalsh
Balmacara
Sligachan
Dornie
Daliburgh
Broadford
Isleornsay
Ardvasar
ISLE OF BARRA
Castlebay

SHETLAND ISLANDS
ISLE OF UNST
Baltasound
Hillswick
MAINLAND
Whiteness
Lerwick
ISLE OF WESTRAY
Pierowall
MAINLAND
ORKNEY ISLANDS
Loch Harray
Stenness
Stromness
Kirkwall
John o' Groats
Bettyhill
Tongue
Wick
Forsinard
Altnaharra
Overscaig
Lairg
Oykel Bridge
Golspie
Bonar Bridge
Dornoch
Tain
Garve
Dingwall
Elgin
Buckie
Cullen
St. Combs
Conon Bridge
A 96
Fochabers
Banff
A 98
A 952
Muir of Ord
Nairn
Rothes
Beauly
Peterhead
INVERNESS
Aberlour
A 9
Advie
Ellon
Drumnadrochit
Grantown-on-Spey
Old Meldrum
Newburgh
Lewiston
Pitcaple
Invermoriston
Mossat
Monymusk
Fort Augustus
Kincraig
Aviemore
ABERDEEN
Maryculter
Kingussie
Ballater
Aboyne
Banchory
A 92
Newtonmore

455

Arisaig
Spean Bridge
Glenfinnan
FORT WILLIAM
Kilchoan
Glenborrodale
Strontian
Onich
Glencoe
Tobermory
Kentallen of Appin
Ballachulish
Dervaig
Duror
ISLE
Port Appin
Salen
Bridge of Orchy
OF
Eriska
Craignure
Connel
Tiroran
Oban
Kilchrenan
A 85
MULL
Bunessan
Clachan Seil
Easdale
Arduaine
STRACHUR
Kilmartin
Lochgoilhead
Carrick
Lochgair
ISLE
Cairnbaan
OF
Colintraive
JURA
Port-Askaig
Tarbert
ISLE
Craighouse
Rothesay
Bridgend
OF
I. OF BUTE
Bowmore
ISLAY
ISLE OF
GIGHA
PENINSULA
Catacol
ISLE
Corrie
Kildalton
OF
Carradale
Brodick
OF
Blackwaterfoot
KINTYRE
ARRAN
Lamlash
Bellochantuy
Whiting Bay
Campbeltown
Kilmory
Turnberry
Girvan
Ardentinny
Drymen
HELENSBURGH
DUNOON
Cove
Kilcreggan
STRATHBLANE
Gourock
Dumbarton
A 8
Greenock
Milngavie
Cumbernauld
Duntocher
Langbank
Hardgate
Erskine
Bearsden
Muirhead
Skelmorlie
Clydebank
GLASGOW
A 80
Airdrie
Renfrew
Coatbridge
Linwood
Paisley
Uddingston
Bellshill
Barrhead
Newarthill
Largs
Bothwell
Motherwell
A 78
East Kilbride
Eaglesham
Seamill
Kilmarnock

ABERDEEN
Kincraig
Kingussie
Maryculter
Newtonmore
Aboyne
Banchory
Ballater
Braemar
Stonehaven
A 9
Clova
Edzell
Kinloch Rannoch
Pitlochry
Kirkmichael
MONTROSE
Bridge of Cally
ABERFELDY
Alyth
Forfar
A 92
KENMORE
Glamis
Meigle
Dunkeld
Kinclaven
KILLIN
Carnoustie
A 85
St. Fillans
Dundee
Lochearnhead
Perth
Inchture
Wormit
Crieff
Comrie
Letham
Cupar
ST. ANDREWS
A 9
Auchterarder
Dunning
Peat Inn
Blackford
Falkland
Kingskettle
Callander
A 84
KINROSS
Lundin Links
Crail
Aberfoyle
Doune
Dunblane
Anstruther
Bridge of Allan
Glenrothes
Leven
Elie
Stirling
Kirkcaldy
M 90
Airth
Dunfermline
Halbeath
Dirleton
North Berwick
Falkirk
Grangemouth
Aberdour
Polmont
Aberlady
Gullane
Dunbar
A 80
South Queensferry
A 90
EDINBURGH
East Linton
Linlithgow
Haddington
Bathgate
Uphall
Gifford
M 8
Pathhead
Howgate
A 68
Lanark
Blyth Bridge
Lauder
Quothquan
PEEBLES
Symington
Walkerburn
GALASHIELS
Kelso
Troon
Broughton
Melrose
PRESTWICK
Dryburgh
AYR
St. Mary's Loch
Hawick
A 74
Sanquhar
Moffat
Beattock
Thornhill
Dalry
New Galloway
Lockerbie
Dumfries
Crocketford
Annan
Newton Stewart
Castle Douglas
Gatehouse of Fleet
Rockcliffe
Kirkcudbright
Auchencairn
Port William
Whithorn (Isle of)

SCOTLAND

Towns

ABERDEEN Grampian 986 ⑦ – pop. 182,071 – ECD : Wednesday and Saturday – ☎ 0224.

See : Marischal College* Y U – Art Gallery and Museum* Y M – ⇷* from the lighthouse X – St. Machar's Cathedral* X B – King's College Chapel* (Crown Tower) X U.

⌷ 19 Golf Rd ☏ 21464 X – ⌷, ⌷ Hazlehead ☏ 35747, W : 3 m. by King's Gate X – ⌷ St. Fittick's Rd, Balnagask ☏ 871286 X.

✈ Aberdeen Airport ☏ 722331 ext 5112/3, NW : 7 m. by A 96 X – **Terminal :** Bus Station, Guild St. (adjacent to Railway Station).

🚗 ☏ 23432.

⛴ to Shetland Islands : Lerwick (P & O Ferries : Orkney and Shetland Services) 2-3 weekly (14 h).

🛈 St. Nicholas House, Broad St. ☏ 23456 (Saturdays ☏ 24890/21814/21810), Telex 73366 – Information Caravan, Stonehaven Rd ☏ 873030.

Edinburgh 124 – Dundee 64.

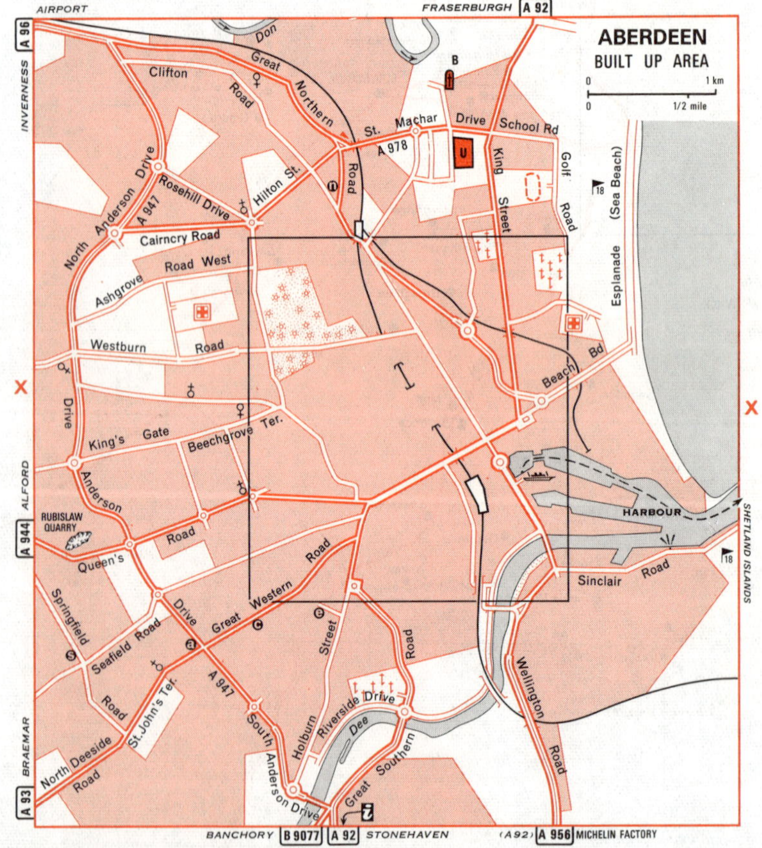

ABERDEEN

Station (B.T.H.), 78 Guild St., AB9 2DN, ☎ 27214, Telex 73161 – Z o
M 5.60/7.50 st. ↓ 2.30 – 57 rm ⌷ 29.70/39.85 st.

Tree Tops, 161 Springfield Rd, AB9 2QH, ☎ 33377, Telex 73794 – X s
⌷ 1.65 – 97 rm 21.85/35.50 st.

Amatola, 448 Great Western Rd, AB1 6NP, ☎ 38724 – X a
M 4.35/5.50 st. ↓ 1.90 – ⌷ 2.00 – 52 rm 20.00/26.00 st.

Caledonian (Thistle), 10-14 Union Ter., AB9 1HF, ☎ 29233, Telex 73758 – Z i
M 3.75/6.00 st. ↓ 1.70 – ⌷ 3.00 – 78 rm 16.00/27.00 st. – P 22.00/28.00 st.

Imperial (Swallow), Stirling St., AB9 2JY, ☎ 29101, Telex 73365 – Z r
109 rm.

P.T.O. ⟶

ABERDEEN

🏨 **Struan**, 239 Great Western Rd., AB1 6PS, 🕾 574484 – TV ⇔wc ☎ P. ⚠ ⓘ VISA **Z a**
M (bar lunch) 2.80/5.00 **st.** ⌗ 1.20 – **16 rm** ⟷ 14.00/26.00 **st.**

🏨 **Northern (Swallow)**, 1 Great Northern Rd., AB9 2UL, 🕾 43342 – ⌷ TV ⇔wc ☎ P. ⛱ **X n**
34 rm.

🏨 **Russel** without rest., 50 St. Swithin St., AB1 6XJ, 🕾 323555 – ☎ P. VISA **Z c**
9 rm ⟷ 9.80/19.55 **st.**

🏠 **Broomfield**, 15 Balmoral Pl., AB1 6HR, 🕾 28758 – P. **X e**
8 rm ⟷ 7.75/12.50 **st.**

XX Fiddler's, 1 Portland St., AB1 2LN, 🕾 52050 – P. **Z n**

XX **Le Dodo**, 15 Crown St., AB1 2HP, 🕾 26916 – ⚠ AE ⓘ VISA **Z v**
closed Saturday and Sunday lunch – **M** a la carte 5.65/10.00.

XX **Malacca** with rm, 349 Great Western Rd., AB1 6NW, 🕾 28901, Telex 73255 – TV ⇔wc
☎ P. AE ⓘ **X c**
M a la carte 5.70/8.90 ⌗ 1.60 – **7 rm** ⟷ 18.40/27.90 **st.**

X **Poldino's**, 7 Little Belmont St., AB1 7JG, 🕾 27777, Italian rest. – ⚠ **YZ u**
closed Christmas Day and 1 January – **M** a la carte 3.70/6.10 **s.** ⌗ 1.95.

at Cults SW: 3 ½ m. on A 93 – **x** – ✉ ✆ 0224 Aberdeen:

🏨 Royal Darroch (Stakis), North Deeside Rd., AB1 9SE, 🕾 48811, Telex 739138 – ⌷ TV
⇔wc ☎ P. ⛱. ⚠ AE ⓘ VISA – **67 rm.**

at Westhill W: 6 ½ m. off A 944 – **x** – ✉ ✆ 0224 Aberdeen:

🏨 **Westhill Inn**, Skene, AB3 6TT, 🕾 740388 – ⌷ TV ⇔wc ⋔wc ☎ P. ⛱. ⚠ AE ⓘ VISA
M 3.00/4.50 **st.** ⌗ 1.50 – **53 rm** ⟷ 15.50/22.50 **st.**

at Bucksburn NW: 4 m. on A 947 by A 96 – **x** – ✉ ✆ 0224 Aberdeen:

🏨 Holiday Inn, Old Meldrum Rd., AB2 9LN, 🕾 73911, Telex 73108, ⚠ – ⌷ TV P. ⛱
99 rm.

at Aberdeen Airport NW: 6 m. off A 96 – **x** – ✉ ✆ 0224 Aberdeen:

🏨 **Aberdeen Airport Skean Dhu**, Argyll Rd., AB2 0DU, 🕾 725252, Telex 739239, ⟱
heated – TV ♿ P. ⚠ AE ⓘ VISA
M 5.00/6.00 **st.** – ⟷ 3.50 – **148 rm** 22.50/45.00 **st.**

at Dyce NW: 6 ½ m. on A 947 by A 96 – **x** – ✉ ✆ 0224 Aberdeen:

🏨 **Dyce Skean Dhu**, Aberdeen Airport East, AB2 0DW, 🕾 723101, Telex 739239 – TV
♿ P. ⛱. ⚠ AE ⓘ VISA
M 4.65/5.85 **st.** ⌗ 2.00 – **148 rm** 26.00/32.00 **st.**

MICHELIN Branch, Wellington Rd., AB9 2JZ, 🕾 875075.

ALFA-ROMEO, SKODA 542 Gt Western Rd 🕾 30181
AUSTIN-MORRIS 92 Crown St. 🕾 50381
AUSTIN-MG-WOLSELEY 16/22 Mid Stocket Rd 🕾 631950
AUSTIN-MORRIS-MG 19 Justice Mill Lane 🕾 52265
DAIMLER-JAGUAR-ROVER-TRIUMPH, ROLLS ROYCE-BENTLEY Forbesfield Rd 🕾 33286
DATSUN 78 Powis Ter. 🕾 41313
FIAT 870 Gt Northern Rd 🕾 695573
FORD Menzies Rd 🕾 879024

FORD 29 Union Glen 🕾 29022
LANCIA 3 Whitehall Rd 🕾 29349
MERCEDES-BENZ, OPEL 366 King St. 🕾 24211
PEUGEOT 519 King St. 🕾 42330
RENAULT 44/48 Rose St. 🕾 54401
SAAB 116/124 Stanley St. 🕾 20911
TALBOT 130 Gt Western Rd 🕾 52391
VAUXHALL 16 Dee St. 🕾 29216
VW, AUDI 94 Hilton Drive 🕾 43327

ABERDOUR Fife – pop. 1,576 – ECD: Wednesday – ✆ 0383.
See : ≼** from the harbour.
Edinburgh 17 – Dunfermline 7.

🏨 **Woodside**, High St., KY3 9SW, 🕾 860328 – TV ⇔wc ⋔wc ☎ P. ⛱. ⚠ AE VISA
closed Christmas and 1 January – **M** a la carte 6.55/8.45 **t.** ⌗ 2.00 – **12 rm** ⟷ 12.10/24.75 **t.**

ABERFELDY Tayside 986 ⑪ – pop. 1,537 – ECD: Wednesday – ✆ 088 72.
☗⁹ 🕾 361, Central Perthshire.
🛈 District Tourist Association, The Square 🕾 276 (May-September).
Edinburgh 74 – Glasgow 72 – Oban 77 – Perth 32.

🛆 **Cruachan**, Kenmore St., PH15 2BL, 🕾 545, ≼, 🚿 – P. ⚠ VISA
March-November – **M** 3.00/4.50 ⌗ 1.90 – **10 rm** ⟷ 7.00/17.00.

🏠 Balnearn, Crieff Rd, PH15 2BJ, 🕾 431, 🚿 – P – **13 rm.**

at Weem N: 1 m. on B 846 – ✉ ✆ 088 72 Aberfeldy:

X **Ailean Chraggan** with rm, PH15 2LD, 🕾 346, ≼, 🚿 – P
April-November – **M** *(closed dinner in winter)* (bar lunch) approx. 6.50 **t.** – ⟷ 4.00 –
4 rm 6.00/12.00.

AUSTIN-MG, FORD Dunkeld St. 🕾 254

ABERFOYLE Central 986 ⑪ – pop. 593 – ECD: Wednesday – ✉ Stirling – ☎ 087 72.
Envir. : Loch Ard** W: 3 ½ m. – Loch Chon** NW: 8 m. – Loch Arklet Reservoir*
NW: 11 m. – ⊞ Main St. ☎ 352 (Easter-September) and ☎ 258 (Easter-mid October).
Edinburgh 55 – Glasgow 27.

　　🏨　Forest Hills ⑤, Lochard Rd, Kinlochard, FK8 3TL, W: 4 m. on B 829 ☎ 087 77
　　(Kinlochard) 277, ≼, « Extensive gardens » – �␣wc ℗. ◪ Æ ◑ VISA
　　Early March-late October – **M** (bar lunch) approx. 5.35 **t.** ▮ 1.00 – **37 rm.**

AUSTIN-MORRIS-MG　Main St. ☎ 342

ABERLADY Lothian – pop. 737 – ECD: Wednesday – ☎ 087 57.
Edinburgh 16 – Haddington 5 – North Berwick 7.

　　🏨　**Kilspindie House**, Main St., EH32 0RE, ☎ 319 – ➣wc ℗
　　M 3.30/5.30 **t.** ▮ 2.00 – **13 rm** � 10.00/22.00 **st.**

ABERLOUR Grampian 986 ⑦ – pop. 763 – ECD: Wednesday – ☎ 034 05.
Edinburgh 187 – Aberdeen 63 – Inverness 54.

　　🏨　**Dowans** ⑤, AB3 9LS, SW: ¾ m. off A 95 ☎ 488, ≼, ⋙ – ➣wc 🝙wc ℗
　　M 3.50/5.50 ▮ 1.75 – **13 rm** ⊠ 11.15/20.25.

AUSTIN-MORRIS-LAND ROVER-MG-RANGE ROVER-ROVER-TRIUMPH-SHERPA 15-19 High St. ☎ 505

ABOYNE Grampian 986 ⑦ – pop. 1,040 – ECD: Thursday – ☎ 0339.
Envir. : Craigievar Castle* (17C) *AC*, NE: 12 m.
⌗₈ Formaston Park ☎ 2328, E: end of Village – ⌗₉ Tarland ☎ 033 981 (Tarland) 413, NW: 5 m.
Edinburgh 137 – Aberdeen 31 – Dundee 80.

　　🏨　Birse Lodge ⑤, Charleston Rd, AB3 5EL, ☎ 2253, ⋙ – ➣wc ☏ ℗
　　Mid March-mid October – **17 rm** ⊠ 12.00/24.00 **t.**

AUSTIN-MORRIS-MG　Main Rd ☎ 2440

ACHILTIBUIE Highland – pop. 300 – ☎ 085 482.
Edinburgh 243 – Inverness 84 – Ullapool 25.

　　🏨　**Summer Isles** ⑤, IV26 2YQ, ☎ 282, ≼ Summer Isles, ⋟ – ➣wc ℗
　　Easter-mid October – **M** (buffet lunch) 3.50/9.00 – **15 rm** ⊠ 10.00/26.00.

ACHNASHEEN Highland 986 ⑥ – pop. 100 – ECD: Wednesday – ☎ 044 588.
Envir. : Glen Docherty** W: 6 m. – Glen Carron* SW: 8 m.
Edinburgh 202 – Inverness 43.

　　🏨　**Ledgowan Lodge** (Best Western) ⑤, IV22 2EJ, on A 890 ☎ 252, ≼, ⋟, ⋙ – ℗. ◪
　　Æ ◑ VISA
　　March-November – **M** 4.50/7.00 **st.** ▮ 2.00 – **17 rm** ⊠ 13.00/26.00 **st.** – P approx. 25.00 **st.**

ADVIE Highland – ✉ Grantown-on-Spey – ☎ 080 75.
Edinburgh 153 – Inverness 46.

　　🏨　**Tulchan Lodge** ⑤, PH26 3PW, on B 9102 ☎ 200, Telex 75405, ≼ Spey Valley, « Tasteful
　　decor », ⋟, ⋙, park – ⇌ ℗
　　closed February and March – **M** 7.50/13.00 ▮ 2.50 – ⊠ 6.00 – **11 rm** 29.00/58.00 –
　　P 55.00.

AIRDRIE Strathclyde 986 ⑮ – pop. 37,740 – ECD: Wednesday – ☎ 023 64.
Edinburgh 32 – Glasgow 14 – Motherwell 6,5 – Perth 53.

　　🏨　**Staging Post** (S & N), 8-10 Anderson St., ML6 6AF, ☎ 67525 – ℗. ◪ VISA
　　closed 1 January – **M** (bar lunch Saturday and Sunday) 6.00/7.00 **t.** ▮ 2.20 – ⊠ 1.70 –
　　8 rm 8.30/16.60 **t.**

FORD South Biggar Rd ☎ 64702

AIRTH Central – pop. 1,027 – ✉ Falkirk – ☎ 032 483.
Edinburgh 27 – Dunfermline 14 – Falkirk 6 – Stirling 8.

　　🏨　**Airth Castle** ⑤, FK2 8JF ☎ 411, ≼, « Former castle in extensive grounds », ✗, ⋙,
　　park – 📺 ℗. ◪ Æ ◑ VISA
　　M a la carte 5.10/12.95 **st.** ▮ 2.60 – **20 rm** ⊠ 23.50/36.00 **st.**

ALTNACEALGACH Highland – ✉ Lairg – ☎ 085 484 Elphin.
Edinburgh 240 – Inverness 81 – Lochinver 23 – Ullapool 22.

　　🏨　**Altnacealgach** ⑤, IV27 4HF, ☎ 240, ≼, ⋟ – ℗
　　April-October – **M** (bar lunch) 3.50/5.50 **t.** ▮ 1.50 – **13 rm** ⊠ 8.75/17.50 **t.** – P 15.50 **t.**

ALTNAHARRA Highland – ☎ 054 981.
Edinburgh 282 – Inverness 123 – Thurso 60.

　　🏨　**Altnaharra** ⑤, IV27 4WE, ☎ 222, ≼, ⋙ – ➣wc ⇌ ℗
　　March-September – **M** (bar lunch) 3.00/7.50 **t.** ▮ 1.50 – **15 rm** ⊠ 9.50/21.00 **t.**

ALYTH Tayside 🖸🖸🖸 ⑪ – pop. 1,701 – ECD: Wednesday – ☎ 082 83.
Envir. : Reekie Linn (waterfall)* N: 5 ½ m.
📍 Pitcrocknie ☏ 2268, E: 1 ½ m.
Edinburgh 63 – Aberdeen 69 – Dundee 16 – Perth 21.

🏨 **Lands of Loyal** ⑤, Loyal Rd, PH11 8JQ, N: ½ m. off B 954 ☏ 2481, ←, « Country house atmosphere », ◱, 🍴, park – ⇔wc 🚗 ℗. AE ⓪
closed 10 days at Christmas – **M** 3.50/5.50 ⌕ 1.80 – ⇌ 2.75 – **14 rm** 8.50/19.00 – P 16.50/ 18.00.

ANNAN Dumfries and Galloway 🖸🖸🖸 ⑲ – pop. 6,051 – ECD: Wednesday – ☎ 046 12.
Envir.: Ruthwell Cross* 8C, W: 7 m.
Edinburgh 82 – Carlisle 19 – Dumfries 16 – Newcastle-upon-Tyne 72.

🏦 Queensberry Arms (Osprey), High St., DG12 6AD, ☏ 2024 – ⇔wc 📞 ℗ – **27 rm.**
AUSTIN-MORRIS, PEUGEOT 25 High St. ☏ 2772   TALBOT Eastriggs ☏ 203
AUSTIN-MORRIS-MG Scotts St. ☏ 2382

ANSTRUTHER Fife 🖸🖸🖸 ⑪ – pop. 3,037 (inc. Kilrenny) – ECD: Wednesday – ☎ 0333 – 📍₉.
See : Harbour*. **Envir. :** St. Monance (church*) SW: 3 m. – Kellie Castle* (16C-17C) *AC*, W : 5 m.
🛈 Scottish Fisheries Museum, St. Ayles ☏ 310628.
Edinburgh 46 – Dundee 23 – Dunfermline 34.

🏨 **Craw's Nest**, Bankwell Rd, KY10 3DS, ☏ 310691, Telex 727396, 🍴 – 📺 ⇔wc 📞 ℗.
◱. ⌺ AE ⓪ *VISA*
M 3.75/6.50 **st.** ⌕ 1.85 – **31 rm** ⇌ 14.00/28.00 **st.**
🛟 Smugglers Inn, High St., KY10 3DQ, ☏ 310506 – �📺wc ℗
9 rm.

ARBROATH Tayside 🖸🖸🖸 ⑪ – pop. 22,586 – ECD: Wednesday – ☎ 0241.
See : Cliffs** (nature trail) – Abbey* *AC*.
📍 Elliot ☏ 2272, S: 1 m.
🛈 Angus District Council, 105 High St., ☏ 72609/76680.
Edinburgh 72 – Aberdeen 51 – Dundee 16.

Hotels see: Carnoustie SW: 7 m.
Montrose NE: 13 ½ m.

AUSTIN-MORRIS-MG-ROVER-TRIUMPH 1 Burnside   BMW Montrose Rd ☏ 72919
Drive ☏ 72921

ARDENTINNY Strathclyde – pop. 150 – ECD: Wednesday – ☎ 036 981.
Edinburgh 107 – Dunoon 13 – Glasgow 64 – Oban 71.

🛟 **Ardentinny** ⑤, PA23 8TR, ☏ 209, ←, 🍴 – ⇔wc ℗. AE
April-October and week ends in winter – **M** approx. 7.50 **st.** ⌕ 1.60 – **8 rm** ⇌ 14.00/ 24.00 **st.**

ARDEONAIG Central – see **Killin**.

ARDROSSAN Strathclyde 🖸🖸🖸 ⑭ – pop. 10,562 – ECD: Wednesday – ☎ 0294.
⛴ to the Isle of Man : Douglas (Isle of Man Steam Packet Co.) 19 May-14 September 1-5 weekly (6 h) – to the Isle of Arran : Brodick (Caledonian MacBrayne) 2-7 daily (55 mn).
Edinburgh 75 – Ayr 18 – Glasgow 32.

Hotels see: Kilmarnock SE: 11 ½ m.
Largs N: 11 ½ m.

ARDUAINE Strathclyde – ECD: Wednesday – ✉ Oban – ☎ 085 22 Kilmelford.
Envir. : Loch Craignish (site**) S: 6 m.
Edinburgh 142 – Oban 20.

🏨 **Loch Melfort** ⑤, PA34 4XG, ☏ 233, ← Sound of Jura, 🍴 – ⇔wc ℗. ⌺ AE
Easter-October – **M** (bar lunch) 6.00/8.00 – ⇌ 1.50 – **28 rm** 17.00/25.00.

ARDVASAR Highland – see **Skye (Isle of)**.

ARISAIG Highland – pop. 177 – ECD: Thursday – ☎ 068 75.
See : Sound of Arisaig*.
Edinburg 172 – Inverness 102 – Oban 88.

🏦 Arisaig, PH39 4NH, ☏ 224, ← – ⇔wc ℗
14 rm.

ARMADALE Highland 🖸🖸🖸 ⑥ – Shipping Services : see **Skye (Isle of)**.

ARRAN (Isle of) Strathclyde 🗺️ ⑭ – pop. 3,576.
See : Kilbrannan Sound** – Sound of Bute *.
🚢 by Caledonian MacBrayne : from Brodick to Ardrossan 2-7 daily (55 mn) – from Lochranza
to Claonaig (Kintyre Peninsula) 6-8 daily (30 mn).

Blackwaterfoot – pop. 203 – ✉️ Blackwaterfoot – ☎ 077 086 Shiskine.
🏌️ ⚑ 226.

🏨 Blackwaterfoot, KA27 8EU, ☎ 202, 🍴 – ⛱️wc – **22 rm.**

Brodick – pop. 630 – ECD : Wednesday – ✉️ ☎ 0770 Brodick.
See : Brodick Bay**.
🏌️ ☎ 2349, ½ m. from Pier.
🎫 The Pier ☎ 2140.

🏨 Douglas, KA27 8AW, ☎ 2155, ≼, 🍴 – ⛱️wc ☎ ℗ – **51 rm.**
🏨 **Kingsley,** KA27 8AJ, ☎ 2226, ≼, 🍴 – ⛱️wc ℗
April-September – **M** 2.75/4.00 t. 🍷 1.45 – **31 rm** ⛱️ 6.75/15.00 t. – P 12.00/13.00 t.
🏠 **Auchrannie** ⚘, KA27 8BZ, ☎ 2234, 🍴 – 🛁wc ℗
June-September – **16 rm** ⛱️ 7.00/17.00 **st.**
🏠 **Kilmichael House** ⚘, KA27 8BY, ☎ 2219, 🍴 – ℗. 🄰 ᴀᴇ ⓪ 𝘝𝘐𝘚𝘈
May-October – **9 rm** ⛱️ 8.50/17.00.
🏠 **Altanna,** KA27 8DW, ☎ 2232, 🍴 – ℗
April-September – **15 rm** ⛱️ 6.25/12.50.
🏠 **Allandale,** KA27 8BJ, ☎ 2278, 🍴 – 📺 ⛱️wc 🛁wc
closed November – **6 rm** ⛱️ 8.50/17.00 t.

Catacol – ✉️ Brodick – ☎ 077 083 Lochranza.
See : Catacol Bay*. **Envir. :** Lochranza (site*) NE : 2 m.

🏨 Catacol Bay, KA27 8AA, ☎ 231, ≼ – ℗. 🄰 𝘝𝘐𝘚𝘈
6 rm ⛱️ 7.50/16.10 **st.**

Corrie pop. 143 – ECD : Wednesday – ✉️ Brodick – ☎ 077 081 Corrie – 🏌️.

🏠 Ingledene, Sannox, KA27 8JB, NW : 1 m. on A 841 ☎ 225, ≼, 🍴 – ℗
season – **14 rm.**

Kilmory – pop. 1,179 – ECD : Wednesday – ✉️ Kilmory – ☎ 077 087 Sliddery.

🏨 **Lagg,** KA27 8PQ, ☎ 255, 🍴 – ⛱️wc ℗. 🄰 ᴀᴇ ⓪
March-October – **M** (bar lunch) 2.50/4.75 t. 🍷 1.95 – **17 rm** ⛱️ 9.00/21.00 t.

Lamlash – pop. 613 – ECD : Wednesday except summer – ✉️ Brodick – ☎ 077 06
Lamlash.
See : Lamlash Bay**.
🏌️ ☎ 296.

🏨 Lamlash, ☎ 208, ⚘, 🍴 – **11 rm.**
🏠 **Glenisle,** Shore Rd, KA27 8LY, ☎ 258, 🍴 – 🛁wc ℗
Mid March-mid October – **22 rm** ⛱️ 6.50/16.00 **st.**

Whiting Bay – pop. 352 – ECD : Wednesday except summer – ✉️ Brodick – ☎ 077 07
Whiting Bay – 🏌️.
See : Whiting Bay*.

🏨 **Whiting Bay** ⚘, KA27 8QJ, ☎ 247, ≼, 🍴 – ⛱️wc ℗. 🄰 ᴀᴇ ⓪ 𝘝𝘐𝘚𝘈
M 2.75/4.50 **st.** 🍷 1.20 – **22 rm** ⛱️ 10.75/25.30 **st.**
🏠 **Burlington,** KA27 8PZ, ☎ 255, ≼, 🍴
Easter-September – **12 rm** ⛱️ 5.00/10.00 **st.**

AUCHENCAIRN Dumfries and Galloway 🗺️ ⑲ – pop. 215 – ✉️ Castle Douglas – ☎ 055 664.
Edinburgh 98 – Dumfries 21 – Stranraer 62.

🏰 **Balcary Bay** ⚘, Balcary, DG7 1QZ, SE : 2 m. off A 711 ☎ 217, ≼ Auchencairn bay,
hills and countryside, 🍴 – ⛱️wc ☎ ℗. 🄰 ᴀᴇ ⓪ 𝘝𝘐𝘚𝘈
April-October – **M** (bar lunch) 7.20 **st.** 🍷 1.85 – **11 rm** ⛱️ 14.00/28.00 **st.** – P 21.00/
24.00 **st.**

AUCHTERARDER Tayside 🗺️ ⑪ – pop. 2,446 – ECD : Wednesday – ☎ 076 46.
🏌️ Orchild Rd ☎ 2804, S : 1 m.
Edinburgh 55 – Glasgow 45 – Perth 14.

🏨 Gleneagles (B.T.H.) ⚘, PH3 1NF, SW : 1 ½ m. ☎ 2231, Telex 76105, ≼, 🍽️, 🄰, 🏌️.
🍴, park – 🛗 📺 ♿ 🚗 ℗. 🏊 – *season* – **210 rm.**
🏨 **Ruthven Tower,** Abbey Rd, PH3 1DN, ☎ 2578, 🍴 – ⛱️wc ℗
M (bar lunch) 2.50/6.70 **st.** 🍷 1.60 – **19 rm** ⛱️ 12.50/29.00 **st.**

Envir. : Cairngorm Mountains ❄******* from the summit (alt. 4084 ft) SE : 8 ½ m. and by chairlift (*AC*) 40 mn Rtn and 45 mn on foot Rtn.

🛈 Main Rd ☏ 810363, Telex 75127 – Aviemore Centre ☏ 810624 (June-September).

Edinburgh 127 – Inverness 32 – Perth 85.

🏨 **Strathspey** (Thistle), PH22 1PG, ☏ 810681, Telex 75213, ≼ Cairngorms – 📶 📺 🅿. ⛷.
🏊 AE ⓓ *VISA*
M a la carte 7.85/10.85 **st.** 🍾 1.75 – **90 rm** ⌕ 22.00/32.00 **st.** – P 23.00 **st.**

🏨 Coylumbridge (Stakis), PH22 1QN, SE : 1 ¾ m. on A 951 ☏ 810661, Telex 75272, ≼
Cairngorms, ⚓, 🚲 – 📺 ♿ 🅿. ⛷. 🏊 AE ⓓ *VISA*
131 rm.

🏨 **Post House** (T.H.F.), PH22 1PJ, ☏ 810771, ≼, 🚲 – 📶 📺 ☐wc ☎ 🅿. ⛷. 🏊 AE ⓓ
VISA
M 5.00/7.00 **st.** 🍾 1.80 – ⌕ 2.25 – **103 rm** 18.00/25.50 **st.**

🏨 Badenoch (Osprey), PH22 1PH, ☏ 810261 – 📶 ☐wc ☎ 🅿
78 rm.

🏨 **High Range**, Grampian Rd, PH22 1PT, ☏ 810636, ≼ – ☐wc 🎏wc 🅿. 🏊 AE ⓓ *VISA*
M (dinner only and Sunday lunch) a la carte 4.80/6.70 🍾 1.70 – **21 rm** ⌕ 10.00/20.00.

🏨 **Lynwilg**, PH22 1QB, S : 1 ½ m. on A 9 ✉ Loch Alvie ☏ 810207 – ☐wc 🚗 🅿. AE ⓓ
Mid February-October – **M** (bar lunch) 6.75 **st.** 🍾 2.00 – **12 rm** ⌕ 12.95/23.25 **st.**

✕ **Bumbles,** 9 New Shopping Development, PH22 1PS, ☏ 810392
closed Wednesday – **M** (buffet lunch) a la carte 5.80/8.40 **t.** 🍾 2.00.

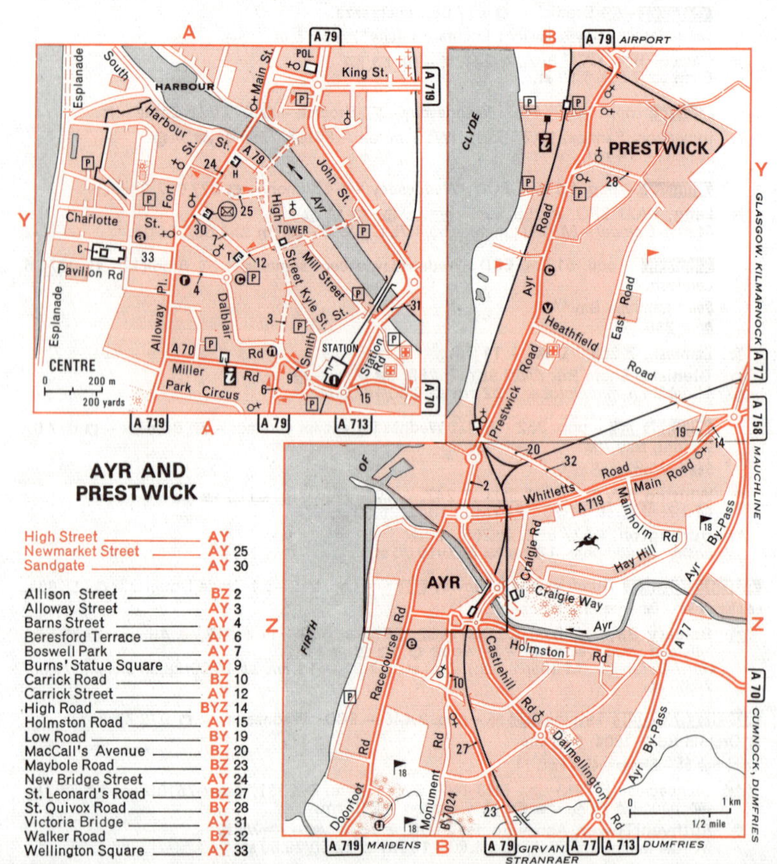

AYR AND PRESTWICK

High Street ———— **AY**
Newmarket Street ———— **AY** 25
Sandgate ———— **AY** 30

Allison Street ———— **BZ** 2
Alloway Street ———— **AY** 3
Barns Street ———— **AY** 4
Beresford Terrace ———— **AY** 6
Boswell Park ———— **AY** 7
Burns' Statue Square ———— **AY** 9
Carrick Road ———— **BZ** 10
Carrick Street ———— **AY** 12
High Road ———— **BYZ** 14
Holmston Road ———— **AY** 15
Low Road ———— **BY** 19
MacCall's Avenue ———— **BZ** 20
Maybole Road ———— **BZ** 23
New Bridge Street ———— **AY** 24
St. Leonard's Road ———— **BZ** 27
St. Quivox Road ———— **BY** 28
Victoria Bridge ———— **AY** 31
Walker Road ———— **BZ** 32
Wellington Square ———— **AY** 33

AYR Strathclyde 𝟵𝟴𝟲 ⑭ – pop. 47,896 – ECD: Wednesday – ☎ 0292
See: Harbour* **AY**. **Envir.**: Alloway* (Burn's Museum *AC*, Burn's birthplace *AC*, Auld brig)
S: 2 ½ m. by B 7024 **BZ**.

⌗, ⌗ Belleisle ☎ 0292 (Alloway) 41258 **BZ** – ⌗ Westwood Av., Whitletts ☎ 63893 **BZ**.

🛈 Tourist Information Bureau, 30 Miller Rd ☎ 68077.

Edinburgh 77 – Glasgow 34.

Plan opposite

🏨 **Caledonian**, Dalblair Rd, KA7 1UG, ☎ 69331 – 🔌 📺 🅿. 🛁. 🔲 AE ⓪ *VISA*   **AY c**
   M (bar lunch Monday to Saturday) a la carte 3.45/10.50 **t.** 🍾 1.60 – **122 rm** ☕ 20.00/
   36.00 **st.**

🏨 **Belleisle House** ⌂, Belleisle Park, KA7 4DU, S: 1 ½ m. on A 719 ☎ 42331, ≼ – 📺
   ⌷wc �🚿wc ☎ 🅿. 🛁. 🔲 AE   **BZ u**
   M 2.75/5.00 **t.** 🍾 1.80 – **16 rm** ☕ 15.00/27.00 **st.**

🏨 Pickwick, 19 Racecourse Rd, KA7 2TD, ☎ 60111, 🚗 – 📺 ⌷wc �🚿wc ☎ 🅿   **BZ e**
   15 rm.

🏨 **Station** (Stakis), Burns Statue Sq., KA7 3AT, ☎ 63268, Telex 778704 – 🔌 📺 ⌷wc ☎
   🅿. 🛁. 🔲 AE ⓪ *VISA*   **AY i**
   M 3.50/5.25 **st.** 🍾 1.55 – **73 rm** ☕ 16.50/26.00 **st.**

🏨 Ayrshire and Galloway (Open House), 1 Killoch Pl., KA7 2EA, ☎ 62626 – ⌷wc 🅿   **AY n**
   24 rm.

🏨 **County** (Open House), 11-13 Wellington Sq., KA7 1HU, ☎ 63368 – 🅿. 🔲 AE ⓪ *VISA*
   M approx. 5.05 **t.** 🍾 2.75 – **31 rm** ☕ 18.00/22.50 **t.**   **AY a**

🏨 **Berkeley**, 1 Barns St., KA7 1XB, ☎ 63658, 🚗 – ⌷wc 🅿. 🔲 *VISA*   **AY r**
   M 3.50/6.00 **t.** 🍾 1.50 – **10 rm** ☕ 15.00/25.00 **t.**

   at Hollybush SE: 6 m. on A 713 – **BZ** – ✉ Ayr – ☎ 029 256 Dalrymple:

🏨 **Hollybush House** ⌂, KA6 7EA, ☎ 214, Telex 777641, ≼, 🎣, 🚗, park – ⌷wc 🅿. 🔲 AE
   VISA
   closed 25 to 27 December – **M** a la carte 3.90/7.50 🍾 1.40 – **12 rm** ☕ 15.20/27.85 **st.**

ALFA-ROMEO, FIAT Galloway Av. ☎ 60416
AUSTIN-MORRIS-MG 7 Fullarton St. ☎ 66944
AUSTIN-MORRIS-MG Maybole Rd ☎ 62991
AUSTIN-DAIMLER-JAGUAR-MORRIS-MG-ROVER-
TRIUMPH 18 Holmston Rd ☎ 68373
CITROEN 216 Prestwick Rd ☎ 67282
DATSUN Alloway Pl. ☎ 63140
RENAULT 84 Prestwick Rd ☎ 81938

SAAB Cambuslea Rd ☎ 66146
TOYOTA 65 Peebles St. ☎ 67606
VAUXHALL 196 Prestwick Rd ☎ 61631
VAUXHALL 12/28 Dalblair Rd ☎ 62215
VOLVO, LANCIA, PORSCHE 16 Smith St. ☎ 60228 and
66007
VW, AUDI-NSU 80 Prestwick Rd ☎ 69522

BALLACHULISH Highland 𝟵𝟴𝟲 ⑩ – pop. 1,089 – ECD: Wednesday – ☎ 085 52.
Envir.: Glen Coe** (glen and waterfall) E: 6 m.

Edinburgh 117 – Inverness 80 – Kyle of Lochalsh 90 – Oban 38.

🏨 **Ballachulish** (Best Western), PA39 4JY, NW: 2 m. on A 828 ☎ 239, ≼ Loch Linnhe
   and mountains, 🚗 – ⌷wc 🅿. 🔲 AE ⓪ *VISA*
   May-7 October – **M** (dinner only) a la carte 5.90/9.85 **st.** 🍾 1.90 – **33 rm** ☕ 13.00/
   30.00 **st.**

BALLATER Grampian 𝟵𝟴𝟲 ⑦ – pop. 982 – ECD: Thursday – ☎ 033 82.
Envir.: NW: Lecht Road ≼** of the Grampian Mountains – Balmoral Castle* (not open) and
park* *AC*, W: 9 m. – ⌗ ☎ 200.

🛈 Station Sq. ☎ 306.

Edinburgh 109 – Aberdeen 41 – Inverness 69 – Perth 67.

🏨 **Tullich Lodge** ⌂, AB3 5SB, E: 1 ½ m. on A 93 ☎ 406, ≼ Dee valley and Grampians,
   🚗 – ⌷wc �🚿wc 🅿. AE ⓪
   April-December – **M** (lunch by arrangement) 6.00/6.50 **st.** 🍾 2.00 – **10 rm** ☕ 18.50/
   33.00 **st.**

🏨 Craigendarroch ⌂, AB3 5XA, W: ¾ m. on A 93 ☎ 217, ≼ Dee valley and Grampians,
   🚗 – ⌷wc 🅿 – **32 rm.**

🏨 **Darroch Learg**, Braemar Rd, AB3 5UX, ☎ 443, ≼ Dee Valley and Grampians, 🚗 –
   ⌷wc 🅿
   March-October – **M** 2.75/5.00 **st.** 🍾 1.60 – **25 rm** ☕ 9.00/18.00 **st.** – P 16.50/18.00 **st.**

🏨 **Craigard**, 3 Abergeldie Rd, AB3 5RR, ☎ 445, ≼, 🚗 – ⌷wc �🚿wc 🅿. 🔲 ⓪
   April-October – **M** (bar lunch) 6.50 **st.** 🍾 1.90 – **16 rm** ☕ 10.00/23.00 **st.**

🏨 **Glen Lui** ⌂, Invercauld Rd, AB3 5RP, ☎ 402, ≼, 🚗 – 🅿
   Easter-October – **M** (bar lunch) 2.00/7.50 **t.** – **7 rm** ☕ 9.00/17.00 **t.**

BALMACARA Highland – pop. 107 – ECD: Wednesday – ✉ Kyle of Lochalsh – ☎ 059 986.
🛈 Lochalsh House, Kyle of Lochalsh ☎ 207.

Edinburgh 197 – Kyle of Lochalsh 4.5.

🏨 **Balmacara**, IV40 8DH, ☎ 283, ≼ – ⌷wc 🅿. AE
   M 2.80/5.50 **t.** 🍾 2.50 – **28 rm** ☕ 11.00/26.00 **t.**

BALNAKEIL Highland.
See : Balnakeil Bay★★. **Envir. :** Smoo Cave★ SE: 3 ½ m. – SW: Dionard Valley★.
Edinburgh 294 – Durness 2 – Inverness 135 – Thurso 83.

BALTASOUND Shetland Islands – see Shetland Islands (Unst).

BANAVIE Highland – see Fort William.

BANCHORY Grampian **986** ⑦ – pop. 2,355 – ECD : Thursday – ☎ 033 02.
Envir. : Crathes Castle★ (16C) *AC*, E : 3 m.
Kinneskie 2365 – Torphins 033 982 (Torphins) 493, NW : 6 m.
Dee St. Car Park 2000 (May-October).
Edinburgh 125 – Aberdeen 17 – Dundee 66 – Inverness 92.

  Raemoir House ⑳, AB3 4ED, N : 2 ½ m. on A 980 2622, ≤, « 18 C mansion in extensive grounds », ⚡, park – ⏢wc **P**. ⓞ
  M a la carte 7.00/8.70 **st.** ⬦ 2.65 – **21 rm** ⬜ 16.00/32.00.

  Banchory Lodge ⑳, AB3 3HS, 2625, ≤, ⬧, ⚡ – ⏢wc **P**. **AE** **VISA**
  closed December and January – **M** 5.00/10.00 **st.** – **20 rm** ⬜ 14.50/29.00 **st.** – P 20.00/25.00 **st.**

  Tor-Na-Coille ⑳, Inch Marlo Rd, AB3 4AB, 2242, ⚡, park – ⦿ **TV** ⏢wc ⊛ **P**. ⓐ. ⬧ **AE** ⓞ **VISA**
  M 3.50/6.50 **t.** ⬦ 1.50 – **25 rm** ⬜ 13.00/29.50 **t.** – P 17.00/22.00 **t.**

AUSTIN-MORRIS High St. 2293   MORRIS-MG North Deeside Rd 2255

BANFF Grampian **986** ⑦ – pop. 3,723 – ECD : Wednesday – ☎ 026 12.
See : Duffhouse★. **Envir. :** Gardenstown (site★) E : 8 m.
Duff House Royal 2278 – Macduff 0261 (Macduff) 32548.
Collie Lodge 2419 (June-September).
Edinburgh 170 – Aberdeen 46 – Fraserburgh 26 – Inverness 74.

  Banff Springs, Golden Knowes Rd, AB4 2JE, W : ¾ m. on A 98 2881, ≤ – **TV** ⏢wc ⦿wc ⊛ **P**. ⓐ. ⬧ **AE** ⓞ **VISA**
  closed 1 to 3 January – **M** 3.00/6.00 **s.** ⬦ 2.00 – **30 rm** ⬜ 12.50/25.00 **s.** – P 21.50 **s.**

  Carmelite House, Low St., AB4 1AY, 2152, ⚡ – **P** – **8 rm.**

AUSTIN-MORRIS High St. 2473   FORD Bridge Rd 2673

BARRA (Isle of) Outer Hebrides (Western Isles) **986** ⑥ – pop. 1,147.

  Castlebay – ✉ ☎ 087 14 Castlebay.
  ⛴ by Caledonian MacBrayne : to Oban 3-4 weekly (5 h to 8 h) – to Lochboisdale (South Uist) (1 h 30 mn).
  336 (May-September).

  Isle of Barra ⑳, PA80 5XW, NW : 2 m. on A 888 383, ≤ sea and mountains – ⏢wc **P**. ⬧ **AE** ⓞ **VISA**
  Mid April-mid October – **M** (bar lunch) 2.35/6.25 **st.** ⬦ 1.25 – **41 rm** ⬜ 17.95/30.30 **st.**

BARRHEAD Strathclyde **986** ⑮ – pop. 18,289 – ECD : Tuesday – ✉ ☎ 041 Glasgow.
Edinburgh 51 – Ayr 30 – Glasgow 8.

  Dalmeny Park, Lochlibo Rd, G78 1LG, SW : ½ m. on A 736 881 9211, « Gardens » –
  TV ⦿wc ⊛ **P**. ⓐ. ⬧ **AE** ⓞ **VISA**
  M a la carte 5.00/8.25 **st.** ⬦ 2.25 – **18 rm** ⬜ 19.00/26.00 **st.**

BATHGATE Lothian **986** ⑮ – pop. 14,224 – ☎ 0506.
Envir. : Cairnpapple Hill (burial cairn★ *AC*, ≤★) N : 3 m.
52232.
Edinburgh 19 – Glasgow 26.

  Golden Circle (Swallow), Blackburn Rd, EH48 2EL, S : 1 ¾ m. on B 792 53771,
  Telex 72606 – ⦿ **TV** ⏢wc ⦿wc ⊛ **P**. ⓐ
  76 rm.

  XX **Balbairdie,** Bloomfield Pl., off George Pl., EH48 1PB, 55448 – ⬧ **AE** ⓞ **VISA**
  closed Sunday – **M** a la carte 6.85/9.50 **s.** ⬦ 2.50.

FORD Torphichen Rd 56685   VW, AUDI-NSU Blackburn Rd 52948

BEARSDEN Strathclyde – pop. 25,013 – ECD : Tuesday and Saturday – ✉ ☎ 041 Glasgow.
Edinburgh 49 – Glasgow 6.

  Burnbrae, (Stakis), Milngavie Rd, G61 3HJ, NE : 1 m. on A 81 942 5951 – **TV** ⏢wc
  ⊛ **P**. ⓐ
  M 7.20 **st.** ⬦ 1.65 – **15 rm** ⬜ 13.00/24.50 **st.**

✗ **La Bavarde,** 9 New Kirk Rd, G61 2SS, ℡ 942 2202 – ⚫ AE ⓪
closed Sunday, Monday, last 3 weeks July and 1 week January – **M** a la carte 5.40/6.50 **t.**
▯ 1.90.

AUSTIN-MG Rannock Drive ℡ 5824   AUSTIN-MORRIS-MG, VANDEN PLAS Kirk Rd ℡ 2225

BEATTOCK Dumfries and Galloway 986 ⑮ – pop. 309 – ✉ Moffat – ✆ 068 33.
Edinburgh 58 – Carlisle 40 – Dumfries 19 – Glasgow 55.

🏨 **Auchen Castle** ⚐, DG10 9SH, N : 2 m. by A 74 ℡ 407, ≼, « 19C mansion in park », ⚲,
🚗 – 📺 ⚏wc �𝄞wc **P.** ⚫ AE ⓪ **VISA**
closed mid December-mid February – **M** 4.50/7.00 **st.** ▯ 2.15 – **30 rm** ⚏ 16.00/28.00 **st.**

✗✗ **Old Brig Inn** with rm, DG10 9PS, ℡ 401 – **P.** AE ⓪
M 4.00/6.50 **s.** – **8 rm** ⚏ 9.00/20.00 **st.**

BEAULY Highland 986 ⑦ – pop. 1,141 – ECD : Thursday – ✆ 046 371.
Envir. : Channory Point ≼* NE : 16 m.
Edinburgh 171 – Inverness 12 – Wick 111.

🏨 **Priory,** The Square, IV4 7BX, ℡ 2309 – ⚏wc ⚲ **P.** ⚫ AE ⓪ **VISA**
M 2.50/6.00 **st.** ▯ 1.60 – **12 rm** ⚏ 11.00/20.50 **st.** – P 17.50/19.00 **st.**

BELLOCHANTUY Strathclyde – see Kintyre (Peninsula).

BELLSHILL Strathclyde – pop. 18,166 – ECD : Wednesday – ✆ 0698.
🏌 ℡ 745124. – Edinburgh 34 – Glasgow 11.

🏨 **Hattonrigg** (S & N), Hattonrigg Rd, ML41RW, ℡ 748488 – ⚏wc ⚲ **P.** ⚑. ⚫ AE ⓪ **VISA**
closed 1 January – **M** *(closed Saturday lunch and Sunday)* 3.50/7.00 **st.** ▯ 1.70 – **8 rm**
⚏ 9.70/19.30 **st.**

AUSTIN-MORRIS-MG 5/27 North Rd ℡ 748516   OPEL-VAUXHALL 296 Main St. ℡ 747645

BETTYHILL Highland 986 ③ – pop. 177 – ✉ Thurso – ✆ 064 12.
See : Cliffs*. **Envir.:** Strathy Point*** NE : 12 m. – Torrisdale Bay** W : 2 m. – Mellvich Bay ≼*
(cliffs) E : 13 ½ m.
Edinburgh 299 – Inverness 140 – Thurso 32.

🏨 **Bettyhill,** KW14 7SP, ℡ 202, ≼, ⚲ – ⚏wc **P.**
March-mid October – **M** (bar lunch Monday to Saturday) 4.00/5.00 **t.** ▯ 1.40 – **21 rm**
⚏ 7.50/18.50 **t.**

BIRSAY Orkney (Orkney Islands) – see Orkney Islands (Mainland).

BLACKFORD Tayside – pop. 529 – ECD : Wednesday – ✉ Auchterarder – ✆ 076 482.
Edinburgh 51 – Glasgow 41 – Perth 18.

⚘ Blackford, Moray St., PH41QF, ℡ 246 – **P.** ⓪
M (bar lunch) 2.25/7.30 **t.** ▯ 1.40 – **6 rm.**

BLACKWATERFOOT Strathclyde – see Arran (Isle of).

BLYTH BRIDGE Borders – pop. 1,000 – ✉ West Linton – ✆ 072 15 Drochil Castle.
Edinburgh 22 – Glasgow 44 – Peebles 8.

✗ **Old Mill Inn,** EH46 7DG, ℡ 220, « Converted water mill », 🚗 – **P.** ⚫ AE **VISA**
M a la carte 7.00/10.20 ▯ 2.50.

BONAR BRIDGE Highland 986 ③ – pop. 519 – ECD : Wednesday – ✆ 086 32 Ardgay – 🏌.
See : Site*.
🅸 Information Centre ℡ 333 (June-September).
Edinburgh 220 – Inverness 61 – Wick 75.

🏨 **Caledonian,** IV24 3EB, ℡ 214, ≼ Kyle of Sutherland and Bonar Bridge, ⚲ – ⚏wc
�𝄞wc **P.** ⚫ AE ⓪ **VISA**
M 3.20/6.50 **st.** ▯ 2.80 – **24 rm** ⚏ 8.50/10.50 **s.**

🏨 **Bridge,** Dornoch Rd, IV24 3EB, ℡ 204, ≼ Bonar Bridge and Kyle of Sutherland – ⚏wc
�𝄞wc **P.** ⚫ AE ⓪ **VISA**
M (bar lunch) a la carte 3.00/8.60 **t.** ▯ 1.75 – **16 rm** ⚏ 10.00/22.00 **t.**

BOTHWELL Strathclyde 986 ⑮ – pop. 4,840 – ✆ 0698.
Edinburgh 38 – Glasgow 8.5.

🏨 Silvertrees, 27 Silverwells Crescent, G71 8DP, ℡ 852311, 🚗 – 📺 ⚏wc ⚲ **P.** ⚑
24 rm.

✗✗ **Da Luciano,** 2 Silverwells Crescent, G71 8SE, ℡ 852722, Italian rest. – **P.** ⚫ AE ⓪ **VISA**
closed Monday – **M** a la carte 5.15/10.10 ▯ 2.00.

BOWMORE Strathclyde 986 ⑭ – see Islay (Isle of).

BRAEMAR Grampian 986 ⑦ – pop. 394 – ECD: Thursday – ☎ 033 83.
Envir.: NW: Cairngorm Mountains ❋*** from the summit (alt. 4084 ft) by chairlift from Avie-
more, *AC*, 40 mn Rtn and 45 mn on foot Rtn – Devil's Elbow** S: 11 m. – Linn of Dee★
W: 6 m.
╔₁₈ ☏ 618, S: ½ m.
⚐ Kindrochit Castle ☏ 600 (May-October).
Edinburgh 92 – Aberdeen 58 – Dundee 52 – Perth 50.

  🏰 Mar Lodge ⚐, AB3 5XG, W: 4 m. ☏ 216, ⬉, « Former Royal Hunting Lodge », ⚲, 🐎,
    park – ⊟wc 🅿
    14 rm.

  🏰 **Invercauld Arms,** AB3 5YR, ☏ 605, Telex 73448, ⬉, ⚲, 🐎 – 🕃 ⊟wc ☎ 🅿. ⚙. ⛤
    AE ① VISA
    April-October – **M** 4.50/7.00 **t.** ⚱ 1.75 – **57 rm** ⊐ 10.00/30.00 **t.** – P 21.00/26.00 **t.**

  ↑ **Callater Lodge,** 9 Glenshee Rd, AB3 5YQ, ☏ 275 – 🅿
    closed mid October-26 December – **9 rm** ⊐ 7.35/14.70 **st.**

VW, AUDI-NSU ☏ 210

BRESSAY (Isle of) Shetland Islands 986 ⑯ – Shipping services: see Shetland Islands.

BRIDGEND Strathclyde – see Islay (Isle of).

BRIDGE OF ALLAN Stirling. (Central) 986 ⑪ – pop. 4,314 – ECD: Wednesday – ☎ 0786.
See: Wallace Monument ⬉*.
╔₉ Sunnylaw ☏ 2332.
Edinburgh 39 – Dundee 52 – Glasgow 30.

  🏰 **Royal** (Best Western), Henderson St., FK9 4MG, ☏ 832284, Telex 778982, 🐎 – 🕃
    ⊟wc ☎ 🅿. ⚙. ⛤ AE ① VISA
    M 3.75/6.50 **st.** ⚱ 1.75 – **32 rm** ⊐ 16.00/30.00 **st.** – P 22.00/24.00 **st.**

BRIDGE OF CALLY Tayside – ✉ Blairgowrie – ☎ 025 086.
Edinburgh 63 – Dundee 23 – Perth 21.

  🏠 **Bridge of Cally,** PH10 7JJ, ☏ 231, ⚲, 🐎 – ⊟wc 🅿. ⛤
    M *(closed Monday, Friday dinner, Sunday from November to December)* (bar lunch)
    7.00 **st.** ⚱ 1.75 – **9 rm** ⊐ 9.50/22.00 **st.**

BRIDGE OF ORCHY Strathclyde – pop. 100 – ☎ 083 84 Tyndrum.
Edinburgh 94 – Ballachullish 25 – Glasgow 63 – Oban 42.

  🏠 Bridge of Orchy, PA36 4AB, ☏ 208, ⬉ – ⊟wc 🅿
    12 rm.

BROADFORD Highland 986 ⑥ – see Skye (Isle of).

BRODICK Strathclyde 986 ⑭ – see Arran (Isle of).

BROUGHTON Borders – pop. 182 – ECD: Wednesday – ✉ Biggar (Lanark) – ☎ 089 94.
Edinburgh 30 – Moffat 24 – Peebles 12.

  ⚘ **Greenmantle,** ML12 6HQ, ☏ 302 – 🅿. ① VISA
    closed 1 January – **M** 3.50/5.00 **t.** ⚱ 1.00 – **6 rm** ⊐ 9.00/25.00 **t.** – P 25.00/35.00 **t.**

BUCKIE Grampian 986 ⑦ – pop. 7,919 – ECD: Wednesday – ☎ 0542.
╔₁₈ Buckpool ☏ 2236 – ╔₁₈ Strathlene ☏ 31798, E: ½ m.
Edinburgh 184 – Aberdeen 60 – Inverness 53.

  🏠 **Cluny,** High St., AB5 1AL, ☏ 32922 – 📺 ⊟wc. ⛤ ①
    M 2.50/5.50 **t.** – **7 rm** ⊐ 11.40/22.00 **t.**

BUCKSBURN Grampian – see Aberdeen.

BUNESSAN Strathclyde – see Mull (Isle of).

BUSBY Strathclyde – see Glasgow.

BUTE (Isle of) Strathclyde 986 ⑭ – pop. 1,834.
See: N: Kyles of Bute** – S: Sound of Bute*.
⛴ by Caledonian MacBrayne and Western Ferries: from Rothesay to Wemyss Bay frequent
services every day (30 mn) – from Rhubodach to Colintraive frequent services every day
(5 mn).

Rothesay – pop. 6,595 – ECD : Wednesday – ✉ ☉ 0700 Rothesay.
See : Site* – Castle* (13C) *AC*.
🏌 ✆ 94.
🛈 The Pier ✆ 2151.

🏨 **Glenburn,** Glenburn Rd. PA20 9JP, ✆ 2500, Telex 778982, ≼, ✗, ☞ – 🏃 ⌷wc ☎ 🅿.
⛲. 🖿 AE ⓪ *VISA*
M 3.75/6.50 st. 🍷 2.00 – **103 rm** ☲ 13.25/29.50 st. – P 18.50/22.00 st.

🏨 Royal (Osprey), Albert Pl. ✆ 3044 – **21 rm.**

🏨 **Craignethan,** 61 Mountstuart Rd, PA20 9AD, ✆ 2079, ☞ – 📺 ⌷wc 🚿wc 🅿. 🖿 *VISA*
M (dinner only) 3.70 t. 🍷 1.90 – **15 rm** ☲ 10.75/21.50 t.

🏨 **Ardmory House** ⚓, 17 Ardmory Rd, PA20 0PG, ✆ 2346, ≼, ☞ – 📺 ⌷wc 🅿. 🖿 AE
⓪ *VISA*
M (bar lunch) 4.00 🍷 1.75 – **10 rm** ☲ 6.50/13.00 – P 11.00.

TRIUMPH 1 East Princess St. ✆ 2317

CAIRNBAAN Strathclyde – pop. 135 – ✉ ☉ 0546 Lochgilphead.
Edinburgh 128 – Glasgow 85 – Oban 34.

🏨 **Cairnbaan Motor Inn,** PA31 8SH, on B 841 ✆ 2488, ≼ – ⌷wc 🅿. 🖿 AE ⓪ *VISA*
M (bar lunch) 4.00/7.00 t. – **24 rm** ☲ 10.00/25.00 t.

CAIRNGORM (Mountains) Inverness. (Highland) 🗺 ⑦.
See : ❋*** from the summit (alt. 4084 ft) by chairlift *AC*, 40 mn Rtn and 45 mn on foot Rtn.

> *Hotels and restaurant see : **Aviemore** NW*
> ***Braemar** SE.*

CAIRNRYAN Wigtown. (Dumfries and Galloway).
⛴ to Larne (Townsend Thoresen : Transport Ferry Service) 4 daily (2 to 2 h 30 mn).

> *Hotels and restaurant see : **Stranraer** S : 6 ½ m.*

CALLANDER Central 🗺 ⑪ – pop. 1,768 – ECD : Wednesday – ☉ 0877.
Envir. : The Trossachs** and Loch Katrine** W : 8 ½ m. – Loch Venacher* W : 4 m.
🏌 ✆ 30090.
🛈 Leny Rd ✆ 30342 (Easter-September).
Edinburgh 51 – Glasgow 43 – Oban 70 – Perth 40.

🏨 **Roman Camp** ⚓, Main St., FK17 8BG, ✆ 30003, « 17C hunting lodge in extensive gardens », ⚓, park – 📺 ⌷wc ☎ 🅿. AE
Easter-late October – M approx. 5.00 🍷 1.50 – **15 rm** ☲ 13.00/31.00.

🏠 **Highland House,** South Church St., ✆ 30269 – ⌷wc 🚿wc
February-October – **10 rm** ☲ 10.00/25.00.

PEUGEOT 124/126 Main St. ✆ 30022

CAMPBELTOWN Strathclyde 🗺 ⑭ – see Kintyre (Peninsula).

CAMPSIE GLEN Central – see Strathblane.

CANNA (Isle of) Highland 🗺 ⑥ – Shipping Services: see Mallaig.

CARNOUSTIE Tayside 🗺 ⑪ – pop. 6,232 – ECD : Tuesday – ☉ 0241.
🏌 ✆ 53249 (Starter's Box).
🛈 24 High St. ✆ 52258 (June-September).
Edinburgh 67 – Dundee 11.

🏨 **Bruce,** 1 Links Par., DD7 7DJ, ✆ 52364, ≼, ☞ – ⌷wc ☎ 🅿
M 4.00/5.75 t. 🍷 2.75 – **32 rm** ☲ 16.00/34.00 t. – P 24.00/28.00 t.

VAUXHALL 37 High St. ✆ 52156

CARRADALE Strathclyde – see Kintyre (Peninsula).

CARRICK Strathclyde – pop. 60 – ✉ ☉ 030 13 Lochgoilhead.
Edinburgh 97 – Glasgow 54 – Oban 65.

🏨 Carrick Castle ⚓, PA24 8AG, ✆ 251, ≼ Loch Goil – 📺 ⌷wc ☎ 🅿
21 rm.

CASTLEBAY Outer Hebrides (Western Isles) 🗺 ⑥ – see Barra (Isle of).

CASTLE DOUGLAS Dumfries and Galloway 🄖🄡🄖 ⑲ – pop. 3,331 – ECD : Thursday – ☎ 0556.
🄵 ☏ 2801.
🄘 Markethill ☏ 2611 (April-September).
Edinburgh 95 – Ayr 50 – Dumfries 18 – Stranraer 58.

   🏨 **Douglas Arms** (Best Western), King St., DG7 1DB, ☏ 2231, Telex 777170 – 🛏wc
     ☏ 🅿. 🅰 🄰🄴 ⓞ 𝘝𝘐𝘚𝘈
     M 6.00/9.00 t. 🅰 2.40 – 🖵 2.60 – **27 rm** 15.00/34.00 st.

   🏠 **King's Arms**, St. Andrews St., DG7 1EL, ☏ 2626 – 🛏wc 🅿. 🄰🄴 ⓞ
     M 2.70/6.00 st. 🅰 2.65 – **17 rm** 🖵 10.35/26.00 st.

AUSTIN-MORRIS-MG Morris House ☏ 2560   VAUXHALL King St. ☏ 2038
TALBOT 227/229 King St. ☏ 2476

CATACOL Strathclyde – see Arran (Isle of).

CLACHAN SEIL Strathclyde – ECD : Wednesday – ✉ Oban – ☎ 085 23 Balvicar.
Edinburgh 133 – Oban 11.

   🏠 **Willowburn** ⌂, PA34 4TJ, ☏ 276, ← Seil Sound, 🚤 – 🛏wc 🅿. 🅰 🄰🄴 ⓞ 𝘝𝘐𝘚𝘈
     closed November – **M** (bar lunch) 4.75/6.50 t. 🅰 1.30 – **11 rm** 🖵 11.00/24.80 t.

CLAONAIG (Cap) Strathclyde – Shipping Services : see Kintyre (Peninsula).

CLEISH Tayside – see Kinross.

CLOVA Tayside – ✉ Kirriemuir – ☎ 057 55.
See : Glen★★.
Edinburgh 86 – Dundee 31 – Perth 44.

   🏨 **Rottal Lodge** 🦌, Rottal, DD8 4QT, SE : 2 ½ m. on B 955 ☏ 224, ←, « Country house
     atmosphere », ✗, 🎣 – 🛏wc 🗮 🅿
     26 April-November – **M** (buffet lunch) 5.20/9.20 t. 🅰 1.40 – **12 rm** 🖵 12.00/24.00 –
     P 25.30/27.60 **t.**

   🏠 Ogilvy Arms ⌂, Glen Clova ☏ 222, ←, 🎣 – 🛏wc 🅿 – **7 rm.**

CLOVENFORDS Borders – see Galashiels.

CLYDEBANK Strathclyde 🄖🄡🄖 ⑮ – pop. 48,300 – ECD : Wednesday – ✉ ☎ 041 Glasgow.
🄵 Dalmuir Park ☏ 952 6372.
Edinburgh 48 – Glasgow 5.

   🏠 Radnor (Osprey), Kilbowie Rd., G81 2AP, ☏ 952 3427 – 🛗 🛏wc ☎ 🅿 – **12 rm.**

   🏠 Boulevard (Open House), 1710 Great Western Rd., G81 2XT, N : 1 ½ m. on A 82 ☏ 0389
     (Duntocher) 72381 – 🅿 – **13 rm.**

DATSUN Kilbowie Rd, Hardgate ☏ 0389 (Duntocher)   PEUGEOT Oceanfield, Great Western Rd ☏ 377 2285
75367

COATBRIDGE Strathclyde 🄖🄡🄖 ⑮ – pop. 52,145 – ECD : Wednesday – ☎ 0236.
🄵 Townhead Rd ☏ 28975. – Edinburgh 36 – Glasgow 9.5.

   🏨 Coatbridge (Open House), Glasgow Rd, ML5 1EL, ☏ 24392 – 📺 🛏wc ☎ 🅿. 🅰
     22 rm.

OPEL, VAUXHALL Main St. ☏ 27201   TALBOT 200 Main St. ☏ 22612

COLINTRAIVE Strathclyde 🄖🄡🄖 ⑭ – pop. 104 – ☎ 070 084.
See : Kyles of Bute★★.
🚢 to Rhubodach (Isle of Bute) (Caledonian MacBrayne and Western Ferries) frequent
services every day (5 mn)
Edinburgh 121 – Glasgow 78 – Oban 80.

   ♨ Faoilinn ⌂, ☏ 277, ←, 🚤 – 🛏wc 🅿 – **7 rm.**

COLL (Isle of) Strathclyde 🄖🄡🄖 ⑩ – pop. 1,019.
🚢 by Caledonian MacBrayne : to Oban via Tobermory (Isle of Mull) : Monday /Saturday
2-4 weekly (3 h 30 mn to 5 h 30 mn) – to Isle of Tiree : 24 weekly (1 h 30 mn).

COLONSAY (Isle of) Strathclyde 🄖🄡🄖 ⑩⑭ – pop. 349.
🚢 to Oban (Caledonian MacBrayne) 3 weekly (2 h 30 mn).

COMRIE Tayside – pop. 1,119 – ECD : Wednesday – ☎ 076 47 – 🄵.
Edinburgh 58 – Glasgow 49 – Oban 70 – Perth 23.

   🏠 **Royal**, Melville Sq., PH6 2DN, ☏ 200, 🎣, 🚤 – 🛏wc ☎ 🅿. 🅰
     M a la carte 5.00/9.15 t. 🅰 1.60 – **16 rm** 🖵 9.00/20.00 t.

   🏠 Comrie, Drummond St., PH6 2DY, ☏ 239 – 🛏wc 🗮wc 🅿
     Easter-late October – **M** 3.25/6.00 st. 🅰 1.30 – **12 rm** 🖵 8.25/31.00 **st.** – P 14.50/16.20 **st.**

CONNEL Strathclyde **986** ⑩ – pop. 300 – ECD : Wednesday – ☎ 063 171.
Envir. : Loch Creran* N : 7 m.
Edinburgh 117 – Glasgow 88 – Inverness 109 – Oban 5.

    Falls of Lora, PA37 1PB, on A 85 ☏ 483, ≤ Loch Etive and mountains – ⌂wc **P**
    April-October – **M** (bar lunch) 2.50/5.50 **t.** ▯ 1.90 – **33 rm** ⌤ 11.00/24.50 **t.**

    Ossian's ⌂, Bonawe Rd, North Connel, PA37 1RB, ☏ 322, ≤, 🚗 – ⌂wc **P**
    Mid April-mid October – **M** (bar lunch) approx. 4.50 ▯ 2.60 – **14 rm** ⌤ 9.75/
    21.00 **st.**

CONON BRIDGE Highland – pop. 914 – ECD : Thursday – ☎ 034 982.
Edinburgh 177 – Inverness 18 – Wick 105.

    Conon, Main St. IV7 8HD, ☏ 206 – **P** – **14 rm.**

CORRIE Strathclyde – see Arran (Isle of).

COVE Strathclyde – pop. 1,343 (inc. Kilcreggan) – ✉ Helensburgh – ☎ 043 684 Kilcreggan.
Edinburgh 83 – Glasgow 40 – Helensburgh 17.

    Knockderry House ⌂, G84 0NX, ☏ 2283, ≤, 🚗 – ⌂wc **P** – **14 rm.**

CRAIGHOUSE Strathclyde **986** ⑭ – see Jura (Isle of).

CRAIGNURE Strathclyde **986** ⑩ – see Mull (Isle of).

CRAIL Fife **986** ⑪ – pop. 1,075 – ECD : Wednesday – ☎ 033 35.
▯₈ Balcomie Clubhouse, ☏ 278.
Edinburgh 52 – Dundee 24 – Dunfermline 39.

    Marine, 54 Nethergate, KY10 3TU, ☏ 207, ≤, 🚗
    April-October, week-ends in winter, Christmas and 1 January – **M** (bar lunch) 2.00/
    6.00 ▯ 1.50 – **11 rm** ⌤ 6.50/13.00.

CRAMOND FORESHORE Lothian – see Edinburgh.

CRIEFF Tayside **986** ⑪ – pop. 5,603 – ECD : Wednesday – ☎ 0764.
Envir.: Drummond Castle Gardens** *AC*, S : 3 ½ m.
▯₈ Peat Rd, Muthill, S : 3 m. on A 822.
🛈 James Sq. ☏ 2578 (9 April-14 October).
Edinburgh 58 – Glasgow 48 – Oban 76 – Perth 17.

    Murraypark ⌂, Connaught Ter., PH7 3DJ, ☏ 3731, 🚗 – ⌂wc 🅿 **P**
    M 4.00/7.00 ▯ 2.00 – **15 rm** ⌤ 8.00/21.00 – P 17.00/20.00.

    Gwydyr, Comrie Rd, PH7 4BP, ☏ 3277, ≤, 🚗 – **P**. *VISA*
    closed 20 December-3 January – **M** *(closed Sunday)* (bar lunch) 3.50 **s.** ▯ 1.80 – **9 rm**
    ⌤ 6.00/11.00 **s.**

    Leven House, Comrie Rd, PH7 4BA, ☏ 2529
    13 rm ⌤ 6.00/12.00 **st.**

LADA Ferntower Rd ☏ 2494   VAUXHALL ☏ 2147
MORRIS-MG-ROVER-TRIUMPH Comrie Rd ☏ 2125

CRINAN Strathclyde – ✉ Lochgilphead – ☎ 054 683.
See : Site** – Crinan Canal*. **Envir. :** N : Loch Craignish (site**) – Tayvallich (harbour*) SW :
7 m. – Keills (site and ≤*) SW : 13 m.
Edinburgh 132 – Glasgow 89 – Oban 34.

        Hotel and restaurant see: **Cairnbaan** SE : 4 m.
                 Kilmartin NE : 6 ½ m.

CROCKETFORD Dumfries and Galloway – pop. 102 – ✉ Dumfries – ☎ 055 669.
Edinburgh 86 – Dumfries 9 – Stranraer 67.

    Galloway Arms, DG2 8RA, ☏ 240 – **P**
    closed mid October-mid November – **M** 3.75/6.00 **st.** ▯ 2.50 – **11 rm** ⌤ 8.50/19.00 **t.** –
    P 16.00/20.00 **t.**

CULLEN Grampian **986** ⑦ – pop. 1,207 – ECD : Wednesday – ☎ 0542.
See : Cullen Bay*, Cullen House* (16C) *AC*.
▯₈ The Links ☏ 40685.
🛈 20 Seafield St. ☏ 40757 (June-September).
Edinburgh 184 – Aberdeen 60 – Banff 14 – Inverness 60.

    Seafield Arms (Best Western), Seafield St., AB5 2SG, ☏ 40791, « Tastefully fur-
    nished » – **P**. ⛾ AE ⓪ *VISA*
    M 3.20/6.30 **st.** ▯ 2.90 – **25 rm** ⌤ 15.50/29.00 **st.**

CULLODEN MOOR Highland 👁👁👁 ⑦ – see Inverness.

CULTS Grampian – see Aberdeen.

CUMBERNAULD Strathclyde 👁👁👁 ⑮ – pop. 31,784 – ECD : Wednesday – ☎ 023 67.
Edinburgh 37 – Glasgow 13 – Stirling 12.

   🏨   Golden Eagle (Osprey), Town Centre, G67 1BX, ☏ 25631 – 🖁 📺 ⊝wc ⋔wc ☎ 🄿
      13 rm.
HONDA, VAUXHALL Carbrain Ring Rd, South Carbrain ☏ 25574

CUPAR Fife 👁👁👁 ⑪ – pop. 6,603 – ECD : Thursday – ☎ 0334.
🏌₁₈ Ladybank ☏ 320, S : 6 m. – 🏌₉ Hill Tarvitt ☏ 3549.
Edinburgh 45 – Dundee 14 – Perth 21.

   ✕   Timothy's, 43 Bonnygate, KY15 4BU, ☏ 2830, Smörrebrod.
AUSTIN-MORRIS-MG-ROVER-TRIUMPH Edenplace   MERCEDES-BENZ James Pl., Ceres Rd ☏ 3346
Garage ☏ 4228   VAUXHALL South Rd ☏ 2481
FORD Bonnygate ☏ 2048

DALIBURGH Outer Hebrides Western Isles – see Uist (South) Isles of.

DALRY Dumfries and Galloway – pop. 432 – ✉ Castle Douglas – ☎ 064 43.
Edinburgh 83 – Dumfries 27 – Glasgow 65 – Stranraer 48.

   🏠   **Lochinvar,** 3 Main St., DG7 3UP, on A 713 ☏ 210 – ⊝wc 🄿
      M (bar lunch) 4.50 **st.** ⋔ 1.10 – **18 rm** ⊑ 7.00/16.00 **st.**

DINGWAL Highland 👁👁👁 ⑦ – pop. 4,232 – ☎ 0349.
Edinburgh 181 – Inverness 21 – Wick 115.

   🏠   National, High St. ☏ 2166 – 🄿
      36 rm.

DIRLETON Lothian – pop. 392 – ☎ 062 085.
See : Castle★ (gardens★) *AC.*
Edinburgh 21 – North Berwick 3.

   🔔   **Castle Inn,** Manse Rd, EH39 5EP, ☏ 221, 🚗 – 🄿
      M (bar lunch) 5.50 **t.** ⋔ 1.20 – **9 rm** ⊑ 8.00/18.00 **t.**
   ✕✕ **Open Arms** (Best Western) with rm, EH39 5EG, ☏ 241, « Tastefully furnished », 🚗 –
      📺 ⊝wc ⋔wc ☎ 🄿. 🄰🄴 ⓪ *VISA*
      M 4.00/8.50 **t.** – **7 rm** ⊑ 22.00/33.00 **t.** – P 33.00 **t.**

DORNIE Highland – pop. 127 – ✉ Kyle of Lochalsh – ☎ 059 985.
Edinburgh 191 – Inverness 74 – Kyle of Lochalsh 8.

   🏠   **Loch Duich,** IV40 8DY, ☏ 213, ≼ Eilean Donan Castle and hills, ⚓, 🚗 – 🄿
      February-October – **M** 2.50/4.25 **t.** ⋔ 1.40 – **19 rm** ⊑ 8.00/16.00 **t.**

DORNOCH Highland 👁👁👁 ③ – pop. 838 – ECD : Thursday – ☎ 086 281.
Env. : Dunrobin Castle gardens★ *AC,* NE : 11 m.
🏌₁₈, 🏌₉ ☏ 219.
🛈 The Square, ☏ 400.
Edinburgh 220 – Inverness 61 – Wick 64.

   🏨   **Dornoch Castle,** Castle St., IV25 3SD, ☏ 216, « Former bishop's palace, part 16C »,
      🚗 – 🖁 ⊝wc 🄿
      May-late September – **M** 5.00/7.00 ⋔ 2.00 – **21 rm** ⊑ 9.00/19.50.
AUSTIN-MORRIS The Square ☏ 232

DOUNE Central 👁👁👁 ⑪ – pop. 3,977 – ECD : Wednesday – ☎ 078 684.
Edinburgh 45 – Glasgow 33 – Perth 32 – Stirling 8.

   🏠   **Woodside,** Callander Rd, on A 24 ☏ 237, 🚗 – ⊝wc 🄿. 🔲
      M a la carte 3.15/11.80 **t.** ⋔ 1.75 – **14 rm** ⊑ 12.00/25.00 **t.**

DRUMNADROCHIT Highland 👁👁👁 ⑦ – pop. 359 – ✉ Milton – ☎ 045 62.
Envir. : Loch Ness★★ E : 1 ½ m. – Urquhart Castle (site★) *AC,* E : 1 ½ m. – Glencannich★ and
Glen Affric★ W : 12 m. by Cannich.
Edinburgh 174 – Inverness 15 – Kyle of Lochalsh 67.

   🏨   **Polmaily House** ⚘, IV3 6XT, W : 2 m. on A 831 ☏ 343, ≼, ✖, ⚖, 🚗 – ⊝wc 🄿.
      🔲 🄰🄴 *VISA*
      May-October – **M** (bar lunch) 3.00/8.50 **st.** ⋔ 2.80 – **10 rm** ⊑ 14.00/16.90 **st.** – P 24.80/
      27.95 **st.**

DRYBURGH Borders 📒 ⑮ – pop. 50 – ⊠ ☎ 083 52 St. Boswells (Roxburgh).
See : Abbey* *AC.* **Envir.** : Scott's View* N : 2 m.
Edinburgh 38 – Hawick 22 – Newcastle-upon-Tyne 69.

  🏛 **Dryburgh Abbey** ⤴, TD6 0RQ, off B 6356 ☎ 2261, ⟨, ⟨, 🚗, park – 🛏wc 🛁wc
    P. 🏖. 🖼 AE ① *VISA*
    M 4.50/7.00 **st.** 🍷 2.10 – **29 rm** ⊇ 15.35/35.00 **st.** – P 23.35/27.75 **st.**

DRYMEN Central 📒 ⑪ ⑮ – pop. 659 – ECD : Wednesday – ☎ 036 06.
🏌 Buchanan Castle ☎ 369.
Edinburgh 60 – Glasgow 17 – Stirling 21.

  🏛 **Buchanan Arms,** Main St., G63 0BQ, ☎ 588, 🚗 – 🛏wc ☎ **P**. 🖼 AE ① *VISA*
    M 4.50/6.35 **t.** 🍷 2.35 – **24 rm** ⊇ 14.45/28.90 **st.**

VOLVO Croftamie ☎ 555

DUMBARTON Strathclyde 📒 ⑭ ⑮ – pop. 25,640 – ECD : Wednesday – ☎ 0389.
Envir. : Loch Lomond** NW : 5 m. – Edinburgh 57 – Glasgow 14.

  🏛 Dumbuck (Open House), Glasgow Rd, G82 1EG, E : ¾ m. on A 814 ☎ 62148 – 📺
    🛏wc ☎ **P** – **25 rm.**

MAZDA Cardross Rd ☎ 63676

DUMFRIES

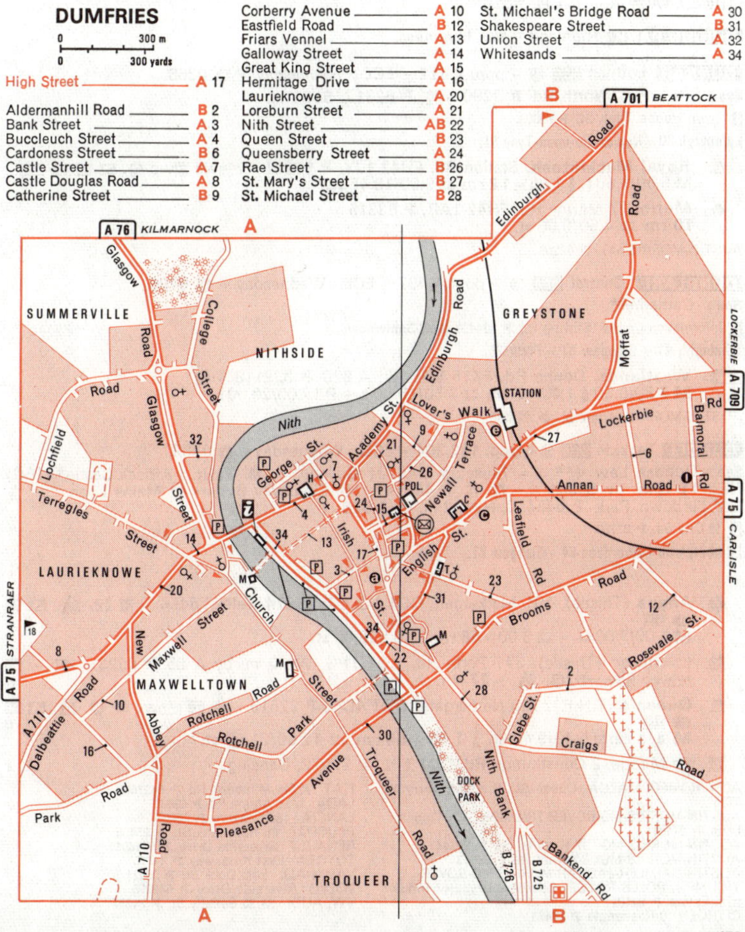

DUMFRIES Dumfries and Galloway **986** ⑲ – pop. 29,382 – ECD: Thursday – ☎ 0387.
Envir. : Caerlaverock Castle* (mediaeval) *AC*, SE: 7 ½ m. by B 725 **B** – New Abbey* *AC*, S: 6 m.
by A 75 **B** and A 710.

⌂₁₈ Laurieston Av. ☏ 3582 **A** – ⌂₉ Lochmaben ☏ 552, NE: 8 m. by A 709 **B**.

🛈 Whitesands ☏ 3862 (April-September).

Edinburgh 77 – Ayr 59 – Carlisle 35 – Glasgow 75 – Manchester 155 – Newcastle-upon-Tyne 88.

Plan on preceding page

🏨 **Cairndale** (Best Western), 136-138 English St., DG1 2DF, ☏ 4111, Telex 777170 – 📶
📺 🛏wc ☏ **P**. 🔊 AE ① *VISA*   **B** c
closed 1 January – **M** 4.50/5.50 t. 🍶 2.10 – ☲ 2.40 – **44 rm** 13.00/27.00 st.

🏨 **Station**, 49 Lovers Walk, DG1 1LT, ☏ 4316 – 📶 📺 🛏wc 🗍wc ☏ **P**. 🔊 AE ① *VISA*   **B** e
M 3.80/6.00 t. 🍶 2.25 – **30 rm** ☲ 14.00/21.00 t. – P 18.00/20.00 t.

🏨 **County**, 79 High St., DG1 2BN, ☏ 5401 – 📶 📺 🛏wc ☏ **P**. 🔊 AE ① *VISA*   **A** a
M 3.80/5.50 st. 🍶 1.80 – **45 rm** ☲ 13.00/25.00 st. – P 17.50/19.50 st.

✗ **Bruno's**, 3 Balmoral Rd, DG1 3BE, ☏ 5757, Italian rest.   **B** i
closed Tuesday – **M** (dinner only) a la carte 4.90/9.90 t. 🍶 2.20.

AUSTIN-DAIMLER-JAGUAR-MORRIS-MG-ROVER-
TRIUMPH Charlotte St. ☏ 4301
AUSTIN-MORRIS-MG ☏ 2862
BMW, MERCEDES-BENZ, VAUXHALL Glencaple
☏ 038 777 (Glencaple) 242
CITROEN, VAUXHALL York Pl. ☏ 5291

FIAT 77 Whitesands ☏ 61378
PEUGEOT St. Mary's Industrial Estate ☏ 2203
RENAULT 33/35 Glasgow St. ☏ 3430
TALBOT Terregles St. ☏ 61997
VW, AUDI-NSU English St. ☏ 5111

DUNAIN PARK Highland – see Inverness.

DUNBAR Lothian **986** ⑮ – pop. 4,611 – ECD: Wednesday – ☎ 0368.
See : Site*. – ⌂₁₈ North Rd ☏ 2280 – ⌂₁₈ ☏ 62317, S: ½ m.

🛈 Town House, High St. ☏ 63353.

Edinburgh 30 – Newcastle-upon-Tyne 91.

♨ **Royal Mackintosh**, Station Rd, EH42 1JY, ☏ 63231 – 🛏wc 🗍wc **P**. 🔊 AE ① *VISA*
M 5.50/7.50 t. 🍶 1.85 – **12 rm** ☲ 9.00/18.15 st.

♠ **Marine**, 7 Marine Rd, EH42 1AR, ☏ 63315
10 rm ☲ 4.50/9.00 st.

AUSTIN-MORRIS-MG ☏ 62255

DUNBLANE Central **986** ⑪ – pop. 4,497 – ECD: Wednesday – ☎ 0786.
See : Cathedral*.

🛈 Information Centre, Stirling Rd ☏ 824428 (May-September).

Edinburgh 41 – Glasgow 31 – Perth 28.

♨ **Westlands**, Doune Rd, FK15 9HT, on A 820 ☏ 822118 – **P**
M 2.80/6.50 🍶 1.40 – **7 rm** ☲ 7.50/15.00 s. – P 17.00/20.00 s.

AUSTIN-MORRIS High St. ☏ 823271

DUNDEE Tayside **986** ⑪ – pop. 182,204 – ECD: Wednesday – ☎ 0382.
See : Dundee Law ⇜** **Z** – Museum and Art Gallery* **Y** M. Envir. : Affleck Castle* (15C)
NE : 11 ½ m. by B 961 **Z** – ⌂₁₈, ⌂₉ ☏ 451147, off Kingsway Bypass at Mains Loan **Z** – ⌂₁₈
Camperdown Park ☏ 645450, NW: 2 m. by A 923 **Z**.

🛈 16 City Sq. ☏ 27723.

Edinburgh 56 – Aberdeen 64 – Glasgow 81.

Plan opposite

🏨 **Angus** (Thistle), 101 Marketgait, DD1 1QU, ☏ 26874, Telex 76456 – 📶 📺. 🛁. 🔊 AE
① *VISA*   **Y** c
M 5.00/7.00 st. – ☲ 3.00 – **58 rm** 18.00/28.00 st.

🏨 **Invercarse** (Thistle), 371 Perth Rd, DD1 1PG, W : 2 m. by A 85 ☏ 69231, 🚲 – 📺
🛏wc 🗍wc ☏ **P**. 🛁 – **27 rm**.   **Z** n

🏨 **Queen's** (T.H.F.), 160 Nethergate, DD1 4DU, ☏ 22515 – 📶 📺 🛏wc ☏ **P**. 🛁. 🔊 AE
① *VISA*   **Y** e
M a la carte 5.40/9.40 st. 🍶 1.65 – **55 rm** ☲ 12.50/21.50 st.

✗✗ **Le Mirage**, 2 Constitution Rd, DD1 1PL, ☏ 27072, Dancing.   **Y** r

ALFA-ROMEO, MAZDA Queen St., Broughty Ferry ☏
77257
AUSTIN-MORRIS-MG-ROVER-TRIUMPH 41 Trades
Lane ☏ 27181
AUSTIN-MORRIS-MG 37 Hospital St. ☏ 88344
AUSTIN-MORRIS-MG 64 Ward Rd ☏ 24013
AUSTIN-DAIMLER-JAGUAR-MORRIS-MG-ROVER-
TRIUMPH, ROLLS ROYCE Baird Av., Dryburgh Indus-
trial Estate ☏ 84101
CITROEN 3 Roseangle ☏ 28483

FIAT 42/44 Milnbank Rd ☏ 642166
LADA Mac Alpine Rd ☏ 88561
LANCIA 166 Seagate ☏ 25007
PEUGEOT 25 Rosebank St. ☏ 25406
RENAULT Riverside Drive ☏ 644401
TOYOTA East Kingsway ☏ 41715
VAUXHALL East Dock St. ☏ 26521
VOLVO Riverside Drive ☏ 643295
VW, AUDI 33/35 Gellatly St. ☏ 24251

474

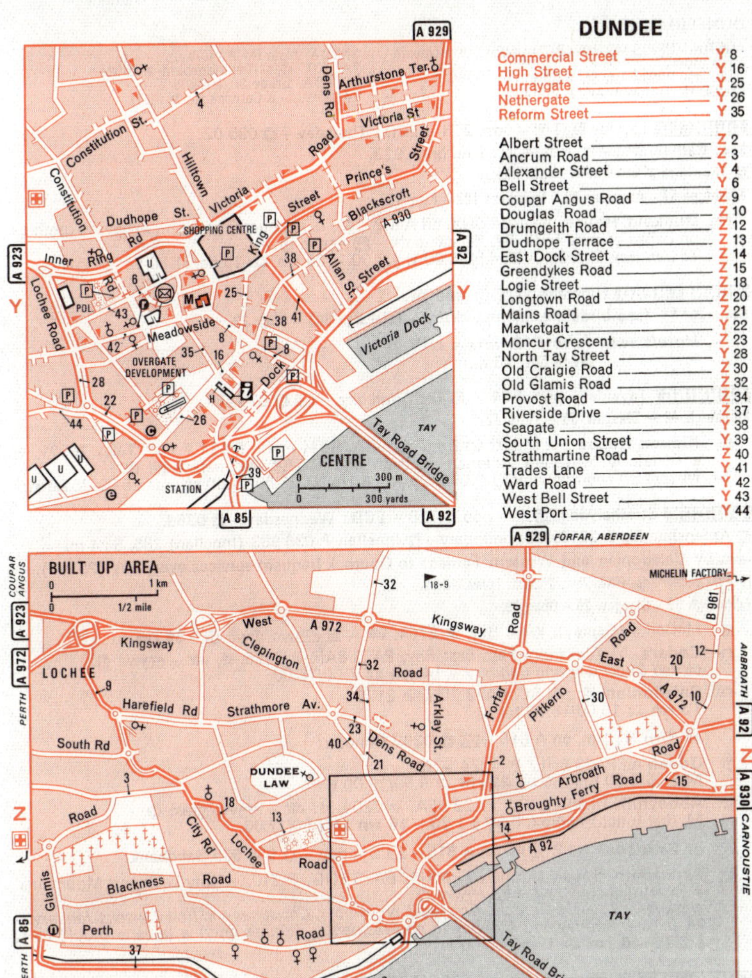

Envir. : Little Loch Broom★ NW : 7 m.

Edinburgh 218 – Inverness 59.

Dundonnell, IV23 2QS, ☎ 204, ≼ Dundonnell Valley – ⊡wc ℗. 🆎 ⑩
M (bar lunch) approx. 6.00 **t.** 🍷 1.80 – **25 rm** ⊡ 10.00/22.00 **t.**

DUNFERMLINE Fife 🔢 ⑪⑮ – pop. 49,897 – ECD : Wednesday – ✆ 0383.

See : Abbey★ *AC.*

🏌 Venturefair ☎ 24969 N : 1 m. – 🏌 Pitreavie, Queensferry Rd ☎ 22591.

🛈 Glen Bridge Car Park ☎ 20999 (Easter-September).

Edinburgh 16 – Dundee 43 – Motherwell 37.

King Malcolm (Thistle), Wester Pitcorthie, KY11 5DS, S : 1 m. off A 823 ☎ 22611 –
📺 ⊡wc ☎ ℗. 🅰 ▦ 🆎 ⑩ *VISA*
M 4.50/6.50 **t.** 🍷 1.80 – ⊡ 3.25 – **48 rm** 21.00/29.00 **t.** – P 28.45/35.25 **t.**

AUSTIN-MORRIS-MG-ROVER-TRIUMPH 18 Halbeath Rd ℡ 31041
OPEL 128 Pittencrieff St. ℡ 22565
PEUGEOT Headwell Av. ℡ 21914

SKODA Main Rd ℡ 24078
TALBOT 45/47 Baldridgeburn ℡ 31821
TOYOTA Bruce St. ℡ 23675
VAUXHALL 3 Carnock Rd ℡ 21511

DUNKELD Tayside 986 ⑪ – pop. 273 – ECD : Thursday – ☎ 035 02.
See : Cathedral*. – ⌐₉ ℡ 524, N : 1 m. on A 923.
🛈 The Cross ℡ 460 (Easter-September).
Edinburgh 57 – Aberdeen 85 – Inverness 102 – Perth 15.

- 🏨 **Dunkeld House** ⑤, PH8 0HX, off A 9 ℡ 243, ≼, « Country house in extensive grounds on banks of river Tay », ※, ⊸, ☞, park – 📺 ⇔wc ℗
  15 January-October – **M** 4.50/8.00 **t.** ⌀ 2.00 – **26 rm** ⊇ 15.65/31.30 **t.**

DUNNET HEAD Highland 986 ③ and ⑳.
See : ❋*** (sea birds' nests) and cliffs. – Edinburgh 303 – Wick 23.

> *Hotels see :* **John O'Groats** E : 16 m.
> **Wick** SE : 23 m.

DUNNING Tayside – pop. 564 – ECD : Thursday – ✉ ☎ 076 484.
Edinburgh 48 – Glasgow 50 – Perth 12.

- 🏤 **Kippen House** ⑤, Muckhart Rd, PH2 0RA, S : ¾ m. on B 934 ℡ 447, Telex 76571, ≼, « Tastefully converted Victorian mansion house », ※, ☞, park – 📺 ℗
  M *(closed Monday lunch)* 5.00/8.00 **t.** – **8 rm** ⊇ 23.50/37.50 **st.** – P 25.00/30.00 **st.**

DUNOON Strathclyde 986 ⑭ – pop. 9,718 – ECD : Wednesday – ☎ 0369.
⌐₁₈ Ardenslate Rd ℡ 2216, NE : boundary – ⌐₉ Innellan ℡ 036 983 (Innellan) 286, S : 4 m.
⛴ by Caledonian and Western Ferries : to Gourock frequent services every day (20 mn).
🛈 Pier Esplanade, PA23 7HL, ℡ 3785, Telex 778867.
Edinburgh 69 – Glasgow 26 – Oban 79.

- 🏨 McColl's (Osprey), West Bay, ℡ 2764, ☞ – ⫴ ⇔wc 🮲wc ℗ – **59 rm.**
- ⌂ **Cedars,** 51 Alexandra Par., East Bay, PA23 8AF, ℡ 2425, ≼, ☞ – ⇔wc 🮲
  closed December and January – **14 rm** ⊇ 7.00/15.00.
- ⌂ **Caledonian,** Argyll St., PA23 7DJ, ℡ 2176
  13 rm ⊇ 10.00/18.00 **t.**

  at Kirn N : 1 m. on A 815 – ✉ ☎ 0369 Dunoon :

- 🏨 **Queen's,** PA23 8HE, ℡ 4224 – ℗
  M 2.25/5.00 **t.** ⌀ 1.50 – **22 rm** ⊇ 9.50/19.00 **t.**
- ⚘ **Abbeyhill,** Dhailling Rd, PA23 8EA, ℡ 2204, ≼, ☞ – ⇔wc 🮲wc ℗
  M *(bar lunch)* approx. 5.50 ⌀ 1.20 – **16 rm** ⊇ 7.50/17.00.

  at Sandbank N : 2 ½ m. on A 815 – ✉ Dunoon – ☎ 036 985 Sandbank :

- 🏤 **Ardnadam House** (formely Firpark), PA23 8QG, ℡ 210, ≼ Holy Loch and Mountains.
  « Tasteful decor », ☞ – 📺 ⇔wc ℗
  closed last 2 weeks October, first week November, Christmas and first 2 weeks January –
  M *(closed Sunday and Monday to non-residents)* (dinner only) a la carte 6.00/9.25 **t.**
  ⌀ 1.75 – **6 rm** ⊇ 12.50/30.00 **st.**

DUNTOCHER Strathclyde – pop. 3,532 – ECD : Wednesday – ✉ Clydebank – ☎ 0389.
Edinburgh 51 – Glasgow 8 – Dumbarton 6.

- 🏨 **Maltings,** Dumbarton Rd, G81 6DP, ℡ 75371 – ⇔wc ☎ ℗. 🅂 🅰🅴 ⓞ 𝘝𝘐𝘚𝘈
  M 4.00/5.00 **st.** ⌀ 2.80 – **27 rm** ⊇ 11.00/18.00 **st.**

DUNVEGAN Highland 986 ⑥ – see Skye (Isle of).

DUROR Strathclyde – pop. 102 – ✉ Appin – ☎ 063 174.
Edinburgh 125 – Fort William 36 – Oban 28.

- 🏨 **Stewart** ⑤, Glen Duror, PA38 4BW, ℡ 268, Telex 727582, ≼ gardens and Cuil Bay,
  ☞, park – ⇔wc ℗. 🅂 🅰🅴 𝘝𝘐𝘚𝘈
  M *(bar lunch)* approx. 6.50 **t.** ⌀ 1.80 – **29 rm** ⊇ 15.50/25.00 **t.** – P 18.00/21.00 **t.**

DYCE Grampian 986 ⑦ – see Aberdeen.

EAGLESHAM Strathclyde – pop. 2,788 – ☎ 035 53.
Edinburgh 47 – Ayr 26 – Glasgow 9.

- 🏨 **Eglington Arms** (Open House), Gilmour St., G76 0LG, ℡ 2631 – 📺 ⇔wc ☎ ℗. 🅂
  🅰🅴 ⓞ 𝘝𝘐𝘚𝘈
  M a la carte 4.00/10.50 **t.** ⌀ 1.50 – **12 rm** ⊇ 18.00/25.00 **st.**

EASDALE Strathclyde – pop. 125 – ECD: Wednesday – ⊠ Oban – ☎ 085 23 Balvicar.
Edinburgh 137 – Oban 15.

- **Dunmor House** ⑤, PA34 4RF, E: ½ m. ☎ 203, ← Firth of Lorn and Islands, 🚗, park –
  ☒wc 🛁wc 🚗 Ⓟ
  May-16 October – **M** (bar lunch) approx. 8.20 **t.** ⌁ 2.50 – **11 rm** ☲ 14.00/31.00 **t.**

EAST KILBRIDE Strathclyde 986 ⑮ – pop. 63,502 – ECD: Wednesday – ☎ 035 52.
🏌 Strathaven Rd ☎ 48638.
Edinburgh 44 – Ayr 34 – Glasgow 8.

- **Bruce** (Thistle), Cornwall St., G74 1AF, ☎ 29771, Telex 778428 – 🛗 📺 Ⓟ
  65 rm.
- **Stuart** (Thistle), 2 Cornwall St., G74 1JS, ☎ 21161 – 🛗 📺 ☒wc 🛁wc 🚗 ♿
  30 rm.
- **Torrance** (Open House), 135 Main St., G74 4LN, ☎ 25241 – ☒wc 🚗 Ⓟ
  26 rm.

AUSTIN-MORRIS-MG Telford Rd ☎ 23455

EAST LINTON Lothian 986 ⑮ – pop. 880 – ECD: Wednesday – ☎ 062 086.
Edinburgh 24 – Newcastle-upon-Tyne 96.

- XX **Harvesters** (Best Western) with rm, Station Rd, EH40 3DP, ☎ 395, Telex 8814912, 🚗 –
  ☒wc Ⓟ. 🅰 AE ⓪ VISA
  closed December and January – **M** 5.50/8.50 **st.** ⌁ 2.20 – **13 rm** ☲ 19.25/36.50 **st.** –
  P 32.25 **st.**

EDAY (Isle of) Orkney Islands 986 ⑯ – Shipping Services: see Orkney Islands (Mainland: Kirkwall).

EDDLESTON Borders – see Peebles.

EDINBURGH Lothian 986 ⑮ – pop. 453,584 – ☎ 031.
See: Castle* (site*, ←**, Regalia*, Scottish United Services Museum*, Scottish National War Memorial) *AC* **DZ** – National Museum of Antiquities** **EY** M¹ – National Gallery** **DY** M² – St. Giles' Cathedral* **EYZ** B – Charlotte Square* **CY** – National Portrait Gallery* *AC* **EY** M¹ – Royal Scottish Museum* **EZ** M³ – Old houses and closes near Lawnmarket, Grassmarket* – Abbey of Holyrood* *AC* **BV** A – Royal Botanic Gardens* **ABV** – Princes Street ←** **DY** – Palace of Holyrood (State apartments*, historic apartments**) *AC* **BV** A – Calton Hill ←* **EY** – Arthur's Seat ←* **BV** – Drama and Music Festival in summer.
Envir.: Roslyn Chapel** (15C) *AC*, S: 6 ½ m. by A 701 **BX** – Leith ←* of the firth of Forth, NE: 2 ½ m. **BV** – Craigmillar Castle* (stronghold) 14C, *AC*, SE: 3 m. **BX** D – Crichton Castle* (16C) *AC*, SE: 13 m. by A7 **BX**.
🏌 Kingston Grange ☎ 664 8580, SE: 3 ½ m. **BX** – 🏌 Silverknowes Parkway ☎ 336 5359, W: 4 m. **AV** – 🏌 Observatory Rd ☎ 667 2837 **BX** – 🏌 Glendevon Park ☎ 337 1096, W: 5 m.
✈ ☎ 333 1000, Telex 727615, W: 6 m. by A 8 **AV** – **Terminal**: Waverley Bridge.
🚗 ☎ 556 5633.
🛈 Scottish Tourist Board, 5 Waverley Bridge, ☎ 332 2433, Telex 72272 – Tourist Information, 5 Waverley Bridge, EH1 1BQ, ☎ 226 6591, Telex 727143.

Glasgow 43 – Newcastle-upon-Tyne 108.

Plans on following pages

- **Caledonian** (B.T.H.), Princes St., EH1 2AB, ☎ 225 2433, Telex 72179 – 🛗 📺 Ⓟ. ♨.
  🅰 AE ⓪ VISA
  M a la carte 8.70/15.80 **st.** ⌁ 2.40 – **212 rm** ☲ 33.55/62.30 **st.**   **CY** n
- **North British** (B.T.H.), Princes St., EH2 2EQ, ☎ 556 2414, Telex 72332 – 🛗 📺. ♨. 🅰
  AE ⓪ VISA
  M a la carte 4.15/10.25 **st.** ⌁ 2.40 – **193 rm** ☲ 22.15/50.60 **st.**   **EY** o
- **George** (County), 19-25 George St., EH2 2PB, ☎ 225 1251, Telex 72570 – 🛗 📺 Ⓟ. ♨.
  🅰 AE ⓪ VISA
  M 5.50/7.70 **st.** ⌁ 1.55 – **194 rm** ☲ 27.00/35.50 **s.**   **DY** z
- **Roxburghe**, 38 Charlotte Sq., EH2 4HG, ☎ 225 3921 – 🛗 📺. ♨. 🅰 AE ⓪ VISA   **DY** o
  M 5.00/6.50 **st.** ⌁ 2.00 – ☲ 1.50 – **78 rm** 20.00/38.00 **st.**
- **Royal Scot** (Swallow), 111 Glasgow Rd, EH12 8NF, W: 4 ½ m. on A 8 ☎ 334 9191,
  Telex 727197 – 🛗 📺 ♿ Ⓟ. ♨   by A 8 **AV**
  258 rm.
- **Post House** (T.H.F.), Corstorphine Rd, EH12 6UA, W: 3 m. on A 8 ☎ 334 8221, Telex
  727103 – 🛗 📺 ☒wc 🚗 ♿ Ⓟ. ♨. 🅰 AE ⓪ VISA   **AV** u
  M 6.50/8.50 **st.** ⌁ 2.00 – ☲ 2.25 – **208 rm** 19.00/28.00 **st.**
- **King James** (Thistle), 107 St. James Centre, Leith St., EH1 3SW, ☎ 556 0111, Telex
  727200 – 🛗 📺 ☒wc 🛁wc 🚗 Ⓟ. ♨. 🅰 AE ⓪ VISA   **EY** u
  M 4.50/6.00 **st.** ⌁ 2.50 – ☲ 3.00 – **160 rm** 23.00/33.50 **st.**

EDINBURGH
0   1 km
0   1 mile
FORTH-ROAD-BRIDGE
A 90
A 902
(A 8)
GLASGOW (M 8)   A 8   (M 9) STIRLING
KILMARNOCK   A 71
LANARK
A 70
CRAMOND
Marine
Drive
West Shore Rd
West Harbour Rd
West
Granton
Rd
Granton
Road
49
Silverknowes
Road
18
Cramond Road South
Main   St.
68
B 9085
Ferry
Road
Hillhouse
Ferry
Road
Telford
A 902
Crewe Road South
Ferry
Road
ROYAL BOTANIC
GARDENS
Queensferry
Road
A 90
Drum Brae North
A 720
Drum Brae South
Clermiston
Road
Craigcrook
Road
BLACKHALL
Road
Craigleith Road
A 90
Queensferry
Road
Road
Ravelston Dykes Rd
Ravelston
Dykes
Ravelston
MURRAYFIELD
54
Road
ZOOLOGICAL
PARK
Corstorphine
Road
A 8
Balgreen
MURRAYFIELD
Glasgow   Road
St.   John's   Rd
Meadow   Pt.   Rd.
Broomhouse Rd
SIGHTHILL
Road
Calder
Longstone   Rd
41
Gorgie
Road
Stateford
Road
Road
Union Canal
Colinton
Road
51
Calder
Road
Wester
Calder
A 71
Water-
of-
Leith
Road
Colinton
Road
Colinton Mains   Dri.
Redford
Road
A 720
Oxgangs
Road
Comiston Rd
5
Comiston
Rd
Hailes
A 720
Road
Gillespie   Rd
Colinton
JUNIPER   Lanark   GREEN

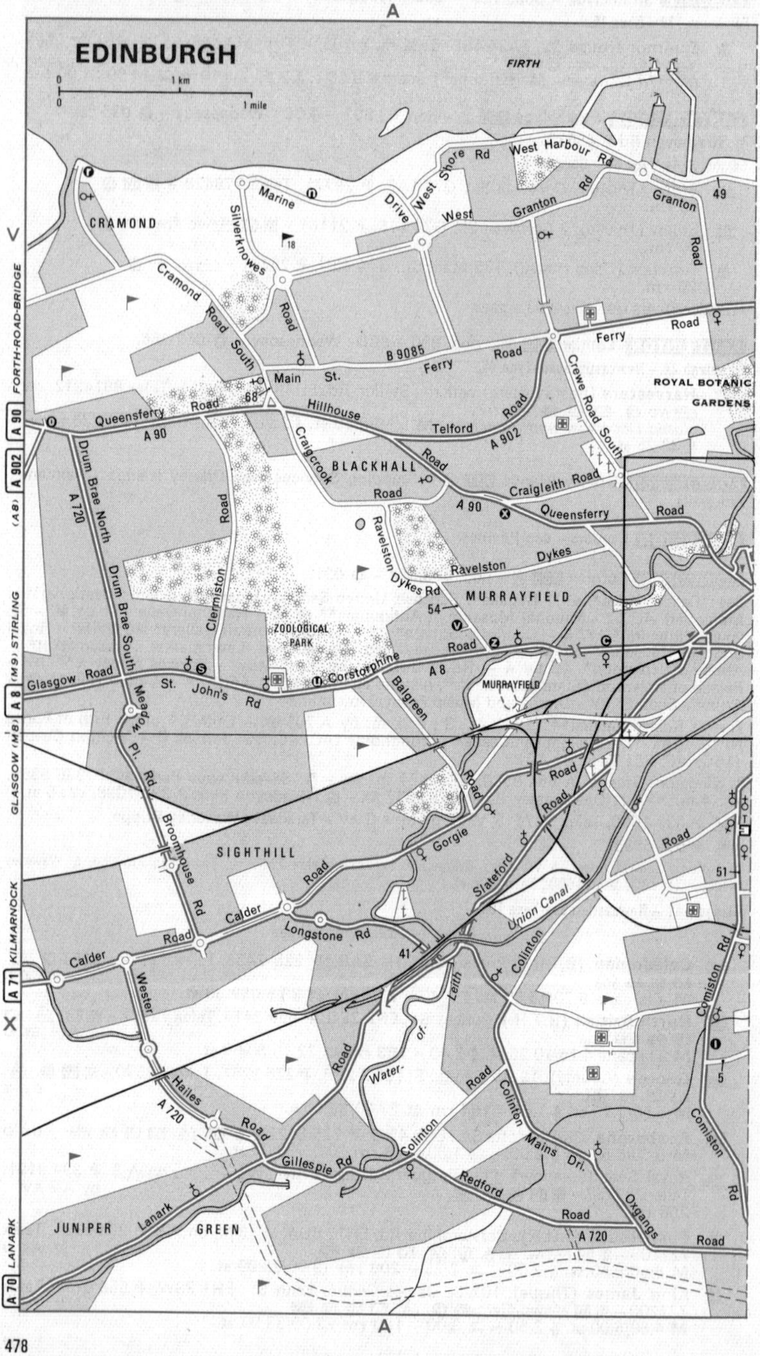

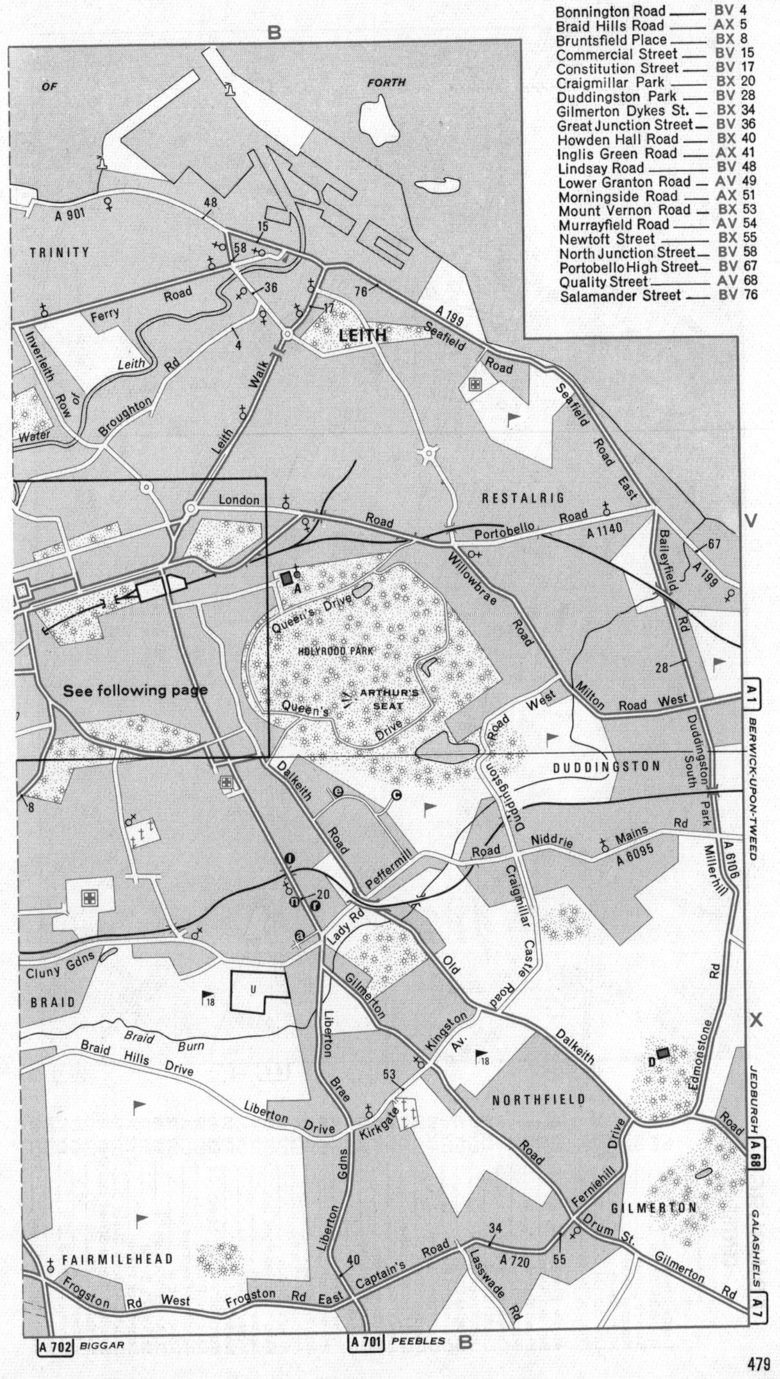

Bonnington Road —— BV 4
Braid Hills Road —— AX 5
Bruntsfield Place —— BX 8
Commercial Street —— BV 15
Constitution Street —— BV 17
Craigmillar Park —— BX 20
Duddingston Park —— BV 28
Gilmerton Dykes St. — BX 34
Great Junction Street — BV 36
Howden Hall Road —— BX 40
Inglis Green Road —— AX 41
Lindsay Road —— BV 48
Lower Granton Road — AV 49
Morningside Road —— AX 51
Mount Vernon Road — BX 53
Murrayfield Road —— AV 54
Newtoft Street —— BX 55
North Junction Street — BV 58
Portobello High Street— BV 67
Quality Street —— AV 68
Salamander Street —— BV 76
B
OF
FORTH
A 901
TRINITY
48
15
58
36
76
Ferry
Road
17
LEITH
A 199
Leith
Rd
Inverleith
Row
4
Seafield
Road
Broughton
Leith
Walk
Seafield
Road
East
Water
London
Road
RESTALRIG
V
Portobello
Road
A 1140
Baileyfield
67
A 199
Rd
A
Queen's
Drive
Willowbrae
Road
28
HOLYROOD PARK
A 1
See following page
ARTHUR'S
SEAT
Milton
BERWICK-UPON-TWEED
Queen's
West
Road
West
Drive
Road
DUDDINGSTON
Duddingston
Park
South
Dalkeith
A 6106
8
Road
Duddingston
Millerhill
Peffermill
Road
Niddrie
Mains
Rd
A 6095
20
Lady Rd
Craigmillar
Castle
Road
Cluny Gdns
Old
D
BRAID
U
Gilmerton
Kingston
Dalkeith
X
18
Liberton
Av.
JEDBURGH
Braid
Burn
Brae
18
Edmonstone
Rd
Braid
Hills
Drive
53
NORTHFIELD
A 68
Liberton
Drive
Kirkgate
Road
GALASHIELS
Liberton
Gdns
Ferniehill
GILMERTON
FAIRMILEHEAD
34
Drum St.
Drive
A 720
55
Gilmerton
A 7
Frogston
Rd
West
Frogston
Rd
East
Captain's
Road
Lasswade
Rd
Rd
A 702
BIGGAR
A 701
PEEBLES
B

EDINBURGH CENTRE

Edinburgh Eurocrest (Crest), Queensferry Rd, EH4 3HL, NW : 2 m. on A 90 ℡ 332 2442, Telex 72541 – ▮ TV ⌷wc ⋔wc ☎ P. ⋛. ⊠ ⁄Æ ① VISA   **AV x**
⊐ 2.80 – **120 rm** 20.60/34.40 **st.**

Carlton, 1 North Bridge, EH1 1SD, ℡ 556 7277 – ▮ TV ⌷wc. ⋛. ⊠ ⁄Æ ① VISA   **EY e**
M approx. 5.50 **st.** – ⊐ 1.85 – **92 rm** 18.70/31.80 **st.**

Barnton (Thistle), 562 Queensferry Rd, EH4 6AS, NW : 4¾ m. on A 90 ℡ 339 1144 –
▮ TV ⌷wc ⋔wc P. ⋛. ⊠ ⁄Æ ① VISA   **AV o**
M 5.00/15.00 **t.** ⚱ 1.75 – ⊐ 3.00 – **48 rm** 20.00/30.00 **st.** – P 28.00/33.50 **st.**

Ellersly House, Ellersly Rd, EH12 6HZ, W : 2½ m. by A 8 ℡ 337 6888, ⇝ – ▮
⌷wc ☎ P. ⊠ ⁄Æ ① VISA ⊐ 19.00/36.00 **st.**   **AV v**
M 5.50 **t.** ⚱ 2.30 – **58 rm** ⊐ 19.00/36.00 **st.**

Howard (Best Western), 34 Gt. King St., EH3 6QH, ℡ 556 1393 – ▮ TV ⌷wc ⋔wc
☎ P. ⊠ ⁄Æ ① VISA   **DY s**
M 4.50/8.50 **st.** ⚱ 2.50 – **26 rm** ⊐ 20.00/36.50 **st.**

Braid Hills, 134 Braid Rd, EH10 6JD, S : 3 m. by A 702 ℡ 447 8888, ⇝ – ⌷wc
☎ P – **51 rm.**   **AX i**

Mount Royal, 53 Princes St., EH2 2DG, ℡ 225 7161 – ▮ ⌷wc ☎   **DY c**
153 rm.

St. Andrew, 8-10 South St., Andrew St., EH2 2AS, ℡ 556 8774 – ▮ ⌷wc ☎   **EY s**
40 rm.

Harp (Osprey), 114-116 St. John's Rd, EH12 8AX, W : 3¾ m. on A 8 ℡ 334 6241 –
⋔wc ☎ P   **AV s**
23 rm.

Murrayfield (Swallow), 18 Corstorphine Rd, EH12 6HN, W : 2½ m. on A 8 ℡ 337 2207 –
TV ⌷wc ☎ P   **AV z**
34 rm.

Old Waverley, 43 Princes St., EH2 2BY, ℡ 556 4648 – ▮ ⌷wc ⋔wc. ⊠ ⁄Æ ①
VISA   **EY r**
M (bar lunch) 6.25 **st.** ⚱ 1.25 – **72 rm** ⊐ 13.30/26.50 **st.**

County, 8 Abercromby Pl., EH3 6LF, ℡ 556 2333, Telex 727127 – ▮ TV ⌷wc ☎ P. ⊠
⁄Æ ① VISA   **EY c**
M 3.50/4.50 **t.** ⚱ 1.90 – **55 rm** ⊐ 19.20/35.00 **t.** – P 25.20/27.20 **t.**

Albany without rest., 39 Albany St., EH1 3QY, ℡ 556 0397 – ⌷wc ⁄Æ VISA   **EY v**
10 rm ⊐ 13.50/20.70 **st.**

Glenisla, 12 Lygon Rd, EH16 5QB, ℡ 667 4098   **BX a**
closed 2 weeks Christmas and 1 January – **9 rm** ⊐ 8.50/15.00 **st.**

Kildonan Lodge, 27 Craigmillar Park, EH16 5PE, ℡ 667 2793 – P   **BX r**
12 rm.

Dorstan Private, 7 Priestfield Rd, EH16 5HJ, ℡ 667 6721 – ⌷wc ⋔ P   **BX e**
closed 14 to 28 October, Christmas and 1 January – **14 rm** ⊐ 6.50/13.50 **s.**

Malcolm, 2 West Coates, EH12 5JQ, W : 2 m. on A 8 ℡ 337 2173 – ⋔wc P   **AV c**
10 rm ⊐ 9.20/17.25 **t.**

Southdown, 20 Craigmillar Park, EH16 5PS, ℡ 667 2410 – P   **BX n**
8 rm.

Prestonfield House ⟨with rm⟩, Priestfield Rd, EH16 5UT, SE : 2½ m. off A 68
℡ 667 8055, Telex 727396, ‹, « *Elegant 17C mansion* », ⇝, park – ⌷wc ⋔ ☎ P. ⊠   **BX c**
⁄Æ ① VISA
M a la carte 9.60/13.80 **t.** ⚱ 2.05 – **5 rm** ⊐ 24.00/32.00 **t.**

Howtowdie, 27a Stafford St., EH3 7BD, ℡ 225 6291 – ⊠ ⁄Æ ① VISA   **CY u**
closed Sunday, 25-26 December and 1-2 January – **M** a la carte 8.25/13.65 **t.** ⚱ 2.15.

Donmaree, with rm, 21 Mayfield Gardens, EH9 2BX, ℡ 667 3641 – ⌷wc ☎ P   **BX i**
20 rm.

Cosmo, 58a North Castle St., EH2 3LU, ℡ 226 6743, Italian rest. – ⊠ VISA   **DY r**
closed Saturday lunch, Sunday, Monday, 1 to 15 July, Christmas and 1 January – **M** a la
carte 7.75/10.65 **t.** ⚱ 2.00.

Ristorante Milano, 7 Victoria St., EHI 2HE, ℡ 226 5260, Italian rest. – ⁄Æ ① VISA   **EZ a**
closed Sunday, Christmas Day and 1-2 January – **M** a la carte 5.65/9.70 **t.** ⚱ 1.80.

Bernard's, 20 Abercromby Pl., EH3 6LB, ℡ 556 2270 – ⊠ ⁄Æ VISA   **DY e**
closed Sunday – **M** a la carte 5.00/10.70 **t.** ⚱ 2.00.

Handsel, 22 Stafford St., EH3 7BH, ℡ 225 5521   **CY e**
closed Sunday and Bank Holidays – **M** a la carte 6.35/9.75 **t.** ⚱ 1.80.

Denzler's, 80 Queen St, EH2 4NF, ℡ 226 5467   **CDY a**
closed Sunday, 24 December-6 January and Bank Holidays – **M** a la carte 4.45/7.20 **t.**
⚱ 2.00.

Lorenzo, 109 Fountainbridge, EH3 9YJ, ℡ 229 2747, Italian rest.   **CZ r**

Cousteau's, 109 Hanover St., EH12 1DR, ℡ 226 3355, Seafood – P. ⊠ ⁄Æ ① VISA
closed Sunday, Monday and 1 to 7 January – **M** a la carte 5.45/7.70 **t.** ⚱ 1.70.   **DY x**

P.T.O. ⟶

XX **Shamiana,** 14 Brougham St., Tollcross, EH3 9JH, ℡ 229 5578, Indian rest. – ⬛ AE ⓪ VISA
　　DZ a
　　closed Sunday, Christmas and 1 January – **M** (dinner only) a la carte 5.85/8.60 **t.** ◊ 1.80.

XX **Flappers,** 8 West Maitland St., EH12 5OS, ℡ 228 1001, Italian rest. – AE
　　CZ c
　　closed Sunday and Saturday lunch – **M** a la carte 5.25/8.55 **t.** ◊ 2.10.

X **Snobs,** 1 Deanbank Lane, EH3 5BS, ℡ 332 0003, Italian rest. – ⬛ AE
　　CY s
　　closed Sunday , Christmas Day and 1 January – **M** a la carte 5.40/8.05 **t.** ◊ 1.90.

X **Casa Siciliana,** 11 Lochrin Ter., Toll Cross, EH3 9QJ, ℡ 229 1690, Italian rest. – AE ⓪
　　DZ n
　　closed Sunday – **M** a la carte 3.50/7.80 ◊ 1.80.

X Henderson's Salad Table, 94 Hanover St., EH2 1DR, ℡ 225 3400, Vegetarian rest.
　　DY n
　　closed Sunday.

X **Le Caveau,** 13b Dundas St., EH3 6QG, ℡ 556 5707, French rest.
　　DY u
　　closed Sunday, first 2 weeks July and Bank Holidays – **M** a la carte 3.95/5.40 **t.**
　　◊ 1.60.

X **Clarinda's,** 29 Waterloo Pl., EH1 3BQ, ℡ 557 1222 – ⬛ VISA
　　EY n
　　M a la carte 4.25/6.00 **t.** ◊ 1.95.

at Cramond Foreshore NW: 5 ¼ m. off A 90 – ✉ ◉ 031 Edinburgh:

🏨 **Commodore** (Stakis), 46 West Marine Drive, EH4 5EP, ℡ 336 1700, ← – ▯ TV ⌷wc
　　☏ Ⓟ. ♿. ⬛ AE ⓪ VISA
　　AV n
　　M 3.50/5.30 **st.** ◊ 1.75 – **50 rm** ⊐ 17.00/29.00 **st.**

X **Cramond Inn,** Cramond Glebe Rd, EH4 6JM, ℡ 336 2035 – Ⓟ. ⬛ AE ⓪ VISA
　　AV r
　　closed Sunday, Christmas Day, 1 January and Bank Holidays – **M** a la carte 5.00/7.15 **t.**
　　◊ 2.50.

MICHELIN Branch, Taxi Way, Hillend Industrial Estate, Hillend, Dunfermline, KY11 5JT,
℡ 0383 (Dunfermline) 822961.

ALFA-ROMEO 22 Canning St. ℡ 229 5561
AUSTIN-DAIMLER-JAGUAR-MORRIS-MG-ROVER-
TRIUMPH, ROLLS ROYCE Gylemuir Rd ℡ 334 9101
AUSTIN-MORRIS-MG Goldenacre Ter. ℡ 552 4695
AUSTIN-MORRIS-MG-ROVER-TRIUMPH Comely
Bank ℡ 332 1344
AUSTIN-MORRIS-MG 77/87 Ferry Rd ℡ 554 6528
AUSTIN-MORRIS-MG-ROVER-TRIUMPH Lanark Rd ℡
443 2936
AUSTIN-MORRIS-MG 107 Glasgow Rd ℡ 334 1351
AUSTIN-MORRIS-MG Falcon Av. ℡ 447 6161
AUSTIN-DAIMLER-JAGUAR-MORRIS-MG-ROVER-
TRIUMPH Westfield Av. ℡ 337 3222
AUSTIN-MORRIS-MG-ROVER-TRIUMPH 70 Slateford
Rd ℡ 337 1252
CITROEN 13 Lauriston Gardens ℡ 229 4207
DATSUN 63/67 London Rd ℡ 661 7966
DATSUN 2 Joppa Rd, Portobello ℡ 669 8411
DATSUN 5 Bankhead Av. ℡ 443 8761
FIAT 8 Glenogle Rd ℡ 556 6404

FIAT 300 Colinton Rd ℡ 441 4567
FIAT 162 St. Johns Rd ℡ 334 6248
FORD Baileyfield Rd ℡ 669 6261
FORD Semple St. ℡ 229 3331
FORD 12 West Mayfield ℡ 667 4475
HONDA, SAAB Westfield Rd ℡ 337 7204
SUBARU Telford Rd ℡ 343 2241
POLSKI-DAF 1/3 Newcraighall Rd ℡ 669 2602
PORSCHE 56 Belford Rd ℡ 225 9266
RENAULT 376 Gilmerton Rd ℡ 664 2900
RENAULT 553 Gorgie Rd ℡ 444 1673
RENAULT Portobello Rd ℡ 669 7481
TALBOT Blackford Av. ℡ 667 5427
TALBOT Lochrin Tollcross ℡ 229 1555
VAUXHALL 39 Fountainbridge ℡ 229 2488
VAUXHALL Seafield Rd ℡ 554 0401
VOLVO 38 Seafield Rd East ℡ 669 8301
VOLVO Saughton Cres. ℡ 337 3282
VW, AUDI-NSU Belford Rd ℡ 225 4664
VW, AUDI-NSU Marionville Rd ℡ 661 7177

EDZELL Tayside – pop. 658 – ECD: Thursday – ◉ 035 64.
See: Castle* (16C) *AC* (Walled garden). **Envir.:** Brechin (Cathedral: round tower*) S:
6 ½ m. – Glen Esk* NW: 11 m.
🏌 ℡ 235 – 🏌 at Brechin ℡ 035 62 (Brechin) 2383, S: 5 ½ m.
Edinburgh 91 – Aberdeen 36 – Dundee 32.

🏠 **Glenesk,** High St., DD9 7TF, ℡ 319, 🚗 – ⌷wc 🏋wc ☏ 🚙 Ⓟ. ♿. AE ⓪
　　M 3.50/5.00 **t.** ◊ 2.00 – **24 rm** ⊐ 10.00/24.00.

EGILSAY (Isle of) Orkney Islands – Shipping Services : see Orkney Islands (Mainland:
Kirkwall).

EIGG (Isle of) Highland 🅶🅸🅶 ⑥ ⑩ – Shipping Services: see Mallaig.

ELGIN Grampian 🅶🅸🅶 ⑦ – pop. 16,407 – ECD: Wednesday – ◉ 0343.
See: Cathedral*. **Envir.:** Burghead (✳** from the lighthouse) NW: 10 m. – Findhorn (site*)
W: 12 m.
🏌 Hardhillock, New Elgin ℡ 2338, S: 1 m. – 🏌 Hopeman ℡ 034 383 (Hopeman) 578, N: 7 m.
🛈 17 High St. ℡ 3388 (May-October).
Edinburgh 191 – Aberdeen 67 – Fraserburgh 61 – Inverness 39.

🏨 Eight Acres, Sheriff Mill, IV30 3UN, W: 1 m. on A 96 ℡ 3077, ←, 🚗 – TV ⌷wc 🏋wc
　　☏ Ⓟ. ♿
　　41 rm.

XX **Enrico's,** 15 Greyfriars St., IV30 1LF, ℡ 2849, Italian rest. – ⓪ VISA
　　closed Sunday, Christmas and 1 January – **M** a la carte 4.05/11.05 **t.**

AUSTIN-MORRIS-MG 27 Greyfriars St. ☎ 7416
DAIMLER-JAGUAR-ROVER-TRIUMPH Station Rd ☎ 2633
DATSUN Borough Briggs Rd ☎ 7473
FIAT School Brae ☎ 3088
FORD 266 High St. ☎ 41121
MAZDA, RELIANT Sheriff Mill ☎ 7121

OPEL 215/219 High St. ☎ 7514
PEUGEOT Bridge Motors ☎ 2955
RENAULT Edgar Rd ☎ 7688
TALBOT East Rd ☎ 3066
VAUXHALL, VOLVO South College St. ☎ 7561
VW, AUDI 41/3 Blackfriars Rd ☎ 2792

ELIE Fife 986 ⑪ – pop. 895 (inc. Earlsferry) – ECD : Wednesday – ✆ 0333.
See : Site and ≼*.
🏌18 🏌9 ☎ 330327.
Edinburgh 42 – Dundee 25 – Kirkcaldy 16.

⌂ **The Elms,** 12 Park Pl., KY9 1DH, ☎ 330404, 🚗
6 rm ⊠ 6.00/12.00 **t.**

ELLON Grampian 986 ⑦ – pop. 2,263 – ECD : Wednesday – ✆ 0358.
🛈 Market St. Car Park ☎ 20730 (June-September).
Edinburgh 140 – Aberdeen 16 – Fraserburgh 26.

🏨 Ellon Ladbroke Mercury Motor Inn, AB4 9NP, ☎ 20666, Telex 739200 – 📺 🛏wc 🚿wc
🅿. 🏊 – **40 rm.**

ERIBOLL (Loch) *** Highland.
Edinburgh 276 – Tongue 21.

Hotels see Tongue E : 21 m.

ERISKA (Isle of) Strathclyde – ✉ Oban – ✆ 063 172 Ledaig.
🏨 **Isle of Eriska** 🦢, PA37 1SD, ☎ 205, ≼ Lismore and mountains, « Country house atmosphere », ✗ 🚗, park – 🛏wc 🕾 🅿. 🅰🅴
March-November – **M** (buffet lunch) 8.50/10.00 **s.** 🍷 2.05 – **24 rm** ⊠ 29.00/58.00 **s.**

ERSKINE Strathclyde – pop. 3,300 – ✆ 041 Glasgow.
Edinburgh 56 – Glasgow 13.

🏨 Glasgow Eurocrest (Crest) 🦢, PA8 6AN, on A 726 ☎ 812 0123, Telex 777713, ≼ – 🛗 📺
♿ 🅿. 🏊. 🅿 🅰🅴 ⓪ VISA
⊠ 2.80 – **198 rm** 19.20/25.90 **st.**

FALKIRK Central 986 ⑮ – pop. 37,579 – ECD : Wednesday – ✆ 0324.
Edinburgh 24 – Dumfermline 19 – Glasgow 23 – Motherwell 26 – Perth 43.

🏨 **Cladhan,** Kemper Av., FK1 1UF, ☎ 27421 – 📺 🛏wc 🚿wc 🕾 🅿. 🏊. 🅿 🅰🅴 ⓪ VISA
M a la carte 4.95/8.10 🍷 1.60 – **33 rm** ⊠ 13.50/19.50 **st.**

🏨 **Park** (Stakis), Camelon Rd, Arnothill, FK1 5RY, ☎ 28331 – 🛗 📺 🛏wc 🚿wc 🕾 🅿. 🏊. 🅿 🅰🅴
⓪ VISA
M 3.85/5.60 **st.** 🍷 1.70 – **54 rm** ⊠ 17.00/28.00 **st.**

AUSTIN-DAIMLER-JAGUAR-MORRIS-MG-ROVER-TRIUMPH Main St. ☎ 22584
FIAT Callendar Rd ☎ 24204
FORD Callendar Rd ☎ 21511
PEUGEOT West End ☎ 23042
SAAB 2 High Station Rd ☎ 22956

TALBOT, LANCIA 95 Glasgow Rd ☎ 22571
TOYOTA Lady'smill ☎ 35935
VAUXHALL Callendar Rd ☎ 21141
VAUXHALL 67/80 Grahams Rd ☎ 21234
VOLVO Victoria Rd ☎ 24693
VW High Station Rd ☎ 24221

FALKLAND Fife 986 ⑪ – pop. 896 – ✆ 033 75.
See : Palace* (16C) *AC.*
🛈 ☎ 397 (13 April-October).
Edinburgh 36 – Dundee 23 – Perth 18.

XX **Covenanter** with rm, KY7 7BU, ☎ 224 – 🅿
closed last 2 weeks July – **M** (*closed Monday*) a la carte 4.40/6.60 **st.** 🍷 1.65 – **4 rm**
⊠ 6.50/13.00 **st.**

FEOLIN Strathclyde 986 ⑭ – Shipping Services : see Jura (Isle of).

FETLAR (Isle of) Shetland Islands 986 ⑯ – Shipping services : see Shetland Islands.

FIONNPHORT Strathclyde 986 ⑩ – Shipping Services : see Mull (Isle of).

FISHNISH Argyll. (Strathclyde) – Shipping Services : see Mull (Isle of).

FOCHABERS Grampian 986 ⑦ – pop. 1238 – ECD : Wednesday – ✆ 0343.
🏌18 Spey Bay ☎ 820424, N : 5 m. – 🏌9 Garmouth ☎ 034 387 (Spey Bay) 388.
Edinburgh 182 – Aberdeen 58 – Fraserburgh 52 – Inverness 48.

🏨 **Gordon Arms,** 89 High St., IV32 7DH, ☎ 820508, 🚗 – 📺 🛏wc 🕾 🅿
M 3.50/8.00 **t.** 🍷 1.60 – ⊠ 2.00 – **17 rm** 11.00/21.00 **t.**

FORFAR Tayside 986 ⑪ – pop. 10,499 – ECD : Thursday – ☎ 0307.

ⅰ₈ Cunninghill ☏ 2120, E : 1 ½ m.

Edinburgh 72 – Aberdeen 52 – Dundee 13 – Perth 30.

    🏛 **Royal,** 31 Castle St., DD8 3AE, ☏ 62691 – ☐wc ☎ 🅿
    M 3.50/5.50 **t.** ⅰ 2.50 – **20 rm** ☞ 10.00/19.00 **t.**

    ♨ County, 7 Castle St., DD8 3AE, ☏ 62878 – **10 rm.**

AUSTIN-MORRIS-MG-ROVER-TRIUMPH-WOLSELEY   TALBOT Lochside Rd ☏ 2676
128 Castle St. ☏ 62542   VW, AUDI Kirriemuir Rd ☏ 2347
DATSUN Lochside Rd ☏ 2281

FORSINARD Highland – ☎ 064 17 Halladale.

Edinburgh 283 – Inverness 124 – Thurso 29 – Wick 62.

    🏚 **Forsinard** ⚘, KW13 6YT, ☏ 221, ≤, ⚓, park – ☐wc 🏚wc 🅿
    M 4.00/7.00 **t.** ⅰ 1.60 – **13 rm** ☞ 13.50/27.00 **t.** – P 24.95 **t.**

FORT AUGUSTUS Highland 986 ⑥ ⑦ – pop. 670 – ECD : Wednesday – ☎ 0320 – ⚑₉.
See : Loch Ness**, (site*, lochs and canal*). **Envir. :** NE : Loch Knockie ≤** from Glendoebeg by A 862.

ℹ Car Park ☏ 6367 (mid May-mid September).

Edinburgh 155 – Inverness 34 – Kyle of Lochalsh 58 – Oban 80.

    🏚 **Inchnacardoch Lodge,** PH32 4BL, on A 82 ☏ 6258, ≤, ⚞ – 🗍 🅿. ☒ AE ⑩ VISA
    M 2.50/4.80 **st.** ⅰ 1.50 – **17 rm** ☞ 10.50/21.00 **st.**

FORTINGALL Tayside – see Kenmore.

FORT WILLIAM Highland 986 ⑩ – pop. 4,214 – ☎ 0397.
Envir. : SE : Glen Nevis*.

ⅰ₈ ☏ 4464, N : 3 m. on A 82.

ℹ Area Tourist Officer ☏ 3581, Telex 778869.

Edinburgh 131 – Glasgow 102 – Inverness 66 – Oban 48.

    🏰 **Inverlochy Castle** ⚘, Inverlochy, PH33 6SN, NE : 3 m. by A 82 ☏ 2177, ≤ garden,
    loch and mountains, « Victorian castle in extensive grounds », ⚔, ⚓, ⚞, park – 📺 🅿. AE
    VISA
    Easter-October – **M** (lunch by arrangement) approx. 18.00 st. ⅰ 3.00 – **13 rm** ☞ 52.00/
    77.00 **st.**

    🏚 **West End,** Auchintore Rd, PH33 6ED, ☏ 2614, ≤ – 🗍 ☐wc 🅿. AE ⑩ VISA
    M a la carte 4.90/7.45 **st.** ⅰ 1.85 – **50 rm** ☞ 9.50/24.00 **st.**

    🏚 **Ladbroke Mercury Motor Inn,** Auchintore Rd, PH33 6TG, on A 82 ☏ 3117, ≤ – 📺
    ☐wc 🅿
    61 rm.

    🏛 **Nevis Bank,** Belford Rd, PH33 6BY, ☏ 2595 – ☐wc 🅿
    M 3.00/4.50 – **20 rm** ☞ 9.00/18.00.

    ↑ Lochiel Villa, Auchintore Rd, PH33 6RQ, ☏ 2379, ≤ – 🅿
    9 rm.

    at Banavie N : 3 m off A 830 by A 82 – ✉ Fort William – ☎ 039 77 Corpach :

    🏛 **Moorings,** PH33 7LY, ☏ 550, ≤, ⚞ – 🗍 🅿
    M *(closed 26 December and 1-2 January)* (bar lunch) 8.25 – **16 rm** ☞ 7.50/18.00 **t.**

AUSTIN-MORRIS-MG-ROVER-TRIUMPH Gordon Sq.   TALBOT Fort William ☏ 4141
☏ 2345

GAIRLOCH Highland 986 ⑥ – pop. 125 – ECD : Wednesday – ☎ 0445.
Envir. : NE : Gruinard Bay*** – Inverewe gardens* (rhododendrons) NE : 6 m.

ℹ Area Tourist Officer, Achtercairn, IV21 2DN, ☏ 2130.

Edinburgh 230 – Inverness 71 – Kyle of Lochalsh 65.

    🏚 **Gairloch,** IV21 2BL, ☏ 2001, ≤ sea and bay, ⚔, ⚓ – 🗍 ☐wc 🚗 🅿. ☒ AE ⑩ VISA
    Mid April-mid October – **M** 2.95/5.70 **st.** ⅰ 2.00 – **49 rm** ☞ 12.90/25.80 **st.**

    🏛 **Gairloch Sands,** IV21 2BJ, ☏ 2131, ≤ sea and bay – ☐wc 🅿. ☒ AE ⑩ VISA
    M (bar lunch) approx. 6.25 **st.** ⅰ 1.25 – **36 rm** ☞ 17.95/30.30 **st.**

GALASHIELS Borders 986 ⑮ – pop. 12,609 – ECD : Wednesday – ☎ 0896.
ⅰ₈ Ladhope, ☏ 3724, NE : ¼ m. – ⅰ₉ Torwoodlee ☏ 2260, N : 1 m. on A 7.

ℹ Volunteer Hall, ☏ 55551 (mid May-September).

Edinburgh 33 – Hawick 17 – Newcastle-upon-Tyne 73.

    🏛 Douglas (Open House), Channel St., TD1 1BJ, ☏ 2189 – 🗍 📺 ☐wc ☎ 🅿
    38 rm.

at Clovenfords W : 3 ½ m. on A 72 – ✉ ☎ 089 685 :

✗ **Thornielee House** with rm, TD1 3LN, SW : 2 ¾ m. on A 72 ℙ 350, ☞ – Ⓟ
  M *(closed Monday to non-residents)* a la carte 3.00/6.75 – **4 rm** ⌷ 10.00/15.00 **t.**

AUSTIN-MORRIS-MG-ROVER-TRIUMPH 3 Market St.   RENAULT Bridge St. ℙ 2363
ℙ 2301   VAUXHALL Albert Pl. ℙ 2729
DATSUN Melrose Rd ℙ 4767

GARVE Highland 🗺 ⑥ – pop. 200 – ECD : Thursday – ☎ 099 74.
Envir. : SE : Blackwater Valley (Falls of Rogie*).

Edinburgh 186 – Inverness 27 – Wick 116.

  🏠 Strathgarve Lodge 🦢, IV23 2PU, ℙ 204, ≼, « Former hunting lodge », ◗, ☞, park –
     ⊖wc Ⓟ
     May-September – **18 rm.**

  🏠 **Inchbae Lodge** 🦢, Ullapool Rd, IV23 2PH, N : 6 m. on A 835 ℙ 099 75 (Aultguish) 269.
     ≼, ◗, ☞ – ⊖wc �📶wc Ⓟ. ⓪
     Mid April-mid October – **M** (bar lunch) approx. 6.00 ▮ 1.70 – **13 rm** ⌷ 10.50/20.50 –
     P 19.00/20.00.

GATEHOUSE OF FLEET Dumfries and Galloway 🗺 ⑲ – pop. 837 – ECD : Thursday –
☎ 055 74 – ⓘ₉.
🅳 Car Park ℙ 212 (April-September).

Edinburgh 109 – Dumfries 32 – Stranraer 44.

  🏠 Cally (T.H.F.) 🦢, DG7 2DL, S : 1 ½ m. off A 75 ℙ 341, Telex 778082, ≼, ✗, ☖ heated,
     ◗, ☞, park – 📱 TV Ⓟ. 🏖. 🅰 AE ⓪ VISA
     M 4.75/6.15 **st.** ▮ 2.00 – **90 rm.**

  🏠 **Murray Arms** (Best Western), High St., DG7 2HY, ℙ 207, ✗, ☞ – ⊖wc. 🅰 AE ⓪
     VISA
     M (bar lunch) 3.50/6.50 **st.** ▮ 2.20 – **26 rm** ⌷ 17.50/37.00 **st.**

  🏠 **Anwoth**, Fleet St., DG7 2JT, ℙ 217 – ⊖wc �📶wc. AE VISA
     M (bar lunch) 2.00/5.00 **t.** ▮ 1.60 – **15 rm** ⌷ 8.00/16.50 – P 12.80/15.00.

GIFFNOCK Strathclyde – see Glasgow.

GIFFORD Lothian – pop. 575 – ECD : Monday and Wednesday – ✉ Haddington – ☎ 062 081
– ⓘ₉.
Edinburgh 20 – Hawick 50.

  ♨ Goblin Ha', Main St., EH41 4QH, ℙ 244, ☞ – Ⓟ
     7 rm.

  ✗✗ Tweeddale Arms, with rm, High St., EH41 4QH, ℙ 240, ☞ – �📶wc Ⓟ
     8 rm.

GIGHA (Isle of) Strathclyde 🗺 ⑭ – pop. 171 – ☎ 058 35.
See : Sound of Gigha*.
⛴ by Caledonian MacBrayne : to Kennacraig **1** daily (1 h 15 mn) – to Port Ellen (Islay)
1-3 daily (1 h 15 mn).

  🏠 **Gigha** 🦢, PA41 7AB, ℙ 254, ≼ Sound of Gigha and Mull of Kintyre, « Tasteful decor »,
     ☞ – ⊖wc Ⓟ
     closed Christmas and 1 January – **M** 3.75/6.50 **t.** – **9 rm** ⌷ 11.50/28.00 **t.**

GIRVAN Strathclyde 🗺 ⑭ – pop. 7,410 – ECD : Wednesday – ☎ 0465.
Envir. : Culzean Castle 18C (site**, interior*) *AC*, N : 9 m.
ⓘ₁₈ Golf Course Rd ℙ 4272.
🅳 Bridge St. ℙ 2056/7.

Edinburgh 98 – Ayr 23 – Glasgow 55 – Stranraer 30.

  🏠 King's Arms (Swallow), Dalrymple St., KA26 0DU, ℙ 3322 – TV ⊖wc ☎ Ⓟ
     39 rm.

GLAMIS Tayside 🗺 ⑪ – pop. 190 – ✉ Forfar – ☎ 030 784.
See: Castle* *AC*.
Edinburgh 66 – Dundee 12 – Forfar 5 – Perth 24.

  ✗✗ **Strathmore Arms**, Main St., DD8 1RS, ℙ 248 – Ⓟ
     closed Sunday and Monday in winter – **M** a la carte 5.85/8.50 **t.** ▮ 2.50.

*Do not always take your holidays in **July** or **August**;*
some districts are more beautiful in other months.

GLASGOW Strathclyde 𝟗𝟖𝟔 ⑭⑮ – pop. 897,483 – ✆ 041.

See : St. Mungo Cathedral*** DZ B – Art Gallery and Museum** CY M – Provand's Lordship* DZ D – Pollock House* (Spanish paintings) AX E.

ⓕ₁₈ Linn Park ☏ 637 5871, S : 4 m. BX – ⓕ₁₈ Cumbernauld Rd ☏ 770 6220 BV – ⓕ₉ Lincoln Av. ☏ 959 2131, W : 4 m. AV – ⓕ₉ Brassey St. ☏ 946 9728 BV.

✈ Glasgow Airport : ☏ 887 1111 ext 504/5 and 552, W : 8 m. by M 8 AV – Terminal : Stand n° 23 Anderston Cross Bus Station, Blythswood St.

✈ see also Prestwick.

🛈 George Sq., G2 1ES, ☏ 221 6136/7 or 221 7371/2, Telex 779504.

Edinburgh 43 – Manchester 213.

Town plans : Glasgow pp. 2-5

🏨🏨🏨 **Albany** (T.H.F.), Bothwell St., G2 7EN, ☏ 248 2656, Telex 77440. ⇐ – ▯ TV ℗. ♨. ☒ AE ⓪ VISA
M a la carte 7.40/12.30 t. ♦ 2.40 – ☲ 2.50 – **243 rm** 27.00/34.50 **st.** — CZ z

🏨🏨🏨 **Central** (B.T.H.), Gordon St., G1 3SF, ☏ 221 9680, Telex 777771 – ▯ TV. ♿. ♨. ☒ AE ⓪ VISA
M a la carte 4.15/7.35 **st.** ♦ 2.40 (see also rest. **Malmaison**) – **211 rm** ☲ 27.00/41.00 **st.** — DZ e

🏨🏨 **North British** (B.T.H.), 50 George Sq., G2 1DS, ☏ 332 6711, Telex 778147 – ▯ TV ⟾ ♨. ☒ AE ⓪ VISA
M a la carte 5.00/9.65 **st.** ♦ 2.20 – **140 rm** ☲ 15.50/29.00 **st.** — DZ u

🏨🏨 Bellahouston (Swallow), 517 Paisley Rd West, G51 1RW, ☏ 427 3146, Telex 778795 –
▯ TV ⟾wc ☎ ℗. ♨
71 rm. — AX a

🏨🏨 Pond (Stakis), 2-4 Shelley Rd, G12 0XP, ☏ 334 8161, Group Telex 778704 – ▯ TV ⟾wc
☎ ℗. ☒ AE ⓪ VISA
134 rm. — AV i

🏨🏨 **Beacons**, 7 Park Ter., G3 6BY, ☏ 332 9438 – ▯ TV ⟾wc ☎. ☒ AE ⓪ VISA — CY c
M a la carte 3.50/9.65 **st.** ♦ 2.40 – **26 rm** ☲ 19.00/26.50 **st.**

🏨🏨 **Tinto Firs** (Thistle), 470 Kilmarnock Rd, G43 2BB, ☏ 637 2353 – TV ⟾wc ☎ ℗. ♨.
☒ AE ⓪ VISA — AX c
M 4.25/5.95 t. ♦ 2.00 – ☲ 3.00 – **30 rm** 18.00/26.00 t.

🏨🏨 Lorne (Open House), 923 Sauchiehall St., G3 7TE, ☏ 334 4891 – ▯ TV ⟾wc ☎ ℗.
♨ — CY a
84 rm.

🏨🏨 Ingram (Stakis), 201 Ingram St., G1 1DQ, ☏ 248 4401 – ▯ TV ⟾wc ☎. ♨ — DZ c
90 rm.

🏨🏨 Shawlands (Open House), 30-36 Shawlands Sq., G41 3NR, off Kilmarnoch Rd
☏ 632 9226 – ▯ TV ⟾wc ☎ ℗. ♨ — AX e
20 rm.

🏨🏨 Glasgow Centre (Centre), Argyle St., G2 8LL, ☏ 248 2355, Telex 779652 – ▯ TV ⟾wc
☎. ☒ AE ⓪ VISA — CZ x
☲ 1.65 – **125 rm** 18.10/23.25 **st.**

🏨🏨 **Royal Stuart**, 316 Clyde St., G1 4NR, ☏ 248 4261, Telex 778833 – ▯ TV ⟾wc ☎.
♨. ☒ AE ⓪ VISA — DZ n
M 3.50/5.50 t. ♦ 1.95 – **112 rm** ☲ 19.00/28.00 t.

🏨 Royal (Osprey), 106 Sauchiehall St., G2 3DE, ☏ 332 3416 – ▯ ⟾wc ♒wc ☎ — DY o
46 rm.

🏨 **Newlands** (S & N), 290 Kilmarnock Rd, G43 2XS, ☏ 632 9171 – ⟾wc ♒wc ☎ – ☒
AE ⓪ VISA — AX n
M *(closed Sunday and 1-2 January)* a la carte 3.25/6.65 t. ♦ 1.95 – **17 rm** ☲ 10.50/
19.50 t.

🏨 Ewington, 132 Queen's Drive, G42 8QW, ☏ 423 1152 – ▯ ⟾wc ♒wc ☎ — BX a
47 rm.

↑ **Dalmeny**, 62 St. Andrews Drive, Nithsdale Cross, Pollockshields, G41 5EZ, ☏ 427 1106 –
⟾wc ♒wc ℗ — AX o
10 rm ☲ 7.50/17.00 **s.**

↑ **Linwood House**, 356 Albert Drive, Pollockshields, G41 5PJ, ☏ 427 1642, ⟗ – ℗ — AX r
16 rm ☲ 6.50/13.00 **st.**

XXXX **Malmaison** (B.T.H.), Hope St., G1 3SF, ☏ 221 9680, French rest. – ☒ AE ⓪ VISA DZ e
closed Saturday lunch, Sunday, Bank Holidays and August – M a la carte 14.40/22.00 **st.**
♦ 2.40.

XXX **Fountain**, 2 Woodside Crescent, Charing Cross, G3 7UL, ☏ 332 6396 – ℗. ☒ AE ⓪
VISA — CY n
*closed Saturday lunch, Sunday, last 2 weeks July, 25-26 December, 1-2 January and
Bank Holidays* – M a la carte 9.15/12.45 **st.** ♦ 2.50.

XXX **Ambassador**, 19-20 Blythswood Sq., G2 4AS, ☏ 221 3530, Dancing – ☒ AE ⓪ VISA
closed Sunday and Bank Holidays – M a la carte 7.40/9.60 **s.** ♦ 2.00. — CY u

GLASGOW
BUILT UP AREA

0   1 km
0   1/2 mile

Aikenhead Road		BX 2
Alexandra Parade		BV 3
Balgrayhill Road		BV 4
Ballater Street		BX 6
Balornock Road		BV 8
Balshagray Avenue		AV 9
Battlefield Road		BX 12
Benalder Street		AV 13
Berryknowes Road		AX 15
Bilsland Drive		BV 16
Blairbeth Road		BX 18
Braidcraft Road		AX 20
Brassey Street		BV 24
Broomloan Road		AV 26
Burnhill Chapel Street		BX 28
Byres Road		AV 30
Caledonia Road		BX 32
Carmunnock Road		BX 33
Cumbernauld Road		BV 40
Edmiston Drive		AV 48
Farmeloan Road		BX 53
Fenwick Road		AX 55
Glasgow Road (PAISLEY)		AX 62

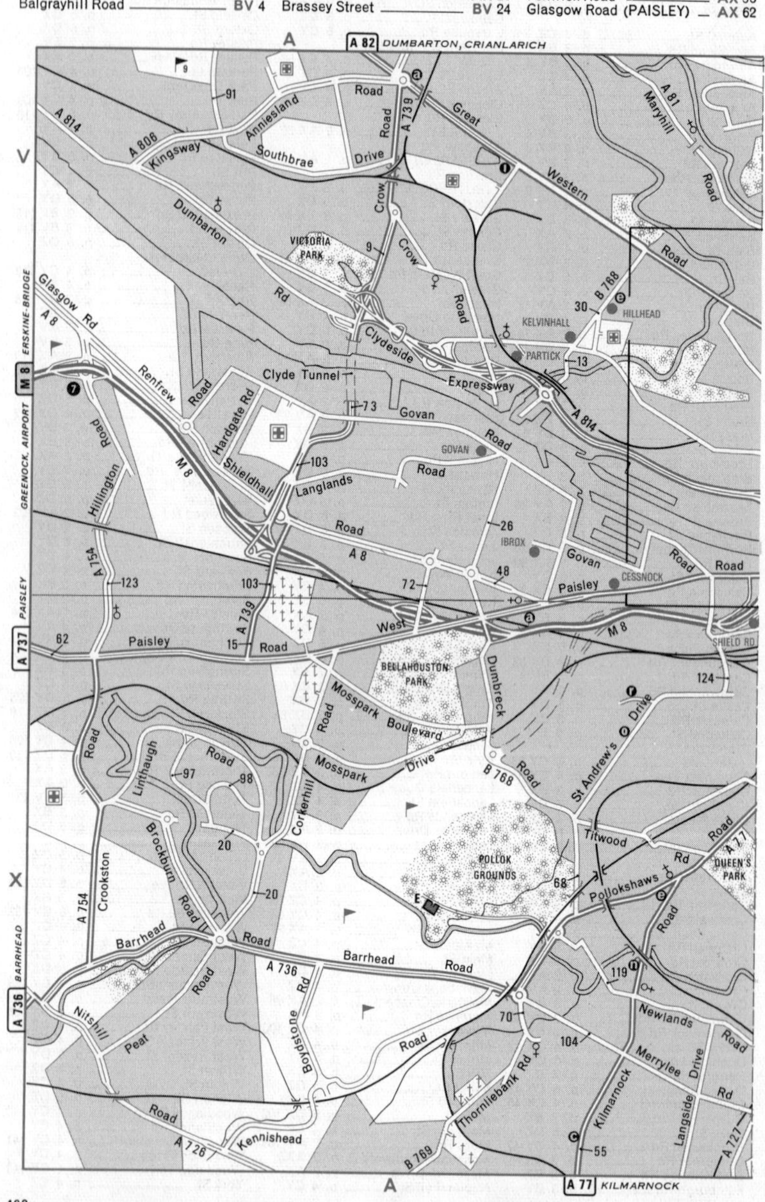

For Street Index see Glasgow p. 1 bis

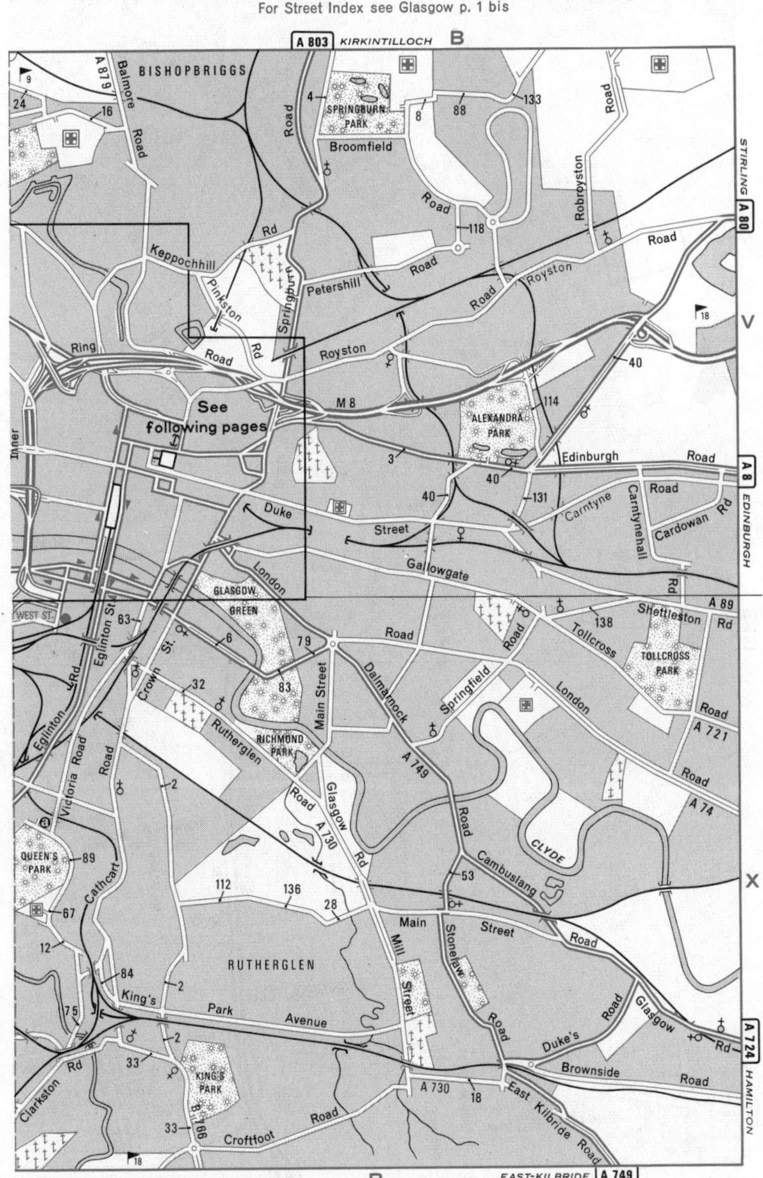

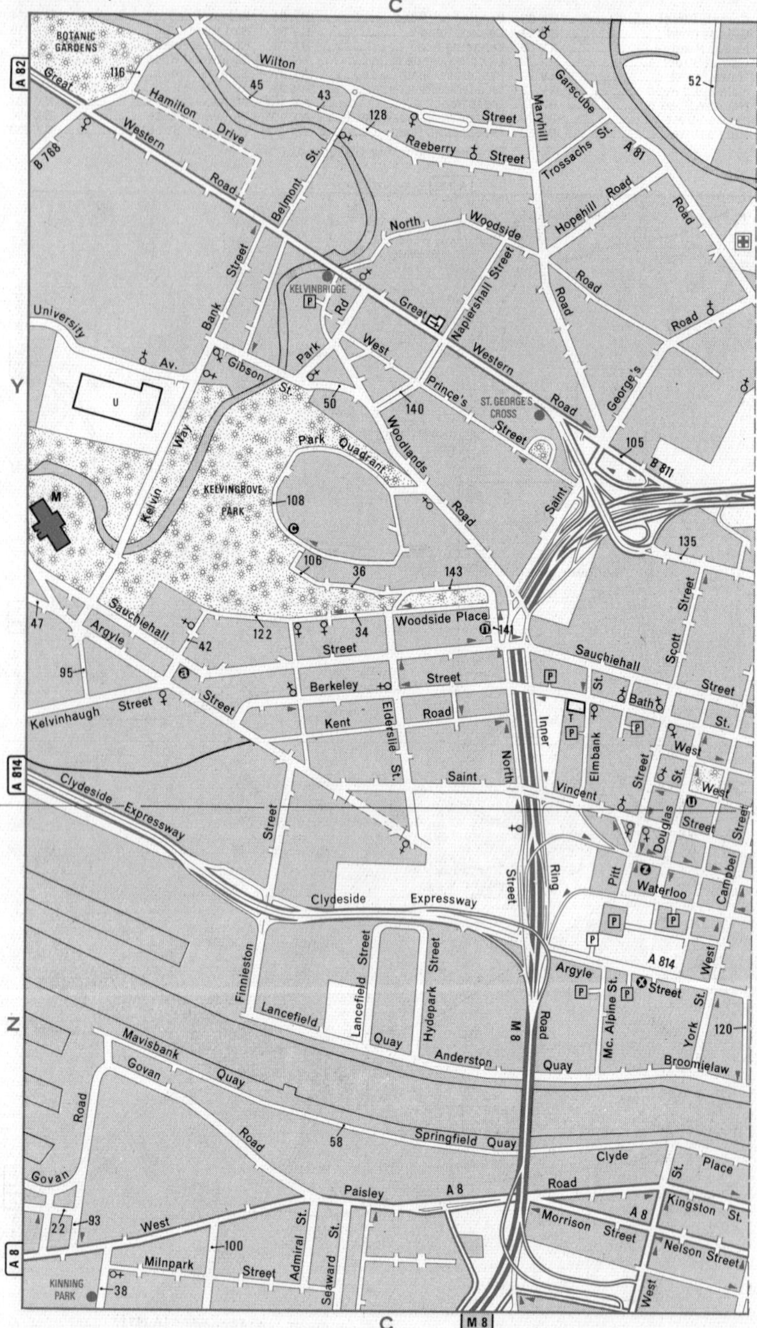
C
Y
Z
BOTANIC
GARDENS
116
A 82
Great
Wilton
45
43
128
Raeberry
Street
Street
Maryhill
Garscube
52
B 768
Western
Hamilton
Drive
Belmont
St.
Street
Trossachs St.
A 81
Hopehill
Road
Road
North
Woodside
Napiershall Street
Road
KELVINBRIDGE
P
Park
Rd
Great
West
Western
Road
University
Bank
Street
Gibson
St.
Prince's
Road
Saint.
George's
Av.
Way
50
140
ST. GEORGE'S
CROSS
105
B 811
U
Kelvin
Park
Quadrant
Woodlands
135
M
KELVINGROVE
PARK
108
C
Road
Saint.
Street
Scott
Sauchiehall
106
36
143
Street
47
Argyle
122
34
Woodside Place
141
Sauchiehall
P
Street
95
Berkeley
Street
Bath
Street
St.
a
42
Kent
Road
P
Elmbank
P
West
St.
Kelvinhaugh
Street
Street
Elderslie
St.
Street
Inner
Street
U
West
Street
A 814
Clydeside
Expressway
Saint
North
Vincent
Douglas
Street
Street
Street
Ring
Pitt
Waterloo
Campbel
Clydeside
Expressway
Finnieston
Lancefield
Street
Hydepark
Street
North
Street
P
P
Argyle
A 814
West
Z
Mavisbank
Lancefield
Quay
Mc. Alpine St.
Street
York
120
Govan
Quay
Road
M 8
Broomielaw
Road
Road
Springfield Quay
Clyde
Place
Govan
58
Road
St.
Govan
Paisley
A 8
Road
Kingston
St.
93
West
Morrison
Street
A 8
22
100
Admiral St.
Seaward
St.
Nelson Street
A 8
Milnpark
Street
West
KINNING
PARK
38
C
M 8

GLASGOW
CENTRE

0   300 m
0   300 yards

Brand Street ______ CZ 22
Bridge Street ______ DZ 25
Claremont Gardens __ CY 34
Claremont Terrace __ CY 36
Commerce Street ___ DZ 37
Cornwald Street ___ CZ 38
Derby Street ______ CY 42
Doune Gardens ____ CY 43
Doune Quadrant ___ CY 45
Dumbarton Road ___ CY 47
Eldon Street ______ CY 50
Ellesmere Street __ CDY 52
General Terminus
  Quay ___________ CZ 58
Glasgow Bridge ___ DZ 60
Gordon Street _____ DZ 65
Jamaica Street ____ DZ 77
John Knox Street __ DZ 80

Kyle Street _______ DY 86
Lorne Street ______ CZ 93
Lymburn Street ___ CY 95
Middlesex Street __ CZ 100
Moir Street _______ DZ 102
New City Road ___ CY 105
Park Gardens _____ CY 106
Park Terrace _____ CY 108
Parliamentary Road _ DY 110
Queen Margaret
  Drive __________ CY 116
Robertson Street __ CZ 120
Royal Terrace ____ CY 122
Stirling Road ____ DY 125
Stockwell Street __ DZ 126
Striven Gardens __ CY 128
Suspension Bridge _ DZ 130
Victoria Bridge __ DZ 132
West Graham Street · CY 135
Woodlands Drive __ CY 140
Woodside Crescent_ CY 141
Woodside Terrace _ CY 143

For Street Index
see Glasgow p. 1 bis

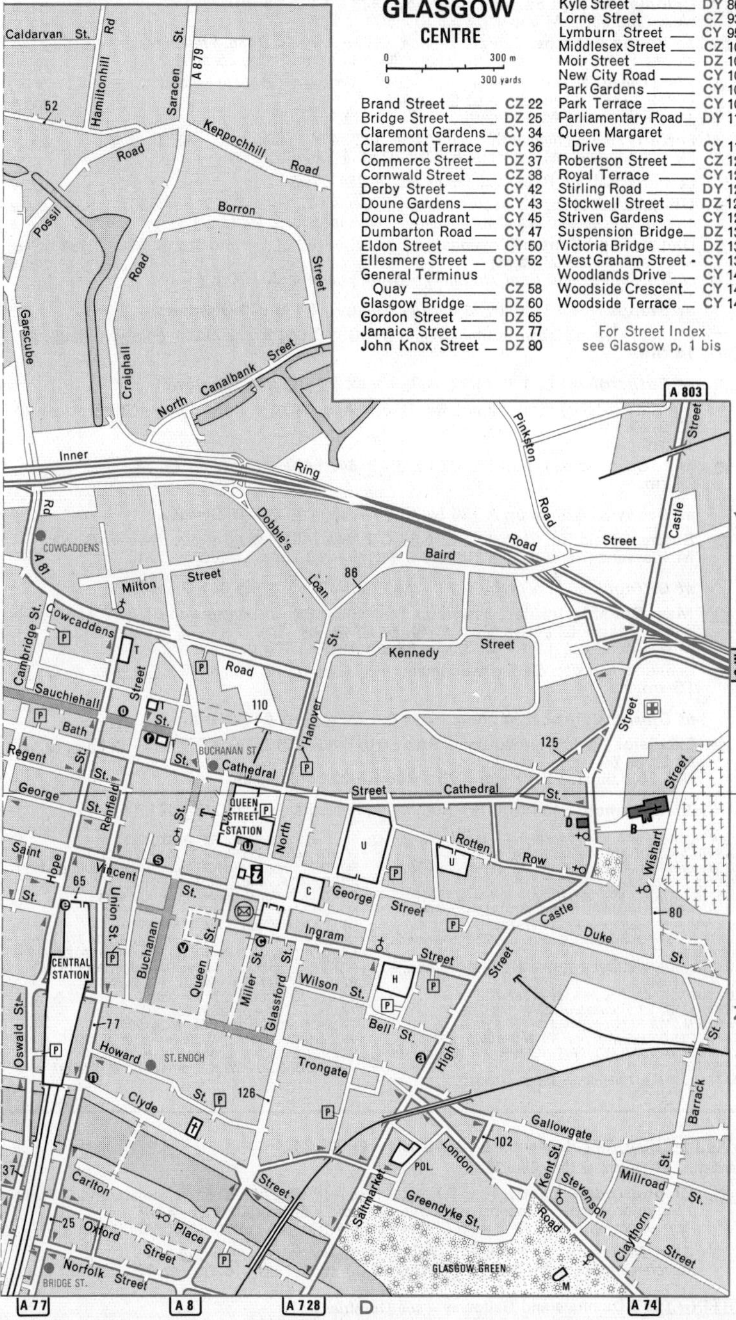

D
Caldarvan St.
Hamiltonhill Rd
Saracen St.
A 879
52
Keppochhill Road
Road
Borron
Possil
Craighall Road
Garscube
North Canalbank Sreet
Inner
Ring
Pinkston Road
A 803
Castle Street
Y
Rd
COWGADDENS
A 81
Dobble's Loan
Baird
Road
Street
M 8
Milton Street
86
Kennedy Street
Cambridge St.
Cowcaddens
Street
Road
St.
110
Hanover St.
Street
125
Sauchiehall Street
Bath
BUCHANAN ST.
St.
St.
Cathedral
Regent St.
St.
George
St.
Renfield St.
Cathedral Street
St.
D
B
Saint
Hope
Vincent
QUEEN STREET STATION
North St.
U
Rotten Row
Wishart Street
80
Street
George Street
Castle
Duke
65
Union St.
Buchanan
St.
C
Ingram
Street
Street
St.
CENTRAL STATION
Queen St.
Miller St.
Glassford St.
Wilson St.
H
Bell St.
Z
Oswald St.
77
Howard
ST. ENOCH
126
Trongate
High
St.
Barrack St.
A 77
A 8
A 728
D
A 74
Clyde
St.
Gallowgate
Kent St.
Millroad St.
Carlton
Street
London Road
102
Stevenson St.
Claythorn Street
25 Oxford Street
Place
Saltmarket
POL.
Greendyke St.
Norfolk Street
BRIDGE ST.
GLASGOW GREEN
M
37

XX **Colonial,** 25 High St., G1 1LX, ☎ 552 1923 – ⟋ AE ⓪ VISA   DZ **a**
closed Sunday – **M** a la carte 5.80/12.50 **t.** ◊ 2.50.

XX **La Bonne Auberge,** 7a Park Terrace, G3 6BY, ☎ 332 9438, French rest. – ⟋ AE ⓪ VISA
closed Sunday and Bank Holidays – **M** a la carte 7.00/9.65 **st.** ◊ 2.40.   CY **c**

XX **Ristorante Mamma Mia,** 828 Great Western Rd, Anniesland Cross, G11 1HA,
☎ 959 7789, Italian rest. – ⟋ AE ⓪ VISA   AV **a**
closed Sunday – **M** a la carte 5.00/6.70 **t.** ◊ 1.70.

XX **Ferrari,** 39 Sauchiehall St., G2 3AT, ☎ 332 8414, Italian rest. – ⟋ AE ⓪ VISA   DY **r**
closed Sunday – **M** a la carte 6.00/8.10 **st.** ◊ 1.80.

X Le Provençal, 21 Royal Exchange Sq. ☎ 221 0798.   DZ **v**

X **Ubiquitous Chip,** 12 Ashton Lane, off Byres Rd, G12 8SJ, ☎ 334 5007   AV **e**
closed Sunday and last 2 weeks July – **M** a la carte 2.45/9.05 ◊ 1.35.

X **Danish Food Centre** (Copenhagen Room), 56-60 St. Vincent St., G2 5TS, ☎ 221 0518,
Smörrebrod – ⟋ AE ⓪ VISA   DZ **s**
closed Sunday and Bank Holidays – **M** a la carte 4.95/7.70 **t.** ◊ 1.65.

at Stepps NE: 5 ¾ m. by M 8 on A 80 – BV – ✉ ✆ 041 Glasgow:

🏨 Garfield (Open House), Cumbernauld Rd, G33 6HW, ☎ 779 2111 – TV ⌷wc ☏ P. ♿
19 rm.

at Rutherglen SE: 1 ½ m. on A 749 – BX – ✉ ✆ 041 Glasgow:

🏨 Burnside (Stakis), East Kilbride Rd, G73 5EA, on A 749, ☎ 634 1276 – TV ⌷wc ☏ P.
⟋ AE ⓪ VISA
16 rm.

🏨 Mill (Open House), Mill St., G73 2AP, ☎ 647 5491 – ⌷wc ☏ P. ♿
29 rm.

at Busby S: 5 ½ m. on A 726 by A 727 – AX – ✉ ✆ 041 Glasgow:

🏨 Busby, 1 Field Rd, Clarkston, G76 8RX, ☎ 644 2661 – ❙◗❙ TV ⌷wc 🕭wc ☏ P. ⟋
M (bar lunch) a la carte 4.15/6.60 **t.** ◊ 1.75 – **14 rm** ☕ 14.00/22.00 **t.**

at Giffnock S: 5 ¼ m. by A 77 – AX – on A 716 – ✉ ✆ 041 Glasgow:

🏨 **Mac Donald** (Thistle), Eastwood Toll, G46 6RA, at intersection of A 77 and A 726
☎ 638 2225 – TV ⌷wc 🕭wc ☏ P. ⟋ AE ⓪ VISA
M 4.50/6.50 **t.** ◊ 1.75 – ☕ 3.00 – **58 rm** 19.00/27.00 **t.**

🏨 Redhurst (Stakis), 27 Eastwoodmains Rd, G46 QE, ☎ 638 6465 – TV ⌷wc ☏ P. ♿
15 rm.

at Glasgow Airport W: 8 m. by M 8 – AV – ✉ ✆ 041 Glasgow:

🏨 **Excelsior** (T.H.F.), Abbotsinch, PA3 2TR, ☎ 887 1212, Telex 777 733 – ❙◗❙ TV ♿ P. ♿.
⟋ AE ⓪ VISA
M 5.25/5.65 **st.** ◊ 2.10 – ☕ 2.75 – **305 rm** 23.00/31.00 **st.**

MICHELIN Branch, Southcroft Rd, Rutherglen Industrial Estate, G73 1UZ, ☎ 647 0261.

ALFA ROMEO, SAAB 60 Tantallon Rd ☎ 637 2206
AUSTIN-MORRIS-MG 76 James St. ☎ 554 7571
AUSTIN-MORRIS-MG St. Andrews Garage, 198 Maxwell Rd ☎ 429 4298
AUSTIN-MORRIS-MG 338 Maryhill Rd ☎ 332 6941
AUSTIN-DAIMLER-JAGUAR-MG-MORRIS-ROVER-TRIUMPH 55 Hamilton Rd ☎ 778 8383
AUSTIN-MG-WOLSELEY 215 Queensborough Gardens ☎ 357 1234
AUSTIN-MORRIS-ROVER-TRIUMPH 21/37 Nithsdale St. ☎ 423 5544
AUSTIN-MG 470 Royston Rd ☎ 552 4718
AUSTIN-MG 32 Finnieston St. ☎ 248 6101
CITROEN 113 St. George Rd ☎ 332 2213
DAF, VOLVO 136 Merrylee Rd ☎ 633 0500
DAIMLER-JAGUAR-ROVER-TRIUMPH 47 Kirklee Rd ☎ 334 2231
DATSUN 77/81 Dumbarton Rd ☎ 334 1241

FIAT 691 Clarkston Rd ☎ 633 1020
FORD 1009 Gallowgate ☎ 554 4321
FORD Temple Industrial Estate, Anniesland ☎ 946 217
FORD 34 Fenwick Rd ☎ 637 7161
FORD 370 Pollokshaws Rd ☎ 423 6644
MORRIS-MG 459 Crow Rd ☎ 954 5041
OPEL 10 Holmbank Av. ☎ 649 9321
OPEL, VAUXHALL 712 Edinburgh Rd ☎ 774 2791
PEUGEOT 28 Old Mearns Rd, Clarkston ☎ 638 6505
PORSCHE Maxwell Av. at Bearsden ☎ 943 1155
RENAULT 117 Berkeley St. ☎ 248 7701
SAAB 162 Crow Rd ☎ 334 4661
TALBOT 268 Ayr Rd ☎ 639 2271
TALBOT 100 Minerva St. ☎ 248 2345
VAUXHALL 640 Pollokshaws Rd ☎ 423 3074
VOLVO 2413/2493 London Rd ☎ 778 8501
VW, AUDI-NSU 512 Kilmarnock Rd ☎ 637 2241

GLENBORRODALE Highland – ✉ Acharacle – ✆ 097 24.
Edinburgh 153 – Inverness 104 – Oban 70.

🏨 **Glenborrodale Castle** (T.H.F.) ⚘, PH36 4JP, ☎ 266, ≼ Loch Sunart and gardens,
« Victorian castle in extensive gardens », park – TV ☏ P. ⟋ AE ⓪ VISA
April-October – **M** a la carte 3.00/8.45 **st.** ◊ 1.90 – **25 rm** ☕ 15.00/28.00 **st.**

🏨 Clan Morrison ⚘, PH36 4JP, ☎ 232, ≼, ⚓, 🚣, park – ⌷wc P.
March-October – **M** (bar lunch) 3.60/9.00 **st.** ◊ 1.50 – **6 rm** ☕ 12.65/25.30 **st.**

GLENCAPLE Dumfries and Galloway – see Dumfries.

GLENCARSE Tayside – see Perth.

GLENCOE Highland 986 ⑩ – pop. 195 – ✉ Ballachulish – ☎ 085 56 Kingshouse.
Envir. : SE: Glen Coe** (glen and waterfall).
🛈 Claymore Filling Station ☏ 085 52 (Ballachulish) 296 (mid May-mid September).
Edinburgh 115 – Glasgow 86 – Oban 40.

  🏛 **King's House** ⌂, PA39 4HY, SE : 12 m. off A 82 ☏ 259, ⪦ Glencoe and Rannoch Moor, ⌐ – ⌷wc **P**. **AE**
    March-October – **22 rm.**

GLENFINNAN Highland 986 ⑩ – pop. 70 – ✉ Fort William – ☎ 039 783 Kinlocheil.
See : Glenfinnan Monument ⪦*.
🛈 ☏ 250 (mid March-mid October).
Edinburgh 149 – Inverness 80 – Kyle of Lochalsh 89 – Oban 66.

  🏛 **Glenfinnan House** ⌂, PH37 4LT, ☏ 235, ⪦ Loch Shiel and Ben Nevis, ⌐, 🛣, park – ⌷wc 🏚wc **P**
    Mid April-mid October – **M** (bar lunch) approx. 5.50 – **19 rm** ⌷ 9.00/18.00 – P 12.00/16.50.

GLENROTHES Fife 986 ⑪ – pop. 27,335 – ECD : Tuesday – ☎ 0592.
🏌 Golf Course Rd ☏ 758686.
🛈 Fife House, North St. ☏ 754411, Telex 727461.
Edinburgh 31 – Dundee 23 – Stirling 35.

  🏛🏛 **Balgeddie House** ⌂, Leslie Rd, KY6 3ET, W : 2 m. off A 911 ☏ 742511, ⪦, « Country house style », 🛣 – ⌷ **TV** ⌷wc ⊗ **P**. 🖾. 🄟 **AE** **VISA**
    closed 1 and 2 January – **M** a la carte 5.85/8.25 ⌀ 1.60 – ⌷ 2.25 – **19 rm** 8.50/20.00.

  🏛🏛 Rothes Arms (Open House), South Parks Rd, KY6 1PB, ☏ 753701 – **TV** ⌷wc ⊗ **P**
    16 rm.

  🏛 Golden Acorn (Osprey), 1 North St., KY7 5NA, ☏ 752292 – 🚿 **TV** ⌷wc 🏚wc ⊗ **P**. 🖾
    24 rm.

VW, AUDI North St. ☏ 752262

GOLSPIE Highland 986 ③ – pop. 1,374 – ECD : Wednesday – ✉ ☎ 040 83.
Edinburgh 248 – Inverness 89 – Wick 47.

  🏛 **Golf Links**, KW10 6TT, ☏ 408, ⪦, ⌐, 🛣 – ⌷wc **P**
    M (bar lunch) 6.50 **st.** ⌀ 2.00 – **10 rm** ⌷ 12.00/26.50 **st.**

GOUROCK Strathclyde 986 ⑭ – pop. 10,922 – ECD : Wednesday – ☎ 0475.
🛳 by Caledonian MacBrayne and Western Ferries : to Dunoon frequent services every day (20 mn).
🛥 to Kilcreggan (Caledonian MacBrayne) Monday/Saturday 6-7 daily (10 mn).
🛈 Municipal Buildings, PA19 1QY, ☏ 31126.
Edinburgh 69 – Ayr 43 – Glasgow 26.

  🏛🏛 Gantock (Stakis), Cloch Rd, PA19 1AR, SW : 2 m. on A 78 ☏ 34671, ⪦ Firth of Clyde – **TV** ⌷wc ⊗ **P**. 🖾. 🄝 **AE** 🄞 **VISA**
    60 rm.

  ⌂ **Claremont**, 34 Victoria Rd, PA19 1DF, ☏ 31687, ⪦
    6 rm ⌷ 5.00/10.00 **st.**

CITROEN Manor Crescent ☏ 32356

GRANGE Fife – see St. Andrews.

GRANGEMOUTH Central 986 ⑮ – pop. 24,569 – ☎ 032 44.
🏌 0324 (Polmont) 711500.
Edinburgh 24 – Dunfermline 17 – Glasgow 25.

  🏛 **Leapark**, 130 Bo'ness Rd, FK3 9BX, ☏ 6733 – **TV** ⌷wc ⊗ **P**. 🖾. 🄝 **AE** 🄞 **VISA**
    M 2.50/3.75 **s.** ⌀ 1.80 – **35 rm** ⌷ 13.00/25.00 **s.**

GRANTOWN-ON-SPEY Highland 986 ⑦ – pop. 1,600 – ECD : Thursday – ☎ 0479.
Envir. : Tomintoul (site*) SE : 13 ½ m.
🏌 ☏ 79, East town boundary.
🛈 54 High St. ☏ 2773/2650 (June-September).
Edinburgh 142 – Inverness 35 – Perth 100.

  🏛🏛 Grant Arms, 25-26 The Square, PH26 3NQ, ☏ 2526, 🛣 – 🚿 ⌷wc 🏚wc ⊗ **P**
    57 rm.

P.T.O. ⟶

⋔ **Holmhill**, Woodside Av., PH26 3JR, ☏ 2645, 🚗 – ℗
   10 rm ⊑ 7.95/15.90 **st.**

⋔ **Ravenscourt**, Seafield Av., PH26 3JR, ☏ 2286, 🚗 – ℗. 𝗩𝗜𝗦𝗔
   closed November and December – **9 rm** ⊑ 8.00/15.00.

⋔ **Dunachton**, off Grant Rd, PH26 3LD, ☏ 2098, 🚗 – ℗
   8 rm ⊑ 6.50/15.00 **st.**

GREAT CUMBRAE ISLAND Strathclyde – pop. 56 – ◉ 047 553 Millport.

🏌 at Millport ☏ 311.

🚢 from Cumbrae Slip to Largs (Caledonian MacBrayne) frequent services every day (10 mn).

🚢 from Millport (Old Pier) to Largs (Caledonian MacBrayne) frequent services every day summer only (30 mn).

🛈 Garrison House at Millport ☏ 356.

GREENOCK Strathclyde 🅱🅱🅱 ⑭ – pop. 69,502 – ECD : Wednesday – ◉ 0475.

🏌 Beith Rd ☏ 24694, S : 2 m.

🛈 Municipal Buildings, PA15 1NB, ☏ 24400.

Edinburgh 66 – Ayr 46 – Glasgow 23 – Oban 97.

🏨 **Tontine** (Best Western), 6 Ardgowan Sq., PA16 8NG, ☏ 23316, 🚗 – 📺 🛏wc 📞 ℗. ♿.
   🔉 𝗔𝗘 ⓞ 𝗩𝗜𝗦𝗔
   M 4.50/6.00 **st.** 🍷 2.40 – **44 rm** ⊑ 20.00/31.00 **st.**

DATSUN 26/30 Brougham St. ☏ 23254   VAUXHALL Pottery St. ☏ 42511
ROVER-TRIUMPH 29 Forsyth St. ☏ 20202   VOLVO 46 Campbell St. ☏ 21610
TALBOT 1 Campbell St. ☏ 24355

GRUINARD BAY *** Highland.

GULLANE Lothian 🅱🅱🅱 ⑮ – pop. 1,701 – ECD : Wednesday – ◉ 0620.

🏌, 🏌, 🏌 ☏ 843115.

Edinburgh 19 – North Berwick 5.

🏨 **Greywalls** ⌘, Duncur Rd, EH31 2EG, ☏ 842144, ≼ gardens and golf course, « Edwardian country house with fine walled gardens », ✗ – 🛏wc 📞 ℗. 🔉 𝗔𝗘 ⓞ 𝗩𝗜𝗦𝗔
   20 April-11 October – **M** 5.00/9.00 **t.** – 🍷 1.80 – **24 rm** ⊑ 25.00/50.00 **st.**

🏠 Bissets, Main St., EH31 2AA, ☏ 842230, 🚗 – 📞 ℗
   24 rm.

HADDINGTON Lothian 🅱🅱🅱 ⑮ – pop. 6,502 – ECD : Thursday – ◉ 062 082.

🏌 Amisfield Park ☏ 3627.

Edinburgh 17 – Hawick 53 – Newcastle-upon-Tyne 103.

⋔ **Browns**, 1 West Rd, ☏ 2254 – 🛏wc ℗. 🔉 𝗔𝗘
   closed last 2 weeks October – **7 rm** ⊑ 8.40/18.00 **s.**

AUSTIN-MORRIS-MG-ROVER-TRIUMPH 46 High St.   TALBOT Knox Pl. ☏ 3277
☏ 3661

HALBEATH Fife – pop. 770 – ✉ ◉ 0383 Dunfermline.

Edinburgh 17 – Dunfermline 3 – Kirkcaldy 10 – Perth 26.

✗ Armando's Hide Away, Kingseat Rd, KY12 0UB, N : ½ m. off A 907, ☏ 25474 – ℗.

HARDGATE Strathclyde – pop. 3,729 – ECD : Wednesday – ✉ Clydebank – ◉ 0389 Duntocher.

Edinburgh 51 – Dumbarton 7 – Glasgow 8.

🏨 **Cameron House**, Glasgow Rd, G81 5PJ, ☏ 73535 – 🛗 📺 🛏wc 🛏wc 📞 ℗. ♿
   M 2.70/5.20 **st.** 🍷 2.20 – **17 rm** ⊑ 15.00/20.00 **st.**

HARRIS (Isle of) Outer Hebrides (Western Isles) 🅱🅱🅱 ② – pop. 2,879.

🚢 by Caledonian MacBrayne : from Kyles Scalpay to the Isle of Scalpay : Monday/Saturday 4-8 daily (10 mn) – from Tarbert to Uig (Isle of Skye) Monday/Saturday 3-6 weekly (2 h direct) via Lochmaddy (May-October) 2-3 weekly – from Tarbert to Lochmaddy (Isle of Uist) May-October : 6 weekly (2 h direct).

Tarbert – pop. 479 – ECD : Thursday – ✉ ◉ 0859 Harris.

🛈 Information Centre ☏ 2011 (May-September).

See : Site*. **Envir. :** Loch Seaforth* NE : 6 m. **Exc. :** Golden Road* from Tarbert to Rode – Rodel (site*) S : 21 ½ m.

🏠 **Harris**, PA85 3DL, ☏ 2154, ⌘, 🚗 – 🛏wc ℗
   closed December and February – **M** 3.50/5.00 **st.** – ⊑ 1.70 – **22 rm** 8.00/18.50 **st.**

HAWICK Borders 986 ⑮ – pop. 16,286 – ECD : Tuesday – ✪ 0450.
Envir. : Jedburgh Abbey★★ *AC*, NE : 10 ½ m. – Hermitage (castle★ : stronghold 14C) *AC*, S : 15 m.
🏌 Vertish Hill 🖅 2293, S : 1 ½ m.
🛈 Common Haugh, Car Park 🖅 2547 (mid May-September).
Edinburgh 50 – Ayr 123 – Carlisle 43 – Dumfries 63 – Motherwell 74 – Newcastle-upon-Tyne 62.

🏰 **Mansfield House**, Weensland Rd, TD9 9EL, NE : 1 m. on A 698 🖅 3988, 🛋, park –
📺 ⊟wc 🕮wc 🕭 🅿. 🄰 AE VISA
closed 24 December-15 January – **M** 4.15/7.25 🍷 2.50 – **9 rm** � 16.75/27.50.

🏠 Crown (Osprey), 22 High St., TD9 9EH, 🖅 3344 – ⊟wc 🅿. 🄲 – **32 rm.**

✕ **Kirklands** 🐾 with rm, West Stewart Pl., TD9 8BH, N : off A 7 🖅 2263 – 📺 ⊟wc 🕮wc
🕭 🅿
closed Christmas – **M** *(closed Saturday lunch and Sunday to non-residents)* a la carte
3.20/5.70 🍷 1.95 – **6 rm** ⊟ 11.50/19.60 **t.**

AUSTIN-MORRIS-MG-ROVER-TRIUMPH Earl St. 🖅 | TALBOT 61 High St. 🖅 2287
3316 | VAUXHALL Bridge St. 🖅 2179
FIAT, VOLVO Croft Rd 🖅 3881 | VW, AUDI Weensland Rd 🖅 3211
FORD Commercial Rd 🖅 2285

HELENSBURGH Strathclyde 986 ⑭ – pop. 12,870 – ECD : Wednesday – ✪ 0436.
Envir. : Loch Lomond★★ NE : 7 ½ m.
🛈 Pier Head Car Park, 🖅 2642 (May-September).
Edinburgh 65 – Glasgow 22.

🏰 Queen's, 114 East Clyde St., G84 7AH, 🖅 3404, ≼ – ⊟wc 🅿 – **24 rm.**

at Rhu NW : 2 m. on A 814 – ⊠ ✪ 043 682 Rhu :

🏠 **Rosslea Hall** 🐾, 🖅 684, ≼, 🛋 – 📺 ⊟wc 🕮wc 🕭 🅿. 🄰 AE ⓞ VISA
closed January – **M** 4.95/6.95 **t.** 🍷 2.50 – **10 rm** ⊟ 17.25/27.60 **st.**

AUSTIN-JAGUAR-MORRIS-MG-ROVER-TRIUMPH | RENAULT 103 East Clyde St. 🖅 6021
135 East Clyde St. 🖅 3344 | TOYOTA 5/7 John St. 🖅 2779
DATSUN 15/27 East Clyde St. 🖅 2233

HILLSWICK Shetland Islands 986 ⑯ – see Shetland Islands (Mainland).

HOLLYBUSH Strathclyde – see Ayr.

HOWGATE Lothian – ⊠ ✪ 0968 Penicuik.
Edinburgh 11 – Peebles 11.

✕ Old Howgate Inn, 7 Wester Howgate, EH26 8QB, 🖅 74244, Smörrebrod – 🅿.

HOY (Isle of) Orkney Islands 986 ⑯ – see Orkney Islands.

INCHNADAMPH Highland 986 ② – ⊠ Lairg – ✪ 057 12 Assynt.
See : ≼★.
Edinburgh 244 – Inverness 85.

🏠 **Inchnadamph** 🐾, IV27 4HL, 🖅 202, ≼ Loch Assynt and mountains, 🐾 – ⊟wc 🅿. ⓞ
March-October – **M** 3.30/4.60 🍷 1.75 – **30 rm** ⊟ 10.00/22.00.

INCHTURE Tayside – pop. 120 – ✪ 082 886.
Edinburgh 55 – Dundee 9 – Perth 13.

✕✕ Maison Bonne Chère (Inchture Hotel), PH14 9RN, 🖅 203 – 🅿.

TALBOT 🖅 401

INVERGARRY Highland 986 ⑥ – pop. 178 – ✪ 080 93.
Envir. : Loch Garry (❋★★ from the A 87) W : 3 m.
Edinburgh 148 – Inverness 41 – Kyle of Lochalsh 51 – Oban 73.

INVERMORISTON Highland 986 ⑥⑦ – pop. 114 – ✪ 0320 Glenmoriston.
See : Loch Ness★★.
Edinburgh 162 – Inverness 27 – Kyle of Lochalsh 55.

🏨 **Glenmoriston Arms**, IV3 6YA, 🖅 51206, Telex 75529, 🐾 – ⊟wc 🅿. 🄰 VISA
M (bar lunch) a la carte 5.00/9.40 **st.** 🍷 1.80 – **6 rm** ⊟ 9.50/21.00 **st.**

INVERNESS Highland 986 ⑦ – pop. 34,839 – ECD : Wednesday – ✪ 0463.
See : Tomnahurich cemetery★ – ≼★ from the Castle Terrace. **Envir. :** Culloden Battlefield, site of
the defeat (1746) of Bonnie Prince Charlie, E : 5 m. by Culcabock Rd.
🏌 🖅 33422, S : 1 m. by Culcabock Rd.
🛬 Dalcross Airport : 🖅 32471, NE : 8 m. by A 96. – 🚗 🖅 32651.
🛈 23 Church St. 🖅 34353, Telex 75114.
Edinburgh 159 – Aberdeen 106 – Dundee 130.

🏨 **Inverness Ladbroke Mercury Motor Inn**, Nairn Rd, IV2 3TR, E: by A 96, junction A 9 and A 96 ℡ 39666, Telex 75377 – 📶 TV 🛏 wc 📞 **P.** 🏊 **84 rm.**

🏨 **Kingsmills** (Best Western), Culcabock Rd, IV2 3LP, ℡ 37166, ≼, 🚗 – TV 🛏 wc 📞 **P.** 🅰 AE ⓪ VISA **s**
M (bar lunch) approx. 6.50 t. 🍷 2.50 – **46 rm** 🛏 22.50/44.00 t.

🏨 **Queensgate**, Queensgate, IV1 1HA, ℡ 37211, Telex 75235, ⚲ – 📶 TV 🛏 wc 📞. 🅰 AE ⓪ **n**
M (dinner only) 5.50 st. 🍷 2.50 – **54 rm** 🛏 18.50/28.10 st.

🏨 **Caledonian**, Church St., IV1 1DX, ℡ 35181 – 📶 TV 🛏 wc 📞 **P.** 🏊 🅰 AE ⓪ VISA **e**
M 5.00/6.00 st. – **120 rm** 🛏 19.00/36.00 st.

🏨 **Royal** (T.H.F.), Academy St., IV1 1JR, ℡ 30665 – 📶 TV 🛏 wc 📞. 🏊 🅰 AE ⓪ VISA **c**
M 3.75/4.85 st. 🍷 1.65 – **48 rm** 🛏 13.50/24.50 st.

🏨 **Glen Mhor**, 9-12 Ness Bank, IV2 4SG, ℡ 34308 – 🛏 wc 📞 **P.** 🅰 AE ⓪ VISA **i**
closed 30 December-3 January – M 5.00/7.50 t. 🍷 2.00 – 🛏 2.00 – **30 rm** 10.30/25.00 t.

🏨 **Cumming's**, 70 Church St., TV1 1EW, ℡ 32531 – 📶 🛏 wc **P** **r**
M 3.75/5.75 st. 🍷 1.80 – **38 rm** 🛏 12.00/27.00 st.

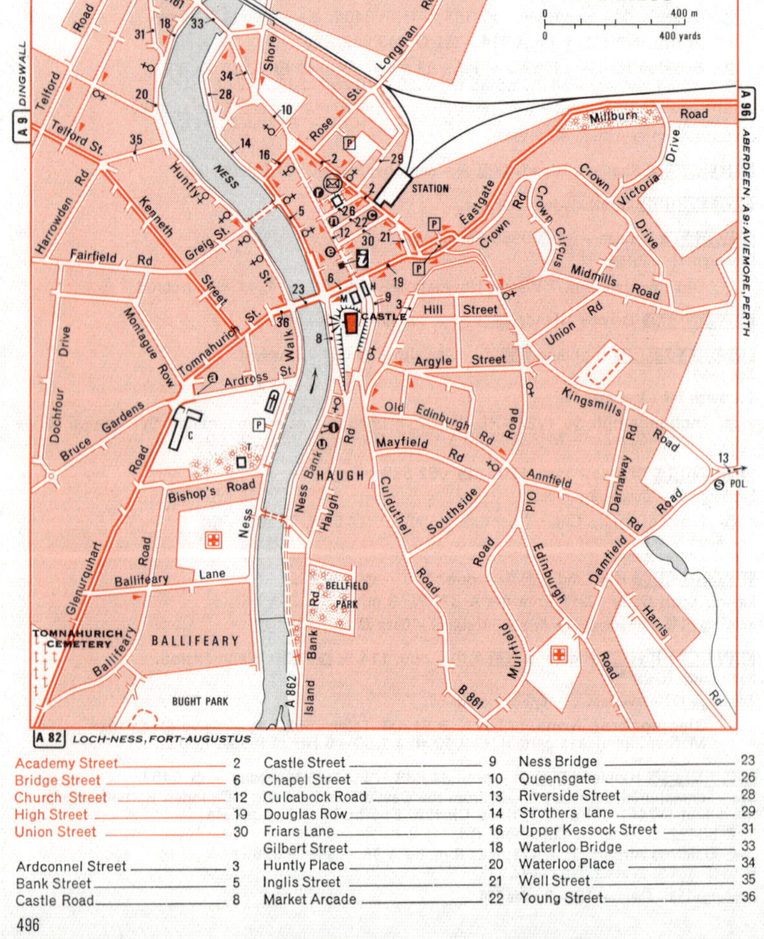

⋔ **Felstead,** 18 Ness Bank, IV2 4SF, ℡ 31634 – Ⓟ   u
May-September – **7 rm** ⌑ 6.00/12.00 **st.**

⋔ **Larchfield,** 14-15 Ness Bank, IV2 4SF, ℡ 33874, ≼ – 𝘝𝘐𝘚𝘈   i
15 rm ⌑ 6.50/13.00.

⋔ **Glencairn,** 19 Ardross St., ℡ 32965 – 🄰 AE ⓪ 𝘝𝘐𝘚𝘈   a
closed mid December-mid January – **10 rm** ⌑ 5.00/10.00 **t.**

at Culloden Moor E: 3 m. off A 96 – ✉ Inverness – ☎ 046 372 Culloden Moor:

🏰 **Culloden House** ⅍, IV1 2NZ, ℡ 461, Telex 75402, ≼, « Elegant installation », 🚗, park – TV Ⓟ. 🄰 AE ⓪ 𝘝𝘐𝘚𝘈
M a la carte 9.50/13.25 ⌗ 2.25 – **21 rm** ⌑ 35.00/50.00.

at Dunain Park SW: 2 ½ m. on A 82 – ✉ ☎ 0463 Inverness:

🏨 **Dunain Park** ⅍, IV3 6JN, ℡ 30512, ≼, « Country house and gardens », park – 🛏wc
Ⓟ
Mid March-mid November – **M** (bar lunch) approx. 10.75 **st.** ⌗ 2.00 – **6 rm** ⌑ 36.70/43.00 **st.**

ALFA-ROMEO VAUXHALL Academy St. ℡ 34311
AUSTIN-MORRIS-MG, BENTLEY, ROLLS ROYCE 36 Academy St. ℡ 34422
BMW Harbour Rd ℡ 36566
DAIMLER-JAGUAR-ROVER-TRIUMPH Strothers Lane ℡ 33701
DATSUN Harbour Rd ℡ 22284

FIAT 8 Tomnahurich St. ℡ 35777
FORD Harbour Rd ℡ 38001
PEUGEOT Harbour Rd ℡ 31536
RENAULT 16 Telford St. ℡ 34367
TALBOT Harbour Rd ℡ 30777
VOLVO Harbour Rd ℡ 30885
VW, AUDI-NSU Harbour Rd ℡ 31313

IONA (Isle of) Strathclyde 𝟿𝟪𝟨 ⑩ – ☎ 068 17.
See: Site* – MacLean's Cross* – St. John's Cross*.

🚢 by Caledonian MacBrayne: to Fionnphort (Isle of Mull) frequent services every day except Sunday in winter (10 mn) – to Oban: summer only 1-2 weekly.

ISLAY (Isle of) Strathclyde 𝟿𝟪𝟨 ⑭ – pop. 3,837.
See: Machir Bay*.
🏌ₗ₈ Port Ellen, ℡ 0496 (Port Ellen) 2310.
✈ Port Ellen Airport: ℡ 0496 (Port Ellen) 2361.
🚢 by Western Ferries: from Port Askaig to Feolin (Isle of Jura) 3-8 daily (5 mn) – from Port Askaig to Kennacraig (Kintyre Peninsula) 1-2 daily (3 h) – by Caledonian MacBrayne: from Port Ellen to Kennacraig Isle of Gigha (2 h to 2 h 30 mn).
🛈 at Bowmore ℡ 049 681 (Bowmore) 254 (April-September).

Bowmore – 947 – ✉ ☎ 049 681 Bowmore.

🛎 **Lochside,** Shore St., PA43 7LB, ℡ 244, ≼, 🍴 – 🛏wc
M (bar lunch) a la carte 6.10/8.50 **st.** ⌗ 1.60 – **7 rm** ⌑ 12.25/28.25 **st.**

⋔ **Bowmore,** Jamieson St., PA43 7HL, ℡ 218
8 rm ⌑ 12.00/24.00 **st.**

Bridgend – ✉ Bridgend – ☎ 049 681 Bowmore.

🛎 **Bridgend,** PA44 7PJ, ℡ 212, 🚗 – Ⓟ
M (bar lunch) 6.00/7.50 **t.** ⌗ 2.50 – **9 rm** ⌑ 10.00/20.00 **st.**

Kildalton NE: 5 m. of Port Ellen – ✉ Port Ellen – ☎ 049 683 Kildalton.

🏨 **Dower House** ⅍, PA42 7EF, ℡ 225, ≼, 🚗 – 🛏wc Ⓟ
M 5.15/7.50 **st.** – **5 rm** ⌑ 8.40/15.60 **st.**

Port Askaig – ECD: Tuesday – ✉ ☎ 049 684 Port Askaig.

🛎 **Port Askaig,** PA46 7RD, ℡ 245, 🚗 – 🛏wc 🚻wc 🚙 Ⓟ
M 4.00/6.00 **st.** – **9 rm** ⌑ 12.00/22.00 **st.**

ISLEORNSAY Highland – see Skye (Isle of).

JOHN O'GROATS Highland 𝟿𝟪𝟨 ③ and ⑳ – pop. 195 – ☎ 095 581.
See: ≼* of Orkney. **Envir.:** Dunnet Head*** (sea bird's nests) NW: 16 m. – Dunnet Bay** W: 11 m. – Duncansby Head (cliffs: birds' nests*) E: 2 ½ m. – Skirza Head (cliffs: birds' nests*) S: 5 m.
🛈 Information Centre, ℡ 373 (May-September).
Edinburgh 299 – Wick 17.

🏨 John O'Groats House ⅍, KW1 4YR, ℡ 203, ≼ – 🚻 Ⓟ
17 rm.

JURA (Isle of) Strathclyde 986 ⑩⑭ – pop. 349.
🚢 from Feolin to Port Askaig (Islay) (Western Ferries) 3-8 daily (5 mn).

Craighouse – ECD: Tuesday – ✉ ◎ 049 682 Jura.
🏠 Jura ⬩, PA60 7XU, ☎ 243, ⪕ Small Isles Bay, ⬩, 🚲 – 🛁wc 🅿 – **18 rm.**

KELSO Borders 986 ⑮ – pop. 4,852 – ECD: Wednesday – ◎ 057 32.
Envir.: Jedburgh Abbey** *AC*, SW: 11 m.
🏌⁹ ☎ 2113.
ℹ Turret House, ☎ 3464 (mid May-September).
Edinburgh 44 – Hawick 22 – Newcastle-upon-Tyne 67.

🏨 **Cross Keys,** 36-37 The Square, TD5 7HL, ☎ 3303 – 🛗 📺 🛁wc 🚿wc ☎ 🅿. 💆. 🔽 AE
① *VISA*
M 3.75/4.90 **t.** 🍷 2.35 – **20 rm** ☲ 14.40/26.80 **t.** – P 20.00/23.00 **t.**
🏨 **Ednam House,** Bridge St., TD5 7HT, ☎ 2168, ⪕, 🚲 – 🛁wc ☎ 🅿. 💆
M 3.00/5.20 **t.** 🍷 1.15 – **32 rm** ☲ 9.95/13.00 **t.** – P 15.50/18.50 **t.**
🏨 **Woodside** ⬩, Edenside Rd, TD5 7SJ, ☎ 2152, ⪕, 🚲, park – 📺 🛁wc 🚿wc ☎ 🅿.
AE ① *VISA*
M (dinner only) 7.50 **st.** 🍷 2.00 – **11 rm** ☲ 18.50/25.00 **st.**

AUSTIN-MG Crawford St. ☎ 2720 TALBOT 47/51 Horsemarket ☎ 2488
AUSTIN-JAGUAR-MORRIS-MG-ROVER-TRIUMPH
Bridge St. ☎ 2345

KENMORE Tayside – pop. 211 – ECD: Thursday – ✉ Aberfeldy – ◎ 088 73.
See: Loch Tay*.
🏌¹⁸ Taymouth Castle ☎ 228.
Edinburgh 80 – Dundee 60 – Oban 71 – Perth 38.

🏨 Kenmore, PH15 2NU, ☎ 205, 🏌¹⁸, ⬩, 🚲 – 🛗 🛁wc ☎ 🅿. 🔽
42 rm.

at *Lawers* SW: 8 m. on A 827 – ✉ Aberfeldy – ◎ 056 72 Killin:
🏠 **Ben Lawers,** PH15 2PA, on A 827 ☎ 436, ⪕, ⬩, 🚲 – 🅿
Easter-October – **7 rm** ☲ 7.50/15.00 **t.**

at *Fortingall* NW: 6 m. off A 827 – ✉ Aberfeldy – ◎ 088 73 Kenmore:
🏠 **Fortingall** ⬩, PH15 2NQ, ☎ 367, ⪕, ⬩, 🚲 – 🛁wc 🅿. 🔽 AE *VISA*
Easter-October – **M** (bar lunch) approx. 8.25 **st.** 🍷 2.50 – **21 rm** ☲ 10.00/24.00 **st.**

KENNACRAIG Strathclyde – Shipping Services: see Kintyre (Peninsula).

KENTALLEN OF APPIN Highland – ✉ Kentallen of Appin – ◎ 063 174 Duror.
Edinburgh 123 – Fort William 34 – Oban 30.

🏠 **Ardsheal House** ⬩, PA38 4BX, SW: ¾ m. off A 828 ☎ 227, ⪕, « Country house in lochside setting », 🏓, 🚲, park – 🛁wc 🅿
Easter-mid October – **M** (bar lunch) 4.00/8.50 🍷 3.00 – **11 rm** ☲ 10.50/24.00 – P 17.00/21.00.

KILCHOAN Highland – pop. 349 – ✉ Acharacle – ◎ 097 23.
Edinburgh 163 – Inverness 114 – Oban 80.

🏠 **Kilchoan** ⬩, PH36 4LH, ☎ 200, ⪕ sea and Isle of Mull, ⬩, 🚲 – 📺 🛁wc ☎ 🅿
M (bar lunch) 2.20/6.00 🍷 1.25 – **7 rm** ☲ 10.00/23.00 **s.**
🏠 **Sonachan** ⬩, PH36 4LN, NW: 3 m. on B 8007 ☎ 211, ⪕ – 🛁wc 🚿 🅿
Easter-October – **M** (bar lunch) approx. 6.50 **st.** 🍷 2.00 – **8 rm** ☲ 12.00/18.50 **s.**

KILCHRENAN Strathclyde – pop. 109 – ECD: Wednesday – ✉ Taynuilt – ◎ 086 63.
See: Loch Awe*.
Edinburgh 116 – Glasgow 88 – Oban 19.

🏨 **Taychreggan** ⬩, Lochaweside, PA35 1HQ, SE: 1 ¼ m. ☎ 211, ⪕ Loch Awe, « Extensive grounds on banks of Loch Awe », ⬩, 🚲, park – 🛁wc 🅿. 🔽 AE ① *VISA*
April-mid October – **M** (buffet lunch) 3.45/6.90 **t.** 🍷 2.45 – **22 rm** ☲ 14.50/32.00 **t.** – P 19.50 **t.**

KILCREGGAN Strathclyde – 1,343 – ✉ Helensburgh – ◎ 043 684.
🚢 to Gourock (Caledonian MacBrayne) Monday/Saturday 6-7 daily (10 mn).
Edinburgh 80 – Glasgow 37 – Helensburgh 15.

🏠 **Kilcreggan** ⬩, Argyle Rd, G84 0JP, ☎ 2243, ⪕, 🚲 – 🛁wc 🚿wc 🅿. 🔽 *VISA*
closed 1 and 2 January – **M** (bar lunch) 4.00/6.00 **st.** 🍷 2.00 – **8 rm** ☲ 11.50/23.00 **st.**

KILDALTON Strathclyde – see Islay (Isle of).

KILLIN Central 986 ⑪ – pop. 600 – ECD : Wednesday – ☎ 056 72.
See : Loch Tay*. Envir. : N : Glen Lyon*.
☇ 𝒯 312.
🛈 Main St. 𝒯 254 (May-September).
Edinburgh 72 – Dundee 65 – Perth 43 – Oban 54.

🏛 **Killin** (Best Western), Main St., FK21 8TP, N : on A 827 𝒯 296, ≼, ⚲, 🚗 – 🛗 🛏wc
🅿. ⚑ AE VISA
M (bar lunch) 3.00/5.25 t. ⚱ 1.85 – **30 rm** ⊆ 8.25/20.35 t. – P 13.60 t.

🏛 Bridge of Lochay, FK21 8TS, N : ½ m. on A 827 𝒯 272, ⚲ – 🛏wc 🅿
Easter-October – **18 rm** ⊆ 8.55/11.30 st. – P 17.00 **st.**

🏠 **Dall Lodge,** FK21 8TN, N : ¼ m. on A 827 𝒯 217, ⚲ – 🅿. VISA
March-October – **10 rm** ⊆ 7.00/14.00 st.

  at Ardeonaig NE : 7 ¼ m. – ✉ ☎ 056 72 Killin :

🏛 **Ardeonaig** ⚜, South Loch Tayside 𝒯 400, ⚲, park – 🛏wc 🛁wc 🅿
Mid January-October – **M** (bar lunch) approx. 7.50 ⚱ 1.90 – **18 rm** ⊆ 9.75/11.00.

AUSTIN-MORRIS 𝒯 319

KILMARNOCK Strathclyde 986 ⑭ ⑮ – pop. 48,787 – ECD : Wednesday – ☎ 0563.
☈ Irvine Rd 𝒯 21644, W : 1 m. – ☈ Caprington, Ayr Rd 𝒯 21915.
Edinburgh 64 – Ayr 14 – Dumfries 58 – Glasgow 21.

🏛🏛 Howard Park (Swallow), 136 Glasgow Rd, KA3 1UT, N : 2 m. on A 77 𝒯 31211, Group
Telex 53168 – 🛗 TV 🛏wc ☎ 🅿. ⚑
50 rm.

KILMARTIN Strathclyde – pop. 327 – ✉ Lochgilphead – ☎ 054 65.
Edinburgh 134 – Glasgow 91 – Oban 29.

✖ Cairn, PA31 8RQ, on A 816 𝒯 254 – 🅿.

KILMORY Strathclyde – see Arran (Isle of).

KINCLAVEN Tayside – pop. 560 – ✉ Stanley – ☎ 025 083 Meikleour.
Edinburgh 54 – Perth 12.

🏛🏛 **Ballathie House** ⚜, PH1 4QN, 𝒯 268, ≼, « Country house in extensive grounds on
banks of river Tay », ✖, ⚲, 🚗, park – TV 🛏wc ☎ 🅿. ⚑ AE
closed December-mid January – **M** 4.00/8.00 t. ⚱ 1.85 – **38 rm** ⊆ 21.00/38.00 **t.**

KINCRAIG Highland – pop. 106 – ECD : Wednesday – ✉ Kingussie – ☎ 054 04.
Edinburgh 121 – Inverness 38 – Perth 79.

♨ **Ossian,** PH21 1NA, off A 9 𝒯 242, ≼, 🚗 – 🅿
closed January – **M** (dinner only) a la carte 4.35/6.95 ⚱ 2.10 – **9 rm** ⊆ 9.50/19.00 **st.**

✖✖ **Invereshie House** ⚜ with rm, PH21 1NA, E : ½ m. off A 9 𝒯 332, ⚲ – 🅿
Easter-October – **M** *(closed lunch to non-residents)* a la carte 6.70/10.50 t. ⚱ 1.70 –
6 rm ⊆ 15.00/30.00 **s.** – P 25.00/28.00 **s.**

KINGHOLM QUAY Dumfries and Galloway – see Dumfries.

KINGSKETTLE Fife. (Fife) – pop. 763 – ☎ 0337 Ladybank.
Edinburgh 46 – Dundee 18 – Kirkcaldy 10.

🏛 **Annfield House** ⚜, KY7 7TW, 𝒯 30245, ≼ countryside, « Country house style », 🚗 –
🛏wc 🅿. ⚑
M *(closed Sunday dinner)* 4.00/6.50 st. ⚱ 1.60 – **9 rm** ⊆ 13.75/25.00 st.

KINGUSSIE Highland 986 ⑦ – pop. 1,104 – ECD : Wednesday – ☎ 054 02.
☈ 𝒯 374, ½ m. from town shops off A 9.
🛈 King St. 𝒯 297 (June-September).
Edinburgh 115 – Inverness 44 – Perth 73.

♨ **Osprey,** PH21 1EN, 𝒯 510 – 🅿. ⚑ AE VISA
closed 24 October-23 December – **M** (dinner only) 6.00 st. ⚱ 1.75 – **9 rm** ⊆ 8.00/
16.00 **st.**

KINLOCHBERVIE Highland – pop. 450 – ECD : Wednesday – ☎ 097 182.
See : Site*.
Edinburgh 282 – Thurso 101 – Ullapool 64.

🏛 **Kinlochbervie** ⚜, IV27 4RP, 𝒯 275, ≼ Loch Inchard and sea, ⚲ – TV 🛏wc ☎ 🅿
closed Christmas Day and 1 January – **M** (bar lunch) 2.00/6.50 ⚱ 2.00 – **10 rm** ⊆ 13.00/
26.00 **s.** – P 21.50 **s.**

KINLOCH RANNOCH Tayside 𝟵𝟴𝟲 ⑪ − pop. 241 − ECD : Wednesday except Summer − ☎ 088 22.

See : Loch★★.

Edinburgh 88 − Inverness 92 − Perth 46.

  🏨 **Dunalastair**, PH15 5PW, ☎ 323, ⚲, 🚗 − 📺 ⛱wc ♿ ⟷ 🅿. ⬛ 🄰🄴 ⓪ 𝘝𝘐𝘚𝘈
     M 2.95/4.95 **st.** ⬗ 1.45 − **23 rm** ⬜ 9.95/24.90 **st.**

KINROSS Tayside 𝟵𝟴𝟲 ⑪ − pop. 2,418 − ECD : Thursday − ☎ 0577.

See : Loch Leven★.

🏌 Beeches Park ☎ 63467.

Edinburgh 25 − Dunfermline 12 − Perth 17 − Stirling 23.

  🏨 **Green** (Best Western), 2 The Muirs, KY13 7AS, ☎ 63467, « Gardens », ⬛, 🏌, ⚲ −
    📺 ⛱wc 🄼wc ☏ 🅿. ⚙. ⬛ 🄰🄴 𝘝𝘐𝘚𝘈
    M (bar lunch) approx. 6.00 **st.** ⬗ 1.50 − **50 rm** ⬜ 17.75/34.00 **st.**

  XX **Windlestrae** with rm, The Muirs, KY13 7AS, ☎ 63217, Telex 76168, 🚗 − 📺 ⛱wc ☏
    🅿. ⬛ 🄰🄴 ⓪ 𝘝𝘐𝘚𝘈
    closed January and first week October − **M** *(closed Tuesday)* a la carte 6.35/9.90 **s.** −
    4 rm ⬜ 17.00/24.00 **s.**

    at Cleish SW : 4 ½ m. by B 996 and B 9097 − ✉ Kinross − ☎ 057 75 Cleish Hills :

  XX **Nivingston House** ⚲ with rm, KY13 7LS, ☎ 216, ≼, 🚗 − 🅿. 🄰🄴 𝘝𝘐𝘚𝘈
    closed Monday and first 2 weeks October − **M** 6.40/10.20 ⬗ 2.80 − **3 rm** ⬜ 10.00/20.00.

AUSTIN, FORD High St. ☎ 62424   MAZDA 10/14 High St. ☎ 62244
DATSUN South St., Milnathort ☎ 62453

KINTYRE (Peninsula) Strathclyde 𝟵𝟴𝟲 ⑭ − pop. 6,051.

🚢 by Caledonian MacBrayne : from Claonaig to Lochranza (Isle of Arran) Easter-October
6-8 daily (30 mn) − from Kennacraig to Port Ellen (Islay) 1-3 daily (2 h to 2 h 30 mn) −
from Kennacraig to Isle of Gigha : 1 daily (1 h 15 mn) − by Western Ferries : from Kennacraig
to Port Askaig (Islay) 1-2 daily (3 h).

  Bellochantuy − ✉ Bellochantuy − ☎ 058 32 Glenbarr.

  🏨 **Putechan Lodge**, PA28 6QE, on A 83 ☎ 266, ≼, « Converted hunting lodge » −
    ⛱wc 🅿. 🄰🄴
    closed 2 January-1 February − **M** a la carte 5.20/7.70 ⬗ 2.00 − **9 rm** ⬜ 12.00/20.00.

  Campbeltown − pop. 5,960 − ECD : Wednesday − ✉ ☎ 0586 Campbeltown.

  See : Site★. Envir. : Machrihanish Bay★ W : 6 m. − Black Bay★ NE : 5 m. − Ugadale Bay★
  NE : 7 m. − Saddell Bay★ NE : 8 m.

  🏌 Machrihanish ☎ 213, W : 5 m.

  ✈ ☎ 2056, Telex 778868.

  Edinburgh 117 − Glasgow 134 − Oban 87.

  🏨 **Ardshiel**, Kilkerran Rd, PA28 6JL, ☎ 2133, 🚗 − 🅿. ⬛ 𝘝𝘐𝘚𝘈
    closed 1 week February and 2 weeks October − **M** 2.80/4.75 **st.** − **11 rm** ⬜ 10.25/
    20.50 **st.**

PEUGEOT Bolgam St. ☎ 2030   VAUXHALL County Garage ☎ 2235

  Carradale − pop. 262 − ECD : Wednesday − ✉ ☎ 058 33 Carradale − 🏌.

  See : Site★, ≼★ over Kilbrannan Sound★★, harbour★, Carradale Bay★.

  Edinburgh 164 − Glasgow 121 − Oban 74.

  🏨 **Carradale**, PA28 6RY, ☎ 223, ≼, 🚗 − 🄼wc 🅿
    March-October − **M** 3.50/5.50 **t.** ⬗ 1.75 − **22 rm** ⬜ 9.50/21.00 **t.** − P 11.00/13.00 **t.**

  Tarbert − pop. 1,391 − ECD : Wednesday− ✉ ☎ 088 02 Tarbert.

  See: West Loch Tarbert★.

  🏌 W : 1 m.

  ✈ ☎ 429 (April-September).

  Edinburgh 139 − Glasgow 96 − Oban 49.

  🏰 **Stonefield Castle** ⚲, PA29 6YJ, N : 2 m. on A 83 ☎ 207, ≼ Loch Fyne and gardens
    « Extensive gardens on the banks of Loch Fyne », ⚒, ⧖ heated, ⚲, park − ⬧ 🅿. ⬛ 🄰🄴
    ⓪ 𝘝𝘐𝘚𝘈
    Easter-October − **M** (bar lunch) approx. 10.80 ⬗ 1.90 − **34 rm** ⬜ 20.00/27.00 **t.**

  🏩 **West Loch**, West Tarbert, PA29 6YS, ☎ 283, ≼ − 🅿
    closed first 3 weeks November − **M** (bar lunch) 8.00 **t.** ⬗ 2.00 − **6 rm** ⬜ 14.00/20.00 **t.** −
    P 18.00 **t.**

  🏚 **Columba**, Pier Rd, PA29 6UL, ☎ 241 − 🅿
    11 rm ⬜ 7.00/14.00.

KIRKCALDY Fife 𝟵𝟴𝟲 ⑪ – pop. 50,360 – ECD: Wednesday – ✆ 0592.
ⓘ₁₈ Balwearie ☏ 60370 – ⓘ₁₈ Dunnikier Way ☏ 61599, North boundary – ⓘ₉ Cardenden ☏ 720575.
N: 5 m.
🛈 Esplanade ☏ 67775 (Easter-September).

Edinburgh 26 – Dundee 28 – Glasgow 52.

🏨 Royal Albert (Stakis), 18 West Albert Rd, KY1 1DL, ☏ 65627 – 📺 ⌨wc ☎ Ⓟ. 🛗
21 rm.

🏨 Station (Osprey), 4 Bennochy Rd, KY1 1YQ, ☏ 62461 – ⌨wc 🚿wc ☎. 🛗 – **35 rm.**

AUSTIN-MORRIS-MG-ROVER-TRIUMPH 39 Rosslyn St. ☏ 51997
AUSTIN-DAIMLER-JAGUAR-MORRIS-MG-ROVER-TRIUMPH Forth Av. ☏ 3703
DATSUN Meldrum Rd ☏ 61353
FORD Dunnikier Way ☏ 52771
OPEL 9 Park Rd ☏ 51932
RENAULT 15 Esplanade ☏ 3123
SAAB 180186 St. Clair St. ☏ 52291
TALBOT Bennochy Rd ☏ 62191
VAUXHALL, CITROEN 24 Victoria Rd ☏ 4755
VOLVO Wemyssfield ☏ 62141

KIRKCUDBRIGHT Dumfries and Galloway 𝟵𝟴𝟲 ⑲ – pop. 2,502 – ECD: Thursday – ✆ 0557 – ⓘ₁₈.
🛈 Harbour Sq. ☏ 30494 (April-September).

Edinburgh 105 – Dumfries 28 – Stranraer 52.

🏨 **Selkirk Arms,** Old High St., DG6 4JG, ☏ 30402, ◪, 🍴 – ⌨wc Ⓟ. 🛗
M (bar lunch) 3.00/5.30 t. ⓘ 1.50 – **27 rm** ⌑ 9.60/23.00 st.

🏨 **Royal,** St. Cuthbert St., DG6 4DY, ☏ 30551 – ⌨wc 🚿wc
M 3.00/5.50 t. ⓘ 1.90 – ⌑ 1.75 – **17 rm** 8.50/16.00 t. – P 16.50/18.50 t.

XX **Ingle,** St. Mary St., DG6 4EQ, ☏ 30606, Italian rest. – ⒶⒺ ⓪
closed Monday from September to June – M (dinner only from September to Easter) a la carte 4.90/9.00 st. ⓘ 2.15.

AUSTIN-MORRIS-MG-ROVER-TRIUMPH Mews Lane ☏ 30 412   DAF Tongland Rd ☏ 30696

KIRKMICHAEL Tayside – pop. 100 – ✉ Blairgowrie – ✆ 025 081 Strathardle.
Envir.: E: Glenshee (❄** by chairlift 15 mn, AC).
Edinburgh 70 – Perth 28 – Pitlochry 12.

🏨 **Log Cabin** ⏳, PH10 7NB, SW: 1 m. ☏ 288, ≤, 🍴, ⌑ heated, ◪ – ⌨wc Ⓟ
M (bar lunch) 3.75/6.00 t. ⓘ 1.75 – **12 rm** ⌑ 12.00/28.00 t. – P 20.00/26.50 t.

KIRKWALL Orkney Islands 𝟵𝟴𝟲 ⑯ – see Orkney Islands (Mainland).

KIRN Strathclyde – see Dunoon.

KYLEAKIN Highland 𝟵𝟴𝟲 ⑥ – Shipping Services: see Skye (Isle of).

KYLE OF LOCHALSH Highland 𝟵𝟴𝟲 ⑥ – pop. 687 – ECD: Wednesday – ✆ 0599.
See: Loch*.
⛴ by Caledonian MacBrayne: to the Kyleakin (Isle of Skye) frequent services every day (5 mn) – to Lochaline: 3 weekly (2 h).
⛴ to Mallaig (Caledonian MacBrayne) 2-3 weekly (2 h); to Isle of Skye (Armadale): 2 weekly winter only (2 h).
🛈 ☏ 4276 (Easter and May-September).

Edinburgh 202 – Dundee 173 – Inverness 85 – Oban 127.

🏨 **Lochalsh** (B.T.H.), Ferry Rd, IV40 8AF, ☏ 4202, ≤ Skye Ferry and hills – 🛗 Ⓟ. 🛗 ⒶⒺ ⓪ 𝐕𝐈𝐒𝐀
M a la carte 8.00/10.70 st. ⓘ 2.30 – **45 rm** ⌑ 24.60/44.00.

AUSTIN-MORRIS-MG The Garage ☏ 4210   TALBOT ☏ 4328

KYLES SCALPAY Highland – Shipping Services: see Harris (Isle of).

LAIDE Highland – ✉ Achnasheen – ✆ 044 582 Aultbea.
See: Gruinard Bay***.
Edinburgh 243 – Inverness 84.

🏠 Ocean View, Sand, IV22 2JQ, ☏ 385, ≤ sea and Summer Isles – Ⓟ
10 rm.

LAIRG Highland 𝟵𝟴𝟲 ③ – pop. 572 – ECD: Wednesday – ✆ 0549.
🛈 Information Centre ☏ 2160 (June-September).
Edinburgh 218 – Inverness 59 – Wick 71.

🏨 **Sutherland Arms,** IV27 4AT, ☏ 2291, ≤, ◪, 🍴 – ⌨wc Ⓟ. 🛗 ⒶⒺ ⓪ 𝐕𝐈𝐒𝐀
May-September – M (bar lunch) approx. 6.25 st. ⓘ 1.25 – **32 rm** ⌑ 13.30/26.50 st.

🏨 **Aultnagar Lodge** ⏳, IV27 4EX, S: 5 m. on A 836 ☏ 054 982 (Invershin) 245, ≤ countryside and hills, ◪, 🍴, park – 🛗 ⌨wc 🚿wc Ⓟ. ⒶⒺ
M 3.00/5.50 ⓘ 1.50 – **26 rm** ⌑ 8.00/9.50.

MORRIS-TRIUMPH ☏ 2465

LAMLASH Strathclyde 986 ⑭ – see Arran (Isle of).

LANARK Strathclyde 986 ⑮ – pop. 8,700 – ECD: Thursday – ☎ 0555.
ᵣ₈ Main St., Carnwath ✆ 251, E: 7 m. – ᵣ₉ Douglas Water, SW: 7 m.
🛈 ✆ 4875 (May-September).
Edinburgh 33 – Carlisle 76 – Glasgow 28.

   🏨 **Cartland Bridge** 🐾, ML11 9UF, N: ¾ m. on A 73 ✆ 4426, 🍴 – ☜ ℗. 🛁. 🅰 AE
     M 3.25/4.00 st. – **15 rm** ⌇ 10.00/20.00 st.

AUSTIN-MORRIS-MG 17/19 Bloomgate ✆ 2371   BMW, LANCIA 30 West Port ✆ 2581
AUSTIN-MG-ROVER-TRIUMPH 178 Hyndford Rd ✆   FORD 144 Hyndford Rd ✆ 4431
2674   VAUXHALL St. Leonard St. ✆ 2185

LANGBANK Strathclyde – pop. 375 – ECD: Saturday – ☎ 047 554.
Edinburgh 59 – Glasgow 16 – Greenock 7.

   🏨 **Gleddoch House** (Best Western) 🐾, PA14 6YE, SE: 1 m. off B 789 ✆ 711, ⇐ Clyde
    and countryside, 🔲, ᵣ₈, 🐾, 🍴, park – TV ☜wc 🚿wc ☎ ℗. 🅰 AE ⓪ VISA
    closed Christmas Day and 1-2 January – M 5.00/8.50 st. ♨ 2.25 – **19 rm** ⌇ 27.00/
    37.50 st.

LARGS Strathclyde 986 ⑭ – pop. 9,771 – ECD: Wednesday – ☎ 0475.
See : Skelmorlie Aisle* in old churchyard.
ᵣ₈ Irvine Rd ✆ 673594 – ᵣ₈ Routenburn, ✆ 673230.
⛴ to Great Cumbrae Island: Cumbrae Slip (Caledonian MacBrayne) frequent services every
day (10 mn).
⛴ to Great Cumbrae Island: Millport Old Pier (Caledonian MacBrayne) frequent services
every day summer only (30 mn).
🛈 Esplanade ✆ 673765.
Edinburgh 72 – Ayr 30 – Glasgow 29.

   🏨 **Marine and Curlinghall,** South Promenade, KA30 8DZ, ✆ 674551, ⇐, 🍴 –
    TV ☜wc ℗. 🛁. 🅰 AE ⓪
    M (bar lunch) 4.50/6.50 t. – **58 rm** ⌇ 15.00/29.00 st.
   🏨 **Mackerston,** Mackerston Pl. ✆ 673264, ⇐, 🍴 – ☜wc 🚿wc ℗. 🅰 AE ⓪ VISA
    M 2.50/4.00 ♨ 1.60 – **60 rm** ⌇ 4.00/14.00.
   🏨 Castle (Osprey), 1 Broomfield, South Promenade, KA30 9HH, ✆ 673302, 🍴 – ☜wc ℗
    40 rm.
   🏨 Royal, The Esplanade, KA30 8LZ, ✆ 674653 – TV ☜wc ☎ ℗
    13 rm.

LAUDER Borders 986 ⑮ – pop. 604 – ECD: Thursday – ☎ 057 82 Lauder.
ᵣ₉ ✆ 381, W : ½ m.
Edinburgh 27 – Hawick 31 – Newcastle-upon-Tyne 78.

   🏨 Carfraemill (Osprey), TD2 6RA, N: 4 m. on junction A 68 and A 697 ✆ 200 – ☜wc
    ☎ ℗
    10 rm.

AUSTIN-MORRIS-MG-WOLSELEY Edinburgh Rd ✆ 228

LAWERS Tayside – see Kenmore.

LECKMELM Highland – pop. 28 – ✉ Garve – ☎ 0854 Ullapool.
Edinburgh 214 – Inverness 55 – Ullapool 4.

   🏨 **Tir Aluinn** 🐾, Loch Broom, IV23 2RJ, ✆ 2074, ⇐ Loch Broom, mountains and hills,
    🐾, 🍴, park – ☜wc ♿ ℗
    June-September – M (bar lunch) approx. 4.00 s. ♨ 1.70 – **16 rm** ⌇ 8.00/18.00 s.

LERWICK Shetland Islands 986 ⑯ – see Shetland Islands (Mainland).

LETHAM Fife – pop. 170 – ✉ Ladybank – ☎ 033 781.
Edinburgh 41 – Dundee 14 – Perth 18.

   🏨 Fernie Castle 🐾, KY7 7RU, NE: ½ m. on A 914 ✆ 209, « Castle with 14C origins »,
    🍴, park – TV ☜wc 🚿wc ☎ ℗
    11 rm.

LEVEN Fife 986 ⑪ – pop. 9,472 – ☎ 0333 – ᵣ₈.
🛈 South St. ✆ 26533.
Edinburgh 34 – Dundee 23 – Glasgow 61.

   🏨 Caledonian (Osprey), High St., KY8 4NG, ✆ 24101 – TV ☜wc ☎ ℗
    36 rm.

AUSTIN-MORRIS-MG The Promenade ✆ 23449   FIAT Scoonie Rd ✆ 26348

LEWIS (Isle of) Outer Hebrides (Western Isles) 986 ② – pop. 15,174 – ECD : Wednesday.

Stornoway – pop. 5,152 – ⊠ ☉ 0851 Stornoway.
See : Broad Bay**. **Envir.** : Tiumpan Head ⊰** NE : 11 m. – Loch Erisort** SW : 12 m. – Callanish Standing Stones** W : 16 m. – East Loch Roag* W : 13 ½ m. – Tolsta (site*) NE : 13 m.
Exc. : Dun Carloway* (stone fort) W : 21 m. – Port of Ness* NE : 25 ½ m. – Valtos* W : 32 m.
✈ ☏ 2256, Telex 75495, E : 2 ½ m. – **Terminal** : British Airways, Cromwell St. – Loganair, Airport.
🛳 to Ullapool (Caledonian MacBrayne) Monday/Saturday 1-2 daily (3 h 15 mn).
🛈 Area Tourist Officer, South Beach St. ☏ 3088, Telex 75125.

🏨 Caberfeidh, PA87 2EU, ☏ 2604 – 🛗 📺 ⇋wc ⓟ – **35 rm.**

🏨 **Caledonian,** South Beach St., PA87 2XY, ☏ 2411, ⊰
M *(closed Sunday)* 2.75/5.15 **t.** – **10 rm** ⇆ 10.20/20.40 **t.**

🏨 Royal (S & N), Cromwell St., PA87 2DG, ☏ 2109, ⊰
16 rm.

AUSTIN-MORRIS-ROVER-TRIUMPH 4 Inaclete Rd ☏ 2346
AUSTIN-MORRIS-MG Bayhead St. ☏ 3246
FORD 80 Keith St. ☏ 3225
TALBOT, RENAULT Bells Rd ☏ 2303
VAUXHALL Bayhead St. ☏ 2888
VW, AUDI Sandwick Rd ☏ 2956

LEWISTON Highland – ☉ 045 62 Drumnadrochit.
Edinburgh 175 – Inverness 16.

🍴 Lewiston Arms, ☏ 225, 🚗 – 📺 ⓟ
8 rm.

LINLITHGOW Lothian – pop. 5,684 – ECD : Wednesday – ☉ 050 683 Philipstoun.
See : Linlithgow Palace* (15C-16C) *AC.*
🏌 ☏ 2585.
🛈 The Vennel Car Park, ☏ 4600 (April-3 October).
Edinburgh 17 – Falkirk 6.

XXX **Champany,** Champany Corner, BH49 7LU, NE : 2 ½ m. on A 904 ☏ 532 – ⓟ. AE ⓪
closed Sunday and 1 to 3 January – **M** a la carte 9.55/24.00 **st.** 🍷 2.60.

LINWOOD Strathclyde – pop. 10,510 – ECD : Tuesday – ☉ 0505 Johnstone.
Edinburgh 54 – Glasgow 11 – Greenock 13.

🏨 Golden Pheasant (Swallow), 1 Moss Rd, PA3 3HP, ☏ 21266 – 📺 ⇋wc 🅿 ⓟ
12 rm.

LISMORE (Isle of) Strathclyde.
🛳 to Oban (Caledonian MacBrayne) Monday/Saturday 2-4 daily (1 h).

Hotels see : Oban.

LOCHALINE Strathclyde 986 ⑩ – pop. 213.
🛳 by Caledonian MacBrayne : to Fishnish (Isle of Mull) 4-11 daily except Sunday from October to May (15 mn) – to Kyle of Lochalsh : 3 weekly (2 h).
Edinburgh 129 – Inverness 105 – Kyle of Lochalsh 115 – Oban 7.

Hotels see : Mull (Isle of).

LOCHBOISDALE Western Isles 986 ⑥ – Shipping Services : see Uist (South) (Isles of).

LOCHCARRON Highland 986 ⑥ – pop. 204 – ☉ 052 02 – 🏌.
Envir. : Shieldaig (site*) NW : 14 ½ m.
Edinburgh 223 – Inverness 64 – Kyle of Lochalsh 23.

🍴 **Lochcarron,** IV54 8YS, ☏ 226, ⊰ – ⇋wc ⓟ
closed Christmas Day and 1 January – **M** *(closed Monday dinner)* (bar lunch) 1.75/6.00 **t.** 🍷 1.35 – **7 rm** ⇆ 10.00/20.00 **t.** – P 15.00/16.00 **t.**

LOCHEARNHEAD Central 986 ⑪ – pop. 175 – ECD : Wednesday – ☉ 056 73.
🛈 ☏ 220 (Easter and mid June-September).
Edinburgh 65 – Glasgow 56 – Oban 57 – Perth 36.

🏨 **Lochearnhead,** FK19 8HB, ☏ 237, ⊰, ✗, 🚗 – ⇋wc ⓟ. 🔌 AE ⓪ *VISA*
February-October – **M** 3.00/5.50 🍷 1.30 – **51 rm** ⇆ 10.00/22.00 – P 17.00/19.00.

🏠 **Mansewood Country House,** FK19 8NS, S : ½ m. on A 84 ☏ 213, 🚗 – ⇋wc 🚿wc ⓟ
closed mid-November-mid December and February – **10 rm** ⇆ 10.05/12.05 **st.**

LOCHGAIR Strathclyde – pop. 100 – ☎ 054 682.
Envir. : Inveraray (site*, castle* 18C) NE : 18 m.
Edinburgh 119 – Glasgow 76 – Oban 43.

🏰 **Lochgair**, PA31 8SA, on A 83 ☎ 233, ⚲, 🚗 – 🛏wc 🅿. AE ⓪
M (bar lunch) approx. 6.25 **s.** 🍷 1.20 – **18 rm** ⚌ 10.95/23.90 **s.**

LOCHGILPHEAD Strathclyde 986 ⑭ – pop. 1,184 – ECD : Tuesday – ☎ 0546.
Envir. : Loch Fyne** E : 4 m. – Crarae Lodge gardens* *AC*, NE : 12 m.
🛈 Colchester Sq. ☎ 2344.
Edinburgh 126 – Glasgow 83 – Oban 36.

Hotel see : Cairnbaan NW : 2 ½ m.

LOCHGOILHEAD Strathclyde – pop. 216 – ✉ ☎ 030 13.
Edinburgh 92 – Glasgow 49 – Oban 60.

XX **Inverlounin House** ⏾ with rm, PA24 8A, S : 1 ½ m. ☎ 211, ≼ loch Goil and mountains,
⚲, 🚗 – 🛏wc 🅿
closed March – **M** 3.50/9.00 **t.** 🍷 2.20 – **4 rm** ⚌ (dinner included) 22.75/38.00 **t.**

LOCH HARRAY Orkney Islands – see Orkney Islands (Mainland).

LOCHINVER Highland 986 ② – pop. 283 – ECD : Tuesday – ✉ Lairg – ☎ 057 14.
See : Site*. Envir. : E : Inver Valley*.
🛈 Information Centre ☎ 330 (June-September).
Edinburgh 259 – Inverness 100 – Wick 118.

🏰 **Culag**, IV27 4LQ, ☎ 209, ≼, ⚲, 🚗 – 🔔 🛏wc 🅿
49 rm.

LOCHMADDY Outer Hebrides (Western Isles) 986 ⑥ – see Uist (North) (Isles of).

LOCHRANZA Strathclyde 986 ⑭ – Shipping Services : see Arran (Isle of).

LOCKERBIE Dumfries and Galloway 986 ⑲ – pop. 2,999 – ECD : Tuesday – ☎ 057 62.
⛳ Corrie Rd ☎ 2463.
Edinburgh 72 – Carlisle 26 – Dumfries 13 – Glasgow 69.

🏰 **Lockerbie House** ⏾, Dryfe Rd, DG11 2RD, N : 1 m. on B 723 ☎ 2610, 🚗, park – 🛏wc
📧 🅿
M (bar lunch) approx. 7.00 **t.** 🍷 1.20 – **30 rm** ⚌ 12.00/20.00 **t.**

🏰 **Dryfesdale House** ⏾, Dryfe Rd, DG11 2SF, NW : 1 m. off A 74 ☎ 2427, ≼, 🚗 – TV
🛏wc 📧 🅿
closed first 2 weeks January – **M** 4.50/6.00 **st.** 🍷 1.70 – **15 rm** ⚌ 12.00/21.50 **st.**

ALFA-ROMEO, SAAB ☎ 2854   COLT High St. ☎ 2648

LOSSIEMOUTH Grampian 986 ⑦ – pop. 5,678 (inc. Branderburgh) – ECD : Thursday –
☎ 034 381.
See : Site**.
⛳, ⛳ Moray ☎ 2018.
Edinburgh 196 – Aberdeen 72 – Fraserburgh 66 – Inverness 44.

Hotel and restaurant see : Elgin S : 5 ½ m.

LUNAN Tayside – see Montrose.

LUNDIN LINKS Fife – pop. 879 – ECD : Thursday – ✉ Leven – ☎ 0333.
⛳ Golf Rd ☎ 320022.
Edinburg 36 – Dundee 25 – Dunfermline 23.

🏠 Elmwood, 12 Links Rd, KY8 6AT, ☎ 320397, 🚗
11 rm.

MAINLAND Orkney Islands 986 ⑯ – see Orkney Islands.

MAINLAND Shetland Islands 986 ⑯ – see Shetland Islands.

MALLAIG Highland 986 ⑥ – pop. 903 – ECD : Wednesday – ✪ 0687.
See : Site* – Harbour* – Sound of Sleat**.
Envir. : Sound of Sleat** – Sound of Arisaig* S : 9 m.
ⓕ Traigh ☎ 068 75 (Arisaig) 2126, S : 9 m.
⛴ to Isle of Skye : Armadale (Caledonian MacBrayne) 1-5 daily (30 mn).
⛴ by Caledonian MacBrayne : to Isles of Eigg, Muck, Rhum, Canna, return Mallaig 3 weekly (except to Muck : 1 weekly only) (6 h to 6 h 30 mn) – to Kyle of Lochalsh 2-3 weekly (2 h).
ⓘ Information Centre, Station Buildings ☎ 2170 (mid May-mid September).
Edinburgh 181 – Inverness 111 – Oban 97.

MARYCULTER Grampian – pop. 813 – ✉ ✪ 0224 Aberdeen.
Edinburgh 118 – Aberdeen 8 – Stonehaven 9.

   ✗ **Maryculter House**, AB1 0BB, W : 1 m. on B 9077 ☎ 732124 – **℗**. ▣ AE ① VISA
     closed Sunday and 1 January – **M** (bar lunch) a la carte 7.30/8.35.

MEIGLE Tayside 986 ⑪ – pop. 375 – ✪ 082 84.
See : Museum (Crosses)*.
Edinburgh 60 – Dundee 13 – Perth 18.

   ✗ **Kings of Kinloch** ⚘ with rm, Coupar Angus Rd, PH12 8QX, W : 1 m. on A 94 ☎ 273, ≼,
     ⛟ – 🛁wc **℗**
     closed last 3 weeks January – **M** 6.00/10.50 t. ⓘ 2.45 – **7 rm** ⇌ 12.00/24.00 **st.**

MELROSE Borders 986 ⑮ – pop. 2,185 – ECD : Thursday – ✪ 089 682.
See : Abbey* *AC*. **Envir. :** Abbotsford House* (Sir Walter Scott's home) *AC*, W : 2 m.
ⓕ Dingleton ☎ 2855, South boundary.
ⓘ Priorwood, near Abbey ☎ 2555 (summer only).
Edinburgh 37 – Hawick 21 – Newcastle-upon-Tyne 69.

   🏨 George and Abbotsford (Swallow), High St., TD6 9PD, ☎ 2308, Group Telex 53168,
     ⛟ – 🛁wc **℗**. ♨
     22 rm.

   🏠 **Burts,** Market Sq., TD6 9PN, ☎ 2285, ⛟ – 🛁wc 🚿wc **℗**. ▣ AE VISA
     M 4.50/6.00 t. ⓘ 1.70 – **21 rm** ⇌ 8.00/19.50 t

AUSTIN-MORRIS-MG Palma Pl. ☎ 2048   TALBOT High St. ☎ 2400
RENAULT Lilliesleaf ☎ 083 57 (Lilliesleaf) 231

MILLPORT Strathclyde 986 ⑭ – Shipping Services : see Great Cumbrae Island.

MILNGAVIE Strathclyde 986 ⑮ – pop. 10,741 – ECD : Tuesday and Saturday – ✉ ✪ 041
Glasgow.
ⓕ Dougalston ☎ 956 5750.
Edinburgh 50 – Glasgow 7.

   🏨 **Black Bull** (Thistle), Main St., G62 6BH, ☎ 956 2291 – 📺 🛁wc ☏ **℗**. ♨. ▣ AE ①
     VISA
     M a la carte 5.35/9.60 **t.** ⓘ 1.65 – ⇌ 1.60 – **27 rm** 19.50/25.00 **t.**

AUSTIN-MORRIS-MG 3 Strathblane Rd ☎ 956 2373   TOYOTA, VAUXHALL Main St. ☎ 956 2255
OPEL Glasgow Rd ☎ 956 1126

MINGARY Strathclyde.
⛴ to Isle of Mull : Tobermory (Caledonian MacBrayne) Monday/Saturday 4 daily (35 mn).
Edinburgh 164 – Inverness 115 – Kilchoan 1.

     Hotels see : Kilchoan W : 1 m.

MOFFAT Dumfries and Galloway 986 ⑮ – pop. 2,031 – ECD : Wednesday – ✪ 0683.
Envir. : E : Moffatwater Valley* – Grey Mare's Tail Waterfall* NE : 11 m.
ⓘ Church Gate ☎ 20620 (April-September).
Edinburgh 58 – Dumfries 21 – Carlisle 42 – Glasgow 54.

   🏨 Moffat Ladbroke Mercury Motor Inn, Church St., DG10 9EP, ☎ 20464 – 📺 🛁wc **℗**
     51 rm.

   🏠 **Annandale**, High St., DG10 9HF, ☎ 20013 – 🛁wc **℗**. ▣ AE ① VISA
     April-November – **M** 3.50/5.90 t. ⓘ 2.20 – **24 rm** ⇌ 10.00/23.00 **st.**

   🏠 **Beechwood Country House** ⚘, up Harthope Pl., off Academy Rd, DG10 9RS,
     ☎ 20210, ⛟ – 🛁wc 🚿wc **℗**. ▣ VISA
     M 3.50/6.00 t. ⓘ 1.80 – **8 rm** ⇌ 8.00/22.00 **t.**

MONKTON Strathclyde – see Prestwick.

MONTROSE Tayside 986 ⑪ – pop. 9,959 – ECD: Wednesday – ☎ 0674.
☞ Broomfield ☏ 2179, E: 1 m. off A 92.
🛈 212 High St., DD10 8PH, ☏ 2000.
Edinburgh 85 – Aberdeen 38 – Dundee 29.

🏨 **Links**, Mid-Links, DD10 8RL, ☏ 2288, 🍽 – 🛏wc ☎ 🅿. 🏌. 🅽 ⓘ 𝘝𝘐𝘚𝘈
   M a la carte 3.90/6.25 **t.** ⏧ 2.55 – **21 rm** ⚏ 15.50/22.00 **st.**

🏨 **Park**, John St., DD10 8RJ, ☏ 3415, Telex 76367, 🚗 – 📺 🛏wc ⋔wc ☎ 🅿. 🏌. AE ⓘ 𝘝𝘐𝘚𝘈
   M a la carte 5.70/10.70 **t.** ⏧ 2.30 – **41 rm** ⚏ 15.50/29.00 **st.**

   at Lunan S: 4 ½ m. by A 92 – ✉ Arbroath – ☎ 024 13 Inverkeilor:

🏛 **Lunan Bay** ⚶, DD10 9TG, ☏ 265, ⋖, 🚗 – 📺 🛏wc ⋙ 🅿. 🏌. 🅽 AE ⓘ 𝘝𝘐𝘚𝘈
   closed 1 to 3 January – **M** a la carte 5.00/12.00 – **8 rm** ⚏ 12.95/16.15 **st.**

AUSTIN-MG-ROVER-TRIUMPH Craigo ☏ 067483 (Hillside) 374 MAZDA ☏ 024 13 (Inverkeilor) 276
DATSUN New Wynd ☏ 3606 TALBOT 99 Bridge St. ☏ 3682

MONYMUSK Grampian – pop. 167 – ☎ 046 77.
Edinburgh 143 – Aberdeen 19 – Old Meldrum 13.

🏛 **Grant Arms** ⚶, The Square, AB3 7HJ, ☏ 226, 🍽 – 🛏wc ⋔wc ☎ 🅿. ⓘ
   April-October – **M** (bar lunch) approx. 7.00 **st.** ⏧ 1.50 – **15 rm** ⚏ 10.00/11.00 **t.**

MOSSAT Grampian – pop. 400 – ✉ Alford – ☎ 033 65 Kildrummy.
Envir.: Kildrummy Castle gardens* *AC*, SW: 2 ½ m.
Edinburgh 137 – Aberdeen 33.

🏨 **Kildrummy Castle** ⚶, AB3 8RA, S: 2 ¼ m. on A 97 ☏ 288, ⋖ gardens and Kildrummy
   Castle, « 19C mansion in extensive park », 🚗 – 🛏wc ⋔wc ☎ 🅿. 🅽 AE ⓘ 𝘝𝘐𝘚𝘈
   closed January and February – **M** 4.25/7.50 **t.** ⏧ 2.00 – **12 rm** ⚏ 14.00/32.00 **t.** –
   P 24.00 **t.**

MOTHERWELL Strathclyde 986 ⑮ – pop. 73,658 (inc. Wishaw) – ☎ 0698.
Edinburgh 35 – Carlisle 84 – Glasgow 12.

🏨 **Garrion** (Open House), 73 Merry St., ML1 1JN, ☏ 64561 – ▐𝟯 📺 🛏wc ⋔wc ☎ 🅿. 🏌
   54 rm.

FORT Windmill Hill St. Rd ☏ 66188 TALBOT 99 Airbles Rd ☏ 65286
MORRIS-MG-PRINCESS 228/232 Hamilton Rd ☏ 64162

MUCK (Isle of) Highland – Shipping Services: see Mallaig.

MUIRHEAD Strathclyde – ✉ ☎ 041 Glasgow.
Edinburgh 41 – Glasgow 6 – Stirling 18.

🏛 Crowwood House (S & N), Cumbernauld Rd, G84 9BS ☏ 779 3861 – 🛏wc ☎ 🅿
   18 rm.

AUSTIN-MORRIS-MG Cumbernauld Rd ☏ 2413

MUIR OF ORD Highland 986 ⑦ – pop. 1,339 – ECD: Thursday – ✉ ☎ 046 382 – ☞
🛈 ☏ 433 435.
Edinburgh 174 – Inverness 14 – Wick 122.

🏨 **Ord House** ⚶, ☏ 492, « Country house atmosphere », 🍽, 🚗, park – 🛏wc 🅿
   May-October – **M** (bar lunch) approx. 7.00 ⏧ 2.40 – **16 rm** ⚏ 15.00/25.00.

MULL (Isle of) Strathclyde 986 ⑩ – pop. 1,569.
See: Coast*.
🚢 by Caledonian MacBrayne: from Craignure to Oban: 2-7 daily except Sunday from
October to May (45 mn) – from Fishnish to Lochaline: 4-11 daily except Sunday from October
to May (15 mn) – from Tobermory to Oban: 3 weekly (4 h 30 mn).
🚤 by Caledonian MacBrayne: from Fionnphort to Isle of Iona frequent services every day
except Sunday in winter (10 mn) – from Tobermory to Mingary Monday/Saturday 4 daily
(35 mn).
🛈 48 Main St. at Tobermory ☏ 2182 (April-September).

   Bunessan – ECD: Wednesday – ✉ Bunessan – ☎ 068 17 Fionnphort.
   Envir.: NE: Loch Scridain* – Fionnphort (site*) W: 6 m.

🏛 **Ardfenaig House** ⚶, PA67 6DX, W: 3 m. by A 849 ☏ 210, ⋖, 🚗 – 🅿
   May-September – **M** (dinner only) 7.00 ⏧ 0.80 – **5 rm** ⚏ 17.00.

   Craignure – ECD: Thursday – ✉ ☎ 068 02 Craignure.
   Envir.: Glen More* SW: 11 m. – Loch Uisg* SW: 13 m.

🏨 **Isle of Mull** ⚶, PA65 6BB, NW: ¾ m. off A 849, ☏ 351, ⋖ mountains, sea and Duart
   Castle – 🛏wc ⚐ 🅿. 🅽 AE ⓘ 𝘝𝘐𝘚𝘈
   May-mid October – **M** (bar lunch) 2.35/6.25 **st.** ⏧ 1.25 – **60 rm** ⚏ 17.95/30.30 **st.**

Dervaig – ⊠ Tobermory – ☎ 068 84 Dervaig.

🏠 **Druimnacroish** ⟋, PA75 6QW, SE : 2 m. off B 8073 ☎ 274, ≼ Bellart Glen, « Converted steading », 🚗 – 🛏wc ⵊ ℗. ⟋ AE ⓞ VISA
Easter–October – **M** (bar lunch) approx. 6.00 **s.** – **7 rm** ⟷ 19.50/39.00 **s.**

Salen pop. 181 – ECD : Wednesday – ⊠ Salen – ☎ 068 03 Aros.
See : Sound of Mull★★. Envir. : Loch Na Keal★★ SW : 2 ½ m.

🏠 Glenforsa ⟋, PA72 6JN, E : 1 ¼ m. by A 849 ☎ 377, ≼ Sound of Mull, « Norwegian wood chalet », ⟋, park – 🛏wc ℗
season – **14 rm.**

Tiroran - ⊠ ☎ 068 15 Tiroran.

🏠 **Tiroran House** ⟋, ☎ 232, ≼, ⟋, 🚗, park – 🛏wc ℗
May–October – **M** (buffet lunch) approx. 7.50 **st.** ⌘ 1.75 – **6 rm** ⟷ 17.00/32.00 **st.**

Tobermory – pop. 641 – ECD : Wednesday – ⊠ ☎ 0688 Tobermory.
See : Site★. Envir. : Calgary Bay★★ SW : 14 m. – Loch Tuath★★ SW : 17 m.

🏠 **Western Isles** ⟋, PA75 6PR, ☎ 2012, ≼ bay and harbour, 🖙, ⟋, 🚗 – 🛏wc ℗. ⟋
AE VISA
closed 3 days at Christmas – **M** (bar lunch) 3.10/5.00 **s.** ⌘ 1.30 – **43 rm** ⟷ 12.00/25.00 **s.**

🏠 **Suidhe**, 59 Main St., PA75 6NT, ☎ 2209, ≼ – 🛏wc
March–October – **9 rm** ⟷ 9.00/22.00 **t.**

NAIRN Highland 🗺 ⑦ – pop. 8,037 – ECD : Wednesday – ☎ 0667.
See : ≼★ from the harbour. Envir. : Fort George★ (Museum of the Queen's Own Highlanders★)
W : 8 ½ m. – Sveno's Stone★ E : 11 m.
🖙18, 🖙9 ☎ 52103 – 🖙18 ☎ 52741.
🛈 Bus Station, King St. ☎ 52753 (mid May–mid September).
Edinburgh 175 – Aberdeen 91 – Inverness 16.

🏠 Newton ⟋, IV12 4RX, off A 96 ☎ 53144, ≼, « Country house in extensive grounds »,
⨯⨯, 🚗, park – ♿ ℗. ⛵
46 rm.

🏠 **Golf View**, Seabank Rd, IV12 4HD, ☎ 52301, ≼, ⨯⨯, ⚊ heated, 🚗 – ♿ TV ℗. ⟋ AE ⓞ VISA
M 4.75/6.75 **t.** ⌘ 2.25 – **57 rm** ⟷ 24.00/40.00 **t.** – P 25.50/29.00 **t.**

🏠 **Royal Marine**, Marine Rd, IV12 4EA, ☎ 53381 ≼, 🚗 – ♿ 🛏wc ⋔wc ℗
April–October – **M** (bar lunch) 6.25 **st.** – **43 rm** ⟷ 23.80/26.50 **st.**

🏠 **Clifton**, Viewfield St., IV12 5HU, ☎ 53119, ≼, 🚗 – 🛏wc ℗
Mid March–October – **M** (bar lunch) approx. 8.50 **t.** ⌘ 1.75 – **19 rm** ⟷ 10.50/29.30 **t.**

🏠 Windsor, Albert St. ☎ 53108 – ℗
48 rm.

AUSTIN-MORRIS-MG-ROVER-TRIUMPH King. St. ☎ 52304   TALBOT Inverness Rd ☎ 52335

NEWARTHILL Strathclyde – pop. 7,003 – ECD : Wednesday – ⊠ Motherwell – ☎ 0698
Holytown.
Edinburgh 31 – Glasgow 13 – Motherwell 3.

🏠 Silverburn (S & N), 2 Loanhead Rd, ML1 5BA, ☎ 732503 – 🛏wc ☎ ℗
12 rm.

NEWBURGH Grampian 🗺 ⑦ – pop. 447 – ECD : Wednesday – ☎ 035 86.
Edinburgh 137 – Aberdeen 13 – Fraserburgh 31.

⨯⨯ **Udny Arms** with rm, AB4 0BL, ☎ 444, ⟋, 🚗 – 🛏wc ⋔wc ℗
M (bar lunch) approx. 7.50 **t.** ⌘ 2.40 – ⟷ 2.00 – **15 rm** 12.50/20.50 **t.**

NEW GALLOWAY Dumfries and Galloway 🗺 ⑲ – pop. 338 – ⊠ Castle Douglas –
☎ 064 42 – 🖙9.
Edinburgh 84 – Dumfries 24 – Glasgow 68 – Stranraer 45.

🏠 **Kenmure Arms**, High St., DG7 3RL, ☎ 360 – ℗. AE VISA
M (bar lunch) 3.00/5.00 **st.** ⌘ 2.20 – **18 rm** ⟷ 6.50/18.00.

NEW SCONE Tayside – see Perth.

Carte	Dans les hôtels et restaurants cités avec des menus à prix fixes, il est généralement possible de se faire servir également à la carte.

 Highland **986** ⑦ – pop. 894 – ECD : Wednesday – ☎ 054 03.
ⓘ₈ ☏ 328.
🛈 Perth Rd ☏ 253 (June-September).

Edinburgh 112 – Inverness 47 – Perth 70.

　🏨 **Ard-na-Coille,** Kingussie Rd, PH20 1AY, ☏ 214, ≼ – ⋔wc ⓟ
　　15 April-29 October – **M** (dinner only) 4.00 **st.** ⬧ 2.00 – **13 rm** ☲ (dinner included)
　　13.35/26.70 **s.**

　🏨 **Glen,** High St., PH20 1DD, ☏ 203 – ⊟wc ⓟ
　　M (bar lunch) 2.00/4.50 **st.** ⬧ 2.00 – **9 rm** ☲ 7.00/18.00 **st.**

 Dumfries and Galloway **986** ⑱ – pop. 1,883 – ECD : Wednesday –
☎ 0671.
🛈 Douglas House ☏ 2549 – Dashwood Sq. ☏ 2431 (April-September).

Edinburgh 127 – Dumfries 50 – Glasgow 84 – Stranraer 26.

　🏰 **Bruce,** Queen St., DG8 6JL, ☏ 2294, ≼ – ⊟wc ☎ ⓟ. ⬧ 🄰🄴 ⓞ 𝗩𝗜𝗦𝗔
　　M 3.50/5.50 **st.** ⬧ 1.50 – **16 rm** ☲ 10.00/20.00 **st.** – P 17.50/20.50 **st.**

　🏛 **Kirroughtree** ✍, DG8 6AN, E : 1 ½ m. by A 75 off A 712 ☏ 2141, ≼, 🚗, park –
　　🆃🆅 ⊟wc ⓟ. ⬧
　　M 4.25/6.00 ⬧ 1.60 – **18 rm** ☲ 7.50/17.00.

　🏛 **Crown,** Queen St., DG8 6JW, ☏ 2727 – ⋔ ⓟ
　　M 2.40/3.75 **s.** ⬧ 1.70 – **12 rm** ☲ 7.50/16.00 **s.**

AUSTIN-MORRIS-MG-ROVER-TRIUMPH 100 Queen 　　　RENAULT Duncan Park, Wigtown ☏ 098 84 (Wigtown)
St. ☏ 2467 　　　　　　　　　　　　　　　　　　3287

 Lothian **986** ⑮ – pop. 4,414 – ECD : Thursday – ☎ 0620.
See : Site*. **Envir. :** Tantallon Castle* (ruins 14C), site* *AC*, E : 2 ½ m.
ⓘ₈ East Links ☏ 2726 – ⓘ₈ West Links, Beach Rd ☏ 2135.
🛈 18 Quality St. ☏ 2197.

Edinburgh 24 – Newcastle-upon-Tyne 101.

　🏛 Nether Abbey, 20 Dirleton Av., EH39 4BQ, ☏ 2802, 🚗 – ⋔wc ⓟ – **18 rm.**

AUSTIN-MG-MORRIS-ROVER-TRIUMPH 　　　　　　　TALBOT 52 Dunbar Rd ☏ 2232
18/24 High St. ☏ 2304

 Orkney Islands – Shipping Services : see Orkney Islands
(Mainland : Kirkwall).

 Strathclyde **986** ⑩ – pop. 6,897 – ECD : Thursday – ☎ 0631.
See : Site*.
ⓘ₈ Glen Cruitten ☏ 2868, E : 1 m.
⛴ by Caledonian MacBrayne : to Craignure (Isle of Mull) 2-7 daily except Sunday from
October to May (45 mn) – to Castlebay (Isle of Barra) 3-4 weekly (5 to 8 h) – to Lochboisdale
(South Uist) 3-6 weekly (5 h to 7 h) – to Tobermory (Isle of Mull) 3 weekly (4 h 30 mn) –
to Isle of Coll : 2-4 weekly (3 h 30 mn to 5 h 30 mn) – to Isle of Tiree : 2-4 weekly (4 to 5 h) –
to Isle of Colonsay : 3 weekly (2 h 30 mn) – to Lismore : Monday/Saturday 2-4 daily (1 h) –
By Western Ferries : to Moville 29 April-September : Sunday 1 daily (4 h).
⛴ to Isle of Iona (Caledonian MacBrayne) summer only 1-2 weekly – to Isle of Mull
(Tobermory) 3 weekly (2 h to 2 h 15 mn) – to Isles of Coll and Tiree : 3 weekly (3 h 45 mn to
4 h 55 mn).
🛈 Boswell House, Argyll Sq. ☏ 3122/3551, Telex 778866.

Edinburgh 122 – Dundee 115 – Glasgow 93 – Inverness 114.

　🏨 **Alexandra,** The Esplanade, PA34 5AA, ☏ 2381, ≼ – 🛗 ⊟wc ⓟ. ⬧ 🄰🄴 ⓞ 𝗩𝗜𝗦𝗔
　　April-mid October – **M** 2.95/6.25 **st.** ⬧ 1.25 – **58 rm** ☲ 13.30/26.50 **st.**

　🏨 **Rowan Tree,** George St., PA34 5HN, ☏ 2954 – ⊟wc ⓟ
　　M a la carte 3.00/5.05 **s.** ⬧ 1.45 – **24 rm** ☲ 10.50/13.00 **s.**

　🏨 **Regent,** The Esplanade, PA34 5PZ, ☏ 2341 – 🛗 ⊟wc. ⬧ 🄰🄴
　　M approx. 6.45 **st.** ⬧ 1.95 – **31 rm** ☲ 11.30/24.70 **st.**

　🏨 **Marine,** The Esplanade, PA34 5QA, ☏ 2211, ≼ – 🛗 ⊟wc ⋔wc ☎ ⓟ. ⓞ
　　Easter-October – **M** (buffet lunch) 3.00/5.75 **s.** – **44 rm** ☲ 11.50/13.50 **s.**

　🏛 **Manor House,** Gallanach Rd, PA34 4LS, ☏ 2087, ≼ – ⊟wc ⋔wc ⓟ. ⬧ ⓞ 𝗩𝗜𝗦𝗔
　　M (bar lunch) 8.00 **st.** ⬧ 1.75 – **11 rm** ☲ 18.00/27.00 **st.**

　🏛 **Soroba House,** Soroba Rd, PA34 4SB, S : 1 m. on A 816 ☏ 2628, 🚗 – ⋔wc ⓟ
　　M 3.50/6.50 ⬧ 1.10 – **12 rm** ☲ 8.20/18.15 – P 16.00/18.50.

AUSTIN-MORRIS-MG-ROVER-TRIUMPH Airds Pl. 　　TALBOT, VAUXHALL Dunollie Rd ☏ 3717
☏ 3173 　　　　　　　　　　　　　　　　　　VOLVO, VW, AUDI-NSU Breadalbane Pl. ☏ 3066
FORD Soroba Rd ☏ 3061

OLD MELDRUM Grampian 🔲🔲🔲 ⑦ – pop. 1,085 – ECD: Wednesday – ☎ 065 12 – 👤.
Envir. : Pitmedden gardens* *AC*, E: 6 m. – Tolquhon Castle* (16C) *AC*, E: 7 ½ m.

Edinburgh 142 – Aberdeen 18 – Fraserburgh 29 – **Inverness 89.**

- ※※ **Meldrum House** 🍴 with rm, AB5 0AE, N: 1 ½ m. off A 947 ☏ 294, ≼, « Large country house, part 13C », 🚗, park – 🛁wc 🚘 **P.** ᴀᴇ ⓞ
  closed 6 January-16 March – **M** 5.00/9.00 🍷 2.00 – **9 rm** ☑ 14.40/37.50 **t.** – P 27.60/35.00 **t.**

ONICH Highland 🔲🔲🔲 ⑩ – pop. 280 – ECD: Saturday – ✉ Fort William – ☎ 085 53.
Edinburgh 122 – Glasgow 93 – Inverness 75 – Oban 39.

- 🏨 **Creag Dhu**, PH33 6RY, on A 82 ☏ 238, ≼ Loch Linnhe and mountains, 🚗 – 🛁wc **P**
  April-October – **M** (bar lunch) approx. 6.75 **st.** 🍷 1.90 – **19 rm** ☑ 12.00/27.00 **st.**

- 🏨 **Onich**, PH33 6RY, on A 82 ☏ 214, ≼ Loch Linnhe and mountains, 🚗 – **P.** ◩ ᴀᴇ
  May-mid October – **M** 3.00/6.00 **st.** 🍷 1.65 – **25 rm** ☑ 9.50/19.00 **st.** – P 17.00/18.50 **st.**

ORKNEY ISLANDS Orkney Islands 🔲🔲🔲 ⑯ – pop. 17,077.
✈ see Mainland: Kirkwall.
⛴, ⛴ see Mainland: Kirkwall and Stromness.

HOY

Old Man of Hoy
See : Rock spike***.

MAINLAND

Birsay – ✉ ☎ 085 672 Birsay.
See : Brough of Birsay (site and ≼**) *AC*. **Envir. :** Kitchener Memorial ❋*** (birds'nests) S: 5 m. – Skara Brae (prehistoric village** *AC*) S : 7 ½ m. – Yesnaby (cliffs** : birds' nests) S: 11 m. – Broch of Gurness* E: 12 m.

Kirkwall – pop. 4,617 – ECD: Wednesday – ✉ ☎ 0856 Kirkwall.
See : Site* – St. Magnus Cathedral**. **Envir. :** Wideford Hill Cairn (Megalithic cairn*, ≼*) W: 2 m.

🏌 Grainbank ☏ 2055, W: 1 m.

✈ ☏ 2421, S : 3 ½ m. – British Airways ☏ 2478 – Loganair ☏ 3025.

⛴ by Orkney Islands Shipping Co.: to Westray via Eday, Stronsay, Sanday, Papa Westray 3 weekly (2 to 6 h) – to North Ronaldsay 1 weekly (2 h 30 mn) – to Shapinsay 2 weekly (30 mn) – to Wyre via Rousay, Egilsay 1 weekly (1 to 4 h) – from Scapa to Flotta (Isle of), Lyness (Isle of Hoy), Longhope (Isle of Hoy) and return 2 weekly (1 to 2 h).

⛴ to Shapinsay (Orkney Islands Shipping Co.) Monday/Saturday 1-3 daily (25 mn).

ℹ Junction Rd ☏ 2856.

- 🏨 **Kirkwall,** Harbour St., KW15 1LF, ☏ 2232, ≼ – 🛗 🛁wc. ◩ ᴀᴇ ⓞ 𝘷𝘪𝘴𝘢
  M 3.50/4.50 **t.** 🍷 1.70 – **38 rm** ☑ 12.00/24.00 **st.**

- 🏨 Lynnfield, Holm Rd, S : 1 m. on A 961 ☏ 2505, 🚗 – **P** – **8 rm.**

- 🏠 **Foveran** 🍴, St. Ola, KW15 1SS, SW: 3 m. on A 964 ☏ 2389, ≼ Scapa Flow – **P.** ◩
  9 rm ☑ 10.50/15.00 **st.**

AUSTIN-MORRIS-MG-ROVER-TRIUMPH 25 Broad St. ☏ 2490
FIAT Junction Rd ☏ 2158
FORD Castle St. ☏ 3212
RENAULT Gt Western Rd ☏ 2601
TALBOT, COLT Gt Western Rd ☏ 2805
VAUXHALL Burnmouth Rd ☏ 2950

Loch Harray – ✉ Loch Harray – ☎ 085 677 Harray.
- 🏨 Merkister, KW17 2LF, ☏ 366, ≼, 🎣, 🚗 – 🛁wc **P**
  19 rm. t.

Stenness – ✉ ☎ 0856 Stromness.
Envir. : Maes Howe Cairn** (Neolithic chambered cairn) *AC*, NE: 1 ½ m. – Ring of Brodgar (stone circle)* NW: 2 ½ m.
- 🏨 **Standing Stones** 🍴, KW16 3JX, ☏ 850 449, ≼ Loch Stenness and Standing Stones, 🎣, 🚗 – **P**
  M (bar lunch) 2.70/6.85 **st.** – **20 rm** ☑ 8.00/16.00.

ORKNEY ISLANDS

Stromness – pop. 1,646 – ECD: Thursday – ✉ ☎ 0856 Stromness.
See : Site*.
Ⓡ Ness ☏ 593.

🛈 Ferry Terminal Building, Pierhead ☏ 716 (June-September).

⛴ to Scrabster (P & O Ferries : Orkney and Shetland Services) Monday/Saturday
1-3 daily (2 h) Sunday in July and August only.

🏠 **Stromness**, 108 Victoria St., KW16 3AA, ☏ 850 298 – ▤ ☐wc ⋔wc
April-October – **M** (buffet lunch) 2.50/5.00 ⏐ 1.50 – ☷ 1.50 – **40 rm** 9.00/14.00.

WESTRAY

Pierowall – ✉ Pierowall – ☎ 085 77 Westray.
🏠 Pierowall, ☏ 208, ⬟, 🚲 – ℗ – **7 rm.**

OVERSCAIG Highland – ✉ Loch Shin – ☎ 054 983 Merkland Lodge.
Edinburgh 235 – Inverness 76.

🏠 Overscaig ⬟, ☏ 245, ⇐ Loch Shin and mountains, ⬟, park – ☐wc ℗. Ⓐ
15 rm.

OYKEL BRIDGE Highland – ✉ Lairg – ☎ 054 984 Rosehall.
Edinburgh 225 – Inverness 66 – Lochinver 31.

🏠 Oykell Bridge ⬟, ☏ 218, ⇐, ⬟, 🚲 – ☐wc 🚗 ℗
16 rm.

PAISLEY Strathclyde 🗺 ⑮ – pop. 95,357 – ECD : Tuesday – ☎ 041 Glasgow.
Ⓡ Barshaw Park ☏ 889 2908, E : 1 m. of Paisley Cross off A 737.
Edinburgh 50 – Ayr 36 – Glasgow 7 – Greenock 16.

🏠 Watermill (Stakis), Lonend, PA1 1SR, ☏ 889 3201 – ▤ 📺 ☐wc 🕾 ℗. Ⓢ Ⓐ ⓪ 𝐕𝐈𝐒𝐀
50 rm.

🏠 **Rockfield**, 125 Renfrew Rd, PA3 4EA, ☏ 889 6182 – 📺 ☐wc ⋔wc 🕾 ℗. Ⓢ Ⓐ ⓪
𝐕𝐈𝐒𝐀
M 4.80/6.50 **t.** ⏐ 1.80 – **12 rm** ☷ 15.45/20.50 **t.**

🏠 Silver Thread (S & N), Lonend, PA1 1TN, on A 726 ☏ 887 2196 – ▤ ☐wc ⋔wc ℗
12 rm.

🏠 **Broadstones Private**, 17 High Calside, PA2 6BY, ☏ 889 4055, 🚲 – ℗
8 rm ☷ 8.50/9.50 **st.**

AUSTIN-MG 46 New Sneddon St. ☏ 889 7882
DATSUN Weir St. ☏ 889 6866
FIAT 4.8 Lochfield Rd ☏ 884 2281
FORD 37/41 Lonend ☏ 887 6231
JAGUAR-ROVER-TRIUMPH 92 Glasgow Rd ☏ 889 8526

OPEL 69 Espedair St. ☏ 889 5254
TALBOT 7 West St. ☏ 889 0011
TOYOTA 53 Love St. ☏ 889 5111
VAUXHALL 15/17 St. James St. ☏ 884 7951

PAPA WESTRAY (Isle of) Orkney (Orkney Islands) – Shipping Services : see Orkney Islands
(Mainland : Kirkwall).

PATHHEAD Lothian – pop. 931 – ECD : Wednesday – ☎ 0875 Ford.
Edinburgh 12 – Haddington 11.

🏠 **Stair Arms** (Open House), EX37 5TX, on A 68 ☏ 320277, 🚲 – 📺 🕾 ℗. Ⓢ Ⓐ ⓪ 𝐕𝐈𝐒𝐀
M a la carte 6.40/8.45 **st.** ⏐ 1.50 – **7 rm** ☷ 15.00/22.50 **st.**

PEAT INN Fife – ✉ Cupar – ☎ 033 484.
Edinburgh 44 – Dundee 21 – Perth 28.

XX **The Peat Inn**, KY15 5LH, ☏ 206 – ℗. Ⓐ
closed Monday, 1 week May, 1 week October and 1 to 18 January – **M** (bar lunch)
a la carte 5.85/7.75 **st.** ⏐ 2.00.

PEEBLES Borders 📖 ⑮ – pop. 5,884 – ECD : Wednesday – ☏ 0721.
Envir. : Neidpath Castle (site*) W : 1 m. – Traquair House* *AC*, SE : 7 ½ m.
🏴 Kirkland St. ☏ 20197 – 🏴 West Linton ☏ 096 86 (West Linton) 589.
🛈 High St. ☏ 20138 (Easter-September). – Edinburgh 23 – Hawick 32 – Glasgow 52.

  🏨 **Peebles Hydro,** Innerleithen Rd, EH45 8LX, ☏ 20602, Telex 72568, ⬳, ✕, ◳, 🚒 –
    ▯ ℗. ♿
    closed 23 to 26 December and 1 to 4 January – **M** 3.75/6.00 **st.** 🍷 2.00 – **144 rm** ⬓
    18.50/33.00 **st.** – P 24.00/30.00 **st.**

  🏨 **Park (Swallow),** Innerleithen Rd, EH45 8BA, ☏ 20451, Group Telex 53168, ⬳, 🚒 –
    TV ⬒wc 🛁wc ☏ ℗ – **23 rm.**

  🏨 **Tontine** (T.H.F.), 39 High St., EH45 8AJ, ☏ 20892 – TV ⬒wc ☏ ℗. ◳ AE ⓞ VISA
    M 4.25/5.60 **st.** 🍷 1.80 – **37 rm** ⬓ 16.50/24.50 **st.**

  🏨 **Cringletie House** 🦢, EH45 8PL, N : 3 m. on A 703 ☏ 072 13 (Eddleston) 233, ⬳,
    « Country house in extensive grounds », ✕, 🚒, park – ▯ ⬒wc ℗
    Mid March-December – **M** 4.50/7.50 **t.** – **16 rm** ⬓ 10.50/27.00 **t.**

  ✕✕ **Dilkusha** with rm, Chambers Ter., EH45 9DZ, ☏ 20590, 🚒 – ℗
    closed February – **M** *(closed Sunday in winter)* a la carte 5.60/8.20 **t.** 🍷 1.80 – **5 rm**
    ⬓ 10.00/17.00 **st.**

    at Eddleston N : 4 ½ m. on A 703 – ✉ Peebles – ☏ 072 13 Eddleston :
  ✕✕ **Horse Shoe Inn,** EH45 8QP, ☏ 225 – ℗. ◳ AE ⓞ VISA
    closed Christmas Day and 1 January – **M** a la carte 5.55/7.35 **t.** 🍷 1.90.

AUSTIN-MORRIS Innerleithen Rd ☏ 20627   LANCIA George St. ☏ 20545
AUSTIN-MORRIS-MG St. Andrews Rd ☏ 20886

PERTH Tayside 𝟵𝟴𝟲 ⑪ – pop. 43,030 – ECD: Wednesday – ☎ 0738.

Envir. : Scone Palace* (furniture) *AC*, N : 4 m. by A 93 **Y**.

⌐ Moncrieffe Island ☏ 25170 by A 90 **z** – ⌐ Cherrybank ☏ 24377, West boundary, by A 9 **z**.

🚗 ☏ 23366.

🛈 The Round House, Marshall Pl. PH2 8NU, ☏ 22900 and 27108, Telex 76421.

Edinburgh 42 – Aberdeen 82 – Dundee 22 – Dunfermline 29 – Glasgow 59 – Inverness 117 – Oban 93.

Plan on preceding page

⚏ **Station** (B.T.H.), Leonard St., PH2 8HE, ☏ 24141, Telex 76481. 🚗 – 🛗 📺 **P**. 🏊. ⌂
Æ ⓪ *VISA*   **Z n**
M a la carte 7.55/14.80 **st.** – **53 rm** ⌑ 23.45/41.00 **st.**

⚏ **Royal George** (T.H.F.), Tay St., PH1 5LD, ☏ 24455 – 📺 🛏wc ☎ 🚗 **P**. 🏊. ⌂ Æ
⓪ *VISA*   **Y c**
M 4.00/5.00 **st.** ⚘ 1.65 – **43 rm** ⌑ 17.00/25.50 **st.**

⚏ **City Mills** (Stakis), West Mill St., PH1 5QP, ☏ 28281. 🚗 – 📺 🛏wc ☎ **P**. 🏊. ⌂ Æ
⓪ *VISA*   **Y a**
M 4.55/5.75 **st.** ⚘ 1.70 – **40 rm** ⌑ 17.50/28.00 **st.**

⌂ **Pitcullen,** 17-18 Pitcullen Crescent, PH2 7HT, NE : ¾ m. on A 94 ☏ 26506 – **P** **Y r**
8 rm ⌑ 5.50/11.00.

XX **Huntingtower** 🍴 with rm, Crieff Rd, PH1 3JT, W : 3 ½ m. off A 85 ☏073 883 (Almond
bank) 241. ⪡, 🚗 – 🛏wc **P**. ⌂ Æ ⓪ *VISA*   on A 85 **Y**
M a la carte 7.35/10.10 **t.** ⚘ 1.70 – **8 rm** ⌑ 18.00/28.00 **st.** – P 22.50/25.00 **st.**

X **Timothy's,** 24 St. John St., PH1 5SP, ☏ 26641, Smörrebrod   **Y e**
closed Sunday, Monday, Christmas Day and 1 January – **M** a la carte 1.95/6.40 **t.** ⚘ 1.85.

at New Scone NE : 2 ½ m. by A 94 – **Y** – ✉ ☎ 0738 Perth :

⚏ **Murrayshall House** 🍴, E : 1 m. ☏ 51171. ⪡, « Country house atmosphere », 🚗, park –
📺 🛏wc ⍾wc ☎ **P**. Æ ⓪ *VISA*
M 3.75/6.00 **t.** – **7 rm** ⌑ 16.50/24.50 **t.**

at Glencarse E : 6 ½ m. off A 85 – **z** – ✉ Perth – ☎ 073 886 Glencarse :

X **Newton House** with rm, PH2 7LX, ☏ 250. 🚗 – ⍾ **P**
closed Monday – **M** 3.50/6.00 ⚘ 2.50 – **7 rm** ⌑ 10.00/18.65.

AUSTIN-MORRIS-MG-ROVER-TRIUMPH 15 King Ed-
ward St. ☏ 26101
BMW, PEUGEOT, ROLLS ROYCE 50/56 Leonard St.
☏ 25481
CITROEN 55/60 South St. ☏ 23335
DATSUN, MERCEDES-BENZ, SAAB 2 Dunkeld Rd ☏
28211
FORD Riggs Rd ☏ 25121

JAGUAR-MORRIS-MG-ROVER-TRIUMPH Glenearn
Rd ☏ 20811
MAZDA 23/29 South Methven St. ☏ 23757
TALBOT Dunkeld Rd ☏ 25252
VAUXHALL Dunkeld Rd ☏ 26241
VOLVO Arran Rd, North Muirton ☏ 22156
VW, AUDI-NSU 58/68 Perth Rd, Scone ☏ 0738 (Scone)
51276

PETERHEAD Grampian 𝟵𝟴𝟲 ⑦ – pop. 14,160 – ECD: Wednesday – ☎ 0779.

Envir. : Bullers of Buchan (cliffs**) S : 6 m. – Cruden Bay (site*) SW : 8 m.

⌐. ⌐ Craigewan ☏ 2149.

Edinburgh 158 – Aberdeen 34 – Fraserburgh 18.

⚏ Palace (Swallow), Prince St., AB4 6PL, ☏ 4821 – 🛗 📺 🛏wc ☎ **P**. 🏊
59 rm.

PIEROWALL Orkney Islands – see Orkney Islands (Westray).

PITCAPLE Grampian – ☎ 046 76.

Edinburgh 145 – Aberdeen 21.

⚏ **Pittodrie House** 🍴, AB5 9HS, SW : 1 ¾ m. off A 96 ☏ 202. ⪡, « Country house with
many antiques ». 🚗, park – 📺 🛏wc ☎ 🚗 **P**. ⌂ Æ ⓪ *VISA*
M 6.35/10.15 **st.** – **11 rm** ⌑ 15.20/31.65 **st.**

PITLOCHRY Tayside 𝟵𝟴𝟲 ⑪ – pop. 2,599 – ECD: Thursday – ☎ 0796.

Envir. : Blair Castle (interior**) *AC*, NW : 7 ½ m. – Linn of Tummel* NW : 4 m. – Quenn's
View (⪡* of Loch Tummel) NW : 6 m. – ⌐ ☏ 2792.

🛈 28 Atholl Rd ☏ 2215.

Edinburgh 68 – Inverness 91 – Perth 26.

⚏ **Atholl Palace** (T.H.F.) 🍴, PH16 5LX, on A 9 ☏ 2400, Telex 76406. ⪡, XX, ⌇ heated,
🚗, park – 🛗 📺 **P**. 🏊. ⌂ Æ ⓪ *VISA*
M 4.60/6.25 **st.** ⚘ 1.65 – **117 rm** ⌑ 17.00/26.50.

⚏ **Green Park,** Clunie Bridge Rd, PH16 5JY, ☏ 2537. ⪡, 🚗 – 🛏wc ⍾wc **P**
Mid March-October – **M** 3.80/7.00 **st.** ⚘ 1.70 – **42 rm** ⌑ 11.00/22.00 **st.**

⚏ **Pine Trees** 🍴, Strathview Ter., PH16 5QR, ☏ 2121. ⪡, ⌇, 🚗, park – 🛏wc ⍾wc
🚗 **P**. ⌂ Æ ⓪ *VISA*
Easter-mid October – **M** a la carte 3.95/6.70 **st.** ⚘ 2.00 – **29 rm** ⌑ 11.00/25.00 **st.**

⚏ Fisher's, 75-79 Atholl Rd, PH16 5BN, ☏ 2000. 🚗 – 🛗 🛏wc 🚗 **P** – **78 rm.**

🏠 **Burnside,** West Moulin Rd, PH16 5EA, ☎ 2203, 🚗 – 🛏wc 🚿wc **Ⓟ**. **AE Ⓓ**
Mid March-mid November – **M** approx. 5.50 **st.** ⏧ 1.90 – **22 rm** ⟷ 10.35/20.50 **st.**

🏠 **Acarsaid,** 8 Atholl Rd, PH16 5BX, ☎ 2389 – 🛏wc 🚿wc **Ⓟ**
Easter-October – **M** (dinner only) 6.50 **t.** ⏧ 1.70 – **20 rm** ⟷ 10.90/23.80 **st.**

🏠 **Craigard,** Strathview Ter., PH16 5AZ, ☎ 2592, 🚗 – 🛏wc 🚿wc **Ⓟ**
April-October – **M** (bar lunch) approx. 5.25 **s.** ⏧ 1.75 – **18 rm** ⟷ 8.30/17.50 **s.**

🏠 Moulin, Kirkmichael Rd, PH16 5EW, N : 1 m. on A 924 ☎ 2196, 🚗 – 🛏wc **Ⓟ**
23 rm.

🏠 **Brae Knowe,** Knockard Rd, PH16 5BS, ☎ 2147, ≼ – 🛏wc 🚿wc **Ⓟ**. **VISA**
April-October – **M** (bar lunch) approx. 5.70 ⏧ 1.80 – **15 rm** ⟷ 12.50/25.00.

🏠 **Port-an-Eilean** ⑊, Strathtummel, PH16 5HJ, NW : 10 m. by A 9 on B 8019, ☎ 088 24
(Tummel Bridge) 233, ≼ Loch Tummel and hills, « Country house on banks of Loch
Tummel », ⑊, 🚗, park – 🛏wc **Ⓟ**
Easter-mid October – **M** a la carte 2.70/4.70 **t.** ⏧ 2.00 – **12 rm** ⟷ 8.00/18.00 – P 14.50/
18.00.

🏠 **Loch Tummel,** Strathtummel, PH16 5RP, NW : 9 ½ m. by A 9 on B 8019 ☎ 088 24
(Tummel Bridge) 272, ≼ Loch Tummel and hills, ⑊ – 🛏wc 🚿wc **Ⓟ**
Easter-October – **M** a la carte 6.45/9.00 **st.** ⏧ 2.10 – **9 rm** ⟷ 11.35/24.90 **st.**

🏠 **Airdaniar,** 160 Atholl Rd, PH16 5QL, ☎ 2266, 🚗 – **Ⓟ**
April-October – **M** (bar lunch) 4.50 **st.** ⏧ 1.50 – **10 rm** ⟷ 9.80/15.60 **st.** – P 13.50 **st.**

🏠 **Claymore,** 162 Atholl Rd, PH16 5AR, ☎ 2888, 🚗 – **Ⓟ**
April-October – **M** (bar lunch) 2.80/7.50 **t.** ⏧ 1.60 – **12 rm** ⟷ 11.80/23.00 **st.**

🏠 **Craig Urrard,** 10 Atholl Rd, PH16 5BX, ☎ 2346, 🚗 – 🚿wc **Ⓟ**
12 rm ⟷ 11.00/24.40.

POLMONT Central – pop. 2,153 – ECD : Wednesday – ⓞ 0324.
🏌 Grangemouth ☎ 711500.
Edinburgh 21 – Falkirk 2.5 – Stirling 14.

🏨 **Inchyra Grange,** Grange Rd, FK2 0YB, ☎ 711911, 🚗 – **TV** 🛏wc 🚿wc ☏ **Ⓟ**. 🅰. 🅺
AE Ⓓ VISA
M 4.25/6.50 **st.** ⏧ 2.40 – **33 rm** ⟷ 17.50/26.50 **t.**

PORT APPIN Strathclyde – ✉ pop. 100 – ECD : Thursday – ⓞ 063 173 Appin.
Edinburgh 136 – Ballachulish 20 – Oban 24.

🏠 **Airds,** PA38 4DF, ☎ 236, ≼ Loch Linnhe and hills of Kingairloch – 🛏wc **Ⓟ**
Easter-mid October – **M** (bar lunch) 3.00/7.00 **st.** – **14 rm** ⟷ 11.00/26.00 **st.** –
P 19.00/21.00 **st.**

PORT ASKAIG Strathclyde 🔢 ⑭ – see Islay (Isle of).

PORT ELLEN Strathclyde 🔢 ⑭ – Shipping Services : see Islay (Isle of).

PORTPATRICK Dumfries and Galloway 🔢 ⑱ – pop. 643 – ECD : Thursday – ✉ Stranraer –
ⓞ 077 681.
Envir.: Logan gardens* *AC*, SE : 13 m. **Exc.:** Mull of Galloway (site and ≼**) SE : 24 ½ m. by
Drummore.
🏌 ☎ 273.
Edinburgh 138 – Ayr 61 – Dumfries 80 – Stranraer 8.

🏨 **Knockinaam Lodge** ⑊, DG9 9AD, SE : 3 ¼ m. off. A 77 ☎ 203, ≼ garden and sea, ⑊,
park – 🛏wc ☏ **Ⓟ**
season – **10 rm.**

🏨 **Portpatrick** (Mt. Charlotte), Heugh Rd, DG9 8TD, ☎ 333, ≼, 💥 ⊐ heated, 🚗 – 🛎
🛏wc **Ⓟ**. 🅺 **AE Ⓓ VISA**
May-mid October – **M** 4.00/4.60 **st.** ⏧ 2.15 – **63 rm** ⟷ 14.50/29.00 **s.** – P 15.00/17.50 **s.**

🏠 **Fernhill,** Heugh Rd, DG9 8TD, ☎ 220, ≼, 🚗 – 🛏wc 🚿wc **Ⓟ**
March-November – **M** (bar lunch) 5.75 **t.** ⏧ 2.00 – **15 rm** ⟷ 11.50/12.50 **t.** – P 13.90/
17.00 **t.**

PORTREE Highland 🔢 ⑥ – see Skye (Isle of).

PORT WILLIAM Dumfries and Galloway – pop. 528 – ECD : Thursday – ⓞ 098 87.
🏌 ☎ 358, SE : 3 m.
Edinburgh 144 – Dumfries 67 – Stranraer 23.

🏠 **Monreith Arms,** The Square, DG8 9SE, ☎ 232 – **Ⓟ**
M a la carte 3.10/5.25 **st.** ⏧ 1.60 – **13 rm** ⟷ 7.00/15.00 **st.** – P 12.50 **st.**

OPEL South St. ☎ 277

PRESTWICK Strathclyde 986 ⑭ – pop. 13,437 – ECD : Wednesday – ☎ 0292.

✈ ☏ 79822 ext. 4011/4051 – **Glasgow Terminal** : Stand no. 23, Anderston Cross Bus Station, Blythswood St.

✈ see also Glasgow.

🛈 Links Rd ☏ 79234 – Prestwick Airport ☏ 77309, Telex 778916.

Edinburgh 73 – Ayr 4 – Glasgow 30.

Plan of Built up Area : see Ayr

🏨 Carlton (Osprey), 187 Ayr Rd, KA9 1TP, ☏ 76811 – TV ⇌wc ☎ ℗   BY **v**
    39 rm.

⌂ Kincraig, 39 Ayr Rd, KA9 1SY, ☏ 79480 – ℗   BY **c**
    7 rm ⊑ 5.50/10.00 **st.**

    at Monkton N : 2 ¾ m. by A 79 – **BY** – ✉ ☎ 0292 Prestwick :

🏨 **Adamton House,** SE : 1 ¼ m. off B 739 ☏ 70678, ⬑, ⚘, park – TV ⇌wc ⋔wc ☎ ℗.
    🖭 AE ⓪ VISA
    M a la carte 4.75/11.10 🍾 2.15 – **30 rm** ⊑ 16.50/27.50 **t.**

AUSTIN-MORRIS-MG   1 Monkton Rd ☏ 77415   OPEL   97/99 Main St. ☏ 70545

QUOTHQUAN Strathclyde – pop. 73 – ✉ ☎ 0899 Biggar.

Edinburgh 30 – Carlisle 72 – Glasgow 37.

🏛 **Shieldhill House** 🦢, ML12 6NA, NE : 1 m. ☏ 20035, ⬑, ⚘ – ⇌wc ⋔wc ℗. 🖭 AE
    ⓪
    M a la carte 4.30/8.25 **t.** 🍾 2.50 – **20 rm** ⊑ 11.50/22.00 **t.** – P 16.00/17.50 **t.**

RAASAY (Isle of) Highland.

🚢 to Isle of Skye : Sconser (Caledonian MacBrayne) Monday/Saturday 3-4 daily (15 mn).

RENFREW Strathclyde 986 ⑭⑮ – pop. 18,595 – ECD : Wednesday – ☎ 041 Glasgow.

Edinburgh 50 – Glasgow 7.

🏨 Normandy (Stakis), Inchinnan Rd, PA4 9EJ, ☏ 886 4100, Telex 778897 – 🛗 TV ⇌wc
    ☎ & ℗. 🏊 . 🖭 AE ⓪ VISA – **142 rm.**

🏨 **Dean Park,** 91 Glasgow Rd, PA4 8YB, ☏ 886 3771, Telex 779032 – TV ⇌wc
    ☎ & ℗. 🏊 . 🖭 AE ⓪ VISA
    M 3.30/4.30 **t.** 🍾 2.10 – **130 rm** ⊑ 16.00/22.50 **t.**

XX **Piccolo Mondo,** 63 Hairst St., PA4 8QY, ☏ 886 3055, Italian rest., Dancing – ℗. 🖭
    AE ⓪ VISA
    closed Sunday – **M** a la carte 5.70/11.00 **t.** 🍾 1.80.

TALBOT   14/18 Fulbar St. ☏ 886 3354   VAUXHALL   Porterfield Rd ☏ 886 2777

RHU Strathclyde – see Helensburgh.

RHUBODACH Strathclyde – Shipping Services : see Bute (Isle of).

RHUM (Isle of) Inverness. (Highland) 986 ⑥ – Shipping Services : see Mallaig.

ROCKCLIFFE Dumfries and Galloway – pop. 170 – ✉ Dalbeattie – ☎ 055 663.

See : Site*.

Edinburgh 95 – Dumfries 18 – Stranraer 69.

🏨 **Baron's Craig** 🦢, DG5 4QF, ☏ 225, ⬑, ⚘, park – ⇌wc ℗
    Easter-October – **M** 5.00/8.00 **t.** 🍾 1.70 – **27 rm** ⊑ 15.35/36.00 **t.** – P 26.00/32.20 **t.**

ROTHES Grampian 986 ⑦ – pop. 1,204 – ECD : Wednesday – ☎ 034 03.

Edinburgh 185 – Aberdeen 61 – Fraserburgh 59 – Inverness 49.

🏨 **Rothes Glen,** IV33 7AH, N : 3 m. on A 941 ☏ 254, ⬑, « Country house atmosphere »,
    ⚘, park – ⇌wc ☎ ℗
    March-mid November – **M** 3.60/7.20 **t.** 🍾 1.95 – **19 rm** ⊑ 16.10/34.60 **t.**

ROTHESAY Strathclyde 986 ⑭ – see Bute (Isle of).

ROUSAY (Isle of) Orkney Islands – Shipping Services : see Orkney Islands (Mainland : Kirkwall).

RUTHERGLEN Strathclyde – See Glasgow.

ST. ANDREWS Fife 🔳🔳🔳 ⑪ – pop. 11,630 – ECD : Thursday – ☎ 033 481 (4 fig.) or 0334 (5 fig.).

See : Cathedral* (St. Rule's tower and Museum *AC*). **Envir.** : Leuchars (church*) NW : 6 m.

🏌 ⚑ 3938, St. Andrews Links – 🏌 ⚑ 4296, St. Andrews Links.

ℹ South St. ⚑ 2021 and 72021.

Edinburgh 49 – Dundee 14 – Stirling 51.

🏨 **Old Course** (B.T.H.) ⧉, Old Station Rd, KY16 9SP, ⚑ 74371, Telex 76280, ≤, 🏌 – 🛗
    📺 ♿ 🅿 ⛵ ⬛ AE ① VISA
    M a la carte 12.30/17.35 **st.** – **68 rm** ⊇ 29.55/50.30.

🏨 **Rufflets** ⧉, Strathkinness Low Rd, KY16 9TX, W : 1 ½ m. on B 939 ⚑ 72594, ≤,
    « Country house in large garden » – 🚿wc 🕾 🚗 🅿. AE ① VISA
    closed mid January-mid February – **M** a la carte 6.00/9.50 **t.** 🍷 2.00 – **22 rm** ⊇ 13.00/29.00 **t.**

🏨 **St. Andrews**, 40 The Scores, KY16 9AS, ⚑ 72611, Group Telex 777205, ≤ – 🛗 📺
    🚿wc 🛁wc 🕾. ⬛ AE ① VISA
    M approx. 6.35 **st.** 🍷 1.75 – **27 rm** ⊇ 15.00/29.00 **st.**

🏨 **Star**, Market St. KY16 9PA, ⚑ 75701, Group Telex 777205 – 📺 🚿wc 🛁wc 🕾. ⬛
    AE ①
    M approx. 6.35 **st.** 🍷 1.75 – **28 rm** ⊇ 13.00/19.50 **st.**

 at Grange S : 1 ½ m. by A 959 – ✉ ☎ 0334 St. Andrews :

XX **Grange Inn**, KY16 8LJ, ⚑ 72670, ≤, « 16C inn », �──, – 🅿. ⬛ AE ① VISA
    M a la carte 6.60/12.30 🍷 2.00.

AUSTIN-MORRIS-MG-WOLSELEY West Port ⚑ 72101

ST. COMBS Grampian – pop. 738 – ECD : Wednesday – ✉ Fraserburgh – ☎ 034 65 Inverallochy.

Edinburgh 166 – Aberdeen 42 – Fraserburgh 6.

🏨 **Tufted Duck** ⧉, AB4 5YS, ⚑ 2481, ≤ – 📺 🚿wc 🛁wc 🕾 🅿. AE ① VISA
    M 4.00/5.25 **t.** 🍷 2.25 – **18 rm** ⊇ 15.50/27.00 **t.**

ST. FILLANS Tayside – pop. 160 – ECD : Wednesday – ☎ 076 485.

🏌 ⚑ 261.

Edinburgh 65 – Glasgow 55 – Oban 64 – Perth 29.

🏨 **Four Seasons**, PH6 2NF, ⚑ 281, ≤ Loch Earn and mountains, « Tasteful decor », �──, –
    📺 🚿wc 🕾 🅿
    April-October – **M** 4.50/5.50 **t.** 🍷 1.40 – **18 rm** ⊇ 18.50/37.00 **st.** – P 22.50/27.50 **st.**

🏨 **Drummond Arms**, PH6 2NF, ⚑ 212, ≤, �──, – 🚿wc 🅿. ⬛ AE ①
    April-October – **M** 3.65/6.70 **st.** 🍷 2.00 – **39 rm** ⊇ 13.80/28.00 **st.**

ST. MARY'S LOCH Borders – ☎ 075 04 Cappercleuch.

See : Loch*.

Edinburgh 56 – Moffat 19 – Selkirk 17.

🏨 **Rodono**, TD7 5LH, ⚑ 232, ≤ St. Mary's Loch and hills, 🎣, �──, – 🅿
    March-November, Christmas and 1 January – **M** 5.75 🍷 2.50 – **10 rm** ⊇ 10.50/21.00 **st.**– P 16.25 **st.**

SALEN Strathclyde 🔳🔳🔳 ⑩ – see Mull (Isle of).

SANDAY (Isle of) Orkney Islands 🔳🔳🔳 ⑯ – Shipping Services : see Orkney Islands (Mainland : Kirkwall).

SANDBANK Strathclyde – see Dunoon.

SANQUHAR Dumfries and Galloway 🔳🔳🔳 ⑮ – pop. 1,991 – ECD : Thursday – ☎ 065 92.

🏌 ⚑ 577, SW : ¼ m.

Edinburgh 57 – Ayr 32 – Dumfries 27 – Glasgow 51.

🏨 **Mennockfoot Lodge**, DG3 5LU, SE : 2 m. on A 76 ⚑ 382, ≤, �──, – 🚿wc 🅿
    M 4.00/5.50 **t.** – **12 rm** ⊇ 11.00/19.00 **t.** – P 18.00/22.00 **t.**

SCALLOWAY Shetland Islands 🔳🔳🔳 ⑯ – see Shetland Islands (Mainland).

SCALPAY (Isle of) Highland.

🚢 to Isle of Harris : Kyles Scalpay (Caledonian MacBrayne) Monday/Saturday 4-8 daily (10 mn).

SCOURIE Highland 🔳🔳🔳 ② – pop. 250 – ✉ Lairg – ☎ 0971.

See : Site*. – Edinburgh 261 – Inverness 102.

🏨 **Scourie** ⧉, IV27 4SX, ⚑ 2396, ≤, 🎣 – 🚿wc 🅿. VISA
    March-21 October – **M** *(closed Friday)* 3.00/5.00 **t.** 🍷 2.20 – **22 rm** ⊇ 9.20/20.85 **t.** – P 12.25/13.50 **t.**

SCRABSTER Highland **986** ③ – Shipping Services: see Thurso.

SEAMILL Strathclyde – ECD: Wednesday – ✉ ✆ 0294 West Kilbride.
Edinburgh 73 – Ayr 22 – Glasgow 30.

  🏯 **Inverclyde,** 31 Ardrossan Rd, KA23 9NA, ☏ 823124 – **Ⓟ**
    M 2.95/5.50 **st.** – **10 rm** ⊑ 9.00/14.00 **st.**

SHAPINSAY (Isle of) Orkney Islands – Shipping Services: see Orkney Islands (Mainland: Kirkwall).

SHETLAND ISLANDS Shetland Islands **986** ⑯ ⑳ – pop. 17,327.
  🛫 see Mainland: Sumburgh.
  🛥 by Shetland Islands Council: from Toft (Mainland) to Ulsta (Yell) May-October 14-20 daily (22 mn) – from Gutcher (Yell) to Belmont (Unst) May-October 9-14 daily (12 mn); to Oddsta (Fetlar) May-October 1-3 daily (25 mn) – from Laxo (Mainland) to Symbister (Whalsay) May-October 5-7 daily (25 mn).
  🛥, 🛥 see also Mainland: Lerwick.

MAINLAND

  Hillswick – ✉ ✆ 080 623 Hillswick.
  See: Site*. **Envir.**: Esha Ness (St. Magnus Bay***) W: 8 m. – E: Sullom Voe**.

  🏨 **St. Magnus Bay** ⑊, ZE2 9RW, ☏ 209, ⟨ St. Magnus Bay, ⟨, ⟨ – 🚽wc **Ⓟ**
    M 3.50/6.00 **s.** 🍷 2.60 – **33 rm** ⊑ 15.00/29.00 **s.**

  Lerwick – pop. 6,127 – ECD: Wednesday – ✉ ✆ 0595 Lerwick.
  See: Site* – Harbour* – Clickhimin Broch*. **Envir.**: W: The Deeps (cliff)*** – Loch of Tingwall* NW: 5 m. – Gulberwick (wick ⟨*) SW: 5 m.
  🏌18 ☏ 059 584 (Gott) 369, N: 3 ½ m.
  🛥 to Aberdeen (P & O Ferries: Orkney and Shetland Services) 2-3 weekly (14 h) – to Bressay (Shetland Islands Council) May-October 8-10 daily (10 mn).
  🛈 Area Tourist Officer, Alexandra Wharf ☏ 3434, Telex 75119.

  🏨 **Kveldsro House,** Greenfield Pl., ZE1 0AN, ☏ 2195, ⟨ – 📺 🚽wc **Ⓟ**
    closed Christmas and 1 January – **M** 5.00/8.00 🍷 2.60 – **14 rm** ⊑ 18.50/34.00.

  🏨 **Lerwick** (Thistle), 15 South Rd, ZE1 0RB, ☏ 2166, Telex 75128, ⟨ Bressay Sound – 📺
    🚽wc 🚽wc ✆ **Ⓟ**. 🅰. 🄰 Ⓐ🄴 ⑩ **VISA**
    M 4.50/7.25 **st.** 🍷 2.95 – ⊑ 3.30 – **24 rm** 27.00/38.00 **t.**

AUSTIN-MORRIS-MG Commercial Rd ☏ 3313   TALBOT 20 Commercial Rd ☏ 2896
RENAULT North Rd ☏ 3315   VAUXHALL 26 North Rd ☏ 2855

  Scalloway – pop. 896 – ECD: Thursday – ✉ ✆ 059 588 Scalloway.
  See: Site and ⟨**.
  🏌9 Berry Farm ☏ 219.

  Sumburgh – ✉ ✆ 095 06 Sumburgh.
  See: Jarlshof (prehistoric village**, site*). **Envir.**: St. Ninian's Isle** NW 9 m. – Levenwick ⟨* N: 9 m.
  🛫 ☏ 654.

  Voe – pop. 220 – ✉ ✆ 080 68 Voe.
  See: Site*. **Envir.**: Dales Voe* N: 5 m. – Walls (site*) SW: 18 ½ m. **Exc.**: W: Voe of Snarraness** – Swarbacks Minn (from B 9071 ⟨**) – Sound of Papa** – The Rona Aith Voe (from B 9071 ⟨**).

  Whiteness – ✉ Whiteness – ✆ 059 584 Gott.
  🏯 **Westings** ⑊, ZE2 9LJ, ☏ 242, ⟨ The Deeps and Islands – 🚽wc **Ⓟ**
    M *(closed Sunday, Monday and lunch to non-residents)* a la carte 3.20/8.10 **t.** – **10 rm** ⊑ 16.50/26.00 **t.**

UNST

  Baltasound – pop. 246 – ✉ ✆ 095 781 Baltasound.
  🏯 Baltasound, ZE2 9DS, ☏ 334, ⟨ – 🚽wc **Ⓟ** – **10 rm.**

SKEABOST Highland – see Skye (Isle of).

SKELMORLIE Strathclyde 🅖🅑🅖 ⑭ – pop. 1,535 – ECD : Wednesday – ☎ 0475 Wemyss Bay.
Edinburgh 73 – Ayr 36 – Glasgow 30.

🏨 **Manor Park** ⏛, PA17 5HE, S : 2 ¾ m. on A 78 ☏ 520832, ← gardens and Firth of Clyde,
« Extensive well kept gardens », park – 📺 🛏wc 🗱wc ☏ 🅿
closed January – **M** 4.75/6.00 t. ▯ 1.80 – **14 rm** ⊇ 14.50/29.00 t.

✗✗ **Redcliffe** with rm, 25 Shore Rd, on A 78 ☏ 521036, ← – 📺 🗱wc ☏ 🅿. 🖭 🅰🅴
M 4.50/5.95 t. ▯ 2.10 – **5 rm** ⊇ 17.00/25.00 st.

SKYE (Isle of) Highland 🅖🅑🅖 ⑥ – pop. 7,364.
See : East coast scenery and Cuillin Hills★★★.
✈ ☏ 34121.
🛳 by Caledonian MacBrayne : from Kyleakin to Kyle of Lochalsh : frequent services every day
(5 mn) – from Armadale to Mallaig : 1-5 daily (30 mn) – from Uig to Lochmaddy (North Uist)
Monday/Saturday 3-6 weekly (2 h direct ; via Tarbert (Isle of Harris) May-October : 3 weekly –
from Sconser to Isle of Raasay : Monday/Saturday 3-4 daily (15 mn) – from Uig to Tarbert :
Monday/Saturday 3-6 weekly (2 h direct) ; via Lochmaddy May-October 3 weekly.

Ardvasar – ✉ ☎ 047 14 Ardvasar.
Envir. : Armadale (site★★) NE : 1 ½ m.

🏛 **Ardvasar** ⏛, IV45 8RS, ☏ 223, ✎ – 🛏wc 🅿
M (bar lunch Monday to Saturday) approx. 5.50 ▯ 2.20 – **11 rm** ⊇ 9.00/22.00.

Broadford – pop. 310 – ECD : Wednesday – ✉ ☎ 047 12 Broadford.
See : Broadford Bay★★ – Red Hills★★. **Envir. :** Elgol (site★★★) SW : 13 ½ m. – Sound of
Sleat★★ SE : by A 851 – Kyleakin (site★) E : 8 m.
🛈 ☏ 361 and 463 (April-October).

🏛 **Broadford**, IV49 9AB, ☏ 204, ←, ✎, 🍴 – 🛏wc 🗱wc 🅿
M (bar lunch) 2.50/7.50 st. ▯ 1.10 – **28 rm** ⊇ 13.50/26.00 s.

VW, AUDI Broadford ☏ 225

Dunvegan – pop. 301 – ✉ ☎ 047 022 Dunvegan.
See : Loch★★ – Dunvegan Castle★ *AC*.

🏛 **Dunvegan**, IV55 8WB, ☏ 202, ← Loch Dunvegan – 🛏wc 🅿. 🖭 🅰🅴 🆅🅸🆂🅰
M 3.50/7.00 t. ▯ 2.00 – **16 rm** ⊇ 14.00/20.00 st.

Isleornsay – ✉ ☎ 047 13 Isleornsay.

🏛 **Kinloch Lodge** ⏛, IV43 8QY, N : 1 ½ m. off A 85 ☏ 214, ← Loch Na Dal, ✎, 🍴 –
🛏wc 🅿
April-October – **M** (bar lunch) approx. 7.00 ▯ 2.20 – **12 rm** ⊇ 10.50/24.00.

Portree – pop. 1,374 – ECD : Wednesday – ✉ ☎ 0478 Portree.
See : Site★ – Sound of Raasay★★★. **Envir. :** Old Man of Storr★★ N : 7 m. – Loch Bracadale★★
SW : 9 m. **Exc. :** Kilt Rock (←★★★), Staffin Bay and Quiraing★★★ N : 18 m.
🛈 Meall House, ☏ 2137, Telex 75202.

🏨 Royal, Bank St., IV51 9BU, ☏ 2525 – 🛏wc 🅿
26 rm.

🏛 **Rosedale**, Beaumont Crest, IV51 9DB, ☏ 2531, ← harbour – 🛏wc
Early May-mid October – **M** (bar lunch) approx. 5.00 t. ▯ 1.60 – **20 rm** ⊇ 10.00/
23.50.

AUSTIN-MORRIS-MG, FORD Dunvegan Rd ☏ 2554   AUSTIN-MORRIS-MG ☏ 2002

Skeabost – ✉ ☎ 047 032 Skeabost Bridge.

🏨 **Skeabost House** ⏛, IV51 9NP, ☏ 202, ← Loch Snizort Beag, « Country house in grounds
bordering Loch Snizort Beag », ✎, 🍴, park – 🛏wc 🅿
Mid April-October – **M** 2.75/5.00 – **22 rm** ⊇ 7.95/21.15.

Sligachan – ✉ ☎ 047 852 Sligachan.
See : Site★★★ – Loch★★. **Envir. :** Loch Harport★★ W : 6 m.

🏨 **Sligachan**, IV47 8SW, ☏ 204, ← mountains and Loch Sligachan, ✎, 🍴 – 🛏wc 🚗 🅿
Easter-mid October – **M** approx. 7.50 st. ▯ 2.75 – **23 rm** ⊇ 13.00/29.00 st.

Uig – pop. 103 – ECD : Wednesday – ✉ ☎ 047 042 Uig.
See : Loch Snizort★★. **Envir. :** Score Bay★ N : 8 m.

🏨 **Uig** ⏛, IV51 9YE, ☏ 205, ← Uig bay and harbour, 🍴 – 🛏wc 🗱wc 🅿. 🖭 🅰🅴 🅾 🆅🅸🆂🅰
Easter-September – **M** (bar lunch) 2.00/5.75 st. ▯ 2.50 – **25 rm** ⊇ 16.10/32.20 st.

SLIGACHAN Highland 🅖🅑🅖 ⑥ – see Skye (Isle of).

 Lothian 📖 ⑮ – pop. 5,056 – ✆ 031 Edinburgh.
See : Forth Bridge ** *AC.* **Envir. :** Hopetoun House ** *AC,* W : 3 m. – Blackness Castle* (15C)
AC, W : 8 ½ m.

Edinburgh 9 – Dunfermline 7 – Glasgow 40.

- **Forth Bridges Lodge** (County), EH30 9SF, junction A 90 and Forth Bridge ☏ 331 1199,
  Telex 727430, ≼ Firth of Forth and Bridges, 🚗 – 📺 🛏 wc ☎ 🅿. 🏊. 🔲 AE ⓘ VISA
  M a la carte 4.05/9.40 **st.** 🍷 1.80 – **98 rm** 18.50/27.00 **s.**

- ✕✕ Hawes Inn (Swallow) with rm, Edinburgh Rd, EH30 9TA, ☏ 331 1990, Group Telex
  53168, 🚗 – ☎ 🅿
  9 rm.

 Highland 📖 ⑩ – pop. 235 – ECD : Thursday – ✆ 039 781.
Envir. : N : Loch Lochy** – Clunes Forest (waterfall)* NW : 3 ½ m.

Edinburgh 133 – Inverness 56 – Kyle of Lochalsh 66 – Oban 58 – Perth 91.

- **Letterfinlay Lodge**, PH34 4DZ, N : 7 m. on A 82 ☏ 039 784 (Invergloy) 222, ≼, 🎣, 🚗 –
  🅿
  M (bar lunch) approx. 6.00 🍷 1.70 – **12 rm** 🛏 10.00/24.00.

- **Spean Bridge**, PH34 4ES, ☏ 250, 🎣 – 🛏 wc 🅿. 🔲 AE VISA
  M (bar lunch) approx. 5.30 **s.** 🍷 1.50 – **28 rm** 🛏 8.50/22.00 **s.**

 Tayside – ✉ Blairgowrie – ✆ 025 085 Glenshee – Winter Sports.
Envir. : Devil's Elbow** N : 6 m. – S : Glenshee (❄** by chairlift 15 mn, *AC*).

Edinburgh 76 – Dundee 36 – Perth 34.

Hotels see : Braemar N : 19 ½ m.

STIRLING

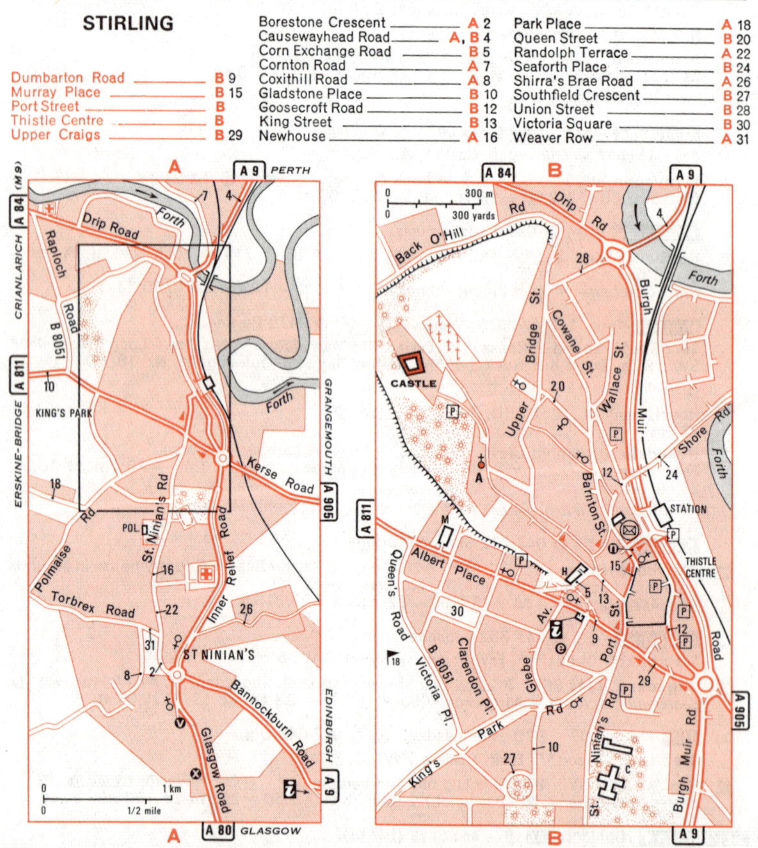

STENNESS Orkney Islands – see Orkney Islands (Mainland).

STEPPS Strathclyde – see Glasgow.

STIRLING Central 986 ⑪ – pop. 29,776 – ECD : Wednesday – ☎ 0786.
See : Stirling Castle★★ *AC* B – Church of the Holy Rude★ B A – **Envir. :** Bannockburn (battlefield)
AC, S : 3 m. by Glasgow Rd A – Doune Castle★ (stronghold 15C) *AC*, NW : 8 m. by A 84 A.
🏌 Queen's Rd ☎ 3801 B – 🏌 Tillicoultry ☎ 741, E : 9 m. by A 9 A.
🚗 ☎ 3085.
🛈 Information Centre, Dumbarton Rd ☎ 5019 – Information Centre, Bannockburn ☎ 0786 (Bannockburn) 814026
(March - September).
Edinburgh 36 – Dunfermline 21 – Falkirk 15 – Glasgow 25 – Greenock 48 – Motherwell 28 – Oban 86 – Perth 33.

Plan opposite

🏨 King Robert (Open House), Glasgow Rd, FK7 0LJ, ☎ 0786 (Bannockburn) 811666 –
📺 🛁wc 🖨 🅿
21 rm.
A x

🏨 Station (Stakis), 56 Murray Pl., FK8 2BX, ☎ 2017 – 📺 🛁wc 🛁wc 🖨 🅿. 🔳 AE ⓪
VISA
M a la carte 3.25/5.15 🍷 1.65 – **25 rm** 🍽 15.50/26.00 **t.**
B n

XX Heritage with rm, 16 Allan Park, FK8 2QG, ☎ 3660, «Tastefully furnished», French
rest. – 🛁wc 🅿. AE
closed Christmas Day and 1 January – **M** 3.50/8.00 – **4 rm** 🍽 14.00/20.00.
B e

X Hollybank, with rm, 54 Glasgow Rd, St. Ninians, FK7 0PH, ☎ 0786 (Bannockburn)
812311, 🚿 – 🅿. ⓪
4 rm.
A v

ALFA-ROMEO,COLT Kerse Rd ☎ 62618
AUSTIN-DAIMLER-JAGUAR-MORRIS-MG-ROVER-
TRIUMPH, ROLLS ROYCE-BENTLEY Wallace St. ☎
62821
CITROEN, VAUXHALL 119/139 Glasgow Rd ☎ 0786
(Bannockburn) 811234
FIAT 44 Causeway Head Rd ☎ 62426

FORD Drip Rd ☎ 4891
OPEL Birkhill Rd, Cambusbarron ☎ 61808
PEUGEOT 124/126 Main St. ☎ 0877 (Callander) 30022
RENAULT Kildean Market ☎ 4793
TALBOT Goosecroft Rd ☎ 4477
VW, AUDI-NSU Drip Rd ☎ 5101

STONEHAVEN Grampian 986 ⑦⑪ – pop. 4,730 – ECD : Wednesday – ☎ 0569.
See : Site★. **Envir. :** Dunnottar Castle (site★★, ruins★) *AC*, S : 1 ½ m.
🏌 Cowie, ☎ 62124.
🛈 The Square ☎ 62806 (May-October).
Edinburgh 109 – Aberdeen 15 – Dundee 50.

🏨 Commodore, Cowie Park, AB3 2PZ, ☎ 62936 – 📺 🛁wc 🖨 🅿. ⛵
36 rm.

🏨 St. Leonard's, 2 Bath St., AB3 2DE, ☎ 62044, 🚿 – 📺 🛁wc 🖨 🅿. ⛵. *VISA*
M 4.50/5.75 **t.** 🍷 2.10 – **12 rm** 🍽 14.00/28.00 **st.**

AUSTIN-MORRIS-MG-ROVER-TRIUMPH 64/74 Barclay St. ☎ 62077

STORNOWAY Western Isles 986 ② – see Lewis (Isle of).

STRACHUR Strathclyde – pop. 700 – ECD : Wednesday – ✉ Cairndow – ☎ 036 986.
See : Loch Fyne★★. **Envir. :** Glen Croe★ NE : 15 m.
Edinburgh 99 – Glasgow 56 – Oban 60.

🏨 Creggans Inn, PA27 8BX, ☎ 279, ‹ Loch Fyne Bay, 🚿 – 🛁wc ♿ 🅿. 🔳 AE *VISA*
M 4.95/6.95 **t.** 🍷 2.50 – **25 rm** 🍽 17.00/29.50 **t.**

at Strathlachlan SW : 6 ½ m. by A 886 on B 8000 – ✉ ☎ 036 986 Strachur :

X Inver Cottage, PA27 8BU, ☎ 396, ‹ Loch Fyne and mountains – 🅿
April-December – **M** a la carte 3.10/7.35 **t.** 🍷 2.50.

STRANRAER Dumfries and Galloway 986 ⑱ – pop. 9,853 – ECD : Wednesday – ☎ 0776.
Envir. : Kennedy Castle gardens★ *AC*, E : 3 ½ m.
🏌 Creachmore, Leswalt ☎ 87245, SW : 2 m.
⛴ to Larne (Sealink) 2-6 daily (2 h 15 mn).
🛈 Port Rodie ☎ 2595.
Edinburgh 128 – Ayr 53 – Dumfries 76.

🏨 North West Castle, Royal Crescent, DG9 8EH, ☎ 2644, 🔳 – 🛗 🛁wc 🖨 🅿
M 2.60/8.00 **st.** 🍷 1.35 – **79 rm** 🍽 10.65/17.10 **st.**

🏨 George (Best Western), George St., DG9 7RJ, ☎ 2487 – 🛗 🛁wc 🖨 🅿. 🔳 AE ⓪ *VISA*
M 4.00/6.00 **t.** 🍷 2.10 – 🍽 2.20 – **28 rm** 11.00/23.00 **st.** – P 18.00/25.00 **st.**

P.T.O. ⟶

STRANRAER

✕ **L'Apéritif,** London Rd, DG9 8EP, ☎ 2991 – Ⓟ
closed Sunday and 15 September-20 October – **M** (bar lunch) 3.50/4.75 **t.** ⌂ 1.70.

AUSTIN-MORRIS-MG-ROVER-TRIUMPH Charlotte St.
☎ 2301
DATSUN Hanover Sq. ☎ 2833

FIAT, VAUXHALL North Strand St. ☎ 2561
MAZDA The Garage, Leswalt ☎ 077687 (Leswalt) 634
TALBOT Leswalt Rd ☎ 3636

STRATHBLANE Central – pop. 755 – ECD: Wednesday – ✉ Glasgow – ☎ 0360 Blanefield.
Edinburgh 48 – Glasgow 11 – Stirling 25.

🏛 **Kirkhouse Inn,** Glasgow Rd, G63 9AA, ☎ 70621 – TV 🛏wc 🐾 Ⓟ. AE ① VISA
M 3.50/10.00 **t.** ⌂ 1.50 – **18 rm** ⌷ 14.00/21.00 **st.** – P 20.00/25.00 **st.**

at Campsie Glen W: 3 ¼ m. on A 891 – ✉ Glasgow – ☎ 0360 Lennoxtown:

✕✕ **Campsie Glen** with rm, G65 7AF, ☎ 310666, 🌲, park – TV 🛏wc Ⓟ. 🔲 AE ① VISA
M 2.50/6.50 **t.** ⌂ 2.00 – **8 rm** ⌷ 15.50/22.50 **t.**

STRATHLACHLAN Strathclyde – see Strachur.

STRATHY Highland – ☎ 064 14.
Envir.: Strathy Point*** N: 3 ½ m.
Edinburgh 301 – Inverness 142 – Thurso 21 – Tongue 23.

Hotel see: Bettyhill SW: 12 m.

STROMNESS Orkney Islands 986 ⑯ – see Orkney Islands (Mainland).

STRONSAY (Isle of) Orkney Islands 986 ⑯ – Shipping Services: see Orkney Islands (Mainland: Kirkwall).

STRONTIAN Highland – pop. 275 – ☎ 0967.
Edinburgh 137 – Inverness 88 – Kyle of Lochalsh 98 – Oban 54.

🏠 **Kilcamb Lodge** 🦢, PH36 4HY, ☎ 2257, ← Loch Sunart, 🌲, park – 🛏wc Ⓟ
M 4.30/5.70 **st.** ⌂ 2.00 – **11 rm** ⌷ 13.25/26.50 – P 16.30/17.55.

SUMBURGH Shetland Islands 986 ⑯ – see Shetland Islands (Mainland).

SYMINGTON Strathclyde – pop. 433 – ECD: Wednesday – ✉ Biggar – ☎ 089 93 Tinto.
Edinburgh 31 – Dumfries 49 – Glasgow 38.

🏠 **Tinto** (Open House), ML12 6LQ, on A 72 ☎ 454, ←, 🌲 – Ⓟ. 🔲 AE ① VISA
M 3.00/4.25 **st.** ⌂ 1.70 – **34 rm** ⌷ 13.50/25.50 **st.** – P 20.75/24.75 **st.**
AUSTIN-MG 61 Biggar Rd ☎ 200

TAIN Highland 986 ③ and ⑦ – pop. 1,942 – ECD: Thursday – ☎ 0862.
Envir.: Portmahomack (←*) E: 10 m.
🏌18 ☎ 2314.
Edinburgh 206 – Inverness 47 – Wick 89.

🏠 Royal, High St., IV19 1AB, ☎ 2013 – 🛏wc Ⓟ. ⛱
21 rm.

AUSTIN-MORRIS-MG-ROVER-TRIUMPH Shore Rd
☎ 2375

TOYOTA Knockbreck Rd ☎ 2175

TALLADALE Highland – ✉ Achnasheen – ☎ 0445 Gairloch.
See: NE: Loch Maree*.
Edinburgh 220 – Gairloch 9 – Inverness 61.

🏠 Loch Maree 🦢, ☎ 2200, ←, 🌲 – Ⓟ
20 rm.

TARBERT Strathclyde 986 ⑭ – see Kintyre (Peninsula).

TARBERT Western Isles 986 ② – see Harris (Isle of).

THORNHILL Dumfries and Galloway 986 ⑮ – pop. 1,510 – ECD: Thursday – ☎ 0848.
Envir.: Drumlanrig Castle* NW: 2 ½ m.
🏌9 ☎ 546.
Edinburgh 62 – Ayr 44 – Dumfries 15 – Glasgow 59.

🏠 **Buccleuch and Queensberry,** Drumlanrig St., DG3 5LU, ☎ 30215 – 🛏wc 🚗 Ⓟ
M a la carte 2.25/5.60 **t.** ⌂ 2.30 – **10 rm** ⌷ 11.75/25.00 **st.** – P 16.85/19.00 **st.**

THURSO Highland 986 ③ – pop. 9,087 – ECD: Thursday – ☎ 0847.
Envir.: Dunnet Head*** (sea birds' nests) NE: 13 m. – Dunnet Bay** NE: 9 m.
18 ☎ 3807, 2 m. from railway station.
from Scrabster to Stromness (Orkney Islands) (P & O Ferries: Orkney and Shetland Services) Monday/Saturday 1-3 daily (2 h) Sunday in July and August only – to Feroes Islands: Torshavn (Strandfaraskip Landsins) summer only 1 weekly (14 h).
Car Park, Riverside ☎ 2371 (May-September).
Edinburgh 290 – Inverness 131 – Wick 21.

Hotels see: John O'Groats NE: 19 m.
Wick SE: 21 m.

CITROEN Couper Sq. Riverside ☎ 2778
RENAULT Bridgend ☎ 4622

TIREE (Isle of) Strathclyde 986 ⑩ – pop. 1,019.
☎ 087 92 (Scarinish) 456/7.
by Caledonian MacBrayne: to Oban via Tobermory 2-4 weekly (4 h to 5 h) – to Isle of Coll: 2-4 weekly (1 h 30 mn).

TOBERMORY Strathclyde 986 ⑩ – see Mull (Isle of).

TONGUE Highland 986 ③ – pop. 129 – ECD: Saturday – ✉ Lairg – ☎ 080 05.
Envir.: Tongue Bay (<* from Coldbackie) N: 2 ½ m. **Exc.**: Loch Eriboll*** W: 21 m. – SW: Ben Loyal and Ben Hope (<*): road from Tongue to Durness.
Edinburgh 255 – Inverness 96 – Thurso 44.

Tongue, IV27 4XD, ☎ 206, <, « Tastefully furnished in Victorian style », – wc
P. AE VISA
M (bar lunch) 3.75/6.20 **st.** 2.10 – **21 rm** 14.25/28.50 **st.**

Ben Loyal, Main St., IV27 4XE, ☎ 216, <, – wc P
M (bar lunch) 2.00/5.00 **t.** 1.00 – **19 rm** 8.30/22.40 **t.** – P 11.00/15.25 **t.**

TROON Strathclyde 986 ⑭ – pop. 11,318 – ECD: Wednesday – ☎ 0292.
18, 18 ☎ 312464.
Municipal Buildings, South Beach ☎ 315131.
Edinburgh 72 – Ayr 7 – Glasgow 29.

Marine, Crosbie Rd, KA10 6HE, ☎ 314444, <, – TV P. AE VISA
M 5.50/7.35 **st.** – **70 rm** 22.00/38.40 **st.**

Sun Court, 19 Crosbie Rd, KA10 6HF, ☎ 312727, <, – wc P. AE
M 4.00/5.50 **st.** 1.50 – **20 rm** 17.00/22.00 **st.**

Piersland Lodge, Craigend Rd, ☎ 314747, – TV wc P
M a la carte 5.25/10.15 **t.** – **11 rm** 11.25/20.75 **t.**

Craiglea, 78-80 South Beach, KA10 6EG, ☎ 311366, <, – TV wc P. AE
M a la carte 4.55/7.95 **t.** 1.70 – **22 rm** 11.00/24.00 **t.** – P 15.00/20.00 **t.**

Ardneil, 51 St. Meddans St., KA10 6NU, ☎ 311611 – wc P
M (bar lunch) 2.75/6.80 **st.** 1.95 – **9 rm** 8.50/19.00 **st.**

XX **L'Auberge de Provence** (at Marine Hotel), Crosbie Rd, KA10 6HE, ☎ 314444, French rest. – P. AE VISA
closed Sunday and Monday – **M** (dinner only) a la carte 7.95/11.55 **t.**

AUSTIN-MORRIS-MG-PRINCESS Dundonald Rd ☎ 314141
AUSTIN-MORRIS-MG-PRINCESS-ROVER-TRIUMPH St. Meddans St. ☎ 312099
FORD 72 Portland St. ☎ 312312
TALBOT Cavendish Pl. ☎ 311001

TURNBERRY Strathclyde – pop. 164 – ECD: Wednesday – ✉ Girvan – ☎ 065 53.
18, 18 ☎ 202.
Edinburgh 93 – Ayr 18 – Glasgow 50 – Stranraer 35.

Turnberry (B.T.H.) , Maidens Rd, KA26 9LT, on A 719 ☎ 202, Telex 777779, < golf course and bay, , 18, – TV P. AE VISA
M a la carte 10.15/14.80 **st.** 2.00 – **122 rm** 31.00/60.00 **st.**

UDDINGSTON Strathclyde – pop. 5,278 – ECD: Wednesday – ✉ Glasgow – ☎ 0698.
Edinburgh 38 – Glasgow 7.5.

Redstones, 8-10 Glasgow Rd, G71 7AS, ☎ 813774 – TV wc P. AE VISA
closed 1 January – **20 rm** 13.75/25.00 **st.** – P 19.50/24.00 **st.**

UIG Highland 986 ⑥ – see Skye (Isle of).

Do not use yesterday's maps for today's journey.

UIST (Isles of) * Western Isles 986 ⑥ – pop. 5,105.
See : Benbecula (≤* from Peinavalla, South Nunton).
✈ ✆ 0870 (Benbecula) 2051.

Daliburgh (South Uist) – pop. 261 – ✉ ☎ 087 84 Lochboisdale.
🏠 Borrowdale, PA81 5SS, ✆ 444 – 🛏wc 🅿
10 rm.

Lochboisdale (South Uist) – pop. 382 – ✉ ☎ 087 84.
Envir. : Sound of Eriskay (≤* from Ludac) S : 9 m. by A 865 and B 888.
🛏 ✆ 253, N : 5 m.
🚢 by Caledonian MacBrayne : to Oban : 3-4 weekly (5 to 7 h) – to Castlebay (Isle of Barra) (1 h 30 mn).
ℹ Information Centre ✆ 286 (May-September).

Lochmaddy (North Uist) – pop. 307 – ECD : Thursday – ✉ ☎ 087 63 Lochmaddy.
See: Site*. **Envir.:** Sound of Berneray** NE : 8 m. by A 865 – Vallay Strand* NW by A 865.
🚢 by Caledonian MacBrayne : to Uig (Isle of Skye) 3-6 weekly Monday/Saturday (2 h direct) ; via Tarbert (Isle of Harris) May-October : 3 weekly – to Tarbert May-October 5-6 weekly (2 h).
ℹ Information Centre ✆ 321 (May-September).
🏠 Lochmaddy, PA28 5AA, ✆ 331, ≤, ⌇ – 🅿
16 rm.

ULLAPOOL Highland 986 ② – pop. 807 – ECD : Tuesday except summer – ☎ 0854.
See : Site*. **Envir. :** Corrieshalloch Gorge*, Falls of Measach* SE : 12 m. – Strath More (≤* from the A 832) SE : 10 m.
🚢 to Isle of Lewis : Stornoway (Caledonian MacBrayne) Monday/Saturday 1-2 daily (3 h 15 mn).
ℹ Information Centre ✆ 2135 (Easter and May-September).
Edinburgh 218 – Inverness 59.

🏨 **Royal,** Garve Rd, IV26 2SY, ✆ 2181, ≤ Loch Broom, hills and gardens, ⌇, ⚞, park –
🅿. 🏊. 🔄 AE
April-October – **M** a la carte 6.50/12.35 t. 🍷 2.00 – **60 rm** � 15.00/38.75 t.
🏨 Ullapool Ladbroke Mercury Motor Inn, North Rd, IV26 2TG, ✆ 2314, ≤ – 🛏wc 🅿
season – **60 rm.**
🏨 **Caledonian,** Quay St., IV26 2UG, ✆ 2306, Telex 778215 – 🛏wc 🅿. 🔄 AE ① *VISA*
Mid April-mid October – **M** (bar lunch) 4.10/6.25 🍷 1.25 – **38 rm** ⊆ 13.30/26.50 st.
🏠 **Ceilidh Place,** 14 West Argyle St., IV26 2TY, ✆ 2103, « Tasteful decor, gaelic art, musical theatrical exhibitions » – 🛏wc 🅿. ①
April-October – **M** (bar lunch) a la carte 5.90/9.25 t. 🍷 2.00 – **13 rm** ⊆ 11.00/25.00 t.
🏠 **Four Seasons,** Garve Rd, IV26 2SY, ✆ 2013, ≤ Loch Broom – 🛏wc 🅿. 🔄 ①
M a la carte 3.70/6.75 🍷 1.50 – **16 rm** ⊆ 12.00/18.00.
🍴 **Ferry Boat Inn,** Shore St., IV26 2UJ, ✆ 2366, ≤ Loch Broom – 🔄
March-November – **M** (bar lunch) approx. 5.40 st. 🍷 2.20 – **12 rm** ⊆ 8.25/16.45 st.

UNST (Isle of) Shetland Islands 986 ⑯ – see Shetland Islands.

UPHALL Lothian – pop. 3,035 – ECD : Wednesday – ☎ 0506 Broxburn.
🛏 ✆ 2404.
Edinburgh 11 – Glasgow 32.

🏨 **Houstoun House** ⌇, EH52 6JS, ✆ 853831, Telex 727148 ≤, « Gardens », park – 📺
🛏wc 🛏wc ☕ 🅿
M 5.00/8.25 st. 🍷 1.70 – ⊆ 1.25 – **29 rm** 20.00/36.00 st.

VOE Shetland Islands – see Shetland Islands (Mainland).

WALKERBURN Borders – pop. 842 – ☎ 089 687.
See : Tweed Valley*.
Edinburgh 32 – Galashiels 9 – Peebles 9.

🍴 **Tweed Valley** ⌇, Galashiels Rd, EH43 6AA, ✆ 220, ⌇, ⚞ – 🅿. 🔄 AE ①
M 2.80/5.65 st. 🍷 1.75 – **14 rm** ⊆ 10.60/17.70 st. – P 17.75/23.40 st.

WEEM Tayside – see Aberfeldy.

WEMYSS BAY Strathclyde 986 ⑭ – pop. 323 – ☎ 0475.
⛴ to the Isle of Bute: Rothesay (Caledonian MacBrayne and Western Ferries) frequent services every day (30 mn).

Hotels see : Largs S: 4 ½ m.
Skelmorlie S: 1 ½ m.

WESTHILL Grampian – see Aberdeen.

WESTRAY (Isle of) Orkney Islands 986 ⑯ – see Orkney Islands.

WHALSAY (Isle of) Shetland Islands 986 ⑯ – Shipping Services: see Shetland Islands.

WHITENESS Shetland Islands – see Shetland Islands (Mainland).

WHITING BAY Strathclyde – see Arran (Isle of).

WHITHORN (Isle of) Dumfries and Galloway – pop. 222 – ☎ 098 85.
See: Harbour*.
Edinburgh 149 – Ayr 74 – Dumfries 72 – Stranraer 32.

Queens Arms, 24 Main St., DG8 8LF, ☎ 369 – wc P
M (bar lunch) approx. 5.25 **t.** 1.70 – **10 rm** 8.00/18.00 **t.**

WICK Highland 986 ③ – pop. 7,617 – ECD: Wednesday – ☎ 0955.
Reiss ☎ 2726, N: 3 m.
✈ ☎ 2215, N: 1 m.
Whitechapel Tourist Organisation off High St. ☎ 2596, Telex 75124.
Edinburgh 282 – Inverness 123.

Wick Ladbroke Mercury Motor Inn, Riverside, KW1 4NL, ☎ 3344 – TV wc P.
30 rm.

AUSTIN-MORRIS-MG-ROVER-TRIUMPH-WOLSELEY Bridge St. ☎ 2195
DATSUN, VAUXHALL Francis St. ☎ 2240
FORD Francis St. ☎ 2103
TALBOT George St. ☎ 2322

WORMIT Fife – pop. 3,750 – ECD: Wednesday – ✉ ☎ 0382 Newport-on-Tay.
Edinburgh 53 – Dundee 4 – St. Andrews 12.

XX **Sandford Hill** with rm, DD6 8RG, S: 2 m. junction A 914 and B 946 ☎ 541802, ←,
– TV wc P.
M a la carte 5.10/9.75 1.60 – **14 rm** 13.00/22.25 **t.**

WYRE (Isle of) Orkney Islands 986 ⑯ – Shipping Services: see Orkney Islands.

YELL (Isle of) Shetland Islands 986 ⑯ – Shipping Services: see Shetland Islands.

Northern Ireland

LICENSING HOURS - WHEN DRINKING ALCOHOLIC BEVERAGES IS PERMITTED IN PUBS AND BARS AND OTHER LICENSED PREMISES (The General Rule).

HEURES PERMISES POUR LA CONSOMMATION DES BOISSONS ALCOOLISÉES (Règle Générale).

ORARI CONSENTITI PER LA CONSUMAZIONE DI BEVANDE ALCOOLICHE (Regola Generale).

AUSSCHANKZEITEN FÜR ALKOHOLISCHE GETRÄNKE (Allgemeine Regelung).

	from / de / dalle / von	to / à / alle / bis	drinking up time consommation jusqu'à consumazione fino alle getrunken werden darf bis	from / de / dalle / von	to / à / alle / bis	drinking up time consommation jusqu'à consumazione fino alle getrunken werden darf bis	
Weekdays (other than Good Friday and Christmas Day) **Jours de semaine** (autres que Vendredi Saint et Jour de Noël)	11.30				23.00	23.30	**Giorni della Settimana** (esclusi Venerdì Santo e Natale) **Wochentags** (außer Karfreitag und Weihnachten)
Good Friday **Vendredi Saint**				17.00	23.00	23.30	**Venerdì Santo** **Karfreitag**
Hotels Rest. — Sundays (except Christmas Day) Dimanche (sauf Jour de Noël)	12.30	14.30	15.00	19.00	22.00		Domeniche (escluso Natale) Sonntags (außer Weihnachten) — **Alberghi Hotels Ristoranti Rest.**
Christmas Day Jour de Noël	12.30				22.00		Natale Weihnachten
Pubs — Sundays and Christmas Day Dimanches et jour de Noël	Closed - Fermés - Chiusi - Geschlossen						**Pubs** — Domeniche e Natale Sonntags und Weihnachten

Hotels may serve alcoholic beverages to non-residents at any time on Christmas Day or Sundays but they have to be accompanied by a meal.

RESIDENTS: There are no drinking restrictions in licensed hotels for residents and their private friends.

Les hôtels peuvent servir des boissons alcoolisées aux non-résidents les dimanches et le jour de Noël mais seulement avec un repas.

RÉSIDENTS: Pas de restriction pour les résidents et leurs invités.

Gli alberghi possono servire bevande alcoliche ai non residenti la domenica ed a Natale ma soltanto con il pasto.

RESIDENTI: Nessuna restrizione per i residenti ed i loro amici.

Hotels dürfen alkoholische Getränke Sonntags und Weihnachten den Besuchern servieren, aber nur in Verbindung mit einer Mahlzeit.

FÜR HOTELGÄSTE und ihre persönlichen Freunde besteht im Hotel selbst keine Beschränkung.

Place with at least :
one hotel or restaurant _______ Larne
one pleasant hotel _______ , with rm.
one quiet, secluded hotel _______
one restaurant with _______ ✿, ✿✿, M
See this town for establishments located in its vicinity _______ BELFAST

La località possiede come minimo :
una risorsa alberghiera _______ Larne
un albergo ameno _______ , with rm.
un albergo molto tranquillo, isolato _______
un'ottima tavola con _______ ✿, ✿✿, M
La località raggruppa nel suo testo le risorse dei dintorni _______ BELFAST

Localité offrant au moins :
une ressource hôtelière _______ Larne
un hôtel agréable _______ , with rm.
un hôtel très tranquille, isolé _______
une bonne table à _______ ✿, ✿✿, M
Localité groupant dans le texte les ressources de ses environs _______ BELFAST

Ort mit mindestens :
einem Hotel oder Restaurant _______ Larne
einem angenehmen Hotel _______ , with rm.
einem sehr ruhigen und abgelegenen Hotel _______
einem Restaurant mit _______ ✿, ✿✿, M
Ort mit Angaben über Hotels und Restaurants in seiner Umgebung _______ BELFAST

Portballintrae
Portstewart
Ballycastle
COLERAINE
Londonderry
A5
A6
Ballymena
Ballygalley
Larne
M22
Craigavon
M1
Saintfield
Hillsborough
Portaferry
ENNISKILLEN
A4
Banbridge
Lisnaskea
A1
Newry
Newcastle

M2
Carrickfergus
NEWTOWNABBEY
Dunadry
Crawfordsburn
Craigavad
BELFAST
Newtownards
M1
M Comber
Grey Abbey
526
A1

NORTHERN IRELAND

Towns

ANTRIM (Coast Road) Antrim 986 ⑭ ⑱.
See : Road*** (A 2) from Larne to Portrush.

BALLYCASTLE Antrim 986 ⑭ – ◎ 026 57.
See : Site**. **Envir. :** Giant's Causeway*** (Chaussée des Géants) basalt formation (from the car-park *AC,* ½ h Rtn on foot) NW : 12 m. – White Park Bay** NW : 8 ½ m. – Carrick-a-Rede (⋖** of Rathlin Island) NW : 5 ½ m.
⛳18 ☎ 62536.
ℹ 61 Castle St. ☎ 62024 (June-August).
Belfast 60 – Ballymena 28 – Larne 40.

⌂⌂ Marine, 1 North St., BT40 6MX, ☎ 62336, ⋖, ⛱ – 🛁wc. 🎤
38 rm.

⌂ **Antrim Arms,** Castle St., BT40 6MX, ☎ 62284 – Ⓟ. AE
M (bar lunch in winter) a la carte 7.50/10.00 **t.** 🍷 1.50 – **16 rm** ☕ 7.50/18.00 **t.**

BALLYGALLEY Antrim – pop. 487 – ✉ Larne – ◎ 057 483.
Belfast 27 – Ballymena 24 – Larne 4.

⌂⌂ Ballygally Castle, 274 Coast Rd, BT40 2QX, ☎ 212, ⋖, 🎾, ⛱ – 🛁wc Ⓟ. 🎤
28 rm.

⌂ Coastway, 352 Coast Rd, BT40 2QQ, ☎ 265, ⋖ – 🚿wc Ⓟ. 🎤
13 rm.

BALLYMENA Antrim 986 ⑱ – pop. 16,487 – ◎ 0266.
Envir. : Glen of Glenariff*** – Glenariff (or Waterfoot) site* NE : 19 m.
⛳18 Broughshane ☎ 026 686 (Broughshane) 207, E : 2 m. on A 42.
Belfast 30 – Dundalk 82 – Larne 20 – Londonderry 50 – Omagh 55.

⌂⌂ Adair Arms, 1-5 Ballymoney Rd, BT43 5BS, ☎ 3674 – 📺 🛁wc 🚿 ☎ Ⓟ. 🎤
28 rm.

ALFA-ROMEO, TALBOT, LOTUS Broadway Av. ☎ 2161
AUSTIN-MORRIS-TRIUMPH Waveney Av. ☎ 3557
AUSTIN-MORRIS-MG 34/36 George St. ☎ 6288
RENAULT 120 Antrim Rd ☎ 2650
VW, AUDI 1/5 Railway St. ☎ 2167

BANBRIDGE Down 986 ⑱ – pop. 6,864 – ◎ 082 06.
⛳9 Huntly Rd ☎ 22342, NW : 1 m.
ℹ Newry Rd ☎ 22143 (July-August).
Belfast 26 – Armagh 20 – Dundalk 26.

⌂ **Belmont,** Rathfriland Rd, BT32 3LH, ☎ 22517, ⛱ – 🚿wc ☎ Ⓟ. AE VISA
M a la carte 4.25/9.85 **st.** 🍷 1.45 – **9 rm** ☕ 10.00/17.00 **st.**

BELFAST Antrim 986 ⑱ and ㊲ – pop. 360,150 – ◎ 0232.
See : City Hall** 1906 BZ **A** – Queen's University** 1906 AZ **U** – Ulster Museum* AZ **M** – Church House* 1905 BZ **B** – Botanic Gardens (hot houses*) AZ – Bellevue Zoological Gardens (site*, ⋖*) *AC,* by A 6 AY.
Envir. : Stormont (Parliament House* 1932, terrace : vista**) E : 4 m. by Belmont Rd AZ – The Giant's Ring* (prehistoric area) S : 5 m. by Malone Rd AZ – Lisburn (Castle gardens ⋖*) SW : 8 m. by A1 AZ.
⛳18 Balmoral ☎ 668540 AZ – ⛳18 Downview Av. ☎ 771770, N : 2 m. AY – ⛳18 240 Upper Malone Rd, Dunmurry ☎ 612695 by A55 AZ. – ⛳18 Shandon Park ☎ 653730, E : 3 m. by A55 AZ.
✈ Belfast Airport : ☎ 29271, NW : 12 m. by A 52 AY.
⛴ to Liverpool (P & O Ferries : Irish Sea Services) 6-8 weekly (10 h).
to Isle of Man : Douglas (Isle of Man Steam Packet Co.) 1-3 weekly summer only (4 h 30 mn).
ℹ Northern Ireland Tourist Board, River House, 48-52 High St., BT1 2DS, ☎ 46609, Telex 748087 – Aldergrove Airport ☎ 084 94 (Crumlin) 52103 – Larne Harbourg, Terminal Building, ☎ 2270.
Dublin 103 – Londonderry 71.

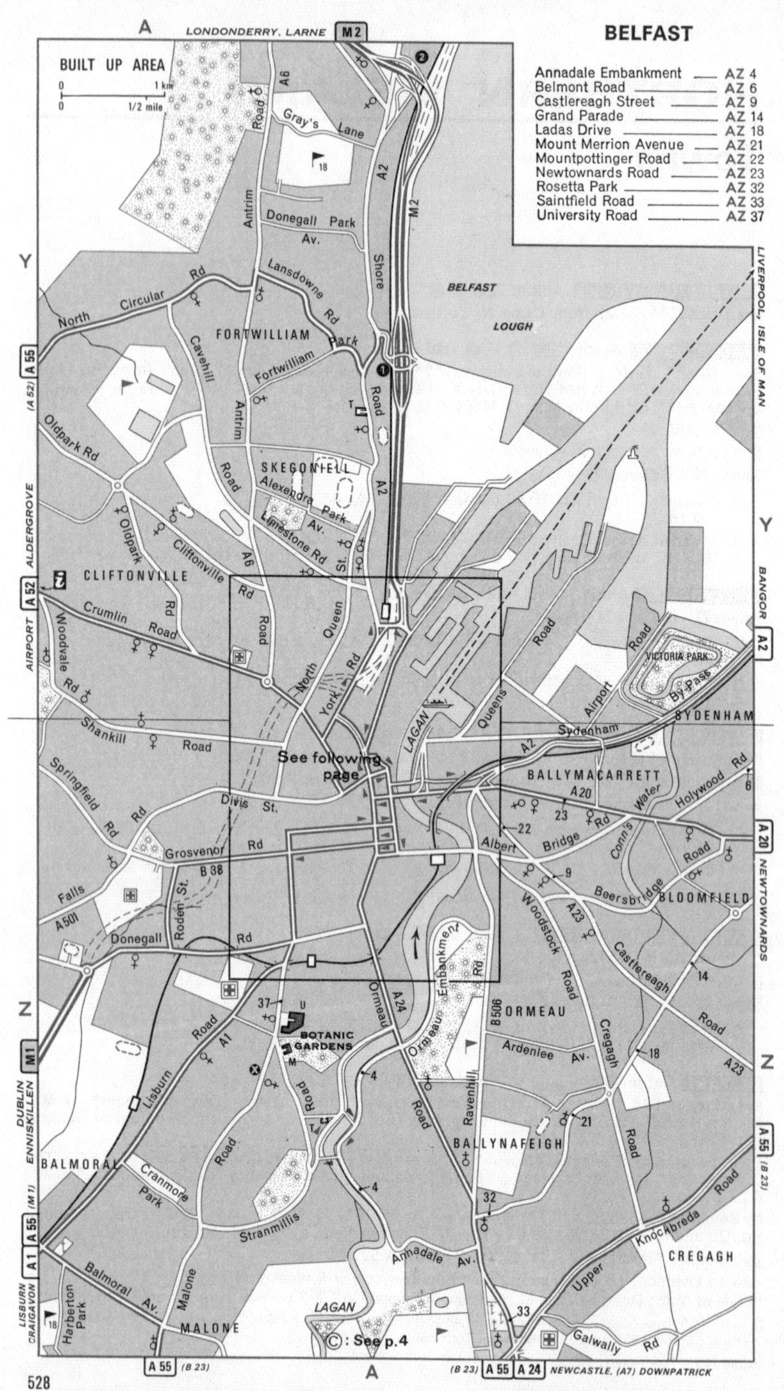

BELFAST
BUILT UP AREA
0   1 km
0   1/2 mile
Annadale Embankment — AZ 4
Belmont Road — AZ 6
Castlereagh Street — AZ 9
Grand Parade — AZ 14
Ladas Drive — AZ 18
Mount Merrion Avenue — AZ 21
Mountpottinger Road — AZ 22
Newtownards Road — AZ 23
Rosetta Park — AZ 32
Saintfield Road — AZ 33
University Road — AZ 37
LONDONDERRY, LARNE
M 2
A
Y
Z
N
A 55
A 52
A 52
ALDERGROVE
AIRPORT
A 52
DUBLIN
ENNISKILLEN
M 1
M 1
LISBURN
CRAIGAVON
A 1
A 55
A 55
B 23
Gray's Lane
Antrim
Donegall Park Av.
Lansdowne Rd
Shore Road
A 6
A 2
M 2
North Circular
Road
FORTWILLIAM
Fortwilliam
Park
Cavehill
Rd
Antrim
Road
Oldpark Rd
Oldpark
Road
Cliftonville
A 6
SKEGONIELL
Alexandra Park
Av.
Limestone Rd
St.
CLIFTONVILLE
Cliftonville
Rd
Crumlin
Road
Woodvale Rd
Shankill
Road
Springfield
Rd
Road
Falls
A 501
Grosvenor
B 38
Roden St.
Donegall
Road
Divis St.
North
Queen
St.
York
Rd
Road
Rd
LAGAN
BELFAST
LOUGH
LIVERPOOL, ISLE OF MAN
BANGOR
A 2
Road
Road
Road
Airport
VICTORIA PARK
By Pass
SYDENHAM
Sydenham
BYDENHAM
Queens
A 2
BALLYMACARRETT
A 20
Conn's Water
Holywood Rd
6
Bridge Rd
23
22
9
Beersbridge
BLOOMFIELD
A 20
NEWTOWNARDS
Albert
Woodstock
Road
A 23
Castlereagh
Road
14
Cregagh
B 506
ORMEAU
Ardenlee Av.
18
A 23
A 55
B 23
Knockbreda Road
Upper
CREGAGH
See following page
37
Lisburn
Road
A 1
Road
BOTANIC GARDENS
U
M
Ormeau
A 24
Ormeau
Embankment
Rd
Road
Ravenhill
BALLYNAFEIGH
21
4
Malone
Road
Road
Road
4
32
Stranmillis
Road
Annadale Av.
LAGAN
33
Galwally Rd
BALMORAL
Cranmore Park
Balmoral Av.
Harberton Park
18
MALONE
©: See p.4
A 55
B 23
A
B 23
A 55
A 24
NEWCASTLE, (A7) DOWNPATRICK
528

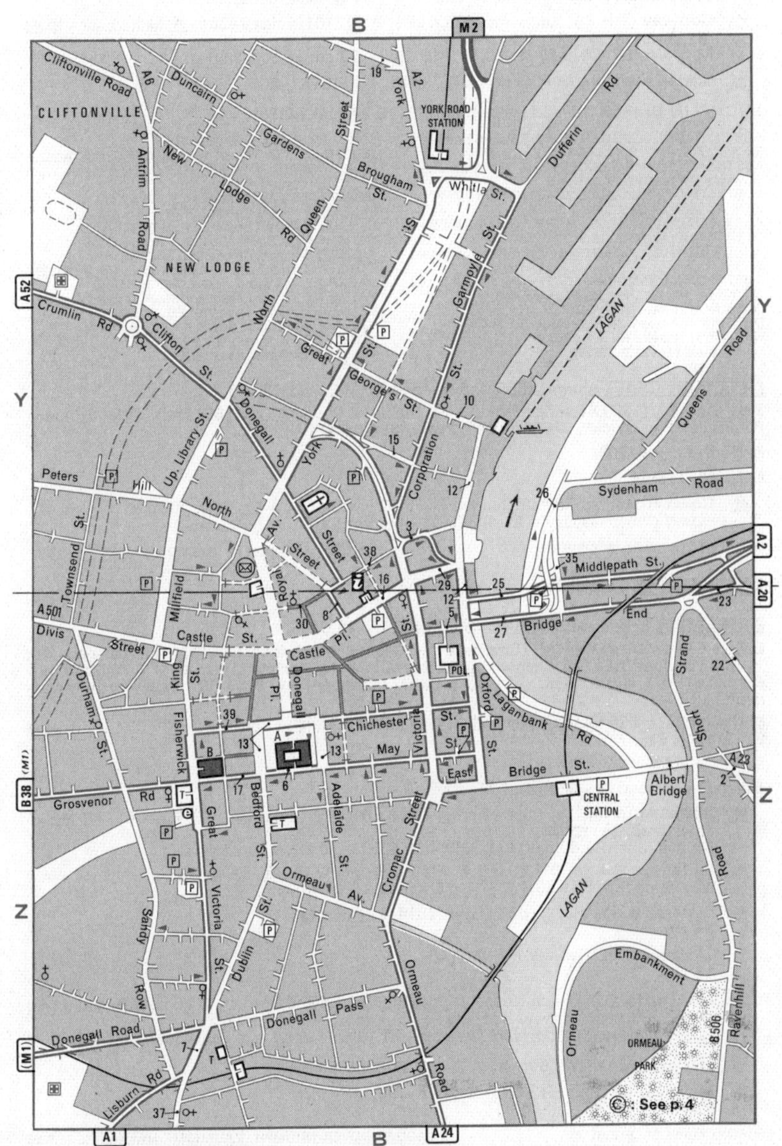

BELFAST
CENTRE
0   400 m
0   400 yards

Castle Place — BZ
Donegal Place — BZ
Royal Avenue — BYZ

Albert Bridge Road — BZ 2

Albert Square — BY 3
Ann Street — BZ 5
Bradbury Place — BZ 7
Bridge Street — BZ 8
Corporation Square — BY 10
Donegall Quay — BYZ 12
Donegall Square — BZ 13
Great Patrick Street — BY 15
High Street — BYZ 16
Howard Street — BZ 17
Limestone Road — BY 19

Mountpottinger Road — BZ 22
Newtownards Road — BZ 23
Queen Elizabeth Bridge — BZ 25
Queen's Quay Road — BY 26
Queen's Bridge — BZ 27
Queen's Square — BY 29
Rosemary Street — BZ 30
Station Street — BY 35
University Road — BZ 37
Waring Street — BY 38
Wellington Place — BZ 39

CLIFTONVILLE
Cliftonville Road
Duncairn
A6
Gardens
New
Lodge
Rd
Queen
Street
Brougham
St.
19
York
A2
M2
YORK ROAD STATION
Whitla St.
Garmoyle St.
Dufferin
Rd
LAGAN
Y
A52
Crumlin Rd
Clifton St.
NEW LODGE
North
Donegall St.
Great George's St.
St.
Corporation
St.
10
Queens
Road
Sydenham Road
26
Peters Hill
Up Library St.
York
North
15
12
A2
A20
Townsend St.
Millfield
Royal Av.
Street
38
16
3
35
Middlepath St.
29
25
23
A501
Divis
Street
Castle St.
30
8
Castle Pl.
12
5
27
Bridge
End
22
Durham St.
King St.
Fisherwick
39
Donegall Pl.
Chichester
May
Victoria St.
Oxford St.
Laganbank Rd
A23
B38 (M1)
Grosvenor Rd
B
13
A
13
6
17
Bedford St.
Adelaide St.
Cromac Street
East Bridge St.
CENTRAL STATION
Albert Bridge
2
Z
Sandy Row
Great Victoria St.
Ormeau Av.
Ormeau
LAGAN
Road
Embankment
Ravenhill Rd
M1
Donegall Road
Lisburn Rd
Dublin
Donegall Pass
Ormeau Road
ORMEAU PARK
B506
7
37
A1
B
A24
POL.
See p. 4

BELFAST

🏨 Belfast Europa (Gd. Met.), Great Victoria St., BT2 7AP, ☎ 45161, Telex 74491, ⟨ – 🛗
� 🅿. ⛱. 🅽 AE ⓪ VISA
200 rm 17.50/30.00 **s.**
BZ e

🏨 Wellington Park, 21 Malone Rd, BT9 6RY, ☎ 669421 – 🛗 🆃🆅 ⌷wc ☎ 🅿. ⛱.
24 rm.
AZ x

🏨 Stormont, 587 Upper Newtownards Rd, BT4 3LP, E: 4 ½ m. by A 2 on A 20 ☎ 658 621 –
🛗 🆃🆅 ⌷wc ☎ 🅿. ⛱. 🅽 AE ⓪ VISA
51 rm ⌷ 19.50/29.00.
on A 20   AZ

at Dunmurry SW: 5 ½ m. on A 1 – AZ – ✉ ☎ 0232 Belfast:

🏨 **Conway** (T.H.F.), Kingsway, BT17 9ES, ☎ 612101, Telex 74281, 🎇 heated, ⟻ – 🛗 🆃🆅
🅿. ⛱. 🅽 AE ⓪ VISA
M a la carte 7.05/9.65 **st.** 🛢 1.80 – ⌷ 2.50 – **77 rm** 18.00/25.50 **st.**

XX Stage Coach Inn, Queensway, BT17 9HG, ☎ 617018 – 🅿.

MICHELIN Branch, 101/3 Limestone Rd, BT15 3AB, ☎ 748255.

AUSTIN-DAIMLER-JAGUAR-MORRIS-MG Saintfield
Rd ☎ 649774
AUSTIN-MORRIS-MG-PRINCESS 276/284 Upper New-
townards Rd ☎ 42456
AUSTIN-DAIMLER-JAGUAR-MG-ROVER-TRIUMPH
10/18 Adelaide St. ☎ 30566
AUSTIN-DAIMLER-JAGUAR-MORRIS-MG-PRINCESS-
TRIUMPH 90/106 Victoria St. ☎ 32361
AUSTIN-MORRIS Upper Newtownards Rd, Dundonald
☎ 2651
AUSTIN-DAIMLER-MORRIS 25/27 Alfred St. ☎ 63056
CITROEN 118/124 Donegall Pass ☎ 23441
DATSUN 226 York St. ☎ 747133
DATSUN 397 Upper Newtownards Rd ☎ 654687
FIAT 47/57 Rosetta Rd ☎ 648049
FORD Lislea Drive ☎ 662231

FORD 58/82 Antrim Rd ☎ 744744
JENSEN, SKODA, TOYOTA 39/49 Adelaide St. ☎ 28225
LANCIA, ROLLS ROYCE-BENTLEY 4 Clarence St. West
☎ 41057
MORRIS-MG 203 Castlereagh Rd ☎ 51111
PEUGEOT 133 Lisburn Rd ☎ 661911
RENAULT 48/50 Corporation St. ☎ 37101
SAAB, FIAT 250/252 Donegall Rd ☎ 21019
TALBOT Annadale Embankment ☎ 642972
TOYOTA 269/285 Upper Newtownards Rd ☎ 655208
VAUXHALL 46 Florenceville Av. ☎ 641350
VAUXHALL 22/28 Brougham St. ☎ 744869
VAUXHALL 17/29 Ravenhill Rd ☎ 51422
VAUXHALL Lisburn Rd, Dunmurry ☎ 614211
VOLVO 27 Pakenham St. ☎ 29399
VW 5/8a Sandown Rd ☎ 653082

CARRICKFERGUS Antrim 🆀🆁🅱 ⑱ and ㉞ – pop. 15,162 – ☎ 023 83.
See : Castle** (13C) *AC* – Sea Front* – St. Nicholas' Church* 12C-18C. **Envir. :** Island Magee
Peninsula (Port Muck*, Isle of Muck*, Power Station ⟨*) NE: 9 m.

🛆 North Rd ☎ 62203.

Belfast 10 – Larne 14.

🏨 **Coast Road,** 28 Scotch Quarter, BT38 7DP, ☎ 61021 – 🆃🆅 ⌷wc 🗍wc ☎
closed Christmas Day – **M** 4.50/5.00 – **20 rm** ⌷ 11.00/22.00.

RENAULT Larne Rd ☎ 63516

TALBOT 72 Belfast Rd ☎ 62299

CASTLEROCK Londonderry – see Coleraine.

COLERAINE Londonderry 🆀🆁🅱 ⑱ – pop. 14,871 – ☎ 0265.
Envir. : Giant's Causeway*** (Chaussée des Géants) basalt formation (from the car-park *AC*,
½ h Rtn on foot) NE: 9 m. – Downhill Castle (Mussenden Temple* 18C : ⟨*** *AC*)NW: 7 m. –
Portrush (site*, ⟨*) N: 6 m. – Dunluce Castle (site*, ⟨*) NE: 8 m. – W : Benevenagh Mountain*.

🛆 Castlerock ☎ 026 584 (Castlerock) 314, W: 5 m. – 🛆, 🛆 at Portrush ☎ 026 582 (Portrush)
822311, N: 6 m.

🄸 Main St. at Castlerock ☎ 258 (July-August).

Belfast 61 – Ballymena 29 – Londonderry 30 – Omagh 62.

🏨 **Bohill Auto Inn** ⌷, Bushmills Rd, BT52 2BB, NE: 2 m. on B 17 ☎ 4406 – 🆃🆅 ⌷wc
🗍wc ☎ 🅿. ⛱. 🅽 ⓪
M (bar lunch) 4.80/6.00 **t.** 🛢 2.60 – ⌷ 2.50 – **30 rm** 9.50/22.50 **t.**

🏨 **Lodge,** Lodge Rd, BT52 1NF, ☎ 4848 – ⌷wc ☎ 🅿. ⛱. 🅽 ⓪ VISA
M a la carte 4.50/9.80 🛢 1.80 – **15 rm** ⌷ 12.50/18.00.

🏨 Gorteen, Lodge Rd, BT52 1LU, ☎ 2814 – ⌷wc 🅿
14 rm.

🏨 Westbrook, 62 Railway Pl., ☎ 3145
16 rm.

XX **MacDuffs,** Blackheath House, Blackhill, BT52 2XQ, S : 8 m. by A 29 on Macosquin Rd
☎ 026 585 (Aghadowey) 433 – 🅿
closed Sunday, Monday and Tuesday – **M** (dinner only) a la carte 5.30/7.90 🛢 1.80.

at Castlerock NW: 6 m. by A 2 – ✉ ☎ 0265 Coleraine:

🏠 Maritima, 43 Main St., BT51 4RA, ☎ 388, ⟨ – 🗍wc
6 rm.

FORD Church St. ☎ 2361

JAGUAR-ROVER-TRIUMPH, VAUXHALL Hanover Pl. ☎ 2386

COMBER Down 986 ⑱ and ㊳ – pop. 5,575 – ✆ 0247.
Belfast 9 – Bangor 9.

XX **Blades,** 39-41 High St., BT23 5HJ, ☎ 872229 – **P**. AE ⓪
closed Sunday, Monday, Tuesday, 4 to 20 November and Christmas Day – **M** (dinner only) a la carte 7.70/11.15 **t.** ⁑ 1.90.

XX **Old Crow,** Glen Rd, BT23 5EL, ☎ 872255 – **P**
closed Sunday lunch, 12 July and Christmas Day – **M** a la carte 5.55/9.85.

CRAIGAVAD Down 986 ㊳ – pop. 679 – ✉ ✆ 023 17 Holywood.
See : Ulster Folk and Transport Museum* (Cultra Manor) AC.
☗ at Hollywood, Nuns Walk, Demesne Rd ☎ 2138, SW : 3 m.
Belfast 8 – Bangor 5.

☖ **Culloden** ⤳, Holywood, BT18 0EY, on A 2 ☎ 5223, ≤, XX, ✿, park – ⧈ TV **P**. ☖. ◰
AE ⓪ VISA
M 5.00 **t.** ⁑ 2.00 – **32 rm** ⌷ 20.00/30.00.

XX Clanbrassil House, Cultra Av., Seafront Rd, BT18 0BB, ☎ 2494, ≤, ✿ – **P**.

CRAIGAVON Armagh – pop. 12,594 – ✉ ✆ 0762 Portadown.
Envir. : Ardress House* 17C (site*, drawing-room plasterwork**) AC, W : 11 m. – Rich Hill (site*, church : scenery*) SW : 9 ½ m. – Armagh (St. Patrick's Protestant Cathedral* 18 C, ≤*, St. Patrick's Catholic Cathedral : interior*) SW : 14 m.
☗ The Demesne, Lurgan ☎ 076 282 (Lurgan) 2087, NE : 3 m.
Belfast 28 – Armagh 13.

☖ Seagoe, Old Lurgan Rd, BT53 5QS, ☎ 33076, ✿ – ⌷wc ☏ **P**. ☖
50 rm.

XX **Green Garter,** Magowan Buildings, West St., Portadown, BT66 6NA, ☎ 35164 – AE ⓪
closed Saturday lunch, Sunday, Monday and 10 to 24 July – **M** a la carte 5.15/9.20 ⁑ 1.80.

CRAWFORDSBURN Down 986 ㊳ – pop. 487 – ✆ 0247 Helen's Bay.
☗ Carnalea ☎ 0247 (Bangor) 65004 – ☗, ☗ Conlig ☎ 0247 (Bangor) 63706.
Belfast 10 – Bangor 3.

☖ **Old Inn,** 15 Main St., BT19 1JH, ☎ 853255, « Part 17C inn », ✿ – TV ⌷wc ☏ **P**
M a la carte 6.00/9.00 **st.** – **24 rm** ⌷ 10.70/21.95 **st.**

DUNADRY Antrim 986 ㉝ – ✆ 084 94 Templepatrick.
Envir. : Antrim (round tower* 10C) NW : 5 m. – Shane's Castle* (16 C ruins) AC, NW : 5 ½ m. (access by miniature railway).
Belfast 15 – Larne 18 – Londonderry 56.

☖ **Dunadry Inn,** 2 Islandreagh Drive, BT41 2HA, ☎ 32474, Telex 747245, ✿ – TV **P**. ☖
◰ AE ⓪ VISA
closed 25 and 26 December – **M** a la carte 7.30/11.10 **st.** – **57 rm** ⌷ 22.30/39.50 **st.**

DUNMURRY Antrim 986 ㊲ – see Belfast.

ENNISKILLEN Fermanagh 986 ⑱ – pop. 6,558 – ✆ 0365.
See : Lough Erne*** (Upper and Lower) – On Lower Lough Erne, by boat AC : Devenish Island (site**, monastic ruins : scenery*) and White Island*. **Envir. :** Castle Coole* 18C (site*) E : 1 m. – Florence Court (site*, park*) AC, SW : 8 m.
☗ Castlecoole ☎ 2900.
🛈 37 Town Hall St. ☎ 3110 (March-October).
Belfast 87 – Londonderry 59.

☖ Killyhevlin, Dublin Rd, BT74 6DX, SE : 1 ¾ m. on A 4 ☎ 3481, ≤, ✿, park – TV ⌷wc ☏ **P**. ☖. AE ⓪ VISA
closed Christmas Day – **M** a la carte 6.90/9.40 – **26 rm.**

☗ Willoughby, 24 Willoughby Pl., BT74 6YX, ☎ 22882 – ◰ AE ⓪ VISA
11 rm.

at Killedeas N : 7 m. on B 82 – ✉ Enniskillen – ✆ 036 562 Irvinestown :

☖ Manor House ⤳, BT74 7LF, ☎ 561, ≤, ✿, park – ⌷wc ☏ **P**
15 rm.

AUSTIN-MG-ROVER-TRIUMPH Dublin Rd ☎ 3475   VAUXHALL Tempo Rd ☎ 4366

GIANT'S CAUSEWAY Antrim 986 ⑭.
See : Giant's Causeway*** (Chaussée des Géants) basalt formation (from the car-park *AC*, ½ h Rtn on foot).
Information Office, Lower Main St., ☎ 026 57 (Bushmills) 31343 (July-August).
Belfast 72 – Ballycastle 13 – **Londonderry 41.**

Hotel see : Portballintrae SW: 4 m.

GLENGORMLEY Antrim – see Newtonabbey.

GLENARIFF (Glen of)*** Antrim.

GREY ABBEY Down 986 ⑱ – ✆ 024 774.
See : Abbey* (Cistercian ruins 12C) *AC*. **Envir.** : Mount Stewart Gardens* *AC*, Temple of the Winds ≤* *AC*, NW: 1 ½ m.
Belfast 18 – Bangor 13.

White Satin Inn, 23-25 Main St., BT22 2NF, ☎ 330, Chinese rest.

HILLSBOROUGH Down – pop. 780 – ✆ 0846.
See : Government House* 18C – the Fort* 17C. **Envir.** : Legananny Dolmen ≤* S: 16 m.
18 at Lisburn ☎ 023 82 (Lisburn) 2186, N: 5 m.
Belfast 13.

White Gables, Dromore Rd, BT26 6HU, ☎ 682755 – wc. **24 rm.**

Number Ten, 10 Ballynahinch St., BT26 6AW, ☎ 682866, French rest. –.

KESH Fermanagh 986 ⑱ – pop. 311 – ✆ 036 563.
Envir. : Lough Erne*** (Upper and Lower) – On Lower Lough Erne, by boat *AC* : Devenish Island (site**, monastic ruins: scenery*) and White Island*.
Belfast 89 – Enniskillen 15 – **Londonderry 52.**

Hotels see : Enniskillen SE: 15 m.

KILLEDEAS Fermanagh – see Enniskillen.

LARNE Antrim 986 ⑱ – pop. 18,242 – ✆ 0574.
Exc. : Antrim Coast Road*** (A 2) from Larne to Portrush.
to Stranraer (Sealink) 2-6 daily (2 h 15 mn) – to Cairnryan (Townsend Thoresen : Transport Ferry Service) 4 daily (2 h to 2 h 30 mn).
18 192 Coast Rd ☎ 057 483 (Ballygally) 248, N: 4 m.
Information Office, Victoria Rd ☎ 2313 (Easter and July-August).
Belfast 23 – Ballymena 20.

King's Arms, Broadway, BT40 2LP, ☎ 3322 – wc. AE VISA
M 4.50/6.00 **st.** 1.60 – **49 rm** 14.00/18.00 **st.**

AUSTIN-MORRIS Point St. ☎ 2091
FORD Glynn Rd ☎ 3311

LISNASKEA Fermanagh 986 ⑱ – pop. 15,990 – ✆ 036 572.
Belfast 83 – **Dundalk 53** – **Omagh 39** – **Sligo 53.**

Ortine, Main St. ☎ 206 – wc. VISA
M 4.50/6.00 **s.** 2.50 – **17 rm** 7.50/14.00 **s.**

LONDONDERRY Derry 986 ⑱ – pop. 31,437 – ✆ 0504.
See : City Walls** 17C – Guildhall* 1908 – Memorial Hall*. **Envir.** Grianan of Aileach* (Republic of Ireland) (stone fort) *** NW : 5 m. – Dungiven (priory : site*) SE : 18 m.
18 Prehen ☎ 42610.
Foyle St. ☎ 61504 (July-August).
Belfast 71 – **Dublin 145.**

Everglades, Prehen Rd, BT47 2PA, S: 1 ½ m. on A 5 ☎ 46722, Telex 748005, –
. AE VISA
M 4.00/6.50 1.00 – 2.50 – **38 rm** 15.00/22.50.

AUSTIN-MORRIS-MG-ROVER-TRIUMPH 78 Strand Rd ☎ 64181
FORD 173 Stroud Rd ☎ 67613
PEUGEOT Campsie ☎ 860588
RENAULT Strand Rd ☎ 68648
VAUXHALL Maydown ☎ 64706
VW, AUDI Bunorana Rd ☎ 65985

MOVILLE Donegal.
to Oban (Western Ferries) 29 April-September: Sunday 1 daily (4 h).

NEWCASTLE Down 986 ㉒ – pop. 4,621 – ✆ 039 67.

Envir. : Tollymore Forest Park* *AC*, NW : 2 m. by B 180 – Dundrum (castle* 13C ruins : top ❄※**, 70 steps) NE : 3 m. – Loughinisland (the 3 churches* : 1000 - 1547 - 1636) NE : 8 m. **Exc. :** SW : Mourne Mountains** (Slieve Donard*, Silent Valley*, Lough Shannagh* : reservoir 1948).

🛈 Information Caravan, The Promenade ☎ 22222 (July-August).

Belfast 30 – Londonderry 101.

🏨 **Slieve Donard** ⟿, Downs Rd, BT33 0AH, ☎ 23681, ≼, ✗, ⊡, 🚗, park – 🛗 📺 🅿. ⚿. ⊠ Æ ① *VISA* **M** 4.50/8.00 – **112 rm** ⊇ 14.00/27.00.

🏠 **Enniskeen** ⟿, 98 Bryansford Rd, BT33 0LF, NW : ¾ m. ☎ 22392, ≼, 🚗, park – 🛏wc ☏ 🅿 *April-October* – **M** 4.00/5.00 **t.** 🍷 2.10 – **13 rm** ⊇ 8.50/18.50 **t.** – P 16.50/18.50 **t.**

NEWRY Down 986 ㉒ – pop. 11,393 – ✆ 0693.

Envir.: Slieve Gullion**, Ring of Gullion : Ballitemple viewpoint**, Bernish Rock viewpoint**, Cam Lough*, Killevy Churches (site*) SW : 5 m. – Derrymore House (site*) *AC*, NW : 2 ½ m. – Rostrevor (Fairy Glen*) SE : 8 ¾ m. – Carlingford Lough* SE : 10 m.

🛈₁₈ Warrenpoint ☎ 069 372 (Warrenpoint) 2219, S : 5 m.

🛈 Council Offices, Monaghan Row ☎ 5411.

Belfast 39 – Armagh 20 – Dundalk 13.

🏠 Ardmore, Belfast Rd, BT34 1QH, ☎ 3161, 🚗 – 🛏wc 🅿. ⚿ **25 rm.**

AUSTIN-MORRIS-MG Railway Av. ☎ 2201
PEUGEOT 18 Edward St. ☎ 2877
RENAULT 52/53 Merchants Quay ☎ 3626

NEWTOWNABBEY Antrim 986 ㊲ – pop. 57,908 – ✉ ✆ 0231 Whiteabbey.

Belfast 6 – Larne 18.

🏨 **Glenavna House** ⟿, 588 Shore Rd, BT37 0SN, Whiteabbey ☎ 64461, ≼, 🚗, park – 📺 🛏wc 🚿wc 🅿. ⚿. ① **M** 4.75/5.50 – **17 rm** ⊇ 14.00/28.00.

at Glengormley W : 7 m. on A 6 by A 2, M 2 – ✉ Newtownabbey – ✆ 023 13 Glengormley :

🏨 **Chimney Corner Motor,** 630 Antrim Rd, BT36 8RH, NW : 2 ¼ m. on A 6 ☎ 44925, 🚗 – 📺 🛏wc ☏ 🅿. ⚿. ⊠ Æ ① *VISA* *closed mid 2 weeks July and 1 week at Christmas* – **M** *(closed Sunday)* 4.50/5.00 🍷 2.00 – **55 rm** ⊇ 15.50/21.00.

PORSCHE 45 Mallusk Rd ☎ 02313 (Glengormley) 7111 TALBOT Glengormley ☎ 2742

NEWTOWNARDS Down 986 ⑱ and ㊳ – pop. 15,387 – ✆ 0247.

Envir. : Scrabo Tower (site*) SW : 1 m.

🛈₁₈ Scrabo ☎ 2355.

Belfast 10 – Bangor 5.

🏨 **Strangford Arms,** 92 Church St., BT23 4AN ☎ 814141 – 📺 🛏wc ☏ 🅿. ⚿. Æ ① *VISA* *closed Easter Monday, Easter Tuesday, 2 weeks July and Christmas Day* – **M** a la carte 6.50/10.50 🍷 1.10 – ⊇ 2.25 – **18 rm** 15.00/26.00 **t.**

FORD Regent St. ☎ 812626
MORRIS Old Cross Garage ☎ 813279
VAUXHALL Portaferry Rd ☎ 813376

OMAGH Tyrone 986 ⑱ – pop. 27,998.

Envir. : Gortin Glen Forest Park*, Gortin Gap* (on B 48) NE : 9 m. – Glenelly Valley* NE : 17 m. by Plumbridge.

🛈₉ Dublin Rd ☎ 3160 – 🛈₉ Fintona ☎ 066 284 (Fintona) 480, S : 5 ½ m.

Belfast 69 – Dublin 113 – Dundalk 64 – Londonderry 32 – Sligo 68.

AUSTIN-MORRIS-MG Dublin Rd ☎ 3116
FIAT 60 Dublin Rd ☎ 2021
FORD Derry Rd ☎ 2788
RENAULT Cookstown Rd ☎ 3451
VAUXHALL Derry Rd ☎ 2782

Les hôtels ou restaurants agréables sont indiqués dans le guide par un signe rouge.

Aidez-nous en nous signalant les maisons où, par expérience, vous savez qu'il fait bon vivre. Votre guide Michelin 1981 sera encore meilleur.

🏨 ⋯ 🏠

XXXXX ⋯ X

PORTAFERRY Down 986 ⑱ – pop. 1,592 – ☼ 024 772.
See : Strangford (site*, Audley's Castle : top ❄**, 44 steps). **Envir. :** Castle Ward 1765 (great hall*) SW : 2 m. – Saul (St. Patrick's Memorial Church : site*, ≤*) SW : 5 m.
Belfast 29 – Bangor 24.

- 🏨 Portaferry, 9 The Strand, BT22 1LA, ☎ 231 – ⌫wc
  9 rm.

- ✗ **Scotsman,** 156-158 Shore Rd, BT22 1LA, ☎ 326
  closed Sunday, Christmas Day, Good Friday lunch and Monday from October-June –
  M a la carte 4.35/6.45 **t.** ⌾ 1.60.

PORTBALLINTRAE Antrim 986 ⑭ – pop. 496 – ✉ ☼ 026 57 Bushmills.
⛳ ☎ 026 57 (Bushmills) 31317.
🛈 Information Office ☎ 3672 (July-August).
Belfast 71 – Larne 54 – **Londonderry 40.**

- 🏨 Beach, Beach Rd, BT57 8RT, ☎ 31214, ≤ – ⌫wc ☏
  28 rm.

PORTSTEWART Londonderry 986 ⑭ – pop. 4,975 – ☼ 026 583.
⛳, ⛳ Strand Rd ☎ 2015, West boundary.
🛈 Town Hall, The Crescent ☎ 2286 (July-August).
Belfast 67 – Coleraine 6.

- 🏨 **Edgewater,** 86-88 Strand Rd, BT55 7LZ, ☎ 2224, ≤ – ⌫wc ☖wc ℗. ⟰
  M 3.25/4.50 ⌾ 2.00 – **18 rm** ⌑ 11.00/20.00 – P 13.50/17.00.

SAINTFIELD Down – pop. 1,500 – ✉ Ballynahinch – ☼ 0238.
⛳ at Ballynahinch ☎ 2365, SW : 5 m.
Belfast 11.

- ✗ **Barn,** 120 Monlough Rd, BT24 7EU, N : 1 ¾ m. ☎ 510396 – ℗
  closed Sunday, Monday, Tuesday, Thursday, 2 weeks May, 12-13 July, 2 weeks September and Christmas week – **M** (dinner only) 8.50 ⌾ 2.20.

Channel Islands

LICENSING HOURS - WHEN DRINKING ALCOHOLIC BEVERAGES IS PERMITTED IN PUBS AND BARS AND OTHER LICENSED PREMISES (The General Rule).

HEURES PERMISES POUR LA CONSOMMATION DES BOISSONS ALCOOLISÉES (Règle Générale).

ORARI CONSENTITI PER LA CONSUMAZIONE DI BEVANDE ALCOOLICHE (Regola Generale).

AUSSCHANKZEITEN FÜR ALKOHOLISCHE GETRÄNKE (Allgemeine Regelung).

ALDERNEY

		from / de / dalle / von	to / à / alle / bis	from / de / dalle / von	to / à / alle / bis		
Monday to Friday (other than Good Friday and Christmas Day) / Lundi au Vendredi (autres que Vendredi Saint et Jour de Noël)	Pubs Hotels	10.00			24.00 * (01.00 in summer)	Pubs Alberghi Hotels	Da Lunedì a Venerdì (esclusi Venerdì Santo e Natale) / Montag-Freitag (außer Karfreitag und Weihnachten)
	Rest.	11.00	15.00	19.00	24.00	Ristoranti Rest.	
Saturday (other than Christmas Day) / Samedi (autre que Jour de Noël)	Pubs Hotels	10.00			24.00	Pubs Alberghi Hotels	Sabato (escluso Natale) / Samstags (außer Weihnachten)
	Rest.	11.00	15.00	19.00	24.00	Ristoranti Rest.	
Sunday, Good Friday and Christmas Day / Dimanche, Vendredi Saint et Jour de Noël	Pubs Hotels	12.00	14.00	20.00	24.00	Pubs Alberghi Hotels	Domenica, Venerdì Santo e Natale / Sonntags, Karfreitag und Weihnachten
	Rest.	11.00	15.00	19.00	24.00	Ristoranti Rest.	

* Summer applies from 1st April to 30th September.

* Période d'été applicable du 1er avril au 30 septembre.

* Stagione estiva applicabile dal 1° aprile al 30 settembre.

* Sommerzeit vom 1. April bis 30. September.

GUERNSEY

		from / de	to / à	from / de	to / à		
Weekdays (other than Good Friday, and Christmas Day) / Jours de semaine (autres que Vendredi Saint et Jour de Noël)	Pubs	10.30			23.00	Pubs	Giorni della settimana (esclusi Venerdì Santo, e Natale)
	Rest.	12.00			23.00	Ristoranti Rest.	Wochentags (außer Karfreitag und Weihnachten)
Sundays	Pubs	Closed - Fermés - Chiusi - Geschlossen				Pubs	Domeniche
Dimanches	Rest.	12.00	14.30	19.30	22.30	Ristoranti Rest.	Sonntags
Good Friday Christmas Day (if not a Sunday)	Pubs	11.00	12.30	19.00	21.30	Pubs	Venerdì Santo e Natale (se non è domenica)
Vendredi Saint et Jour de Noël (si non un dimanche)	Rest.	12.00	14.30	19.00	21.30	Ristoranti Rest.	Karfreitag und Weihnachten (falls nicht Sonntag)
		dalle / von	alle / bis	dalle / von	alle / bis		

JERSEY

		from / de	to / à	from / de	to / à		
Weekdays (other than Good Friday and Christmas Day) / Jours de semaine (autres que Vendredi Saint et Jour de Noël)	Pubs	9.00			23.00	Pubs	Giorni della settimana (esclusi Venerdì Santo e Natale)
	Rest.	9.00			1.00	Rist. Rest.	Wochentags (außer Karfreitag und Weihnachten)
Sundays, Good Friday and Christmas Day	Pubs	11.00	13.00	16.30	23.00	Pubs	Domeniche, Venerdì Santo e Natale
Dimanches, Vendredi Saint et Jour de Noël	Rest.	11.00			1.00	Rist. Rest.	Sonntags, Karfreitag und Weihnachten
		dalle / von	alle / bis	dalle / von	alle / bis		

Residents: no restrictions on licensed premises.
Hotels with a pub or restaurants attached are obliged to keep official licensing hours.
Résidents: pas de restriction dans les lieux ayant une licence.
Hôtels: s'ils possèdent un pub ou un restaurant, ils doivent respecter les horaires légaux.
Per i residenti: nessuna restrizione nei locali con licenza.
Alberghi: possono possedere un pub od un ristorante. Devono rispettare gli orari legali.
Für Hotelgäste: keine Beschränkung in den lizensierten Hotels.
Die Hotels können ein « Pub » oder ein Restaurant besitzen, müssen aber die jeweils geltenden Vorschriften beachten.

Place with at least :
one hotel or restaurant .... ● Catel
one pleasant hotel .... 🏠 , ✕ with rm.
one quiet, secluded hotel .... 🛥
one restaurant with .... ✿, ✿✿, M
See this town for establishments
  located in its vicinity ....

Localité offrant au moins :
une ressource hôtelière .... ● Catel
un hôtel agréable .... 🏠 , ✕ with rm.
un hôtel très tranquille, isolé .... 🛥
une bonne table à .... ✿, ✿✿, M
Localité groupant dans le texte
  les ressources de ses environs ....

La località possiede come minimo :
una risorsa alberghiera .... ● Catel
un albergo ameno .... 🏠 , ✕ with rm.
un albergo molto tranquillo, isolato .... 🛥
un'ottima tavola con .... ✿, ✿✿, M
La località raggruppa nel suo testo
  le risorse dei dintorni ....

Ort mit mindestens :
einem Hotel oder Restaurant .... ● Catel
einem angenehmen Hotel .... 🏠 , ✕ with rm.
einem sehr ruhigen und abgelegenen Hotel .... 🛥
einem Restaurant mit .... ✿, ✿✿, M
Ort mit Angaben über Hotels und Restaurants
  in seiner Umgebung ....

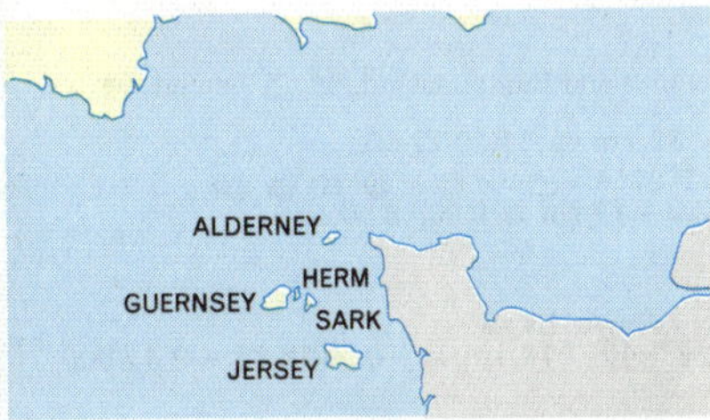
ALDERNEY
GUERNSEY
HERM
SARK
JERSEY

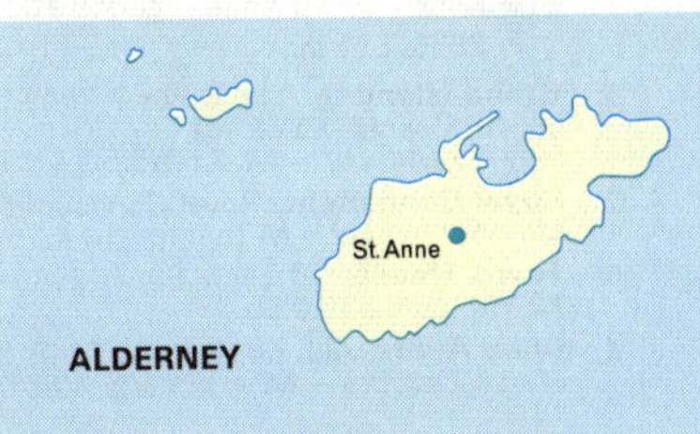
St. Anne
ALDERNEY

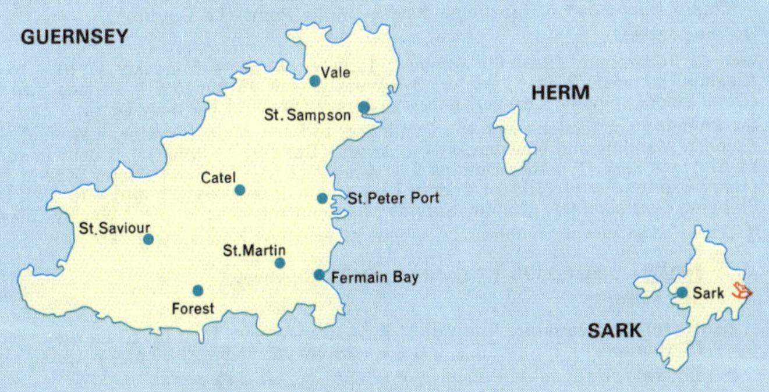
GUERNSEY
Vale
St. Sampson
HERM
Catel
St. Peter Port
St. Saviour
St. Martin
Fermain Bay
Forest
Sark
SARK

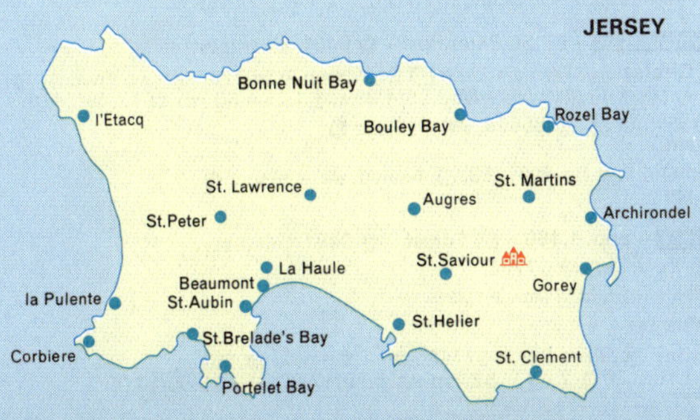
JERSEY
Bonne Nuit Bay
l'Etacq
Bouley Bay
Rozel Bay
St. Lawrence
St. Martins
Augres
St. Peter
Archirondel
St. Saviour
La Haule
Beaumont
Gorey
St. Aubin
la Pulente
St. Helier
St. Brelade's Bay
Corbiere
St. Clement
Portelet Bay

CHANNEL ISLANDS

Towns

ALDERNEY 59 ③ and 230 ⑨ – pop. 1,686 – ECD: Wednesday – ✆ 048 182.
See : Telegraph Bay* (cliffs*) – Clonque Bay* – Braye Bay*.
✈ 🕿 2886 – Booking Office: Aurigny Air Services.
🚢 Shipping connections with the Continent : to Saint-Malo (Condor : hydrofoil) – to Jersey (Condor : hydrofoil) 2 weekly summer only (2 h).
🛈 States Offices, Queen Elizabeth II St. 🕿 2811.

St. Anne – ✉ St. Anne – ✆ 048 182 Alderney.
🛈 🕿 2835, E : 1 m.

🏨 **Grand Island** ⬠, The Butes 🕿 2848, ⮜ harbour and Burhou Island, ✗, ⌇ heated, 🚗 –
⌂wc 🕮wc 🅿. 🔌 ⓞ *VISA*
May-19 October – **M** 3.50/5.50 🍷 1.50 – **32 rm** ☷ 11.30/22.60.

🏨 **Royal Connaught,** Royal Connaught Sq. 🕿 2756 – ⌂wc 🕮wc 🅿. 🔌 ⓞ *VISA*
May-September – **M** (bar lunch) 4.75 🍷 1.00 – **17 rm** ☷ 9.00/18.00.

🏠 **Town House,** 10 High St. 🕿 2330
12 rm ☷ 6.50/10.50.

✗ **Chez André** with rm, Victoria St. 🕿 2777 – ⌂wc. 🔌 ⓞ
March-October – **M** a la carte 4.65/7.90 🍷 1.40 – **14 rm** ☷ 10.50/16.25 – P 17.00/18.25.

GUERNSEY 59 ④ and 230 ⑨ ⑩ – pop. 51,458 – ✆ 0481.
See : Icart Point ⮜*** – Cobo Bay** – Fort Pézéries ⮜** – Fort Doyle ⮜* – Fort Saumarez ⮜*
– Moulin Huet Bay* – Rocquaine Bay* – Moye Point (Le Gouffre*).
✈ see Forest.
🚢 to Portsmouth (Sealink) summer : 1 daily ; winter 4-5 weekly (7 h) – to Weymouth (Sealink) summer : 2 daily ; winter : 3-5 weekly (4 h 45 mn to 6 h 30 mn) – to Saint-Malo (Commodore Shipping Co.) cars only – to Jersey (Sealink) 1-2 daily (2 h).
🚢 Shipping connections with the Continent : to Saint-Malo (Condor : hydrofoil) – to Carteret (Service Maritime and Hovercross) – to Jersey (Condor : hydrofoil) 1-3 daily in summer direct (1 h) or via Sark (1 h 15) ; October 2-6 weekly (1 h) – to Herm (Herm Seaway Marine Ltd) (Herm Express Ferry) (Trident Charter Co.) frequent services (25 mn) – to Sark (Isle of Sark Shipping Co.) summer : Monday/Saturday frequent services ; winter 3 weekly (35 mn to 1 h).
🛈 States Tourist Information Bureau, Crown Pier, St. Peter Port 🕿 23552, Telex 41612.

Catel – pop. 6,317 – ✉ Catel – ✆ 0481 Guernsey.
St. Peter Port 2.

🏨 **Hotel de Beauvoir,** Rue Cohu, 🕿 54750 – ⌂wc 🕮wc 🅿. 🔌 AE *VISA*
M (bar lunch) 2.50/4.50 **s.** 🍷 0.95 – **29 rm** ☷ 11.50/21.00 **s.** – P 18.00/27.00 **s.**

🏠 **Lilyvale,** Hougue du Pommier, 🕿 56868, ⌇, 🚗 – 🅿
17 May-September – **13 rm** ☷ 10.00/23.00 **s.**

✗ **Le Friquet Country** with rm, rue du Friquet 🕿 56422, ⌇ heated, 🚗 – ⌂wc 🕮wc 🅿
closed Monday from mid October-mid April – **M** a la carte 4.45/6.00 🍷 1.40 – **13 rm** ☷ 10.00/20.00 – P approx. 13.00.

Fermain Bay – ✉ St. Peter Port – ✆ 0481 Guernsey.

🏨 **Le Chalet** ⬠, Fermain Lane ✉ St. Martin 🕿 35716 – ⌂wc 🕮wc ☎ 🅿. 🔌 AE ⓞ *VISA*
20 April-20 September – **M** 3.25/4.25 **s.** 🍷 1.25 – **50 rm** ☷ 12.45/24.00 – P 15.50/17.10.

🏨 **La Favorita** ⬠, 🕿 35666, 🚗 – ⌂wc 🅿
30 rm.

🏨 **Fermain,** Fort Rd 🕿 37763, ⌇ heated, 🚗 – ⌂wc 🅿
33 rm.

Forest – pop. 1,460 – ✉ Forest – ✆ 0481 Guernsey.
✈ La Villiaze 🕿 37766.
🛈 The Airport, La Villiaze 🕿 63422.
St. Peter Port 4.

🏨 **Manor** ⬠, Petit Bôt 🕿 37788, 🚗 – 🛗 ⌂wc 🅿. *VISA*
M 2.75/3.50 🍷 1.40 – **62 rm** ☷ 6.50/12.00 – P 12.00/14.00.

St. Martin – pop. 6,161 – ECD : Thursday – ✉ St. Martin – ☎ 0481 Guernsey.
See : Church* 11C.

St. Peter Port 2.

St. Margaret's Lodge, Forest Rd ☏ 35757, ⌇ heated, 🛏 – 📺 **P**. 📷 AE ⓓ VISA
M (see rest. **Anniversary Room**) – **42 rm** ⊇ 20.50/34.00 s. – P approx. 25.00 s.

Bella Luce, La Fosse ☏ 38764, ⌇ heated, 🛏 – 📺 ⊟wc 🚿wc **P**
M 2.50/5.50 ▯ 1.20 – **25 rm** ⊇ 17.50/32.00 – P 21.00/24.00.

Green Acres, Les Hubits ☏ 35711, ⌇ heated, 🛏 – ⊟wc ☎ **P**
M 2.00/3.50 s. ▯ 1.00 – **48 rm** ⊇ 9.50/19.00 s. – P 12.50/16.75 s.

Idlerocks, Jerbourg Point ☏ 37711, ⩽ islands, ⌇ heated – ⊟wc 🚿wc **P**. 📷 ⓓ VISA
M 4.00/7.00 s. ▯ 0.80 – **20 rm** ⊇ 12.00/27.00 s. – P 16.50/18.50 s.

Captain's, La Fosse ☏ 38990 – **P**
Mid May-September – **M** (bar lunch) 2.50/3.00 – **11 rm** ⊇ 9.00/18.00.

Anniversary Room (at St. Margaret's Lodge Hotel), Forest Rd ☏ 35757 **P**. 📷 AE ⓓ VISA
M a la carte 4.50/5.70 ▯ 0.80.

AUSTIN-MORRIS-MG-WOLSELEY ☏ 37661   FERRARI, FIAT Forest Rd ☏ 35753

St. Peter Port – pop. 16,303 – ECD : Thursday – ✉ St. Peter Port – ☎ 0481 Guernsey.
See : St. Peter's Church* 14C z A – Castle Cornet* (❊*) AC z – Hauteville House (Victor Hugo Museum* : 5 pearl-embroidered tapestries**) AC z M – Victoria Tower : top ❊**, 100 steps Y. **Envir. :** Les Vauxbelets (Little Chapel*) SW : 2 ½ m. by Mount Durand z – Saumarez Park* W : 2 ½ m. by Grange Rd z.

🛈 Crown Pier ☏ 23552, Telex 41612.

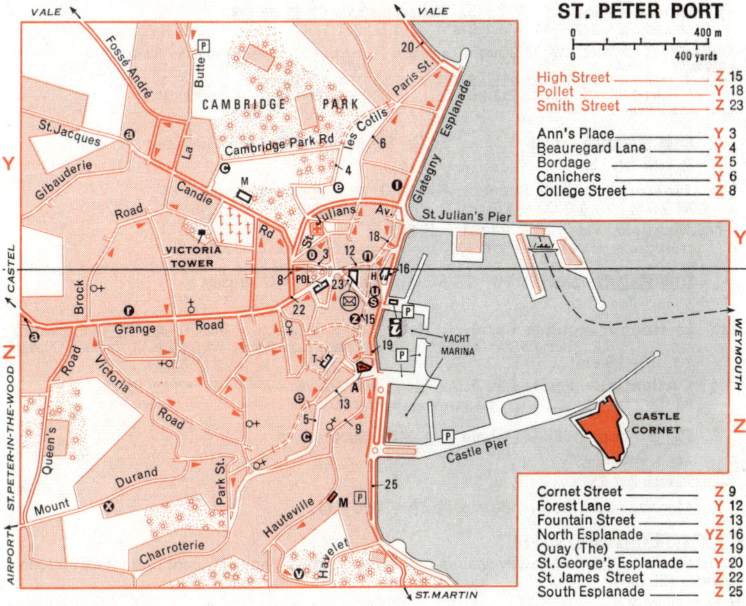

Duke of Richmond, Cambridge Park ☏ 26221, Telex 4191462, ⌇ heated – 📺. 📷 AE ⓓ VISA   Y c
M 3.75/6.00 s. ▯ 1.20 – **75 rm** ⊇ 18.00/30.00 s. – P 20.50/28.50 s.

Old Government House, Ann's Pl. ☏ 24921, Telex 4181144, ⩽ harbour and sea, ⌇ heated, 🛏 – 📺 **P**. 📷 AE ⓓ VISA   Y o
M a la carte 3.50/4.50 s. ▯ 1.75 – **72 rm** ⊇ 19.25/38.50 s. – P 26.25/28.75 s.

Royal, Glategny Esplanade ☏ 23921, Telex 4191221, ⩽, ⌇ heated, 🛏 – 📺 **P**. 📷 AE ⓓ VISA   Y i
M 3.50/4.00 s. ▯ 1.25 – **79 rm** ⊇ 20.00/40.00 s. – P approx. 27.00 s.

P.T.O. ⟶

Summerland House, Mount Durand ☎ 24196, ❦ – ☐wc 🅟. 🆎 *VISA* Z x
M 2.75/3.75 ⚱ 1.20 – **21 rm** ☷ 16.00/29.00.

La Collinette, St. Jacques ☎ 22585, ⚊ heated, ❦ – 📺 ☐wc 🛁wc ☎. 🅟. 🆎 ⓸ *VISA* Y a
M 3.00/4.50 ⚱ 1.00 – **29 rm** ☷ 12.00/24.00.

De Havelet, Havelet ☎ 22199, ❦ – ☐wc ☎. 🆎 ⓸ *VISA* Z v
M a la carte 2.05/3.75 ⚱ 1.10 – **35 rm** ☷ 11.70/26.40 **s.** – P 14.50/16.25 **s.**

Moore's, Pollet ☎ 24452 – 🛗 ☐wc 🛁 ☎. 🆎 *VISA* Y n
M 3.25/4.25 **s.** ⚱ 1.00 – **40 rm** ☷ 12.45/24.00 – P 15.50/17.10.

Dunchoille, Guelles Rd ☎ 22912, ❦ – ☐wc 🛁wc 🅟   N : by la Butte Y
M (bar lunch) approx. 5.00 ⚱ 0.95 – **24 rm** ☷ 7.00/16.00 – P 15.50/17.50.

Grange Lodge, The Grange ☎ 25161, ⚊ heated, ❦ – ☐wc 🅟. *VISA* Z r
13 March-October – M (bar lunch) approx. 3.50 ⚱ 0.90 – **35 rm** ☷ 9.50/19.00.

Baltimore House, Les Gravées ☎ 23641, ❦ – 🛁. 🆎 ⓸ *VISA* Z a
closed November and December – **13 rm** ☷ 7.95/10.50 **s.**

La Frégate ⚓ with rm, Les Côtils ☎ 24624, ≼ town and harbour, « Country house atmosphere », ❦ – ☐wc ☎ 🅟. 🆎 ⓸ *VISA* Y e
M a la carte 4.75/9.60 ⚱ 1.40 – ☷ 2.00 – **13 rm** 13.50/25.00 – P 21.50/24.10.

Le Nautique, Quay Steps ☎ 21714, ≼ – 🆎 ⓸ *VISA* Z s
closed Sunday from December to February – M a la carte 5.50/11.20 ⚱ 1.30.

Le Français, Le Marchand House, Market St. ☎ 20963, French rest. – 🆎 ⓸ *VISA* Z e
closed Saturday lunch, Sunday, 15 January-15 February and Bank Holidays – M a la carte 5.50/7.15 ⚱ 1.40.

Tudor House, The Bordage, ☎ 25528, Chinese rest. – 🆎 ⓸ *VISA* Z c
M a la carte 2.90/5.35 ⚱ 1.25.

Bistro Borsalino, North Esplanade ☎ 27529, Bistro – 🆎 ⓸ *VISA* Z u
closed Sunday – M a la carte 5.40/7.35 ⚱ 1.50.

Nino's, Lefebvre St. ☎ 23052, Italian Bistro – 🆎 ⓸ *VISA* Z z
closed January – M a la carte 4.80/6.60 ⚱ 1.15.

BMW, MERCEDES-BENZ, VW 16 Glategny Esplanade ☎ 23916
DAIMLER-JAGUAR-ROVER-TRIUMPH, ASTON MARTIN, ROLLS ROYCE Rue du Pré ☎ 24261
FORD Les Banques ☎ 24774

PEUGEOT Lower Colbourne Rd ☎ 20115
RENAULT Upland Rd ☎ 26846
TALBOT, LANCIA Doyle Rd ☎ 24025
VOLVO La Plaque Lane ☎ 64104

St. Sampson – pop. 6,534 – ✉ St. Sampson's – ☎ 0481 Guernsey.
St. Peter-Port 3.5.

Pinetops, Pointues Rocques, ☎ 44020, ❦ – ☐wc 🅟
M 2.75/3.75 ⚱ 1.00 – **15 rm** ☷ (dinner included) 12.00/26.40.

Mayfield, Vale Rd, ☎ 44891 – 🛁 🅟
closed Christmas – **17 rm** ☷ (dinner included) 6.20/8.60 **s.**

St. Saviour – pop. 2,116 – ✉ St. Saviour – ☎ 0481 Guernsey.
St. Peter Port 4.

La Hougue Fouque Farm ⚓, Route-des-Bas-Courtil ☎ 63800, ❦ – ☐wc 🛁wc 🅟
closed 15 October-15 November – M (closed Monday in winter) a la carte 5.00/6.45 ⚱ 1.40 – **19 rm** ☷ 10.00/21.00.

L'Atlantique, Perelle Bay ☎ 64056, ⚊ heated, ❦ – ☐wc 🅟. 🆎 ⓸ *VISA*
M 3.60/5.00 **s.** ⚱ 1.10 – **13 rm** ☷ 18.40/24.70 **s.**

Vale – pop. 7,558 – ✉ Vale – ☎ 0481 Guernsey.
See : Castle ≼*.
St. Peter-Port 4.5.

Marina, Yacht Marina, Beaucette, ☎ 47066 – 🅟.

HERM ISLAND 59 ⑤ and 230.
🚢 to Guernsey (Herm Seaway Marine Ltd) (Herm Express Ferry) (Trident Charter Co) frequent services (25 mn).
🛈 Herm Office ☎ 5.

JERSEY 59 ⑤⑥ and 230 ⑪ – pop. 72,629 – ☎ 0534.

See : Devil's Hole* (site**) *AC* private access, ¾ h Rtn on foot by a steep road – Grosnez Castle ⦅* – La Hougue Bie Tumulus* (prehistoric tomb) *AC* – St. Catherine's Bay* – Fliquet Bay (St. Catherine's Breakwater ⦅**) – Sorel Point ⦅* – Noirmont Point ⦅* – Jersey zoo (site*) *AC*.

✈ Ports of Jersey Airport ☏ 41272, Telex 41528.

⛴ Shipping connections with the Continent: to St-Malo (Emeraude Ferries) – to Saint-Malo (Commodore Shipping Co.) cars only – to Portsmouth (Sealink) summer: 1 daily; winter: 4-5 weekly (9 h 30 mn) – to Weymouth (Sealink) summer 2 daily; winter 3-5 weekly (6 h 30 mn to 9 h) – to Guernsey (Sealink) 1-2 daily (2 h).

⛴ Shipping connections with the Continent: to Saint-Malo (Condor: hydrofoil) – to Granville (Navifrance: Vedettes Armoricaines and Vedettes Vertes Granvillaises) – to Carteret (Service Maritime and Hovercross).

to Guernsey (Condor: hydrofoil) summer 1-3 daily (1 h); October 2-6 weekly (1 h) – to Sark (Condor: hydrofoil) summer Monday/Saturday 1-3 daily (45 mn) – to Alderney (Condor: hydrofoil) summer 2 weekly (2 h).

🛈 States of Jersey Tourism Committee, Weighbridge, St-Helier ☏ 21281 and 31958.

Archirondel – ✉ Gorey – ☎ 0534 Jersey.

St. Helier 5.

🏨 **Les Arches,** ☏ 53839, Telex 4192085, ⦅, ⊡ heated, 🍴 – ⊟wc 🚿wc ☎ Ⓟ. ⛱. ⊠
AE VISA
M 5.50/7.50 **s.** 🍾 1.75 – **51 rm** � 17.50/19.50 **s.** – P approx. 25.00 **s.**

Augres – ✉ Trinity – ☎ 0534 Jersey.

St. Helier 4.

🏨 **Oaklands Lodge,** Trinity Hill, on A 8 ☏ 61735 – 📺 ⊟wc ☎ Ⓟ. ⊠ VISA
M *(closed Saturday lunch)* a la carte 4.00/6.00 🍾 1.00 – **10 rm** ⊟ 18.00/28.00 **s.**

Beaumont – ✉ Beaumont – ☎ 0534 Jersey.

St. Helier 3.

⋔ **Seawold,** St. Aubins Rd, ☏ 20807, ⊡ heated – 📺 ⊟wc 🚿wc Ⓟ
22 rm ⊟ (dinner included) 10.50/21.00.

Bonne Nuit Bay – ✉ St. John – ☎ 0534 Jersey.

St. Helier 6.

🏨 **Cheval Roc** ⋟, ☏ 62865, ⦅ Bonne Nuit Bay, ⊡ heated – ⊟wc 🚿wc Ⓟ. VISA
11 May-23 October – M 3.00/4.00 **s.** 🍾 1.10 – **45 rm** ⊟ 12.00/24.00 **s.** – P 16.00/20.00 **s.**

🏨 **Bonne Nuit,** ☏ 61644, ⦅, 🍴 – ⊟wc ☎ Ⓟ. ⊠ AE ⓪ VISA
April-mid October – M 6.00/8.00 🍾 2.00 – **34 rm** ⊟ 12.00/36.00 **s.** – P 17.00/19.75 **s.**

Bouley Bay – ✉ Trinity – ☎ 0534 Jersey. – St. Helier 5.

🏨 **Water's Edge** ⋟, ☏ 62777, ⦅ Bouley Bay, « Tasteful decor », ⊡ heated, 🍴 – 🛗 📺 Ⓟ.
⊠ AE ⓪ VISA
April-3 January – M 4.00/6.00 🍾 1.75 – **56 rm.**

Corbiere – ✉ St. Brelade – ☎ 0534 Jersey.

St. Helier 8.

🏨 Le Chalet ⋟, ☏ 41216, ⦅, ⊡ – ⊟wc 🚿wc ☎ Ⓟ – **31 rm.**

🍴 **Sea Crest** with rm, Petit Port ☏ 42687, ⦅, ⊡, 🍴 – 📺 ⊟wc ☎ Ⓟ. ⊠ VISA
M a la carte 4.80/7.80 🍾 2.50 – **7 rm** ⊟ 14.00/28.00.

L'Etacq – ✉ St. Ouens – ☎ 0534 Jersey.

St. Helier 7.5.

🍴 **Lobster Pot,** Mont du Vallet ☏ 82888 – Ⓟ. ⊠ AE ⓪ VISA
closed Sunday dinner – M a la carte 5.60/8.00 🍾 1.40.

Gorey – ✉ St. Martin – ☎ 0534 Jersey.

See : Mont Orgueil Castle* (⦅**, tableaux*) *AC*. – St. Helier 4.

🏨 **Old Court House,** Gorey Village ☏ 54444, Telex 4192032, ⊡ heated, 🍴 – 📺 ⊟wc
☎ Ⓟ.⊠ AE ⓪ VISA
closed 20 December-January – M 4.50/4.85 **s.** 🍾 1.45 – **27 rm** ⊟ 22.00/44.00 **s.** –
P 25.00 **s.**

🏨 **Trafalgar Bay,** Gorey Village ☏ 53216, 🍴 – ⊟wc Ⓟ
May-September – M (bar lunch) approx. 4.25 **s.** 🍾 1.50 – **40 rm** ⊟ 7.50/21.00 **s.**

at Gorey Pier – ✉ St. Martin – ☎ 0534 Jersey:

🏨 **Dolphin,** ☏ 53370, Telex 41385 – 🚿wc. ⊠ AE VISA
M 3.75/4.50 **s.** – **17 rm** ⊟ 13.50/27.50 **s.** – P 19.00/21.00 **s.**

XX **Moorings** with rm, ☏ 53633 – ⌷wc ☏. ⟋ AE
M a la carte 6.15/8.20 **s.** ⌕ 1.60 – **10 rm** ⌷ 10.90/14.90 **s.** – P 19.15 **s.**

X **Seascale** with rm, ☏ 54395 – ⌷wc ⌷wc
closed January and February – **M** *(closed Sunday dinner and Monday lunch)* a la
carte 4.95/8.05 ⌕ 1.80 – **10 rm** ⌷ 9.85/21.00.

La Haule – ⊠ St. Brelade – ☉ 0534 Jersey.

🏨 **La Place** ⅍, Route du Coin ☏ 44261, ⌇ heated – TV P. ⟋ AE ⑩ VISA
April-October – **M** 4.00/4.50 ⌕ 1.40 – **42 rm** ⌷ 18.50/37.00 – P 24.50/25.50.

🏠 **Au Caprice**, St. Aubins Bay ☏ 20334, ⋖
March-October – **14 rm** ⌷ (dinner included) 7.80/18.00 **s.**

Portelet Bay – ⊠ St. Brelade – ☉ 0534 Jersey.
St. Helier 5.

🏨 **Portelet**, ☏ 41204, ⋖, %, ⌇ heated – TV ⌷wc ☏ P. ⟋ AE ⑩ VISA
2 April-11 October – **M** 3.50/4.50 ⌕ 1.50 – **85 rm** ⌷ 13.50/19.00 **s.** – P 20.75/22.00 **s.**

La Pulente – ⊠ St. Brelade – ☉ 0534 Jersey.
St. Helier 7.

🏨 **Atlantic** ⅍, ☏ 44101, Telex 4192341, ⋖, %, ⌇ heated, ⊠ – ▥ TV P. ⌂. ⟋ AE ⑩ VISA
closed 15 January-1 March – **M** 4.00/7.50 **s.** ⌕ 2.80 – **42 rm** ⌷ 17.90/29.20 **s.** – P approx.
35.90 **s.**

Rozel Bay – ⊠ St. Martin – ☉ 0534 Jersey.
St. Helier 6.

🏨 **Le Couperon de Rozel**, ☏ 62190, ⌇ heated – ⌷wc P. ⟋ AE ⑩ VISA
May-October – **M** 4.00/5.00 ⌕ 1.30 – **24 rm** ⌷ 10.50/21.00 – P 20.00/25.00.

X Le Bistro Frère de Borsalino, Gorselands ☏ 61000, ⋖ – P.

St. Aubin – ⊠ St. Aubin – ☉ 0534 Jersey.
St. Helier 4.

X **Old Court House Inn** with rm, St. Aubin's Harbour, ☏ 41156 – TV ⌷wc ☏
M a la carte 3.80/10.70 **s.** ⌕ 1.50 – **9 rm** ⌷ 10.00/25.00 **s.**

St. Brelade's Bay – pop. 8,224 – ⊠ St. Brelade – ☉ 0534 Jersey.
See : Site*.
St. Helier 6.

🏨 L'Horizon, ☏ 43101, Telex 4192281, ⋖, ⟋ – ▥ TV P. ⌂. ⟋ AE ⑩ VISA
M 6.25/7.50 ⌕ 1.15 *(see also rest.* **Star Grill***)* – **90 rm.**

🏨 **Chateau Valeuse**, rue de la Valeuse ☏ 43476, ⌇ heated, ⊠ – P. VISA
closed January-20 February – **M** 4.00/6.00 ⌕ 2.80 – **26 rm** ⌷ 11.00/26.00 **s.** –
P 14.00/18.00 **s.**

XX **Star Grill** (at l'Horizon Hotel), ☏ 43101, ⋖ – P. ⟋ AE ⑩ VISA
M a la carte 5.50/8.70 ⌕ 1.15.

FORD Airport Rd ☏ 43222   SAAB Route de Noirmont ☏ 41911

St. Clement – pop. 5,329 – ⊠ St. Clement – ☉ 0534 Jersey.
St. Helier 2.

🏨 **Shakespeare**, Samares Coast Rd, ☏ 51915 – ⌷wc ⌷wc P. ⟋ AE VISA
closed mid December-mid February – **M** a la carte 4.80/7.50 ⌕ 1.00 – **23 rm** ⌷ 8.50/17.30.

St. Helier – pop. 28,135 – ECD : Thursday and Saturday – ⊠ St. Helier – ☉ 0534
Jersey.

See : Fort Regent ✳*** (Militia Museum) *AC* z – Elizabeth Castle ✳* *AC* z – Rocher
des Proscrits (au Havre des Pas) z.

Plan opposite

🏨 **De la Plage**, Havre des Pas ☏ 23474, Telex 4192356, ⋖ – ▥ TV P. ⟋ AE ⑩ VISA   **z s**
M a la carte 2.40/10.90 ⌕ 1.05 – **97 rm** ⌷ 19.50/42.50 **s.** – P 21.50/25.75 **s.**

🏨 **Beaufort**, Green St. ☏ 32471, Telex 4192160 – ▥ TV P. ⟋ AE ⑩ VISA   **z r**
M 3.50/6.00 **s.** – **50 rm** ⌷ 16.00/26.00 **s.** – P 19.00 **s.**

🏨 **Apollo**, 9 St. Saviour's Rd ☏ 25441, Telex 4192086 – ▥ TV ⌷wc ☏ P. ⟋ AE ⑩ VISA
M 3.00/4.50 **s.** ⌕ 1.30 – **53 rm** ⌷ 19.50/39.00 **s.**   **z e**

🏨 Royal Yacht, Weighbridge ☏ 20511, Telex 41385 – ▥ ⌷wc ⌷wc – **47 rm.**   **z c**

🏨 **Savoy**, Rouge Bouillon ☏ 30012, ⌇ heated – ⌷wc P. ⟋ VISA   **Y i**
April-October and Christmas – **M** 3.00/4.50 **s.** ⌕ 1.05 – **67 rm** ⌷ 10.25/23.50 **s.** –
P 14.75/16.25 **s.**

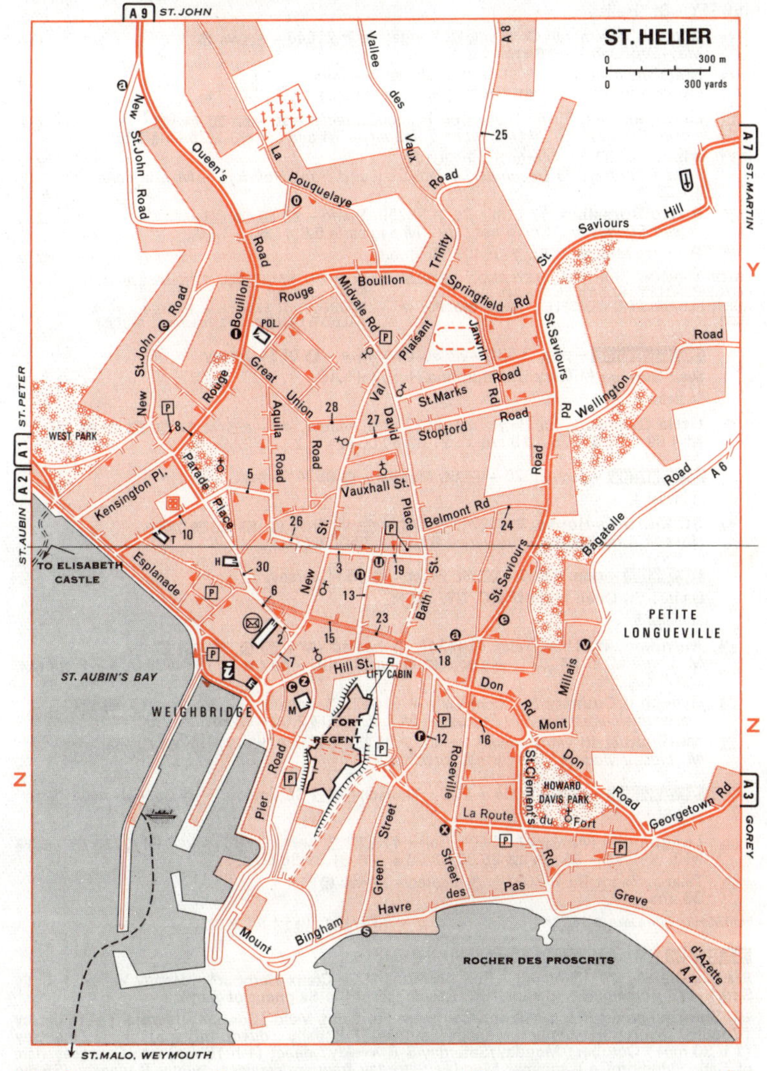

Mont Millais, Mont Millais ℡ 30281, ⌗ – ⌂wc Ⓟ **Z v**
M 2.00/3.00 ⌗ 1.20 – **50 rm** ⌂ 13.00/29.00 **s.** – P 11.00/15.50 **s.**

Mountview, 49 New St., John's Rd ℡ 30080 – ⌗ ⌂wc ⌗wc Ⓟ **Y e**
April-October – M 3.50/5.50 **s.** ⌗ 1.25 – **35 rm** ⌂ 15.50/25.00 **s.** – P approx. 18.50 **s.**

Uplands, St. John's Rd, ℡ 30151, ⌗ heated, ⌗ – ⌂wc Ⓟ **Y a**
April-October – M (bar lunch) 2.00/4.00 **s.** ⌗ 1.30 – **28 rm** ⌂ 9.00/18.00 **s.** – P approx. 12.50 **s.**

P.T.O. →

543

JERSEY - St. Helier

↑ Almorah, 1 Almorah Crescent, La Pougelaye ℡ 21648 – ⌂wc ℗ Y o
May-September – **16 rm**.

↑ **Merton**, 48 Roseville St. ℡ 20044, 🍴 – ⌂wc Z x
Easter-mid October – **46 rm** �! (dinner included) 10.00/22.00 **s.**

ⅩⅩ **La Capannina**, 65-67 Halkett Pl. ℡ 34602, Italian rest. – 🚫 AE ⓞ *VISA* Z n
closed Sunday and 24 December-5 January – **M** a la carte 3.75/6.65 🍷 1.50.

ⅩⅩ **Mauro's**, 37 La Motte St. ℡ 20147 Z a
closed Sunday, 23 December, 4 February and Bank Holidays – **M** a la carte 4.95/9.35
🍷 1.25.

Ⅹ **Bistro Borsalino**, 12 Cattle St. ℡ 35299, Bistro – 🚫 AE ⓞ *VISA* Z u
closed Sunday and Christmas Day – **M** a la carte 6.60/7.60 🍷 1.50.

Ⅹ Pedro's, Mulcaster St. ℡ 35405, Seafood. Z z

ASTON-MARTIN, BRITISH LEYLAND, ROLLS-
ROYCE-BENTLEY 87 Bath St. ℡ 31341
AUSTIN-MORRIS-MG-WOLSELEY Havre des Pas ℡
33233

CITROEN, VAUXHALL 27 New St. ℡ 24541
FORD ℡ 31361
PEUGEOT 17 Esplanade ℡ 33623
TALBOT, LANCIA 1/2 Victoria St. ℡ 37357

St. Lawrence – pop. 3,535 – ✉ St. Lawrence – ☏ 0534 Jersey.
See : German Military Underground Hospital* *AC.*
St. Helier 3.

🏛 **Little Grove** ⚘, rue de Haut ℡ 25321, 🏊 heated, 🍴 – ⌂wc ☎ ℗. 🚫 AE ⓞ *VISA*
M 4 00/5.00 🍷 1.25 – **18 rm** �! 21.00/50.00 **s.** – P 27.00/32.00 **s.**

St. Martins – pop. 2,626 – ✉ St. Martins – ☏ 0534 Jersey.
St. Helier 4.

↑ **St. Martin's House**, ℡ 53271, 🏊, 🍴 – ⌂wc 🚿wc ℗. 🚫 AE ⓞ *VISA*
closed Christmas and 1 January – **9 rm** �! 7.50/16.00.

St. Peter – pop. 4,000 – ✉ St. Peter – ☏ 0534 Jersey.
Envir. : St. Ouen Manor* *AC,* NW : 2 m.
St. Helier 5.

🏛 **Mermaid**, ℡ 41255, Telex 4192249, 🏊 heated, 🍴 – 📺 ℗. 🚗. 🚫 AE *VISA*
M 3.50/4.50 **s.** 🍷 1.25 (see also rest. **Mermaid Grill**) – **68 rm** �! 19.00/38.00 **s.** – P approx.
25.00 **s.**

🏛 **Greenhill Country** ⚘, Coin Varin ℡ 81042, 🏊 heated – ⌂wc 🚿wc ℗. AE *VISA*
closed mid December-mid February – **M** 3.00/5.00 🍷 2.00 – **18 rm** �! 22.00/44.00.

ⅩⅩ **Mermaid Grill** (at Mermaid Hotel), ℡ 41255, Telex 419249 – ℗. 🚫 AE *VISA*
M *(closed Monday)* a la carte 6.30/8.30 **s.**

St. Saviour – pop. 11,064 – ECD : Thursday – ✉ St. Saviour – ☏ 0534 Jersey.
St. Helier 1.

🏛 **Longueville Manor**, ℡ 25501, Telex 41306, 🏊 heated, 🍴, park – 📺 ℗. 🚫 AE ⓞ *VISA*
M 5.50/7.75 – **35 rm** �! 26.00/49.00 **s.** – P 31.50/36.50 **s.**

🏛 Talana, Bagot Rd ℡ 30317, 🏊 heated – ⌂wc ℗
36 rm.

PORSCHE Fire Oaks ℡ 26156 RENAULT Bagot Rd ℡ 32571

SARK 59 ④⑤ and 230 ⑩ – pop. 590 – ☏ 048183.
See : La Coupée*** (isthmus) – Port du Moulin** – Creux Harbour* – Happy Valley* – Little
Sark* – La Seigneurie* (manor 18C, Residence of the Seigneur of Sark).

🚢 Shipping connections with the Continent : to Saint-Malo (Condor : hydrofoil) – to Jersey
(Condor : hydrofoil) summer Monday/Saturday 1-3 daily : direct (45 mn) or via Guernsey
(1 h 30 mn) ; October : Monday/Saturday 3-6 weekly : direct (1 h 15 mn) – to Guernsey (Isle
of Sark Shipping Co.) summer Monday/Saturday frequent services ; winter 3 weekly (35 mn
to 1h) – to Guernsey (Condor : hydrofoil) summer Monday/Saturday 1-2 daily (35 mn to 1h).

🛈 Sark Publicity Officer ℡ 135.

🏛 **Petit Champ** ⚘, ℡ 46, ‹ countryside and sea, 🏊 heated, 🍴 – ⌂wc 🚿wc. 🚫 ⓞ *VISA*
Easter-September – **M** (booking essential) 6.60/7.50 **s.** 🍷 1.00 – **17 rm** �! 9.00/19.50 **s.**

Ⅹ **Aval du Creux** with rm, Harbour Hill ℡ 2036, 🍴 – 🚿wc
May-October – **M** a la carte 5.40/10.50 🍷 1.10 – **10 rm** �! (dinner included) 12.60/
29.20 – P 16.60/17.60.

Isle of Man

LICENSING HOURS-WHEN DRINKING ALCOHOLIC BEVERAGES IS PERMITTED IN PUBS AND BARS (The General Rule).

HEURES PERMISES POUR LA CONSOMMATION DES BOISSONS ALCOOLISÉES (Règle Générale).

ORARI CONSENTITI PER LA CONSUMAZIONE DI BEVANDE ALCOOLICHE (Regola Generale).

AUSSCHANKZEITEN FÜR ALKOHOLISCHE GETRÄNKE (Allgemeine Regelung).

		from / de / dalle / von	to / à / alle / bis	from / de / dalle / von	to / à / alle / bis		
WEEKDAYS / JOURS DE SEMAINE	SUMMER ÉTÉ	10.30			22.45	ESTATE SOMMER	GIORNI DELLA SETTIMANA / WOCHENTAGS
	WINTER - HIVER Monday to Thursday / Lundi au Jeudi	12.00			22.00	INVERNO-WINTER Da lunedì a giovedì / Montag - Donnerstag	
	Friday and Saturday / Vendredi et Samedi	12.00			22.45	Venerdì e sabato / Freitag und Samstag	
SUNDAYS / DIMANCHES	SUMMER ÉTÉ	12.00	13.30	20.00	22.00	ESTATE SOMMER	DOMENICHE / SONNTAGS
	WINTER HIVER	Closed - Fermés - Chiusi - Geschlossen				INVERNO WINTER	

RESIDENTS (hotels): no restrictions in licensed hotels even on Sundays.

SUMMER: from Maundy Thursday (the Thursday before Good Friday) to 30 September.

RÉSIDENTS (hôtels) : aucune restriction dans les lieux autorisés recevant le résident, même les dimanches.

ÉTÉ: du Jeudi Saint au 30 septembre.

RESIDENTI (alberghi): nessuna restrizione nei locali autorizzati che ospitano il residente, anche la domenica.

ESTATE: dal giovedi precedente il Venerdi Santo al 30 settembre.

FÜR HOTELGÄSTE keine Beschränkung (auch nicht an Sonntagen) in den lizensierten Hotels selbst.

SOMMER: Von Gründonnerstag bis 30. September.

ISLE OF MAN

Towns

BALLASALLA – ☎ 062 482 Castletown. – Douglas 8.5.

XXX **Coach House,** Silverburn Bridge ℡ 2343 – **P**. AE VISA
closed Sunday, last 2 weeks October and first week November – **M** a la carte 5.70/
10.20 ⌀ 1.90.

MERCEDES-BENZ, VW, AUDI-NSU Douglas Rd ℡ 2884

BALLAUGH – pop. 524 – ✉ Kirkmichael – ☎ 062 489 Sulby.
Envir. : Curragh Wildlife Park* *AC*. NE: 1 ½ m.
Douglas 18.

🏛 **Ravensdale Castle** 🐾, Ballaugh Glen ℡ 7330, ⛴, 🌲, park – 🚻wc **P**. ⑩
M (bar lunch) a la carte 4.95/7.15 ⌀ 1.50 – **11 rm** ⌑ 10.00/26.00.

FIAT, POLSKI, SAAB, POLONEZ Main Rd ℡ 7229

CASTLETOWN 986 ㉒ – pop. 2,820 – ECD: Thursday – ☎ 062 482.
See : Rushen Castle** (13C) *AC :* keep ✳*. – Port Erin (site*) W: 4 ½ m.
🏌 Fort Island ℡ 2201, E : 2 m.
🛈 Town Hall, ℡ 3518.
Douglas 10.

🏨 **Castletown Golf Links** 🐾, Fort Island E: 2 m. ℡ 2201, Telex 627636, ≼ sea and golf
links, ✗, ⛴ heated, 🏌, 🌲 – **P**
April-mid October – **M** a la carte 4.50/5.50 **t.** ⌀ 1.10 – **80 rm** ⌑ 16.00/30.00 **t.** – P 21.00/
22.00 **t.**

See : Manx Museum** – The Promenades* – A 18 Road** from Douglas to Ramsey.

Envir. : Snaefell ❈*** (by electric railway from Laxey) *AC*, NE : 7 m. – Laxey (waterwheel* : Lady Isabella) NE : 6 m. – St. John's (Tynwald Hill) NW : 8 m. – Peel : Castle* (ruins 13C-16C) AC, NW : 11 ½ m.

ᵍₒₗf Pulrose Park ☏ 5952, 1 m. from Douglas Pier – ᵍₒₗf Howstrake at Onchan, N : 1 m.

✈ Ronaldsway Airport, ☏ 0624 82 (Castletown) 3311, SW : 7 m. – **Terminal :** Lord St., Douglas.

⛴ by Isle of Man Steam Packet Co. to Ardrossan : 9 May-14 September 1-5 weekly (6 h) – to Belfast : 25 May-16 September 1-3 weekly (4 h 30 mn) – to Dublin : 24 May/20 September 1-3 weekly (4 h 30 mn) – to Fleetwood : 27 May-19 September 2-5 weekly (3 h 15 mn) – to Heysham (Manx Line) summer : 1-3 daily ; winter : 9 weekly (3 h) – to Liverpool : 1-6 daily (4 h 15 mn).

⛴ to Llandudno (Isle of Man Steam Packet Co.) summer only 2-4 weekly (3 h).

🛈 13 Victoria St. ☏ 4323 – 79 Main Rd at Onchan ☏ 22311/5564.

🏨 **Palace,** Central Promenade ☏ 4521, Telex 627742, ≤, ⌇ heated – ▮ 📺 ⊟wc ☏ **P.** ⚄
AE ⓪ VISA
M 4.00/5.00 t. ⌾ 2.30 – **139 rm** ⊏⊐ 30.75/40.00 t.

AUSTIN-MORRIS Victoria Rd ☏ 3141.	FORD Douglas ☏ 3211
AUSTIN-DAIMLER-JAGUAR-MG-ROVER-TRIUMPH-WOLSELEY, ROLLS ROYCE Westmoreland Rd ☏ 23481	MAZDA, VOLVO Alexander Drive ☏ 21830
	OPEL-VAUXHALL The Milestone, Peel Rd ☏ 3791
DATSUN Hill St. ☏ 4428	RENAULT Peel Rd ☏ 3342

Republic of Ireland

LICENSING HOURS - WHEN DRINKING ALCOHOLIC BEVERAGES IS PERMITTED IN PUBS AND BARS AND OTHER LICENSED PREMISES (The General Rule).

HEURES PERMISES POUR LA CONSOMMATION DES BOISSONS ALCOOLISÉES (Règle Générale).

ORARI CONSENTITI PER LA CONSUMAZIONE DI BEVANDE ALCOOLICHE (Regola Generale).

AUSSCHANKZEITEN FÜR ALKOHOLISCHE GETRÄNKE (Allgemeine Regelung).

	from / de / dalle / von	to / à / alle / bis	from / de / dalle / von	to / à / alle / bis	
Weekdays / Jours de semaine — APRIL to OCTOBER / AVRIL à OCTOBRE	10.30			23.30	da APRILE a OTTOBRE / APRIL - OKTOBER — Giorni della settimana
NOVEMBER to MARCH / NOVEMBRE à MARS	10.30			23.00	da NOVEMBRE a MARZO / NOVEMBER - MÄRZ — Wochentags
Sundays and St. Patrick's Day (17 March) / Dimanches et Jour de la St-Patrick (17 mars)	12.30	14.00	16.00	22.00	Domeniche e giorno di St. Patrick (17 Marzo) / Sonntags und am St. Patricks Tag (17. März)
Good Friday and Christmas Day / Vendredi Saint et Jour de Noël	Closed - Fermés - Chiusi - Geschlossen				Venerdì Santo e Natale / Karfreitag und Weihnachten

DUBLIN AND CORK : Pubs close on weekdays from 14.30 - 15.30 hours.

RESIDENTS : there are no time restrictions in licensed hotels apart from Good Friday when alcoholic beverages may only be served with meals.

RESTAURANTS: not attached to a hotel or other establishment with a full licence may only sell wine (i.e. no spirits or beer).

DUBLIN AND CORK : Pubs fermés entre 14 h 30 et 15 h 30 les jours de semaine.

RESIDENTS : aucune restriction, sauf le Vendredi Saint où les boissons alcoolisées ne sont servies qu'à l'occasion des repas.

RESTAURANTS : si non installés dans un hôtel ou autre établissement ayant une licence complète, ne peuvent vendre que du vin, à l'exclusion de toute autre boisson alcoolisée.

DUBLIN E CORK : Pubs chiusi dalle 14.30 alle 15.30 durante la settimana.

RESIDENTI : nessuna restrizione, escluso il Venerdì Santo in cui le bevande alcooliche sono servite soltanto in occasione dei pasti.

RISTORANTI : se non si trovano in un albergo o in un altro esercizio munito di licenza completa, possono vendere soltanto del vino, con esclusione di tutte le altre bevande alcooliche.

DUBLIN UND CORK : Pubs sind wochentags von 14.30 bis 15.30 Uhr geschlossen.

FÜR HOTELGÄSTE : keine Beschränkung, außer für Karfreitag, an dem alkoholische Getränke nur zu den Mahlzeiten serviert werden.

IN RESTAURANTS dürfen, außer Wein, keine alkoholischen Getränke ausgegeben werden. Ausnahmen sind hier Hotelrestaurants oder Restaurants anderer lizensierter Betriebe.

Mali
Rosapenna
DUNFANAGHY
Gortahork
Rathmullan
Faha
Dunglow
Letterkenny
Raphoe
Ballybofey
Lifford
Killybegs
Donegal
N 15
Rossnowlagh
Bundoran
SLIGO
N 59
N 16
Ballina
Riverstown
ACHILL ISLAND
Pontoon
Newport
Boyle
Carrick-on-Shannon
Castlebar
Lough Gowna
Westport
Castlerea
Virginia
Renvyle
Strokestown
Leenane
Longford
Moyard
Letterfrack
Cong
N 4
Clifden
Clonbur
Ballyconneely
Cashel Bay
Oughterard
Mullingar
T 40
Moycullen
Athlone
Carraroe
Moate
Spiddal
GALWAY
Bearna
Ballinasloe
Banagher
Monasterevi
Ballyvaughan
Emo
Liscannor
N 18
Scarriff
Roscrea
Ennis
Quin
Abbeyleix
N 7
Bunratty
Killaloe
Shannon Airport
Limerick
Thurles
Ballybunion
Adare
Kilkenny
N 21
Listowel
Cashel
Templeglantine
Glen of Aherlow
Tipperary
Castlegregory
Charleville
(Rath Luirc)
Cahir
Clonmel
New Ross
Ballyferriter
N 24
Dingle
Inch
Kanturk
Fermoy
WATERFORD
Caragh Lake
Killarney
Lismore
Tramore
Valentia
Island
Glenbeigh
Glencar
Mallow
Ballyduff
Dunmore East
Cahersiveen
N 22
Waterville
Sneem
KENMARE
Macroom
Blarney
Youghal
N 25
Ballinskelligs
Parknasilla
Ardmore
Caherdaniel
Garryvoe Strand
Castletownbere
Shanagarry

Redcastle
M 22
M 1
onaghan
Cootehill
Carrickmacross
Kingscourt
DUNDALK
A 1
N 1
Slane
Drogheda
Bettystown
Navan
Ashbourne
Straffan
Newbridge
(Droichead Nua)
Curragh
Annamoe M
GLENDALOUGH
Rathnew
Castledermot
Wicklow
Rathdrum
Carlow
Avoca
Woodenbridge
N 11
Arklow
Gorey
Courtown
Enniscorthy
N 25
Wexford
Rosslare
Rosslare Harbour
Tomhaggard

Place with at least :
one hotel or restaurant
Longford
one pleasant hotel
with rm.
one quiet, secluded hotel
one restaurant with
M
See this town for establishments
located in its vicinity
SLIGO

Localité offrant au moins :
une ressource hôtelière
Longford
un hôtel agréable
with rm.
un hôtel très tranquille, isolé
une bonne table à
M
Localité groupant dans le texte
les ressources de ses environs
SLIGO

La località possiede come minimo :
una risorsa alberghiera
Longford
un albergo ameno
with rm.
un albergo molto tranquillo, isolato
un'ottima tavola con
M
La località raggruppa nel suo testo
le risorse dei dintorni
SLIGO

Ort mit mindestens :
einem Hotel oder Restaurant
Longford
einem angenehmen Hotel
with rm.
einem sehr ruhigen und abgelegenen Hotel
einem Restaurant mit
M
Ort mit Angaben über Hotels und Restaurants
in seiner Umgebung
SLIGO

Malahide
N 1
N 4
Howth
DUBLIN
N 7
Dun Laoghaire
Kill
Dalkey
Killiney M
Blessington
Bray
N 11
Greystones
Delgany

Gougane Barra
N 71
N 25
Glengarriff
CORK
Cobh
Ballylickey
BANDON
Crosshaven
Ballycotton
Bantry
Kinsale
N 71
Ballinascarty
Ballydehob
Courtmacsherry
Schull
Skibbereen
Baltimore

REPUBLIC OF IRELAND

Towns

ABBEYLEIX Laois 986 ㉖ – pop. 1,919 – ECD : Wednesday – ☉ 0502 – ⓠ.
Envir. : Dunamase Rock (castle** 13C-16C ruins), site**, ☀** NE : 13½ m.
Dublin 64 – Kilkenny 21 – Limerick 65 – Tullamore 30.

  🏠 Hibernian House, ☎ 31252 – Ⓟ
      10 rm.

FORD Market Sq. ☎ 31125

ACHILL ISLAND Mayo 986 ㉑ – pop 1,163.
See : Achill Sound* – The Atlantic Drive*** SW : Coast Rd from Cloghmore to Dooega – Kee
(the strand*) – Lough Keel*.
ⓠ Achill Sound, Westport, in Keel.
🚩 ☎ Achill Sound 51 (June-August).

      at Achill Sound – ✉ ☉ Achill Sound :
  🏠 **Achill Sound,** ☎ 6 – ⌁wc Ⓟ
    April-September – **M** (bar lunch) approx. 4.75 **t.** ⓑ 2.00 – **36 rm** ⌷ 8.00/14.00 **t.**

ADARE Limerick 986 ㉕ – pop. 2,604 – ☉ 061.
See : ⟨* from the bridge of the River Maigue.
ⓠ ☎ 94204.
🚩 ☎ 94255 (July-August).
Dublin 131 – Killarney 59 – Limerick 10.

  🏰 Dunraven Arms, Main St., ☎ 94209, « Gardens » – ⌁wc Ⓟ
    22 rm.

ANNAMOE Wicklow – ✉ ☉ 0404 Wicklow.
Envir. : Glendalough (ancient monastic city** : site***, St. Kervin's Church*) and Upper
Lake* in Glendalough Valley*** SW : 5 m. – Lough Tay** NW : 8 m.
Dublin 29 – Wexford 72.

  XX **Armstrong's Barn,** on T 61 ☎ 5194, 🍴 – Ⓟ. Ⓐ𝖤 **VISA**
    18 March-22 December – **M** *(closed Sunday and Monday)* (dinner only) 12.00 **t.**
    ⓑ 2.00.

ARAN ISLANDS ** Galway 986 ⑰.
By boat or aeroplane from Galway City or by boat from Kilkieran, or Fisherstreet (Clare).
See : Inishmore Island (Kilronan harbour*).
🚩 ☎ Kilronan 29 (July - August).

      Hotels see : Galway.

ARDMORE Waterford 986 ㉙ – pop. 1,076 – ☉ 024.
See : Site*, round tower* 10C, cathedral ruins* 12C, ⟨*.
Dublin 138 – Cork 33 – Waterford 44.

  🏠 Cliff House, ☎ 4106, ⟨, 🍴 – Ⓟ
    21 rm.

ARKLOW Wicklow 986 ㉖ – pop. 6,948 – ECD : Wednesday – ☉ 0402.
🚩 ☎ 2492.
🚩 ☎ 2484 (June-August).
Dublin 47 – Kilkenny 68 – Waterford 66 – Wexford 49.

  🏰 **Arklow Bay,** Ferrybank, Brittas Bay Rd N : ½ m. off L 29 ☎ 2289, Telex 4858, 🍴 –
    ⌁wc Ⓟ. Ⓐ𝖤 ⓪
    M 4.00/7.00 **t.** – **28 rm** ⌷ 11.25/24.00 **t.** – P 23.75 **t.**

FIAT Ferrybank ☎ 2481   RENAULT, VAUXHALL Wexford Rd ☎ 2013
FORD Gorey Rd ☎ 2076

ASHBOURNE Meath – ☺ 01 Dublin.

Dublin 13 – Drogheda 24 – **Dundalk 42.**

× Ashbourne House, with rm, on T 2 ☏ 350167, 🚗 – Ⓟ
10 rm.

ATHLONE Westmeath 🅆 ㉑ – pop. 9,825 – ECD : Thursday – ☺ 0902.
Envir. : Clonmacnoise (mediaeval ruins) SW : 8 m. – N : Lough Ree*.**

🛈 17 Church St. ☏ 2866.

Dublin 75 – **Galway 57 – Limerick 75 – Roscommon 20 – Tullamore 24.**

🏨 Royal Hoey, Mardyke St. ☏ 2924, 🚗 – ▐ 🛏wc 🛁wc ☎ Ⓟ. 🛴
47 rm.

🏨 Prince of Wales, Church St. ☏ 2626 – 🛏wc ☎ Ⓟ. 🛴
50 rm.

DATSUN Dublin Rd ☏ 4009
FORD Magazine Rd ☏ 2007
OPEL Dublin Rd ☏ 4095

PEUGEOT Industrial Est. ☏ 2619
VW, AUDI-NSU, MERCEDES-BENZ, TOYOTA
Lakeview ☏ 2734

AVOCA Wicklow 🅆 ㉖ – pop. 2,266 – ☺ 0402.
See : Vale of Avoca* from Arklow to Rathdrum on T 7.

🏌 ☏ 5202.

Dublin 47 – **Waterford 72 – Wexford 55.**

🏨 Vale View, N : 1 ¾ m. on T 7 ☏ 5178, ⩠ – 📺 🛏wc ☎ Ⓟ
10 rm.

BALLINA Mayo 🅆 ㉑ – pop. 4,616 – ECD : Thursday – ☺ 096.
**Envir. : Rosserk Abbey* (Franciscan Friary 15 C) N : 4 m. – Ballycastle (cliffs* NW : 3 m.
near L 133) NW : 15 m. – Downpatrick Head* NW : 18 m.**

🏌 ☏ 21050, E : 1 m.

🛈 ☏ 21544 (June - August).

Dublin 147 – **Galway 73 – Roscommon 63 – Sligo 37.**

🏨 **Downhill** 🦢, Sligo Rd ☏ 21033, 🏊, 🚗 – 🛏wc 🛁wc ☎ Ⓟ. 🔺 AE ⓪ VISA
M 4.00/8.00 **st.** ⧍ 2.00 – **60 rm** 🍽 18.00/30.00 **st.**

🏚 **Mount Falcon Castle** 🦢, S : 4 m. on Foxford-Ballina Rd ☏ 21172, « Country house
atmosphere », ✕✕, 🦢, park – 🛏wc Ⓟ
closed 1 week at Christmas – **M** (residents only) 4.00/6.25 **t.** ⧍ 2.00 – **11 rm** 🍽 11.50/
23.00 **t.** – P 20.50 **t.**

🏚 **Bartra House,** Pearse St. ☏ 22570 – 🛏wc. 🔺 ⓪ VISA
closed 24 to 26 December – **M** 3.75/7.50 **t.** ⧍ 1.40 – **34 rm** 🍽 9.50/20.50 **t.** –
P 20.00/22.00 **st.**

DATSUN Bachelor Walk ☏ 53
FIAT Ballina ☏ 21288
FORD Pearse St. ☏ 21066
OPEL Killala Rd ☏ 63

PEUGEOT, VAUXHALL Sligo Rd ☏ 430
RENAULT Lord Edward St. ☏ 21037
VW, AUDI-NSU Pearse St. ☏ 91

BALLINASCARTY Cork – ✉ Clonakilty – ☺ 023 Bandon.
Dublin 188 – **Cork 27.**

🏨 **Ardnavaha House** 🦢, SE : 2 m. by L 63 ☏ 49135, ⩠, ✕✕, 🏊 heated, 🦢, 🚗, park –
🛏wc ☎ Ⓟ
May-September – **M** a la carte 4.15/11.00 **t.** ⧍ 2.75 – **24 rm** 🍽 15.00/24.00 **t.**

BALLINASLOE Galway 🅆 ㉑ – pop. 5,969 – ECD : Thursday – ☺ 0905.

🏌 ☏ 2126.

🛈 ☏ 2332 (May-September).

Dublin 91 – **Galway 41 – Limerick 66 – Roscommon 36 – Tullamore 34.**

🏨 Hayden's, Dunlo St. ☏ 2347, Telex 33147, 🚗 – ▐ 🛏wc ☎ Ⓟ
54 rm.

FORD ☏ 2204
PEUGEOT, VW, AUDI-NSU Dunlo St. ☏ 2290

RENAULT Brackernagh ☏ 2420

BALLINSKELLIGS Kerry 🅆 ㉙ – pop. 355.
See : Augustinian Monastery ⩠*.
Dublin 238 – **Killarney 48.**

🏨 Waterville Beach 🦢, NE : 2 ¾ m. on Waterville Rd ☏ 23, ⩠ coast and mountains, ✕✕, 🦢,
park – 🛏wc ☎ Ⓟ. 🛴
45 rm.

Prices	For full details of the prices quoted in the guide, consult pp. 16 and 17.

BALLYBOFEY Donegal – pop. 2,214 – ECD : Wednesday – ✉ Lifford.

ⁱ₈ ☏ 93.

Dublin 148 – Londonderry 30 – Sligo 58.

🏨 **Jackson's,** Glenfinn St. ☏ 21 – ⊟wc 🅿
M 3.50/5.50 **st.** ⌀ 1.15 – **42 rm** ⊠ 8.80/16.80 **st.**

RENAULT ☏ 122

BALLYBUNION Kerry 🄨🄫🄬 ㉕ – ⊙ 068.

ⁱ₈ ☏ 20.

🅱 ☏ 27202 (June-September).

Dublin 174 – Killarney 40 – Limerick 53.

🔱 **Marine,** Sandhill Rd ☏ 27139 – 🅿
closed 1 to 15 November – **M** a la carte 6.00/10.00 **t.** ⌀ 2.20 – ⊠ 2.95 – **23 rm** 7.50/15.00 **t.**

⟑ **Eagle Lodge,** ☏ 27224 – ⊞wc 🅿
Easter-October – **11 rm** ⊠ 5.00/12.00 **t.**

BALLYCONNEELY Galway.

Dublin 187 – Galway 55.

✗ **Fishery,** ☏ 31, Seafood – 🅿. ⚎
June-September – **M** a la carte 4.35/13.50 **t.** ⌀ 2.00.

BALLYCOTTON Cork 🄨🄫🄬 ㉙ – ⊙ 021 Cork.

Dublin 165 – Cork 27 – Youghal 17.

🏛 **Bay View,** ☏ 62746, ⟨, 🚗 – ⊟wc 🅿
M (bar lunch Monday to Saturday) 4.00/7.00 **st.** ⌀ 1.30 – ⊠ 2.25 – **23 rm** 4.50/11.00 **st.**

BALLYDEHOB Cork.

Dublin 220 – Cork 59 – Killarney 58.

🏛 **Audley House** ⟍, Foilnanuck S : 2 ¾ m. ☏ 51, ⟨ Roaring water bay and Islands, 🚗 –
⊟wc 🅿
M 5.50/8.50 **st.** ⌀ 1.75 – **10 rm** ⊠ 11.00/18.00 **st.**

✗ **Basil Bush,** Main St. ☏ 10
closed Sunday and December-January – **M** a la carte 5.15/9.50 **t.** ⌀ 1.75.

BALLYDUFF Waterford.

Dublin 150 – Cork 30 – Waterford 51.

🏛 **Blackwater Lodge** ⟍, SW : 1 ½ m. ☏ 35, ⟨, ⟍ – ⊟wc 🅿
February-September – **M** (bar lunch) 6.60 **st.** ⌀ 2.00 – **10 rm** ⊠ 9.00/16.00 **t.** –
P 14.00 **t.**

BALLYFERRITER Kerry.

Envir. : Kilmalkedar (church* 12C) NE : 4 ½ m. – Gallarus Oratory* 8C, NE : 2 m.

Dublin 224 – Killarney 59 – Limerick 103.

🏛 **Dun an Oir** ⟍, NW : 2 m. ☏ 33, Telex 8273, ⟨, ✗, ⟍ heated, ⟦₉ – ⊟wc ⊞wc 🅿
May-October – **M** 5.00/7.50 **t.** ⌀ 1.75 – **22 rm** ⊠ 13.20/19.20 **t.**

BALLYLICKEY Cork – pop. 350 – ✉ ⊙ Bantry.

Dublin 216 – Cork 55 – Killarney 45.

🏨 **Ballylickey House** ⟍, ☏ 71, ⟨, ⟍ heated, ⟍, 🚗, park – ⊟wc ⊛ 🅿. ⚎ ⓪
Easter-September – **M** (buffet lunch) 6.50/9.00 **st.** ⌀ 2.50 – **25 rm** 15.00/30.00 **st.**

🏛 Seaview ⟍, ☏ 73, ⟨, 🚗 – ⊟wc ⊞wc 🅿
12 rm.

🔱 Green Acre Lodge, ☏ 182, 🚗 – 🅿
10 rm.

BALLYVAUGHAN Clare – pop. 200 – ✉ Galway (Galway).

Envir. : SW : Coast road L 54 from Ailladie to Fanore : Burren District (Burren limestone terraces**) – Corcomroe Abbey* (or Abbey of St. Maria de Petra Fertilis : 12C Cistercian ruins) NE : 6 m.

Dublin 149 – Ennis 34 – Galway 29.

🏛 **Gregans Castle** ⟍, SW : 3 ¼ m. on T 69 ☏ 5, Telex 8110, ⟨ – ⊟wc 🅿. ⚎ **VISA**
Mid March-October – **M** (bar lunch) 8.50 **t.** ⌀ 2.50 – **16 rm** ⊠ 13.00/26.00 **t.**

BALTIMORE Cork – pop. 200 – ☻ 028.
Dublin 221 – Cork 60 – Killarney 75.

🏠 **Baltimore House** ⟡, ☏ 27, ⩻ Baltimore Bay and islands, 🛏 – ⌷wc Ⓟ
   M (bar lunch) 6.50 **st.** 🍷 2.50 – **19 rm** ⌷ 8.00/15.00 **st.**

🏠 **Corner House,** The Square, ☏ 43 – 🅰 AE *VISA*
   9 rm ⌷ 6.00/11.00.

BANAGHER Offaly – pop. 1,052.
See : ⩻* from the bridge of Shannon. **Envir.:** Clonfert (St. Brendan's Cathedral : west door*
12C, east windows* 13C) NW : 4 ½ m. – Birr : Castle Demesne (arboretum*, gardens*, teles-
cope of Lord Rosse) *AC*, SE : 8 m.
Dublin 83 – Galway 54 – Limerick 56 – Tullamore 24.

🏠 Brosna, Main St. ☏ 50, 🛏 – ⌷wc Ⓟ
   14 rm.

BANDON Cork 🅖🅑🅜 ㉙ – pop. 2,257 – ECD : Thursday – ☻ 023.
🆑 ☏ 41111.
Dublin 180 – Cork 19 – Killarney 51.

🏠 Munster Arms, Oliver Plunkett St., ☏ 41562 – TV ⌷wc 🛁wc ☎ Ⓟ. 🏖
   37 rm.

   at Innishannon NE : 4 ½ m. on T 65 – ✉ Innishannon – ☻ 021 Cork :

🏠 Innishannon ⟡. S : ¾ m. on L 41 ☏ 75121, ⬟, 🛏 – ⌷wc Ⓟ
   10 rm.

DATSUN Convent Rd, Clonakilty ☏ 43374   OPEL Irishtown ☏ 41264
FIAT, LANCIA ☏ 41514   RENAULT ☏ 41617
FORD 72 Main St. ☏ 41522   TALBOT ☏ 41264

P 20.00/27.50	**Full Board prices** given are intended as a rough guide. If you are planning a stay, make enquiries at the hotel.

BANTRY Cork 🅖🅑🅜 ㉙ – pop. 2,579 – ECD : Wednesday.
See : Bantry Bay** – Bantry House (interior**, ⩻*) *AC*. **Envir. :** Glengarriff (site***) NW :
8 m. – NE : Shehy Mountains**.
🆘 ☏ 229 (June-September).
Dublin 218 – Cork 57 – Killarney 48.

🏨 **Westlodge,** SW : 1 ½ m. on T 65 ☏ 360, Telex 8477, ✗, 🅰 – 🛗 ⌷wc ☎ Ⓟ. 🅰 AE Ⓞ
   VISA
   M 4.25/8.50 **t.** 🍷 2.00 – **60 rm** ⌷ 15.50/18.00 **t.** – P 25.00 **t.**

🏠 **Eve's Pine Lodge,** N : 1 m. on T 65 ☏ 249, ⩻ – ⌷wc Ⓟ. 🅰 AE Ⓞ *VISA*
   M (bar lunch) 6.50 **s.** 🍷 1.50 – **10 rm** ⌷ 11.80/16.00 **s.**

🏠 Bantry Bay, Wolfe Tone Sq., ☏ 62
   17 rm.

RENAULT Barrack St. ☏ 92   TALBOT The Square ☏ 23

BEARNA Galway.
Dublin 135 – Galway 3.

✗✗ Ty Ar Mor, Sea Point ☏ 65031, ⩻ Bearna harbour and Galway Bay, Seafood – Ⓟ.

BETTYSTOWN Meath – ✉ ☻ 041 Drogheda.
🆘 ☏ 7134.
Dublin 28 – Drogheda 6.

🏠 Village, NW : ¾ m. on L125 ☏ 27136, 🛏 – ⌷wc ☎ Ⓟ
   10 rm.

✗✗ **Coastguard Inn,** ☏ 27115, ⩻ – Ⓟ. AE *VISA*
   closed Sunday, Monday and Christmas – **M** (dinner only) a la carte 7.80/10.75 **t.** 🍷 1.40.

BLACKROCK Cork – see Cork.

BLARNEY Cork 🅖🅑🅜 ㉙ – pop. 1,128 – ✉ ☻ 021.
See : Castle* 15C (top ⁕*, 112 steps) *AC*.
Dublin 167 – Cork 6.

🏨 Blarney, ☏ 85281, 🛏 – ⌷wc 🛁wc ☎ ♿ Ⓟ
   76 rm.

BLESSINGTON Wicklow – pop. 637 – ✆ 045 Naas.
Envir.: Lackan ≼* SE : 4 ½ m. – SE : Poulaphuca Lake* (reservoir).
Dublin 20.

    Downshire House, Main St. ☎ 65199, ⛟ – ⌂wc ☎ **P**. ⚒
    closed mid December-mid January – **M** 5.00/8.00 **t.** ⬦ 1.75 – ⌷ 3.50 – **25 rm** 12.00/
    18.00 **t.** – P 25.50/28.50 **t.**

BOYLE Roscommon ⑼⑻⑹ ㉑ – pop. 1,727.
See : Cistercian Abbey* 12C.
Envir. : NE : Lough Key*.

⛳ Knockadoo, Roscommon Rd.

🛈 ☎ 145 (May-September).

Dublin 107 – Ballina 40 – Galway 74 – Roscommon 26 – Sligo 24.

    Forest Park, Carrick Rd E : ½ m. on T 3 ☎ 229, ⛟ – ⌂wc ☎ **P**. AE
    closed Good Friday and Christmas – **M** 3.50/7.00 **st.** – **13 rm** ⌷ 11.50/19.50 **st.**

FORD Elphin St. ☎ 22

BRAY Wicklow ⑼⑻⑹ ㉖ – pop. 15,550 – ECD : Wednesday – ✆ 01 Dublin.
⛳ Woodbrook ☎ 862073, N : 1 m. – ⛳ ☎ 862484.

🛈 ☎ 867128 (June-August).

Dublin 13 – Wicklow 20.

    Esplanade, Strand Rd ☎ 862056 – **P**
    18 rm.

    XX **Lacy's** with rm, Strand Rd, Sea Front, ☎ 862127 – ◪ ⓪ *VISA*
    closed 25 to 27 December – **M** *(closed Sunday dinner)* a la carte 8.20/12.75 **t.** ⬦ 2.10 –
    10 rm ⌷ 9.50/14.50 **t.**

BUNCRANA Donegal ⑼⑻⑹ ⑭ – pop. 5,458.
Envir. : Lough Naminn* NE : 7 m. – Carndonagh (Donagh Cross*) NE : 15 m.
⛳ Ballyliffin ☎ Clonmany 19, N : 12 m. – ⛳ ☎ 1.

🛈 ☎ 158 (June-August).

Dublin 161 – Donegal 64 – **Londonderry 16.**

BUNDORAN Donegal ⑼⑻⑹ ⑰ – pop. 1,337 – ECD : Thursday – ✆ 072.
Envir. : S : Lough Gill*** (Innisfree*), Park's Castle (site**).
⛳ Great Northern Hotel, ☎ 41302.

🛈 ☎ 41350 (May-September).

Dublin 145 – Sligo 21.

    Maghery House, Brighton Ter. ☎ 41234 – ⋔wc **P** – **32 rm.**

VW, AUDI-NSU ☎ 41300

BUNRATTY Clare ⑼⑻⑹ ㉕ – ✉ ✆ 061 Limerick.
See : Castle (great hall*) *AC* – Folk Park* *AC*.
Dublin 129 – Ennis 15 – Limerick 8.

    Fitzpatrick's Shannon Shamrock Inn, ☎ 61177, Telex 6214, ◪, ⛟ – ⌂wc ☎ **P**
    81 rm.

CAHERDANIEL Kerry – pop. 357.
Envir. : Sheehan's Point ≼*** W : 5 m. – Staigue Fort* (prehistoric stone fort : site*, ≼*)
AC, NE : 5 m.
Dublin 238 – Killarney 48.

    Derrynane ⌂, SE : 1 m. on T 66 ☎ 36, ≼ Kenmare river Bay, ✗, ⌷ heated, ⚓ – ⌂wc
    ⋔wc ☎ **P**. ◪ AE ⓪
    Easter-October – **M** 4.15/7.50 **t.** ⬦ 2.50 – **62 rm** ⌷ 14.90/22.60 **t.**

CAHERSIVEEN (CAHIRCIVEEN) Kerry ⑼⑻⑹ ㉙ – pop. 1,547 – ECD : Thursday.
Envir. : Remains of Carhan House (birthplace of Daniel O'Connell) NE : 1 m.
🛈 ☎ 113 (June-September).

Dublin 228 – Killarney 38 – Limerick 105.

    Evan's, O'Connell St. ☎ 10 – ⌂wc ⇦. ◪ *VISA*
    March-September – **M** a la carte 6.40/8.40 **t.** – **12 rm** ⌷ 5.50/12.00 **t.**

RENAULT ☎ 91

CAHIR Tipperary 986 ㉙ – pop. 1,747 – ECD : Thursday.

See : Castle* (12C-15C) the most extensive mediaeval castle in Ireland.

▗ Cahir Park, ℡ 474, S : 1 m.

▤ ℡ 453 (June-August).

Dublin 112 – Cork 49 – Kilkenny 41 – Limerick 38 – Waterford 39.

    Kilcoran Lodge, SW : 5 m. on T 6 ℡ 261, ≤, ⚓, ⚒, park – ⊜wc **P**. ⚙
23 rm.

    Earl of Glengall, The Square ℡ 205 – ▦ AE ⓞ VISA
closed Sunday – **M** (buffet lunch) a la carte 5.25/9.50 **t.** ▯ 1.30.

BRITISH LEYLAND ℡ 483   SAAB ℡ 432

CARAGH LAKE Kerry 986 ㉙.

See : Lough Caragh*.

Dublin 212 – Killarney 22 – Tralee 25.

    Ard-na-Sidhe ⚘, ℡ 5, ≤, « Country house atmosphere with tasteful decor », ⚓, ⚒,
park – **P**. AE ⓞ VISA
May-end September – **M** approx. 9.50 **st.** ▯ 2.70 – **22 rm** ⊇ 11.00/13.00 **st.**

    Caragh Lodge ⚘, ℡ 15, ≤, « Fine gardens and lakeside setting », ✖, ⚓, ⚒, park –
⊜wc **P**
April-mid September – **M** (dinner only, residents only) 7.00 **t.** – **10 rm** ⊇ 9.50/
22.00 **t.**

CARLOW Carlow 986 ㉖ – pop. 9,588 – ECD : Thursday – ☎ 0503.

▗18 Oak Park ℡ 41695.

▤ ℡ 41554 (July-August).

Dublin 52 – Kilkenny 25 – **Tullamore 44** – Wexford 46.

    Royal, Dublin St. ℡ 41621 – ⊜wc **P**. ⚙. AE VISA
closed 25 to 27 December – **M** 4.25/6.50 **st.** ▯ 1.65 – **36 rm** ⊇ 9.50/19.50 **st.**

    Carlow Lodge, Kilkenny Rd S : 2 m. on N 9/T 51 ℡ 42002 – ⊜wc ☏ **P**
10 rm.

BMW, TOYOTA Dublin Rd ℡ 41572   TALBOT, PEUGEOT Tullow Rd ℡ 41391
BRITISH LEYLAND Pollerton Rd ℡ 41141   VAUXHALL Dublin Rd ℡ 41938
FIAT, LANCIA Tullow Rd ℡ 41955   VW, AUDI-NSU, MAZDA, MERCEDES-BENZ Green
FORD Court Place ℡ 41665   Lane ℡ 41047
OPEL Tullow Rd ℡ 41303

CARRAROE Galway – ☎ 091 Galway.

Dublin 159 – Galway 27.

    Carraroe, ℡ 72105, ≤ – ⊜wc ☏ **P**. AE
29 May-September – **M** 4.15/7.50 **t.** – **24 rm** ⊇ 11.30/22.60 **t.**

CARRICKMACROSS Monaghan 986 ㉒ – pop. 4,846 – ECD : Wednesday – ☎ 042.

▗ Nuremore H. ℡ 61438.

Dublin 56 – Dundalk 14.

    Nuremore ⚘, SE : 1 m. by T 2 ℡ 61438, ≤, ▣, ▗, ⚓, ⚒, park – ⊜wc 🚻wc ☏ **P**
39 rm.

CARRICK-ON-SHANNON Leitrim 986 ㉑ – pop. 6,429 – ECD : Wednesday.

▗ ℡ 157.

▤ ℡ 170 (May-September).

Dublin 97 – Ballina 50 – Roscommon 26 – **Sligo 34.**

    Bush, Main St. ℡ 14, Telex 4394, ⚒ – ⊜wc 🚻wc ☏ **P**
28 rm.

    County, Bridge St. ℡ 42 – ⊜wc 🚻wc **P**. AE
closed 25 to 27 December – **M** a la carte approx. 2.90 **t.** – **18 rm** ⊇ 9.00/21.50 **st.**

    Cartown House, Leitrim Rd N : 1 ½ m. on T 54 ℡ 103, ⚒ – ☏ **P**
11 rm.

BRITISH LEYLAND Cartober ℡ 80

CASHEL Tipperary 986 ㉕ – pop. 2,692 – ECD : Wednesday – ☎ 062.

See : St. Patrick's Rock*** (or Rock of Cashel) : site and ecclesiastical ruins 12C-15C (⁂**)
AC – Hore Abbey* ruins 13C – St. Dominick's Abbey* ruins 13C.

▤ Town Hall ℡ 61333.

Dublin 101 – Cork 60 – Kilkenny 34 – **Limerick 36** – Waterford 44.

CASHEL

- 🏨 Cashel Palace ⑤, Main St. ☏ 61411, « Interesting art collection », 🍴 – Ⓟ
  20 rm.

- 🏨 Cashel Kings, Dublin Rd, NE: 1 m. on N 8 ☏ 61477, Telex 4404, ← Cashel Rock and mountains – 🚽wc 🅿 Ⓟ
  40 rm.

- XX **Chez Hans**, Rockside ☏ 61177, « Converted 19C church » – Ⓟ
  closed Sunday, Monday, October and Christmas – **M** (dinner only) 10.00 **t.**

FORD Cahir Rd ☏ 310   TALBOT, FIAT ☏ 61155

CASHEL BAY Galway.

Envir. : N : Connemara** – SE : Kilkieran Peninsula**.

Dublin 173 – Galway 41.

- 🏨 **Cashel House** ⑤, ☏ 9, Telex 8812, « Country house set in attractive gardens », 🍴, 🐎,
  🍴 – 🚽wc Ⓟ. **VISA**
  March-October – **M** (bar lunch) a la carte 5.10/8.00 **t.** 🍷 1.60 – **23 rm** ☑ 10.00/28.00 **t.** –
  P 19.90/24.50 **t.**

- 🏨 **Zetland** ⑤, ☏ 8, Telex 8853, ←, 🐎, 🍴 – 🚽wc Ⓟ. 🅂 🅰🅴 ⓪ **VISA**
  Easter-October – **M** approx. 7.70 🍷 2.75 – **19 rm** ☑ 10.65/32.25.

CASTLEBAR Mayo 🄆🄆🄆 ㉑ – pop. 5,979 – ECD : Thursday – ☎ 094.

Envir. : Ballintuber Abbey* (13C-15C) S : 7 m.

🏌 ☏ 111.

🛈 ☏ 21207 (June-September).

Dublin 152 – Ballina 25 – Galway 48 – Sligo 54.

- 🏨 **Breaffy House** ⑤, SE : 2 ¾ m. on T 39 ☏ 22033, 🐎, park – 📶 🚽wc 🅿 Ⓟ. 🏖. 🅂
  🅰🅴 ⓪ **VISA**
  closed 18 to 27 December – **M** 5.00/8.75 **t.** 🍷 1.90 – **43 rm** ☑ 19.00/30.00 **t.** –
  P 27.00 **t.**

CITROEN, DATSUN Breaffy Rd ☏ 21975   RENAULT Spencer St. ☏ 21355
FIAT Turlough Rd ☏ 22144   VW, AUDI-NSU, MERCEDES-BENZ Spencer Park ☏
FORD 3 Ellison St. ☏ 21611   238

CASTLEDERMOT Kildare 🄆🄆🄆 ㉖ – pop. 583 – ☎ 0503 Carlow.

Envir.: Baltinglass (abbey ruins : scenery *) NE : 7 m.

Dublin 44 – Kilkenny 33 – Wexford 54.

- 🏨 Kilkea Castle ⑤, Kilkea NW : 3 ½ m. ☏ 45156, Telex 5388, ←, « 12C castle », 🏊 heated,
  🍴, 🐎, park – Ⓟ. 🏖 – **50 rm.**

BRITISH LEYLAND, PEUGEOT ☏ 44114

CASTLEGREGORY Kerry – pop. 804 – ☎ 066.

Dublin 201 – Killarney 36 – Limerick 80.

- X **Tralee Bay** with rm, SE : 2 ¾ m. ☏ 39138, ← – 🚽wc Ⓟ
  Easter-October – **M** (bar lunch) a la carte 8.00/15.00 🍷 3.00 – **13 rm** ☑ 11 00/
  27.00 **t.**

CASTLEKNOCK Dublin – see Dublin.

CASTLEREA Roscommon 🄆🄆🄆 ㉑ – pop. 1,752 – ECD : Monday.

🏌 Clonalis, ☏ 68.

Dublin 110 – Galway 49 – Roscommon 17 – Sligo 42.

- 🏨 Tully's, Main St. ☏ 163 – 🚽wc 🚿wc – **19 rm.**

CASTLETOWNBERE Cork 🄆🄆🄆 ㉙ – pop. 812.

🏌 Berehaven ☏ 24.

Dublin 247 – Cork 86 – Killarney 68.

- 🏨 **Cametringane House** ⑤, ☏ 27, ←, 🍴 – 🚽wc 🅿 Ⓟ. 🅰🅴
  M 3.00/6.00 **t.** 🍷 2.00 – **18 rm** ☑ 6.00/13.00 **t.**

- 🏨 Beara Bay, Main St. ☏ 130 – 🚽wc 🚿wc Ⓟ – **18 rm.**

CHARLEVILLE (RATH LUIRC) Cork 🄆🄆🄆 ㉙ – pop. 2,232 – ECD : Thursday – ☎ 063.

Envir. : Kilmallock (Dominican Friary ruins 13C, SS. Peter and Paul church 14C : scenery*)
NE : 6 m. – Kilfinnane (site*) E : 11 m.

🏌 ☏ 257.

Dublin 138 – Cork 38 – Killarney 57 – Limerick 24.

- 🏨 Deerpark, Limerick Rd N : ½ m. on T 11 ☏ 581 – 🚽wc 🅿 Ⓟ – **10 rm.**

FORD Limerick Rd ☏ 561

CLIFDEN Galway 986 ㉑ – pop. 790 – ECD : Thursday.
Envir. : E : Connemara** : Ballynahinch Lake*, The Twelve Pins* (mountains), Lough Inagh*, Kylemore Lake*, Kylemore Abbey (site**), Streamstown Bay* NW : 2 m. – Cleggan (site**) NW : 6 m.

Ⅰ8 Connemara, Ballyconneely ☏ Ballyconneely 5.

☒ ☏ 103 (May-September).

Dublin 181 – Ballina 77 – Galway 49.

- **Alcock and Brown,** The Square ☏ 134 – ⇋wc ☎ ℗. AE ⓪
  Easter-September – **M** 2.95/5.85 **t.** ⓵ 1.50 – ⊠ 1.80 – **20 rm** 9.75/15.60 **t.** – P 18.00 **t.**
- **Abbeyglen House** ⑤ Sky Rd W : ½ m. ☏ 33, ≤, ⸙, ⎯ heated, ⚘, park – ⇋wc ☎ ℗. AE *VISA*
  closed November-15 December and 15 January-Easter – **M** 6.00/8.00 **t.** ⓵ 2.50 – **30 rm** ⊠ 25.00 **t.**
- Clifden Bay, Main St. ☏ 128, ⚘ – ⇋wc **44 rm.**
- **Rock Glen Country House** ⑤, S : 1 ½ m. on Roundstone Rd ☏ 16 – ⇋wc ℗
  Easter-October – **M** (bar lunch) approx. 7.00 **t.** ⓵ 2.40 – **20 rm** ⊠ 7.50/18.00 **t.** – P 15.00/16.00 **t.**
- **Celtic,** Main St. ☏ 115, ⚘ – ⇋wc
  closed 11 to 27 December – **M** (bar lunch) approx. 7.00 **t.** ⓵ 1.65 – **20 rm** ⊠ 10.00/20.00 **t.**

CLONBUR Galway.
Envir. : W : Joyces Country : by road L 100 from Clonbur to Leenane : Lough Nafovey*, ⁂* from the bridge on Lough Mask**.

Dublin 161 – Galway 29 – Wesport 32.

- **Fairhill,** ☏ 6 – ℗
  Easter-October – **9 rm** ⊠ 5.00/10.00 **t.**

CLONDALKIN Dublin 986 ㉖ and ㊲ – see Dublin.

CLONMEL Tipperary 986 ㉙ – pop. 11,622 – ECD : Thursday – ✆ 052.
See : The Main Guard* 1674. **Envir. :** Ahenny (2 high crosses*) NE : 16 m. – S : Nire Valley* (≤**).

Ⅰ8 Lyranearla, ☏ 21138.

Dublin 108 – Cork 59 – Kilkenny 31 – Limerick 48 – Waterford 29.

- **Minella** ⑤, Coleville Rd SE : 1 m. on L 27 ☏ 22388, ⚘, ⇶, park · – ⇋wc ⇋wc ☎ ℗. ⚴. ◪ AE ⓪ *VISA*
  M 4.00/8.00 **st.** ⓵ 1.50 – **34 rm** ⊠ 13.00/23.00 **s.**
- **Clonmel Arms,** Sarsfield St. ☏ 21233 – ▮◌ ⇋wc ⇋wc ☎ ℗. ⚴. ◪ AE ⓪ *VISA*
  M 4.00/6.50 **st.** ⓵ 1.50 – ⊠ 2.75 – **41 rm** 10.00/20.00 **st.**
- **Inislounaght House** ⑤, Marlfield W : 1 ½ m. off N 24 ☏ 22847, ≤, « Country house atmosphere », ⚘, ⇶ – ⇋wc ℗
  15 March-15 October – **M** (dinner only) 8.25 **st.** ⓵ 2.50 – **6 rm** ⊠ 14.00/21.00 **st.**

CITROEN, VOLVO Thomas St. ☏ 22430
DATSUN Anglesea St. ☏ 21238
FIAT, OPEL Main St. ☏ 22972
FIAT Parnell St. ☏ 21615
FORD Davis Rd ☏ 21199

RENAULT Dungarvon Rd ☏ 22399
TALBOT Cashel Rd ☏ 22387
TOYOTA Chasel Rd ☏ 21652
VW, AUDI-NSU Upper Irishtown ☏ 22199

COBH Cork 986 ㉙ – pop. 6,076 – ECD : Wednesday – ✆ 021.
Dublin 170 – Cork 15 – Waterford 76.

- Commodore, Westbourne Pl. ☏ 811277, Telex 8447, ≤, ◪ – ▮◌ ⇋wc ☎. ⚴ **50 rm.**

CONG Mayo – ✆ 094 Castlebar.
See : Lough Corrib*** – Ashford Castle (site*). **Envir. :** Ross Abbey**, Franciscan Friary (tower ⁂*, 80 steps) SE : 9 m.

Dublin 160 – Ballina 49 – Galway 28.

- **Ashford Castle** ⑤, ☏ 22644, Telex 4749, ≤ Lough Corrib and countryside, « Tastefully converted castle », ⸙, ⌊9, ⚘, ⇶, park – ▮◌ ℗. ◪ AE ⓪ *VISA*
  May-December – **M** 6.50/14.00 ⓵ 3.00 – **78 rm** ⊠ 24.85/44.80 **t.**

COOTEHILL Cavan 986 ㉒ – pop. 3,273 – ECD : Tuesday.
Envir. : Bellamont Forest* N : 1 ½ m.

Dublin 68 – Dundalk 33.

- White Horse, Market St. ☏ 24 – ☎ ℗ **32 rm.**

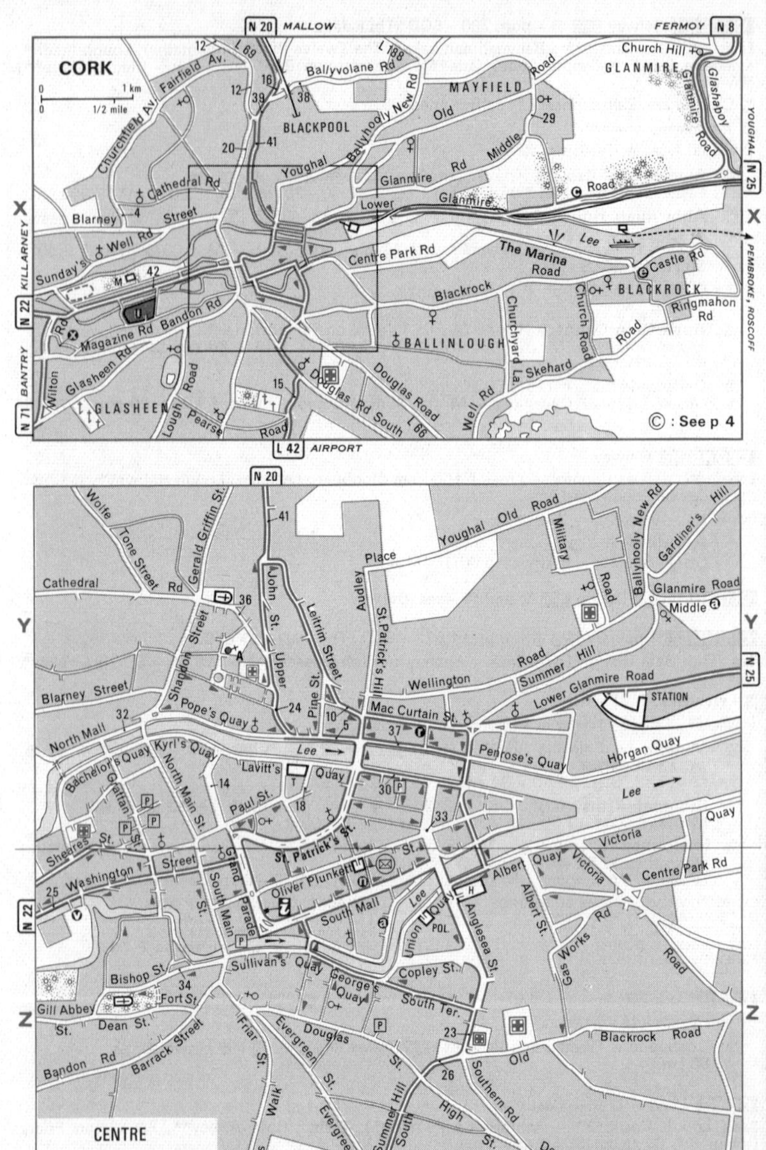

Oliver Plunkett Street	Z		Dublin Street	X 16		Newsom's Quay	Y 32
St. Patrick's Street	YZ		Emmet Place	Y 18		Parnell Place	Y 33
			Great William O'Brien Street	X 20		Proby's Quay	Z 34
Baker's Road	X 4		Infirmary Road	Z 23		Roman Street	Y 36
Camden Place	Y 5		John Redmond Street	Y 24		St. Patrick's Quay	Y 37
Coburg Street	Y 10		Lancaster Quay	Z 25		Spring Lane	X 38
Commons Road	X 12		Langford Row	Z 26		Thomas Davis Street	X 39
Corn Market Street	Y 14		Lower Mayfield Road	X 29		Watercourse Road	X 41
Curragh Road	X 15		Merchant's Quay	Y 30		Western Road	X 42

CORK Cork 📖 ㉙ – pop. 128,645 – ✆ 021.

See : St. Patrick's Street* YZ – St. Ann's Shandon Church* 18C (steeple ❄* AC, 134 steps) Y A –
University College* 1845 X U – The Marina ≼* X.

🏌 Little Island ☏ 821263 E : 5 m. by N 25 X – 🏌 Monkstown ☏ 841225, S : 7 m. by L 66 X.

✈ ☏ 25341, S : 4 m. by L 42 X – **Terminal**: Bus Station, Parnell Pl.

⛴ to Pembroke (B. & I. Line) 4-6 weekly (10 h).

Shipping connections with the Continent : to Roscoff (Brittany Ferries).

🛈 Cork City, 42 Grand Parade ☏ 23251 – Cork Airport, ☏ 22923 (June-September).

Dublin 161.

Plan opposite

🏨 **Jury's,** Western Rd ☏ 26651, Telex 6073, 🚗 – 📺 ♿ 🅿. 🔺 AE ⓞ VISA   Z v
   M 5.25/8.00 t. 🍶 2.00 – ☕ 3.25 – **150 rm** 25.50/35.90 t.

🏨 **Silver Springs,** E : 2 ½ m. on N 25 ☏ 51231, Telex 6111, 🚗 – 🛗 📺 🅿. 🏊. 🔺 AE ⓞ
   VISA   X c
   M 5.00/8.50 t. 🍶 1.50 – **72 rm** ☕ 22.00/32.50.

🏨 **Imperial,** South Mall ☏ 23304 – 🛗 🅿. 🏊. 🔺 AE ⓞ VISA   Z n
   closed 25 and 26 December – M 4.50/6.00 t. 🍶 2.50 – **84 rm** ☕ 21.00/30.00 t.

🏨 ✾ **Arbutus Lodge,** Middle Glanmire Rd, Montenotte ☏ 501237, Telex 32079, 🚗 – 📺
   ⊟wc ⋔wc ☎ 🅿. AE ⓞ VISA   Y a
   closed 24 December-1 January – M *(closed Sunday dinner to non-residents)* a la carte
   10.25/15.25 st. 🍶 2.00 – **20 rm** ☕ 23.50/35.75 st.
   Spec. Seasonal specialities.

🏨 **Metropole,** MacCurtain St. ☏ 508122, Telex 32077 – 🛗 ⊟wc ☎ 🚗. 🏊. 🔺 AE ⓞ
   VISA   Y r
   M 4.00/7.50 t. – ☕ 3.00 – **125 rm** 18.00/24.20 t. – P 26.00/30.75 t.

🏠 **Airport Motel,** Kinsale Rd S : 3 ½ m. on L 42 ☏ 961616 – 📺 ⊟wc ☎ 🅿 by L42 X
   M (bar lunch) approx. 5.50 st. 🍶 3.00 – **20 rm** ☕ 17.00/24.00 st.

🏠 **Glengarriffe,** Orchard Rd, Victoria Cross ☏ 417851, ✖, ⊿, 🚗 – ⊟wc 🅿   X x
   closed Sunday, 23 December-16 January and Bank Holidays – M 4.50/8.50 t. 🍶 3.00 –
   20 rm ☕ 15.00/30.00 t. – P 27.00/30.00 t.

🏠 Moore's, Morrisons Island ☏ 227361 – ⊟wc   Z a
   39 rm.

   at Blackrock E : 3 ¼ m. South of the River – ✉ ✆ 021 Cork :

✖ Pier Head Inn, ☏ 31616.   X e

   at Glounthaune E : 7 m. on N 25 – X – ✉ ✆ 021 Cork :

🏨 **Ashbourne House,** ☏ 821320, « Extensive gardens », ✖, ⊿ heated – ⊟wc ⋔wc ☎
   🅿. 🔺 AE ⓞ VISA
   closed 23 to 30 December – M 4.50/8.00 st. 🍶 1.80 – ☕ 3.00 – **26 rm** 15.00/27.00 st. –
   P 24.00 st.

   at Douglas SE : 2 m. on L 66 – X – ✉ ✆ 021 Cork :

✖✖ **Briar Rose,** Douglas Rd ☏ 294794 – 🅿. VISA
   closed Saturday lunch and Sunday – M a la carte 6.50/9.00 t. 🍶 2.00.

   at Killeens NW : 3 ¾ m. on L 69 – X – ✉ ✆ 021 Cork :

🏠 Sunset Ridge Motel, Blarney Rd ☏ 85271 – ⊟wc ☎ 🅿
   10 rm.

AUSTIN-ROVER-TRIUMPH Ivy Lawn, Douglas Rd ☏ 504055
BMW, CITROEN, VW, AUDI-NSU, MERCEDES-BENZ Douglas Rd ☏ 34805
BRITISH LEYLAND Victoria Cross ☏ 41851
BRITISH LEYLAND 26 St. Patricks Quay ☏ 26657
DATSUN Convent Rd ☏ 43374
DATSUN Blackrock Rd ☏ 32888
DATSUN, VOLVO ☏ 25008
FIAT 24 Watercourse Rd ☏ 503228
FIAT 11 South Terrace ☏ 507344
FORD Dennehys Cross ☏ 42846

FORD Monaghan Rd ☏ 503381
MAZDA, MERCEDES, VW, AUDI-NSU Kinsale Rd ☏ 21713
OPEL 26 St. Patricks Quay ☏ 26657
PEUGEOT, TOYOTA Emmett Pl. ☏ 23296
RENAULT Douglas Rd ☏ 31861
RENAULT Tivoli ☏ 503397
RENAULT Mill St. ☏ Millstreet 42
SAAB St. Patricks Quay ☏ 501291
TALBOT Mallow Rd ☏ 503271
VAUXHALL Douglas Rd ☏ 32861

COURTMACSHERRY Cork – pop. 210 – ✉ ✆ 023 Bandon.

Envir. : Timoleague (Franciscan Abbey* 16C) W : 1 ½ m.

Dublin 190 – Cork 29.

🏨 **Courtmacsherry** ⚓, ☏ 46198, ≼, 🚗, park – ⊟wc 🅿
   Easter-September – M (bar lunch Monday to Saturday) 4.50/7.50 t. 🍶 2.00 – **17 rm** ☕
   10.00/25.00 t.

🏠 **Lislee House** ⚓, SW : 2 m. ☏ 40126, ≼, « Country house atmosphere », ⊿, 🚗 – 🅿
   M (dinner only) 9.50 st. 🍶 1.75 – **7 rm** ☕ 12.50/25.00 st.

COURTOWN Wexford 986 ㉖ – pop. 291 – ☎ 055 Gorey.
18 Courtown Harbour ☎ 21566.
Dublin 62 – Waterford 59 – Wexford 42.

- **Courtown,** Courtown ☎ 25108, ⛱ – ⛀wc ⛆wc Ⓟ. AE ◑ VISA
  Easter-26 October – **M** 4.50/8.50 **t.** 🌢 1.90 – **26 rm** ☕ 13.00/23.00 **t.**

CROSSHAVEN Cork 986 ㉙ – pop. 1,222 – ✉ ☎ 021.
Dublin 173 – Cork 12.

- Grand, ☎ 831444, ≤, ⛱ – TV Ⓟ
  25 rm.
- **Whispering Pines,** ☎ 831448, ≤, ⚓ – ⛀wc ⛆wc Ⓟ
  10 rm ☕ 8.80/15.60 **t.**
- Cobbles, Church Bay Rd ☎ 831 525 – Ⓟ.

CURRAGH Kildare – ✉ Kildare – ☎ 045.
18 ☎ 41238.
Dublin 31 – Kilkenny 54 – Tullamore 33.

- **Jockey Hall,** ☎ 41416 – Ⓟ. 🅂 AE VISA
  closed Sunday, Good Friday and 24-25 December – **M** (dinner only) a la carte 8.20/12.50 **st.** 🌢 1.95.

DALKEY Dublin 986 ㊲ – ☎ 01 Dublin.
Dublin 11.

- **Guinea Pig,** 17 Railway Rd ☎ 859055
  M (dinner only) a la carte 9.70/12.75 **t.** 🌢 1.50.

FIAT Convent Rd ☎ 802046

DELGANY Wicklow – pop. 4,517 – ✉ Bray – ☎ 01 Dublin.
Dublin 19.

- Glenview 🐎, Glen of the Downs NW : 2 m. on N 11 by L 164 ☎ 862896, ≤, 🌳 – Ⓟ. 🏋
  23 rm.
- **Delgany Inn,** ☎ 875701 – ⛀wc ☎. AE VISA
  closed Christmas Day – **M** *(closed Sunday dinner)* a la carte 7.45/12.95 **t.** 🌢 2.30 – ☕ 2.00 – **10 rm** 9.00/18.00 **t.**

DINGLE Kerry 986 ㉙ – pop. 1,401 – ECD : Thursday.
See : Dingle Bay*. Envir. : NE : Conair Pass ☼* – Fahan : Belvedere (coast road) ≤* SW : 7 ½ m.
ℹ ☎ 88 (June-September).
Dublin 216 – Killarney 51 – Limerick 95.

- **Sceilig** 🐎, ☎ 104, Telex 6900, ≤, 🎾, ⛱ heated – ⛀wc ☎ ♿ Ⓟ. 🅂 AE ◑ VISA
  14 March-October – **M** 4.50/7.95 **t.** 🌢 2.30 – **79 rm** ☕ 20.20/28.40 **t.**
- **Alpine,** Mail Rd ☎ 15 – ⛆wc Ⓟ
  March-October – **15 rm** ☕ 5.50/10.50 **t.**
- **Doyle's Seafood Bar,** John St. ☎ 144, Seafood – AE VISA
  13 March-October – **M** *(closed Sunday)* a la carte 5.40/7.40 **st.** 🌢 2.00.
- **Whelan's,** Main St. ☎ 41 – VISA
  18 March-October – **M** *(closed Thursday)* a la carte 4.65/6.50 **t.** 🌢 2.30.

DONEGAL Donegal 986 ⑰ – pop. 1,725 – ECD : Wednesday.
See : Franciscan Priory (site*, ≤*).
18 Murvagh ☎ Ballintra 54, S : 8 m.
ℹ ☎ 148 (June-September).
Dublin 164 – Londonderry 48 – Sligo 40.

- **Hyland Central,** The Diamond ☎ 27, Telex 33522, 🌳 – |◆| ⛀wc ☎. AE VISA
  closed Christmas – **M** 4.50/7.50 **t.** – **44 rm** ☕ 13.00/26.00 **t.** – P 24.00 **t.**
- Abbey, The Diamond ☎ 14 – ⛀wc ☎
  19 rm.
- National, Main St. ☎ 35, ⚓
  16 rm.

BMW, PEUGEOT, VAUXHALL, VOLVO Milford ☎ 7
DATSUN Dunkineely ☎ 14
DATSUN Kerrykell ☎ 3
FORD The Glebe ☎ 17
RENAULT ☎ 117
ROVER-TRIUMPH Quay St. ☎ 39

DOUGLAS Cork – see Cork.

See : St. Lawrence's Gate* 13C.

Envir. : Mellifont Abbey** (Cistercian ruins 1142) NW : 4 ½ m. – Monasterboice (3 tall crosses** 10C) NW : 5 ½ m. – Dowth Tumulus ※* W : 4 m. – Duleek (priory* 12C ruins) SW : 5 m. – Newgrange Tumulus* (prehistoric tomb) *AC*, SW : 7 m.

ⁱ⁸ Baltray 𝒫 8860, E : 3 m.

🛈 𝒫 7070 (June-August).

Dublin 29 – Dundalk 22 – Tullamore 67.

   🏨 Boyne Valley, SE : 1 ½ m. on T 1 𝒫 7737, Telex 31334, 🚗, park – 🛏wc 🛁wc ☎
    🅿
    21 rm.

   🏠 **Glenside House,** Smithstown SE : 3 m. on T 1 𝒫 7449, 🚗 – 🛏wc 🅿. AE
    closed 16 December-1 January – **M** *(closed Sunday dinner)* 3.75/6.00 t. 🍷 1.80 – **9 rm**
    ☲ 9.00/16.00 **st.** – P 16.00 **t.**

FIAT, LANCIA North Rd 𝒫 7920   PEUGEOT Palace St. 𝒫 7303
FORD North Rd 𝒫 8951   RENAULT Dublin Rd 𝒫 36076
OPEL Dublin Rd 𝒫 8511   TOYOTA North Rd 𝒫 8566

See : National Gallery*** BY **M¹** – Castle (State apartments*** *AC*) BY – Christ Church Cathedral** 12C BY A – National Museum (Irish antiquities, Art and Industrial)** BY **M²** – Trinity College* (Library**) BY – National Museum (Zoological Collection)* BY **M¹** – Municipal Art Gallery* BX **M³** – O'Connell Street* (and the General Post Office) BXY – St. Stephen's Green* BZ – St. Patrick's Cathedral (interior*) BZ B – Phoenix Park (Zoological Gardens*) AY.

Envir. : St. Doolagh's Church* 13C (open Saturday and Sunday, afternoon only) NE : 7 m. by L 87 AY – Castletown House* 18C (Georgian mansion) *AC*, W : 11 m. by N 4 AY – Maynooth : St. Patrick's College : museum Ecce Homo* 12 C, leaf of ivory diptych Northern French* 14C – College Chapel : interior wainscots*) W : 15 m. by N 4 AY.

ⁱ⁸ Rathfarnham 𝒫 907461, S : 3 m. by N 81 AZ – ⁱ⁸ Nutley House, Donnybrook 𝒫 693438, S : 3 m. AZ – ⁱ⁸ Lower Churchtown Rd 𝒫 976090 S : by T 43 AZ.

✈ 𝒫 379900, N : 5 ½ m. by N 1 AY – **Terminal :** Busaras (Central Bus Station) Store St.

🚢 to Liverpool (B & I Line) 2-3 weekly (7 h) – to the Isle of Man : Douglas (Isle of Man Steam Packet Co.) 24 May-20 September 1-3 weekly (4 h 30 mn).

🛈 51 Dawson St. 𝒫 747733 – Dublin Airport 𝒫 376387 and 375533.

Belfast 103 – Cork 161 – Londonderry 145.

Plans on following pages

  🏨 **Jury's,** Pembroke Rd, Ballsbridge 𝒫 767511, Telex 5304, 🔲, ⌇ heated, 🚗 – 🛗 📺 ♿
   🅿. 🪑. 🔲 AE ⓞ VISA   AZ c
   M 6.00/8.50 **t.** 🍷 2.00 – ☲ 4.00 – **314 rm** 28.50/39.90 **t.**

  🏨 **Shelbourne** (T.H.F.), 27 St. Stephen's Green 𝒫 766471, Telex 5184 – 🛗 📺 🅿. 🪑. 🔲 AE
   ⓞ VISA   BZ s
   M 4.30/6.50 **t.** 🍷 1.60 – ☲ 3.50 – **176 rm** 30.50/45.50 **t.**

  🏨 **Royal Hibernian** (T.H.F.), 46-48 Dawson St. 𝒫 772991, Telex 5220 – 🛗. 🪑. 🔲 AE ⓞ
   VISA   BY o
   M 6.50/8.25 **st.** 🍷 1.70 – ☲ 3.50 – **110 rm** 27.50/34.00 **t.**

  🏨 Burlington, Upper Leeson St. 𝒫 785711, Group Telex 5517, 🔲 – 🛗 📺 🅿   BZ c
   420 rm.

  🏨 Royal Dublin, 40 Upper O'Connell St. 𝒫 749351, Telex 4288 – 🛗 🅿   BX s
   101 rm.

  🏨 Tara Tower, Merrion Rd SE : 4 m. on T 44 𝒫 694666, Group Telex 5517 – 🛗 📺 🛏wc
   ☎ 🅿   on T 44 AZ
   83 rm.

  🏨 Skylon, Upper Drumcondra Rd N : 2 ½ m. on N 1 𝒫 379121, Group Telex 5517 – 🛗
   🛏wc ☎ 🅿   AY e
   88 rm.

  🏨 **Ashling,** Parkgate St. 𝒫 772324, Telex 5891 – 📺 🛏wc 🛁wc ☎ 🅿. AE   AY r
   closed 24 to 26 December – **M** 5.40/8.00 **st.** 🍷 1.70 – **42 rm** ☲ 17.00/29.00 **st.** – P 30.40 **st.**

  🏨 Buswells, 25-26 Molesworth St. 𝒫 764013 – 🛗 🛏wc ☎   BY u
   53 rm.

  🏨 **Central,** Exchequer St. 𝒫 778341 – 🛗 🛏wc 🛁wc ☎ 🅿. 🪑. 🔲 AE ⓞ VISA BY v
   M 4.50/7.50 **t.** 🍷 2.00 – **84 rm** ☲ 18.00/27.00 **t.**

  🏨 Mount Herbert (wine licence only), 7 Herbert Rd, Ballsbridge 𝒫 684321, 🚗 –
   🛏wc ☎ 🅿   AZ a
   84 rm.

P.T.O. ⟶

DUBLIN

MONAGHAN N 2
A
AIRPORT N 1 BELFAST, LONDONDERRY
BUILT UP AREA
0 1 km
0 1/2 mile
MALAHIDE L 87
COOLOCK
Ballymun Avenue
Finglas
Old Finglas Rd
GLASNEVIN
Ballymun Rd
Griffith
Swords Road
Collins
Avenue
Malahide Road
HOWTH L 86
Ratoath
Tolka
BOTANIC GARDENS
Royal
Mobhi Rd
DRUMCONDRA
Avenue
Road
Howth Road
Clontarf Rd
NAVAN N 3
CABRA
Faussagh Av.
Navan Road
PHIBSBOROUGH
Iona Road
Canal
Drumconda
Clonliffe Road
Tolka
Fairview
FAIRVIEW PARK
Cabra Road
Road
Old Cabra Rd
North Circular
ZOOLOGICAL GARDENS
East Wall Road
Tolka Quay
LIVERPOOL
MULLINGAR
Main
PHŒNIX PARK
Road
46
Seville Pl.
Sheriff Street
Conyngham Road
102 5
N 4
LIFFEY
LIFFEY
St. John's Road West
92 Usher's Quay
James St.
Thomas St.
50
N 7
Mount Brown
Canal
Dolphin's Barn St.
Mount St.
75
Dodder
Beach Road
LIMERICK
Grand
Davitt Road
Dolphin Rd
Parnell
Haddington Rd
3
79
SANDYMOUNT
HOLYHEAD
Road
60
Merrion
HERBERT PARK
N
Crumlin Road
T 54
Sundrive
Clogher Road
HAROLD'S CROSS
Ranelagh Road
Anglesea Rd
25
Ailesbury Rd
T 44
DUN-LAOGHAIRE
Kildare Road
SUNDRIVE PARK
Road
77 29
Clonskeagh
Stillorgan Rd
CRUMLIN
Road
Lower Leinster Rd
Harold's
Rathgar Rd
RATHMINES
Milltown Road
Dodder
18
Kimmage Road West
Kimmage Road
73
84 83
© : See p. 4
BLESSINGTON N 81
A
ENNISKERRY T 43
BRAY N 11

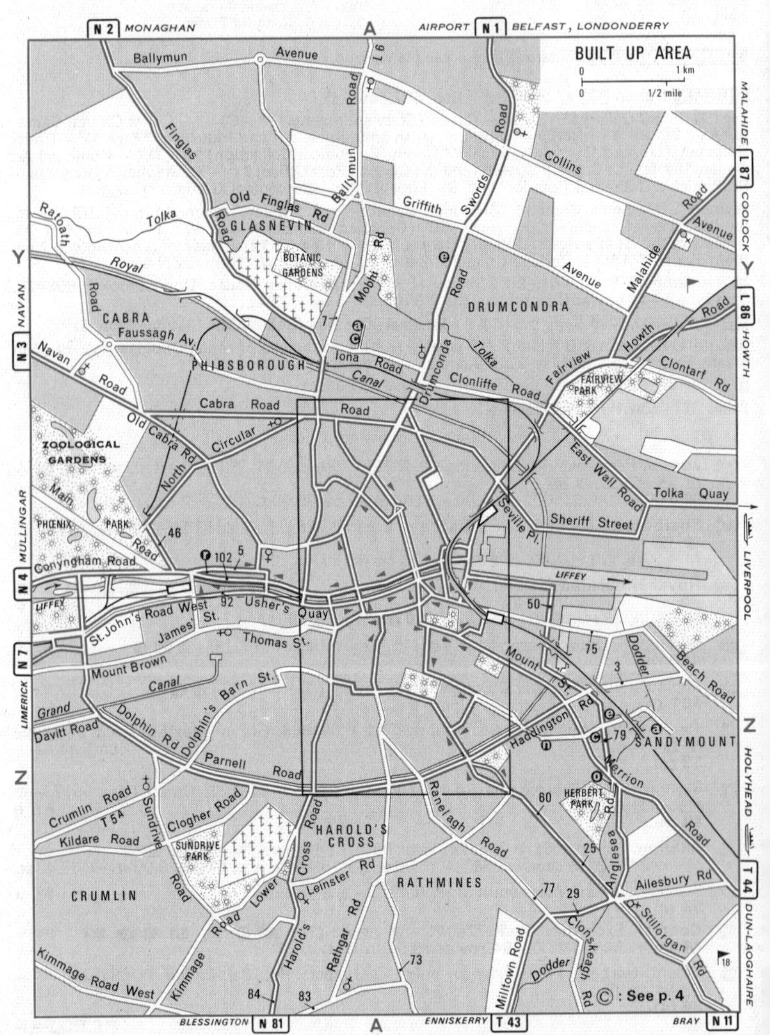

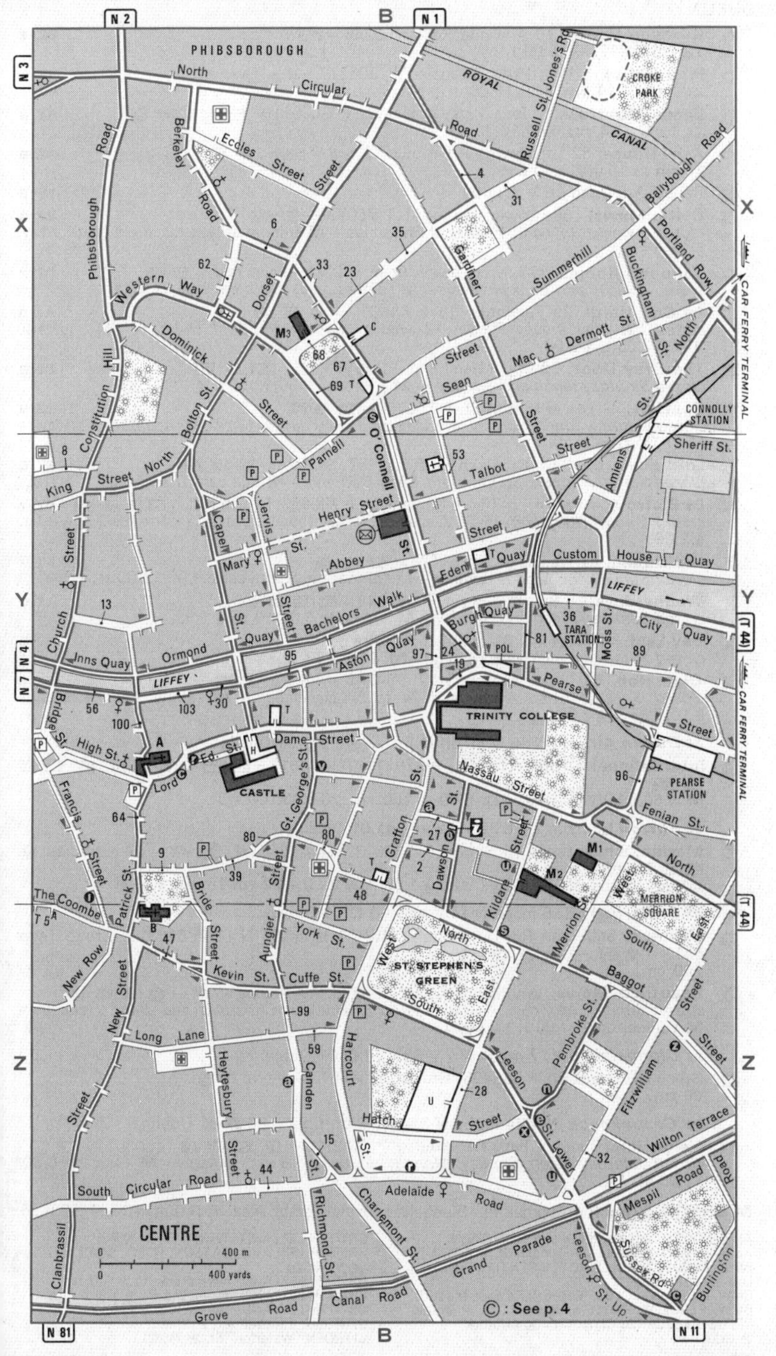

N 2
N 3
B
N 1
PHIBSBOROUGH
ROYAL
CROKE PARK
CANAL
Russell St.
Jones's Rd.
Ballybough Road
North
Circular
Road
Eccles
Street
Berkeley
Street
Dorset
Street
Gardiner
Summerhill
Buckingham
Portland Row
X
Phibsborough
Road
Phibsborough
Hill
6
62
33
23
35
31
4
CAR FERRY TERMINAL
Western
Way
Dominick
Constitution Hill
M3
68
67
69 T
C
Street
Sean
Mac
Dermott St.
St. North
CONNOLLY STATION
Bolton St.
Street
O'Connell
St.
Sheriff St.
Y
8
King
Street
North
Constitution Hill
Church
Street
Capel
Street
Jervis
St.
Parnell
Henry Street
Abbey
Mary
Street
53
Talbot
Street
Street
Amiens
St.
13
Ormond
Quay
Bachelors
Walk
Eden
Quay
T
Quay
Custom
House
Quay
LIFFEY
City
Quay
44
Inns Quay
LIFFEY
95
Aston
Quay
97
24
19
Burgh Quay
POL.
81
36
TARA STATION
Moss St.
89
Pearse
N 7
N 4
56
100
103
30
T
Dame
Street
Gt. George's St.
97
TRINITY COLLEGE
Nassau
Street
96
PEARSE STATION
Street
CAR FERRY TERMINAL
Bridge St.
Francis
Street
High St.
A
Lord
Ed. St.
H
CASTLE
64
Fenian St.
Pearse
Street
9
80
80
Grafton
Street
27
2
Kildare
Street
Dawson
St.
Z
M1
M2
North
MERRION SQUARE
West
South
East
Merrion
St.
Patrick St.
Bride
Street
39
48
B
47
York
St.
Aungier
Street
Kevin
St.
Cuffe St.
a
St. STEPHEN'S GREEN
West
North
East
South
South
Baggot
Street
The Coombe
T 5
A
New Row
New Street
Heytesbury
Street
Camden
Street
99
59
15
44
a
Harcourt
St.
U
28
32
Leeson
Street
Pembroke St.
Fitzwilliam
Wilton Terrace
N 81
South
Circular
Road
CENTRE
400 m
400 yards
Richmond St.
Charlemont St.
Hatch
Adelaide
Road
Grand
Parade
Canal
Road
Grove
Road
Leeson
St. Up.
Mespil
Road
Sussex Rd.
Burlington
Road
B
N 11
©: See p. 4
Clanbrassil
Street
Long Lane
Z
X
Y
44
N

⋔ **Kilronan House,** 70 Adelaide Rd ☎ 755266 – 🛏wc   **BZ r**
12 rm 🖙 12.00/16.00 **t.**

⋔ **Iona House,** 5 Iona Park, Glasnevin ☎ 306217, 🚗 – 🛏wc ☎   **AY c**
🖙 2.00 – **14 rm** 8.50/13.00.

⋔ **Egans Montrosa,** 7 Iona Park, Glasnevin ☎ 303611 – 🛏wc 🛏wc 🅿   **AY a**
🖙 1.95 – **18 rm** 6.60/10.30 **t.**

⋔ **Ariel House,** 52 Lansdowne Rd ☎ 685512, 🚗 – 🛏wc ☎ 🅿   **AZ e**
16 rm 🖙 10.00/17.40 **t.**

XXX Bailey, 2-3 Duke St. ☎ 770600.   **BY a**

XX **Celtic Mews,** 109a Lower Baggot St. ☎ 760796 – AE VISA   **BZ z**
closed 2 weeks July and 1 week at Christmas – **M** (dinner only) a la carte 9.50/11.20 **st.**
🍾 2.00.

XX **Tandoori Rooms,** 27 Lower Leeson St. ☎ 762286, Indian rest. – AE ①   **BZ x**
closed Sunday and Bank Holidays – **M** (dinner only) a la carte 9.95/14.70 **t.**

XX **Le Coq Hardi,** 29 Pembroke Rd ☎ 689070 – 🅿 AE VISA   **AZ n**
closed Saturday lunch, Sunday, 2 weeks January and Bank Holidays – **M** a la carte
9.70/13.00 **t.** 🍾 2.00.

XX **The Grey Door,** 23 Upper Pembroke St. ☎ 763286 – 🔌 AE VISA   **BZ n**
closed Saturday lunch and Sunday – **M** a la carte 9.50/12.50 **t.** 🍾 2.00.

XX **Snaffles,** 47 Lower Leeson St. ☎ 760790 – AE ① VISA   **BZ u**
closed Saturday lunch, Sunday, Monday dinner, 10 days at Christmas and Bank Holidays –
M 18.00 **st.** 🍾 1.50.

XX **Lord Edward,** 23 Christchurch Pl. ☎ 752557, Seafood – AE ① VISA   **BY c**
closed Saturday lunch, Sunday and Bank Holidays – **M** a la carte 7.40/13.50 **t.** 🍾 1.60.

XX **Le Bistro** (Castle Inn), 5-7 Lord Edward St. ☎ 780663, French rest. – 🔌 AE ① VISA   **BY r**
closed Good Friday and 25-26 December – **M** (bar lunch) a la carte 10.30/14.80 **t.**
🍾 2.50.

X **Old Dublin,** 91 Francis St. ☎ 751173 – 🔌 AE VISA   **BY i**
closed Sunday and Monday dinner – **M** (dinner only) a la carte 8.00/13.00 **st.** 🍾 2.40.

X **Wednesdays,** 15 Ballsbridge Ter. ☎ 681049 – 🔌 AE ① VISA   **AZ o**
closed Saturday lunch and Sunday – **M** a la carte 8.00/10.55 🍾 1.95.

X **Bay Leaf,** 41 Pleasants St. ☎ 753257, Bistro   **BZ a**
closed Saturday lunch and Sunday – **M** 3.10/8.50 **st.**

X **Olde Hob,** 68 Lower Leeson St. ☎ 764745 – 🔌 AE ① VISA   **BZ e**
closed Sunday, Good Friday and 24 to 27 December – **M** (dinner only) a la carte
6.10/7.85 **s.** 🍾 2.00.

at Dublin Airport N : 6 ½ m. off N 1 – **AY** – ✉ ✪ 01 Dublin :

🏨 **International Airport** (T.H.F.), ☎ 379211, Telex 4612 – 📺 🛏wc ☎ &. 🅿. ⚒. 🔌 AE
① VISA
M 3.60/5.50 **t.** 🍾 1.45 – 🖙 2.50 – **150 rm** 20.00/30.00 **t.**

at Sutton NE : 9 m. by L 86 – **AY** – ✉ ✪ 01 Dublin :

🏨 **Marine,** Sutton Cross, Dublin Rd ☎ 322613, Telex 4858, ≤, 🔌, 🚗 – 📺 🛏wc ☎ 🅿.
🔌 AE ① VISA
closed Christmas – **M** 6.50/7.50 **t.** 🍾 1.60 – 🖙 2.50 – **22 rm** 16.00/24.00 **st.**

at Stillorgan SE : 6 m. on N 11 – **AZ** – ✉ ✪ 01 Dublin :

🏨 Montrose, Stillorgan Rd, Donnybrook NW : 1 ½ m. on N 11 ☎ 693311, Group Telex
5517 – 🛗 📺 🛏wc ☎ 🅿. ⚒
200 rm.

XX **Beaufield Mews,** Woodlands Av. ☎ 880375, «Antiques», 🚗 – 🅿. AE ① VISA
closed Sunday, Monday, 1 week Easter, 1 week at Christmas and Bank Holidays –
M (dinner only) 7.00 **t.** 🍾 2.00.

at Clondalkin SW : 7 m. on N 7 – **AZ** – ✉ ✪ 01 Dublin :

🏨 Green Isle, Naas Rd ☎ 593406, Group Telex 5517 – 🛏wc ☎ 🅿. ⚒
66 rm.

at Castleknock NW : 4 m. by N 3 – **AY** – on L 92 – ✉ ✪ 01 Dublin :

XX **Weigh Inn,** Phoenix Park Racecourse ☎ 300042 – 🅿. 🔌 AE ①
closed Saturday lunch, Sunday, Monday dinner and Bank Holidays – **M** a la carte 6.80/
11.00 **st.** 🍾 1.75.

MICHELIN Branch 4 Spilmak Pl., Bluebell Industrial Estate, Naas Rd, Dublin 12, ☎ 509096.

ALFA-ROMEO   457 North Circular Rd ☎ 749588
ALFA-ROMEO   52/55 Lower Camden St. ☎ 783377
BMW, PEUGEOT, ROLLS ROYCE-BENTLEY, VOLVO
Lad Lane ☎ 763921
BMW, DATSUN, VOLVO Ballygall Rd East ☎ 342577
BMW, PEUGEOT, TOYOTA Rathgar Av. ☎ 979456
BRITISH LEYLAND, CITROEN Donnybrook
☎ 693055

BRITISH LEYLAND   Temple Rd ☎ 885085
BRITISH LEYLAND, DATSUN, FORD, SAAB 5/7 New
St. ☎ 780033
BRITISH LEYLAND   Northbrook Rd ☎ 970811
BRITISH LEYLAND   Richmond Rd ☎ 379162
BRITISH LEYLAND   Donnybrook ☎ 694359
CITROEN   Bluebell Av. ☎ 507887
CITROEN   Waterford St. ☎ 745821

CITROEN, MERCEDES, PEUGEOT, TOYOTA 54 Glasnevin Hill ℡ 373771
DATSUN, VOLVO Howth Rd ℡ 314066
DATSUN, VOLVO North Rd ℡ 343970
DATSUN Parkgate St. ℡ 782929
DATSUN 10 B Russel St. ℡ 723833
FIAT Milltown Rd ℡ 971098
FIAT Stillorgan Rd ℡ 886977
FIAT, LANCIA Dublin Rd, Bray ℡ 867671
FIAT, LANCIA Sandyford Rd ℡ 982389
FIAT, LANCIA 56 Howth Rd ℡ 332301
FIAT Church Pl. ℡ 973999
FIAT North Rd ℡ 342977
FIAT, LANCIA 84 Prussia St. ℡ 721622
FIAT Taney Rd ℡ 987166
FIAT, LANCIA Herberton Rd ℡ 754216
FORD 151 South Circular Rd ℡ 764131
FORD Malahide ℡ 450284
FORD 172/175 Parnell St. ℡ 747831
FORD Naas Rd ℡ 505721
FORD 40/51 Benburb St. ℡ 771521
OPEL, PEUGEOT Beach Rd ℡ 686011
OPEL 146 Cabra Rd ℡ 301222
OPEL Emmet Rd, Inchicore ℡ 755535
OPEL New Rd ℡ 592438
OPEL Lower Rathmines Rd ℡ 976661
PEUGEOT 109 Dorset St. ℡ 301400
PEUGEOT, VOLVO Maxwell Rd ℡ 973338

PEUGEOT Stillorgan Rd ℡ 885179
PEUGEOT 23 Parkgate St. ℡ 710333
PEUGEOT, VOLVO Maxwell Rd ℡ 973338
RENAULT 232 Nth Circular Rd, Grangegorman ℡ 300799
RENAULT 19 Conyngnam Rd ℡ 775677
RENAULT 27 Upper Drumcondra Rd ℡ 373706
RENAULT Newlands Cross ℡ 593751
RENAULT Malahide Rd ℡ 339948
RENAULT Merrion Rd ℡ 693911
RENAULT Crumlin Rd ℡ 752297
SAAB Upper Rathmines Rd ℡ 971227
SAAB 457 North Circular Rd ℡ 306925
SKODA-MERCEDES, TOYOTA Kilbarrack Rd ℡ 322701
SKODA, TOYOTA Smithfield Market ℡ 721222
TALBOT North Rd ℡ 343033
TALBOT South Circular Rd ℡ 780800
VAUXHALL 46 Manor St. ℡ 723490
VAUXHALL Longmile Rd ℡ 508227
VAUXHALL Swords Rd ℡ 379933
VW, AUDI-NSU, MAZDA, MERCEDES-BENZ 218/224 North Circular Rd ℡ 722011
VW, AUDI-NSU, MERCEDES-BENZ Deans Grange ℡ 893611
VW, AUDI-NSU, MAZDA, MERCEDES-BENZ Ballybough Rd ℡ 749991
VW, AUDI-NSU, MERCEDES-BENZ Harolds Cross Rd ℡ 975757

DUNDALK Louth 986 ㉒ – pop. 21,672 – ECD : Thursday – ☎ 042.
Envir. : N : Slieve Gullion** (Northern Ireland), Ring of Gullion : Cam Lough*, Ballintemple viewpoint**, Killevy Churches (site*), Bernish Rock viewpoint** – Carlingford Lough* NE : 10 m.

⌐₁₈ Blackrock, ℡ 35379, S : 3 m.

Dublin 51 – Belfast 52 – Londonderry 96.

血 Imperial, Park St. ℡ 32241, Telex 33860 – 🛗 🛏wc ☎ 🅿. ⚒ – **50 rm.**

血 Ballymascanlon House, NE : 3 ½ m. by T 1 on T 62 ℡ 71124, Telex 33860, ⚔, 🏊, 🚗, park – 🛏wc 🛏wc ☎ 🅿. ⚒. 🏊 AE ⓪ VISA
closed Christmas Day – **M** 4.50/7.00 t. 🍷 2.00 – **44 rm.**

at Rockmarshall E : 7 m. by T 1 on T 62 – ✉ ☎ 042 Dundalk :

XX **Angela's,** Jenkinstown ℡ 76193 – 🅿. 🏊 AE ⓪ VISA
closed Sunday and 2 weeks mid October – **M** (dinner only) 10.00 **st.** 🍷 2.20.

BRITISH LEYLAND The Ramparts ℡ 35514
DATSUN Dublin Rd ℡ 31595
FIAT, LANCIA Park St. ℡ 34820
FORD Dublin St. ℡ 31171
MAZDA, MERCEDES, VW, AUDI-NSU Quay St. ℡ 32279

OPEL Newry Rd ℡ 34297
PEUGEOT, VAUXHALL Newry Rd ℡ 35053
RENAULT Newry Rd ℡ 34604
TALBOT Dublin Rd ℡ 35422
TOYOTA Dublin Rd ℡ 35088

DUNFANAGHY Donegal 986 ⑬ – pop. 2,464 – ✉ Letterkenny – ⌐₁₈.
Envir: Doe Castle* 16C ruins (site*, ≼*) SE : 7 ½ m.

🛈 ℡ 63.

Dublin 172 – Donegal 54 – Londonderry 43.

☝ Carrig Rua, ℡ 14, ≼ – 🅿 – **18 rm.**

at Port-na-Blagh E : 1 ½ m. on T 72 – ✉ Letterkenny :

血 Shandon ⑤, Marble Hill Strand NE : 2 ½ m. ℡ 15, ≼ Bay and hills, ⚔, 🏊, 🚗 – 🛗 🛏wc ☎ 🅿
63 rm.

血 **Port-na-Blagh,** ℡ 11, ≼ Sheephaven Bay and harbour, ⚔, 🏊 – 🛏wc 🅿
Easter-19 September – **M** 4.50/6.00 🍷 2.25 – **58 rm** 🍵 7.50/20.00 t. – P 11.50/13.50 t.

DUNGLOW Donegal 986 ⑰ – pop. 2,956 – ✉ Lifford.
🛈 ℡ 72 (July-August).

Dublin 210 – Donegal 46 – Londonderry 61.

血 Ostan na Rosann, ℡ 91, ≼, 🏊 – 🛏wc ☎ 🅿. ⚒ – **48 rm.**

DUN LAOGHAIRE Dublin 986 ㉖ and ㊲ – pop. 53,171 – ☎ 01 Dublin.
See : Windsor Terrace ≼* over Dublin Bay. **Envir. :** Killiney Bay** SE : 2 m. by T 44.

⌐₁₈ Eglinton Park ℡ 801055.

⛴ to Fishguard (Sealink) 1 daily (5 h 30 mn) – to Holyhead (Sealink) 2-4 daily (3 h 30 mn).

🛈 ℡ 805760 and 806547.
Dublin 9.

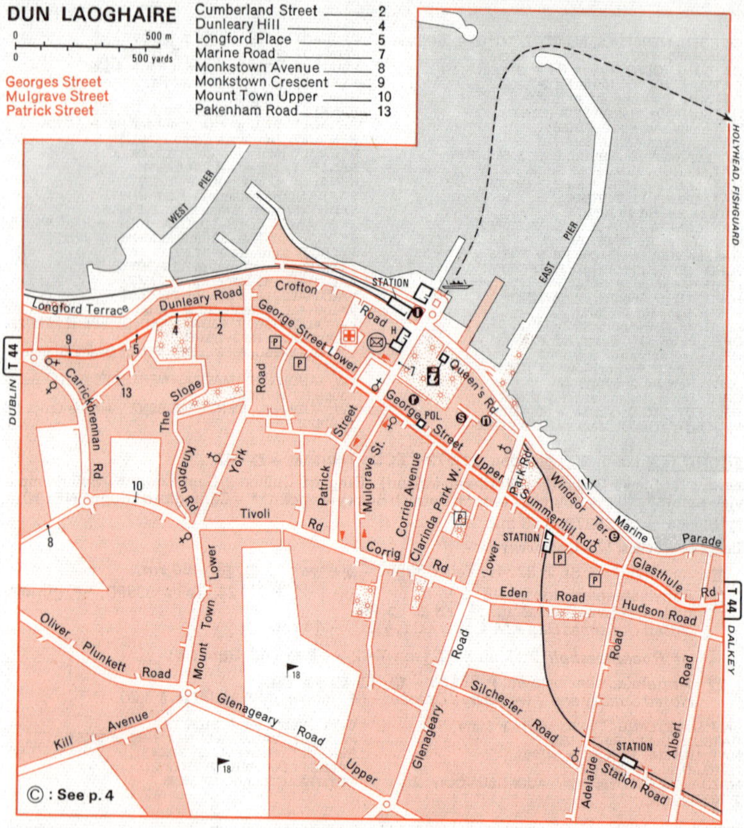

Royal Marine, Marine Rd Tel. 801911, – P. **M** 5.00/8.00 **t.** 1.50 – **115 rm** 17.50/27.50 **t.** r

Pierre, Seafront Tel. 800291 – wc P **40 rm.** n

Mirabeau, Marine Parade, Sandy Cove Tel. 809873 – AE VISA e
closed Sunday, Christmas and Bank Holidays – **M** (dinner only) a la carte 8.65/16.75 **t.** 2.50.

Na Mara, Mallin Station Tel. 806767, Seafood – AE VISA i
closed Sunday and Monday – **M** a la carte 7.00/11.50 **t.** 2.00.

Salty Dog, 3a Haddington Terrace off Adelaide St. Tel. 808015 – AE VISA s
closed Sunday, Monday, 1 week at Easter and 1 week at Christmas – **M** (dinner only) a la carte 7.40/11.65 1.65.

FORD 127 Lower Georges St. Tel. 800372
PEUGEOT Glenageary Rd Tel. 852405
RENAULT Rochestown Av. Tel. 852555
TALBOT Crofton Pl. Tel. 800341
TOYOTA, VOLVO Glasthule Rd Tel. 802991

DUNMORE EAST Waterford 986 30 – **pop. 656** – **051 Waterford.**
Dublin 109 – Waterford 10.

Ocean, Dock Rd Tel. 83136 – wc P
16 rm.

Haven, Tel. 83150, – wc wc P. AE VISA
Easter-September – **M** (bar lunch) approx. 7.00 **t.** 1.70 – **20 rm** 10.00/22.00 **t.**

Leggereste un giornale di ieri ?...
Utilizzate allora la guida dell'anno !

EMO Laois – pop. 200 – ⊠ ✪ 0502 Port Laoise.
Dublin 49 – Limerick 74 – Tullamore 20.

   Montague Motel, E: 1 ¾ m. on N 7 ☎ 26154 – ➦wc ☎ ♿ ℗. ⛲ – **20 rm.**

ENNIS Clare ⑨⑧⑥ ㉕ – pop. 5,972 – ECD: Thursday – ✪ 065.
See : Franciscan Friary★ (13C ruins). **Envir. :** Killone Abbey (site★) S : 4 m. – Dysert O'Dea (site★) NW : 6 ½ m. – Kilmacduagh monastic ruins★ (site★) NE : 16 ½ m.
₁₈ ☎ 21070.
🛈 Bank Pl. ☎ 21366.
Dublin 144 – Galway 41 – Limerick 23 – Roscommon 85 – Tullamore 93.

   Old Ground (T.H.F.), O'Connell St. ☎ 21127, Telex 8103, 🚗 – ℗. ⛲. ◩ AE ⓪ VISA
   M 5.00/8.00 t. ⌕ 1.70 – **63 rm** ⊇ 22.00/31.50 **st.** – P 27.00 **st.**

FORD Lifford ☎ 21035   VW, AUDI-NSU, MAZDA, VAUXHALL Mill Rd ☎
RENAULT Tulla Rd ☎ 22758   21505
TOYOTA Gort Rd ☎ 21904

ENNISCORTHY Wexford ⑨⑧⑥ ㉖ – pop. 10,845 – ECD : Thursday – ✪ 054.
₉ ☎ 2191.
🛈 Castle Hill ☎ 2341 (July-August).
Dublin 77 – Kilkenny 36 – Waterford 36 – Wexford 14.

   Murphy Floods, 27 Main St., Market Sq. ☎ 2592, Telex 8586 – 🏠wc ☎. ◩ AE
   closed Good Friday and Christmas Day – M 3.85/6.05 **st.** ⌕ 1.50 – **22 rm** ⊇ 9.90/
   20.60 **st.** – P 16.00/18.00 **st.**

DATSUN Templeshannon ☎ 2742   FORD Dublin Rd ☎ 2337
FIAT Ballycorney ☎ 8554   TALBOT Templeshannon Quay ☎ 2575

ENNISKERRY Wicklow ⑨⑧⑥ ㉖ – pop. 772 – ✪ 01 Dublin.
See : Site★ – Powerscourt Demesne (gardens★★★, Araucaria Walk★) *AC.* **Envir. :** Powerscourt Waterfall★ *AC,* S : 4 m. – Lough Tay★★ SW by T 43, T 61, L 161.
Dublin 17.

   Hotels and restaurant see : Bray NE : 3 m.

FAHAN Donegal – pop. 332 – ⊠ Lifford.
₁₈ Lisfannon, ☎ Buncrana 12.
Dublin 156 – Londonderry 11 – Sligo 95.

   Roneragh House, with rm, ☎ 14, ≤ Lough Swilly, 🚗 – 🏠wc ☎ ℗ – **10 rm.**

FERMOY Cork ⑨⑧⑥ ㉙ – pop. 22,156 – ECD : Wednesday – ✪ 025.
₁₈ ☎ 31472.
🛈 ☎ 31110 (June-September).
Dublin 139 – Cork 22 – Limerick 45.

   St. Annes, 2 Abbercrombie Pl. ☎ 31205, 🚗 – ℗ – **7 rm.**

GALWAY Galway ⑨⑧⑥ ㉑ – pop. 27,726 – ECD : Monday – ✪ 091.
See : Lynch's Castle★ 16C.
Envir. : NW : Lough Corrib★★★ – Claregalway (Franciscan Friary★ 13C) NE : 7 m. – Abbey-knockmoy (Cistercian Monastery★ 12C ruins) NE : 18 m. – Tuam (St. Mary's Cathedral : chancel arch★ 12C) NE : 20 m.
₁₈ Salthill ☎ 62422, W : 3 m.
🛈 ☎ 63081.
Dublin 132 – Limerick 57 – Sligo 88.

   Great Southern, Eyre Sq. ☎ 64041, Telex 8364, ◩ – 🛗. ⛲. ◩ AE ⓪ VISA
   M 5.00/8.00 t. ⌕ 2.50 – **120 rm** ⊇ 24.00/42.50 **t.**

   Corrib Great Southern, Dublin Rd E : 2 m. on T 4 ☎ 65281, Telex 8844, ≤, ◩ – 🛗 ℗
   113 rm.

   Ardilaun House ⌖, Taylor's Hill ☎ 21433, Telex 8873, 🚗 – ➦wc 🏠wc ☎ ℗. ◩ AE
   ⓪ VISA
   closed 3 days at Christmas – M 4.80/8.00 t. ⌕ 1.60 – **73 rm** ⊇ 17.00/27.00 t. –
   P 23.00/27.00.

   Galway Ryan, Dublin Rd E : ½ m. on T 4 ☎ 63181, Telex 8349, 🚗 – 🛗 ➦wc 🏠wc ☎
   ℗ – **96 rm.**

   Adare House, 9 Father Griffin Pl., Lower Salthill ☎ 62638 – ◩ AE ⓪ VISA
   10 rm ⊇ 6.50/15.00 **t.**

P.T.O. ⟶

at Salthill SW : 2 m. – ✉ Salthill – ☎ 091 Galway :

🏠 Rockbarton Park, Rockbarton Park ☏ 61717 – ⊜wc ⋔wc ☎ 🅿
11 rm.

🏠 **Banba,** ☏ 63075 – ☎ 🅿 *VISA*
M *(closed lunch from September to July)* 4.25/6.75 **st.** – **31 rm** ⇌ 9.50/19.00 **st.**

🏠 Lochlurgain, ☏ 64627 – **19 rm.**

BMW, CITROEN, OPEL, VOLVO Tuam Rd ☏ 65451	SAAB Spanish Par. ☏ 62167
BRITISH LEYLAND ☏ 62364	TALBOT, DATSUN Headford Rd ☏ 65296
DATSUN Bishop St., Tuam ☏ 24126	VAUXHALL College Rd ☏ 62044
FIAT, LANCIA Tuam Rd ☏ 63037	VOLVO Salthill ☏ 62833
FORD Headford Rd ☏ 67691	VW, AUDI-NSU, MERCEDES-BENZ Lower Salthill ☏
PEUGEOT, TOYOTA Bohermore ☏ 63664	62583
RENAULT Tuam Rd ☏ 64066	

GARRYVOE STRAND Cork – pop. 50 – ✉ Castlemartyr – ☎ 021 Cork.

Dublin 161 – Cork 23 – Waterford 62.

🏠 **Garryvoe,** ☏ 62718 – ⊜wc ⋔wc ☎. ◪ AE ⓞ *VISA*
closed Christmas Day – **M** 4.00/7.00 **st.** ⌁ 1.40 – ⇌ 2.25 – **20 rm** 6.00/11.50 **st.**

GLENBEIGH Kerry 𝟿𝟪𝟨 ㉙ – pop. 266.

⌊₁₈ Dooks ☏ 5, N : 3 m.

Dublin 211 – Killarney 21.

🏛 **Glenbeigh,** NE : ½ m. on T 66 ☏ 4, ⬿, 🚣 – ⊜wc ⋔ 🅿. AE ⓞ *VISA*
April-October – **M** (bar lunch) a la carte 7.00/9.90 **t.** ⌁ 1.75 – **21 rm** ⇌ 10.50/30.00 **t.**

🏠 **Falcon Inn,** SW : 1 m. on T 66 ☏ 56, ⬳ – 🅿. AE *VISA*
Easter-September – **M** a la carte approx. 4.10 **t.** – **15 rm** ⇌ 10.00/18.00 **t.**

XX **Towers** with rm, ☏ 12, ⬿, 🚣, Ballad Singing, Seafood – ⊜wc ☎ 🅿. ◪ AE ⓞ *VISA*
closed mid October-mid November – **M** a la carte 5.50/15.00 **t.** – **21 rm** ⇌ 11.50/33.00 **t.**

GLENCAR Kerry.

Dublin 215 – Cork 80 – Killarney 25.

🏛 **Glencar** ⬳, ☏ 102, ⬳ , XX, ⬿, 🚣, park – ⊜wc 🅿. AE
March-September – **M** (dinner only) 8.00 **t.** ⌁ 3.00 – **30 rm** ⇌ 11.00/23.00 **t.**

GLENDALOUGH Wicklow 𝟿𝟪𝟨 ㉖ – pop. 184 – ☎ 0404.

See : Ancient monastic city** (site***, St. Kervin's Church*) and Upper Lake* in Glendalough Valley***.

Dublin 34 – Wexford 71.

🏠 **Royal** ⬳, ☏ 5135, 🚣 – ▤ ⊜wc 🅿
April-September – **M** 4.85/7.80 **t.** ⌁ 2.50 – **28 rm** ⇌ 9.75/24.55 **t.** – P 21.60 **t.**

at Laragh E : 1 ½ m. on T 61 – ✉ Glendalough – ☎ Wicklow :

X Laragh Inn, ☏ 5141 – 🅿.

GLENGARRIFF Cork 𝟿𝟪𝟨 ㉙ – pop. 244.

See : Site***. **Envir. :** S : Garinish Island (20 mn by boat *AC*) : Italian gardens* – Martello Tower ❋** *AC*.

⌊₉ ☏ 29, E : 1 m.

🛈 ☏ 84 (June-September).

Dublin 224 – Cork 63 – Killarney 37.

🏠 Casey's, ☏ 10, 🚣 – ⊜wc 🅿 – **20 rm.**

GLEN OF AHERLOW Tipperary – ✉ ☎ 062 Tipperary.

See : Glen of Aherlow* (statue of Christ the King**).

Dublin 118 – Cahir 6 – Tipperary 9.

🏨 **Aherlow House** ⟿, ☏ 56153, ≼ countryside and Galtee mountains, park – ⇱wc ⋔wc
P. **AE** ⑩ **VISA**
M 4.25/8.50 **st.** ▯ 2.00 – **11 rm** ⊆ 12.50/26.00 **st.**

🏨 Glen, ☏ 56146, ⬧, ⊞ – ⋔wc ⊛ **P** – **12 rm.**

GLOUNTHAUNE Cork – see Cork.

GOREY Wexford – pop. 5,853 – ECD : Wednesday – ☎ 055.

Dublin 58 – Waterford 55 – Wexford 38.

🏨 Marlfield House ⟿, Courtown Rd E : ¾ m. ☏ 21124, ≼, « Tastefully decorated Regency
house », ⊠, ⊞, park – ⇱wc ⊛ **P**. **VISA**
closed 10 December-14 February – **M** 4.00/10.00 **t.** ▯ 2.00.

GORTAHORK Donegal – pop. 3,000 – ✉ Letterkenny – ☎ Falcarragh.

Envir.: W : Bloody Foreland Head*.

Dublin 182 – Londonderry 53 – Sligo 113.

🏨 **McFaddens,** ☏ 17 – ⇱wc **P**. **AE** ⑩ **VISA**
M 3.90/7.70 **st.** ▯ 1.75 – **35 rm** ⊆ 7.70/18.70 **t.** – P 14.50/16.00 **t.**

🏠 An Shorlan, ☏ 72, ≼ – **P**
12 rm ⊆ 4.50/9.00 **st.**

GOUGANE BARRA Cork – ✉ Macroom – ☎ Ballingeary.

See : Lake (site*). **Envir. :** SE : Shehy Mountains**.

Dublin 206 – Cork 45.

🏨 Gougane Barra ⟿, ☏ 31, ≼ lough and mountains, ⬧ – ⇱wc **P**
33 rm.

GREYSTONES Wicklow 🗺️ ㉖ – pop. 4,517 – ECD : Wednesday – ☎ 01 Dublin.

ᴛ₁₈ ☏ 874614.

Dublin 18.

🏨 **La Touche,** Trafalgar Rd ☏ 874401, ⊠, ⊞ – ⇱wc ⊛ **P**. **AE** ⑩ **VISA**
M 5.00/8.00 **t.** ▯ 1.90 – **52 rm** ⊆ 14.00/26.00 **t.** – P 20.00/25.00 **t.**

BRITISH LEYLAND, VOLVO ☏ 874494   DATSUN, SAAB ☏ 874510

HOWTH Dublin 🗺️ ㉒㉖ and ㊲ – pop. 6,990 – ✉ ☎ 01 Dublin.

See : Howth Summit ≼** – Cliff Walk ≼** – Harbour* – St. Mary's Abbey* (ruins 13C,
15C), site* – Howth Gardens (rhododendrons*, site*, ≼*) *AC.*

ᴛ₁₈ Deer Park Hotel, ☏ 322624 – ᴛ₉ Hill of Howth ☏ 322624, NE : 8 m.

Dublin 10.

✗✗ **King Sitric,** East Pier ☏ 325235, Seafood – ⧄ **AE** ⑩ **VISA**
closed Sunday, 10 days at Christmas and Bank Holidays – **M** (dinner only) a la carte
7.45/16.50 **t.** ▯ 2.00.

✗ **Abbey Tavern,** Abbey St. ☏ 322006, Ballad singing, Seafood – ⧄ **AE** ⑩ **VISA**
closed Sunday in winter – **M** (dinner only) a la carte 10.70/14.25 **t.** ▯ 1.75.

INCH Kerry – ✉ Annascaul.

Dublin 210 – Dingle 16 – Killarney 30 – Tralee 25.

🏠 **Inch Heights** ⟿, W : ¼ m. off L 103 ☏ 12, ≼ Dingle Bay and McGillycuddy's Reeks – **P**
11 rm ⊆ 6.00/12.00 **st.**

INNISHANNON Cork – see Bandon.

KANTURK Cork 🗺️ ㉙ – ECD : Wednesday.

Dublin 161 – Cork 33 – Killarney 31 – Limerick 44.

🏨 **Assolas Country House** ⟿, E : 3 ¼ m. by L 38 and L 186 ☏ 15, ≼, « Country house
atmosphere », ⊠, ⬧, ⊞, park – ⇱wc ⋔wc **P**
Easter-mid October – **M** (bar lunch residents only) 7.50 **t.** ▯ 2.60 – **7 rm** ⊆ 10.00/22.50 **t.**

MERCEDES-BENZ, TOYOTA, VW, AUDI-NSU ☏ 35

KELLS Kilkenny – pop. 423.

See : Augustinian Priory** 14C. **Envir. :** Kilree's Church (site*, round tower*) S : 2 m.

Dublin 86 – Kilkenny 9 – Waterford 23.

    ***Hotels see : Kilkenny** N : 9 m.*

KENMARE Kerry 🆈🆇🆈 ㉙ – pop. 903 – ECD : Thursday – ☉ 064 Killarney – 🐟.
Envir. : Kenmare River Valley** E : by L 62.

🛈 🕾 41233 (June-September).

Dublin 210 – Cork 58 – Killarney 20.

🏨 Riversdale House, S : ¾ m. on T 65 🕾 41299, Telex 8243, ≤, ✖, 🎣, 🚗, park – 🛏wc
🕿 🅿
40 rm.

🏨 **Kenmare Bay,** Sneem Rd, W : ½ m. by T 65 on T 66 🕾 41300, Telex 8180, ≤, 🚗 –
🛏wc 🚹wc 🕿 🅿. 🔄 AE ⓞ VISA
M 4.25/7.50 t. ▯ 2 25 – ⌲ 3.00 – **50 rm** 16.50/22.00 t.

✖ **Purple Heather Bistro,** Henry St. 🕾 41016, Seafood
Easter-mid October – **M** *(closed Sunday)* a la carte 5.55/9.25 t.

at Templenoe W : 4 m. on T 66 – ✉ Kenmare – ☉ 064 Killarney :

✖ **Rockvilla** with rm, Sneem Rd 🕾 41331 – 🅿
March-October – **M** a la carte 4.00/6.00 t. ▯ 1.00 – **8 rm** ⌲ 5.00/10.00 t.

BRITISH LEYLAND Shelbourne St. 🕾 41355   FORD Henry St. 🕾 17

KILKENNY Kilkenny 🆈🆇🆈 ㉖ – pop. 9,838 – ECD : Thursday – ☉ 056.
See : St. Canice's Cathedral** 13C – Grace's Castle (Courthouse)* – Castle (park*, ≤*). **Envir. :**
Jerpoint Abbey**(ruins 12C-15C) SE : 12 m. – Callan (St. Mary's Church* 13C-15C) SW :
13 m.

🏌 Glendine 🕾 22125, N : 1 m.

🛈 The Parade 🕾 21755.

Dublin 77 – Cork 90 – Killarney 118 – Limerick 68 – Tullamore 51 – Waterford 30.

🏨 **Newpark,** Castlecomer Rd N : ¾ m. on T 6 🕾 22122, ✖, 🚗, park – 🛏wc 🚹wc 🕿 🅿.
🔄. AE ⓞ VISA
M 4.75/9.00 t. – ⌲ 3.50 – **45 rm** 14.50/22.00 t.

🏨 **Springhill,** Waterford Rd, S : 2 m. on T 14 🕾 21122 – 🛏wc 🕿 🅿. 🔄. AE VISA
M 4.20/8.30 st. ▯ 1.50 – **48 rm** ⌲ 14.00/24.00 st. – P 25.00/28.00 st.

DATSUN Castlecomer 🕾 41358   RENAULT Irishtown 🕾 21494
FIAT Waterford Rd 🕾 22195   TALBOT Green St. 🕾 21304
FORD Patrick St. 🕾 21016   VAUXHALL Upper John St. 🕾 21140
PEUGEOT Waterford Rd 🕾 21782

KILKIERAN (Peninsula) ** Galway 🆈🆇🆈 ㉑.

KILL Kildare – ☉ 045 Naas.
🐟 at Naas 🕾 97509, SW : 3 m.

Dublin 17.

🏨 **Cill Dara,** on N 7 🕾 97064 – 🛏wc 🕿 🅿. AE ⓞ VISA
M 8.00/10.00 t. – ⌲ 3.50 – **36 rm** 14.00/20.00 t.

KILLALOE Clare 🆈🆇🆈 ㉕ – pop. 875 – ECD : Wednesday – ☉ 061.
See : Site*. **Envir. :** N : Lough Derg Coast Road** (L12) to Tuamgraney, Lough Derg***
(Holy Island : site**) – Nenagh : Butler Castle (keep* 13C) NE : 9 m.

🛈 🕾 76155 (July-August).

Dublin 109 – Ennis 32 – Limerick 13 – Tullamore 58.

🏨 **Lakeside** 🦢, 🕾 76122, ≤, 🚗 – 🛏wc 🚹wc 🕿 🅿. 🔄 AE ⓞ VISA
M 3.50/7.50 t. ▯ 1.20 – **28 rm** ⌲ 9.50/19.00 t.

KILLARNEY Kerry 🆈🆇🆈 ㉙ – pop. 7,184 – ECD : Thursday – ☉ 064.
Envir. : SW : Killarney District, Ring of Kerry : Lough Leane***, Muckross House (gardens***),
Muckross Abbey* (ruins 13C), Tork Waterfall (Belvedere : ≤**, 251 steps), Lady's View
Belvedere** – Gap of Dunloe**.

🏌. 🏌 Mahoney's Point 🕾 31034, W : 3 m.

🛈 Town Hall, 🕾 31633.

Dublin 190 – Cork 55 – Limerick 69 – Waterford 116.

🏰 **Dunloe Castle** 🦢, Beaufort W : 6 ½ m. off T 67 🕾 32223, Telex 8233, ≤, ✖, 🎾,
🎣, 🚗, park – 🛗 ♿ 🅿. 🔄. AE ⓞ VISA
Mid April-October – **M** a la carte 9.00/14.20 st. ▯ 2.70 – **140 rm** ⌲ 26.00/48.00 st.

🏰 **Europe** 🦢, Fossa, W : 3 ½ m. on T 67 🕾 31900, Telex 8213, ≤ lake and mountains, ✖,
🎾, 🎣, 🚗, park – 🛗 ♿ 🅿. 🔄. AE ⓞ VISA
March-October – **M** 7.00/9.50 st. ▯ 2.80 – **180 rm** ⌲ 20.00/48.00 st. – P 36.00/56.00 st.

🏰 **Great Southern,** 🕾 31262, Telex 6998, ✖, 🎾, 🚗, park – 🛗 🅿. 🔄. 🔄 AE ⓞ VISA
M 4.60/8.50 t. ▯ 2.00 – ⌲ 3.00 – **180 rm** 23.30/38.60 t. – P 31.15/40.25 st.

🏨 **Aghadoe Heights** ⑤, NW: 3 ½ m. by T 67 ℙ 31766, Telex 6942, ≼ countryside, lake and
mountains, 🛋 – 📺 🛁wc ☎ 🅿. 🏖. 🖪 AE ⓪ *VISA*
closed 20 December-14 January – **M** 4.25/7.50 **t.** ⱷ 1.95 – ⌲ 3.20 – **46 rm** 17.50/26.50 **t.** –
P 25.00/29.50 **t.**

🏨 Castlerosse ⑤, W: 2 m. on T 67 ℙ 31144, Telex 4404, ≼, ✗, ♨, ⚲, 🛋 – 🛁wc ☎
🅿
40 rm.

🏨 **Cahernane** ⑤, Kenmare Rd, S: 1 m. on T 65 ℙ 31895, Telex 8123, ≼, ✗, ⚲, 🛋 –
🛁wc 🛁wc ☎ 🅿. AE ⓪ *VISA*
Easter-September – **M** (bar lunch) 4.25/7.25 **t.** ⱷ 1.75 – **37 rm** ⌲ 12.00/23.00 **t.**

🏨 **International**, Kenmare Pl. ℙ 31816, Telex 8125 – 🛁wc ☎. 🖪 AE ⓪ *VISA*
M 3.75/6.00 ⱷ 1.20 – ⌲ 2.75 – **105 rm** 13.25/26.50 **t.**

🏨 Three Lakes, Kenmare Pl. ℙ 31479 – 🛗 🛁wc ☎ 🅿
70 rm.

🏨 **Dromhall**, Muckross Rd ℙ 31431 – 🛁wc 🛁wc 🅿
Easter-October – **M** 3.50/5.50 **t.** – **63 rm** ⌲ 10.00/18.00 **t.**

🏨 **Linden House**, New Rd ℙ 31379 – 🛁wc 🛁wc 🅿
closed mid December-mid January – **M** *(closed November-January and Wednesday,
Friday to non-residents)* (dinner only) 5.00 **t.** ⱷ 1.40 – **11 rm** ⌲ 7.50/10.00 **t.**

🏨 **Whitegates**, Muckross Rd S : ¾ m. on T 65 ℙ 31164, 🛋 – 🛁wc 🅿. 🖪 AE ⓪ *VISA*
M a la carte 5.70/9.80 **t.** ⱷ 1.80 – ⌲ 2.20 – **14 rm** 6.50/13.50 **t.**

🏠 Carriglea House ⑤, Muckross Rd S : 1 ½ m. on T 65/N 71 ℙ 31116, ≼, 🛋 – 🛁wc
🛁wc 🅿
9 rm.

🏠 Castle Lodge, Muckross Rd ℙ 31545 – 🅿
12 rm.

🏠 **Gardens** ⑤, Countess Rd off Muckross Rd ℙ 31147, 🛋 – 🅿
February-October – **16 rm** ⌲ 5.50/12.00 **t.**

🏠 **Loch Lein Farm** ⑤, Fossa, W : 4 m. on T 6 ℙ 31260, ≼, 🛋 – 🛁wc 🅿
Easter-October – **10 rm** ⌲ 7.50/16.00.

🏠 **Tuscar House**, Fossa, W : 3 ¾ m. on T 67 ℙ 31978, 🛋 – 🅿. 🖪 AE ⓪ *VISA*
10 rm ⌲ 6.00/10.00 **st.**

BRITISH LEYLAND Muckross Rd ℙ 31237
FIAT New St. ℙ 31416
FORD New Rd ℙ 31087

TALBOT, DATSUN Park Rd ℙ 31355
VW, AUDI-NSU, MERCEDES-BENZ 94 New St. ℙ 31190

KILLEENS Cork – see Cork.

KILLINEY Dublin 🟨🟨🟨 ㊲ – ✆ 01 Dublin.
See : Killiney Bay★★.
🚩 ℙ 851983.
Dublin 12.

🏨 **Fitzpatrick's Castle**, Killiney Hill Rd off Dalkey Av. ℙ 851533, Telex 30353, ✗, 🖪,
🛋 – 🅿. 🏖. 🖪 AE ⓪ *VISA*
M 5.00/7.50 **t.** ⱷ 2.00 – ⌲ 3.50 – **48 rm** 22.50/33.00 **t.**

🏨 **Court**, Station Rd, Killiney Bay ℙ 851622, ≼, 🛋 – 🛁wc ☎ 🅿. 🏖. AE
M 5.50/10.00 **t.** ⱷ 2.20 – ⌲ 3.50 – **10 rm** 17.00/34.00 **t.**

XXX **Rolland**, Killiney Hill Rd ℙ 851329, French rest. – 🅿. AE *VISA*
closed Sunday and Monday – **M** (dinner only) a la carte 7.30/14.25 **t.**

KILLYBEGS Donegal 🟨🟨🟨 ⑰ – pop. 1,094.
See : Fishing harbour★ – Carpet factory.
Envir. : NW: Glen Bay★★ – Glencolumbkille (site★★, folk village) NW : 14 m. – Portnoo (site★)
N : 16 ½ m.
Dublin 181 – Londonderry 65 – Sligo 57.

🏨 **Killybegs**, ℙ 120, ≼ – 🛁wc ☎ 🅿. AE ⓪ *VISA*
15 June-August – **M** 4.00/6.75 **t.** ⱷ 1.60 – **30 rm** ⌲ 11.50/24.00 – P 20.00 **t.**

KINGSCOURT Cavan 🟨🟨🟨 ㉒ – pop. 1,016.
Dublin 50 – Dundalk 31 – Tullamore 64.

🏨 **Cabra Castle** ⑤, NE : 2 m. on L 14 ℙ 60, ≼, « Converted 17 C castle », 🚩, 🛋, park –
🛁wc 🅿. 🏖
M 4.00/7.00 ⱷ 2.50 – **20 rm** ⌲ 12.00/22.00 – P 18.00/22.00 **t.**

RENAULT Corrygarry ℙ 83

TALBOT ℙ 26

KINSALE Cork 🗺️ ㉙ – pop. 1,622 – ECD : Thursday – ☎ 021 Cork.
See : St. Multose's Church* 12C.
ⓖ Ringenane ☎ 72197.
🛈 ☎ 72234 (June - September).
Dublin 178 – Cork 17.

 🏨 **Acton's** (T.H.F.), The Pier ☎ 72135, ⊲, ⊒ heated, 🍴 – 📶 Ⓟ. 🌅 AE ⓪ VISA
  M 5.00/6.75 **st.** ⧓ 2.10 – **59 rm** ⊑ 15.50/30.50 **t.**

 ♨ Blue Haven, Pearse St. ☎ 72209, 🍴
  11 rm.

 XX **The Vintage,** 50 Main St. ☎ 72502
  April-October – **M** *(closed Tuesday and Wednesday)* (dinner only) a la carte 6.50/11.00 **t.**
  ⧓ 1.75.

 ✕ **The Bistro,** Guardwell ☎ 72470
  closed Sunday, Monday and 20 December-20 January – **M** (dinner only) a la carte 6.90/
  12.50 **st.**

 ✕ The Man Friday, Village of Scilly ☎ 72260.

LAHINCH Clare 🗺️ ㉕ – pop. 455.
Envir. : Cliffs of Moher*** (O'Brien's Tower ≼** N : 1 h Rtn of foot) NW : 5 ½ m.
ⓖ, ⓖ, ☎ Lahinch 3.
🛈 ☎ 48 (June - August).
Dublin 162 – Galway 49 – Limerick 41.

LARAGH Wicklow – see Glendalough.

LEENANE Galway 🗺️ ㉑.
See : ≼* on Killary Harbour*. **Exc. :** SE : Joyces Country : by road L 100 from Leenane to
Clonbur : Lough Nafooey*, ≼* from the bridge on Lough Mask**.
Dublin 173 – Ballina 56 – Galway 41.

 🏨 Leenane, ☎ 8, ≼, ✕, 🍴 – 🚽wc ☎ Ⓟ
  38 rm.

LETTERFRACK Galway – ☎ Moyard.
Dublin 189 – Ballina 69 – Galway 57.

 🏨 **Rosleague Manor** ⚓, W : 1 ¼ m. on T 71 ☎ 7, ≼, « Country house furnished
  with antiques », 🍴 – 🚽wc Ⓟ
  Easter-October – **M** (bar lunch) 7.50 **t.** ⧓ 2.15 – **16 rm** ⊑ 10.00/23.00 **t.** – P 20.00/
  23.00 **t.**

LETTERKENNY Donegal 🗺️ ⑱ – pop. 4,930 – ECD : Monday.
See : St. Eunan's Cathedral ≼*. **Envir. :** Grianan of Aileach* (stone fort) ≼*** NE : 18 m. –
Gartan Lake* NW : 8 ½ m.
ⓖ ☎ 144, NE : 1 m.
🛈 Derry Rd ☎ 348.
Dublin 150 – Londonderry 21 – Sligo 72.

 🏨 Ballyraine, Port Rd NE : 1 ½ m. on T 72 by T 59 ☎ 411, Telex 33406, 🍴 – 🚽wc ☎ Ⓟ.
  🏕
  56 rm.

 🏠 Gallagher's, 100 Main St. ☎ 8 – 🚽wc Ⓟ
  19 rm.

ALFA-ROMEO, RENAULT Ballymacool ☎ 256   TALBOT Ramelton Rd ☎ 22
BRITISH LEYLAND Port Rd ☎ 60   TOYOTA ☎ 671
FIAT, LANCIA Railway Rd ☎ 791

LIFFORD Donegal 🗺️ ⑱ – pop. 1,121.
Dublin 133 – Donegal 34 – Londonderry 14 – Omagh 20.

 🏨 **Inter County,** Coneyburrow Rd ☎ 153 – 🚽wc ☎ Ⓟ. AE ⓪ VISA
  M 3.00/5.00 **t.** – **36 rm** ⊑ 10.50/20.00 **t.**

Envir. : Monasteranenagh Abbey* (ruins 12C) S : 14 m. by N 20 Z.

📇 Castletroy ☏ 45261, N : 2 ½ m. by N 7 Z – 📇 Ballyclough ☏ 44083, S : 3 m. by N 20 Z.

✈ Shannon Airport : ☏ 061 (Shannon) 61222 and 61444, W : 16 m. by N 18 Y – **Terminal :** Limerick Railway Station.

🛈 62 O'Connell St. ☏ 47522.

Dublin 121 – Cork 62.

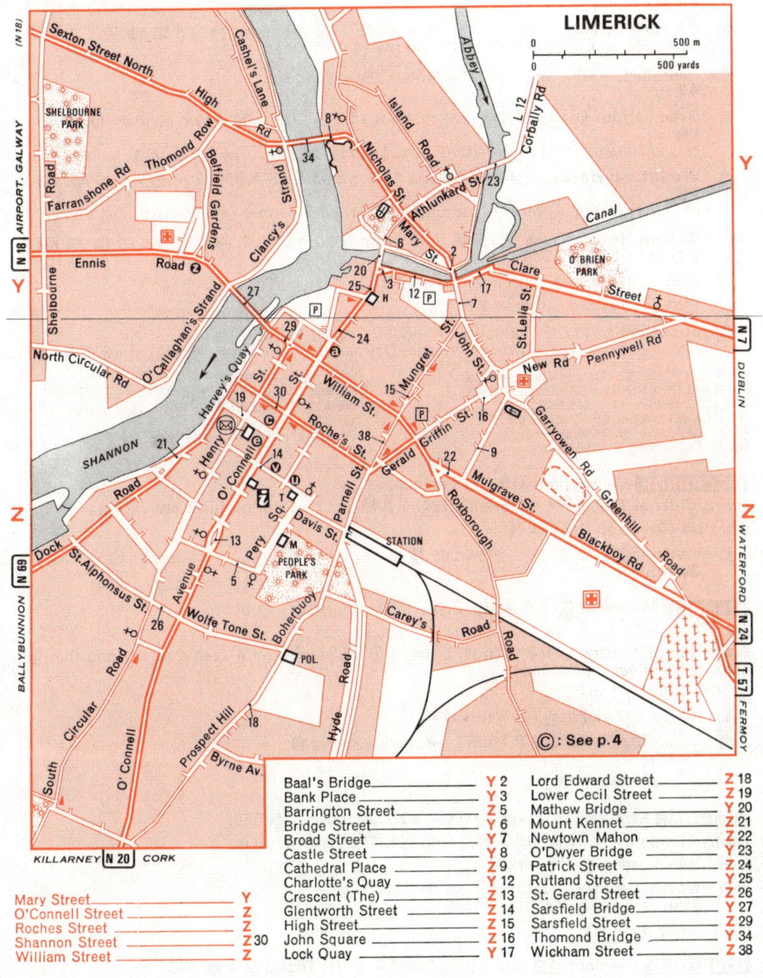

Baal's Bridge	Y 2		Lord Edward Street	Z 18	
Bank Place	Y 3		Lower Cecil Street	Z 19	
Barrington Street	Z 5		Mathew Bridge	Y 20	
Bridge Street	Y 6		Mount Kennet	Z 21	
Broad Street	Y 7		Newtown Mahon	Z 22	
Castle Street	Y 8		O'Dwyer Bridge	Y 23	
Cathedral Place	Z 9		Patrick Street	Z 24	
Charlotte's Quay	Y 12		Rutland Street	Y 25	
Crescent (The)	Z 13		St. Gerard Street	Z 26	
Glentworth Street	Z 14		Sarsfield Bridge	Y 27	
High Street	Z 15		Sarsfield Street	Z 29	
John Square	Z 16		Thomond Bridge	Y 34	
Lock Quay	Y 17		Wickham Street	Z 38	

Mary Street	Y
O'Connell Street	Z
Roches Street	Z
Shannon Street	Z 30
William Street	Z

🏨 Jury's, Ennis Rd ☏ 47266, Telex 8266, 🍴 – 📺 ♿ 🅿 **Y Z** 96 rm.

🏨 **Limerick Inn** ⓢ, Ennis Rd NW : 4 m. on N 18 ☏ 51544, Telex 32222 – 📺 ♿ 🅿 on N 18 **Y** 🆎 ① 𝘝𝘐𝘚𝘈 M 4.50/10.00 **st.** 🍷 2.00 – 🍽 3.00 – **133 rm** 17.00/26.50 **st.**

🏨 Limerick Ryan, Ennis Rd NW : 1 ¼ m. on N 18 ☏ 53922, Telex 6920, 🍴 – 🛗 🚻wc on N 18 **Y** 🅿 – **184 rm.**

🏨 **Royal George,** O'Connell St. ☏ 44566, Telex 6910 – 🛗 🚻wc 🅿 🆎 ① **Z c** 𝘝𝘐𝘚𝘈 *closed Good Friday and Christmas Day* – M 3.75/8.00 **st.** – 🍽 2.35 – **52 rm** 11.35/20.95 **t.**

🏨 **Two Mile Motor Inn,** Ennis Rd NW: 3 ½ m. on N 18 ℡ 53122 – 🛏wc 🛁wc ☎ 🅿. ⚐.
🔺 AE ⑩ VISA
on N 18 **Y**
M 4.00/7.00 **t.** – ⌁ 3.00 – **46 rm** 12.00/18.00 **t.** – P 26.00 **t.**

🏨 **Parkway Motor Inn,** Dublin Rd, E: 1 ½ m. on N 7 ℡ 47599, Telex 6850 – 🛏wc 🛁wc
☎ 🅿. ⚐. 🔺 AE ⑩ VISA
on N 7 **Z**
closed 25 and 26 December – **M** 3.50/8.00 **t.** – ⌁ 3.25 – **103 rm** 13.00/20.20 **t.**

🏨 Glentworth, Glentworth St. ℡ 43822 – 🛗 🛏wc ☎. ⚐
Z u
63 rm.

🏨 **Cruise's Royal,** 5-7 O'Connell St. ℡ 44977 – 🛗 🛏wc ☎. ⚐. 🔺 AE ⑩ VISA
Z a
M 4.50/8.00 **t.** ⚑ 2.00 – ⌁ 3.00 – **80 rm** 14.00/19.00 **t.**

🏛 Hanratty's, 4 Glentworth St. ℡ 43466 – 🛏wc 🛁wc ☎
Z v
43 rm.

🏛 **Green Hills,** Ennis Rd NW: 2 ¼ m. on N 18 ℡ 53033 – 📺 🛏wc 🛁wc ☎ 🅿. 🔺 AE ⑩
VISA
on N 18 **Y**
closed Christmas Day – **M** 4.00/7.50 **t.** ⚑ 1.50 – **25 rm** ⌁ 14.20/25.00 **t.**

🏛 **Woodfield House,** Ennis Rd NW : 1 ¼ m. on N 18 ℡ 53022 – 🛏wc ☎ 🅿. 🔺 AE
VISA
on N 18 **Y**
M *(closed Sunday dinner)* (bar lunch) 6.95 **t.** ⚑ 1.75 – ⌁ 2.75 – **25 rm** 9.50/15.95 **t.**

🏠 **Clifton House,** Ennis Rd, NW: 1 ¼ m. on N 18 ℡ 51224, 🚗 – 🛏wc ☎ 🅿. AE VISA
23 rm ⌁ 8.75/15.95 **t.**
on N 18 **Y**

✕✕ Merryman, 5 Glentworth St. ℡ 43466.
Z v

✕✕ Ted's, 102 O'Connell St. ℡ 47412.
Z e

✕✕ **Jonathan's,** 112 O'Connell St. ℡ 46050 – 🔺 AE ⑩ VISA
Z c
closed Sunday, Good Friday, Christmas Day and Bank Holidays – **M** a la carte 8.45/12.40 **t.**

BMW, CITROEN 2a Georges Quay ℡ 43133
BRITISH LEYLAND Punch's Cross ℡ 45566
DATSUN Dublin Rd ℡ 44305
FIAT, LANCIA Coonagh Cross ℡ 51577
FORD Mulgrave St. ℡ 45844
FORD Lansdowne ℡ 52244

OPEL Ennis Rd ℡ 53211
RENAULT Dooradoyle ℡ 45486
TALBOT Dublin Rd ℡ 49455
TOYOTA Ennis Rd ℡ 46111
VAUXHALL, VOLVO Henry St. ℡ 45577

LISCANNOR Clare – pop. 319 – ✆ Lahinch.
Envir.: Cliffs of Moher★★★ (O'Brien's Tower ✳★★ N: 1 h. Rtn on foot) NW: 3 m.
Dublin 165 – Galway 52 – Limerick 44.

🏛 Liscannor 🦢, ℡ 96, ⪻ – 🛏wc ☎ 🅿
36 rm.

LISMORE Waterford 🅈🅇🅴 ㉙ – pop. 884 – ECD: Thursday – ✆ 058.
See: Castle (site★).
Envir.: SE: Blackwater Valley★★ (from Lismore to the mouth, by a scenic road along the right bank of the River Blackwater).
🎣 ℡ 54026, N: 1 m.
Dublin 143 – Cork 37 – Killarney 74 – Waterford 44.

🏛 Ballyrafter House 🦢, ℡ 54002, 🚗, park – 🛏wc 🅿
14 rm.

TOYOTA Lismore ℡ 54147

LISTOWEL Kerry 🅈🅇🅴 ㉕ – pop. 3,021 – ECD: Monday – ✆ 068.
Envir.: Carrigafoyle Castle★ 15C-16C (top ✳★, 106 steps) N: 9 m.
Dublin 168 – Killarney 37 – Limerick 47.

🏠 **North County,** 67 Church St. ℡ 21238
8 rm ⌁ 5.50/10.00.

FORD Market St. ℡ 6

LONGFORD Longford 🅈🅇🅴 ㉑㉒ – pop. 3,876 – ECD: Thursday – ✆ 043.
🏌 Glack, ℡ 6310.
🎣 ℡ 6566 (May - September).
Dublin 74 – Roscommon 19 – Sligo 57 – Tullamore 47.

🏛 Longford Arms, Main St. ℡ 6296 – 🛏wc ☎ 🅿. ⚐
40 rm.

✕ Weavers Loft, Ballymahon St. ℡ 6184.

BRITISH LEYLAND Richmond St. ℡ 6217
DATSUN Drumlish ℡ 24104
FORD Dublin Rd ℡ 6421
PEUGEOT Dublin Rd ℡ 6496

PEUGEOT, VW, AUDI-NSU Dublin Rd ℡ 6321
RENAULT Athlone Rd ℡ 6615
TALBOT Dublin Rd ℡ 6221
TOYOTA Lanesboro ℡ 21159

LOUGH GOWNA Cavan – pop. 125.

Dublin 81 – Tullamore 54.

☼ **Robin Hill** ⌂, ☏ 21, 🚗 – Ⓟ
closed Monday – **M** (dinner only) 5.50 **st.** – **5 rm** ⌸ 5.50 **st.**

MACROOM Cork 986 ㉙ – pop. 2,256 – ECD : Wednesday.

🏌 ☏ 72.

Dublin 186 – Cork 25 – Killarney 30.

🏨 Castle, Main St. ☏ 74, 🚗 – 🛁wc 🚗
31 rm.

FORD Main St. ☏ 29   TOYOTA Emmet Pl. ☏ 23296

MALAHIDE Dublin 986 ㉒ and ㉝ – pop. 3,834 – ✪ 01 Dublin.

Envir.: Swords (St. Columba's Church : towers*) W : 2 ½ m. – Lusk (church : round towers*)
NW : 8 m.

🏌 ☏ 350248.

Dublin 9 – Drogheda 24.

✕✕ **Johnny's**, 9 James Ter. ☏ 450314 – 🅂 🄰🄴 ⓞ 𝘝𝘐𝘚𝘈
closed Sunday, Monday, Easter week, 9 September-mid October and Christmas week –
M (dinner only) a la carte 6.60/13.50 **t.** ▯ 2.60.

MALIN Donegal – pop. 2,723 – ✉ Lifford.

Dublin 176 – Londonderry 31.

☼ Malin, ☏ 6 – 🛁wc Ⓟ
17 rm.

MALLOW Cork 986 ㉙ – pop. 5,901 – ECD : Wednesday – ✪ 022.

🏌 ☏ 21145, SE : 1 ½ m. of Mallow Bridge.

Dublin 149 – Cork 21 – Killarney 40 – Limerick 41.

🏨 **Longueville House** ⌂, W : 3½ m. by T 72 ☏ 27156, ≤, « Georgian mansion in extensive grounds », ⌂, 🚗, park – 🛁wc 🚿wc Ⓟ
Easter-mid October – **M** (bar lunch) (booking essential) 10.00 **st.** ▯ 2.00 – **18 rm** ⌸ 10.50/
25.00 **st.**

BRITISH LEYLAND Victoria Cross ☏ 41851   OPEL Castlecor ☏ 28137
FIAT Shortcastle ☏ 21711   RENAULT Ballydaheen ☏ 21107

MOATE Westmeath 986 ㉑㉒ – pop. 1,378 – ECD : Wednesday – ✪ 0902.

🏌 ☏ 31271, N : 1 m.

Dublin 65 – Galway 67 – Roscommon 30 – Tullamore 14.

🏨 Grand, Main St. ☏ 31104 – 🛁wc Ⓟ. 🏊
10 rm.

MONAGHAN Monaghan 986 ⑱ – pop. 5,256 – ECD : Thursday – ✪ 047.

See : St. Macartan's Cathedral* 19C.

🏌 ☏ 135, 3 m. Cotehill Rd.

🅩 ☏ 81122 (May-September).

Dublin 80 – Dundalk 31.

🏨 **Hillgrove**, Old Armagh Rd E : ¾ m. off T 2 ☏ 81288, ✕ – 🛁wc 🚿wc ☎ Ⓟ
M 3.75/6.00 **t.** ▯ 2.00 – **29 rm** ⌸ 10.00/20.00 **t.**

🏨 Four Seasons, N : 1 m. on T 2 ☏ 81888 – 🛁wc ☎ Ⓟ
25 rm.

🏨 Westenra Arms, The Diamond ☏ 81517 – ☎ Ⓟ
25 rm.

BRITISH LEYLAND Old Cross Sq. ☏ 82011   VAUXHALL 15 Farney St. ☏ 61637
FORD Dawson St. ☏ 81399   VW, AUDI-NSU, MERCEDES-BENZ North
TALBOT Glaslough St. ☏ 81843   Rd ☏ 81044

MONASTEREVIN Kildare 986 ㉖ – pop. 1,897 – ECD : Thursday – ✪ 045.

Envir. : Dunamase Rock (Castle** 13C-16C ruins), site**, ※ ** SW : 12 m.

Dublin 41 – Kilkenny 44 – Limerick 80 – Tullamore 23.

🏨 Hazel, SW : ¼m. on N 7 ☏ 25373, 🚗 – 🛁wc 🚿wc ☎ Ⓟ
10 rm.

FIAT ☏ 25331

☞ *To go a long way quickly, use* Michelin maps *at a scale of 1/1 000 000.*

MOYARD Galway – pop. 382.
Dublin 187 – Galway 55.

   Crocnaraw ⚘, ₱ 9, ⬚, « Country house atmosphere », ⬚, ⬚, park – ⬚wc ℗
10 rm.

MOYCULLEN Galway – pop. 1,547 – ☎ 091 Galway.
Dublin 139 – Galway 7.

   Knockferry Lodge ⚘, Knockferry (on Lough Corrib) NE : 6 m. ₱ 80122, ⬚, ⬚ – ⬚wc
℗
Easter-September – **M** (dinner only) 5.75 **st.** ⬚ 1.40 – **10 rm** ⬚ 6.00/12.00 **st.**

MULLINGAR Westmeath 986 ㉖ – pop. 6,790 – ECD : Wednesday – ☎ 044.
Envir. : N : Lough Derravaragh* – Lough Owel* – Multyfarman (Franciscan College park :
Stations of the Cross*) – NE : Lough Lene* – Fore (St. Feichin's Church and ruined Priory*)
13C – S : Lough Ennel*.

⛳₁₈ Belvedere ₱ 8366, S : 3 m.

☒ Clonard House, Dublin Rd ₱ 8650 and 8761.

Dublin 48 – Dundalk 58 – Tullamore 21.

   Greville Arms, Pearse St. ₱ 8563 – ⬚wc ⬚wc ⬚ ℗. ⬚ AE ⓪ VISA
closed 24 to 26 December – **M** 6.00/8.00 **st.** ⬚ 2.25 – **28 rm** ⬚ 14.00/25.00 **st.**

BRITISH LEYLAND Harbour St. ₱ 8508   RENAULT Lynn Rd ₱ 8977
DATSUN Dublin Bridge ₱ 8755   VAUXHALL Patrick St. ₱ 8365
FIAT Dublin Rd ₱ 8806   VW, AUDI-NSU Millmount Rd ₱ 8437
FORD Castle St. ₱ 8347

NAVAN Meath 986 ㉒ – pop. 10,099 – ECD : Thursday – ☎ 046.
Envir. : Bective Abbey* (12C ruins) S : 3 m.

⛳₁₈ Bellinter Park ₱ 25244.

Dublin 30 – Drogheda 16 – Dundalk 34.

   Ardboyne, Dublin Rd SE : 1 m. on N 3 ₱ 23119 – ⬚wc ⬚ ℗. ⬚ – **26 rm.**

FORD Academy St. ₱ 21129   RENAULT Cannon Row ₱ 21312
MAZDA, MERCEDES, PEUGEOT, VW, AUDI-NSU Du-   TALBOT Dublin Rd ₱ 21212
blin Rd ₱ 21929   TOYOTA Kells Rd ₱ 21336

NEWBRIDGE (DROICHEAD NUA) Kildare 986 ㉖ – pop. 5,053 – ECD : Tuesday – ☎ 045 Naas.
Envir. : Kildare (St. Brigid's Cathedral* 13C-19C and round tower* 9C-10C) SW : 5 m – Tully
(National Stud*, Japanese gardens* *AC*) SW : 6 m. via Kildare – Old Kilcullen (site*, ❋*)
S : 7 ½ m.

⛳₉ Cill-Dara, ₱ Kildare 21433, Kildare Town, SW : 5 m.

Dublin 28 – Kilkenny 57 – Tullamore 36.

   Keadeen, Ballymany SW : 1 m. on N 7 ₱ 31666, Telex 4326, ⬚, park – 📺 ℗. ⬚. ⬚
AE VISA
closed 24 and 25 December – **M** 7.50/12.50 **st.** ⬚ 1.50 – **22 rm** ⬚ 25.00/35.00 **st.**

DATSUN, PEUGEOT Ballymany ₱ 31281   FIAT, LANCIA ₱ 31725

NEWPORT Mayo 986 ㉑ – pop. 1,387.
See : St. Patrick's Church*, modern Irish-Romanesque style (site*). **Envir. :** Burrishoole Abbey
(site*) NW : 2 m.

Dublin 164 – Ballina 37 – Galway 60.

   Newport House ⚘, ₱ 12, ⬚, ⬚, park – ⬚wc ⬚wc ℗. ⬚ AE ⓪ VISA
April-September – **M** 5.25/8.00 **st.** ⬚ 1.50 – **20 rm** ⬚ 14.50/26.00 **st.** – P 22.50/25.00 **st.**

BRITISH LEYLAND Castlebar St. ₱ 3   TOYOTA, VOLVO ₱ 57

Envir. : St. Mullins Monastery (site*) N : 9 m. – John F. Kennedy Memorial Park* 1968 (arboretum, ≼*) S : 7 ½ m. – SW : River Barrow Valley*.

┌9 Tinneranny ☏ 21433.

🛈 ☏ 21857 (July-August).

Dublin 88 – Kilkenny 27 – Waterford 15 – Wexford 23.

🏨 **New Five Counties,** Wexford Rd S : 1 m. on N 25 ☏ 21703, Telex 8771, 🛋 – 🛏wc ☎ 🅿. 🛁. 🖭 AE ⓪ VISA
M 4.75/8.00 **st.** ⌁ 1.50 – 🍴 2.20 – **37 rm** 13.00/21.00 **st.** – P 23.25 **st.**

🏠 **Inishross,** 96 Mary St. ☏ 21335 – 🅿
7 rm 🍴 5.50/10.00 **st.**

BRITISH LEYLAND South St. ☏ 21205   FORD Waterford Rd ☏ 21403
FIAT Rosebercon ☏ 21122   RENAULT The Quay ☏ 21415
FORD The Quay ☏ 21235

OUGHTERARD Galway 986 ㉑ – pop. 628 – ☎ 091 Galway.
See : The northern scenic road (cul-de-sac) ≼** on Lough Corrib***. **Envir.:** Aughnanure Castle* (16C) SE : 3 m. – Leckavrea Mountain* NW : 13 m. – Gortmore (≼** S : on Kilkieran Bay, ≼* NW : on the Twelve Pins) SW : 16 m.

┌9 ☏ 82131.

Dublin 149 – Galway 17.

🏨 **Sweeney's Oughterard House** ⏾, W : ½ m. on T 71 ☏ 82207, Telex 8370, « Country house set in attractive gardens », 🌳, 🛋 – 🛗 🛏wc ☎ 🅿. AE
M a la carte 4.85/9.75 **t.** – 🍴 2.00 – **31 rm** 22.00/40.00.

🏨 **Connemara Gateway Motor Inn** (T.H.F.) ⏾, SE : 1 m. on T 71 ☏ 82328, ≼, ⏋ –
🛏wc 🅿. 🖭 AE ⓪ VISA
April-October – M 5.00/7.50 **st.** ⌁ 1.95 – **48 rm** 🍴 14.00/21.00 **t.**

🏠 **Corrib,** ☏ 82329 – 🛏wc 🛁wc ☎ 🅿. 🖭 AE ⓪ VISA
M (bar lunch) 7.80 **t.** ⌁ 2.00 – **26 rm** 🍴 14.40/26.40 **t.**

🏠 **Currarevagh House** ⏾, NW : 4 m. ☏ 82313, « Country house atmosphere », 🌳, 🛋, park – 🛏wc 🅿
Easter-early October – M 3.50/7.00 **t.** ⌁ 1.70 – **15 rm** 🍴 11.50/25.00 **t.** – P 19.50 **t.**

PARKNASILLA Kerry – pop. 250 – ☎ 064 Sneem.
┌9 Parknasilla, ☏ 3.

Dublin 224 – Cork 72 – Killarney 34.

🏨 **Great Southern** ⏾, ☏ 45122, Telex 6899, ≼ Kenmare river, bay and mountains, ✖,
⏋, ┌9, 🌳, 🛋, park – 📺 🅿. 🖭 AE ⓪ VISA
Easter-December – M 12.50 **st.** ⌁ 2.50 – 🍴 2.90 – **59 rm** 19.10/32.20 – P 31.00/
35.00 **st.**

PONTOON Mayo – ✉ ☎ Foxford.
See : ⁂* – moraines*.
Envir. : Glen Nephin ≼* W : 6 m.
Dublin 141 – Ballina 11 – Galway 59.

🏠 Pontoon Bridge ⏾, NE : 1 m. on L 22 ☏ 20, ≼, ✖, 🌳, 🛋 – 🛏wc ☎ 🅿
24 rm.

PORT NA BLAGH Donegal 986 ⑬ – see Dunfanaghy.

QUIN Clare – pop. 300 – ☎ 065 Ennis.
Envir.: Tulla (site*, ancient church ⁂**) NE : 6 m.
Dublin 139 – Ennis 6 – Limerick 18.

🏠 Ballykilty Manor ⏾, SW : 1 m. ☏ 25627, 🌳, park – 🛏wc 🅿 – **11 rm.**

RAPHOE Donegal – pop. 1,257.
Envir.: Beltany Stone Circle* (site*) from the road 10 mn on foot, S : 2 m.
Dublin 139 – Donegal 29 – Londonderry 20 – Sligo 69.

🏛 **Central,** The Diamond ☏ 8 – 🛁wc
closed 24 to 31 December – M 2.40/3.50 **t.** – **10 rm** 🍴 6.00/12.75 **t.**

RATHDRUM Wicklow 986 ㉖ – pop. 2,304 – ECD : Wednesday – ☎ 0404 Wicklow.
Dublin 39 – Kilkenny 65 – Wicklow 11.

🏠 **Avonbrae House,** ☏ 6198, ✖, ⏋, 🛋 – 🛁wc 🅿. AE
Mid March-mid November – **8 rm** 🍴 9.50/16.00 **st.**

RATH LUIRC Cork 986 ㉙ – see Charleville.

 Donegal 986 ⑭⑱ – pop. 486 – ⊠ Letterkenny – ॎ.
Envir.: Mulroy Bay** NW: 8 m. – Fanad Head ⩻* N: 20 m.

Dublin 165 – Londonderry 36 – Sligo 87.

 🏰 **Rathmullan House** ⌂, N: ½ m. on L 77, ℡ 4, ⩻ Lough Swilly and hills, « Country house atmosphere », ✗, ⌁, 🚗, park – ⌂wc 🛏wc ℗. ⚡ AE ⓪
Easter-September – **M** (buffet lunch) a la carte 5.00/7.50 **st.** ⌁ 2.10 – ⌁ 1.00 – **21 rm** 9.50/29.00 **st.**

 🏰 **Fort Royal** ⌂, N: 1 m. off L 77 ℡ 11, ⩻, ✗, ॎ, 🚗, park – ⌂wc ℗
Easter-September – **M** 4.00/6.50 **t.** ⌁ 1.50 – **27 rm** ⌁ 10.00/24.00 **t.** – P 16.50/19.50 **t.**

 Wicklow 986 ㉖ – pop. 954 – ⊠ ✆ 0404 Wicklow.
Dublin 31 – Waterford 82 – Wexford 65.

 🏰 Hunter's, N: ¾ m. on L 29 ℡ 4106, ✗, ⌁, 🚗 – ⌂wc ℗
 17 rm.

 Donegal – pop. 467 – ⊠ ✆ Moville.
Dublin 162 – Londonderry 17.

 🏰 Redcastle ⌂, ℡ 73, ⩻, ॎ, ⌁, park – ⌂wc ℗. ⚓ – **20 rm.**

 Galway.
See: Castle ⩻*.
Dublin 194 – Ballina 74 – Galway 62.

 🏰 Renvyle House, ℡ 3, ⩻, ✗, ⌁, 🚗, park – ⌂wc ☎ ℗
 75 rm.

 Sligo – pop. 2.100 – ✆ 071 Sligo.
Dublin 119 – Roscommon 30 – Sligo 13.

 🏰 **Coopershill** ⌂, NE: 2 m. ℡ 75108, « Country house atmosphere », ⌁, 🚗, park – ℗. ⚡ AE *VISA*
 Easter-October – **M** (dinner only) 6.00 **t.** – **6 rm** ⌁ 7.50/12.00 **t.**

 Louth – see Dundalk.

 Donegal – ⊠ Letterkenny – ✆ Downings.
ॎ₁₈ ℡ 4.
Dublin 175 – Londonderry 46 – Sligo 97.

 🏰 Rosapenna Golf ⌂, ℡ 4, ⩻, ✗, ॎ₁₈, park – ⌂wc ☎ 🚗 ℗
 40 rm.

 Tipperary 986 ㉕ – pop. 3,855 – ECD: Wednesday.
ॎ ℡ 311, 2 m. on Dublin Rd.
Dublin 78 – Kilkenny 36 – Limerick 43 – Tullamore 28.

 🏰 **Pathé**, Castle St. ℡ 241 – ⌂wc ℗. ⚡ AE ⓪ *VISA*
 closed Christmas Day – **M** 3.50/7.00 **st.** ⌁ 1.25 – **23 rm** ⌁ 10.00/20.00 **st.**

CITROEN Grove St. ℡ 351
PEUGEOT, RENAULT Abbey Garage ℡ 38
TOYOTA Birr Rd ℡ 444

VAUXHALL Limerick Rd ℡ 403
VW, AUDI-NSU, MERCEDES-BENZ ℡ 76

 Sligo 986 ⑰ – see Sligo.

ROSSLARE Wexford 🆖🆖🆖 ㉚ – pop. 588 – ☎ 053.

🏌 ☎ 32113.

Dublin 104 – Waterford 50 – Wexford 12.

🏨 **Kelly's Strand,** Main Rd ☎ 32114, ✖, ☒, ☒ heated, ☞ – 🛗 🅿
Mid February-mid December – **M** 5.25/8.25 **t.** ⫶ 2.50 – **97 rm** ☄ 12.50/29.00 **t.**

🏠 Golf, Strand Rd ☎ 32179, ✖, ☞ – 🚻wc 🅿
25 rm.

ROSSLARE HARBOUR Wexford 🆖🆖🆖 ㉚ – pop. 725 – ☎ 053 Wexford.

🚢 Shipping connections with the Continent : to Cherbourg and Le Havre (Irish Continental Line) – to Fishguard (Sealink) 1-2 daily except Sunday mid September-mid June (3 h 30 mn).

🛈 ☎ 33232 (June - August).

Dublin 105 – Waterford 51 – Wexford 13.

🏨 Great Southern, ☎ 33233, Telex 8788, ✖, ☒ – 🅿 – **100 rm.**

ROSSNOWLAGH Donegal – ☎ 072 Bundoran.

Dublin 157 – Donegal 9 – Sligo 33.

🏨 Sand House ⏚, ☎ 65343, ← bay, beach and mountains, 🏌, ☜ – 🅿 . ᴀᴇ ⓪
Easter-September – **M** 4.50/8.50 **t.** ⫶ 2.00 – **40 rm** ☄ 15.50/25.00 **t.** – P 18.00/19.50 **t.**

SALTHILL Galway 🆖🆖🆖 ㉕ – see Galway.

SCARRIFF Clare 🆖🆖🆖 ㉕ – pop. 619.

Envir.: E: Lough Derg*** (Holy Island : site**) – SE: Lough Derg Coast Road** (L 12) to Tuamgraney.

Dublin 119 – Ennis 21 – Limerick 20.

🏠 **Clare Lakelands,** Main St., ☎ 18, ☜ – 🚻wc 🏛wc ☏ 🅿
closed 23 to 31 December – **M** 3.50/7.00 **t.** ⫶ 2.00 – **24 rm** ☄ 12.50/24.50 **t.** – P 18.00/22.00 **t.**

SCHULL (SKULL) Cork 🆖🆖🆖 ㉙ – pop. 457 – ☎ 028.

Dublin 226 – Cork 65 – Killarney 64.

🏠 East End, Main St. ☎ 28101, ☞ – 🏛wc 🅿 – **17 rm.**

SHANAGARRY Cork – ✉ ☎ 021 Cork.

Dublin 163 – Cork 25 – Waterford 64.

✖✖ ✿ **Ballymaloe House** ⏚ with rm, NW : 1 ¾ m. on L 35 ☎ 62531, ←, « Farmhouse atmosphere », ✖, ☒, 🏌, ☜, ☞, park – 🚻wc 🏛wc 🅿
closed 2 weeks late November, 24 to 26 December and 2 weeks mid January – **M** (buffet lunch) 4.00/10.00 **t.** ⫶ 1.75 – ☄ 1.20 – **23 rm** 12.50/22.05 **t.**
Spec. Ballymaloe cheese fondue, Tournedos with mushrooms, Plaice in Ballybane sauce.

SHANNON AIRPORT Clare 🆖🆖🆖 ㉕ – pop. 3,657 – ☎ 061.

🏌 ☎ Shannon 61020.

✈ ☎ 61222 and 61444 – Terminal : Limerick Railway Station ☎ 42433.

🛈 ☎ 61664.

Dublin 136 – Ennis 16 – Limerick 15.

🏨 **Shannon International** without rest., ☎ 61122, Telex 4018 – 🅿 . ☒ ᴀᴇ ⓪ 𝗩𝗜𝗦𝗔
126 rm ☄ 19.50/29.00 **t.**

SHEEHAN'S POINT Kerry.

See : ←***.

Hotels see : Caherdaniel E : 5 m.
Waterville N : 6 m.

SKIBBEREEN Cork 🆖🆖🆖 ㉙ – pop. 2,104 – ECD : Thursday – ☎ 028.

Envir : Roaringwater Bay* W : 5 m.

🏌 ☎ 82.

🛈 Main St. ☎ 21766.

Dublin 213 – Cork 52 – Killarney 67.

🏨 **Liss Ard House** ⏚, S : 1 m. on L 60 ☎ 21511, Telex 32137, ←, « Country house atmosphere », ☜, ☞, park – 🚻wc 🏛wc ☏ 🅿 . ᴀᴇ ⓪ 𝗩𝗜𝗦𝗔
M (buffet lunch Monday to Saturday) 8.50 **t.** ⫶ 2.75 – ☄ 2.00 – **10 rm** 10.00/18.50 **t.**

🏠 Eldon, Bridge St. ☎ 21300 – 🚻wc ☏ 🅿 – **26 rm.**

FORD 14 North St. ☎ 38
MAZDA, VW, AUDI-NSU ☎ 111

RENAULT Townsend St. ☎ 21091

SLANE Meath – pop. 483 – ✆ 041 Drogheda.
See: Hill of Slane (site*, ⩽ *).
Dublin 42 – Drogheda 8 – Dundalk 26.

XXX **Slane Castle,** W: 1 m. on T 26 ✆ 24207, Telex 31868, Dancing – **P**. AE
closed Monday, Tuesday and 21 to 31 December – **M** (lunch by arrangement only) a la carte 6.75/10.05 **t.**

SLIEVERUE Waterford – see Waterford.

SLIGO Sligo 986 ⑰ – pop. 14,080 – ✆ 071.
See : Sligo Abbey* (13C ruins) – Court House*. **Envir. :** E: Lough Gill*** (Innisfree*), Park's Castle (site**), Lough Colgagh**, Drumcliff (High Cross) ⩽* on Benbulbin Mountains N : 4 m. – Glencar Lough* NE: 6 m. – Carrowmore (Megalithic cemetery*) SW : 2 m.
🛈 Stephen St. ✆ 2436.
Dublin 131 – Belfast 128 – Dundalk 106 – Londonderry 88.

🏨 **Sligo Park,** Pearse Rd S: 1 ½ m. on T 3 ✆ 3291, Telex 4397, 🚗 – ♿ **P**. 🏊. 🖾 AE ⓪ VISA
M 4.50/7.50 **t.** ⱥ 1.25 – ⌓ 3.00 – **60 rm** 16.50/22.50 **t.**

🏨 **Ballincar House** 🦢, Rosses Point Rd NW : 2 ½ m. on L 16 ✆ 5361, ⩽, 🚗 – ⌐wc ⋔wc ☎ **P**. AE
M 4.00/8.00 **t.** ⱥ 2.15 – **17 rm** ⌓ 11.50/22.00 **t.**

🏨 Innisfree, Lord Edward St. ✆ 2101, Telex 33506, 🚗 – 🛗 ⌐wc ⋔wc ☎ **P**. 🏊
52 rm.

🏨 Silver Swan, Hyde Bridge ✆ 3231 – ⌐wc ⋔wc ☎ **P**. 🏊
24 rm.

at Rosses Point NW : 5 m. on L 16 – ✉ ✆ 071 Sligo:

🏨 Yeats Country Ryan, ✆ 77211, Telex 6403, ⩽, ✗ – 🛗 ⌐wc **P**. 🏊
80 rm.

✗ **Moorings,** ✆ 77112, Seafood
closed Sunday and 23 December for 4 weeks – **M** (bar lunch) a la carte 7.50/12.00 **t.** ⱥ 1.75.

AUDI-NSU Ballisodare ✆ 71291
BMW Carton Hill ✆ 2193
BRITISH LEYLAND Teeling St. ✆ 2248

FIAT, LANCIA Ballinode ✆ 2188
FORD Wine St. ✆ 2610
RENAULT Mail Coach Rd ✆ 2091

SNEEM Kerry 986 ㉙ – pop. 285 – ✆ 064.
Dublin 226 – Killarney 36.

🏩 **Cantharella Country Motel,** ✆ 45187, ⌘ – ⌐wc ⋔wc **P**. AE
April-October – **M** a la carte 6.00/7.20 **t.** ⱥ 1.75 – ⌓ 2.00 – **16 rm** 6.50/11.00 **t.**

✗ **Blue Bull,** ✆ 45231 – 🖾 AE
closed Monday dinner and Easter to May – **M** (bar lunch) a la carte 6.75/10.35 **t.** ⱥ 1.50.

SPIDDAL Galway 986 ㉑ – pop. 819 – ✆ 091 Galway.
Dublin 143 – Galway 11.

🏠 Bridge House, Main St. ✆ 83118 – ⌐wc ⋔wc **P**
14 rm.

STILLORGAN Dublin 986 ㊲ – see Dublin.

STRAFFAN Kildare – ✉ Celbridge – ✆ 01 Dublin.
Dublin 16 – Limerick 108.

🏨 **Barberstown Castle** 🦢, N : ¾ m. on L 2 ✆ 288206, ⩽ – ⌐wc **P**. 🖾 AE ⓪ VISA
M 7.00/15.00 **t.** ⱥ 1.50 – **12 rm** ⌓ 14.10/33.75 **t.**

STROKESTOWN Roscommon – pop. 563.
Dublin 88 – Roscommon 12 – Sligo 46.

🏠 Percy French, Bridge St. ✆ 46 – ⋔wc **P**
22 rm.

TALBOT ✆ 29

SUTTON Dublin – see Dublin.

TEMPLEGLANTINE Limerick – pop. 855.
Dublin 154 – Killarney 36 – Limerick 33.

⛲ Devon, ✆ 7 – ⌐wc **P** – **10 rm.**

TEMPLENOE Kerry – see Kenmare.

See : Catholic Cathedral (interior*). **Envir.** : Holycross Abbey** (12C) *AC*, SW: 4 ½ m.

🛆 ☏ 87.

Dublin 93 – Cork 73 – Kilkenny 29 – Limerick 39.

🏠 **Anner**, Dublin Rd E : ½ m. on T 19 ☏ 21799, 🚗 – 🛏wc 🅿
15 rm.

BRITISH LEYLAND Kicham St. ☏ 21288
FIAT ☏ 21377
FORD The Mall ☏ 83

MAZDA, VW, AUDI-NSU Racecourse Rd ☏ 695
TOYOTA Stradavoher ☏ 21188

TIPPERARY Tipperary 🗺️ ㉕ – pop. 16,874 – ECD : Wednesday – ☎ 062.

Envir. : S : Glen of Aherlow* (statue of Christ the King ⩿ **).

🛆 Rathanny ☏ 51119, S : 2 m.

🛈 ☏ 51457 (July-August).

Dublin 113 – Cork 57 – Limerick 24 – Waterford 53.

↑ **Ach-na-sheen House**, Waterford Rd ☏ 51298 – 🛏wc 🅿
10 rm 🍽 5.50/14.00 **st.**

TOMHAGGARD Wexford – ✉ ☎ 053 Wexford.

Dublin 101 – Waterford 47 – Wexford 9.

🏰 **Bargy Castle** ⑊, NE : ½ m. ☏ 35203, « 12C castle with country house atmosphere »,
✕, 🚗, park – 🛏wc 🅿
20 rm.

TRALEE Kerry 🗺️ ㉙ – pop. 12,287 – ECD : Wednesday – ☎ 066.

🛆 Mount Hawke ☏ 21150.

🛈 The Mall ☏ 21288.

Dublin 185 – Killarney 20 – Limerick 64.

🏰 **Ballyseede Castle** ⑊, SE : 2 ¾ m. by N 21 ☏ 21585, ⩿, « Part 15C and 17C castle »,
🚗, park – 🛏wc 🅿 🅿
13 rm.

🏰 **Earl of Desmond**, SE : 2 ¾ m. on N 21 ☏ 21299, ✕, 🍸 – 🛏wc 🚾 ♿ 🅿. 🏊. 🖥 AE
⑩ VISA
M 3.75/8.00 **st.** 🍷 2.50 – **52 rm** 🍽 14.00/24.00 **st.** – P 23.75/26.75 **st.**

🏰 Manhattan, SE : 1 ½ m. on N 21 ☏ 21233, 🚗 – 🛏wc 🚾 🅿 – **16 rm.**

BRITISH LEYLAND 100 Rock St. ☏ 21113
FIAT Ashe St. ☏ 21124
FORD Edward St. ☏ 21555
MAZDA, VW, AUDI-NSU The Market and Rock St.
☏ 21193

OPEL ☏ 22366
PEUGEOT, TOYOTA Denny St. ☏ 21688
TALBOT Rathass ☏ 22411

TRAMORE Waterford 🗺️ ㉚ – pop. 3,792 – ✉ ☎ 051 Waterford.

🛆 ☏ 81247.

🛈 ☏ 81572 (June - August).

Dublin 107 – Cork 72 – Waterford 8.

🏰 **Grand**, Market Sq. ☏ 81414, Telex 4404 – 📶 🛏wc 🚾wc ♿ 🅿. 🏊. 🖥 AE ⑩ VISA
M 4.00/7.00 **st.** 🍷 1.40 – 🍽 3.00 – **48 rm** 8.00/16.00 **st.** – P 22.00/23.00 **st.**

🎏 Shalloe's Cliff, Strand St. ☏ 81723 – 🅿 – **21 rm.**

VALENTIA ISLAND Kerry 🗺️ ㉙.

Dublin 242 – Killarney 52 – Limerick 119.

↑ **Valentia Heights** ⑊, ☏ 38, ⩿ Valentia harbour and islands – 🛏wc 🅿
April-September – **10 rm** 🍽 9.00/18.00 **st.**

VIRGINIA Cavan 🗺️ ㉒ – pop. 1,651.

Envir. : Kells (St. Columba's House* 9C – St. Columba's Church : old tower* 1783 – Churchyard
(high crosses*) SE : 11 m.

🛆 ☏ 35.

Dublin 52 – Dundalk 39 – Roscommon 56 – Tullamore 59.

🏰 **Park** ⑊, ☏ 35, ⩿, « Country house atmosphere », ✕, 🛆, 🚗, 🍸, park – 🛏wc 🚾wc 🅿.
🏊. 🖥 AE ⑩ VISA
closed mid December-mid January – **M** 5.00/7.50 **st.** 🍷 1.45 – **26 rm** 🍽 15.25/28.00 **t.** –
P 22.00 **t.**

Do not lose your way in Europe, use the Michelin

Main Roads maps, scale : **1 inch : 16 miles.**

WATERFORD Waterford 986 ㉚ – pop. 31,968 – ☎ 051.

See : Franciscan ruins of the French Church* 13C-16C (Grey Friars Street).

⌕ Newrath ☏ 4182.

🛈 41 The Quay ☏ 75788.

Dublin 99 – Cork 77 – Limerick 77.

- **Tower**, The Mall ☏ 75801, Telex 8699 – 🛗 ℗. ♨. ⟷ 𝔸𝔼 ⓓ 𝗩𝗜𝗦𝗔
  M 4.60/8.00 **st.** ⌂ 1.75 – ⌧ 3.25 – **100 rm** 14.50/24.70 **st.**

- Ardree, Ferrybank ☏ 73491, Telex 8684, ⟵ Waterford and estuary, ✗, ⚘ – 🛗 ℗. ♨
  100 rm.

- **Dooley's**, The Quay ☏ 73531 – ⌸wc ☎. ⟷ 𝔸𝔼 𝗩𝗜𝗦𝗔
  closed 25 to 27 December – **M** 5.40/8.00 **t.** ⌂ 2.00 – **31 rm** ⌧ 12.00/21.00 **t.**

  at Slieverue N : 2 m. on N 25 – ✉ ☎ 051 Waterford :

- Diamond Hill, ☏ 75543, ⚘ – ℗
  8 rm ⌧ 5.50/11.00 **st.**

BRITISH LEYLAND Bakehouse Lane ☏ 75831
BRITISH LEYLAND Arundel Sq. ☏ 75339
DATSUN Slieverue ☏ 73676
FIAT Catherine St. ☏ 74988
FIAT, LANCIA Wellington St. ☏ 32813
FORD The Mall and Cork Rd ☏ 32891
PEUGEOT, OPEL Morgan St. ☏ 74232

RENAULT 3 Michael St. ☏ 76181
TALBOT Railway Sq. ☏ 75939
TOYOTA William St. ☏ 74037
VAUXHALL Cork Rd ☏ 75844
VW, AUDI-NSU, MAZDA, MERCEDES-BENZ 22/24 The Quay ☏ 74918

WATERVILLE Kerry 986 ㉙ – pop. 547.

Envir. : Sheehan's Point ⟨*** S : 6 m.

🛈 ☏ 60 (June-September).

Dublin 238 – Killarney 48.

- **Waterville Lake** ⚲, ☏ 7, Telex 8246, ⟵ lake and mountains, ✗, ⌕, ⚲, ⚘ – 🛗 ♿ ℗. ⟷
  𝔸𝔼 ⓓ 𝗩𝗜𝗦𝗔
  April-mid October – **M** 5.70/9.00 **st.** ⌂ 3.00 – **100 rm** ⌧ 24.65/40.80 **st.**

- **Butler Arms**, ☏ 5, ✗, ⚲, ⚘ – ⌸wc ℗. 𝔸𝔼 ⓓ
  Easter-mid October – **M** (bar lunch) 8.10 **st.** ⌂ 3.00 – **40 rm** ⌧ 10.00/23.00 **st.**

- Villa Maria, ☏ 83 – ⋔wc ℗
  13 rm.

WESTPORT Mayo 986 ㉑ – pop. 3,023 – ECD : Wednesday.

See : Westport House* *AC*. **Envir. :** Croagh Patrick Mountain* (statue of St. Patrick ⟨*, pilgrimage) SW : 6 m. – Roonah Quay ⟨* on Clare Island W : 15 m.

⌕ Carrowholly ☏ 547.

🛈 The Mall ☏ 269.

Dublin 163 – Galway 50 – Sligo 65.

- Westport, The Demesne ☏ 351, Telex 6397 – ⌸wc ☎ ℗
  49 rm.

FIAT, Fairgreen ☏ 15
OPEL Belclare ☏ 284

VW, AUDI-NSU Mill St. ☏ 106

WEXFORD Wexford 986 ㉚ – pop. 11,849 – ECD : Thursday – ☎ 053.

Envir. : Johnstown Castle (the park-arboretum*) SW : 4 m.

⌕ Mulgannon ☏ 22238, SE : 1 m.

🛈 Crescent Quay ☏ 23111.

Dublin 92 – Kilkenny 50 – Waterford 38.

- **Talbot**, Trinity St. ☏ 22566, Telex 8658, ⟷ – 🛗 ℗. ♨. ⟷ 𝔸𝔼 ⓓ 𝗩𝗜𝗦𝗔
  M 6.50/9.50 **t.** ⌂ 2.00 – ⌧ 3.50 – **116 rm** 11.50/25.00 **t.**

- **White's**, Abbey St. ☏ 22311, Telex 8630 – 🛗 ℗. ♨. ⟷ 𝔸𝔼 ⓓ 𝗩𝗜𝗦𝗔
  M 6.50/7.00 **t.** – ⌧ 3.00 – **97 rm** 16.00/25.00 **t.** – P 24.00/26.00 **t.**

- **Ferrycarrig Castle** ⚲, Ferrycarrig Bridge NW : 2 ¾ m. on N 11 ☏ 22999, ⟨, ✗ – 🛗
  ⌸wc ☎ ℗. 𝔸𝔼 ⓓ 𝗩𝗜𝗦𝗔
  April-October – **M** (bar lunch) 6.00 **t.** ⌂ 2.15 – ⌧ 2.00 – **40 rm** 13.20/22.80 **t.**

- **Kincone Lodge Motor**, N : ¾ m. on L 29 ☏ 23661 – ⌸wc ⋔wc ℗. 𝔸𝔼 𝗩𝗜𝗦𝗔
  closed Christmas – **M** (bar lunch) a la carte 7.50/9.75 **t.** – **17 rm** ⌧ 13.50/18.50 **t.**

- **Whitford House**, New Line Rd, SW : 2 m. on L 159 ☏ 23405, ⟷ – ⌸wc ⋔wc ℗
  22 rm ⌧ 6.75/14.00 **st.**

BMW, OPEL Ferrybank ☏ 22107
BRITISH LEYLAND Ballycanew, Gorey ☏ 21282
DATSUN Enniscorthy ☏ 8554
DATSUN Blackwater ☏ 29110
FORD Ferrybank ☏ 23329
PEUGEOT, RENAULT The Faythe ☏ 22998

TALBOT Redmond Rd ☏ 23133
TOYOTA Custom House Quay ☏ 22165
VAUXHALL Ardcavan ☏ 22561
VW, AUDI-NSU, MERCEDES-BENZ Westgate ☏ 22011
VW, AUDI-NSU, MAZDA, MERCEDES Drinagh ☏ 22377

Envir. : Ashford (Mount Usher or Walpole's Gardens* *AC*, NW : 4 m.

Dublin 33 – Waterford 84 – Wexford 67.

Grand, Main St. ☎ 2337 – ⌷wc **P**
22 rm.

Knockrobin House ⤴ with rm, NW : 1 ½ m. on Dublin Rd ☎ 2344, 🚗 – ⌷wc **P**
AE
March-October – **M** (dinner only and Sunday lunch) a la carte approx. 11.00 **st.** ⌷ 1.60 –
4 rm ⌷ 9.00/18.00 **st.**

FIAT Bollarney ☎ 2212   VW, AUDI-NSU The Glebe ☎ 2126
FORD Whitegates ☎ 2331

WOODENBRIDGE Wicklow – ✉ ☎ 0402 Arklow.

Avoca, Arklow ☎ 5202.

Dublin 48 – Waterford 71 – Wexford 54.

Woodenbridge, ☎ 5146, ⤴, 🚗 – **P**. 🔺 AE ⓪
closed Good Friday and Christmas Day – **M** 3.50/6.50 **st.** ⌷ 1.75 – **12 rm** ⌷ 8.50/
15.00 **st.**

See : St. Mary's Collegiate Church* 13C. **Envir. :** Ardmore (site*, round tower* 10C, cathedral
ruins* 12C, ≼*) E : 5 ½ m.

Knockaverry ☎ 2447.

☐ ☎ 2390 (June-September).

Dublin 146 – Cork 30 – Waterford 47.

Hilltop, W : 1 ½ m. on N 25 ☎ 2577 – ⌷wc ☎ **P**
April-October – **M** 3.80/7.50 **st.** ⌷ 2.00 – **50 rm** ⌷ 15.00/24.00 **st.**

Aherne's Seafood Bar, 163 North Main St. ☎ 2424 – **P**. AE VISA
closed Sunday lunch and Monday dinner – **M** a la carte 5.50/9.45 **t.** ⌷ 1.20.

FIAT North Main St. ☎ 2470   RENAULT North Abbey ☎ 2354

TRAFFIC SIGNS
A few important signs

SIGNALISATION ROUTIÈRE
Quelques signaux routiers importants

SEGNALETICA STRADALE
Alcuni segnali importanti

VERKEHRSZEICHEN
Die wichtigsten Straßenverkehrszeichen

Please note : The maximum speed limits in Great Britain are 70 mph (112 km/h) on motorways and dual carriageways and 60 mph (96 km/h) on all other roads, except where a lower speed limit is indicated. In the Republic of Ireland the wearing of seat belts is mandatory.

N.B. N'oubliez pas qu'il existe des limitations de vitesse en Grande-Bretagne : 70 mph (112 km/h) sur routes à chaussée séparée et autoroutes, 60 mph (96 km/h) sur autres routes, sauf indication d'une vitesse inférieure. En République d'Irlande, le port de la ceinture de sécurité est obligatoire.

N.B. In Gran Bretagna esistono dei limiti di velocità : 70 mph (112 km/h) sulle strade a doppia carreggiata e autostrade, 60 mph (96 km/h) sulle altre strade, salvo che sia indicata una velocità inferiore. Nella Repubblica d'Irlanda é obbligatorio l'uso delle cinture di sicurezza.

Zur Beachtung : In Großbritannien gelten folgende Geschwindigkeitsbegrenzungen : 70 mph (112 km/h) auf Autobahnen und Straßen mit getrennten Fahrbahnen, 60 mph (96 km/h) auf allen anderen Straßen, wenn keine niedrigere Geschwindigkeit angezeigt ist. In der Republik Irland besteht Gurtanlegepflicht.

Warning signs — *Signaux d'avertissement*
Segnali di avvertimento — *Warnzeichen*

T junction
Jonction avec autre route
Confluenza con altra strada
Straßeneinmündung

Right-hand lane closed
Voie de droite barrée
Corsia di destra sbarrata
Rechte Fahrbahn gesperrt

Roundabout
Sens giratoire
Senso rotatorio
Kreisverkehr

Quayside or river bank
Débouché sur un quai ou une berge
Banchina o argine senza sponda
Ufer

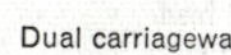

Dual carriageway ends

Fin de chaussée à deux voies

Fine di doppia carreggiata

Ende der zweispurigen Fahrbahn

Two-way traffic crosses one-way road
Voie à deux sens croisant voie à sens unique
Strada a due sensi che incrocia una strada a senso unico
Straße mit Gegenverkehr kreuzt Einbahnstraße

Change to opposite carriageway

Déviation sur chaussée opposée

Deviazione sulla carreggiata opposta

Überleitung auf Gegenfahrbahn

Level crossing with automatic half barriers ahead
Passage à niveau automatique
Passaggio a livello automatico con semi-barriere
Bahnübergang mit automatischen Halbschranken

Distance to give way sign ahead
Cédez le passage à 50 yards
Dare la precedenza a 50 iarde
Vorfahrt gewähren in 50 yards Entfernung

Height limit
Hauteur limitée (en pieds et pouces)
Altezza limitata (piedi e pollici)
Maximale Höhe (in Fuß und Zoll)

Ralentir maintenant

Rallentare subito

Geschwindigkeit verringern

Opening or swing bridge
Pont mobile
Ponte mobile
Bewegliche Brücke

Signs giving orders
Signaux de prescriptions absolues
Segnali di prescrizione (di divieto o d'obbligo)
Gebots- und Verbotszeichen

End of speed limit
Fin de limitation de vitesse
Fine di limitazione di velocità
Ende der Geschwindigkeitsbeschränkung

School crossing patrol
Sortie d'école
Uscita di scolari
Achtung Schule

No stopping (« clearway »)

Arrêt interdit

Fermata vietata

Halteverbot

All vehicles prohibited
(plate gives details)
Circulation interdite à tous véhicules
(plaque donnant détails)
Divieto di transito a tutti i veicoli (la
placca sottostante fornisce dei dettagli)
Verkehrsverbot für Fahrzeuge aller Art
(näherer Hinweis auf Zusatzschild)

Give priority to vehicles from opposite
direction
Priorité aux véhicules venant de face
Dare la precedenza ai veicoli che proven-
gono dal senso opposto
Dem Gegenverkehr Vorrang gewähren

Voie à stationnement réglementé

Sosta regolamentata

Fahrbahn mit zeitlich begrenzter
Parkerlaubnis

Width limit
Largeur limitée (en pieds et pouces)
Larghezza limitata (piedi e pollici)
Breite begrenzt (in Fuß und Zoll)

Plate below sign at end of prohibition
Fin d'interdiction
Fine del divieto posta sotto il segnale
Ende einer Beschränkung

Information signs
Signaux de simple indication
Segnali di indicazione
Hinweiszeichen

One-way street
Rue à sens unique
Via a senso unico
Einbahnstraße

No through road
Voie sans issue
Strada senza uscita
Sackgasse

Accès à une chaussée à deux voies

Accesso ad una carreggiata a due corsie

Zufahrt zu einer zweispurigen Fahrbahn

Ring road
Voie de contournement
Strada di circonvallazione
Ringstraße

Warning signs on rural motorways
Signaux d'avertissement sur autoroutes
Segnali di avvertimento su autostrade
Warnzeichen auf Autobahnen

Maximum advised speed
Vitesse maximum conseillée
Velocità massima consigliata
Empfohlene Höchstgeschwindigkeit

1 Lane closed
1 voie barrée
1 Corsia sbarrata
1 Fahrstreifen gesperrt

Count-down markers at exit from motorway or primary route

Balises situées sur autoroute ou route principale et annonçant une sortie

Segnali su autostrada annuncianti un'uscita

Hinweise auf Abfahrten an Autobahnen und Hauptverkehrsstraßen

Road clear

Route libre

Strada libera

Straße frei

Direction to service area, with fuel, parking, cafeteria and restaurant facilities.

Indication d'aire de service avec carburant, parc à voitures, cafeteria et restaurant.

Indicazione di area di servizio con carburante, parcheggio, bar e ristorante

Hinweis auf Tankstelle, Parkplatz, Cafeteria und Restaurant

Warning signs on urban motorways
Signaux d'avertissement sur autoroutes urbaines
Segnali di avvertimento su autostrade urbane
Warnzeichen auf Stadtautobahnen

_1_   _2_   _3_

  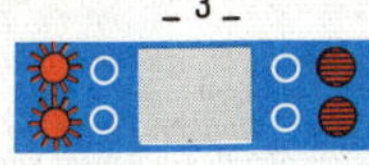

The insets show (flashing amber lights) (1) advised maximum speed, (2) lane to be used; (3) (flashing red lights), you must stop.

L'ensemble de ces panneaux indique : (1) la vitesse maximale conseillée, (2) la voie à utiliser (signaux lumineux jaunes) ; (3) l'arrêt obligatoire (signaux lumineux rouges).

L'insieme di questi segnali indica : (1) la velocità massima consigliata, (2) la corsia da imboccare (segnali luminosi gialli) ; (3) la fermata obbligatoria (segnali luminosi rossi).

Diese Schilder (mit blinkenden Ampeln) weisen hin auf : 1. die empfohlene Höchstgeschwindigkeit, 2. die zu befahrende Fahrbahn (gelbes Licht) und 3. Halt (rotes Licht).

In town — *En ville*
In città — in der Stadt

SIGNALISATION SHOWN ON OR ALONG KERBS

SIGNALISATION MATÉRIALISÉE SUR OU AU LONG DES TROTTOIRS

SEGNALI TRACCIATI SOPRA O LUNGO I MARCIAPIEDI

ZEICHEN AUF ODER AN GEHWEGEN

OTHER ROAD SIGNS

AUTRES PANNEAUX

ALTRI CARTELLI INDICATORI

ZUSÄTZLICHE VERKEHRSZEICHEN

No waiting during every working day
Stationnement interdit tous les jours ouvrables
Sosta vietata nei giorni feriali con indicazioni complementari
Parkverbot an Werktagen

Stationnement interdit de 8 h 30 à 18 h 30 du lundi au samedi
Sosta vietata da lunedì a sabato dalle 8,30 alle 18,30
Parkverbot Montag bis Samstag von 8.30 bis 18.30 Uhr

No loading or unloading during every working day
Livraisons interdites tous les jours ouvrables
Carico e scarico vietato nei giorni feriali con indicazioni complementari
Be- und Entladen verboten an allen Werktagen

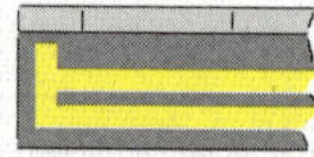

No waiting during every working day and additional times
Stationnement interdit tous les jours ouvrables plus autres périodes indiquées sur panneaux
Divieto di sosta tutti i giorni feriali e negli altri periodi indicati sul cartello
Parkverbot an Werktagen und den auf Zusatzschildern angegebenen Zeiten

---

No loading or unloading during every working day and additional times
Livraisons interdites tous les jours ouvrables plus autres périodes indiquées sur panneaux
Divieto di carico e scarico tutti i giorni feriali e negli altri periodi indicati sul cartello
Be- und Entladen verboten an Werktagen und den auf Zusatzschildern angegebenen Zeiten

---

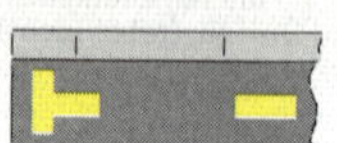

No waiting during any other periods
Stationnement interdit à toute autre période
Sosta vietata in determinate ore
Parkverbot zu bestimmten Zeiten

No loading or unloading during any other periods
Livraisons interdites à toute autre période
Divieto di carico e scarico in determinate ore
Be- und Entladeverbot zu bestimmten Zeiten

Livraisons interdites de 8 h 30 à 18 h 30 du lundi au samedi
Carico e scarico vietato da lunedì a sabato dalle 8,30 alle 18,30
Be- und Entladen verboten von Montag bis Samstag von 8.30 bis 18.30 Uhr

---

Stationnement interdit en permanence

Divieto permanente di sosta

Parkverbot zu jeder Zeit

Livraisons interdites en permanence

Divieto permanente di carico e scarico

Be- und Entladeverbot zu jeder Zeit

Stationnement limité à 20 mn de 8 h à 18 h
Sosta limitata a 20 mn dalle 8 alle 18
Höchstparkdauer 20 min. in der Zeit von 8.00 bis 18.00 Uhr

Livraisons interdites du lundi au vendredi de 8 h à 9 h 30 et de 16 h 30 à 18 h 30
Carico e scarico vietato da lunedì a venerdì dalle 8 alle 9,30 e dalle 16,30 alle 18,30
Be- und Entladeverbot Montag bis Freitag von 8.00 bis 9.30 und von 16.30 bis 18.30 Uhr

---

Remember : speed limit in Great Britain 70 mph and in Eire 60 mph.

Direction signs on the road network
Panneaux de direction sur le réseau routier
Cartelli direzionali sulla rete stradale
Richtungsschilder auf den Straßen

Michelin maps

Cartes Michelin

Carte Michelin

Michelin-Karten

Motorways and A (M) class roads

Sur autoroutes et routes classées A (M)

Sulle autostrade e strade classificate A (M)

Autobahn M und Schnellstraße A (M)

Primary routes

Apart from motorways, « Primary routes » provide the major road network linking towns of local and national traffic importance

Sur grands itinéraires routiers « Primary routes »

En complément du système autoroutier, les grands itinéraires constituent un réseau de routes recommandées reliant les villes selon leur importance dans le trafic national

Sui principali itinerari stradali (Primary routes)

I principali itinerari, unitamente alle autostrade, costituiscono una rete di strade consigliate che collegano le città secondo la loro importanza nel traffico nazionale

Empfohlene Fernverkehrsstraßen (Primary routes)

Sie bilden ein überregionales Straßennetz, das verkehrswichtige Orte verbindet ; sie ergänzen das Autobahnnetz

Other A class roads

Sur autres routes classées A

Sulle altre strade classificate A

Andere Straße der Kategorie A

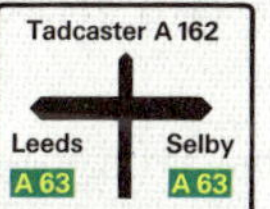

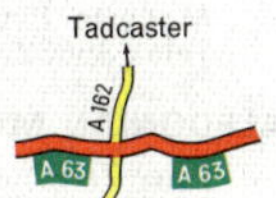

B class roads

Sur routes classées B

Sulle strade classificate B

Straße der Kategorie B

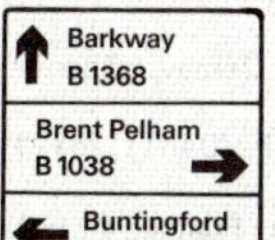

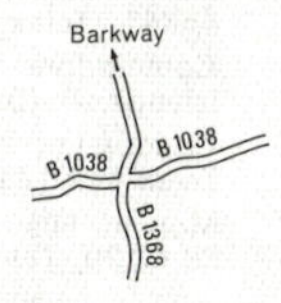

Unclassified roads — Local direction sign

Sur routes non classées — Signalisation locale

Sulle strade non classificate — Segnaletica locale

Nicht klassifizierte Straßen — Örtliche Richtungsschilder

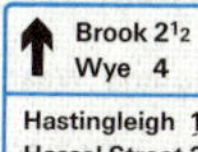

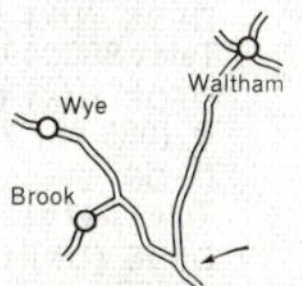

ADDRESSES OF SHIPPING COMPANIES AND THEIR PRINCIPAL AGENTS

ADRESSES DES COMPAGNIES DE NAVIGATION ET DE LEURS PRINCIPALES AGENCES

INDIRIZZI DELLE COMPAGNIE DI NAVIGAZIONE E DELLE LORO PRINCIPALI AGENZIE

ADRESSEN DER SCHIFFAHRTSGESELLSCHAFTEN UND IHRER WICHTIGSTEN AGENTUREN

BALTIC SHIPPING CO.

C.T.C. Lines (UK), 1-3 Lower Regent St., London, SW1Y 4NN, ☏ (01) 930 5833, Telex 917193.

Oy Saimaa Lines, P. Makasiinikatu, 7A P.O. Box 008 SF-00131, Helsinki 13, Finland, Telex 122384.

Baltic Shipping Co, 35 Herzen St., Leningrad 19 00 00, U.S.S.R. ☏ 211 77 76, Telex 551.

B & I LINE

British & Irish Steam Packet Co., Ltd, 155 Regent St., London, W1R 7FD, ☏ (01) 734 4681, Telex 23523.

6-8 Temple Row, Birmingham, B2 5HG, ☏ (021) 236 5552.

16 Westmoreland St., Dublin 2, Eire, ☏ (01) 778271, Telex 5651.

46 Patrick St., Cork, Eire, ☏ (021) 504100, Telex 6137.

Reliance House, Water St., Liverpool, L2 8TP, ☏ (051) 227 3131, Telex 627839.

28 Cross St., Manchester, M2 3NH, ☏ (061) 834 1332.

BRITISH RAIL see SEALINK and SOLENT SEASPEED

BRITTANY FERRIES

Millbay Docks, Plymouth, PL1 3EF, Devon, ☏ (0752) 21321.

Norman House, Albert Johnson Quay, Portsmouth, PO2 7AE, Hampshire, ☏ (0705) 27701.

Gare Maritime, 35400 St-Malo, France, ☏ (99) 56.42.29, Telex 950487.

Gare Maritime, Roscoff, Port du Bloscon 29211, France, ☏ (98) 69-07-20, Telex 940360.

Tourist House, 42 Grand Parade, Cork ☏ (021) 507666, Telex 32088.

Modesto Pineiro & Co., 27 Paseo de Pereda, Santander, Spain, ☏ (942) 214500, Telex 35832.

CALEDONIAN MACBRAYNE LTD.

Ferry Terminal, Gourock, PA19 1QP, Strathclyde, Scotland, ☏ (0475) 33755, Telex 779318.

COMMODORE SHIPPING CO. AND CONDOR LTD.

Commodore House, Bulwer Av., St. Sampsons, Guernsey, Channel Islands, ☏ (0481) 46841, Telex 419 1289.

Commodore Shipping Services Ltd., 28 Conway St., St. Helier, Jersey, Channel Islands, ☏ (0534) 36331, Telex 419 2079.

Condor Ltd, 4 North Quay, P.O. Box 33, St. Peter Port, Guernsey ☏ (0481) 26121, Telex 419 1417.

Morvan Fils, 4, rue des Cordiers et Gare Maritime, 35400 St-Malo, France, ☏ (99) 56.42.29, Telex 950486.

DFDS DANISH SEAWAYS

DFDS (UK) Ltd., Mariner House, Pepys St., London, EC3N 4BX, ☏ (01) 481 3211, Telex 883049.

DFDS (UK) Ltd., Tyne Commission Quay, North Shields, NE29 6EE, Tyne and Wear, ☏ (089 45) 78115, Telex 537285.

DFDS Ekspedition Englandskajen, DK-6700 Esbjerg, Denmark, ☏ (05) 12.17.00, Telex 54151.

DFDS (UK) Ltd., Parkeston Quay, Harwich, CO12 4SY, Essex, ☏ (025 55) 4411, Telex 98582.

EMERAUDE FERRIES

Gare Maritime du Naye, 35400 St. Malo, France ℡ (99) 56.61.46, Telex 950271.
Marine Management, 17a York St., St. Helier, Jersey ℡ (0534) 74458, Telex 419 2029.

FRED. OLSEN-BERGEN LINE

Fred. Olsen-Bergen Lines, 229 Regent St., London, W1R 8AP, ℡ (01) 437 9888.
Fred. Olsen Co, Reisebyra, Prinsensgt. 2B, Oslo, Norway, ℡ 41.50.70.
Fred. Olsen-Bergen Lines, P.O. Box 82, 4601 Kristiansand, Norway, ℡ 26500.
Fred. Olsen-Bergen Line, P.O. Box 4121, 5015 Dreggen, Bergen, Norway, ℡ 21.00.20.

HERM SEAWAY MARINE LTD, HERM EXPRESS FERRY AND TRIDENT CHARTER CO.

Herm Seaway Marine Ltd, Castle Emplacement, St. Peterport, Guernsey ℡ (0481) 24161 and 26829.
Herm Express Ferry, Crown Pier, St. Peterport, Guernsey ℡ 0481 (21342).
Trident Charter Co., Weigh Bridge, St. Peterport, Guernsey ℡ 0481 (21379).

HOVERLLOYD LTD.

49 Charles St., London W1X 8AE, ℡ (01) 493 5525.
International Hoverport, Pegwell Bay, Ramsgate, CT12 5HS, Kent, ℡ 0843 (Thanet) 54881.
International Hoverport, 62226 Calais Cedex, France, ℡ 96-67-10.
Hoverlloyd Ltd., 24 rue de St-Quentin, 75010 Paris, France, ℡ 278.75.05.

HOVERTRAVEL LTD.

Quay Road, Ryde, Isle of Wight, ℡ (0983) 65241.
Clarence Pier, Southsea, Portsmouth, PO5 3AD, Hampshire, ℡ (0705) 29988.

IRISH CONTINENTAL LINE LTD.

19/21 Aston Quay, Dublin 2, Eire, ℡ (01) 774331, Telex 30355.
Agent: P & O Ferries (Normandy Ferries), Gare Maritime, Route du Môle Central, 76061 Le Havre, France, ℡ (35) 26.57.26, Telex 190736.
Truckline Ferries, Quai de Normandie, 50100 Cherbourg, ℡ (33) 53.46.30, Telex 171432.
Transport et Voyages, 8, rue Auber, 75441 Paris Cedex 09, ℡ 266.90.90, Telex 660400.

ISLE OF MAN STEAM PACKET CO. LTD.

P.O. Box 5, Douglas, Isle of Man, ℡ (0624) 3824, Telex 629414.
McBride's Shipping Agencies Ltd., 241A West George St., Glasgow, G2 4QR, Scotland, ℡ (041) 248 5161, Telex 77181.
W.E. Williames & Co. Ltd., 35/39 Middlepath St. Belfast, Northern Ireland, ℡ (0232) 55411, Telex 747166.
British & Irish Steam Packet Co. Ltd., 16 Westmoreland St., Dublin, Eire ℡ (01) 778271
India Buildings, 40 Brunswick St., Liverpool 2, ℡ (051) 236 3214, Telex 629415.

ISLE OF SARK SHIPPING CO. LTD.

White Rock, St. Peter Port, Guernsey, Channel Islands, ℡ (0481) 24059, Telex 419 1549.
The Avenue, Rue Lucas, Sark, Channel Islands, ℡ 10.

ISLES OF SCILLY STEAMSHIP CO. LTD.

St. Mary's, Isles of Scilly, ℡ 072 04 (Scillonia) 22357/8.
16 Quay St., TR18 4BD, Penzance, Cornwall, ℡ (0736) 2009/4013.

MANX LINE

Manx Line Ltd., Sea Terminal, Douglas, Isle of Man ℡ (0624) 24241.
The Harbour, Heysham, Lancashire ℡ (0524) 53802.

NORFOLK LINE

Atlas House, Southgates Rd, Great Yarmouth, Norfolk, ℡ (0493) 56133, Telex 97449.
Norfolk Line BV, P.O. Box 84214, 2508 AE Scheveningen, Netherlands, ℡ (070) 514601, Telex 31515.

NORTH SEA FERRIES LTD.

King George Dock, Hedon Rd, Hull, HU9 5QA, North Humberside, ℙ (0482) 795141, Telex 52349.

Noordzee Veerdiensten B.V., Beneluxhaven, Netherlands, Europoort, P.O. Box 1123 Rozenburg 3180 AC, ℙ (01819) 62077, Telex 26571.

Prins Fillipsdok, Lanceloot Blondeellaan, 8380 Zeebrugge, Belgium, ℙ (050) 545601, Telex 81469.

OLAU-LINE LTD.

Sherness Docks, Sheerness, ME12 1SN, Kent, ℙ (079 56) 4981, Telex 965605.

Olau-Line (Nederland) B.V., Buitenhaven, Postbus 231, Vlissingen (Flushing), Netherlands, ℙ (01184) 65400, Telex 55317.

ORKNEY ISLANDS SHIPPING CO. LTD.

4 Ayre Road, Kirkwall, Orkney Islands, Scotland, ℙ (0856) 2044.

P & O FERRIES LTD., IRISH SEA SERVICES

94 High St., Belfast BT1 2DH, Northern Ireland, ℙ (0232) 23636 and 34534.

Seaway House, St. Nicholas Pl., Liverpool, L3 0AA, ℙ (051) 236 5464.

P & O NORMANDY FERRIES

Arundel Towers, Portland Terrace, Southampton, SO9 4AE, Hampshire, ℙ (0703) 34141, Telex 47485.

Eastern Docks, Dover, ℙ (0304) 205069, Telex 965726.

9 Place de la Madeleine, 75008 Paris, France, ℙ 266.40.17.

Route du Môle Central, BP. 1031, 76061 Le Havre, France, ℙ (35) 26.57.26.

Gare Maritime, Quai de Chanzy, 62204 Boulogne Sur-Mer, France, ℙ (21) 31.78.00.

P & O FERRIES, ORKNEY & SHETLAND SERVICES

P.O. Box 5, Ferry Terminal, Jamiesons Quay, Aberdeen, AB9 8DL, Scotland, ℙ (0224) 572615.

Scrabster Ferry Terminal, Highland, Scotland, ℙ (0847) 2052.

Harbour Street, Kirkwall, Orkney Islands, Scotland, ℙ (0856) 3330.

Holmsgarth Terminal, Lerwick, Shetland Islands, Scotland, ℙ (0595) 4848.

Ferry Terminal, Stromness, Orkney Islands, Scotland, ℙ (0856) 850 655.

PRINS FERRIES

Prins Ferries (Lion Ferry AB, Halmstad, Sweden), 13-14 Queen St., London, W1X 8BA, ℙ (01) 629 7961 and 491 7641, Telex 264311.

Hadag Seetouristik und Fahrdienst AG, Johannisbollwerk 6-8,2000 Hamburg 11, Germany, ℙ (040) 31.24.21, Telex 02 13846.

Karl Geuther & Co, Martinistrasse 58, 2800 Bremen 1, Germany ℙ (0421) 31 49 70, Telex 02 45502.

POLISH BALTIC SHIPPING

Gdynia America Shipping Lines (London) Ltd., Branch Office, Cerdic House, Ferry Terminal, The Docks, Felixstowe, JP11 8TX.

Konopnickiej Street 1, Kolobrzeg, Poland.

Franck and Tobisen, Esplanaden 18, Dk-1263, Copenhagen, ℙ (01) 130255, (01) 226066, Telex 27515.

POLISH OCEAN LINES

Stelp and Leighton Agencies Ltd., 238 City Rd, London, EC1V 2PR, ℙ 01-251 3389, Telex 884477 – 34 Bruton St., London W1, ℙ 493 0374.

Polish Ocean Lines, Gdynia.

RED FUNNEL SERVICES

12 Bugle St., Southampton, SO9 4LJ, Hampshire, ℙ (0703) 26211.

Fountain Pier, West Cowes, Isle of Wight, ℙ (098 382) 2101 and 2704.

SEALINK (British Rail)

Sealink Car Ferry Centre, P.O. Box 303, 52 Grosvenor Gardens, London, SW1W 0AG, ℙ (01) 730 3440.

12 boulevard de la Madeleine, 75009 Paris, France, ℙ 073.56.70.

Gare Maritime, B.P. 327/1, 62200 Boulogne-sur-Mer, France, ℙ (21) 30-25-11.

Gare Maritime, 62100 Calais, France, ℙ (21) 34.64.12 (passengers) 34.48.40 (cars).

SEALINK (British Rail) *(continued)*

Jean-Claude Tellier, Agent Maritime, Quai de l'Ancien Arsenal, 50100 Cherbourg, France, ℡ 010.33-53-24-27.

c/o Chef de Gare Principal (SNCF), Dieppe Maritime, 76200 Dieppe BP 85, France, ℡ (35) 84.24.89 (cars) 84.24.68/69 (passengers)

A.L.A. Steamship Co., Gare Maritime, 59140 Dunkerque, France, ℡ (20) 66.80.01.

Régie des Transports Maritimes, 5 Natienkaai, Oostende, Belgium, Telex 81033.

Harwich Ferry Agency, Hoek Van Holland, Netherlands, ℡ 01747-2351.

The Agent, British Rail, Rosslare Harbour, Co. Wexford, Eire, ℡ (053) 33115.

British Rail, North Wall, Dublin 1, Eire, ℡ (0001) 742931.

British Rail, 24 Donegall Place, Belfast, BT1 5BH, Northern Ireland, ℡ (0232) 27525.

Sealink Car Ferry Office, Holyhead, Gwynedd, ℡ (0407) 2304.

Sealink (Scotland) Ltd. Stranraer Harbour, DG9 8EJ, Strathclyde, ℡ (0776) 3531.

Central Reservations Office, Isle of Wight Car Ferry Services, Portsmouth Harbour Station Portsmouth, PO1 3EU, ℡ (0705) 812 011 and Car Ferry Terminal, Fishbourne Lane, Fishbourne, Isle of Wight, ℡ (0983) 882432.

Sealink, Lymington Pier, Lymington, SO4 80E, Hampshire, ℡ (059 07) 3301.

Shipping Manager, British Rail, Weymouth Quay, Weymouth, Dorset, ℡ (030 57) 6363.

Sealink, The Jetty, St. Peter Port, Guernsey, ℡ (0481) 24742, Telex 41249.

Sealink, 9 Bond St. St. Helier, Jersey, ℡ (0534) 23412, Telex 41262.

SEASPEED HOVERCRAFT

Reservations Offices: Maybrook House, Queens Gardens, Dover, CT17 9UQ, Kent, ℡ (0304) 208288 or (01) 606 3681, at Birmingham, ℡ (021) 236 0701 and at Manchester, ℡ (061) 228 2041.

Hoverport, 62203 Boulogne, ℡ (21) 317122.

Hoverport, 62225 Calais, ℡ (21) 346570.

Also the Sealink Offices above.

SEAJET

18 Marine Parade, BN2 1TL, Brighton, Sussex, ℡ (0273) 696977, Telex 877468.

8 Bd Général de Gaulle, 76200 Dieppe, ℡ (35) 82.82.82, Telex 180392.

SERVICE MARITIME

Service Maritime, 50270 Carteret, France, ℡ (33) 54.87.21 et 54.80.72 Barneville Telex 170477.

SHETLAND ISLANDS COUNCIL

Grantfield, Lerwick, Shetland, ZE1 ONT, ℡ (0595) 2024, Telex 75218.

SOLENT SEASPEED

Crosshouse Rd, Southampton, SO1 9GZ, Hampshire, ℡ (0703) 21249.

Medina Rd, Cowes, PO31 7BV, Isle of Wight, ℡ (098 382) 2337.

STRANDFARASKIP LANDSINS

3800 Torshavn, Isles of Faeroes ℡ Faeroes 14550, Telex 81295.

P.O. Box 5, P & O Ferry Terminal, AB9 8DL, Aberdeen ℡ (0224) 572615.

TOR LINE LTD.

34 Panton St., London, SW1Y 4DY, ℡ (01) 930 0881, Telex 25882.

Tor Line Travel Services, Hotellplatsen 2, 41106 Goteborg, Sweden, ℡ (031) 17.20.50.

Passenger Terminal, No 2 Gate, IP11 8HD, Felixstowe ℡ (039 42) 78777, Telex 987542.

TOWNSEND THORESEN

127 Regent Street, London, W1R 8LB, ℡ (01) 734 4431 and 473 7800, Telex 23802.

Car Ferry Centre, 1 Camden Crescent, Dover, CT16 1LD, Kent, ℡ (0304) 202822 and 204040, Telex 96200 - Reservations: ℡ 20 3388.

Car Ferry House, Canute Road, Southampton, SO9 5GP, Hampshire, ℡ (0703) 34444, Telex 47637.

Continental Ferry Port, Mile End, Portsmouth, ℡ (0705) 815231.

The Ferry Centre, The Docks, P.O. Box 7, Felixstowe, IP11 8TS, Suffolk, ℡ (039 42) 78711, Telex 98236.

Car Ferry Terminal, Doverlaan 7, B-8380 - Zeebrugge, Belgium, ℡ (050) 54-48-73, Telex 81306.

P.T.O. ⟶

TOWNSEND THORESEN *(continued)*

41 place d'Armes, 62106 Calais, France, ℗ (21) 34.41.90, Telex 810750.

41 boulevard des Capucines, 75002 Paris, France, ℗ 261.51.75, Telex 21679.

Gare Maritime, 50101 Cherbourg, France, ℗ (33) 44..20.13, Telex 170765.

Quai de Southampton, 76600 Le Havre, France, ℗ (35) 21.36.50, Telex 190757.

The Harbour, Larne, Co. Antrim, Northern Ireland, ℗ (0574) 4321.

Lighterage Wharf, Cairnryan, near Stranraer, Scotland, ℗ (058 12) 276.

Beneluxhaven, Europoort, Netherlands, ℗ West Rozenburg 2366, Telex 22640.

VEDETTES ARMORICAINES S.A.

1er Bassin, Port de Commerce, P.O. Box 88, 29268 Brest Cedex, France, ℗ (98) 44.44.04 et 44.42.47, Telex 940210 F.

12 rue Georges-Clemenceau, P.O. Box 24, 50400 Granville, France, ℗ (33) 50.09.87 et 50.12.75, Telex 170449.

Vedettes Armoricaines S.A. and Sea Express, Gare Maritime de la Bourse, 35400 Saint-Malo, ℗ (99) 56.48.88 et 40.93.27.

VEDETTES VERTES GRANVILLAISES

1-3 rue Le Campion, 50400 Granville, France, ℗ (33) 50 16 36, Telex 170002.

Marine Management Ltd, 17 York St., St. Helier, Jersey, ℗ 77458/74467, Telex 41429.

WESTERN FERRIES LTD.

Kennacraig, Tarbert (Loch Fyne) Strathclyde Scotland, ℗ (088 073) 271/2.

Keneavey Travel, Moville, Donegal, Northern Ireland, ℗ Moville 65.

North Pier, Oban, Strathclyde, Scotland, ℗ (0631) 3949.

NOTES

MANUFACTURE FRANÇAISE DES PNEUMATIQUES MICHELIN
© Michelin et Cie, propriétaires-éditeurs, 1980
Société en commandite par actions au capital de 700 millions de francs
R.C. Clermont-Fd B 855 200 507 - Siège Social Clermont-Fd (France)

ISBN 2 06 006 500 — 3

S.C.I.A., La Chapelle d'Armentières-20450 — Imp. Blanchard, 92350 Le Plessis-Robinson-77 795
Printed in France 12.79.80 — Dépôt légal, 1er trimestre 1980

GREAT BRITAIN and IRELAND

Main Roads map
14 miles to 1 inch

986

NEW PUBLICATIONS 1980

Maps at a scale
of: 1/400 000 (1 in: 6.30 miles)

403 **404**

England
West and South West
Wales

England
Midlands and South East

To follow later: Maps 401 and 402

Enlarged inset maps
at: 1/200 000 (1 in: 3.15 miles)
of BIRMINGHAM
MANCHESTER
LIVERPOOL
index with
map co-ordinates

Enlarged inset maps
at: 1/200 000 (1 in: 3.15 miles)
of LONDON
BIRMINGHAM
MANCHESTER
index with map co-ordinates
*Map of shipping services,
transporting vehicles, with the continent*

Green Tourist Guides

English editions

AUSTRIA - GERMANY - ITALY
PORTUGAL - SPAIN - SWITZERLAND

LONDON - NEW YORK CITY - PARIS

BRITTANY - CHATEAUX OF THE LOIRE
DORDOGNE - FRENCH RIVIERA - NORMANDY
PROVENCE